RETAIL MANAGEMENT

A Strategic Approach

THIRTEENTH EDITION
GLOBAL EDITION

Barry Berman
Hofstra University

Joel R. Evans
Hoftsra University

Patrali Chatterjee
Montclair State University

Pearson

Harlow, England • London • New York • Boston • San Francisco • Toronto • Sydney • Dubai • Singapore • Hong Kong
Tokyo • Seoul • Taipei • New Delhi • Cape Town • São Paulo • Mexico City • Madrid • Amsterdam • Munich • Paris • Milan

To Linda; Glenna, Paul, Danielle, Sophie, and Joshua;
and Lisa, Ben, Philip, Emily, and Levi

To Linda, Jennifer and Phil, and Stacey and Adam

To Amit; Amal, Bharati, and Parnali; and Trisha and Raaka

Thank you for support and encouragement.

Vice President, Business Publishing: Donna Battista
Director of Portfolio Management: Stephanie Wall
Portfolio Manager: Daniel Tylman
Editorial Assistant: Linda Albelli
Project Manager, Global Edition: Nitin Shankar
Acquisitions Editor, Global Edition: Tahnee Wager
Senior Project Editor, Global Edition: Daniel Luiz
Managing Editor, Global Edition: Steven Jackson
Manager, Media Production, Global Edition: M. Vikram Kumar
Senior Manufacturing Controller, Production, Global Edition: Trudy Kimber
Vice President, Product Marketing: Roxanne McCarley
Director of Strategic Marketing: Brad Parkins
Strategic Marketing Manager: Deborah Strickland
Product Marketer: Becky Brown
Executive Field Marketing Manager: Adam Goldstein
Field Marketing Manager: Lenny Ann Kucenski
Field Marketing Assistant: Kristen Compton
Product Marketing Assistant: Jessica Quazza

Vice President, Production and Digital Studio, Arts and Business: Etain O'Dea
Director of Production, Business: Jeff Holcomb
Managing Producer, Business: Ashley Santora
Content Producer: Linda Albelli
Operations Specialist: Carol Melville
Creative Director: Blair Brown
Manager, Learning Tools: Brian Surette
Content Developer, Learning Tools: Sarah Peterson
Managing Producer, Digital Studio, Arts and Business: Diane Lombardo
Digital Studio Producer: Darren Cormier
Digital Studio Producer: Alana Coles
Full-Service Project Management and Composition: Nathaniel Jones, SPi Global
Interior Design: SPi Global
Cover Design: Lumina Datamatics, Inc.
Cover Art: Shutterstock/Creative Lab

Acknowledgments of third-party content appear on page[s] 560–576, which constitute an extension of this copyright page.

Pearson Education Limited
KAO Two
KAO Park
Harlow
CM17 9NA
United Kingdom

and Associated Companies throughout the world

Visit us on the World Wide Web at: www.pearsonglobaleditions.com

ISBN 10: 1-292-21467-8
ISBN 13: 978-1-292-21467-2

British Library Cataloguing-in-Publication Data
A catalogue record for this book is available from the British Library.

10 9 8 7 6 5 4 3 2 1
20 19 18 17

Typeset in Palatino LT Pro Roman by SPi Global.

Printed and bound by Vivar, Malaysia.

Brief Contents

Contents

Preface

We are quite proud and *very* thankful to have produced a book that has been so enduringly popular. The book has been adopted by universities and colleges around the world, and it has been translated into Chinese and Russian.

Both Joel and I (Barry) are pleased to welcome a new co-author for this edition. Dr. Patrali Chatterjee (Ph.D. in Management with a major in Marketing) is a Full Professor of Marketing in the Feliciano School of Business at Montclair State University. She is currently an officer for the American Collegiate Retailing Association (ACRA). She has published her research in several academic journals and been featured in business media, as well. Professor Chatterjee has also consulted for several *Fortune 500* companies.

As we move further into the twenty-first century, our goal is to seamlessly meld the traditional framework of retailing with the realities of the competitive environment and the emergence of high-tech as a backbone for retailing. *Retail Management: A Strategic Approach* is a cutting-edge text, while retaining the coverage and features most desired by professors and students. To remain timely, we regularly post material about current events at our blog (**www.bermanevansretail.com**), which already has more than 1,500 posts and viewers from 180 countries.

Our enthusiasm for teaching and writing remains quite high. We all teach a full schedule of undergraduate and graduate courses in the Zarb School of Business at Hofstra University (Barry and Joel) and the Feliciano School of Business at Montclair State University (Patrali); both schools are fully accredited by AACSB International. We have been all been active in and supportive of ACRA. Barry has served as president and is in the ACRA Hall of Fame, while Joel has edited several conference proceedings and Patrali is an officer on the board.

The concepts of a strategic approach and a retail strategy remain our cornerstones. We were the first authors to take this primary orientation to the teaching of retail management. With a strategic approach, the fundamental principle is that the retailer has to plan for and adapt to a complex, changing environment. Both opportunities and constraints must be considered. A retail strategy is the overall plan or framework of action that guides a retailer. Ideally, it will be at least one year in duration and outline the mission, goals, consumer market, overall and specific activities, and control mechanisms of the retailer. Without a pre-defined and well-integrated strategy, the firm may flounder and be unable to cope with the environment that surrounds it. Through our text, we want the reader to become a good retail planner and decision maker and be able to adapt to change.

Retail Management is designed as a one-semester text for students of retailing or retail management. Due to the flexible pedagogical elements that accompany the book and the ability of the instructor to cover all or selected chapters in the book, *Retail Management* has been used by four-year and two-year schools, in undergraduate and graduate courses, and by business schools and nonbusiness schools. In many cases, students will have already been exposed to marketing principles. We feel retailing should be viewed as one form of marketing and not distinct from it.

NEW TO THE THIRTEENTH EDITION

Since the first edition of *Retail Management: A Strategic Approach*, we have sought to be as contemporary and forward-looking as possible. We are proactive rather than reactive in our preparation of each edition. That is why we still take this adage of Walmart's founder, the late Sam Walton so seriously: "Commit to your business. Believe in it more than anybody else."

For the Thirteenth Edition, there are many changes in *Retail Management*:

1. All data and examples are as current as possible and reflect the current economic and world situations as much as possible. We believe it is essential that our book take into account the economic environment that has dramatically affected so many businesses and consumers.
2. There is now extensive coverage of omnichannel retailing—an evolving practice whereby the best retailers understand and seamlessly integrate all of their interactions across channels (including stores, online, mobile, social media, and more).

3. ALL NEW CHAPTER-OPENING VIGNETTES—each relating to the evolving nature of retailing. We had a lot of fun writing these vignettes:
   Chapter 1: Multichannel versus Omnichannel Experiences
   Chapter 2: The Role of Digital and Traditional Channels in Delivering in-Store Service
   Chapter 3: Brand Intimacy: How Consumers Form Bonds with Brands
   Chapter 4: Tesla Motors Seeks to Bypass the Franchise Dealer Network
   Chapter 5: The Evolution of Factory Outlets
   Chapter 6: Buy Online, Pick Up In Store Programs
   Chapter 7: Online Groceries: Traditional Grocer's New Threat
   Chapter 8: Lip Service Versus Real Customer Service
   Chapter 9: Trading-Area Analysis for Traditional and Destination Retailers
   Chapter 10: The Impact of Store Closings on Shopping Centers
   Chapter 11: Strategies to Reduce Retail Employee Turnover
   Chapter 12: Incremental Versus Zero-Based Budgeting
   Chapter 13: Facial Recognition: The Faceoff Against Retail Credit Card Fraud
   Chapter 14: Amazon's Dash Button
   Chapter 15: American Eagle Outfitters New Distribution Center
   Chapter 16: Strategies to Reduce Markdowns
   Chapter 17: Retailer Price Matching Programs
   Chapter 18: The In-Store Service Imperative
   Chapter 19: Apps with Generation Z Appeal
   Chapter 20: Customer Satisfaction Suffers: American Customer Satisfaction Data

4. ALL NEW BOXES! **They now include thought-provoking questions**. Topics include:
   a. *Technology in Retailing*
      Chapter 1: Generating Location-Sensitive Offers
      Chapter 2: Automated Customized Service
      Chapter 3: Retail Planning Software
      Chapter 4: Loyalty Programs
      Chapter 5: Sephora's Phygital Makeover
      Chapter 6: Bringing Concierge Service to Online Shopping
      Chapter 7: Recommendation Engines
      Chapter 8: Mobile Beacons and Data Collection
      Chapter 9: GIS Systems
      Chapter 10: Lease Management Software
      Chapter 11 Job Listing Web Sites
      Chapter 12: The Impact of Self-Scanning on Impulse Sales
      Chapter 13: Energy Management
      Chapter 14: Store Planning Software
      Chapter 15: Retailers Taking the Right Steps to Fight Shrinkage
      Chapter 16: Point-of-Sale (POS) Systems
      Chapter 17: Oracle Markdown Software
      Chapter 18: 3D Afoot
      Chapter 19: Smartphone Couponing
      Chapter 20: Retail Planning Using EXCEL

   b. *Retailing Around the World*
      Chapter 1: Debenhams Goes East: The Continuing Expansion of the UK Department Store Retailer
      Chapter 2: Lane Crawford; Selling Luxury Goods in Hong Kong
      Chapter 3: Handling Payments from Global Customers
      Chapter 4: KFC in China
      Chapter 5: McDonald's Investments in Russia
      Chapter 6: The Global Retail E-Commerce Index
      Chapter 7: Global Adaptation
      Chapter 8: Studying a Consumer's Purchase Journey
      Chapter 9: Doomed Locations?
      Chapter 10: Pop-Up Stores
      Chapter 11: Recruiting of Retail Executives

Chapter 12: Ikea's Global Results
Chapter 13: Countries' Payment-Related Issues
Chapter 14: Young Chinese Favor Global Brands
Chapter 15: Processing Foreign Credit Cards
Chapter 16: Gray Market Sourcing
Chapter 17: Game Stores: Africa's Largest Discounter
Chapter 18: Hyatt Hotels Promotes Global Social Responsibility
Chapter 19: Burberry's Chinese Promotional Strategy
Chapter 20: Best Buy's Failure in China

c. *Ethics in Retailing*
Chapter 1: Environmental Sustainability
Chapter 2: Community Champions in the UK
Chapter 3: Deceptive Price Advertising
Chapter 4: Unethical Behavior by Franchisors
Chapter 5: Bargaining Power by Category Killers
Chapter 6: Sales Tax Collection By Online Retailers
Chapter 7: Selling Add-Ons
Chapter 8: Retail Security Breaches
Chapter 9: Gentrification Issues
Chapter 10: Shopping Center Leases
Chapter 11: Zero-Hour Contracts
Chapter 12: Restrictive Loan Covenants
Chapter 13: Corporate Responsibility at Target
Chapter 14: What's a Fair Return Policy
Chapter 15: Upcycling: A Form of Green Marketing
Chapter 16: Markdown Allowances
Chapter 17: Trust and Fairness in Revenue Management
Chapter 18: Product Reviews on the Web
Chapter 19: Using of Promotional Goods
Chapter 20: Why Do Poor Ethics Occur?

d. *Careers in Retailing*
Chapter 1: Hiring From Within Versus Best Person for the Job
Chapter 2: Category Managers
Chapter 3: "Builders," "Maintainers," and "Undertakers"
Chapter 4: Succession Planning
Chapter 5: Considering Being a Retail Buyer as a Career
Chapter 6: Web Developers
Chapter 7: Marketing Research as a Career
Chapter 8: Careers in Customer Relationship Management
Chapter 9: Trading-Area Analysis Careers
Chapter 10: Site-Selection Based Careers
Chapter 11: Buyer Training
Chapter 12: Retail Financial Analyst
Chapter 13: Security Personnel
Chapter 14: Buying for a Retailer's Private-Label Program
Chapter 15: Opportunistic Buying by Discounters
Chapter 16: Retailing Accounting Careers
Chapter 17: Carol Meyrowitz of TJX
Chapter 18: Joseph Bona's Design Career Path
Chapter 19: Omnichannel Promotions Manager
Chapter 20: Retail Audit Personnel

5. ALL NEW! 30 shorter cases, as well as 8 comprehensive cases. Every case is based on real companies and real situations. Cases include:
a. Short cases:

Part One
1. Retailers MUST Be Future-Oriented
2. Stores that Accommodate Those with Physical Limitations

3. Is the Proliferation of Job Titles Helping or Hurting?
4. Competition and Quick Foodservice

Part Two
1. Do Power Players Rule?
2. Will the Favorites of Today Remain Popular?
3. Omnichannel Strategies of Top Retailers
4. Omnichannel Food Retailing Still Needs Work

Part Three
1. Eating Patterns in America
2. The Convenience Economy Comes of Age
3. Are Hot Retailers of 2015 Still Hot?
4. Navigating the Shopper Universe Through Big Data

Part Four
1. Are Smaller and Faster Better?
2. Organize, Optimize, Synchronize
3. Removing Barriers to Cross-Border Commerce
4. Warehouse Management: Right Time, Right Place

Part Five
1. Assistant Store Manager
2. Manager, Training and Development
3. Senior Manager of Digital Operations
4. Retail Shrinkage: A Significant Problem

Part Six
1. Buyer of Sports Equipment
2. Adapting to the Internet of Things (IoT)
3. High Marks by Suppliers and Wholesalers for Convenience Stores
4. Data-Driven Pricing

Part Seven
1. Keep It Simple
2. More than Price
3. Enhancing the In-Store Experience Through Facial Recognition Software
4. Revitalizing Customer Loyalty

Part Eight
1. Envision the Future: Part 1
2. Envision the Future: Part 2

a. Part Cases:
Part One: Ideas Worth Stealing
Part Two: What Consumers Find Expendable Vs. Untouchable
Part Three: How Do You Attract and Satisfy Millennials?
Part Four: Autenticidad en Acción: Mexican Delights the Real Deal
at Food City Remodel
Part Five: Predicting Retail Trends
Part Six: Knocking Off the Knockoffs
Part Seven: Inside the Mind of Shake Shack's Founder
Part Eight: Achieving Excellence in Retailing

6. MANY photos and images have been replaced or updated throughout.
7. The hundreds of PowerPoint slides that accompany the book have been fully revised; **AND** there are descriptions related to each slide.
8. Our blog (www.bermanevansretail.com) has been updated. We have a current (multiple posts each week), dynamic, multimedia, interactive blog just for students and professors interested in retailing. There is a lot of cool stuff there. Please join us at (www.bermanevansretail.com). Our blog has a lot of career material. There are more than 325 career-related posts at the blog.

Substantive Changes for the Thirteenth Edition by Chapter

▶ **Chapter 1 (An Introduction to Retailing).** The importance of omnichannel retailing is highlighted. We describe Home Depot's overall strategy and its approach to the complex marketplace. And to properly capture the importance of the economic situation facing retailers today, we update the chapter appendix to reflect the state of economy after the worldwide recession period: "Understanding the Recent Economic Environment in the United States Around the Globe." The appendix covers the U.S. economy, the global effects of the downturn, the effect of the current economic climate on retailing, and strategic options for retailers.

▶ **Chapter 2 (Building and Sustaining Relationships in Retailing).** There is more coverage of "value" and "relationships" in retailing—with both customers and other channel members. Retailer interactions with customers depend on the customer base and customer service, and they have an impact on customer satisfaction; and there are different types of loyalty programs. Emerging technologies often enable retailers to form stronger relationships; and retailer ethics can stimulate or deter shoppers. The end-of-chapter appendix ("Planning for the Unique Aspects of Service Retailing") reflects current thinking on service retailing.

▶ **Chapter 3 (Strategic Planning in Retailing).** There is greater attention to strategic planning in today's marketplace, with numerous examples. The software that supplements the section of this chapter devoted to a strategic planning template—*Computer-Assisted Strategic Retail Management Planning*—has been updated and is available for download at our blog (**www.bermanevansretail.com**). The chapter appendix ("The Special Dimensions of Strategic Planning in a Global Retailing Environment") notes the challenges for retailers operating outside their home markets and various trends in global retailing.

▶ **Chapter 4 (Retail Institutions by Ownership).** All of the data on retail ownership formats (independents, chain-owned, franchisee-operated, leased departments, owned by manufacturers or wholesalers, or consumer-owned) have been updated. The appendix on franchising opportunities ("The Dynamics of Franchising") presents current information on various aspects of franchising.

▶ **Chapter 5 (Retail Institutions by Store-Based Strategy Mix).** All of the data on store-based retail strategies have been updated – 14 strategic formats in all that are divided into food-based and general-merchandise-based categories. There are numerous new examples.

▶ **Chapter 6 (Web, Nonstore-Based, and Other Forms of Nontraditional Retailing).** The emerging and critical omnichannel perspective of retailing is discussed in more detail in this chapter than in Chapter 1; and single-channel, multichannel, and omnichannel retailing are contrasted. The coverage of online retailing reflects the present state of the Web and mobile channels, and includes many examples. There is a fully updated and refocused appendix on retail supply chains ("Omnichannel Retailing") and its impact.

▶ **Chapter 7 (Identifying and Understanding Consumers).** There is a strong emphasis on the retailing ramifications of the empowered consumer, as well as consumer characteristics, attitudes, and behavior. We include current demographic data on U.S. and foreign consumers, consumer profiles, and shopping attitudes and behavior.

▶ **Chapter 8 (Information Gathering and Processing in Retailing).** This chapter looks at information flows in a retail distribution channel and notes the ramifications of inadequate research. We then describe the retail information system, database management, and data warehousing. The barcode discussion is enhanced.

▶ **Chapter 9 (Trading-Area Analysis).** There is new material on geographic information systems, as well as many new retail applications. We have increased the coverage of the TIGER digital mapping system, which is the basis for most geographic information systems' software.

▶ **Chapter 10 (Site Selection).** We include many new retail applications and examples.

▶ **Chapter 11 (Retail Organization and Human Resource Management).** There is more emphasis on employee turnover and the human resource environment in retailing, as well as updated coverage of women and minorities in retailing. We also have substantially revised some of the organization charts.

▶ **Chapter 12 (Operations Management: Financial Dimensions).** We have new material on incremental and zero-based budgeting, as well as updated information on key business ratios, financial trends, and resource allocation.

▶ **Chapter 13 (Operations Management: Operational Dimensions).** There is a new discussion of digital payment systems, as well as updated material on operations issues in retailing.

▶ **Chapter 14 (Developing Merchandise Plans).** Innovative practices are highlighted. We place greater emphasis on a merchandising-based philosophy and the activities necessary to carry it out. There is updated coverage of merchandising practices, the popularity of private brands (including a new quiz), and category management.

▶ **Chapter 15 (Implementing Merchandise Plans).** There is enhanced coverage of the power of large retailers, RFID (radio frequency identification), logistics, and inventory management.

▶ **Chapter 16 (Financial Merchandise Management).** There is updated coverage of financial merchandise management, including unanticipated markdowns.

▶ **Chapter 17 (Pricing in Retailing).** We focus on the retailer's need to provide value to customers, regardless of its price orientation—and the growing power of the consumer due to online comparison shopping.

▶ **Chapter 18 (Establishing and Maintaining a Retail Image).** We place more focus on the total retail experience (both in the store and online), retail positioning, and atmospherics and Web-based retailers, as well as how to increase shopping time.

▶ **Chapter 19 (Promotional Strategy).** There are many new applications and examples—especially with regard to mobile apps and social media—and a strong strategic emphasis on the retail promotional strategy.

▶ **Chapter 20 (Integrating and Controlling the Retail Strategy).** There is an in-depth discussion on integrating the retail strategy in today's high-tech marketplace, as well as how to assess a strategy, with a detailed example based on TJX.

▶ **Appendix (Careers in Retailing).** We emphasize the strong long-term possibilities (through 2024) for careers in retailing. There is a new table citing 10 retail positions with unique responsibilities.

BUILDING ON THE E-VOLUTION OF *RETAIL MANAGEMENT: A STRATEGIC APPROACH*

From a retailer perspective, we see four formats—all covered in *Retail Management*—competing in the new millennium (cited in descending order of importance):

▶ **Combined "bricks-and-mortar" and "clicks-and-mortar" retailers.** These are store-based retailers that also offer online shopping, thus providing customers the ultimate in choice and convenience. Virtually all of the world's largest retailers, as well as many medium and small firms, fall into this category; and they are omnichannel retailers. This is clearly the fast-growing format in retailing. Even Amazon.com, a long-time online only retailer, is now opening some physical stores.

▶ **Clicks-and-mortar retailers.** These are the online-only retailers that have emerged. Rather than use their own physical store facilities, these companies promote a "virtual" shopping experience: wide selections, convenience, and—sometimes—low prices. Among the firms in this category are Priceline—the discount airfare and hotel retailer—and Zappos –the retailer of shoes, apparel, and a whole lot more.

▶ **Direct marketers with clicks-and-mortar retailing operations.** These are firms that have relied on traditional nonstore media such as print catalogs, direct selling in homes, and TV infomercials to generate business. Almost of them have added Web sites to enhance their businesses. Leaders include Lands' End and QVC. These direct marketers will continue to see a dramatic increase in the proportion of sales coming from the Web.

▶ **Bricks-and-mortar retailers.** These are companies that rely on their physical facilities to make sales. They do not sell online but use the Web for providing information and customer service and for image building. Auto dealers typically offer product information and customer service online but conduct their sales transactions at retail stores. Firms in this category represent the smallest grouping of retailers. Many will need to rethink their approach as online competition intensifies.

We now have access to more information sources, from global trade associations to government agencies. The information in *Retail Management*, Thirteenth Edition, is more current than ever because we are using the original sources themselves and not waiting for data to be published months or a year after being compiled. We are also able to include a greater range of real-world examples because of the information at company Web sites.

Will this help you? Yes. You will benefit because our philosophy has always been to make *Retail Management* as reader-friendly, up-to-date, and useful as possible. In addition, we want students to benefit from our experiences—in this case, our E-xperiences.

Retail Management: A Strategic Approach, Thirteenth Edition, incorporates many E-features in the book; and at our lively and constantly updated blog (**www.bermanevansretail.com**).

Our blog includes many features that are intended to enrich both the student's and professor's understanding and appreciation of retailing. These include:

- More than 1,600 blog posts and counting. To stay current, we post multiple times EVERY week!
- A multimedia approach—with embedded videos, colorful infographics (charts with data), photos, and links to a huge number of real world sources.
- Post categories keyed to each of 8 parts of the book.
- Additional post categories on such important issues as: Careers in Retailing, Global Retailing, Nontraditional Retailing, Online Retailing, Privacy and Identity Theft, Social Media and Retailing, and Strategy Mix.

But, that's not all! Our Web site has career material; and each chapter of the book ends with a Web-based exercise.

BUILDING ON A STRONG TRADITION

Besides introducing the E-features just mentioned, *Retail Management*, Thirteenth Edition, carefully builds on its heritage as the market leader in strategic retail management. These features have been retained from earlier editions of *Retail Management*:

- A strategic decision-making orientation, with many illustrative flow charts, figures, tables, and photos. The chapter coverage is geared to the six steps used in developing and applying a retail strategy, which are first described in Chapter 1.
- Full coverage of all major retailing topics—including merchandising, consumer behavior, information systems, omnichannel retailing, store location, operations, logistics, service retailing, the retail audit, retail institutions, franchising, human resource management, computerization, and retailing in a changing environment.
- A real-world approach focusing on both small and large retailers.
- Real-world boxes on current retailing issues in each chapter. These boxes further illustrate the concepts presented in the text by focusing on real firms and situations.
- A numbered summary keyed to chapter objectives, a key terms listing, and discussion questions at the end of each chapter.
- Both short cases involving a wide range of retailers and retail practices and comprehensive cases.
- Up-to-date information from such sources as *Advertising Age, Businessweek, Chain Store Age, Direct Marketing, Entrepreneur, Fortune, Inc., International Journal of Retail & Distribution Management, Journal of Retailing, Multichannel Merchant, Progressive Grocer, Retailing Today, Shopping Centers Today, Standard & Poor's, Stores*, and *Wall Street Journal*.
- End-of-chapter appendixes on service retailing (following Chapter 2), global retailing (following Chapter 3), and franchising (following Chapter 4).
- End-of-text appendix "Careers in Retailing" and a glossary.

HOW THE TEXT IS ORGANIZED

Retail Management: A Strategic Approach has eight parts. Part One introduces the field of retailing, the basics of strategic planning, the importance of building and maintaining relations, and the decisions to be made in owning or managing a retail business. In Part Two, retail institutions are examined in terms of ownership types, as well as store-based, nonstore-based, electronic, and nontraditional strategy mixes. The wheel of retailing, scrambled merchandising, the retail life cycle, and the Web are covered. Part Three focuses on target-marketing and information-gathering methods, including discussions of why and how consumers shop and the retailing information system and data warehouse. Part Four presents a four-step approach to location planning: trading-area analysis, choosing the most desirable type of location, selecting a general locale, and deciding on a specific site.

Part Five discusses the elements involved in managing a retail business: the retail organization structure, human resource management, and operations management (both financial and operational). Part Six deals with merchandise management—developing and implementing merchandise plans, the financial aspects of merchandising, and pricing. In Part Seven, the ways to communicate with customers are analyzed, with special attention paid to retail image, atmosphere, and promotion. Part Eight deals with integrating and controlling a retail strategy.

At the end of the text, Appendix: Careers in Retailing highlights career opportunities in retailing. There is also a comprehensive Glossary.

INSTRUCTOR RESOURCES

At Pearson's Higher Ed catalog, www.pearsonglobaleditions.com/berman, instructors can easily register to gain access to a variety of instructor resources available with this text in downloadable format. If assistance is needed, our dedicated technical support team is ready to help with the media supplements that accompany this text. Visit https://support.pearson.com/getsupport for answers to frequently asked questions and toll-free user support phone numbers. The following supplements are available with this text: • Instructor's Resource Manual • Test Bank • TestGen® Computerized Test Bank • PowerPoint Presentations. This title is available as an E-book and can be purchased at most E-book retailers.

Recommended Syllabi

A course in retail management is taught in a number of ways and according to different term calendars. Accordingly, here are two different recommended syllabi to assist instructors in their course preparation. These syllabi suggest coverage for schools on both the semester and quarter system.

These syllabi are merely recommended. We recognize that greater or lesser emphasis may be placed on particular retailing topics.

Recommended Syllabus for a 14-Week Semester Course

Week	Amount of Coverage	Topics	Text Chapters
1	½ week	An introduction to retailing	1
1–2	1 week	Relationship retailing/strategic planning in retailing	2, 3
2–3	1½ weeks	Retail institutions categorized by ownership, strategy mix, Web, nonstore, and other forms of nontraditional retailing	4, 5, 6
4	½ week	Understanding consumer behavior	7
4–5	1 week	Information systems and marketing research in retailing	8
5–6	1½ weeks	Trading-area analysis and site selection	9, 10
7–8	1½ weeks	Retail organization and human resource management; and operations management	11, 12, 13
8–9	1 week	Buying and handling merchandise	14, 15
9–10	1 week	Financial merchandise planning and management	16
10–11	1 week	Pricing in retailing	17
11–12	1 week	Establishing and maintaining a retail image	18
12–13	1 week	Promotional strategy	19
14	1 week	Integrating and controlling the retail strategy	20

Recommended Syllabus for a 10-Week Semester Course

Week	Amount of Coverage	Topics	Text Chapters
1	½ week	An introduction to retailing	1
1–2	1 week	Strategic planning in retailing	2, 3
2–3	1½ week	Retail institutions characterized by ownership, strategy mix, Web, nonstore, and other forms of nontraditional retailing	4, 5, 6
4	½ week	Understanding consumer behavior	7
4	½ week	Information systems and marketing research in retailing	8
5	1 week	Trading-area analysis and site selection	9, 10
6	1 week	Retail organization and human resource management; and operations management	11, 12, 13
7	1 week	Merchandise management	14, 15, 16
8	1 week	Pricing in retailing	17
9	1 week	Establishing and maintaining a retail image, and promotional strategy	18, 19
10	1 week	Integrating and controlling the retail strategy	20

CONCLUDING REMARKS

As always, we are extremely "hands on" in developing and maintaining all instructor materials and teaching resources. Please feel free to send us feedback regarding any aspect of *Retail Management* or its package. We promise to reply to any correspondence.

Sincerely,

Barry Berman (E-mail at **barry.berman@hofstra.edu**),
Zarb School of Business, Hofstra University, Hempstead, NY 11549

Joel R. Evans (E-mail at **joel.r.evans@hofstra.edu**),
Zarb School of Business, Hofstra University, Hempstead, NY, 11549

Patrali Chatterjee (E-mail at **chatterjeep@mail.montclair.edu**,
Feliciano School of Business, Montclair State University, Montclair, NJ 07043

Global Edition Acknowledgments

For their contributions to the content of the Global Edition, Pearson would like to thank Diane and Jon Sutherland, and for their feedback, Ronan Jouan de Kervenoael, Sabancı Üniversitesi; Hasan Gilani, University of Brighton; Khaled Haque; and Stephanie Phang, Tunku Abdul Rahman University College.

Barry Berman
Hofstra University

Joel R. Evans
Hoftsra University

Patrali Chatterjee
Montclair State University

Part 1

An Overview of Strategic Retail Management

Source: nasirkhan/Shutterstock. Reprinted by permission.

Welcome to *Retail Management: A Strategic Approach*, 13th edition. We hope you find the book is informative, timely, action-oriented, and reader-friendly. Visit our popular blog (www.bermanevansretail.com) for interactive, useful, up-to-date features that complement the text—including chapter hotlinks, a study guide, and much more!

In Part One, we explore the field of retailing, establishing and maintaining relationships, and the basic principles of strategic planning and the decisions made in owning or managing a retail business.

Chapter 1 describes retailing, shows why it should be studied, and examines its special characteristics. We note the value of strategic planning, including a detailed review of Home Depot (a titan of retailing). The retailing concept is presented, along with the total retail experience, customer service, and relationship retailing. The focus and format of the text are comprehensive. An appendix, "Understanding the Recent Economic Environment in the United States and Around the Globe," appears at the end of this chapter.

Chapter 2 looks at the complexities of retailers' relationships—with both customers and other channel members. We examine value and the value chain, customer relationships and channel relationships, the differences in relationship building between goods and service retailers, the impact of technology on retailing relationships, and the interplay between ethical performance and relationships in retailing. The chapter ends with an appendix on planning for the unique aspects of service retailing.

Chapter 3 shows the usefulness of strategic planning for all kinds of retailers. We focus on the planning process: situation analysis, objectives, identifying consumers, overall strategy, specific activities, control, and feedback. We also look at the controllable and uncontrollable parts of a retail strategy. Strategic planning is shown as a series of interrelated steps that are continuously reviewed. A detailed computerized strategic planning template, available at our Web site, is described. At the end of the chapter, there is an appendix on the strategic implications of global retailing.

1 An Introduction to Retailing

Chapter Objectives

1. To define retailing, consider it from various perspectives, demonstrate its impact, and note its special characteristics

2. To introduce the concept of strategic planning and apply it

3. To show why the retailing concept is the foundation of a successful business, with an emphasis on the total retail experience, customer service, and relationship retailing

4. To indicate the focus and format of the text

Digital technologies such as Web 2.0, social media, and mobile media have dramatically altered how businesses and consumers get information, make decisions, communicate, transact, and own versus share possessions around the world. In this always-connected, 24/7/365 competitive retailing landscape, consumers choose how, when, and where they want to interact with retailers. Retailers are expected to be proactive and adaptive in anticipating their consumers' needs at the time and utilize an omnichannel approach to provide the customer with a seamless shopping experience, whether the customer is shopping online from a desktop or a mobile device, by telephone, or in a bricks-and-mortar store. Accordingly, in *Retail Management: A Strategic Approach,* we begin each chapter with a discussion of omnichannel perspectives relevant to the retailing topics in that chapter.

How do we distinguish between multichannel and omnichannel experiences? Multichannel retailing is associated with a retailer having separate channels—store and Web—as alternatives. A traditional multichannel retail environment has few linkages among these channel alternatives. Simply put, although shoppers can purchase an item through either channel, important linkages among channels may not exist. For example, consumers may not be able to view store inventories online, can be charged different prices in each channel, cannot arrange for store pickup on a Web order, may not return Web purchases to a local store, and a store and Web site can have separate customer databases.

In contrast, omnichannel retailing delivers a consistent, uninterrupted, and seamless brand experience regardless of channel or device (store, laptop computer, iPad, smartphone, etc.). Omnichannel retailing assumes that there are various shopping journey maps that use mobile, Web, and stores quite differently. As an example, product discovery can be Web or social-media–based, information search can use the Web or in-store observation, and consumers can purchase an item via a mobile device but seek to return it to a store. Omnichannel retailing is by nature seamless and integrated.

At www.bermanevansretail.com, we've set up a dynamic retailing blog with all sorts of interesting and current information—retailer links, career opportunities, news about the retail industry and individual retailers, and more. Check it out!

Many different kinds of retailers, both large and small, utilize multiple technologies, employ social and mobile media to communicate with customers, reinforce their images, introduce new locations and merchandise, sell products, run special promotions, and so much more.

Source: iQoncept/Shutterstock. Reprinted by permission.

Overview

Retailing encompasses the business activities involved in selling goods and services to consumers for their personal, family, or household use. It includes every sale to the *final* consumer—ranging from cars to apparel to meals at restaurants to movie tickets. Retailing is the last stage in the distribution process from supplier to consumer.

Today, retailing is at a complex crossroad. On the one hand, retail sales are at their highest point in history (despite a dip during the 2008–2010 "Great Recession"). Walmart is the leading company in the world in terms of sales, but Amazon.com, predominately an online retailer with few physical stores as of this writing has an annual growth rate of 25 percent compared to 1 percent for Walmart.[1] New technologies are improving retail productivity. There are many opportunities to start a new retail business—or work for an existing one—and to become a franchisee. Global retailing possibilities abound, especially for pure online retailers that can replicate their business models globally without the capital costs of store-based retailing.

On the other hand, retailers face numerous challenges. The rise of the U.S. dollar against major currencies in recent years has had a major impact on retailers, their suppliers, and consumers around the world. Many consumers are bored with shopping for products or do not have much time for it and are spending more for experiences. Some locales have too many stores, and retailers often spur one another into frequent price cutting (and low profit margins). Customer service expectations are high at a time when more retailers offer self-service, automated systems, and omnichannel ordering and pick-up services. Although online E-commerce accounts for only 7.1 percent of U.S. retail sales, today it is growing at a faster rate and displacing sales revenues at stores. Some retailers are still grappling with their omnichannel strategy in terms of capital and human resource investments for in-store versus digital formats; coordinating merchandising, pricing, and logistics across channels; and the relative emphasis to place on image enhancement, customer information and feedback, and sales transactions. The widespread proliferation of mobile and social media technologies has been difficult for many retailers to adapt to in their strategies all over the world. These are among the key issues that retailers must resolve:

> How can we better serve our customers while earning a fair profit?
>
> How can we stand out in a highly competitive environment where consumers have so many choices?
>
> How can we better coordinate our merchandising, pricing, and service strategy across all our channels when costs, profit margins, and target segments differ across the channels?
>
> How can we grow our business while retaining a core of loyal customers?

Retail decision makers can best address these questions by fully understanding and applying the basic principles of retailing in a well-structured, systematic, and focused retail strategy. That is the philosophy behind *Retail Management: A Strategic Approach.*

Visit Amazon.com's Web site (www.amazon.com) and see what drives one of the world's "hot" retailers.

Can retailers flourish in today's tough marketplace? You bet! Just look at your favorite restaurant, gift shop, and food store. Look at the success of retailers such as Costco, Starbucks, L Brands (whose major brands include Victoria's Secret and Bath & Body Works), and Amazon.com. What do they have in common? A desire to please the customer and a strong market niche. To prosper in the long term, they all need a strategic plan and a willingness to adapt—both central thrusts of this book. See Figure 1-1.

In this chapter, we look at the framework of retailing, the value of developing and applying a sound retail strategy, and the focus and format of the text. A special appendix at the end of this chapter examines the impact of the global economic environment on retailers in the United States and around the world.

THE FRAMEWORK OF RETAILING

To appreciate the role of retailing and the range of retailing activities, let's view it from three perspectives:

1. Suppose we manage a manufacturing firm that makes cosmetics. How should we sell these items? We could distribute via big chains such as Sephora or small neighborhood stores, have our own sales force visit people in their homes as Mary Kay does, or set up our own

FIGURE 1-1

A Willingness to Adapt Is Essential for Retailers

The most successful retailers over the long run are those which recognize that consumers and the marketplace are constantly evolving. They do research to get feedback and then act accordingly.

Source: iQoncept/ Shutterstock. Reprinted by permission.

stores (if we have the ability and resources to do so). We could sponsor TV infomercials or magazine ads, complete with a toll-free phone number.

2. Suppose we have an idea for a new way to teach first-graders how to use computer software for spelling and vocabulary. How should we implement this idea? We could lease a store in a strip shopping center and run ads in a local paper, rent space in a local YMCA and rely on teacher referrals, or do mailings to parents and visit children in their homes. In each case, the service is offered "live." But there is another option: We could use an animated Web site to teach children online.

3. Suppose that we, as consumers, want to buy apparel. What choices do we have? We could go to a department store or an apparel store. We could shop with a full-service retailer or a discount store. We could go to a shopping center or order from a catalog. We could patronize retailers that carry a wide range of clothing (from outerwear to jeans to suits) or firms that specialize in one clothing category (such as leather coats). We could surf the Web and visit retailers around the globe. We could also look at Facebook and see what other consumers are saying about various retailers.

Service businesses such as Jiffy Lube (www .jiffylube.com) are engaged in retailing.

There is a tendency to think of retailing as primarily involving the sale of tangible (physical) goods. However, retailing also includes the sale of services and digital goods. And this is a big part of retailing! A service may be the shopper's primary purchase (such as a haircut) or it may be part of the shopper's purchase of a good (such as furniture delivery). Sales in many physical goods—product categories such as books, movies, and music—are now dominated by their digital applications in the format of downloads. Obviously, retailing does not have to involve a store. Mail and phone orders, direct selling to consumers in their homes and offices, Web transactions, kiosks, and vending machine sales all fall within the scope of retailing. In fact, retailing does not even have to include a "retailer." Manufacturers, importers, nonprofit firms, wholesalers, and individual artisans on online platforms, such as Etsy.com, act as retailers when they sell to final consumers.

Let's now examine various reasons for studying retailing and its special characteristics.

Reasons for Studying Retailing

Retailing is an important field to study because of its impact on the economy, its functions in distribution, and its relationship with firms selling goods and services to retailers for their resale or use. These factors are discussed next. A fourth factor for students of retailing is the broad range of career opportunities, as highlighted with a "Careers in Retailing" box in each chapter, Appendix A at the end of this book, and our blog (www.bermanevansretail.com). See Figure 1-2.

Learn more about the exciting array of retailing career opportunities (www.allretailjobs.com).

THE IMPACT OF RETAILING ON THE ECONOMY   Retailing is a major part of U.S. and world commerce. Retail sales and employment are vital economic contributors, and retail trends often mirror trends in a nation's overall economy.

According to the Department of Commerce, annual U.S. retail store sales in 2015 were $4.785 trillion—representing one-third of the total economy. During that year, more than one-fifth of the world's retail sales occurred in the United States.[2] The weighted-average share of retail E-commerce in overall U.S. retail sales has been steadily growing from 3.4 percent in 2007 to 7.1 percent in 2015.[3] Share of online retail sales is slightly higher in Europe at 7.5 percent and highest in the Asia-Pacific region at 10.2 percent. Telephone and mail-order sales by nonstore retailers, vending machines, and direct selling generate hundreds of billions of dollars in additional yearly revenues. Personal expenditures on financial, medical, legal, educational, and other services account for another several hundred billion dollars in annual retail revenues.

Durable goods stores—including motor vehicles and parts dealers; furniture, home furnishings, electronics and appliance stores; and building materials and hardware stores—make up 30 percent of U.S. retail store sales. Nondurable goods and services stores—including general merchandise stores; food and beverage stores; health- and personal-care stores; gasoline stations; clothing and accessories stores; sporting goods, hobby, book, and music stores; eating and drinking places; and miscellaneous retailers—together account for 70 percent of U.S. retail store sales.

The world's 250 largest retailers generate more than $4.6 trillion in annual revenues. They represent 29 nations. Seventy-six of the largest 250 retailers are based in the United States, 28 in Japan, 17 in Germany, 16 in Great Britain, and 15 in France. Five of the 250 top retailers are nonstore retailers.[4] The 10 largest retailers in the United States generate nearly one trillion dollars in annual domestic revenues and more than 1.2 trillion dollars in total worldwide sales. They operate over 32,000 U.S. stores. See Table 1-1. Visit our blog (www.bermanevansretail.com) for additional information on retailing.

Retailing is a major source of jobs. In the United States alone, 15 million people—about one-tenth of the total labor force—work for traditional retailers (including food and beverage service firms, such as restaurants). Yet this figure understates the true number of people who work in retailing because it does not include the several million persons employed by other service firms, seasonal employees, proprietors, and unreported workers in family businesses or partnerships.

FIGURE 1-2

Encouraging People to Consider a Career in Retailing

To attract and retain high-quality, motivated workers, retailers should properly train them, empower them to be responsive to reasonable requests that may "break the rules" (without always having to ask the boss), and reward—and visibly recognize—superior performance. A key aspect of a meaningful reward system is an employee's opportunities for upward mobility in terms of a better job and a bigger paycheck (promoting from within).

Source: Dusit/Shutterstock. Reprinted by permission.

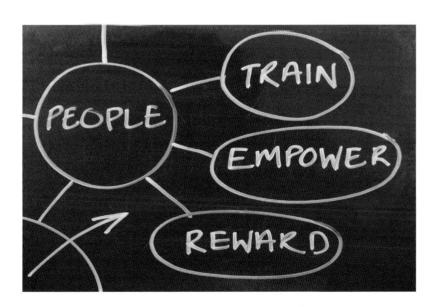

TABLE 1-1 The 10 Largest Retailers Based in the United States

Rank	Company	Web Address	Major Retail Emphasis	2015 U.S. Sales (millions)	2015 Number of U.S. Stores	2015 Worldwide Sales (millions)
1	Walmart	www.walmart.com	Full-line discount stores, supercenters, membership clubs	$353,108	5,182	$500,108
2	Kroger	www.kroger.com	Supermarkets, convenience stores, jewelry stores	103,878	3,747	103,878
3	Costco	www.costco.com	Membership clubs	83,545	476	116,671
4	Home Depot	www.homedepot.com	Home centers	79,297	1,965	88,621
5	Walgreen Boots Alliance	www.walgreens.com	Drugstores	76,604	8,052	92,670
6	Target	www.target.com	Full-line discount stores, supercenters	73,226	1,774	73,226
7	CVS Health	www.cvshealth.com	Drugstores	72,151	9,659	73,546
8	Amazon.com	www.amazon.com	Web merchant	61,619	N/A	104,060
9	Albertsons	www.albertsons.com	Supermarkets, drugstores	58,443	2,311	58,443
10	Lowe's	www.lowes.com	Home centers	57,486	1,805	59,051

Source: Based on material in David P. Schulz, "Stores Top 100 Retailers," *STORES Magazine* (July 2016). Reprinted by permission Copyright 2016. STORES Magazine.

The *Occupational Outlook Handbook* (www.bls.gov/oco) is a great source of information on employment trends.

Retailing is the largest private-sector employer in the United States. According to the National Retail Federation, anyone whose employment results in a consumer product—from those who supply raw materials to manufacturers to truck drivers who deliver goods—counts on retail for their livelihood. With 35 million stores and the vast number of suppliers, the retail industry is responsible for 42 million jobs, and $1.6 trillion in labor income, and it accounts for $2.6 trillion of the U.S. gross domestic product (GDP).[5]

From a cost perspective, retailing is a significant field of study. In the United States in 2015, on average, 36 cents of every dollar spent in department stores, 47 cents spent in women's apparel stores, and 28 cents spent in pharmacies and drugstores go to the retailers to cover operating costs, activities performed, and profits. Costs include rent, displays, wages, ads, and maintenance. Only a small part of each dollar is profit. Profit margins in the retail sector vary. Whereas audio/video and consumer electronics stores have pre-tax profit margins of 4.2 percent, the pre-tax profit margins averaged 2.1 percent for department stores in 2015.[6] In its fiscal year ending January 31, 2016, Walmart, the world's largest retailer, had after-tax profits of 3.1 percent of sales.[7] Figure 1-3 shows costs and profits for Walgreens Boots Alliance, an international drugstore chain.

  CAREERS IN RETAILING   Hiring from within Versus Best Person for the Job

Two opposing human resources strategies in retailing are (1) limiting promotions to only those working within the firm versus (2) recruiting personnel from competing companies. The promote-from-within strategy reduces employee turnover, encourages employee loyalty, and develops specific career paths for current employees. It also minimizes the difficulty in training new employees on company policies.

The hire-from-outside strategy seeks the best person for the position regardless of employment history with the given retailer. This strategy encourages firms to adopt new ways of thinking and enables a retailer to attract personnel with skills and contacts developed at their prior firms.

Under what conditions should a retailer use the hire-from-outside strategy? How can a retailer using this strategy reduce the poor morale from existing staff?

FIGURE 1-3

The High Costs and Low Profits of Retailing— Where the Typical $100 Spent with Walgreens Boots Alliance Goes

Source: Computed and estimated by the authors from *Walgreens Boots Alliance 2016 Reports.*

Manufacturer's costs and profits

Retailer's operating, personnel, advertising, and other costs

Retailer's income taxes

Retailer's after-tax profits

$73.92 $21.87 $0.79 $3.42

RETAIL FUNCTIONS IN DISTRIBUTION Retailing is the last stage in a **channel of distribution**—all the businesses and people involved in the physical movement and transfer of ownership of goods and services from producer to consumer. A typical distribution channel is shown in Figure 1-4. Retailers often act as the contact between manufacturers, wholesalers, and the consumer. Many manufacturers would like to make one basic type of item and sell their entire inventory to as few buyers as possible, but consumers usually want to choose from a variety of goods and services and purchase a limited quantity. Retailers collect an assortment from various sources, buy in large quantity, and sell in small amounts. This is the **sorting process**. See Figure 1-5.

Another job for retailers is communicating both with customers and with manufacturers and wholesalers. Shoppers learn about the availability and characteristics of goods and services, store hours, sales, and so on from retailer ads, salespeople, and displays. Manufacturers and wholesalers are informed by their retailers with regard to sales forecasts, delivery delays, customer complaints, defective items, inventory turnover, and more. Many goods and services have been modified due to retailer feedback.

For small suppliers, retailers can provide assistance by transporting, storing, marking, advertising, and pre-paying for products. Small retailers may need the same type of help from their suppliers. The tasks performed by retailers affect the percentage of each sales dollar they need to cover costs and profits.

Retailers also complete transactions with customers. This means having convenient locations, filling orders promptly and accurately, and processing credit purchases. Some retailers also provide customer services such as gift wrapping, delivery, and installation. To make themselves even more appealing, many firms now engage in **omnichannel retailing**, whereby a retailer sells to consumers through multiple retail formats (points of contact). Most large retailers operate both physical stores and Web sites to make shopping easier and to accommodate consumer desires. Some firms provide information and sell to customers through multiple touch points: retail stores, mail order, Web sites, tablets, smartphones, and a toll-free phone number. See Figure 1-6.

Sherwin-Williams (www .sherwin-williams.com) is not only a manufacturer but also a retailer.

For these reasons, products are usually sold through retailers not owned by manufacturers (wholesalers). This lets the manufacturers reach more customers, reduce costs, improve cash flow, increase sales more rapidly, and focus on their area of expertise. Select manufacturers, such

FIGURE 1-4

A Typical Channel of Distribution

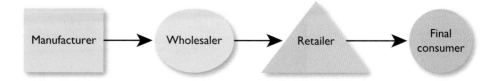

Manufacturer → Wholesaler → Retailer → Final consumer

FIGURE 1-5

The Retailer's Role in the Sorting Process

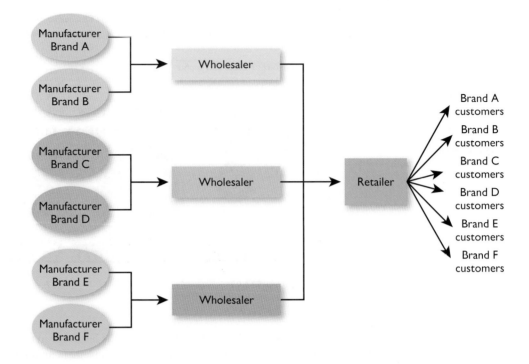

as Sherwin-Williams, Coach, and Nike, operate retail facilities (besides selling at independent retailers). In running their stores, these firms complete the full range of retailing functions and compete with conventional retailers.

THE RELATIONSHIPS AMONG RETAILERS AND THEIR SUPPLIERS Relationships among retailers and suppliers can be complex. Because retailers are part of a distribution channel, manufacturers and wholesalers must be concerned about the caliber of displays, customer service, store hours, and retailers' reliability as business partners. Retailers are also major customers of goods and services for resale, store fixtures, computers, management consulting, and insurance.

These are some issues over which retailers and their suppliers have different priorities: control over the distribution channel, profit allocation, the number of competing retailers handling suppliers' products, product displays, promotion support, payment terms, and operating flexibility. Due to the growth of large chains, retailers have more power than ever. Unless suppliers know retailer needs, they cannot have good rapport with them; so long as retailers have a choice of suppliers, they will choose those offering more.

FIGURE 1-6

The Multiple Retail Channels of WOM (World of Music)

WOM (World of Music) is a German-based retailer with physical facilities and a strong online presence https://wom.de/?lang=en). It offers many genres of music CDs and DVDs, movies, books, games, sheet music, and more—and even ships to the United States.

Source: Jules Selmes/Pearson Education Ltd. Reprinted by permission.

Channel relations tend to be smoothest with **exclusive distribution**, whereby suppliers make agreements with one or a few retailers that designate the latter as the only ones in specified geographic areas to carry certain brands or products. This stimulates both parties to work together to maintain an image, assign shelf space, allot profits and costs, and advertise. It also usually requires that retailers limit their brand selection in the specified product lines; they might have to decline to handle other suppliers' brands. From the manufacturers' perspective, exclusive distribution may limit their long-run total sales.

Channel relations tend to be most volatile with **intensive distribution**, whereby suppliers sell through as many retailers as possible. This often maximizes suppliers' sales and lets retailers offer many brands and product versions. Competition among retailers selling the same items is high; retailers may use tactics not beneficial to individual suppliers, because they are more concerned about their own results. Retailers may assign little space to specific brands, set very high prices on them, and not advertise them.

With **selective distribution**, suppliers sell through a moderate number of retailers. This combines aspects of exclusive and intensive distribution. Suppliers have higher sales than in exclusive distribution, and retailers carry some competing brands. It encourages suppliers to provide some marketing support and retailers to give adequate shelf space. See Figure 1-7.

The Special Characteristics of Retailing

Three factors that most differentiate retailing from other types of business are noted in Figure 1-8 and discussed here. Each factor imposes unique requirements on retail firms.

The average amount of a sales transaction for retailers is much less than for manufacturers. The average sales per customer transaction in retailing is low. The average supermarket transaction is about $30.00.[8] In comparison, Home Depot's average sales transaction in 2015 was $58.55.[9] The average sales transaction per shopping trip is well under $100 for department stores and specialty stores. This low amount creates a need to tightly control the costs associated with each transaction (such as credit verification, sales personnel, and bagging); to maximize the number of customers drawn to the retailer, which may place more emphasis on ads and special promotions; and to increase impulse sales by more aggressive selling. However, cost control can be tough. For instance, inventory management is often expensive due to the many small transactions to a large number of customers. A typical supermarket has several thousand customer transactions *per week,* which makes it harder to find the proper in-stock level and product selection. Thus, retailers are expanding their use of computerized inventory systems.

FIGURE 1-7

Comparing Exclusive, Intensive, and Selective Distribution

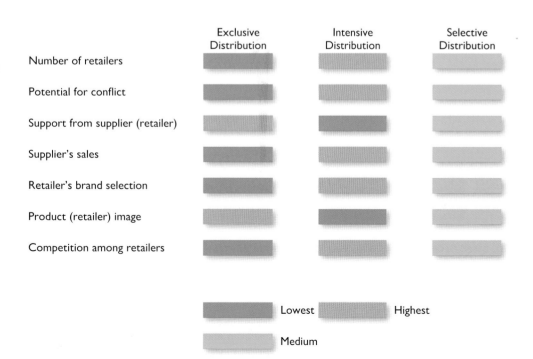

FIGURE 1-8
Special Characteristics Affecting Retailers

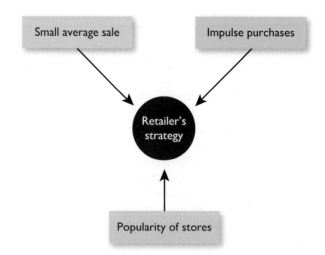

Final consumers make many unplanned or impulse purchases. Surveys show that a large percentage of consumers do not look at ads before shopping, do not prepare shopping lists (or do deviate from the lists once in stores), and make fully unplanned purchases. This behavior indicates the value of in-store displays, attractive store layouts, and well-organized stores, catalogs, and Web sites. Candy, cosmetics, snack foods, magazines, and other items are sold as impulse goods when placed in visible, high-traffic areas in a store, catalog, or Web site. Because so many purchases are unplanned, the retailer's ability to forecast, budget, order merchandise, and have sufficient personnel on the selling floor is more difficult.

Macy's (www.macys .com) has a Web site to accompany its traditional stores and catalogs.

Despite the inroads made by nonstore retailers, most retail transactions (more than 90 percent) are still conducted in stores—and will continue to be in the future. Many people like to shop in person; want to touch, smell, and/or try on products; enjoy browsing for unplanned purchases; feel more comfortable taking a purchase home with them than waiting for a delivery; and desire privacy while at home. This store-based shopping orientation has implications for retailers; they must work to attract shoppers to stores and consider such factors as store location, transportation, store hours, proximity of competitors, product selection, parking, and ads.

THE IMPORTANCE OF DEVELOPING AND APPLYING A RETAIL STRATEGY

A **retail strategy** is the overall plan guiding a retail firm. It influences the firm's business activities and its response to market forces, such as competition and the economy. Any retailer, regardless of size or type, should utilize these six steps in strategic planning:

1. Define the type of business in terms of the goods or service category and the company's specific orientation (such as full service or "no frills").
2. Set long-run and short-run objectives for sales and profit, market share, image, and so on.

RETAILING AROUND THE WORLD

Debenhams Goes East: The Continuing Expansion of the UK Department Store Retailer

UK-based Debenhams has 248 department stores in 28 countries. It is actively looking to expand its overseas business to around 30 percent of its total business. It is achieving this through a combination of franchise expansion, enhanced distribution, and online sales. Debenhams opened its largest global franchise store in Abu Dhabi and its largest-ever store in Moscow. In 2016, Debenhams focused on the Australian and Vietnamese markets. In Australia, they partnered with Pepkor and in Vietnam with VinDS. Debenhams is targeting key markets in Northern Europe, Central Europe, the Middle East, and the Far East.

Identify examples of large or emerging markets in your region that are either weak or under-represented in terms of department stores. Identify likely franchise partners.

3. Determine the customer market to target on the basis of its characteristics (such as gender and income level) and needs (such as product and brand preferences).
4. Devise an overall, long-run plan that gives general direction to the firm and its employees.
5. Implement an integrated strategy that combines such factors as store location, product assortment, pricing, and advertising and displays to achieve objectives.
6. Regularly evaluate performance and correct weaknesses or problems when observed.

To illustrate these points, the background and strategy of the Home Depot Corporation—one of the world's foremost retailers—are presented. Then the retailing concept is explained and applied.

The Home Depot Corporation: Successfully Navigating the Omnichannel Landscape[10]

See the target marketing approach of Home Depot (www.homedepot.com).

COMPANY BACKGROUND Home Depot is the world's largest home improvement retail chain and the ninth largest retailer globally in terms of revenues. It was established in 1978 by Bernie Marcus (a pharmacist by training), Arthur Blank (educated as an accountant), Ken Langone (an investment banker), and Pat Farrah (who had a merchandising background). The first two Home Depot stores opened on June 22, 1979, in Atlanta, Georgia, with the vision of "one-stop shopping for the do-it-yourselfer." Today, Home Depot operates nearly 2,275 stores with over 370,000 employees in the United States, Canada, Mexico, Puerto Rico, Virgin Islands, and Guam—as well as an online business.

Home Depot targets the do-it-yourself (DIY) and professional contractor markets with its selection of 40,000 to 600,000 SKUs (stock-keeping units, or machine-readable barcodes), including lumber, flooring, plumbing supplies, garden products, tools, paint, and appliances. Home Depot also offers installation services for carpeting, cabinetry, and other products. The Home Depot went public in 1981, experienced tremendous growth in the 1980s and 1990s, and celebrated the opening of its 100th store in 1989. One-third of Home Depot's total sales in FY 2016 came from California, Florida, New York, and Texas.

Home Depot seeks to provide excellent customer service through consistent high-quality products, customer service, and competitive pricing. Accordingly, every customer has a bill of rights at Home Depot, and this entitles the customer to the right assortment, quantities, and prices, along with trained associates on the sales floor who want to take care of customers. Home Depot's vision is driven by a set of eight core values: excellent customer service, building strong relationships, taking care of its employees, giving back, doing the "right" thing, creating shareholder value, respecting all people, and exhibiting entrepreneurial spirit.

THE HOME DEPOT CORPORATION'S STRATEGY: KEYS TO SUCCESS Throughout its existence, Home Depot has adhered to a consistent, far-sighted, customer-oriented strategy—one that has paved the way for its long-term achievements.

GROWTH STRATEGY Home Depot's current strategy of product authority (continually analyzing customer data to better understand consumer preferences), providing a seamless and friction-free experience no matter where customers shop, and investing to build a best-in-class supply chain network support its dominant position in its industry. Disciplined capital allocation, continuous optimization of productivity, and efficient operations allow Home Depot to lower its operating costs and increase shareholder wealth.

Although the company operates in markets that are highly competitive in terms of customer service, store location, price, and quality, Home Depot has the resources to compete on the basis of price, service, and product variety. Competitors include major chains such as Lowe's, Menard, True Value, Ace Hardware, and numerous local retailers. It also faces competition from pure-online retailers—for example, Amazon—as it moves into adjacent product categories in its quest for growth.

TARGETED APPEAL TO MULTIPLE SEGMENTS Home Depot serves three major market segments:

1. Do-it-yourself customers are mostly homeowners and end-users who purchase products to complete their projects and repairs by themselves.
2. Do-it-for-me customers are homeowners who purchase their products and hire a third party to complete their repairs and projects. To these customers, Home Depot is able to offer installation programs and design services on carpets, countertops, home appliances, and many others.

3. Professional customers are general contractors, repair people, and small business owners. To these customers, Home Depot offers value-added services such as dedicated staff, designated parking, and bulk pricing. This segment accounts for one-third of sales revenues and represents a more recurring and larger sales opportunity compared to the first two retail customer segments.

DISTINCTIVE COMPANY IMAGE Home Depot communicates its vision and image as a one-stop shopping experience for the do-it-yourselfer through the extensive width and depth of its product portfolio and its store size. Its first stores in Atlanta, Georgia, at around 60,000 square feet each, were cavernous warehouses that dwarfed the competition and stocked 25,000 SKUs (much more than the average hardware store at that time). Empty boxes piled high on the shelves gave the illusion of even more depth in inventory. Although Home Depot still leverages its store size as a competitive advantage, it is losing its importance in the omnichannel marketplace. Stores of various sizes are continuously redesigned to allow customers to interact more with products and to allow the chain to more efficiently stock products.

"Big Orange" is the nickname by which Home Depot is known all over the world. The bright orange logo was inspired by crates used to transport freight, keeping in line with the "depot" theme. Stamped at an upright angle to symbolize success and in bright orange to help simulate activity, the logo appears on signs, equipment, and employee aprons. The Home Depot introduced the slogan "More saving. More doing" in the March 18, 2009, circular, replacing "You can do it. We can help" which had been used since 2003. Another slogan used in the past 25 years is "The Home Depot, Low prices are just the beginning" in the early 1990s. The company advertises through TV, flyers, radio, online, and social and mobile media.

STRONG CUSTOMER SERVICE FOR ITS RETAIL CATEGORY Home Depot's philosophy of customer service—"whatever it takes"—means cultivating a relationship with customers rather than merely completing a transaction. The founders define themselves to be "in the people business." From the start, associates offered excellent customer service, guiding customers through projects. After undergoing rigorous product knowledge training, store associates began offering clinics so customers could learn how to do it themselves. The Home Depot revolutionized the home improvement industry by bringing the know-how and the tools to the consumer, thus *empowering* them and saving them money.

MULTIPLE POINTS OF CONTACT Home Depot reaches its customers through extensive advertising, stores in 49 states, a toll-free telephone service center (open 7 days a week, 17 hours a day), a Web site, and the use of Facebook, Twitter, LinkedIn, Pinterest, and other social-media sites. The retailer has applied the same customer service philosophy to its multichannel initiatives. The E-commerce channel is an increasingly vital sales driver for Home Depot, accounting for nearly 7.2 percent of overall sales revenues. Despite the many advantages of Web-only sales, Home Depot was early in recognizing that brick-and-mortar stores play a vital role in driving conversion rates. Stores often double as fulfillment centers. About 40 percent of Web site (homedepot .com) orders are fulfilled through its stores. Millions of deliveries are made from stores each year.

Three multichannel programs enable Home Depot to effectively leverage its store network: buy online, ship to store (BOSS); buy online, pick up in store (BOPIS); and buy online, return in store (BORIS). These omnichannel initiatives enable quicker order pickups and returns, reduce customer time, and save on storage and costs. Its fastest growing E-commerce channel is BOPIS. E-commerce sales also have a higher average ticket size than the average $55 to $65 in-store purchases, and a higher percentage of BOPIS sales also tends to improve store productivity metrics. Orders placed online and delivered to a purchaser's home have the largest average ticket size because these orders typically consist of bulkier items that cannot be picked up in the store and are far more costly than smaller items typically purchased in a store.

EMPLOYEE RELATIONS Home Depot employed 385,000 associates as of the beginning of 2016. Employees are expected to share the same vision as Home Depot. Employees are provided with many in-house workshops, such as "customers-first" training program and company-sponsored programs, to give associates a better understanding of their products and services. Home Depot believes its employees are satisfied with the compensation and offers employees the opportunity to purchase stock options at a discounted price. Employees are also eligible for medical, dental, vision, and life insurance—depending on their status and tenure at the company.

INNOVATION   The home improvement industry experiences continuous innovation. Home Depot introduces new products and services, such as 3D printing, thus allowing it to adapt to the change in equipment and consumer preferences. Home Depot's focus on solving customer problems has been a source of innovation and strategic movement into adjacent markets for services by providing design and installation services for its products as well as third-party resellers, equipment rental (e.g., carpet cleaning, small trucks to transport equipment), and home inspection products (water, air quality and radiation).

Home Depot collaborates with new and existing manufacturers to enable it to be a one-stop-shopping destination for home improvement products. It recently broadened the number of brands it offers in its appliances department by including Whirlpool, Frigidaire, and Electrolux. Additionally, it also introduced innovative new products to its DIY and professional customers in most of its departments.

COMMITMENT TO TECHNOLOGY   Home Depot has consistently invested in backend, as well as customer-interactive, technologies. It currently operates 18 remote distribution centers in the United States, and 33 bulk distribution centers within the United States, Canada, and Mexico. The company continuously updates its distribution centers through building logistic competencies and improving its inventory management system. Over the past few years, Home Depot has centralized its inventory planning and implemented new forecasting technology. Currently, 91 percent of its U.S. store products are ordered through a central replenishment system and it hopes to increase the number in the coming years.

Home Depot is successfully implementing three multiyear internal initiatives: (1) *ProjectSync*—a major supply chain synchronization to reduce average lead time from supplier to shelf; (2) *COM*—Home Depot's order management platform, which provides greater visibility into and improved execution of special orders for a more seamless and friction-free experience for customers; and (3) *FIRST phones*—in-store mobile enablement for inventory management, product look-up, and business analytics. It even offers line-busting features to speed up checkout for associates and customers.

COMMUNITY INVOLVEMENT   Home Depot believes in creating shareholder value while being responsible and balancing the needs of its communities. Through The Home Depot Foundation, community impact grants, and associates' volunteer time, the retailer strives to have a positive impact on communities in the United States, Canada, and Mexico. It invites community participation in practical and educational programs in stores that benefit children and adults. The commitment to environmental sustainability is demonstrated through its sale of energy-efficient and sustainable products, recycling practices, and business principles. Home Depot promotes an environmentally friendly atmosphere by protecting its employees' health and safety requirements. It has also created a supplier social responsibility program intended to ensure that suppliers observe a high standard of social responsibility.

ADAPTATION TO A GLOBAL, OMNICHANNEL WORLD   Due to the difficult economic, political, and social conditions in recent years, even outstanding retailers, such as Home Depot, have been affected. In 2012, Home Depot closed all seven of its stores in China.

The company outsources some of its products from third-party manufacturers in third-world countries with unstable political environments. It may be exposed to trade embargos, increases in tariff rates, different tax regulations, and double taxation by the countries that do not have respective treaties in place to avoid double taxes. Yet, many governments in these countries may have incentive programs applicable for Home Depot as an employer of local labor.

Home Depot has capitalized on the digitization in retailing by enabling a secure multichannel shopping experience—mobile, in-store, at home, or even on the job site. Its global sales revenues have grown substantially to almost $89 billion in fiscal 2016, and its operating income increased by 12 percent from the prior year to reach $11.8 billion. Home Depot's performance was boosted by the demand for home improvement products, a better housing market, and rising consumer employment.

Growth in the number of big-ticket transactions boosted sales. The company's multiyear productivity enhancement plan also provided some profitability upside. The Home Depot has been one of the best-performing stocks in the consumer discretionary sector and the Dow Jones Industrial Average over the past five years. The stock returned an annualized average of 28.5 percent—almost three times that provided by the S&P 500 Index's 9.6 percent over the same period.

FIGURE 1-9
**Applying the
Retailing Concept**

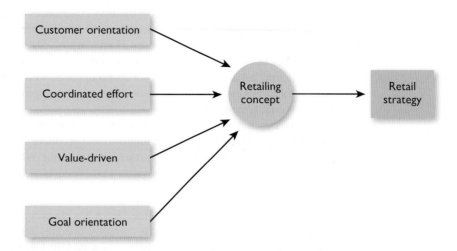

Although the strong U.S. dollar affected Home Depot's sales growth in the Canadian and Mexican markets, they account for 10 percent of overall sales and are less significant. CEO Craig Menear has ambitious goals for FY 2018; his target is $101 billion in sales, with a 14.5 percent operating margin and a 35 percent return on invested capital. In 2015, Home Depot acquired Interline Brands, whose product portfolio of home repair and maintenance products is complementary to Home Depot's offerings in home remodeling products and is largely viewed as a good strategic fit. Home Depot expects additional revenue from existing customers' purchase of repair and maintenance products, which are recurring purchases, and a sales upside from Interline Brands' customer base, which will get a tremendous boost from Home Depot's E-commerce capabilities.

The Retailing Concept

As just described, Home Depot has a sincere long-term desire to please customers. It uses a customer-centered, chainwide approach to strategy development and implementation, is value-driven, and has clear goals. Together, these four principles form the **retailing concept** (depicted in Figure 1-9), which should be understood and applied by all retailers:

1. *Customer orientation.* The retailer determines the attributes and needs of its customers and endeavors to satisfy these needs to the fullest.
2. *Coordinated effort.* The retailer integrates all plans and activities to maximize efficiency.
3. *Value driven.* The retailer offers good value to customers, whether it be upscale or discount. This means having prices appropriate for the level of products and customer service.
4. *Goal orientation.* The retailer sets goals and then uses its strategy to attain them.

Unfortunately, this concept is not grasped by every retailer. Some are indifferent to customer needs, plan haphazardly, have prices that do not reflect the value offered, and have unclear goals. Some are not receptive to change, or they blindly follow strategies enacted by competitors. Some do not get feedback from customers; they rely on supplier reports or their own past sales trends.

ETHICS IN RETAILING | Environmental Sustainability |

Suppose a large supermarket chain is revising its approach regarding environmental sustainability. Hallmarks of the new strategy are to encourage customers to purchase reusable plastic shopping bags (available at cost at all registers); to use high-efficiency lighting, heating, and air-conditioning systems; and to reformulate its private-label products to have minimal negative environmental impact (such as selling grains and nuts via bins instead of prepackaged bottles). The chain plans to heavily promote this strategy via in-store displays, through its Web site, and in its freestanding inserts that are distributed by local newspapers.

Aside from the positive societal impact, the store sees several advantages to this strategy. One, it will appeal to shoppers concerned with environmental responsibility. Two, this environmental strategy can position the store favorably with respect to competition. And three, the societal strategy is an excellent way to reposition its private-label products versus national brands.

Discuss additional pros and cons of this strategy.

The retailing concept is straightforward. It means communicating with shoppers and viewing their desires as critical to the firm's success; having a consistent strategy (such as offering designer brands, plentiful sales personnel, attractive displays, and above-average prices in an upscale store); offering prices perceived as "fair" (a good value for the money) by customers; and working to achieve meaningful, specific, and reachable goals. However, the retailing concept is only a strategic guide. It does not deal with a firm's internal capabilities or competitive advantages but offers a broad planning framework.

Let's look at three issues that relate to a retailer's performance in terms of the retailing concept: the total retail experience, customer service, and relationship retailing.

THE TOTAL RETAIL EXPERIENCE   The rapid adoption of E-commerce and the proliferation of smart mobile devices makes it seem possible to *purchase anything, anytime, and have it delivered anywhere.* Such thinking has fundamentally changed consumers' shopping habits and expectations. Almost every customer encounters a total retail experience in his or her retail journey. Imagine using a mobile app to purchase a refrigerator while attending a ball game. By the time you get home, the refrigerator has been scheduled for delivery. Everything, from the activation of the mobile app to receiving the purchase at home, plays a role in the customer's total retail experience.

Most retailers are aware that price has been, and always will be, a key motivator in shopping behavior. It is important for retailers to remember, however, that they must provide an appropriate customer experience at every touchpoint with the customer to sustain her or his continued loyalty. More than ever, shopping is about how to "engage" the customer and how the shopping experience makes the customer feel. It is also about driving customer engagement in new and different ways to deliver relevant experiences that customers can share with others on social media. The shift in consumer expectations is compelling retailers to look at aspects of "who" as opposed to "what" they want to be—the competition is now for share of lifetime spending, as opposed to share of wallet.[11] Retailers with genuine character and interest in listening to and solving their customers' needs, core values, and concern for community are likely to profit the most.

The **total retail experience** includes all the elements in a retail offering that encourage or inhibit consumers during their contact or journey with a retailer. See Figure 1-10. Many elements, such as the number of salespeople, displays, prices, brand names, mobile app or Web page design, accurate product and pricing information, and inventory on hand, are controllable by a retailer. Others, such as the adequacy of parking, the speed of a consumer's Internet connection, and sales taxes, are not. If some part of the total retail experience is unsatisfactory,

FIGURE 1-10

Creating a Unique Shopping Experience

At this Hong Kong shopping center, an exciting and distinctive customer experience was formed by featuring an enormous dinosaur skeleton in the middle of the shopping center.

Source: Cheuk-king Lo/ Pearson Education Ltd. Reprinted by permission.

consumers may be "turned off" and not make a purchase—they may even decide not to patronize a retailer again if they attribute the failure to be controllable by the retailer. Given the widespread use of mobile devices in-store and the propensity to share information, one bad retail experience can be quickly shared with many other current and potential consumers via social media.

In planning its strategy, a retailer must be sure that all strategic elements are in place. For the shopper segment to which it appeals, the total retail experience must be aimed at fulfilling that segment's expectations. A discounter should have ample stock on hand when it runs sales but not plush carpeting; a full-service store should have superior personnel but not personnel who are perceived as haughty by customers. Various retailers have not learned this lesson, which is why some theme restaurants are in trouble. The novelty has worn off, and many people believe the food is only fair while prices are high.

A big challenge for retailers is generating customer "excitement" because many people are bored with shopping or have little time for it. For example, Build-A-Bear Workshop is the leading and only global company that offers an interactive make-your-own stuffed animal retail-entertainment experience. The company currently operates more than 400 Build-A-Bear Workshop stores worldwide, including company-owned stores in the United States, Puerto Rico, Canada, Great Britain, and Ireland, and franchise stores in Europe, Asia, Australia, Africa, Mexico, and the Middle East.

Since 2007, the interactive experience has been enhanced—all the way to CyBEAR® space—with the launch of Bearville.com, its entertainment destination and virtual world. In September 2015, Build-A-Bear Workshop launched a new store format and brand refresh as a "multigenerational" brand for millennial parents who first engaged with Build-A-Bear Workshop when they were children.

Guests who visit a Build-A-Bear Workshop store still enter a recognizable and distinctive teddy-bear–themed environment consisting of eight stuffed animal-making stations: Choose Me, Hear Me, Stuff Me, Stitch Me, Fluff Me, Dress Me, Name Me, and Take Me Home. Store associates, known as Master Bear Builder associates, can share the experience with guests at each phase of the bear-making process or they can do it for the guests.[12] In addition, guests can enjoy the brand's "play beyond the plush" with entertainment offerings such as the Bearville Alive YouTube channel, which features original video content and the launch of mobile apps tied to complementary products (an enterprise-selling solution), and creates the memories with their friends and family that they can share through social media.[13]

Build-A-Bear Workshop (www.buildabear.com) even offers a great online shopping experience.

CUSTOMER SERVICE **Customer service** refers to the identifiable, but sometimes intangible, activities undertaken by a retailer in conjunction with the basic goods and services it sells. It has a strong impact on the total retail experience. Among the factors comprising a customer service strategy are store hours, parking, shopper-friendly store layout, credit acceptance, helpful salespeople, amenities such as gift wrapping, clean restrooms, reasonable delivery policies, the time shoppers spend in checkout lines, and customer follow-up. This list is not all-inclusive, and it differs in terms of the retail strategy undertaken. Customer service is discussed further in Chapter 2.

At Lands' End (www.landsend.com), customer service means "Guaranteed. Period."

Satisfaction with customer service is affected by expectations (based on the type of retailer) and past experience. People's assessment of customer service depends on their perceptions—not necessarily reality; different people may evaluate the same service quite differently. The same person may even rate a firm's customer service differently over time due to its intangibility, although the service stays constant. Interestingly, despite a desire to provide excellent customer service, a number of outstanding retailers now wonder if "the customer is always right." Are there limits?

RELATIONSHIP RETAILING The best retailers know it is in their interest to engage in **relationship retailing**, whereby they seek to establish and maintain long-term bonds with customers, rather than act as if each sales transaction is a completely new encounter. This means concentrating on the total retail experience, monitoring satisfaction with customer service, and staying in touch with customers. Figure 1-11 shows a customer respect checklist that retailers could use to assess their relationship efforts.

As do the retailers profiled in this book, we want to engage in relationship retailing. So please visit our blog (www.bermanevansretail.com).

To be effective in relationship retailing, a firm should keep two points in mind. First, it is harder to lure new customers than to make existing ones happy; a "win–win" approach is critical. For a retailer to "win" in the long run (attract shoppers, make sales, earn profits), the customer

FIGURE 1-11

A Customer Respect Checklist

✓ When interacting with customers, do employees always say "How may I help you," "Please," and "Thank you"?

✓ Are employees properly trained to service the retailer's customers?

✓ Do employees listen carefully when customers state their preferences and not push goods and services that are beyond the shoppers' interest or budget?

✓ Are employees patient and not condescending when talking to customers?

✓ Is the customer's time valued?

✓ Do the hours that the retailer is open correspond with the hours sought by customers?

✓ Do the retailer and its employees honor all promises that are made to customers—and strive not to mislead shoppers?

✓ Do employees avoid being confrontational with customers if the latter make a complaint about merchandise or service?

✓ Are customer phone calls, E-mails, and other contacts with the retailer directed to the right employees and handled promptly?

✓ For a retailer that operates both store and online businesses, are policies clearly stated and distinctions between the two formats with regard to purchase, shipping, and return policies noted in the store and online?

✓ Does the retailer monitor online customer reviews and social media discussions and work to resolve any problems that are noted there?

✓ Does the retailer treat every customer respectfully, regardless of age, gender, race, ethnicity, and other factors?

✓ Does the retailer recognize and reward its most loyal customers?

✓ Does the retailer's employee review process include how well the employees are rated by customers?

must also "win" in the short run (receive good value, be treated with respect, feel welcome by the firm). Otherwise, that retailer loses (shoppers patronize competitors) and those customers lose (by spending time and money to learn about other retailers). Second, due to advances in computer technology, it is now much easier to develop a customer database with information on people's attributes and past shopping behavior. Ongoing customer contact can be better, more frequent, and more focused. This topic is covered further in Chapter 2.

TECHNOLOGY IN RETAILING   Generating Location-Sensitive Offers

Newer technologies such as GPS navigation, Global System for Mobiles (GSM), Bluetooth, and RFID tracking now enable retailers to track the exact location of a customer. "Geofencing" technology works outside the store, whereas "iBeacons" allow retailers to target a customer within a store.

The various advantages to a retailer that uses these technologies are plentiful. From a promotional perspective, a retailer can send a mobile coupon valid for three hours to a lapsed customer who had not purchased an item within 30 days. With iBeacons, customers receive targeted information based on their aisle position in a store. Thus, a shopper could receive a mobile coupon for a cereal brand when in the cereal aisle. Unlike traditional coupons that must be clipped and returned; mobile coupons can be scanned from smartphones.

Discuss three other retailer uses of location-sensitive technology-based promotions.

THE FOCUS AND FORMAT OF THE TEXT

There are various approaches to the study of retailing: an institutional approach, which describes the types of retailers and their development; a functional approach, which concentrates on the activities that retailers perform (such as buying, pricing, and personnel practices); and a strategic approach, which centers on defining the retail business, setting objectives, appealing to an appropriate customer market, developing an overall plan, implementing an integrated strategy, and regularly reviewing operations.

We will study retailing from each perspective but will focus on a *strategic approach*. Our basic premise is that the retailer has to plan for and adapt to a complex, changing environment. Opportunities as well as threats must be considered. By engaging in strategic retail management, the retailer is encouraged to study competitors, suppliers, economic factors, consumer changes, marketplace trends, legal restrictions, and other issues. A firm prospers if its competitive strengths match the opportunities in the environment, weaknesses are eliminated or minimized, and plans look to the future (as well as the past). Refer to the appendix at the end of this chapter; it examines the impact of the current economic situation on retailers and consumers alike.

Retail Management: A Strategic Approach is divided into eight parts. The rest of Part One looks at building relationships and strategic planning in retailing. Part Two examines retailing institutions on the basis of their ownership; store-based strategy mix; and Web, nonstore-based, and other nontraditional retailing formats. Part Three deals with consumer behavior and information gathering in retailing. Parts Four through Seven discuss the specific elements of a retailing strategy: planning the store location; managing a retail business; planning, handling, and pricing merchandise; and communicating with the customer. Part Eight shows how a retailing strategy may be integrated, analyzed, and improved. These topics have special end-of-chapter appendices: the impact of the economy (Chapter 1), service retailing (Chapter 2), global retailing (Chapter 3), franchising (Chapter 4), and multichannel retailing (Chapter 6). There is also an end-of-text appendix on retailing careers and a glossary.

To underscore retailing's exciting nature, four real-world boxes appear in each chapter: "Careers in Retailing," "Ethics in Retailing," "Retailing Around the World," and "Technology in Retailing."

Chapter Summary

In this and every chapter, the summary is related to the objectives stated at the beginning of the chapter.

1. *To define retailing, consider it from various perspectives, demonstrate its impact, and note its special characteristics.* Retailing comprises the business activities involved in selling goods and services to consumers for personal, family, or household use. It is the last stage in the distribution process. Today, retailing is at a complex crossroad, with many challenges ahead.

Retailing may be viewed from multiple perspectives. It includes tangible and intangible items, does not have to involve a store, and can be done by manufacturers and others—as well as retailers.

Annual U.S. store sales are approaching $5 trillion, with other forms of retailing accounting for hundreds of billions of dollars more. The world's 250 largest retailers account for more than $4.6 trillion in yearly revenues. About 15 million people in the United States work for retailers (including food and beverage service firms), which understates the number of those actually employed in a retailing capacity. Retail firms receive up to 40 cents or more of every sales dollar as compensation for operating costs, the functions performed, and the profits earned.

Retailing encompasses all of the businesses and people involved in physically moving and transferring ownership of goods and services from producer to consumer. In a distribution channel, retailers perform valuable functions as the contact for manufacturers, wholesalers, and final consumers. They collect assortments from various suppliers and offer them to customers. Retailers also communicate with both customers and other channel members. They may ship, store, mark, advertise, and pre-pay for items. In addition, they complete transactions with customers and often provide customer services. They may also offer multiple formats (multichannel retailing) to facilitate shopping.

Retailers and their suppliers have complex relationships because retailers serve in two capacities. They are part of

CHAPTER 1 • AN INTRODUCTION TO RETAILING   **39**

a distribution channel aimed at the final consumer, and they are major customers for suppliers. Channel relations are smoothest with exclusive distribution; they are most volatile with intensive distribution. Selective distribution is a way to balance sales goals and channel cooperation.

Retailing has several special characteristics. The average sales transaction is small, consumers make many unplanned purchases, and most customers visit a store location.

2. *To introduce the concept of strategic planning and apply it.* A retail strategy is the overall plan guiding the firm. It has six basic steps: defining the business, setting objectives, defining the customer market, developing an overall plan, enacting an integrated strategy, and evaluating performance and making modifications. For example, Home Depot's strategy has been particularly well designed and enacted, even though it has been affected by the tough economy in recent years.

3. *To show why the retailing concept is the foundation of a successful business, with an emphasis on the total retail experience, customer service, and relationship retailing.*

The retailing concept should be understood and used by all retailers. It requires a firm to have a customer orientation, use a coordinated effort, and be value driven and goal oriented. Despite its straightforward nature, many firms do not adhere to one or more elements of the retailing concept.

The total retail experience consists of all elements in a retail offering that encourage or inhibit consumers during their contact with a retailer. Some elements are controllable by the retailer; others are not. Customer service includes identifiable, but sometimes intangible, activities undertaken by a retailer in association with the basic goods and services sold. It has an effect on the total retail experience. In relationship retailing, a firm seeks long-term bonds with customers rather than acting as if each sales transaction is a totally new encounter with them.

4. *To indicate the focus and format of the text.* Retailing may be studied by using an institutional approach, a functional approach, and/or a strategic approach. Although all three approaches are covered in this textbook, our focus is on the strategic approach. The underlying principle is that a retail firm needs to plan for and adapt to a complex, changing environment.

Key Terms

retailing (p. 23)
channel of distribution (p. 27)
sorting process (p. 27)
omnichannel retailing (p. 27)

exclusive distribution (p. 29)
intensive distribution (p. 29)
selective distribution (p. 29)
retail strategy (p. 30)

retailing concept (p. 34)
total retail experience (p. 35)
customer service (p. 36)
relationship retailing (p. 36)

Questions for Discussion

1. What is the average amount that you spend in a retail store per transaction? What factors are likely to influence your supermarket transaction spend compared to other retailing spending?
2. Why might a supplier opt for exclusive channel distribution with retailers?
3. Why might a new manufacturer want their products to be sold in the maximum number of retail outlets? Is this a good idea?
4. One retailer wants to be part of a selective distribution channel. Another wants to be part of an exclusive distribution channel. What might be the reasons for these choices?
5. Describe how the special characteristics of retailing offer unique opportunities and problems for local gift shops.
6. What is the purpose of developing a formal retail strategy? How could a strategic plan be used by a restaurant chain?

7. What are the six key steps of strategic planning that should be used by a retailer?
8. Explain the retailing concept. Apply it to your school's bookstore.
9. Define the term *total retail experience.* Then describe a recent retail situation in which your expectations were surpassed, and state why.
10. Do you believe that customer service in retailing is improving or declining? Why?
11. How could a small Web-only retailer engage in relationship retailing?
12. What checklist item(s) in Figure 1-11 do you think would be most difficult for Home Depot, the global home improvement retailer, to address? Why?

Web-Based Exercise

Visit the website of *Global Retailing* (http://globalretailmag.com/). Describe the elements of the site and give several examples of what you could learn there.

APPENDIX Understanding the Recent Economic Environment in the United States and Around the Globe

In this appendix, we present a brief overview of the U.S. and global economic climate. We then discuss some of the strategic options that retailers are pursuing and should pursue to sustain their business amid the current economic conditions.

The Current Economic Situation in the United States

In 2016, the Census Bureau reported that the average U.S. family's income was $57,243.When adjusted for inflation, the median income level was 1.3 percent lower than its high in January 2008, but well above its low in August 2011.[1] Median income has climbed since the August 2011 low point. A significant factor in the increase in real income is low prices for energy, gasoline, and heat.

The percentage of Americans living in poverty is about 15 percent of the population as of 2014, nearly 1 million Americans.[2] Especially noteworthy has been the growing gap between the "best-off" and "worst-off" Americans. The Pew Research Center found that the percentage of adults in the highest-income groups grew from 14 percent in 1971 to 21 percent in 2015. During the same time, the percentage of households in the lowest two categories increased from 25 to 29 percent. And middle-income households as a percentage of all households declined from 61 percent to 50 percent over the same time interval.[3]

One widely accepted measure of income inequality is the Gini index, which ranges from zero (if all households have the same earnings) to 100 (when all income goes to one person). The U.S. Gini index is 45.0, which is in the same range as Jamaica (45.5), Peru (45.3), and Cameroon (44.6).[4] Countries with a more equal distribution of income as shown by their Gini indices include Sweden (24.9), Denmark (24.8), Ukraine (24.6), and Slovenia (23.7). The distribution of wealth in the United States is even more unequal. An Organization for Economic Co-operation and Development (OECD) report study found that the wealthiest 10 percent of all U.S. households account for 76 percent of all the wealth in the country.[5]

As of 2016, the U.S. unemployment rate was 4.9 percent. This rate is low, but it must be tempered with some additional insights. First, only 63 percent of adult Americans are in the labor force. This low labor force participation rate is due to large numbers of Baby Boomers who have retired, younger residents attending college or graduate school, and people giving up on finding work. Second, long-term unemployment is high, as 2.1 million U.S. residents have been unemployed for over 6 months.[6] And third, the 4.9 percent unemployment rate does not reflect those who are no longer seeking employment or those underemployed (such as being in a part-time job).

The personal savings rate, the percent of each paycheck that is not spent, was at 5.4 percent as of the end of April 2016. Because consumer spending constituted 68.5 percent of the U.S. economy in the fourth quarter of 2015 (up from 65.3 percent at the end of 2000), this is an important number to monitor.[7] Historically, the savings rate has varied from 4.6 percent as of the end of January 2013 to 5.9 percent as of the end of March 2016. At the end of December 2012, the savings rate was 6.5 percent.[8] The low savings rate highlights the role of the consumer as an important factor in economic growth.

As of May 2016, consumer confidence, measured by the University of Michigan's Index of Consumer Sentiment was 94.7. There were only four months since its January 2007 peak in which this number was higher. One reason for the higher consumer optimism is the continuing anticipation of low inflation due to low interest rates.[9] Better consumer confidence is generally associated with greater amounts of consumer spending as consumers feel good about their job prospects and job security.

With some exceptions, the housing market is showing signs of improvement. A 2016 study showed that 1 in every 122 housing units had at least one foreclosure filing (such as a default notice, scheduled auction, or bank repossession) in 2015. This was the second year in a row where the foreclosure rate was less than 1 percent of all U.S. housing units. The improvement in foreclosure rates was not uniform across the country, however. States with high foreclosure rates in 2015 were New Jersey, Florida, Maryland, Nevada, and Illinois.[10]

The Impact of the Downturn on Economies Around the World

The worldwide economic climate is not as strong as in the United States. Growth in emerging and developing economies has declined for the fifth year in a row. These economies still make up 70 percent of total global economic growth.[11] According to the International Monetary Fund, three factors continue to affect the global economy: a slowdown in China's economy, lower prices for oil and other commodities, and a possible tightening of the monetary policy in the United States.[12]

In mid-2016, another factor could be added to the preceding list: the decision of Great Britain to exit the European Union (also referred to as *Brexit,* meaning "British exit"). This decision will have a significant impact on European economies for several years, and have a smaller effect on the United States and Asia. In addition, the Euro-zone financial crises in Greece, Belgium, Italy, Ireland, and Spain—due to large national debt—affect businesses and consumers there and elsewhere.

The Effect of the Current Economic Climate on Retailing

The data on income and wealth disparity present two distinct market segments: the affluent and the "getting by" groups. Affluent groups are attracted to high-quality specialty retailers, fashion designers, and designer brands. In contrast, the getting-by segment may purchase less expensive products, try and use private-label brands, and postpone purchases. Both groups have become more value-conscious as a result of the "Great Recession." Among the retailers that are doing well in this economic climate are deep-discount retailers with their low prices, specialty retailers of food products, retailers that attract customers with fresh merchandise in a treasure-hunt experience, and retailers that use opportunistic purchasing of closeouts.

Off-price apparel chains, such as Marshalls, Burlington Coat Factory (now called simply "Burlington"), and T. J. Maxx, have drawn new shoppers because more people have become value-driven. In addition, these off-price chains have had significant buying opportunities due to overstocked channel members and cancellations of purchases from bankrupt retailers. In an effort to increase sales, traditional department stores have developed their off-price outlets, such as Saks Fifth Avenue's Off Saks, Nordstrom's The Rack, and Macy's Backstage. These outlets receive goods from two sources: closeout and less-than-full merchandise cartons from their own stores, and merchandise specially purchased for sales at these outlets.

Since 2008, a number of large retailers have declared bankruptcy. These include American Apparel (2015), Circuit City (2008), Linens-N-Things (2008), A&P (2015), Radio Shack (2015), Blockbuster (2010), Borders (2011), Sbarro (2011 and again in 2014), Friedman's (2008), Brookstone (2014), and Quiksilver (2015). Numerous other retailers have suffered losses and had to run frequent sales to generate business or to close unprofitable stores.

Prior to 2005, U.S. firms had an unlimited amount of time to file a restructuring plan after filing for bankruptcy. Since then, these filings have had to be submitted within 18 months. Under earlier laws, retailers had 2 years or more (via extensions) to determine which store locations to keep. Today, retailers in bankruptcy protection must make store-closing decisions within 210 days. Retailers in bankruptcy now are required to pay suppliers and utilities during their bankruptcies. Under the older laws, suppliers and utilities had to wait until a company emerged from bankruptcy before being paid. Also, due to concerns from lenders who were burnt with mortgage-backed securities, troubled retailers have found it much more difficult to get financing. As a result of these factors, many retailers that entered bankruptcy over the past decade were unable to restructure and were therefore forced to close. A study by AlixPartners found that only 49 of 93 retailers were able to emerge from a Chapter 11 bankruptcy as a going concern.[13]

Great Atlantic & Pacific Tea (A&P) filed for Chapter 11 bankruptcy two times in a 5-year time period: December 2010 and July 2015. As a result of its first bankruptcy, A&P became a privately held company after obtaining financing from Goldman Sachs and others. In addition to the stores operating under its A&P name, the firm operated supermarkets under the Best Cellars,

Waldbaum's, Food Emporium, Super Fresh, Food Basics, and Pathmark brands in six Northeast states. Some analysts attributed the chain's problems to the loss of sales to supercenters such as Walmart, membership clubs like Costco, and higher-end retailers such as Whole Foods. Others cited problems such as A&P's high debt, low-profit margins, and inability to finance store renovations for its dated store fixtures and interiors.[14] A&P sold off all its stores, remaining merchandise, and fixtures as of late 2015, and went out of business.

Some analysts believe that retailers that are not leaders in their respective industry segments remain at least somewhat vulnerable to bankruptcy or liquidation. This is especially the case for retailers that used heavy debt to fund their expansion during the period when interest rates were low and credit availability was high—a temporary occurrence.

Strategic Options for Retailers

Let's look at several strategic options that are available to retailers to increase their performance during these economic times:

- *Rethink existing store formats.* A 2015 Nielsen study found that over 18,000 new retail stores opened in the United States. Of this number, 88 percent were small-format stores: dollar, convenience, and drug.[15] These smaller stores have lower inventory requirements due to a more limited selection and lower rents, and they are more adaptable to urban locations.

- *Close unprofitable stores.* Online sales (especially by Amazon), as well as their own poor sales performance, have forced many retailers to close unprofitable stores. As of January 2016, Sears had just over 700 stores, down from 866 in 2006. Kmart was at 952 stores versus over 1,400 stores in 2006. Other major retailers that have been closing stores include Macy's, J. C. Penney, Walmart, and Target.[16] The store closings of anchor tenants (such as department stores) can have a major impact on adjacent retailers, especially when the closed store was a major source of customer traffic.

- *Reexamine the role of price.* Value-oriented shoppers (particularly the "worst-off" Americans) have become more price-conscious. The greater concern for price is due to a number of factors: increased price transparency (due to the ease of checking prices via the Web); the absence of sales tax when consumers purchase goods from some out-of-state retailers; and the popularity of off-price chains, factory outlets, and sites such as eBay. Traditional retailers can respond by price-matching selected competitors (currently done by Best Buy, Target, Home Depot, Walmart, and other retailers) and by unbundling prices (offering separate prices for the product, delivery, and installation). Some retailers also offer price guarantees in which they will reimburse consumers if the price of an item is reduced within a certain number of days after purchase.

- *Increase promotional coupons.* The number of print and/or digital coupon users have remained steady over the past 4 years, but the digital paperless coupon user base has grown 27 percent since 2012 to 68.4 million users in 2015. The print coupon user base at 116.3 million still dominates.[17] NCH Marketing Services reports that free-standing inserts (FSI) account for 92 percent of coupons distributed and represent nearly 50 percent of coupons redeemed, whereas digital coupons account for less than 1 percent of distribution but represent nearly 12 percent of redemptions.[18] Annually, marketers distribute about 320 billion coupons. More than 62 percent of coupons are for nonfood items. Less than 1 percent (2.84 billion) of the coupons are redeemed, mostly for food.[19] According to NCH Marketing Services, more than three-quarters of U.S. consumers regularly use coupons. The use of mobile phones for in-store coupons is spurring a push toward retailer app-based digital couponing platforms, such as Target's Cartwheel, CVS's Pharmacy App, and Walmart's Savings Catcher.[20]

- *Begin the holiday season earlier.* One estimate is that stores typically place orders up to 4 to 7 months in advance. Thus, due to the combined effects of a recession, poor credit availability, and/or an atmosphere of consumer caution, stores may acquire 15 to 20 percent or more excess holiday inventory. As a result, many retailers promote major holidays well ahead of time and conduct special sales events even before a holiday season begins. Many retailers now reduce prices on Christmas items before Thanksgiving.

‣ *Re-introduce layaway plans.* The concept of layaways started during the Great Depression as a way of enabling customers to purchase items without using a credit card. Through a layaway plan, a customer pays the product's total cost (plus a small fee) in installments before being allowed to take the item home. In a traditional layaway program, a customer has 30 days to pay for an item after making an initial payment. Although layaway programs deny instant gratification to the purchaser, the customer receives the attraction of credit cards (being able to purchase an item without paying the full price up front), but without the risk of overextending his or her credit. Until the 2008–2009 economic downturn, Kmart was the only major U.S. retailer with a layaway program. Now, Sears, T. J. Maxx, Marshalls, Burlington, Toys "R" Us, and Walmart—along with many regional chains and local stores—offer layaway programs.

2 Building and Sustaining Relationships in Retailing

Chapter Objectives

1. To explain what *value* really means and highlight its pivotal role in retailers' building and sustaining relationships

2. To describe how both customer relationships and channel relationships may be nurtured in today's highly competitive marketplace

3. To examine the differences in relationship building between goods and service retailers

4. To discuss the impact of technology on relationships in retailing

5. To consider the interplay between retailers' ethical performance and relationships in retailing

In this chapter, we emphasize the importance of *value* and *relationships* for retailers. Retailers focus on providing a great customer experience through all touchpoints–in-store, online, mobile, and customer call centers to create a superior experiential value—the intangible psychological and emotional value that attracts new customers and retains existing ones to stay competitive in the industry. Research shows that creating experiential value leads to long-term relationships and higher spending with a retailer in the future.[1]

Retailers face considerable challenges in maintaining long-term customer relationships when consumers expect retailers to "know" what customers have done online and respond to their individual demands with personalized assistance and tailored in-store experiences! According to TimeTrade's "Annual State of Retail" survey (http://timetrade.com)[2] based on input from 5,000 consumers and 100 senior retail executives, 59 percent of respondents want store associates to know the items in their online shopping carts![3] However, just 24 percent of retailers currently have that ability—and only 12 percent are looking to implement it within the next 18 months.

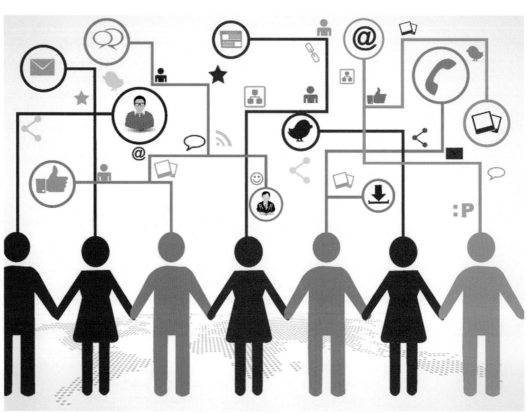

Source: Allies Interactive/ Shutterstock. Reprinted by permission.

Some retailers are trying to distinguish themselves from competitors by deploying technology that positions them as collaborators in the consumer's retail choice. These retailers focus on ensuring seamless connections between digital and traditional channels to delivering prompt, personalized in-store service. For example:

> EyeQ uses a combination of in-store digital signage, advanced facial recognition software, and the capabilities of Watson, IBM's cognitive computing system. When a shopper stops to look at an EyeQ digital sign, the sign uses sophisticated facial recognition software, and based on facial features and appearance, tailors its product recommendations to the viewer's age and gender. If the shopper gives the system her or his Twitter username, Watson can capture the shopper's most recent 200 tweets, run them through its natural language processing capabilities, and slot the customer into a basic personality type. Based on that data, not only can the system change the products being recommended, but it can also alter the whole experience—background colors, video, music, and so on. Personalization does not require the customer to identify himself or herself. The system, even without a consumer opting in or providing personal information, can identify a repeat visitor by the unique media access control address his or her mobile device sends out to find available Wi-Fi. Every time the shopper visits the store, the system learns more about her or him, updates parameters, and provides relevant recommendations.[4]

When shopping in-store, consumers most highly value "prompt service" (54 percent), "a personalized experience" (30 percent), and "smart recommendations" (30 percent). The lack of prompt assistance will drive most consumers (85 percent) to leave a dressing room—and the store—and abandon intended purchases. In sum, customers want to have access to retailers on a 24-hour-a-day basis through multiple media platforms—and to be able to offer comments, feedback, questions, complaints, and praise that will get prompt and helpful responses from retailers.[5]

Overview

To prosper, a retailer must properly apply the concepts of *value* and *relationship* so (1) customers strongly believe the firm offers a good value for the money and (2) both customers and channel members want to do business with that retailer. Some firms grasp this well. Others still have some work to do. Consider GameStop Corp., a global family of specialty retail brands that make the most popular technologies affordable through retail stores and repair centers.

GameStop (www .gamestop.com) is— first and foremost—a customer-driven retailer.

As the world's largest videogame retailer, GameStop Corp. sells new and pre-owned video-game hardware, physical and digital videogame software, and videogame accessories, as well as new and pre-owned mobile and consumer electronics products and other merchandise at its Game-Stop, EB Games, and Micromania stores. Buying customers' unwanted games and consoles, irrespective of where they were initially purchased, and selling them as "pre-owned" after repair-ing and certifying them, creates value for the selling customer and the purchasing customer (by reducing the cost associated with used goods), as well as being environmentally friendly due to its recycling efforts. As of June 2016, GameStop operated about 7,100 stores in the United States, Australia, Canada, and Europe, primarily located in shopping malls and strip centers. In July 2015, the company acquired Geeknet, Inc. (www.thinkgeek.com),which specializes in selling collect-ibles, apparel, gadgets, electronics, toys, and other products for technology enthusiasts, general consumers, and wholesale customers. Geeknet's network includes www.kongregate.com, a browser-based game site; *Game Informer* magazine, the world's leading print and digital video-game publication; and iOS and Android mobile applications.[6]

As discussed at the beginning of the chapter, consumers expect more for less, especially from their stores than from their online or mobile shopping experience.[7] Time- and budget-constrained consumers will spend less time shopping, make fewer trips, visit fewer stores, and shop more purposefully. Different strokes will satisfy different folks. Consumers will shop for different for-mats for a variety of needs. Specifically, they will split the commodity shopping trip from the value-added shopping trip. Consumers are becoming more skeptical of pricing and advertising

FIGURE 2-1

The Key to Long-Term Customer Satisfaction: Meeting Expectations

In today's highly competitive retailing enviornment, companies must do everything they can to generate and maintain a distinctive edge. To attract customers and gain their loyalty, it is no longer enough to "satisfy" them; they need to be "wowed." This requires (a) an in-depth understanding of target shoppers' desires; (b) the proper mix of merchandise, customer service, and prices for those shoppers; and (c) supportive, ongoing customer interaction. These are not easy tasks.

Source: iQoncept/ Shutterstock.com. Reprinted by permission.

tactics and more concerned about the environmental impact of their consumption. Under the barrage of sales, price has lost its meaning and gimmicks have lost their appeal. To regain consumer confidence, pricing by retailers and manufacturers alike will become transparent, more sensible, and more sophisticated. See Figure 2-1.

This chapter looks at value and the value chain, relationship retailing with regard to customers and channel partners, the differences in relationship building between goods and service retailers, technology and relationships, and ethics and relationships. An appendix on service retailing is found at the end of this chapter.

VALUE AND THE VALUE CHAIN

A channel of distribution involves multiple parties: manufacturer, wholesaler, retailer, and customer. These parties are most apt to be satisfied with their interactions when they have similar beliefs about the value provided and received, and they agree on the appropriate payment for that level of value.

From the perspective of the manufacturer, wholesaler, and retailer, **value** is embodied by a series of activities and processes—a value chain—that *provides* a certain value for the consumer. It is the totality of the tangible and intangible product and customer service attributes offered to shoppers. The level of value relates to each firm's desire for a fair profit and its niche (such as discount versus upscale). Firms may differ in rewarding the value each provides and in allocating the activities undertaken.

From the customer's perspective, **value** is the *perception* a shopper has of a value chain. It is the customer's view of all benefits from a purchase (formed by the total retail experience). Value is based on perceived benefits received versus the price paid. It varies by type of shopper. For example, price-oriented shoppers want low prices, service-oriented shoppers will pay more for superior customer service, and status-oriented shoppers will pay a lot to patronize prestigious stores.

Why is *value* such a meaningful concept for every retailer in any kind of setting?

▶ Customers must always believe they get their money's worth, whether the retailer sells $45,000 Patek Phillipe watches or $40 Casio watches.
▶ A strong retail effort is required so that customers perceive the level of value provided in the manner the firm intends.
▶ Value is desired by all customers; however, it means different things to different customers.
▶ Consumer comparison shopping for prices is easy through ads and the Web. Thus, prices have moved closer together for different types of retailers.
▶ Retail differentiation is essential so a firm is not perceived as a "me too" retailer.

▶ A specific value/price level must be set. A retailer can offer $100 worth of benefits for a $100 item or $125 worth of benefits (through better ambience and customer service) for the same item with a $125 price. Either approach can work if properly enacted and marketed.

A retail **value chain** represents the total bundle of benefits offered to consumers through a channel of distribution. It comprises shopping location and parking, retailer ambience, the level of customer service, the products/brands carried, product quality, the retailer's in-stock position, shipping, prices, the retailer's image, and other elements. As a rule, consumers are concerned with the results of a value chain, not the process. Food shoppers who buy online via Peapod care only that they receive the goods ordered at the promised time, not about the steps needed for the home delivery of food at the neighborhood level.

Some elements of a retail value chain are visible to shoppers, such as display windows, store hours, sales personnel, and point-of-sale equipment. Other elements are not visible, such as store location planning, credit processing, company warehouses, and many merchandising decisions. In the latter case, various cues are surrogates for value: upscale store ambience and plentiful sales personnel for high-end retailers; shopping carts and self-service for discounters.

There are three aspects of a value-oriented retail strategy: expected, augmented, and potential. An *expected retail strategy* represents the minimum value chain elements a given customer segment (e.g., young women) expects from a type of retailer (e.g., a mid-priced apparel retailer). In most cases, the following are expected value chain elements: store cleanliness, convenient hours, well-informed employees, timely service, popular products in stock, parking, and return privileges. If applied poorly, expected elements cause customer dissatisfaction and relate to why shoppers avoid certain retailers.

An *augmented retail strategy* includes the extra elements in a value chain that differentiate one retailer from another. As an example, how is Saks different from Sears? The following are often augmented elements: exclusive brands, superior salespeople, loyalty programs, delivery, personal shoppers and other special services, and valet parking. Augmented features complement expected value chain elements, and they are the key to continued customer patronage with a particular retailer.

A *potential retail strategy* comprises value chain elements not yet perfected by a competing firm in the retailer's category. For example, what customer services could a new upscale apparel chain offer that no other chain offers? In many situations, the following are potential value chain elements: 24/7 store hours (an augmented strategy for supermarkets), unlimited customer return privileges, full-scale product customization, instant fulfillment of rain checks through in-store orders accompanied by free delivery, in-mall trams to make it easier for shoppers to move through enormous regional shopping centers, and a doorman. The first firms to capitalize on potential features typically gain a head start over their adversaries. Barnes & Noble and Borders accomplished this by opening the first book superstores, and Amazon.com became a major player by opening the first online bookstore. Yet, even as pioneers, firms must excel at meeting customers' basic expectations and offering differentiated features from competitors if they are to grow, which is why Borders eventually had to close all its stores—it did not adapt fast enough.

Peapod (www.peapod .com) offers a unique value chain with its home delivery service.

Compare T. J. Maxx (www.tjmaxx.com) and Lord & Taylor (www .lordandtaylor.com).

Today, Barnes & Noble (www.bn.com) relies on its stores and its Web site for revenues.

  CAREERS IN RETAILING   Category Managers

Buyers are often contrasted with category managers. Buyers usually evaluate suppliers, negotiate purchases, and match inventory levels with sales prospects. They need to understand and properly respond to sales trends, seasonality, fashion influences, and price concerns among shoppers.

Whereas a buyer may be responsible for a range of products for a supermarket such as prepackaged lettuce, spinach, and carrots; a category manager's responsibility can extend to all produce. Category managers also have greater sales and marketing responsibilities. This includes space allocation, assortment planning, display planning, and discussing joint promotions with key suppliers. A good category manager for a supermarket should think in terms of meal solutions versus frozen foods.

Discuss the differences between the meal solutions versus frozen foods orientation.

■

There are five potential pitfalls to avoid in planning a value-oriented retail strategy:

▶ *Planning value with just a price perspective.* Value is tied to two factors: benefits and prices. All major discounters now accept credit cards because shoppers want to purchase with them.
▶ *Providing value-enhancing services that customers do not want or will not pay extra for.* Ikea knows most of its customers want to save money by assembling furniture themselves.
▶ *Competing in the wrong value/price segment.* Neighborhood retailers generally have a tough time competing in the low-price part of the market. They are better off providing augmented benefits and charging somewhat more than large chains.
▶ *Believing augmented elements alone create value.* Many retailers think that if they offer a benefit not available from competitors that they will automatically prosper. Yet, they must never lose sight of the importance of expected benefits. A movie theater with limited parking will have problems even if it features first-run movies.
▶ *Paying lip service to customer service.* Most firms say, and even believe, customers are always right. Yet, they may act contrary to this philosophy—by having a high turnover of salespeople, charging restocking fees for returned goods that have been opened, and not giving rain checks for out-of-stock items.

To sidestep these pitfalls, a retailer could use the checklist in Figure 2-2, which poses a number of questions that must be addressed. The checklist can be answered by an owner/corporate president, a team of executives, or an independent consultant. It should be reviewed yearly or more often if a major development, such as the emergence of a strong competitor, occurs.

RETAILER RELATIONSHIPS

In Chapter 1, we introduced the concept of *relationship retailing,* whereby retailers seek to form and maintain long-term bonds with customers, rather than act as if each sales transaction is a new encounter with them. For relationship retailing to work, enduring value-driven relationships are needed with other channel members, as well as with customers. Both jobs are challenging. See Figure 2-3. Visit our blog for posts related to relationship retailing issues (www.bermanevansretail .com).

FIGURE 2-2
A Value-Oriented Retailing Checklist
Answer yes or no to each question.

✓ Is value defined from a consumer perspective?

✓ Does the retailer have a clear value/price point?

✓ Is the retailer's value position competitively defensible?

✓ Are channel partners capable of delivering value-enhancing services?

✓ Does the retailer distinguish between expected and augmented value chain elements?

✓ Has the retailer identified meaningful potential value chain elements?

✓ Is the retailer's value-oriented approach aimed at a distinct market segment?

✓ Is the retailer's value-oriented approach consistent?

✓ Is the retailer's value-oriented approach effectively communicated to the target market?

✓ Can the target market clearly identify the retailer's positioning strategy?

✓ Does the retailer's positioning strategy consider trade-offs in sales versus profits?

✓ Does the retailer set customer satisfaction goals?

✓ Does the retailer periodically measure customer satisfaction levels?

✓ Is the retailer careful to avoid the pitfalls in value-oriented retailing?

✓ Is the retailer always looking out for new opportunities that will create customer value?

FIGURE 2-3

The Many Relationships in Retailing

In most instances, the retail supply chain is quite complex. It requires that the many relationships be satisfying to all parties, including both various channel members and customers.

Source: johnkworks/ Shutterstock. Reprinted by permission.

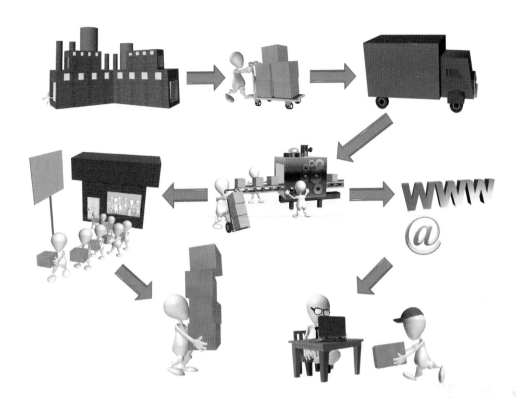

Customer Relationships

Loyal customers are the backbone of a business. Thus, it is important that retailers retain their loyal customers through repeated sales in a trusting relationship. Loyalty has two unique dimensions—attitudinal and behavioral—and each contributes differently to retailers' revenues, profits, and market share.[8] Customers who are *attitudinally loyal* will have a higher tendency to spread positive word-of-mouth recommendations to friends and family on social media, have a higher commitment to the retailer, and not be reluctant to pay more for products at a particular retailer.

Customers who are *behaviorally loyal* will have a higher tendency to continue purchasing from a particular retailer. Behavioral loyalty may also be a manifestation of inertia (or inertial loyalty) due to high switching costs associated with changing retailers. Although both attitudinal and behavioral loyalty are important to achieve business goals and to sustain the position in the marketplace, a retailer's positioning strategy (discussed in Chapter 3) will influence which dimension needs to be strategically managed. Attitudinal loyalty should be emphasized if the objective is to charge higher prices, whereas behavioral loyalty should be more important if the objective is to increase market share or profits.[9]

In a competitive industry such as retailing, many consumers show divided behavioral loyalty to more than one retailer for a single category need. Here's why: You have satisfied customers. "That's good, right? Well, yes for the short term the customer[s] will continue purchasing. While a loyal customer is a satisfied customer, the converse is not necessarily true. Real loyalty [or attitudinal loyalty]—much harder to earn than mere satisfaction—tells you that your customer wants to stick with you over the long haul and will share that feeling with others."[10] Retailers need to develop and strategically manage loyalty programs to cultivate behavioral loyalty (discussed later in this chapter). But in the long term, it's not necessarily enough. Customers who spend a lot can defect to the retailer providing lower prices or better service and enroll in multiple loyalty programs. Attitudinal loyalty derives not from hum-drum "good" transactions but from exceeding customer expectations on a repeated basis and delightful experiences that make shoppers so emotionally devoted that they want to share their experience by telling others.

In relationship retailing, there are four factors to keep in mind: the customer base, customer service, customer satisfaction, and loyalty programs and defection rates. Let's explore these next.

THE CUSTOMER BASE   Retailers must regularly analyze their customer base in terms of population and lifestyle trends, attitudes toward and reasons for shopping, the level of loyalty, and the mix of new versus loyal customers.

As reported by the Census Bureau, the U.S. population is aging. One-fourth of households consist of only one person, one-seventh of people move annually, most people live in urban and suburban areas, middle-class income has been rising very slowly, and African American, Hispanic American, and Asian American segments are expanding. Thus, gender roles are changing, shoppers demand more, consumers are more diverse, there is less interest in shopping, and time-saving goods and services are desired.

Future retail trends will be driven by the Millennials (Generation Y), who have surpassed Baby Boomers as the largest generation. According to the Pew Research Center, there are about 75 million Americans born between the early 1980s and the late 1990s; and they defy easy categorization, for they are the most racially diverse generation the United States has experienced.[11] Millennials have an elevated sense of idealism and are concerned how brands and retailers perform on social responsibility, sustainability, gender equality, and fair trade.

In their quest for growth in market share and sales revenue, many retailers typically focus on one side of customer value—*delivering value.* The customer is king (or queen) and everything must be done to deliver superior value and to delight him (or her). Astute retailers balance this view with the other side of customer value—*receiving value.* This is achieved by attracting and retaining those customers who provide value in the form of profits to the firm through their transactions.

It is worth more to nurture relationships with some shoppers than with others. These are the retailer's **core customers**—its best customers—loyal, satisfied customers who get high value from the retailer and generate high profits for the retailer. These core customers are the most desirable, are resistant to competitors' enticements of better deals, and deliver long-term profits. At the other extreme are the "lost causes" who don't value the retailer's goods or services and are not profitable.[12] They cost the retailer more than they are worth because they frequently complain and return products, spread bad word of mouth, misuse promotions, and lower staff morale through their interactions. It does not make economic sense for the retailer to acquire them in the first place. Losing these customers may reduce market share but lead to improved profitability and higher levels of retailer performance. "Free-riders" (customers who are highly satisfied with the company but not highly profitable) and vulnerable customers (profitable but not satisfied with the retailer) can be managed through customer relationship management strategies. Charging higher prices and reducing services for free-riders can increase profitability. It is important for retailers to identify unmet needs of vulnerable customers and consider whether it will be profitable to satisfy them; otherwise, competitors will poach them away.

Retailers need to identify their best customers and see what characteristics differentiate these profitable customers from all the rest. Next, the retailer should determine whether it makes economic sense to pursue a differentiated offering to free-riders and vulnerable customers and to fine-tune strategies for the consumers who are most likely to yield profitable customers.

A retailer's desired mix of new versus loyal customers depends on that firm's stage in its life cycle, goals, and resources, as well as competitors' actions. A mature firm is more apt to rely on core customers and supplement its revenues with new shoppers. A new firm faces the dual tasks of attracting shoppers and building a loyal following; it cannot do the latter without the former. If goals are growth-oriented, the customer base must be expanded by adding stores, increasing advertising, and so on; the challenge is to do this in a way that does not deflect attention from core customers. Although it is more costly to attract new customers than to serve existing ones, core customers are not cost-free; they must be service properly. If competitors try to take away a retailer's existing customers with price cuts and special promotions, that retailer might pursue the competitors' customers in the same way. Again, regardless of what action is taken, all retailers must be careful not to alienate core customers.

CUSTOMER SERVICE   As described in Chapter 1, *customer service* refers to the identifiable, but sometimes intangible, activities undertaken by a retailer in conjunction with the goods and services it sells. It has an impact on the total retail experience. Consistent with a value chain philosophy, retailers must apply two elements of customer service. **Expected customer service** is the service level that customers want to receive from any retailer, such as basic employee courtesy. **Augmented customer service** includes the activities that enhance the shopping experience and give retailers a competitive advantage.

AutoZone (www
.autozone.com) has a
unique style of customer
service.

Nordstrom (www
.nordstrom.com) strongly
believes in empowering
its employees to better
serve customers.

The attributes of personnel who interact with customers (such as politeness and knowledge), as well as the number and variety of customer services offered, have a strong effect on the relationship created. Although planning a superior customer service strategy can be complex, a well-executed strategy can pay off in a big way.

Some retailers realize customer service is better if they utilize **employee empowerment**, whereby workers have the discretion to do what they believe is necessary—within reason—to satisfy the customer, even if this means bending the rules. The founders of Home Depot made a strategic decision to train employees to form enduring customer relationships rather than push for incremental sales gains. As a result, the retailer grew very quickly because of its outstanding customer service. Home Depot's core value, "Taking care of our people," states that the company encourages associates to speak up and take risks, recognizes and rewards good work performance, and leads and develops employees so that they may grow. Home Depot believes that the key to its success and its competitive advantage in the marketplace is treating people well—starting with employees, who in turn ensure that customers are treated well. However, Home Depot's American Customer Satisfaction Index rating tumbled to the bottom in the home-improvement category when it faced a high-profile credit-card security breach in the fall of 2014.[13] That rating has risen since then.

To apply customer service effectively, a firm must first develop an overall service strategy and then plan individual services. Figure 2-4 shows one way a retailer may view the customer services it offers.

DEVELOPING A CUSTOMER SERVICE STRATEGY.   A retailer must make the following vital decisions.

What customer services are expected and what customer services are augmented for a particular retailer? Examples of expected customer services are credit for a furniture retailer, new-car preparation for an auto dealer, and a liberal return policy for a gift shop. Those retailers could not stay in business without these services. Because augmented customer services are extra elements, a firm could serve its target market without such services, but using them will enhance its competitive standing. Examples are home delivery for a supermarket within a 1-hour window, an extended warranty for a used auto dealer, and free gift wrapping for a toy store. Each firm needs to learn which customer services are expected and which are augmented for its situation. Services that are viewed as expected customer services for one retailer, such as delivery, may be viewed as augmented for another. See Figure 2-5.

What level of customer service is proper to complement a firm's image? An upscale retailer would offer more customer services than a discounter because people expect the upscale firm to have a wider range of customer services as part of its basic strategy. Performance would also be different. Customers of an upscale retailer may expect elaborate gift wrapping, valet parking, an in-store restaurant, and a ladies' room attendant, whereas discount shoppers may expect cardboard gift boxes, self-service parking, a lunch counter, and an unattended ladies' room. Customer service categories are the same; performance is not.

Should there be a choice of customer services? Some firms let customers select from various levels of customer service; others provide only one level. A retailer may honor several credit cards or only its own. Trade-ins may be allowed on some items or all. Warranties may have optional extensions or fixed lengths. A firm may offer 1-, 3-, and 6-month payment plans or insist on immediate payment.

FIGURE 2-4

**Classifying
Customer Services**

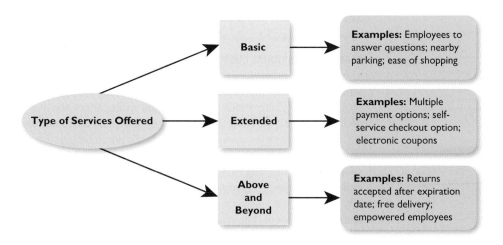

(a)   (b)

FIGURE 2-5

Providing Extra Value for Customers

Retailers that offer extra services to customers often stand out in the marketplace. For example, a given retailer could offer free repairs on the products it sells (a) and also allow consumers to tag QR codes via their smartphones so they can learn more about products within the store (b).

Sources: (a) Lena Pan/Shutterstock. Reprinted by permission. (b) rangizzz/Shutterstock. Reprinted by permission.

Should customer services be free? Two factors cause retailers to charge for some customer services: First, delivery, gift wrapping, and some other customer services are labor intensive, and second, people are more apt to be home for a delivery or service call if a fee is imposed. Without a fee, a retailer may have to attempt a delivery twice. In settling on a free or fee-based strategy, a firm should (1) determine which customer services are expected (these are often free) and which are augmented (these may be offered for a fee); (2) monitor competitors and profit margins; and (3) study the target market. In setting fees, a retailer must also decide if its goal is to break even or to make a profit on certain customer services.

How can a retailer measure the benefits of providing customer services against the cost of the services? The aim of customer services is to enhance the shopping experience in a way that attracts and retains shoppers—while maximizing sales and profits. Thus, augmented services should not be offered unless they increase total sales and profits. A retailer should plan augmented customer services based on its experience, competitors' actions, and customer comments; when the costs of providing these customer services increase, higher prices should be passed on to the consumers.

How can customer services be terminated? When a customer service strategy is set, shoppers are apt to react negatively to any customer service reduction. Yet, some costly augmented customer services may have to be dropped. In that case, the best approach is to be forthright by explaining why the customer services are being terminated and how customers will benefit via lower prices. Sometimes a firm may use a middle ground, charging for previously free customer services (such as clothing alterations) to allow those who want the services to still receive them.

> Amazon.com (www .amazon.com) offers free 2-day delivery to its Prime customers.

PLANNING INDIVIDUAL CUSTOMER SERVICES.   After a broad customer service plan is outlined, individual customer services need to be planned. A department store may offer credit, layaway, gift wrapping, a bridal registry, free parking, a restaurant, a beauty salon, carpet installation, dressing rooms, clothing alterations, restrooms and sitting areas, the use of baby strollers, home delivery, and fur storage. See Table 2-1 for a range of typical customer services.

Most retailers let customers make credit purchases; and many firms accept personal checks with proper identification. Consumers' use of credit rises as the purchase amount goes up. Retailer-sponsored credit cards have three key advantages: (1) The retailer saves the fee it would pay for outside card sales, (2) people are encouraged to shop with a given retailer because its card is usually not accepted elsewhere, and (3) contact can be maintained with customers and information learned about them. There are also disadvantages to retailer cards: Startup costs are high, the firm must worry about unpaid bills and slow cash flow, credit checks and follow-up tasks must be

TABLE 2-1   Typical Customer Services

Typical	Miscellaneous	
• Credit	• Bridal registry	• Rest rooms
• Delivery	• Interior designers	• Restaurant
• Alterations and installations	• Personal shoppers	• Babysitting
• Packaging (gift wrapping)	• Ticket outlets	• Fitting rooms
• Complaints and returns handling	• Parking	• Beauty salon
• Gift certificates	• Water fountains	• Fur storage
• Trade-ins	• Baby strollers	• Shopping bags
• Trial purchases	• Company-sponsored social media	• Information
• Special sales for regular customers		• Layaways
• Extended store hours		
• Mail and phone orders		

performed, and customers without the firm's card may be discouraged from shopping at that particular retail store. Bank and other commercial credit cards enable small and medium retailers to offer credit, generate added business for all types of retailers, appeal to mobile shoppers, provide advertising support from the sponsor, reduce bad debts, eliminate startup costs for the retailer, and provide data. Yet, the cards charge a transaction fee and do not yield loyalty to a retailer.

Most bank cards and retailer cards involve a **revolving credit account**, whereby a customer charges items and is billed monthly on the basis of the outstanding cumulative balance. An **option credit account** is a form of revolving account; no interest is assessed if a person pays a bill in full when it is due. When a person makes a partial payment, he or she is assessed interest monthly on the unpaid balance. Some credit card firms (such as American Express) and some retailers offer an **open credit account**, whereby a consumer must pay the bill in full when it is due. Partial, revolving payments are not permitted. A person with an open account also has a credit limit (although it may be more flexible).

For a retailer that offers delivery, there are three decisions: the transportation method, equipment ownership versus rental, and timing. The transportation method can be car, van, truck, rail, mail, and so forth. The costs and appropriateness of the methods depend on the products. Regarding transportation equipment ownership, large retailers often find it economical to own their delivery vehicles. This also lets them advertise the company name, have control over schedules, and use their employees for deliveries. Small retailers serving limited trading areas may use personal vehicles. Many small, medium, and even large retailers use shippers such as UPS if consumers live away from a delivery area and shipments are not otherwise efficient. And finally, for the timing of delivery, the retailer must decide how quickly to process orders and how often to deliver to different locales.

For some firms, alterations and installations are expected services—although more retailers now charge fees. However, many discounters have stopped offering alterations of clothing and installations of appliances on both a free and a fee basis. They feel the services are too ancillary to their business and not worth the effort. Other retailers offer only basic alterations: shortening pants, taking in the waist, and lengthening jacket sleeves. They do not adjust jacket shoulders or width. Some appliance retailers may hook up washing machines but not do plumbing work.

Within a store, packaging (gift wrapping)—as well as complaints and returns handling—can be centrally located or decentralized. Centralized packaging counters and complaints and returns areas have advantages: They may be located in otherwise dead spaces, the main selling areas are not cluttered, specialized personnel can be used, and there is a common policy. The advantages of decentralization are that shoppers are not inconvenienced, they are kept in the selling area (where a salesperson may resolve a problem or offer different merchandise), and extra personnel are not required. In either case, clear guidelines as to the handling of complaints and returns are needed.

A Hong Kong Luxury Retailer

Lane Crawford (www.lanecrawford.com) is a Hong Kong-based luxury retailer of apparel, home furnishings, bedding, and kitchen-related goods. It features such brands as Armani, Valentino, Alexander McQueen, Jimmy Choo, and Alessi. According to its president, the firm's typical customer is female, aged 25 to 35, and interested in ready-to-wear apparel. Lane Crawford has store locations in Beijing, Chengdu, Hong King, and Shanghai; and it practices an omnichannel approach. This strategy integrates stores and a Web-based experience. The Web presence also allows Lane Crawford to serve a much broader geographic base. How should Lane Crawford grow its business?

Source: Christopher Horton, "When It Comes to Luxury, China Still Leads," *The New York Times*, April 5, 2016, http://www.nytimes.com.

Gift cards encourage shopping with a given retailer. Many firms require gift cards to be spent and not redeemed for cash. Trade-ins also induce new and regular shoppers to visit the store or its Web site. People may feel they are getting a bargain. Trial purchases let shoppers test products before purchases are final.

Retailers increasingly offer special customer services to their regular customers. Sales events (not open to the general public) and extended hours are provided. Mail and phone orders are handled for convenience.

Other useful customer services include a bridal registry, interior designers, personal shoppers, ticket outlets, free (or low-cost) and plentiful parking, water fountains, pay phones, baby strollers, company-sponsored social media, restrooms, a restaurant, babysitting, fitting rooms, a beauty salon, fur storage, shopping bags, information counters, and layaway plans.

A retailer's willingness to offer some or all of these services indicates to customers a concern for them. Therefore, firms need to consider the impact of excessive self-service. Research shows that some shoppers think self-service technologies (SSTs) are used by service providers to cut costs rather than extend customer service. Thus, service managers need to provide a clear reason for using SSTs to stimulate customers' attribution of higher benefits and convenience.[14]

CUSTOMER SATISFACTION   **Customer satisfaction** occurs when the value and customer service provided through a retailing experience meet or exceed consumer expectations. If the expectations of value and customer service are not met, the consumer will be dissatisfied. "Retail satisfaction consists of three categories: *shopping systems satisfaction*, which includes availability and types of outlets; *buying systems satisfaction*, which includes selection and actual purchasing of products; and *consumer satisfaction*, which is derived from the use of the product. Dissatisfaction with any of the three aspects could lead to customer disloyalty, decrease in sales, and erosion of the market share."[15]

Only "very satisfied" customers are likely to remain loyal in the long run. How well are retailers doing in customer satisfaction? Many have much work to do. The American Customer Satisfaction Index (www.theacsi.org) annually questions thousands of people to link customer expectations, perceived quality, and perceived value to satisfaction. Overall, department and discount stores generally have scores from 66 to 82, supermarkets from 67 to 86, and specialty retail stores from 65 to 81 (on a scale of 100). Gasoline stations usually rate lowest in the retailing category (with scores around 70). To improve matters, retailers should consider engaging in the activities shown in Figure 2-6.

Most consumers do not complain to the retailer when dissatisfied; they just shop elsewhere. Why don't shoppers complain more? (1) Most people feel complaining produces little or no positive results, so they do not bother to complain, and (2) complaining is not easy. Consumers have to find the party to whom they should complain, access to that party may be restricted, and written forms may have to be completed.

To obtain more feedback, retailers must make it easier for shoppers to complain, make sure shoppers believe their concerns are addressed, and sponsor ongoing customer satisfaction surveys. As suggested by software firm StatPac, retailers should ask such questions as these and then take corrective actions:

Try out some of StatPac's surveys (www.statpac.com/online-surveys/examples.htm) for measuring customer satisfaction.

1. "Overall, how satisfied or dissatisfied are you with the store?"
2. "How satisfied or dissatisfied are you with the *price* of the items you purchased?"
3. "How satisfied or dissatisfied are you with the *quality* of the merchandise?"
4. "Please tell us something we could do to improve our store."[16]

FIGURE 2-6

Turning around Weak Customer Service

All of these solutions incur costs. Thus, the retailer must weigh the benefits of improving their services versus the additional costs.

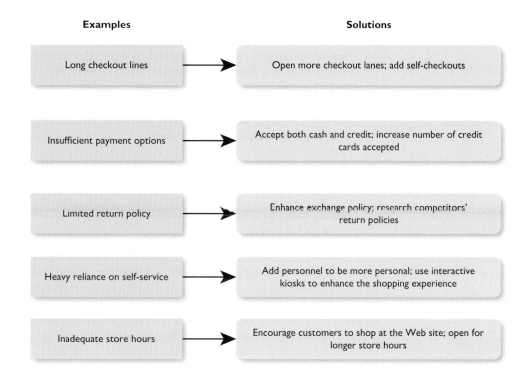

Examples	Solutions
Long checkout lines	Open more checkout lanes; add self-checkouts
Insufficient payment options	Accept both cash and credit; increase number of credit cards accepted
Limited return policy	Enhance exchange policy; research competitors' return policies
Heavy reliance on self-service	Add personnel to be more personal; use interactive kiosks to enhance the shopping experience
Inadequate store hours	Encourage customers to shop at the Web site; open for longer store hours

LOYALTY PROGRAMS AND DEFECTION RATES **Consumer loyalty (frequent shopper) programs** reward a retailer's best customers, those with whom it wants long-lasting relationships. These programs have been shown to enhance consumers' purchase frequencies and volumes. An example of a loyalty program is after your membership card is punched nine times, indicating that you've had nine pancake breakfasts, your tenth pancake breakfast is free. Loyalty programs vary dramatically, based on number of visits, reward timing, reward type, reward value, behavior before and after redemptions, accumulation of credits toward the award, the behavioral unit used to track purchase behavior (e.g., points, miles flown, nights stayed, dollars, number of purchases/visits, etc.), the redemption policy of rewards, and the reward program enrollment fee. Academic research shows that consumers who pay a fee to participate in loyalty programs have more favorable attitudes toward the programs and higher behavioral loyalty, focus more on the benefits associated with program enrollment, and perceive the programs as a better value than consumers who enroll in a loyalty program for free.[17]

For retailers, fee-based programs increase consumer revenue after enrollment (in addition to the revenue generated from the fee). In general, the higher the program fee, the lower the consumers' willingness to join. When membership fees are nominal (or free), simple dollar and point accrual work best, as these programs lead to the highest joining intentions and keep the consumer focused on cost/benefit assessments of the program (rather than the price of the program).[18] Simple accrual systems allow for easy conversions and should make the ultimate reward seem closer to obtaining and more attractive, enhancing the cost/benefit ratio for customers. Retailers who offer higher fee-based loyalty programs are more likely to attract members when they offer complex accruals—the accrual of multiple points per dollar spent to encourage consumers to consider the benefits of reward membership holistically.

Retailers in categories with less differentiation (e.g., airlines and supermarkets) offer loyalty programs with the goal of increasing repeat business and profitability. In these cases, a decision to join a loyalty program may have a big impact by increasing customer perceptions of switching costs that increase behavioral loyalty. Firms can collect customer contact and socio-demographic information when they sign up, and track browsing and purchase behavior that they can use to personalize offers and strengthen the exchange with customers.[19]

From the shopper's perspective, there are five types of reward categories:[20]

1. *Economic rewards* include price reductions and purchase vouchers. These rewards attract price-sensitive customers and induce them to buy more. Dunkin Donuts DDPerks program members receive a free beverage after earning 200 Points ($40 in spending) on qualifying

purchases. Members receive promotional E-mails with dollars off selected food or beverage items automatically applied when they use the mobile app or loyalty card in stores.[21]

2. *Hedonistic rewards* include things such as points that can be exchanged for spa services or participation in games or sweepstakes. These rewards have more emotional value and will attract people who shop for pleasure.

3. *Social-relational rewards* include things such as mailings about special events or the right to use special waiting areas at airports. Consumers who want to be identified with a privileged group will value these kinds of rewards.

4. *Informational rewards* include things such as personalized beauty advice or information on new goods or services. These rewards will attract consumers who like to stick with one brand or store.

5. *Functional rewards* include things such as access to priority checkout counters or home delivery. Consumers who want to reduce the time they spend shopping will value these most. Dunkin Donuts DDperks rewards members can use the On-The-Go mobile app to order ahead and skip the line at the store.

What do good customer loyalty programs have in common? Their rewards are useful and appealing, and they are attainable in a reasonable time. Referrals (through social media or direct invites) are rewarded, as well as frequent shopping behavior (the greater the purchases, the greater the benefits). Each year, Starbucks Rewards members start at the Green Level and earn two stars for each $1 spent until they accumulate 300 stars for Gold status. The latter members earn free beverages for every 125 stars and other benefits until the end of the year.[22] Rewards that are unique to particular retailers and not redeemable elsewhere are more effective. Rewards stimulate both short- and long-run purchases. Customer communications are personalized. Frequent shoppers feel "special." Participation rules are publicized and rarely change.

When a retailer studies customer defections (by tracking databases or surveying consumers), it can learn how many customers it is losing and why they no longer patronize a firm. Customer defections may be viewed in absolute terms (people who no longer buy from the firm at all) and in relative terms (people who shop less often or who have reduced their average purchase quantity). Each retailer must define its acceptable defection rate. Furthermore, not all shoppers are "good" customers. A retailer may feel it is okay if shoppers who always look for sales, return items without receipts, and expect fee-based services to be free decide to defect. Unfortunately, too few retailers review defection data or survey defecting customers because of the complexity of doing so and an unwillingness to hear "bad news."

Starbucks (www .starbucks.com/card/ rewards) has a strong loyalty program for its customers.

Channel Relationships

Within a value chain, the members of a distribution channel (manufacturers, wholesalers, and retailers) jointly represent a **value delivery system**, which comprises all the parties that develop, produce, deliver, and sell and service particular goods and services. These are the ramifications for retailers:

▶ Each channel member is dependent on the others. When consumers shop with a certain retailer, they often do so because of the retailer as well as the products it carries.

▶ All activities in a value delivery system must be enumerated and responsibility assigned.

▶ Small retailers may have to use suppliers outside the normal distribution channel to get items they want and gain adequate supplier support. Large firms may be able to buy directly from manufacturers; smaller firms may have to buy through wholesalers handling such accounts.

▶ A value delivery system is as good as its weakest link. No matter how well a retailer performs its activities, it will still have unhappy shoppers if suppliers deliver late or do not honor warranties.

▶ The nature of a given value delivery system must be related to target market expectations.

▶ Channel member costs and functions are influenced by each party's role. Long-term cooperation and two-way information flows foster efficiency.

▶ Value delivery systems are complex due to the vast product assortment of superstores, the many forms of retailing, and the use of multiple distribution channels by some manufacturers.

▶ Nonstore retailing (such as mail order, phone, and Web transactions) requires a different delivery system than store retailing.

▶ Due to conflicting goals about profit margins, shelf space, and so on, some channel members are adversarial—to the detriment of the value delivery system and channel relationships.

When they forge strong positive channel relationships, members of a value delivery system better serve each other and the final consumer. Here's how: Walmart and Sam's Club work closely with suppliers to drive out unnecessary costs in order to pass savings to their shoppers.[23]

FIGURE 2-7

Elements Contributing to Effective Channel Relationships

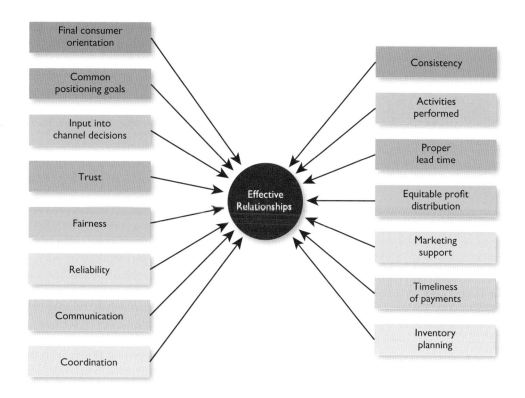

Ace (www.acehardware.com) prides itself on strong relationships with its suppliers.

Ace Hardware's cooperative structure allows its buyers to negotiate with the power of over 4,800 locations, so that store owners have a significant advantage over nonaffiliated stores.[24]

One relationship-oriented practice that some manufacturers and retailers use, especially supermarket chains, is *category management*, whereby channel members collaborate to manage products by category rather than by individual item. Successful category management is based on these actions: (1) Retailers listen better to customers and stock what they want, (2) Profitability is improved because inventory more closely matches demand, (3) By being better focused, shoppers find each department to be more desirable, (4) Retail buyers have more responsibility and accountability for category results, (5) Retailers and suppliers share data and are more computerized, (6) Retailers and suppliers plan together. See Figure 2-7 for various factors that contribute to effective channel relationships, Category management is discussed further in Chapter 14.

THE DIFFERENCES IN RELATIONSHIP BUILDING BETWEEN GOODS AND SERVICE RETAILERS

Consumer interest in services makes it crucial to understand the differences in relationship building between retailers that market services and those that market goods. This applies to store-based and nonstore-based firms, those offering only goods *or* services, and those offering goods *and* services.

Goods retailing focuses on the sale of tangible (physical) products. **Service retailing** involves transactions in which consumers do not purchase or acquire ownership of tangible products. Some retailers engage in either goods retailing (such as hardware stores) or service retailing (such as travel agencies); others offer a combination of the two (such as Best Buy selling PCs and offering fee-based Geek Squad services). The latter format is growing. Consider how many drugstores have equipment to process digital photos, how many department stores have cafés, how many hotels have gift shops, and so on.

Service retailing encompasses such diverse businesses as personal services, hotels and motels, auto repair and rental, and recreational services. In addition, although several services have not been commonly considered a part of retailing (such as medical, dental, legal, and educational services), they should be when they entail final consumer sales. There are three basic kinds of service retailing:

  ▶ **Rented-goods services**, whereby consumers lease and use goods for specified periods of time. Tangible goods are leased for a fixed time, but ownership is not obtained and the goods must be returned when the rental period is up. Examples are Hertz car rentals, carpet cleaner machine rentals from a supermarket, and video rentals at Redbox kiosks.

▶ **Owned-goods services**, whereby goods owned by consumers are repaired, improved, or maintained. In this grouping, the retailer providing the service never owns the good involved. Illustrations include watch repair, lawn care, and an annual air-conditioner tune-up.

▶ **Nongoods services**, whereby intangible personal services are offered to consumers who then experience the services rather than possess them. The seller offers personal expertise for a specified time in return for a fee; tangible goods are not involved. Some examples are accountants, stockbrokers, travel agents, real-estate brokers, and personal trainers.

Please note: The terms *customer service* and *service retailing* are not interchangeable. Customer service refers to the activities undertaken *in conjunction with* the retailer's main business; they are part of the total retail experience. Service retailing refers to situations in which services *are sold to* consumers.

Four unique aspects of service retailing impact relationship building and customer retention: (1) The intangibility of many services makes a consumer's choice of competitive offerings more difficult than with goods, (2) the service provider and his or her services are sometimes inseparable (thus localizing marketing efforts), (3) the perishability of many services prevents storage and increases risks, and (4) the human nature involved in many services makes them more variable.

Cheap Tickets (www
.cheaptickets.com) makes
itself more tangible
through its descriptive
name.

The *intangible* (and possibly abstract) nature of some services makes it harder for a firm to develop a clear consumer-oriented strategy, particularly because many retailers (such as opticians, repairpeople, and landscapers) start service businesses on the basis of their product expertise. The *inseparability* of the service provider and his or her services means the owner-operator is often indispensable and good customer relations are pivotal. *Perishability* presents a risk that in many cases cannot be overcome. Thus, revenues from an unrented hotel room are forever lost. *Variability* means service quality may differ for each shopping experience, store, or service provider. See Figure 2-8.

FIGURE 2-8

The Unique Characteristics of Service Retailing and How to Manage Them

Unique Characteristics **How to Manage Them**

Intangibility →

- Display/distribute customer testimonials.
- Explain in detail how the service will be performed and what the expected results will be.
- Have strong, clearly stated guarantees of performance.
- Be competitively priced.

Inseparability →

- Prominently promote the major points of distinction with competing firms.
- At the time a service is completed, encourage customers to schedule appointments for a follow-up service visit or call.
- If possible, rotate the employees who interact with customers each time they buy a service so that customers do not leave if a popular employee goes elsewhere.
- Call customers after a service is performed to demonstrate the firm's interest in them.

Perishability →

- Carefully plan each work day to optimize service visits or calls.
- Be prepared to do alternative tasks if the weather is bad.
- Offer appropriate other services that are popular during off-seasons.
- Be willing to work longer hours during peak periods and fewer hours during slower times.

Variability →

- Develop and implement systematic procedures for performing each service—including a series of steps to be undertaken every time the same service is requested.
- Train employees well.
- Computerize as many steps as possible, such as inputting customer information, verifying that each step has been completed, and billing.
- Regularly observe employee actions to be sure they are done correctly.

FIGURE 2-9

**Selected Factors
Affecting Consumer
Perceptions of
Service Retailing**

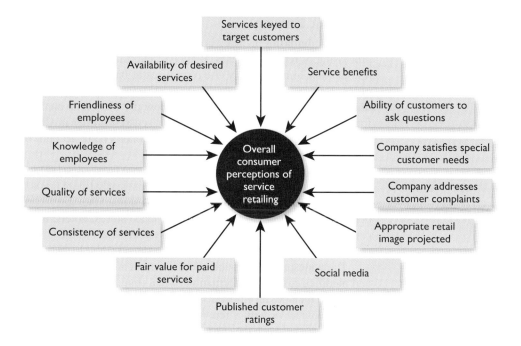

Service retailing is much more dependent on personal interactions and word-of-mouth communication than goods retailing. According to Professor Leonard Berry, building customer–firm relationships benefits both parties: "For services that are personally important, variable in quality, and/or complex, many customers will desire to be relationship customers." For example, financial, insurance, and hairstyling services have characteristics "that would cause many customers to desire continuity with the same provider, a proactive service attitude, and customized service delivery."[25]

Figure 2-9 highlights several factors that consumers may consider in forming their perceptions about the caliber of the service retailing experience offered by a particular firm. The appendix at the end of this chapter presents an additional discussion on the unique aspects of operating a service retailing business.

TECHNOLOGY AND RELATIONSHIPS IN RETAILING

Technology is beneficial to retailing relationships if it facilitates a better communication flow between retailers and their customers, as well as between retailers and their suppliers, and there are faster, more dependable transactions.

These two points are key in studying technology and its impact on relationships in retailing:

1. In each firm, the roles of technology and "humans" must be clear and consistent with the goals and style of that business. Although technology can facilitate customer service, it may become overloaded and break down. It is also viewed as impersonal by some consumers. New technology must be set up efficiently with minimal disruptions to suppliers, employees, and customers.
2. Shoppers expect certain operations to be in place, so they can rapidly complete credit transactions, get feedback on product availability, and so on. Firms have to deploy some advances (such as a computerized checkout system) simply to be competitive. By enacting other advances, they can be distinctive. For instance, consider the paint store with computerized paint-matching equipment for customers who want to touch up old paint jobs or who threw out their old paint can without saving the custom color number.

Throughout this book, we devote a lot of attention to technological advances via our "Technology in Retailing" boxes and in-chapter discussions. Here, we look at technology's effects in terms of electronic banking and customer–supplier interactions.

Electronic Banking

Electronic banking involves both the use of automatic teller machines (ATMs) and the instant processing of retail purchases. It allows centralized recordkeeping and lets customers complete transactions 24 hours a day, 7 days a week at bank and nonbank locations—including home or office. Besides its use in typical financial transactions (such as check cashing, deposits, withdrawals, and transfers), many retailers now use electronic banking. These retailers accept some form of electronic debit payment plan (discussed further in Chapter 13), whereby the purchase price is immediately deducted from a consumer's bank account by computer and transferred to the retailer's account.

Worldwide, there are more than 3 billion ATMs—450,000 in the United States alone—and people make several billion ATM transactions yearly (there are 800 transactions, on average, per month per ATM machine).[26] These automated machines are located in banks, shopping centers, department stores, supermarkets, convenience stores, hotels, and airports, as well as on college campuses and other sites. With sharing systems, such as the Cirrus, Maestro, and Plus networks, consumers can make transactions at ATMs outside their local banking areas and around the world.

The widespread acceptance of the smart card, which contains an electronic strip that stores and modifies customer information in real time, is important for retailers and shoppers alike. A smart card includes an embedded integrated circuit chip and communicates with a reader through physical contact or with a remote contactless electromagnetic field that energizes the chip and transfers data between the card and the reader.[27]

The adoption of Apple Pay, Android Pay, and Samsung Pay apps since 2014 through NFC-enabled mobile devices allow for contactless payments. Contactless payment transactions do not require physical contact between the consumer payment device and the physical point-of-sale (POS) terminal. The consumer holds the NFC-enabled mobile device in close proximity (less than 2 to 4 inches) to the merchant POS terminal and the payment account information is communicated wirelessly (via radio frequency).[28]

Customer and Supplier Interactions

Technology is changing the nature of retailer–customer and retailer–supplier interactions. See Figure 2-10. If properly implemented, benefits accrue to all parties. If not, there are negative ramifications. Here are several illustrations.

Retailers widely use point-of-sale scanning equipment. Why? By electronically scanning products (rather than having cashiers "ring up" each product), retailers can quickly complete transactions, amass sales data, give feedback to suppliers, place and receive orders faster, reduce costs, and adjust inventory. There is a downside to scanning: the error rate. This can upset consumers, especially if they perceive scanning as inaccurate. Yet, according to research on scanning, scanner errors in reading prices occur very infrequently; although consumers believe most errors result in overcharges, overcharges and undercharges are equally likely. One way to assure consumers is to display more information at the point of purchase.

One type of point-of-sale system involves self-scanning (which is discussed further in Chapter 13). Here's how a basic customer-operated point-of-sale system—a self-scanning checkout—works: Shoppers do not interact with a human cashier (although a supervisor is usually nearby to assist the customer) because these shoppers scan merchandise themselves, insert coupons in designated slots, use an electronic cash register to process a cash, credit, or debit payment, and bag their merchandise themselves. The display at a self-scanning checkout is typically touchscreen and visual. Items are placed on a flatbed scanner that reads each item's barcode; for produce, the item category is entered, the item weighed, and the price then processed by the scanner. If the shopper forgets to scan an item, an alarm will alert the supervisor.[29]

The combination of self-scanning and mobile technologies in the form of scan-as-you-shop yield a form of self-checkout. Also, customers can scan items as they select items from store shelves and add to their cart using a smartphone app. They can tap to redeem the digital coupons offered by the retailer's loyalty program that they had selected earlier. Those customers can pay at a self-checkout unit using cash or saved payment data from their mobile wallet, get a receipt, and get cash back—as in an ATM—before exiting the store. It is an easier, quicker, and automated experience for customers and allows retailers to standardize payments, reward redemptions, and

FIGURE 2-10

Advances in Technology Aid Retailer Interactions

Retailer interactions with their customers and suppliers are faster and more multiplatform than ever. Communications "anywhere, anytime" are now a reality. The new world of technology affects both large and small retailers.

Source: Samer/Shutterstock. Reprinted by permission.

personalize product recommendations based on prior purchases via mobile marketing campaigns to the individual customer.[30]

Other technological innovations also influence retail interactions. Here are three examples:

Neiman Marcus pioneered the electronic gift card (www .neimanmarcus.com).

▷ Many retailers think they have the answer to the problem of finding the perfect gift—the electronic gift card. Sales revenues in the gift card industry are over $100 billion annually. Almost 93 percent of consumers have received or given a gift card each year. Gift cards spur buyers into making new purchases, often within the first 90 days, and most consumers spend more than the gift card amount.[31] Some retailers now offer a gift-card exchange to customers who can swap physical gift cards issued by other firms (sometimes competitors) at a discount.[32] Retailers promote and sell gift cards as a means to increase sales, improve cash flow, and manage inventory. Retailers may even offer virtual gift cards through Web sites and mobile apps delivered to recipients by E-mail, text, Facebook post, or tweet.

▷ Interactive electronic kiosks (discussed in Chapter 6) are widely used and accounted for more than 40 percent of the $1.2 billion global interactive kiosk market as of 2014.[33] Smart kiosks equipped with sensors are able to collect and analyze data from customers, display product recommendations, and place orders to customers engaged through the entire path to purchase. Reasons for smart kiosk popularity include increased customer preference for self-service (e.g., hotels, airports, restaurants); a better interaction of customers with kiosks in stores to place online orders (e.g., Lands' End, Staples); access to product information (e.g., Staples); and the ability to customize products (e.g., Dr. Scholl's FootMapping kiosks). Smart kiosks reduce or eliminate the need for in-store personnel to do mundane tasks, thus reducing costs. However, mobile apps pose a threat to kiosks. Many tasks performed at kiosks can be done using smartphone apps that require very low investments for retailers.

Automated Customized Service

A new tabletop technology promises to feed customers' phones while they're feeding their appetites. Called Entercharge, the tabletop smart system was introduced in 2016 and underwent testing at 30 Los Angeles restaurants. The device won the Master-Card Challenge at the 2014 Fintech Hackathon, then spent a year in the pilot stage, conducting initial testing at a trendy downtown L.A. juice bar, Green Grotto. While Entercharge functions as a phone-charging station, the version debuting in spring 2016 uses iBeacons and Bluetooth for bill payment and customer couponing via smartphones. In addition, Entercharge will establish a "smart restaurant" experience, where the kiosk recognizes returning diners' phones and creates a personalized dining experience.

What do you think of this new technology? Why?

Source: "STORES Trends: April 2016," Susan Reda, April 2016, *STORES Magazine.* Based on material from STORES magazine. Reprinted by permission. Copyright 2016. STORES Magazine.

Some kiosk-mobile–integrated uses like Amazon Lockers use mobile apps to communicate passcodes and locations to customers and kiosks as dispensing or collection centers that interact with them.[34]

▶ More retailers are using Web portals to exchange information with suppliers. For example, ChainDrugStore.net serves a network of pharmacy stakeholders through its industry Web site, hub.pharmacyfocus.com, to provide efficient pharmacy purchasing, dispensing, reimbursement, and contracting. These portals provide a set of online tools designed to streamline communications, drive analytics and proprietary business intelligence, and manage the day-to-day data requirements of a pharmacy network. They work with more than 300 manufacturers, wholesalers, and managed care organizations to positively impact pharmacy purchasing, dispensing, reimbursement, and contracting strategy by secure online communications, analytics, and proprietary business intelligence tools. ChainDrugStore.net is the link with more than 100,000 stores and pharmacies.[35]

ETHICAL PERFORMANCE AND RELATIONSHIPS IN RETAILING

Ethical challenges fall into three interconnected categories: *Ethics* relates to the retailer's moral principles and values. *Social responsibility* involves acts benefiting society. *Consumerism* entails protecting consumer rights. "Good" behavior depends not only on the retailer but also on the expectations of the community in which it does business.

Throughout our book, "Ethics in Retailing" boxes and chapter discussions provide an opportunity to look at ethical issues. Here, we study the broader impact of ethics, social responsibility, and consumerism. Visit our blog for posts on ethical challenges (www.bermanevansretail .com).

Ethics

In dealing with their constituencies (customers, the general public, employees, suppliers, competitors, and others), retailers have a moral obligation to act ethically. Furthermore, due to the media attention paid to firms' behavior and the high expectations people have today, a failure to be ethical may lead to adverse publicity, lawsuits, the loss of customers, and a lack of self-respect among employees.

When a retailer has a sense of **ethics**, it acts in a trustworthy, fair, honest, and respectful manner with each of its constituencies. Executives must articulate to employees and channel partners which kinds of behavior are acceptable and which are not. The best way to avoid unethical acts is for firms to have written ethics codes, to distribute them to employees and channel partners, to monitor behavior, and to punish poor behavior—and for top managers to be highly ethical in their own conduct. See Figure 2-11.

Society often may deem certain behavior to be unethical even if laws do not forbid it. Most observers would agree that practices such as these are unethical (and sometimes illegal, too):

▶ Raising prices on scarce products after a natural disaster such as a hurricane.
▶ Not having adequate merchandise on hand when a sale is advertised.
▶ Charging high prices in low-income areas because consumers there do not have the transportation mobility to shop out of their neighborhoods.

FIGURE 2-11

"Ethics" in Retailing

Some retailers are less ethical than they should be. They need to do better. Use this photo as an example. It is pretty easy to read the large print in the store sign: "WEEKEND SALE. ENTIRE STORE. TAKE 40% OFF." It is almost impossible to read the small print at the bottom: "excludes dress shirts, neckware, handbags, & accessories."

Source: Chin-Hong, Cheah/ Shutterstock.com. Reprinted by permission.

> ▷ Selling alcohol and tobacco products to children.
> ▷ Having a salesperson pose as a market researcher when engaged in telemarketing.
> ▷ Defaming competitors.
> ▷ Selling refurbished merchandise as new.
> ▷ Pressuring employees to push high-profit items, even if these items are not the best products.
> ▷ Selling information from a customer database to other parties.

The Direct Marketing Association makes its complete ethics code available at its Web site (www.dmaresponsibility .org/Guidelines).

Many trade associations promote ethics codes to member firms. For example, here are some provisions of the Direct Marketing Association's ethics code:

Article 1: "All offers should be clear, honest, and complete."

Article 8: "All contacts should disclose the name of the sponsor and each purpose of the contact; no one should make offers or solicitations in the guise of one purpose when the intent is a different purpose."

Article 24: "No sweepstakes promotion should represent that a recipient or entrant has won a prize or that any entry stands a greater chance of winning a prize than any other entry when this is not the case."

Article 32: "Firms should be sensitive to the issue of consumer privacy."[36]

Social Responsibility

A retailer exhibiting **social responsibility** acts in the best interests of society—as well as itself. The challenge is to balance corporate citizenship with a fair level of profits for stockholders, management, and employees. Some forms of social responsibility are virtually cost-free, such as having employees participate in community events or disposing of waste products in a more careful way. Some are more costly, such as making donations to charitable groups or giving away goods and services to a school. Still others mean going above and beyond the letter of the law, such as having free loaner wheelchairs for persons with disabilities besides legally mandated wheelchair accessibility to retail premises.

Most retailers know socially responsible acts do not go unnoticed. Although the acts may not stimulate greater patronage for firms with weak strategies, they can be a customer inducement for those otherwise viewed as "me too" entities. It may also be possible to profit from good deeds. If a retailer donates excess inventory to a charity that cares for the ill, it can take a tax deduction equal to the cost of the goods plus one-half the difference between the cost and the retail price. To do this, a retailer must be a corporation and the charity must use the goods and not sell or trade them.

The Ronald McDonald House program (www .rmhc.org) is one of the most respected community outreach efforts in retailing.

There are some fine examples of socially responsible retailers. Ronald McDonald House Charities (RMHC) has been McDonald's Charity of Choice since 1974. During its national fundraisers, RMHC has collected over $200 million in donations from customers at participating restaurants. Portions of the operating costs of RMHC are funded by McDonald's owners/operators. McDonald's founded Ronald McDonald House so families can stay at a low-cost facility instead of a costly hotel when seriously ill children get medical treatment away from home. Ronald McDonald House Charities has served 5.7 million children and their families in its 334 RMHC facilities.[37]

Target and CVS are among the firms that no longer sell cigarettes. Walmart has specific environmental goals related to reducing waste sent to landfills, obtaining electricity from renewable energy resources, reducing emissions, and developing a more sustainable food system.[38] In 1999, Whole Foods Market was the first supermarket chain to collaborate with the Marine Stewardship Council, the leading certification program for sustainable wild-caught seafood. Whole Foods has also stopped selling especially vulnerable species of fish.

Consumerism

Consumerism involves the activities of government, business, and other organizations to protect people from practices infringing on their rights as consumers. These actions recognize that consumers have basic rights that should be safeguarded. As President Kennedy said more than 50 years ago, consumers have the *right to safety* (protection against unsafe conditions and hazardous goods and services); the *right to be informed* (protection against fraudulent, deceptive, and incomplete information, advertising, and labeling); the *right to choose* (access to a variety of goods, services, and retailers); and the *right to be heard* (consumer feedback, both positive and negative, to the firm and to government agencies).

Here are some reasons that retailers and their channel partners need to avoid business practices violating these rights and to do all they can to understand and protect them:

Learn more about ADA (www.ada.gov).

▶ Some retail practices are covered by legislation. One major law is the **Americans with Disabilities Act (ADA)**, which mandates that persons with disabilities be given appropriate access to retailing facilities. As Title III of the Act states (www.ada.gov/cguide.htm), "Public accommodations [retail stores] must comply with basic nondiscrimination requirements that prohibit exclusion, segregation, and unequal treatment. They also must comply with specific requirements related to architectural standards for new and altered buildings; reasonable modifications to policies, practices, and procedures; effective communication with people with hearing, vision, or speech disabilities; and other access requirements. Additionally, public accommodations must remove barriers in existing buildings where it is easy to do so without much difficulty or expense, given the public accommodation's resources." The ADA affects entrances, vertical transportation, width of aisles, and store displays. See Figure 2-12.

▶ People are more apt to patronize firms perceived as customer-oriented and not to shop with ones seen as "greedy."

▶ Consumers are more knowledgeable, price-conscious, and selective than in the past. Online customer reviews and social media now attract a lot of shopper interest.

▶ Large retailers may be viewed as indifferent to consumers. They may not provide enough personal attention for shoppers or may have inadequate control over employees.

ETHICS IN RETAILING | Community Champions in the UK

UK high-street supermarkets have been taking the lead in working with local communities. Tesco has in-store food collection points for donations to local food banks, while Asda, Aldi, and Sainsbury's donate their surplus food stocks to charities. Marks and Spencer has set up clothes recycling schemes. Many of the retailers have been involved in one-off schemes such as Morrisons donating $23 million of gardening equipment to over 26,500 schools. Tesco shoppers who bought new school uniforms saw a second school uniform donated to a child in the region of the world where the uniform was manufactured. Marks and Spencer's Global Community Programme provided training to people in regions where products were sourced by the chain.

Suggest a suitable "community champion" for a supermarket retailer in your country.

FIGURE 2-12

Understanding the Americans with Disabilities Act

The Americans with Disabilities Act requires that retailers provide reasonable access—both inside and outside—their stores. As highlighted here, aisles must be wide enough to accommodate shoppers who use scooters or wheelchairs to maneuver around.

Source: Paul Vasarhelyi/ Shutterstock. Reprinted by permission.

▷ For some shoppers, the increasing use of self-service causes frustration.
▷ Innovative technology is unsettling to many consumers, who must learn new shopping behavior (such as how to use electronic video kiosks).
▷ Retailers are in direct customer contact, so they are often blamed for and asked to resolve problems caused by manufacturers (such as defective products).

One troublesome issue for consumers involves how retailers handle *customer privacy*. A consumer-oriented approach, with elements such as these, can reduce negative shopper feelings:

1. Consumers should be clearly informed about the way that each company handles its customers' data. This involves transparency (full disclosure).
2. Consumers should be able to decide what kinds of information they want to receive from the company being asked to opt-in (choose to received information) rather than having to opt-in (by actively informing a firm that no information should be sent).
3. Consumers should feel confident that their personal are protected and kept secure by the company, and that only limited information is passed on to third parties (such as shippers).
4. Consumers should able to correct any personal data stored on them that they believe to be incorrect.
5. Consumer feedback on their personal private information should be promptly and properly addressed by the company.[39]

To avoid customer relations problems, many retailers have devised programs to protect consumer rights without waiting for government or consumer pressure to do so. Here are some examples.

More than 45 years ago, the Giant Food supermarket chain built on the consumer bill of four rights stated by President Kennedy, which it still follows today: (1) the right to safety; (2) the right to be informed; (3) the right to choose; and the (4) right to be heard. It has added a fifth right: the right to redress, which offers shoppers a money-back guarantee policy on products.[40]

In recent years, wireless phone service retailers have become much more aggressive in competing with one another—especially the big four of AT&T, Verizon, T-Mobile, and Sprint. They run television and other ads all the time. In an attempt to stand out, especially against giants AT&T and Verizon, T-Mobile decided to add a consumerism thrust to its company positioning by devising the industry's first customer bill of rights. T-Mobile's consumer bill of rights focuses on such issues as not having to sign a service contract, offering the ability to grade to a new phone at any time, allowing unused data to carry over, allowing free roaming around the world, and more.[41]

A number of retailers have enacted programs to test merchandise for such attributes as value, quality, misrepresentation of contents, safety, and durability. Sears, Walmart, Macy's, and Target are just a few of those doing testing. Among the other consumerism activities undertaken by many retailers are setting clear procedures for handling customer complaints, sponsoring consumer education programs, and training personnel to interact properly with customers.

Consumer-oriented activities are not limited to large chains; small firms can also be involved. A local toy store can separate toys by age group. A grocery store can set up displays featuring environmentally safe detergents. A neighborhood restaurant can cook foods in low-fat vegetable oil. A sporting goods store can give a money-back guarantee on exercise equipment, so people can try it at home.

Chapter Summary

1. *To explain what* value *really means and highlight its pivotal role in retailers' building and sustaining relationships.* Sellers undertake a series of activities and processes to provide a given level of value for the consumer. Consumers then perceive the value offered by sellers, based on the perceived benefits received versus the prices paid. Perceived value varies by type of shopper.

    A retail value chain represents the total bundle of benefits offered by a channel of distribution. It comprises shopping location, ambience, customer service, the products/brands carried, product quality, the in-stock position, shipping, prices, the retailer's image, and so forth. Some elements of a retail value chain are visible to shoppers; others are not. An expected retail strategy represents the minimum value chain elements a given customer segment expects from a given retailer type. An augmented retail strategy includes the extra elements that differentiate retailers. A potential retail strategy includes value chain elements not yet perfected in the retailer's industry category.

2. *To describe how both customer relationships and channel relationships may be nurtured in today's highly competitive marketplace.* For relationship retailing to work, enduring relationships are needed with other channel members as well as with customers. More retailers now realize loyal customers are the backbone of their business.

    To engage in relationship retailing with consumers, these factors should be considered: the customer base, customer service, customer satisfaction, and loyalty programs and defection rates. In terms of the customer base, all customers are not equal. Some shoppers are worth more nurturing than others; they are a retailer's core customers.

    Customer service has two components: expected services and augmented services. The attributes of personnel who interact with customers, as well as the number and variety of customer services offered, have a big impact on the relationship created. Some firms have improved customer service by empowering personnel, giving them the authority to bend some rules. In devising a strategy, a retailer must make broad decisions and then enact specific tactics as to credit, delivery, and so forth.

Customer satisfaction occurs when the value and customer service provided in a retail experience meet or exceed expectations. Otherwise, the consumer will be dissatisfied.

Loyalty programs reward the best customers—those with whom a retailer wants to develop long-lasting relationships. To succeed, they must complement a sound value-driven retail strategy. By studying defections, a firm can learn how many customers it is losing and why they no longer patronize the firm.

Members of a distribution channel jointly represent a value delivery system. Each one depends on the others; and every activity must be enumerated and responsibility assigned. Small retailers may have to use suppliers outside the normal channel to get the items they want and gain supplier support. A delivery system is as good as its weakest link. A relationship-oriented technique that some manufacturers and retailers are trying, especially supermarket chains, is category management.

3. *To examine the differences in relationship building between goods and service retailers.* Goods retailing focuses on selling tangible products. Service retailing involves transactions where consumers do not purchase or acquire ownership of tangible products.

    There are three kinds of service retailing: rented-goods services, where consumers lease goods for a given time; owned-goods services, where goods owned by consumers are repaired, improved, or maintained; and nongoods services, where consumers experience personal services rather than possess them. *Customer service* refers to activities that are part of the total retail experience. With service retailing, services are sold to the consumer.

    The unique features of service retailing that influence relationship building and retention are the intangible nature of many services, the inseparability of some service providers and their services, the perishability of many services, and the variability of many services.

4. *To discuss the impact of technology on relationships in retailing.* Technology is advantageous when it leads to an improved information flow between retailers and suppliers, and between retailers and customers, and to faster, smoother transactions.

Electronic banking involves both the use of ATMs and the instant processing of retail purchases. It allows centralized records and lets customers complete transactions 24 hours a day, 7 days a week, at various sites. Technology is also changing the nature of supplier–retailer–customer interactions via point-of-sale equipment, self-scanning, electronic gift cards, interactive kiosks, and other innovations.

5. *To consider the interplay between retailers' ethical performance and relationships in retailing.* Retailer challenges fall into three related categories: *Ethics* relates to a firm's moral principles and values. *Social responsibility* has to do with benefiting society. And *consumerism* entails the protection of consumer rights. "Good" behavior is based not only the firm's practices but also on the expectations of the community in which it does business.

Ethical retailers act in a trustworthy, fair, honest, and respectful way. Firms are more apt to avoid unethical behavior if they have written ethics codes, communicate them to employees, monitor and punish poor behavior, and have ethical executives. Retailers perform in a socially responsible manner when they act in the best interests of society through recycling and conservation programs and other efforts. Consumerism activities involve government, business, and independent organizations. Four consumer rights are basic: to safety, to be informed, to choose, and to be heard.

Key Terms

value (p. 46)
value chain (p. 47)
core customers (p. 50)
expected customer service (p. 50)
augmented customer service (p. 50)
employee empowerment (p. 51)
revolving credit account (p. 53)
option credit account (p. 53)

open credit account (p. 53)
customer satisfaction (p. 54)
consumer loyalty (frequent shopper) programs (p. 55)
value delivery system (p. 56)
goods retailing (p. 57)
service retailing (p. 57)
rented-goods services (p. 57)

owned-goods services (p. 58)
nongoods services (p. 58)
electronic banking (p. 60)
ethics (p. 62)
social responsibility (p. 63)
consumerism (p. 64)
Americans with Disabilities Act (ADA) (p. 64)

Questions for Discussion

1. Value is embodied by a series of activities and processes—a value chain. This provides a certain value to the consumer. What does the value chain comprise, and what features are readily recognizable as far as consumers are concerned?
2. There are five potential pitfalls to avoid in planning a value-oriented retail strategy. Discuss these three:
   a. Planning value with just a price perspective.
   b. Providing value-enhancing services that customers do not want or will not pay extra for.
   c. Competing in the wrong value/price segment.
3. How do new and mature retailing businesses differ in terms of their treatment of core customers?
4. How would you differentiate between expected and augmented customer service provisions? Why does customer service rely on the abilities of employees?
5. How would you measure the level of customer satisfaction with your favorite restaurant?
6. As a retailer, how would you reward social media referrals by customers?
7. What are the unique aspects of service retailing? Give an example of each.
8. What are the pros and cons of ATMs? As a retailer, would you want an ATM in your store? Why or why not?
9. Will the time come when most consumer purchases are made with self-scanners? Explain your answer.
10. Describe three unethical, but legal, acts on the part of retailers that you have recently encountered. How have you reacted in each case?
11. Differentiate between social responsibility and consumerism from the perspective of a retailer.
12. How would you deal with consumer concerns about privacy in their relationships with retailers?

Web-Based Exercise

Chinese shopping behavior focusses on price, and mainstream retailers tend to emphasize deals and promotions to avoid profit reduction through haggling. Do some research on Chinese retail consumers and suggest how retailers could manage their relationship with consumers. How do Chinese consumers view their relationships with retailers?

APPENDIX Planning for the Unique Aspects of Service Retailing

We present this appendix because service retailing in the United States and around the world is growing steadily and represents a large portion of overall retailing. U.S consumers spend 60 percent of their after-tax income on such services as travel, recreation, personal care, education, medical care, and housing. Over 84 percent of the labor force works in services. Consumers spend billions of dollars each year to rent such products as power tools and party goods (coffee urns, silverware, wine glasses, etc.). There are 86,000 beauty and barber shops; 480,000 restaurants; and 53,000 commercial child care and 21,000 nonprofit child care facilities.[1] Although automation has substantially reduced manufacturing labor costs, many services remain labor-intensive due to their personal nature.

Here, we look at the abilities required to be a successful service retailer, how to improve the performance of service retailers, and the strategy of a Baldrige Award winner.

Abilities Required to Be a Successful Service Retailer

The personal abilities required to succeed in service retailing are usually quite distinct from those in goods retailing, as shown here:

► With service retailing, the major value provided to the customer is some type of retailer service, not the ownership of a physical product produced by a manufacturer.

► Specific skills are often required, and these skills may not be transferable from one type of service to another. Television repair technicians, beauticians, and accountants cannot easily change businesses or transfer skills. The owners of appliance stores, cosmetics stores, and toy stores (all goods retailers) would have an easier time than service retailers in changing and transferring their skills to another area.

► More service operators must possess licenses or certification to run their businesses. Barbers, real-estate brokers, dentists, attorneys, plumbers, and others must pass exams in their fields.

► Owners of service businesses must enjoy their jobs and have the aptitude for them. Because of the close personal contact with customers, these elements are essential and hard to fake.

Many service retailers can operate on lower overall investments and succeed on less yearly revenues than goods retailers. A firm with four outdoor tennis courts can operate with one worker who functions as clerk/cashier and maintenance person. A tax-preparation firm can succeed with one accountant. A watch repair business needs one repairperson. In each case, the owner may be the only skilled worker. Operating costs can be held down accordingly. On the other hand, a goods retailer needs a solid product assortment and inventory on hand, which may be costly and require storage facilities.

The time commitment of a service retailer differs by type of business opportunity. Some businesses, such as a self-service laundromat or a movie theater, require a low time commitment. Other businesses, such as house painting or a travel agency, require a large time commitment because personal service is the key to profitability. More service firms are in the high rather than the low time-investment category.

Improving the Performance of Service Retailers

Service tangibility can be increased by stressing service provider reliability, promoting a continuous theme (the Hertz #1 Club Gold), describing specific results (a car tune-up improving gas consumption by 1 mile per gallon), and offering warranties (hotels giving automatic refunds to unhappy guests). Airlines have Web sites where customers can select flights and make their reservations interactively. These sites are a tangible representation of the airlines and their logos.

Demand and supply can be better matched by offering similar services to market segments with different demand patterns (e.g., tourists versus residents). This can be done by offering new services with demand patterns that are countercyclical from existing services (cross-country skiing during the winter at Denver golf resorts); new services that complement existing ones (beauty salons adding tanning booths); special deals during nonpeak times (midweek movie theater prices); and new services not subject to existing capacity constraints (a 10-table restaurant starting a home catering service).

Standardizing services reduces their variability, makes it easier to set prices, and improves efficiency. Services can be standardized by clearly defining each task, determining the minimum and maximum times needed to complete each task, selecting the best order for tasks to be done, and noting the optimum time and quality of the entire service. Standardization has been successfully applied to such firms as quick-auto-service providers (oil change and tune-up firms), legal services (for house closings and similar proceedings), and emergency medical care centers. If services are standardized, there is often a trade-off (e.g., more consistent quality and convenience in exchange for less of a personal touch).

Besides standardizing services, retailers may be able to make services more efficient by automating them and substituting machinery for labor. Thus, real-estate attorneys often use word-processing templates for common paragraphs in house closings. This means more consistency in the way documents look, time savings, and neater documents with fewer errors. Among the service firms that automate at least part of their operations are banks, car washes, bowling alleys, airlines, phone services, real-estate brokers, and hotels.

One way that services can increase customer loyalty is by better understanding and reacting to shopper complaints. This strategy enables a service operator to rectify problem areas that would otherwise be unknown. It also makes it possible for the service operator to offer restitution to the consumer so that he/she will remain loyal. Unfortunately, too often, a dissatisfied customer will find it easier to switch to a competitor (or complain to friends and family) as opposed to complaining to the service operator. Retailers can reduce the negative effect of a service-related failure by (1) apologizing, (2) reviewing the complaint, (3) fixing the problem and following up to show concern, (4) documenting the problem so that the poor situation will not recur, and (5) communicating with these customers and treating them in a fair manner. Employee politeness and sincerity are closely related to customer satisfaction following a service failure.[2]

The location of a service retailer must be carefully considered. Sometimes, as with TV repairs, house painting, and lawn care, the service is "delivered" to the customer. The firm's location becomes a client's home, and the actual retail office is rather insignificant. Many clients might never even see a service firm's office; they make contact by phone or personal visits, and customer convenience is optimized. The firm incurs travel expenses, but it also has low (or no) rent and does not have to maintain store facilities, set up displays, and so on. Other service retailers are visited on "specific-intent" shopping trips. Although a customer may be concerned about the convenience of a service location, he or she usually does not select a skilled practitioner such as a doctor or a lawyer based on the location. It is common for doctors and attorneys to have offices in their homes or near hospitals or court buildings. A small store can often be used because little or no room is needed for displaying merchandise. A travel agency may have six salespeople and book millions of dollars in trips, but fit into a 500-square-foot store.

Satisfaction-based pricing recognizes and reduces customer perceptions of uncertainty that service intangibility magnifies. It involves service guarantees, benefit-driven pricing, and flat-rate pricing.[3] Relationship pricing encourages long-term relationships with valuable customers. It entails long-term contracts and price bundling. Efficiency pricing shares cost savings with customers that arise from the firm's efficiently executing service tasks. It is related to the concept of cost leadership.

Negotiated pricing occurs when a retailer works out pricing arrangements with individual customers because a unique or complex service is involved and a one-time price must be agreed on. Unlike traditional pricing (whereby each consumer pays the same price for a standard service), each consumer may pay a different price under negotiated pricing (depending on the nature of the unique service). A moving company charges different fees, depending on the distance of the move, who packs the breakable furniture, the use of stairs versus an elevator, access to highways, and the weight of furniture.

Contingency pricing is an arrangement whereby the retailer does not get paid until after the service is performed and payment is contingent on the service's being satisfactory. A real-estate broker earns a fee only when a house purchaser (who is ready, willing, and able to buy) is presented to the house seller. Several brokers may show a house to prospective buyers, but only the broker who actually sells the house earns a commission. This technique presents risks to a retailer because considerable time and effort may be spent without payment. A broker may show a house 25 times, not sell it, and therefore not be paid.

Dynamic pricing uses data from customers, as well as ongoing analyses of reservations (such as airlines and hotels), to vary prices on a customer-by-customer basis. Prices can differ for the same service, such as airline travel, based on when a customer makes a reservation (early or late), the time of day and day of the week of the flight, and whether the service provider feels it needs to reduce price to fill otherwise empty facilities (seats on a plane or at a show).[4]

One customer type is often beyond the reach of some service firms: the do-it-yourselfer. And the number of do-it-yourselfers in the United States is growing, as service costs increase (and due to the slow-growth economy). The do-it-yourselfer performs repairs on his or her car, paints the house, mows the lawn, and makes all vacation plans. Goods-oriented discount retailers do well by selling supplies to these people, but service retailers suffer because labor is done by the customer.

The Strategy of Pal's Sudden Service: Baldrige Award Winner[5]

The Baldrige Award is given by the president of the United States to businesses—manufacturing and service, small and large—and to education and healthcare organizations that apply and are judged to be outstanding in seven areas: leadership; strategic planning; customer and market focus; measurement, analysis, and knowledge management; human resource focus; process management; and results. One of the few retailers to win the award is Pal's Sudden Service—based in Kingsport, Tennessee—a privately owned, quick-service restaurant chain with 26 locations and about 1,000 employees (as of 2016). The firm distinguishes itself by offering competitively priced food of consistently high quality, delivered quickly, cheerfully, and without error.

At Pal's, customer waiting time from placing an order to picking it up is four times faster than the second-fastest quick-serve U.S. restaurant; at the drive-up window, where orders are placed, the average turnaround time is 12 seconds. Despite the speedy service, Pal's makes an error only once in every 3,600 orders. That is 10 times better than the average fast-food restaurant.

Hop over to Pal's Sudden Service (www.palsweb .com). See why it's a big winner!

Pal's has a process for every organizational and operational activity. Its Business Excellence Process is the key integrating force and ensures that customer needs are met in each transaction. Carried out under the leadership of Pal's top executives and its owner-operators, this process spans all facets of operations from strategic planning (done annually) to online quality control.

The company's success in significantly reducing turnover among frontline production and service personnel, most of whom are between the ages of 16 and 18 and work part-time, is a big advantage. Job candidates must pass a 60-question psychometric test before being considered for training. Owner-operators and assistant managers have primary responsibility for training, based on a four-step model: Show it, do it, evaluate it, and perform it again. New employees get 120 hours of training before working on their own and must be certified for each specific job task. At the assistant manager level, job turnover is 1.4 percent; at the front-line level it is just 32 percent.

3

Strategic Planning in Retailing

Strategic planning in retailing is a complex process with a number of intertwined factors, both controllable and uncontrollable. Previously, retailers were focused on in-store marketing by trying to influence consumers' buying decisions as they shopped—typically through flashy product displays, special promotions at the end of the aisle, and attention-grabbing packaging on the shelf.

Today, many consumers approach their shopping differently, and retailers need to plan and adapt their strategies accordingly. Consumers not only go online to shop; they also go online to begin the shopping process and sometimes just to hear what others have to say. The dominance of the online channel in some retail categories such as consumer electronics, travel, and entertainment has damaged, and in some cases obliterated, business models of established retailers and led to the popularity of pure online firms. In other product categories, where the online channel has been less disruptive, the ongoing digitization due to mobile and social-media technologies is forcing additional planning and investment in retailers' omnichannel strategies as consumers use channels and devices (laptops, smartphones, and tablets) interchangeably and seamlessly during their search and purchase process. Retailers have no control over this usage. Developing long-term relationships with customers or brand intimacy is the key. *Brand intimacy* describes an essential relationship between a person and a brand (this can include retailers). Brand intimacy transcends usage, purchase, and loyalty. According to brand agency MBLM, the Brand Intimacy Agency (www.mblm.com), intimate brands create enhanced business performance.

Chapter Objectives

1. To show the value of strategic planning for all types of retailers

2. To explain the steps in strategic planning for retailers: situation analysis, objectives, identification of consumers, overall strategy, specific activities, control, and feedback

3. To examine the individual controllable and uncontrollable elements of a retail strategy, and to present strategic planning as a series of integrated steps

4. To demonstrate how a strategic plan can be prepared

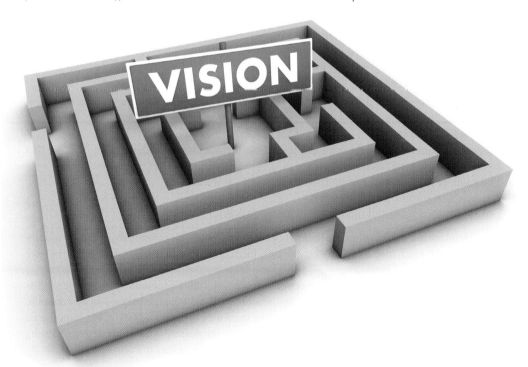

Source: niroworld/Shutterstock.
Reprinted by permission.

So, which brands succeed at developing intimate connections? That depends on gender. Women connect with a broad and more mature staple of brands that involve more aspects of their daily lives. Among female consumers, Apple is the most intimate brand followed by Disney, Amazon, Whole Foods, and Toyota, according to MBLM. The top five brands for men are Harley-Davidson, Apple, Toyota, Nintendo, and Lexus. Rina Plapler, a MLBM partner, insists that how people form bonds with brands transcends gender. "It's important to see the types of brands that women tend to connect with and how age and income influence brand choices. It helps retailers to better promote goods and services and form deep brand attachments."

Age and income play a large role in determining brand preferences. Among female Millennials ages 18 to 34, the top five brands are Apple, Amazon, Sephora, Target, and Whole Foods; 18- to 34-year-old men select Nintendo, Samsung, PlayStation, Xbox, and YouTube as their top five. Women earning $34,000 to $49,000 are most connected, with L'Oréal, Revlon, and Dove in their top five. Among those with incomes of $50,000 to $75,000, leaders include Apple, Starbucks, Olay, Coca-Cola, and Netflix. And for those earning $75,000 to $150,000, Apple, Sephora, Amazon, Target, and Clinique top the list.[1]

Overview

In this chapter, we cover strategic retail planning—the foundation of our book—in detail. As noted in Chapter 1, a **retail strategy** is the overall plan or framework of action that guides a retailer. Ideally, it will cover at least 1 year and outline the retailer's mission, goals, consumer market, overall and specific activities, and control mechanisms. Without a defined and well-integrated strategy, a firm may be unable to cope with the marketplace. The U.S. Small Business Administration recommends that every business, irrespective of whether it intends to seek financial support from lenders or investors, should have comprehensive and thoughtful business plan. It serves as a roadmap for the next 3 to 5 years and helps thoughtful and objective decision making on many key business elements, including:

(1) What you will need to do to get started and what resources (time, money, etc.) you will need to expend. (2) What it will take for your business to make a profit and how long that will take. (3) What information potential customers, vendors, and investors will need to know in order for you to effectively market your business. Many other factors critical to business success depend on your plan: outside funding, credit from suppliers, management of your operation and finances, promotion and marketing of your business, and achievement of your goals and objectives. The U.S. Small Business Association provides a step-by-step interactive guide Business Plan Tool to help entrepreneurs get started on their planning process.[2]

OnStrategy (http://onstrategyhq.com) has a lot of useful planning tools for retailers at its Web site. Click on "Resources."

The process of strategic retail planning has several attractive features:

1. It provides a thorough analysis of the requirements for doing business for different types of retailers.
2. It outlines retailer goals.
3. A firm determines how to differentiate itself from competitors and develop an offering that appeals to a group of customers.
4. The legal, economic, and competitive environment is studied.
5. A firm's total efforts are coordinated.
6. Crises are anticipated and often minimized or avoided.

Strategic planning can be done by the owner of a firm, professional management, or a combination of the two. Even among family businesses, the majority of high-growth companies have strategic plans.

The steps in planning and enacting a retail strategy are interdependent; a firm often starts with a general plan that gets more specific as options and payoffs become clearer. In this chapter, we cover each step in developing a retail strategy, as shown in Figure 3-1. Given the importance of global retailing, a chapter appendix explores the special dimensions of strategic planning in a global environment. Visit our blog (www.bermanevansretail.com) for several links on strategic planning.

FIGURE 3-1

Elements of a Retail Strategy

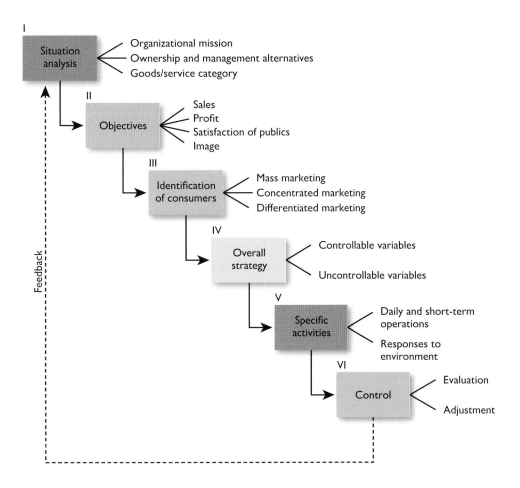

SITUATION ANALYSIS

Situation analysis is a candid evaluation of the opportunities and threats facing a prospective or existing retailer. It seeks to answer two general questions: What is the firm's current status? In which direction should it be heading? Situation analysis means being guided by an organizational mission, evaluating ownership and management options, and outlining the goods/service category to be sold.

A good strategy anticipates and adapts to both the opportunities and threats in a changing business environment. **Opportunities** are marketplace openings that exist because other retailers have not yet capitalized on them. Ikea does well because it is the pioneer firm in offering a huge selection of furniture at discount prices. **Threats** are environmental and marketplace factors that can adversely affect retailers if they do not react to them (and, sometimes, even if they do). Single-screen movie theaters have virtually disappeared because they have been unable to fend off multiscreen theaters. Movies available via pay-per-view services and streaming movies by subscription services like Netflix and Amazon are additional threats to the movie theater industry.

A firm needs to spot trends early enough to satisfy customers and stay ahead of competitors, yet not so early that shoppers are not ready for changes or that false trends are perceived. Merchandising shifts—such as stocking fad items—are more quickly enacted than changes in a firm's location, price, or promotion strategy. A new retailer can adapt to trends easier than existing ones with established images, ongoing leases, and space limitations. Well-prepared small firms can compete with large retailers due to their nimbleness.

In situation analysis, especially for a new retailer or one thinking about a major strategic change, an honest, in-depth self-assessment is vital. It is all right for a person or company to be ambitious and aggressive, but overestimating one's abilities and prospects may be harmful—if it results in entry into the wrong retail business, inadequate resources, or misjudging competitors.

Organizational Mission

An **organizational mission** is a retailer's commitment to a type of business and to a distinctive role in the marketplace. It is reflected in the firm's attitude toward consumers, employees, suppliers, competitors, government, and others. A clear mission lets a firm gain a customer following and distinguish itself from competitors. Figure 3-2 highlights some inspirational quotes from prominent executives that retailers should keep in mind when devising their missions.

One major decision is whether to base a business around the goods and services sold or around consumer needs. A person opening a hardware business must decide if, in addition to hardware products, a line of bathroom vanities should be stocked. A traditionalist might not carry vanities because they seem unconnected to the proposed business. But if the store is to be a do-it-yourself home improvement center, vanities are a logical part of the mix. That store would carry any relevant items the consumer wants.

A second major decision is whether a retailer wants a place in the market as a leader or a follower. It could seek to offer a unique strategy, such as Taco Bell becoming the first national

FIGURE 3-2

Leadership Lessons from Retail Executives

Source: Based on material from National Retail Federation (www.nrfc.com/careers), "21 Leadership Lessons from Retail Executives," https://nrf.com/sites/default/files/Leadership_Lessons.pdf. Reprinted by permission.

CAREERS IN RETAILING

"Builders," "Maintainers," and "Undertakers"

The skill set of retail executives needs to match the needs of the organization, as well as the life-cycle stage of the firm (growing, mature, or decline). Multiple-unit organizations (such as Saks Fifth Avenue and Off Saks, a discount unit of the parent organization) may have different objectives (such as moderate growth at Saks Fifth Avenue versus higher growth at Off Saks, based on sales per store unit as well as additional units). Likewise, an emerging retail format, Peapod (a home delivery service for groceries) requires different manager types than a traditional supermarket (such as corporate owner Stop & Shop). Fast-growing units should be headed by "builders," mature units by "maintainers, and declining businesses by "undertakers," who specialize in selling off or redeploying assets in other locations and business units.

Develop job descriptions for the three different types of managers.

quick-serve Mexican food chain. Or it could emulate practices of competitors but do a better job executing them, such as a local fast-food Mexican restaurant offering five-minute guaranteed service and a cleanliness pledge.

A third decision involves market scope. Large chains often seek a broad customer base (due to their resources and recognition). It is often best for small retailers and startups to focus on a narrower customer base, so they can compete in a local versus a regional marketplace.

Although the development of an organizational mission is the first step in the planning process, a firm's mission should be continually reviewed and adjusted to reflect changing company goals and a dynamic retail environment. Here is an example of how Amazon's organizational mission has evolved since it launched online in July 1995.

> Its initial mission was to use the Internet to transform book buying into the fastest, easiest, and most enjoyable shopping experience possible.[3] Since then, Amazon has grown in sales revenues ($100 billion in 2015)[4] and in product offerings to be the seventh largest retailer in the world. As a result, its mission statement has become much broader, but the focus and commitment to customer satisfaction and the delivery of an educational shopping experience has remained.[5]

See how the Neiman Marcus Web site (www .neimanmarcus.com) is consistent with its upscale mission.

Ownership and Management Alternatives

An essential aspect of situation analysis is assessing ownership and management alternatives, including whether to form a sole proprietorship, partnership, or corporation—and whether to start a new business, buy an existing business, or become a franchisee.[6] Management options include owner-manager versus professional manager and centralized versus decentralized structures. There is no one best ownership type for a retailer; the type of legal structure impacts taxation, personal liability, record keeping, and the ability to raise money. The limitations of a particular form of ownership can often be overcome. For instance, a sole proprietor can buy insurance coverage to reduce liability exposure. Astute entrepreneurs re-evaluate their choice of entity as their business evolves. The Small Business Association (SBA) and an experienced attorney or tax advisor are valuable sources of information and advice for a business.[7]

A **sole proprietorship** is an unincorporated retail firm owned by one person. All benefits, profits, risks, and costs accrue to that individual. It is simple to form, fully controlled by the owner, operationally flexible, easy to dissolve, and subject to single taxation by the government. It makes the owner personally liable for legal claims from suppliers, creditors, and others; it can also lead to limited capital and expertise.

A **partnership** is an unincorporated retail firm owned by two or more persons, each with a financial interest. Partners share benefits, profits, risks, and costs. Advantages include the following: Responsibility and expertise are divided among multiple principals, there is a greater capability for raising funds than with a proprietorship, the format is simpler to form than a corporation, and it is subject to single taxation by the government. Depending on the type of partnership, it can make owners personally liable for legal claims, can be dissolved due to a partner's death or a disagreement, it binds all partners to actions made by any individual partner acting on behalf of the firm, and it usually has less ability to raise capital than a corporation.

A **corporation** is a retail firm that is formally incorporated under state law. It is a legal entity apart from individual officers (or stockholders). Funds can be raised through the sale of stock; legal claims against individuals are not usually allowed; ownership transfer is relatively easy; the firm is more assured of long-term existence (if a founder leaves, retires, or dies); the use of professional managers is encouraged; and unambiguous operating authority is outlined. Depending on the type of corporation, it is subject to double taxation (company earnings and stockholder dividends), faces more government rules, can require a complex process when established, may be viewed as impersonal, and may separate ownership from management. A closed corporation is run by a limited number of persons who control ownership; stock is not available to the public. In an open corporation, stock is traded and available to the public.

Sole proprietorships account for 74 percent of U.S. retail firms filing tax returns, partnerships for 6 percent, and corporations for 20 percent. Yet, sole proprietorships account for just 5 percent of total U.S. retail store sales, partnerships for 10 percent, and corporations for 85 percent.[8]

Starting a new business—being entrepreneurial—offers a retailer flexibility in location, operating style, product lines, customer markets, and other factors, and involves planning and implementing a strategy that is fully tailored to the owner's desires and strengths. There may be high construction costs, a time lag until the business is opened and then until profits are earned, beginning with an unknown name, and having to form supplier relationships and amass an inventory of goods. Figure 3-3 presents a checklist to consider when starting a retail business.

Buying an existing business allows a retailer to acquire an established company name, a customer following, a good location, trained personnel, and facilities; to operate immediately; to generate ongoing sales and profits; and to possibly get good lease terms or financing (at low

FIGURE 3-3

A Checklist to Consider When Starting a New Retail Business

Source: Adapted by the authors from *Small Business Management Training Instructor's Guide,* No. 109 (Washington, DC: U.S. Small Business Administration, n.d.).

Name of Business _____

A. Self-Assessment and Business Choice
✓ Evaluate your strengths and weaknesses.
✓ Commitment paragraph: Why should you be in business for yourself? Why open a new business rather than acquire an existing one or become a member of a franchise chain?
✓ Describe the type of retail business that fits your strengths and desires. What will make it unique? What will the business offer customers? How will you capitalize on the weaknesses of competitors?

B. Overall Retail Plan
✓ State your philosophy of business.
✓ Choose an ownership form (sole proprietorship, partnership, or corporation).
✓ State your long- and short-run goals.
✓ Analyze your customers from their point of view.
✓ Research your market size and store location.
✓ Quantify the total retail sales of your goods/service category in your trading area.
✓ Analyze your competition.
✓ Quantify your potential market share.
✓ Develop your retail strategy: store location and operations, merchandising, pricing, and store image and promotion.

C. Financial Plan
✓ What level of funds will you need to get started and to get through the first year? Where will they come from?
✓ Determine the first-year profit, return on investment, and salary that you need/want.
✓ Project monthly cash flow and profit-and-loss statements for the first two years.
✓ What sales will be needed to break even during the first year? What will you do if these sales are not reached?

D. Organizational Details Plan
✓ Describe your personnel plan (hats to wear), organizational plan, and policies.
✓ List the jobs you like and want to do and those you dislike, cannot do, or do not want to do.
✓ Outline your accounting and inventory systems.
✓ Note your insurance plans.
✓ Specify how day-to-day operations would be conducted for each aspect of your strategy.
✓ Review the risks you face and how you plan to cope with them.

FIGURE 3-4

A Checklist for Purchasing an Existing Retail Business

NAME OF BUSINESS _____

✓ Why is the seller placing the business up for sale?

✓ How much are you paying for goodwill (the cost of the business above its tangible asset value)?

✓ Have sales, inventory levels, and profit figures been confirmed by your accountant?

✓ Will the seller introduce you to his or her customers and stay on during the transition period?

✓ Will the seller sign a statement that he or she will not open a directly competing business in the same trading area for a reasonable time period?

✓ If sales are seasonal, are you purchasing the business at the right time of the year?

✓ In the purchase of the business, are you assuming existing debts of the seller?

✓ Who receives proceeds from transactions made prior to the sale of the business but not yet paid by customers?

✓ What is the length of the lease if property is rented?

✓ If property is to be purchased along with the business, has it been inspected by a professional engineer?

✓ How modern are the storefront and store fixtures?

✓ Is inventory fresh? Does it contain a full merchandise assortment?

✓ Are the advertising policy, customer service policy, and pricing policy of the past owner similar to yours? Can you continue old policies?

✓ If the business is to be part of a chain, is the new unit compatible with existing units?

✓ How much trading-area overlap is there with existing stores?

✓ Has a lawyer examined the proposed contract?

✓ What effect will owning this business have on your lifestyle and on your family relationships?

interest rates) from the seller. A few disadvantages are that fixtures may be older, there is less flexibility in enacting a strategy tailored to the new owner's desires and strengths, and the growth potential of the business may be limited. One issue that must be examined in purchasing is the valuation of a firm's existing inventory. Figure 3-4 shows a checklist to consider when purchasing an existing retail business.

By being a franchisee, a retailer can combine independent ownership with franchisor support such as strategic planning assistance; a known company name and loyal customer following; cooperative advertising and buying; and a regional, national, or global (rather than local) image. However, a franchisee contract may specify rigid operating standards, limit the product lines sold, and restrict supplier choice; the franchisor company is usually paid continuously (royalties); advertising fees may be required; and there is a possibility of termination by the franchisor if the agreement is not followed satisfactorily.

Strategically, the management format also has a dramatic impact. With an owner-manager, planning tends to be less formal and more intuitive, and many tasks are reserved for that person (such as employee supervision and cash management). With professional management, planning tends to be more formal and systematic. Yet, professional managers are more constrained in their authority than an owner-manager. In a centralized structure, planning clout lies with top management or ownership; managers in individual departments have major input into decisions with a decentralized structure.

A comprehensive discussion of independent retailers, chains, franchises, leased departments, vertical marketing systems, and consumer cooperatives is included in Chapter 4.

Goods/Service Category

Entrepreneur magazine (www.entrepreneur.com) addresses many of the issues facing new and growing firms as they plan their strategies.

Before a prospective retail firm can fully design a strategic plan, it selects a **goods/service category**—the line of business—in which to operate. Figure 3-5 shows the diversity of goods/service categories. Chapter 5 examines the attributes of food-based and general merchandise store retailers. Chapter 6 focuses on Web, nonstore, and other forms of nontraditional retailing.

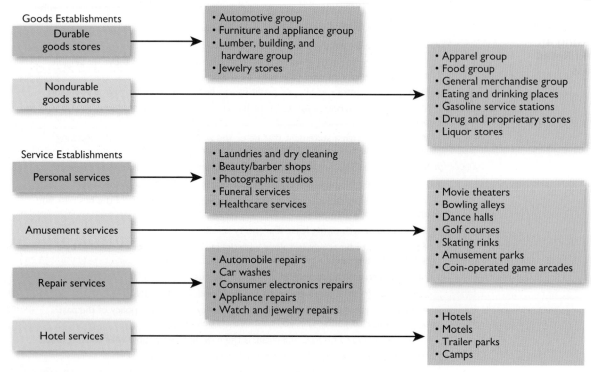

FIGURE 3-5
Selected Kinds of Retail Goods and Service Establishments

It is advisable to specify both a general goods/service category and a niche within that category. Mercedes dealers are luxury auto retailers catering to upscale customers. Wendy's is a chain known for its quality fast food with a menu emphasizing hamburgers. Motel 6 is a chain whose strength is inexpensive, clean, and centrally located hotel rooms with few frills.

A potential retail business owner should select a type of business that will allow him or her to match personal abilities, financial resources, and time availability with the requirements of that kind of business. Visit our blog (www.bermanevansretail.com) for links to many retail trade associations that represent various goods/service categories.

Personal Abilities

Personal abilities depend on an individual's aptitude—the preference for a type of business and the potential to do well; education—formal learning about retail practices and policies; and experience—practical learning about retail practices and policies.

An individual who wants to run a business, shows initiative, and has the ability to react quickly to competitive developments will be suited to a different type of situation than a person who depends on others for advice and does not like to make fast decisions. The first individual could be an independent operator in a dynamic business such as apparel; the second might seek partners or a franchise and a stable business, such as a stationery store. Some people enjoy customer interaction; they would dislike the impersonality of a self-service operation. Others enjoy the impersonality of mail-order or Web retailing.

In certain fields, education and experience requirements are specified by law. Stockbrokers, real-estate brokers, beauticians, pharmacists, and opticians must all satisfy educational or experience standards to show competency. For example, real-estate brokers are licensed after a review of their knowledge of real-estate practices and their ethical character. The legal designation "broker" does not depend on the ability to sell or have a customer-oriented demeanor.

Some skills can be learned; others are inborn. Accordingly, potential retail owners have to assess their skills and match them with the demands of a given business. This involves careful reflection about oneself. Partnerships may be best when two or more parties possess complementary skills. A person with selling experience may join with someone who has the operating skills to start a business. Each partner has valued skills, but he or she may be unable to operate a retail entity without the expertise of the other.

Financial Resources

Many retail enterprises, especially new, independent ones, fail because the owners do not adequately project the financial resources needed to open and operate the firm. Table 3-1 outlines some of the typical investments for a new retail venture.

Novice retailers tend to underestimate the value of a personal drawing account, which is used for the living expenses of the owner and his or her family in the early, unprofitable stage of a business. Because few new ventures are immediately profitable, the budget must include such expenditures. In addition, the costs of renovating an existing facility often are miscalculated. Underfunded firms usually invest in only essential renovations. This practice reduces the initial investment, but it may give the retailer a poor image. Merchandise assortment, as well as the types of goods and services sold, also affects the financial outlay. Finally, the use of a partnership, corporation, or franchise agreement will affect the investment.

Table 3-2 illustrates the financial requirements for a hypothetical used-car dealer. The initial personal savings investment of $300,000 would force many potential owners to rethink the choice of product category and the format of the firm: (1) The plans for a 40-car inventory reflect this owner's desire for a balanced product line. If the firm concentrates on subcompact, compact, and intermediate cars, it can reduce inventory size and lower the investment, (2) the initial investment can be reduced by seeking a location whose facilities do not have to be modified, and (3) fewer financial resources are needed if a partnership or corporation is set up with other individuals, so that costs—and profits—are shared.

Wells Fargo (www .wellsfargo.com/biz) offers financial support and advice for small firms.

The U.S. Small Business Administration (www.sba.gov) assists businesses by guaranteeing thousands of loans each year. Such private companies as Wells Fargo and American Express also have financing programs specifically aimed at small businesses.

Time Demands

Time demands on retail owners (or managers) differ significantly by goods or service category. They are influenced both by consumer shopping patterns and by the ability of the owner or manager to automate operations or delegate activities to others.

Many retailers must have regular weekend and evening hours to serve time-pressed shoppers. Gift shops, toy stores, and others have extreme seasonal shifts in their hours. Mail-order firms and those selling through the Web, which can process orders during any part of the day, have more flexible hours.

Some businesses require less owner involvement, including gas stations with no repair services, coin-operated laundries, and movie theaters. The emphasis on automation, self-service,

TABLE 3-1 Some Typical Financial Investments for a New Retail Venture

Use of Funds	Source of Funds
Land and building (lease or purchase)	Personal savings, bank loan, commercial finance company
Inventory	Personal savings, manufacturer credit, commercial finance company, sales revenues
Fixtures (display cases, storage facilities, signs, lighting, carpeting, etc.)	Personal savings, manufacturer credit, bank loan, commercial finance company
Equipment (cash register, marking machine, office equipment, computers, etc.)	Personal savings, manufacturer credit, bank loan, commercial finance company
Personnel (salespeople, cashiers, stockpeople, etc.)	Personal savings, bank loan, sales revenues
Promotion	Personal savings, sales revenues
Personal drawing account	Personal savings, life insurance loan
Miscellaneous (equipment repair, credit sales [bad debts], professional wholesaler credit, bank services, repayment of loans)	Personal savings, manufacturer and credit plan, bank loan, commercial finance company

Note: Collateral for a bank loan may be a building, fixtures, land, inventory, or a personal residence.

TABLE 3-2 Financial Requirements for a Used-Car Dealer

Total investments (first year)

Lease (10 years, $60,000 per year)	$ 60,000
Beginning inventory (40 cars, average cost of $10,000)	400,000
Replacement inventory (40 cars, average cost of $10,000)*	400,000
Fixtures and equipment (painting, paneling, carpeting, lighting, signs, heating and air-conditioning system, electronic cash register, service bay)	60,000
Replacement parts	75,000
Personnel (one mechanic)	45,000
Promotion (brochures and newspaper advertising)	35,000
Drawing account (to cover owner's personal expenses for one year; all selling and operating functions except mechanical ones performed by the owner)	40,000
Accountant	15,000
Miscellaneous (loan payments, etc.)	100,000
Profit (projected)	40,000
	$1,270,000

Source of funds

Personal savings	$ 300,000
Bank loan	426,000
Sales revenues (based on expected sales of 40 cars, average price of $13,600)	544,000
	$1,270,000

* Assumes that 40 cars are sold during the year. As each type of car is sold, a replacement is bought by the dealer and placed in inventory. At the end of the year, inventory on hand remains at 40 units.

standardization, and financial controls lets the owner reduce her or his time. Other businesses, such as hair salons, restaurants, and jewelry stores, require more active owner involvement.

Intensive owner participation can be the result of several factors:

▶ The owner may be the key service provider, with patrons attracted by his or her skills (the major competitive advantage). Delegating work to others will lessen consumer loyalty.
▶ Personal services are not easy to automate.
▶ Due to limited funds, the owner and his or her family must often undertake all operating functions for a small retail firm. Spouses and/or children work in 40 percent of family-owned businesses.
▶ In a business that operates on a cash basis, the owner must be around to avoid being cheated.

Off-hours activities are often essential. At a restaurant, some foods must be prepared in advance of the posted dining hours. An owner of a small computer store cleans, stocks shelves, and does the books during the hours the firm is closed. A prospective retail owner also has to examine his or her time preferences regarding stability versus seasonality, ideal working hours, and personal involvement.

OBJECTIVES

Kroger (www.kroger.com) is one of the leading food-based retailers in the United States.

After situation analysis, a retailer sets **objectives**, the long-run and short-run performance targets it hopes to attain. This helps in strategy and translates the organizational mission into action. A firm can pursue goals related to one or more of these areas: sales, profit, satisfaction of publics, and image. Some retailers strive to achieve all these goals; others attend to a few and want to achieve them really well. Think about the array of goals for the Kroger Company: competitive pricing while maintaining profitability, long-term sales growth, and reducing operations costs.[9]

Sales

Sales objectives are related to the volume of goods and services a retailer sells. Growth, stability, and market share are the sales goals most often sought.

Some retailers set sales growth as a top priority. They want to expand their business; therefore, they may place less emphasis on short-run profits. The assumption is that current investments will yield future sales and profits. A firm that does well often becomes interested in opening new units, expanding channel coverage and enlarging revenues. However, management skills and the personal touch are sometimes lost with overly fast expansion.

Stability is the goal of retailers that emphasize maintaining their sales volume, market share, price lines, and so on. Small retailers often seek stable sales that enable the owners to make a satisfactory living every year without downswings or upsurges. And certain firms develop a loyal customer following and are intent not on expanding but on continuing the approach that attracted the original consumers.

For some firms, market share—the percentage of total retail-category sales contributed by a given company—is another goal. It is often an objective only for large retailers or retail chains. The small retailer is more concerned with competition across the street than with total sales in a metropolitan area.

Sales objectives may be expressed in dollars and units. To reach dollar goals, a retailer can engage in a discount strategy (low prices and high unit sales), a moderate strategy (medium prices and medium unit sales), or a prestige strategy (high prices and low unit sales). In the long run, having unit sales as a performance target is vital. Dollar sales by year may be difficult to compare due to changing retail prices and inflation; unit sales are easier to compare. A firm with sales of $350,000 3 years ago and $500,000 today might assume it is doing well, until unit sales are computed: 10,000 then and 8,000 now.

Profit

With profitability objectives, retailers seek at least a minimum profit level during a designated period, usually a year. Profit may be expressed in dollars or as a percentage of sales. For a firm with yearly sales of $5 million and total costs of $4.2 million, pre-tax dollar profit is $800,000 and profits as a percentage of sales are 16 percent. If the profit goal is equal to or less than $800,000, or 16 percent, the retailer is satisfied. If the goal is higher, the firm has not attained the minimum desired profit and is dissatisfied.

Firms with large capital expenditures in land, buildings, and equipment often set return on investment (ROI) as a goal. Return on investment is the relationship between profits and the investment in capital items. A satisfactory rate of return is pre-defined and compared with the actual return at the end of the year or other period. For a retailer with annual sales of $5 million and expenditures (including payments for capital items) of $4 million, the yearly profit is $1 million. If the total capital investment is $10 million, ROI is $1 million/$10 million, or 10 percent per year. The goal must be 10 percent or less for the firm to be satisfied.

Operating efficiency may be expressed as 1– (operating expenses/company sales). The higher the result, the more efficient the firm. A retailer with sales of $2 million and operating costs of $1 million has a 50 percent efficiency rating ([1– ($1 million/$2 million)]). Of every sales dollar, 50 cents goes for nonoperating costs and profits, and 50 cents for operating expenses. The retailer might set a goal to increase efficiency to 60 percent. On sales of $2 million, operating costs would have to drop to $800,000 ([1– ($800,000/$2 million)]). Sixty cents of every sales dollar would then go for nonoperating costs and profits, and 40 cents for operations, which would lead to better profits. If a firm cuts expenses too much, customer service may decline; this in turn might lead to a decline in sales and profit.

Satisfaction of Publics

Retailers typically strive to satisfy their publics; that is, their stockholders, customers, suppliers, employees, and government. *Stockholder satisfaction* is a goal for any publicly owned retailer. Some firms set policies leading to small annual increases in sales and profits (because these goals can be sustained over the long run and indicate good management) rather than ones based on innovative ideas that may lead to peaks and valleys in sales and profits (indicating risky decisions). Stable earnings lead to stable dividends.

Customer satisfaction with the total retail experience is a well-entrenched goal at most firms now. Policies of *caveat emptor* ("Let the buyer beware") or "the absence of complaints indicates that customers are satisfied" will not work in today's competitive marketplace. Retailers must listen to criticism and adapt. If shoppers are pleased, other goals are more easily reached. Yet, for many retailers, other objectives rate higher than customer satisfaction in their list of priorities.

Good supplier relations is also a key goal. Retailers must understand and work with their suppliers to secure favorable purchase terms, new products, good return policies, prompt shipments, and cooperation. Relationships are very important for small retailers due to the many services that suppliers offer them.

Cordial labor relations is another goal that is often critical to retailers' performance. Good employee morale means less absenteeism, better treatment of customers, and lower staffing turnover. Relations can be improved by effective selection, training, and motivation.

Because all levels of government impose rules affecting retailing practices, another goal should be to *understand and adapt to government rules.* In some cases, firms can influence rules by acting as members of large groups, such as trade associations or chambers of commerce.

Image (Positioning)

An **image** represents how a given retailer is perceived by consumers and others. A firm may be seen as innovative or conservative, specialized or broad-based, discount-oriented or upscale. The key to a successful image is that consumers view the retailer in the manner the firm intends.

Through **positioning**, a retailer devises its strategy in a way that projects an image relative to its retail category and its competitors and that elicits a positive consumer response. A firm selling women's apparel, for example, could generally position itself as an upscale or mid-priced specialty retailer, a traditional department store, a discount department store, or a discount specialty retailer, and it could specifically position itself with regard to other retailers carrying women's apparel.

Two opposite positioning philosophies have gained popularity in recent years: mass merchandising and niche retailing. **Mass merchandising** is a positioning approach whereby retailers offer a discount or value-oriented image, a wide and/or deep merchandise selection, and large store facilities. Walmart has a wide, deep merchandise mix, whereas Dick's Sporting Goods has a narrower, deeper assortment. These firms appeal to a broad customer market, attract a lot of customer traffic, and generate high stock turnover. Because mass merchants have relatively low operating costs, achieve economies in operations, and appeal to value-conscious shoppers, their continuing popularity is forecast.

Babies "R" Us (www.babiesrus.com) has a very focused strategy and an online tie-in with Toys "R" Us.

In **niche retailing**, retailers identify specific customer segments and deploy unique strategies to address the desires of those segments rather than the mass market. Niching creates a high level of loyalty and shields retailers from more conventional competitors. Babies "R" Us appeals to parents with very young children, whereas Catherines Stores has fashions for plus-size women. A niche retailing approach will have a strong future because it lets retailers stress factors other than price and have a better focus. See Figure 3-6.

Because both mass merchandising and niche retailing are now popular, some observers call this the era of **bifurcated retailing**. They believe this may mean the decline of middle-of-the-market retailing. Firms that are neither competitively priced nor particularly individualistic may have more difficulty competing.

Trader Joe's (www.traderjoes.com) is a shopping haven for consumers looking for distinctive, fairly priced food items.

Let's further examine the concept of positioning through these two examples:

▶ The bebe apparel chain designs, develops, and produces contemporary women's apparel and accessories targeted to 18- to 35-year-old sophisticated, hip, body-conscious women who seek current fashion trends to suit their lifestyle needs.[10]

▶ The underpinning of Trader Joe's food stores' strategy is to provide "value." The firm offers everyday low prices on all the items it sells without the need for "loyalty" cards, clubs, or gimmicks. Trader Joe's focuses on what matters: "great food + great prices = value."[11]

TECHNOLOGY IN RETAILING | Retail Planning Software

Devising retail plans is now easier with the increased sophistication of planning software. Popular software include Sales and Marketing Pro (www.bplans.com), MPlans (www.mplans.com), and SmartTools: Fast Marketing Plan (http://www.marketingprofs.com/smarttools). A lot of retail planning software contains templates that suggest how each element of a plan can be completed. Some templates include blog posts, articles, case studies, and checklists; help in enabling users to easily prepare PowerPoint presentation; and much more.

As a startup retailer, how would you use such software? ◼

FIGURE 3-6
Niche Retailing

In this scenario, retailers choose to specialize and target a specific customer group. Examples include Babies "R" Us (apparel for very young children), Mercedes (luxury autos for upscale customers), and SeniorStore.com (products oriented to those age 50 and older).

Source: Chatchawan/ Shutterstock. Reprinted by permission.

Figure 3-7 shows a retail positioning map based on two shopping criteria: (1) price and service and (2) product lines offered. Our assumption: There is a link between price and service (high price equals excellent service). Upscale department stores (Neiman Marcus) offer outstanding customer service and carry prestigious designer apparel. Traditional department stores (Sears) focus more on appliances, tools, auto repair, and private-label apparel. Discount department stores (Walmart) carry a broad variety of product lines and rely on self-service. Membership clubs (Costco) have a limited selection in a number of product categories. They have very low prices

FIGURE 3-7
Selected Retail Positioning Strategies

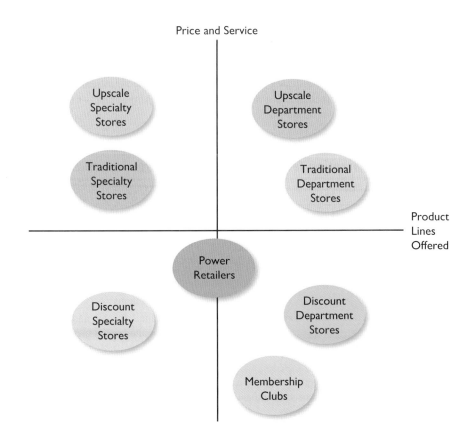

and warehouse type surroundings. Upscale specialty stores (Tiffany) offer outstanding customer service and focus on one general product category. Traditional specialty stores (Gap) have a trained sales staff to help customers and focus on apparel needs for the entire family. Discount specialty stores (Old Navy) rely more on self-service and focus on one general product category. Power retailers (Ikea) offer moderate service, low prices, and a huge assortment within one general product category.

Selection of Objectives

A firm that sets clear goals and devises a strategy to attain them improves its chances of success. An example of a retailer with clear goals and a proper strategy to attain them is Papa John's, the 4,900-outlet pizza chain that has stores in all 50 U.S. states and 37 countries. As reported at its Web site (www.papajohns.com), Papa John's focuses on customers. It seeks to generate strong brand loyalty via "(a) authentic, superior-quality products, (b) legendary customer service, and (c) exceptional community service."

IDENTIFICATION OF CONSUMER CHARACTERISTICS AND NEEDS

The customer group sought by a retailer is called the **target market**. In selecting its target market, a firm may use one of three techniques: **mass marketing**, selling goods and services to a broad spectrum of consumers; **concentrated marketing**, zeroing in on one specific group; or **differentiated marketing**, aiming at two or more distinct consumer groups, with different retailing approaches for each group.

Supermarkets and drugstores define their target markets broadly. They sell a wide assortment of medium-quality items at popular prices. In contrast, a small upscale men's shoe store appeals to a specific consumer group by offering a narrow, deep product assortment at above-average prices (or in other cases, below-average prices). A retailer aiming at one segment does not try to appeal to everyone.

Department stores are among those seeking multiple market segments. They cater to several customer groups, with unique goods and services for each. Apparel may be sold in a number of distinct boutiques in the store. Large chains frequently have divisions that appeal to different market segments. Darden Restaurants operates Olive Garden (Italian), LongHorn Steakhouse (emphasis on beef entrées), Capital Grill (American-style with "relaxed elegance"), Seasons 52 (seasonal grill and wine bar), Bahama Breeze (Caribbean-style), Eddie V's (seafood), and Yard House (food and craft beer) restaurants for customers with different food preferences.

After choosing the target market, a firm can determine its best competitive advantages and devise a strategy mix. See Table 3-3. The significance of **competitive advantages**—the distinct competencies of a retailer relative to competitors—must not be overlooked. Some examples will demonstrate this:

TABLE 3-3 Target Marketing Techniques and Their Strategic Implications

	Target Market Techniques		
Strategic Implications	Mass Marketing	Concentrated Marketing	Differentiated Marketing
Retailer's location	Near a large population base	Near a small or medium population base	Near a large population base
Goods and service mix	Wide selection of medium-quality items	Selection geared to market segment—high- or low-quality items	Distinct goods/services aimed at each market segment
Promotion efforts	Mass advertising subscription	Direct mail, E-mail, and segmented social media	Different for each segment
Price orientation	Popular prices	High or low	High, medium, and low—depending on market segment
Strategy	One general strategy for a large homogeneous (similar) group of consumers	One specific strategy directed at a specific, limited group of customers	Multiple specific strategies, each directed at different (heterogeneous) groups of consumers

FIGURE 3-8

La Boqueria Market: A Shopper's Delight

La Boqueria Market in Barcelona is Spain's most famous indoor marketplace. It is especially popular with tourists and local residents who are attracted by the fresh foods and wide variety: "It's been here since medieval times and is the largest market in Spain. The iconic Modernist stained glass entrance attracts millions of visitors every year to this Aladdin's cave of tantalizing food, exotic fruits, and spices." People eat, shop, and gossip together doing what the Spanish excel at—living life and enjoying a sense of community" (www.barcelona-tourist-travelguide.com/la-boqueria.html).

Source: Roman Borodaev/Shutterstock. Reprinted by permission.

Is the T. J. Maxx Web site (www.tjmaxx.com) on target for the customers it wants to reach?

- ▹ Tiffany seeks affluent, status-conscious consumers. It puts stores in prestigious shopping areas, offers high-quality products, uses elegant ads, has extensive customer services, and has rather high prices.
- ▹ Kohl's targets middle-class, value-conscious shoppers. It locates mostly in suburban shopping areas, offers national brands and Kohl's brands of medium quality, features good values in ads, has some customer services, and charges below-average to average prices.
- ▹ T. J. Maxx, an off-price store chain, aims at extremely price-conscious consumers. It locates in low-rent strip shopping centers or districts, offers national brands (sometimes overruns and seconds) of average to below-average quality, emphasizes low prices, offers few customer services, and sets very low prices.

The key to the success of each of these retailers is its ability to define customers and cater to their needs in a distinctive manner. See Figure 3-8. Retailers are better able to select a target market and satisfy customer needs if they have a good understanding of consumer behavior. This topic is discussed in Chapter 7.

OVERALL STRATEGY

Next, a retailer develops an in-depth overall strategy. This involves two components: the aspects of business the firm can directly affect and those to which the retailer must adapt. The former are called **controllable variables**, and the latter are called **uncontrollable variables**. See Figure 3-9.

A strategy must be devised with both variables in mind. The ability of retailers to grasp and predict the effects of controllable and uncontrollable variables is greatly aided by the use of suitable data. In Chapter 8, information gathering and processing in retailing are described.

Controllable Variables

The controllable parts of a retail strategy consist of the categories in Figure 3-9: store location, managing a business, merchandise management and pricing, and communicating with the customer. A good strategy integrates these areas, which are covered in depth in Chapters 9 through 19.

FIGURE 3-9

Developing an Overall Retail Strategy

Controllable variables
• Store location
• Managing a business
• Merchandise management and pricing
• Communicating with the customer

Retail strategy

Uncontrollable variables
• Consumers
• Competition
• Technology
• Economic conditions
• Seasonality
• Legal restrictions

STORE LOCATION A retailer has several store location decisions to make. The initial one is whether to use a store or nonstore format. Then, for store-based retailers, a general location and a specific site are determined. Competitors, transportation access, population density, the type of neighborhood, nearness to suppliers, pedestrian traffic, and store composition are considered in selecting a location. See Figure 3-10.

The terms of tenancy (such as rent and operating flexibility) are reviewed and a build, buy, or rent decision is made. The locations of multiple outlets are considered if expansion is a goal.

MANAGING A BUSINESS Two major elements are involved in managing a business: the retail organization and human resource management, and the operations management. Tasks, policies, resources, authority, responsibility, and rewards are outlined via a retail organization structure. Practices regarding employee hiring, training, compensation, and supervision are instituted through human resource management. Job descriptions and functions are communicated, along with the responsibility of all personnel and the chain of command.

Operations management oversees the tasks that satisfy customer, employee, and management goals. Financial aspects of operations involve asset management, budgeting, and resource allocation. Other elements include store format and size, personnel use, store maintenance, energy management, store security, insurance, credit management, computerization, and crisis management.

MERCHANDISE MANAGEMENT AND PRICING In merchandise management, the general quality of the goods and services offering is set. Decisions are made as to the width of assortment (the number of product categories carried) and the depth of assortment (the variety of products in any category). Policies are set with respect to introducing new items. Criteria for buying decisions

FIGURE 3-10

Retailing Opportunities in Mexico City, Mexico

Mexico City is the second-most-populated urban area in the world with more than 20 million people residing there. In addition, numerous tourists visit every year. As a result, Mexico City is home to a wide variety of retail store location formats – from big shopping centers to local shopping markets and food stands. Both domestic and foreign retailers compete here.

Source: 123rf.com. Reprinted by permission.

Handling Payments from Global Customers

Rituals, a cosmetics and fragrance company based in the Netherlands, has nearly 400 stores in 21 countries and recently opened a New York location. It planned to open 80 new stores worldwide in 2016 alone and uses payments company Adyen systems for both online and in-store payments. Adyen has facilitated Ritual's entering new countries and accepting new forms of payment. Rituals currently accepts 20 different forms of payment, including major credit cards, country-specific payment alternatives, and

bank transfers. Adyen's systems take care of back-office issues and put all the data into one interface. Reconciliation statements are consolidated each week.

What are the characteristics of a good global currency payment system for retail customers, as well as retailers?

Source: Based on material in STORES magazine. "Clearing the Path to Purchase," *STORES Magazine* (August 2015). Reprinted by permission. Copyright 2016 STORES Magazine.

(how often, what terms, which suppliers) are set. Forecasting, budgeting, and accounting procedures are outlined, as is the level of inventory for each type of merchandise. Finally, the retailer devises procedures to assess the success or failure of each item sold.

With regard to pricing, a retailer chooses from among several techniques; and it decides what range of prices to set, consistent with the firm's image and the quality of goods and services offered. The range of prices within each product category is determined, such as stocking carry-on luggage from $39 to $99. The use of markdowns is planned in advance: how often goods will be on sale and at what reduction from the usual selling price.

COMMUNICATING WITH THE CUSTOMER   An image can be created and sustained by applying various techniques.

Physical attributes, or atmosphere, of a store and its surrounding area influence consumer perceptions. The impact of a storefront (building exterior or home page for a Web retailer) should not be undervalued, as it is the first physical element seen by customers. Once inside, layouts and displays, floor colors, lighting, scents, music, and sales personnel also contribute to a retailer's image. Customer services and community relations generate a favorable image.

The right use of promotional tools enhances sales performance. Tools range from inexpensive flyers for a take-out restaurant to an expensive national ad campaign for a franchise chain. Three forms of paid promotion are available: advertising, personal selling, and sales promotion. A retailer can gain free publicity if stories about it are written, televised, broadcast, or blogged.

Uncontrollable Variables

The preceding discussion outlined controllable parts of a retail strategy, but uncontrollable variables must also be kept in mind. Uncontrollable parts of a strategy consist of the factors shown in Figure 3-9: consumers, competition, technology, economic conditions, seasonality, and legal issues. Farsighted firms adapt the controllable parts of their strategies to take into account factors beyond their immediate control.

CONSUMERS   A skillful retailer knows it cannot alter demographic trends or lifestyle patterns, impose tastes, or "force" goods and services on people. The firm learns about its target market and forms a strategy consistent with consumer trends and desires. It cannot sell goods or services that are beyond the desired price range of customers, that are not wanted, or that are not displayed or advertised in the proper manner.

COMPETITION   There is often little that retailers can do to limit the entry of competitors. In fact, a retailer's success may encourage the entry of new firms or cause established competitors to modify their strategies to capitalize on the popularity of a successful retailer. A major increase in competition should lead a company to re-examine its strategy, including its target market and merchandising focus, to ensure that it holds a competitive edge. A continued willingness to satisfy customers better than any competitor is fundamental. Retailers should define competition broadly. Sales of perishables at Target, home cleaning supplies by Staples, and home delivery of groceries by AmazonFresh all constitute competitive threats to a supermarket chain.

TECHNOLOGY Computer systems are available for inventory control and checkout operations. There are more high-tech ways to warehouse and transport merchandise. Toll-free 800 numbers are popular for consumer ordering. And, of course, there is the Web. Nonetheless, some advancements are expensive and may be beyond the reach of small retailers. For example, although small firms might have computerized checkouts, they will probably be unable to use fully automated inventory systems. As a result, their efficiency may be less than that of larger competitors. They must adapt by providing more personalized service.

ECONOMIC CONDITIONS Economic conditions are beyond any retailer's control, no matter how large it is. Unemployment, interest rates, inflation, tax levels, and the annual economic growth (known as gross domestic product, or GDP) are just some economic factors with which a retailer copes. In outlining the controllable parts of its strategy, a retailer needs to consider forecasts about international, national, state, and local economies.

SEASONALITY A constraint on certain retailers is their seasonality, as well as the possibility that unpredictable weather will play havoc with sales forecasts. Retailers selling sports equipment, fresh food, travel services, and car rentals cannot control the seasonality of demand or bad weather. They can diversify offerings to carry a goods/service mix with items that are popular in different seasons. Thus, a sporting goods retailer can emphasize ski equipment and snowmobiles in the winter, baseball and golf equipment in the spring, scuba equipment and fishing gear in the summer, and basketball and football supplies in the fall.

LEGAL RESTRICTIONS Table 3-4 shows how each controllable aspect of a retail strategy is affected by the legal environment.

The FTC has a publication on why "Competition Counts" (www.ftc .gov/tips-advice/ competition-guidance/ competition-counts).

Retailers that operate in more than one state are subject to federal laws and agencies. The Sherman Act and the Clayton Act deal with monopolies and restraints of trade. The Federal Trade Commission deals with unfair trade practices and consumer complaints. The Robinson-Patman Act prohibits suppliers from giving unjust merchandise discounts to large retailers that could adversely affect small ones. The Telemarketing Sales Rule protects consumers.

At the state and local levels, retailers have to deal with many restrictions. Zoning laws prohibit firms from operating at certain sites and demand that building specifications be met. Blue laws limit the times during which retailers can conduct business. Construction, smoking, and other codes are imposed by the state and city. Licenses to operate some businesses are under state or city jurisdiction.

For more information, contact the Federal Trade Commission (www.ftc.gov), state and local bodies, the Better Business Bureau (www.bbb.org), the National Retail Federation (www.nrf .com), or a group such as the Direct Marketing Association (www.the-dma.org).

Integrating Overall Strategy

What do you think about the overall strategy of Kmart (www.kmart.com)?

At this point, the firm has set an overall strategy. It has chosen a mission, an ownership and management style, and a goods/service category. Goals are clear. A target market has been designated and studied. Decisions have been made about store location, managing the business, merchandise management and pricing, and communications. These factors must be coordinated to have a consistent, integrated strategy and to account for uncontrollable variables (consumers, competition, technology, economy, seasonality, and legal restrictions). The firm is then ready to do the specific tasks to carry out its strategy productively.

SPECIFIC ACTIVITIES

Short-run decisions are now made and enacted for each controllable part of the strategy in Figure 3-9. These actions are known as **tactics** and encompass a retailer's daily and short-term operations. They must be responsive to the uncontrollable environment. Here are some tactical moves a retailer may make:

Stores (www.stores.org) tracks all kinds of tactical moves made by retailers.

▶ *Store location.* Trading-area analysis gauges the area from which a firm draws its customers. The level of competition in a trading area is studied regularly. Relationships with nearby retailers are optimized. A chain carefully decides on the sites of new outlets. Facilities are actually built or modified.

TABLE 3-4 The Impact of the Legal Environment on Retailing*

Controllable Factor Affected	Selected Legal Constraints on Retailers
Store location	*Zoning laws* restrict the potential choices for a location and the type of facilities constructed.
	Blue laws restrict the days and hours during which retailers may operate.
	Environmental laws limit the retail uses of certain sites.
	Door-to-door (direct) selling laws protect consumer privacy.
	Local ordinances involve fire, smoking, outside lighting, capacity, and other rules.
	Leases and mortgages require parties to abide by stipulations in tenancy documents.
Managing the business	*Licensing provisions* mandate minimum education and/or experience for certain personnel.
	Personnel laws involve nondiscriminatory hiring, promoting, and firing of employees.
	Antitrust laws limit large firm mergers and expansion.
	Franchise agreements require parties to abide by various legal provisions.
	Business taxes include real-estate and income taxes.
	Recycling laws mandate that retailers participate in recycling for various materials.
Merchandise management and pricing	*Trademarks* provide retailers with exclusive rights to the brand names they develop.
	Merchandise restrictions forbid some retailers from selling specified goods or services.
	Product liability laws allow retailers to be sued if they sell defective products.
	Lemon laws specify consumer rights if products, such as autos, require continuing repairs.
	Sales taxes are required in most states, although *tax-free days* have been introduced in some locales to encourage consumer shopping.
	Unit-pricing laws require price per unit to be displayed (most often applied to supermarkets).
	Collusion laws prohibit retailers from discussing selling prices with competitors.
	Sale prices must be a reduction from the retailer's normal selling prices.
	Price discrimination laws prohibit suppliers from offering unjustified discounts to large retailers that are unavailable to smaller ones.
Communicating with the customer	*Truth-in-advertising* and *truth-in-selling laws* require retailers to be honest and not omit key facts.
	Truth-in-credit laws require that shoppers be informed of all terms when buying on credit.
	Telemarketing laws protect the privacy and rights of consumers regarding telephone sales.
	Bait-and-switch laws make it illegal to lure shoppers into a store to buy low-priced items and then to aggressively try to switch them to higher-priced ones.
	Inventory laws mandate that retailers must have sufficient stock when running sales.
	Labeling laws require merchandise to be correctly labeled and displayed.
	Cooling-off laws let customers cancel completed orders, often made by in-home sales, within three days of a contract.

* This table is broad and omits a law-by-law description. Many laws are state or locally oriented and apply only to certain locales; the laws in each area differ widely. The intent here is to give the reader some understanding of the current legal environment as it affects retail management.

  ETHICS IN RETAILING   Deceptive Price Advertising

The Federal Trade Commission's (www.ftc.gov) "Guide against Deceptive Pricing" lists several forms of deceptive price advertising: former price comparisons, comparable value price advertising, advertising price reductions based on suggested selling prices, and bargain offers. The guide states that the former price for a good should be an actual price at which it was offered to the public on a regular basis for a reasonably substantial time. Price-based advertising is deceptive in these situations: A men's clothier uses shows manufacturers' suggested prices online, so it appears that its prices are discounted from the clothier's regular prices (which they are not). A department store promotes kitchen appliances at 20 percent off a manufacturer's suggested list price, although that price does not correspond to the actual selling price in its geographic area.

Discuss how a large Web-based retailer can avoid false advertising litigation.

> ▶ *Managing the business.* There is a clear chain of command from managers to workers. An organization structure is set into place. Personnel are hired, trained, and supervised. Financial management tracks assets and liabilities. The budget is spent properly. Operations are systemized and adjusted as required.
> ▶ *Merchandise management and pricing.* Assortments in departments and the space allotted to each department require constant decisions. Innovative firms look for new merchandise and clear out slow-moving items. Purchase terms are negotiated and suppliers sought. Selling prices reflect the firm's image and target market. Price ranges offer consumers some choice. Adaptation is needed to respond to higher supplier prices and react to competitors' prices.
> ▶ *Communicating with the customer.* The storefront and display windows, store layout, and merchandise displays need regular attention. These elements help gain consumer enthusiasm, present a fresh look, introduce new products, and reflect changing seasons. Ads are placed during the proper time and in the proper media. The deployment of sales personnel varies by merchandise category and season.

The essence of retailing excellence is building a sound strategy and fine-tuning it. A firm that stands still is often moving backward. Tactical decision making is discussed in detail in Chapters 9 through 19.

CONTROL

In the **control** phase of strategic planning for retailers, a review takes place (Step VI in Figure 3-1), as the strategy and tactics (Steps IV and V) are assessed against the business mission, objectives, and target market (Steps I, II, and III). This procedure is called a *retail audit*, which is a systematic process for analyzing the performance of a retailer. The retail audit is covered in Chapter 20.

The strengths and weaknesses of a retailer are revealed as performance is reviewed. The aspects of a strategy that have gone well are maintained; those that have gone poorly are revised, consistent with the mission, goals, and target market. The adjustments are reviewed in the firm's next retail audit.

FEEDBACK

At each strategic stage, an observant management receives signals or cues, known as **feedback**, as to the success or failure of that part of the strategy. Again, refer to Figure 3-1. Positive feedback includes high revenue, a high percentage of customers renewing annual membership in a membership (warehouse) club, and low employee turnover and absenteeism. Negative feedback includes falling sales revenue, low membership renewals, and high employee turnover and absenteeism. Retail executives look for positive and negative feedback so they can determine the causes and then capitalize on opportunities or rectify problems.

A STRATEGIC PLANNING TEMPLATE FOR RETAIL MANAGEMENT

A detailed, user-friendly strategic planning template, *Computer-Assisted Strategic Retail Management Planning*, appears at our Web site (www.pearsonhighered.com/bermanevans). This template, based on Figure 3-1, enables you to build a strategic plan. You may apply the template to one of the scenarios provided—or devise your own scenario. You have the option of printing each facet of the planning process individually, or printing the full plan as an integrated whole.

Table 3-5 highlights the steps used in *Computer-Assisted Strategic Retail Management Planning* as the basis for preparing a strategic plan. Table 3-6 presents an example of how the template may be used.

TABLE 3-5 Outline of the Computerized Strategic Planning Template

1. **Situation Analysis**
   - Current organizational mission
   - Current ownership and management alternatives
   - Current goods/service category

2. **SWOT Analysis**
   - Strengths: Current and long term
   - Weaknesses: Current and long term
   - Opportunities: Current and long term
   - Threats: Current and long term

3. **Objectives**
   - Sales
   - Profit
   - Positioning
   - Satisfaction of publics

4. **Identification of Consumers**
   - Choice of target market
     - Mass marketing
     - Concentrated marketing
     - Differentiated marketing

5. **Overall Strategy**
   - Controllable variables
     - Goods/services strategy
     - Location strategy
     - Pricing strategy
     - Promotion strategy
   - Uncontrollable variables
     - Consumer environment
     - Competitive environment
     - Legal environment
     - Economic environment
     - Technological environment

6. **Specific Activities**
   - Daily and short-term operations
   - Responses to environment

7. **Control**
   - Evaluation
   - Adjustment

TABLE 3-6 Sample Strategic Plan: A High-Fashion Ladies Clothing Shop

Sally's is a small, independently owned, high-fashion ladies clothing shop in a suburban strip mall. It is a full-price, full-service retailer for fashion-forward shoppers. It carries sportswear from popular designers, has a personal shopper for good customers, and has an on-premises tailor. Sally's is updating its strategic plan to secure more funding for an expected expansion.

1. **Situation Analysis**
   - Current organizational mission: A high-fashion clothing retailer selling high-quality and designer-label clothing and accessories in an attractive full-service store environment.
   - Current ownership and management alternatives: Sole proprietor, independent store.
   - Current goods/service category: Ladies coats, jackets, blouses, and suits from major designers, as well as a full line of fashion accessories (such as scarves, belts, and hats).

Continued

TABLE 3-6 Sample Strategic Plan: A High-Fashion Ladies Clothing Shop (*continued*)

2. **SWOT Analysis**
   - Strengths
     - Current
       - Loyal customer base.
       - Excellent reputation for high-fashion clothing and accessories within the community.
       - Little competition within a target market concerned with high fashion.
       - Acceptance by a target market more concerned with fashion, quality, and customer service than with price.
       - Unlike consumers favoring classic clothing, Sally's fashion-forward customers spend a considerable amount of money on clothing and accessories per year.
       - Sally's highly regarded personal shopper (who assembles clothing based on customer preferences, visits customers, and arranges for a tailor to visit customers).
     - Long term
       - Fashion-forward image with the store's target market.
       - Exclusive relationships with some well-known and some emerging designers.
       - Low-rent location in comparison to a regional shopping center.
       - Excellent supplier relationships.
       - Loyal employees.
       - Excellent relationships within the community.
   - Weaknesses
     - Current
       - Difficulty in recruiting appropriate part-time personnel for peak seasonal periods.
       - Small store space limits selection. Too often, the tailor does major alterations.
       - Long delivery times for certain French and Italian designers.
       - Lack of a computer-based information system that would better enable it to access key information concerning inventory, sales, customer preferences, and purchase histories.
       - Limited expertise in social media.
     - Long term
       - Limited bargaining power with vendors due to small orders. This affects prices paid, as well as access to "hot-selling" clothing.
       - Suburban strip mall location reduces its trading area. There is little tourist trade.
       - Over-reliance on the owner-manager, and on several key employees.
       - No long-term management succession plan.
   - Opportunities
     - Current
       - Hire another experienced tailor to create a custom-made clothing department.
       - Hire an assistant to better coordinate trunk and fashion shows. This would solidify Sally's reputation among fashion-forward shoppers and in the community.
       - Take over an empty adjacent store to increase size by 50 percent.
       - Enhance the Web site. This would enable it to appeal to a larger trading area, promote more events (such as a fashion show), and provide links to designers.
     - Long term
       - Larger store increases the ability to expand the number of designers, as well as the product lines carried. This would improve Sally's bargaining power with suppliers.
       - Custom-made clothing department to appeal to customers who dislike "ready-to-wear apparel" and to customers with highly individualized tastes.
       - Expanded market due to enhanced Web site.
   - Threats
     - Current
       - Rumors that Bloomingdale's, a fashion-based department store, may soon locate a new store within 10 miles of Sally's. This could affect relationships with suppliers as well as customers. Bloomingdale's offers one-stop shopping and has a flexible return policy for unaltered merchandise with its labels intact.
       - Local recession's impact on revenues.
     - Long term
       - Many customers in their 50s and 60s. Some are close to retirement; others intend to spend more time in Florida and Arizona during the winter. The retailer needs to attract and retain younger shoppers.

Continued

TABLE 3-6 Sample Strategic Plan: A High-Fashion Ladies Clothing Shop (*continued*)

3. Objectives
- Sales: Achieve sales volume of $4 million per year.
- Profit: (a) Achieve net profit before tax of $300,000. (b) Increase inventory turnover from 4 times a year to 6 times a year. (c) Increase gross margin return on inventory (GMROI) by 50 percent through more effective inventory management.
- Positioning: (a) Reposition store to appeal to younger shoppers without losing current clientele. (b) Increase acceptance by younger shoppers. (c) Establish more of a Web presence.
- Satisfaction of publics: (a) Maintain store loyalty among current customers. (b) Increase relationship with younger designers selling less costly, younger apparel. (c) Maintain excellent relationship with employees.

4. Identification of Consumers
- Choice of target market approach
  - Mass marketing: This is not a mass-market retailer.
  - Concentrated marketing: This is Sally's current target market strategy.
  - Differentiated marketing: Sally's might consider attracting multiple target markets: its current fashion-forward customers seeking designer apparel and accessories in a full-service environment; younger, professional customers who desire more trendy clothing; and fashion-forward customers who desire custom-made clothing.

5. Overall Strategy
- Controllable variables
  - Goods/service strategy: Merchandise is fashion-forward from established and emerging designers. Fashion accessories include such items as scarves, belts, and hats. The retailer has no plans to sell ladies' shoes or pocketbooks. Most of the designer merchandise is selectively distributed. A planned custom-made clothing department would enable Sally's to attract hard-to-fit and hard-to-please shoppers. Custom-made clothing shoppers would have a wide variety of swatches and fashion books from which to choose.
  - Location strategy: Sally's currently occupies a single location in a suburban strip mall. This site has comparatively low rent, is within 10 miles of 80 percent of the store's customers, has adequate parking, and has good visibility from the road.
  - Pricing strategy: Sally's charges list price for all of its goods. Included in the price are full-tailoring service, as well as a personal shopper for major customers. Twice a year, the store has a 50 percent off sale on seasonal goods. This is followed by 70 percent off sales to clear the store of remaining off-season inventory.
  - Promotion strategy: Sally's sales personnel are well-trained and highly motivated. They know key customers by name and by their style, color, and designer preferences. Sally's plans to upgrade its regular fashion and trunk shows where new styles are exhibited to current customers and potential customers. Sally's also maintains a customer database. The best customers are called when suitable merchandise arrives and are allowed to preview it. Some other customers are contacted by mail. The improved Web site will feature the latest styles, the Web address of major designers, color availability, and more. Sally's has a display listing in the Yellow Pages.
- Uncontrollable variables
  - Consumer environment: Business is subject to the uncertainty of the acceptance of new fashions by the target market. Although Sally's wants to attract two additional segments (custom-made clothing buyers and younger buyers), there is no assurance that it will be successful with these target markets. The store needs to be careful that in seeking these new segments, it does not alienate its current shoppers.
  - Competitive environment: The rumored opening of a fashion-oriented department store in the area would significantly affect sales.
  - Legal environment: Sally's is careful in fully complying with all laws. Unlike some competitors, it does not eliminate sales taxes for cash purchases or ship empty boxes out-of-state to avoid sales tax.
  - Economic environment: Local recessions can reduce sales substantially.
  - Technological environment: Sally's is in the process of investigating a new retail information system to track purchases, inventories, credit card transactions, and more.

6. Specific Activities
- Daily and short-term operations: Sally's matches competitors' prices, promptly corrects alteration issues, has longer store hours in busy periods, and offers exclusive merchandise.
- Responses to environment: Sally's acts appropriately with regard to trends in the economy, competitor actions, and so forth.

7. Control
- Evaluation: A new retail information system will better enable Sally's to ascertain fashion trends, adjust inventories to reduce markdowns, and contact customers with specific offerings. Sales by color, size, style, and designer will be more carefully monitored.
- Adjustment: The retail information system will enable Sally's store to reduce excess inventories, maximize sales opportunities, and better target individual customers.

Chapter Summary

1. *To show the value of strategic planning for all types of retailers.* A retail strategy is the overall plan that guides a firm. It consists of situation analysis, objectives, identification of a customer market, broad strategy, specific activities, control, and feedback. Without a well-conceived strategy, a retailer may be unable to cope with environmental factors.

2. *To explain the steps in strategic planning for retailers.* Situation analysis is the candid evaluation of opportunities and threats. It looks at the firm's current marketplace position and where it should be heading. This analysis includes defining an organizational mission, evaluating ownership and management options, and outlining the goods/service category.

   An organizational mission is a commitment to a type of business and a place in the market. Ownership/management options include sole proprietorship, partnership, or corporation; starting a business, buying an existing one, or being a franchisee; owner management or professional management; and being centralized or decentralized. The goods/service category depends on personal abilities, finances, and time resources.

   A firm may pursue one or more of these goals: sales (growth, stability, and market share); profit (level, return on investment, and efficiency); satisfaction of publics (stockholders, consumers, and others); and image/positioning (customer and industry perceptions).

   Next, consumer characteristics and needs are determined, and a target market is selected. A firm can sell to a broad spectrum of consumers (mass marketing); zero in on one customer group (concentrated marketing); or aim at two or more distinct groups of consumers (differentiated marketing), with separate retailing approaches for each.

   A broad strategy is formed. It has controllable variables (factors a firm can directly affect) and uncontrollable variables (factors a firm cannot control and to which it must adapt).

   After a general strategy is set, a firm makes and implements short-run decisions (tactics) for each controllable part of that strategy. Tactics must be forward-looking and respond to the environment.

   Through a control process, strategy and tactics are evaluated and revised continuously. A retail audit systematically reviews a strategy and its execution on a regular basis. Strengths are emphasized and weaknesses minimized or eliminated.

   An alert firm seeks out signals or cues, known as feedback, that indicate the level of performance at each step in the strategy.

3. *To examine the individual controllable and uncontrollable elements of a retail strategy, and to present strategic planning as a series of integrated steps.* There are four major controllable factors in retail planning: store location, managing the business, merchandise management and pricing, and communicating with the customer. The principal uncontrollable factors affecting retail planning are consumers, competition, technology, economic conditions, seasonality, and legal restrictions.

   Each stage in the strategic planning process needs to be performed, undertaken sequentially, and coordinated in order to have a consistent, integrated, unified strategy.

4. *To demonstrate how a strategic plan can be prepared.* A comprehensive, user-friendly strategic planning template, *Computer-Assisted Strategic Retail Management Planning,* appears at our Web site. This template uses a series of drop-down menus to build a strategic plan.

Key Terms

retail strategy (p. 72)
situation analysis (p. 73)
opportunities (p. 73)
threats (p. 73)
organizational mission (p. 73)
sole proprietorship (p. 75)
partnership (p. 75)
corporation (p. 76)
goods/service category (p. 77)

objectives (p. 80)
image (p. 82)
positioning (p. 82)
mass merchandising (p. 82)
niche retailing (p. 82)
bifurcated retailing (p. 82)
target market (p. 84)
mass marketing (p. 84)
concentrated marketing (p. 84)

differentiated marketing (p. 84)
competitive advantages (p. 84)
controllable variables (p. 85)
uncontrollable variables (p. 85)
tactics (p. 88)
control (p. 90)
feedback (p. 90)

Questions for Discussion

1. Strategic planning can be done by the owner of a firm, professional management, or a combination of both. Why is strategic planning attractive?
2. How might a retailer go about identifying and quantifying the key opportunities and threats it faces?
3. What are the pros and cons of setting up a new retail operation as a sole proprietor?
4. Develop a checklist of likely financial investments for a new retail venture. What are the most common funding methods for these investments?
5. Why do retailers frequently underestimate the financial and time requirements of a business?
6. Draw and explain a positioning map showing the kinds of retailers selling tablets such as the iPad and Kindle Fire.
7. Discuss local examples of retailers applying mass marketing, concentrated marketing, and differentiated marketing.
8. A footwear retailer located in a seasonal coastal resort wants to choose the most appropriate ways to target their market. Which would you choose, mass, concentrated or differentiated marketing? Explain each approach as well as the reason for your choice of targeting method.
9. A competing bicycle store has a better location than yours. It is in a modern shopping center with a lot of customer traffic. Your store is in an older neighborhood and requires customers to travel farther to reach you. How could you use a merchandising, pricing, and communications strategy to overcome your disadvantageous location?
10. Describe how a retailer can use fine-tuning in strategic planning.
11. How are the control and feedback phases of retail strategy planning interrelated? Give an example.
12. Should a catalog-based men's wear retailer use the strategic planning process differently from an Internet retailer? Why or why not?

Web-Based Exercise

Visit the Web site of Angie's List (www.angieslist.com): "More than three million households nationwide check Angie's List reviews to find the best local service providers, like roofers, plumbers, handymen, mechanics, doctors, and dentists." Describe and evaluate the company's strategy based on the information you find there. Why do you think Angie's List has been so successful?

APPENDIX The Special Dimensions of Strategic Planning in a Global Retailing Environment

There are about 270 countries and dependent areas—with more than 7.3 billion people and a $115 trillion economy—in the world. The United States accounts for less than 5 percent of the world's population and about 16 percent of the worldwide economy. Although the United States is a huge marketplace, there are also many other opportunities. Annual worldwide retailing sales have reached about $25 trillion—and they are growing. When we talk about the global environment of retailing, we mean both U.S. firms operating in foreign markets and foreign retailers operating in U.S. markets.

Michigan State University has a Web site (www.globaledge.msu.edu) that is an excellent source of information on global business practices.

The global strategic planning challenge is clear: "It is time to focus on a portfolio of countries—with different levels of risk, at different stages of maturity, and with distinctive consumer profiles—to balance short- and long-term opportunities."[1]

Yearly, A. T. Kearney ranks 30 developing nations on a 0- to 100-point Global Retail Development Index (GRDI) scale. Higher-ranked countries represent better opportunities to enter or expand in that market. The GRDI scores are based on four attributes: market attractiveness (25 percent), country and business risk (25 percent), market saturation (25 percent), and time pressure (25 percent).[2] Table A3-1 shows the GRDI scores for the top 10 performing foreign countries.

When embarking on an international retailing strategy, firms should consider the various factors shown in Figure A3-1.

Opportunities and Threats in Global Retailing

For participating firms, there are wide-ranging opportunities and threats in global retailing.

Opportunities

▶ Foreign markets may be used to complement domestic sales.
▶ Foreign markets may represent growth opportunities if domestic markets are saturated or stagnant.
▶ A retailer may be able to offer goods, services, or technology not yet available in foreign markets.
▶ Competition may be less in some foreign markets.

TABLE A3-1 Top Ten Scoring Countries for 2015 Global Retail Development Index

Country	Market Attractiveness	Country Risk	Market Saturation	Time Pressure	GRDI Score
China	66.7	55.7	42.3	96.6	65.3
Uruguay	93.3	60.4	68.0	38.9	65.1
Chile	98.2	100.0	13.0	37.9	62.3
Qatar	100.0	89.4	34.3	12.8	59.1
Mongolia	22.4	19.9	93.1	100.0	58.8
Georgia	36.5	39.1	78.8	79.2	58.4
United Arab Emirates	97.6	84.0	16.5	33.9	58.0
Brazil	98.0	60.4	45.2	28.0	57.9
Malaysia	75.6	68.8	29.3	52.7	56.6
Armenia	35.4	37.1	82.1	66.3	55.2

Source: A. T. Kearney, "2015 Global Retail Development Index." Reprinted by permission.

FIGURE A3-1

Factors to Consider When Engaging in Global Retailing

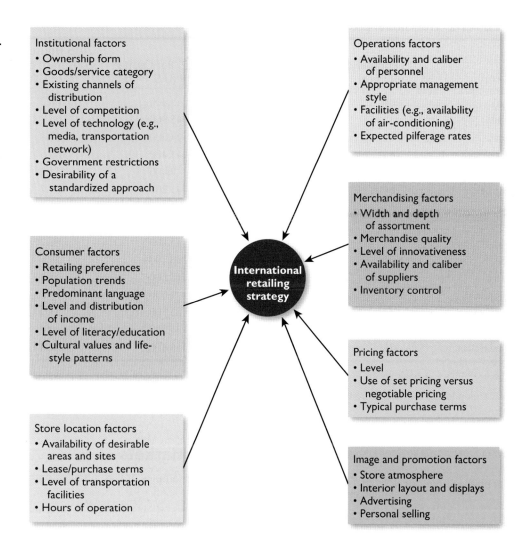

> There may be tax or investment advantages in foreign markets.
> Due to government and economic shifts, many nations are more open to the entry of foreign firms.
> Communications are easier than before. The Internet enables retailers to reach customers and suppliers well outside their domestic markets.

Threats

> There may be cultural differences between domestic and foreign markets.
> Management styles may not be easily adaptable.
> Foreign governments may place restrictions on some operations.
> Personal income may be poorly distributed among consumers in foreign markets.
> Distribution systems and technology may be inadequate (e.g., poor roads and lack of refrigeration). This may minimize the effectiveness of the Web as a selling tool.
> Institutional formats vary greatly among countries.
> Currencies are different. The countries in the European Union have sought to alleviate this problem through the euro, a common currency, in most of their member nations.

Standardization: An opportunity and a threat

In devising a global strategy, a retailer must pay attention to the concept of *standardization.* Can the home market strategy be standardized and directly applied to foreign markets, or do personnel, physical facilities, operations, advertising messages, product lines, and other factors have to be adapted to local conditions and needs? Table A3-2 shows how the economies differ in 15 countries.

TABLE A3-2 The Global Economy, Selected Countries

Country	2015 Population (millions)	2015 Population Growth Rate (%)	2015 Per Capita GDP (U.S. PPP$)	2015 Household Consumption (as % of GDP)	2015 Unemployment Rate (%)
Brazil	204	0.77	15,800	68.2	6.4
Canada	35	0.75	45,900	56.7	6.9
China	1,367	0.45	14,300	38.1	4.2
France	66	0.43	41,400	55.6	9.9
Germany	81	-0.17	47,400	54.2	4.8
Great Britain	64	0.54	41,200	64.7	5.4
India	1,252	1.22	6,300	59.7	7.1
Indonesia	256	0.92	11,300	56.8	5.5
Italy	62	0.27	35,800	60.7	12.2
Japan	127	-0.16	38,200	59.6	3.3
Mexico	122	1.18	18,500	67.3	4.5
Philippines	101	1.61	7,500	71.5	6.5
Russia	142	-0.04	23,700	53.2	5.4
South Korea	49	0.14	36,700	49.0	3.5
United States	321	0.78	56,300	68.8	5.2

GDP is a country's gross domestic product. Per capita GDP is expressed in terms of purchasing power parity.

Source: Compiled by the authors from *CIA World Factbook*, 2016, https://www.cia.gov/library/publications/resources/the-world-factbook *2015.*

U.S. Retailers in Foreign Markets

Discussed here are three of the many examples of U.S. retailers with high involvement in foreign markets.

Toys "R" Us has more than 750 Toys "R" Us, Babies "R" Us, and Side-by-Side stores abroad. In addition to company-owned stores, Toys "R" Us licenses 250 stores in 20 countries and jurisdictions. In these markets, such as Indonesia, South Africa, Turkey, and United Arab Emirates, the firm emphasizes licensing rather than direct corporate ownership. Why? This enables it to better tap the local knowledge of franchisees in certain markets while still setting corporate policies.[3] Toys 'R" Us also has an online presence in 19 countries and jurisdictions.

The majority of McDonald's restaurants are outside the United States. Sales at McDonald's foreign outlets in over 100 foreign nations account for two-thirds of total revenues. Besides Europe, McDonald's has outlets in such nations as Argentina, Australia, Austria, Brazil, Canada, China, Colombia, Egypt, Greece, India, Japan, Malaysia, Mexico, New Zealand, Pakistan, Russia, South Africa, South Korea, Spain, and Uruguay. To appeal to foreign tastes, McDonald's adapts its menu around the world. For example, its French units sell macaroons, offer blue-cheese burgers, and offer a wide choice of sauces for french fries.[4]

Amazon.com has rapidly expanded globally by introducing dedicated Web sites for specific nations. They include Canada (www.amazon.ca), China (www.joyo.com), France (www.amazon.fr), Germany (www.amazon.de), Great Britain (www.amazon.co.uk), Japan (www.amazon.co.jp), and Spain (www.amazon.es). Although these sites all have the familiar Amazon Web design, they differ by language, products offered, and currency.

Foreign Retailers in the U.S. Market

Although the revenues of U.S.-based retailers owned by foreign firms are hard to measure, they equal several hundred billion dollars annually. Foreign ownership in U.S. retailers is highest for general merchandise stores, food stores, and apparel and accessory stores. Examples of U.S.-based retailers owned by foreign firms are shown in Table A3-2. A large number of foreign retailers have entered the United States to appeal to the world's most affluent mass market. Here are three examples.

The Netherlands' Royal Ahold and Belgium-based Delhaize Group recently merged into Ahold Delhaize. Royald Ahold operates Stop and Shop, Giant Foods, and Martin's Food Markets. It also owns Peapod, the online food retailer. Delhaize Group's U.S. operations include Food Lion and Hannaford supermarkets. The combined operation will result in the creation of one of the largest grocery chains in the United States, with over 6,500 stores. The merger is subject to approval by the Federal Trade Commission.

PricewaterhouseCoopers publishes many resources for global retailing executives (http://www.pwc.com/gx/en/industries/retail-consumer.html).

Luxottica, an Italian firm, operates more than 7,200 optical and sunglass stores in over 150 countries in North America, Asia-Pacific, the Middle East, Latin America, and Europe. It has the highest market share in the U.S. optical retail market with its LensCrafters, Pearle Vision, and Sunglass Hut stores. Luxottica also operates leased departments at Sears Optical and at Target Optical stores in the United States. Luxottica's annual total 2015 revenue (including eyeglass and sunglass manufacturing) exceeded $10 billion (U.S.).[5]

Ikea is a Swedish-based home-furnishings retailer operating more than 300 stores in 37 nations. In 1985, Ikea opened its first U.S. store in Pennsylvania. Since then, it has added nearly 40 other U.S. stores in such cities as Baltimore, Chicago, Elizabeth (New Jersey), Hicksville (Long Island, New York), Houston, Los Angeles, San Diego, Seattle, and Washington, DC. The firm offers durable, stylish, ready-to-assemble furniture at low prices. Stores are huge, have enormous selections, include a playroom for children, and other amenities. Today, Ikea generates 94 percent of its sales from international operations, and 15 percent of total company sales are from its North American stores.[6]

Although the revenues of U.S.-based retailers owned by foreign firms are hard to measure, they reach several hundred billion dollars annually. Foreign ownership in U.S. retailers is highest for general merchandise stores, food stores, and apparel and accessory stores. Examples of U.S.-based retailers owned by foreign firms are shown in Table A3-3.

TABLE A3-3 Selected Ownership of U.S. Retailers by Foreign Firms

U.S. Retailer	Principal Business	Foreign Owner	Country of Owner
Aldi	Limited assortment food stores	Aldi Sud	Germany
Crate & Barrel	Housewares stores	The Otto Group	Germany
Food Lion	Supermarkets	Ahold Delhaize	Netherlands/Belgium
Giant Food	Supermarkets	Royal Ahold	Netherlands/Belgium
Hannaford	Supermarkets	Ahold Delhaize	Netherlands/Belgium
LensCrafters	Optical stores	Luxottica	Italy
Lord & Taylor	Department stores	Hudson's Bay Co.	Canada
Peapod	Online grocery delivery	Ahold Delhaize	Netherlands/Belgium
Saks Fifth Avenue	Department stores	Hudson's Bay Co.	Canada
7-Eleven	Convenience stores	Seven & I Holdings	Japan
Sofitel	Economy motels	Accor S.A.	France
Stop & Shop	Supermarkets	Ahold Delhaize	Netherlands/Belgium
Sunglass Hut	Sunglass stores	Luxottica	Italy
Trader Joe's	Limited assortment food stores	Aldi Nord	Germany

PART 1 Short Cases

Case 1: Retailers MUST Be Future-Oriented*

When children's organic food manufacturer Happy Family wanted to reimagine the retail aisle, the stakes were high. "We looked at how people shop this section," says Riddhish Kankariya, Happy Family's vice-president of strategy and insights. "Do they shop based on brand, on organic versus non-organic, on type of food, or on age?"

To answer those questions, Happy Family turned to virtual reality, creating four scenarios to gather data from 800 shoppers. "There is no way, if we had not done this virtually, that we'd have been able to get these numbers," Kankariya adds. While it may seem that Happy Family reached into the future, virtual and augmented reality are already transforming retail from store design to signage.

"It's definitely one of the hottest technologies right now," says David Evans, commercial director of Kantar Retail Virtual Reality. "It's hot in the marketplace, but it's not a fad. VR has been around for a long time, so it's had time to mature." "Retailers need to look at virtual reality not as some addition, but as how the Web is going to evolve," notes Mary Spio, founder of CEEK VR. "When we first started working with brands to do online video, we had Web 1.0—just text, pictures. The brands that embraced video early could attract a wider user base. That's the same way that retailers can and should look at virtual reality."

The world has been waiting for hardware to catch up—and some major manufacturers released virtual reality devices in 2016. As that happens, more customers may expect virtual and augmented reality when shopping online. "The next step will be to move to V-commerce, which will become a part of the omnichannel strategy," says Mark Hardy, CEO of InContext Solutions, which focuses on shopper insights via virtual reality. "'Can I jump in and look at the ingredients or parts of the product? Can I actually put it on and see what it looks like in a different scenario? It will help with some of the shortfalls in E-commerce, upselling, cross-selling, and providing a more engaging and individualized experience."

Happy Family's research is just the beginning of how companies use—and plan to use—virtual reality. Working with InContext, Kankariya sees more possibilities. "When we showed the virtual technology to our CEO and founder, her first thought was, 'There are so many ways we can use this to test packaging or design. So many ways of engaging with our audience,'" he remarks.

"At the macro level," says Hardy, "it starts with store design, the flow, the adjacencies, and extends down to the micro level, product, category, displays, and signage. There are two levels for retailers wanting to create a new store. They can take the current footprint and play around with it, to reinvent the experience in current stores. Or they can create an entire new building footprint." There are reasons to do so virtually. "If you create it in a physical world, your competition knows what you're doing before you understand the impact of the strategy."

And without having to build fixtures or stock a single product, retailers can allow "customers" to "shop" a virtual store while measuring their behavior and what, how and why they buy.

Augmented reality "is adding a layer of the virtual realm to your reality, immediately delivering an enhanced experience that provides unprecedented value," comments Yoni Nevo, CEO of augmented-reality-visualization platform Cimagine. "It can give the consumer contextual information, showing products before purchase, thus enabling the consumer to have confidence to make a more informed decision to buy faster. The ability to add the virtual layer to a user's reality provides significant value to brands, retailers, and manufacturers."

Questions

1. What do you think are the best uses of VR for retailers today? What are the limitations?
2. Is the typical retailer ready for VR? Why or why not?
3. How can VR enhance a firm's ability to generate a great total retail experience and relationship retailing?
4. Even if a retailer is not ready for VR, what can it learn from this case?

Case 2: Stores That Accommodate Those with Physical Limitations*

Fifty million people, age 65 and older, represent one-seventh of the U.S. population, according to the U.S. Department of Health and Human Services Administration for Community Living.

"We account for all of the requested shoppers when designing a new space, which can vary depending on the retailer, location, and demographics," states Christopher Studach, creative director at King Retail Solutions. "In the case of seniors, there are several elements that we consider when designing. One key area is good lighting that improves product visibility and readability. Seniors can also have a difficult time with contrast, so large swings from light to dark areas within the store can cause frustration and risks for senior shoppers."

According to Studach, King Retail Solutions also focuses on the size, location, and makeup of categories that are of special interest to seniors, particularly lifestyle and health-related categories, with the goal of providing an easy way to locate hard-to-find items. "For example," he notes, "how many times have you searched with frustration for that one small package of vitamin K that is thoughtfully buried among hundreds of similar small packages?"

A current trend among retailers, he adds, is to use every inch of space for merchandising, but for areas in which seniors have particular interest, it's important to consider product height and not force seniors to stoop or bend down to merchandise placed too low, and also to try to place heavier products at a height that makes them easier to load into a cart. "Designer trends tend to lean toward ghostly pale text in graphics and signs, sometimes with barely legible font sizes. When considering a senior

*Based on material from Sandy Smith, "The Future Is Now," *STORES Magazine*, April 2016, pp. 20–23. Reprinted by permission. Copyright 2016. STORES Magazine.

*Based on material from Bob Ingram, *"All Access: Stores That Accommodate Those with Physical Limitations," *Progressive Grocer*, April 2016, pp. 144–147. Reprinted by permission.

shopper, we need to back off from that trend and have a better font size and contrast. The goal should be to convey a genuine sense of compassion through functionality as well as aesthetics," says Studach.

David Yehuda, president of DY Design Inc., stresses that efficient store design benefits all customers, regardless of age or disability, and makes their shopping experience more pleasant and comfortable. "Layouts and traffic flow are designed for the ease of all customers, as well as the efficiency of the store and its products," he says. "Placing enough room between the checkouts, utilizing signage with letters large enough to be seen and read by all, and applying lighting that illuminates signage, in addition to giving the products a punch of color and vibrancy, are all important."

Yehuda believes that applying universal design principles benefits the senior population as well as people in other life stages and age groups. "Specifying slip-resistant flooring is another smart consideration for the young to the old," he notes, "with toddlers running around and seniors often walking with canes or using walkers or wheelchairs."

Good design choices are recommended by the designer and need to be approved by the store owner, Yehuda points out. Regulations, codes, and laws at the local, state, and federal levels exist and influence these decisions, ensuring, for example, that wheelchair users have enough space to navigate through doors comfortably and safely. "Entryways are of huge importance," he stresses. "If an entryway does have stairs, a ramp must be installed. Also required are handicapped toilets, which must be clearly marked and come equipped with handrails, an important safety measure."

Improved technology in the future will afford seniors—and all shoppers—quicker and easier access to check prices and check out their food items, he says, and store designers will use their creativity to develop innovative graphics and store décor from natural and sustainable building materials.

Questions

1. Relate the material in this case to the value chain and the value delivery chain.
2. Are services related to physical accommodations typically considered as expected customer services or augmented customer services? Why does this distinction matter?
3. What are the ethical implications of the issues raised in this case?
4. Develop a 5-point physical accommodation plan for an apparel store chain.

Case 3: Is the Proliferation of Job Titles Helping or Hurting?*

The phrase is familiar: "Too many chiefs, not enough Indians." In retailing, where so many firms employ thousands of people, the adage hardly seems applicable. Then again, the CEO and other C-suite regulars are now sharing the "chief" prefix with a growing list of colleagues. Macy's has a chief digital officer, Kohl's has a chief customer officer, and Target has a chief information security officer. In recent years, there's been a rise in the number of chief customer and chief digital officers hired; some

predict that an upsurge in chief content and chief social officer appointments is next.

Retail experts say these new positions reflect the fast-paced change within an industry jumping headfirst into digital transformation. The newly appointed chiefs are tasked with creating business agility, tearing down function-focused silos, and applying their skills to the ever-mounting mission of exceeding customer expectations.

Nevertheless, there are those who are wary. Is the influx of new titles creating more silos than it is removing? Do the new chiefs have a boardroom seat? Will these roles be required 10 years from now—or is this a fad? Not all the newly minted chiefs are regulars in the executive boardroom, but most are reporting to the CEO in some capacity.

"Data show that from the mid-1980s to 2010, the average C-suite doubled. Today that continues," says Eamonn Kelly, a director with Deloitte Consulting. "Almost all the growth has been in functional, specialized areas. The goal is to transform a business to remain competitive and to focus on the customer holistically. Still achieving that coherence and alignment across multiple strategies is a challenge."

Maryam Morse, national retail practice leader for Hay Group, maintains that the retail executive team "needs to be close to where innovation and change are happening, and, thus, we're seeing more positions at the top. It's not about E-commerce or technology. It's about putting the customer at the core of decision making."

It's become commonplace to link industry trends to the transformation of the customer experience and the rise of digital technology. Several years ago when the role of marketing began taking on amplified importance, the position of chief marketing officer quickly took root and discussions about collaborating with the CIO reached a fevered pitch. Overnight, it seemed, CMOs were tasked with leading dramatic change within their organizations while technology continued to evolve at a rapid-fire pace.

At many companies, the CMO realized that delivering a seamless experience to today's customer—making shopping more personalized and communicating with engaging content—would require more exacting functional expertise.

"Different skill sets and organizational structures are needed in a digitally driven world," says Susan Hart, co-leader of Spencer Stuart's global retail, apparel, and luxury goods practice. "The idea that one single person can do it all may require a change in perception. That's part of why we're seeing not just a chief digital officer, but a chief content officer and a chief analytics officer. Tasking people to take on these specialized roles is intended to move the retailer closer to the customer."

"The number of new chiefs in retail is more a reaction to new developments in the industry than expanding the C-suite," comments Tom Cole, partner in the retail and consumer group at Kurt Salmon. "There are perhaps more pyramid heads than in the past, but they're still reporting up to the CEO or the COO." He adds that naming chiefs goes a long way toward clarifying responsibilities. "It designates who's at the top of the pyramid and it sends a clear signal—both internally and externally—about the importance of the role inside that retail company."

Morse concurs. "Titles reflect company strategy. Elevating 'customer experience' or 'security' responsibility to a 'chief' sends a message about where the retailer is making its bets and what it values."

*Based on material from Susan Reda, "Chief Concerns," *STORES Magazine,* June 2015, pp. 22–24. Reprinted by permission.

Questions

1. Why do you think that there has been a proliferation of job titles? Is this good or bad? Why?
2. State how the issues raised in this case relate to a retailer's conducting a situation analysis.
3. Should retailers have a Chief of Digital Operations position? Explain your answer.
4. Do you agree or disagree with this statement? "Elevating 'customer experience' or 'security' responsibility to a 'chief' sends a message about where the retailer is making its bets and what it values." Why?

Case 4: Competition and Quick Foodservice*

Consumers have a need for convenient, quick, high-quality prepared foods. As traditional convenience store (c-store) products slip in demand, c-store operators must place a stronger emphasis on prepared foods to improve profits. A growing number of c-store chains are providing high-quality, quick food supported by appealing, food-forward marketing. For quick-service restaurants (QSRs), this means many c-stores are now direct competitors.

Grocery stores are also focusing on prepared foods. Grocery retailers were once very different from restaurants, serving customers' needs for in-home meal preparation. But today, prepared, ready-to-eat meals and snacks are readily available in this channel. Grocery stores' prepared meals offer quality and are growing in variety.

C-stores and grocery stores, historically different, now compete in the same space as traditional QSRs for the same customer and the same occasion. Most customers use multiple channels to purchase food for immediate consumption. Fewer than one in four U.S. consumers are exclusive QSR users for these meal occasions. Those who are exclusive QSR customers are just as likely to dine in or take away as other QSR users. Off-premise visits made by exclusive QSR buyers are likely vulnerable to shifts to other channels. The extent of the customer-sharing, as seen through NPD research, demonstrates the channel blurring happening among retail and traditional quick foodservice segments.

Quick and convenient food from c-stores and grocery stores incrementally adds customers to the fast food/foodservice market. Further, the number of fast-food purchases made by customers using these outlets is more than six visits higher in an average four-week period. Traditional QSRs offering morning meals are most likely to feel the impact of c-stores on their customer base. These occasions are likely in-and-out, grab-and-go visits where convenience and fast service trump QSR chain preference.

Between-meal purchases/snacks is another competitive time of the day. C-stores hold their highest share of these product categories: coffee, snacks, breakfast foods, and soft drinks. Product offerings vary, with some c-store chains emphasizing prepared foods more than others. Grocery stores hold a high share of purchases of chicken, side dishes, and salads. They provide a ready-to-consume meal for the family —easy, convenient, and an opportunity to meet the needs of multiple family members.

Retail foodservice at c-stores and grocery stores is growing and expected to continue to grow. This growth delivers new and very different insights about the structure of the quick foodservice market from a consumer perspective. Consumers have a need for convenient, quick, high-quality prepared foods and whichever channel fills that need is where they will visit.

The challenge for all retailers offering quick-serve food is to find the best way to stand out among a diverse set of competitors in order to grow market share. Figures 1 through 3 provide more information on the competitive battle. Note: Wawa is a c-store chain.

Questions

1. How should the organizational missions of convenience stores and QSRs differ? Why?
2. What are the competitive advantages of convenience stores versus QSRs? Explain your answer.
3. Comment on the information in Figures 1 and 2. What are the strategic implications?
4. What could Dunkin' Donuts, McDonald's, and Wawa learn from the information in Figure 3? What are the strategic implications?

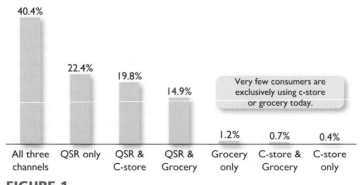

FIGURE 1

Where Do Consumers Go to Buy Fast Food Away from Home?

Source: NPD Group/QSR Plus Retail Market Monitor, March–June 2015. Reprinted by permission of Convenience Store News © 2016 (www.csnews.com)

---

*Based on material from Bonnie Riggs, "The Competition for Quick Foodservice Heats Up," *Convenience Store News*, January 2016, pp. 72, 74. Reprinted by permission. Convenience Store News © 2016 (www.csnews.com)

FIGURE 2

Food Category Purchase by Channel

Source: NPD Group/
QSR Plus Retail Market
Monitor, March–June 2015.
Reprinted by permission of
Convenience Store News
© 2016 (www.csnews.com)

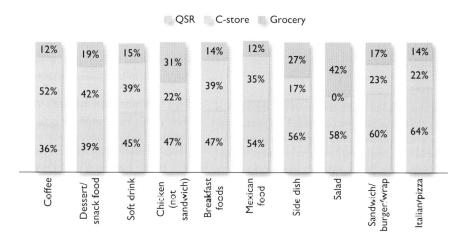

FIGURE 3

What Types of Food Are Bought at Dunkin' Donuts, McDonald's, and Wawa? (Reported for Previous Visit in Philadelphia Area)

Source: NPD Group/
QSR Plus Retail Market
Monitor, March–June 2015.
Reprinted by permission of
Convenience Store News
© 2016 (www.csnews.com)

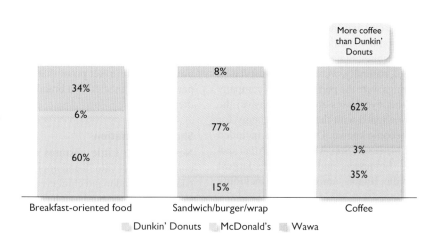

PART 1 Comprehensive Case

Ideas Worth Stealing*

Introduction

Feeling a day late and a dollar short for the retail innovation party? Not to worry; *STORES* has you covered. This year's roster of the top "ideas worth stealing" offers copious opportunities for catching up. Retailers, small and large, have had a banner season of creatively making things work in this increasingly demanding industry—and many of their inspired concepts can be scaled up or down to fit other companies. Here, we celebrate their successes while broadening the guest list of possibility. Cheers!

Coalesce Product, Lifestyle, and Experience

Consider looking at marketing through a different lens. Warby Parker's #seesummerbetter campaign encouraged consumers to "enjoy the ride" of the season by downloading a map of must-see destinations across the United States, along with a Spotify playlist. Woven throughout, naturally, were the hottest styles in sunglasses. The free offerings were the perfect fit for a company founded on the premise that eyeglasses are too expensive; the fun, quirky graphics were aligned with the creative energy for which the company has become known. Destinations included Cadillac Ranch in Amarillo, Texas; Stax Museum of American Soul Music in Memphis, Tennessee; and the world's largest ketchup bottle in Collinsville, Illinois, among others (including the company's stores).

Warby Parker, incidentally, was named *Fast Company*'s Most Innovative Company of 2015, lauded for being the first great made-on-the-Internet brand. Warby Parker continues to expand its bricks-and-mortar presence with great success—so a road trip or two may well be in order.

Empower Success for Others

A sizable part of business is competition—but not all. Rent the Runway and global financial services provider UBS teamed up in 2015 to help women entrepreneurs across the country build high-growth, high-impact businesses through Project Entrepreneur.

Launched in September 2015 as the first initiative of the nonprofit Rent the Runway Foundation, Project Entrepreneur is a venture competition open to those beyond ideation and intending to build a high-growth company using an existing prototype or beta technology. The top 200 finalists attended an April 2016 workshop in New York, with three winning teams awarded $10,000 each and given a spot in a 5-week accelerator program. A series of free educational summits also took place.

Rent the Runway CEO Jennifer Hyman notes that despite the many entrepreneurial women founding businesses, only 4 percent generate $500,000 or more in annual revenue. There's still space on the far side of the glass ceiling, and efforts like this can help lead to breakthrough.

Give Customers an Insider's View

New York's Fashion Week is the place where trendsetters come together. Now a fashionista in Iowa or Montana can do the same—without leaving the couch.

When Lauren Conrad's collection for Kohl's made its debut at the September 2015 Fashion Week, the actress-turned-designer's company wanted to bring along a few thousand friends. Using Conrad's active and robust social media presence (nearly 11 million followers among several social-media sites) to issue invites, Kohl's hosted the fashion show on the video streaming site Periscope. Those watching could chat and comment live, or they could shop: The fashion items were instantly available for online purchase.

Traffic to Kohl's Web site increased 600 percent during the show, and viewers even got a backstage peek before show time. It is just further proof that today's consumers want to feel personally connected to a brand, and to feel that the brand likes them back.

Show Appreciation

Never forget: Little gestures can go a long way in helping employees feel valued and appreciated. Barbara Bradley Baekgaard, co-founder and chief creative officer of Vera Bradley, has maintained a personal touch throughout the impressive growth of her handbag, luggage, and accessories to $509 million in annual sales.

She recently told *Fortune:* "My father always said, 'In business, you sell yourself first, your company second, and the product third; and he was right. Business is all about forming relationships and having a company that reflects your values.'"

So how does that play out? Baekgaard told the magazine that when the company first started, the leadership would put $50 cash in employees' birthday cards and instructed, "This has to be spent on you." As the company has expanded to 3,000 employees, there's still a $50 bill in each card. "Finance asks every year if we can just put the money in people's paychecks, and I say no," she said. "When you have found money in cash, it's just more meaningful."

Give Associates an Insider's View

Kohl's gets another mention here, hosting a question-and-answer session with designer Vera Wang, who visited the retailer's new Innovation Center near headquarters in Menomonee Falls, Wisconsin. Associates in IT, store design, purchasing, and supply chain operations—who began moving into the new center in the summer—had the chance to interact with Wang and Kevin Mansell, Kohl's chairman, president, and CEO.

The event, which Kohl's called an opportunity to learn from the industry's top talent, is part of Kohl's multiyear Greatness Agenda strategy, which has "Winning Teams" as one of the core components. It is a realization that the retailer of the

---

*Based on material from Sandy Smith and Fiona Soltes, "20 Ideas Worth Stealing in 2016," *STORES Magazine,* January 2016, pp. 32–40. Reprinted by permission. Copyright 2016. STORES Magazine.

future will rely more heavily on associates than ever. Investing in developing their skills—and giving them access to top-notch experts—develops a lot more commitment than comes with just a steady paycheck.

Build Lasting Relationships through Innovative Memberships

At their best, neighborhood coffee shops are all about community, the chance to see familiar faces over a steaming hot cup o' joe. One New York City coffee shop, however, has expanded that idea—forgive us— quite a latte. Greenwich Village's Fair Folks & a Goat is based on a subscription model: $25 a month gets members as many coffees, teas, and lemonades as they desire.

The shop, which opened in 2012, also features clothing, art, home design pieces, and other items that consumers don't have to be members to purchase. Members do receive discounts on select merchandise, as well as invitations to various events and "access to a community and a home away from home." A second location has been added in the East Village, and the community continues to expand; referred friends receive a free month's membership. We can raise a mug to that.

Relearn to Sell Commodities

It's been said that we live in a disruptive environment. Who knew that a bra needed disrupting? Fashion label Chromat and designer Becca McCharen have been doing just that.

McCharen's background in architecture and urban design is focused on the human body, specifically in making architecturally structured foundations for garments like bras, swimwear, sportswear, and lingerie. Sure, it may be the more outlandish designs—such as architectural cages—that get the attention, especially when they appear on Beyoncé during a Super Bowl performance or at the Video Music Awards, but it's the functional aspects of some pieces that deserve notice.

In 2015, Chromat teamed with Intel to create two pieces using the technology company's Curie Module: a bra that opens vents to cool down the body when it senses heat and sweat, and a 3D-printed dress that measures adrenaline levels and expands to mimic the "fight or flight" mode. It is proof that, in this disruptive age, even the most basic products are going high-tech and retailers will need to rethink sales strategies.

Foster Community with Shared Memories and Stories

A long time ago, in a boardroom far, far away, a Target leader must have fondly remembered space adventures gone by. In addition to hosting a "Shop the Force" event to promote Lucasfilm's "Star Wars: Episode VII—The Force Awakens" with toys, apparel, and other items related to the film starting at midnight on September 4, 2015, the retailer offered a "Share the Force" experience both online and in stores.

In stores, consumers were given the opportunity to enjoy photo ops, giveaways, and demos of Star Wars toys on September 5. Online at SharetheForce.com, those consumers were able to turn memories into "holograms" among the stars. The collected memories will eventually be archived at Lucasfilm (which is owned by Disney). It is a place, as Darth Vader might say, we can all meet again, at last. The circle is now complete.

Fight Unfairly for Shelf Space

There is no doubt that getting a new product onto a store's shelves is a daunting task. Without proper placement, the product simply won't succeed. But barkTHINS, a chocolate snack, did anything but play fair: It used samples of its product to sweet-talk its way onto the store shelves.

Working with brand growth strategists at Switch, barkTHINS hired area brand managers, typically health-conscious chocolate lovers, in select markets. The company not only stocked the area brand managers with samples of the product, but brand managers were allowed to negotiate with retailers when necessary. BarkTHINS was able to keep an eye on the progress of the area brand managers using a dashboard to monitor account visits, demos performed, and incremental retail sales. In today's competitive environment, different strategies are required.

Confront Gender Stereotypes and Sexism

Nearly two-thirds of Brazilian women don't agree with the way they are portrayed in advertising, according to a creative activism group. That's likely impacted by the fact that only 10 percent of the country's advertising creatives are women. So what do you do with a product like beer? It depends: Is it Cerveja Feminista?

This "feminist beer," introduced in 2015 by a group called 65/10 in conjunction with Beauvoir Brewing, is as much a conversation starter as it is a beverage. It's a red ale, somewhere between the darker beers typically associated with men and the blonder brews associated with women. The label is in no way gender-specific. But the conversation is rich. Cerveja Feminista has been covered by *Fast Company, The Independent,* and others, in stories that speak as much about women's treatment as the beer. A Brazilian a woman is killed every 90 minutes by domestic violence. The group 65/10 asserts that when women are objectified, they are considered possessions—which eventually leads to brutality.

Shake Up Perceptions

As an upscale retailer well entrenched in successful marketing initiatives, Nordstrom would be forgiven for playing it safe, especially where new technology is concerned. That relationship with the tried and true became somewhat complicated in 2015: To promote its summer sale, Nordstrom took to the roof with a 3D installation, mimicking its Leith leopard-print body dress as part of one giant Instagram post.

A 55-foot version of the dress, including a 25-foot-long wooden hanger, was installed on the roof of Nordstrom's Seattle flagship location. The entire installation—which included a woman walking across the roof wearing the leopard dress—was filmed by drones and posted live on social-media accounts. A time-lapse video of the installation was also created and shared via Instagram. This type of comprehensive social-media campaign may not have resonated with its typical affluent customer, but Nordstrom was laying the groundwork to develop the next generation of shoppers.

Make the Most of Instagram

A picture is worth a thousand . . . sales? Visual commerce platform Curalate has joined forces with eBay Enterprise to launch Like2Buy, which lets users click directly from Instagram photos to E-commerce product pages.

The best part? The easy-to-deploy system works for publishers of all sizes, so the partnership gives users fast access to more than 100,000 publishers in the eBay Enterprise Affiliate Network. One publisher, according to Curalate, found that 60 percent of visitors clicked through to relevant content, as well as spent 37 percent more time on the site than that publisher's average mobile visitor.

eBay Enterprise considers the effort a "huge opportunity" to remove barriers from the buying experience, since 30 percent of total E-commerce spending is driven by mobile devices. It's exactly what we all need: More reasons to spend time perusing photos.

Craft an Experience—and Listen for Cues

Step into an Alton Lane showroom and you might find yourself casually having a drink and an engaging conversation about your hobbies.

The premium tailored apparel retailer is creating a bit of a revolution in bespoke menswear, attempting to know its customers well enough to create "the best experience possible," according to CEO and co-founder Colin Hunter. "We want our team to be observant hosts and hostesses, so we try to pick up on the small cues that naturally come up in conversation."

Style preferences, clothing needs, and personal interests all help determine the best offerings. As for the customer data, that's taken care of through NetSuite's integrated customer relationship management, financial, inventory, and order management software. Hunter considers the partnership a "game-changer," allowing Alton Lane to track and access data as effortlessly as striking up a chat.

Take Advantage of Cutting-Edge Technology

Maybe it's time for the Internet of Things (IoT) to move to the storefront. London's Dandy Lab has done just that, using Cisco's IoT technology and third-party software. The storefront was originally designed as a home for small independent British fashion designers, and while that is still at the base of the products, technology is used to drive sales.

Because people like a good story with their purchases, a customer can pick up a product, place it on a near-field communication terminal, and see more about the brand on a large flat screen. Tablet-sized screens are embedded into the walls, displaying price, product details, and stock levels when an item is held in front of the screen. Another area allows a customer to show a product, color, or pattern and receive advice on other items that might pair—or clash—with it. In today's increasingly wired world, the Dandy Lab serves as something of a playground for retail's next big wave.

Create a New Definition of "Showrooming"

Beijing-based Li Ning Company Limited (named for its founder, famed Chinese Olympic gymnast Li Ning) recently upped its game with a new model: physical showrooms where sporting goods customers can touch and feel products, but not buy.

The shift to online-only purchasing, as part of a strategy to overcome losses in recent years, has allowed the popular brand to keep thousands of locations open but distribute goods from a single warehouse, according to Bloomberg. That means reductions in costs plus improvements in inventory management.

During the first month the strategy garnered the equivalent of $3.5 million in sales.

Li Ning is not alone in its approach. According to Bloomberg, Haier Electronics also featured display-only inventory in a number of its stores across China, and Hong Kong-based online clothing retailer Grana opened showrooms in Singapore, Australia, and the United States in 2016.

Get Exposure in New Ways

When HGTV wanted to furnish its 2015 Urban Oasis, it turned to Overstock.com's shelves. Overstock provided furniture, home décor, sporting goods, clothing, and accessories for the 1,300-square-foot bungalow in Asheville, North Carolina. It wasn't just the contest winner who came out on top. The Urban Oasis giveaway received Overstock contributions for its $500,000 grand-prize package awarded to one lucky viewer, and Overstock got additional exposure from the heavily promoted giveaway.

Overstock received an added bonus: Since it provided more than furnishings (including a kayak), Overstock got to show its extensive lifestyle products. In addition to the television show, which offered a tour of the bungalow, and advertising, a dedicated Web page featured copious images of the products used to pull the look together.

This is just one step in a blossoming relationship between Overstock and HGTV. The two also paired up on the TV shows "Vacation House for Free" and "Holiday House 2015." The retailer took full advantage, creating dedicated Web pages that allowed viewers to shop and purchase the looks used on the programs.

Strategize Traditional Standbys

With the ever-increasing customization of retail, traditional ad circulars can seem a bit too one-size-fits-all. But personalized digital media company Catalina has introduced My Favorite Deals, allowing those circulars to be tailored for individual shoppers based on past purchases.

Delivered in-store, online, through E-mail, and on cell phones, My Favorite Deals brings five or more of the most relevant offers to shoppers, increasing sales, driving retail trips, and building loyalty. Catalina found that 66 percent or more of weekly shoppers don't buy a single item from a typical circular; with My Favorite Deals, retailers have seen an increase of up to 1.5 percent in sales to targeted shoppers and an incremental lift of 1.5 to 5 percent in sales of promoted items.

Better yet, Catalina touts, My Favorite Deals needs no hardware or system changes for retailers, and the firm's network already includes more than 28,000 U.S. grocery, drug, and mass merchandise stores.

Take Advantage of "X" Month

It seems like every day, week, and month offers some special theme. When it came time for Family Meals Month, midwestern grocer Hy-Vee was ready to provide a solution to one of the greatest barriers to family meals: someone to plan and cook them.

The Dinner Crasher promotion selected a family shopping in selected stores to have a Hy-Vee chef and dietician "crash" dinner and create a custom dinner experience. After the family was selected in the store, dietary needs and preferences were discussed with the crash taking place later that week.

The takeaway for savvy retailers here is the notion of capitalizing on a themed day/week/month with a promotion that both offers customer appreciation and solves issues: a win-win.

Questions

1. What can *any* retailer learn from this case?
2. Relate the material in this case to the concept of the total retail experience.
3. What uncontrollable factors will affect a retailer's ability to undertake the suggestions cited in the case? How would you handle them?
4. Comment on this observation: "In business, you sell yourself first, your company second, and the product third."
5. Target has a Web site (https://corporate.target.com/about/shopping-experience/) about the shopping experience it provides. Relate what you find at this site to Target's overall retail strategy, based on the steps discussed in Chapter 3.
6. What kind of loyalty program(s) should Nordstrom offer? Present details in your answer.
7. What recommendations would you suggest for any retailer as it looks to the future? Trader Joe's (www.traderjoes.com) is a shopping haven for consumers looking for distinctive, fairly priced food items.

Part 2

Situation Analysis

Source: nasirkhan/Shutterstock.
Reprinted by permission.

In Part Two, we talk about the organizational missions, ownership and management alternatives, goods/service categories, and objectives of a broad range of retail institutions. By understanding the unique attributes of these institutions, better retail strategies can be developed and implemented.

Chapter 4 examines the characteristics of retail institutions on the basis of ownership type: independent, chain, franchise, leased department, vertical marketing system, and consumer cooperative. We also discuss the methods used by manufacturers, wholesalers, and retailers to obtain control in a distribution channel. A chapter appendix has additional information on franchising.

Chapter 5 describes retail institutions in terms of their strategy mix. We introduce three key concepts: the wheel of retailing, scrambled merchandising, and the retail life cycle. Strategic responses to the evolving marketplace are noted. Several strategy mixes are then studied, with food and general merchandise retailers reviewed separately.

Chapter 6 focuses on nonstore retailing, electronic retailing, and nontraditional retailing approaches. We cover direct marketing, direct selling, vending machines, the Web, video kiosks, and airport retailing. The dynamics of Web-based retailing are featured. A chapter appendix covers the emerging area of omnichannel retailing in more depth.

4 Retail Institutions by Ownership

Chapter Objectives

1. To show the ways in which retail institutions can be classified

2. To study retailers on the basis of ownership type and to examine the characteristics of each

3. To explore the methods used by manufacturers, wholesalers, and retailers to exert influence in the distribution channel

Store-based retail firms may operate as few as one facility—such as a local pizza shop—or as many as several thousand locations—such as the Subway fast-food chain with more than 44,000 outlets around the world. Differences in scale, product portfolio mix, and product life cycle stage of the products carried; consumers' pre-purchase, purchase, and post-purchase information and service needs; distribution channel structure; and laws and regulations contribute a retailer's choice of ownership structure.

Most states have laws restricting the ability of auto dealers to sell new cars directly to consumers. These laws require that new cars be sold only through franchised dealers. Franchise agreements typically give a dealer an exclusive right to operate in a specific geographic area. Geographic protection enables a retailer to invest in a franchised location with the knowledge that its facilities will not directly compete with nearby dealers. Geographic protection also protects traditional dealers from direct price competition.

Source: Keith Bell/Shutterstock.
Reprinted by permission.

110

In contrast to the auto franchising model, Tesla Motors bypasses the franchise dealer network by selling cars directly to the consumer through Tesla-owned and operated retail centers. Tesla says it operates a different business than a traditional car manufacturer. (1) Unlike traditional dealers, Tesla does not stock unordered cars in inventory. It only builds cars based on customer orders. (2) Since Tesla's technology is innovative, it needs time to explain product features. Dealers would not have salespeople that were as informed as Tesla's or as willing to answer all questions. (3) Regular dealers often make more money by selling extended warranties and via financing than on the actual sale of the car. Tesla does not offer these services. (4) Automotive antitrust laws were designed to prevent manufacturers from competing with existing dealers. Tesla has no existing dealers. (5) Tesla pays sales personnel a salary; dealers pay them on a commission basis. The commission structure may encourage salespeople to seek higher prices from consumers and/or to sell them more costly cars and accessories than needed. And (6) Tesla says direct distribution lowers costs over dealer franchised networks.[1]

Overview

A **retail institution** is the basic format or structure of a business. In the United States, there are 2.4 million retail firms (including those with no payroll, whereby only the owner and/or family members work for the firm), and they operate 3.2 million establishments. An institutional discussion shows the relative sizes and diversity of different kinds of retailing, and indicates how various retailers are affected by the external environment. Institutional analysis is important in strategic planning when selecting an organizational mission, choosing an ownership alternative, defining the goods/service category, and setting objectives.

We examine retail institutions from these perspectives: ownership (discussed in this chapter); store-based strategy mix (Chapter 5); and nonstore-based, electronic, and nontraditional retailing (Chapter 6). Figure 4-1 shows a classification method for various retail institutions. An institution may be placed in more than one category: A department store may be part of a chain, have a store-based strategy, accept mail-order sales, and operate a Web site.

Please interpret the data in Chapters 4, 5, and 6 carefully. Some institutional categories are not mutually exclusive; thus, care should be taken in combining statistics so that double counting does not occur. We have drawn in the data in these chapters from a number of government and nongovernment sources. Although data are as current as possible, not all information corresponds to a common date. *Census of Retail Trade* data are collected only twice a decade. Furthermore, our numbers are based on the broad interpretation of retailing used in this book, which includes auto repair shops, hotels and motels, movie theaters, real-estate brokers, and others who sell to the final consumer.

RETAIL INSTITUTIONS CHARACTERIZED BY OWNERSHIP

Retail firms may be independently owned, chain-owned, franchisee-operated, leased departments, owned by manufacturers or wholesalers, or consumer-owned.

Although retailers are primarily small (three-quarters of all stores are operated by firms with one outlet and more than one-half of all firms have two or fewer paid employees), there are also very large retailers. The five leading U.S.-based retailers annually total $700 billion in U.S. sales alone and employ about 3 million people in the United States. Ownership opportunities abound. According to the U.S. Census Bureau (www.census.gov), women own one million retail firms, African Americans (men and women) 120,000 retail firms, Hispanic Americans (men and women) 185,000 retail firms, and Asian Americans (men and women) 200,000 retail firms.

Each ownership format serves a marketplace niche, if the strategy is executed well:

▸ Independent retailers capitalize on a highly targeted customer base and please shoppers in a friendly, informal way. Word-of-mouth communication is important. These retailers should not try to serve too many customers or enter into price wars.

▸ Chain retailers benefit from their widely known image and from economies of scale and mass promotion possibilities. They should maintain their image chainwide and not be inflexible in adapting to changes in the marketplace.

FIGURE 4-1

A Classification Method for Retail Institutions

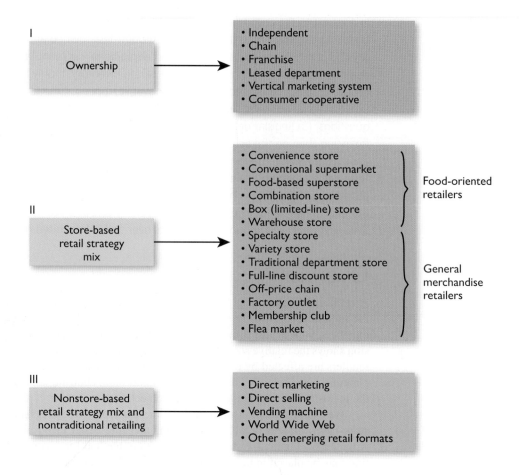

I Ownership
- Independent
- Chain
- Franchise
- Leased department
- Vertical marketing system
- Consumer cooperative

II Store-based retail strategy mix
- Convenience store
- Conventional supermarket
- Food-based superstore
- Combination store
- Box (limited-line) store
- Warehouse store
} Food-oriented retailers
- Specialty store
- Variety store
- Traditional department store
- Full-line discount store
- Off-price chain
- Factory outlet
- Membership club
- Flea market
} General merchandise retailers

III Nonstore-based retail strategy mix and nontraditional retailing
- Direct marketing
- Direct selling
- Vending machine
- World Wide Web
- Other emerging retail formats

▷ Franchisors have strong geographic coverage—due to franchisee investments—and the motivation of franchisees as owner-operators. They should not get bogged down in policy disputes with franchisees or charge excessive royalty fees.

▷ Leased departments enable store operators and outside parties to join forces and enhance the shopping experience, while sharing expertise and expenses. They should not hurt the image of the store or place too much pressure on the lessee to generate store traffic.

▷ A vertically integrated channel gives a firm greater control over sources of supply, but it should not provide consumers with too little choice of products or too few outlets.

▷ Cooperatives provide members with cost savings due to pooled purchasing and joint ownership of a warehouse. They should not expect too much involvement by members or add facilities that raise costs too much.

Independent

An **independent** retailer owns one retail unit. We estimate that there are 2.3 million independent U.S. retailers—accounting for about one-quarter of total store sales. Seventy percent of independents are run by the owners and their families; and those firms generate just 3 percent of U.S. store sales (averaging under $100,000 in annual revenues) and have no paid workers (there is no payroll).

The high number of independents is associated with the **ease of entry** into the marketplace, due to low capital requirements and no, or relatively simple, licensing provisions for many small retail firms. The investment per worker in retailing is usually much lower than for manufacturers, and licensing is pretty routine. Each year, tens of thousands of new retailers, mostly independents, open in the United States.

The ease of entry—which leads to intense competition—is a big factor in the high rate of failures among newer firms. One-third of new U.S. retailers do not survive the first year, and two-thirds do not continue beyond the third year. Most failures involve independents. Annually,

The Business Owner's Toolkit (www.toolkit.com) is an excellent resource for the independent retailer.

CAREERS IN RETAILING

Succession Planning

In *succession planning*, a retailer develops a detailed plan as to a future change in leadership. Succession planning is crucial for any business that can unexpectedly lose a key executive due to illness, early retirement, incapacity, or accident. The need for succession planning is especially crucial for independent retailers because only one-third of family-owned businesses survive from one generation to the next. Here are some tips for a family-owned retailer: (1) Involve the successor in planning and decision making during a transition period, (2) Determine whether the successor needs more training and compensation, (3) Draft a legal document outlining all terms of succession.

List other items that need to be discussed in the succession plan.

Source: "Management Succession Planning," http://www .referenceforbusiness.com/encyclopedia/Man-Mix/Management-Succession-Planning.html. (Accessed July 20, 2016).

■

thousands of U.S. retailers (of all sizes) file for bankruptcy protection—besides the thousands of small firms that simply close.[2]

The U.S. Small Business Administration (SBA) has a Small Business Development Center (SBDC) to assist current and prospective small business owners (www.sba.gov/content/small-business-development-centers-sbdcs). There are 63 lead SBDCs (at least one in every state) and more than 900 local SBDCs, satellites, and specialty centers. The purpose is to assist "small businesses with financial, marketing, production, organization, engineering, and technical problems and feasibility studies." Centers offer free counseling, seminars and training sessions, conferences, and information through the Internet, as well as in person and by phone. The SBA also has a lot of free downloadable information at its Web site (www.sba.gov). See Figure 4-2.

FIGURE 4-2

Useful Online Information for Retailers

Go to www.sba.gov/starting-managing-business and download any of the U.S. Small Business Administration publications at this Web site. They're free!

COMPETITIVE ADVANTAGES AND DISADVANTAGES OF INDEPENDENTS   Independent retailers have various advantages and disadvantages. The following are among the advantages:

Read the Aunt Annie's story (http://www.annies .com/our-mission/about- annies)—a success story from a farmer's market to a worldwide chain.

▶ There is flexibility in choosing retail formats and locations and in devising strategy. Because only one location is involved, detailed specifications can be set for the best site and a thorough search undertaken. Uniform location standards are not needed, as they are for chains, and independents do not have to worry about stores being too close together. Independents have great latitude in selecting target markets. Because they often have modest goals, small segments may be selected rather than the mass market. Assortments, prices, hours, and other factors are then set consistent with the segment.

▶ Investment costs for leases, fixtures, workers, and merchandise can be held down; and there is no duplication of stock or personnel. Responsibilities are clearly delineated within a store.

▶ Independents frequently act as specialists in a niche of a particular goods/service category. They are then more efficient and can lure shoppers interested in specialized retailers.

▶ Independents exert strong control over their strategies, and the owner-operator is often on the premises. Decisions are centralized and layers of management personnel are minimized.

▶ There is a certain image attached to independents, particularly small ones that chains cannot readily capture. This is the image of a personable retailer with a comfortable atmosphere in which to shop.

▶ Independents can easily sustain consistency in their efforts since only one store is operated.

▶ Independents have "independence." They do not have to fret about stockholders, board of directors meetings, and labor unrest. They are often free from unions and seniority rules.

▶ Owner-operators typically have a strong entrepreneurial drive. They have made a personal investment and there is a lot of ego involvement. Research shows that independent retailers are more likely to "put customers' interests first." Their personal interaction with customers, flat organizational structure, and limited resources lead to efficient and effective customer-oriented planning that improves profitability.[3]

These are some of the disadvantages of independent retailing:

▶ In bargaining with suppliers, independents may not have much power because they often buy in small quantities. Suppliers may even bypass them. Reordering may be difficult if minimum order requirements are high. Some independents, such as hardware stores, belong to buying groups to increase their clout.

▶ Independents generally cannot gain economies of scale in buying and maintaining inventory. Due to financial constraints, small assortments are bought several times per year. Transportation, ordering, and handling costs per unit are high.

▶ Operations are labor intensive, sometimes with little computerization. Ordering, taking inventory, marking items, ringing up sales, and bookkeeping may be done manually. This is less efficient than computerization. In many cases, owner-operators are unwilling or unable to spend time learning how to set up and apply computerized procedures.

▶ Due to the relatively high costs of TV ads and the broad geographic coverage of magazines and some newspapers (too large for firms with one outlet), independents are limited in their access to certain media. Yet, there are various promotion tools available for creative independents (see Chapter 19).

▶ A crucial problem for independents is overdependence on the owner. All decisions may be made by that person, and there may be no management continuity when the owner-boss is ill, on vacation, or retires. Financial concerns like how to pay bills, collect accounts receivable, and make payroll or the bank loan can overwhelm an independent retailer. This can also affect employee morale and long-run success.[4]

▶ A limited amount of time is allotted to long-run planning because the owner is intimately involved in daily operations of the firm.

Chain

A **chain** retailer operates multiple outlets (store units) under common ownership; it usually engages in some level of centralized (or coordinated) purchasing and decision making. In the United States, there are more than 110,000 retail chains that operate about 1 million establishments.

There are about 1,465 PetSmart stores in the United States, Canada, and Puerto Rico and an online business (www.petsmart .com). See if there is one near you.

The relative strength of chain retailing is great, even though the number of firms is small (less than 5 percent of all U.S. retail firms). Chains today operate about 30 percent of retail establishments, and because stores in chains tend to be considerably larger than those run by independents, chains account for roughly three-quarters of total U.S. store sales and employment. Although the majority of chains have 5 or fewer outlets, the several hundred firms with 100 or more outlets account for more than 60 percent of U.S. retail sales. Some big U.S. chains have at least 1,000 outlets each. There are also many large foreign chains, as seen in Figure 4-3.

Chain dominance varies by type of retailer. Chains generate at least 75 percent of total U.S. category sales for department stores, discount department stores, and grocery stores. On the other hand, stationery, beauty salon, furniture, and liquor store chains produce far less than 50 percent of U.S. retail sales in their categories.

COMPETITIVE ADVANTAGES AND DISADVANTAGES OF CHAINS There are numerous competitive advantages for chain retailers:

Sears' own Kenmore brand (www.kenmore.com) is so powerful that many different appliances are sold under the Kenmore name.

▹ Many chains have bargaining power due to their purchase volume. They receive new items when introduced, have orders promptly filled, get sales support, and obtain quantity discounts. Large chains may also gain exclusive rights to certain items and have private-label goods produced under the chains' brands.
▹ Chains achieve cost efficiencies when they buy directly from manufacturers and in large volume, ship and store goods, and attend trade shows sponsored by suppliers to learn about new offerings. They can sometimes bypass wholesalers, which results in lower supplier prices.
▹ Efficiency is gained by sharing warehouse facilities, purchasing standardized store fixtures, and so on; by centralized buying and decision making; and by other practices. Chains typically give headquarters' executives broad authority for personnel policies and for buying, pricing, and advertising decisions.
▹ Chains use computers in ordering merchandise, taking inventory, forecasting, ringing up sales, and bookkeeping. This increases efficiency and reduces overall costs.
▹ Chains, particularly national or regional ones, can take advantage of a variety of media, from TV to magazines to newspapers to online blogs.
▹ Most chains have defined management philosophies, with detailed strategies and clear employee responsibilities. There is continuity when managerial personnel are absent or retire because there are qualified people to fill in and succession plans in place. See Figure 4-4.
▹ Many chains expend considerable time on long-run planning and assign specific staff to planning on a permanent basis. Opportunities and threats are carefully monitored.

Chain retailers also have a number of disadvantages:

▹ After chains are established, flexibility may be limited. New nonoverlapping store sites may be hard to find. Consistent strategies must be maintained throughout all units, including prices, promotions, and product assortments. It may be difficult to adapt to local diverse markets.
▹ Investments are higher due to multiple leases and fixtures. There is higher investment in inventory due to the number of store branches that must be stocked.
▹ Managerial control is complex, especially for chains with geographically dispersed branches. Top management cannot maintain the control over each branch that independents have over

TECHNOLOGY IN RETAILING   Loyalty Programs

The simplest loyalty program is a variation of "buy 10, get 1 free." Paper-based cards are the simplest to implement, but they don't provide retailers with a customer database to track purchases. The second program provides rebates to customers based on their cumulative purchases. A major disadvantage is that the retailer's database contains no information on a customer except purchase activity. However, most major retailers have rewards trackers in their mobile apps. The most sophisticated programs track consumers by segment based on purchase history. Digitally enabled rewards program can customize promotions. They can also induce customers to upgrade to more profitable goods or services, decrease time between visits, or reward customers for feedback on social media.

Provide an example of a retailer using each type of loyalty program.

FIGURE 4-3

Pimke: An International Retail Fashion Chain

Pimkie, based in France, operates about 800 women's apparel stores in more than 25 foreign countries. It targets women "who love fashion." It also operates several country Web sites, available through www .pimkie.com.

Source: Jules Selmes/Pearson Education Ltd. Reprinted by permission.

their single outlet. Lack of communication and delays in making and enacting decisions are particularly problematic.

▶ Personnel in large chains often have limited independence because there are several management layers and unionized employees. Some chains empower personnel to give them more authority.

Franchising[5]

The International Franchise Association (www .franchise.org) is a leading source of information about franchising.

Franchising involves a contractual arrangement between a *franchisor* (a manufacturer, wholesaler, or service sponsor) and a retail *franchisee*, which allows the franchisee to conduct business under an established name and according to a given pattern of business. The franchisee typically pays an initial fee and a monthly percentage of gross sales in exchange for the exclusive rights to sell goods and services in an area. Small businesses benefit by being part of a large, chain-type retail institution.

In **product/trademark franchising**, a franchisee acquires the identity of a franchisor by agreeing to sell the latter's products and/or operate under the latter's name. The franchisee operates rather autonomously. There are some operating rules, but the franchisee sets hours, chooses a location, and determines facilities and displays. Product/trademark franchising represents 60 percent of retail franchising sales. Examples are auto dealers and many gasoline service stations.

With **business format franchising**, there is a more interactive relationship between a franchisor and a franchisee. The franchisee receives assistance on site location, quality control,

FIGURE 4-4

Louis Vuitton: A Powerhouse of Upscale Retailing

Louis Vuitton is a huge chain with luxury stores in dozens of different markets around the world (including this futuristic-looking store in Singapore. Its Web site (www.louisvuitton .com) may be accessed in several different languages.

Source: Mix and Match/ Shutterstock. Reprinted by permission.

accounting systems, startup practices, management training, and responding to problems besides the right to sell goods and services. Prototype stores, standardized product lines, and cooperative advertising foster a level of coordination previously found only in chains. Business format franchising arrangements are common for restaurants and other food outlets, real-estate, and service retailing. Due to the small size of many franchisees, business formats account for about 80 percent of franchised outlets, although just 40 percent of total sales (including auto dealers). See Figure 4-5.

McDonald's (www.aboutmcdonalds.com/mcd/franchising.html) is a good example of a business format franchise arrangement. The firm provides franchisee training at Hamburger University, a detailed operating manual, regular visits by service managers, and brush-up training. In return for a 20-year franchising agreement with McDonald's, a traditional franchisee generally must put up a minimum of $500,000 of nonborrowed personal resources and typically pays ongoing royalty fees totaling at least 12.5 percent of gross sales to McDonald's.

SIZE AND STRUCTURAL ARRANGEMENTS[6]   Although auto and truck dealers provide more than one-half of all U.S. retail franchise sales, few sectors of retailing have been unaffected by franchising's growth. In the United States, there are more than 3,000 retail franchisors doing business with 350,000+ franchisees. They operate 850,000 franchisee- and franchisor-owned outlets, employ several million people, and generate one-third of total store sales. In addition, hundreds of U.S.-based franchisors have foreign operations, with tens of thousands of outlets.

About 85 percent of U.S. franchising sales and franchised outlets involve franchisee-owned units; the rest involve franchisor-owned outlets. If franchisees operate one outlet, they are independents; if they operate two or more outlets, they are chains. Today, a large number of franchisees operate as chains.

As Figure 4-6 shows, three structural arrangements dominate retail franchising:

1. *Manufacturer-retailer.* A manufacturer gives independent franchisees the right to sell goods and related services through a licensing agreement.
2. *Wholesaler-retailer.*
    a. *Voluntary.* A wholesaler sets up a franchise system and grants franchises to individual retailers.
    b. *Cooperative.* A group of retailers sets up a franchise system and shares the ownership and operations of a wholesaling organization.
3. *Service sponsor-retailer.* A service firm licenses individual retailers so they can offer specific service packages to consumers.

FIGURE 4-5

Selected Factors for Prospective Franchisees to Consider

Owning a franchise comes with defined costs, franchisor controls, and contractual obligations.

Source: Based on material from the Federal Trade Commission, "A Consumer's Guide to Buying a Franchise," www.ftc.gov/tips-advice/business-center/guidance/consumers-guide-buying-franchise

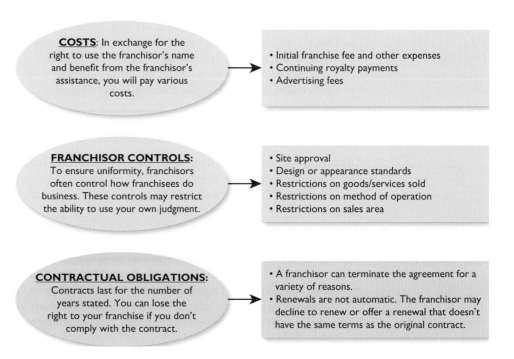

COSTS: In exchange for the right to use the franchisor's name and benefit from the franchisor's assistance, you will pay various costs.
- Initial franchise fee and other expenses
- Continuing royalty payments
- Advertising fees

FRANCHISOR CONTROLS: To ensure uniformity, franchisors often control how franchisees do business. These controls may restrict the ability to use your own judgment.
- Site approval
- Design or appearance standards
- Restrictions on goods/services sold
- Restrictions on method of operation
- Restrictions on sales area

CONTRACTUAL OBLIGATIONS: Contracts last for the number of years stated. You can lose the right to your franchise if you don't comply with the contract.
- A franchisor can terminate the agreement for a variety of reasons.
- Renewals are not automatic. The franchisor may decline to renew or offer a renewal that doesn't have the same terms as the original contract.

FIGURE 4-6

Structural Arrangements in Retail Franchising

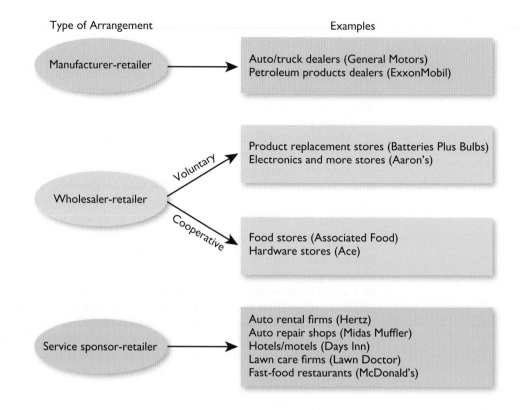

COMPETITIVE ADVANTAGES AND DISADVANTAGES OF FRANCHISING *Franchisees* receive several benefits by investing in successful franchise operations:

- They own a retail enterprise with a relatively small capital investment.
- They acquire well-known names and goods/service lines.
- Standard operating procedures and management skills may be taught to them.
- Cooperative marketing efforts (such as regional or national advertising) are facilitated.
- They obtain exclusive selling rights for specified geographical territories.
- Their purchases may be less costly per unit due to the volume of the overall franchise.

Some potential problems do exist for franchisees:

- Oversaturation could occur if too many franchisees are in one geographic area.
- Due to overzealous selling by some franchisors, franchisees' income potential, required managerial ability, and investment may be incorrectly stated.
- They may be locked into contracts requiring purchases from franchisors or certain vendors.
- Cancellation clauses may give franchisors the right to void agreements if provisions are not satisfied.
- In some industries, franchise agreements are of short duration.
- Royalties are often a percentage of gross sales, regardless of franchisee profits.

The preceding factors contribute to **constrained decision making**, whereby franchisors limit franchisee involvement in the strategic planning process.

The Federal Trade Commission (FTC) has a rule as to disclosure requirements and business opportunities (www.ftc.gov/tips-advice/business-center/guidance/amended-franchise-rule-faqs) that applies to all U.S. franchisors. It is intended to provide adequate information to potential franchisees prior to their investment. Although the FTC does not regularly review disclosure statements, nearly 20 states check them and may require corrections. Several states (including Arkansas, California, Hawaii, Illinois, Indiana, Maryland, Michigan, Minnesota, Mississippi, Nebraska, South Dakota, Virginia, Washington, and Wisconsin) have fair practice laws that do not let franchisors terminate, cancel, or fail to renew franchisees without just cause. The FTC has a franchising Web site (https://goo.gl/ivfnSW), as highlighted in Figure 4-7.

Want to learn more about what it takes to be a franchisee? Check out the Jazzercise Web site (www.jazzercise.com/Franchisee-Links/Franchisee-Costs).

FIGURE 4-7

The FTC on Franchise and Business Opportunities

At the FTC's franchising site, https://goo.gl/ivfnSW, there are many free downloads about opportunities—and warnings are included, as well.

Franchisors accrue lots of benefits by having franchise arrangements:

- A national or global presence is developed more quickly and with less franchisor investment.
- Franchisee qualifications for ownership are set and enforced.
- Agreements require franchisees to abide by stringent operating rules set by franchisors.
- Money is obtained when goods are delivered rather than when they are sold.
- Because franchisees are owners and not employees, they have more incentive to work hard.
- Even after franchisees have paid for their outlets, franchisors receive royalties and may sell products to the individual proprietors.

Franchisors also face potential problems:

- Franchisees harm the overall reputation if they do not adhere to company standards.
- A lack of uniformity among outlets adversely affects customer loyalty.
- Intrafranchise competition is not desirable.
- The resale value of individual units is injured if franchisees perform poorly.
- Ineffective franchised units directly injure franchisors' profitability that results from selling services, materials, or products to the franchisees and from royalty fees.
- Franchisees, in greater numbers, are seeking to limit franchisors' rules and regulations.

Further information on franchising is in the appendix at the end of this chapter. Also, visit our blog for a lot of posts on this topic (www.bermanevansretail.com).

Leased Department

A **leased department** is a department in a retail store—usually a department, discount, or specialty store—that is rented to an outside party. The leased department proprietor is responsible for all aspects of its business (including fixtures) and normally pays a percentage of sales as rent. The host retailer earns a steady income renting out extra space and the leased department gets market access at a smaller footprint at a lower negotiated cost. The store sets operating restrictions for the leased department to ensure overall consistency and coordination.[7]

Leased departments (sometimes called "stores within a store" or kiosks with even smaller footprints) are used by store-based retailers to broaden their offerings into product categories that often are on the fringe of the store's major product lines. They are most common for in-store beauty salons; banks; photographic studios; and shoe, jewelry, cosmetics, watch repair, and shoe repair departments. Leased departments are also popular in shopping center food courts. They account for $20 billion in annual department store sales. More luxury brands, such as Gucci and Dior, are leasing out departments to have greater control over the way their products are sold. Data on overall leased department sales are not available.

The stores-within-a-store concept provides host retailers and their lessees with opportunities to cross-market their brands and reach new demographics. Leased spaces can add excitement to the customers' shopping experience, add variety to the retailer's product assortment, and encourage customers to linger longer and make impulse purchases. The success and failure of this strategy for the retailer depends on the choice of the right retail partners, making sure they complement the host retailer and have the potential to attract a new customer base for the host retailer. The strategy must also be supported by an appropriate level of advertising by both the host retailer and retail partners to generate awareness of the locations of the leased department stores. A successful example is Sephora, which has operated leased departments in J.C. Penney stores since 2006. Sephora's presence has helped energize and reinvent Penney's image.

CVS (www.cvs.com/ target) has flourished with its leased department relationship at Target.

Here are other examples: CVS bought the rights to run Target's pharmacies and health clinics at 1,660 locations for $1.9 billion; it rebranded them as CVS with added digital healthcare tools. This increased CVS's retail footprint by 20 percent and helped capture pharmacy purchases made in general merchandise stores. Target can offer customers integrated pharmacy services with CVS expertise, and focus on improving performance in its core product areas.[8] Finish Line offers an exclusive shoe line in its almost 600-branded shops at Macy's department stores. As a result, Finish Line has enjoyed strong sales and Macy's has seen an increase in foot traffic.[9]

For retailers facing declining sales, leasing out space may be part of a retrenchment strategy, to reduce their footprint while generating stable income. Sears hosts the trendy Forever 21, a women's fashions business. Walmart Realty says it has almost 400 in-store leases ready for some well-matched retailer that sees a benefit in letting "Walmart's repeat customers become [their] repeat customers." Retailers in Europe and Asia have used the concept extensively—nearly all major Chinese retailers are really a conglomeration of ever-changing smaller stores that stand up in competition or are pruned from the landscape.[10]

COMPETITIVE ADVANTAGES AND DISADVANTAGES OF LEASED DEPARTMENTS From the *stores' perspective*, leased departments offer a number of benefits:

▸ The market is enlarged by providing one-stop customer shopping.
▸ Personnel management, merchandise displays, and reordering are undertaken by lessees.
▸ Regular store personnel do not have to be involved.
▸ Leased department operators pay for some expenses, thus reducing store costs.
▸ A percentage of revenues is received regularly.

There are also some potential pitfalls from the stores' perspective:

▸ Leased department operating procedures may conflict with store procedures.
▸ Lessees may adversely affect stores' images.
▸ Customers may blame problems on the stores rather than on the lessees.

For *leased department operators*, there are these advantages:

▸ Stores are known, have steady customers, and offer immediate sales for leased departments.
▸ Some costs are reduced through shared facilities, such as security equipment and display windows.

> Their image is enhanced by their relationships with popular stores.
> The operators have greater control over their own image and selling strategy than if the retailers act as the resellers.

Lessees face these possible problems:

> There may be inflexibility as to the hours they must be open and the operating style.
> The goods/service lines are usually restricted.
> If they are successful, stores may raise rent or not renew leases when they expire.
> In-store locations may not generate the sales expected.

An example of a thriving long-term lease arrangement is one between Luxottica and Macy's. Luxottica started with Sunglass Hut shops in Macy's stores in 2009 to offer optical products and services to Macy's customers. Sunglass Hut shops have grown to 670 Macy's locations; and in April 2016, Luxottica agreed to establish LensCrafters shops in 500 Macy's locations.[11]

Vertical Marketing System

A **vertical marketing system** consists of all the levels of independently owned businesses along a channel of distribution. Goods and services are normally distributed through one of these systems: independent, partially integrated, and fully integrated. See Figure 4-8.

FIGURE 4-8

Vertical Marketing Systems: Functions and Ownership

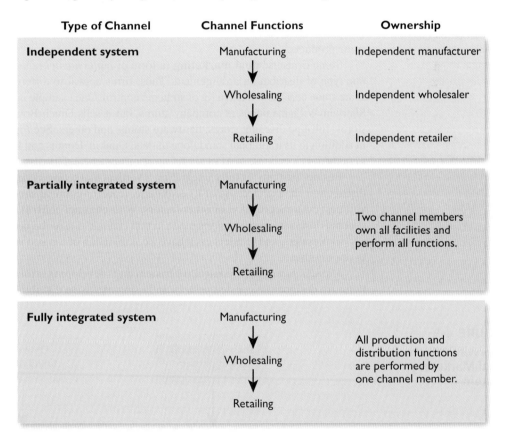

Type of Channel	Channel Functions	Ownership
Independent system	Manufacturing ↓ Wholesaling ↓ Retailing	Independent manufacturer / Independent wholesaler / Independent retailer
Partially integrated system	Manufacturing ↓ Wholesaling ↓ Retailing	Two channel members own all facilities and perform all functions.
Fully integrated system	Manufacturing ↓ Wholesaling ↓ Retailing	All production and distribution functions are performed by one channel member.

ETHICS IN RETAILING

Unethical Behavior by Franchisors

Although the Federal Trade Commission (www.ftc.gov) has specific requirements that govern legal behavior by franchises, there are some gray areas (legal activities that may be unethical) concerning franchisor strategies. For example, many contracts between franchisors and franchisees do not give a franchisee an exclusive territory. Also, franchisees may be required to buy goods from the franchisor. And some franchisors may retain the most profitable locations as company-operated units, rather than sell them to franchisees.

Comment on the above from the perspective of franchisor-franchisee relationships

In an *independent vertical marketing system*, there are three levels of independently owned firms: manufacturers, wholesalers, and retailers. Such a system is most often used if manufacturers or retailers are small, intensive distribution is sought, customers are widely dispersed, unit sales are high, company resources are low, channel members seek to share costs and risks, and task specialization is desirable. Independent vertical marketing systems are used by many stationery stores, gift shops, hardware stores, food stores, drugstores, and many other firms. They are the leading form of vertical marketing system.

With a *partially integrated system*, two independently owned businesses along a channel perform all production and distribution functions. It is most common when a manufacturer and a retailer complete transactions and shipping, storing, and other distribution functions in the absence of a wholesaler. This system is most apt if manufacturers and retailers are large, selective or exclusive distribution is sought, unit sales are moderate, company resources are high, greater channel control is desired, and existing wholesalers are too expensive or unavailable. Partially integrated systems are often used by furniture stores, appliance stores, restaurants, computer retailers, and mail-order firms.

Kroger, the food retailer, manufactures 5,000 food and nonfood products in its 38 plants (www.thekrogerco.com/about-kroger/operations/manufacturing).

Through a *fully integrated system*, one firm performs all production and distribution functions. The firm has total control over its strategy, direct customer contact, and exclusivity over its offering; it also keeps all profits. This system can be costly and requires a lot of expertise. In the past, vertical marketing was employed mostly by manufacturers, such as Avon and Sherwin-Williams. At Sherwin-Williams, its own 4,100 paint stores account for nearly 60 percent of total company sales.[12] Today, more retailers (such as Kroger) use fully integrated systems for at least some products.

Some firms use **dual marketing** (a form of *multichannel retailing*) and engage in more than one type of distribution arrangement. Thus, firms appeal to different consumers, increase sales, share some costs, and retain a lot of strategic control. One example is Sherwin-Williams which sells Sherwin-Williams paints at company stores, but it sells Dutch Boy paints in home-improvement stores, full-line discount stores, hardware stores, and others. See Figure 4-9. As another example, in addition to its traditional standalone outlets, Dunkin' Donuts and Baskin-Robbins share facilities in numerous locations, so as to attract more customers and increase the revenue per transaction.

Besides partially or fully integrating a vertical marketing system, a firm can exert power in a distribution channel because of its economic, legal, or political strength; superior knowledge and abilities; customer loyalty; or other factors. With **channel control**, one member of a distribution channel dominates the decisions made in that channel due to the power it possesses. Manufacturers, wholesalers, and retailers each have a combination of tools to improve their positions relative to one another.

Manufacturers exert control by franchising, developing strong brand loyalty, pre-ticketing items (to designate suggested prices), and using exclusive distribution with retailers that agree to

FIGURE 4-9
Sherwin-Williams' Dual Marketing System

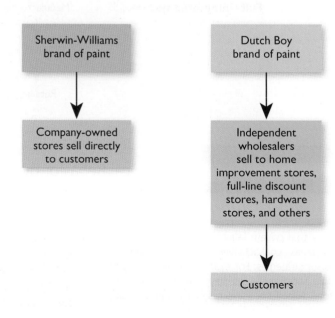

certain standards in exchange for sole distribution rights in an area. *Wholesalers* exert influence when they are large, introduce their own brands, sponsor franchises, and are the most efficient members in the channel for tasks such as processing reorders. *Retailers* exert clout when they represent a large percentage of a supplier's sales volume and when they foster their own brands. Private brands let retailers switch vendors with no impact on customer loyalty, as long as the same product features are included.

Strong long-term channel relationships often benefit all parties. They lead to scheduling efficiencies and cost savings. Advertising, financing, billing, and other tasks are greatly simplified.

Consumer Cooperative

A **consumer cooperative** is a retail firm owned by its customer members. A group of consumers invests, elects officers, manages operations, and shares the profits or savings that accrue.[13] In the United States, there are several thousand such cooperatives, from small buying clubs to Recreational Equipment Inc. (REI), with $2.5 billion in annual sales. Consumer cooperatives have been most popular in food retailing. Yet, the 500 or so U.S. food cooperatives account for less than 1 percent of total grocery sales.

As an REI member (www .rei.com/membership/ benefits), look at what $20 will get you!

Consumer cooperatives exist for these basic reasons: Some consumers feel they can operate stores as well as or better than traditional retailers. They think existing retailers inadequately fulfill customer needs for healthful, environmentally safe products. They also assume existing retailers make excessive profits and that they can sell merchandise for lower prices.

Recreational Equipment Inc. sells outdoor recreational equipment to 5.5 million members and other customers. It has about 140 stores, a mail-order business, and a Web site (www.rei.com). Unlike other cooperatives, REI is run by a professional staff that adheres to policies set by the member-elected board. There is a $20 one-time membership fee, which allows customers to shop at REI, vote for directors, and share in profits (based on the amount spent by each member). REI's goal is to distribute a regular dividend to members.

Cooperatives are only a small part of retailing because they involve consumer initiative and drive, consumers are usually not expert in retailing functions, cost savings and low selling prices are often not as expected, and consumer boredom in running a cooperative frequently occurs.

RETAILING AROUND THE WORLD

| KFC in China |

Recently, KFC (originally called Kentucky Fried Chicken) opened a futuristic restaurant in Shanghai's National Exhibition and Convention Center. It was designed to be digitalized. KFC refers to this store as "Original +"—the firm's designated name for KFC's traditional fried chicken recipe. The highlight of this store is the presence of two voice-activated robots named "dumi." They enable customers to order and pay for their meal. The robots,

developed by Baidu (a China-based company), turn their bodies and heads when interacting with a customer. The robots cannot accept payment, but they can display a QR (quick response) code. The customer can pay by scanning the code with a mobile payment app.

Are these robots just a novelty or the wave of the future? Explain your answer.

◼

Chapter Summary

1. *To show the ways in which retail institutions can be classified.* There are 2.4 million retail firms in the United States operating 3.2 million establishments. They can be grouped on the basis of ownership, store-based strategy mix, and nonstore-based and nontraditional retailing. Many retailers can be placed in more than one category. This chapter deals with retail ownership. Chapters 5 and 6 report on the other classifications.

2. *To study retailers on the basis of ownership type, and to examine the characteristics of each.* About 70 percent of U.S. retail establishments are independents, each with one store. This is mostly due to the ease of entry. Independents' competitive advantages include their flexibility, low investments, specialized offerings, direct strategy control, image, consistency, independence, and entrepreneurial spirit. Disadvantages include limited

bargaining power, few economies of scale, labor intensity, reduced media access, overdependence on owner, and limited planning.

Chains are multiple stores under common ownership, with some centralized buying and decision making. They account for 30 percent of U.S. retail outlets but 75 percent of retail sales. The advantages of chain stores are bargaining power, functional efficiencies, multiple-store operations, computerization, media access, well-defined management, and planning. The problems they often are inflexibility, high investments, reduced control, and limited independence of personnel.

Franchising embodies arrangements between franchisors and franchisees that let the latter do business under established names and according to detailed rules. It accounts for one-third of U.S. store sales. Franchisees benefit from small investments, popular company names, standardized operations and training, cooperative marketing, exclusive selling rights, and volume purchases. They may face constrained decision making, resulting in oversaturation, lower-than-promised profits, strict contract terms, cancellation clauses, short-term contracts, and royalty fees. Franchisors benefit by expanding their businesses, setting franchisee qualifications, improving cash flow, outlining procedures, gaining motivated franchisees, and receiving ongoing royalties. They may suffer if franchisees hurt the company image, do not operate uniformly, compete with one another, lower resale values and franchisor profits, and seek greater independence.

Leased departments are in-store locations rented to outside parties. They usually exist in categories on the fringe of their stores' major product lines. Stores gain from the expertise of lessees, greater traffic, reduced costs, merchandising support, and revenues. Potential store disadvantages are conflicts with lessees and adverse effects on store image. Lessee benefits are well-known store names, steady customers, immediate sales, reduced expenses, economies of scale, an image associated with the store, and more control over their strategy. Potential lessee problems are operating inflexibility, restrictions on items sold, lease nonrenewal, and poorer results than expected.

Vertical marketing systems consist of all the levels of independently owned firms along a channel of distribution. Independent systems have separately owned manufacturers, wholesalers, and retailers. In partially integrated systems, two separately owned firms, usually manufacturers and retailers, perform all production and distribution functions. With fully integrated systems, single firms do all production and distribution functions. Some firms use dual marketing, whereby they are involved in more than one type of system.

Consumer cooperatives are owned by their customers who invest, elect officers, manage operations, and share savings or profits. They account for a tiny piece of retail sales. Cooperatives are formed because consumers think they can do retailing functions, traditional retailers are inadequate, and prices are high. They have not grown much because consumer initiative is required, expertise may be lacking, expectations have frequently not been met, and boredom occurs.

3. *To explore the methods used by manufacturers, wholesalers, and retailers to exert influence in the distribution channel.* Even without an integrated vertical marketing system, channel control can be exerted by the most powerful firm(s) in a channel. Manufacturers, wholesalers, and retailers each have ways to increase their impact. Retailers' influence is greatest when they are a large part of their vendors' sales and private brands are used.

Key Terms

retail institution (p. 111)
independent (p. 112)
ease of entry (p. 112)
chain (p. 114)
franchising (p. 116)

product/trademark franchising (p. 116)
business format franchising (p. 116)
constrained decision making (p. 118)
leased department (p. 120)
vertical marketing system (p. 121)

dual marketing (p. 122)
channel control (p. 122)
consumer cooperative (p. 123)

Questions for Discussion

1. How would you define the term "retail institution"? What is implied by this term?
2. In most markets, independents are the most common form of retailer. Why is this the case?
3. Comparatively speaking, why do independents have much less power when it comes to negotiating with suppliers and other businesses?
4. How can an independent retailer avoid becoming over-reliant on the owner?
5. To what extent do you agree that independents put their customers first?
6. What competitive advantages and disadvantages do regional chains have in comparison with national chains?
7. What are the similarities and differences between chains and franchising?
8. From the *franchisee's* perspective, under what circumstances would product/trademark franchising be advantageous? When would business format franchising be better?

9. Why would a supermarket want to lease space to an outside operator rather than run a business, such as dry cleaning, itself? What would be its risks in this approach?
10. What are the pros and cons of Sherwin-Williams using dual marketing?
11. How could a small independent restaurant increase its channel power?
12. Would REI be as successful if it operated as a traditional chain? Explain your answer.

Web-Based Exercise

Visit the Web site of 7-Eleven (www .franchise.7-eleven.com), one of the leading retail franchisors in the world. Based on the information you find there, would you be interested in becoming a 7-Eleven franchisee? Why or why not?

APPENDIX # The Dynamics of Franchising

This appendix is presented because of franchising's strong retailing presence and the exciting opportunities in franchising. Over the past two decades, annual U.S. franchising sales have more than tripled! Here, we go beyond the discussion of franchising in Chapter 4 and provide information on managerial issues in franchising and on franchisor–franchisee relationships.

Consider this, for example: In 1999, Tariq and Kamran Farid opened their first Edible Arrangements store in East Haven, Connecticut. The initial franchised store opened during 2001 in Waltham, Massachusetts. Now, due to franchising, Edible Arrangements has over 1,200 stores worldwide, mostly franchised. The firm was recently ranked number 9 on *Forbes* magazine's "Top Franchises for the Money" and number 1 in its category in "*Entrepreneur* Magazine's Franchise 500" (for nine consecutive years) and also regularly appears in *Entrepreneur*'s "Top 50 of the "Fastest-Growing Franchises," and "America's Top Global Franchises,"[1]

Look at the "Franchise" section of Edible Arrangements' Web site (www.ediblearrangements .com).

How about Dunkin' Donuts? It is the number 1 retailer of hot and iced regular coffee-by-the-cup in the United States and the largest coffee and baked goods chain in the world. Dunkin' Donuts sells over 1.7 billion cups of coffee per year with 70 varieties of donuts and over a dozen coffee beverages (as well as bagels, breakfast sandwiches, and other baked goods).There are over 8,000 franchised Dunkin' Donuts in the United States and an additional 3,200 shops in over 32 countries throughout the world. Financial requirements are a minimum net worth of $500,000 and a minimum liquid capital of $250,000.[2]

U.S. franchisors are situated in over 170 countries, a number that is rising due to these factors: U.S. firms see the foreign market potential. Franchising is accepted as a retailing format in more nations. And trade barriers are fewer due to such pacts as the North American Free Trade Agreement, which makes it easier for firms based in the United States, Canada, and Mexico to operate in each other's marketplaces.

The following Web sites will give you more information on franchising:

▶ Federal Trade Commission (https://www.ftc.gov/tips-advice/business-center/guidance/consumers-guide-buying-franchise)
▶ International Franchise Association (http://www.franchise.org/)
▶ Small Business Administration (https://www.sba.gov/starting-business/how-start-business/business-types/franchise-businesses)

Managerial Issues in Franchising

Franchising appeals to franchisees for several reasons. Most franchisors have easy-to-learn, standardized operating methods that they have perfected. Also, new franchisees do not have to learn from their own trial-and-error method. Additionally, franchisors often have facilities where franchisees are trained to operate equipment, manage employees, keep records, and improve customer relations; there are usually follow-up field visits.

A new outlet of a nationally advertised franchise (such as Burger King) can attract a large customer following rather quickly and easily because of the reputation of the firm. And not only does franchising result in good initial sales and profits but it also reduces franchisees' risk of failure *if the franchisees affiliate with strong, supportive franchisors.*

Investment and startup costs for a franchised outlet can be as low as a few thousand dollars for a personal service business to as high as several million dollars for a hotel. In return for its expenditures, a franchisee gets exclusive selling rights for an area; a business format franchisee gets training, equipment and fixtures, and support in site selection; as well as supplier negotiations, advertising, and so on. Besides receiving fees and royalties from franchisees, franchisors may sell goods and services to them. This may be required—more often, for legal reasons, such purchases are at the franchisees' discretion (subject to franchisor specifications). Each year, franchisors sell billions of dollars' worth of items to franchisees.

Table A4-1 shows the franchise fees, startup costs, and royalty fees for new franchisees at 10 leading franchisors in various business categories. Financing support—either through in-house financing or third-party financing—is offered by most of the firms cited in Table A4-1. In addition, with its guaranteed loan program, the U.S. Small Business Administration is a good financing option for prospective franchisees, and some banks offer special interest rates for franchisees affiliated with established franchisors.

Franchised outlets can be bought (leased) from franchisors, master franchisees, or existing franchisees. Franchisors sell either new locations or company-owned outlets (some of which may have been taken back from unsuccessful franchisees). At times, they sell rights in entire regions or counties to master franchisees, which deal with individual franchisees. Existing franchisees usually have the right to sell their units if they first offer them to their franchisor, if potential buyers meet all financial and other criteria, and/or if buyers undergo training. Of interest to prospective franchisees is the emphasis a firm places on franchisee-owned outlets versus franchisor-owned ones.

One last point regarding managerial issues in franchising concerns the failure rate of new franchisees. For many years, it was believed that success as a franchisee was a "sure thing"—and much safer than starting a business—due to the franchisor's well-known name, its experience, and its training programs. However, some recent research has shown franchising to be as risky as opening a new business. Why? Some franchisors have oversaturated the market and not provided promised support, and unscrupulous franchisors have preyed on unsuspecting investors.

Figure A4-1 has a checklist by which potential franchisees can assess opportunities. In using the checklist, franchisees should also obtain full prospectuses and financial reports from all franchisors under consideration, and talk to existing franchise operators and customers.

Franchisor–Franchisee Relationships

Taco John's (www.tacojohnsfranchise.com), with 415 stores, prides itself on its supportive relationships with franchisees.

Many franchisors and franchisees have good relationships because they share goals for company image, operations, the goods and services offered, cooperative ads, and sales and profit growth.

Nonetheless, for several reasons, tensions do sometimes exist between various franchisors and their franchisees:

▸ The franchisor–franchisee relationship is not one of employer to employee. Franchisor controls are often viewed as rigid.
▸ Many agreements are considered too short by franchisees.
▸ The loss of a franchise often means eviction, and the franchisee gets nothing for "goodwill."
▸ Some franchisors believe their franchisees do not reinvest enough in their outlets or care enough about the consistency of operations from one outlet to another.
▸ Franchisors may not give adequate territorial protection and may open new outlets or allow other franchisees to locate near existing ones.

TABLE A4-1 The Costs of Becoming a New Franchisee with Selected Franchisors (as of 2016)

Franchising Company	Total Startup Costs (Including Franchise Fee)	Franchise Fee	Royalty Fee as a % of Sales	Date Founded	Date Franchising Started
Aamco Transmissions	$227,400–$333,000	$39,500	7.5	1963	1963
H&R Block	$31,500–$149,200	$2,500	30	1955	1956
Carvel Ice Cream	$250,000–$383,100	$30,000	$2.29/gallon	1934	1947
Fantastic Sams	$137,100–$261,500	$30,000	$292–$452/wk	1974	1976
Jazzercise	$3,330–$77,750	$1,250	20	1969	1982
Pearle Vision	$410,199–$614,400	$30,000	7	1961	1980
Petland	$273,500–$1,024,000	$35,000	4.5	1967	1971
Subway	$80,700–$263,150	$15,000	8	1965	1974
Super 8 Motels	$134,195–$4,251,000	$25,000–$25,500	5.5	1974	1976
UPS Store	$167,825–$353,580	$29,950	8.5	1980	1980

Source: Computed by the authors from "2016 Franchise 500 Rankings," www.entrepreneur.com/franchise500

FIGURE A4-1

A Checklist of Questions for Prospective Franchisees Considering Franchise Opportunities

✓ What are the required franchise fees: initial fee, advertising appropriations, and royalties?

✓ What degree of technical knowledge is required of the franchisee?

✓ What is the required investment of time by the franchisee? Does the franchisee have to be actively involved in the day-to-day operations of the franchise?

✓ How much control does the franchisor exert in terms of materials purchased, sales quotas, space requirements, pricing, the range of goods sold, required inventory levels, and so on?

✓ Can the franchisee tolerate the regimentation and rules of the franchisor?

✓ Are the costs of required supplies and materials purchased from the franchisor at market value, above market value, or below market value?

✓ What degree of name recognition do consumers have of the franchise? Does the franchisor have a meaningful advertising program?

✓ What image does the franchise have among consumers and among current franchisees?

✓ What are the level and quality of services provided by the franchisor: site selection, training, bookkeeping, human relations, equipment maintenance, and trouble-shooting?

✓ What is the franchisor's policy in terminating franchisees? What are the conditions of franchise termination? What is the rate of franchise termination and nonrenewal?

✓ What is the franchisor's legal history?

✓ What is the length of the franchise agreement?

✓ What is the failure rate of existing franchises?

✓ What is the franchisor's policy with regard to company-owned and franchisee-owned outlets?

✓ What policy does the franchisor have in allowing franchisees to sell their business?

✓ What is the franchisor's policy with regard to territorial protection for existing franchisees? With regard to new franchisees and new company-owned establishments?

✓ What is the earning potential of the franchise during the first year? The first five years?

▷ Franchisees may refuse to participate in cooperative advertising programs.
▷ Franchised outlets up for sale must usually be offered first to franchisors, which also have approval of sales to third parties.
▷ Some franchisees believe franchisor marketing support is low.
▷ Franchisees may be prohibited from operating competing businesses.
▷ Restrictions on suppliers may cause franchisees to pay more and have limited choices.
▷ Franchisees may band together to force changes in policies and exert pressure on franchisors.
▷ Sales and profit expectations may not be realized.

Tensions can lead to conflicts—even litigation. Potential negative franchisor actions include ending agreements; reducing marketing support; and adding red tape for orders, data requests, and warranty work. Potential negative franchisee actions include ending agreements, adding competitors' items, not promoting goods and services, and not complying with data requests.

Although franchising has been characterized by franchisors having more power than franchisees, this inequality is being reduced. First, franchisees affiliated with specific franchisors have joined together. For example, the Association of Kentucky Fried Chicken Franchisees and National Coalition of Associations of 7-Eleven Franchisees represent thousands of franchisees. Second, large umbrella groups, such as the American Franchisee Association (www.franchisee.org) and the American Association of Franchisees & Dealers (www.aafd.org), have been formed. Third, many franchisees now operate more than one outlet, so they have greater clout. Fourth, there has been a substantial rise in litigation.

Better communication and better cooperation help resolve problems. Two progressive tactics are the International Franchise Association (www.franchise.org/mission-statementvisioncode-of-ethics), which has an ethics code for its franchisor and franchisee members, founded on the principle that each franchisor–franchisee relationship requires mutual commitment by both parties. The National Franchise Mediation Program seeks to resolve franchisor–franchisee disagreements. All mediation efforts are voluntary, confidential, nonbinding, and informal: "Typically, disputes that are mediated are concluded expeditiously at moderate cost compared to disputes that are arbitrated or litigated. Since its inception in 1993, a success rate of approximately 90 percent has been achieved in mediations in which the franchisee agreed to participate and in which a mediator was needed. Many cases are resolved without intervention of a mediator."[3]

The Business Owner's Toolkit (www.bizfilings.com/toolkit) is an excellent resource for the independent retailer.

Retail Institutions by Store-Based Strategy Mix

Chapter Objectives

1. To describe the wheel of retailing, scrambled merchandising, and the retail life cycle, and to show how they can help explain the performance of retail strategy mixes

2. To discuss ways in which retail strategy mixes are evolving

3. To examine a wide variety of food-oriented retailers involved with store-based strategy mixes

4. To study a wide range of general merchandise retailers involved with store-based strategy mixes

In virtually every retail format, there is a great deal of competition. Here, we cover a total of 14 different retail formats—six are food-oriented and eight are focused more on nonfood goods and services. What is clear is that more shoppers than ever are interested in low prices, and many retail formats have adapted accordingly. One such format is the factory outlet.

In the past, manufacturers set up factory outlet stores to recoup some of the costs associated with the manufacturing of defective merchandise. Many of the goods sold in these stores were broken lots (incomplete selections), seconds (minor rips in clothing or scratches on appliances), and gently used products that were returned by retailers and final consumers.

This manner of business was a far cry from the current factory outlet approach operated by retailers such as Brooks Brothers, Ralph Lauren, Gap, and Coach. Today's outlets may be located in shopping centers, and feature attractive atmosphere, well-trained salespeople, and fitting rooms. Today, there are even large shopping areas that feature nothing but factory outlet stores, such as the Kittery Outlets in Maine, in which there are more than 120 outlets. Another selling point for factory outlets now is that most accept credit cards and have return and exchange privileges.

Factory outlet stores usually receive items from two sources: planned and opportunistic. The *planned sources* consist of goods made especially for outlets (often with lower-quality fabrics and less tailoring). These sources enable outlet stores to have a wide selection of merchandise throughout the year. This kind of merchandise also helps outlet stores attract a more price-conscious shopper. *Opportunistic purchases* are based on closeouts, returns from department

Source: Monkey Business Images/Shutterstock. Reprinted by permission.

stores, overstocks, and broken lots. A major benefit of these goods is that they encourage shoppers to treasure hunt (visit the store frequently).

Some firms prefer to sell at factory outlets rather than at closeout retailers such as Marshall's, Off Saks (discount unit of Saks Fifth Avenue), and The Rack (discount unit of Nordstrom's). Selling through company-owned and operated factory outlets gives the seller greater control over both the final selling price and the store locations where the discounted goods are sold. Some firms, however, are concerned that sales of heavily discounted goods at factory outlet locations will anger traditional department and specialty stores.

Overview

In Chapter 4, retail institutions were described by ownership. In this chapter, we cover three key concepts in planning a retail strategy: wheel of retailing, scrambled merchandising, and retail life cycle. We then look at how retail strategies are evolving and study the strategies of several store-based formats. Chapter 6 deals with nonstore-based, electronic, and nontraditional strategies.

CONSIDERATIONS IN PLANNING A RETAIL STRATEGY MIX

A retailer may be categorized by its **strategy mix**, the firm's particular combination of store location, operating procedures, goods/services offered, pricing tactics, store atmosphere and customer services, and promotional methods.

Store location refers to the use of a store or nonstore format, placement in a geographic area, and the kind of site (such as a shopping center). *Operating procedures* include the personnel employed, management style, store hours, and other factors. The *goods/services offered* may encompass many product categories or just one; quality may be low, medium, or high. *Pricing* refers to the use of prestige pricing (creating a quality image), competitive pricing (setting prices at the level of rivals), or penetration pricing (underpricing other retailers). *Store atmosphere and customer services* are reflected by the physical facilities and personal attention, return policies, delivery, and more. *Promotion* involves activities in such areas as advertising, displays, personal selling, and sales promotion. By combining the elements, a retailer can devise a unique strategy.

To flourish today, a retailer should strive to be dominant in some way. The firm may then reach **destination retailer** status, whereby consumers view the company as distinctive enough to be loyal to it and go out of their way to shop there. We tend to link "dominant" with "large geographic footprint." Yet, both small and large retailers can be influential in different ways, by dominating their consumer's choices based on time, money spent, or status upheld. As shown here, there are many ways to be a destination retailer, and combining two or more approaches can yield even greater appeal for a given retailer:

- ▸ Be price-oriented and cost-efficient to attract price-sensitive shoppers.
- ▸ Be upscale to attract full-service, status-conscious consumers.
- ▸ Be convenient to attract those consumers who want shopping ease, nearby locations, or extended hours.
- ▸ Offer a dominant assortment in the product lines carried to appeal to customers interested in variety and in-store shopping comparisons.
- ▸ Offer superior customer service to attract those frustrated by the decline in retail service.
- ▸ Be innovative or exclusive and provide a unique way of operating (such as kiosks at airports) or carry products/brands not stocked by others to reach people who are innovators or bored.

Before looking at specific strategy mixes, let's consider three concepts that help explain the use of these mixes: the wheel of retailing, scrambled merchandising, and the retail life cycle—as well as the ways in which retail strategies are evolving.

The Wheel of Retailing

According to the **wheel of retailing** theory, retail innovators often first appear as low-price operators with low costs and low profit margin requirements. Over time, the innovators upgrade the products they carry and improve their facilities and customer service (by adding better-quality

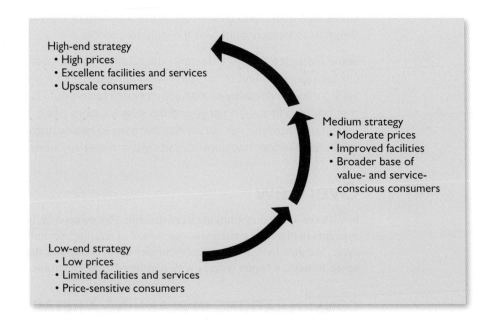

items, locating in higher-rent sites, providing credit and delivery, and so on), and prices rise. As innovators mature, they become vulnerable to new discounters with lower costs—hence, the wheel of retailing.[1] See Figure 5-1.

The wheel is based on four principles: (1) Many price-sensitive shoppers will trade customer services, wide selections, and convenient locations for lower prices. (2) Price-sensitive shoppers are often not loyal and will switch to retailers with lower prices. In contrast, prestige-oriented customers enjoy shopping at retailers with high-end strategies. (3) New institutions are frequently able to have lower operating costs than existing formats. (4) As retailers move up the wheel, they typically do so to increase sales, broaden the target market, and improve their image.

For example, when traditional department store prices became too high for many consumers, the growth of the full-line discount store (led by Walmart) was the result. The full-line discount store stressed low prices because of such cost-cutting techniques as having a small sales force, situating in lower-rent store locations, using inexpensive fixtures, emphasizing high stock turnover, and accepting only cash or check payments for goods. Then, as full-line discount stores prospered, they typically sought to move up a little along the wheel. This meant enlarging the sales force, improving locations, upgrading fixtures, carrying a greater selection of merchandise, and accepting credit. These improvements led to higher costs, which led to somewhat higher prices. The wheel of retailing again came into play as newer discounters, such as off-price chains, factory outlets, and permanent flea markets, expanded to satisfy the needs of the most price-conscious consumer. More recently, we have witnessed the birth of discount Web retailers, some of which have very low costs because they do not have "brick-and-mortar" facilities.

Where would you place CarMax (www.carmax .com) along the wheel of retailing?

As indicated in Figure 5-1, the wheel of retailing reveals three basic strategic positions: low end, medium, and high end. The medium strategy may have some problems if retailers in this position are not perceived as distinctive. In a mature format such as department stores, competitors at the higher-end and lower-end can steal market share from a middle-of-the-road retailer such as Sears. Its merchandising strategy of selling a vast array of mid-priced goods and services, and a failure to anticipate and react as department stores have diverged into two separate approaches (one at the low end and one at the high end), is threatening its survival as a retailer.[2] Figure 5-2 shows the opposing alternatives in considering a strategy mix.

The wheel of retailing suggests that established firms should be wary of adding services or converting a strategy from low end to high end. Because price-conscious shoppers are not usually loyal, they are apt to switch to lower-priced firms. Furthermore, retailers may then eliminate the competitive advantages that initially led to profitability. This occurred with the retail catalog showroom, a now defunct retail format.

FIGURE 5-2

Retail Strategy Alternatives

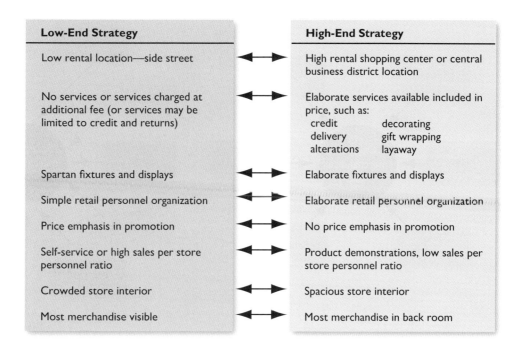

Low-End Strategy	High-End Strategy
Low rental location—side street	High rental shopping center or central business district location
No services or services charged at additional fee (or services may be limited to credit and returns)	Elaborate services available included in price, such as: credit / decorating / delivery / gift wrapping / alterations / layaway
Spartan fixtures and displays	Elaborate fixtures and displays
Simple retail personnel organization	Elaborate retail personnel organization
Price emphasis in promotion	No price emphasis in promotion
Self-service or high sales per store personnel ratio	Product demonstrations, low sales per store personnel ratio
Crowded store interior	Spacious store interior
Most merchandise visible	Most merchandise in back room

Scrambled Merchandising

Whereas the wheel of retailing focuses on product quality, prices, and customer service, scrambled merchandising involves a retailer increasing its width of assortment (the number of different product lines carried). **Scrambled merchandising** occurs when a retailer adds goods and services that may be unrelated to each other and to the firm's original business. See Figure 5-3.

Scrambled merchandising is popular for many reasons: Retailers want to increase overall revenues; fast-selling, highly profitable goods and services are usually the ones added; consumers make more impulse purchases; people like one-stop shopping; different target markets may be reached; and the impact of seasonality and competition is reduced. In addition, the popularity of a retailer's original product line(s) may decline, causing it to scramble to maintain and grow the customer base. For example, although Starbucks' in-store coffee sales are still strong, it now faces more competition in the coffee market from Dunkin' Donuts (www .dunkindonuts.com), McDonald's (www.mcdonalds.com), and other chains that have upgraded their offerings. Today, Starbucks (www.starbucks.com) carries many items outside its original coffee business, including pastries, hot breakfasts, salads, sandwiches, smoothies, and even wine at some locations.

How much of a practitioner of scrambled merchandising is Brookstone (www .brookstone.com)?

Scrambled merchandising is contagious. Drugstores, bookstores, florists, kitchenware stores and gift shops are all affected by supermarkets' scrambled merchandising. A significant amount of U.S. supermarket sales are from general merchandise, health and beauty aids, and other non-grocery items, such as pharmacy items, magazines, flowers, and kitchen items. In response, drugstores and others are pushed into scrambled merchandising to fill the sales void caused by supermarkets. Drugstores have added toys and gift items, greeting cards, batteries, and cameras. This then creates a void for additional retailers, which are also forced to scramble.

RETAILING AROUND THE WORLD

McDonald's Investments in Russia

McDonald's (www.mcdonalds.com) is expanding in Russia. It signed an agreement with Alexander Govor, a Siberian business-man, to grow beyond the Ural region. McDonald's has worked with other Russian partners in the past, such as awarding the right to open stores in transportation hubs to Razvitie ROST company. To increase sales at existing restaurants, McDonald's now accepts Mir credit cards. To reduce the impact of currency swings and import restrictions, McDonald's plans to obtain all poultry, beef, and potatoes from Russian sources as of 2018.

Describe other strategies that can be used to increase McDonald's presence in Russia.

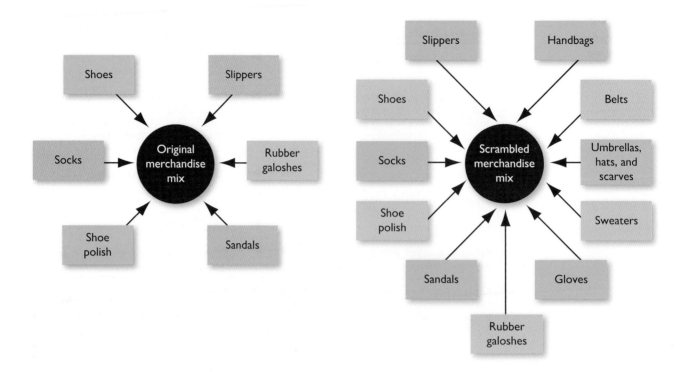

FIGURE 5-3
Scrambled Merchandising by a Shoe Store

The prevalence of scrambled merchandising means greater competition among different types of retailers, and distribution costs are affected as sales are dispersed over more retailers. There are other limitations to scrambled merchandising, including the potential lack of retailer expertise in buying, selling, and servicing unfamiliar items; the costs associated with a broader assortment (including lower inventory turnover); and the possible harm to a retailer's image if scrambled merchandising is ineffective.

The Retail Life Cycle

The **retail life cycle** concept states that retail institutions—like the goods and services they sell—pass through identifiable life stages: introduction (early growth), growth (accelerated development), maturity, and decline. The direction and speed of institutional changes can be interpreted from this concept.[3] Take a look at Figure 5-4. The figure shows the five stages of the retail life cycle, with a brief description of each. Examples of each stage are shown at the bottom of the figure.

Let's examine the retail life cycle as it applies to individual institutional formats and highlight specific examples. During the first stage of the cycle, *introduction*, there is a strong departure from the strategy mixes of existing retail institutions. A firm in this stage significantly alters at least one element of the strategy mix from that of traditional competitors. Sales and then profits often rise sharply for the first firms in the new category. At this stage, long-run success is not assured. There are risks that new institutions will not be accepted by shoppers, and there may be large initial losses due to heavy investments.

One retail format in the innovation stage is the online flash-sale retail Web site. Many flash-sale Web sites specialize in selling few items in limited sizes and colors of high-end brand apparel at significantly lower-prices for a short time—often a few hours—to bargain-seeking customers who subscribe to their service.

The early category leader was Gilt Groupe (www.gilt.com), which was launched in the United States in 2007 and is owned by Hudson's Bay. Others include Rue La La (www.rulelala.com), Ideel (www.ideel.com), Haute Look (www.hautelook.com), The RealReal (www.therealreal.com), and Zulily (www.zulily.com), which caters to mothers and young children and is the only publicly traded company in this category.[4] During the economic downturn starting in 2008, store sales of high-end brands dropped dramatically, which resulted in manufacturers and retailers needing to

FIGURE 5-4

The Retail Life Cycle

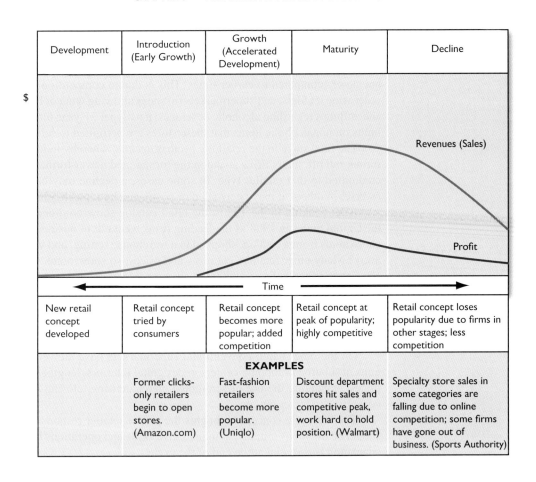

Development	Introduction (Early Growth)	Growth (Accelerated Development)	Maturity	Decline
New retail concept developed	Retail concept tried by consumers	Retail concept becomes more popular; added competition	Retail concept at peak of popularity; highly competitive	Retail concept loses popularity due to firms in other stages; less competition

		EXAMPLES		
	Former clicks-only retailers begin to open stores. (Amazon.com)	Fast-fashion retailers become more popular. (Uniqlo)	Discount department stores hit sales and competitive peak, work hard to hold position. (Walmart)	Specialty store sales in some categories are falling due to online competition; some firms have gone out of business. (Sports Authority)

find buyers quickly to unload excess inventory of high-end products. This provided the perfect opportunity for flash sales to emerge and succeed in the market.

The economy and consumers' financial situations have since improved and demand for high-end items has increased. Some high-end brands scaled back production during the recession and are now more conservative about increasing production despite higher demand. Given the lower volume of liquidated high-end goods, and the purchasing power of off-price retailers such as T. J. Maxx, which can make early buys, some flash-sale sites are struggling to get inventory. Sparser selections and higher shipping rates compared to larger apparel retailers have led to a slowdown in growth.[5] Flash sites are adapting by merging with larger players, diversifying into multiple product categories such as art, household goods (Beyond the Rack), and consignments (The RealReal) or to a hybrid retail model—offering curated collections (Trunk Club) or personal closet service (Gilt Groupe).[6]

See Intouch Interactive's (www.intouchinteractive .com) future view for video kiosks.

In the *growth stage*, both sales and profits exhibit rapid growth. Existing firms expand geographically, and newer companies of the same type enter. Toward the end of accelerated development, cost pressures (to cover a larger staff, a more complex inventory system, and extensive controls) may begin to affect profits.

The interactive electronic video kiosk is an institution in the growth stage. Today, kiosks sell everything from clothing to magazines to insurance to personal computers (PCs). Kiosks come in many forms: self-checkout machines; ticketing kiosks (at amusement parks, parking facilities, movie theaters, etc.); check-in kiosks (at hotels); food-ordering kiosks; postal kiosks (to mail packages and letters); and miscellaneous kiosks (such as DVD rental). According to one research report, U.S. retail revenues generated by kiosks exceeded $1 trillion as of 2015.[7] This format is examined further in Chapter 6.

The third stage of the retail life cycle, *maturity*, is characterized by slow sales growth for the institutional type. Although overall sales may continue to go up, that rise is at a much lower rate than during prior stages. Profit margins may have to be reduced to stimulate purchases. Maturity is brought on by market saturation caused by the high number of firms in an institutional format, competition from newer institutions, changing societal interests, and inadequate management skills to lead mature or larger firms. Once maturity is reached, the goal is to sustain it as long as possible and not to fall into decline.

The beer, wine, and liquor store—a specialty store—is in the maturity stage; sales are rising, but slowly compared to earlier times. This is due to competition from membership clubs, mail-order wine retailers, and supermarkets (in states allowing wine or liquor sales); changing lifestyles and attitudes regarding alcoholic beverages; a national 21-year-old drinking age requirement; and limits on nonalcoholic items that these stores are permitted to sell in some locales.

The final stage in the retail life cycle is *decline*, whereby industrywide sales and profits for a format fall off, many firms abandon the format, and newer formats attract consumers previously committed to that retailer type. In some cases, a decline may be hard or almost impossible to reverse. In others, it may be avoided or postponed by repositioning the institution.

After peaking in the 1980s, the retail catalog showroom declined thereafter; it vanished in the United States in 1998 as the leading firms went out of business. With this format, consumers chose items from a catalog, shopped in a warehouse setting, and wrote up orders. Why did it fade away? Many other retailers cut costs and prices, so showrooms were no longer low-price leaders. Catalogs had to be printed far in advance. Many items were slow-sellers or had low margins. Some people found showrooms crowded and disliked writing orders, a lack of displays reduced browsing, and the paucity of apparel goods held down revenues. *Note:* Great Britain's Argos chain (www.argos.co.uk), part of Home Retail Group, operates 845 catalog showrooms, making it the largest general goods retailer in Great Britain.[8]

On the other hand, conventional supermarkets have slowed their decline by placing new units in suburban shopping centers, redesigning interiors, lengthening store hours, offering lower prices, expanding the use of scrambled merchandising, closing unprofitable smaller units, and converting to larger outlets.

The life-cycle concept highlights the proper retailer response as formats evolve. Expansion should be the focus initially, administrative skills and operations become critical in maturity, and adaptation is essential at the end of the cycle.

HOW RETAIL INSTITUTIONS ARE EVOLVING

Forward-looking firms know their individual strategies must adapt as retail institutions evolve over time. Complacency is not appropriate. Many retailers have witnessed shrinking profit margins due to intense competition and consumer interest in lower prices. This puts pressure on them to tighten internal cost controls and to promote higher-margin goods and services while eliminating unprofitable items. Let's examine how firms are reacting to this formidable challenge through mergers, diversification, and downsizing, as well as cost containment and value-driven retailing.

Mergers, Diversification, and Downsizing

Some retail firms use mergers and diversification to sustain sales growth in a highly competitive environment (or when the institutional category in which they operate matures). For stronger firms, this trend is expected to carry over into the future.

Mergers involve the combination of separately owned retail firms. Some mergers take place between retailers of different types, such as the ones between Sears (the department store chain) and Kmart (the full-line discount store chain) and between upscale Saks Fifth Avenue and Lord & Taylor (both owned by mainstream Hudson's Bay). Other mergers occur between similar types of retailers, such as two banks (Bank of America acquiring Commerce Bank) and supermarket chain Royal Ahold merging with Delhaize Group. By merging, firms can jointly maximize resources, enlarge their customer base, improve productivity and bargaining power, limit weaknesses, and gain competitive advantages. It is a way for resourceful retailers to grow more rapidly and for weaker ones to enhance their long-term prospects for survival (or sell assets).

With **diversification**, retailers become active in businesses outside their normal operations, perhaps adding stores in different goods/service categories. That is why Bed Bath & Beyond now owns and operates Christmas Tree Shops (a bargain store chain), Harmon, and Harmon Face Values (discount store chains that emphasize cosmetics and health-and-beauty aids), as well as buybuy BABY (a store chain with 20,000-plus items targeted to parents of infants and young children).

With its various retail chains, Bed Bath & Beyond (http://goo.gl/93ZQFN) is a retailing dynamo.

Although the size of some retail chains has grown due to mergers and diversification, not all firms have done well with that approach. Even though stronger firms are expanding, we are also witnessing **downsizing**—whereby unprofitable stores are closed or divisions are sold off—by retailers unhappy with performance. Because Kmart's diversification efforts had poor results, it closed or sold its ventures outside the general merchandise store field (including Borders bookstores, Builders Square, Office Max, Payless shoe stores, and Sports Authority). It also closed many Kmart stores after merging with Sears.

The interest in downsizing will likely continue. Various retailers have overextended themselves and do not have the resources or management talent to succeed without retrenching. In their quest to open new stores, certain firms have chosen poor sites (having already saturated the best locations). Retailers such as Barnes & Noble are more interested in operating fewer, but larger, stores and more effectively using the Web. Supermarket retailers are finding they can do better if they are regional rather than national.

Cost Containment and Value-Driven Retailing

With a cost-containment approach, retailers strive to hold down both initial investments and operating costs. Many use this strategy due to intense competition from discounters, the need to control complicated chain or franchise operations, high land and construction costs, the volatility of the economy, and a desire to maximize productivity. The mature, highly saturated market; a slow-growth environment; competitive pressure to serve customers through multiple channels; and firms' inability to raise prices make it imperative for retailers to drive down costs. They must examine every aspect of their businesses to streamline processes and costs. See Figure 5-5.

Ocean State Job Lot has a cost-containment approach that even extends to its austere Web site (www .oceanstatejoblot.com).

Cost containment can be accomplished by one or more of these approaches:

▹ Standardize operating procedures, store layouts, store size, and product offerings.
▹ Use secondary sites, freestanding units, and locations in older strip centers or occupy sites abandoned by other retailers (second-use locations).
▹ Place stores in smaller communities where building regulations are less strict, labor costs are lower, and construction and operating costs are reduced.
▹ Use inexpensive construction materials, such as bare cinder-block walls and concrete floors.
▹ Use plainer fixtures and lower-cost displays.
▹ Buy refurbished equipment.
▹ Join cooperative buying and advertising groups.
▹ Encourage manufacturers to finance inventories.
▹ Use shipping techniques that reduce inventory carrying costs.

FIGURE 5-5

Cutting Costs Wherever Possible

Given the thin profit margins for supermarkets and many other retailers, every penny of costs saved really matters. With regard to shopping carts, there are two associated costs that retailers want to reduce: paying employees to scour the parking lot to collect stray carts and the replacement costs of stolen and damaged carts.

Source: StacieStauffSmith Photos/Shutterstock. Reprinted by permission.

A driving force behind cost containment is the quest to provide good value to customers. However, value is typically subjective. It can be based on price, quality, service, convenience, or a combination of them. Price usually has a big role in what shoppers purchase and the firms they patronize. The pricing strategies of some retailers—especially discount retailers—encourage people to look for bargains and to be wary of sale prices. Smart shoppers have learned that price may not be a true measure of quality. They can get good quality with everyday low pricing.[9]

RETAIL INSTITUTIONS CATEGORIZED BY STORE-BASED STRATEGY MIX

Selected aspects of the strategy mixes of 14 store-based retail institutions, divided into food-oriented and general merchandise groups, are highlighted in this section and in Table 5-1. Although not all-inclusive, these strategy mixes provide a good overview of store-based strategies. Please note that *width of assortment* is the number of different product lines carried by a retailer; *depth of assortment* is the selection within the product lines stocked.

TABLE 5-1 Selected Aspects of Store-Based Retail Strategy Mixes

Type of Retailer	Location	Merchandise	Prices	Atmosphere and Services	Promotion
Food-Oriented					
Convenience store	Neighborhood	Medium width and low depth of assortment; average quality	Average to above average	Average	Moderate
Conventional supermarket	Neighborhood	Extensive width and depth of assortment; average quality; manufacturer, private, and generic brands	Competitive	Average	Heavy use of newspapers, flyers, and coupons; self-service
Food-based superstore	Community shopping center or isolated site	Full assortment of supermarket items, plus health and beauty aids and general merchandise	Competitive	Average	Heavy use of newspapers and flyers; self-service
Combination store	Community shopping center or isolated site	Full selection of supermarket and drugstore items or supermarket and general merchandise; average quality	Competitive	Average	Heavy use of newspapers and flyers; self-service
Box (limited-line) store	Neighborhood	Low width and depth of assortment; few perishables; few national brands	Very low	Low	Little or none
Warehouse store	Secondary site, often in industrial area	Moderate width and low depth; emphasis on manufacturer brands bought at discounts	Very low	Low	Little or none
General Merchandise					
Specialty store	Business district or shopping center	Very narrow width and extensive depth of assortment; average to good quality	Competitive to above average	Average to excellent	Heavy use of displays; extensive sales force
Traditional department store	Business district, shopping center, or isolated store	Extensive width and depth of assortment; average to good quality	Average to above average	Good to excellent	Heavy ad and catalog use, direct mail; personal selling
Full-line discount store	Business district, shopping center, or isolated store	Extensive width and depth of assortment; average to good quality	Competitive	Slightly below average to average	Heavy use of newspapers; price-oriented; moderate sales force
Variety store	Business district, shopping center, or isolated store	Good width and some depth of assortment; below-average to average quality	Average	Below average	Use of newspapers; self-service

Continued

TABLE 5-1 Selected Aspects of Store-Based Retail Strategy Mixes (*continued*)

Type of Retailer	Location	Merchandise	Prices	Atmosphere and Services	Promotion
Off-price chain	Business district, suburban shopping strip, or isolated store	Moderate width but poor depth of assortment; average to good quality; lower continuity	Low	Below average	Use of newspapers; brands not advertised; limited sales force
Factory outlet	Out-of-the-way site or discount mall	Moderate width but poor depth of assortment; some irregular merchandise; lower continuity	Very low	Very low	Little; self-service
Membership club	Isolated store or secondary site (industrial park)	Moderate width but poor depth of assortment; lower continuity	Very low	Very low	Little; some direct mail; limited sales force
Flea market	Isolated site, racetrack, or arena	Extensive width but poor depth of assortment; variable quality; lower continuity	Very low	Very low	Limited; self-service

Food-Oriented Retailers

The following food-oriented strategic retail formats are described next: convenience store, conventional supermarket, food-based superstore, combination store, box (limited-line) store, and warehouse store.

CONVENIENCE STORE A **convenience store** is typically a well-located, food-oriented retailer that is open long hours and carries a moderate number of items. The store facility is small (only a fraction of the size of a conventional supermarket) and has average to above-average prices and average atmosphere and customer services. The ease of shopping at convenience stores and the impersonal nature of many large supermarkets make convenience stores particularly appealing to their customers, many of whom are male.

7-Eleven (www.7-eleven.com) leads the convenience store category.

There are more than 154,000 U.S. convenience stores (excluding stores where food is a small fraction of revenues), and total annual sales are $215 billion (excluding gasoline).[10] 7-Eleven (www.7-eleven.com), Circle K (www.circlek.com), Casey's General Store (www.caseys.com), and Wawa (www.wawa.com) are major food-based U.S. convenience store chains. Speedway (www.speedway.com) is a leading gasoline service-station–based convenience store chain with 2,770 outlets.[11]

Items such as milk, eggs, and bread once represented the major portion of convenience store sales; today, healthy food options such as packaged salads and fresh whole or cut fruits and vegetables are generating the fastest growth in sales.[12] Sandwiches, tobacco products, snack foods, soft drinks, general merchandise, beer and wine, ATMs, and lottery tickets are also key items. Lately, many convenience stores are adding prepared foods. Gasoline generates 30 percent or more of total sales at most of the convenience stores that carry it.

This format's advantages are its usefulness when a person does not want to travel to or shop at a supermarket, when fill-in items and gas are needed, when store hours are long, and when drive-thru windows are available. Many shoppers visit multiple times a week, and the average transaction is small. Due to limited space, stores get frequent deliveries and have high handling costs. Buyers are less price-sensitive than at other food-oriented stores.

The convenience stores industry does have problems: Some areas are saturated with stores; some stores have become too big, making shopping less convenient; supermarkets now offer longer hours and more nonfood items; a decrease in tobacco purchasing, which is a big sales category; and some chains have had financial woes.

The Food Marketing Institute (www.fmi.org) is the leading industry association for food retailers.

CONVENTIONAL SUPERMARKET A **supermarket** is a self-service food store with grocery, meat, and produce departments and a minimum annual sales of $2 million. Included are conventional supermarkets, food-based superstores, combination stores, box (limited-line) stores, and warehouse stores. See Figure 5-6.

A **conventional supermarket** is a departmentalized food store with a wide range of food and related products; sales of general merchandise are rather limited. This institution started more than 85 years ago when it was recognized that large-scale operations would let a retailer combine volume sales, self-service, and low prices. Self-service enabled supermarkets to cut costs as well as increase volume. Personnel costs were reduced, and impulse buying increased. The car and the refrigerator contributed to the supermarket's success by lowering travel costs and adding to the life span of perishables.

For several decades, overall supermarket sales have been about 70 to 75 percent of U.S. grocery sales, with conventional supermarkets now yielding a fraction of total supermarket sales. There are over 26,000 conventional units, with annual sales of $420 billion.[13] Chains account for the great majority of sales. Among the leaders are Kroger (www.kroger.com), Safeway (www .safeway.com), and Publix (www.publix.com), although a number of these firms' stores are now food-based superstores. Many independent supermarkets are affiliated with cooperative or voluntary organizations such as IGA (www.iga.com) and Supervalu (www.supervalu.com).

Conventional supermarkets generally rely on high inventory turnover (volume sales). Their profit margins are low. In general, average gross margins (selling price less merchandise cost) are 20 to 22 percent of sales, and net profits are 1 to 3 percent of sales.

These supermarkets face intense competition from other food stores: Convenience stores offer easier shopping; food-based superstores and combination stores have more product lines and greater variety within them, as well as better margins; and box and warehouse stores have lower operating costs and prices. Delivery-based food services such as Fresh Direct and AmazonFresh offer the convenience of online ordering and in-home scheduled delivery. Membership clubs (discussed later), with low prices, also provide competition—especially now that they have many expanded food lines. Variations of the supermarket are covered next.

FOOD-BASED SUPERSTORE A **food-based superstore** is larger and more diversified than a conventional supermarket but usually smaller and less diversified than a combination store. This format originated in the 1970s as supermarkets sought to stem sales declines by expanding store size and the number of nonfood items carried. Some supermarkets merged with drugstores or general merchandise stores, but more grew into food-based superstores. There are 12,000 food-based U.S. superstores, with sales of $280 billion.[14]

A food-based superstore occupies at least 30,000 to 50,000 square feet of space, and 20 to 25 percent of sales are from general merchandise, such as garden supplies, flowers, small appliances, and DVDs. It caters to complete grocery needs, along with fill-in general merchandise.

CAREERS IN RETAILING   Considering being a Retail Buyer as a Career

If you answer YES to the following questions, you may want to consider a career as a retail buyer. They purchase goods for resale, work for a broad range of retailers, attend trade shows, predict sale and fashion trends, forecast sales, negotiate purchase terms with vendors, and constantly adjust price levels to match demand for specific products.

- Do you have a passion for a given merchandise category such as high fashion clothing, appliances, watches?

- Would you enjoy attending trade shows where new styles and technologies are shown?
- Do you have excellent analytical skills?
- Do you love to negotiate with people?

How would a buyer's responsibilities for high-fashion clothing differ from sporting goods?

Like combination stores, food-based superstores are efficient, offer a degree of one-stop shopping, stimulate impulse purchases, and feature high-profit general merchandise. They also have other advantages: It is easier and less costly to redesign and convert supermarkets into food-based superstores than into combination stores. Many people feel more comfortable shopping in true food stores than in huge combination stores. Management expertise is more focused.

Numerous U.S. supermarket chains have turned more to food-based superstores. They have expanded and remodeled existing supermarkets and built new stores. Many independents have also converted to food-based superstores.

Meijer's (www.meijer.com) combination stores are quite popular with shoppers. They carry 120,000 items.

COMBINATION STORE   A **combination store** unites supermarket and general merchandise in one facility, with general merchandise accounting for 25 to 40 percent of sales. The format began in the late 1960s and early 1970s, as common checkout areas were used for separately owned supermarkets and drugstores or supermarkets and general merchandise stores. The natural offshoot was integrating operations under one management. The thousands of U.S. combination stores (including supercenters) have annual sales of several hundred billion dollars.[15] Combination store leaders are Meijer (www.meijer.com), Fred Meyer (www.fredmeyer.com), and Albertson's (www.albertsons.com).

Combination stores are large, from 30,000 up to 100,000 or more square feet. This means operating efficiencies and cost savings. Most consumers like one-stop shopping and will travel the extra distance to patronize them. Impulse sales are high. General merchandise often has better margins than food items. Supermarkets and drugstores have commonalities in customers served and the low-price, high-turnover items sold. Drugstore and general merchandise customers are drawn to the store more frequently.

A **supercenter** is a combination store blending an economy supermarket with a discount department store. It is the U.S. version of the even larger **hypermarket** (the European institution pioneered by firms such as Carrefour [www.carrefour.com] that did not succeed in the United States). As a rule, the majority of supercenter sales are from nonfood items. Stores usually range from 75,000 to 150,000 square feet in size, and they stock up to 50,000 or more items—much more than the 30,000 or so items carried by other combination stores. Walmart and Target both operate a growing number of supercenters.

BOX (LIMITED-LINE) STORE   The **box (limited-line) store** is a food-based discounter that focuses on a small selection of items, moderate hours of operation (compared with other supermarkets), few services, and limited manufacturer brands. This type of store carries under 2,000 items, few refrigerated perishables, and few sizes and brands per item. Items are displayed in cut cases, and prices are shown on shelves or overhead signs. Customers bag their own purchases. Box stores rely on low-priced, private-label brands. Their prices are 20 to 30 percent below those in supermarkets.

The box store originated in Europe and was exported to the United States in the mid-1970s. The growth of these stores has not been as anticipated, and sales have actually fallen modestly in recent years. Some other food stores have matched box-store prices. Many people are loyal to manufacturer brands, and box stores cannot fulfill one-stop shopping needs. There are 2,500 box stores in the United States, with sales of $14 billion.[16] The leading box store operators are Save-A-Lot (http://save-a-lot.com) and Aldi (www.aldi.com).

WAREHOUSE STORE   A **warehouse store** is a food-based discounter that offers a moderate number of food items in a no-frills setting. It appeals to one-stop food shoppers, concentrates on special purchases of popular brands, uses cut-case displays, offers little service, posts prices on shelves, and locates in secondary sites. These stores began in the late 1970s. There are now 1,700 U.S. stores with $70 billion in annual sales.[17]

The largest warehouse store is known as a superwarehouse. There are more than 600 of them in the United States. They have annual sales exceeding $20 million each, and they contain a variety of departments, including produce. High ceilings accommodate pallet loads of groceries. Shipments are made directly to the store. Customers pack their own groceries in these types of stores. Superwarehouses are profitable at gross margins far lower than for conventional supermarkets. The leading super warehouse chain is Cub Foods (www.cub.com).

Many people do not like shopping in warehouse settings. Also, because products are usually acquired through special deals, brands may be temporarily or permanently out of stock. Table 5-2 shows selected characteristics for the food-oriented retailers just described.

General Merchandise Retailers

We now look at the general merchandise retail formats highlighted in Table 5-1: specialty store, traditional department store, full-line discount store, variety store, off-price chain, factory outlet, membership club, and flea market.

SPECIALTY STORE   A **specialty store** concentrates on selling one type of goods or service line, such as young women's apparel. It usually carries a narrow but deep assortment in the chosen category and tailors the strategy to a given market segment. This enables the store to maintain a better selection and sales expertise than its competitors, which are often department stores. Investments are controlled, and there is a certain amount of flexibility. Among the most popular categories of specialty stores are apparel, personal care, auto supply, home furnishings, electronics, books, toys, home improvement, pet supplies, jewelry, and sporting goods.

Consumers often shop at specialty stores because of the knowledgeable sales personnel, the variety of choices within a given category, customer service, intimate store size and atmosphere

TABLE 5-2 Selected Characteristics of Food-Oriented Retailers, 2016

Factor	Convenience Stores	Conventional Supermarkets	Food-Based Superstores	Combination Stores	Box (Limited-Assortment) Stores	Warehouse Stores
Average store selling area (sq. ft.)	5,000 or less	15,000–20,000	30,000–50,000+	30,000–100,000+	5,000–9,000	15,000+
Number of checkouts per store	1–3	6–10	10+	10+	3–5	5+
Gross margin	25–30%	20–22%	20–25%	25%	10–12%	12–15%
Number of items stocked per store	3,000–4,000	15,000–60,000	30,000+	30,000+	Under 2,000	2,500+
Major emphasis	Daily fill-in needs; dairy, sandwiches, tobacco, gas, beverages, magazines	Food; only 5–10% of sales from general merchandise; may have deli, bakery, and pharmacy	Positioned between supermarket and combo store; 20–25% of sales from general merchandise; has specialty departments and extra services	One-stop shopping; general merchandise 25–40% of sales (higher at supercenters)	Low prices; few or no perishables	Low prices; variable assortments; may or may not stock perishables

(although this is not true of the category killer store), the lack of crowds (also not true of the category killer store), and the absence of aisles of unrelated merchandise that they must pass through. Some specialty stores have elaborate fixtures and upscale merchandise for affluent shoppers, whereas others are discount-oriented and aim at price-conscious consumers. See Figure 5-7.

Total specialty store sales are tough to determine because these retailers sell virtually all kinds of goods and services, and aggregate specialty store data are not compiled by the government. Specialty store leaders include Home Depot (home improvement), Best Buy (consumer electronics), Staples (office supplies), Toys "R" Us (toys), GameStop (videogames), and Bed Bath & Beyond (household furnishings and small appliances).

One type of specialty store—the category killer—has gained particular strength. A **category killer** (also known as a **power retailer**) is an especially large specialty store. It features an enormous selection in its category and relatively low prices. Consumers are drawn from wide geographic areas. Home Depot (www.homedepot.com), Barnes & Noble (www.barnesandnoble.com), Sephora (www.sephora.com), and Staples (www.staples.com) are among the chains almost fully based on the concept. Not only is Sephora the leading chain of perfume and cosmetics stores in France but it also has more than 1,900 stores in 29 countries around the world (including 360 stores located in North America). Sephora's stores sell a broad range of brands in such product categories as makeup, skin care, fragrances, bath and body lotions, lip care, and hair care. In addition, Sephora has its own private label.[18]

The focus of specialty stores is sometimes as narrow as the Joy of Socks (www.joyofsocks.com).

Nonetheless, smaller specialty stores (even ones with under 1,000 square feet of space) can prosper if they are highly focused, offer strong customer service, and avoid imitating larger firms. Shoppers looking to purchase products quickly may not want to spend the time and effort to search through multiple categories and brands at a huge category-killer store and instead may prefer to shop at a smaller specialty store. Some categories of merchandise, such as high-tech consumer electronics products, require greater support from specially trained, knowledgeable employees than the support typically offered at category-killer stores.

Any size specialty store can be adversely affected by seasonality or a decline in the popularity of its product category. This type of store may also fail to attract consumers who are interested in one-stop shopping for multiple product categories.

TRADITIONAL DEPARTMENT STORE A **department store** is a large retail unit with an extensive assortment (width and depth) of goods and services that is organized into separate departments for purposes of buying, promotion, customer service, and control. It has the most selection of any general merchandise retailer, often serves as the anchor store in a shopping center or district, has strong credit card penetration, and is usually part of a chain. To be classified as a department store, a retailer must sell a wide range of products (such as apparel, furniture, appliances, and home furnishings), and selected other items (such as paint, hardware, toiletries, cosmetics, photo equipment, jewelry, toys, and sporting goods) with no one merchandise line predominating.

Two basic types of retailers meet the preceding criteria: the traditional department store and the full-line discount store. Together, they generate about $680 billion in U.S. revenues annually.[19] The traditional department store is discussed next, followed by coverage on the full line discount store.

FIGURE 5-7

The Vast Assortment of Specialty Stores

Due to their emphasis on mainly one product category, specialty retailers often carry a huge selection of items with that category.

Source: S_E/Shutterstock. Reprinted by permission.

Belk, Inc. (www.belk .com) is the nation's largest privately owned department store company, with nearly 300 fashion department stores in 16 states.

At a **traditional department store**, merchandise quality ranges from average to quite good. Pricing is moderate to above average. Customer service ranges from medium levels of sales help, credit, delivery, and so forth to high levels of each. For example, Macy's (www.macys.com) targets middle-class shoppers interested in assortment and moderate prices, whereas Bloomingdale's (www.bloomingdales.com) aims at upscale consumers through more trendy merchandise and higher prices. Few traditional department stores sell all of the product lines that the category used to carry. Many place greater emphasis on apparel and may not carry such lines as furniture, electronics, and major appliances.

Over its history, the traditional department store has contributed many innovations, such as advertising prices, enacting a one-price policy (whereby all shoppers pay the same price for the same item), developing computerized checkouts, offering money-back guarantees, adding branch stores, decentralizing management, and moving into suburban shopping centers. However, in recent years, the performance of traditional department stores has lagged far behind that of full-line discount stores. Today, traditional department store sales ($170 billion annually) represent one-quarter of total department store sales. These are some reasons for traditional department stores' difficulties:

▶ Price-conscious consumers are more attracted to discounters and online stores than to traditional department stores.
▶ These stores no longer have exclusive brands for many of the items they sell.
▶ The growth of shopping centers has aided specialty stores because consumers can engage in one-stop shopping at several specialty stores in the same shopping center. Department stores do not dominate the smaller stores around them as they once did.
▶ Specialty stores often have better assortments in the lines they carry.
▶ Customer service has deteriorated. Often, store personnel are not as loyal, helpful, or knowledgeable as in prior years.
▶ Some stores are too big and have a lot of unproductive space and low-turnover merchandise.
▶ Many department stores have had a weak focus on market segments and a fuzzy image.
▶ Such chains as Sears have repeatedly changed strategies, confusing consumers as to their image. (Is Sears a traditional department store chain or a full-line discount store chain?)
▶ Some companies are not as innovative in their merchandise decisions as they once were.

Traditional department stores need to clarify their niche in the marketplace (retail positioning); place greater emphasis on customer service and sales personnel; present more exciting, better-organized store interiors; use space better by downsizing stores and eliminating slow-selling items; and open outlets in smaller, less developed towns and cities (as Sears has done). They can also centralize more buying and promotion functions, do better research, and reach customers more efficiently (by such tools as targeted mailing pieces). See Figure 5-8.

FIGURE 5-8

Galeria Kaufhof: A Leading Department Store Chain

Galeria Kaufhof, a subsidiary of the Canadian Hudson's Bay Company, operates 100 department stores in 80 German cities, such as Stuttgart. The chain generates several billion Euros in revenue each year.

Source: Jules Selmes/Pearson Education Ltd. Reprinted by permission.

Sephora's "Phygital" Makeover

Sephora's new flagship store in San Francisco melds consumers' physical and digital worlds in a way that shoppers haven't seen until now. It's being called a "phygital" makeover. Visitors may digitally interact at the Beauty Workshop, where makeup enthusiasts can stream YouTube how-to videos at 12 designated stations. It's also possible for visitors to sit down with Sephora's glam squad for a workshop-style session and try out new products—all while using the screens to inspire and engage. Another aspect of the new flagship is a digital Beauty Board, where the latest user-generated beauty trends and looks are shown on a shoppable screen. Beauty bloggers have proven to be especially engaged; the trend is not as prominent among fashionistas.

How quickly do you think other retailers will follow Sephora's "phygital" lead? Why?

Source: Based on material in STORES magazine. Susan Reda, "STORES Trends: March 2016," *STORES Magazine*, March 2016. Reprinted by permission, Copyright 2016. STORES magazine.

FULL-LINE DISCOUNT STORE   A **full-line discount store** is a type of department store with these features:

- It conveys the image of a high-volume, low-cost outlet selling a broad product assortment for less than conventional prices.
- It is more apt to carry the range of general merchandise once expected only at department stores, including electronics, furniture, and appliances—as well as auto accessories, gardening tools, and housewares.
- Shopping carts and centralized checkout service are provided.
- Customer service is not usually provided within store departments but at a centralized area. Products are normally sold via self-service with minimal assistance in any single department.
- Nondurable (soft) goods often feature private brands, whereas durable (hard) goods emphasize well-known manufacturer brands.
- Less fashion-sensitive merchandise is often carried.
- Buildings, equipment, and fixtures are less expensive; and operating costs are lower than for traditional department stores and specialty stores.

Annual U.S. full-line discount store revenues are $510 billion (including general merchandise-based supercenters and leased departments), roughly 75 percent of all U.S. department store sales. Together, Walmart (www.walmart.com) and Target (www.target.com) operate 7,400 full-line discount stores (including supercenters) in the United States alone.[20]

The success of full-line discount stores is due to many factors. They have a clear customer focus: middle-class and lower-middle-class shoppers looking for good value. The stores feature popular brands of average- to good-quality merchandise at competitive prices. They have expanded their goods and service categories and often have their own private brands. Full-line discount stores have worked hard to improve their image and provide more customer services. The average outlet (not the supercenter) tends to be smaller than a traditional department store, and sales per square foot are usually higher, which improves productivity. Some full-line discount stores are located in small towns where competition is less intense. Facilities may be newer than those of many traditional department stores.

The greatest challenges facing full-line discount stores are the competition from other retailers (especially lower-priced store discounters, category killer stores, and Web-based retailers such as Amazon.com and eBay), too rapid expansion of some firms, saturation of prime locales, and the dominance of Walmart and Target (as Kmart has fallen dramatically from its heyday). The industry has undergone a number of consolidations, bankruptcies, and liquidations.

VARIETY STORE   A **variety store** handles an assortment of inexpensive and popularly priced goods and services, such as apparel and accessories, costume jewelry, notions and small wares, candy, toys, and other items in the price range. There are open displays and few salespeople. The stores do not carry full product lines, may not be departmentalized, and do not deliver products. Although the conventional variety store format has faded away, there are two successful spin-offs from it: dollar discount stores and closeout chains.

Dollar discount stores sell similar items to those in conventional variety stores but in plainer surroundings and at much lower prices. They generate $40 billion in yearly sales. Dollar General and Dollar Tree (which acquired Family Dollar in 2015) are the two leading dollar discount store chains. The two firms operate over 26,000 stores and have about $35 billion in annual sales. *Closeout chains* sell similar items to those in conventional variety stores but feature closeouts and overruns. They account for $8 billion in sales annually. Big Lots (www.biglots.com) is the leader in that category with about 1,460 stores and annual sales of $5.2 billion.[21]

The conventional variety store format (which included Woolworths and McCrorys) pretty much disappeared from the U.S. marketplace in the mid-1990s after a long, successful run. What happened? There was heavy competition from specialty stores and discounters, most of the stores were older facilities, and some items had low profit margins. At one time, Woolworths had 1,200 variety stores with annual sales of $2 billion.

OFF-PRICE CHAIN   An **off-price chain** features brand-name (sometimes designer) apparel and accessories, footwear (primarily women's and family), linens, fabrics, cosmetics, and/or house-wares and sells them at everyday low prices in an efficient, limited-service environment. It frequently has community dressing rooms, centralized checkout counters, no gift wrapping, and extra charges for alterations. The chains buy merchandise opportunistically, as special deals occur. Other retailers' canceled orders, manufacturers' irregulars and overruns, and end-of-season items are often purchased for a fraction of their original wholesale prices. The total sales of U.S. off-price apparel stores are $55 billion. The biggest chains are T. J. Maxx (www.tjmaxx.com) and Marshalls (www.marshalls.com) (both owned by TJX), Ross Stores (www.rossstores.com), and Burlington Coat Factory, now advertised as Burlington (www.burlingtoncoatfactory.com).

Off-price chains aim at the same shoppers as traditional department stores do—but with prices reduced by 40 to 50 percent. Shoppers are also lured by the promise of new merchandise on a regular basis. See Figure 5-9.

The most crucial strategic element for off-price chains involves buying merchandise and establishing long-term relationships with suppliers. To succeed, the chains must secure large quantities of merchandise at reduced wholesale prices and have a regular flow of goods into the stores. Sometimes manufacturers use off-price chains to sell samples, products that are not doing well when they are introduced, and remaining merchandise near the end of a season. At other times, off-price chains employ a more active buying strategy. Instead of waiting for closeouts and canceled orders, they convince manufacturers to make merchandise during off-seasons and will pay cash for items early. Off-price chains are less demanding in terms of the support requested from suppliers; they do not return products and they pay promptly.

Off-price chains face some market pressure because of competition from other institutional formats that run frequent sales throughout the year, such as temporary pop-up stores and factory outlets. In addition, they have disadvantages associated with discontinuity of merchandise, poor

TJX (www.tjx.com) operates two of the biggest off-price apparel chains: T. J. Maxx and Marshalls.

FIGURE 5-9

Off-Price Retailing

Off-price retailing attracts shoppers who are most interested in popular brands at discounted prices. These prices may be reduced by up to 50 percent (or more) from those of traditional department stores.

Source: Bikeworldtravel/ Shutterstock. Reprinted by permission.

management at some firms, insufficient customer service for some shoppers, and the shakeout of underfinanced companies.

FACTORY OUTLET   A **factory outlet** is a manufacturer-owned store that sells closeouts, discontinued merchandise, irregulars, canceled orders, and sometimes in-season, first-quality merchandise. Manufacturers' interest in outlet stores has risen for four basic reasons:

1. Manufacturers can control where their discounted merchandise is sold. By placing outlets in out-of-the-way spots with low sales penetration of the firm's brands, outlet revenues do not affect relationships with key specialty and department store accounts.
2. Outlets are profitable despite prices being up to 60 percent less than customary retail prices. Profits are due to low operating costs—few services, low rent, limited displays, and plain store fixtures—and selling more merchandise made especially for outlet stores.
3. The manufacturer decides on store visibility, sets promotion policies, removes labels, and ensures that discontinued items and irregulars are disposed of properly.
4. Because many specialty and department stores are increasing private-label sales, manufacturers need revenue from outlet stores to sustain their own growth.

More factory stores now locate in clusters or outlet malls to expand customer traffic, and they use cooperative ads. The states with a large number of outlet centers are California, Florida, Texas, Pennsylvania, and New York. The largest U.S. factory outlet mall is Woodbury Common Premium Outlets (located in Central Valley, New York) with 904,000 gross leasable square feet.

There are more than 200 outlet malls nationwide.[22] Firms with a major presence include Phillips-Van Heusen Corp. (Tommy Hilfiger, Calvin Klein, and Arrow); Ascena Retail Group (Dress Barn, Maurices, Justice, Lane Bryant, and Catherines); Gap Inc. (Gap and Banana Republic); JAG Footwear; and Carter's, Inc. (children's clothing). Worldwide factory outlet sales equaled $46 billion in 2015.

Large outlet centers are in Connecticut, Florida, Georgia, New York, Pennsylvania, Tennessee, and other states. There are more than 15,000 U.S. factory outlet stores representing hundreds of manufacturers, many in outlet malls. These stores have $27 billion in U.S. yearly sales, with three-quarters from apparel and accessories. Firms with a mall presence include Bass (footwear); Polo Ralph Lauren (apparel); Levi's (apparel); Nike (apparel and footwear); Samsonite (luggage); and Totes (rain gear).

When deciding whether to utilize factory outlets, manufacturers must be cautious. They must evaluate their own retailing expertise, the investment costs, the impact on existing retailers that buy from them, and the response of consumers. Manufacturers do not want to jeopardize their products' sales at full retail prices.

MEMBERSHIP CLUB   A **membership (warehouse) club** straddles the line between wholesaling and retailing. It appeals to price-conscious consumers, who must be members to shop there. Some members are small business owners and employees who pay a membership fee to buy merchandise at wholesale prices. They make purchases for use in operating their firms or for personal use and yield 60 percent of club sales. Most members are final consumers who buy for their own use; they represent 40 percent of club sales. They must pay an annual fee to be a member. Prices may be slightly more than for business customers. There are over 1,500 U.S. membership clubs, with annual sales to final consumers of $75 billion. Costco www.costco.com) and Sam's Club (www.samsclub.com) generate over 90 percent of industry sales.[23]

ETHICS IN RETAILING

Bargaining Power by Category Killers

Category killers such as Home Depot, Sephora, and Barnes & Noble have bargaining power with their suppliers, particularly small ones. Here are some examples of misuse of bargaining power: (1) Requiring preferential terms such as slotting fees, quantity discounts, markdown allowances, and extended payment terms. (2) Asking suppliers for special SKU designations so consumers cannot demand price adjustments based on price-matching guarantees. (3) Demanding that suppliers have private-label goods sold under the retailer's name as a condition for purchasing the supplier's other brands. (4) Requiring suppliers to ship goods directly to customers.

As a small retailer, how would you react to the bargaining power of category killers?

The operating strategy of today's membership club centers on large stores (up to 100,000 or more square feet), inexpensive sites, opportunistic buying (with some product discontinuity), a fraction of the items stocked by full-line discount stores, little advertising, warehouse-style fixtures, wide aisles to give forklift trucks access to shelves, concrete floors, limited delivery, and low prices. A typical club carries general merchandise, such as consumer electronics, appliances, computers, housewares, tires, and apparel (35 to 60 percent of sales); food (20 to 35 percent); and sundries, such as health and beauty aids, tobacco, liquor, and candy (15 to 30 percent). It may have a pharmacy, photo developing, a car-buying service, a gas station, and other items once seen as frills for this format. Inventory turnover is several times that of a department store.

The major retailing challenges relate to the allocation of efforts between business and final consumer accounts (without antagonizing one group or the other and without presenting a blurred image), the lack of interest by many consumers in shopping at warehouse-type stores, the power of the two industry leaders, and the potential for saturation caused by overexpansion.

FLEA MARKET   At a **flea market**, many retail vendors sell a range of products at discount prices in plain surroundings. It is rooted in the centuries-old tradition of street selling—shoppers touch and sample items, and haggle over prices. Vendors used to sell only antiques, bric-a-brac, and assorted used merchandise. Today, they also frequently sell new goods, such as clothing, cosmetics, watches, consumer electronics, housewares, and gift items. See Figure 5-10.

Many flea markets are in nontraditional sites such as racetracks, stadiums, and arenas. Some are at sites abandoned by other retailers. Typically, vendors rent space; depending on location, a flea market might rent individual spaces for $30 to $100 or more a day. Some flea markets impose a parking fee or admission charge for shoppers.

There are a few hundred major U.S. flea markets, but overall sales data are not available. The credibility of permanent flea markets, consumer interest in bargaining, a broader product mix, availability of brand-name goods, and low prices all contribute to the format's appeal. A popular site is the Rose Bowl Flea Market (www.rgcshows.com/rosebowl.aspx), which is open the second Sunday of each month. It regularly features 2,500 vendors and attracts 20,000 shoppers a day. The only restricted items are "food, animals, guns, ammunition, pornography, and services requiring physical contact." A vendor space costs from $60 to $250 for 1 day.

At a flea market, price haggling is common, cash is the predominant currency, and many vendors gain their first real experience as retail entrepreneurs. One twenty first-century trend involves nonstore, Web-based flea markets such as eBay (www.ebay.com), eBid (www.ebid .com), OnlineAuction (www.onlineauction.com), and Skoreit! (www.skoreit.com). Online auction sites account for several billion dollars in sales annually and are popular among bargain hunters.

FIGURE 5-10

The Eclectic Nature of Flea Markets

These days, you can find almost anything at a flea market; and that is true around the globe. Shown here are a large number of homemade chess boards displayed for sale on a table at the Mauerpark Sunday Flea Market in Berlin, Germany

Source: Eldad Carin/ Shutterstock. Reprinted by permission.

Many traditional retailers believe flea markets represent an unfair method of competition because the quality of merchandise may be misrepresented, consumers may buy items at flea markets and return them to other retailers for higher refunds, suppliers are often unaware their products are sold there, sales taxes can be easily avoided, and operating costs are quite low. Flea markets may also cause traffic congestion.

The high sales volume from off-price chains, factory outlets, membership clubs, and flea markets is explained by the wheel of retailing. These institutions are low-cost operators appealing to price-conscious consumers who are not totally satisfied with other retail formats that have upgraded their merchandise and customer service, raised prices, and moved along the wheel.

Chapter Summary

1. *To describe the wheel of retailing, scrambled merchandising, and the retail life cycle, and to show how they can help explain the performance of retail strategy mixes.* A retail strategy mix involves a combination of factors: location, operations, goods/services offered, pricing, atmosphere and customer services, and promotion. To flourish, a firm should seek to be dominant in some way and reach destination retailer status.

Three important concepts help explain the performance of diverse retail strategies. According to the wheel of retailing, retail innovators often first appear as low-price operators with low costs and low profit margins. Over time, they upgrade their offerings and customer services and raise prices. They are then vulnerable to new discounters with lower costs that take their place along the wheel. With scrambled merchandising, a retailer adds goods and services that are unrelated to each other and its original business to increase overall sales and profits. Scrambled merchandising is contagious and often used in self-defense. The retail life cycle states that institutions pass through identifiable stages of introduction, growth, maturity, and decline. Strategies change as institutions mature.

2. *To discuss ways in which retail strategy mixes are evolving.* Many institutions are adapting to marketplace dynamics. These approaches have been popular for various firms, depending on their strengths, weaknesses, and goals: *mergers*, by which separately owned retailers join together; *diversification*, by which a retailer becomes active in businesses outside its normal operations; and *downsizing*, whereby unprofitable stores are closed or divisions sold. Sometimes, single companies use all three approaches. More firms also utilize cost containment and value-driven retailing. They strive to hold down both investment and operating costs. There are many ways to do this.

3. *To examine a wide variety of food-oriented retailers involved with store-based strategy mixes.* Retail institutions may be classified by store-based strategy mix and divided into food-oriented and general merchandise. Fourteen store-based strategies are covered in this chapter.

Food-oriented store-based retailers include the following: A *convenience store* is well located, is open long hours, and offers a moderate number of fill-in items at average to above-average prices. A *conventional supermarket* is departmentalized and carries a wide range of food and related items, there is little general merchandise, and prices are competitive. A *food-based superstore* is larger and more diversified than a conventional supermarket but smaller and less diversified than a combination store. A *combination store* unites supermarket and general merchandise in a large facility and sets competitive prices; the food-based *supercenter (hypermarket)* is a type of combination store. A *box (limited-line) store* is a discounter focusing on a small selection, moderate hours, few services, and few name brands. A *warehouse store* is a discounter with a moderate number of food items in a no-frills setting that can be large.

4. *To study a wide range of general merchandise retailers involved with store-based strategy mixes.* A *specialty store* concentrates on one goods or service line and has a tailored strategy; the *category killer* is a special kind of specialty store. A *department store* is a large retailer with an extensive assortment of goods and services. The *traditional department store* has a range of customer services and average to above-average prices. A *full-line discount store* is a department store with a low-cost, low-price strategy. A *variety store* has inexpensive and popularly priced items in a plain setting. An *off-price chain* features brand-name items and sells them at low prices in an austere environment. A *factory outlet* is manufacturer-owned and sells closeouts, discontinued merchandise, and irregulars at very low prices. A *membership club* appeals to price-conscious shoppers who must be members to shop. A *flea market* has many vendors offering items at discount prices in nontraditional venues.

Key Terms

strategy mix (p. 131)
destination retailer (p. 131)
wheel of retailing (p. 131)
scrambled merchandising (p. 133)
retail life cycle (p. 134)
mergers (p. 136)
diversification (p. 136)
downsizing (p. 137)
convenience store (p. 139)

supermarket (p. 139)
conventional supermarket (p. 140)
food-based superstore (p. 140)
combination store (p. 141)
supercenter (p. 141)
hypermarket (p. 141)
box (limited-line) store (p. 141)
warehouse store (p. 142)
specialty store (p. 142)

category killer (power retailer) (p. 143)
department store (p. 143)
traditional department store (p. 144)
full-line discount store (p. 145)
variety store (p. 145)
off-price chain (p. 146)
factory outlet (p. 147)
membership (warehouse) club (p. 147)
flea market (p. 148)

Questions for Discussion

1. Describe how a small shoe store could be a destination retailer.
2. What does it mean to become a destination retailer? How is this achieved?
3. Price-sensitive shoppers are one of the most fickle target groups. What makes them difficult to convert to loyal customers? How could you retain them?
4. Briefly explain and provide local examples of the four stages of the retail life cycle.
5. Choose a local example of a retailer and explain how they could avoid terminal decline and reset themselves into a new growth period.
6. Contrast the strategy mixes of convenience stores, conventional supermarkets, food-based superstores, and warehouse stores. Is there room for each? Explain your answer.
7. Is the trend towards mergers of retailers an important aspect of your local retail environment?
8. What are the pros and cons of Sephora carrying more than 200 brands of personal-care products?
9. Contrast the strategy mixes of specialty stores, traditional department stores, and full-line discount stores.
10. What must the off-price chain do to succeed in the future?
11. Do you expect factory outlet centers to keep growing? Explain your answer.
12. Comment on the decision of many membership clubs to sell gasoline.

Web-Based Exercise

Using your own knowledge, identify examples of local retailers at the four main stages of the wheel of retailing. Use a search engine to find their Web sites. Compare the theory with practice by assessing whether the Web sites suggest the kinds of behaviors covered in the chapter.

6 Web, Nonstore-Based, and Other Forms of Nontraditional Retailing

As both multichannel and Web-only retailers look to ramp up their online revenues, many of them may be missing out on a huge opportunity. Why? A big challenge is for these retailers to effectively coordinate their E-commerce efforts with their social-media activities. Too often, the two formats are not integrated well—and sometimes not interrelated at all.

Omnichannel retailers have integrated operations across all of their multiple channels and seek to maximize a firm's total performance across these channels. One popular logistics strategy in omnichannel marketing is for shoppers to buy online and pick up the item(s) at the store. This enables them to receive products immediately without incurring shipping charges. What are the advantages for the retailer? Consumers buying online and picking up the merchandise allows the retailer to sell related items (batteries, cables, extended warranties, etc.) as well as trade up customers to more related, higher-margin goods when they arrive at the store.

Kohl's is among a number of retailers that has a buy online, pick up in-store program. "We see it as an advantage. [Convenience is] part of our core DNA, so having someone be able to place an order and then just drive in and pick it up—we've seen very positive reactions from our customers," says Krista Berry, executive vice-president and chief digital officer for Kohl's.

Chapter Objectives

1. To contrast single-channel, multichannel, and omnichannel retailing

2. To look at the characteristics of the three major retail institutions involved with nonstore-based strategy mixes—direct marketing, direct selling, and vending machines—with an emphasis on direct marketing

3. To explore the emergence of electronic retailing through the Web

4. To discuss two other nontraditional forms of retailing: video kiosks and airport retailing

Source: Photosani/Shutterstock. Reprinted by permission.

Kohl's buy online, pick up in-store program was initially limited to desktop and laptop computer users. However, after the service went mobile, it reached the more than 7 million shoppers who had already downloaded the Kohl's app. Kohl's can use the app's wallet function to deliver personalized messages and offers that can be scanned and redeemed in stores.

According to consultant Paul McFarren, "The size of the retail operation is an important factor" in implementing the buy online, pick up in-store feature. "Retailers need a sophisticated inventory management program that is able to accurately depict the number of units in stock at each store location. Retailers also need adequate personnel to set aside online purchases at the store level".[1]

Overview

In this chapter, we contrast single-channel, multichannel, and omnichannel retailing. We also look at nonstore-based retailing, electronic retailing, and two other types of nontraditional retailing: video kiosks and airport retailing. These formats affect current and new store retailers. Visit our blog (www.bermanevansretail.com) for posts on these topics.

When it begins, a retailer often relies on **single-channel retailing**, whereby it sells to consumers through one retail format. That one format may be store-based (a corner shoe store) or nonstore-based (catalog retailing, direct selling, or Web retailing). As the firm grows, it may turn to **multichannel retailing**, whereby a retailer sells to consumers through multiple retail formats.

To optimize efficiency and enhance customer experiences, the best retailers turn to **omnichannel retailing**, and deliver a consistent, uninterrupted, and seamless experience regardless of channel or device. As noted in Chapter 1, omnichannel retailing assumes that various shoppers' journeys use mobile, Web, and stores differently. Product discovery can be Web– or social-media–based, information search can use the Web or in-store observation, and consumers can buy via a mobile device and return the product to a store. For example, according to recent research, Web users are most apt to discover small businesses online than via any other mode, including word-of-mouth.[2]

The differences between multichannel and omnichannel retailing must be understood. Although both types of retailers sell through multiple channels, there is seldom integration or coordination among the separate channels or devices at a multichannel retailer. In addition to competing against other retailers, such a company may find its channels are competing against each other. Prices, SKU designations, and customer return policies may differ across channels at a multichannel retailer. A multichannel retailer also seeks to maximize the performance of each separate channel. For that firm, a store manager and a Web executive may compete against each other. Sometimes, multichannel retailers do not allow consumers to buy goods online and return them to a local store. They are also less likely to have integrated databases that can determine a customer's purchases across channels.

Omnichannel retailing, on the other hand, focuses on consumers' use of multiple devices and channels throughout the consumer's retail journey to a single purchase. A multichannel approach may reward customers for purchases through each separate channel, but an omnichannel approach rewards customers for purchases made through all channels. An example of an omnichannel strategy is a retailer's Web site or mobile app containing information on in-store product availability, the aisle location of specific goods, the ability to reserve the goods online for in-store pickup, and text notifications with promotional codes to be redeemed in local stores. Omnichannel retailers also encourage in-store shoppers access to "endless aisles" that use kiosks to place online orders for store pickup or to be shipped home. See Table 6-1.

From its roots as a full-line discount store chain, Walmart (www.walmart.com) has become a master of omnichannel retailing.

Retail leader Walmart sells at stores (including Walmart, Sam's Club, and Neighborhood Market), multiple Web sites (including www.walmart.com), and a Web-to-store format whereby customers purchase online and pick up products at the nearest store. Figure 6-1 shows examples of single-channel, multichannel, and omnichannel retailing. An end-of-chapter appendix explores omnichannel retailing in more detail.

Why have we introduced this concept here? Because even though some nonstore-based firms are "pure players" (single-channel retailers), a rapidly growing number of firms have combined store and nonstore retailing to actively pursue multichannel retailing—and then, ominchannel

TABLE 6-1 **Consumer Engagement (percent of respondents rating as extremely or very important)**

In an era when folks have more options than ever about where to spend their food dollars—along with more ways to share and amplify their opinions of the same—showing customers love and admiration with more purposeful, impactful consumer engagement strategies has never been more critical.

	Percent
Customer Relationship Marketing	81.8%
Social Media	57.6
Loyalty Incentive Programs	46.3
Blogs	23.9
Online Surveys	21.2
Comment Cards	16.4
Toll-Free Hotlines	12.1

Source: "Progressive Grocer's 83rd Annual Report of the Grocery Industry," *Progressive Grocer*, April 2016, p. 50. Reprinted by permission.

retailing. As new digital channels emerge and customer preferences for various channels evolve, more retailers are exploring new ways to reach the right customer with the right message through the right channel at the right time. The best retailers know that the secret to omnichannel retailing success is to invest in new channels, develop a channel integration roadmap, more intensely use customer analytics, enhance Web sites, and develop better marketing communications.[3]

The still-popular eBay (www.ebay.com) is a pure Web retailer.

Retailers—single-channel, multichannel, and omnichannel—engage in **nonstore retailing** when they use strategies that are not store-based to reach consumers and complete transactions. Nonstore retailing sales in the United States exceed $530 billion. The fastest-growing form of direct marketing involves electronic (including mobile) retailing. U.S. Web retailing sales were $319 billion in 2015. Web-influenced offline sales were $1.55 trillion in that same year.[4] See Figure 6-2.

Nontraditional retailing also comprises video kiosks and airport retailing—two key formats not fitting neatly into "store-based" or "nonstore-based" retailing. Sometimes they are store-based; other times they are not. What they have in common is their departure from traditional retailing strategies.

FIGURE 6-1

Approaches to Retailing Channels

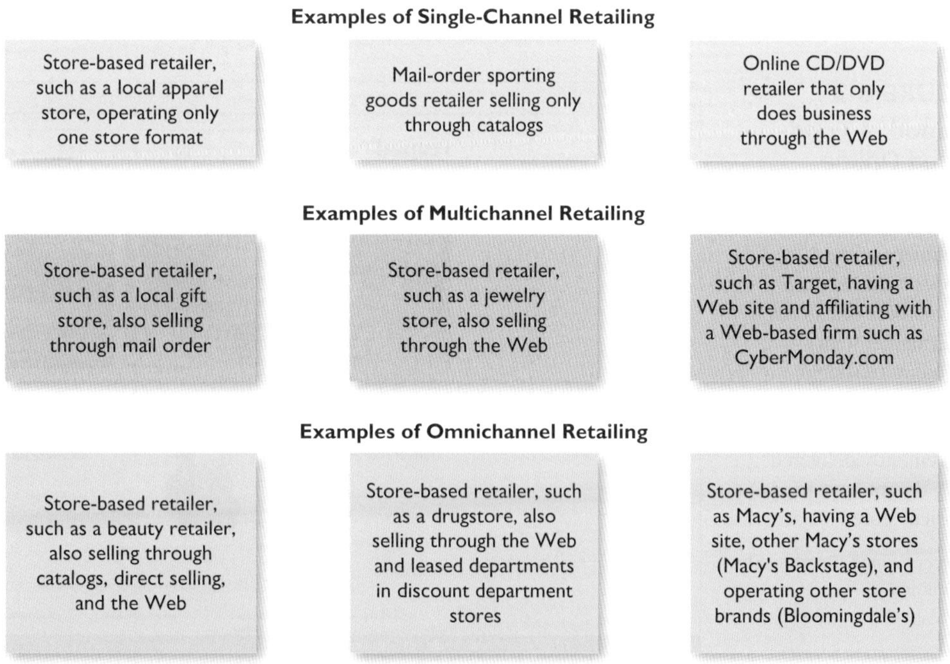

Examples of Single-Channel Retailing

Store-based retailer, such as a local apparel store, operating only one store format

Mail-order sporting goods retailer selling only through catalogs

Online CD/DVD retailer that only does business through the Web

Examples of Multichannel Retailing

Store-based retailer, such as a local gift store, also selling through mail order

Store-based retailer, such as a jewelry store, also selling through the Web

Store-based retailer, such as Target, having a Web site and affiliating with a Web-based firm such as CyberMonday.com

Examples of Omnichannel Retailing

Store-based retailer, such as a beauty retailer, also selling through catalogs, direct selling, and the Web

Store-based retailer, such as a drugstore, also selling through the Web and leased departments in discount department stores

Store-based retailer, such as Macy's, having a Web site, other Macy's stores (Macy's Backstage), and operating other store brands (Bloomingdale's)

Multichannel Retailing for ALL Retailers

Today, every retailer needs to at least engage in multichannel retailing to offer consumers more shopping options and information. For example, the food-based retailer depicted here should have a Web site. The site could provide information such as store location, store hours, a menu, directions, and contact information. It could also enable consumers to order online and pick up at the store or schedule a delivery.

Source: Wavebreak Premium/Shutterstock. Reprinted by permission.

Direct magazine (www.directmag.com) is a vital source of direct marketing information.

DIRECT MARKETING

In **direct marketing**, a customer is first exposed to a good or service through a nonpersonal medium (direct mail, TV, radio, magazine, newspaper, computer, tablet, or mobile device) and then orders by mail, phone, or fax (and increasingly by computer, smartphone, or tablet. Annual U.S. sales are more than $475 billion (including the Web), and more than half of American adults make at least one such purchase a year. Japan, Germany, Great Britain, France, and Italy are among the direct-marketing leaders outside the United States. Popular products are gift items, apparel, magazines, books and music, sports equipment, home accessories, food, and insurance.

In the United States, direct-marketing customers are more apt to be middle class. Mail shoppers are more likely to live in areas away from malls. And, because they want to avoid traffic and save time, phone shoppers are more likely to live in upscale metropolitan areas. The share of direct-marketing purchases made by men has grown: The average consumer who buys direct spends several hundred dollars per year, and he or she wants convenience, unique products, and good prices.

Direct marketers can be divided into two categories: general and specialty. *General* direct-marketing firms, such as Neiman Marcus (with its mail-order and Web businesses) and QVC (with its cable TV and Web businesses), offer a full line of products and sell everything from clothing to housewares. *Specialty* direct marketers focus on more narrow product lines. L.L. Bean, Publishers Clearinghouse, and Franklin Mint are among the thousands of U.S. specialty firms. See Figure 6-3.

FIGURE 6-3

Peapod: A Food-Based Online Retailer

Through Peapod, a subsidiary of Stop & Shop, consumers can place online orders for supermarket items—including fresh and packaged foods—and have these items conveniently delivered. They do not have to visit a physical store.

Source: Peapod. Reprinted by permission.

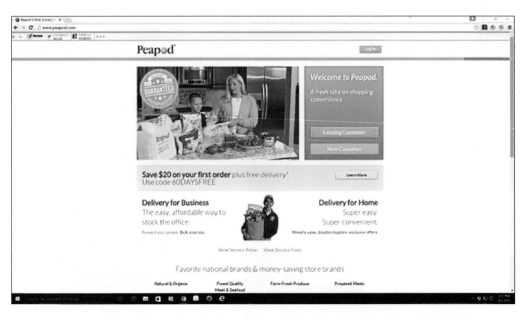

Direct marketing has a number of strategic business advantages:

- Many costs are reduced—even low startup costs are possible; inventories are reduced; no displays are needed; a prime location is unnecessary; regularly staffed store hours are not important; a sales force may not be needed; and business may be run out of a garage or basement.
- It is possible for direct marketers to have lower prices (due to reduced costs) than store-based retailers. A huge geographic area can be covered inexpensively and efficiently.
- Customers shop conveniently—without crowds, parking congestion, or checkout lines. And they do not have safety concerns about shopping early in the morning or late at night.
- Specific consumer segments are pinpointed through targeted mailings.
- Consumers may sometimes legally avoid sales tax by buying from direct marketers not having retail facilities in their state (however, some states want to eliminate this loophole).
- A store-based firm can supplement its regular business and expand its trading area (even becoming national or global) without adding outlets.

Direct marketing also has its limits, but they are not as critical as those for direct selling:

- Products cannot be examined before purchase. Thus, the range of items purchased is more limited than in stores, and firms need liberal return policies to attract and keep customers.
- Firms may underestimate costs. Catalogs can be costly. Computer systems must track shipments, purchases, and returns, and keep lists current. A 24-hour phone staff may be needed.
- Even successful catalogs often draw purchases from less than 10 percent of recipients.
- Clutter exists. Each year, billions of E-mails and catalogs are mailed in the United States alone.
- Printed catalogs are prepared well in advance, causing difficulties in price and style planning.
- Some firms have given the industry a bad name due to delivery delays and shoddy goods.

The full "30-day rule" is available online (https://goo.gl/BL2WGD).

The Federal Trade Commission's "30-day rule" is a U.S. regulation that affects direct marketers. It requires firms to ship orders within 30 days of their receipt or notify customers of delays. If an order cannot be shipped in 60 days, the customer must be given a specific delivery date and offered the option of canceling an order or waiting for it to be filled. The rule covers mail, phone, fax, and computer orders.

Despite its limitations, long-run growth for direct marketing is projected. Consumer interest in convenience and the difficulty in setting aside shopping time will continue. More direct marketers will offer 24-hour ordering and improve their efficiency. Greater product standardization and the prominence of well-known brands will reduce consumer perceptions of risk when buying from a catalog or the Web. Technological breakthroughs, such as purchases on smartphones, will attract more and more consumer shopping.

Due to its vast presence and immense potential, our detailed discussion is intended to give you an in-depth look into direct marketing. Let's study the domain of direct marketing, database retailing, emerging trends, steps in a direct marketing strategy, and key issues facing direct marketers.

  CAREERS IN RETAILING   Web Developers

If you go to a retailer's Web site and it offers one-click payment, shows inventory availability at a local store, remembers your home address, and contains product reviews from users, then thank the retailer's Web site team. Web experts create an overall Web design, write code, incorporate sound and videos, check download times, plan for search engine optimization, and ensure that site features operate on different devices (smartphones, tablets, and laptops) and with different operating systems. Each device and operating system needs a similar appearance because many people channel hop from laptop, tablet, and smartphones in their purchase journey.

The Bureau of Labor Statistics predicts that, from 2016 to 2024, the demand for Web developers will grow by 27 percent. During this period, 39,500 new jobs will be created. The median salary for Web developers is over $63,000.

How would a Web developer's job vary if she or he worked for a retailer versus a manufacturer?

Source: "Web Developer Careers," http://money.usnews.com/careers/best-jobs/web-developer.

The Domain of Direct Marketing

As defined earlier, *direct marketing* is a form of retailing in which a consumer is exposed to a good or service through a nonpersonal medium and then orders by mail, phone, fax, computer, or mobile media. It may also be viewed as a "data-driven, cross media, interactive, multichannel process for building and cultivating mutually beneficial relationships between companies and their customers and prospects."[5]

Accordingly, we *do* include these following forms of direct marketing: any catalog; any mail, TV, radio, magazine, newspaper, phone directory, fax, or other ad; any computer-based or mobile app transaction; or any other nonpersonal contact that stimulates customers to place orders by mail, phone, fax, or computer (including interactive TV and mobile).

We *do not* include these as forms of direct marketing: (1) Direct selling—consumers are solicited by in-person sales efforts or seller-originated phone calls and the firm uses personal communication to initiate contact. (2) Conventional vending machines, whereby consumers are exposed to nonpersonal media but do not complete transactions via mail, phone, fax, or computer; they do not interact with the firm in a manner that allows a database to be generated and kept.

Direct marketing *is* involved in many computerized kiosk transactions; when items are shipped to consumers, there is a company–customer interaction and a database can be formed. Direct marketing is also in play when consumers originate phone calls, based on catalogs or ads they have seen.

The Customer Database: Key to Successful Direct Marketing

Because direct marketers often initiate contact with customers (in contrast to store shopping trips that are initiated by the consumer), it is imperative that they develop and maintain a comprehensive customer database. They can then pinpoint their best customers, make offers aimed at specific customer needs, avoid costly mailings to nonresponsive shoppers, and track sales by customer. A good database is the major asset of most direct marketers, and *every* thriving direct marketer has a strong database.

Database retailing is a way to collect, store, and use relevant information about customers. Such information typically includes a person's name, address, background data, shopping interests, and purchase behavior. Although databases are often compiled through large computerized information systems, they may also be used by small firms that are not overly computerized.

Reports on database retailing show that collecting individual-level customer data (ILCD) about online and store-based shopping behavior helps retailers more efficiently select and contact customers. Gathering ILCD also assists retailers in personalizing content and offers, enhancing customer experience, and improving purchase conversion of individual consumers or business buyers via individually interactive media (IIM) and other touchpoints. When a company can link customer purchases to the offers that spurred them, the data provide valuable clues for personalizing the goods, services, and promotional offers that should be offered next to those particular customers and prospects. Knowing more about target audiences' particular attitudes, propensities, and household composition provides clues about the channels, messages, and timing for the next offer.[6] Database retailing is discussed further in Chapter 8.

Emerging Trends

Several trends are relevant for direct marketing: the evolving activities of direct marketers, changing consumer lifestyles, increased competition, the greater use of omnichannel retailing, the newer roles for catalogs and TV, technological advances, and the interest in global direct marketing. Online retailing is discussed in depth later in this chapter.

EVOLVING ACTIVITIES OF DIRECT MARKETERS   Over the past several decades, these direct marketing activities have evolved:

- Web and mobile technology has moved to the forefront in all aspects of direct marketing—from lead generation to order processing.
- Multiple points of customer contact are offered by most firms today.
- There is an increased focus on database retailing.
- The emergence of database–driven direct marketing services is helping newer and smaller firms enter and diversify into new markets at a lower cost than in the past years.[7]
- Firms now have well-articulated and widely communicated privacy policies.

CHANGING CONSUMER LIFESTYLES   Consumer lifestyles in the United States have shifted, mostly due to the numerous women who are now in the labor force and the longer commuting time to and from work for suburban residents. Many consumers no longer have the time or inclination to shop at stores. They are attracted by the ease of purchasing through direct marketing. Some of the factors consumers consider in selecting a direct marketer are:

- Company reputation (image)
- Ability to shop whenever the consumer wants
- Types of goods and services as well as the assortment and brand names carried
- Availability of a toll-free phone number or Web site for ordering
- Credit card acceptance
- Speed of promised delivery time
- Competitive prices
- Satisfaction with past purchases and good return policies
- Customer reviews and comments at retail sites and through social media

Spiegel (www.spiegel.com) has largely been a direct marketer since the early 1900s. It faces more competition now than ever before.

INCREASED COMPETITION AMONG FIRMS   As direct marketing sales have risen, so has competition; although there are a number of big firms, such as Guthy/Renker (www.guthy-renker.com), which has marketed such products as Proactiv acne solution, there are also thousands of small ones. According to the Direct Marketing Association, there are thousands of U.S. mail-order (and E-mail–based) companies alone.

Intense competition exists because entry into direct marketing is easier and less costly than entry into store retailing. A firm does not need a store; can operate with a small staff; can use low-cost 1-inch magazine ads, send brochures to targeted shoppers, and have an inexpensive Web site. It can also keep a low inventory and place orders with suppliers after people buy items (so long as it meets the "30-day rule").

About one of every two new direct marketers fail. Direct marketing lures small firms that may poorly define their market niche, offer nondistinctive products, have limited experience, misjudge the needed effort, have trouble with supplier continuity, and get consumer complaints.

GREATER USE OF MULTICHANNEL AND OMNICHANNEL RETAILING   Today, many stores add to their revenues by using ads, brochures, catalogs, and Web sites to obtain mail-order, phone, and computer-generated sales. They see that direct marketing is efficient, targets specific segments, appeals to people who might not otherwise shop with those firms, and needs a lower investment to reach other geographic areas than opening branch outlets.

Neiman Marcus Group is a good example of a luxury store-based retailer that has flourished with its distinctive omnichannel approach. It uses its strong print catalog experience to drive omnichannel efforts. Its catalogs, such as "The Book" for Neiman Marcus and "BG Magazine" for Bergdorf Goodman, play an important role in bringing the firm to life in a very tactile way to customers. Neiman Marcus started selling online through its Web site in 1999; today it accounts for 24 percent of total business. The company still asserts that there is a niche in the market for catalog services, and that catalogs play a role in moving customers across the demographic spectrum through the purchase cycle. Neiman Marcus has successfully leveraged data and insights gained from its catalogs, its vendor relationships, and its fulfillment infrastructure in its E-commerce efforts.[8]

NEWER ROLES FOR CATALOGS AND TV   Direct marketers are recasting how they use their catalogs and their approach to TV retailing. We are witnessing three key changes in long-standing catalog tactics: (1) Many firms now print "specialogs" in addition to or instead of the annual catalogs showing all their products. With a **specialog**, a retailer caters to a particular customer segment, emphasizes a limited number of items, and reduces production and postage costs (a specialog is much shorter than a general catalog). Each year, such firms as L.L. Bean and Travelsmith send out separate specialogs by market segment or occasion. (2) To help defray costs, some companies accept ads from noncompeting firms that are compatible with their image. (3) To stimulate sales and defray costs, some catalogs are sold in bookstores, supermarkets, and airports, as well as at company Web sites. The percentage of consumers buying a catalog who actually make a purchase is far higher than that for those who get catalogs in the mail.

Television retailing has two major components (not including interactive TV shopping, which is now emerging): shopping networks and infomercials. On a *shopping network*, programming focuses on merchandise presentations and sales (often by phone). The two biggest players are cable giants QVC and Home Shopping Network (HSN), with combined annual worldwide revenues of $12.4 billion. QVC has access to a global TV audience of 350 million households, HSN to 94 million. They feature jewelry, women's clothing, and personal-care items and do not focus on leading brands. Most items must be bought when they are shown to encourage shoppers to act quickly. Both firms have active Web sites (www.qvc.com and www.hsn.com) and mobile apps. Nearly half of their U.S. sales revenues (40 percent HSN and 49 percent QVC in 2015) are E-commerce orders, with mobile accounting for half of QVC's E-commerce revenues.[9]

An **infomercial** is a program-length TV commercial (typically, 30 minutes) for a specific good or service that airs on cable or broadcast television, often at a fringe time. As they watch an infomercial, shoppers call in orders, which are delivered to them. Infomercials work well for products that benefit from demonstrations. Good infomercials present detailed information, include customer testimonials, are entertaining, and are divided into timed segments (since the average viewer watches only a few minutes at a time) with ordering information displayed in every segment. Infomercials account for several billion dollars in annual U.S. revenues. Popular infomercials include those for the Total Gym, Life Lock, Proactiv Acne Treatment, Shark Rocket, and Copper Chef. The Electronic Retailing Association (www.retailing.org) is the trade association for infomercial firms.

George Foreman became a very rich man through his infomercials for grills (www.georgeforemancooking.com).

TECHNOLOGICAL ADVANCES The technology revolution has improved operating efficiency as well as enhanced sales opportunities:

▶ Market segments are better targeted. Through selective binding, bigger catalogs are sent to the best customers and shorter catalogs to new prospects.
▶ Advances in computerized database technology has made it both easier and less costly to selectively reach individual customers.
▶ Firms inexpensively use computers to enter mail and phone orders, arrange for shipments, and monitor inventory on hand.
▶ Huge, automated distribution centers efficiently accumulate and ship orders.
▶ Customers dial toll-free phone numbers or visit Web sites to place orders and get information. The cost per call for the direct marketer is quite low.
▶ Consumers can conclude transactions from more sites, including kiosks at airports and train stations.
▶ Cable and satellite programming and the Web offer 24-hour shopping and ordering.
▶ In-home, at-work, and leisure-time Web-based shopping transactions can be conducted.

Lands' End has Web sites to service customers around the world, such as its French site (www.fr.landsend.com). Because of Lands' End's customer commitment, this site is in French.

MOUNTING INTEREST IN GLOBAL DIRECT MARKETING More retailers are engaged with global direct marketing because of the growing consumer acceptance of nonstore retailing in other countries. Among the U.S.-based direct marketers with a significant international presence are Brookstone, Eddie Bauer, Lands' End, and Williams-Sonoma.

Outside the United States, annual direct-marketing sales (by both domestic and foreign firms) amount to hundreds of billions of dollars. Direct-marketing trade associations—each representing many member firms—exist in such diverse countries as Australia, Brazil, China, France, Germany, Japan, Russia, and Spain. In Europe alone, there are well over 10,000 direct-marketing companies; and the emerging Indian direct-marketing arena features numerous firms, domestic and international.[10]

ETHICS IN RETAILING

Sales Tax Collection by Online Retailers

A recurring issue underlying all Web-based transactions concerns the legal responsibility of online sellers to collect sales tax. The general guideline is that online retailers are not required to collect sales tax in states where they have no physical presence. A number of states have recently enacted laws that require large online retailers to collect sales tax from all purchasers in those states. Under the current sales tax collection process, Web-based retailers with no presence in a state have a significant price advantage equal to the sales tax. This is especially the case in those states where the sales tax states equals or exceeds 7 percent.

As a store-based retailer, how you deal with this issue?

The Steps in a Direct-Marketing Strategy

A direct marketing strategy has eight steps: business definition, generating customers, media selection, presenting the message, customer contact, customer response, order fulfillment, and measuring results, and maintaining the database. See Figure 6-4.

BUSINESS DEFINITION   First, a company makes two decisions as to its business definition: (1) Is the firm going to be a pure direct marketer or is it going to engage in multichannel or omnichannel retailing? If the firm chooses one of the latter two strategies, it must clarify the role of direct marketing in its overall retail strategy. (2) Is the firm going to be a general direct marketer and carry a broad product assortment or will it specialize in one product category?

GENERATING CUSTOMERS   A mechanism for generating business is devised next. A firm can:

▸ Buy a printed mailing list or an E-mail list from a broker. For one mailing, a list usually costs up to $50 to $100 or more per 1,000 names and addresses; if printed, it is supplied in mailing-label format. Lists may be broad or broken down by gender, location, and so on. In purchasing a list, the direct marketer should check its currency.
▸ Download a mailing list from the Web that is sold by a firm such as infoUSA (www.infousa.com), which has data on the home addresses of 100 million U.S. households. With a download, a retailer can use the list multiple times, but it is responsible for selecting names and printing labels.
▸ Send out a blind mailing to all the residents in a particular area. This method can be expensive (unless done through E-mail) and may receive a very low response rate.
▸ Advertise in a newspaper, magazine, Web site, or other medium, and ask customers to order by mail, phone, fax, or computer.
▸ Contact consumers who have bought from the firm or requested information. This is efficient, but it takes a while to develop a database. To grow, a firm cannot rely solely on past customers.

MEDIA SELECTION   Several media are available to the direct marketer:

▸ Printed and/or online catalogs
▸ Direct mail ads and brochures
▸ Inserts with monthly credit card and other bills ("statement stuffers")
▸ Freestanding displays with coupons, brochures, or catalogs (such as magazine subscription cards at the supermarket checkout counter)
▸ Ads or programs in the mass media—newspapers, magazines, radio, TV
▸ Banner ads or hotlinks on the Web
▸ Video kiosks

In choosing among media, the costs, distribution, lead time, and other factors should be considered.

PRESENTING THE MESSAGE   The next step in a direct-marketing strategy is the firm prepares and presents its message in a way that engenders interest, creates (or sustains) the proper image,

FIGURE 6-4
Executing a Direct Marketing Strategy

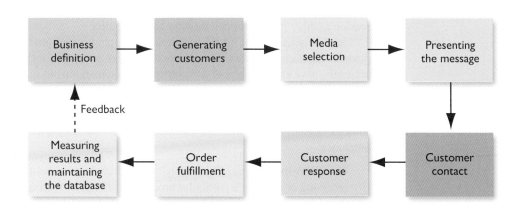

points out compelling reasons to purchase, and provides data about goods or services (such as prices and sizes). The message must also contain ordering instructions, including the payment method; how to designate the chosen items; shipping fees; and a firm's address, phone number, and Web address.

The message, and the media in which it is presented, should be planned in the same way that a traditional retailer plans a store. The latter uses a storefront, lighting, carpeting, the store layout, and displays to foster an image. In direct marketing, the headlines, message content, use of color, paper quality, personalization of mail, space devoted to each item, return policy, product guarantees, and other elements affect a firm's image.

CUSTOMER CONTACT   For each campaign, a direct marketer decides whether to contact all customers in its database or to seek specific market segments (with different messages and/or media for each). It can classify prospective customers as *regulars* (those who buy continuously); *nonregulars* (those who buy infrequently); *new contacts* (those who have never been sought before by the firm); and *nonrespondents* (those who have been contacted but never made a purchase).

Regulars and nonregulars are the most apt to respond to a firm's future offerings, and they can be better targeted because the firm has their purchase histories. For example, customers who have bought clothing before are prime prospects for specialogs. New contacts probably know less about the firm. Messages to them must build interest, accurately portray the firm, and present meaningful reasons for consumers to buy. This group is important if growth is sought.

Nonrespondents who have been contacted repeatedly without purchasing are unlikely to ever buy. Unless a firm can present a very different message, it is inefficient to pursue this group. Firms such as Publishers Clearinghouse send mailings to millions of people who have never bought from them; this is okay because they sell inexpensive impulse items and need only a small response rate to succeed.

CUSTOMER RESPONSE   Customers respond to direct marketers in one of three ways: (1) They buy through the mail, phone, fax, computer, or smartphone. (2) They request further information, such as a catalog. (3) They ignore the message. Purchases are generally made by no more than 2 to 3 percent of those contacted. The rate is higher for specialogs, mail-order clubs (e.g., for books), and firms focusing on repeat customers.

ORDER FULFILLMENT   A system is needed for order fulfillment. If orders are received by mail or fax, the firm must sort them, determine if payment is enclosed, see whether the item is in stock, mail announcements if items cannot be sent on time, coordinate shipments, and replenish inventory. If phone orders are placed, a trained sales staff must be available when people may call. Salespeople answer questions, make suggestions, enter orders, note the payment method, see whether items are in stock, coordinate shipments, and replenish inventory. If orders are placed by computer or smartphone, there must be a process to promptly and efficiently handle credit transactions, issue receipts, and forward orders to a warehouse. In all cases, names, addresses, and purchase data are added to the database for future reference.

Order fulfillment can also be conducted through "drop shipping," wherein manufacturers and wholesalers handle packaging, shipping, and inventory storage functions. Drop shipping occurs when retailers have a lot of channel power relative to suppliers or when niche goods with low demand are sought by consumers. Although consumers may not know that items are drop shipped (because the invoice is from the retailer), they still expect the same level of prompt and accurate service as other goods shipped directly by the retailer.

In peak seasons, additional warehouse, shipping, order processing, and sales workers supplement regular employees. Direct marketers that are highly regarded by consumers fill orders promptly, have knowledgeable and courteous personnel, do not misrepresent quality, and provide liberal return policies.

MEASURING RESULTS AND MAINTAINING THE DATABASE   The last step in a direct-marketing strategy is analyzing results and maintaining the database. Direct marketing often yields clear outcomes:

► *Overall response rate:* The number and percentage of people who make a purchase after receiving or viewing a particular brochure, catalog, or Web site
► *Average purchase amount:* By customer location, gender, and so forth

> *Sales volume by product category:* Revenues correlated with the space allotted to each product in brochures, catalogs, and so forth
> *Value of list brokers:* The revenues generated by various mailing lists

After measuring results, the firm reviews its database and makes sure that new shoppers are added, address changes are noted for existing customers, purchase and consumer information is current and available in segmentation categories, and nonrespondents are purged (when desirable). This stage provides feedback for the direct marketer as it plans each new campaign.

Key Issues Facing Direct Marketers

In planning and applying their strategies, direct marketers must keep certain issues in mind. Many consumer perceptions of aspects of direct marketing are negative. Nonetheless, in most cases, leading direct marketers are rated well by consumers. Factors leading to dissatisfaction include:

> *Delivery problems.* Customer dissatisfaction includes late delivery or nondelivery, deceptive claims, broken or damaged items, receiving the wrong items, and the lack of information.
> *Clutter or "junk" mail.* Most U.S. households report that they do open direct mail, but they would like to receive less of it. Firms are concerned about clutter and difficulty in being distinctive.
> *Privacy concerns.* Many consumers are concerned that their names and other information are being sold by list brokers and retailers. They feel this is an invasion of privacy and that their decision to purchase does not constitute permission for the retailer to make secondary use of their personal data. To counteract this, members of the Direct Marketing Association remove people's names from list circulation if they make a request.[11]

Multichannel and omnichannel retailers need a consistent image for both store-based and direct-marketing efforts. They must also recognize the similarities and differences in each approach's strategy. Postal rates and paper costs makes mailing catalogs, brochures, and other promotional materials costly for some firms. Numerous direct marketers are turning more to newspapers, magazines, cable TV, and the Web.

Direct marketers must monitor the legal environment. They must be aware that, in the future, more states will probably require residents to pay sales tax on out-of-state direct-marketing purchases; the firms will have to remit the tax payments to affected states. New laws will be contested by some retailers.

DIRECT SELLING

Direct selling includes both personal contact with consumers in their homes (and other nonstore locations such as offices) and phone solicitations initiated by a retailer. See Figure 6-5. Cosmetics, jewelry, vitamins, household goods and services (such as carpet cleaning), vacuum cleaners, and magazines and newspapers are among the items sometimes sold in this way. The industry has $35 billion in annual U.S. sales and employs more than 18.2 million people (more than 90 percent of whom work part time). Annual foreign direct-selling revenues are an additional $185 billion, generated by more than 100 million salespeople.[12] Table 6-2 shows a U.S. industry overview.

FIGURE 6-5
Direct Selling via Telemarketing

With telemarketing, trained salespeople interact with customers virtually anywhere. They describe product features, answer questions, arrange for payment and shipping, and follow-up to see if customers are satisfied after purchasing. However, today, many people feel that telemarketing is too intrusive.

Source: Andresr/Shutterstock. Reprinted by permission.

TABLE 6-2 A Snapshot of the U.S. Direct Selling Industry

Major Product Groups (as a percent of sales dollars)	
Home and family care products/home durables	16.3
Wellness (weight loss products, vitamins, etc.)	33.5
Personal care	17.1
Services (travel, real-estate) and other	21.9
Clothing and accessories	8.8
Leisure/educational (books, encyclopedias, toys/games, etc.)	2.4
Sales Strategy (method used to generate sales, as a percent of sales dollars)	
Individual/one-to-one selling	71.0
Party plan/group sales	20.4
Other	8.6
Demographics of Salespeople (as a percent of all people engaged in direct selling)	
Female/male	77.4/22.6

Source: Based on "U.S. Direct Selling in 2015: An Overview," http://www.dsa.org/docs/default-source/research/dsa_2015factsheetfinal.pdf?sfvrsn=8; www.dsa.org/research/industry-statistics. Reprinted by permission of the Direct Selling Association.

The Direct Selling Association (www.dsa.org) is working hard to promote the image and professionalism of this retail format.

A direct-selling strategy emphasizes convenient shopping and a personal touch, and detailed demonstrations can be made. Consumers often relax more at home than in stores. They are also apt to be attentive and are not exposed to competing brands (as in stores). For some, such as older consumers and those with young children, in-store shopping is difficult due to limited mobility. For the retailer, direct selling has less overhead cost because stores and fixtures are not necessary.

Despite its advantages, direct selling in the United States is growing slowly:

▸ Online transactions are easier and offer many more seller product options for shoppers.
▸ More women work, and they may not be interested in or available for at-home selling.
▸ The desire for full-time careers and job opportunities in other fields have reduced the pool of people interested in direct-selling jobs.
▸ A firm's market coverage is limited by the size of its sales force.
▸ Sales productivity is low because the average transaction is small and most consumers are unreceptive—many will not open their doors to salespeople or talk to telemarketers.
▸ Sales force turnover is high because employees are often poorly supervised part-timers.
▸ To stimulate sales personnel, compensation is usually 25 to 50 percent of the revenues they generate. This means average to above-average prices.
▸ There are legal constraints due to deceptive and high-pressure sales tactics. One is the FTC's Telemarketing Sales Rule (https://www.consumer.ftc.gov/articles/0198-telemarketing-sales-rule). It mandates that firms must disclose their identity and that the call's purpose is selling.
▸ Because *door-to-door* has a poor image, the industry prefers the term *direct selling*.

Firms are reacting to these issues. Avon, for example, places greater emphasis on workplace sales, offers free training to sales personnel, rewards the best workers with better territories,

 TECHNOLOGY IN RETAILING | Concierge Service Comes to Online Shopping

With the latest products in home automation, such as turbo bikes and camera drones, even tech-savvy consumers may have difficulty figuring out how to use their new toys. Most people can relate to this problem. For example, you purchase a new smartphone and realize that it may be *too* smart. Enter Enjoy.com, an online retailer that hand-delivers a product, sets it up, and gives a tutorial; the entire visit may last up to an hour. Enjoy.com contacts customers ahead of time to understand exactly what help the shopper wants. It's the perfect marriage of online shopping's convenience and the hands-on experience with a trusted tech expert that an in-store experience provides. Thus far, Enjoy.com has been limited to San Francisco and New York City, where it is a shipping option for partners such as AT&T.

Describe the pros and cons of this service to the high-tech retailer as well as its consumers.

Source: Based on material in Sandy Smith, "Bring Concierge Service to Online Shopping," *STORES Magazine,* January 2016. Reprinted by permission.

pursues more global sales, and places cosmetics kiosks in shopping centers. Mary Kay hires community residents as salespeople and has a party atmosphere rather than a strict door-to-door approach; this requires networks of family, friends, and neighbors. And every major direct-selling firm has a Web site to supplement revenues.

Among the leading direct sellers are Avon and Mary Kay (cosmetics), Amway (household supplies), Tupperware (plastic containers), Shaklee (health products), Fuller Brush (small household products), and Kirby (vacuum cleaners). Some stores, such as J. C. Penney, also use direct selling. Penney's decorator consultants sell a complete line of furnishings, not available in its stores, to consumers in their homes (http://goo.gl/MkpvjI).

VENDING MACHINES

A **vending machine** is a cash- or card-operated retailing format that dispenses goods (such as beverages) and services (such as electronic arcade games). It eliminates use of sales personnel and allows 24-hour sales. Machines can be placed wherever convenient for consumers—inside or outside stores, in motel corridors, at train stations, or on street corners. See Figure 6-6.

Although there have been many attempts to "vend" clothing, magazines, and other general merchandise, the vast majority of the $65 billion in annual U.S. vending machine sales involve cold beverages, candy, snacks, and confections. The greatest sales at are public places such as service stations and at offices; colleges, universities, and elementary schools; factories; and hospitals and nursing homes.[13] Newspapers on street corners and sidewalks, various machines in hotels and motels, and candy machines in restaurants and at train stations are visible aspects of vending but account for a small percentage of U.S. vending machine sales. Leading vending machine operators are Aramark Corporation and Canteen.

The Canteen Corporation (www.canteen.com) has vending machines at thousands of client locations.

Items priced above $1.50 have not sold well; too many coins are required, and some vending machines do not have dollar bill changers. Consumers are reluctant to buy more expensive items that they cannot see displayed or have explained. However, their expanded access to and use of debit cards are having an impact on resolving the payment issue, and the video-kiosk type of vending machine lets people see product displays and get detailed information (and then place a credit or debit card order). Popular brands and standardized nonfood items are best suited to increasing sales via vending machines.

To improve productivity and customer relations, vending operators are being innovative. Popular products such as french fries are made fresh in vending machines. Machine malfunctions are reduced by applying electronic mechanisms to cash-handling controls. Microprocessors track consumer preferences, trace malfunctions, and record receipts. Some machines have voice synthesizers that are programmed to say "Thank you, come again" or "Your change is 25 cents."

Operators must still deal with theft, vandalism, items out of stock, above-average prices, and a perception that vending machines should be used only when a fill-in convenience item is needed.

FIGURE 6-6

Vending Machines: Popular around the Globe

Vending machines can popup everywhere, including this food-and-beverage vending machine in a gym.

Source: Jon Barlow/Pearson Education Ltd. Reprinted by permission.

Major regulatory issues confronting the industry concern cigarette sales and beverages sold at public schools. Prior to age restrictions on cigarettes, cigarette sales at vending machines made up 25 percent of vending machine sales. They now comprise 1 percent of vending machine sales. New regulations imposed starting in the 2014–15 school year by the Healthy, Hunger-Free Kids Act of 2010 limit sodium, sugar, and calories in all snack items sold at school vending machines.

ELECTRONIC RETAILING: THE EMERGENCE OF THE WORLD WIDE WEB

We are living through exciting changes from the days when retailing simply meant visiting a store, shopping from a printed catalog, greeting the Avon lady in one's home, or buying candy from a vending machine. Who would have thought a generation or so ago that a person would have his or her own personal computer with which to research ("surf" the Web) a stock, learn about a new product, search for bargains, save a trip to the store, and complain about customer service? These activities are taken for granted today. Let's look at the Web (or the World Wide Web, as it was initially called) from a retailing perspective, remembering that selling on the Web is a form of direct marketing.

Our discussion begins with defining two terms that may be confusing: The **Internet** is a global electronic superhighway of computer networks that use a common protocol and that are linked by telecommunications lines and satellites. It acts as a single, cooperative virtual network and is maintained by universities, governments, and businesses. The **World Wide Web (Web)** is one way to access information on the Internet, whereby people work with easy-to-use Web addresses (sites) and pages. Users see words, charts, pictures, and video, and hear audio—which turn their computers, smartphones, and tablets into interactive multimedia centers. People can easily move from site to site by pointing at the proper spot on the screen and clicking a mouse button, or by touching the screen. Browsing software, such as Google Chrome, Microsoft Edge, Mozilla Firefox, and Apple Safari—as well search engines such as Google, Bing, and Safari—facilitate "Web surfing."

Both the *Internet* and the *Web* convey the same theme: online interactive retailing. Because almost all online retailing is done via the Web, our discussion focuses on these topics: the role of the Web, the scope of Web retailing, characteristics of Web users, factors to consider in planning whether to have a Web site, and examples of Web retailers. Visit our blog (www.bermanevansretail .com) for lots of information on E-retailing.

The Role of the Web

From the vantage point of the retailer, the World Wide Web can serve manyone or more roles:

- ▷ Project a retail presence and enhance the retailer's image.
- ▷ Generate sales as the major source of revenue for an online retailer or as a complementary source of revenue for a store-based retailer.
- ▷ Reach geographically dispersed consumers, including foreign ones.
- ▷ Provide information to consumers about products carried, store locations, usage information, answers to common questions, customer loyalty programs, and so on.
- ▷ Promote new products and fully explain and demonstrate their features.
- ▷ Furnish customer service in the form of E-mail, hotlinks, and other communications.
- ▷ Be more "personal" with consumers by letting them point and click on topics they choose.
- ▷ Conduct a retail business in a cost-efficient manner.
- ▷ Obtain customer feedback and reviews, and encourage "conversations" via social media.
- ▷ Foster two-way communication through social media.
- ▷ Promote special offers and send coupons to Web customers.
- ▷ Indicate employment opportunities.
- ▷ Present information to potential investors, potential franchisees, and the media.

The role a retailer assigns to the Web depends on (1) whether its major goal is to communicate interactively with consumers, sell goods and services, or engage in both of these activities; (2) whether it is predominantly a traditional store-based retailer that wants to have a Web presence or a newer firm that wants to derive most or all of its sales from the Web; and (3) the level of resources the retailer wants to commit to site development and maintenance. Worldwide, there are millions of Web sites and 650,000+ retailers that each generate at least $1,000 in annual sales.

The Global Retail E-Commerce Index

As Table 6-3 shows, the Global Retail E-Commerce Index highlights investment opportunities around the world. The 2015 index gives the highest score to the United State due to its continued growth, improving economy, and higher levels of consumer confidence. China, which scored highest in 2014, dropped one position in 2015 due to weaker E-commerce growth and concerns over infrastructure investments and consumer spending. Brazil dropped in rank due to logistics issues, and Argentina declined due to government regulations. A co-author of the study noted that the future of E-commerce is not online, but in omnichannel offerings that link online with store based shopping.

What are the implications of Table 6-2?

Source: Hana Ben-Shabat, Parvaneh Nilforoushan, Christine Yuen, and Mike Moriarty **A.T.** Kearney, "Global Retail E-Commerce Keeps On Clicking: The 2015 Global Retail E-Commerce Index," https://goo.gl/RnKo5Q. Reprinted by permission.

Internet Retailer (www .internetretailer.com) tracks online retailing.

The Scope of Web Retailing

The potential for online retailing is enormous: As of mid-2016, there were 314 million Web users in North America, 604 million in Europe, 1.6 billion in Asia, 344 million in Latin America/Caribbean, 330 million in Africa, and 123 million in the Middle East.[14] Well over 90 percent of U.S. Web users have made at least one online purchase; and 80+ percent have made at least one online purchase in the last 6 months. A decade ago, U.S. shoppers generated 75 percent of worldwide online sales; the amount is now one-quarter and falling—as online shopping has grown around the globe. Today, Chinese online shoppers spend more than anywhere else.

Forrester, a leading Internet research firm, projects that U.S. shoppers will spend $530.1 billion online by 2020. This represents a 57 percent growth from online sales in 2015.[15] The high growth of the Web will not be the death knell of store-based retailing. Instead, it will constitute another choice for shoppers, like other forms of direct marketing. There is much higher sales growth for "clicks-and-mortar" Web retailing (multichannel and omnichannel retailing) than "bricks-and-mortar" stores (single-channel retailing) and "clicks-only" Web firms (single-channel retailing). Many shoppers seek a "seamless omnichannel experience," which enables them to buy online, and pick it up in a local store.

Despite economic challenges worldwide, global online revenues have increased steadily to $2.05 trillion in 2016 and are expected to reach $3.6 trillion in 2019.[16] U.S. online retail revenues were $340.61 billion[17] and mobile revenues were $89 billion in 2015.[18] U.S. retail E-commerce sales as a percent of total retail sales has been increasing since 2006, and has a far higher growth rate than overall retail sales.[19] Mobile commerce surged ahead of computer commerce in terms of time spent shopping for the first time in early 2015 (59 percent compared to 41 percent for computer); however, it still lags computers in share of online spending (15 percent to 85 percent).[20] Figure 6-7 indicates the percentage of global consumers who have ever made online purchases by selected product category. Table 6-3 shows the most attractive countries in the world for online retailing, as determined by A. T. Kearney's Global Retail E-Commerce Index.

FIGURE 6-7

Global Consumers' Online Retail Purchases, 2016 (selected product categories)

Source: Chart developed by the authors based on data from *Nielsen Global Connected Commerce Survey*, Q4, 2015 and authors' estimates.

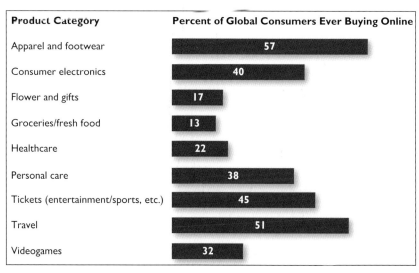

Product Category	Percent of Global Consumers Ever Buying Online
Apparel and footwear	57
Consumer electronics	40
Flower and gifts	17
Groceries/fresh food	13
Healthcare	22
Personal care	38
Tickets (entertainment/sports, etc.)	45
Travel	51
Videogames	32

TABLE 6-3 A. T. Kearney's 2015 Global Retail E-Commerce Index™

Rank	Change in rank	Country	Online market size (40%)	Consumer behavior (20%)	Growth potential (20%)	Infrastructure (20%)	Online market attractiveness score
1	+2	United States	100.0	83.2	22.0	91.5	**79.3**
2	−1	China	100.0	59.4	86.1	43.6	**77.8**
3	+1	United Kingdom	87.9	98.6	11.3	86.4	**74.4**
4	−2	Japan	77.6	87.8	10.1	97.7	**70.1**
5	+1	Germany	63.9	92.6	29.5	83.1	**66.6**
6	+1	France	51.9	89.5	21.0	82.1	**59.3**
7	−2	South Korea	44.9	98.4	11.3	95.0	**58.9**
8	+5	Russia	29.6	66.4	51.8	66.2	**48.7**
9	+15	Belgium	8.3	82.0	48.3	81.1	**45.6**
10	−1	Australia	11.9	80.8	28.6	84.8	**43.6**
11	−1	Canada	10.6	81.4	23.6	88.9	**43.1**
12	+2	Hong Kong	2.3	93.6	13.0	100.0	**42.2**
13	+6	Netherlands	8.9	98.8	8.1	84.6	**41.8**
14	−3	Singapore	1.3	89.4	15.7	100.0	**41.5**
15	+13	Denmark	8.1	100.0	15.1	75.5	**41.4**
16	0	Sweden	8.8	97.2	11.8	77.7	**40.9**
17	Not ranked	Mexico	10.0	53.3	58.6	68.0	**40.0**
18	Not ranked	Spain	13.2	73.1	20.2	80.1	**39.9**
19	+1	Chile	2.7	71.8	49.3	73.2	**39.9**
20	+6	Norway	8.2	99.4	5.6	76.3	**39.5**
21	−13	Brazil	19.6	57.4	28.0	72.4	**39.4**
22	−7	Italy	12.3	71.6	27.8	70.7	**38.9**
23	+8	Switzerland	7.1	89.6	7.4	82.5	**38.8**
24	−1	Venezuela	1.7	54.1	79.4	55.7	**38.5**
25	−4	Finland	6.4	98.3	3.8	77.3	**38.4**
26	−8	New Zealand	1.7	86.4	25.9	75.4	**38.2**
27	Not ranked	Austria	5.9	85.3	19.0	74.8	**38.1**
28	Not ranked	Saudi Arabia	1.1	46.6	67.3	74.6	**38.1**
29	−17	Argentina	5.7	70.3	43.9	64.3	**38.0**
30	−3	Ireland	4.9	74.4	27.6	74.1	**37.2**

Note: Scores are rounded. 100 is the highest and 0 is the lowest for each dimension.
Source: Hana Ben-Shabat, Parvaneh Nilforoushan, Christine Yuen, Mike Moriarty, and A. T. Kearney, "Global Retail E-Commerce Keeps on Clicking: The 2015 Global Retail E-Commerce Index," https://goo.gl/RnKo5Q. Reprinted by permission.

Despite the foregoing data, the Web accounts for only 8 percent or so of U.S. retail sales! It will not be the death knell of store-based retailing; rather, it will service as another choice for shoppers, like other forms of direct marketing. There is much higher sales growth for "clicks-and-mortar" Web retailing (multichannel and omnichannel retailing) than "bricks-and-mortar" stores (single-channel retailing) and "clicks-only" Web firms (single-channel retailing). Store-based retailers account for more than three-quarters of U.S. online sales.

Consumers may switch between retail formats—online or in-store based on their shopping orientation at each purchase occasion. "Order online, pick up in store" is a very profitable retail option. Retailers need to respond to consumers' changing habits. British retailer John Lewis used augmented reality to create an "endless showroom" to help its in-store customers browse through thousands of products in all varieties, sizes, colors, and fabrics—available in the store and online—and to get contextual information. This "endless showroom" enables the customers to make a more informed decision and buy faster. The future may mean that less stock is displayed in-store, but it is displayed with more flair as more space is available to create displays that make the consumer go Wow![21]

Characteristics of Web Users

Web users in the United States have these characteristics, which are highlighted in Figure 6-8:

▸ *Gender.* There are about as many males as females on the Web; however, females are somewhat more likely to shop online.

▸ *Age.* Those who are ages18 to 29 are most likely to use the Web; those who are age 65 and older are least likely.

▸ *Community type.* Suburban and urban residents are slightly more apt to use the Web than rural residents.

▸ *Income.* Nearly four-fifths of households with an annual income under $30,000 use the Web; in contrast, 99 percent of households with an annual income of at least $75,000 use the Web.

▸ *Education.* Those who have attended college are more likely to use the Internet than those who have not, especially those with a high school degree or less.

Following are some key factors for online shoppers regarding their continued patronage. (1) *Web site design/interaction:* All Web site elements (excluding customer service)—including navigation, information search, product and price offerings, product availability, order processing, and shipment tracking—impact the informational and experiential value customers seek. (2) *Reliability:* Customers want what they order based on the textual and visual description on the retailer'a Web site and delivery of the right product at the right price (billed correctly, etc.) in good condition within the promised time frame. (3) *Service:* Customer service expectations include insightful and supportive responses to inquiries and returns/complaints quickly during and after the sale. (4) *Privacy/security:* Shoppers want to know that their personal data are protected and to be assured that credit-card payments are secure during and after the sale.[22]

More Web users can be enticed to shop more often if they are assured of privacy, retailers are perceived as trustworthy, sites are easy to maneuver, there are strong money-back guarantees, they can return a product to a store, shipping costs are not hidden until the end of the purchase process, transactions are secure, they can speak with sales representatives, download time is fast, and the retailer has smartphone and tablet apps available.

Factors to Consider in Planning Whether to Have a Web Site

The Web offers many *advantages* for retailers. It is usually less costly to operate a Web site than a store. The potential marketplace is huge and dispersed, yet relatively easy to reach. Web sites can be quite exciting, due to their multimedia capabilities. People can visit Web sites at any time, and their visits can be as short or as long as they desire. Information can be targeted, so that, for example, a person visiting a toy retailer's Web site could click on the icon labeled "Educational Toys—ages 3 to 6." A customer database can be established and customer feedback obtained.

FIGURE 6-8

A Snapshot of U.S. Web Users

Sources: Charts developed by the authors based on data in "Demographics of Internet Users," www.pewinternet.org (Accessed August 1, 2016), and authors' estimates.

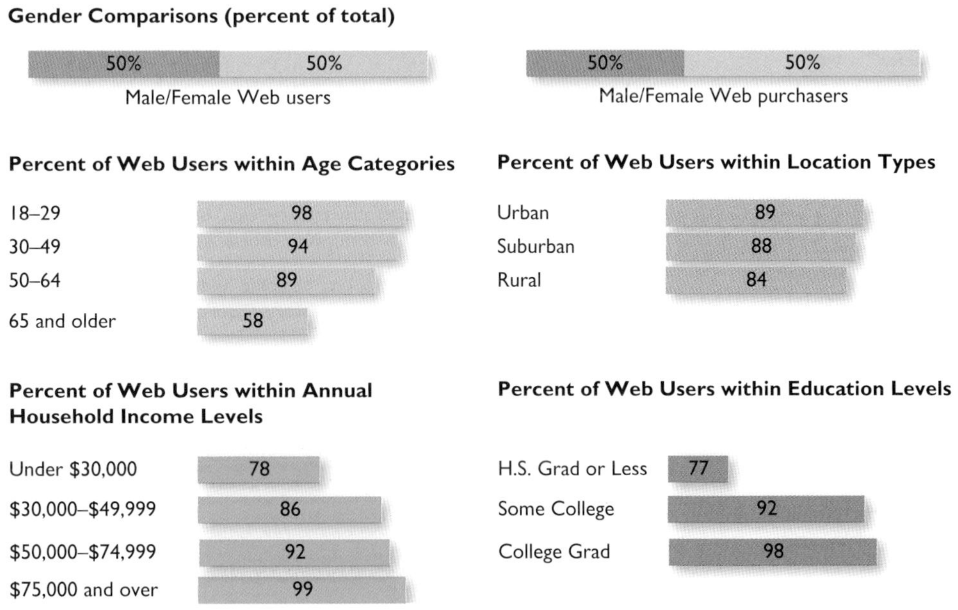

Gender Comparisons (percent of total)

50%	50%

Male/Female Web users

50%	50%

Male/Female Web purchasers

Percent of Web Users within Age Categories

18–29	98
30–49	94
50–64	89
65 and older	58

Percent of Web Users within Location Types

Urban	89
Suburban	88
Rural	84

Percent of Web Users within Annual Household Income Levels

Under $30,000	78
$30,000–$49,999	86
$50,000–$74,999	92
$75,000 and over	99

Percent of Web Users within Education Levels

H.S. Grad or Less	77
Some College	92
College Grad	98

The Web also has *disadvantages* for retailers. For example, if consumers do not know the Web address, it may be hard to find. For various reasons, some people are not yet willing to buy online. There is tremendous clutter with regard to the number of Web sites. Because Web surfers are easily bored, a Web site must be regularly updated to ensure repeat visits. The more multimedia features a Web site has, the slower it may be for people with weak Internet connections to access. Some firms have been overwhelmed with customer service requests and questions from E-mail. It may be hard to coordinate store and Web transactions. There are few standards or rules as to what may be portrayed at Web sites. Consumers expect online services to be free and are reluctant to pay for them.

There is a large gulf between full-scale, integrated Web selling and a basic "telling"—rather than "selling"—Web site. A "telling" site emphasizes information about the retailer and where its stores are located; little attention is devoted to facilitating transactions. A "selling" site includes the features of a telling site, but is also a dynamic transaction-oriented approach. Many retailers have responded by simply transferring their existing strategies to an online channel. Instead, they should follow the nine stages highlighted in Figure 6-9.

In addition, to achieve profitable growth in this challenging environment, A. T. Kearney offers "10 Steps to Reach Online Sales Excellence." These steps show how to shape and implement a strategy to address both the strengths and weaknesses of online retailing in an omnichannel setting. A. T. Kearney clients have seen revenue growth of 40 to 50 percent above the industry average when utilizing this approach:[23]

► *Shape your offering.* (1) Define your omnichannel strategy. (2) Shape your assortment to target your customer. (3) Optimize pricing strategies.
► *Showcase your assortment.* (4) Create interactive and responsive product presentations. (5) Customize the online user experience. (6) Promote your online channel.
► *Deliver customer value.* (7) Enhance order fulfillment. (8) Boost after-sales services.
► *Develop your organization.* (9) Analyze your business using big-data methods. (10) Shape your organization.

FIGURE 6-9

The Stages in Devising and Implementing an Online Retailing Strategy

Sources: Figure developed by the authors based on tips at "Six Things to Consider If You Are New to ECommerce," www .networksolutions.com (Accessed August 1, 2016); "10 Factors to Consider When Selling on the Web," www.powerhomebiz.com (accessed on August 1, 2016); Diane Buzzeo, "Retail Online Integration: Four Steps Every Online Retailer Can Take Right Now to Drive Sales," www.retailonlineintegration .com (accessed June 20, 2011); and The SnapRetail BlogOnline: Marketing Strategy, Tactics, and Tips for Small Businesses, http://www.snapretail.com/ blog (Accessed August 1, 2016).

1. Be sure there is a customer base interested in you having an online retail business: Who will shop online? Why? What do they want in online shopping?

2. Two options when starting are (a) becoming a bricks-and-clicks retailer or (b) beginning as an online retailer. *Note:* The first option has a customer following and name recognition—at least among its store-based customers.

3. Select a distinctive and easy-to-remember Web address (URL). This may be difficult given that many addresses have already been taken. So be creative.

4. Design the Web site using do-it-yourself software—or have the site professionally designed by a specialist—and prepare content to appear on the site. The design must encourage people to spend time at the Web site and to make purchases. Make the site easy to navigate and have your competitive advantages stand out. Use photos with good resolution. Have highly visible "about us," "products," "buy," "add to cart," and "shipping" buttons. Regularly update content.

5. Make shopping easy and secure. Offer multiple payment options, with PayPal the simplest format for smaller retailers (it processes leading credit/debit cards). Have an SSL (secure sockets layer) certificate and display it to allay privacy fears. Describe the policies for cancellations, returns, and shipping. Send E-mails confirming orders and let customers track their orders.

6. Have logistics in place for storing, shipping, and returning merchandise. Have shippers lined up. Monitor order fulfillment and inventory. Coordinate store and online sales, if engaged in both.

7. Promote the Web site as much as possible—online and offline. Make sure the site is search engine optimized (SEO) for Google, Bing, etc., with regard to key words, headings, and so forth. Use opt-in E-mail to stay in touch with customers.

8. After the online business is running well, become more engaged with social media. This presents many opportunities and provides ongoing customer feedback.

9. Measure Web site performance and revise the strategy as needed. If shopping cart abandonment (whereby the shopper stops before paying) is high, the causes must be remedied.

Sign up for eMarketer's free daily newsletter with regular summaries of E-retailing news (www.emarketer.com/Newsletter.aspx).

Web retailers should carefully consider these recommendations, which build on the preceding list. They are compiled from several industry experts:

- Develop (or exploit) a well-known, trustworthy retailer name.
- Tailor the product assortment for Web shoppers, and keep freshening the offerings.
- With download speed in mind, provide pictures and ample product information.
- Enable shoppers to make as few clicks as possible to get information and place orders.
- Provide the best possible search engine at the firm's Web site.
- Capitalize on information about customers and relationships.
- Integrate online and offline businesses, and look for partnering opportunities.
- With permission, save customer data to make future shopping trips easier.
- Indicate shipping fees upfront and be clear about delivery options.
- Do not promote items that are out of stock; and let shoppers know immediately if items will not be shipped for a few days.
- Offer online order tracking.
- Use a secure order entry system for shoppers.
- Prominently state the firm's return and privacy policies.

See the checklist in Figure 6-10.

A firm cannot just put up a site and wait for consumers to visit it in droves and then expect them to happily come back. In many cases: (1) It is still difficult for people to find exactly what they are looking for. (2) The inability of the digital interface to convey spatial, haptic (sense of touch), and olfactory cues is a limitation if purchasing products that have experiential attributes. Some large retailers provide virtual online experiences in the form of 3D images and videos—applications that render augmented reality depictions of products; however, this technology is in its early stage of development and needs to be user-friendly. (3) Customer service may be lacking. (4) Friction and barriers between Web sites and their store operations may occur: "Send someone a gift from CompanyA.com and the recipient may be surprised to find it can't be returned or exchanged

FIGURE 6-10

A Checklist of Retailer Decisions in Utilizing the Web

✓ What are the company's Web goals? At what point is it expected that the site will be profitable?
✓ What budget will be allocated to developing and maintaining a Web site?
✓ Who will develop and maintain the Web site—the retailer itself or an outside specialist?
✓ Should the firm set up an independent Web site for itself or should it be part of a "cybermall"?
✓ What features will the Web site have? What level of customer service will be offered?
✓ What information will the Web site provide?
✓ How will the goods and services assortment differ at the Web site from the firm's store?
✓ Will the Web site offer benefits not available elsewhere?
✓ Will prices reflect a good value for the consumer?
✓ How fast will the user be able to download the text and images from the Web site, and point and click from screen to screen?
✓ How often will Web site content be changed?
✓ What staff will handle Web inquiries and transactions?
✓ How fast will turnaround time be for Web inquiries and transactions?
✓ How will the firm coordinate store and Web transactions and customer interactions?
✓ What will be done to avoid crashes and slow site features during peak shopping hours and seasons?
✓ How will online orders be processed?
✓ How easy will it be for shoppers to enter and complete orders?
✓ What online payment methods will be accepted?
✓ What search engines (such as Yahoo!) will list the retailer's Web site?
✓ How will the site be promoted: (a) on the Web and (b) by the company?
✓ How will Web data be stored and arranged? How will all of the firm's information systems be integrated?
✓ How will Web success be measured?
✓ How will the firm determine which Web shoppers are new customers and which are customers who would otherwise visit a company store?
✓ How will the firm ensure secure (encrypted) transactions?
✓ How will consumer privacy concerns be handled?
✓ How will returns and customer complaints be handled?

at a Company A store." (5) Privacy policies may not be consumer-oriented. Many online retailers are aggressive in their use of ad-retargeting technology, in which a customer who orders from a Web site, clicks on an E-mail newsletter, fills out a survey, or merely browses the Web site finds his or her E-mail box stuffed with junk mail.[24]

Mobile Apps Enabling Online Retailing

The retail industry has been an early adopter of mobile technology; certainly many retailers have made mobile applications central to their strategies, operations, and customer communications. Almost 30 percent of transactions at U.S. online retailers and travel firms are driven by mobile apps.[25] Astute retailers recognize that their mobile app strategy is more than transferring Web site features and functions to the mobile platform; one in five mobile apps are tried once and never opened again.

Any retail mobile app should have the following basic elements: (1) *An efficient customer login* that provides clear reasons for requiring customers to register, collecting minimal information to personalize customer experiences, and assuring protection of the information. (2) *An account management system* that allows customers to check and manage their accounts and check rewards information quickly, and that provides links to the mobile site for more complex information requests. (3) *Notifications* that engage customers and nurture loyalty; 140-character messaging with personalized data, offers, or reward updates serve as reminders to click on the app and connect with the retailer. (4) *A "browse products" service* that allows customers to browse products and check inventory online; omnichannel retailers should enable geotargeting so users selecting store pickup automatically default to a local store's on-hand inventory. (5) *A native shopping cart and payment system* that allows customers to buy from the mobile app and close the deal, instead of bouncing them to the mobile Web site, which can add delays and increase purchase abandonment. (6) *A store locator* that gives targeted information about the local store address (connected to a mobile phone mapping app), telephone numbers, and hours.[26]

Examples of Web Retailing in Action

Amazon.com (www.amazon.com) is one of the largest retailers of any type by revenue; it is the largest pure Web retailer in the world, with revenues exceeding $107 billion in 2015, and has tens of millions of customers who buy from the firm each year.[27] Amazon.com has three distinct lines: Business Prime, Marketplace, and Amazon Web Services (AWS). They differ in their customer base: AWS serves enterprise customers, Marketplace serves third-party retailers, and Prime serves the best retail customers.

Amazon.com started in 1995 as just an online bookseller. Its core business has greatly evolved. Amazon Prime is subscription-based—a "physical-digital hybrid" including not just free 2-day delivery of over 30 million items in 35 cities around the world but it also offers music, photo storage, the Kindle Owners' Lending Library, and streaming films and TV shows. For example, Prime Video offers exclusive, original, Emmy-award winning shows. Amazon characterizes Prime Video as "feeding the Prime flywheel." Amazon customers who watch Prime Video are more likely to convert from a free trial to a paid membership, and more likely to renew their annual subscriptions. In 2015, Amazon initiated Prime Day, when Prime members can buy select products at discounted price. It is also an effective way to increase Prime customer acquisition and retention.

Through the Amazon Marketplace, more than 70,000 third-party sellers offer their products on Amazon (for a listing fee), increasing the assortment variety for Amazon customers and leveraging Amazon's logistics capability for product delivery. Amazon.com has also produced cutting-edge, popular products—Kindle (E-book readers); Firestick and Fire-TV (streaming video and music from Amazon, Netflix, YouTube, and others); Dash (one-touch product ordering from Amazon; and Echo (a voice-enabled wireless speaker that operates as a home-automation hub).[28]

At the opposite end of the spectrum from Amazon.com is the specialty business of Seamless .com (www.seamless.com). Seamless offers small and large businesses an organized and cost-cutting way to order food for delivery and pick up from more than 12,000 restaurants and over 80 cuisine types. It provides interactive tools for the entire process—consolidated ordering and invoicing, the monitoring of food and catering expenses, and expense documentation that clients can use for tax purposes. Seamless is the nation's largest online and mobile food ordering company with more than one million members. It has made ordering food fast and easy for individual employees and business administrators by featuring interactive menus, ratings and reviews, and

FIGURE 6-11

CarMax: A Popular Site for Auto Shoppers

Source: Carmax. Reprinted by permission.

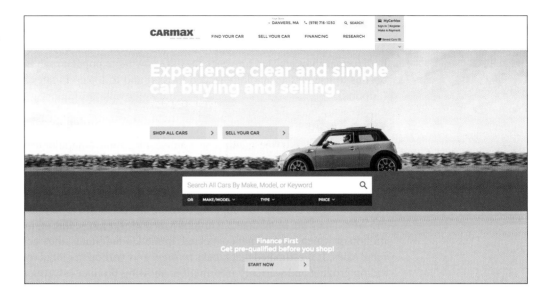

new restaurants. Office administrators can set ordering "rules" based on expense account allowances for each employee or department on computers or using their mobile applications on multiple platforms. Seamless serves New York; Washington, D.C.; Boston; Chicago; San Francisco; Los Angeles; Philadelphia; London; and other U.S. cities.[29]

CarMax (www.carmax.com), as highlighted in Figure 6-11, is a leading bricks-and-clicks retailer that sells new and used cars and buys used cars. It has 150 retail outlets. On the Web site, shoppers can find the cars with the specific features that they want to buy, find out the exact prices of those cars (CarMax has no-haggle pricing), find the location of the nearest dealers, and schedule appointments to see the value of used cars that customers want to sell to Carmax.[30]

Dollar Tree (www.dollartree.com), as depicted in Figure 6-12, is another bricks-and-clicks retailer with a unique online strategy. It has one of the few sites where customers can shop for items priced at $1—the amount of every Dollar Tree product. On the Web site, customers can find information on Dollar Tree's Value Seekers Club, access ads and catalogs, read a company blog, shop, and more. Because of its low-price policy, customers can order online and pick up in the store for no delivery fee, but they must pay a delivery fee if they want items shipped to them.

Other interesting Web retailing illustrations include eBay (www.ebay.com), Priceline.com (www.priceline.com), and uBid.com (www.ubid.com), all of which offer online auctions. Even the nonprofit Goodwill has an auction Web site (www.shopgoodwill.com) to sell donated items.

FIGURE 6-12

Dollar Tree: Consumer Oriented Shopping Options

In addition to its physical stores, Dollar Tree has a popular Web site where consumers can shop online. Purchases can be picked up in a nearby store or shipped via UPS.

Source: Dollar Tree. Reprinted by permission.

OTHER NONTRADITIONAL FORMS OF RETAILING

Two other nontraditional institutions merit discussion: video kiosks and airport retailing. Although both formats have existed for years, they are now more popular than ever. They appeal to retailers' desires to use new technology (video kiosks) and to locate in sites with high pedestrian traffic (airports).

Video Kiosks

The **video kiosk** is a freestanding, interactive, electronic computer terminal that displays products and related information on a video screen. It often has a touch screen for consumers to make selections. Retail store kiosks locate items in the store and enhance customer service. They also let consumers place orders, complete transactions (typically with a credit card), cross-sell products, sell tickets, and arrange for shipping. Kiosks can be linked to retailers' computer networks or to the Web. There are more than 2.5 million video kiosks in use throughout the world, more than one million of which are Internet connected. In the United States, they generate $20 billion in annual retail sales. It is estimated that kiosks *influence* $1 trillion in global retail sales annually—by providing product and warranty information, showing product assortments, displaying out-of-stock products, and listing products by price. Transactions at self-service kiosks are growing by more than 7 percent in North America, which accounts for the majority of kiosk sales, followed by the Pacific Rim, Europe, and the rest of the world.[31]

The Kiosk Industry Association (http://kioskindustry.org) tracks trends involving video kiosks.

How exactly do video kiosks work? They are self-contained, computer-style terminals through which self-service shoppers can access information and facilitate transactions. Video kiosks can enable self–check-ins at airports, demonstrate products in stores, dispense tickets, offer DVD rentals, take and transmit meal orders, and a whole lot more. Kiosk systems use hardware designs that can include numerous peripherals, such as touch screens, printers, and barcode and QR code scanners. Consumers can use on-screen keyboards for data entry, along with card readers and barcode scanners. A thermal printer is the most common output device. Interactive kiosks may have a customized, hardened enclosure or be a standard PC that has been repurposed (for example, IBM's Anyplace Kiosk). Almost all video kiosks are interactive.[32]

Video kiosks can be placed almost anywhere (from a store aisle to the lobby of a college dormitory to a hotel lobby), require few employees, and are an entertaining and easy way to shop. Many shopping centers and individual stores are putting their space to better, more profitable use by setting up video kiosks in previously underutilized areas. These kiosks carry everything from gift certificates to concert tickets to airline tickets. For example, Staples has launched omnichannel stores that feature endless-aisle kiosks and consultation areas for small-business customers—or what the company calls "the future of retail." Staples said the stores allow it to leverage its real-estate and digital capabilities. The pilot stores, in Norwood, Massachusetts, and Dover, Delaware, also serve as test labs for new goods and services. The move is part of an effort to reduce the size of its stores by 15 percent.[33]

The average hardware cost to a retailer per video kiosk is several thousand dollars plus ongoing content development and kiosk maintenance. Hardware prices range from under $500 per kiosk to $10,000 to $15,000 or more per kiosk, depending on its functions—the more features, the higher the price.[34]

Airport Retailing

In the past, the leading airport retailers were fast-food outlets, tiny gift stores, and newspaper/magazine stands. Today, airports are a major mecca of retailing. At virtually every large airport, as well as at many medium ones, there are full-blown shopping areas. And most small airports have at least a fast-food retailer and vending machines for newspapers, candy, and so forth.

The potential retail market is huge. Worldwide, more than 1,200 commercial airports handle nearly 5 billion passengers each year—with North America accounting for one-third of global passenger traffic. U.S. airports alone fly millions of passengers each day and employ nearly 2 million people (who often buy something for their personal use at the airport). There are more than 400 primary commercial U.S. airports. Overall, airport retailing generates $45 billion in global sales annually, and many airports generate annual retail revenues of at least $50 million.[35] Retail sales at duty-free shops throughout the world are forecast to reach $74 billion in 2019. The largest categories of goods sold are personal care and drinks.[36] See Figure 6-13.

FIGURE 6-13
Airport Retailing: Popular Worldwide

Source: Gareth Dewar/ Pearson Education Ltd. Reprinted by permission.

New York's Kennedy Airport (http://www.ifly. com/john-f-kennedy -international-airport/shops- stores) typifies the retailing environment at the world's major airports.

Airline-related sales at most major airports account for 40 percent of revenue; the remaining 60 percent is derived from other sources (predominantly retail sales). Most airport hubs are nearing full-flight utilization; the only way they can grow is by increasing retail income. Airports in the Middle East and Singapore are designed to be luxury retail and family experience destinations. The Ark at New York's Kennedy Airport offers luxury accommodations for pets.[37] Airport stores target teenagers, women, and bargain shoppers; retailers typically pay 10 percent more rent for the airport shopping area. Domestic leisure travelers spend more than an hour, on average, waiting in airports after passing security and are likely to buy food and beverages and to shop than those who spend less time at the airport. Sales at airports are expected to increase by 73 percent from 2013 to 2019.[38]

Some of the distinctive features of airport retailing are:

▷ There is a large group of prospective shoppers. In an average year, a big airport may have 20 million or more people passing through its concourses. In contrast, a typical regional shopping mall attracts 5 million to 6 million annual visits.
▷ Air travelers are a temporarily captive audience at the airport who are looking to fill their waiting time, which could be up to several hours. They tend to have above-average incomes.
▷ Sales per square foot of retail space are much higher than at regional malls. Rent is about 20 to 30 percent higher per square foot for airport retailers.
▷ Airport stores are smaller, carry fewer items, and have higher prices than traditional stores.
▷ Replenishing merchandise and stocking shelves may be difficult at airport stores because they are physically removed from delivery areas and space is limited.
▷ The sales of gift items and forgotten travel items, from travelers not having the time to shop elsewhere, are excellent. Brookstone, which sells garment bags and travel clocks at airport shops, calls these products "'I forgot'" merchandise.
▷ Passengers are at airports at all times of the day. Thus, longer store hours are possible.
▷ International travelers are often interested in duty-free shopping.
▷ There is much tighter security at airports than before, which has had a dampening effect on some shopping.

Chapter Summary

1. *To contrast single-channel, multichannel, and omnichannel retailing.* A new retailer often relies on single-channel retailing, whereby it sells to consumers through one retail format. As the firm grows, it may turn to multichannel retailing and sell to consumers through multiple retail formats. This allows the firm to reach different customers, share costs among various formats, and diversify its supplier base. To optimize efficiency and enhance customer experiences, the best retailers turn to omnichannel retailing.

2. *To look at the characteristics of the three major retail institutions involved with nonstore-based strategy mixes—direct marketing, direct selling, and vending machines—with an emphasis on direct marketing.* Firms employ nonstore retailing to reach customers and complete transactions. Nonstore retailing encompasses direct marketing, direct selling, and vending machines.

In direct marketing, a consumer is exposed to goods or services through a nonpersonal medium and orders by mail, phone, fax, or computer. Annual U.S. retail sales from direct marketing (including the Web) exceed $475 billion. Direct marketers fall into two categories: general and specialty. Among the strengths of direct marketing are its reduced operating costs, large geographic coverage, customer convenience, and targeted segments. Among the weaknesses are a shopper's inability to examine items before purchase, printing and mailing costs, the low response rate, and marketplace clutter. Under the "30-day rule," there are legal requirements that a firm must follow regarding shipping speed. The long-run prospects for direct marketing are strong due to consumer interest in reduced shopping time, 24-hour ordering, the sales of well-known brands, improvements in operating efficiency, and technology.

The key to direct marketing is the customer database, with database retailing being a way to collect, store, and use relevant data. Several trends are vital to direct marketers: consumer attitudes and activities, changing lifestyles, more competition, the use of multichannel and omnichannel retailing, the roles for catalogs and TV, technology advances, and growth in global direct marketing. Specialogs and infomercials are used more by direct marketers.

A direct marketing plan has eight stages: business definition, generating customers, media selection, presenting the message, customer contact, customer response, order fulfillment, and measuring results and maintaining the database. Firms must consider that many people dislike shopping this way, feel overwhelmed by the amount of direct mail, and are concerned about privacy.

Direct selling includes personal contact with consumers in their homes (and other nonstore sites) and seller phone calls. It yields $35 billion in annual U.S. retail sales, covering many goods and services. The strategy mix stresses convenience, a personal touch, demonstrations, and relaxed consumers. U.S. sales are not going up much due to the rise in working women, the labor intensity of the business, sales force turnover, government rules, and the poor image of some firms.

A vending machine uses coin- and card-operated dispensing of goods and services. It eliminates salespeople, allows 24-hour sales, and may be put almost anywhere. Beverages and food represent the vast majority of the $65 billion in annual U.S. vending revenues. Efforts in other product categories have met with customer resistance, and items priced above $1.50 have not done well.

3. *To explore the emergence of electronic retailing through the Web.* The Internet is a global electronic superhighway that acts as a single, cooperative virtual network.

The World Wide Web (the Web) is a way to access information on the Internet, whereby people turn computers into interactive multimedia centers. The Web can serve various retailer purposes, from projecting an image to presenting information to investors. The purpose chosen depends on the goals and focus. There is a great contrast between store retailing and Web retailing.

The growth of Web-based retailing has been enormous. Annual U.S. revenues from retailing on the Web are expected to reach $530 billion in 2020. Nonetheless, the Web still garners a small percentage of total U.S. retail sales.

Females spend somewhat more time shopping on the Web than males do. Internet usage declines by age group and increases by income and education level. Shoppers are attracted by Web site design, reliability, customer service, and security. Nonshoppers worry about the trustworthiness of online firms, want to see and handle products first, and do not like shipping cost surprises.

The Web offers these positive features for retailers: It can be inexpensive to have a Web site. The potential marketplace is huge and dispersed, yet easy to reach. Sites can be quite exciting. People can visit a site at any time. Information can be targeted. A customer database can be established and customer feedback obtained. Yet, if consumers do not know a firm's Web address, it may be hard to find. Many people will not buy online. There is clutter with regard to the number of retail sites. Because Web surfers are easily bored, a firm must regularly update its site to ensure repeat visits. The more multimedia features a site has, the slower it may be to access. Some firms have been deluged with customer service requests. Improvements are needed to coordinate store and Web transactions. There are few standards or rules as to what may be portrayed at Web sites. Consumers expect online services to be free and are reluctant to pay for them.

A well-developed Web strategy would move through nine stages, from determining the customer base to measuring performance. A systematic approach is vital.

4. *To discuss two other nontraditional forms of retailing: video kiosks and airport retailing.* The video kiosk is a freestanding, interactive computer terminal that displays products and other information on a video screen; it often has a touch screen for people to make selections. Although some kiosks are in stores to upgrade customer service, others let consumers place orders, complete transactions, and arrange shipping. Kiosks can be put almost anywhere, require few personnel, and are an entertaining and easy way for people to shop. They yield $20 billion in annual U.S. revenues.

Due to the huge size of the air travel marketplace, airports are popular as retail shopping areas. Travelers (and workers) are temporarily captive at the airport, often with a lot of time to fill. Sales per square foot, as well as rent, are high. Gift items and "'I forgot' merchandise" sell especially well. Globally, annual retail revenues are $45 billion at airports.

Key Terms

single-channel retailing (p. 152)
multichannel retailing (p. 152)
omnichannel retailing (p. 152)
nonstore retailing (p. 153)
direct marketing (p. 154)

database retailing (p. 156)
specialog (p. 157)
infomercial (p. 158)
direct selling (p. 161)
vending machine (p. 163)

Internet (p. 164)
World Wide Web (Web) (p. 164)
video kiosk (p. 172)

Questions for Discussion

1. Contrast omnichannel and multichannel retailing. What do you think are the advantages of each?
2. Do you think that nonstore retailing is gaining traction in your own country? Explain your answer.
3. Direct marketing may be advantageous to sellers, but what are the key advantages of this type of relationship for consumers? Why might they choose it?
4. List all of the variations and versions of direct marketing.
5. What is database retailing, and how does it work? Explain how a retailer makes use of the database.
6. Why is reliability one of the four major concerns for retailers' Web sites?
7. Differentiate between direct selling and direct marketing. What are the strengths and weaknesses of each?
8. Select a product not heavily sold through vending machines, and present a brief plan for doing so.
9. From a consumer's perspective, what are the advantages and disadvantages of the Web?
10. From a retailer's perspective, what are the advantages and disadvantages of having a Web site?
11. What must retailers do to improve customer service on their online stores?
12. What future role do you see for video kiosks? Why?

Web-Based Exercise

Visit the "Charts & Data" section of Internet Retailer's Web site (www.internetretailer.com) by clicking on the tab. Describe four key current facts that a retailer could learn from this section of the site.

APPENDIX Omnichannel Retailing*

As noted at the beginning of this chapter, a retail firm relies on single-channel retailing if it sells to consumers through one format such as the Web or a store. In multichannel retailing, a firm has separate channels such as a store and the Web. In a traditional multichannel retail environment, consumers may not be able to view store inventories online, can be charged different prices in each channel, cannot arrange for store pickup on a Web order, or return Web-ordered purchases to a local store. With multichannel retailing, the Web site and store customer databases are separate.

In contrast, omnichannel retailing delivers a consistent, uninterrupted, and seamless experience regardless of channel or devices. Omnichannel retailing assumes customers go through the shopping journey very differently by using different combinations of mobile, PC, tablet, and store activities. As an example, product discovery can be Web or social media-based, consumers can receive product information via the Web or through in-store observation, and consumers can buy an item via a mobile device but seek to pick it up and return it to a store (if unhappy). This appendix focuses on omnichannel retailing because so many firms are combining store and nonstore retailing—as well as using multiple store formats.

Planning and maintaining a well-integrated omnichannel strategy is not easy. At a minimum, it requires setting up an infrastructure that can effectively link multiple channels. A retailer that accepts a Web purchase for exchange at a retail store needs an information system to verify the purchase, the price paid, the payment method, and the transaction date. That firm also needs a mechanism for delivering goods regardless of which channel is used by a customer to purchase.

A December 2015 study of North American retailers sheds some light on the progress these firms have made in adopting omnichannel strategies. When asked about the effectiveness of their "buy online, pickup in the store" strategy, only 18 percent of respondents stated that this was available and working, whereas 24 percent stated that it was available but needed improvement. Similarly, 16 percent of the respondents reported that returns were accepted across channels, with 46 percent of respondents stating that this service was available but needed improvement.[1]

Home Depot, which annually generates billions of dollars in online sales, is a retailer that has been increasing its omnichannel presence. "We not only offered more spring season products online, but also leveraged digital media channels to highlight local in-store assortments," CEO Craig Menear told investors and analysts on a conference call, referring to Home Depot's mobile app's in-store product location capabilities.[2]

These are some strategic and operational issues for omnichannel retailers to address:

▶ What omnichannel cross-selling opportunities exist? A firm could list its Web site on business cards, store invoices, and shopping bags. It could also list the nearest store locations when a consumer inputs a ZIP code at the Web site.
▶ How should the product assortment/variety strategy be adapted to each channel? How much merchandise overlap should exist across channels?
▶ How well can a distribution center handle direct-to-store and direct-to-consumer shipping?
▶ Should prices be consistent across channels (except for shipping and handling, as well as closeouts)?
▶ How can a consistent image be devised and sustained across all channels?
▶ What is the role of each channel? Some consumers prefer to search the Web to determine pricing and product information, and then they purchase in a store due to their desire to see the product, try it on, and gain the immediacy that accompanies an in-store transaction.
▶ What are the best opportunities for leveraging a firm's assets with an omnichannel strategy? Many catalog retailers have logistics systems that can be easily adapted to Web-based sales.
▶ Do relationships with current suppliers prevent the firm from expanding into new channels?

---

* The material in this appendix is updated and adapted by the authors from Barry Berman and Shawn Thelen, "A Guide to Developing and Managing a Well-Integrated Multichannel Retail Strategy," *International Journal of Retail & Distribution Management*, 32(3), 2004, pp. 147–156. Used by permission of Barry Berman and Shawn Thelen.

Advantages of Omnichannel Retail Strategies

There are several advantages to a retailer's enacting an omnichannel approach, including the selection of specific channels based on their unique strengths, opportunities to leverage assets, and opportunities for increased sales and profits by appealing to omnichannel shoppers.

Selecting Among Channels Based on Their Unique Strengths

A retailer with an omnichannel strategy can use the most appropriate channels to sell particular goods or services or to reach different target markets. Because each channel has a unique combination of strengths, an omnichannel retailer has the best opportunities to fulfill its customers' shopping desires.

Store-based shopping enables customers to see an item, feel it, smell it (e.g., candles or perfumes), try it out, and then pick it up and take it home on the same shopping trip without incurring shipping and handling costs. Catalogs offer high visual impact, a high-quality image, and portability (they can be taken anywhere by the shopper). The Web offers high-quality video and audio capabilities, an interactive format, a personalized customer interface, virtually unlimited space, the ability for a customer to verify in-stock position and order status, and, in some cases, tax-free shopping. Mobile marketing devices are always on, always connected, and always with the customer; they can be easily personalized and can generate location-sensitive offers.[3]

In-store kiosks are helpful for shoppers not having Web access. They can lead to less inventory in the store (and reduce the need to stock low-turnover items in each store), can facilitate self-service by providing information, and can offer high video/audio quality.

To plan an appropriate channel mix and the role of each channel, retailers must recognize how different channels complement one another. Best Buy (www.bestbuy.com), Costco (www.costco .com), Staples (www.staples.com), Home Depot (www.homedepot.com), and Walmart (www .walmart.com) are just a few of the retailers that have a broader selection of items on the Web to encourage consumers to shop online.

Opportunities to Leverage Assets

Omnichannel retailing presents opportunities for firms to leverage both tangible and intangible assets. A store-based retailer can leverage tangible assets by using excess capacity in its warehouse to service catalog or Web sales; that same firm can leverage its well-known brand name (an intangible asset) by selling online in geographic areas where it has no stores. Store-based retailers can also arrange to ship goods ordered online or through mobile devices from closely located stores rather than a centralized distribution center.

Opportunities for Increased Sales and Profits by Appealing to Omnichannel Shoppers

Omnichannel consumers, on average, spend more and have a higher lifetime value to retailers than single-channel consumers. For example, Macy's found that its omnichannel customers are eight times as valuable as customers who confine their shopping experience to a single channel. Similarly, Target found that its omnichannel customers are its most valuable, as they spend three times more as those who shop in a single channel.[4]

Developing a Well-Integrated Omnichannel Strategy

A well-integrated omnichannel strategy requires linkages among all the channels. Customers should be able to easily make the transition from looking up products on the Web or in a catalog to picking up the products in a retail store. If these linkages are not properly established, sales can be lost. There should be a good deal of commonality in the description and appearance of each item regardless of channel. For example, in-store personnel should be able to verify a Web or catalog purchase and arrange for returns or exchanges.

Characteristics common to superior omnichannel strategies include the following: integrated promotions across channels; product consistency across channels; an integrated information system that shares customer, pricing, and inventory data across multiple channels; a store pickup process for items purchased on the Web or through a catalog; and the search for omnichannel opportunities with appropriate partners.

Integrating Promotions across Channels

Cross-promotion enables consumers to use each promotional forum in its best light. Following is a list of some cross-promotion tactics:

▶ Include the Web site address on shopping bags, in catalogs, and in newspaper ads.
▶ Provide in-store kiosks so customers can order out-of-stock merchandise without a shipping fee.
▶ Include store addresses, phone numbers, hours, and directions on the Web site and in catalogs.
▶ Make it possible for customers to shop for items on the Web using the catalog order numbers.
▶ Distribute store coupons by direct mail, online. and mobile sources; offer catalogs in stores and at the Web site.
▶ Encourage in-store shoppers to use their smartphones to scan barcodes and get more product information.
▶ Target single-channel customers with promotions from other channels.
▶ Send store-based shoppers targeted E-mails on their mobile device (on an opt-in basis) for selected goods and services.
▶ Have a strong social media presence.

Ensuring Product Consistency across Channels

Too little product overlap across channels may result in an inconsistent image. However, too much overlap may result in a loss of sales opportunities. Omnichannel retailers often use the Web to offer very specialized merchandise that cannot be profitably offered in stores. This maximizes store space while, at the same time, fulfills specialized needs of niche market segments.

Having an Information System That Effectively Shares Data across Channels

To best manage an omnichannel system, a retailer needs an information system that shares customer, pricing, and inventory information across channels:

▶ After a customer creates an online bridal registry account at Crate & Barrel, he or she can visit any of the chain's stores and seamlessly synchronize the store's scanners with their online accounts. This makes it easy for customers to add new items to their registry while in the store. Customers can also use an in-store computer to modify their product choices.[5]
▶ Rebecca Minkoff—a chain specializing in accessible luxury handbags, accessories, footwear, and apparel—utilizes apps to create user profiles that link what customers view online with what the customers try on and purchase in stores.[6]
▶ Macy's recently combined its online and offline marketing operations to create one inventory system across channels. This system displays sales data, stock-on-hand, and on-order data.[7]

Enacting a Store-Pickup Process for Items Purchased on the Web or through a Catalog

In-store pickup requires that a retailer's inventory database be integrated and that the firm has a logistics infrastructure that can select and route merchandise to customers. Increasingly, shoppers are ordering big-ticket items such as digital cameras, computers, and appliances online but picking them up at nearby stores. Consumers favor this approach to avoid shipping and handling charges, to reduce their having to navigate through a big-box store, and to avoid wasting time looking for items that may be out of stock.

Store pickup often enables shoppers to get items on the same day they make a purchase. Many customers also favor in-store pickup so that they can more easily return goods that do not meet their expectations.

Searching for Omnichannel Opportunities with Appropriate Partners

The retailer needs to understand that in almost all cases an omnichannel strategy requires added resources and competencies that are significantly greater than those demanded by a single-channel strategy. Some retailers may conclude that they do not have these competencies or resources; others look for strategic partnerships with firms having complementary resources.

Special Challenges

An omnichannel strategy is not right for every retailer. Not all retailers possess the financial and managerial resources to do pursue omnichannel opportunities. A big challenge for many retailers, particularly small- to middle-size ones, is the consolidation of their disparate retail management systems into one customer-focused system. A 2015 study of retail CEOs found that 75 percent of the respondents did not restructure operations to provide customers with seamless shopping.[8]

Many of today's leading retailers began with one channel—typically bricks-and-mortar—and then added phone sales, Web sales, and mobile sales. As a result, these retailers usually devised separate information systems for each channel. Thus, each channel had a distinct information system with its own set of customer, product, sales, and inventory data. With a move to an omnichannel strategy, these retailers' overall information centers had to be unified. In this way, they could determine whether a large Web site or catalog user base exists within the trading area of a proposed retail location.

Omnichannel retailers need to maintain the same branding identity for their products across diverse channels. Graphic designers need to establish specific guidelines and templates so that type fonts, colors, and key design elements are shared across channels. To complicate matters, products often look different in a catalog versus on a computer screen due to Web sites and smartphones having lower resolutions than print. The same can be said for variations in colors. This may especially affect the purchase of apparel or furniture.

A final potential difficulty is the management of a retailer's distribution center. Such a center requires efficient procedures for handling both large orders that are shipped directly to stores and small shipments that are made to thousands or tens of thousands of customers. The system for handling large store-based retail purchase orders (which are often full caseloads) is quite different from shipping individual items to a customer's home.

PART 2 Short Cases

Case 1 Do Power Players Rule?*

A power player is any U.S. retailer with sales equal to or greater than 10 percent of those of the category leader.

Department Stores

Department stores have survived the rise of sectors specializing in narrower product ranges, as well as the challenges of discount stores and other off-price retailers, and finally E-commerce. Gerald Storch, CEO of Hudson's Bay, parent of Saks Fifth Avenue and Lord & Taylor, says, "Increasingly, consumers don't think of stores as physical locations, they think of stores as brands. The opportunity is to customize on a mass scale so you simulate the selling experience on a mobile device."

Drugstores

National healthcare questions have been driving a lot of what has been going on in the drugstore industry. CVS is moving on several fronts: It broadened its pharmacy reach by acquiring Omnicare, which distributes prescription drugs to nursing homes, assisted living facilities, and so on. CVS has unveiled the makeover of the Navarro Discount Pharmacy sites it acquired. Carrying the banner "CVS pharmacy y mas," the South Florida stores feature bilingual associates and 1,500+ "trusted Hispanic products." It also acquired Target's pharmacy businesses for about $1.9 billion.

General Apparel

Fast fashion has been rising among the ranks of apparel retailers. "There is an underlying sense of rebellion that comes through in today's fashion," notes Marshal Cohen, chief industry analyst with NPD Group. "The fashion industry has undergone one of the most dramatic makeovers in recent history, no doubt influenced by the Millennial consumer."

Home Improvement and Hardware

These have had to deal with some flooring issues. First, it was hardwood laminate flooring that was said to emit formaldehyde in excess of California state standards. Soon after, came a study of vinyl floor tiles, which found that 58 percent of samples bought from large home improvement dealers contained phthalates, several forms of which have been banned from children's products since 2009. The Home Depot clicked on several fronts, including online.

Jewelry and Accessories

Signet, which bills itself as the world's largest retailer of diamond jewelry, acquired Zale Corp. The company now operates stores and kiosks under a variety of banners, including Kay, Jared, and a number of regional brands in its Sterling division, along with Zale, Peoples, and Piercing Pagoda in its Zale division. Zale operations have been growing same-store sales faster than the company as a whole, and Signet expects that to continue.

Mass Merchants

Amazon has joined the ranks of mass merchant power players, selling everything from digital downloads to consumer electronics, toilet paper, books, and groceries. Its limited face-to-face interaction with consumers belies Amazon's vast physical presence around the country, where a network of fulfillment centers puts it near to customers. Amazon's mass market tactics include spreading same-day delivery to more segments of the population.

Supermarkets

Although mergers and acquisitions have been a way of life, grocery remains the most fragmented segment of retailing. Albertsons took over the remnants of Safeway's network, covering much of North America, and Kroger completed its first full year with Harris Teeter stores under its wing. Then, after A&P and its affiliate brands were forced into bankruptcy in 2015, it was ultimately decided to sell off all the store locations to several major chains.

Women's Apparel

The biggest news was a deal that closed in August 2015—Ascena Retail Group's acquisition of Ann Taylor and Loft parent company Ann Inc. Ascena paid $2 billion to bring Ann Inc. into a diverse stable of brands that included Lane Bryant, Dress Barn, Maurices, and Justice.

Questions

1. How can an independent retailer compete with power retailers?
2. What is the greatest opportunity for each of the retail categories described in this case?
3. What is the greatest threat for each of the retail categories described in this case?
4. What are the pros and cons of Signet's mix of retail jewelry chains: Zale, Kay, Jared, and other units?

Case 2 Will the Favorites of Today Remain Popular?*

While competition constantly shifts, the top tier of consumers' favorite online retailers is stable. There was little movement among the top 10 in a 2015 consumer survey by Prosper Insights & Analytics; the full list includes only six relative newcomers. This allows for greater insights about what motivates shoppers, where they like to shop, and what methods retailers are using to draw them in—and it's all been represented in recent research.

So what does it all say—and more importantly, what does it all mean? Pam Goodfellow, director of consumer insights for Prosper, provides a deeper look at two recent surveys: one assessed shoppers' favorite online retail sites; the other looked at consumer behavior. Each provides a clear message about where online retailing is today, as well as the fact that consumers still have their "favorites."

"These are some of the biggest names in retail anyway," Goodfellow says. "These are safer retailers for a lot of

---

* Based on material from David P. Schulz, "Power Players 2015," *STORES Magazine*, July 2015. Reprinted by permission. Copyright STORES magazine.

* Based on material from Sandy Smith, "The Favorite 50," *STORES Magazine*, September 2015, pp. 21–26. Reprinted by permission. Copyright STORES magazine.

consumers to visit. Younger consumers are a little more trusting when it comes to online shopping. For Baby Boomers or someone a little older, consumers see these as safe retailers when it comes to online shopping."

It's no surprise that Amazon continues to dominate among all age groups, even increasing its share slightly. Millennials ranked it even higher. Walmart.com ranks second, although its share dropped slightly from 2014; Walmart ranks higher among Millennials than it does among Baby Boomers. Does this mean Amazon has a lock on online retailing? Goodfellow points to Walmart's status as the top bricks-and-mortar retailer. Still, "Walmart has its issues competing with Amazon," she says. "For the foreseeable future, Amazon will be the one to beat. But that's the interesting part of retail: It's always changing."

There are newcomers that hope to chip away at big retailers' dominance. Take Jet, which is tackling both Amazon and warehouse clubs. But Amazon has something that could make that tough. "Amazon has collected a loyal shopper base," Goodfellow says. "Its customer service speaks for itself." Even if Amazon Prime Day drew mixed reviews, "It shows that Amazon is trying different things and still testing." A final thought on Amazon: It increased its share slightly. Goodfellow believes "this shows that people are still discovering Amazon."

It might be easy to gloss over Best Buy's move to number three on the list of favorites. The increase was relatively small, though it could signal a solution to an even bigger concern: showrooming. "That had a lot of analysts wondering what the future was going to look like for Best Buy," Goodfellow says. "With a focus on customer service and the price matching that it's now doing, it has brought some consumers back into the fold."

Those shopping at Best Buy and Walmart are apt to have triggers that drive them to the two Web sites: coupons for Walmart shoppers and a cable TV ad for Best Buy shoppers. Most triggering events—such as an online ad or text message—are apt to move a Walmart or Best Buy shopper to the online store more than Amazon shoppers who are more apt to be triggered by reading an article.

Data show several key insights about shoppers in general. It's probably no surprise that Best Buy shoppers are the most mobile-savvy. But what may be surprising is those same shoppers are more likely to compare prices or ask for a price match, and are the most likely to look at another retailer's Web site while in the store.

Questions

1. What must retailers that are the "favorites of today" do to remain popular?
2. What criteria do you use in deciding on your favorite stores? Why?
3. Take a look at the Jet Web site (https://jet.com). Do you think it will succeed? Why or why not?
4. Describe what you think are Best Buy's greatest strengths and weaknesses as a specialty retail chain.

Case 3 Omnichannel Strategies of Top Retailers*

It's no longer bricks-and-mortar versus E-commerce—omnichannel is the path to success. Consumers have myriad ways to shop, and retailers must keep up. "New [technology]

tools transform the way consumers want to shop," says Anne Zybowski, a vice-president at Kantar Retail. In response, retailers are re-thinking operations, from infrastructure and inventory systems to delivery and marketing. As measured by *STORES*' annual "Top 100 Retailers" report, by Kantar, the evolution of retailing displays the survival skills of long-time firms. Chart-topping stalwarts—Walmart, Kroger, Costco, Home Depot, Target, Walgreen, and CVS—have maintained dominance by meeting consumers' changing desires, including for online shopping and digital interaction.

Amazon's ascent continues, and although E-commerce has not proven to knock bricks-and-mortar off its pedestal, the old "location, location, location" mantra doesn't carry the same weight that it once did. Instead, the two channels continue to converge: Store operators are seeing much digital success, whereas online merchants—including Amazon—are expanding with showrooms, pop-up shops, and other ways of meeting shoppers face-to-face.

"Omnichannel remains aspirational. Today's omni-shoppers know what they want," Zybowski says, "retailers to offer whatever, wherever, whenever they want. When it comes to value, they want [to have] their cake and eat it too—they don't expect to pay more for convenience." The challenge is meeting consumers' reset expectations. "Retailers must learn how to fundamentally transform their business models, ones built for maximum efficiency and scale, and transform them into more nimble, effective ones," Zybowski adds.

Tom Cole, of Kurt Salmon Associates, says mobile is key in omnichannel's push to seamless consumer experiences, although the mobile transactions' volume is still low. Retailers need to build to omnichannel via legacy systems already in place. "Omnichannel is the new reality whether they engage or not. If you're available where and when consumers look for you, great. If not, you lose to someone who is," says Marge Laney, of Alert Technologies. "Online-only retailers lack the high engagement that the in-store experience can deliver. Offline-only retailers don't deliver the comfortable experience that consumers utilize to make their shopping itineraries."

"Digital is the connective tissue between online and in-store," says Claude de Jocas, intelligence group director for L2. "Stores have been cast as a liability in an Amazon era, but they've been making a comeback as something that's critical to a retail strategy."

Nordstrom is advanced in all facets of its omnichannel approach. The retailer has nearly 1 million followers who can shop via Instagram; its network of fulfillment centers is growing. Nordstrom has also launched a "scan-and-shop" feature within its catalog app that links readers of the print catalog to E- and M-commerce sites. "We hope that scan and shop creates a more seamless shopping experience for our customers who enjoy browsing our catalogs but also enjoy the many benefits technology affords the experience to make it more personal," says spokesman Dan Evans, Jr.

Nordstrom is also connecting with teen shoppers via digital mall Wanelo; and in spring 2015, it unveiled a test of a "click-and-collect" service that included curbside pickup. This complements a more traditional buy online, pick up in-store program that Nordstrom has had since 2008. A third service, TextStyle, was launched in late May 2015 and involves all of Nordstrom's

* Based on material from David P. Schulz, "The Future Is Now," *STORES Magazine,* July 2015, pp. 54–56, 58. Reprinted by permission. Copyright 2016. STORES Magazine.

full-line stores; it allows customers to make purchases from their personal stylist or sales associate using text messages.

Questions

1. Do you agree or disagree with this statement: "It's no longer bricks-and-mortar versus E-commerce—omnichannel is the path to success." Explain your answer.
2. How has Walmart evolved over the years to address changing consumer desires, new technologies, and new competitors?
3. What are keys to succeeding with an omnichannel strategy?
4. What could other retailers learn from Nordstrom's current omnichannel strategy?

Case 4 Omnichannel Food Retailing Still Needs Work*

Grocery buying is changing due to the emergence of omnichannel retailing. Consumers want options, and grocers need to be ready to provide them. Thus, experts say retailers will have to deal with selling price, venue, payment, and customer experience in all transactional channels. Doing so effectively is easier said than done, however.

One who understands that well is Jim Wisner, formerly a VP at Jewel Food Stores and Shaw's Supermarkets. He states that omnichannel retailing is being able to operate, in any fashion, when and where the customer wants to interact. That can involve customer service via social media, online chat, E-mail, or phone; browsing or shopping in-store or online; receiving products via home delivery or in-store pickup, or old-fashioned aisle browsing; or making coupons or discounts similar across channels. "As much as the ultimate goal needs to be a complete integration of 'all things at all times,'" says Wisner, now president of Wisner Marketing, "it is important to make sure that each individual piece can operate functionally and effectively on its own. Pasting an online shopping portal to a Web site that hasn't been redesigned in years or mobile-optimized won't attract shoppers."

DyShaun Muhammad, VP of consultancy Catapult, offers these three key steps for retailers:

Educate Yourself

Get to know shoppers, especially those who are most valuable. What really drives a shopper to actually buy a particular category from you? What are the barriers to his or her doing more transactions with you? Where do tools like mobile apps, flexible fulfillment, digital couponing, and more traditional merchandising tools fit in his or her path to purchase for your priority categories? How could you best deploy these tactics to better deliver your retail proposition to drive stronger affinity and share with the shopper? How could your vendors help?

Evaluate Your Ecosystem

Once you have a good understanding of shoppers' needs and key drivers, you must assess your own ecosystem. Do you have the technology, logistics, data, and organizational resources to operate against a unified view of shoppers and their activity across channels? What are the gaps in your systems that impede delivering the quality of experiences that will drive the desired level of shopper loyalty and conversion? What frustrations are shoppers communicating to your customer service teams or via social channels?

Experiment to Find What Works

At this point, you can then engage in the hard work of determining which things to experiment against, where to invest, and how to restructure your organization to deliver. It can't be done all at once, but each step needs to be able to deliver meaningful value for shoppers and make it easier for them to accomplish their shopping goals with you.

As with any major new initiative, obstacles stand in the way of smooth implementation. Wisner, Muhammad, and others point to organizational silos in different departments as one challenge to overcome. "There are operational, organizational, and experiential issues to resolve," affirms Channie Mize, general manager for the retail sector for Periscope, a McKinsey solution. "It's easier to do multichannel, but that creates silos and doesn't extend to customer service. Also, branding may not be consistent across the channels with a multichannel versus omnichannel approach.

"In more traditional multichannel environments," Mize continues, "the chief merchant officer controls the merchandising in the physical stores, while the CIO, or 'head of online,' controls the offering in the online stores. They each have different agendas tied to different or misaligned incentive structures. This can cause the same retailer to cannibalize itself across channels, which inherently provides for less than optimal results for the customer."

Questions

1. Why is omnichannel retailing a bigger challenge for food retailers than general merchandise retailers?
2. Apply DyShaun Muhammad's three key steps to your favorite supermarket.
3. Comment on this statement: "It's easier to do multichannel, but that creates silos and doesn't extend to customer service. Also, branding may not be consistent across the channels with a multichannel versus omnichannel approach."
4. What are *your* top five recommendations as to how to best perform as an omnichannel retailer?

---

* *Source:* Based on material in John Karolefski, "Omnichannel Retailing: A Work in Progress," *Progressive Grocer,* January 2016, pp. 91–95. Reprinted by permission.

PART 2   Comprehensive Case

What Consumers Find Expendable versus Untouchable*

Introduction

Consumers say they can cut back on most purchases: What won't they give up? If retailers had to guess the one item most consumers say they can't live without, they'd probably answer "Smartphone." And for the most part, they would be right. Although Internet service actually tops the list of "untouchables," it's hardly a leap to say that the two are intimately linked. Eight in 10 consumers consider Internet service non-negotiable; 58 percent feel that way about their smartphones.

What Are Consumers Finding Expendable?

Beyond an online connection and a way to access it from the palm of their hands, consumers are proving to be a relatively agnostic bunch. Hyperinformed, price-savvy, and emboldened by a post-recessionary survivor attitude, consumers assert that things like a new pair of jeans, dining in upscale restaurants, and buying high-end cosmetics or a luxury handbag are expendable.

Much like their grandparents or great-grandparents, many of whose attitudes to shopping were shaped by the Great Depression, the spending behaviors of today's shoppers are liable to be clouded by the recent Great Recession for some time. Still, even though they consider many products to be expendable, they have no problem spending on the latest smartphone or on-demand video streaming. Therein lies the rub.

The good news is that the economy has been bouncing back—recent Wall Street hysteria over China and volatile oil prices notwithstanding. Although financial experts don't think consumers will revert to their spendthrift ways, the latest installment of "Expendables vs. Untouchables" research, compiled by Prosper Insights and Analytics exclusively for *STORES*, shows clear signs of consumer spending optimism. See Tables 1 and 2.

Among the indicators: In 2009 (the first time *STORES* reported on this research), fitness and gym memberships were on the chopping block, with 86 percent of respondents citing them as expendable. In 2015, that figure slipped to 79 percent—72 percent among the 18- to 34-year-old cohort. In 2013, 73 percent of adults age 18 and older said that they planned to forego vacations; in 2015, that figure fell to 66 percent.

Shopping rebounded a bit as well. When consumers were asked how the current state of the U.S. economy has affected household spending plans, 40 percent indicated that they planned to spend less overall; 23 percent said they would be dining out less frequently. In 2014, 45 percent that they planned to spend less overall and 28 percent expected to dine out less often—notable shifts in shopper attitudes. When asked to describe their feelings about the chances for a strong economy during the next 6 months, 46 percent of adults age 18 and older said they were either confident or very confident. See Table 3.

The data, which reflect the feedback of nearly 7,000 consumers across the country, are part of the December 2015 Monthly Consumer Survey taken by Prosper during the first 2 weeks of the month.

Ongoing Recovery

"Year over year, the changes have been slim, but when you compare the December 2015 survey to data compiled in December 2008, it's evident that consumer attitudes toward spending are heading in the right direction," says Chrissy Wissinger, director of communications at Prosper.

---

* Based on material from Susan Reda, "Expendable vs. Untouchable," *STORES Magazine*, February 2016, pp. 22–25. Reprinted by permission. Copyright 2016. STORES Magazine.

TABLE 1 Expendable Shopping

Given the current economic situation, what **can** *you* live without/consider to be expendable? (Top 12 responses are shown.)

	Adults 18+
Luxury handbag	89%
High-end jewelry	88
Club/social memberships (country club, golf club, etc.)	88
Costume jewelry	88
Maid service	87
High-end cosmetics	87
Gourmet foods	87
Specialty shopping for apparel	87
Facial	86
Fine dining sit-down restaurant	85
Extra-curricular leagues	85
Satellite radio	85

Source: Prosper Marketing Consumer Survey, December 2015. Reprinted by permission of *STORES Magazine*.

TABLE 2 Untouchable Shopping

Given the current economic situation, we want to know what *you* **cannot** live without/consider to be untouchable. (Top 12 responses are shown.)

	Adults 18+
Internet service	80%
Mobile smartphone	58
Cable/satellite TV (basic)	50
Hair cut/color	42
Discount shopping for apparel	36
Charitable contribution	35
Vacation	34
Casual sit-down restaurant (Applebee's, Olive Garden, etc.)	32
Fast-food restaurant	31
Cable/satellite TV (premium)	31
On-demand video streaming (Netflix, Hulu, etc.)	29
Fast-casual restaurant (Panera. etc.)	27

Source: Prosper Marketing Consumer Survey, December 2015. Reprinted by permission of *STORES Magazine*.

"Communication trumps just about everything else for today's consumer. They don't want to be without Internet service or their smartphone, and the idea of streaming video on demand via Netflix or Hulu has become more important every year since we began watching the category. Consumers seem more comfortable with their financial situation," Wissinger says. "They've made cutbacks over time and now they're making tradeoffs in how they spend."

NRF Chief Economist Jack Kleinhenz said he's seen a trend toward more dollars being spent on services versus goods—a shift supported by these data. "Consumers are spending on services such as smartphone plans and on-demand streaming, and there's some pent-up demand for vacations and entertainment in the form of movie tickets and eating out."

However, "2016 was not expected to be very different from 2015 in terms of economic growth," Kleinhenz adds. "Overall consumer spending looks good, employment is solid, and there don't appear to be any significant recession risks cropping up now. But that said, there are a number of underpinnings that need to be closely monitored. Consumer spending has varied in certain regions of the country. Changes in housing and healthcare continue to bear watching, as does the aging of the Baby Boomer generation and the rise of Millennials."

Mash-Up

It is generally acknowledged that consumers' propensity to spend varies by age, as do the types of products they purchase. Age-wise, Millennials are on the cusp of what experts deem to be the sweet-spot for spending—setting up homes, starting a family, and so on—but that's just not typically been the reality.

Burdened by student debt, many in this age group spend money primarily on mobile devices and media content. They are champions of the sharing economy and sustainability, content to rent rather than own everything from special occasion apparel and jewelry to cars. The research aligns: 18- to 34-year-old respondents are more likely than any other group to

TABLE 3 Economic Impact on Shopping

Is the current state of the U.S. economy affecting your household spending plans in any of the following ways? (Top six responses shown.)

	Adults 18+	18–34	35–54	55+
Spending less overall	40%	37%	42%	42%
Shopping for sales more often	32	29	32	33
Using coupons more often	27	26	28	28
Comparative shopping online more often	24	26	25	21
Dining out less frequently	23	19	24	24
State of the U.S. economy not affecting spending plans	28	24	27	34

Source: Prosper Marketing Consumer Survey, December 2015. Reprinted by permission of *STORES Magazine*.

consider on-demand video streaming untouchable—42 percent, compared with 29 percent of 35- to 54-year-olds. They also are less apt to give up their daily cup of gourmet coffee, their gym membership, and their costume jewelry as compared with other adults.

"Millennials are now the largest generation of potential shoppers and they have certain traits that are shaping their buying habits. They've lived through the Great Recession and it has had an effect on them: They tend to be frugal," says Paula Rosenblum, co-founder and managing partner at RSR Research. "If you ask them if purchasing jeans is expendable, they'll say 'Sure,' because they can buy another pair from H&M for $20. This generation has grown up with fast fashion; and when you are buying from those types of retailers, everything becomes expendable."

Rosenblum is quick to point out that although Millennials may be frugal, they are interested in quality, as exemplified by their desire to have the latest smartphone and a willingness to invest in items that inspire and speak to their social consciousness. "Part of the reason why department stores and some specialty retailers are in a world of hurt is because Millennials don't want to go into stores and wander; and they definitely don't want to wear logos emblazoned on their chest. They favor curated assortments that are in line with who they are." As a result, some long-established retailers "are going to have to find a way to reinvent themselves if they expect to return to relevancy," states Rosenblum.

Older and Wiser?

Baby Boomers and beyond are obviously in a somewhat different frame of mind when it comes to determining what's expendable and untouchable. Having spent years amassing stuff, they'd prefer to spend money on an experience. Organic and gourmet foods are off the table for the 55 and older crowd, with 87 and 93 percent checking the expendable box on these potential purchases, respectively. And although this age group is a target market for the makers of anti-aging products, a commanding 92 percent say they can live without high-end cosmetics.

There is a silver lining: Among consumers age 55 and older, 45 percent designate charitable contributions as untouchable. When they dine out, they tend to favor casual sit-down restaurants such as Applebee's, TGI Friday's, and Ruby Tuesday. (It helps that some of these places offer special senior discounts.) This age group is also more inclined than any other to consider their vacations to be something they can't live without. That's not surprising when you consider how spread out families tend to be today; traveling is one way to reconnect with the grandkids.

Older consumers are in sync with the younger generation when it comes to Internet service. In fact, 87 percent cite their connection as untouchable, which might have something to with live chatting with grandkids and monitoring retirement funds. However, 62 percent of older consumers say that basic cable television is something they can't live without (while many Millennials are turning to streaming media for their entertainment, sports, etc.); 33 percent have the same feeling for premium cable or satellite television. It appears that once you reach age 55, the lion's share of entertainment takes place in the living room recliner, remote in hand—83 percent of these consumers deem movie/theater tickets to be expendable for them.

Tracking Trends

Digging into the research by household income and gender yields interesting insights. Among consumers with a household income of $150,000 or more, 53 percent indicate that having their hair cut or colored is an untouchable item—a greater percentage than any other income or age group; 21 percent say maid service is untouchable; and 22 percent feel the same way about lawn care service. One might expect that more affluent consumers would be further inclined to consider fine dining untouchable, but that's not the case. Their propensity to spend on fine dining is actually on par with other income segments; they also don't show a particular proclivity for shopping at department or specialty stores. See Table 4.

The one category that stands out among this income group is the vacation. On average, 34 percent of all respondents consider it to be untouchable; the percentage jumps to 36 percent

TABLE 4 Higher-Income Shopping

What do higher-income households consider **untouchable**? Here are some notable instances where their responses varied widely from those of adults 18+.

	Household income $50K-$100K	Household income 100K +	Overall Adults 18+ (All incomes)
Hair cut/color	47%	53%	42%
Maid service	14	21	13
Charitable contribution	40	40	35
Mobile smartphone	63	65	58
Vacation	46	50	34
Cable/satellite TV (basic)	56	58	50
Cable/satellite TV (premium)	36	40	31
Internet service	86	85	80
Fitness/gym memberships	25	30	21

Source: Prosper Marketing Consumer Survey, December 2015. Reprinted by permission of *STORES Magazine.*

for the 55-and-older group, but for those with a household income of $150,000 and up, 50 percent refuse to give up their vacation time. Perhaps the most telling indicator of how well-heeled consumers are feeling about spending in the near future is the feedback provided to the question, "Have you cut back on any of the items [included in the survey]?" Slightly more than 7 out of every 10 respondents (71 percent) answered "no."

Gender Trends

The differences between men's and women's perception of what's expendable or untouchable are generally not dramatic, but they can be eye-opening: 16 percent of men consider gourmet food untouchable; only 11 percent of women feel the same way. Then again, it would be interesting to determine how each defines "gourmet." Nearly 40 percent of men cite a haircut as untouchable; among women, 45 percent say taking care of their hair is something they're not willing to forego. Women are more inclined to feel that charitable contributions are untouchable; men are more likely to consider a new pair of jeans to be an item they can't live without.

The research provides a curious snapshot of gender differences when it comes to dining outside the home. Men and women are on the same page regarding eating at fast-casual restaurants such as Panera Bread; but men are more likely to view both fine dining and casual sit-down establishments such as Applebee's as untouchable. When it comes to fast food, 71 percent of women feel it's expendable. Men are not quite as willing to give up their Big Mac and fries; 34 percent say there's no way they'll give up their fast-food fix.

Some of the greatest discrepancies between men and women are apparent in the responses provided when asked about changes they've made recently. Nearly 4 in 10 women feel they've become more practical and realistic in their purchases; and 46 percent indicate that they focus more on what they need rather than what they want. That's in sharp contrast to how men responded; 33 percent say they've become more practical and 34 percent focus more on needs than wants.

The challenge for retailers is trying to make sense of all of these data and make the most of this moment in time. Reading between the lines, it's clear that regardless of age, income, or gender, consumers do not appear to have strong ties to stores or brands compared to the past. They're looking for value and they take some pride in being thrifty—except when they're upgrading their smartphone, in which case, all budget bets are off.

Questions

1. Differentiate between expendable and untouchable shopping. Why is this distinction important to retailers?
2. As an independent jewelry retailer, what could you learn from Table 1? How should you adapt to this?
3. Do you think that the revenues of retail cooperatives will go up during weak economic times and decline during strong economic times? Explain your answer.
4. Relate the discussion in this case to the wheel of retailing and scrambled merchandising highlighted in Chapter 5.
5. Are the research data reported in this case good and/or bad for specialty retailers? Explain your answer.
6. Present an omnichannel retailing strategy for a retailer of your choosing based on the information in this case.
7. Are the research data reported in this case good and/or bad for online retailers? Explain your answer. As an airport retailer, what could you learn from this case? How should you adapt to this information?

Part 3

Targeting Customers and Gathering Information

In Part Three, we first present various key concepts for retailers to better identify and understand consumers and develop an appropriate target market plan. Information-gathering methods—which can be used in identifying and understanding consumers as well as in developing and implementing a retail strategy—are then described.

Chapter 7 discusses many influences on retail shoppers: demographics, lifestyles, needs and desires, shopping attitudes and behavior, retailer actions that influence shopping, and environmental factors. We place these elements within a target marketing framework because it is critical for retailers to recognize what makes their customers and potential customers tick—and to act accordingly.

Chapter 8 deals with information gathering and processing in retailing. We first consider the information flows in a retail distribution channel and review the difficulties that may arise from basing a retail strategy on inadequate information. Then we examine in depth the retail information system, its components, and recent advances in information systems—with particular emphasis on data warehousing and data mining. The last part of the chapter describes the marketing research process.

7 Identifying and Understanding Consumers

Chapter Objectives

1. To discuss why it is important for a retailer to properly identify, understand, and appeal to its customers

2. To enumerate and describe a number of consumer demographics, lifestyle factors, and needs and desires—and to explain how these concepts can be applied to retailing

3. To examine consumer attitudes toward shopping and consumer shopping behavior, including the consumer decision process and its stages

4. To look at retailer actions based on target-market planning

5. To note some of the environmental factors that affect consumer shopping

Source: Photobank gallery/ Shutterstock. Reprinted by permission.

Identifying the characteristics of their customers and understanding their behavior patterns are vital tasks for retailers to be able to devise and implement the correct strategy and tactics. As digital technologies increasingly influence higher proportions of consumer purchase decisions online and in-store, retailers have the opportunity to collect and analyze significant amounts of data on customer opinions, preferences, and choices at every interaction. They can harness the data deluge to derive actionable insights, make better decisions, and take the right action at the right place at the right time.

How fast is the online tide, in terms of retailer and customer usage, rising for food items? Does that translate to a mushrooming online grocery business? The answer: It depends. New research from a company called Brick Meets Click, released in mid-2016, finds that consumers are rapidly making online grocery shopping part of their routine. One in five consumers is now an active user of online grocery services, with "active" users spending an average of 16 percent of their weekly grocery dollars online. The company also reports that 21 percent of surveyed shoppers bought groceries online in the preceding month—up from 11 percent in 2013.

Among the competitors in this area are Amazon Fresh, Fresh Direct, Net Grocer, and Peapod. Although they differ in their approach, each enables shoppers to choose from a personalized Web site that facilitates the reordering of merchandise on a week-to-week basis. They also promise delivery within a 1- to 2-hour delivery window.

Steven Pinder, a retail strategist at Kurt Salmon, is more skeptical about future growth in online groceries. He acknowledges its foothold in urban markets, but Pinder feels adoption rates are slowing. "Bottom line: No one has figured out how to address some of the major inhibitors with online grocery," he says. "Shoppers still can't test the fruit, substitutions are clunky, and shelf in-stocks are problematic."[1]

Overview

The success of a retail strategy depends on how well a firm identifies and understands its customers and how well it forms a strategy mix to appeal to them. This entails identifying consumer characteristics, needs, and attitudes; recognizing how people make decisions; and then devising the proper target-market plan. See Figure 7-1. It also means studying environmental factors that affect decisions. Consider this:

Today's consumers are more empowered than ever before. They have numerous options with regard to when they shop, where they shop, and how they go about shopping. As a result, consumers now have higher expectations about the retailers with which they do business. In such a competitive environment, retailers must better understand and service their customers.

In this chapter, we explore—from a retailing perspective—the impact on shoppers of each of the elements shown in Figure 7-2: demographics, lifestyles, needs and desires, shopping attitudes

FIGURE 7-1

Recognizing Consumer Diversity in the Marketplace

Good retailers realize that customers (and potential customers) have varying backgrounds, interests, fashion sense, shopping behavior, and so on—even the young adult market. Thus, the best retail strategies cater to the needs and desires of a specific group of customers.

Source: Kurhan/Shutterstock. Reprinted by permission.

FIGURE 7-2

What Makes Retail Shoppers Tick

and behavior, retailer actions that influence shopping, and environmental factors. We also look at the impact of digital/mobile advances. By studying these elements, a retailer can devise the best possible target-market plan and do so in the context of its overall strategy.

Please note: We use *consumer*, *customer*, and *shopper* interchangeably in this chapter.

CONSUMER DEMOGRAPHICS AND LIFESTYLES

At *The Rite Site* (www .easidemographics.com), retailers can access lots of useful demographic data. Take a look at the free reports.

Demographics are objective, quantifiable, easily identifiable, and measurable population data. **Lifestyles** are ways in which individual consumers and families (households) live and spend time and money. Visit our Web site (www.bermanevansretail.com) for posts on these topics.

Consumer Demographics

Consumers, both as groups and as individuals, can be identified by such demographics as gender, age, population growth rate, life expectancy, literacy, language spoken, household size, marital and family status, income, retail sales, mobility, place of residence, occupation, education, and ethnic/racial background. These factors affect retail shopping and retailer actions.

A retailer should have some knowledge of overall trends, as well as the demographics of its own target market. Table 7-1 indicates broad demographics for 10 nations around the world, and Table 7-2 shows U.S. demographics by region. Regional data are useful since most retailers are local and regional.

In understanding U.S. demographics, it is helpful to know these facts:

▸ The typical household has an annual income of $54,000, according to the Federal Reserve. The top one-fifth of households earns approximately $100,000 or more; the lowest one-fifth earns approximately $20,000 or less.[2] If income is high, people are apt to have **discretionary income**—money left after paying taxes and buying necessities.

▸ About 12 percent of people move each year; two-thirds of all moves are in the same county.

▸ There are about 6.5 million more U.S. females than males; 57 percent of adult females are in the labor force.[3]

▸ Most U.S. employment is in services. In addition, there are now more professionals and white-collar workers than before and fewer blue-collar and agricultural workers.

▸ Approximately 32 percent of all U.S. adults age 25 and older have at least a 4-year college degree.[4]

▸ The population comprises many ethnic and racial groups. African Americans, Hispanic Americans, and Asian Americans account for one-third of U.S. residents—a steadily rising figure. Each of these groups represents a large potential target market; their total annual buying power is more than $3.4 trillion.[5]

TABLE 7-1 Population Demographics: A Global Perspective—Selected Countries

Country	Male/ Female (%)	Age Distribution (%)			2015 Population Growth (%)	Life Expectancy in Years	Literacy Rate (%)	Principal Languages Spoken
		0–14 Years	15–64 Years	65 Years and Over				
Canada	49.5/50.5	16	66	18	0.75	81.7	99	English, French
China	51.3/48.7	17	73	10	0.45	75.4	96	More than a dozen versions of Chinese
Great Britain	49.5/50.5	17	65	18	0.54	80.5	99	English, Welsh
India	51.9/48.1	28	66	6	1.22	68.5	71	Hindi, English, 14 other official languages
Italy	49.0/51.0	14	65	21	0.27	82.2	99	Italian, German, French, Slovene
Japan	48.7/51.3	13	60	27	−0.16	84.7	99	Japanese
Mexico	49.0/51.0	28	65	7	1.18	75.7	95	Spanish
Poland	48.5/51.5	15	69	16	−0.09	77.4	99	Polish
South Africa	49.7/50.3	28	66	6	1.33	62.3	94	Afrikaans, IsiZulu, IsiXhosa, 8 other official languages
United States	49.2/50.8	19	66	15	0.78	79.7	99	English, Spanish

The literacy rate is the percentage of people who are 15 and older who can read and write.

Sources: Compiled by the authors from *World Factbook*, www.cia.gov/library/publications/the-world-factbook. (Accessed April 09, 2016).

Although the preceding gives an overview of the United States, demographics vary by area (as Table 7-2 indicates). Within a state or city, some locales have larger [or smaller] populations and more [or less] affluent, older [younger], and better-educated [or less-educated] residents.

TABLE 7-2 Selected 2010 U.S. Demographics by Region

Region	Percent of Household Income	Percent of Population	Percent Ages 18–24	Percent Ages 62 and Older	Population. Square Mile
ENC	15.0	15.6	9.7	16.0	160
ESC	6.0	5.5	9.4	16.7	106
M	7.1	7.3	9.9	15.5	30
MA	13.2	14.5	9.6	17.4	388
NE	4.7	5.2	9.6	17.3	215
P	16.2	16.7	10.7	14.7	55
SA	19.4	17.6	9.7	17.4	238
WNC	6.6	6.9	9.7	16.7	42
WSC	11.8	10.7	10.0	14.2	94

ENC (East North Central) = Illinois, Indiana, Michigan, Ohio, Wisconsin
ESC (East South Central) = Alabama, Kentucky, Mississippi, Tennessee
M (Mountain) = Arizona, Colorado, Idaho, Montana, Nevada, New Mexico, Utah, Wyoming
MA (Middle Atlantic) = New Jersey, New York, Pennsylvania
NE (New England) = Connecticut, Maine, Massachusetts, New Hampshire, Rhode Island, Vermont
P (Pacific) = Alaska, California, Hawaii, Oregon, Washington
SA (South Atlantic) = Delaware, District of Columbia, Florida, Georgia, Maryland, North Carolina, South Carolina, Virginia, West Virginia
WNC (West North Central) = Iowa, Kansas, Minnesota, Missouri, Nebraska, North Dakota, South Dakota
WSC (West South Central) = Arkansas, Louisiana, Oklahoma, Texas

Source: Computed and estimated by the authors from U.S. Bureau of the Census, http://2010.census.gov/2010census.

Because most retailers are local or operate in only part of a region, they must compile data about the people living in their trading areas and those most apt to shop there. *For a given business and location*, the characteristics of the target market (the customer group to be sought by the retailer) can be studied on the basis of some combination of these demographic factors—and a retail strategy planned accordingly:

- ▶ *Market size.* How many people are in the potential target market?
- ▶ *Gender.* Is the potential target market more male or female, or are they equal in proportion?
- ▶ *Age.* What are the prime age groups to which the retailer wants to appeal?
- ▶ *Household size.* What is the average household size of potential consumers?
- ▶ *Marital and family status.* Are potential consumers single or married? Do families have children?
- ▶ *Income.* Is the potential target market lower income, middle income, or upper income? Is discretionary income available for luxury purchases?
- ▶ *Retail sales.* What is the area's sales forecast for the retailer's goods/services category?
- ▶ *Birthrate.* How important is the birthrate for the retailer's goods/services category?
- ▶ *Mobility.* What percent of the potential target market moves into and out of the trading area yearly?
- ▶ *Where people live.* How large is the trading area from which potential customers can be drawn?
- ▶ *Employment status.* Does the potential target market include working women?
- ▶ *Occupation.* In what industries and occupations are people in the area working? Are they professionals, office workers, or of some other designation?
- ▶ *Education.* Are potential customers college educated?
- ▶ *Ethnic/racial background.* Does the potential target market cover a distinctive racial or ethnic group?

Consumer Lifestyles

Great Britain's *Customer Insight Magazine* (www .customer-insight.co.uk) provides a good perspective on emerging consumer trends.

Consumer lifestyles are based on social and psychological factors and are influenced by demographics. As with demographics, a retailer should first have some knowledge of consumer lifestyle concepts and then determine the lifestyle attributes of its own target market.

These *social factors* are useful in identifying and understanding consumer lifestyles.

- ▶ A **culture** is a distinctive heritage shared by a group of people that passes on a series of beliefs, norms, and customs. The U.S. culture stresses individuality, success, education, and material comfort; there are also various subcultures (such as African-, Asian-, and Hispanic-Americans) due to the many countries from which residents have come.
- ▶ **Social class** involves an informal ranking of people based on income, occupation, education, and other factors. People often have similar values in each social class.
- ▶ **Reference groups**, of which there are several types, influence people's thoughts and behavior. For example, a group that someone wishes she or he belonged to but does not is called an *aspirational group;* a group that a person does belong to is referred to as a *membership group;* and a *dissociative group* is one in which a person belongs but wishes he or she did not.

RETAILING
AROUND
THE WORLD

Global Adaptation

In domestic markets, retailers have had to adapt to changes in demographics. Tradition target groups have aged, and new groups have developed. Music, fashion, luxury goods, and health products are all examples of rapidly changing markets. Proportions of gender, race, religion, and ethnicity are constantly changing and need to be addressed for the retailer to thrive. These constant changes and adaptations have made some of the more established retailers better placed to cater for a global market. Other older retailers have floundered and failed overseas.

Why might some retailers succeed and other fail to understand the importance of demographics?

Face-to-face groups, such as families, have the most impact. In reference groups are opinion leaders whose views are respected and sought.

 ▷ The **family life cycle** describes how a traditional family moves from bachelorhood to children to solitary retirement. At each stage, attitudes, needs, purchases, and income change. Retailers must also be alert to the many adults who never marry, divorced adults, single-parent families, and childless couples. The **household life cycle** incorporates life stages for both family and nonfamily households.

 ▷ *Time utilization* refers to activities in which a person engages and the time allocated to them. The broad categories are work, transportation, eating, recreation, entertainment, parenting, sleeping, and (retailers hope) shopping. Today, the number of dual-earner households continues to increase; many people have multiple jobs to maintain the rise in standards of living. This affects retailers in that consumers have less discretionary time and therefore allocate less time to shopping.

These *psychological factors* help in identifying and understanding consumer lifestyles:

Consumer psychology can be studied with tools such as the Keirsey Temperament Sorter. Take the online test (www.keirsey.com/sorter/instruments2.aspx) to learn about yourself.

 ▷ A **personality** is the sum total of an individual's traits, which make that individual unique. Traits include a person's level of self-confidence, innovativeness, autonomy, sociability, emotional stability, and assertiveness.

 ▷ **Class consciousness** is the extent to which a person desires and pursues social status. It helps determine the use of reference groups and the importance of prestige purchases. A class-conscious person values the status of goods, services, and retailers.

 ▷ **Attitudes (opinions)** are the positive, neutral, or negative feelings a person has about different topics. Attitudes are also feelings consumers have about a given retailer and its activities. Does the consumer feel a retailer is desirable, unique, and fairly priced?

 ▷ **Perceived risk** is the level of risk a consumer believes exists regarding the purchase of a specific good or service from a given retailer, whether or not the belief is correct. There are six types: *functional* (Will a good or service perform well?); *physical* (Can a good or service hurt me?); *financial* (Can I afford it?); *social* (What will peers think of my shopping here?); *psychological* (Am I doing the right thing?); and *time* (How much shopping effort is needed?). Perceived risk is high if a retailer or its brands are new, a person is on a budget or has little experience, there are many choices, and an item is socially visible or complex. See Figure 7-3. Firms can reduce perceived risk with information.

 ▷ *The importance of a purchase* to the consumer affects the amount of time he or she will spend to make a decision and the range of alternatives considered. If a purchase is important, perceived risk tends to be higher, and the retailer must adapt to this.

FIGURE 7-3

The Impact of Perceived Risk on Consumers

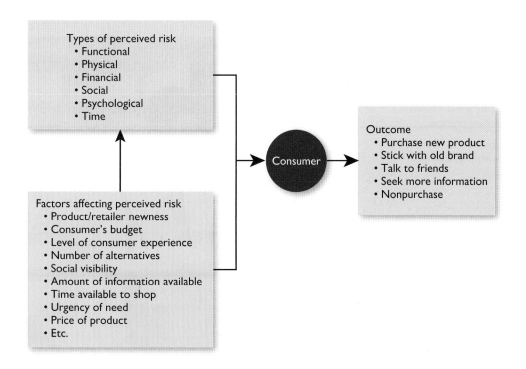

A retailer can develop a lifestyle profile of its target market by answering these questions and then using the answers in developing its strategy:

▶ *Culture:* What values, norms, and customs are important to the potential target market?
▶ *Social class:* Are potential consumers lower, middle, or upper class? Are they socially mobile?
▶ *Reference groups:* To whom do people look for purchasing advice? Does this differ by good or service category? How can a firm target opinion leaders?
▶ *Family (or household) life cycle:* In what stage(s) of the cycle are most potential customers?
▶ *Time utilization:* How do people spend time? How do they feel about their shopping time?
▶ *Personality:* Do potential customers have identifiable personality traits?
▶ *Class consciousness:* Are potential consumers status-conscious? How does this affect purchases?
▶ *Attitudes:* How does the potential target market feel about the retailer and its offerings in terms of specific strategy components?
▶ *Perceived risk:* Do potential customers feel risk in connection with the retailer? Which goods and services have the greatest perceived risk?
▶ *Importance of the purchase:* How crucial are the goods/services offered to potential customers?

Retailing Implications of Consumer Demographics and Lifestyles

Demographic and lifestyle factors need to be considered from several perspectives. Here are some illustrations. By no means do the examples cover the full domain of retailing.

GENDER ROLES   The many working women who put in 60 to 70 hours or more each week between their job and home responsibilities have altered lifestyles. Compared with women who have not worked outside the home, they tend to be more self-confident and individualistic, more concerned with convenience, more interested in sharing household tasks with spouses or significant others, more knowledgeable and demanding, more interested in leisure activities and travel, more involved with self-improvement and education, more appearance-conscious, and more indifferent to small price differences among retailers. They are less interested in unhurried shopping.

Due to the number of working women, male lifestyles are also changing. More men now take care of their children, shop for food, do laundry, wash dishes, cook, vacuum, and clean the bathroom. Male grocery and mass merchandise shoppers in the United States are steadily increasing, especially with Millennials.[6] The generational shift from traditional roles is bolstered by mobile E-commerce and millennial men's savviness with smartphones and shopping apps. In the future, there will be still more changes in men's and women's roles. The clout and duties of husbands and wives will be shared more often. Retailers need to appreciate this trend. See Figure 7-4.

FIGURE 7-4
Blurring Gender Roles

Due to changing lifestyles, more men and women now shop together.

Source: iofoto/Shutterstock. Reprinted by permission.

Selling Add-Ons

A commonality among car dealerships, home builders, and electronics retailers is the high profit they make on add-ons relative to the primary purchase. Car dealers earn more from financing, extended warranties, trade-ins, and upgrades (such as remote starters and alarm systems) than on the basic car. New home builders generate large profits on upgrades (appliances, doors, and kitchen cabinets). Electronics retailers often charge high prices for extended warranties, as well as batteries and cables. What disturbs many consumers is that although the price of a car, home, or laptop is transparent and heavily promoted in the ads and on Web sites, the price of ancillaries is often not listed. These customers want the price of add-ons to be transparent before the purchase.

How can a consumer minimize the issues with the sale of add-ons?

CONSUMER SOPHISTICATION AND CONFIDENCE   Many shoppers are now more knowledgeable and cosmopolitan; more aware of trends in tastes, styles, and goods and services; and more sophisticated. Nonconforming behavior is accepted when consumers are self-assured and better appreciate the available choices. Confident shoppers experiment more. For example, today, it may be considered an asset to be viewed as "cheap," which to some shoppers means "smart." Thus, for example, Ikea offers style at low prices, partly since consumers are responsible for self-assembly of the furniture they buy. Unlike other fashion-based apparel retailers, Zara has little in-store stock and updates its fashion apparel often. These combined strategies motivate Zara customers to visit its stores often. This also encourages shoppers to immediately buy an item since they fear that it may quickly sell out and not be available on subsequent store visits.[7]

POVERTY OF TIME   The increase in working women, the desire for personal fulfillment, the job commute, and the need for some people to have second jobs has led to many consumers feeling time-pressured. Retailers can react to time-pressured consumers through various strategies. Included in those strategies are offering pre-wrapped gift items, store pick-up windows for purchases ordered on the Web, home delivery of groceries ordered online, in-home delivery and installation of appliances (on one home visit), and longer store hours (including 24/7). See Figure 7-5.

COMPONENT LIFESTYLES   In the past, shoppers were typecast, based on demographics and lifestyles. It is widely recognized that shopping is less predictable and more individualistic now, and shopper profiling based traditional segmentation strategies may have low predictive ability for a majority of retailers. This shopping profile is more situation-based, hence, the term *component lifestyle.*

FIGURE 7-5

Addressing the Poverty of Time

The 24/7, anywhere, anything nature of online shopping is a big attraction for people who are pressed for time.

Source: iofoto/Shutterstock. Reprinted by permission.

So-called hybrid consumers are increasingly opting both to trade up to premium products for high-involvement, discretionary spending, and to trade down to budget options for low-involvement necessities in various product and service categories.[8] Retailers with mid-priced alternatives are losing share in their polarized consumption basket. It becomes increasingly more complicated for retailers when consumers mix luxury and budget products within the same category. Why will they buy a luxury auto and then go to Costco for replacement tires? Why will they spend several dollars for coffee at Starbucks but feel $1.49 is too high for a fast-food hamburger? The rapid growth of store brands underscores how many retailers are responding by managing a brand portfolio that includes multiple value propositions, such as a generic, a standard, and a premium brand.

Consumer Profiles

Considerable research has been aimed at describing consumer profiles in a way that is useful for retailers. Here are three examples:

VALS (www .strategicbusinessinsights .com/vals) classifies lifestyles into several profiles. Visit the site to learn about the profiles and take the "VALS Survey" to see where you fit.

▶ Boston Proper is an online and catalog retailer that appeals to a customer group that is not well served. The retailer's target market is women aged 35 to 60. It features Bohemian-inspired fashions as well as classy, casual, and sports apparel. When Chico's acquired Boston Proper in 2011, the retailer operated online and through catalog sales exclusively. Under Chico's leadership, Boston Proper launched its first stores in 2013 and now has 13 locations in Florida, Georgia, North Carolina, and Texas. Chico's plans to open hundreds of Boston Proper stores throughout the United States.[9]

▶ About one-sixth of the people who live in the United States self-identify as Hispanic or Latino—up by 2.5 percent from 2010 to 2015, compared to the 2005 to 2010 figure of 51 million people. Hispanic women will make up about 30 percent of the total U.S. female population by 2060. This group is especially important because it represents close to one-fifth of the total women's fashion-based footwear market, according to research by NPD Group. One strategy used by retailers seeking to attract this market is to use Hispanic celebrities in product branding. Television star Sofia Vergara, on *Forbes*'s list of the wealthiest women, helped launch a product line for Kmart. Similarly, Latina singer Thalia was involved in a Macy's brand launch.[10]

▶ Claritas Prizm segmentation system for marketing (owned by the Nielsen Company) divides American households into various lifestyle categories. These are the four wealthiest groups: (1) Upper crust—America's wealthiest lifestyle consisting of opulent empty-nesting couples over the age of 50. (2) Networked neighbors—The nation's second wealthiest lifestyles representing suburban wealth. This group embraces technology. (3) Movers and shakers—Dual-income couples who are highly educated, typically between the ages of 45 and 64. Many of these group members are business professionals. (4) Young digerati—Tech-savvy individuals who reside in fashionable urban neighborhoods and love trendy restaurants and clothing boutiques.[11]

CONSUMER NEEDS AND DESIRES

Lane Bryant (www .lanebryant.com), a retailer of fashionable plus-size women's apparel, seeks to satisfy both consumer needs and desires, especially the latter.

When deriving a target market profile, a retailer should identify key consumer needs and desires. To a retailer, *needs* are a person's basic shopping requirements consistent with his or her present demographics and lifestyle. *Desires* are discretionary shopping goals that affect attitudes and behavior. A person may *need* a new car to get to and from work, and he or she might seek a dealer with Saturday service hours. A person may *desire* a Porsche and a free loaner car when the vehicle is serviced but be satisfied with a Toyota that can be serviced on weekends and fits within a budget.

When a retail strategy aims to satisfy consumer needs and desires, it appeals to consumer **motives**, or the reasons for their behavior. These are just a few of the questions to resolve:

▶ How far will customers travel to get to the retailer? How important is convenience?
▶ What hours are desired? Are evening and weekend hours required?
▶ What level of customer services is preferred?
▶ How extensive a goods/service assortment is desired?
▶ What level of goods/service quality is preferred?
▶ How important is price?
▶ What retailer actions are necessary to reduce perceived risk?
▶ Do different market segments have special needs? If so, what are they?

Let's address the last question by looking at three particular market segments that attract retailer attention: in-home shoppers, online/mobile shoppers, and outshoppers.

1. *In-Home Shopping:* The in-home shopper is not always a captive audience. Shopping is often discretionary, not necessary. Convenience in ordering an item, without traveling for it, is important. These shoppers are often active store shoppers as well as affluent, well educated, self-confident, younger, and venturesome. They like in-store shopping but have low opinions of local shopping. Catalog shoppers have more flexible time requirements. In households with young children, in-home shopping is more likely if the woman works part time or not at all than full-time working mothers. In-home shoppers may be unable to comparison shop; may not be able to touch, feel, handle, or examine products firsthand; are concerned about service (such as returns); and may not have a salesperson to answer questions.

Check out the Pew Internet & American Life Project Web site (www.pewinternet.org) to find out more about Web users.

2. *Online/Mobile Shopping:* People who shop online are often well educated and have above average incomes (as stated in Chapter 6). As we noted earlier, online shopping encompasses more than just purchasing online. Using the Toys "R" Us Web site, shoppers can research items, check out prices, and place orders. Shoppers can have items shipped to them or can pick them up in-store. The retailer has two strong E-commerce Web sites: www.Toysrus.com and www.Babiesrus.com. These sites offer customers a large online choice of toys and baby products, provide free shipping on items costing $19 or more, and allow in-store pickup for online purchases. In addition to its Web sites, Toys "R" Us has over 1,600 company-operated stores and an additional 250 licensed stores in 39 countries and jurisdictions.[12]

3. *Outshopping:* Out-of-hometown shopping, **outshopping**, is important for both local and surrounding retailers. The former want to minimize this behavior, whereas the latter want to maximize it. Outshoppers are often young, members of a large family, and new to the community. Income and education vary by situation. Outshoppers differ in their lifestyles from those who patronize hometown stores. They enjoy fine foods, like to travel, are active, like to change stores, and read out-of-town newspapers. They also downplay hometown stores and compliment out-of-town stores. These are vital data for suburban shopping centers. Outshoppers have the same basic reasons for out-of-town shopping whether they reside in small or large communities—easy access, liberal credit, store diversity, product assortments, prices, the presence of large chains, entertainment facilities, customer services, and product quality.

SHOPPING ATTITUDES AND BEHAVIOR

In this section, we look at people's attitudes toward shopping, where they shop, and the way in which they make purchase decisions. The top of Table 7-3 shows how shoppers around the world say they would change their retail behavior if they needed to reduce their spending; the bottom of the table indicates how global shoppers say they would alter their behavior if they have extra money to spend. Notice the differences among people living in different regions of the world.

Attitudes toward Shopping

Research has been done on people's attitudes and motivations toward shopping. Such attitudes have a big impact on the ways in which people act in a retail setting. Retailers must strive to turn around some negative perceptions that now exist. We will highlight some research findings here.

SHOPPING ENJOYMENT   Generally, people today do not enjoy shopping as much as they did before. However, some consumers enjoy shopping and consider it a pleasant experience. Consumers who seek relaxation and/or fun while shopping may prefer goods and services associated with higher prices, such as national brands and popular department stores. Although research on the relationship between shopping enjoyment, time spent, and size in the context of physical stores has been ambiguous, perceived shopping enjoyment has a significant positive effect on Web visit duration and purchase conversion.

So, what does stimulate a pleasurable shopping experience—a challenge that retailers must address to increase share of wallet and loyalty? Customers derive shopping enjoyment from their assessment of accessibility and in-store atmospherics that include music, lighting, store design, window displays, visual merchandising, and personnel. Drivers of shopping enjoyment differ by gender—men seek fast, efficient shopping, whereas women often prefer a relaxing atmosphere. In the online retailing environment, use of 3D virtual models, close-up pictures, zoom-in functions, and mix-and-match capabilities enhance the online shopping experience.[13]

TABLE 7-3 Global Shopping Behavior (61 countries)

How Consumers Intend to Save Money—Retail-Related (% agreeing they will spend less)

	Africa/Middle East	Asia Pacific	Europe	Latin America	North America
Apparel	47%	49%	56%	50%	46%
Branded groceries	26	28	49	47	26
Entertainment venues	41	45	51	53	31
Replacing household items	23	27	31	31	16
Takeout food	48	33	38	36	43
Technology	33	33	36	39	22
Vacations	17	44	32	24	35

Selected Ways People Spend Their Discretionary Spending by Region (% spending)

	Africa/ Middle East	Asia Pacific	Europe	Latin America	North America
Apparel	25%	41%	34%	25%	23%
Entertainment venues	18	34	26	24	35
Home improvement	9	37	6	9	16
Retirement	7	16	6	6	16
Saving	38	61	36	30	45
Technology	16	34	17	17	15
Vacations	18	18	31	29	16

Source: Compiled by the authors based on data from Nielsen, "Who's Spending and Saving Around the World?" February 10, 2016, http://goo.gl/d5gfZh

ATTITUDES TOWARD SHOPPING TIME Time pressure and emergency purchase situations are important situational influences that impact retail shopping enjoyment and outcomes. Demographic changes, including the high proportion of dual-income households and the increase in the number of earners managing multiple jobs due to wage stagnation, have contributed to chronic time pressure. Research shows that shoppers are task-oriented, under time pressure, and likely to rely on economic cues such as unit-price data in making product selections.[14] Further, retail assortment size and complexity can create perceived time pressure when shopping online or in-store. Retailers have often increased their assortments to keep up with changing customer trends and face the challenging tradeoff of whether "more is better" or "less is better" in terms of assortments. Thus, retailers should not only invest more in store atmospherics (such as music, color, lighting, smell, and visual merchandising) but also pay equal attention to the efficiency of store location, parking, and sales personnel assistance that may reduce shoppers' chronic time pressure."[15]

CAUTIOUS OPTIMISM AND DISPARITY IN WEALTH EFFECT There is a disparity in wealth across income tiers. Higher-income consumers are more likely to own stocks; and when their investments gain, they spend more at luxury retailers. Lower-income consumers are less likely to own stocks and the lack of wage growth means that they haven't seen any improvement in their financial standing over the last several years. For them, memories of the recession linger, which has led to more cautionary spending habits and the propensity to save the extra cash from lower mortgage and energy costs. These consumers have traded down to less expensive brands and shop more at discount stores to secure the most value for their dollar; sometimes, they postpone or forgo discretionary big-ticket items. This has led to bifurcated retailing, with high-end and low-end retailers doing better than middle-of-the road retailers.[16]

WHY PEOPLE BUY OR DO NOT BUY ON A SHOPPING TRIP It is critical for retailers to determine why shoppers leave without making a purchase. Some consumers at online stores place items in their virtual shopping carts but later abandon them, which can lead to lost sales for high-demand, fast-fashion products.[17] Research on shopper behavior indicates that shopping goals determine the consumer's retail journey through both physical and online stores. Shopping goals differ across consumers and across shopping occasions for each consumer based on the complexity of product purchase, as well as the time horizon within which the purchase decision needs to be made. On some shopping trips, consumers might conduct a goal-directed search to browse and collect information; whereas on other occasions, they might compare items and complete the purchase. On yet other shopping occasions, they might just enjoy experiential browsing or window shopping. Consumers' shopping goals may also change in response to the shopping environment such as product presentations or demonstrations, sensory stimuli such as smell or music,[18] prices, promotions, salesperson interaction, and the behavior of other shoppers in the store.

ATTITUDES BY MARKET SEGMENT   There is considerable academic and commercial research on shopper segmentation. Researchers have segmented shoppers in terms of consumer characteristics (geo-demographics and psychographics), purchase quantity/variety/frequency, promotion sensitivity and usage, search behavior, shopping values, multichannel usage behavior, and post-purchase behavior.[19] One recent study, examining "smart" shopping activities, identified three smart grocery shopper segments: involved, spontaneous, and apathetic.

Involved shoppers are apt to be Baby Boomers and prioritize saving time and effort, be attracted by retailers that provide good product assortment and price-saving opportunities in the form of sales, coupons, or bulk pricing. They spend more time planning stores to visit, but engage in minimal information search on products and brand alternatives, hence in-store purchase activities of hedonic value (sampling, in-store café) are essential. *Spontaneous* shoppers are primarily Baby Boomers and least likely to engage in pre-purchase planning and information search, but they care more about saving time and effort than apathetic shoppers. The majority of *apathetic* shoppers are Generation Xers, those less likely to be time conscious and more likely to have a low marketplace knowledge. This group holds the inherent belief that they are smart shoppers. Although they are most likely to engage in online pre-purchase information search than the other segments, they are price-conscious but do not plan or respond to in-store promotional stimuli.

ATTITUDES TOWARD PRIVATE BRANDS   Many consumers believe private (retailer) brands are as good as or better than manufacturer brands. Private label dollar-based market shares exceed one-sixth of U.S. and Canadian revenues. Although these market shares are less than in Western Europe (where private-label sales are over 30 percent), the majority of American and Canadian consumers have positive perceptions of private-label goods: 75 percent of Americans and 73 percent of Canadians view private-label products as a good alternative to national brands; 74 percent of Americans and 66 percent of Canadians state they are a good value; and 67 percent of Americans and 61 percent of Canadians feel they are at parity with national brands on quality.[20]

Where People Shop

Why do some people shop at both upscale Tiffany (www.tiffany.com) and at a membership club such as BJ's (www.bjs.com)?

Consumer patronage differs sharply by type of retailer. Thus, it is vital for firms to recognize the venues where consumers are most likely to shop and plan accordingly.

Many consumers do **cross-shopping**, whereby they (1) shop for a product category at more than one retail format during the year or (2) visit multiple retailers on one shopping trip. The first scenario occurs because these consumers feel comfortable shopping at different formats during the year, their goals vary by occasion (they may want bargains on everyday clothes and fashionable items for weekend wear), they shop wherever sales are offered, and they have a favorite format for themselves and another one for other household members. Visiting multiple outlets on one trip occurs because consumers want to save travel and shopping time. The increased use of retail apps on mobile phones during in-store shopping induces more cross-shopping as retailers compete to deploy geo-targeted promotions that activate at competitors' stores, which attracts people to visit competitors' stores. According to a survey by the National Retail Federation, the most planned activity for smartphone users is researching products and comparing prices (38 percent of smartphone owners). The second most planned activity on smartphones (28 percent of smartphone owners) is looking up information, such as location, store hours, and directions.[21]

TABLE 7-4 Where Do You Purchase Motor Fuel in a Given Month (besides gasoline-based convenience stores)?*

	Total	By Income: Less than $35,000	By Income: $35,000 – $49,999	$50,000 – $74,999	$75,000 – $99,999	$100,000 or more
Purchase at other outlets (net)	75.7%	67.8%	74.2%	78.4%	78.5%	83.9%
Gas-only location	49.0%	40.0%	46.4%	52.4%	55.2%	56.5%
Supercenter/mass merchandiser (Walmart, Target, etc.)	21.5%	25.0%	22.6%	23.3%	16.6%	16.1%
Wholesale club (BJ's, Costco, Sam's Club, etc.)	17.0%	8.4%	13.7%	18.5%	26.0%	24.9%
Supermarket	16.8%	13.4%	16.9%	19.5%	19.3%	15 5%
Truck stop plaza	7.1%	6.9%	5.2%	8.6%	8.3%	6.2%
Other	0.5%	1.6%	0	0.3%	0	0
I only purchase motor fuel at a convenience store	24.3%	32.2%	25.8%	21.6%	21.5%	16.1%

*Multiple responses accepted. Base: 1,234 people buying gas at least one time in the prior month.

Source: Based on material in "Category Data: Motor Fuels," *Convenience Store News*, February 2016, p. 30. Reprinted by permission. Convenience Store News (c) 2016 (www.csnews.com).

Here are some cross-shopping examples:

▶ Some supermarket customers also regularly buy items carried by the supermarket at convenience stores, full-line department stores, drugstores, and specialty food stores.

▶ Some department-store customers also regularly buy items carried by the department store at factory outlets and full-line discount stores.

▶ The majority of Web shoppers also buy from catalog retailers, mass merchants, apparel chains, and/or department stores.

▶ Cross-shopping is high for apparel, home furnishings, shoes, sporting goods, personal-care items, and motor fuel. Table 7-4 shows cross-shopping for motor fuel purchases.

The Consumer Decision Process

Besides identifying target market traits, a retailer should know how people make decisions. This requires familiarity with **consumer behavior**, which is the process by which people determine whether, what, when, where, how, from whom, and how often to purchase goods and services. Such behavior is influenced by a person's background and traits.

The decision process must be grasped from two different perspectives: (1) what good or service the consumer is thinking about buying and (2) where the consumer is going to buy that item (if the person opts to buy). A consumer can make these decisions separately or jointly. If made jointly, she or he relies on the retailer for support (information, assortments, and informed sales personnel) over the full decision process. If the decisions are made independently—what to buy versus where to buy—the person gathers information and advice before visiting a retailer and views the retailer merely as a place to buy (and probably more interchangeable with other firms).

CAREERS IN RETAILING   Marketing Research as a Career

Those with superior analytical skills and degrees (in marketing, market research, statistics, or the social sciences) sometimes seek positions in marketing research at major retailers and at market research consulting firms. Retail chains and franchises often have their own market research staffs. Research studies involving consumer behavior may be done continually or one-time occasions. Continual studies may focus on customer satisfaction, sales forecasts, and loyalty program tracking. One-time studies involve research on strategies to solve problems (such as poor sales) and/or to assess opportunities (national or global expansion plans). Examples include store layout planning to maximize sales potential, real-estate site selection, and private-label brand recognition.

What are the pros and cons of a retailer's conducting consumer research in-house versus outsourcing these activities?

The U.S. government facilitates consumer decision making for such products as food by providing free online information (http://publications.usa.gov/USAPubs.php?CatID=6).

In choosing whether or not to buy a given item (*what*), the consumer considers features, durability, distinctiveness, value, ease of use, and so on. In choosing the retailer to patronize for that item (*where*), the consumer considers location, assortment, credit availability, sales help, hours, customer service, and so on. Thus, the manufacturer and retailer have distinct challenges: The manufacturer wants people to buy its brand *what*) at any location carrying it (*where*). The retailer wants people to buy the product, not necessarily the manufacturer's brand (*what*), at its store or nonstore location (*where*).

The **consumer decision process** has two parts: the process itself and the factors affecting the process. There are six steps in the process: stimulus, problem awareness, information search, evaluation of alternatives, purchase, and post-purchase behavior. The consumer's demographics and lifestyle affect the process. The complete process is shown in Figure 7-6.

The best retailers assist shoppers at each stage in the process: stimulus (online ads), problem awareness (stocking new models), information search (point-of-sale displays and good sales-people), evaluation of alternatives (noticeable differences among products), purchase (acceptance of credit cards), and post-purchase behavior (extended warranties and money-back returns). The greater the role a retailer assumes in the decision process, the more loyal the consumer will be.

Each time a person buys a good or service, he or she goes through a decision process. In some cases, all six steps in the process are utilized; in others, only a few steps are employed. For example, a consumer who has previously and satisfactorily bought luggage at a local store may not use the same extensive process as one who has never bought luggage.

The decision process outlined in Figure 7-6 assumes that the end result is a purchase. However, at any point, a potential customer may decide not to buy; the process then stops. A good or service may be unneeded, unsatisfactory, or too expensive. Before discussing the ways in which retail consumers use the decision process, we explain the entire process.

Stimulus. A **stimulus** is a cue (social or commercial) or a drive (physical) meant to motivate or arouse a person to act. When a person talks with friends, fellow employees, and others, a social cue is received. The special attribute of a social cue is that it involves an interpersonal, noncommercial source. A commercial cue is a message sponsored by a retailer or some other seller. Ads, sales pitches, and store displays are commercial stimuli. Such cues may not be regarded as highly as social ones by consumers because they are seller-controlled. A third type of stimulus is a physical drive. It occurs when one or more of a person's physical senses are affected. Hunger, thirst, cold, heat, pain, or fear could cause a physical drive. A potential consumer may be exposed to any or all three types of stimuli. If aroused (motivated), he or she goes to the next step in the process. If a person is not sufficiently aroused, the stimulus is ignored—terminating the process for the given good or service.

Problem awareness. At **problem awareness**, the consumer not only has been aroused by social, commercial, and/or physical stimuli but she or he also recognizes that the good or service

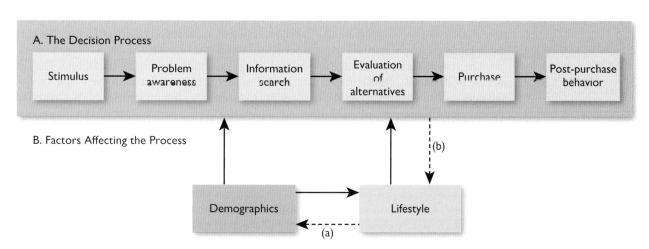

Note: Solid arrows connect all the elements in the decision process and show the impact of demographics and lifestyle upon the process. Dashed arrows show feedback. (a) shows the impact of lifestyle on certain demographics, such as family size, location, and marital status. (b) shows the impact of a purchase on elements of lifestyle, such as social class, reference groups, and social performance.

FIGURE 7-6

The Consumer Decision Process

under consideration may solve a problem of shortage or unfulfilled desire. It may be hard to learn why a person is motivated to move from stimulus to problem awareness. Many people shop with the same retailer or buy the same good or service for different reasons; they may not know their own motivation, and they may not tell a retailer their reasons for shopping there or buying a certain item.

Recognition of shortage occurs when a person discovers a good or service should be repurchased. A good could wear down beyond repair, or the person might run out of an item such as milk. Service may be necessary if a good (such as a car) requires a repair. Recognition of unfulfilled desire takes place when a person becomes aware of a good or service that has not been bought before or a retailer that has not been patronized before. An item (such as contact lenses) may improve a person's lifestyle or self-image in an untried manner, or it may offer new features (such as a voice-activated laptop). People are more hesitant to act on unfulfilled desires. Risks and benefits may be tougher to see. When a person becomes aware of a shortage or an unfulfilled desire, he or she acts only if it is a problem worth solving. Otherwise, the process ends.

Information search. If problem awareness merits further thought, information is sought. An **information search** has two parts: (1) determining the alternatives that will solve the problem at hand (and where they can be bought) and (2) ascertaining the characteristics of each alternative.

First, the person compiles a list of goods or services that address the shortage or desire being considered. This list does not have to be formal. It may be a group of alternatives the person thinks about. A person with a lot of purchase experience normally uses an internal memory search to determine the goods or services—and retailers—that are satisfactory. A person with little purchase experience often uses an external search to develop a list of alternatives and retailers. This search can involve commercial sources such as retail salespeople, noncommercial sources such as *Consumer Reports*, and social sources such as friends. Second, the person gathers information about each alternative's attributes. An experienced shopper searches his or her memory for the attributes (pros and cons) of each alternative. A consumer with little experience or a lot of uncertainty searches externally for information.

The extent of an information search depends, in part, on the consumer's perceived risk regarding a specific good or service. Risk varies among individuals and by situation. For some, it is inconsequential; for others, it is important. The retailer's role is to provide enough information for a shopper to feel comfortable in making decisions, thus reducing perceived risk. Point-of-purchase ads, product displays, and knowledgeable sales personnel can provide consumers with the information they need.

When the consumer's search for information is completed, she or he must decide whether a current shortage or unfulfilled desire can be met by any of the alternatives. If one or more are satisfactory, the consumer moves to the next step in the decision process. The consumer stops the process if no satisfactory goods or services are found.

Evaluation of alternatives. Next, a person selects one option. This is easy if one alternative is better on all features. An item with great quality and a low price is a certain pick over expensive, average-quality ones. Yet, a choice may not be that simple, and the person then does an **evaluation of alternatives** before making a decision. If two or more options seem attractive, the person sets the criteria to evaluate and their importance. Alternatives are ranked and a choice is made.

The criteria for a decision are those good or service attributes considered relevant. They may include price, quality, fit, durability, and so on. The person sets standards for these characteristics and rates each alternative according to its ability to meet them. The importance of each criterion is also set, and attributes are often of differing importance to each person. One person may consider price as most important while another places more weight on quality and durability.

At this point, the person ranks alternatives from most favorite to least favorite and selects one. Sometimes, it is hard to rate attributes because they are technical, intangible, new, or poorly labeled. When this occurs, shoppers often use price, brand name, or store name to indicate quality and choose based on this criterion. After a person ranks alternatives, he or she chooses the most satisfactory one. In situations where no alternative is adequate, a decision not to buy is made.

Purchase act. A person is now ready for the **purchase act**—an exchange of money or a promise to pay for the ownership or use of a good or service. Important decisions are still made in this step. For a retailer, the purchase act may be the most crucial aspect of the decision process because the consumer is mainly concerned with three factors, as highlighted in Figure 7-7:

1. *Place of purchase:* This may be a store or a nonstore location. Many more items are bought at stores than through nonstore retailing, although the latter method is growing quickly. The place of purchase is evaluated in the same way as the good or the service: alternatives are listed, their traits are defined, and they are ranked. The most desirable place is then chosen.

Nonprofit Consumer World is an online, noncommercial guide with more than 2,000 sources to aid the consumer's information search (www.consumerworld.org).

FIGURE 7-7

Key Factors in the Purchase Act

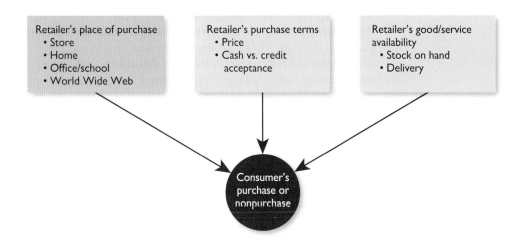

Criteria for selecting a store retailer include store location, store layout, service, sales help, store image, and prices. Criteria for selecting a nonstore retailer include image, service, prices, hours, interactivity, and convenience. A consumer will shop with the firm that has the best combination of criteria, as defined by that consumer.

2. *Purchase terms:* These include the price and method of payment. Price is the dollar amount a person must pay to achieve the ownership or use of a good or service. Method of payment is the way the price may be paid (cash, short-term credit, long-term credit).

3. *Availability:* This relates to stock on hand and delivery. Stock on hand is the amount of an item that a place of purchase has in stock. Delivery is the time span between placing an order and receiving an item and the ease with which an item is transported to its place of use.

If a person is pleased with all aspects of the purchase act, the good or service is bought. If there is dissatisfaction with the place of purchase, the terms of purchase, or availability, the consumer may not buy, although she or he may be satisfied with the item itself.

Post-purchase behavior. After buying a good or service, a consumer may engage in **post-purchase behavior**, which falls into either of two categories: further purchases or re-evaluation. Sometimes, buying one item leads to further purchases and decision making continues until the last purchase. A car purchase leads to insurance; a retailer using scrambled merchandising may stimulate a shopper to further purchase after the primary good or service is bought.

A person may also re-evaluate a purchase. Is performance as promised? Do actual attributes match the expectations the consumer had? Has the retailer acted as expected? Satisfaction typically leads to contentment, a repurchase when a good or service wears out, and positive ratings to friends. Dissatisfaction may lead to unhappiness, brand or store switching, and unfavorable conversations with friends and negative online postings. The latter situation (dissatisfaction) may result from **cognitive dissonance**—doubt that the correct decision has been made. A consumer may regret that the purchase was made at all or may wish that another choice had been made. To overcome cognitive dissonance and dissatisfaction, the retailer must realize that the decision process does not end with a purchase. After-care (by phone, a service visit, or E-mail) may be as important as anything a retailer does to complete the sale. When items are expensive or important, after-care takes on greater significance because the person really wants to be right. Also, the more alternatives from which to choose, the greater the doubt after a decision is made and the more important the after-care. Department stores pioneered money-back guarantees so customers could return items if cognitive dissonance occurred.

Realistic sales presentations and ad campaigns reduce post-sale dissatisfaction because consumer expectations do not then exceed reality. If overly high expectations are created, a consumer is more apt to be unhappy because performance is not at the level promised. Combining an honest sales presentation with good customer after-care reduces or eliminates cognitive dissonance and dissatisfaction.

Types of Consumer Decision Making

Every time a person buys a good or service or visits a retailer, she or he uses a form of the decision process. The process is often undertaken subconsciously, and a person is not aware of its use. Also, as was shown in Figure 7-6, the process is affected by consumer characteristics. Older people may not spend as much time as younger ones in making some decisions due to experience. Well-educated consumers may consult many information sources—increasingly, the Web—before making a decision. Upper-income consumers may spend less time deciding because they can afford to buy again if they are dissatisfied. In a family with children, each member may have input into a decision, which lengthens the process. Class-conscious shoppers may be interested in social sources, including social media. Consumers with low self-esteem or high perceived risk may use all the steps in detail. People under time pressure may skip steps to save time.

The use of the decision process differs by situation. The purchase of a new home usually means a thorough use of each step in the process; perceived risk is high regardless of the consumer's background. In the purchase of a fast-food meal, the consumer often skips certain steps; perceived risk is low regardless of the person's background. There are three types of decision processes: extended decision making, limited decision making, and routine decision making.

Extended decision making occurs when a consumer makes full use of the decision process. Much time is spent gathering information and ranking alternatives—what to buy and where to buy—before a purchase. The potential for cognitive dissonance is great. In this category are expensive, complex items with which a person has had little or no experience. Perceived risk of all kinds is high. Items requiring extended decision making include a house, a first car, and life insurance. At any point in the process, a consumer can stop, and for expensive, complex items, this occurs often. Consumer traits (such as age, education, an income) have the most impact.

Because their customers tend to use extended decision making, such retailers as real-estate brokers and auto dealers emphasize personal selling, printed materials, and other communication to provide as much information as possible. A low-key informative approach may be best, so shoppers do not feel threatened. Various financing options may be offered. In this way, the consumer's perceived risk is minimized.

With **limited decision making**, a consumer uses all the steps in the purchase process but does not spend a great deal of time on each of them. It requires less time than extended decision making because a person typically has some experience with both the brand and retailer choice of the purchase. This category includes items that have been bought before but not regularly. Risk is moderate, and the consumer spends some time shopping. Priority may be placed on evaluating known alternatives according to a person's desires and standards, although information search is vital for some. Items requiring limited decision making include a second car, clothing, a vacation, and gifts. Consumer attributes affect decision making, but the impact lessens as perceived risk falls and experience rises. Income, purchase importance, and motives play strong roles.

This form of decision making is relevant to such retailers as department stores, specialty stores, and nonstore retailers that want to sway behavior and that carry goods and services that people have bought before. The shopping environment and assortment are very important. Sales personnel should be available for questions and to differentiate among brands or models.

Routine decision making takes place when the consumer buys out of habit and skips steps in the purchase process. He or she wants to spend little or no time shopping, and the same brands are usually repurchased (often from the same retailers). This category includes items bought regularly. They have little risk due to consumer experience. The key step is problem awareness. When the consumer realizes a good or service is needed, a repurchase is often automatic. Information search, evaluation of alternatives, and post-purchase behavior are unlikely. These steps are not undertaken so long as a person is satisfied. Items involved with routine decision making include groceries, newspapers, and haircuts. Consumer attributes have little impact. Problem awareness almost inevitably leads to a purchase.

This type of decision making is most relevant to such retailers as supermarkets, dry cleaners, and fast-food outlets. For them, the following strategic elements are crucial: a good location, long hours, clear product displays, and, most important, product availability. Ads should be reminder-oriented. The major task is completing the transaction quickly and precisely.

Impulse Purchases and Customer Loyalty

Impulse purchases and customer loyalty merit special attention. **Impulse purchases** arise when consumers buy products and/or brands they had not planned on buying before entering a store, reading a mail-order catalog, seeing a TV shopping show, turning to the Web, and so forth. At least part of consumer decision making is influenced by the retailer. There are three kinds of impulse shopping:

► *Completely unplanned.* Before coming into contact with a retailer, a consumer has no intention of making a purchase in a goods or service category.
► *Partially unplanned.* Before coming into contact with a retailer, a consumer has decided to make a purchase in a goods or service category but has not chosen a brand or model.
► *Unplanned substitution.* A consumer intends to buy a specific brand of a good or service but changes his or her mind about the brand after coming into contact with a retailer.

With the partially unplanned and substitution kinds of impulse purchases, some decisions take place before a person interacts with a retailer. In these cases, a shopper may be involved with extended, limited, or routine decision making. Completely unplanned shopping often relates to routine or limited decision making; there is little or no time spent shopping; the key step is problem awareness.

Traditional store-based strategies to sell impulse goods were to place magazines, gift cards, batteries, and candies near cash registers. This strategy is not as successful as in the past as more consumers are making purchases online or ordering goods for home delivery through grocery lists that do not include these items.[22]

In studying impulse buying, these are some of the consumer attitudes and behavior patterns that retailers should take into consideration:

► In-store browsing is positively affected by the amount of time a person has to shop.
► Some individuals are more predisposed toward making impulse purchases than others.
► The leading reason given by consumers for impulse shopping is to take advantage of a low price/bargain. Impulse purchases should no longer be viewed of as frivolous behavior—increasingly, it is savvy opportunism. See Figure 7-8.
► Impulse shopping is affected by how stores are arranged. Old Navy reconfigured many of its stores so shoppers could move through the stores more easily and be exposed to more products.
► Impulse shopping is influenced by whether consumers believe that discounts are real.
► Impulse purchasing is not confined to stores. Web-based impulse purchases can be increased through various strategies. These include having an attractive and informative Web site, making it easy to buy items (such as Amazon's one-click purchasing), offering free shipping, and targeting shoppers based on past purchases, where they live, and media consumption.[23]

FIGURE 7-8

Stimulating Impulse Shopping

Could you resist spending more if an in-store circular featured deals such as the ones shown here?

Source: trekandshoot/ Shutterstock. Reprinted by permission.

TECHNOLOGY IN RETAILING

Recommendation Engines

One of the major applications of big data is personalized recommendations. It can be used on Web sites and, in the store setting, offer targeted offers and discounts. Recommendations are based on a customer's purchasing history or the histories of other consumers just like them. The computerized system predicts what the customer is likely to buy next and makes the recommendation to them. Analysts suggest that Amazon recommendations generate a revenue uplift of between 10 and 30 percent. Some retailers use third-party recommendation engines, but they will increasingly develop their own.

Analyze your own purchasing habits. What data would a third-party need to predict your next purchase?

L. L. Bean (www.llbean .com) has some of the most loyal customers around. See why.

When **customer loyalty** exists, a person regularly patronizes a particular retailer (store or nonstore) that he or she knows, likes, and trusts. This lets consumers reduce decision making because they do not have to invest time learning about and choosing the retailer from which to purchase. Loyal customers tend to be time-conscious (e.g., shop locally); do not often engage in outshopping; and spend more per shopping trip. In a service setting, such as an auto repair shop, customer satisfaction often leads to shopper loyalty; price has less bearing on decisions. Applying the retailing concept enhances the chances of gaining and keeping customers. This means being customer-oriented, coordinated, value-driven, and goal-oriented. Relationship retailing also helps!

The degree of customer loyalty to retailers can be classified according to five groupings: false loyalty, inertial loyalty, latent loyalty, premium loyalty, and reciprocal loyalty. In *false loyalty*, customers buy from a retailer only when it is offering special sales or promotions. With *inertia loyalty*, customers are loyal to a retailer mainly by the convenience of its location for store-based retailers or the ease of ordering and delivery for Web-based retailers. *Latent loyal* customers are loyal to a retailer, but they are light shoppers. With *premium loyalty*, people are heavy shoppers and advocates for the retailer among friends and family. The most loyal shoppers are *reciprocal loyal*. They have a strong relationship with a retailer by being advocates, through high purchase activity and by membership and participation in reward programs.[24]

Unfortunately, a number of retailers use a one-size-fits-all loyalty program, typically monetary rewards to stimulate repeat visits. Price reductions often do not alter long-run purchase behavior for people who desire more personal service or convenience. After buying from a retailer because of a limited-time price reduction, some shoppers are apt to return to their usual retailers. A better strategy to sustain customer loyalty is to offer tailored rewards, based on what particular shoppers desire. Tailored promotions include merchandise and service upgrades, free shipping by online stores, and messages through cell phone apps, as well as being more effective in enhancing customer engagement and loyalty.[25]

RETAILER ACTIONS

As noted in Chapter 3, in *mass marketing*, a firm such as a supermarket or a drugstore sells to a broad spectrum of consumers; it does not really focus efforts on any one kind of customer. In *concentrated marketing*, a retailer tailors its strategy to the needs of one distinct consumer group, such as young working women; it does not attempt to satisfy people outside that segment. With *differentiated marketing*, a retailer aims at two or more distinct consumer groups, such as men and boys, with a different strategy mix for each; it can do this by operating more than one kind of outlet (such as separate men's and boys' clothing stores) or by having distinct departments grouped by market segment in a single store (as a department store might do). In deciding on a target market approach, a retailer considers its goods/service category and goals, competitors' actions, the size of various segments, the efficiency of each target market alternative for the particular firm, the resources required, and other factors. See Figure 7-9.

After choosing a target-market method, the retailer selects the target market(s) to which it wants to appeal; identifies the characteristics, needs, and attitudes of the target market(s); seeks to understand how its target customers make purchase decisions; and acts appropriately. The process to devise a target market strategy is shown in Figure 7-10. Next, we present several examples of retailers' target-market activities.

We now present several examples of retailers' target market activities.

FIGURE 7-9

Concentrated Marketing in Action

The eatery shown here appeals to young professionals interested in casual dining and an enjoyable experience. The menu is tailored for this group.

Source: Monkey Business Images/Shutterstock. Reprinted by permission.

Retailers with Mass Marketing Strategies

Walgreens drugstore chain and Kohl's Department Stores engage in mass marketing. We will discuss both.

Walgreens Boots Alliance is a global company, with over 13,100 drugstores (Walgreens, Duane Reade, Boots, and Alliance Healthcare) in 11 countries. The firm attracts a broad array of customers. Three-quarters of the U.S. population live within 5 miles of a Walgreens or Duane Reade pharmacy. To attract a broad customer base, Walgreens Boots Alliance has convenient store locations, offers a broad array of consumer goods in addition to pharmacy and health care needs, and has online access. The retailer's Web sites have an average of 68 million visits per month.[26]

Find out why Kohl's is appealing (www.kohls.com).

Kohl's is a popular general merchandise retailer capitalizing on mass marketing. Key components of Kohl's mass marketing approach include: the sale of moderately priced private-label merchandise; exclusive and national brand apparel; and footwear and accessories for women, men, and children. Kohl's has a consistent merchandise mix across all stores (except for some differences due to meeting regional preferences).[27]

Retailers with Concentrated Marketing Strategies

Next, we will discuss Dollar Tree and Claire's Stores. Both engage in concentrated marketing.

Dollar Tree's Family Dollar (www.familydollar.com) has carved out a distinctive, narrow niche for itself.

With the acquisition of Family Dollar, Dollar Tree is the leading operator of discount variety stores in the U.S. with 13,000 stores in 48 states and 5 Canadian providences. Its Dollar Tree stores target lower-middle-income customers in suburban locations. These stores sell all items for $1. Dollar Tree has been adding freezers and coolers to drive customer traffic. Its Family Dollar division sells general merchandise to a lower-income customer in urban and rural locales. Family Dollar stores offer multiple price points, serving customers as their "neighborhood discount store," with great values on everyday items and a convenient shopping experience.[28]

Claire's Stores, Inc. operates close to 3,000 stores under the Claire's and Icing brand names. The Claire's stores specialize in fashionable jewelry and accessories (including earrings, necklaces,

| Determine Target Market Approach | → | Select Specific Target Market(s) | → | Study Characteristics, Needs, and Attitudes of Target Market(s) | → | Examine How Consumers Make Decisions—by Product Category | → | Develop and Enact Appropriate Retail Strategy Mix(es) for the Target Market(s) Chosen |

FIGURE 7-10

Devising a Target Market Strategy

bracelets, body jewelry, and rings) for young women, teens, tweens, and kids. The Icing stores sell fashion and hair accessories for women (including jewelry, cosmetics, and watches).[29]

Retailers with Differentiated Marketing Strategies

L Brands (www.lbrands .com) is another retailer practicing differentiated marketing—with its Victoria's Secret, Pink, Bath & Body Works, La Senza, and Henri Bendel units.

Last, we'll focus on Foot Locker, Inc. and Gap Inc. Both engage in differentiated marketing.

Besides its mainstream Foot Locker stores, the parent company (Foot Locker, Inc.) also operates chains geared specially toward women and children. Lady Foot Locker offers athletic footwear and apparel brands, as well as casual wear and apparel designed for running, walking, toning, and fitness. Kids Foot Locker carries "the largest selection of brand-name athletic footwear, apparel, and accessories for young athletes. Its stores feature an environment geared to appeal to both parents and children."[30]

Gap Inc. applies differentiated marketing through its Gap ("clean, classic clothing and accessories to help customers express their individual sense of style"—including Gap, Gap Kids, Baby Gap, Gap Maternity, Gap Body, and GapFit collections); Banana Republic (clothing, shoes, handbags, and fashion accessories with detailed craftsmanship and luxurious materials); Old Navy (less-expensive fashions and accessories than the Gap, but highly styled); Athleta (women's active and fitness apparel); and Intermix (styles from emerging and established designers).[31]

ENVIRONMENTAL FACTORS AFFECTING CONSUMERS

Several environmental factors influence shopping attitudes and behavior, including:

- ▶ State of the economy
- ▶ Consumer confidence about the future
- ▶ Country of residence (industrialized versus developing)
- ▶ Cost of living in the person's region or city of residence
- ▶ Rate of inflation (how quickly prices are rising)
- ▶ Infrastructure where people shop, such as traffic congestion, the crime rate, and the ease of parking
- ▶ Price wars among retailers
- ▶ Emergence of new retail formats
- ▶ Emergence of new technologies
- ▶ Trend toward more people working at home
- ▶ Government and community regulations regarding shopping hours, new construction, consumer protection, and so forth
- ▶ Evolving societal values and norms
- ▶ Digital presence and convenience of shopping at the retailer's Web site or mobile app

Although all of these elements may not necessarily have an impact on any particular shopper, they do influence the retailer's overall target market.

When planning the retail strategy that they offer their customers, companies should consider the customers' standard of living, including family size; discretionary income after spending for health, recreation, and social services; and consumer confidence in their financial future. Unemployment, low wages, crowded living conditions, and physical calamities may bring a drop in the standard of living; and an increase in social benefits and higher wages may bring a rise. The standard of living varies from nation to nation, and international comparisons are sometimes made by analyzing per capita income or any number of other indicators.

Chapter Summary

1. *To discuss why it is important for a retailer to properly identify, understand, and appeal to its customers.* To properly develop a strategy mix, a retailer must identify the characteristics, needs, and attitudes of consumers; understand how consumers make decisions; and enact

the proper target-market plan. It must study environmental influences, too.

2. *To enumerate and describe a number of consumer demographics, lifestyle factors, and needs and desires—and to*

explain how these concepts can be applied to retailing. Demographics are easily identifiable and measurable population statistics. Lifestyles are the ways in which consumers live and spend time and money.

Consumer demographics include gender, age, life expectancy, literacy, languages spoken, income, retail sales, education, and ethnic/racial background. These data usually have to be localized to be useful for retailers. Consumer lifestyles comprise social and psychological elements and are affected by demographics. Social factors include culture, social class, reference groups, the family life cycle, and time utilization. Psychological factors include personality, class consciousness, attitudes, perceived risk, and purchase importance. As with demographics, a firm can set a lifestyle profile of its target market by analyzing these concepts.

There are several demographic and lifestyle trends that apply to retailing. These involve gender roles, consumer sophistication and confidence, the poverty of time, and component lifestyles. Research has enumerated consumer profiles in a useful way for retailers.

In preparing a target market profile, consumer needs and desires should be identified. *Needs* are basic shopping requirements, and *desires* are discretionary shopping goals. A retail strategy geared toward satisfying consumer needs is appealing to their motives—the reasons for behavior. The better needs and desires are addressed, the more apt people are to buy.

3. *To examine consumer attitudes toward shopping and consumer shopping behavior, including the consumer decision process and its stages.* Many people do not enjoy shopping and no longer feel high prices reflect value. Different segments have different attitudes. More people now believe private brands are of good quality. Consumer patronage differs by retailer type. People often cross-shop, whereby they shop for a product category at more than one retail format during the year or visit multiple retailers on the same shopping trip.

Retailers should be aware of consumer behavior—the process individuals use to decide whether, what, when,

where, how, from whom, and how often to buy. The consumer's decision process has two perspectives: (a) the good or service the consumer thinks of buying and (b) where the consumer will buy that item. These decisions can be made separately or jointly.

The consumer decision process consists of stimulus, problem awareness, information search, evaluation of alternatives, purchase, and post-purchase behavior. It is influenced by a person's background and traits. A stimulus is a cue or drive meant to motivate a person to act. At problem awareness, the consumer not only has been aroused by a stimulus but also recognizes that a good or service may solve a problem of shortage or unfulfilled desire. An information search determines the available alternatives and their characteristics. Alternatives are then evaluated and ranked. In the purchase act, a consumer considers the place of purchase, terms, and availability. After a purchase, there may be post-purchase behavior in the form of additional purchases or re-evaluation. The consumer may have cognitive dissonance if there is doubt that a correct choice has been made.

In extended decision making, a person makes full use of the decision process. In limited decision making, each step is used, but not in depth. In routine decision making, a person buys out of habit and skips steps. Impulse purchases occur when shoppers make purchases they had not planned before coming into contact with the retailer. With customer loyalty, a person regularly patronizes a retailer.

4. *To look at retailer actions based on target market planning.* Retailers can deploy mass marketing, concentrated marketing, or differentiated marketing. Several examples are presented.

5. *To note some of the environmental factors that affect consumer shopping.* Consumer attitudes and behavior are swayed by the economy, inflation, the infrastructure where people shop, and other factors. Retailers also need to consider how the standard of living is changing.

Key Terms

demographics (p. 190)
lifestyles (p. 190)
discretionary income (p. 190)
culture (p. 192)
social class (p. 192)
reference groups (p. 192)
family life cycle (p. 193)
household life cycle (p. 193)
personality (p. 193)
class consciousness (p. 193)

attitudes (opinions) (p. 193)
perceived risk (p. 193)
motives (p. 196)
outshopping (p. 197)
cross-shopping (p. 199)
consumer behavior (p. 200)
consumer decision process (p. 201)
stimulus (p. 201)
problem awareness (p. 201)
information search (p. 202)

evaluation of alternatives (p. 202)
purchase act (p. 202)
post-purchase behavior (p. 203)
cognitive dissonance (p. 203)
extended decision making (p. 204)
limited decision making (p. 204)
routine decision making (p. 204)
impulse purchases (p. 204)
customer loyalty (p. 206)

Questions for Discussion

1. Comment on this statement: "A competitive retail sector, facing an uncertain economic future, is being challenged by consumers to compete for their business. In this environment, only the fittest and those really listening to what their customers really want are likely to survive."
2. Analyze the global population data in Table 7-1 from a retailing perspective.
3. How could a self-service frozen yogurt chain use the U.S. population data presented in Table 7-2?
4. Explain how a retailer selling expensive bicycles could reduce the six types of perceived risk.
5. Why is it important for retailers to know the difference between needs and desires?
6. Why do some consumers engage in outshopping? What could be done to encourage them to shop closer to home?
7. Identify the product categories with high cross-shopping. What is the reason for this?
8. The consumer decision process can be either short and decisive or long and involved, depending on the product or service and the involvement of the retailer. Outline this process and illustrate it with an example of a short decision process and a longer one.
9. Outline how a retailer could maximize the tendency for many consumers to buy impulsively.
10. Some retailers engage in differentiated marketing by having distinctively separated brands to cater for different customer targets. Give local examples and explain why this is necessary.
11. Sacla is a global Italian food brand (http://www.sacla .com/). Visit its Web site and identify its target market strategy.
12. Why is it valuable for retailers to understand the complexity of the standard-of-living concept?

Web-Based Exercise

The German discount retailer Aldi is considering breaking into the Italian market. Aldi Süd is carrying out extensive research in Italy. Read the article at the *Global Retail Brands* Web site (http://globalretailmag.com) titled "Five Facts That Make Italy Alluring to Aldi and a Potential Threat to Lidl." Review it and suggest how Aldi could circumvent the problems and establish itself in Italy.

8 Information Gathering and Processing in Retailing

The best retailers recognize that their decisions should be made after gathering and analyzing key information rather than making decisions based on intuition or "gut feelings." We are seeing more and more often that feedback can play a vital ongoing role in this process—even with regard to acquiring competitive intelligence.

Although many retailers just pay lip service to customer satisfaction, others employ real service efforts. "Lip service retailers" publicly state that customer service is important but do not empower employees; or they believe that customer service is going well so long as there are no complaints; or they refuse to fund service guarantee programs based on cost considerations. In contrast, real service is based on having high customer long-term loyalty based on delighting customers.

One way of distinguishing between the two is to see how far a retailer would go for its customers. Would it go as far as reporters and other employees at the *Boston Globe* recently did? After hearing repeated subscriber complaints about "widespread delivery problems," the *Boston Globe* management asked for volunteers in the newsroom to deliver the Sunday paper. The response was positively overwhelming. Editors, reporters, Web producers, and employees in marketing and advertising arrived at the newspaper's three distribution centers, stacked the Sunday edition in their own cars, and fanned out across the city to deliver the

Chapter Objectives

1. To discuss how information flows in a retail distribution channel

2. To show why retailers should avoid strategies based on inadequate information

3. To look at the retail information system, its components, and the recent advances in such systems

4. To describe the marketing research process

Source: Kheng Guan Toh/ Shutterstock. Reprinted by permission.

papers. One reporter said, "It was pretty incredible that so many people were willing to give up their sleep because we care so much about our readers."

There are other stories of retail employees going beyond customer expectations to delight customers. In one incident, a Nordstrom tailor did alterations on a garment not purchased at Nordstrom's so a bridesmaid's dress would properly fit. In another instance, a bellhop at a Ritz Carlton drove to the airport to meet up with a guest who left some valuables behind in a hotel room. How far would your retailers go to satisfy customers after receiving feedback from them?[1]

Overview

When a retailer sets a new strategy or modifies an existing one, gathering and analyzing information is crucial because it reduces the chances of wrong decisions. The firm can study the attributes and buying behavior of current and potential customers, alternative store and nonstore sites, store management and operations, product offerings, prices, and store image and promotion to prepare the best plan. See Figure 8-1.

iTools (www.itools.com) offers very useful research tools, including multiple search engines, a dictionary, a thesaurus, a language translator, and more.

Research activity should, to a large degree, be determined by the risk involved. Although it may be risky for a department store to open a new branch store, there is much less risk if that retailer is deciding whether to carry a new line of sweaters. In the branch store situation, thousands of research dollars and months of study may be necessary. In the case of the new sweaters, limited research may be sufficient.

Information gathering and processing should be conducted in an ongoing manner, yielding enough data for planning and analysis. Consider this example: More and more, retailers are gathering in-store geofencing and mobile beacon data, and then merging these data with information from their more traditional sources. With geofencing technology, retailers can track customers away from the store. iBeacon technology enables retailers to track customers inside the store.

They are also studying clickstream data which track behavior from Web sites, E-mail interactions, and point-of-sale data to integrate online and offline behavioral information to obtain customer insights and personalize shopper experience across multiple channels.[2]

This chapter first looks at the information flows in a retail distribution channel and notes the ramifications of inadequate research. We then describe the retail information system, database management and data warehousing, and the marketing research process in detail.

FIGURE 8-1

Be Informed, But Not Overloaded

Today, more information is available—for both large and small retailers—than ever before. So, even though it is imperative to gather and analyze sufficient data to make the best decisions, retailers also must be careful not to become overwhelmed by the data.

Source: Angela Waye/ Shutterstock. Reprinted by permission.

CAREERS IN RETAILING

Customer Relationship Management

Customer relationship managers typically rely on Universal Product Code–generated data (UPC) in conjunction with the retailer's POS system. An important use of point-of-sale (POS) equipment is to set up customers' accounts and collect and analyze their purchase history. Point-of-sale systems often look at core customer data. These customers are quite loyal to a retailer. An effective customer relationship management program relies on timely data, enabling a retailer to offer special sales and services to the best customers, suggest new items based on purchase history, and have special coupon offers to former core customers with diminished activity. As an example, a supermarket retailer can offer different coupons to consumers whose purchase history favors packaged goods versus those who favor organics.

What information skills should a customer relationship manager possess?

INFORMATION FLOWS IN A RETAIL DISTRIBUTION CHANNEL

In an effective retail distribution channel, information flows freely and efficiently among the three main parties: supplier (manufacturer and/or wholesaler), retailer, and consumer. This enables the parties to better anticipate and address each other's performance expectations. We highlight the flows in Figure 8-2 and describe the information needs of the parties next.

A *supplier* needs to know different kinds of information. From the retailer, the supplier needs estimates of category sales, inventory turnover rates, feedback on competitors, the level of customer returns, and so on. From the consumer, the retailer needs to know about attitudes toward given styles and models, the extent of brand loyalty, the willingness to pay a premium for superior quality, and the like.

A *retailer* also needs to know different kinds of information. From the supplier, the retailer needs advance notice of new models and model changes, training materials for complex products, sales forecasts, justification for price hikes, and so on. From the consumer, the retailer wants to know why people shop with the retailer, what they like and dislike about the retailer, where else people shop, and so on.

And the *consumer* needs different types of information. From the supplier, the consumer needs assembly and operating instructions, the extent of warranty coverage, where to send a complaint, and so forth. From the retailer, the consumer needs to know how various alternatives compare, where specific merchandise is stocked in the store, the methods of payment accepted, the rain check policy when a sale item is out of stock, and so on.

Retailers often play a crucial role in collecting data for other members of the value delivery chain because they have the most direct contact with shoppers. They can assist other channel members by:

▷ Permitting data to be gathered on their premises. Many research firms like to conduct surveys at shopping centers because of the large and broad base of shoppers.
▷ Gathering specific data requested by suppliers, such as how shoppers react to displays.
▷ Passing along information on the attributes of consumers buying particular brands and models. Because many credit transactions involve retailer cards, these retailers can link purchases with consumer age, income, occupation, and other factors.

For the best information flows, collaboration and cooperation are necessary—especially between suppliers and retailers. This is not always easy. Managing supply chain systems,

FIGURE 8-2

How Information Flows in a Retail Distribution Channel

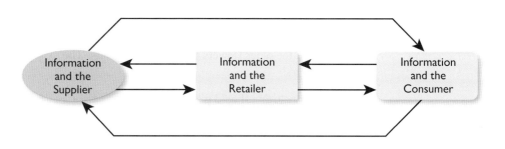

processes, and infrastructure and the associated changes to transform legacy store-based operations to omnichannel is complex and difficult. The lack of visibility across supply chain functions, as well as fragmented, incomplete, insufficient data, and/or manual processes of pre-existing systems and infrastructure, are not ideally suited for omnichannel functions. This results in the limited ability of existing retailers to compete effectively with new retailers deploying systems designed for omnichannel operations.[3]

Fortunately, many retailers are working to improve their information-sharing efforts. And as in many aspects of retailing, Walmart is leading the way. Thousands of suppliers have online access to Walmart's database through its password-protected online Retail Link system, which handles hundreds of thousands of information queries weekly. Retail Link was developed to promote more collaboration in inventory planning and product shipping, and it is a linchpin of Walmart's information efforts.[4]

AVOIDING RETAIL STRATEGIES BASED ON INADEQUATE INFORMATION

Retailers may rely on nonsystematic or incomplete ways of gathering information due to time and costs, as well as a lack of research skills. But the results can be devastating. For example:

▶ *Using intuition.* A movie theater charges $10 for tickets at all times. The manager feels that because all patrons are seeing the same movie, prices should be the same for a Monday matinee as a Saturday evening. Yet, by looking at data stored in the theater's information system, she would learn attendance is much lower on Mondays. Because people prefer Saturday evening performances, they will pay $10 to see a movie then. Weekday customers have to be lured, and a lower price is a way to do so.

▶ *Continuing what was done before.* A toy store orders conservatively for the holiday season because prior year sales were weak. The store sells out 2 weeks before the peak of the season, and more items cannot be received in time for the holiday. The owner assumed that last year's poor sales would occur again. Yet, a consumer survey would reveal a sense of optimism and an increased desire to give gifts.

▶ *Copying a successful competitor's strategy.* A local bookstore decides to cut the prices of best-sellers to match the prices of Amazon.com. The local store then loses a lot of money and goes out of business because its costs are too high to match the chain. The firm lost sight of its natural strengths (personal service, a customer-friendly atmosphere, and long-time community ties).

▶ *Devising a strategy after speaking to a few individuals about their perceptions.* A family-run gift store decides to have a family meeting to determine the product assortment for the next year. Each family member gives an opinion, and an overall "shopping list" is then compiled. Sometimes, the selections are right on target; other times, they result in a lot of excess inventory. The family would do better by also attending trade shows and reading industry publications.

▶ *Automatically assuming that a successful business can easily expand.* A Web retailer does well with small appliances and portable TVs. It has a good reputation and wants to add other product lines to capitalize on customer goodwill. However, adding custom furniture yields poor results. The firm did not first conduct research, which would have indicated that people buy standard, branded merchandise via the Web but are reluctant to buy custom furniture that way.

▶ *Not having a good read on consumer perceptions.* A florist cuts the price of 2-day-old flowers from $17 to $5 a dozen because they have a shorter life expectancy, but they don't sell. The florist assumes bargain-hunting consumers will want the flowers as gifts or for floral arrangements. What the florist does not realize (due to a lack of research) is that people perceive the older flowers to be of poor quality. The extremely low price actually turns off customers!

What conclusion should we draw from these examples? Inadequate information can cause a firm to devise and enact a bad strategy. These situations can be avoided by using a well-conceived retail information system and properly executing marketing research.

ETHICS IN RETAILING

Retail Security Breaches

Retailers used to be most concerned about truck hijacking and robberies; today, they are most concerned about cyber theft. Unlike stolen inventory, with cyber theft, data can be passed along electronically and anonymously among thieves. Among the retailers that have had significant credit-card account information theft are: Target, CVS, Wendy's, and Home Depot. The average size of a single credit-card data breach incident has increased a lot in recent years. Cyber theft has costs for retailers, credit-card issuers, and consumers. Even though consumer liability is limited, payment processors are passing more costs onto retailers. The greater U.S. retailer use of credit cards with embedded chips can reduce fraud and breaches—as they have done in Europe—since these embedded cards are more secure in the store.

How else should retailers better keep customers' credit-card information secure?

THE RETAIL INFORMATION SYSTEM

A retail information system requires a lot of background information, which makes the SecondaryData.com Web site (www.secondarydata.com/marketing/retailing.asp) valuable.

Data gathering and analysis should not be regarded as a one-shot resolution of a single retailing issue. They should be part of an ongoing, integrated process. A **retail information system (RIS)** anticipates the information needs of retail managers; collects, organizes, and stores relevant data on a continuous basis; and directs the flow of information to the proper decision makers.

These topics are covered next: Building and using a retail information system, database management, and gathering information via the UPC (Universal Product Code) and EDI (electronic data interchange).

Building and Using a Retail Information System

Figure 8-3 presents a general RIS. A retailer begins with its business philosophy and goals, which are affected by environmental factors (such as competitors and the economy). The philosophy and goals provide guidelines that direct strategic planning. Some aspects of plans are routine and need little re-evaluation. Others are nonroutine and need evaluation each time they arise.

After a strategy is outlined, data must be collected, analyzed, and interpreted. If data already exist, they are retrieved from files. When new data are acquired, files are updated. All of this occurs in the information control center. Based on data in the control center, decisions are enacted.

Performance is fed back to the information control center and compared with pre-set criteria. Data are retrieved from files or further data collected. Routine adjustments are made promptly. Regular reports and exception reports (to explain deviations from expected performance) are shown to the right parties. Managers may react in a way affecting company philosophy or goals (such as revamping a passé image or forgoing short-run profits to buy a new computer system).

FIGURE 8-3

A Retail Information System

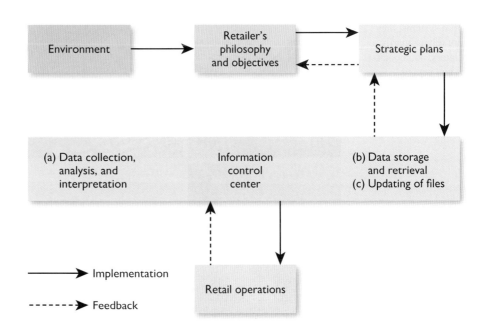

All types of data should be stored in the control center for future and ongoing use, and the control center should be integrated with the firm's short- and long-run plans and operations. Information should not be gathered sporadically and haphazardly but systematically.

A good RIS has several strengths. Information gathering is organized and company focused. Data are regularly collected and stored so opportunities are foreseen and crises averted. Strategic elements can be coordinated. New strategies can be devised more quickly. Quantitative results are accessible, and cost/benefit analysis can be done. Information is routed to the right personnel. Yet, deploying a retail information system may require high initial time and labor costs, and complex decisions may be needed to set up such a system.

In building a retail information system, a number of decisions have to be made:

▶ *How active a role should be given to the RIS?* Will it be used to proactively search for and distribute any relevant data or will it be used to reactively respond to requests from managers when problems arise? The best systems are more proactive because they anticipate events.

▶ *Should an RIS be managed internally or be outsourced?* Although many retailers engage in RIS functions, some use outside specialists. Either style can work, so long as the RIS is guided by the retailer's information needs. Several firms have their own RIS and use outside firms for specific tasks (such as conducting surveys or managing networks).

▶ *How much should an RIS cost?* Retailers typically spend 0.5 to 2.5 percent of their sales on an RIS. This lags behind most of the suppliers from which retailers buy goods and services.[5]

▶ *How technology-driven should an RIS be?* Although retailers can gather data from trade associations, surveys, and so forth, more firms now rely on technology to drive the information process. With the advent of low-cost personal computers and tablets, inexpensive networks, cloud computing, and low-priced software, technology is easy to use. Even a neighborhood deli can generate sales data by product and offer specials on slow-sellers. See Figure 8-4.

Retail Info Systems News (http://risnews.edgl.com) provides good insights for retailers.

FIGURE 8-4

It's Time to Turn from the Old Ways of Collecting and Storing Data

With all of the inexpensive, easy-to-use technology and related software on the market today, even the smallest retailers are able to utilize computerized retail information systems; they should not rely primarily on calculators, notebooks, and pens and pencils.

Source: Olga Constantin/ Shutterstock. Reprinted by permission.

> ▶ *How much data are enough?* The purpose of an RIS is to provide enough information, on a regular basis, for a retailer to make the proper strategy choices—not to overwhelm retail managers. This means performing a balancing act between too little information and information overload. To avoid overload, data should be carefully edited to eliminate redundancies.

> ▶ *How should data be disseminated throughout the firm?* This requires decisions as to who receives various reports, frequency of data distribution, and access to databases. When a firm has multiple divisions or operates in several regions, information access and distribution must be coordinated.

> ▶ *How should data be stored for future use?* Relevant data should be stored in a way that makes information retrieval easy and allows for adequate longitudinal (period-to-period) analysis.

Larger retailers tend to have a chief information officer (CIO) oversee the RIS. Their information systems departments often have formal, written annual plans. Computers are used by virtually all firms that conduct information systems analysis, and many firms use the Web for some RIS functions. Further growth in the use of retail information systems is still expected. There are many differences in information systems among retailers, in terms of revenues and retail format.

Thirty-five years ago, most computerized retail systems were used only to reduce cashier errors and improve inventory control. Today, they often form the basis for a retail information system and are used in surveys, ordering, merchandise transfers between stores, and other tasks. These activities are conducted by both small and large retailers. Most small and medium retailers—as well as large retailers—have computerized financial management systems, analyze sales electronically, and use computerized inventory management systems. Here are illustrations of how retailers are using the latest technology advances to computerize their information systems.

To see the various applications of Retail Pro, visit www.retailpro.com/solutions.

Retail Pro, Inc. markets Retail Pro management information software to retailers. This software is used at stores around the world. Although popular with large retailers, Retail Pro software also appeals to smaller and specialty retailers due to flexible pricing based on the number of users and stores, the type of hardware, payment fraud protection with its partner Cayan POS, customer personalization, and business optimization technology for an omnichannel strategy.[6]

MicroStrategy typically works with larger retailers—including about two-thirds of the top 500 retailers in the world—to provide merchandising optimization, loss prevention, and customer insight analytics; mobile technology for customer engagement; sales training; product information; and store operations and security solutions.[7]

Database Management

In **database management**, a retailer gathers, integrates, applies, and stores information related to specific subject areas. It is a major element in a retail information system, and may be used with customer databases, vendor databases, product category databases, and so on. A firm may compile and store data on customer attributes and purchase behavior, compute sales figures by vendor, and store records by product category. Each of these would represent a separate database. Among retailers that have databases, most use them for frequent shopper programs, customer analysis, promotion evaluation, inventory planning, trading area analysis, joint promotions with manufacturers, media planning, and customer communications.

Database management should be approached as a series of five steps:

1. Plan the particular database and its components and determine information needs.
2. Acquire the necessary information.
3. Retain the information in a usable and accessible format.
4. Update the database regularly to reflect demographic trends, recent purchases, and so forth.
5. Analyze the database to determine company strengths and weaknesses.

Information can come from internal and external sources. A firm can develop databases internally by keeping detailed records and sorting them. It could generate databases *by customer*— purchase frequency, items bought, average purchase, demographics, and payment method; *by vendor*—total retailer purchases per period, total sales to customers per period, the most popular items, retailer profit margins, delivery time, and service quality; and *by product category*—total category sales per period, item sales per period, retailer profit margins, and the percentage of items discounted.

As retailers align their strategies around customer needs and experiences across multiple channels, the need to extract and integrate high-quality, context-specific information from the big

Pitney Bowes (www
.pitneybowes.com/us) offers
a number of useful products
to help firms build and
manage their databases.

data deluge is paramount. Customer information management providers such as Pitney Bowes, a leader in this field, leverage their expertise and data collected from their multiple clients and industries to facilitate cross-channel and cross-border commerce. Pitney Bowes' Single Customer View service provides a fully integrated 360-degree view of customers to employees. This is done by converting company-dispersed customer interaction data into integrated databases; adding geodemographic context to customer profiles to uncover timely, actionable insights to help craft memorable customer experiences; dynamically tracking customer lifetime value; improving the efficiency of customer acquisitions; and, in some cases, ensuring compliance with national and international regulations.[8]

To effectively manage a retail database, these are vital considerations:

▶ What are the firm's database goals?
▶ Who will be responsible for data management?
▶ What type of information will be collected and produced? What will be its format (images, data files, and so on)? Where do you plan to store the data?
▶ Is every database initiative analyzed to see if it is successful?
▶ Is there a mechanism to flag data that indicates potential problems or opportunities?
▶ Are customer purchases of different items or from different company divisions cross-linked?
▶ How will data be communicated?
▶ Is there a clear privacy policy that is communicated to those in a database? Are there opt-out provisions for those who do not want to be included in a database?
▶ Is the database updated each time there is a customer interaction?
▶ Are customers, personnel, suppliers, and others invited to update their personal data?
▶ Is the database periodically checked to eliminate redundant files?
▶ Roughly how long should the data be retained? Is it permanent? Will it be updated?[9]

Let's now discuss two aspects of database management: Data warehousing is a mechanism for storing and distributing information. Data mining and micromarketing are ways in which information can be utilized. Figure 8-5 shows the interplay of data warehousing with data mining and micromarketing.

DATA WAREHOUSING   One advance in database management is **data warehousing**, whereby copies of all the databases in a firm are maintained in one location and are accessible to employees at any locale. A data warehouse is a comprehensive compilation of the data used to support management decision making. According to government sources,

FIGURE 8-5

Retail Database Management in Action

The data warehouse is where information is collected, sorted, and stored centrally. Information is disseminated to retailer personnel, as well as to channel partners (such as alerting them to what merchandise is hot and what is not hot) and customers (such as telling them about order status). In data mining, retail executives and other employees—and sometimes channel partners—analyze information by customer type, product category, and so forth in order to determine opportunities for tailored marketing efforts. With micromarketing, the retailer applies differentiated marketing. Focused retail strategy mixes are planned for specific customer segments—or even for individual customers.

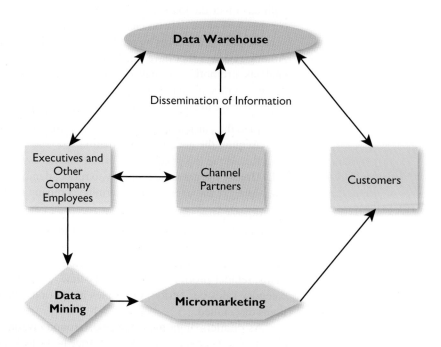

Teradata Magazine (www
.teradatamagazine.com)
explores data warehousing
in depth.

The fundamental attributes of a data warehouse are: *Subject-Oriented*—A data warehouse is organized around high-level business groupings called subjects [such as sales]. *Integrated*—The data in the warehouse must be integrated and consistent. If two different source systems store conflicting data, the differences need to be resolved during the process of transforming the source data and loading it into the data warehouse. *Time-Variant*—A key characteristic distinguishing warehouses is the currency of the data. Operational systems require real-time views of data, while data warehouse applications generally deal with longer term, historical data. They can also provide access to a greater volume of more detailed information over a longer time period. *Nonvolatile*—Data in the warehouse is read-only; updates or a refresh of the data occur on a periodic incremental or full refresh basis.[10]

A data warehouse has these components: (1) the data warehouse, where data are actually stored; (2) software to copy original databases and transfer them to the warehouse; (3) interactive software to process queries; and (4) a directory for the categories of data kept in the warehouse.

Data warehousing has several advantages. Executives and other employees are quickly, easily, and simultaneously able to access data wherever they may be. There is more companywide entrée to new data when they are first available. Data inconsistencies are reduced by consolidating records in one location. Better data analysis and manipulation are possible because information is stored in one location.

Computerized data warehouses were once costly to build (an average of $2.2 million in the 1990s) and, thus, feasible only for the largest retailers. Rapid progress in Web 2.0 and cloud technologies now makes it possible for startup businesses, especially online-only retailers, to access data warehouse as a service (DWaaS). It is a cloud-based outsourcing model in which DWaaS service providers such as Google (BigQuery), Microsoft (Azure), and Amazon Web Services (AWS) configure and manage the hardware, software platforms, and resources a data warehouse requires. The small business user uploads its own data and queries it on the Web through application programming interfaces (APIs), and pays based on usage for the managed service.[11] The user has no upfront costs to create, staff to manage, or software or hardware to upgrade, and can easily and quickly scale up from small to large in terms of usage and storage. Oracle, NCR-Teradata, and IBM provide enterprise-level data warehousing, and DWaaS provides the same to mid-size and large firms. Cabela's, Hudson's Bay, and 7-Eleven are just a few of the multitude of retailers that use data warehousing.[12]

Dollar Tree's Family Dollar (www.familydollar.com) discount stores is one of the retailers positioning itself for long-term growth and developing an efficient collaborative business intelligence program with suppliers by using a constantly updated retail data warehousing structure developed by Retail Solutions (RSi, www.retailsolutions.com). Real-time store-level inventory and point-of-sale data at the store/item and category level are provided through a Retail Management Solution after cleansing, validation, and standardization through a single portal to Family Dollar and its suppliers. Family Dollar can analyze performance by store cluster, price point, and product mix, and identify lost sales opportunities. Suppliers can fine-tune forecasting and product allocations, and identify distribution voids (e.g., phantom inventory). The micro-level information provides suppliers with greater understanding of consumer demand. Increased collaboration with Family Dollar lowers inventory-holding costs while providing consumers with the highest service levels.[13]

DATA MINING AND MICROMARKETING **Data mining** is the in-depth analysis of information to gain specific insights about customers, product categories, vendors, and so forth. The goal is to learn if there are opportunities for tailored marketing efforts that would lead to better retailer performance. One application of data mining is **micromarketing**, whereby the retailer uses differentiated marketing and develops focused retail strategy mixes for specific customer segments, sometimes fine-tuned for the individual shopper.

For an in-depth discussion,
go to The Balance (www
.thebalance.com/retail-
industry-4073977) and type
"data mining" in the search
engine.

Data mining relies on special software to sift through a data warehouse to uncover patterns and relationships among different factors. The software allows vast amounts of data to be quickly searched and sorted. That is why many firms, such as supermarkets, have made the financial commitment to data mining. The entry of well-funded online players such as Amazon, Google, and others has made the competition for grocery share of wallet even more fierce. Grocery has a distinct advantage over other forms of retail to leverage predictive analytics because consumers typically make frequent shopping trips according to SAS, a provider of business analytics software and services. Frequent-shopper card data help grocers track customer purchases over time and understand a shopper's evolving buying behavior. By using behavioral analytics and value segmentation for multiple shoppers within a single household, combined with demographic data, retailers can create a more complete picture of that household's needs and habits, personalize the shopping experience with micro-targeted promotions to increase the amount of groceries purchased, improve profit margins, and increase consumer satisfaction.[14]

Gathering Information through the UPC and EDI

To be more efficient with their information systems, most retailers rely on the Universal Product Code (UPC) and many now utilize electronic data interchange (EDI).

With the **Universal Product Code (UPC)**, products (or tags attached to them) are marked with a series of thick and thin vertical lines, representing each item's identification code. An item's UPC includes both numbers and lines. The lines are "read" by scanners at checkout counters. Cashiers do not enter transactions manually—though they can, if needed. Because the UPC itself is not readable by humans, the retailer or vendor must attach a ticket or sticker to a product specifying its size, color, and other information (if not on the package or the product). Given that the UPC does not include price information, this too must be added by a ticket or sticker.

By using UPC-based technology, retailers can record data instantly on an item's model number, size, color, and other factors when it is sold, as well as send the data to a computer that monitors unit sales, inventory levels, and so forth. The goals are to produce better merchandising data, improve inventory management, speed transaction time, raise productivity, reduce errors, and coordinate information.

Since its inception more than 40 years ago, UPC technology has improved substantially. It is now the accepted retailing standard. Several billion scans occur every day. The UPC allows all stores in the retail sector to identify products and capture information about them. Stores can control inventory more efficiently, provide a faster and more accurate checkout for customers, and easily gather inventory data for accurate and immediate marketing reports. Virtually every time sales or inventory data are scanned by a computer, UPC technology is involved. More than 200,000 U.S. manufacturers and retailers belong to GS1 US (formerly known as the Uniform Code Council), a group that has taken the lead in setting and promoting inter-industry product identification and communication standards.[15] Figure 8-6 shows how far UPC technology has come.

Regular UPC tags may result in errors when scanned by customers for product information lookup and be a disadvantage in mobile commerce. To meet the needs of mobile-centric customers, manufacturers and brand owners are adopting GS1 US Mobile Scan that imprints packages with an imperceptible digital watermark (DWcode), that, when scanned with a smartphone app, is linked to a mobile-optimized Web address. This provides contextual product information provided by the brand. Retailers benefit from faster retail checkout, better supply chain efficiency, and an enhanced in-store experience resulting from more information at product locations in aisles and inventory. Consumers, anywhere in the world, get information transparency by scanning the UPC or package imprinted with a DWcode with their Internet-enabled smartphones. Consumers are then able to see a Web page with real-time, brand-authorized product information, pricing, special offers, instructional videos, rich media, and additional shopping assistance.[16]

GXS is one of the leaders in EDI technology (http://edi.gxs.com).

With **electronic data interchange (EDI)** and *Internet electronic data interchange (I-EDI)*, retailers and suppliers regularly exchange information through their computers with regard to inventory levels, delivery times, unit sales, and so on of particular items. As a result, both parties enhance their decision-making capabilities, better control inventory, and are more responsive to demand. UPC scanning is often the basis for product-related EDI data. Hundreds of thousands of firms around the world (led by U.S.-based firms) use some form of the EDI system. Retailers use EDI to replace paper-based documents such as purchase orders, invoices, inventory reports, shipping notifications, routing requests, and routing instructions to electronic documents sent from one computer system to another instantaneously.

Unlike in some other industries, the supply chain in the retail industry is very complicated, and has to be flexible and responsive to fluctuations in demand levels, which can differ for each SKU (stock-keeping unit); and the number of SKUs may increase each year. A retail supply chain cannot afford occasional order delays or "stock-outs"; this it leads to lost sales and raises the risk of sending customers to the competition. Vendor-managed inventory (VMI) systems, one of EDI's applications, shorten the replenishment cycle and ensure that accurate and timely information is passed on electronically at every stage of the fulfillment cycle by streamlining direct store delivery

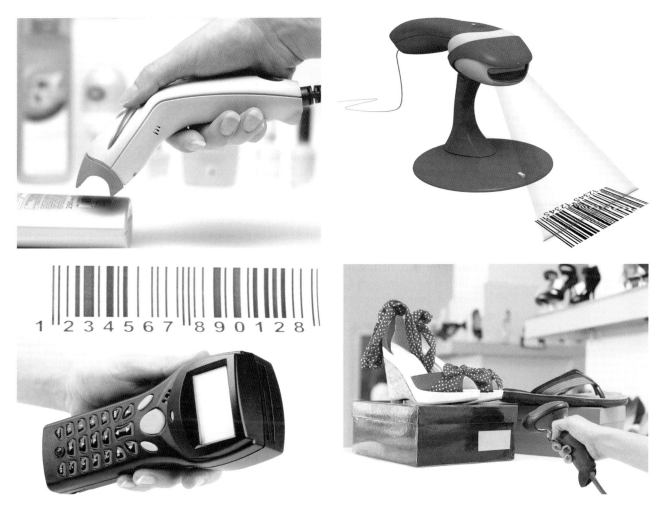

FIGURE 8-6

Applying UPC Technology to Gain Better Information

Portable UPC scanners are lightweight, highly mobile, and come in various shapes and colors. They all have the same purpose—to "read" the information on the UPC label, transmit the data to a computer, compile and store the data, and provide up-to-the-minute and detailed reports to retail employees who analyze the data and act accordingly.

Sources: Voznikevich Konstantin/Shutterstock, erzetic/Shutterstock, Ruslan Kuzmenkov/Shutterstock, and Photobac/Shutterstock. Reprinted by permission.

and lowering delivery and labor costs. This ensures that customers always get products when they want them (e.g., during promotion events or holidays when demand is very high), yet reduces oversupply when demand wanes. Vendor-managed inventory helps retailers strengthen relationships with customers and vendors by reducing check-in times, keeping products stocked consistently, and reducing human errors.[17]

Many retailers now require potential suppliers to have an EDI solution—either their own or via a third-party provider—before they are selected ("onboarded") as a vendor. Many small and medium-sized suppliers and retailers choose cloud-based, third-party EDI solutions for more flexibility and faster integration, quicker onboarding of suppliers, reduction of operating costs, elimination of manual ordering, and better order management.[18] The EDI system is covered further in Chapter 15, along with collaborative planning, forecasting, and replenishment.

THE MARKETING RESEARCH PROCESS

Marketing research in retailing entails the collection and analysis of information relating to specific issues or problems facing a retailer. At farsighted firms, marketing research is just one element in a retail information system. At others, marketing research may be the only type of data gathering and processing.

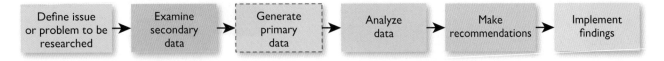

FIGURE 8-7

The Marketing Research Process in Retailing

The **marketing research process** embodies a series of activities: defining the issue or problem to be studied, examining secondary data, generating primary data (if needed), analyzing data, making recommendations, and implementing findings. It is not a single act; rather, it is a systematic process. Figure 8-7 outlines the research process. Each activity is done sequentially. Secondary data are not examined until after an issue or problem is defined. In Figure 8-7, the dashed line around the primary data stage means these data are generated only if secondary data do not yield actionable information. The process is described next.

Issue (problem) definition involves a clear statement of the topic to be studied. What information does the retailer want to obtain to make a decision? Without clearly knowing the topic to be researched, irrelevant and confusing data could be collected. Here are examples of issue definitions for a shoe store. The first one seeks to compare three locations and is fairly structured; the second is more open-ended: (1) "Of three potential new store locations, which should we choose?" (2) "How can we improve the sales of our men's shoes?"

When **secondary data** are involved, a retailer looks at data that have been gathered for purposes other than addressing the issue or problem currently under study. Secondary data may be internal (such as company records) or external (such as government reports and trade publications). When **primary data** are involved, a retailer looks at data that are collected to address the specific issue or problem under study. This type of data may be generated via survey, observation, experiment, and simulation.

Convenience Store News conducted a study of what time of day people most often visit convenience stores. Its 2016 "Realities of the Aisle" consumer research studied 1,501 people who shopped at least one time in the prior month. By the time you read this, the data in Table 8-1 will be secondary data in nature.[19]

Secondary data are sometimes relied on; other times, primary data are crucial. In some cases, both are gathered. It is important that retailers keep these points in mind: (1) There is great diversity in the possible types of data collection (and in the costs). (2) Only data relevant to the issue being studied should be collected. (3) Primary data are usually acquired only if secondary data are inadequate (thus, the dashed box in Figure 8-7). Both secondary and primary data are described further in the next sections.

TABLE 8-1 An Illustration of Secondary Data

At what time(s) of day do you typically shop at convenience stores?

| | TOTAL | BY GENDER | |
		MALE	FEMALE
6 A.M. – 8:59 A.M.	33.5%	36.6%	29.2%
9 A.M. – 10:59 A.M.	27.0%	26.5%	27.9%
11 A.M. – 1:59 P.M.	32.8%	31.0%	35.4%
2 P.M. –3:59 P.M.	33.8%	31.1%	37.5%
4 P.M. – 6:59 P.M.	50.1%	48.6%	52.2%
7 P.M. – 10 P.M	34.8%	34.5%	35.1%
After 10 P.M.	13.3%	13.0%	13.8%
Don't know	4.3%	4.1%	4.5%

Multiple responses accepted.

Source: "Bring Your 'A' Game," *Convenience Store News*, February 2016, p. 26. Reprinted with permission. Convenience Store News (c) 2016 (www.csnews.com)

These kinds of secondary and primary data can be gathered for the shoe store issues recently stated:

Issue (Problem) Definition	Information Needed to Solve Issue (Problem)
1. Which store location?	1. Data on access to transportation, traffic, consumer profiles, rent, store size, and types of competition are gathered from government reports, trade publications, and observation by the owner for each of the three potential store locations.
2. How to improve sales of shoes?	2. Store sales records for the past 5 years by product category are gathered. A consumer survey in a nearby mall is conducted.

After data are collected, data analysis is performed to assess that information and relate it to the defined issue. Alternative solutions are also clearly outlined. For example:

Issue (Problem) Definition	Alternative Solutions
1. Which store location?	1. Each site is ranked for all the criteria (access to transportation, traffic, consumer profiles, rent, store size, and types of competition).
2. How to improve sales of shoes?	2. Alternative strategies to boost sales are analyzed and ranked.

At this point, the pros and cons of each alternative are enumerated. See Table 8-2. Recommendations are then made as to the best strategy for the firm. Of the available options, which is best? Table 8-2 also shows recommendations for the shoe-store issues discussed in this section.

Last, but not least, the recommended strategy is implemented. If research is to replace intuition in strategic retailing, a decision maker must follow the recommendations from research studies, even if those results seem to contradict his or her own ideas.

Let's now look at secondary data and primary data in greater depth.

TABLE 8-2 Research-Based Recommendations

Issue (Problem)	Alternatives	Pros and Cons of Alternatives	Recommendation
1. Which store location?	Site A	Best transportation, traffic, and consumer profiles. Highest rent. Smallest store space. Extensive competition.	Site A: the many advantages far outweigh the disadvantages.
	Site B	Poorest transportation, traffic, and consumer profiles. Lowest rent. Largest store space. No competition.	
	Site C	Intermediate on all criteria.	
2. How to improve sales of shoes?	Increased assortment	Will attract and satisfy many more customers. High costs. High level of inventory. Reduces turnover for many items.	Lower prices and increase ads: additional customers offset higher costs and lower margins; combination best expands business.
	Drop some lines and specialize	Will attract and satisfy a specific consumer market. Excludes many segments. Costs and inventory reduced.	
	Slightly reduce prices	Unit sales increase. Markup and profit per item decline. Will increase traffic and new customers. High costs.	
	Advertise		

Secondary Data

ADVANTAGES AND DISADVANTAGES   Secondary data have several advantages:

Through Public Register Online (www .annualreportservice .com), a retailer can learn about other firms around the globe. Get an annual report here. (A free login is required.)

▶ Data assembly is inexpensive. Company records, trade journals, and government publications are all rather low cost. No data collection forms, interviewers, and tabulations are needed.

▶ Data can be gathered quickly. Company records, library sources, and Web sites can be accessed immediately. Many firms store reports in their retail information systems.

▶ There may be several sources of secondary data—with many perspectives.

▶ A secondary source may possess information that would otherwise be unavailable to the retailer. Government publications often have statistics no private firm could acquire.

▶ When data are assembled by a source such as *Progressive Grocer*, Nielsen, *Stores*, or the government, results are usually quite credible.

▶ The retailer may have only a rough idea of the topics to investigate. Secondary data can then help define issues more specifically. In addition, background information about a given issue can be gathered from secondary sources before undertaking a primary study.

Secondary data also have several potential disadvantages:

▶ Available data may not suit the purposes of the current study because they have been collected for other reasons. Neighborhood statistics may not be found in secondary sources.

▶ Secondary data may be incomplete. A service station owner would want car data broken down by year, model, and mileage driven, so as to stock parts. A motor vehicle bureau could provide data on the models but not the mileage driven.

▶ Information may be dated. Statistics gathered every 2 to 5 years may not be valid today. The *U.S. Census of Retail Trade* is conducted every 5 years. Furthermore, there is often a time delay between the completion of a census and the release of information.

▶ The accuracy of secondary data must be carefully reviewed. A retailer needs to decide if the data have been compiled in an unbiased way. The purpose of the research, the data collection tools, and the method of analysis should each be examined—if they are available for review.

▶ Some secondary data sources are known for poor data collection methods; they should be avoided. When data conflict, the source with the best reputation for accuracy should be used.

▶ In retailing, many secondary data projects are not retested and the user of secondary data has to hope results from one narrow study are applicable to his or her firm.

Whether secondary data resolve an issue or not, their low cost and availability require that primary data not be amassed until after studying secondary data. Only if secondary data are not actionable should primary data be collected. We now cite secondary data sources for retailers.

SOURCES   There are many sources and types of secondary data. The major distinctions are between internal and external sources.

Internal secondary data are available within the company, sometimes from the data bank of a retail information system. Before searching for external secondary data or primary data, the retailer should look at information available inside the firm.

TECHNOLOGY IN RETAILING   Mobile Beacons and Data Collection

Many large retailers have experimented with mobile beacons in stores to deliver highly targeted promotions and collect data on customer purchase journeys. Understanding how beacon technology works and what customers can do to protect identifiable information is required. Beacons use battery-powered Bluetooth Low Energy transmitters to send static pieces of data within a short distance (a few inches to 35 feet) to receivers (typically, a customer's smartphone app). The typical beacon promotion or message consists of an alphanumeric code identifying the retailer), a major ID (particular store of the retailer), minor ID (unique for every location within a store), and coded promotion messages. Beacons cannot transmit or collect data or track customers if the customer does not have the retailer's app on a smartphone or it is turned off.

How should retailers best use beacons?

■

At the beginning of the year, most retailers forecast and develop budgets for the next 12 months. This helps outline planned spending for that year. A firm's prior budget and its success in reaching budgetary goals are good sources of secondary data in forming a new budget.

Retailers use sales and profit-and-loss reports to judge performance. Many have data from electronic registers that can be studied by store, department, and item. By comparing data with prior periods, a firm gets a sense of growth or contraction. Overdependence on sales data may be misleading. Sales should be examined along with profit-and-loss data to indicate strengths and weaknesses in operations and management and to help lead to improvements.

Through customer billing reports, a retailer learns about inventory movement, sales by different personnel, and sales volume. For credit customers, sales by location, repayment time, and types of purchases can be reviewed. Purchase invoices show the retailer's own buying history and enables the retailer to evaluate itself against budgetary goals. See Figure 8-8.

Inventory records indicate the merchandise carried throughout the year and the turnover of these items. Knowing the lead time to place and receive orders from suppliers, as well as the extra inventory kept on hand to prevent running out at different times over the year, aids planning.

If a firm does primary research, the resultant report should be kept for future use (hopefully in the retail information system). When used initially, a report involves primary data. Later reference to it is secondary in nature since the report is no longer used for its primary purpose.

Written reports on performance are another source of internal secondary data. They may be prepared and filed by senior executives, buyers, sales personnel, or others. All phases of retail management can be improved through formal report procedures.

FIGURE 8-8

Internal Secondary Data: A Valuable Source of Knowledge

Every retailer retains a variety of records that indicate past performance, typically by season, product category, and store unit (if a chain)—and, increasingly, by specific customer and product item. This information is useful in comparing past and current performance and in making future forecasts.

Source: Nataliiap/ Shutterstock. Reprinted by permission.

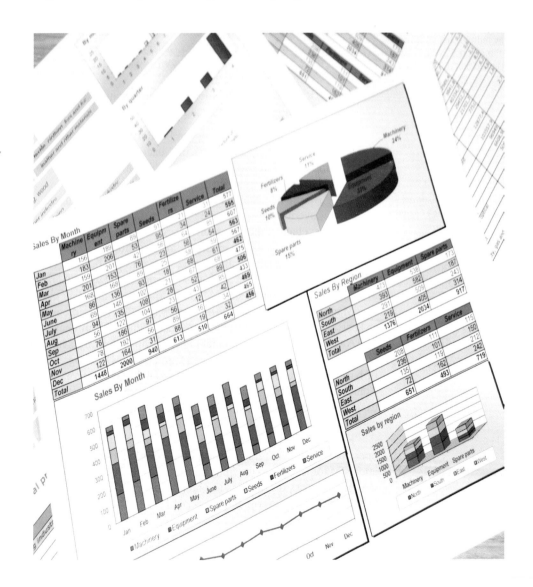

External secondary data are available from sources outside the firm. They should be consulted if internal information is insufficient for a decision to be made on a defined issue. These sources are comprised of government and nongovernment categories.

To use external secondary data well, appropriate online databases should be consulted. They contain all kinds of written materials, usually by subject or topic heading, for a specified time. Here are several databases, chosen for their retailing relevance. They are typically available through the Internet (for online access, you must use your company, college, or local library Web connection—direct entry to the sites is password-protected):

- Academic Search Premier/EBSCOhost
- Business Source Premier/EBSCOhost
- Dow Jones Factiva
- Gale's Business & Company Resource Center
- Gale Virtual Reference Library
- Ingenta Connect
- LexisNexis Academic Universe
- Mergent Online
- Plunkett Research Online
- Standard & Poor's NetAdvantage

The government distributes many materials. Here are publications chosen for their retailing value. They are available in a business library or other large library or through the Web:

- *Annual Retail Trade Survey*
- *Consumer Expenditure Survey* (Quarterly)
- *U.S. Census of Retail Trade* (Every 5 years ending in 2 and 7)
- *U.S. Census of Service Industries* (Every 5 years ending in 2 and 7)
- *Monthly Retail Trade and Food Services Sales*
- *U.S. Survey of Current Business*
- *Other* (Registration data such as births, deaths, automobile registrations, etc. Available through federal, state, and local agencies.)

Government agencies, such as the Federal Trade Commission, provide online pamphlets on topics such as franchising, unit pricing, deceptive ads, and credit policies. The Small Business Administration provides smaller retailers with online literature and advice. Pamphlets are distributed free or sold for a nominal fee.

Nongovernment secondary data come from many sources, often cited in reference guides. Major nongovernment sources are regular periodicals; books, monographs, and other nonregular publications; channel members; and commercial research houses.

Regular periodicals are available at most libraries or by personal subscription. A growing number are also available online; some Web sites provide free information, whereas others charge a fee. Periodicals may have a broad scope (such as *Fortune*) and discuss diverse business topics, or they may be narrower (such as *Chain Store Age*) and deal mostly with retail topics.

Many firms publish books, monographs, and other nonregular retailing materials. Some, such as Pearson Higher Education (www.pearsonhighered.com), have textbooks and practitioner books. The American Marketing Association (www.ama.org) offers information to enhance readers' business knowledge. The Better Business Bureau (www.bbb.org) wants to improve the public's image of business and expand industry self-regulation. The International Franchise Association (www.franchise.org) and the National Retail Federation (www.nrf.com) describe industry practices and trends, and they act as spokespersons to advocate the best interests of members. Other associations can be uncovered by consulting Gale's *Encyclopedia of Associations*.

Retailers may also get information from channel partners such as ad agencies, franchise operators, manufacturers, and wholesalers. When those firms do research for their own purposes and offer some or all of the findings to their retailers, external secondary data are involved. Channel partners pass on findings to enhance their own sales and retailer relations. They usually do not charge for the information.

The last external source is the commercial research house that conducts ongoing studies and makes results available to many clients for a fee. This source is secondary if the retailer is a subscriber and does not request tailored studies. Information Resources Inc., Nielsen, and Standard Rate & Data Service provide subscriptions at lower costs than a retailer would incur if data were collected only for its use.

The U.S. Census Bureau has a Web site (www.census.gov/econ/www/retmenu.html) listing recent retailing reports, which can be viewed and downloaded.

Looking for secondary data on direct marketing? Check out these sites: (https://thedma.org/knowledge-center) or E-commerce (http://baymard.com/research).

Our blog (www.bermanevansretail.com) has posts on online sources of free external secondary data—both government and nongovernment.

Primary Data

ADVANTAGES AND DISADVANTAGES   After exhausting available secondary data, a defined issue may still be unresolved. In this instance, primary data (collected to resolve a specific topic at hand) are needed. When secondary data are sufficient, primary data are not collected. There are several advantages associated with primary data:

- They are collected to fit the retailer's specific purpose.
- Information is current.
- The units of measure and data categories are designed for the issue being studied.
- The firm either collects data itself or hires an outside party. The source is known and controlled, and the methodology is constructed for the specific study.
- There are no conflicting data from different sources.
- When secondary data do not resolve an issue, primary data are the only alternative.

There are also several possible disadvantages often associated with primary data:

- They are normally more expensive to obtain than secondary data.
- Information gathering tends to be more time-consuming.
- Some types of information cannot be acquired by an individual firm.
- If only primary data are collected, the perspective may be limited.
- Irrelevant information may be collected if the issue is not stated clearly enough.

In sum, a retailer has many criteria to weigh when evaluating the use of primary data. In particular, specificity, currency, and reliability must be balanced against high costs, time, and limited access to materials. A variety of primary data sources for retailers are discussed next.

SOURCES   The first decision is to determine who collects the data. A retailer can do this itself (internal) or hire a research firm (external). Internal collection is usually quicker and cheaper. External collection is usually more objective and formal. Second, a sampling method is specified. Instead of gathering data from all stores, all products, and all customers, a retailer may obtain accurate data by studying a sample of them. This saves time and money. With a **probability (random) sample**, every store, product, or customer has an equal or known chance of being chosen for study. In a **nonprobability sample**, stores, products, or customers are chosen by the researcher—based on judgment or convenience. A probability sample is more accurate but is also more costly and complex. Third, the retailer chooses among four methods of data collection: survey, observation, experiment, and simulation. All of the methods are capable of generating data for each element of a strategy.

Want to learn about conducting an Internet survey? Go to this Business Research Lab Web site (www.busreslab.com/onlinesurvey.htm).

SURVEY   With a **survey**, information is systematically gathered from respondents by communicating with them. Surveys are used in many retail settings. In a low-key, interactive manner, Sunglass Hut surveys its shoppers and encourages them to share their experiences through an interactive device known as Social Sun. Food Lion uses in-store surveys to learn how satisfied customers are and what their attitudes are on various subjects.

A survey may be conducted in person, over the phone, by mail, or online. Typically, a questionnaire is used. A *personal survey* is face-to-face, flexible, and able to elicit lengthy responses; unclear questions can be explained. It may be costly, and interviewer bias is possible. A *phone survey* is fast and rather inexpensive. Responses are often short, and nonresponse may be a problem. A *mail survey* can reach a wide range of respondents, has no interviewer bias, and is not costly. Slow returns, high nonresponse rates, and participation by incorrect respondents are potential problems. An *online survey* is interactive, can be adapted to individuals, and yields quick results. Yet, only certain customers shop online or answer online surveys. The technique chosen depends on the goals and requirements of the research project.

A survey may be nondisguised or disguised. In a nondisguised survey, the respondent is told the real purpose of the study. In a disguised survey, the respondent is not told the true purpose so that person does not answer what he or she thinks a firm wants to hear. Disguised surveys use word associations, sentence completions, and projective questions (such as, "Do your friends like shopping at this store?"). See Table 8-3.

TABLE 8-3 A Nondisguised Survey

Have any of the following elements influenced your decision to visit a convenience store?

	Total	By Age: 18-24	25-34	35-44	45-54	55+
Word-of-mouth	15.7%	18.8%	18.8%	18.8%	13.3%	11.4%
Coupon	12.3%	14.7%	12.2%	12.7%	12.5%	10.7%
Mobile app offer from c-store	10.9%	18.3%	16.4%	11.5%	12.9%	2.1%
Radio or TV advertisement	9.5%	9.4%	14.3%	11.5%	6.3%	6.6%
Billboard	7.5%	7.9%	12.9%	8.5%	6.3%	3.8%
Promotion or message on social media (Facebook, Twitter, etc.)	7.3%	9.9%	15.0%	7.6%	3.7%	2.8%
Print circular	5.7%	2.1%	7.7%	7.6%	5.2%	5.0%
Text message	5.7%	8.4%	11.8%	4.8%	3.3%	2.4%
E-mail	4.9%	3.7%	7.3%	4.5%	5.5%	3.6%
Other	3.6%	1.0%	1.4%	2.7%	4.8%	6.2%

Multiple responses accepted.

Source: "Bring Your 'A' Game," *Convenience Store News*, February 2016, p. 28. Reprinted with permission. Convenience Store News (c) 2016 (www.csnews.com)

The **semantic differential**—a listing of bipolar adjective scales—is a survey format that may be disguised or nondisguised. A respondent is asked to rate one or more retailers on several criteria, each evaluated by bipolar adjectives (such as unfriendly–friendly). By computing the average rating of all respondents for each criterion, an overall profile emerges. Figure 8-9 shows a semantic differential comparing two furniture retailers. Retailer A is a prestigious, high-quality store and retailer B is a mid-quality, family-run store. The semantic differential graphically portrays their images.

OBSERVATION The form of research in which present behavior or the results of past behavior are noted and recorded is known as **observation**. Because people are not questioned, observation may not require respondent cooperation, and survey biases are minimized. Observation may be used in real situations. The key disadvantage of observation is that attitudes are not elicited.

FIGURE 8-9

A Semantic Differential for Two Furniture Stores

Please check the blanks that best indicate your feelings about Stores A and B.

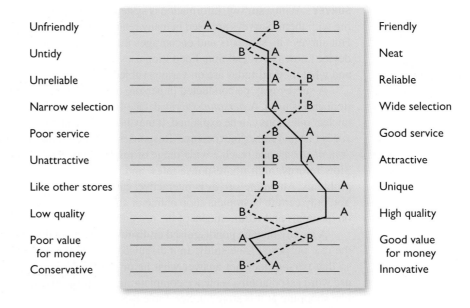

Retailers use observation to determine the quality of sales presentations (by having researchers pose as shoppers), to monitor related-item buying, to determine store activity by time and day, to make pedestrian and vehicular traffic counts (to measure the potential of new locations), and to determine the proportion of patrons using mass transit.

With **mystery shoppers**, retailers or their market research partners hire people to pose as customers and observe a service or a brand through visits, telephone calls, or Web site interactions. These mystery shoppers may evaluate operations, customer service experience, compliance with service standards, product availability, price, service calls, sales presentations, and how well store environments and displays are maintained. Some firms prefer video mystery shopping to address complex and challenging aspects of a service business.[20]

Observation may be disguised or nondisguised, structured or unstructured, direct or indirect, and human or mechanical. In disguised observation, the shopper or company employee is not aware he or she is being watched by a two-way mirror or hidden camera. In nondisguised observation, the participant knows he or she is being observed—such as a department manager watching a cashier's behavior. Structured observation calls for the observer to note specific behavior. Unstructured observation requires the observer to note all of the activities of the person being studied. With direct observation, the observer watches people's present behavior. With indirect observation, the observer examines evidence of past behavior, such as food products in consumer pantries. Human observation is carried out by people. It may be disguised, but the observer may enter biased notations and overlook behavior. Mechanical observation, such as a camera filming in-store shopping, eliminates viewer bias and does not miss behavior.

EXPERIMENT   An **experiment** is a type of research in which one or more elements of a retail strategy mix are manipulated under controlled conditions. An element may be a price, a shelf display, store hours, or some other feature. If a retailer wants to find the effects of a price change on sales, only one item's price is varied. Other strategic elements (location, quantity, etc.) stay the same, so the true price effect is measured.

An experiment may use survey or observation techniques to record data. In a survey, questions are asked about the experiment: Did you buy Brand Z because of its new shelf display? Are you buying more ice cream because it's on sale? In observation, behavior is watched during the experiment: Sales of Brand Z rise by 20 percent when a new display is used. Ice cream sales go up 25 percent during a special sale.

Surveys and observations are experimental if they occur under controlled situations. When surveys ask broad attitude questions or unstructured behavior is observed, experiments are not involved. Experimentation can be difficult because many uncontrollable factors (such as weather, competition, and the economy) come into play. A well-controlled experiment yields good data.

The major advantage is an experiment's ability to show cause and effect (a lower price results in higher sales). It is also systematically structured and enacted. The major potential disadvantages are high costs, contrived settings, and uncontrollable factors.

SIMULATION   A type of experiment whereby a computer program is used to manipulate the elements of a retail strategy mix rather than test them in a real setting is called **simulation**. Two

RETAILING AROUND THE WORLD

Studying a Consumer's Purchase Journey

A large-scale study of shopping behavior in the Netherlands found that Dutch consumers pursue different paths in the purchase journey—getting information, making a purchase, receiving delivery, and returning goods—based on the product purchased. Fifty-three percent of food shoppers relied on product information only in the store. In contrast, 17 percent of electronics product customers used store information exclusively. Customers utilize different retail formats to make purchases. Eighty-four percent made grocery purchases only in stores, compared with 59 percent of electronics purchases.

Seventy-six percent of grocery purchases were picked up in the store versus 46 percent for electronic travel items. Last, 70 percent of grocery returns are in-store versus 48 percent of electronics returns.

Discuss the impact of these findings on an electronics retailer pursuing an omnichannel retail strategy.

Source: Based on material from Karina van den Oever, Kenny Brams, Matthew Kentridge, and Jos Leijnse, in A. T. Kearney, "Back to the Basics in Omnichannel Retailing: Delighting Your Customers," October 2014. Reprinted by permission.

kinds of simulation are now being applied in retail settings: those based on mathematical models and those involving "virtual reality."

In the first kind of simulation, a model of the expected controllable and uncontrollable retail environment is constructed. Factors—such as effects of a price cut or longer store hours—are manipulated by computer (rather than the marketplace) so their effect on the overall strategy and specific elements of it are determined. No consumer cooperation is needed, and combinations of factors can be analyzed in a controlled, rapid, inexpensive, and risk-free manner. This format is gaining popularity as reliable software is increasingly available. However, it is still somewhat difficult to use.

In the second kind of simulation, a retailer devises or buys interactive software that lets participants simulate actual behavior in as realistic a format as possible. This approach creates a "virtual shopping environment." For example, Facebook's Oculus Rift VR headset now makes it possible to render virtual shopping environments at lower costs; and the glasses can be enhanced with eye-tracking capability to make it an efficient shopper research tool. SMI studies on the virtual shopper journey using EEGs (which test the electrical activity of the brain) have had participants use eye-tracking and real-time consumer behavior in a virtual setting to assess the impact of in-store campaigns on buying decisions and how consumers interact with merchandise displays and package design before deciding to buy. Participants virtually interact with signs and products displayed in the VR headset as a natural experience; findings can be used to devise real-life store campaigns. The simulated space can easily compare several conditions (A/B testing) of in-store campaigns and shelf placements.[21]

Chapter Summary

1. *To discuss how information flows in a retail distribution channel.* In an effective retail distribution channel, information flows freely and efficiently among the three main parties (supplier, retailer, and consumer). As a result, the parties can better anticipate and address each other's performance expectations. Retailers often have a vital role in collecting data because they have the most direct contact with shoppers.

2. *To show why retailers should avoid strategies based on inadequate information.* Whether developing a new strategy or modifying an existing one, good data are necessary to reduce a retailer's chances of making incorrect decisions. Retailers that rely on nonsystematic or incomplete research, such as intuition, increase their probabilities of failure.

3. *To look at the retail information system, its components, and the recent advances in such systems.* Useful information should be acquired through an ongoing, well-integrated process. A retail information system anticipates the data needs of retail managers; continuously collects, organizes, and stores relevant data; and directs the flow of information to decision makers. Such a system has several components: environment, retailer's philosophy, strategic plans, information control center, and retail operations. The most important component is the information control center. It directs data collection, stores and retrieves data, and updates files.

Database management is used to collect, integrate, apply, and store information related to specific topics (such as customers, vendors, and product categories). Database information can come from internal (company-generated) and external (purchased from outside firms) sources. A key advance in database management is data warehousing, whereby copies of all the databases in a firm are kept in one location and can be accessed by employees at any locale. It is a huge repository separate from the operational databases that support departmental applications. Through data mining and micromarketing, retailers use data warehouses to pinpoint the specific needs of customer segments.

Retailers have increased the use of computerized retail information systems, and the Universal Product Code (UPC) is the dominant technology for processing product-related data. With electronic data interchange (EDI) and Internet electronic data interchange (I-EDI), the computers of retailers and suppliers regularly exchange information, sometimes through the Web.

4. *To describe the marketing research process.* Marketing research in retailing involves these sequential activities: defining the issue or problem to be researched, examining secondary data, gathering primary data (if needed), analyzing the data, making recommendations, and implementing findings. It is systematic in nature and not a single act.

Secondary data (gathered for other purposes) are inexpensive, can be collected quickly, may have several sources, and may yield otherwise unattainable information. Some sources are very credible. When an issue is ill defined, a secondary data search can clarify it. There are also potential pitfalls: These data may not suit the purposes of the study, units of measurement may not be specific enough, information may be old or inaccurate, a source may be disreputable, and data may not be reliable.

Primary data (gathered to resolve the specific topic at hand) are collected if secondary data do not adequately address the issue. They are precise and current, data are collected and categorized with the units of measures desired, the methodology is known, there are no conflicting results, and the level of reliability can be determined. When secondary data do not exist, primary data are the only option. The potential disadvantages are the cost, time, limited access, narrow perspective, and amassing of irrelevant information.

Key Terms

retail information system
  (RIS) (p. 215)
database management (p. 217)
data warehousing (p. 218)
data mining (p. 219)
micromarketing (p. 219)
Universal Product Code
  (UPC) (p. 220)
electronic data interchange (EDI)
  (p. 220)

marketing research in
  retailing (p. 221)
marketing research process (p. 222)
issue (problem) definition (p. 222)
secondary data (p. 222)
primary data (p. 222)
internal secondary data (p. 224)
external secondary data (p. 226)
probability (random)
  sample (p. 227)

nonprobability sample
  (p. 227)
survey (p. 227)
semantic differential (p. 228)
observation (p. 228)
mystery shoppers (p. 229)
experiment (p. 229)
simulation (p. 229)

Questions for Discussion

1. Relate the information flows in Figure 8-2 to a bakery near your college or university.
2. Why is gathering and analyzing information crucial to a retailer that is launching a new strategy or modifying an existing one?
3. What information does a customer actually demand from a retailer?
4. What information could a retailer supply to other channel members?
5. In database management, a retailer gathers, integrates, applies, and stores information related to specific subject areas. Outline how this should be carried out. What are the information sources? Provide detailed examples.
6. One application of data mining is micromarketing. What is micromarketing, and how might a retailer use it?

7. Cite the major advantages and disadvantages of secondary data.
8. As a fitness club owner, what kinds of secondary data would you use to learn more about your industry and consumer trends in working out?
9. Cite the benefit of each primary data method: survey, observation, experiment, and simulation.
10. Develop a 10-item semantic differential for a local furniture store to judge its image. Who should be surveyed? Why?
11. Why would a retailer use mystery shoppers rather than other forms of observation? Are there any instances when you would not recommend their use? Why or why not?
12. Why do you think "virtual shopping" has not taken off faster as a research tool for retailers?

Web-Based Exercise

One of the key strategic issues facing traditional retailers is failing to have an effective plan to provide an "always open" environment. Customers demand an "always open" retailer. How is this being handled in your country? Use the Internet to identify solutions being used by retailers.

PART 3   Short Cases

Case 1: Eating Patterns in America*

Household changes will shape the future of eating for years to come. The "typical" U.S. consumer and the households in which they live are very different from those of 20 years ago. The changes are reflected across the spectrum of eating patterns today—who, what, when, where, how, and why.

Single-person U.S. households are 38 million strong and growing—the highest in history—This represents 55 percent of all adult only households. The typical size of an American family is 2.5 persons per household, with more than one-quarter with children headed by single moms. Smaller households, in many cases, are a long-term choice for adults choosing not to be married and/or have fewer children. This change has wide-ranging implications for retailers and manufacturers in terms of marketing, merchandising, new product development, packaging, and positioning.

By 2044, the U.S. Census Bureau projects that more than one-half of Americans will be in a minority group; by 2060, nearly one in five of the total population is projected to be foreign-born. The Hispanic population has accounted for more than half of the 27-million U.S. population increase in the last decade. Hispanics currently represent 18 percent of the total U.S. population. Although Hispanics will continue to be a very large and growing group, Asians are one of the fastest-growing ethnic populations, currently representing 8 percent of the U.S. population.

The Millennial generation is more diverse than the preceding generations, with 44 percent being part of a minority race or ethnic group. Even more diverse than Millennials are the youngest Americans—those younger than 5 years of age. In 2014, this group became majority-minority for the first time, with 50 percent being part of a minority race or ethnic group.

The share of the U.S. population that is considered middle income has been shrinking over the last four decades. In the past, those in the middle-income group typically moved up into higher income levels; today, however, the opposite is true. Declining or stagnant wages, coupled with a growing income gap during the past 15 years, have resulted in many families slipping out of the middle class.

If past trends continue, it's unlikely that recovery from the Great Recession will lead to a rebound in the share of adults in middle-income households. Since the middle class has fueled spending on everything from housing to cars to food purchasing, a smaller middle class has a wide-ranging impact on the economy. See Figure 1.

This overview presents just a few of the changing consumer dynamics that will shape the retail marketplace in the future—both near and long term. Retailers need to be aware of changes in consumer behaviors in order to modify their marketing tactics and strategies, and to meet the needs and wants of today's consumers.

Questions

1. According to the information in the case, how are American demographics changing?
2. As a supermarket retailer, how would you address the rise in U.S. single-person households?
3. As a local gift shop, how would you address the rise of Hispanics in the United States?
4. What are the implications of Figure 1 for retailers?
5. What demographic trends not mentioned in this case should retailers address? How?

Case 2: The Convenience Economy Comes of Age*

Among the transformations on the retail landscape in the recent past, perhaps none was more profound than proliferation of the "convenience economy," in which everything is at the consumer's disposal at the click of a button, according to Chris Bryson, CEO of Unata, a leading omnicommerce solutions provider. He

FIGURE 1

The Shrinking Middle Class

Source: Based on material in Bonnie Riggs, "Eating Patterns in America: The State of the Consumer," *Convenience Store News,* March 2016, pp. 58, 60. Reprinted by permission. Convenience Store News (c) 2016 (www.csnews.com)

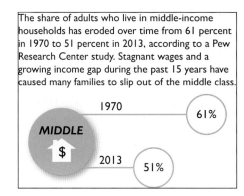

The share of adults who live in middle-income households has eroded over time from 61 percent in 1970 to 51 percent in 2013, according to a Pew Research Center study. Stagnant wages and a growing income gap during the past 15 years have caused many families to slip out of the middle class.

MIDDLE $
1970 — 61%
2013 — 51%

---

* Based on material in Bonnie Riggs, "Eating Patterns in America: The State of the Consumer," *Convenience Store News,* March 2016, pp. 58, 60. Reprinted by permission Convenience Store News (c) 2016 (www.csnews.com).

* Based on material in Jim Dudlicek, "Fridge's Dare [The Convenience Economy Comes of Age]," *Progressive Grocer,* February 2016, p. 28. Reprinted by permission.

states, "2015 was the year UberX went from a smaller, unknown player to a force driving change across sectors. We're at a point where new business ideas are often described as 'Uber for __.'"

The convenience economy's biggest shift, Bryson says, "came when major players like Starbucks started embracing it with the "Order Ahead mobile app," which has led to "widespread adoption of this kind of immediate customer transaction, and reinforced the need for quick and convenient service on a daily basis," and with it, a huge shift in consumer expectations across all sectors.

Retailers of all stripes "are suddenly playing catchup, learning how they can incorporate real-time, on-demand transactions into their strategies," notes Bryson, who founded Unata in 2011. The company's roster of grocery clients includes Longo's, Grocery Gateway, Lowes Foods, Lunds and Byerlys, and Raley's. When asked to elaborate on some examples of the convenience economy now catching his eye, and which are the most important, Bryson ticks off a shortlist of standouts, including the following.

- UberX/UberEATS: "Consumers don't have to call to order their car/food, take out their wallets to pay, or wait very long for their car/food to arrive. They can watch the driver travel and arrive live on a map, with the ability to communicate with their driver at the click of a button."
- Starbucks: "The Order Ahead app is simple and easy to use, and saves the customer minutes on a daily basis—which becomes especially valuable on rushed mornings. They are reinforcing this type of customer experience on a daily basis."
- Ritual: "This is a Toronto-based app—expanding in the United States—that lets consumers order lunch ahead of time from various restaurants near their location. The app notifies consumers exactly when they should leave their current locale so they arrive at the restaurant just when food is ready for pickup, ensuring the food remains as hot and fresh as possible. Ritual is a simple and clean user experience that lets customers order food in a couple of clicks and saves them 5 to 10 minutes a day of waiting time."
- Amazon Echo and Dash with Prime: "With both Amazon Echo and Dash, consumers don't have to write a shopping list, go to their computers, or even pull out their phones to make an order, or take out their wallets to pay. With Dash buttons, they can order at the click of one button; and with Echo, Amazon has taken the click out entirely. It's the easiest possible way for consumers to online shop. Combined with Amazon Prime, consumers don't have to wait long to get things that they've ordered."

Although it's still unclear what the shopper of the future will find the most convenient way to shop for groceries, Bryson says, "The convenience economy so far tells us that the fewer clicks needed, the more adoption there will be, which is why we have our eye on Amazon Echo. We've seen how quickly Uber has changed the landscape, and we expect it to continue to change just as quickly in ways we don't yet know over the next few years. Retailers need to focus on setting up their systems so they can easily flex, adapt, iterate, and connect with new systems."

Questions

1. What is the convenience economy? Give your own examples.
2. Is the convenience economy good or bad for retailers? Why?
3. What would restaurants have to do to be able to efficiently and effectively use the Ritual app?
4. What is your favorite example of a retailer that has become more convenient in recent years? Explain your answer.

Case 3: Are Hot Retailers of 2015 Still Hot?*

Differentiation is important for the nation's fastest-growing ("hot") retailers. These retailers typically come in a variety of different flavors, but one thing they have in common is that they all do things a little differently—and this helps them get (and often) stay ahead of the pack.

Chart-topper Hudson's Bay is "hot" because at least one man in retailing thinks there is still a place for the traditional department store. Hudson's Bay Executive Chairman Richard Baker, who bought Lord & Taylor 9 years ago, has assembled a conglomerate operating in three countries on two continents.

Runner-up NoMoreRack.com, founded in November 2010 and offering deep discounts on an array of general merchandise, was rebranded as Choxi in 2015 after Nordstrom objected to its name (due to possible confusion with its Nordstrom Rack off-price division). The new name is a mixture of "chock full" and "choice." It is not a real word in any language — which can assist a firm expanding globally.

Number 3, Zulily, has elevated the flash sale model to new heights. The company's early strength was in infant clothing, toys, and accessories with a very strict no-returns policy. In May 2015, Zulily began a test program that allows some customers to return some brands of apparel and home linens.

"The Hot 100 is a mix of companies that have balance sheets that allow them to make acquisitions or grow organically," explains Bryan Gildenberg, the chief knowledge officer at Kantar Retail, providers of the Hot 100 data. "Hot 100 retailers can grow more quickly because they understand why people are buying. They understand the dynamics of their audience."

Among those following the acquisition trail is Number 4, G-III Apparel Group. Best known as a soft-goods vendor to major department and specialty stores, it also operates its own retail stores under the Wilsons Leather, Bass, G. H. Bass & Co., Vilebrequin, and Calvin Klein Performance banners.

Ranking as Number 5 is Wayfair, the umbrella company for five different home furnishings and décor E-commerce brands. The firm had a particularly good holiday selling season 2 years ago, with the active customers in its direct retail business reaching 3.2 million at year-end, up 54 percent from a year earlier.

Two years ago, Number 7 on the list, Office Depot purchased a major rival in OfficeMax and not too long afterward put itself in position to be taken over by Staples, potentially reducing the number of office supply superstore operators to just one. If the Staples takeover cleared regulatory hurdled, Wall

---

* Based on material in David P. Schulz, "Hot 100 Retailers 2015," *STORES Magazine,* August 2015, pp. S4–S6. Reprinted by permission. Copyright 2016. STORES Magazine.

Street analysts said they expected at least 1,000 office supply stores to be closed around the country. (*Authors' note:* Due to U.S. government objections, the two companies called off their merger in early 2016. For both firms, their physical stores are vulnerable to online retailers such as Amazon.com.)

Both Number 8, Signet Jewelers, and Number 9, Men's Wearhouse, acquired major rivals in Zale and JoS. A. Bank, respectively. Signet has put together the only national group of mall-based popular-priced jewelry stores, and Men's Wearhouse has achieved pretty much the same among men's apparel retailers after turning the tables on JoS. A. Bank, which had tried to take over Men's Wearhouse.

Together, supermarkets and apparel stores account for nearly half of the Hot 100 entries. Most of the Hot 100 supermarkets have "core categories that are growing very quickly," Gildenberg says, such as an emphasis on natural and organic foods or a store full of ethnic products.

Questions

1. What do hot retailers have in common? Explain your answer.
2. Why do you believe that so many supermarkets and apparel stores seem to be hot retailers?
3. Cite one retailer mentioned in this case that you think is still hot. Do some research to prove that this retailer is still hot.
4. Cite one retailer mentioned in this case that you think is no longer hot. Do some research to prove that this retailer is not hot today.

Case 4: Navigating the Shopper Universe through Big Data*

Taking on the challenge of understanding the motivations behind why shoppers buy what they buy, and how they buy it, could pay off in manifold ways. "There are lifestyle tensions that impact shopping behavior for each shopper segment, but these tensions often extend beyond the store: time stress, financial pressure, and information overload," explains John Essegian, executive vice-president at TNS Global. "Retailers can increase their market share with each segment by understanding and addressing these important lifestyle tensions."

TNS Shopper Universe is a large syndicated database that maps competition for Grocery, Mass/Supercenter, Club, Convenience, Dollar Store, Drug, Natural/Organic, Pet, and Home Improvement retailers. It shows how shoppers perceive the marketplace, shopper segmentation for targeting, and occasion-based need segmentation detailing what's most motivating to shoppers on each trip. The database provides retailers and manufacturers with a comprehensive understanding of this broad marketplace, and the key drivers of choice for shoppers.

"Shoppers' functional needs are generally well met," Essegian says. "Yet, opportunities exist to engage shoppers more emotionally, such as helping them simplify their lives, leveraging modern technology, and creating a more experiential shopping trip." TNS identifies nine occasion-based need states. Just over half of shopping trips, defined by consumer needs, are more experience-driven, whereas the rest tend to be task-focused.

Experience-Driven Needs

The experience-focused need states break down as follows: (1) *Smart Family Fun:* These consumers want shopping to be fun, relaxing, and productive (so they can take care of family needs). They expect enjoyment to be facilitated by technology aids, a convenient and pleasant in-store experience, and good value. (2) *Only the Best:* Needs on these shopping trips are for top-tier brands, often outside the mainstream, including fresh, healthy, and natural products. (3) *Rewarding Experience:* This shopping is uplifting and inspiring, thanks to the combination of the retailer's values, great staff, and interesting and unique products. (4) *Food Safari:* Shoppers want this kind of trip to be more than just stocking up on staples; they want a little adventure and exploration. It's a chance to try new and different products such as exotic, gourmet, organic, and healthy items.

Task-Driven Needs

Task-focused need states shake out as follows: (1) *Weekly Grocery Shopping:* These shoppers want every item their family needs for the week under one roof. The store needs to have a wide selection of packaged and fresh food items. This shopper looks to coupons and quality store brands to help stay on budget. (2) *Hassle-Free Value:* The shopping trip should be easy and efficient, providing good deals and incentives while covering all brand needs, from premium to quality store brands. (3) *Personal Care Plus:* These shoppers are looking for a store with a good selection of personal care and household items that they can shop at any time of the day or night. They also want a good selection of snacks and beverages. (4) *All-Around Value:* These shoppers want a place for stocking up and bargain hunting, with everyday low prices, great specials, and economical package sizes. Hours should be convenient, and it should be a place that kids enjoy. (5) *Grab and Go:* This is about fulfilling an immediate need to quickly and easily grab a snack, beverage, or fill-in item at a store located on the shopper's normal route.

Most generalists, such as grocery, mass, and club retailers, have an incentive to align to both task-driven and experiential need states. Specialty stores tend to be more associated with experiential shopping. While each segment participates, to at least some degree, more engaged shoppers tend to have more experiential needs.

Questions

1. What is the TNS Shopper Universe? Why is it a valuable tool for retailers?
2. Describe the consumer segments included as experience-driven.
3. Describe the consumer segments included as task-driven.
4. Which customer segments noted in this case are most important for a convenience store? Explain your answer.

---

* Based on material in Jim Dudlick, "Harnessing Big Data: Navigating the Shopper Universe," *Progressive Grocer 2016 Category Management Handbook.* Reprinted by permission.

Part 3   Comprehensive Case

How Do You Attract and Satisfy Millennials?*

Introduction

How do you connect with a generation that defies easy categorization?

The members of Generation Y (Millennials) have perplexed many knowledgeable retailers for more than a decade. There is a stereotype that all Millennials are broke 20-somethings who live with their parents, but that's only a small segment of the cohort. Many Millennials are homeowners, married with children, and more concerned about their investments and saving for college than playing videogames.

If there's one thing all Millennials have in common, it's an immersion in the digital world. If they weren't fully born in the digital age, they spent formative years and entered early adulthood in a rapidly changing environment of phones, computers, and devices that connect them to each other and the world.

Large and Diverse

Generation Y will drive the future of retail, and experts say retailers' success will hinge on how they understand and give this cohort the experience it desires. Millennials, roughly defined as those born between the early 1980s and the late 1990s, have surpassed Baby Boomers as the largest generation. The Pew Research Center estimates that there are roughly 75 million Americans between the ages of 18 and 34, and they represent a wide array of characteristics and preferences.

Although a younger segment may meet the "broke and living at home" stereotype, it doesn't characterize the generation as a whole, says researcher Jason Dorsey; all discussions around Millennials have to start with knowing their diversity: "A [Millennial] could be married in a two-income household with two kids or living at home with mom or three roommates. You can't speak to them in the same way!"

A 2015 report by *Oracle* (the software firm) breaks Millennials into five different groups:

- "Up and Comers" represent a diverse group of males with high incomes but low awareness levels.
- "Mavens" are 30-something high earners with a child.
- "Eclectics" are female free spirits on the lookout for the perfect deal and a high level of Amazon awareness.
- "Skeptics" tend to be gamers focused on social media, sci-fi films, and fast food.
- "Trendsetters," the youngest segment of the generation, keep up with the latest and greatest and purchases across a wide variety of brands.

Millennials are also the most racially diverse generation, with 43 percent identified as non-Caucasian. Multiculturalism and a high acceptance of interracial marriage are blurring the lines between cultural and racial demographics.

Ryan McConnell, senior vice-president and head of North American subscription services for the Futures Company, calls the cohort "the Big Blend." He says categorization along the lines of things like race, gender, and sexual orientation is disappearing. "If you're big on categorization, you're forcing people into boxes," he says, "and that doesn't bode well among Millennials."

Conflicting data and the complexity of the generation has spawned myths about who the Millennials are. A 2013 Accenture report found that the biggest misconceptions related to Millennials' preferences in retail were that they only shop online, have no loyalty, and treat retailers the same as people on social networks. Retailers are discovering, however, that they can be the complete opposite.

Unified by Digital

Many Millennials have spent their adulthood ordering goods and services, paying their bills, and banking online. They interact with the world through social media; and when it comes to retail, they have no tolerance for companies that lag behind in technology.

A survey by research firm BI Intelligence found that 40 percent of Millennials would give up cash completely if they could rely on plastic or mobile payments. More than 90 percent of those aged 18 to 34 have used a self-service kiosk, according to a 2015 study by location-based mobile platform company Retale, versus 81 percent of those 35 and older; 72 percent of respondents choose self-checkout because they have a limited number of items, while 55 percent do so because there is no line. *Authors' Note*: These numbers do not total to 100 percent due to multiple responses.

Interestingly, 20 percent of Millennials (8 percent more than other generations) said they choose self-service to avoid interacting with cashiers, and yet, the Accenture study found that 82 percent of Millennials prefer visiting bricks-and-mortar stores.

The 18-to 34-year-olds certainly interact through social media. A recent Deloitte (financial consulting) survey found that 47 percent use social media while shopping, compared with only 19 percent for all other age groups. Another survey by Web analytics company SDL revealed Millennials check their smartphones an average of 43 times daily, and five out of six connect with companies via social media.

Waiting isn't an option. Same-day delivery would make 64 percent of Millennials more likely to make a purchase online, according to a survey by Coldwell Banker Commercial Affiliates, compared with 56 percent of Gen Xers and 40 percent of Baby Boomers.

"Time and quality of life can be more important than money for Millennials," says Willy Kruh, global chairman of consumer markets at KPMG. "If you don't grab them in three seconds, and if you can't [provide] next-day delivery, they're gone."

Millennials are constantly bombarded with so much information over so many devices and media that "you have to get them with bite-sized information," he says. "You also have to

* Based on material in Craig Guillot, "Millennial Moment," *STORES Magazine*, January 2016, pp. 26–30. Reprinted by permission. Copyright 2016. STORES Magazine.

design your Web site in that fashion. They want everything, including the [purchase process], to be short and fast."

Conscientious Consumers

Young people in every generation show an elevated sense of idealism, but Millennials have a tendency to put their money where their mouth is. Concepts such as social responsibility, sustainability, gender equality, and fair trade are more than just buzzwords.

A 2015 Nielsen survey revealed three in four Millennials would be willing to pay extra for "sustainable offerings." They're more likely than other generations to wonder where their products come from, how they're made, and how retailers view social issues.

Exclusivity and equality are non-negotiable. Generation Y is overwhelmingly progressive, socially liberal, and in favor of gay marriage and women's reproductive rights. "If you are putting out a message that you are not open for everyone, if you're not accepting of different cultures, different lifestyles, and different ways of being, then there's going to be a real problem" for retailers, says Ryan McConnell.

A brand survey by digital ad agency Moosylvania revealed that the top five Millennial brands in 2015 were Nike, Apple, Samsung, Sony, and Walmart. Of respondents to that survey, 40 percent said social responsibility played into their criteria, whereas 39 percent said the company "shared similar interests."

A Pew survey on demographics also found Millennials are less anchored to traditional institutions. Nearly 30 percent claim to have no religious affiliation, compared with 21 percent of Gen Xers and 16 percent of Baby Boomers. On the issue of politics, 50 percent consider themselves to be independent, compared with 39 percent of Gen Xers and 37 percent of Baby Boomers.

Millennials place more emphasis on happiness and experience than on possessions. The generation is leading the "sharing economy" through things such as peer-to-peer lending, crowdfunding, and companies that rent products or offer short-term use. They're more likely to use services such as Airbnb and Uber and sites like Neighborgoods, where consumers can rent or borrow products from one another.

Although a PricewaterhouseCoopers study found that only 44 percent of consumers overall are familiar with the sharing economy and just 19 percent have engaged in such a transaction, those most excited about the sharing economy once they've tried it are those aged 18 to 24, households with income between $50,000 and $75,000, and those with kids in the house under age 18.

Many Millennials have shifted to a more simplistic lifestyle; 78 percent of respondents in the PricewaterhouseCoopers report said sharing reduces clutter and waste. "Millennials aren't as into accumulating things," Willy Kruh states. "They don't see things such as a car as status symbols. They're much happier to lease it or rent it, and that preference is having huge reverberations in many industries, including retail."

PricewaterhouseCoopers reports that "today's consumers are finding more satisfaction and status in experiences, rather than static material possessions." McConnell says Millennials tend to worry less about being flashy and more about being "authentic." "They have more value for a minimalist lifestyle

than [Boomers and Gen Xers]. They realize there's a burden that comes with ownership," he says.

Because Millennials spend more than any other group on leisure activities while seemingly struggling in other aspects of life, they're perceived as bad with money. The reality is they're more apt to pay with available funds than use credit cards, according to a study by software firm Segmint. Rob Heiser, CEO of Segmint, says Millennials are actually very conscious about how they spend their money. "Deeper insights into data reveal that many Millennials make spending decisions after much research and consideration, rather than impulse."

Higher Expectations

Christopher Donnelly, senior managing director for retail at Accenture, says Millennials are "fundamentally not much different than anyone else, except they like doing things digitally." That digital preference has raised the bar for the customer experience. Much of the generation has always been able to find out anything about any product and order from any merchant in the world. A study by SDL revealed that nearly 60 percent of Millennials surveyed expect to engage with a company whenever they choose, by any channel they desire.

Sarah Clark, vice-president of product at Mitek Systems, says Millennials are leading the adoption of mobile payment in retailing. Mitek's survey with Zogby Analytics found that 86 percent of Millennials have used their smartphone to make a purchase, with 40 percent having spent $100 or less. Nearly one-half of the respondents have made the decision on where to shop based on a mobile app's features and functionality. They'd also like to make things even easier, with 68 percent saying they'd prefer to always use their smartphone camera for a mobile capture instead of manually typing information.

"It's a wake-up call to retailers to continue to focus on the mobile experience," Clark says. "Making things easier is extremely important," as is adopting new technologies as soon as they appear. Retailers that wait for months or years to engage in the new ways may be seen as too out of touch. Millennials "adapt [to technology] very quickly and they expect that retailers will do the same," she says.

Loyalty: Embracing Change

Millennials have grown up in a world where loyalty is seemingly going by the wayside. Lifelong careers are gone; Alexandra Levit, co-author of a Harris Interactive study about the future of Millennials' careers, said the average Millennial may work up to 15 jobs in his or her lifetime.

Futures Company's Ryan McConnell believes that very few Millennials are willing to stick with a retailer simply for the sake of legacy (past purchase behavior); they need to be motivated by service, brand affiliation, a "message," or price. "Their loyalty can vary by industry," he says. "You might find loyalty for companies such as Apple, but they'll quickly go somewhere else and follow their friends."

Willy Kruh of KPMG says Millennials may be the "least loyal generation" unless a company shows it's "listening to them" and engage in "evolution." Then, they can become "very loyal."

A November 2015 survey by global strategic branding and design firm Landor Associates found that Millennials seek long-term relationships with brands that embrace change in ways they feel are authentic, foster trust, and are respectful of heritage and values. The survey revealed that Millennials expect brands to be "agile and navigate a tension between change and continuity." Landor CEO Lois Jacobs comments, "As digital natives, Millennials are used to the rapid speed of the market and they expect brands to be as well." She adds, "They have shifted the marketing landscape. We no longer live in an era of mass marketing."

According to Ryan McConnell, Millennials have a strong sense of individualism, which is a big shift from previous generations when they were in their late teens and twenties. There's less of a need to be or look exactly like their friends. "Today, what's really hip or cool is being different. There aren't any [unifying] styles," he says. "There's an incredible inclusiveness about this generation that accepts different lifestyles and ways of expressing yourself."

Most Millennials are more trusting of their friends and social media networks than traditional advertising, says Kruh. Nearly 90 percent of respondents in McCarthy Group's Engaging Millennials Study did not like traditional ads, and that lack of trust extended to both people and institutions. The Pew demographics survey found that when they were asked if people can generally be trusted, only 19 percent of Millennials said yes, compared with 31 percent of the Gen Xers and 40 percent of the Baby Boomers.

And even though 8 in 10 Millennials say they're generally optimistic about their future, 51 percent of them believe they will get no benefits from Social Security, whereas 39 percent predict they will get benefits at reduced levels.

They're Not All Broke

Every generation likes to think it had it tougher than those who come later. However, Millennials do have a huge mountain to climb on almost every economic front. They have lower levels of wealth and personal income than Gen Xers and Baby Boomers did at the same stage in their lives; and they are spending far more on things like their rent and food than previous generations did.

Young households are also carrying far higher levels of student loan debt. "These things can be a massive drag on spending," says researcher Dorsey." It changes the options they have."

Millennials are what previous generations might call "late bloomers." They are more likely to live at home longer, and they wait longer to get married, longer to have kids, and longer to buy a house. According to a report from Goldman Sachs, nearly 30 percent of them live at home with their parents. Furthermore, only 23 percent of Millennials were married and living in their own households in 2012, as compared with 43 percent of that age group in 1981 and 56 percent in 1968.

That doesn't mean they don't have money to spend, however. On an individual basis, they may spend less on certain things than previous generations, but their sheer numbers can make up for it in total volume. Kruh says Millennials think with a "different cost-benefit analysis." Experience is essential, and not always about whether they can afford it or not. Millennials living at home also have a big impact on how their parents shop, by exposing them to new technologies and their values around sustainability.

The biggest factors are their core buying power and the fact that there will be a "tremendous wealth transfer" in the future from Baby Boomers to Millennials. According to Accenture, Generation Y is in line to inherit more than $30 trillion from Baby Boomers over the next few decades. As a result, researcher Dorsey says because of their current ages, life expectancy, and purchasing patterns, Millennials actually represent "the greatest lifetime value of any customer segment you can win in retail." See Figure 1.

Questions

1. What do all Millennials have in common? Is this good or bad for retailers? Why?
2. What do you think is the most misunderstood aspect of the Millennial generation? Why?
3. As a furniture retailer, how would you appeal to "Mavens"?
4. As a consumer electronics retailer, how would you appeal to "Up and Comers"?
5. Based on the information in this case, what are the three most important lessons for store-based retailers? Explain your answers.
6. Based on the information in this case, what are the three most important lessons for online retailers? Explain your answers.
7. From a retailer perspective, comment on the findings shown in Figure 1.

FIGURE 1

What's Untouchable?

Source: Based on material in Susan Reda, "Expendable vs. Untouchable," *STORES Magazine,* February 2016, www.nrf.com/untouchables. Copyright 2016. STORES Magazine. Reprinted by permission.

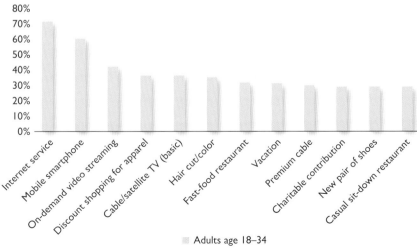

Adults age 18–34

Part 4

Choosing a Store Location

After a retailer has conducted a situation analysis, set its goals, identified consumer characteristics and needs, and gathered adequate information about the marketplace, it is ready to develop and enact an overall strategy. In Parts Four through Seven, we examine the elements of such a strategy: choosing a store location, managing a business, merchandise management and pricing, and communicating with the customer. Part Four concentrates on store location.

Besides dealing with the crucial nature of store location for retailers, **Chapter 9** outlines a four-step approach to location planning. In this chapter, we focus on Step 1, trading-area analysis. Among the topics we look at are the use of geographic information systems, the size and shape of trading areas, how to determine trading areas for existing and new stores, and the major factors to consider in assessing trading areas. Several data sources are described.

Chapter 10 covers the last three steps in location planning: deciding on the most desirable type of location, selecting a general location, and choosing a particular site within that location. We first contrast isolated store, unplanned business district, and planned shopping center locales. Criteria for rating each location are then outlined and detailed.

9 Trading-Area Analysis

Retailers choose store locations based on a wide range of factors, including attributes of various trading areas, nearness to other units operated by the same firm and to stores operated by competing firms, population characteristics, and more. Likewise, consumers choose the locations where they like to shop based on various factors, including overall appeal of the area, distance to the store, availability of a choice of retailers and brands, ease of parking, and more.

Trading-area analysis for a traditional retailer and a destination retailer are very different. Key issues in trading-area analyses by a traditional retailer are its size, competitor locations, affinities with other retailers, and travel time. Differences in sales tax between adjacent areas, tolls, and traffic congestion can also have a major effect on a traditional store's trading area. The normal rules associated with a trading-area analysis—regarding the population size of two cities, travel time, and square footage of selling space—may not directly apply to a destination retailer.

A destination retailer, such as Ikea or CarMax, often has a huge trading area based on the massive selection, large store size, value proposition, and unique merchandise. Destination retailers generate their own traffic and are not as dependent on the influence of other retailers; therefore, they can thrive in inexpensive locales. Unlike traditional retailers, many shoppers go only to that store on a shopping trip. Hence, there is no spillover traffic to adjacent retailers; and destination stores can thrive in inexpensive locales.

Source: Naki Kouyioumtzis/ Pearson Education Ltd. Reprinted by permission.

Nonetheless, a concern of some property owners is renting space to a destination retailer that might have difficulty being successful at that location on such a large scale. Several former destination retailers have gone out of business (e.g., Sports Authority and Borders) or lost their effectiveness (e.g., Best Buy, Staples, and Toys "R" Us). Some of these stores suffered due to competition from Web-based retailers that were able to offer large selections of merchandise at lower prices, from price competition by discounters such as Walmart, and/or from digital books that enabled customers to conveniently download and bypass traditional booksellers.

Overview

Because over 90 percent of all retail revenues are made at stores (including buying online and picking up in the store), the selection of a store location is one of the most significant strategic decisions in retailing. Consider the detailed planning of Aldi, the German-based discount food chain with more than 30 million customers of 1,500 stores in 32 U.S. states. Aldi's U.S. expansion plans include opening shopping-mall–based U.S. supermarkets. Except for its shopping mall sites, the 20,000-square-foot Aldi store is typical of the retailer. It works closely with developers to provide a good presentation of the store and preserve historic aspects of the original redeveloped properties. Unlike in Europe, supermarkets in malls are uncommon in the United States. Malls offer many benefits, including pass-through regular mall traffic and captive mall employees, as well as the opportunity to introduce Aldi to a whole new group of customers.[1]

This chapter and the next explain why the proper store location is so crucial, as well as the steps a retailer should take in choosing a store location and deciding whether to build, lease, or buy. Visit our blog (www.bermanevansretail.com) for store location posts.

THE IMPORTANCE OF LOCATION TO A RETAILER

A lot of helpful information on location planning is available at this Web site (www.thebalance.com/choosing-a-retail-store-location-2890245).

Location decisions are complex. Costs can be quite high, there is little flexibility once a site is chosen, and locational attributes have a big impact on a strategy. One of the oldest retailing adages is that "location, location, location" is the major factor leading to a firm's success or failure. See Figure 9-1.

A good location may be substantial enough to allow a retailer to succeed even if its strategy mix is mediocre. A hospital gift shop may do well, although its assortment is limited, its prices are high, and it does not advertise. On the other hand, a poor location may be such a liability that even superior retailers cannot overcome it. A mom-and-pop store may do poorly if it is across the street from a category-killer store; although the small firm features personal service, it cannot match the selection and prices. At a different site, however, it might prosper.

The choice of a location requires extensive decision making due to the number of criteria considered, including population size and traits, the competition, transportation access, parking

FIGURE 9-1

The Importance of Store Location

The IFC shopping center (http://ifc.com.hk/en/mall) is located at the Hong Kong train station in China. It generates a huge amount of pedestrian traffic and has both outside entrances and entrances inside the station. There are more than 200 stores, as well dining and entertainment options. It is also a place for sightseeing in Hong Kong.

Source: Naki Kouyioumtzis/Pearson Education Ltd. Reprinted by permission.

availability, the nature of nearby stores, property costs, the length of the agreement, legal restrictions, and other factors.

A store location typically necessitates a sizable investment and a long-term commitment. Even a retailer that minimizes its investment by leasing (rather than owning a building and land) can incur large costs. Besides lease payments, the firm must spend money on lighting, fixtures, a storefront, and so on.

Although leases of less than 5 years are common in less desirable retailing locations, leases in good shopping centers or shopping districts are often 5 to 10 years or more. It is not uncommon for a supermarket lease to be 15 or 20 years. Department stores and large specialty stores on major downtown thoroughfares occasionally sign leases longer than 20 years.

Due to its fixed nature, the investment, and the length of the lease, store location is the least flexible element of a retail strategy. A firm cannot easily move to another site or convert to another format. Also, a retailer may be barred from subleasing to another party during the lease period; if a company breaks a lease, it may be responsible to the property owner for financial losses. In contrast, ads, prices, customer services, and assortment can be modified as the environment (consumers, competition, the economy) changes.

Even a retailer that owns its building and land may also find it hard to change locations. It has to find an acceptable buyer, which might take several months or longer, and it may have to assist the buyer with financing. It might also incur a loss, should it sell during an economic downturn.

A firm moving from to another locale faces three potential problems. (1) Some loyal shoppers and employees may be lost; the greater the distance between the old and new sites, the bigger the loss. (2) A new site may not have the same traits as the prior one. (3) Most store fixtures and renovations at a site cannot be transferred; their value is lost if they have not been fully depreciated.

Store location affects long- and short-run planning. In the *long run*, the choice of location influences the overall strategy. A retailer must be at a site that is consistent with its mission, goals, and target market for an extended time. It also must regularly study and monitor the status of the location as to population trends, the distances people travel to the store, and competitors' entry and exit—and adapt accordingly.

In the *short run*, a location has an impact on specific elements of a strategy mix. A retailer in a downtown area with many office buildings may have little pedestrian traffic on weekends. It may be futile to try to sell items such as major appliances there. (Such items are often bought jointly by adult household members.) The retailer could either close on weekends and not stock certain products or remain open and try to attract customers to the area by aggressive promotion or pricing. If the retailer closes on weekends, it adapts its strategy mix to the attributes of the location. If it stays open, it invests additional resources in an attempt to alter shopping habits. A retailer that strives to overcome its location, by and large, faces greater risks than one that adapts.

Retailers should follow these four steps in choosing a store location:

1. Evaluate alternate geographic (trading) areas in terms of the characteristics of residents and existing retailers.
2. Determine whether to locate as an isolated store in an unplanned business district or in a planned shopping center within the geographic area.
3. Select the general isolated store, unplanned business district, or planned shopping center location.
4. Analyze alternate sites contained in the specified retail location type.

The selection of a store location is a process involving each of these steps. This chapter focuses on Step 1; Chapter 10 examines Steps 2, 3, and 4.

TRADING-AREA ANALYSIS

The first step in choosing a retail store location is to describe and assess alternate trading areas and then choose the best one. A **trading area** is a geographical area containing the customers and potential customers of a particular retailer or group of retailers for specific goods and/or services. The size of a trading area typically reflects the boundaries within which it is profitable to sell and/or deliver products.[2] After a trading area is selected, it should be reviewed regularly.

RETAILING
AROUND
THE WORLD

Doomed Locations?

In the United Kingdom, My Local, the 120-branch convenience store run by supermarket chain Morrisons, went into administration at the end of June 2016. Initially, 90 of the stores, employing nearly 1700, were closed, and the rest were bought by other retailers. Morrisons had acquired the sites from the doomed movie rental retailer Blockbuster when that company finally collapsed in 2013. The problem was that few of the sites acquired by Morrisons in the deal were prime convenience store locations.

Examine your own retail market. Can you identify retail locations that seem to constantly change hands as a succession of retailers fail to make the site work? Why might this be the case, and what kind of retailer might work instead?

A thorough analysis of trading areas provides several benefits:

▶ Consumer demographic and socioeconomic characteristics are examined. For a new store, the study of proposed trading areas reveals opportunities and the retail strategy needed to succeed. For an existing store, it can be determined if the current strategy still matches consumer needs.

▶ The focus of promotional activities is ascertained, and the retailer can look at media coverage patterns of proposed or existing locations. If 95 percent of customers live within 3 miles of a store, it would be inefficient to advertise in a paper with a citywide audience.

▶ A chain retailer learns whether the location of a proposed new store will reach additional customers or take business from existing stores. Suppose a supermarket chain has a store in Jackson, Mississippi, with a trading area of 2 miles, and it considers adding a new store, three miles from the Jackson branch. Figure 9-2 shows the distinct trading areas and expected store overlap. The shaded portion represents the **trading-area overlap**, where the same customers are served by both branches. The chain must look at the overall net increase in sales if it adds the proposed store (total revised sales of existing store + total sales of new store − total previous sales of existing store).

▶ Chains anticipate whether competitors want to open nearby stores if the firm does not do so itself. That is why TJX has two of its chains, T. J. Maxx and Marshalls, situate within 1.5 miles of each other in more than 100 U.S. markets, even though they are both off-price apparel firms.

▶ The best number of stores for a chain to operate in a given area is calculated. How many outlets should a retailer have in a region to provide good service for customers (without raising costs too much or having too much overlap)? When CVS pharmacy entered Atlanta, it opened nine new drugstores in one day. This gave it enough coverage of the city to service residents,

FIGURE 9-2

The Trading Areas of Current and Proposed Supermarket Outlets

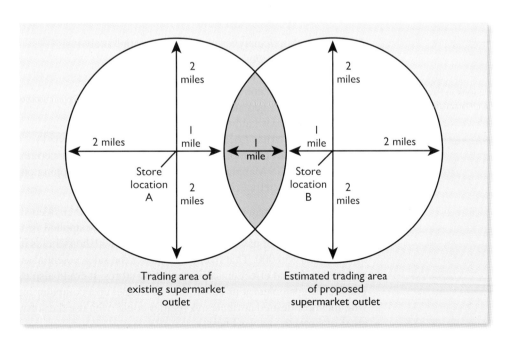

without placing stores too close together. A major competitive advantage for Canadian Tire Corporation is that four-fifths of the Canadian population lives within a 15-minute drive of a Canadian Tire store.

▶ Geographic weaknesses are highlighted. Suppose a suburban shopping center does an analysis and finds that most of those residing south of town do not shop there, and a more comprehensive study reveals that people are afraid to drive past a dangerous railroad crossing. Due to its research, the shopping center could exert political pressure to make the crossing safer.

▶ The impact of the Internet is taken into account. Store-based retailers must examine trading areas more carefully than ever to see how their customers' shopping behavior is changing due to the Web.

▶ Other factors are reviewed. The competition, financial institutions, transportation, labor availability, supplier location, legal restrictions, and so on can each be learned for the trading area(s) examined.

The Use of Geographic Information Systems in Trading-Area Delineation and Analysis

Increasingly, retailers are using **geographic information system (GIS)** software, which combines digitized mapping with key locational data to graphically depict trading-area characteristics such as population demographics; data on customer purchases; and listings of current, proposed, and competitor locations. Commercial GIS software lets firms quickly research the attractiveness of different locations and access computer-generated maps. Before, retailers often placed different color pins on paper maps to show current and proposed locales—and competitors' sites—and had to collect and analyze data.[3]

Most GIS software programs are extrapolated from the decennial *Census of Population* and the U.S. Census Bureau's national digital map (known as TIGER—topologically integrated geographic encoding and referencing).[4] TIGER incorporates all streets and highways in the United States. TIGER files may be accessed online free using its web-based platform TIGERweb or as Shapefiles downloads. TIGERweb's Web Map Service (WMS) maps may be adapted to reflect census tracts, railroads, highways, waterways, and other physical attributes of any U.S. area, but they do not show retailers or other commercial entities. Many versions of the TIGER data are available for download and adaptation based on level of detail.[5] See Figure 9-3 shows the breadth of TIGER services.

Learn more about TIGER mapping at this Web site (www.census.gov/geo/maps-data/data/tiger.html).

Mapping software from private firms have many more enhancements than TIGER does. These firms often offer free demonstrations, but they expect to be paid for their software. Although GIS applications differ by vendor, they generally can be accessed or bought for as little as $100 (or less) or for as much as several thousand dollars. They are designed to work with personal computers, and allow for some manipulation of trading-area data.

Private firms that offer mapping software include:

Take a look at ArcGIS from Esri (www.arcgis.com/home).

▶ Alteryx (http://analytics.alteryx.com/spatial-analytics)
▶ Autodesk (http://usa.autodesk.com)
▶ Caliper Corporation (www.caliper.com)
▶ Esri (www.esri.com)
▶ geoVue (www.geovue.com)
▶ Kalibrate (www.kalibrate.com/market-intel-cloud)
▶ Nielsen's Claritas Location Mapping (http://goo.gl/iiNj8T)
▶ Pitney Bowes Location Intelligence (www.pitneybowes.com/us/location-intelligence.html)
▶ Tele Mart GIS Mapping (www.tele-mart.com/gis-mapping.php)
▶ Tetrad (www.tetrad.com)

Many of these companies have free demonstrations at their Web sites.

Geographic information system software can be applied in various ways. A chain retailer could learn which of its stores have trading areas with households having a median annual income of more than $50,000. That firm could derive the sales potential of proposed new store locations and their potential effect on sales at existing stores. It could also use software to learn the demographics of customers at its best locations and set up a computer model to find potential locations with the most desired attributes. A retailer could even use the software to pinpoint its geographic areas of strength and weakness.

FIGURE 9-3

TIGER GIS in Action

The U.S. Census Bureau's TIGERweb site offers a lot of useful information and mapping options for users. For more retailing-based information, GIS software is often used by retailers—in addition to TIGER data. Because the GIS software is rather inexpensive, even small retailers are capable of using it. In this figure are four screen shots that illustrate the value of TIGERweb: (A) Image of the TIGERweb home page; (B) Image highlights the available TIGERweb applications; (C) Shows an example of census tracts and other data based on the 2010 *Census of Population;* (D) Image indicates how easy it is to print a GIS map withTigerWeb.

Source: U.S. Census Bureau: TIGERweb, https://tigerweb .geo.census.gov (July 28, 2016).

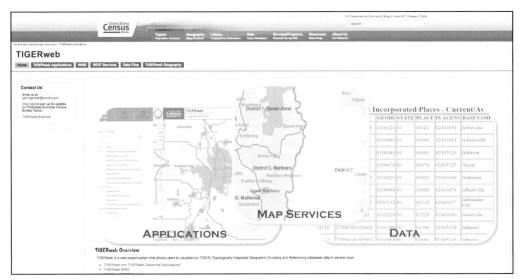

(A)

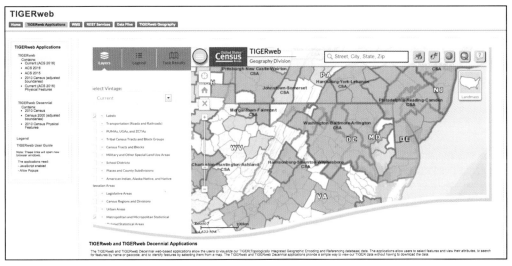

(B)

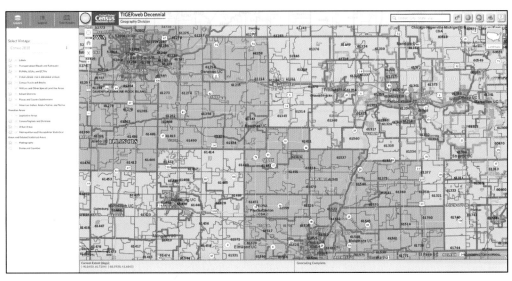

(C)

(Continued)

**FIGURE 9-3
(Continued)**

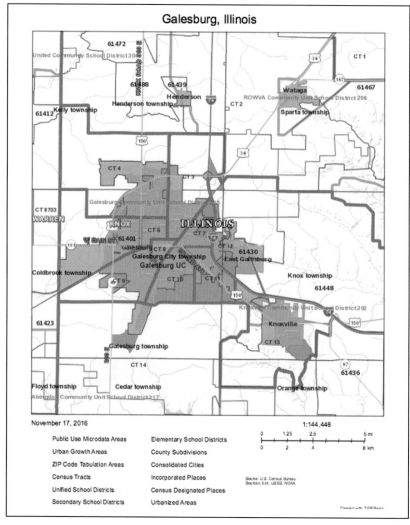

(D)

Pitney Bowes offers a wide range of MapInfo GIS software (http://goo .gl/hN7SkV). Click "Try It Free" on the left toolbar.

These three examples show how retailers benefit from GIS software:

▶ Starbucks uses GIS software from Esri to create and use store location data, maps, and models through employee desktops, in browsers, or on mobile devices. A new capability of this software is its ability to generate "heat maps" that depict the distribution of Starbucks locations. The points on the GIS maps can be grouped on a small scale to analyze regional patterns and on a large scale to view patterns within a metropolitan area. The heat maps depict the density of Starbucks locations. The Esri-based software provides Starbucks with data on population demographics, population density, auto traffic patterns, public transportation, and the types

TECHNOLOGY IN RETAILING   GIS Systems

GIS mapping software enables retailers and real-estate developers to better assess store locations. Geographic information systems now incorporate both store and online data to develop a target market profile. An omnichannel perspective can be undertaken by seeing the impact of additional stores in a market area on online sales. GIS software allows sales data to be exported to an Excel spreadsheet format for more intensive data analysis. GIS systems include lifestyle and demographic customer data to better assess locations. The software can help reduce cannibalism among store units and show the impact of drive time on stores' trading-area overlap. GIS helps assess compatible retailers. The system also show a market's overall size, as well as population projections.

Could a retailer accomplish the above without using a GIS system? Explain your answer.

of nearby stores. Starbucks uses the data in making decisions about new store openings as well as menu options tailored to the store.[6]

▸ Walgreens has used GIS technology since 2000. Its new system, called WalMap, contains interactive maps that can be used to determine the best place to locate a new store on the basis of demographic trends, competitor locations, and sales trend data. This software, which can be viewed on an iPad, contains location-specific data so store managers and Walgreens' corporate-level real-estate team can use the information. With the use of mobile devices, managers no longer have to print out maps to access important information.[7]

▸ GFK GeoMarketing offers GIS software services that assist international retailers that want to expand overseas. The software helps find best locations for store networks, identifying regional target groups, and determining product demand. RegioGraph helps retailers analyze and visualize their data on digital maps.[8]

The Size and Shape of Trading Areas

Each trading area has three parts: The **primary trading area** encompasses 50 to 80 percent of a store's customers. It is the area closest to the store and possesses the highest density of customers to population and the highest per capita sales. There is little overlap with other trading areas. The **secondary trading area** contains an additional 15 to 25 percent of a store's customers. It is located outside the primary area, and customers are more widely dispersed. The **fringe trading area** includes all the remaining customers, and they are the most widely dispersed. A store could have a primary trading area of 4 miles, a secondary trading area of 5 miles, and a fringe trading area of 10 miles. The fringe trading area typically includes some outshoppers who travel greater distances to patronize certain stores.

Figure 9-4 shows the makeup of trading areas and their segments. In reality, trading areas do not usually follow such circular patterns. They adjust to the physical environment. The size and

FIGURE 9-4

The Segments of a Trading Area

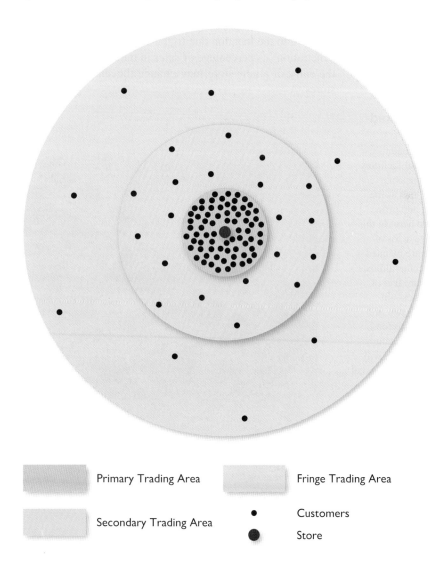

Primary Trading Area

Secondary Trading Area

Fringe Trading Area

• Customers

● Store

Visit this site to see the complexity of factors in site selection (http://siteselection.com/).

shape are affected by store type, store size, location of competitors, housing patterns, travel time and traffic barriers (such as toll bridges), and media access. These factors are discussed next.

Two stores can have different trading areas even if they are in the same shopping district or shopping center. Situated in one shopping center could be a branch of an apparel chain with a distinctive image and customers willing to travel up to 20 miles and a shoe store regarded as average and customers willing to travel up to 5 miles. When one store has a better assortment, promotes more, and/or creates a stronger image, it may then become a **destination store** and generate a trading area much larger than that of a competitor with a "me-too" appeal. To be a desination retailer, Dunkin' Donuts uses the slogan "America Runs on Dunkin'." A **parasite store** does not create its own traffic and has no real trading area of its own. It depends on people who are drawn to the location for other reasons. A magazine stand in a hotel lobby and a snack bar in a shopping center are parasites. People patronize the shops but they did not come to the location of these shops specifically to make a purchase.

The extent of a store/center trading area is affected by its own size. As a store or center gets larger, its trading area usually increases, because store or center size generally reflects the assortment of goods and services. Yet, trading areas do not grow proportionately with store or center size. As a rule, supermarket trading areas are bigger than those of convenience stores. Customers go to the supermarket because it offers a better product selection; they go to the convenience store because of the need for a couple of "fill-in" items. In a regional shopping center, department stores usually have the largest trading areas, followed by apparel stores; gift stores have comparatively small trading areas. See Figures 9-5 and 9-6.

Whenever potential shoppers are situated between two competing stores, the trading area is often reduced for each store. The size of each store's trading area normally increases as the distance between stores grows (target markets do not overlap as much). On the other hand, when stores are very near one another, the size of each store's trading area does not necessarily shrink. This store grouping may actually increase the trading area for each store if more consumers are attracted to the location due to the variety of goods and services. However, each store's market penetration (its percentage of sales in the trading area) may be low with such competition. Also, the entry of a new store may change the shape or create gaps in the trading areas of existing stores.

FIGURE 9-5

Planning a Mixed-Use Center

A mixed-use center combines retail facilities with other types of businesses, such as the hotel, bank, and office space shown here. In this instance, five acres of retail space are planned—which amount to almost 220,000 square feet of retail properties—in addition to the two full acres allocated to food. As a result, the retailers (nonfood and food) will attract local workers, hotel guests, and other tourists and shoppers (some of whom will be willing to travel to the center because of its size and variety).

Source: Donald Joski/ Shutterstock. Reprinted by permission.

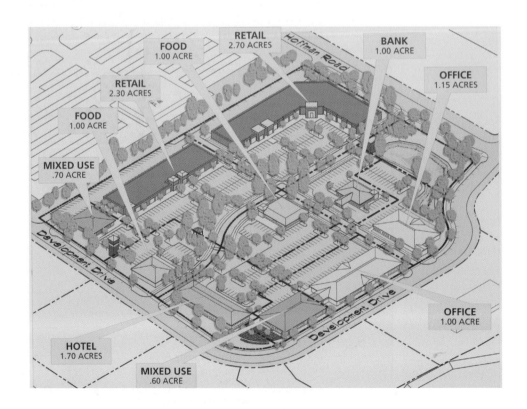

FIGURE 9-6

Informal Retailing: A Local Neighborhood Draw

At times, many people think of themselves as "retailers" with valuable mementos and other used (vintage) items to sell. But garage sales are usually not a draw outside of the immediate surrounding neighborhood. Shown here is a garage sale in Ottawa, Canada.

Source: Paul McKinnon/ Shutterstock. Reprinted by permission.

In many urban communities, people are clustered in multiunit housing near the center of commerce. With such population density, it is worthwhile for a retailer to be quite close to consumers; trading areas tend to be small because there are several shopping districts in close proximity to one another, particularly for the most densely populated cities. In many suburbs, most people live in single-unit housing, which is more geographically spread out. To produce satisfactory sales volume in suburbia, a retailer needs to attract shoppers from a greater distance.

The influence of travel or driving time on a trading area may not be clear from the population's geographic distribution. Physical barriers (toll bridges, poor roads, railroad tracks, one-way streets) usually reduce trading areas' size and contribute to their odd shapes. Economic barriers, such as different sales taxes in two towns, also affect the size and shape of trading areas.

In a community where a newspaper or other local media are available, a retailer could afford to advertise and enlarge its trading area. If local media are not available, the retailer would have to weigh the costs of advertising in countywide or regional media against the possibilities of a bigger trading area.

Delineating the Trading Area of an Existing Store

The size, shape, and characteristics of the trading area for an existing store—or shopping district or shopping center—can usually be delineated quite accurately. Store records (secondary data) or a special research study (primary data) can measure the trading area. And many firms offer computer-generated maps that can be tailored to individual retailers' needs.

Store records can reveal customer addresses. For credit customers, the data can be obtained from a retailer's billing department; for cash customers, addresses can be acquired by analyzing deliveries, cash sales slips, store contests (sweepstakes), and checks. In both instances, the task is relatively inexpensive and quick because the data were originally collected for other purposes and are readily available.

Because many big retailers have computerized credit-card systems, they can define primary, secondary, and fringe trading areas in terms of the following:

▷ The frequency with which people from various geographic locales shop at a particular store

▷ The average-dollar purchases at a store by people from given geographic locales

▷ The concentration of a store's credit-card holders from given geographic locales

MetroCount (www
.metrocount.com) offers
software to provide
vehicular traffic counts.
Click on "Products."

Visit this site (https://
goo.gl/TLUQvh) to study
your area's lifestyles and
purchasing preferences.
Enter your ZIP code to
begin.

Although it is easy to get data on credit-card customers, the analysis may be invalid if cash customers are not also studied. Credit use may vary among shoppers from different locales, especially if consumer traits in the locales are dissimilar. A firm reduces this problem if both cash and credit customers are studied.

A retailer can also collect primary data to determine trading-area size. It can record license plate numbers of cars parked near a store, find general addresses of those vehicle owners by contacting the state motor vehicle office, and then note them on a map. Typically, only the ZIP code and street of residence are given to protect people's privacy. In license plate analysis, nondrivers and passengers—customers who walk to a store, use mass transit, or are driven by others—should not be omitted. To collect data on these people, questions must often be asked (survey).

If a retailer desires more demographic and lifestyle information about consumers in particular areas, it can buy the data. PRIZM (now owned by Nielsen) is a system for identifying communities by lifestyle clusters. It identifies 66 neighborhood types, including "Upward Bound," "Blue-Chip Blues," and "Suburban Sprawl." This system was originally based on ZIP codes; it now also incorporates census tracts, block groups and enumeration districts, phone exchanges, and postal routes. Online PRIZM reports can be downloaded for as little as a few hundred dollars; costs are higher if reports are tailored to the individual retailer.

No matter how a trading area is delineated, a time bias may exist. A downtown business district is patronized by different customers during the week (those who work there) than on weekends (those who travel there to shop). Special events may attract people from great distances for only a brief time. Thus, an accurate estimate of a store's trading area requires complete and continuous investigation.

After delineating a trading area, the retailer should map people's locations and densities—either manually or with GIS software. In the manual method, a paper map of the area around a store is used. Different color dots or pins are placed on this map to represent *population* locations and densities, incomes, and other factors. *Customer* locations and densities are then indicated; primary, secondary, and fringe trading areas are denoted by ZIP code. Customers can be lured by promotions aimed at particular ZIP codes. With GIS software, vital customer data (such as purchase frequencies and amounts) are combined with other sources (such as census data) to yield computer-generated digitized maps depicting primary, secondary, and fringe trading areas.

Delineating the Trading Area of a New Store

A new store opening in an established trading area can use the methods just cited. The discussion in this section refers to a trading area with less-defined shopping and traffic patterns. Such an area must normally be evaluated in terms of opportunities rather than current patronage and traffic (pedestrian and vehicular) patterns. Accordingly, additional tools must be utilized.

Trend analysis—projecting the future based on the past—can be used by examining government and other data for predictions about population location, auto registrations, new housing starts, mass transportation, highways, zoning, and so on. With consumer surveys, data can be gathered about the time and distance people would be willing to travel to various retail locations, factors attracting people to a new store, addresses of those most apt to visit a new store, and other topics. Either technique may be a basis for delineating alternate new store trading areas.

Three computerized trading-area models are available for assessing new store locations:

1. An **analog model** is the simplest and most popular trading-area analysis tool. Potential sales for a new store are estimated on the basis of revenues for similar stores in existing areas, the competition at a prospective location, the new store's expected market share at that location, and the size and density of the location's primary trading area.
2. A **regression model** uses a series of mathematical equations showing the association between potential store sales and several independent variables at each location, such as population size, average income, the number of households, nearby competitors, transportation barriers, and traffic patterns.
3. A **gravity model** is based on the premise that people are drawn to stores that are closer and more attractive than competitors' stores. The distance between consumers and competitors, the distance from consumers to a given site, and store image can be included in this model.

Computerized trading-area models offer several benefits to retailers: (1) They operate in an objective and systematic way. (2) They offer insights as to how each locational attribute should be weighted. (3) They are useful in screening a large number of locations. (4) They can assess management performance by comparing forecasts with results.

More specific methods for delineating new trading areas are described next.[9]

REILLY'S LAW   The traditional means of trading-area delineation is **Reilly's law of retail gravitation**.[10] It establishes a point of indifference between two cities or communities, so the trading area of each can be determined. The **point of indifference** is the geographic breaking point between two cities (communities) at which consumers are indifferent to shopping at either. According to Reilly's law, more people go to a larger city or community because there are more stores; the assortment makes travel time worthwhile. Reilly's law rests on these assumptions: Two competing areas are equally accessible from a major road, and retailers in the two areas are equally effective. Other factors (such as population dispersion) are held constant or ignored.

The law may be expressed algebraically as:[11]

$$D_{ab} = \frac{d}{1 + \sqrt{P_b/P_a}}$$

where

D_{ab} = Limit of city (community) A's trading area, measured in miles along the road to city (community) B

d = Distance in miles along a major roadway between cities (communities) A and B

P_a = Population of city (community) A

P_b = Population of city (community) B

A city with a population of 90,000 (A) would draw people from three times the distance as a city with 10,000 (B). If the cities are 20 miles apart, the point of indifference for the larger city is 15 miles, and for the smaller city, it is 5 miles:

$$D_{ab} = \frac{20}{1 + \sqrt{10,000/90,000}} = 15 \text{ miles}$$

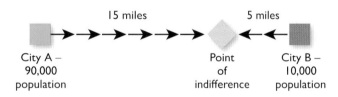

| 15 miles | | 5 miles |

City A –
90,000
population

Point
of
indifference

City B –
10,000
population

Reilly's law is an important contribution to trading-area analysis because of its ease of calculation. It is most useful when other data are not available or when compiling other data is costly. Nonetheless, Reilly's law has three limitations: (1) Distance is measured only by major thoroughfares; some people will travel shorter distances along streets that cross major thoroughfares. (2) Travel time does not necessarily reflect the distance traveled. Many people are more concerned about time than distance. (3) Actual distance may not correspond with the perceptions of distance. A store with few services and crowded aisles is apt to be a greater perceived distance from a person than a similarly located store with a more pleasant atmosphere.

Learn more about how to use the Huff model (http://goo.gl/48QvHc).

HUFF'S LAW   **Huff's law of shopper attraction** delineates trading areas on the basis of the product assortment (of the items desired by the consumer) carried at various shopping locations, travel times from the shopper's home to alternative locations, and the sensitivity of the kind of shopping to travel time. Assortment is rated by the total square feet of selling space a retailer expects all firms in a shopping area to allot to a product category. Sensitivity to the kind of shopping entails the trip's purpose (restocking versus shopping) and the type of good/service sought (such as clothing versus groceries).[12]

Huff's law is expressed as:

$$P_{ij} = \frac{\dfrac{S_j}{(T_{ij})^\lambda}}{\displaystyle\sum_{j}^{n} \dfrac{S_j}{(T_{ij})^\lambda}}$$

where

P_{ij} = Probability of a consumer's traveling from home i to shopping location j

S_j = Square footage of selling space in shopping location j expected to be devoted to a particular product category

T_{ij} = Travel time from consumer's home i to shopping location j

λ = Parameter used to estimate the effect of travel time on different kinds of shopping trips

n = Number of different shopping locations

Note that λ must be determined through research or by a computer program.

Assume a leased department operator studies three possible locations with 200, 300, and 500 total square feet of store space allocated to men's cologne (by all retailers in the areas). A group of potential customers lives 7 minutes from the first location, 10 minutes from the second, and 15 minutes from the third. The operator estimates the effect of travel time to be 2. Therefore, the probability of consumers' shopping is 43.9 percent for Location 1, 32.2 percent for Location 2, and 23.9 percent for Location 3:

$$P_{i1} = \frac{(200)/(7)^2}{(200)/(7)^2 + (300)/(10)^2 + (500)/(15)^2} = 43.9\%$$

$$P_{i2} = \frac{(300)/(10)^2}{(200)/(7)^2 + (300)/(10)^2 + (500)/(15)^2} = 32.2\%$$

$$P_{i3} = \frac{(500)/(15)^2}{(200)/(7)^2 + (300)/(10)^2 + (500)/(15)^2} = 23.9\%$$

If 200 shoppers for men's cologne live 7 minutes from Location 1, about 88 of them will shop there.

These points should be considered in using Huff's law:

▷ To determine Location 1's trading area, similar computations would be made for shoppers living at a driving time of 10, 15, 20 minutes, and so on. The number of shoppers at each distance who would shop there are then summed. Thus, stores in Location 1 could estimate their total market, trading-area size, and primary, secondary, and fringe areas for a product category.

▷ If new retail facilities in a product category are added to a locale, the percentage of shoppers living at every travel time from that location who would shop there goes up.

▷ The probability of people shopping at a location depends on the effect of travel time. If a product is important, such as dressy watches, consumers are less travel sensitive. A λ of 1 leads to these figures: Location 1, 31.1 percent; Location 2, 32.6 percent; and Location 3, 36.3 percent (based on the space in the cologne example). Location 3 would be popular for the watches due to assortment.

▷ All the variables are rather hard to calculate; for mapping purposes, travel time must be converted to miles. Travel time also depends on the transportation form used.

▷ Since people buy different items on different shopping trips, the trading area varies by trip.

Today, the Huff model is utilized in such GIS software as Esri's ArcGIS Business Analyst.

OTHER TRADING-AREA RESEARCH   Over the years, many researchers have examined trading-area size in a variety of settings. They have introduced additional factors and advanced statistical techniques to explain the consumer's choice of shopping location. Here are some examples.

In his model, Gautschi added to Huff's analysis by including shopping-center descriptors and transportation conditions. Weisbrod, Parcells, and Kern studied shopping-center appeal on the basis of expected population changes, store characteristics, and the transportation network. Bell,

Ho, and Tang devised a model with fixed and variable store-choice factors. Rogers examined the role of human decision making versus computer-based models in site choice. Rajagopal studied shopping attractions, routes to shopping, and establishing customer-centric strategies. Dolega, Pavlis, and Singleton extended the retail store attractiveness and catchment model from a single store or shopping center to a national network of retail centers.[13]

CHARACTERISTICS OF TRADING AREAS

After the size and shape of alternative trading areas are determined, the characteristics of those areas are studied. Of special interest are the attributes of residents and how well they match the firm's definition of its target market. An auto repair franchisee may compare opportunities in several locales by reviewing the number of car registrations; a hearing aid retailer may evaluate the percentage of the population 60 years of age or older; and a bookstore retailer may be concerned with residents' education level.

Tetrad (http://www.tetrad.com/franchising/) has useful tools for scrutinizing potential franchise locations.

Among the trading-area factors that should be studied by most retailers are the population size and characteristics, availability of labor, closeness to sources of supply, promotion facilities, economic base, competition, availability of locations, and regulations. The **economic base** is an area's industrial and commercial structure—the companies and industries that residents depend on to earn a living. The dominant industry (company) in an area is important because its drastic decline may have adverse effects on a large segment of residents. An area with a diverse economic base, where residents work for a variety of nonrelated industries, is more secure than an area with one major industry. Table 9-1 summarizes a number of factors to consider in evaluating retail trading areas.

Much of the data needed to describe an area can be obtained from the U.S. Bureau of the Census, the *American Community Survey*, *Editor & Publisher Market Guide*, *Standard Rate & Data Service*, regional planning boards, public utilities, chambers of commerce, local government offices, shopping-center owners, and renting agents. In addition, GIS software shows data on potential buying power in an area, the location of competitors, and highway access. Both demographic and lifestyle information may also be included in this software.

Although the yardsticks in Table 9-1 are not equally important in all location decisions, each should be considered. The most important yardsticks should be "knockout" factors: If a location does not meet minimum standards on key measures, it should be immediately dropped from further consideration.

These are examples of desirable trading-area attributes, according to these two retailers:

▶ Duluth Trading Company (www.duluthtrading.com), the Wisconsin-based omnichannel retailer of inventive and functional workwear for men and women, has evolved from a small mail-order business to a national retailer with nine stores and two outlets, and is expanding to other states. Duluth Trading analyzes dozens of markets to identify those with the strongest network potential based on trading-area analysis, customer segmentation, and proprietary retail modeling. Requirements for a Duluth store include a 10,000- to 15,000-square-foot space with a prominent interstate in the vicinity as well as access and visibility from a freeway, preferably near other male-oriented stores, with ample and convenient parking. Furthermore, to support its positioning that shopping at Duluth is an experience not just a purchase, it seeks "special, character-filled places and spaces, including downtown heritage locations suitable for renovation."[14]

▶ Texas-based Container Store (www.containerstore.com) sells high-end storage and organization products. It notes that one bad store location imposes "costs for 5 to 15 years" and opportunity losses of almost five good stores. It uses predictive analytics with cutting-edge location intelligence data to identify optimal locations for stores. Location intelligence leverages data from multiple sources relevant to Container Store customers and its lines of business (e.g., number of people in a geographic area who drink wine or donate to charity). In addition, it uses census-based data GIS (incomes, demographics in a neighborhood, etc.); information from consumer credit-card transactions (for example, annual spending in various product categories in an area); social-media information from LinkedIn (jobs and skills within an area) and Facebook (opinions of businesses in the area); mobile beacon data from telecommunications companies on when and how often consumers visit stores in a neighborhood; and traffic density information (how long customers may sit in traffic) to evaluate prospective sites. The retailer may decide not to invest in real estate at all and instead develop an online strategy.[15]

TABLE 9-1 Chief Factors to Consider in Evaluating Retail Trading Areas

Population Size and Characteristics

Total size and density	Total disposable income
Age distribution	Per capita disposable income
Average educational level	Occupation distribution
Percentage of residents owning homes	Trends

Availability of Labor

Management

Management trainee

Clerical

Closeness to Sources of Supply

Delivery costs	Number of manufacturers and wholesalers
Timeliness	Availability and reliability of product lines

Promotion Facilities

Availability and frequency of media

Costs

Waste

Economic Base

Dominant industry	Freedom from economic and seasonal fluctuations
Extent of diversification	Availability of credit and financial facilities
Growth projections	

Competitive Situation

Number and size of existing competitors	Short-run and long-run outlook
Evaluation of competitor strengths/weaknesses	Level of saturation

Availability of Store Locations

Number and type of locations	Zoning restrictions
Access to transportation	Costs
Owning versus leasing opportunities	

Regulations

Taxes	Minimum wages
Licensing	Zoning
Operations	

ETHICS IN RETAILING

Gentrification Issues

Prior to an area being rediscovered by young urban professionals, retail tenants often consisted of small independent retailers paying low rents. Many storefronts were unattractive, and there were few big retail chains. Ironically, neighborhood gentrification is often accompanied by retail vacancies, with some of the retailers responsible for the gentrification of the area being the first to move. In some cases, property owners wanted existing tenants to pay higher rents. In other instances, those owners sought to vacate the retail space in order to sell the building. Some experts say there is a retail lag when a neighborhood undergoes gentrification because of retailer reluctance to open new stores until redevelopment is more certain. One solution is to offer store-opening incentives for anchor retailers. This has been done in Washington, D.C., and Chicago.

Discuss the pros and cons of city incentives to attract anchor retail tenants.

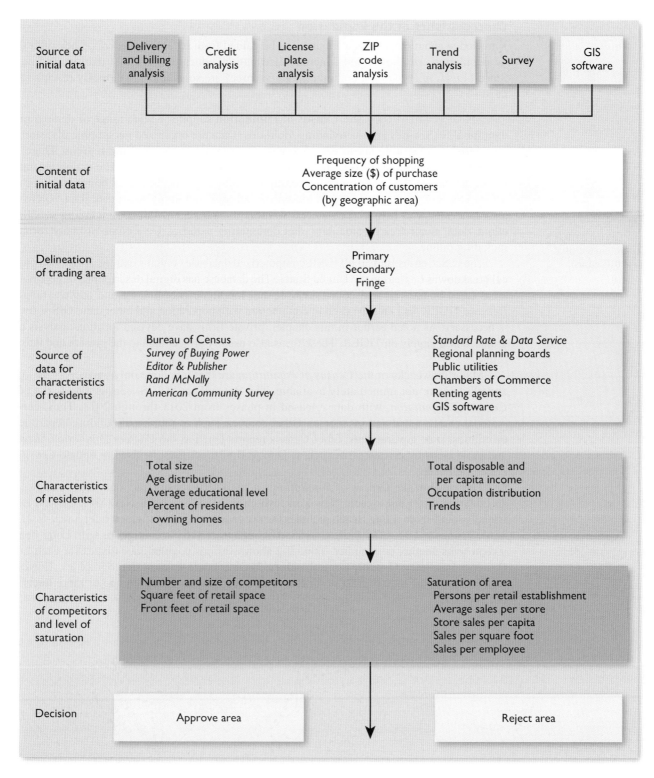

FIGURE 9-7
Analyzing Retail Trade Areas

Several stages of the process for gathering data to analyze trading areas are shown in Figure 9-7, which includes not only resident attributes but also those of competition. By studying these factors, a retailer sees how desirable an area is for a new retail business. We next discuss three elements in trading-area selection: population factors, economic base characteristics, and competition and saturation.

Characteristics of the Population

Knowledge about population attributes can be gained from secondary sources. They offer data on population size, households, income distribution, education, age distribution, and more. Since *Census of Population* and other public sources are so valuable, we briefly discuss them next.

CENSUS OF POPULATION   The **Census of Population** supplies a wide range of demographic data for all U.S. cities and surrounding vicinities. Data are organized geographically, starting with blocks and continuing to census tracts, cities, counties, states, and regions. There are less data for blocks and tracts than for larger units due to privacy issues. The major advantage of census data is the data on small geographic units. After trading-area boundaries are set, a firm can look at data by geographic unit in an area and study aggregate data. There are also data categories helpful for retailers wanting market segmentation—including racial and ethnic data, small-area income data, and commuting patterns. Data come in many formats, including online.

The U.S. Census Bureau's TIGER computerized database contains extremely detailed physical breakdowns of areas in the United States. The database has digital descriptions of geographic areas (area boundaries and codes, latitude and longitude coordinates, and address ranges). Because TIGER data must be used in conjunction with population and other data, GIS software is necessary. As noted earlier in this chapter, private firms have devised location analysis programs, based largely on TIGER. These firms also usually project data to the present and into the future.

Major drawbacks of the *Census of Population* are that it is done only once every 10 years and all data are not immediately available. The last full set of U.S. census data is the 2010 *Census of Population*, with data released in phases from 2011 through 2013. Thus, census material can be dated and inaccurate. Other sources, such as municipal building departments or utilities, state governments, other Census reports (such as the *Current Population Survey*), and projections by private firms such as Dun & Bradstreet must be used to update *Census of Population* data.

The value of the *Census of Population*'s actual 2010 census tract data can be shown by an illustration of Long Beach, New York, which is 30 miles east of New York City on Long Island's south shore. Long Beach includes the six census tracts highlighted in Figure 9-8: 4164, 4165, 4166, 4167.01, 4167.02, and 4168. Although tract 4163 is contiguous with Long Beach, it represents another community. Table 9-2 shows various population statistics for each Long Beach census tract. Overall, Long Beach is above average in most demographics. However, resident attributes in each tract do differ; thus, a retailer may locate in one or more tracts but not in others.

Find in-depth data regarding the 2010 U.S. Census (www.census .gov/2010census).

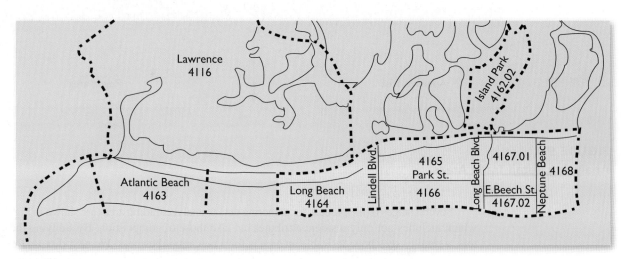

FIGURE 9-8

The Census Tracts of Long Beach, New York

Suppose a local bookstore wants to evaluate two potential trading areas based on the demographic data of the census tracts described in Table 9-2. Trading-area A corresponds with tracts 4164 and 4166. Area B corresponds to tracts 4167.01 and 4168. Population data for these areas (extracted from Table 9-2) are presented in Table 9-3. Area A is somewhat different from Area B, despite their proximity:

- The population in Area B is 20 percent larger.
- Although the population in both areas fell from 2000 to 2010, Area B dropped by a smaller percentage.
- In Areas A and B, the percentage aged 25 and older with college degrees is about equal.
- The annual median income and the proportion of workers who are managers or professionals are a bit higher for Area B.

The bookstore would have a tough time selecting between the areas because they are so similar. Thus, the firm might also consider the location of the sites available in Area A and Area B, relative to the locations of its existing stores, before making a final decision. It should also consider the differences between the census tracts in each proposed location. For example, in Area A, a much lower percentage of people are college graduates in tract 4164 than tract 4166.

OTHER PUBLIC SOURCES   There are many other useful, easily accessible public sources for current population information, in addition to the *Census of Population*—especially on a city or county basis. These sources typically update their data annually. They also provide some data not available from the *Census of Population*—total annual retail sales by area, annual retail sales for specific product categories, and population projections. The biggest disadvantage of these sources

TABLE 9-2 Selected Characteristics of Long Beach, New York, Residents by Census Tract, 2000 and 2010

	Tract Number					
	4164	4165	4166	4167.01	4167.02	4168
Total Population						
2000	7,406	6,231	6,326	4,471	4,443	6,585
2000 population 25 and older	5,772	4,073	4,904	3,163	3,739	5,173
2010	7,140	6,158	5,392	4,329	4,155	6,101
2010 population 25 and older	5,471	4,295	4,230	3,149	3,615	4,968
2010 median age (years)	44.4	52.7	44.6	41.6	46.6	48.2
Number of Households						
2000	3,138	2,002	2,592	1,601	2,440	3,165
2010	3,096	2,009	2,571	1,593	2,474	3,066
2010 average size	2.31	3.07	2.10	2.72	1.68	1.99
Education						
College graduates (% of population 25 and older), 2010	38.4	26.7	60.8	41.4	57.4	53.6
Income						
Median household income, 2010	$92,167	$84,208	$97,922	$96,713	$70,335	$99,150
Annual household of $50,000 or more (% of households)	76.1	70.4	79.6	78.9	68.2	75.8
Selected Occupations						
Managerial, professional, and related occupations (% of employed persons 16 and older), 2010	39.4	35.1	56.3	45.6	57.4	54.6

Sources: 2010 Census of Population; and authors' computations.

TABLE 9-3 Selected 2010 Population Statistics for Long Beach, New York. Trading-Areas A and B

	Area A (Tracts 4164 and 4166)	Area B (Tracts 4167.01 and 4168)
Total population, 2010	12,532	10,430
Population change, 2000–2010 (%)	−8.7	−5.7
College graduates, 25 and older, 2010 (%)	48.2	48.9
Median household income, 2010	$94,778	$98,317
Managerial and professional specialty occupations (% of employed persons 16 and older), 2010	47.1	51.5

is their use of geographic territories that are often much larger than a store's trading area and that cannot be broken down easily.

One newer national source of annual population data is the *American Community Survey*, which provides "demographic, social, economic, and housing data" for about 1,000 geographical areas. The survey has an excellent, user-friendly Web site (www.census.gov/acs/www). On the state and local levels, public data sources include planning commissions, research centers at public universities, county offices, and many other institutions.

Let us demonstrate the usefulness of public sources through the following example. (*Note:* We obtained all of the information for our example on the Internet—free!)

Suppose a prospective new car dealer investigates three counties near Chicago: DuPage, Kane, and Lake. The dealer decides to focus on one source of data available in print and online versions: *Northern Illinois Market Facts* (prepared by the Center for Government Studies, Northern Illinois University). Table 9-4 lists selected population and retail sales data for these counties.

What can the dealer learn? DuPage is by far the largest county; Kane is the smallest. Yet, the population growth rate from 2000 to 2010 was much higher for Kane. Lake has the highest median household income; DuPage has more adult college graduates. Per capita, DuPage residents account for 60 percent more retail sales than Kane residents and 21 percent more than Lake's. Lake and DuPage residents both allot more than one-fifth of spending to autos and gas stations; Kane residents account for the highest percentage of retail spending at apparel and food stores.

A Cadillac dealer using the data might select DuPage or Lake; a Ford dealer might choose Kane. But because the data are broad, several subsections of Kane may really be better choices to subsections in DuPage or Lake for the Cadillac dealer. Competition in each area also must be noted.

A location decision for a fast-food franchise often requires less data than for a bookstore or an auto dealer. Fast-food franchisors often seek communities with many people who live or work within three or four miles of their stores. But bookstore owners and auto dealers cannot locate merely based population density; they must consider a more complex set of population factors.

ECONOMIC BASE CHARACTERISTICS

The economic base reflects a community's commercial and industrial infrastructure and residents' sources of income. A firm seeking stability normally prefers an area with a diversified economic base (a large number of nonrelated industries) to one with an economic base keyed to a single major industry. The latter area is more affected by a strike, declining demand for an industry, and cyclical fluctuations.

In assessing a trading area's economic base, a retailer should investigate the percentage of the labor force in each industry, transportation, banking facilities, the impact of economic fluctuations, and the future of individual industries (firms). Data can be obtained from such sources as Easy Analytic Software, *Editor & Publisher Market Guide*, regional planning commissions, industrial development organizations, and chambers of commerce.

Easy Analytic Software (www.easidemographics.com) offers several inexpensive economic reports. It also produces "Census 2010 Reports" that can be downloaded free (after a simple sign-in), including Quick Reports, Quick Tables, Quick Maps, Site Analysis, Rank Analysis, and Profile Analysis.

Editor & Publisher Market Guide offers annual economic base data for cities, including employment sources, transportation networks, financial institutions, auto registrations, newspaper

TABLE 9-4 Selected Data Relating to Three Illinois Counties (2010, unless otherwise specified)

	County		
	DuPage	Kane	Lake
Total population	954,215	525,966	732,619
Annual population growth, 2000–2010	0.54%	2.67%	1.29%
Number of households	356,437	179,532	254,774
People 20 and over (%)	73.0%	68.2%	69.9%
Median household income	$ 67,066	$65,752	$ 70,368
Households with $50,000 or more in annual income	65.60%	63.90%	66.30%
College graduates, 25 and older (%)	45.10%	32.30%	42.00%
Total retail sales	$15,887,679,750	$5,456,897,250	$10,039,810,776
Annual per-capita retail sales	$ 16,650	$10,375	$ 13,704
Employment in retail trade	102,500	49,655	76,489
Total Retail Sales by Category			
Apparel	$ 651,765,882	$ 360.637,354	$ 331,022,264
Automotive and gas stations	$ 3,688,040,975	$ 983,556,420	$ 2,116,536,291
Eating, drinking, and hotel	$ 1,549,645,160	$ 564,361,518	$ 967,057,080
Food (grocery)	$ 1,767,206,180	$ 770,014,224	$ 1,178,051,352
General merchandise	$ 1,708,044,850	$ 676,918,242	$ 1,239,591,348
Home improvement and hardware	$ 680,355,295	$ 330,306,648	$ 539,940,203
Household goods	$ 917,954,830	$ 233,528,904	$ 734,084,238
Pharmaceutical	$ 2,377,903,780	$ 788,423,034	$ 1,786,125,122
Other	$ 2,546,799,835	$ 752,131,380	$ 1,147,281,354
Percentage of Total Retail Sales by Category			
Apparel	4.1%	6.6%	3.3%
Automotive and gas stations	23.2%	18.0%	21.1%
Eating, drinking, and hotel	9.8%	10.3%	9.6%
Food (grocery)	11.1%	14.1%	11.7%
General merchandise	10.7%	12.4%	12.4%
Home improvement and hardware	4.3%	6.1%	5.4%
Household goods	5.8%	4.3%	7.3%
Pharmaceutical	15.0%	14.5%	17.8%
Other	16.0%	13.7%	11.4%

circulation, and shopping centers. It also has data on population size and total households. The data in this guide cover broad geographic areas. The bookstore noted earlier might find the data on shopping centers to be helpful. The auto dealer would find the information on the transportation network, the availability of financial institutions, and the number of passenger cars to be useful. *Editor & Publisher Market Guide* is best used to supplement other sources.

The Nature of Competition and the Level of Saturation

A trading area may have residents who match desired characteristics of the desired market and a strong economic base, yet be a poor site for a new store if competition is too intense. A locale with a small population and a narrow economic base may be a good place if competition is less.

When examining competition, these factors should be analyzed: the number of existing stores, the size distribution of existing stores, the rate of new store openings, the strengths and weaknesses of all stores, the short-run and long-run trends, and the level of saturation.

Over the past 30 years, more U.S. retailers have entered foreign markets due to not as much competition. That is why Walmart is now in 28 countries, including Argentina, Brazil, China, Mexico, and Nigeria; Home Depot is in Canada, Guam, Mexico, and the Virgin Islands; and Baskin-Robbins has stores in Australia, Greece, Indonesia, Malaysia, Russia, and Thailand. Yet, in the future, even these locales may become oversaturated due to all the new stores. Furthermore, although the Northeast population in the United States has been declining relative to the Southeast and the Southwest—and is often considered to be saturated with stores—its high population density (the number of persons per square mile) is crucial for retailers. According to the *2010 U.S. Census*, in New Jersey, there were 1,196 people per square mile; in Massachusetts, 840; in Florida, 351; in Louisiana, 105; in Arizona, 57; and in Utah, 34.

An **understored trading area** has too few stores selling a specific good or service to satisfy the needs of its population. An **overstored trading area** has so many stores selling a specific good or service that some retailers cannot earn an adequate profit. A **saturated trading area** has the proper amount of stores to satisfy the needs of its population for a specific good or service, and to enable retailers to prosper.

Despite the large number of areas in the United States that are overstored, there still remain plentiful opportunities in understored communities. In some product categories, such as furniture, there can be a devastating plunge in sales and store closings in many areas during a housing recession. An economic recovery, low interest rates, improving employment, and rising home sales can stoke demand for household furniture. Today, new furniture stores are opening at an unprecedented rate in understored areas due to 83 million Millennials at their peak spending age and 76 million Baby Boomers who need new furniture appropriate for downsized homes and lifestyles.[16]

MEASURING TRADING-AREA SATURATION   Because any trading area can support only a given number of stores or square feet of selling space per goods/service category, these ratios can help quantify retail store saturation:

- Number of persons per retail establishment
- Average sales per retail store
- Average sales per retail store category
- Average store sales per capita or household
- Average sales per square foot of selling area
- Average sales per employee

The saturation level in a trading area can be measured against a goal or compared with other trading areas. An auto accessory chain could find that its current trading area is saturated by computing the ratio of residents to auto accessory stores. On the basis of this calculation, the owner could then decide to expand into a nearby locale with a lower ratio rather than to add another store in its present trading area.

Data for saturation ratios can be obtained from retailer records on its performance, city and state records, phone directories, surveys, economic census data, *Editor & Publisher Market Guide*,

    CAREERS IN RETAILING   Trading-Area Analysis

Real-estate careers in retailing are common in large chains as well in franchises. Personnel in this area have two major responsibilities: (1) trading-area analysis—identifying retail areas that are understored relative to their potential and (2) site selection—selecting specific sites and negotiating terms of occupancy. This box focuses on trading-area analysis. Site-selection careers are discussed in Chapter 10. Trading-area personnel can work in a large retailer's real-estate department, marketing research companies, or in consulting companies and real-estate firms. Trading-area analysis is typically an inside job that relies on GIS to map a location's existing customers relative to current stores, determines drive times to existing locations, shows competitor locations, and highlights barriers (such as tolls, bridges, etc.).

What college courses should a student interested in a trading-area analysis career pursue?

■

County Business Patterns, trade publications, and other sources. Sales by category, population size, and number of households per market area can be found with other sources.

When investigating an area's saturation for a specific good or service, ratios must be interpreted carefully. Differences among areas are not always reliable indicators of saturation. For instance, car sales per capita are different for a suburban area than an urban area because suburbanites have a much greater need for cars. Each area's level of saturation should be evaluated against distinct standards—based on optimum per-capita sales figures in that area.

In calculating saturation based on sales per square foot, a new or growing retailer must take its proposed store into account. If that store is not part of the calculation, the relative value of each trading area is distorted. Sales per square foot decline most if new outlets are added in small communities. The retailer should also consider if a new store will expand the total consumer market for a good or service category in a trading area or just increase its market share in that area without expanding the total market.

Next are three examples of how retailers factor trading-area saturation into their decisions:

▸ Urban Outfitters (www.urbn.com) is an omnichannel lifestyle specialty retailer that operates Urban Outfitters (average store 9,000 square feet); Free People (average store 1,800 square feet); Anthropologie, Terrain, and BHLDN (average store 7,000 square feet); as well as E-commerce Web sites, mobile applications, and catalogs. It competes with online and offline stores, including those that sell its wholesale Free People products and chain fashion specialty and department stores in competitive domestic and international markets. Declines in discretionary spending on fashion, overstored U.S. retail space (where there is five times more space per person compared to that of Great Britain, France, and Japan),[17] and more comparison shopping online can force markdowns—a promotional sales environment—that negatively affect profit margins.

▸ The retail drugstore industry is highly competitive. Prescription drug sales account for more than half of sales revenues in the industry, but profit margins are low due to insurers and Medicare/Medicaid. Rite Aid (www.riteaid.com), the third-largest drugstore chain (with 4,560 stores) competes with other retail drugstore chains, independently owned drugstores, supermarkets, mass merchandisers, discount stores, wellness offerings, dollar stores, and mail-order pharmacies. Consolidation in the drugstore industry, the aggressive discounting of generic drugs by supermarkets and mass merchandisers (e.g., Walmart), and the increase of promotional incentives to drive prescription sales further increase competitive pressures. To expand overall profitability and higher market share, Rite Aid acquired pharmacy benefit manager (PBM) Envision Rx to access prescription files to see what are likely to be customer generators for higher margin "front-end" (e.g., nonprescription) goods and services (such as photo printing) and mini-clinics in stores. Rite Aid is rebuilding its real-estate portfolio by adding stores to fill out understored trading areas, in addition to store remodels and relocations.[18]

▸ *Marketing Guidebook* (www.marketingguidebook.com) has data for retailers selling food—including population size, number of households, total food store sales, number of food stores by type of retailer (such as supermarkets versus membership clubs), and more—that can be used to measure the level of saturation by U.S. city and community.

Look at the *Marketing Guidebook* demo (www .marketingguidebook .com/demo.html) to see the saturation levels of supermarkets. There is a free login required.

Chapter Summary

1. *To demonstrate the importance of store location for a retailer and to outline the process for choosing a store location.* Location choice is critical due to complex decision making, high costs, lack of flexibility once a site is chosen, and the impact of a site on the strategy. A good location may let a retailer succeed even if its strategy mix is relatively mediocre.

   The selection of a store location includes (1) evaluating alternative trading areas, (2) determining the best type of location, (3) picking a general site, and (4) settling on a specific site. This chapter looked at Step 1. Chapter 10 details Steps 2, 3, and 4.

2. *To discuss the concept of a trading area and its related components.* A trading area is the geographical area from which customers are drawn. When shopping locales are nearby, they may have trading-area overlap.

Many retailers utilize geographic information system (GIS) software to delineate and analyze trading areas. The software combines digitized mapping with key data to depict trading areas. This allows retailers to research alternative locations and display findings on computerized maps. Vendors market GIS software, based on TIGER mapping by the U.S. government.

Each trading area has primary, secondary, and fringe components. The farther people live from a shopping area, the less apt they are to travel there. The size and shape of a trading area depend on store type, store size, competitors, housing patterns, travel time and traffic barriers, and media availability. Destination stores have larger trading areas than do parasite stores.

3. *To show how trading areas may be delineated for existing and new stores.* The size, shape, and characteristics of the trading area for an existing store or group of stores can be learned accurately—based on store records, contests, license plate numbers, surveys, and so on. Time biases must be considered in amassing data. Results should be mapped and customer densities noted.

Potential trading areas for a new store must often be described in terms of opportunities rather than current patronage and traffic. Trend analysis and consumer surveys may be used. Three computerized models are available for planning a new store location: analog, regression, and gravity. They offer several benefits.

Two techniques for delineating new trading areas are Reilly's law, which relates the population size of different cities to the size of their trading areas; and Huff's law, which is based on each area's shopping assortment, the distance of people from various retail locales, and sensitivity to travel time.

4. *To examine three major factors in trading-area analysis: population characteristics, economic base characteristics, and competition and the level of saturation.* The best sources for population data are the *Census of Population* and other publicly available sources. Census data are detailed and specific, but become dated. Information from public sources such as the *American Community Survey* may be more current but report on broader geographic areas.

An area's economic base reflects the community's commercial and industrial infrastructure, as well as residents' income sources. A retailer should look at the percentage of the labor force in each industry, the transportation network, the banking facilities, the potential impact of economic fluctuations on the area, and the future of individual industries. Easy Analytic software and *Editor & Publisher Market Guide* are good sources of data on the economic base.

A trading area cannot be properly analyzed without studying the nature of competition and the level of saturation. An area may be understored (too few retailers), overstored (too many retailers), or saturated (the proper number of retailers). Saturation may be measured in terms of the number of persons per store, average sales per store, average store sales per capita or household, average sales per square foot of selling space, and average sales per employee.

Key Terms

trading area (p. 242)
trading-area overlap (p. 243)
geographic information system
     (GIS) (p. 244)
primary trading area (p. 247)
secondary trading area (p. 247)
fringe trading area (p. 247)

destination store (p. 248)
parasite store (p. 248)
analog model (p. 250)
regression model (p. 250)
gravity model (p. 250)
Reilly's law of retail gravitation (p. 251)
point of indifference (p. 251)

Huff's law of shopper attraction
     (p. 251)
economic base (p. 253)
Census of Population (p. 256)
understored trading area (p. 260)
overstored trading area (p. 260)
saturated trading area (p. 260)

Questions for Discussion

1. Comment on this statement: "A poor location may be such a liability that even superior retailers cannot overcome it." Is it always true? Give examples.
2. If a retailer has a new 10-year store lease, does this mean the next time it studies the characteristics of its trading area should be 5 years from now? Explain your answer.
3. What is trading-area overlap? Are there any advantages to a chain retailer's having some overlap among its various stores? Why or why not?
4. Describe three ways in which a consumer electronics store chain could use geographic information system

(GIS) software in its trading-area analysis.
5. How could an off-campus store selling textbooks and supplies near a college campus determine its primary, secondary, and fringe trading areas? Why should the store obtain this information?
6. How could a parasite store increase the size of its trading area?
7. Compare the analog and regression models of assessing new locations.
8. Computerized trading-area models like Reilly's Law offer significant advantages to retailers. These models

are objective and consider all of the factors in a systematic manner. Retailers can use a model to screen those locations and shortlist them. Explain the relationship between the law of gravitation and the point of indifference with regard to store location.

9. Why is it critical for a retailer to examine a location's economic base in its decision to open a store?

10. Visit the Web site of the Department of Singapore Statistics (http://www.singstat.gov.sg) and look up the population trends for 2016. As a retailer, where would you find information to help you determine ideal locations?

11. A fast-food brand is contemplating trading area saturation before committing to locate in several cities in an overseas market. What should it consider?

12. How could a Web-based retailer determine the level of saturation for its product category? What should this retailer do to lessen the impact of the level of saturation it faces?

Web-Based Exercise

Visit the Web site of *Retail Focus* (http://www.retail-focus .co.uk/). What could a retailer learn from the News and Features sections of the magazine? Which Web site feature do you like best? Why?

10 Site Selection

Chapter Objectives

1. To thoroughly examine the types of locations available to a retailer: isolated store, unplanned business district, and planned shopping center

2. To note the decisions necessary in choosing a general retail location

3. To describe the concept of the one-hundred percent location

4. To discuss several criteria for evaluating general retail locations and the specific sites within them

5. To contrast alternative terms of occupancy

In recent years, shopping centers have faced intense competition from big-box stores in isolated or strip locations, outlet shopping areas, and online retailers—including those with traditional store locales. As a result, more shopping-center operators are utilizing social media to lure and retain customers.

Research by the Georgia Institute of Technology found that about one-third of malls nationwide are considered dead; only one-third are considered truly healthy.[1] The large continuing number of store closings threaten to affect the vitality of existing shopping centers where the closings are located. Among retailers that have implemented and announced store closings in the last few years are Macy's, Sears, Target, J. C. Penney, and Office Depot.

Many closed locations are in shopping centers where the retailer has been an anchor tenant, in terms of square footage and its ability to attract customers to the mall. Analysts cite several reasons for the store closings: overstoring, the popularity of the Web (especially Amazon), the increased competition for shoppers by different store formats, and the attractiveness of small-store formats (based on fewer product selections).

An important concern when a major traffic-generating store closes is its impact on the remaining retail tenants. In addition to image issues associated with an anchor-store vacancy is its effect on store traffic. This is especially significant when the closed store had a prominent position in the mall. Typically, traffic-generating stores are placed at opposite ends of a mall to attract customer traffic. Stores closest to the vacant store may suffer the most.

Source: Kavalenkava Volha/Shutterstock. Reprinted by permission.

There are also challenges when renting a store's vacated space. New tenants may require a significant rent reduction in comparison to the previous tenant. Many department stores are huge and have multiple levels; other store formats cannot easily adapt to that space.

Overview

The Small Business Administration offers lots of advice on site selection (www.sba.gov/content/tips-choosing-business-location).

After a retailer investigates alternative trading areas (Step 1), it determines what type of location is desirable (Step 2), selects the general location (Step 3), and evaluates alternative specific store sites (Step 4). Steps 2, 3, and 4 are discussed in this chapter.

Identifying the right location at the right price is critical to success for any retailer. In addition to careful planning and conservatively budgeting space needs and requirements, retailers also need to consider the following five steps in site selection:[2]

1. Know the characteristics of customer segments shopping at the location. This is critical in site selection. Retailers such as Starbucks and Target use specific location and shopper profiles that incorporate numerous data points. Firms can use scoring systems to rate "quality" of alternative retail sites on factors such as visibility, access, population size, household income, and traffic. Predictive analytics can be used to forecast sales performance at low, medium, and high location quality retail sites.[3] A minimum acceptable score can be applied as the baseline and other sites can be evaluated based on marginal contribution to predicted store performance. Retailers need to take into consideration the limitations of secondary data and model assumptions that may not be applicable to their particular business. Most importantly, they must physically verify the store location.[4]

2. Seek out locales with the highest sales potential. The rent charged for a site should reflect the sales revenue that can be generated there. Marginal analysis of rent paid versus increase in store performance can be used to rule out high-rent sites that are not worth the investment.

3. Understand the current state of the retail leasing market to see whether a landlord's rent is fair (reasonable). Evaluating multiple qualified locations as backups is a prudent practice. Not only does this help in negotiating for the most preferred choice but if the preferred choice does not work out it helps alleviate uncertainty and frustration.

4. Research co-tenants in a shopping center or shopping district to see if they are compatible and attract customers likely to patronize the new retailer. Pedestrian and vehicular traffic counts indicate whether co-tenants are good for the newly arriving retailer. Anchor stores determine the basic customer profile of the location, but the type of smaller tenants is equally important.

5. Consider the long-term commitment. Leases typically are in force for at least 5 years—and many times, longer than that.

TYPES OF LOCATIONS

There are three different location types: isolated store, unplanned business district, and planned shopping center. Each has its own attributes as to the composition of competitors, parking, nearness to nonretail institutions (such as office buildings), and other factors. Step 2 in the location process is to determine which type of location to use.

The Isolated Store

An **isolated store** is a freestanding retail outlet located on either a highway or a street. There are no adjacent retailers with which this type of store shares traffic. The advantages of this type of retail location are many:

- There is no competition in close proximity.
- Rental costs are relatively low.
- There is flexibility; no group rules affect operations, and larger space may be obtained.
- Isolation is good for stores involved in one-stop or convenience shopping.
- Better road and traffic visibility is possible.
- Facilities can be adapted to individual specifications.
- Easy parking can be arranged.
- Cost reductions are possible, leading to lower prices.

There are also various disadvantages to this retail location type:

- ▶ Initial customers may be difficult to attract.
- ▶ Many people will not travel very far to get to one store on a continuous basis.
- ▶ Most people like variety in shopping.
- ▶ Advertising expenses may be high.
- ▶ Costs such as outside lighting, security, grounds maintenance, and trash collection are not shared.
- ▶ Other retailers and community zoning laws may restrict access to desirable locations.
- ▶ A store must often be built rather than rented.
- ▶ As a rule, unplanned business districts and planned shopping centers are much more popular among consumers; they generate most of retail sales.

Large-store formats (such as Walmart supercenters and Costco membership clubs) and convenience-oriented retailers (such as 7-Eleven) are usually the retailers best suited to isolated locations due to the challenge of attracting a target market. A small specialty store would probably be unable to develop a customer following; people would be unwilling to travel to a store that does not have a large assortment of products or a strong image for merchandise and/or prices.

Years ago, numerous shopping centers forbade discounters because discounting was frowned on by anchor retailers. This forced discounters to seek isolated sites or to build their own centers; and they have been successful. Today, diverse retailers are in isolated locales as well as at business district and shopping center sites. Retailers using a mixed-location strategy include McDonald's, Target, Sears, Starbucks, Toys "R" Us, Walmart, and 7-Eleven. Some retailers, including many gas stations and convenience stores, still emphasize isolated locations. See Figure 10-1.

The Unplanned Business District

An **unplanned business district** is a type of retail location where two or more stores situate together (or in close proximity) in such a way that the total arrangement or mix of stores is not due to prior long-range planning. Stores locate based on what is best for them, not the district. For example, four shoe stores may exist in an area with no pharmacy. There are four kinds of unplanned business districts: central business district, secondary business district, neighborhood business district, and string. A discussion of each follows.

CENTRAL BUSINESS DISTRICT   A **central business district (CBD)** is the hub of retailing in a city. It is synonymous with the term *downtown*. The CBD exists where there is the greatest density of office buildings and stores. Both vehicular and pedestrian traffic are very high. The core of a CBD is often no more than a square mile, with cultural and entertainment facilities surrounding it. Shoppers are drawn from the whole urban area and include all ethnic groups and all classes of people. The central business district has at least one major department store and a number of

FIGURE 10-1

An Isolated Store Location

Gas stations often situate in locations where they are not adjacent to other retailers. Favorite spots include side roads off major highways and corners of streets that have a lot of vehicular traffic. These gas stations typically have a small convenience store (operated by the gas stations) on the premises.

Source: dean bertoncelj/ Shutterstock. Reprinted by permission.

specialty and convenience stores. The arrangement of stores follows no pre-set format; it depends on history (first come, first located), retail trends, and luck.

Here are some strengths that allow central business districts to draw a large number of shoppers:

- ▶ Excellent goods/service assortment
- ▶ Access to public transportation
- ▶ Variety of store types and positioning strategies within one area
- ▶ Wide range of prices
- ▶ Variety of customer services
- ▶ High level of pedestrian traffic (see Figure 10-2)
- ▶ Nearness to commercial and social facilities

In addition, chain headquarters stores are often situated in central business districts.

These are some of the inherent weaknesses of the CBD:

- ▶ Inadequate parking, as well as traffic and delivery congestion
- ▶ Travel time for those living in the suburbs
- ▶ Frail condition of some cities—such as aging stores—compared with their suburbs
- ▶ Relatively poor image of central cities to some potential consumers
- ▶ High rents and taxes for the most popular sites
- ▶ Movement of some popular downtown stores to suburban shopping centers
- ▶ Discontinuity of offerings (such as four shoe stores and no pharmacy)

The central business district remains a major retailing force, although its share of overall sales has fallen over the years, as compared with the planned shopping center. Besides the weaknesses cited, much of the drop-off of business is due to suburbanization. In the first half of the twentieth century, most urban workers lived near their jobs. Gradually, many people moved to suburbs—where they are often served by planned shopping centers.

A number of CBDs are doing well, however, and many others are striving to return to their prior stature. They use such tactics as modernizing storefronts and equipment, forming merchants' associations, modernizing sidewalks and adding brighter lighting, building vertical malls (with several floors of stores), improving transportation networks, closing streets to vehicular traffic (sometimes with disappointing results), bringing in "razzmatazz" retailers such as Apple stores, and integrating a commercial and residential environment known as *mixed-use facilities*. The renewed popularity of living in urban areas by Millennials and Baby Boomers creates retail needs that go beyond those of the transient daytime population. Vibrant urban shopping districts with mixed-use properties, access to public transport, and entertainment districts appeal to diverse lifestyles and are a competitive advantage for cities.[5]

A good example of the value of a revitalized CBD is Philadelphia, where there has been a strong long-term effort under way to make the central city more competitive with suburban

FIGURE 10-2

The Central Business District and Pedestrian Traffic

One of the main advantages of the central business district—such as the Japanese CBD shown here—is the massive amount of pedestrian traffic that passes by retailers. This includes tourists, residents, and commuters who work in the CBD.

Source: Spencer Hoo/Shutterstock. Reprinted by permission.

shopping centers. Consider these facts about Philadelphia's central business district: $1.5 billion is being spent in streetscape, façade, and public-area improvements to construct 5.5 million square feet of leasable space. Also, some 27,000 new housing units will be added by 2019, converting vacant office buildings, factories, and empty lots into condos, apartments, and single-family housing. This will result in a transformation of neighborhoods, an increase in population, and revitalized retail development. Empty Nesters and Millennials, who make up 40 percent of Philadelphia's center city population, work and live in the city; and the average household income has been rising. The influx of such retailers as high-end furniture maker Thos. Moser, Vince, Under Armor, Lululemon, Nordstrom Rack, and Bloomingdale's Outlet is extending the area to nearby neighborhoods and ancillary corridors. Many successful E-commerce sites, including Warby Parker, Bonobos, and Athleta, are establishing brick-and-mortar stores here.[6]

Boston's Faneuil Hall is another long-term CBD renovation success. When developer James Rouse took over the site originally called Quincy Market, it had three 150-year-old, block-long former food warehouses that were abandoned for nearly a decade. Rouse used landscaping, fountains, banners, open-air courts, street performers, and colorful graphics to enable Faneuil Hall "America's First Open Marketplace" to capture a festive spirit. Faneuil Hall now combines shopping, eating, and entertainment. Today, it has 100 shops and Bull Market pushcart vendors, 13 full-service restaurants, 35 food stalls, and regular events and entertainment. It attracts 18 million shoppers and visitors yearly.[7]

Grand Central Terminal (www.grandcentralterminal.com) is all dressed up and open for shopping and dining.

Other major CBD revitalization projects have included Annapolis Town Centre (Maryland), Branson Landing (Missouri), City Center District (Dallas), Harborplace Baltimore, Peabody Place (Memphis), Pioneer Place (Portland, Oregon), Grand Central Terminal (New York City), Tower City Center (Cleveland), and Union Station (Washington, D.C.).

SECONDARY BUSINESS DISTRICT A **secondary business district (SBD)** is an unplanned shopping area in a city or town that is usually bounded by the intersection of two major streets. Cities—particularly larger ones—often have multiple SBDs, each with at least a junior department store (a branch of a traditional department store or a full-line discount store) and/or some larger specialty stores, besides many smaller stores. This format is now more important because cities have "sprawled" over larger geographic areas.

The kinds of goods and services sold in an SBD mirror those in the CBD. However, a secondary business district has smaller stores, less width and depth of merchandise assortment, and a smaller trading area (consumers will not travel as far), and it sells a higher proportion of convenience-oriented items.

The SBD's major strengths include a good product selection, access to thoroughfares and public transportation, less crowding and more personal service than in a central business district, and placement nearer to residential areas than a CBD. The SBD's major weaknesses include the discontinuity of offerings, the sometimes high rent and taxes (but not as high as in a CBD), traffic and delivery congestion, aging facilities, parking difficulties, and fewer chain outlets than in the CBD. These weaknesses have generally not affected the SBD as much as the CBD—and parking problems, travel time, and congestion are less for the SBD.

NEIGHBORHOOD BUSINESS DISTRICT A **neighborhood business district (NBD)** is an unplanned shopping area that appeals to the convenience shopping and service needs of a single residential area. An NBD contains several small stores, such as a dry cleaner, a stationery store, a barber shop and/or a beauty salon, a liquor store, and a restaurant. The leading retailer tends to be a

---

ETHICS IN RETAILING   Shopping Center Leases

There are a number of issues related to retail leasing in a shopping center that pose ethical issues for the developer, major tenants, smaller retailers, and consumers. Some issues are due to the bargaining power possessed by large retail tenants. Others are because of the data available to developers and by bank financing requirements. Large retailers may seek to reduce competition via lease terms that restrict specific types of retailers.

This often restricts category killers or discount stores from opening units in a regional shopping center. In a percentage lease, a shopping-center developer knows the net sales of all tenants. Financing of shopping centers is based on the credit rating of retail tenants, which typically excludes small independent retailers.

Comment on the ethical considerations presented.

supermarket or a large drugstore. This type of business district is situated on the major street(s) of its residential area.

A neighborhood business district offers a good location, long store hours, good parking, and a less hectic atmosphere than a central business district or secondary business district. On the other hand, there is a more limited selection of goods and services, and prices tend to be higher because competition is less than in a CBD or SBD.

STRING A **string** is an unplanned shopping area comprising a group of retail stores, often with similar or compatible product lines, located along a street or highway. There is little extension of shopping onto perpendicular streets. A string may start with an isolated store, success then breeding competitors. Car dealers, antique stores, and apparel retailers often situate in strings.

A string location has many of the advantages of an isolated store site (lower rent, more flexibility, better road visibility and parking, and lower operating costs), along with some disadvantages (less product variety, increased travel for many consumers, higher advertising costs, zoning restrictions, and the need to build premises). Unlike an isolated store, a string store has competition at its location. This draws more people to the area and allows for some sharing of common costs. It also means less control over prices and less loyalty toward each outlet. An individual store's increased traffic flow, due to being in a string rather than an isolated site, may be greater than the customers lost to competitors. This explains why four gas stations locate on opposing corners.

Figure 10-3 shows a map with various unplanned business districts and isolated locations.

The Planned Shopping Center

A **planned shopping center** consists of a group of architecturally unified commercial establishments on a site that is centrally owned or managed, designed and operated as a unit, based on balanced tenancy, and accompanied by parking facilities. Its location, size, and mix of stores are

FIGURE 10-3

Unplanned Business Districts and Isolated Locations

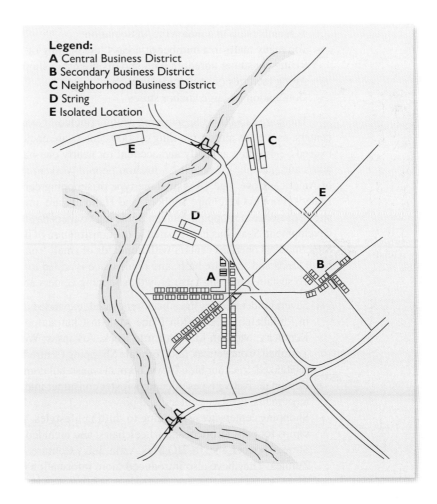

Legend:
A Central Business District
B Secondary Business District
C Neighborhood Business District
D String
E Isolated Location

Shopping centers in some form have existed for more than 1,000 years. Learn more about this phenomenon (https://goo.gl/Dy69sO).

related to the trading area served. Through **balanced tenancy**, the stores in a planned shopping center complement each other as to the quality and variety of their product offerings, and the kind and number of stores are linked to overall population needs. To ensure balanced tenancy, management of a planned center usually specifies the proportion of total space for each kind of retailer, limits product lines that can be sold by every store, and stipulates what kinds of firms can acquire unexpired leases. At a well-run center, a coordinated and cooperative long-run retailing strategy is followed by all stores.

The planned shopping center has several positive attributes:

▷ Well-rounded assortments of goods and services based on long-range planning
▷ Strong suburban population
▷ Interest in one-stop, family shopping
▷ Cooperative planning and sharing of common costs
▷ Creation of distinctive, but unified, shopping center images
▷ Maximization of pedestrian traffic for individual stores
▷ Access to highways and availability of parking for consumers
▷ More appealing than city shopping for some people
▷ Generally lower rent and taxes than CBDs (except for enclosed regional malls)
▷ Generally lower theft rates than CBDs
▷ Popularity of malls—both *open* (shopping area off-limits to vehicles) and *closed* (shopping area off-limits to vehicles and all stores in a temperature-controlled facility)
▷ Growth of discount malls and other newer types of shopping centers

There are also some limitations associated with the planned shopping center:

▷ Landlord regulations that reduce each retailer's flexibility, such as required hours
▷ Generally higher rent than an isolated store
▷ Restrictions on the goods/services that can be sold by each store
▷ A competitive environment within the center
▷ Required payments for items that may be of little or no value to an individual retailer, such as membership in a merchants' association
▷ Too many malls in a number of areas ("the malling of America")
▷ Rising consumer boredom with and disinterest in shopping as an activity
▷ Aging facilities of some older centers
▷ Domination by large anchor stores

Shopping Centers Today (www.icsc.org/sct/index.php) is the bible of the industry.

There are 115,000 U.S. shopping centers (including convenience, power, lifestyle, and theme centers, as well as airport retailing); 1,000 centers are enclosed malls. Shopping center revenues exceed $2.4 trillion annually and account for nearly one-half of U.S. retail-store sales (including autos and gasoline). About 12.5 million people work in shopping centers. Eighty-five percent of Americans over age 18 visit some type of shopping center in an average month. Nordstrom, Macy's, Foot Locker, Gap, Sephora, and Hallmark are among the vast number of chains with a strong presence at shopping centers. Some big retailers have also been involved in shopping-center development. Sears has participated in the construction of dozens of shopping centers, and Publix Supermarkets operates centers with hundreds of small tenants. Each year, numerous new centers of all kinds and sizes are built, and retail space is added to existing centers.[8] See Figure 10-4.

To sustain their long-term growth, shopping centers are engaging in these practices:

▷ Several older centers have been renovated, expanded, and/or repositioned. Cherry Hill Mall in Philadelphia; Hamilton Place Mall in Chattanooga; Kentucky Oaks Mall in Paducah, Kentucky; McCain Mall in Little Rock, Arkansas; Westfield Trumbull Shopping Center in Trumbull, Connecticut; and Yorkdale Shopping Centre Mall in Toronto, Canada, have all been revitalized. Visit our blog (www.bermanevansretail.com) for information on shopping centers.
▷ Certain derivative types of centers foster consumer interest and enthusiasm. Three of these—megamalls, lifestyle centers, and power centers—are discussed a little later in this chapter.
▷ Shopping centers are responding to shifting lifestyles. They have made parking easier; added ramps for baby strollers and wheelchairs; and included distinctive retailers such as the Apple Store, Apricot Lane, BCBG Max Azria, Juicy Couture, MaxMara, Michael Kors, Rue 21, and Zumiez. They have also introduced more information booths and center directories.

FIGURE 10-4

The Dynamics of a Planned Shopping Center

Many planned shopping centers have created a customer-friendly experience with a balanced selection of retailers, innovative walking patterns, well-known retailers, and a unique interior.

Source: YIUCHEUNG/ Shutterstock. Reprinted by permission.

▸ The retailer mix has broadened at many centers to attract people wanting one-stop shopping. More centers now include banks, stockbrokers, dentists, doctors, beauty salons, TV repair outlets, and/or car rental offices. Centers may also include "temporary tenants" (retailers that lease space, often in mall aisles or walkways, and sell from booths or moving carts). Tenants benefit from the lower rent and short-term commitment; centers benefit by creating more shopping excitement and diversity. Consumers then discover new vendors in unexpected places.

▸ Open-air malls are gaining popularity because they are less expensive to build, which means lower rents and common-area costs. Many people also like the outdoor shopping experience. A popular example is the Mall at Partridge Creek, an open-air regional center in Clinton Township, Michigan. It is anchored by Nordstrom, Carson's, and a 14-screen cinema. The center has 90 stores and restaurants. What gives it a special flair? "Partridge Creek has amenities unique to malls in Michigan, including: Bocce ball courts, free Wi-Fi, pop-jet fountains, a TV court, and a 30-foot fireplace."[9] Free events—including concerts, Wellness Wednesdays, and walking clubs—create community involvement and offer retailers opportunities to engage with shoppers.

▸ More center developers are striving to build their own brand loyalty. Simon and Westfield are among those that have spent millions of dollars to boost their images by promoting their own names—with the Simon Mall name prominently featured at its shopping centers. Simon (www.simon.com) owns and/or manages 230 properties in North America, Europe, and Asia.[10]

▸ Some shopping centers use frequent-shopper programs to retain customers and track spending. Simon Insiders earn VIP parking spots and invitations to private mall events in addition to cash back when they spend more than $1,000 in a month at Simon Property Group malls.[11]

There are three types of planned shopping centers: regional, community, and neighborhood. Their characteristics are noted in Table 10-1, and they are described next.

  **CAREERS IN RETAILING**   Site-Selection Careers

Unlike trading-area analysis work that can be done at a desk with a computer, site-selection jobs require travel to proposed sites. These personnel need to compile traffic counts, assess the composition of adjacent stores, judge parking adequacy, and determine store visibility. Since these employees are involved with negotiating leases, they need strong bargaining skills and legal knowledge. Some long-term leases have escalator clauses that raise rents over time and may require retail tenants to pay all or part of increases in real-estate taxes and insurance. Some large chains use their legal staff for complex negotiations. Smaller firms hire attorneys to negotiate.

Assess your own negotiation skills. Provide examples to document your answer.

TABLE 10-1 Typical U.S. Regional, Community, and Neighborhood Types of Planned Shopping Centers

Features of a Typical Center	Type of Center		
	Regional	Community	Neighborhood
Total site area (acres)	40–100+	10–40	3–5
Total sq. ft. leased to retailers	400,001–2,000,000+	100,001–400,000	30,000–100,000
Principal tenant	One, two, or more full-sized department stores	Branch (traditional or discount), department store, variety store, and/or category killer store	Supermarket or drugstore
Number of stores	40–125 or more	15–40	5–20
Goods and services offered	Largest assortment for customers, focusing on goods that encourage careful shopping and services that enhance the shopping experience (such as a food court)	Moderate assortment for customers, focusing on a mix of shopping- and convenience-oriented goods and services	Lowest assortment for customers, emphasizing convenience-oriented goods and services
Minimum number of people living/working in trading area needed to support center	100,000+	20,000–100,000	3,000–50,000
Trading area in driving time	Up to 30 minutes	Up to 20 minutes	Fewer than 15 minutes
Location	Outside central city, on arterial highway or expressway	Close to one or more populated residential area(s)	Along a major thoroughfare in a single residential area
Layout	Mall, often enclosed with anchor stores at major entrances/exits	Strip or L-shaped	Strip
Percentage of these three center types	3	22	75
Percentage of these three center types' selling space	20	36	44

Note: The percentage data in the table refer *only* to these three specific types of planned shopping centers.

Source: Authors' estimates, based on material compiled and adapted from International Council of Shopping Centers, "U.S. Shopping Center Classification and Definitions," June 2016, http://www.icsc.org

REGIONAL SHOPPING CENTER   A **regional shopping center** is a large, planned shopping facility appealing to a geographically dispersed market. It has at least one or two department stores (each with at least 100,000 square feet) and 40 to 125 or more smaller retailers. A regional center offers a very broad and deep assortment of shopping-oriented goods and services intended to enhance the consumer's visit. The market is 100,000+ people who live or work up to a 30-minute drive away. On average, people travel under 20 minutes. A significant trend among regional shopping centers is to add category killers as anchor tenants to replace closed department stores. General Growth Properties has filled 79 of 83 vacant department store locations with such tenants as H&M, Dick's Sporting Goods, and Wegman's Food Markets.[12]

The regional center is the result of a planned effort to re-create the shopping variety of a central city in suburbia. Some regional centers have become the social, cultural, and vocational focal point of a suburban area. They may be used as a town plaza, a meeting place, a concert hall, and a place for a brisk indoor walk. Despite the declining overall interest in shopping, on a typical visit to a regional shopping center, many people spend an average of an hour or more there.

The first outdoor regional shopping center opened in 1950 in Seattle, anchored by a branch of Bon Marche, then a leading downtown department store. Southdale Center (outside Minneapolis), built in 1956 for Target Corporation (then Dayton Hudson), was the first fully enclosed, climate-controlled mall. Today, there are about 1,250 U.S. regional centers of various kinds, and this format has popped up around the world (where small stores still remain the dominant force) from Australia to Brazil to India to Malaysia.

One type of regional center is the **megamall**, an enormous planned shopping center with 800,000+ square feet of retail space, multiple anchor stores, up to several hundred specialty stores, food courts, entertainment facilities, and a trade area size of up to 25 miles. It seeks to heighten interest in shopping and expand the trading area. There are 625 U.S. megamalls in the United States.[13] The largest is the Mall of America (www.mallofamerica.com) in Bloomington, Minnesota. It has three anchors (Macy's, Nordstrom, and Sears), 520 specialty stores, a 14-screen movie theater, a health club, 50 restaurants, a Nickelodeon Universe indoor amusement park, an aquarium, and 12,550 parking spaces—with 4.2 million square feet of building space. The mall has stores for every budget, attracts between 35 to 40 million visitors yearly (40 percent of visitors are tourists). Beijing, China's Jinyuan Yansha shopping center (nicknamed the "Great Mall of China") is the largest megamall in the world. It is 1.5 times the size of Mall of America, with over 1,000 shops and 6 million square feet of space. See Figure 10-5 for another leading megamall.

COMMUNITY SHOPPING CENTER   A **community shopping center** is a moderate-sized, planned shopping facility with a branch department store (traditional or discount) and/or a category killer store, as well as several smaller stores (similar to those in a neighborhood center). It offers a moderate assortment of shopping- and convenience-oriented goods and services to consumers from one or more nearby, well-populated, residential areas. About 20,000 to 100,000 people who live or work within a 10- to 20-minute drive are served by this location. There are 10,000 community shopping centers in the United States.

Better long-range planning occurs for a community shopping center than a neighborhood shopping center. Balanced tenancy is usually enforced, and cooperative promotion is more probable. Store composition and the center's image are kept pretty consistent with pre-set goals.

Two noteworthy variations of the community center (not included in Table 10-1) are the power center and the lifestyle center. A **power center** is a shopping site with (1) up to a half-dozen or so category-killer stores and a mix of smaller stores or (2) several complementary stores specializing in one product category. A power center usually occupies 200,000 to 600,000 square feet on a major highway or road intersection. It seeks to be quite distinctive to draw shoppers and better compete with regional centers. There are 2,250 U.S. power centers.[14] An example of a power

Mall of America's attractions (www.mallofamerica.com/attractions) are as impressive as the mall itself.

Brixmor is a leading retail-estate developer with several power centers. Visit its properties online (http://properties.brixmor.com).

FIGURE 10-5

The West Edmonton Mall

The very popular West Edmonton Mall, located in Alberta, Canada, is one of the world's largest shopping centers. It has more than 800 stores, 100+ dining venues, two hotels, and a variety of entertainment attractions, including the roller coaster shown here.

Source: 2009fotofriends/Shutterstock. Reprinted by permission.

FIGURE 10-6

The Neighborhood Shopping Center

As the anchor store in a neighborhood shopping center, a supermarket attracts nearby residents and workers with a wide range of goods and services.

Source: Zentangle/ Shutterstock. Reprinted by permission.

center is 280 Metro Center in Colma, California. The center's tenants include such category-killer retailers as Marshalls, Nordstrom Rack, Old Navy, David's Bridal, and Pier 1 Imports.

A **lifestyle center** is an open-air shopping site that typically includes 150,000 to 500,000 square feet of space dedicated to upscale, well-known specialty stores as well as dining and entertainment. The focus is often on apparel, home products, books, music, and restaurants. Popular stores at lifestyle centers include Ann Taylor, Banana Republic, Bath & Body Works, Gap, Pottery Barn, Talbots, Victoria's Secret, and Williams-Sonoma. Examples of lifestyle shopping centers include Aspen Grove in Littleton, Colorado; Deer Park Town Center in Illinois; Rookwood Commons in Cincinnati, Ohio; and CocoWalk in Coconut Grove, Florida. At present, there are about 460 such centers in the United States.[15]

NEIGHBORHOOD SHOPPING CENTER A **neighborhood shopping center** is a planned shopping facility, with the largest store being a supermarket or a drugstore. Other retailers often include a bakery, laundry, dry cleaner, stationery store, barbershop or beauty parlor, hardware store, restaurant, liquor store, and gas station. This center focuses on convenience-oriented goods and services for people living or working nearby. It serves 3,000 to 50,000 people who are within a 15-minute drive (usually less than 10 minutes). See Figure 10-6.

A neighborhood center is usually arranged in a strip. Initially, it is carefully planned and tenants are balanced. Over time, the planned aspects may lessen and newcomers may face fewer restrictions. Thus, a liquor store might replace a barbershop—leaving a void. A center's ability to maintain balance depends on its attractiveness to potential tenants (expressed by the extent of store vacancies). In number, but not in selling space or sales, neighborhood centers account for 75 percent of all U.S. regional, community, and other shopping centers.

THE CHOICE OF A GENERAL LOCATION

The last part of Step 2 in location planning requires a retailer to select a locational format: isolated, unplanned district, or planned center. The decision depends on the firm's strategy and a careful evaluation of the advantages and disadvantages of each alternative.

Next, in Step 3, the retailer chooses a broadly defined site. Two decisions are needed here. First, the specific kind of isolated store, unplanned business district, or planned shopping center location is selected. If a firm wants an isolated store, it must decide on a highway or side street. Should it desire an unplanned business area, it must decide on a central business district, a secondary business district, a neighborhood business district, or a string. A retailer seeking a planned area must choose a regional, community, or neighborhood shopping center—and decide whether to use a derivative form such as a megamall or power center. Here are the preferences of two retailers:

Guitar Center (www .guitarcenter.com) has a well-conceived location plan.

▶ Guitar Center, privately owned by CNL-KKR, operates more than 260 Guitar Center stores in 44 states and 120 Music & Arts stores in 19 states. Among the Guitar Center stores, 62 percent are primary format units, 33 percent are secondary format units, and 5 percent are tertiary format units. The retailer selects the store format based on the size of the market in which it is located. Primary format stores range in size from 13,000 to 30,000 square feet and serve major metropolitan population centers. Secondary format stores range from 8,000 to 14,000 square feet and serve metropolitan areas not served by primary format stores. Tertiary market stores of 5,000 square feet serve smaller populations.[16]

▶ Apple Stores are usually located at high-traffic locations in premium shopping malls and urban shopping districts in about a dozen countries, including the United States. Apple owns and operates 400 of its own stores, thereby attracting new customers by ensuring a high-quality buying experience. Stores are designed to simplify and enhance the presentation and marketing of Apple products and related items. Store configurations of various sizes have evolved to address market-specific demands.[17]

The second decision is that a firm must select its general store placement. For an isolated store, this means choosing a specific highway or side street. For an unplanned district or planned center, this means selecting a specific district (e.g., downtown Los Angeles) or center (e.g., La Gran Plaza in Fort Worth, Texas).

In Step 3, the retailer narrows down the decisions made in the first two steps and then chooses a general location. Step 4 requires the firm to evaluate specific alternative sites, including their position on a block (or in a center), the side of the street, and the terms of tenancy. Factors to be considered in assessing and choosing a general location and a specific site within that location are described together in the next section because many strategic decisions are similar for these two steps.

LOCATION AND SITE EVALUATION

Assessment of general locations and the specific sites within them requires extensive analysis. In any area, the optimum site for a particular store is called the **one-hundred percent location**. Because different retailers need different kinds of sites, a location labeled as 100 percent for one firm may be less desirable for another. An upscale ladies' apparel shop would seek a location unlike one sought by a convenience store. The apparel shop would benefit from pedestrian traffic, closeness to major department stores, and proximity to other specialty stores. The convenience store would rather be in an area with ample parking and vehicular traffic. It does not need to be near other stores.

Figure 10-7 has a location/site evaluation checklist. A retailer should rate each alternative location (and specific site) on all the criteria and develop overall ratings for them. Two firms may rate the same site differently. This figure should be used in conjunction with the trading-area data in Chapter 9, not instead of them.

Pedestrian Traffic

The most crucial measures of a location's and site's value are the number and type of people passing by. Other things being equal, a site with the most pedestrian traffic is often best.

Not everyone passing a location or site is a good prospect for all types of stores, so many firms use selective counting procedures, such as counting only those with shopping bags. Otherwise, pedestrian traffic totals may include many nonshoppers. It would be improper for an appliance retailer to count as prospective shoppers all people passing a downtown site on the way to work. Much downtown pedestrian traffic may be from those who are there for nonretailing activities.

FIGURE 10-7

A Location/Site Evaluation Checklist

Rate each of these criteria on a scale of 1 to 10, with 1 being excellent and 10 being poor.

Pedestrian Traffic	Number of people	_____
	Type of people	_____
Vehicular Traffic	Number of vehicles	_____
	Type of vehicles	_____
	Traffic congestion	_____
Parking Facilities	Number and quality of parking spots	_____
	Distance to store	_____
	Availability of employee parking	_____
Transportation	Availability of mass transit	_____
	Access from major highways	_____
	Ease of deliveries	_____
Store Composition	Number and size of stores	_____
	Affinity	_____
	Retail balance	_____
Specific Site	Visibility	_____
	Placement in the location	_____
	Size and shape of the lot	_____
	Size and shape of the building	_____
	Condition and age of the lot and building	_____
Terms of Occupancy	Ownership or leasing terms	_____
	Operations and maintenance costs	_____
	Taxes	_____
	Zoning restrictions	_____
	Voluntary regulations	_____
Overall Rating	General location	_____
	Specific site	_____

A proper pedestrian traffic count should encompass these four elements:

▶ Separation of the count by age and gender (with very young children not counted).
▶ Division of the count by time (this allows the study of peaks, low points, and changes in the gender of the people passing by the hour).
▶ Pedestrian interviews (to find out the proportion of potential shoppers).
▶ Spot analysis of shopping trips (to verify the stores actually visited).

Vehicular Traffic

The quantity and characteristics of vehicular traffic are very important for retailers that appeal to customers who drive there. Convenience stores, outlets in regional shopping centers, and car washes are retailers that rely on heavy vehicular traffic. Automotive traffic studies are essential in suburban areas, where pedestrian traffic is often limited.

As with pedestrian traffic, adjustments to the raw count of vehicular traffic must be made. Some retailers count only homeward-bound traffic, some exclude vehicles on the other side of a divided highway, and some omit out-of-state cars. Data may be available from the state highway department, the county engineer, or the regional planning commission.

Besides traffic counts, the retailer should study the extent and timing of congestion (from traffic, detours, and poor roads). People normally avoid congested areas and shop where driving time and driving difficulties are minimized.

Parking Facilities

Many U.S. retail stores include some provision for nearby off-street parking. In many business districts, parking is provided by individual stores, arrangements among stores, and local government. In planned shopping centers, parking is shared by all stores there. The number and quality of parking spots, their distances from stores, and the availability of employee parking should all be evaluated. See Figure 10-8.

FIGURE 10-8

The Importance of Parking

In comparison with urban shopping districts, suburban shopping centers tend to have plentiful free parking—with no time limits. However, most shoppers want to be close as possible to a shopping center or store entrance. As shown in this aerial view of a regional shopping center, that is not always possible, particularly during busy periods such as holidays.

Source: Dinga/Shutterstock. Reprinted by permission.

The need for retailer parking facilities depends on the store's trading area, the type of store, the proportion of shoppers using a car, the existence of other parking, the turnover of spaces (which depend on the length of a shopping trip), the flow of shoppers, and parking by nonshoppers. A shopping center normally needs 4 to 5 parking spaces per 1,000 square feet of gross floor area, a supermarket 10 to 15 spaces, and a furniture store 3 or 4 spaces.

Free parking sometimes creates problems. Commuters and employees of nearby businesses may park in spaces intended for shoppers. This problem can be lessened by validating shoppers' parking stubs and requiring payment from nonshoppers. Another problem may occur if the selling space at a location increases due to new stores or the expansion of current ones. Existing parking may then be inadequate. Double-deck parking or parking tiers save land and shorten the distance from a parked car to a store—a key factor because customers at a regional shopping center may be unwilling to walk more than a few hundred feet from their cars to the center.

Transportation

Mass transit, access from major highways, and ease of deliveries must be examined. For example, in a downtown area, closeness to mass transit is important for people who do not own cars, who commute to work, or who would not otherwise shop in an area with traffic congestion. The availability of buses, taxis, subways, trains, and other kinds of public transit is a must for any area not readily accessible by vehicular traffic.

Locations dependent on vehicular traffic should be rated on nearness to major thoroughfares. Driving time is a consideration for many people. Also, drivers heading eastbound on a highway often do not like to make a U-turn to get to a store on the westbound side of that highway.

RETAILING AROUND THE WORLD

Pop-Up Stores

Pop-up stores are typically leased for short time periods. Such stores have one of two themes: to show exciting new products and styles or to sell-off surplus inventory. Alex Eagle (www.alexeagle.co.uk) used a pop-up store for a one-week period in Tuscany, located at an exclusive hotel, to highlight a new collection of clothes. Orlebar Brown's (www.orlebarbrown.com) pop-up store in Somerset, England, offered its high-end men's clothing at up to 70 percent off usual prices. Pop-up stores benefit both the retailer and the property owner. The retailer can use the store without having to sign a long-term lease. The property owner can secure rental income for a space that would otherwise be vacant.

How would your site-selection process differ for a pop-up versus a traditional store?

The transportation network should be studied for delivery truck access. Some thoroughfares are excellent for cars but ban large trucks or cannot bear their weight.

Store Composition

The number and size of stores should be consistent with the type of location. A retailer in an isolated site wants no stores nearby; a retailer in a neighborhood business district wants an area with 10 to 15 small stores; and a retailer in a regional shopping center wants a location with many stores, including large department stores (to generate customer traffic).

If the stores at a given location (be it an unplanned district or a planned center) complement, blend, and cooperate with one another, and each benefits from the others' presence, **affinity** exists. When affinity is strong, the sales of each store are greater, due to the high customer traffic, than if the stores are apart. The practice of similar or complementary stores locating near each other is based on two factors: First, customers like to compare the prices, styles, selections, and services of similar stores. Second, customers like one-stop shopping and like to purchase at different stores on the same trip. Affinities can exist among competing stores as well as among complementary stores. More people travel to shopping areas with large selections than to convenience-oriented areas, so the sales of all stores are enhanced.

One measure of compatibility is the degree to which stores exchange customers. Stores in these categories are very compatible with each other and have high customer interchange:

▸ Supermarket, drugstore, bakery, fruit-and-vegetable store, meat store
▸ Department store, apparel store, hosiery store, lingerie shop, shoe store, jewelry store

Retail balance, the mix of stores within a district or shopping center, should also be considered. (1) Proper balance occurs when the number of store facilities for each merchandise or service classification is equal to the location's market potential, (2) a range of goods and services is provided to foster one-stop shopping, (3) there is an adequate assortment within any category, and (4) there is a proper mix of store types (balanced tenancy).

Specific Site

Selecting the specific site for the retail store depends on visibility; placement in the location, size, and shape of the lot; size and shape of the building; and condition and age of the lot and building.

Visibility is a site's ability to be seen by pedestrian or vehicular traffic. A site on a side street or at the end of a shopping center is not as visible as one on a major road or at the center's entrance. High visibility increases store awareness.

Placement in the location is a site's relative position in the district or center. A corner location may be desirable because it is situated at the intersection of two streets and has "corner influence." It is usually more expensive because of the greater pedestrian and vehicular passersby due to traffic flows from two streets, increased window display area, and less traffic congestion through multiple entrances. Corner influence is greatest in high-volume locations. That is why some Pier 1 stores, Starbucks restaurants, and other retailers seek corner sites. See Figure 10-9.

A *convenience*-oriented firm, such as a stationery store, is very concerned about the side of the street, the location relative to other convenience-oriented stores, nearness to parking, access to a bus stop, and the distance from residences. A *shopping*-oriented retailer, such as a furniture store, is more interested in a corner site to increase window display space, proximity to wallpaper and other related retailers, the accessibility of its pick-up platform to consumers, and the ease of deliveries to the store.

When a retailer buys or rents an existing building, its size and shape should be noted. Condition and age of the lot and the building should be studied, as well. A department store, of course, requires much more space than a boutique. It may desire a square site, whereas the boutique might prefer a rectangular one. Any site should be viewed in terms of total space needs: parking, walkways, selling, nonselling, and so on.

Due to the saturation of many desirable locations and the lack of available spots in others, some firms have turned to nontraditional sites—often to complement their existing stores. T.G.I. Friday's, Staples, and Bally have airport stores. Subway has outlets in many Walmarts, and Subway and some other fast-food retailers share facilities to provide more variety and to share costs.

FIGURE 10-9

Corner Influence and Louis Vuitton

Consider the potential pedestrian and vehicular traffic—and the eyecatching appeal—generated by this corner Louis Vuitton store in Hong Kong.

Source: Coleman Yuen/ Pearson Education Asia Ltd. Reprinted by permission.

Terms of Occupancy

Terms of occupancy—ownership versus leasing, type of lease, operations and maintenance costs, taxes, zoning restrictions, and voluntary regulations—must be evaluated for each prospective site.

OWNERSHIP VERSUS LEASING   A retailer with adequate funding can either own or lease premises. Ownership is more common in small stores, in small communities, or at inexpensive locations. It has several advantages. There is no chance that a property owner will not renew a lease or double the rent when a lease expires. Monthly mortgage payments are stable. Operations are flexible; a retailer can engage in scrambled merchandising and break down walls. It is also likely that property value will appreciate over time, resulting in a financial gain if the business is sold. Ownership disadvantages are high initial costs, long-term commitment, and inability to readily change sites. Home Depot owns about 90 percent of its store properties.[18]

The National Trust for Historic Preservation (www.preservationnation .org) has revitalized communities across the United States.

If a retailer chooses ownership, the next decision is whether to construct a new facility or buy an existing building. Considerations include purchase price and maintenance costs, zoning restrictions, age and condition of existing facilities, adaptability of existing facilities, and time to erect a new building. To encourage building rehabilitation in towns with 5,000 to 50,000 people, Congress enacted the Main Street America program (www.mainstreet.org) of the National Trust for Historic Preservation. It has a network of statewide, citywide, and regional programs actively serving more than 2,000 towns, which benefit from planning support, tax credits, and low-interest loans.

The great majority of stores in central business districts and regional shopping centers are leased (with Home Depot sometimes being one of the exceptions), mostly due to the high investment for ownership. Department stores tend to have renewable 20- to 30-year leases, supermarkets usually have renewable 15- to 20-year leases, and specialty stores often have 5- to 10-year leases with options to extend. Some leases give the retailer the right to end an agreement before the expiration date—under given circumstances and for a specified retailer payment.

Leasing minimizes initial investment, reduces risk, provides access to prime sites that cannot add more stores, leads to immediate occupancy and traffic, and reduces long-term commitment. Many retailers feel they can open more stores or spend more on their strategies by leasing. Firms that lease accept limits on operating flexibility, restrictions on subletting and selling the business, possible nonrenewal problems, rent increases, and not gaining from rising real-estate values.

Through a *sale-leaseback*, some large retailers build stores and then sell them to real-estate investors who lease the property back to the retailers on a long-term basis. Retailers using sale-leasebacks build stores to their specifications and have bargaining power in leasing—while lowering capital expenditures.

TYPES OF LEASES Property owners do not rely solely on constant rent leases, partly due to their concern about interest rates and the related rise in operating costs. Terms can be quite complicated.[19]

The simplest, most direct arrangement is the **straight lease**—a retailer pays a fixed dollar amount per month over the life of the lease. Rent usually ranges from $1 to $75 annually per square foot, depending on the site's desirability and store traffic. At some sites, rents can be much higher. On New York's Fifth Avenue, the average yearly rental rate ranges up to $3,500 per square foot! This is the world's highest retail rental rate.[20]

A **percentage lease** stipulates that rent is related to sales or profits. This differs from a straight lease, which requires constant payments. A percentage lease protects a property owner against inflation and lets it benefit if a store is successful; it also allows a tenant to view the lease as a variable cost—rent is lower when its performance is weak and higher when performance is good. The percentage rate varies by type of shopping district or center and by type of store.

Percentage leases have variations. With a specified minimum, low sales are assumed to be partly the retailer's responsibility; the property owner receives minimum payments (as in a straight lease) no matter what the sales or profits. With a specified maximum, it is assumed that a very successful retailer should not pay more than a maximum rent. Superior merchandising, promotion, and pricing should reward the retailer. Another variation is a sliding scale: The ratio of rent to sales changes as sales rise. A sliding-down scale has a retailer pay a lower percentage as sales go up and is an incentive to the retailer.

A **graduated lease** calls for precise rent increases over a stated period of time. Monthly rent may be $4,800 for the first 10 years and $5,600 for the last 10 years of a lease. Rent is known in advance by the retailer and the property owner; it is based on expected sales and cost increases. There is no need to audit sales or profits, as with percentage leases. This lease is often used with small retailers.

A **maintenance-increase-recoupment lease** has a provision allowing rent to increase if a property owner's taxes, heating bills, insurance, or other expenses rise beyond a certain point. This provision most often supplements a straight rental lease agreement.

A **net lease** calls for all maintenance costs (such as heating, electricity, insurance, and interior repair) to be paid by the retailer. It frees the property owner from managing the facility and gives the retailer control over store maintenance. It supplements a straight lease or a percentage lease.

OTHER CONSIDERATIONS After assessing ownership and leasing opportunities, a retailer must look at the costs of operations and maintenance. The age and condition of a facility may cause a retailer to have high monthly costs, even though the mortgage or rent is low. Furthermore, the costs of extensive renovations should be calculated.

Differences in sales taxes (those that customers pay) and business taxes (those that retailers pay) among alternative sites must be weighed. Business taxes should be broken down into real-estate and income categories. The highest statewide sales taxes are in California (7.5 percent) and in Indiana, Mississippi, New Jersey, Rhode Island, and Tennessee (7 percent); Alaska, Delaware, Montana, New Hampshire, and Oregon have no state sales tax.

There may be zoning restrictions as to the kind of stores allowed, store size, building height, type of merchandise carried, and other factors that have to be hurdled (or another site chosen). For example, many communities believe their local retail economies can handle only so many new

TECHNOLOGY IN RETAILING | Lease Management Software

Software firms such as Accruent (www.accruent.com), LeaseEagle (www.leaseagle.com), and VisualLease (www.visuallease.com) have automated details involved with complex retail leases. Many retailers as well as owners of retail properties use lease management software to reconcile a property owner's billings with specific lease clause stipulations, calculate CPI (consumer price index—a measure of inflation) escalations, track expense increases on year-to-year basis for further review; monitor critical dates for lease payment and lease renewal, and generate sales reports required for percentage leases.

What types of retailers should consider using lease management software? Why?

stores without causing some existing firms to fail. Thus, they have passed zoning regulations or store size caps that forbid retail stores from exceeding a given size. This helps local communities sustain the vitality of small, pedestrian-oriented business districts, keep commercial retail space affordable, and nurture local retailers. Size caps can prevent traffic congestion and overburdened public infrastructure. They require all retailers, including retail chains such as Walmart, to build stores that are properly sized for the community. Cities that have adopted size caps find that, in some cases, retailers that typically build larger stores will opt not to open; in other cases, they will design smaller stores. Size caps also ensure that retail space is affordable for local business. [21]

Voluntary restrictions are prevalent in planned shopping centers and may include required membership in merchant groups, uniform hours, and shared security forces. Leases in regional centers have had clauses protecting anchor tenants from too much competition from discounters. Clauses may also involve limits on product lines, fees for common services, and so on. Anchors are protected because developers need long-term commitments to finance the centers. The Federal Trade Commission discourages "exclusives," whereby only a certain retailer can carry specified merchandise, and "radius clauses," whereby a tenant agrees not to have another store within a certain distance.

Because of overbuilding, some retailers are in a good position to bargain over the terms of occupancy. This differs from city to city and from shopping location to shopping location.

Overall Rating

The last task in choosing a store location is to compute overall ratings:

1. Each location under consideration is given an overall rating based on the criteria in Figure 10-7.
2. The overall ratings of alternative locations are compared, and the best location is chosen.
3. The same procedure is used to evaluate the alternative sites within the location.

Lease agreements used to be so simple that they could be written on a napkin—not today (https://goo.gl/cvVn4D).

It is often difficult to compile and compare composite evaluations because some attributes may be positive whereas others are negative. The general location may be a good shopping center, but the site in the center may be poor, or an area may have excellent potential but it takes 2 years to build a store. The attributes in Figure 10-7 should be weighted according to their importance. An overall rating should also include *knockout factors*—those that preclude consideration of a site. Possible knockout factors are a short lease, little or no evening or weekend pedestrian traffic, and poor tenant relations with the landlord.

Chapter Summary

1. *To thoroughly examine the types of locations available to a retailer: isolated store, unplanned business district, and planned shopping center.* After a retailer rates alternative trading areas, it decides on the type of location, selects the general location, and chooses a particular site. There are three basic locational types.

   An *isolated store* is freestanding, not adjacent to other stores. It has no competition, low rent, flexibility, road visibility, easy parking, and lower property costs. It also has a lack of traffic, no variety for shoppers, no shared costs, and zoning restrictions.

   An *unplanned business district* is a shopping area with two or more stores located together or nearby. Store composition is not based on planning. There are four categories: central business district, secondary business district, neighborhood business district, and string. An unplanned district generally has these favorable points:

variety of goods, services, and prices; access to public transit; nearness to commercial and social facilities; and pedestrian traffic. Yet, its shortcomings have led to the growth of the planned shopping center: inadequate parking, older facilities, high rents and taxes in popular CBDs, discontinuity of offerings, traffic and delivery congestion, high theft rates, and some declining central cities.

   A *planned shopping center* is centrally owned or managed and well balanced. It usually has one or more anchor stores and many smaller stores. The planned center is popular, due to extensive goods and service offerings, expanding suburbs, shared strategic planning and costs, attractive locations, parking facilities, lower rent and taxes (except for regional centers), lower theft rates, the popularity of malls (although some people are now bored with them), and the lesser appeal of inner-city shopping. Negative aspects include operations inflexibility, restrictions on merchandise carried, and anchor-store domination. There are three forms: regional, community, and neighborhood centers.

2. *To note the decisions necessary in choosing a general retail location.* First, the specific form of isolated store, unplanned business district, or planned shopping center location is determined, such as whether to be on a highway or side street; in a CBD, an SBD, an NBD, or a string; or in a regional, community, or neighborhood shopping center. Then the general store location is specified—singling out a particular highway, business district, or shopping center.

3. *To describe the concept of the one-hundred percent location.* Extensive analysis is required in assessing each general location and specific sites within it. Importantly, the optimum site for a given store must be determined. This is the one-hundred percent location; it differs by retailer.

4. *To discuss several criteria for evaluating general retail locations and the specific sites within them.* Pedestrian traffic, vehicular traffic, parking facilities, transportation, store composition, the attributes of each specific site, and terms of occupancy should be studied. An overall rating is then computed for each location and site, and the best one selected.

   Affinity occurs when the stores at the same location complement, blend, and cooperate with one another; each benefits from the others' presence.

5. *To contrast alternative terms of occupancy.* A retailer can opt to own or lease. If it leases, terms are specified in a straight lease, percentage lease, graduated lease, maintenance-increase-recoupment lease, and/or net lease. Operating and maintenance costs, taxes, zoning restrictions, and voluntary restrictions also need to be reviewed.

Key Terms

isolated store (p. 265)
unplanned business district (p. 266)
central business district (CBD)
  (p. 266)
secondary business district (SBD)
  (p. 268)
neighborhood business district
  (NBD) (p. 268)
string (p. 269)

planned shopping center (p. 269)
balanced tenancy (p. 270)
regional shopping center (p. 272)
megamall (p. 273)
community shopping center (p. 273)
power center (p. 273)
lifestyle center (p. 274)
neighborhood shopping center (p. 274)
one-hundred percent location (p. 275)

affinity (p. 278)
retail balance (p. 278)
terms of occupancy (p. 279)
straight lease (p. 280)
percentage lease (p. 280)
graduated lease (p. 280)
maintenance-increase-recoupment
  lease (p. 280)
net lease (p. 280)

Questions for Discussion

1. A convenience store chain has had some success in choosing locations in unplanned business districts of smaller cities. Explain the four variants of these districts.
2. From the retailer's perspective, what are the key disadvantages of locating in a secondary business district?
3. Outline the typical stores that you are likely to find in a neighborhood business district, and explain why.
4. Why might it be advantageous for a competing fuel station to open across the road to an existing one?
5. Explain why the owners of a shopping mall would want to achieve a balanced tenancy. What are the limitations of an overly planned shopping center?
6. Evaluate a regional shopping center near your campus.

7. Explain why a one-hundred percent location for a mid-priced apparel chain may not be a one-hundred percent location for an upscale local apparel store.
8. What criteria should a small retailer use in selecting a general store location and a specific site within it? A large retailer?
9. What difficulties are there in using a rating scale such as that shown in Figure 10-7? What are the benefits?
10. How do the parking needs for a fast-food restaurant, a watch repair store, and a luggage store differ?
11. Under what circumstances would it be more desirable for a retailer to buy or lease an existing facility rather than to build a new store?
12. What are the pros and cons of a net lease for a prospective retail tenant? For the landlord?

Web-Based Exercise

Visit the Web site of real estate firm CBRE (http://news.cbre .co.uk/) and search for the article "EMEA Region Accounts for 50% of the Top Ten Global Retail Locations for Brand Presence." What does it tell you about global retail trends?

PART 4 Short Cases

Case 1: Are Smaller and Faster Better?*

As the grocery industry diversifies, whose lunch will get eaten? The first 365 formatted stores from Whole Foods Market opened in mid-2016. Kroger opened the first Main & Vine in February 2016. Fresh Formats, an Ahold company, debuted bfresh stores in fall 2015; and Fresh Thyme Farmer's Market, which opened its first store in 2014, is on course to operate 60 units by 2019. Each of these concepts operates in smaller footprint settings. There's an emphasis on fresh foods (especially a large selection of produce), along with organic items and artisanal specialties, and price points are rooted in value.

Google Express launched in 2016 by offering same-day delivery of fruit, vegetables, meat, and more in select San Francisco and Los Angeles neighborhoods; Whole Foods invested in Instacart; and Kroger is expanding online ordering and in-store pick-up. Amazon's Prime Pantry and AmazonFresh initiatives are taking a bite out of the food retailing apple, and a growing number of subscription services—including Blue Apron, Plated, and HelloFresh—are angling for a slice of the pie by offering meal-in-a-box solutions.

With numerous competitors eating off every section of their plate, could traditional supermarkets be in real danger? The consensus among supermarket industry experts is "no"—but it comes with a caveat. "If you define traditional supermarkets in terms of Kroger, then they look quite well," says John Rand, senior vice-president of retail insights for Kantar Retail. "If you define it in terms of some other chains, then they look less well. Some of the top supermarkets in the country are super regionals, chains such as Publix, H-E-B, and Wegmans. These guys are growing faster than average, so they're doing just fine."

Steven Pinder, retail strategist at Kurt Salmon, says consumers "are shifting and changing . . . spending habits across the platforms available to us, but we're not doing so in grocery nearly as quickly or as much as in other formats. Consumers' adoption of technology and omnichannel shopping behavior is not taking off in this segment the way those things have in others."

Not everyone, however, is optimistic about the fate of the 45,000-square-foot supermarket, with its predictable fresh perimeter and center store setup featuring aisles of packaged and canned items, frozen foods, and household essentials. "The conventional supermarket is a dinosaur," says Phil Lempert, a food industry analyst. "It doesn't serve the needs of today's shopper who is looking for more exciting offerings." Lempert identifies two types of food stores that are clicking with shoppers: small stores concentrating on fresh items, and "grocerants"—stores that blend grocery and restaurant. Operators providing sit-down restaurants on premises "are also on the rise. Stores like Hy-Vee or Wegmans are saying, 'We're all things food — sit down and eat a meal now, then take home some fresh items to make dinner tomorrow.'"

Against the backdrop of a fast-changing marketplace, some legacy banners are ceding share to smaller, more nimble entrants. Others, such as Walmart and Kroger, the two biggest in terms of supermarket sales, are refusing to let others eat their lunch. AlthoughWalmart has pulled the plug on its 12,000-square-foot Walmart Express food and merchandise pilot stores, it is committed to the food-dominant, 40,000-square-foot Neighborhood Market format. Along with the Main & Vine project, Kroger operates Turkey Hill Markets and Mariano's.

Experts say it's incumbent on retailers to choose a niche. Rand divides supermarkets into three segments: premium, mainstream, and value. *Premium* supermarkets are projected to pull in about 19 percent of grocery sales from 2015 to 2020; *mainstream* will account for nearly 33 percent, and the *value* segment will be the largest at nearly 48 percent.

Questions

1. How is trading-area analysis different for a small store than a large store? Explain your answer.
2. How should a food-delivery service such as AmazonFresh define its trading area? Is it going to be bigger or smaller than a traditional supermarket's trading area? Why?
3. What are the pros and cons of locating in a mixed-use center?
4. What type of retail location is best suited to a small store? Why?

Case 2: Organize, Optimize, Synchronize*

To get closer to its customers, American Eagle Outfitters (AEO) conducted several site assessments that factored in its customer population, order profiles, transportation, and labor costs. Christine Miller, the firm's director of operations, says AEO established a strategy based on what its road map would look like for the next 5 years: A second fulfillment center with omnichannel capabilities was needed to support AEO's continued growth, as well as to get physically closer to customers. "Most of our customer base, online and in stores, is on the East Coast," Miller says, "and we needed to be closer to our customers."

The firm also needed to improve direct-to-consumer fulfillment time. With the Kansas facility in the middle of the country, getting to either coast took too long: On average, Miller says AEO took anywhere from 5 to 7 days to deliver an order. "Reducing that time was definitely something that was a goal for us and a challenge, just based on having that one facility in the middle of the country," she says.

After securing the Hazleton, Pennsylania location, AEO selected the Vargo Solutions company to design the operations of the 1 million-square-foot facility—everything from processes to equipment. Vargo synchronizes operations in fulfillment centers with its continuous order-fulfillment system. Carlos Ysasi, Vargo's vice-president of systems engineering, says the key to efficiency was creating "channel-immune" distribution centers that use one inventory, one workforce, and one fulfillment engine to meet the inventory needs of physical stores and E-commerce. "Having separate distribution centers for the channels doubles your costs."

---

*Based on material in Susan Reda, "Supermarket Showdown," *STORES Magazine*, April 2016, pp. 24–27. Reprinted by permission. Copyright 2016. STORES Magazine.

*Based on material in Craig Guillot, "Organize, Optimize, Synchronize," *STORES Magazine*, February 2016, pp. 50–52. Reprinted by permission. Copyright 2016. STORES Magazine.

Before, workers unloaded incoming trailers to build, move, and reorganize pallets, which Ysasi says "required everything to be touched multiple times," and every process had a buffer system that needed a lot of space. The new system lets cartons be quickly placed on the conveyor and "pulled" anywhere needed in the facility. The facility is also free of mobile equipment. There is no need for pallet storage or for pallets to move in the center. Material handling maximizes up-time and optimizes energy efficiency.

Vargo's continuous order fulfillment enterprise system extends functionality beyond traditional warehouse execution systems. The system can control all work resources, including machinery and associates, and organize, optimize, sequence, and synchronize everything across the work process.

All inventory at the Hazleton facility is loaded directly onto conveyors in the receiving mezzanine and sent to two sorters with automatic variable-speed controls that adjust the through-put demands. The sorters can automatically detect surges or declines in flows and adjust speed to more efficiently accommodate activity. Inventory is then routed to pick modules in a four-level, 400-foot-long picking structure in a 288,000-square-foot section of the facility. Operators pull products from the conveyors using a radio frequency picking process. Along the entire route, conveyors are controlled by photo eyes that sense totes, so the conveyor remains off when a product doesn't need to move anywhere.

Sections of motorized roller conveyors are divided into small zones that can be independently powered and operated, creating an on-demand system that increases energy savings and decreases noise. Miller says the system also saves space and is easier to use. "There's not a big motor hanging from the conveyors every 10 feet," she says. "We were able to lower them and there's a big ergonomic benefit for the workers. There's also less maintenance, and they're efficient because they only run when needed."

With the new distribution center, 90 percent of direct orders are fulfilled in 2 to 3 days.

Questions

1. Comment on this statement: "AEO established a strategy based on what its road map would look like for the next 5 years."
2. Explain the concept of "channel-immune" distribution centers. How does this fit with retailers' store location decisions?
3. What factors should be considered in determining where to locate distribution centers? Explain your answer.
4. What factors should be considered in determining how much inventory to carry at the store rather than at a distribution center? Why?

Case 3: Removing Barriers to Cross-Border Commerce*

If you ask online retailers what methods of payment they accept, most would say credit cards. But a study of global E-commerce payments found that in many parts of the world, credit cards

account for a very small portion of payments made online. The conclusion? Retailers need to expand significantly the number of payment options they accept if they want to compete successfully in the global market.

"The 2015 Global E-Commerce Payments Guide," by payments company Adyen, found that cross-border E-commerce is growing at a rate more than double that of domestic E-commerce; the global market is expected to reach more than $2 trillion by 2017. Yet, credit cards won't be used to pay for many online purchases. The study found that in China, 1 percent of online shoppers pay with international credit-card brands; in Germany, only 25 percent use credit cards in making an online purchase.

"The main payment method differs a lot around the world, and, in order, for a retailer to support a global customer base, it must be able to accept a wide range of payment options," says Adyen's chief commercial officer Roelant Prins. It is not always easy for retailers to accept a wide range of payments because each form comes with its own technical and security concerns. "You need for multiple people inside your organization—from technology support to customer support to marketing—to be aware of differences in payment options and how they work. There is a huge mindset that people pay by credit card. But if you want to expand internationally, that is not always the case. You must be prepared for alternative systems."

For example, China is the largest retail E-commerce market in the world. Yet, with just 1 percent of online purchases made via international credit cards, Asian payment company Alipay has about a 48 percent market share; interbank network UnionPay accounts for about 14 percent. Tenpay, a mobile payment program, accounts for 19 percent of the market.

China isn't the only market with a growing interest in mobile shopping. The rate of online payments using mobile devices continues to rise around the world, according to Adyen's Mobile Payments Index, which now accounts for more than 25 percent of all online payments made during the first quarter of this year.

Europe leads the world in adopting mobile payments; 29 percent of online purchases are made via a mobile device. The United States showed considerable growth as well, increasing nearly 5 percentage points to 27 percent over one 6-month period in 2015 alone. During 2015, Asian markets saw more than 20 percent of online transactions conducted on mobile devices for the first time.

To deal with the complexity, Prins recommends retailers hire a payments firm with global expertise. Even retailers that do not want to leave their current payments processors can use existing processors for domestic payments and use a global specialist for foreign sales. In Europe, for example, consumers are often directed to a separate site to make payments rather than pay directly to the retailer. Settlement can also be different in the speed at which retailers receive money and the costs they pay to settle a transaction.

Fraud is also a concern, as online sales from certain parts of the world represent a much greater payment fraud threat than transactions from other areas. Retailers need help in assessing and mitigating fraud risk from various foreign transactions.

---

* Based on material in Lauri Giesen, "Clearing the Path to Purchase," *STORES Magazine*. August 2015, pp. 48–50. Reprinted by permission. Copyright 2016. STORES Magazine.

Questions

1. What is the most surprising thing that you learned from reading this case? Explain your answer.
2. What are the implications of this case for a U.S. retailer that wants to open in Europe?
3. What are the implications of this case for an online retailer that wants to sell its products globally?
4. Discuss the pros and cons of this statement: "Even retailers that do not want to leave their current payments processors can use existing processors for domestic payments and use a global specialist for foreign sales."

Case 4: Warehouse Management: Right Time, Right Place*

There's an evolution from the existing physical and technical warehouse management infrastructure to capabilities offering multiple methods to store, pick, and process orders. Dan Grimm, solution strategist at JDA, sees progress in a number of areas of warehouse management systems (WMS), including value-added services (VAS), food safety, the use of voice, and mobile technology. A VAS (and food safety) example Grimm provides is capturing temperature in the nose, middle, and tail of a trailer to be sure it's in the range for refrigerated or frozen food, and indicating whether products can go to the store, require more testing, or are rejected. This means standard methods are followed. One warehouse trend is the use of voice to replace paper and RF (radio frequency) technology, giving retailers better productivity.

Mobility, Grimm notes, has given warehouse supervisors the abilities to do their job and be on the floor. "The new mobile technology lets them have real-time visibility, make changes from a tablet device, and be on the floor with employees, all at once." Trends he anticipates are omnichannel fulfillment and multiple methods to store, pick, and process orders; warehouse optimization by having better visibility of demand within the network; and in-store logistics in which retailers adapt WMS to be used in stores.

Eric Lamphier, a senior director at Manhattan Associates, says labor management (LM) issues have been addressed by his firm by embedding an LM module inside the WMS solution and making the module part of every conversation, including sales, implementation, support, and upgrades. Food retailers' "pioneering efforts in this area have paid off. Our focal point has been tablet capabilities delivered via a hybrid mobile app that provides distribution center managers with real-time data about the operation."

---

* Based on material in Bob Ingram "Right Time, Right Place," *Progressive Grocer*, September 2015, pp. 169–172. Reprinted by permission. Copyright 2016. STORES Magazine.

Reducing total cost of ownership is an ongoing challenge, according to Lamphier, who says Manhattan Associates is continuing to advance its Management Center module, which handles installation, cloning, monitoring, patching, and synchronization for all platform solutions. "These capabilities have been shown to lower implementation times and costs so our customers can realize benefits more rapidly."

Lamphier notes that E-commerce order-fulfillment expectations, approaches, and standard operating procedures have evolved rapidly over the past decade and require sophisticated, nonstop integration between warehouse management and the Enterprise Order Management suite. "We expect the future to be full of these projects as investments go mainstream, and upgrade and replacement cycles transpire."

At HighJump, territory manager Roger Falkenstein says online firms meet the E-commerce challenge by turning the store environment into a distribution center, resulting in such new requirements as supporting consumer-grade devices, displaying product images to help locate mixed-SKU item locations, enabling workflows for item substitutions, handling variable-weight and -temperature items, and fostering interaction between store associates and customers to manage special needs, exceptions, and various delivery methods. "We've taken our traditional warehouse platform and built applications to support store requirements and to drive efficiency, control, and visibility throughout the in-store fulfillment process."

A remaining challenge, as Falkenstein sees it, is the training of high-turnover staff. Driving efficiency is a priority, and grocers are looking for user-friendly tools to train employees quickly. "HighJump's philosophy is to have simple instructions, "directing users step by step with optimized workflows and minimized walk times. This helps keep the learning curve low and labor costs at a profitable level."

Questions

1. A new technology allows retailers to be sure the temperature in a delivery trailer is in the proper range for refrigerated or frozen food, and whether products can go on to the store, require more testing, or are rejected. Relate this to store location planning.
2. Comment on this statement: A key future trend will involve omnichannel fulfillment and multiple methods to store, pick, and process orders.
3. Should a retailer use its excess in-store inventory to fulfill online orders or stick to warehouse fulfillment for online orders? Explain your answer.
4. As a local pharmacy located in a neighborhood shopping center, what lessons could you learn from this case?

PART 4 # Comprehensive Case

Autenticidad en Acción: Mexican Delights the Real Deal at Food City Remodel*

Introduction

When it comes to food, today's consumers are more sophisticated and knowledgeable than ever. For a truly rewarding grocery store experience, shoppers want freshness, diversity, and authenticity. In response, grocery retailers have "upped" their games in those areas, even some value/price operators.

Food City Overview

A case in point is Food City, the 47-unit Mexicentric banner owned by Chandler, Arizona–based Bashas' Family of Stores. Its latest remodel—in South Tucson, where the store shares a bustling shopping center on Interstate 19 with Target, Home Depot, and others—reflects Food City's commitment to freshness, authenticity, and, as evidenced by the mariachi band serenading shoppers, a fun community experience.

From food to experience to outreach, Food City lives up to its Spanish headline of Autenticidad en Acción, which translates as "authenticity in action." Food City has "a colorful new look that we have been rolling out in our store remodels since 2014," explains Mike Solis, the banner's director of operations. "Along with the refreshed décor, we have emphasized the areas that differentiate Food City from the rest of the market and best meet the needs of our customers."

Authenticity and connection to community have been on display from the start. When the remodel of the North Tucson store was formally unveiled in December 2015, shoppers enjoyed food samples along with performances by Ballet Folklórico Tapatío dancers and music, including Tucson's acclaimed mariachi vocalist Monica Treviño.

The store's signature offerings include the deli department's Cocina (literally, "kitchen"), offering authentic Mexican dishes to eat in or to take home; a bakery with the traditional pan dulce (sweet bread) and other ethnic selections; a tortillería, with on-site production of corn and flour tortillas; and a full-service meat department with authentic cuts, value-added offerings, and seafood. The remodel also delivered a reconfigured center store for more shopper-friendly navigation.

"Our strategy is to reinvest in our stores by upgrading and remodeling them to better serve the needs of our customers," Solis says. "We completed 10 Food City store remodels in 2014 and an additional 12 store remodels in 2015. We had even more store remodels planned for 2016."

Fresh, Fresh, Fresh

Changes at the Irvington Road store are evident at the front door, with the produce department pulled forward to a more prominent position. "We moved it right to the entrance," Solis explains. "It's a huge draw to drive traffic. Our attention at the entrance is fresh, fresh, fresh." A wide variety of colorful produce is joined by a wall of spices offering a vast array of authentic selections.

Some shoppers think the store is bigger than it is, Solis notes. "The color package for the remodel is more open and vibrant." We've gotten comments like 'Have you made the store larger?'" That visibility extends to the revamped deli and prepared food area, the aforementioned Cocina. Solis says the Cocina area used to be framed by a "hacienda-type fixture" that is being removed in the ongoing remodelings. "It has really opened things up," he says. "Right from the entrance, you can see these departments and the bright colors."

Further enhancing the visibility in the store was the consolidation of the seating in a larger fixed dining area, rather than spread around the deli department; the new configuration allows visitors an unobstructed view through produce to the deli and bakery. "It's become a destination to stay and eat a meal," Solis says of the dining area, noting that "a lot of people do take food home." The Cocina offers daily breakfast and lunch specials as well as family meal deals. On Sundays mornings, it hosts a three-hour live mariachi performance.

Authenticity is on full display in the Cocina. "We're known for our authentic Mexican foods, offered daily," Solis declares. On the menu on the day of *Progressive Grocer*'s visit were red and green chilies, carnitas (pork), caldos (Mexican soup), menudo (tripe soup), tamales, burritos, and carne asada (considered by certain locals as the best in town).

"Our chicken category is a substantial part of our business," Solis says. The Cocina offers several varieties—fried, grilled, and rotisserie, plus pollo ranchero (peppers and tomatoes) and pollo chipotle (pepper cream sauce). Seafood includes ceviche (citrus-cured seafood), shrimp cocktail, and camaron aguachiles (shrimp in lime and chiles), the last of which Solis says is "very unique and very authentic."

A dedicated case offers fresh salsas, pico de gallo, and guacamole, some items made in house. Another huge draw for the deli is aguas frescas—icy house-made fruit beverages in flavors such as cantaloupe, lemonade, pineapple, and watermelon, plus horchata, a creamy rice-milk beverage. "We really hang our hat on the authenticity of our aguas frescas," Solis says. "It definitely sets us apart from the others." The beverage lineup also includes champurrado, a popular Hispanic hot chocolate, available ready to drink in the deli; there's also a do-it-yourself mix sold in the center of the store.

Sweet Showcase

Authenticity continues into the store's scratch-bakery selections. "We do doughnuts, but it's on a much smaller scale. Here, it's all about the pan dulce," Solis says, referring to traditional Mexican sweet bread. It's offered in many varieties, including shell-shaped conchas, sweet and savory empanadas, telleras (sandwich rolls), and bollilos (crusty bread rolls). There are also cortadillos (sliced cakes in dozens of varieties) and mantecadas, which Solis describes as "like a cupcake without any icing, but so moist, a unique flavor. It's a great item for us."

---

* Based on material in Jim Dudlicek, "Store of the Month: Autenticidad en Acción," *Progressive Grocer,* March 2016, pp. 24–36. Reprinted by permission.

Full-size and single-serve cakes come in traditional tres leches, strawberry, chocolate, fan (custard), and chocoflan— the last of which delivers rich custard over a chocolate-cake base. The bakery's signature cakes are in such flavors as dulce de leche, cappuccino, piña colada, strawberry, and cookies and cream— all topped with huge strawberries. Parfait cups and gelatin with fruit round out the sweet selections.

As in the Cocina, the bakery's kitchen is on full display. "That's one of the things we've been focusing on," Solis says of that enhanced visibility for shoppers. The redesign flip-flopped the positions of the self-serve and service bakery counters to further open up the kitchen, which also put the cake-decorating station at the front counter. Solis notes, "It's a showcase for people to see the works of art we do on our cakes."

The in-store tortillería, or tortilla bakery, has been a part of Food City stores for many years. "We run 19 of these machines throughout the company," Solis says of the mini production plant. "Our flour tortillas are head and shoulders above anything else in the market."

With a 10-day shelf life, the tortillas come in assorted sizes and thicknesses for tacos, burritos, and other applications. The store also makes tortillas with manteca (lard) in the flour for a more traditional flavor profile. Meanwhile, corn tortillas come in different varieties for table use and frying. The store also makes tortilla chips for sale and serving in the Cocina.

Speaking of corn, Food City is into masa (corn flour) in a big way, as it is used widely in the local Hispanic community in preparing tamales and menudo. These dishes are made more often for the fall and winter holidays, so masa sales double, and even sometimes triple, during these periods, Solis notes. The store performs regular demonstrations on the sales floor to show uses and applications for different varieties of the masa. "We sell a lot of it," Solis says. "This is one of the top-selling stores for masa out of all of the units that we have."

For shoppers going that extra mile toward authenticity at home, Food City also sells nixtamal, the corn kernels that are ground to make the masa, which are also used to make menudo and posole (meat stew with hominy).

Consistency and Variety

There's more authenticity on display in the meat department, which offers a full-service butcher counter, seafood, a wide selection of Mexican cheeses, the store's signature chorizo (Mexican sausage), and marinated beef and chicken ready for the grill.

The service counter will cut meat to any thickness, but as Solis observes, "Our customers like thinner-cut meat." That's evidenced by the many cased offerings under the Food City label, like beef flaps for carne asada, merchandised alongside shrink-wrapped trays of cut vegetables for fajitas.

Cuts more familiar to folks outside the Hispanic community are joined by local favorites such as oxtails, beef shanks, and beef short ribs, which Solis says are popular for making soups during colder months, along with neck bones, hearts and cheek meat.

The butcher counter also features a "phenomenal" variety of Mexican cheeses, Solis notes, offering samples of queso fresco, panela, cotija, and Oaxaca, the last a popular melting cheese (named for the Mexican province) used to make quesadillas. Of the value-added chorizo (sausage), Solis says, "It's our in-house recipe, a real signature item."

Seafood selections—expected to get an annual boost during Lent—include tilapia, catfish, swai, cod, red snapper, and shrimp. "Tilapia is by far our best-selling seafood, whole or fillets," Solis says.

Fresh chicken cuts are joined by pre-cooked breaded chicken wings, nuggets, and patties. "Chicken is a big category for us," Solis reiterates, noting Food City's "consistency and variety." Solis points out the $19.99 value pack, which offers select cuts of beef, pork, and chicken, plus ground beef, valued at up to $25. "Our prices really address the price-conscious consumer throughout the entire store," he says. Meanwhile, a coffin freezer offers "menudo packs"—bags of beef tripe or beef and pig feet, ready for use by folks making the traditional Mexican dish at home.

The remodel allowed for a larger meat department, Solis notes. "Based on the volume of sales at this store, we shifted down" farther along the perimeter, he says. "It definitely helped with our pork and chicken sections."

Improving Shopability

The center of the store was reconfigured as part of the remodel, which Solis says required a period of adjustment as shoppers and associates got used to the new order of things. "We really changed the flow of the categories," he says, explaining that this has helped to enhance "shopability around the perimeter."

Among the key shifts: The beer and salty snack aisles were moved to the far end of the store for placement with the carbonated soft drinks. Additionally, the store got rid of its warehouse shelving in favor of standard gondolas. End-of-aisle displays are massively merchandised. "We have a limited variety of SKUs in the center of the store, but we have what our consumers like, and at a great value," Solis says.

The store's Hispanic aisle offers "groupings of our Mexican-branded products in several different categories," Solis explains. This row features everything from canned goods to crackers to religious figurines. There are myriad varieties of pepper — "a strong category for us," Solis affirms—along with chili pastes and powders. There are also aloe vera drinks and coconut waters, which he notes "have exploded in popularity." And for those who don't want to buy authentic ingredients or pick some up ready to eat from the Cocina, there's even canned menudo.

Cross-merchandising efforts throughout the store include store-brand bread with peanut butter and jelly on one end, and mayo and mustard on the other, and jarred nopalitos (cactus) displayed near the eggs, a pairing popular among Hispanics for Lent, Solis notes. Prominently displayed atop cases around the perimeter are 40-quart stockpots used for making menudo and tamales.

"The most rewarding part of the grand reopening has to be the excitement of our members [employees] and customers, who are enjoying the new look and feel of the store," Solis declares. Associates' excitement is no doubt increased by their ability to deliver the real deal to those who know the difference. "We really give the authenticity to the Hispanic consumer," Solis says. "They can have all their needs met here."

Figure 1 shows the supermarket grid layout that highlights the remodeling.

FIGURE 1

Food City Remodeling

Source: Based on material in Jim Dudlicek, "Store of the Month: Autenticidad en Acción," *Progressive Grocer,* March 2016, pp. 34–35. Reprinted by permission.

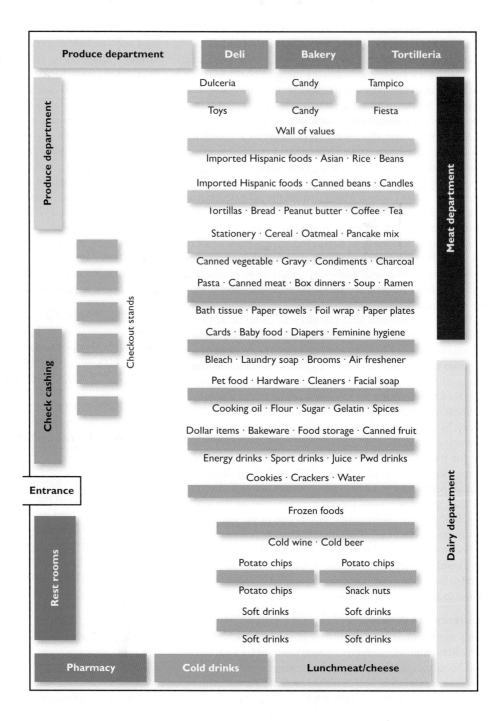

More about the Food City Chain

Arizona's Food City is a low-price format supermarket chain offering a full range of ethnic and Hispanic food varieties along with traditional grocery store items. The community-focused grocery store chain is known for holding car-seat and water-safety events, mobile dental clinics, back-to-school immunizations, backpack giveaways, and other cultural celebrations that are very important to the Hispanic community.

Investing heavily in the neighborhoods that it serves, Food City also holds annual signature events such as the Copa Food City Soccer Tournament and the Food City Tamale Festival. In addition, the banner supports many holidays and special events important to its shoppers, including Mexican concerts, Three Kings Day, Children's Day, Mexico's Independence Day (September 16), and Día de los Muertos (Day of the Dead).

Dating back more than 60 years, Food City was acquired in 1993 by Bashas' Grocery Store, which has since grown the brand from a single store to 47 locations, many of which are in metro Phoenix and southern Arizona, home to a significant Hispanic community.

Striving to hire people from its surrounding communities, Food City has saved and created thousands of jobs in many economically challenged neighborhoods. Its diverse employee base allows it to serve consumers in their native language, creating a gratifying family shopping experience.

Visit the chain at www.myfoodcity.com.

Questions

1. How important are store locations in Food City's overall retailing strategy? Explain your answer.
2. Enumerate several criteria that Food City should consider when choosing a new location to open a supermarket.
3. Outside of Arizona, where should Food City consider opening supermarkets? Why?
4. How does the location of a supermarket affect that store's interior layout and merchandise mix? Refer to Figure 1 in your answer.
5. Discuss the pros and cons of the remodeled supermarket described in the case being located in a shopping center with Target and Home Depot.
6. What store exterior factors most influence Food City's ability to draw vehicular traffic? Why?
7. How vital do you think each factor in the Figure 10-7 location checklist is for Food City? Why?

Managing a Retail Business

Source: nasirkhan/Shutterstock. Reprinted by permission.

In Part Five, the elements of managing a retail enterprise are discussed. We first look at the steps in setting up a retail organization and the special human resource management environment of retailing. Operations management is then examined—from both financial and operational perspectives.

Chapter 11 reports how a retailer can use its organizational structure to assign tasks, policies, resources, authority, responsibilities, and rewards to satisfy the needs of the target market, employees, and management. We also show how human resource management can be applied so that the structure works properly. Human resource management consists of recruiting, selecting, training, compensating, and supervising personnel.

Chapter 12 focuses on the financial dimensions of operations management in enacting a retail strategy. We discuss these topics: profit planning, asset management (including the strategic profit model, other key ratios, and financial trends in retailing), budgeting, and resource allocation.

Chapter 13 presents the operational aspects of operations management. We cover these specific concepts: operations blueprint; store format, size, and space allocation; personnel utilization; store maintenance, energy management, and renovations; inventory management; store security; insurance; credit management; computerization; and crisis management.

11 Retail Organization and Human Resource Management

Chapter Objectives

1. To study the procedures involved in setting up a retail organization

2. To examine the various organizational arrangements utilized in retailing

3. To consider the special human resource environment of retailing

4. To describe the principles and practices involved with the human resource management process in retailing

Superior human resource management in retailing not only requires that a firm hire and train good employees but the firm must also keep them motivated. With the high employee turnover rate in retailing, this is not an easy task. One estimate is that the cost of replacing a $10 per hour retail employee averages more than $3,300.[1] Since the turnover rate among some retailers can easily exceed 70 percent per year, costs related to employee turnover can amount to a very large expenditure.

Strategies a retailer can use to reduce turnover among low-wage employees include:

▶ *Promote from within.* This rewards long-time employees In addition, it lets short-term employees directly observe role models who have advanced to managerial positions.
▶ *Be understanding.* Grant exceptions to occasional lateness or absenteeism if there is good cause (sickness, family crisis, etc.).
▶ *Make the job relevant to company goals.* Show employees the value of short waiting lines, clean facilities, and customer-service–centric employees.

Source: S.john/Shutterstock.
Reprinted by permission.

> *Minimize boredom by rotating jobs.* Stockroom persons could work the cash registers at busy times or assist elderly or infirm customers with their packages.

> *Invest in training.* Make sure the trainer respectfully instructs and corrects the new employee.

Overview

Managing a retail business comprises three steps: setting up an organization structure, hiring and managing personnel, and managing operations—financially and nonfinancially. The first two steps of this procedure are covered in this chapter. Chapters 12 and 13 deal with operations management.

SETTING UP A RETAIL ORGANIZATION

Through a **retail organization**, a firm structures and assigns tasks (functions), policies, resources, authority, responsibilities, and rewards to efficiently and effectively satisfy the needs of its target market, employees, and management. Figure 11-1 shows various needs that should be taken into account when planning and assessing an organization's structure.

As a rule, a firm cannot survive unless its organization structure satisfies the target market, no matter how well employee and management needs are met. A structure that reduces costs

FIGURE 11-1

Selected Factors That Must Be Considered in Planning and Assessing a Retail Organization

TARGET MARKET NEEDS

Are there sufficient personnel to provide appropriate customer service?

Are personnel knowledgeable and courteous?

Are store facilities well maintained?

Are the specific needs of branch store customers met?

Are changing needs promptly addressed?

EMPLOYEE NEEDS

Are positions challenging and satisfying enough?

Is there an orderly promotion program from within?

Is the employee able to participate in the decision making?

Are the channels of communication clear and open?

Is the authority-responsibility relationship clear?

Is each employee treated fairly?

Is good performance rewarded?

MANAGEMENT NEEDS

Is it relatively easy to obtain and retain competent personnel?

Are personnel procedures clearly defined?

Does each worker report to only one supervisor?

Can each manager properly supervise all the workers reporting to him or her?

Do operating departments have adequate staff support (e.g., marketing research)?

Are the levels of organization properly developed?

Are the organization's plans well integrated?

Are employees motivated?

Is absenteeism low?

Is there a system to replace personnel in an orderly manner?

Is there enough flexibility to adapt to changes in customers or the environment?

FIGURE 11-2

The Process of Organizing a Retail Firm

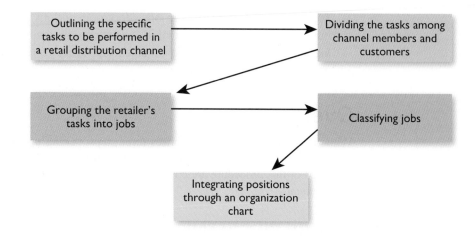

via centralized buying but leads to a firm's insensitivity to geographic differences in customer preferences will lose market share. Although many retailers perform similar tasks (buying, pricing, displaying, and wrapping merchandise), there are many ways of organizing to conduct these functions. The process of setting up a retail organization, shown in Figure 11-2, is described next.

Specifying Tasks to Be Performed

The tasks in a distribution channel must be enumerated and then keyed to the chosen strategy mix for effective retailing to occur:

- Buying merchandise on behalf of the retailer
- Shipping merchandise to the retailer
- Receiving merchandise and checking incoming shipments
- Setting prices and marking merchandise
- Inventory storage and control
- Preparing merchandise and window displays
- Facilities maintenance (e.g., keeping the store clean)
- Customer research and exchanging information
- Customer contact (e.g., Web site, personal selling)
- Facilitating shopping (e.g., convenient location, short checkout lines)
- Customer follow-up and complaint handling
- Personnel management
- Repairs and alteration of merchandise
- Billing customers and credit operations
- Handling receipts and financial records
- Gift wrapping
- Delivery to customers (e.g., multichannel or omnichannel retailing)
- Returning unsold or damaged merchandise to vendors
- Sales forecasting and budgeting
- Coordination

Dividing Tasks among Channel Members and Customers

Although the preceding tasks are typically performed in a distribution channel, they do not all have to be done by a retailer. Some can be completed by the manufacturer, wholesaler, specialist, or consumer. Figure 11-3 shows the types of activities that could be carried out by each party. Following are some criteria to consider in allocating the functions related to consumer credit.

Sysco is a wholesaler serving 425,000 restaurants, hotels, schools, and other locales. It offers them a wide range of support services (www.sysco.com/customer-solutions.html).

- A task should be done by the person who is most competent, and it should be carried out only if desired by the target market.
- For some retailers, liberal credit policies may provide significant advantages over competitors. For others, a cash-only policy may reduce their overhead and lead to lower prices.
- Credit collection may require a legal staff and detailed digitized records—most affordable by medium or large retailers. Smaller retailers are likely to rely on bank credit cards.

FIGURE 11-3

The Division of Tasks in a Distribution Channel

Performer	Tasks
Retailer	Can perform all or some of the tasks in the distribution channel, from buying merchandise to coordination.
Manufacturer or Wholesaler	Can take care of few or many functions, such as shipping, marking merchandise, inventory storage, displays, research, etc.
Specialist(s)	Can undertake a particular task: buying office, delivery firm, warehouse, marketing research firm, ad agency, accountant, credit bureau, computer service firm.
Consumer	Can be responsible for delivery, credit (cash purchases), sales effort (self-service), product alterations (do-it-yourselfers), etc.

▷ There is a loss of control when an activity is delegated. A credit collection agency, pressing for past-due payments, may antagonize customers.

▷ The retailer's institutional framework can affect task allocation. Franchisees are readily able to get together to have their own private-label brands. Independents cannot do this as easily.

▷ Task allocation depends on the savings gained by sharing or shifting tasks. The credit function is better performed by an outside credit bureau if it has expert personnel and ongoing access to financial data, uses tailored computer software, pays lower rent (due to an out-of-the-way site), and so on. Many retailers cannot attain these savings themselves.

Grouping Tasks into Jobs

This site (www .thebalance.com/retail-job-search-4073851) highlights the range of jobs available in retailing.

After the retailer decides which tasks to perform, they are grouped into jobs. The jobs must be clearly structured. Here are examples of grouping tasks into jobs:

Tasks	Jobs
Displaying merchandise, customer contact, gift wrapping, customer follow-up	Sales personnel
Entering transaction data, handling cash and credit purchases, gift wrapping	Cashier(s)
Receiving merchandise, checking incoming shipments, marking merchandise, inventory storage and control, returning merchandise to vendors	Inventory personnel
Window dressing, interior display setups, use of mobile displays	Display personnel
Billing customers, credit operations, customer research	Credit personnel
Merchandise repairs and alterations, resolution of complaints, customer research	Customer service personnel
Cleaning store, replacing old fixtures	Janitorial personnel
Employee management, sales forecasting, budgeting, pricing, coordinating tasks	Management personnel

While grouping tasks into jobs, specialization should be considered so each employee is responsible for a limited range of functions (as opposed to performing many diverse tasks). Specialization has the advantages of clearly defined tasks, greater expertise, reduced training, and

ETHICS IN RETAILING | Zero-Hour Contracts |

According to the UK Office of National Statistics, the number of UK workers on zero-hour contracts increased by 20 percent in 2016 to just over 900,000. This represents nearly 3 percent of the employed UK workforce. The zero-hour contract workers are not offered guaranteed hours or sick pay. Retailers are amongst those most likely to offer their employees zero-hour contracts. On average, the retailer workers work for around 25 hours per week. However, over 30 percent of them would like to work longer and more predictable hours if they were given the option. The British Retail Consortium claims that zero-hours contracts are not widely used in the retail sector but that certain chains and brands only use this form of employment.

Why might a retailer opt for zero-hour contracts? What advantages does it offer them?

hiring people with narrow education and experience. Problems can result due to extreme specialization: poor morale (boredom), people not being aware of their jobs' importance, and the need for more employees. Specialization means assigning explicit duties to individuals so a job position encompasses a homogeneous cluster of tasks.

Once tasks are grouped, job descriptions are constructed. These outline the job titles, objectives, duties, and responsibilities for every position. They are used as a hiring, supervision, and evaluation tool. Figure 11-4 contains a job description for a store manager.

Classifying Jobs

Jobs are then broadly grouped into functional, product, geographic, or combination classifications. *Functional classification* divides jobs by task—such as sales promotion, buying, Web design, and store operations. Expert knowledge is used. *Product classification* divides jobs on a goods or service basis. A department store hires different personnel for clothing, furniture, appliances, and so forth. This classification recognizes differences in personnel requirements for different products.

Geographic classification is useful for chains operating in different areas. Employees are adapted to local conditions, and they are supervised by branch managers. Some firms, especially larger ones, use a *combination classification*. If a branch unit of a chain hires its selling staff, but buying personnel for each product line are hired by headquarters, the functional, product, and geographic formats are combined.

Developing an Organization Chart

The format of a retail organization must be designed in an integrated, coordinated way. Planning leaders in the organization need to clearly articulate accountability and decision-making authority for each position or role on the organizational chart, span of control (number of subordinates

FIGURE 11-4

A Job Description for a Store Manager

JOB TITLE: Store manager for 34th Street Branch of Pombo's Department Stores

POSITION REPORTS TO: Senior vice-president

POSITIONS REPORTING TO STORE MANAGER: All personnel in the 34th Street store

OBJECTIVES: To properly staff and operate the 34th Street store

DUTIES AND RESPONSIBILITIES:
- Sales forecasting and budgeting
- Personnel recruitment, selection, training, motivation, and evaluation
- Merchandise display, inventory management, and merchandise reorders
- Transferring merchandise among stores
- Handling store receipts, preparing bank transactions, opening and closing store
- Reviewing customer complaints
- Reviewing computer data forms
- Semi-annual review of overall operations and reports for top management

COMMITTEES AND MEETINGS:
- Attendance at monthly meetings with senior vice-president
- Supervision of weekly meetings with department managers

under a manager's direct control) for each position, and lateral relationships between positions. Aligning individual employee goals with organizational goals and communicating to employees how the organizational structure will meet strategic objectives and goals and create sustained economic value is key. Managers and their direct reports must jointly identify common goals, define each individual's responsibilities and expectations, and understand how they will be evaluated. Joint goal setting and shared responsibility toward achieving them will increase employee motivation and perceived empowerment, and provide a common direction toward achievement of organizational goals.

The **hierarchy of authority** outlines the job interactions within a company by describing the reporting relationships among employees (from lowest level to highest level). Coordination and control are provided by this hierarchy. A firm with many workers reporting to one manager has a *flat organization*. Its benefits are good communication, quicker problem handling, and better employee identification with a job. The major problem tends to be the number of people reporting to one manager. A *tall organization* has several management levels, resulting in close supervision and fewer workers reporting to each manager. Problems include a long communication channel, the impersonal impression given to workers regarding access to upper-level personnel, and inflexible rules.

With these factors in mind, a retailer devises an **organization chart**, which graphically displays its hierarchical relationships. Table 11-1 lists the principles to consider in establishing an organization chart. Figure 11-5 shows examples of basic organization charts.

ORGANIZATIONAL PATTERNS IN RETAILING

An independent retailer has a simple organization. It operates only one store, the owner/manager usually supervises all employees, and workers have access to the owner/manager if there are problems. In contrast, a chain must specify how tasks are delegated, coordinate multiple stores, and set common policies for employees. As examples, the organizational arrangements used by independent retailers, department stores, chain retailers, and diversified retailers are discussed next.

Organizational Arrangements Used by Small Independent Retailers

Small independents use uncomplicated arrangements with only two or three levels of personnel (owner/manager and employees), and the owner/manager personally runs the firm and oversees workers. There are few employees, little specialization, and no branch units. This does not mean fewer activities must be performed but that many tasks are performed relative to the number of workers. Each employee must allot part of his or her time to several duties.

Figure 11-6 shows the organizations of two small firms. In A, a boutique is organized by function. Merchandising personnel buy and sell goods and services, plan assortments, set up displays,

TABLE 11-1 Principles for Organizing a Retail Firm

An organization should show interest in its employees. This can be done through job rotation, promotion from within, participatory management, recognition, job enrichment, and so forth.

Employee turnover, lateness, and absenteeism should be monitored, because they may indicate personnel problems.

The line of authority should be traceable from the highest to the lowest positions. In this way, employees know to whom they report and who reports to them (*chain of command*).

A subordinate should report to only one direct supervisor (*unity of command*). This avoids the problem of workers receiving conflicting orders.

There is a limit to the number of employees a manager can directly supervise (*span of control*).

A person responsible for a given objective needs the power to achieve it.

Although a supervisor can delegate authority, he or she is still responsible for subordinates.

The greater the number of organizational levels, the longer the time for communication to travel and the greater the coordination problems.

An organization has an informal structure aside from a formal organization chart. Informal relationships exercise power in the firm and may bypass formal relationships and procedures.

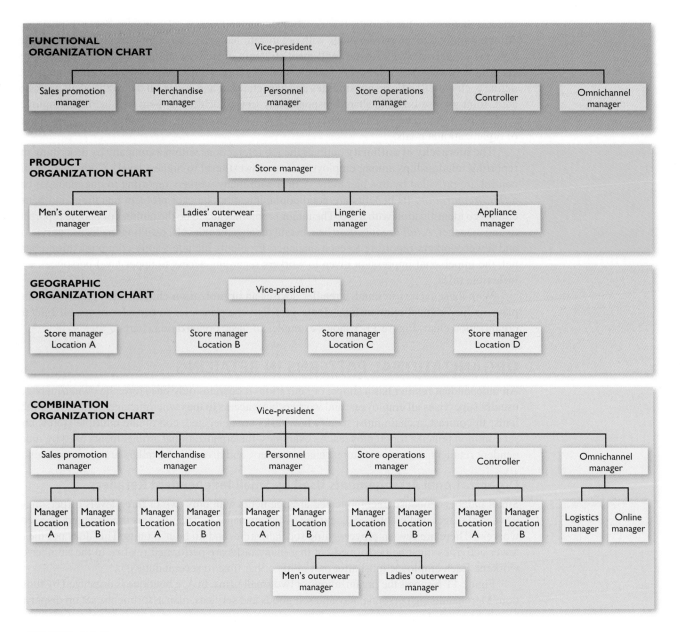

FIGURE 11-5
Different Forms of Retail Organization

and prepare ads. Operations personnel are involved with store maintenance and operations. In B, a furniture store is organized on a product-oriented basis, with personnel in each category responsible for selected activities. All products get proper attention, and some expertise is developed. This is important because different skills are necessary to buy and sell each type of furniture.

Organizational Arrangements Used by Department Stores

Many department stores continue to use an organizational arrangement that is an adaptation of the **Mazur plan**, which divides all retail activities into four functional areas.[2] In twenty-first century terms, these are store management, communications, merchandising, and financial accounting. Figure 11-7 shows the modern version of the Mazur plan, as devised by the authors of this book:

1. *Store management:* Operations, customer service, human resources, inventory, "backroom" activities, and store maintenance
2. *Communications:* Public relations, advertising, window and interior displays, promotions, and online efforts

FIGURE 11-6

Organization Structures Used by Small Independents

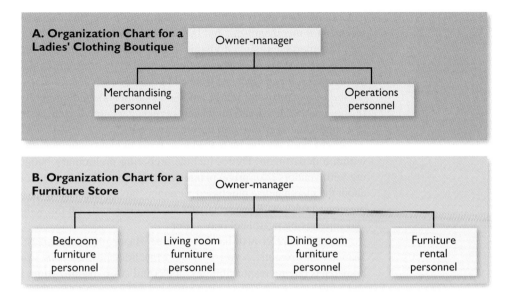

3. *Merchandising:* Buying, selling, stock planning and forecasting, and product-positioning (image-related) with regard to the mix of goods and services offered by the retailer
4. *Financial accounting (overseen by controller):* Accounting, inventory control, credit, and auditing

These areas are organized into *line* (direct authority and responsibility) and *staff* (advisory and support) components. Thus, in Figure 11-7, the omnichannel manager reports directly to the

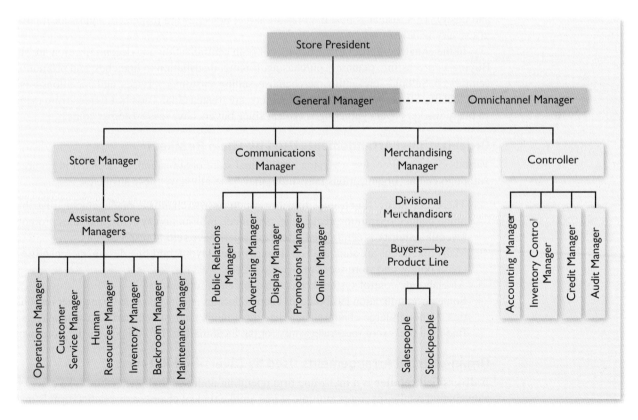

FIGURE 11-7

A Modern Version of the Mazur Organizational Plan for Department Stores

Source: Chart developed by the authors.

general manager and is a staff person; and a controller and a communications manager often staff services for merchandisers; but in their disciplines, personnel are organized on a line basis.

The merchandising division is responsible for buying and selling. It is headed by a merchandising manager, who is often viewed as the most important of the area executives. She or he supervises buyers, devises financial goals for each department, coordinates merchandise plans (so there is a consistent image among departments), and interprets the effects of economic data. In some cases, divisional merchandise managers are utilized, so the number of buyers reporting to a single manager does not become unwieldy.

In the basic Mazur plan, the buyer has complete accountability for expenses and profit goals within a department. Duties include preparing preliminary budgets, studying trends, negotiating with vendors over price, planning the number of salespeople, and informing sales personnel about the merchandise purchased. Grouping buying and selling activities into one job (buyer) may present a problem. Because buyers are not constantly on the selling floor, training, scheduling, and supervising personnel may suffer.

Branch store growth has led to three Mazur plan derivatives: *main store control*, by which headquarters executives oversee and operate branches; *separate store organization*, by which each branch has buying responsibilities; and **equal store organization**, by which buying is centralized and branches become sales units with equal operational status. The latter is the most popular format.

In the main store control format, most authority remains at headquarters. Merchandise planning and buying, advertising, financial controls, store hours, and other tasks are centrally managed to standardize the performance. Branch store managers hire and supervise employees, but daily operations conform to company policies. This works well if there are few branches and the preferences of customers are similar to those at the main store. As branch stores increase, buyers, the advertising manager, and others may be overworked and give little attention to branches. Because headquarters personnel are not at the branches, differences in customer preferences may be overlooked.

The separate store format places merchandise managers in branches, which have autonomy for merchandising and operations. Customer needs are quickly noted, but task duplication is possible. Coordination can also be a problem. Transferring goods between branches is more complex and costly. This format is best if stores are large, branches are dispersed, and/or local customer tastes vary widely.

In the equal store format, the benefits of both centralization and decentralization are sought. Buying—forecasting, planning, purchasing, pricing, distribution to branches, and promotion—is centralized. Selling—presenting merchandise, selling, customer services, and operations—is managed locally. All stores, including headquarters, are treated alike. Buyers are freed from managing so many workers. Data gathering is critical since buyers have less customer contact.

Organizational Arrangements Used by Chain Retailers

Various chain retailers use a version of the equal store organization, as depicted in Figure 11-8. Although chains' organizations may differ, they generally have these attributes:

▶ There are many functional divisions, such as merchandise management, distribution, omnichannel, operations, real-estate, personnel, information systems, and sales promotion.
▶ Overall authority is centralized. Store managers have selling responsibility.
▶ Many operations are standardized (fixtures, store layout, building design, merchandise lines, credit policy, and store service).
▶ An elaborate control system keeps management informed.
▶ Some decentralization lets branches adapt to locales and increases store manager responsibilities. Although large chains standardize most items their outlets carry, store managers often fine-tune the rest of the strategy mix for the local market. This empowers the store manager.

Organizational Arrangements Used by Diversified Retailers

A **diversified retailer** is a multi-line firm operating under central ownership. Like other chains, a diversified retailer operates multiple stores; unlike typical chains, a diversified firm is involved with different types of retail operations. Here are two examples:

To discover more about Kroger, go to this section of its Web site (www .thekrogerco.com/ about-kroger/operations).

▶ Kroger Co. (www.kroger.com) operates supermarkets, warehouse stores, supercenters, convenience stores, and jewelry stores; it also has a manufacturing group. The firm owns multiple store chains in each of its retail categories. See Figure 11-9.

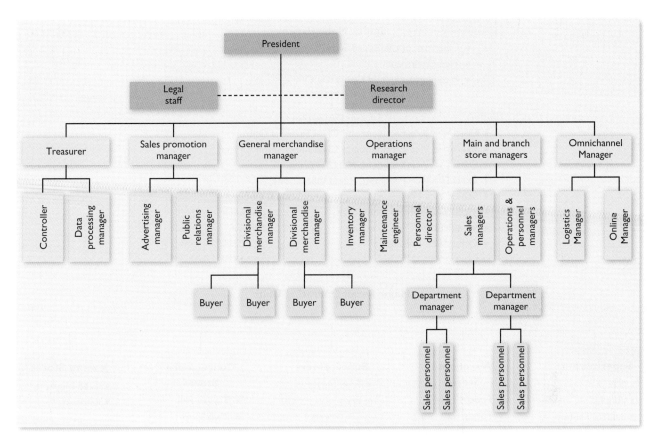

FIGURE 11-8
The Equal Store Organizational Format Used by Many Chain Stores

> Japan's Aeon Co. (www.aeon.info/en) comprises superstores, supermarkets, discount stores, home centers, specialty stores, convenience stores, financial services stores, restaurants, and more. Besides Japan, Aeon has facilities in numerous other countries. It is also a shopping center developer.

Due to multiple strategy mixes, diversified retailers face complex organizational considerations. Interdivision control is needed, with operating procedures and goals clearly communicated. For example, (1) interdivision competition must be coordinated, (2) resources must be divided among divisions, (3) potential image and advertising conflicts must be avoided, and (4) management skills must adapt to different operations.

HUMAN RESOURCE MANAGEMENT IN RETAILING

Human resource management involves recruiting, selecting, training, compensating, and supervising personnel in a manner consistent with the retailer's organization structure and strategy mix. Personnel practices depend on the line of business, number of employees, store location, and other factors. Because good personnel are needed to develop and carry out strategies, and labor costs can amount to 50 percent or more of expenses, the value of human resource management is clear.

Retailing in the United States employs 25 million people. Thus, there is a constant need to attract new employees—and retain existing ones. For example, as many as 2 million fast-food workers are aged 16 to 20, and they stay in their jobs for short periods. In general, retailers need to reduce the turnover rate; when workers quickly exit a firm, the results can be disastrous. See Table 11-2. Turnover in retail averages around 66 percent for part-time hourly, whereas it drops to 27 percent for full-time employees with benefits such as health insurance.[3]

Consider the approaches of Target, Zappos, and Wegmans Food Markets:

> Target is committed to employee development and retention. Target challenges employees to innovate, collaborate, and efficiently and intelligently provide the best possible shopping

Retail Management Advisor offers several employee development tips (www .the-retail-advisor.com/ increasing_employee_ performance.html).

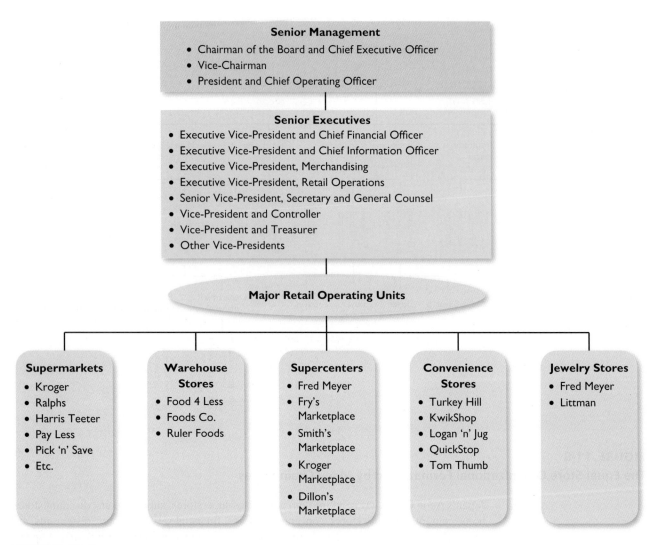

FIGURE 11-9

The Organizational Structure of Kroger Co. (Selected Store Chains and Positions)

Note: Most Kroger supermarkets are food-based combination stores.

Source: Chart developed by the authors based on material in the *Kroger Co. 2015 Annual Report.* and the *2015 Kroger 2015 Fact Book.*

experience to customers. It believes empowering and training employees and providing them with opportunities for professional growth will help its business stay competitive. Every entry-level employee, whether hourly or full time, is mentored by the store team leader. Campus

TABLE 11-2 The True Costs of Employee Turnover

Using fill-in employees until permanent replacements are found.

Severance pay for exiting employees.

Hiring new employees: advertising, interviewing time, travel expenses, testing, screening.

Training costs: trainers, training materials and technology, trainee compensation, supervisor time (on-the-job training).

Mistakes and lower productivity while new employees gain experience.

Customer dissatisfaction due to the departure of previous employees and the use of inexperienced workers.

Loss of continuity among co-workers.

Poor employee morale when turnover is high.

Lower employee loyalty to retailer when turnover is high.

recruits are encouraged to join the summer internship program in Minneapolis where they are trained in leadership skills as well as their functional area (planning, software training, etc.) to be a successful member of a Target store/distribution center, corporate, or technology leadership team. Company benefits include health coverage, a pension, a 401(K) plan, tuition reimbursement, life insurance, a paid vacation, and an annual bonus.[4]

▷ Zappos, an online retailer of shoes, apparel, and accessories (owned by Amazon.com Inc. since 2009) says its goal is to be the online service leader. Employees call themselves "Zapponians" and claim they "Live to Deliver WOW" in support of the first core value of the firm. Employees get benefits such as vacation and sick days, a retirement plan, life and disability insurance, medical and dental coverage, maternity and paternity leave, tuition reimbursement, discounts (40%) on Zappos merchandise, and free shipping. Zappos helps employees stay fit by having an on-site fitness center, a yoga studio, weight management programs, and fitness challenges. To help employees achieve a work–life balance, Zappos pays for dry cleaning, car washes, and oil changes; it even has an on-site library and life coach, health screening, and a nap room! Company happy hours, fun events, and healthy on-site catering build team and family spirit.[5]

▷ Wegmans Food Markets is the only retailer on the *Forbes* "100 Best Companies to Work For" list every year since 1998.[6] It offers health insurance to part-timers, telecommuting, job sharing and compressed work weeks, tuition reimbursement, paid vacations, and substantial training. Full-time employee turnover is low. Wegmans has multiple paths to career success via lateral learning, cross-training, internships, and management training. Wegmans cares about the well-being of employees and empowers them to make decisions that customers and the company.[7]

The Special Human Resource Environment of Retailing

The Bureau of Labor Statistics compiles current employment data on such jobs as retail sales worker supervisors and managers (www.bls.gov/oco).

Retailers face a human resource environment characterized by a large number of inexperienced workers, long hours, highly visible employees, a diverse work force, many part-time workers, and variable customer demands. These factors complicate employee hiring, staffing, and supervision.

The need for a large retail labor force often means hiring those with little or no prior experience. Sometimes, a position in retailing represents a person's first "real job." People are attracted to retailing because they find jobs near to home, and retail positions (such as cashiers, stock clerks, and some types of sales personnel) may require limited education, training, and skill. Also, the low wages paid for some positions result in the hiring of inexperienced people. Thus, high employee turnover and cases of poor performance, lateness, and absenteeism may result.

The long working hours in retailing, which may include weekends, turn off certain prospective employees. Many retailers now have longer hours because more shoppers want to shop during evenings and weekends. Accordingly, some retailers require at least two shifts of full-time employees.

Retailing employees are highly visible to the customer. Thus, when personnel are selected and trained, special care must be taken as to their manners and appearance. Some small retailers do not place enough emphasis on employee appearance (neat grooming and appropriate attire).

RETAILING AROUND THE WORLD

Recruiting Retail Executives

RWR Group (www.johnmcaldwell.com/rwr-group), HGA (http://hga-group.com), and Carter Murray (www.cartermurray.com) specialize in the global recruitment of retail executives. Why? Demand factors include the need for multinational executives to effectively manage global retail operations. The supply stems from retail executives seeking foreign experience to better prepare for high-level positions, as well as individuals wanting the excitement of living in a foreign country. Some executive search firms such as HGA Group specialize in a field of retailing; others such as RWR Group are involved in executive placement in a wide variety of retail fields. All of these companies have offices in major cities throughout the world. Carter Murray, as an example, has offices in London, Singapore, Hong Kong, New York, Germany, and Australia.

Discuss the advantages to both a company and a prospective employee of using a global executive recruitment firm.

◾

It is common for retailers to have a diverse labor force, with regard to age, work experience, gender, race, and other factors. This means that firms must train and supervise their workers so they interact well with one another—and are sensitive to the perspectives and needs of each other. Home Depot's recruitment strategy includes partnerships with several national nonprofit, government, and educational organizations to reach out to the communities it serves and to attract a broad range of qualified candidates with diverse backgrounds, including AARP, NAACP, National Urban League, National Society of Hispanic MBAs, National Black MBA Association Inc., and several U.S. military groups. In addition, Home Depot provides resources to help recruits succeed through Associate Resource groups and online tools such as "Military Skills Translator" to help veterans identify positions and job descriptions that leverage skills acquired in the military.[8]

Due to long operating hours, retailers regularly hire part-time workers. In many supermarkets, more than half the workers are part-time, and problems may arise. Some part-time employees are more lackadaisical, late, absent, or likely to quit than full-time employees. They must be closely monitored. Like other firms, retailers hire a large number of Millennials. Although this group is generally technologically advanced, Millennials often have different work values than older employees. A recent Gallup Poll found that Millennials are the least engaged group in the work force.[9] Here are a number of ways to better motivate Millennials:[10]

▸ Show the firm's commitment to society and respected charities by supporting volunteerism.
▸ Train managers to communicate frequently and openly with Millennials.
▸ Get Millennials actively involved in solving important problems.
▸ Provide Millennials with mentors.
▸ Accommodate Millennials' needs with flexible hours.

Variations in customer demand by day, time period, or season may cause difficulties. A number of U.S. shoppers make major supermarket trips on Saturday or Sunday. So, how many employees should there be Monday through Friday and how many on Saturday and Sunday? Differences by time of day (morning, afternoon, evening), season, and holidays also affect planning. When stores are very busy, even administrative and clerical employees may be needed on the sales floor.

As a rule, retailers should consider these points:

▸ Recruitment and selection procedures must efficiently generate sufficient applicants.
▸ Some training must be short because workers are inexperienced and temporary.
▸ Compensation must be perceived as "fair" by employees.
▸ Advancement opportunities must be available to employees who view retailing as a career.
▸ Employee appearance and work habits must be explained and reviewed.
▸ Diverse workers must be taught to work together well and amicably.
▸ Morale problems may result from high turnover and the many part-time workers.
▸ Full- and part-time workers may conflict, especially if some full-timers are replaced.

Various retail career opportunities are available to women and minorities. There is still some room for improvement, however.

See how Avon offers "inspiring work" and is "empowering women" (www.avoncompany.com/careers).

WOMEN IN RETAILING   Retailers have made a lot of progress in career advancement for women. According to the "2020 Women on Boards," Ann Inc., Avon, Chico's, Children's Place, Estee Lauder, HSN (Home Shopping Network), Macy's, Ulta, and Williams-Sonoma Inc. are among the U.S. public firms with 40 percent or more of corporate officers who are women.[11] The "2013 Catalyst Census: *Fortune 500* Women's Representation by NAICS Industry" report notes that retailing has the highest percentage of women as corporate officers among the 18 industry groups.

Women have more career options in retailing than ever before, as the following examples show. Mary Kay Ash (Mary Kay cosmetics), Debbi Fields (Mrs. Fields' Cookies), and Lillian Vernon (the direct marketer) have founded retailing empires. As of 2016, women were chief executive officers in 21 of *Fortune 500* companies overall and/or chairpersons of the board of such U.S.-based retailers as Enterprise, Home Shopping Network, Ross Stores, Sam's Club, and Victoria's Secret.[12] Let's look at a brief profile of two of these.

As part of her legacy, Mary Kay Ash left behind a charitable foundation (www.mkacf.org).

Rosalind Brewer is president and CEO of Sam's Club. She started her career with Walmart in 2006 as regional vice-president of operations. She then was promoted to division president of Walmart Southeast, and then president of Walmart East. In 2012, Brewer was named president and CEO of Sam's Club. She earned her bachelor's degree in chemistry from Spelman College. In 2015, *Forbes* referred to Rosalind Brewer as one of the "World's 100 Most Powerful Women."[13]

At Enterprise Holdings Inc., the parent company of Enterprise, Alamo, and National car-rental service providers with more than $19 billion in annual revenues, Pamela Nicholson has been president and CEO since 2013. She is the highest-ranking woman among the world's largest travel companies and has been named to *Fortune's* list of "America's 50 Most Powerful Women in Business" every year since 2007. Nicholson graduated from the University of Missouri with a bachelor of arts degree and began her career with Enterprise Rent-A-Car in 1981 as a management trainee. She has grown the U.S. and international businesses and has been working on a deal with Nissan for a car-sharing businesses for students at 90 college campuses.[14]

Despite recent progress, women still account for a small percentage of corporate officers at publicly owned retailers. These initiatives can help to increase the number of female executives:

▸ Meaningful training programs
▸ Advancement opportunities
▸ Telecommuting and flex time—the ability of employees to adapt their work hours
▸ Job sharing among two or more employees who each work less than full-time
▸ Onsite child care

Fortune annually lists the best employers among public firms (http://fortune.com/best-companies).

MINORITIES AND DIVERSITY IN RETAILING   *Fortune's* 2016 "100 Best Companies to Work For" study listed the top companies' minority statistics. Among retailers with a high percent of minorities are Ikea (52 percent minorities), Nordstrom (50 percent), Whole Foods (43 percent), CarMax (41 percent), Nugget Market (40 percent), Build-A-Bear (35 percent), Container Store (30 percent), Wegmans Food Markets (21 percent), and REI (17 percent).[15]

As with women, retailers have done many good things in the area of minority employment, but there is still more to be accomplished. Consider these positive examples:

▸ CarMax strongly believes in having a diverse work force—and not just because it wants to be a good corporate citizen. CarMax knows that employee diversity contributes to its already strong competitive advantages. Through such diversity, CarMax has a broader view of the marketplace and attracts a greater range of customers. It continuously strives to treat every job applicant, employee, customer, and supplier with respect and fairness—regardless of gender, race, sexual orientation, age, and various other factors.[16]
▸ Walmart is committed to embracing diversity on all aspects of its organization; from its associates to its supplier partners. Through its Supplier Diversity Program,[17] Walmart works with over 3,000 suppliers owned and operated by minorities, women, veterans, and disabled people. In fiscal 2016, Walmart purchased $14.7 billion from women and minority-owned businesses.
▸ Walgreens shows its commitment to diversity as part of a multipronged effort. It includes dealing with a minimum of 8 percent certified minority business firms and 2 percent other certified diversified businesses; and it encourages prime suppliers to use diverse suppliers.[18]

The following list suggests some ways for retailers to even better address the needs of minority workers:

McDonald's (www.aboutmcdonalds.com/mcd/corporate_careers) actively encourages diversity and understanding.

▸ Have clear policy statements from top management as to the value of employee diversity.
▸ Engage in active recruitment programs to stimulate minority applications.
▸ Offer meaningful training programs.
▸ Provide advancement opportunities.
▸ Have zero tolerance for insensitive workplace behavior.

The Human Resource Management Process in Retailing

The **human resource management process** consists of these interrelated personnel activities: recruitment, selection, training, compensation, and supervision. The goals are to obtain, develop, and retain employees. When applying the process, diversity, labor laws, and privacy should be reflected.

Diversity involves two premises: (1) employees must be hired and promoted in a fair and open way, without regard to gender, ethnic background, and other related factors; and (2) in a diverse society, the workplace should be representative of such diversity.

There are several aspects of labor laws for retailers to satisfy:

▸ Do not hire underage workers.
▸ Do not pay workers "off the books" ("under the table").

▸ Do not require workers to engage in illegal acts (such as bait-and-switch selling).
▸ Do not discriminate in hiring or promoting workers.
▸ Do not violate worker safety regulations.
▸ Do not disobey the Americans with Disabilities Act.
▸ Do not deal with suppliers that disobey labor laws.

Retailers must also be careful not to violate employees' privacy rights. Only necessary data about workers should be gathered and stored, and such information should not be freely disseminated.

We now discuss each human resource management activity for sales and middle-management jobs. For further insights, go to our blog (www.bermanevansretail.com).

RECRUITING RETAIL PERSONNEL   **Recruitment** is the activity whereby a retailer generates a list of job applicants. Table 11-3 indicates the features of several key recruitment sources. In addition to these sources, the Web now plays a bigger role in recruitment. Many retailers have a career or job section at their Web site, and some sections are as elaborate as the overall sites. Visit Target's Web site (www.target.com), for example. Scroll down to the bottom of the home page and click on "more" and then "careers."

With entry-level sales jobs, retailers rely on educational institutions, ads, walk-ins (or write-ins), Web sites (including social media), and employee referrals. With middle-management positions, retailers rely on employment agencies, competitors, ads, and employee referrals. A retailer's usual goal is to generate a list of potential employees, which is reduced during selection. Firms that accept applications only from those meeting minimum standards save a lot of time and money.

SELECTING RETAIL PERSONNEL   The company next selects new employees by matching the traits of potential employees with specific job requirements. Job analysis and description, the application blank, interviewing, testing (optional), references, and a physical exam (optional) are tools in the process; they should be integrated.

In **job analysis**, information is amassed on each job's functions and requirements: duties, responsibilities, aptitude, interest, education, experience, and physical tasks. It is used to select

TABLE 11-3 Recruitment Sources and Their Characteristics

Sources	Characteristics
Outside the Company	
Educational institutions	a. High schools, business schools, community colleges, universities, graduate schools
	b. Good for training positions; ensure minimum educational requirements are met; especially useful when long-term contacts with instructors are developed
Other channel members, competitors	a. Employees of wholesalers, manufacturers, ad agencies, competitors; leads from each of these
	b. Reduce extent of training; can evaluate performance with prior firm(s); must instruct in company policy; some negative morale if current employees feel bypassed for promotions
Advertisements	a. Newspapers, trade publications, professional journals, Web sites
	b. Large quantity of applicants; average applicant quality may not be high; cost/applicant is low; additional responsibility placed on screening; can reduce unacceptable applications by noting job qualifications in ads
Employment agencies	a. Private organizations, professional organizations, government, executive search firms
	b. Must be carefully selected; must be determined who pays fee; good for applicant screening; specialists in personnel
Unsolicited applicants	a. Walk-ins, write-ins
	b. Wide variance in quality; must be carefully screened; file should be kept for future positions
Within the Company	
Current and former employees	a. Promotion or transfer of existing full-time employees, part-time employees; rehiring of laid-off employees
	b. Knowledge of company policies and personnel; good for morale; honest appraisal from in-house supervisor
Employee recommendations	a. Friends, acquaintances, relatives
	b. Value of recommendations depend on honesty and judgment of current employees

personnel, set performance standards, and assign salaries. Thus, department managers often act as the main sales associates for their areas, oversee other sales associates, have some administrative duties, report to the store manager, are eligible for bonuses, and receive $25,000 to $45,000+ annually.

Job analysis should lead to written job descriptions. A **traditional job description** contains a position's title, relationships (superior and subordinate), and specific roles and tasks. Figure 11-4 showed a store manager description. Yet, using a traditional description alone has been criticized. It may limit a job's scope, as well as its authority and responsibility; not let a person grow; limit activities to those listed; and not describe how jobs are coordinated. To complement a traditional description, a **goal-oriented job description** enumerates basic functions, the relationship of each job to overall goals, the interdependence of positions, and information flows. See Figure 11-10.

FIGURE 11-10

A Goal-Oriented Job Description for a Management Trainee

Attributes Required	Ability	Desire	In the Retailing Environment
ANALYTICAL SKILLS: ability to solve problems; strong numerical ability for analysis of facts and data for planning, managing, and controlling.			Retail executives are problem solvers. Knowledge and understanding of past performance and present circumstances form the basis for action and planning.
CREATIVITY: ability to generate and recognize imaginative ideas and solutions; ability to recognize the need for and be responsive to change.			Retail executives are idea people. Successful buying results from sensitive, aware decisions, while merchandising requires imaginative, innovative techniques.
DECISIVENESS: ability to make quick decisions and render judgments, take action, and commit oneself to completion.			Retail executives are action people. Whether it's new fashion trends or customer desires, decisions must be made quickly and confidently in this ever-changing environment.
FLEXIBILITY: ability to adjust to the ever-changing needs of the situation; ability to adapt to different people, places, and things; willingness to do whatever is necessary to get the task done.			Retail executives are flexible. Surprises in retailing never cease. Plans must be altered quickly to accommodate changes in trends, styles, and attitudes, while numerous ongoing activities cannot be ignored.
INITIATIVE: ability to originate action rather than wait to be told what to do and ability to act based on conviction.			Retail executives are doers. Sales volumes, trends, and buying opportunities mean continual action. Opportunities for action must be seized.
LEADERSHIP: ability to inspire others to trust and respect your judgment; ability to delegate and to guide and persuade others.			Retail executives are managers. Running a business means depending on others to get the work done. One person cannot do it all.
ORGANIZATION: ability to establish priorities and courses of action for self and/or others; skill in planning and following up to achieve results.			Retail executives are jugglers. A variety of issues, functions, and projects are constantly in motion. To reach your goals, priorities must be set and work must be delegated to others.
RISK TAKING: willingness to take calculated risks based on thorough analysis and sound judgment and to accept responsibility for the results.			Retail executives are courageous. Success in retailing often comes from taking calculated risks and having the confidence to try something new before someone else does.
STRESS TOLERANCE: ability to perform consistently under pressure, to thrive on constant change and challenge.			Retail executives are resilient. As the above description should suggest, retailing is fast-paced and demanding.

An **application blank** is usually the first tool used to screen applicants; it provides data on education, experience, health, reasons for leaving prior jobs, outside activities, hobbies, and references. It is usually short, requires little interpretation, and can be used as the basis for probing in an interview. With a **weighted application blank**, factors having a high relationship with job success are given more weight than others. Retailers using such a form analyze current and past employee performance and determine the criteria (education, experience, etc.) best correlated with job success (as measured by longer tenure, better performance, etc.). After weighted scores are awarded to all job applicants (based on data they provide), a minimum total score becomes a cutoff point for hiring. An effective application blank aids retailers in lessening turnover and selecting high achievers.

An application blank should be used along with a job description. Those meeting minimum job requirements are processed further; others are immediately rejected. In this way, the application blank provides a quick and inexpensive method of screening.

The interview seeks information that can be amassed only by personal questioning and observation. It lets an employer determine a candidate's verbal ability, note his or her appearance, ask questions keyed to the application, and probe career goals. Interviewing decisions must be made about the level of formality, the number and length of interviews, the location, the person(s) to do the interviewing, and the interview structure. These decisions often depend on the interviewer's ability and the job's requirements.

Small firms tend to hire applicants based on their performance during interviews. Large firms may have multiple stages: candidates who excel at the interview stage may then be required to take psychological tests (to measure personality, intelligence, interest, and leadership), and/or achievement tests (to measure learned knowledge).[19]

Tests must be administered by qualified people. Standardized exams should not be used unless proven effective in predicting job performance. Achievement tests deal with specific skills or information (such as the ability to make a sales presentation), are easier to interpret than psychological tests, and show direct relationships between knowledge and ability. In administering tests, firms must not violate federal, state, and local laws. The federal Employee Polygraph Protection Act bars firms from using lie detector tests in most hiring situations (drugstores are exempt).

CVS (https://jobs.cvshealth .com) encourages potential employees to apply online.

To save time and operate more efficiently, some retailers—large and small—use computerized application blanks and testing. Advance Auto Parts, Babies "R" Us, Best Buy, CVS, Family Tree, Lowe's, and PetSmart are among those with in-store kiosks that allow people to apply for jobs, complete applications, and answer questions. This speeds the process and attracts applicants.

Many retailers get references from applicants that can be checked either before or after an interview. References are contacted to see how enthusiastically they recommend an applicant, check the applicant's honesty, and ask why an applicant left a prior job. Mail and phone checks are inexpensive, fast, and easy.

Some firms require a physical exam because of the physical activity, long hours, and tensions involved in many retailing positions. A clean bill of health means the candidate is offered a job. Again, federal, state, and local laws must be followed.

Each step in the selection process complements the others; together they give the retailer a good information package for choosing personnel. As a rule, retailers should use job descriptions,

TECHNOLOGY IN RETAILING — Job-Listing Web Sites

A number job-listing sites exist, such as www.workinretail .com, http://retail.jobs.careercast.com, www.findtherightjob.com, www.job-application.com, and www.snagajob.com. Although each site has unique features, together they generally offer job descriptions, locations, and more. Job seekers can print out this information; view available positions at multiple retailers; and look up minimum age requirements, hours of operation, and compensation. Some sites provide E-mail alerts about available positions in their geographic areas. Others let job seekers selectively look for jobs in specific fields. Still others allow job applicants to post their résumés. For retailers, these sites also have advantages, including access to a larger applicant pool, the ability to compile and screen applicants on a database, and better matching candidate qualifications with a retailer needs.

Discuss the pros and cons of a job applicant using a job-listing Web site to post résumés.

■

application blanks, interviews, and reference checks. Follow-up interviews, psychological and achievement tests, and physical exams depend on the retailer and the position. Inexpensive tools (such as application blanks) are used in the early screening stages; more costly, in-depth tools (such as interviews) are used after reducing the applicant pool. Equal opportunity, nondiscriminatory practices must be followed.

TRAINING RETAIL PERSONNEL Every new employee should receive **pre-training**, an indoctrination on the firm's history, culture, and policies, job orientation on hours, compensation, the chain of command, and job duties. The term **onboarding** describes the process of integrating new employees into an organization and its culture, and understanding the expectations of their new job. New employees should be introduced to co-workers; encouraged to build relationships with a diverse network of colleagues; and provided with tools, resources, and knowledge to become successful and productive. A well-designed onboarding process may evolve over an entire year—from new employee orientation to continuous improvement. It should be modified for specific job roles and locations and make the employee feel welcome.[20]

Training programs teach new (and existing) personnel how best to perform their jobs or how to improve themselves. Training can range from 1-day sessions on operating a computerized cash register, personal selling techniques, or compliance with affirmative action programs to 2-year programs for executive trainees on all aspects of the retailer and its operations:

▹ For each new employee, Container Store provides extensive formal training, which includes understanding its "Employee First Culture," systems training, and classes on how to perform multiple jobs. Each first-year, full-time employee receives about 260 hours of training. The New Store Trainer program has three phases: pre-training (3 weeks prior to opening), post-support (week of and after grand opening), and post-training (a few weeks after post-support). The training ensures that employees are knowledgeable and empowered to offer the customer service the retailer is known for in the industry.[21]
▹ Best Buy uses an online "Learning Lounge" (www.bestbuylearninglounge.com) to facilitate employee training for new and continuing workers, to keep employees current on the firm's best practices, and to let employees easily communicate with one another. The password-protected portal is under the auspices of Best Buy's Retail Training & Development group, whose slogan is "grow. perform. succeed."

Training should be an ongoing activity. New equipment, legal changes, new product lines, job promotions, low employee morale, and employee turnover necessitate not only training but also retraining. Macy's has a program called "Clienteling," which tutors sales associates on how to have better long-term relations with specific repeat customers. Core vendors of Macy's teach sales associates about the features and benefits of new merchandise when it is introduced.[22]

There are several training decisions, as shown in Figure 11-11. They can be divided into three categories: identifying needs, devising appropriate training methods, and evaluation.

FIGURE 11-11
A Checklist of Selected Training Decisions

✓ When should training occur? (At the time of hiring and/or after being at the workplace?)
✓ How long should training be?
✓ What training programs should there be for new employees? For existing employees?
✓ Who should conduct each training program? (Supervisor, co-worker, training department, or outside specialist?)
✓ Where should training take place? (At the workplace or in a training room?)
✓ What material (content) should be learned? How should it be taught?
✓ Should audiovisuals be used? If yes, how?
✓ Should elements of the training program be computerized? If yes, how?
✓ How should the effectiveness of training be measured?

TABLE 11-4 The Characteristics of Retail Training Methods

Method	Characteristics
Lectures	Factual, uninterrupted presentations of material; can use professional educator or expert in the field; no active participation by trainees
Demonstrations	Good for showing how to use equipment or do a sales presentation; applies relevance of training; active participation by trainees
Videos	Highly visual, good for demonstration; can be used many times; no active participation by trainees
Programmed instruction	Presents information in a structured manner; requires response from trainees; provides performance feedback; adjustable to trainees' pace; high initial investment
Conferences	Useful for supervisory training; conference leaders must encourage participation; reinforce training
Sensitivity training	Extensive interaction; good for supervisors as a tool for understanding employees
Case studies	Actual or hypothetical problems presented, including circumstances, pertinent information, and questions; learning by doing; exposure to a wide variety of problems
Role-playing	Trainees placed into real-life situations and act out roles
Behavior modeling	Trainees taught to imitate models shown in videos or in role-playing sessions
Competency-based instruction	Trainees given a list of tasks or exercises that are presented in a self-paced format

Short-term *training needs* can be identified by measuring the gap between the skills that workers already have and the skills desired by the firm (for each job). This training should prepare employees for possible job rotation, promotions, and changes in the company. A longer training plan lets a firm identify future needs and train workers appropriately.

There are many *training methods* for retailers: lectures, demonstrations, videos, programmed instruction, conferences, sensitivity training, case studies, role-playing, behavior modeling, and competency-based instruction. Some techniques may be computerized, as evidenced by more and more firms.. The attributes of the various training methods are noted in Table 11-4. Retailers often use more than one technique to reduce employee boredom and to cover the material better.

Computer-based training software is available from a variety of vendors. For example, TiER1 Performance Solutions has numerous modules that have been used to train retail employees in such areas as point-of-sales systems, labor scheduling, customer service, manager training, store operations, merchandise management, and more. Among its many clients are CDW, Kroger, Macy's, McDonald's, Petco, and Wendy's.

For training to succeed, a conducive environment is needed, based on several principles:

Take a look at RetailTraining.com's training solutions (www.retailtraining.com).

- All people can learn if taught well; there should be a sense of achievement.
- A person learns better when motivated; intelligence alone is not sufficient.
- Learning should be goal-oriented.
- A trainee learns more when he or she participates and is not a passive listener.
- The teacher must provide guidance, as well as adapt to the learner and to the situation.
- Learning should be approached as a series of steps rather than a one-time occurrence.
- Learning should be spread out over a reasonable period of time rather than be compressed.
- The learner should be encouraged to do homework or otherwise practice.
- Different methods of learning should be combined.
- Performance standards should be set and good performance recognized.

A training program must be regularly evaluated. Comparisons can be made between the performance of those who receive training and those who do not, as well as among employees receiving different types of training for the same job. *Evaluations* should always be made in relation to stated training goals. In addition, training effects should be measured over different time intervals (such as immediately, 30 days later, and 6 months later), and proper records maintained.

COMPENSATING RETAIL PERSONNEL   Total **compensation**—direct monetary payments (salaries, commissions, and bonuses) and indirect payments (paid vacations, health and life insurance, and retirement plans)—should be fair to both the retailer and its employees. To better motivate employees, some firms also have a profit-sharing plan. Smaller retailers often pay salaries, commissions, and/or bonuses and have fewer fringe benefits. Bigger ones generally pay salaries, commissions, and/or bonuses and offer more fringe benefits.

This site (www.dol.gov/whd/minwage/america.htm) shows the minimum wage in every state.

Although the hourly federal minimum wage has been $7.25 since July 2009, 45 states have their own laws—29 are higher than the federal minimum and two are lower. In 2016, the highest minimum wage was in Washington, D.C. ($11.50), and in these states: California and Massachusetts ($10.00); Alaska, ($9.75); and Connecticut, Rhode Island, and Vermont ($9.60). Some states and cities are phasing in a minimum wage as high as $15.00 per hour. The minimum wage has the most impact on retailers hiring entry-level, part-time workers. Full-time, career-track retailing jobs are typically paid an attractive market rate; to attract part-time workers in good economic times, retailers must often pay salaries above the minimum.

At some firms, compensation for certain positions is set through collective bargaining. According to the U.S. Bureau of Labor Statistics, 825,000 retail employees are represented by labor unions. Yet, union membership varies greatly. Unionized grocery stores account for more than one-half of total U.S. supermarket sales, whereas independent supermarkets are not usually unionized.

With a *straight salary*, a worker is paid a fixed amount per hour, week, month, or year. Advantages are retailer control, employee security, and known expenses. Disadvantages are retailer inflexibility, the limited productivity incentive, and fixed costs. Clerks and cashiers are usually paid salaries. With a *straight commission*, earnings are directly tied to productivity (such as sales volume). Advantages are retailer flexibility, the link to worker productivity, no fixed costs, and employee incentive. Disadvantages are the retailer's potential lack of control over the tasks performed, the risk of low earnings to employees, cost variability, and the lack of limits on worker earnings. Sales personnel for autos, real-estate, furniture, jewelry, and other expensive items are often paid a straight commission—as are direct-selling personnel.

To combine the attributes of salary and commission plans, retailers may pay employees a *salary plus commission*. Shoe salespeople, major appliance salespeople, and some management personnel are among those paid this way. Sometimes, bonuses supplement salary and/or commission, usually for outstanding performance. At Finish Line footwear and apparel stores, regional, district, and store managers receive salaries and earn bonuses based on sales, payroll size, and theft goals. In certain cases, executives are paid via a "compensation cafeteria" and choose their own combination of salary, bonus, fringe benefits, life insurance, stock, and retirement benefits.

Sears (http://jobs.sears.com/why-choose-us/benefits) has a good benefits package.

A thorny issue facing retailers today involves the benefits portion of employee compensation, especially as related to pensions and health care. It is a challenging time due to intense price competition, the use of part-time workers, and escalating medical costs as retailers try to balance their employees' needs with company financial needs.

SUPERVISING RETAIL PERSONNEL **Supervision** is the manner of providing a job environment that encourages employee accomplishment. The goals are to oversee personnel, attain good performance, maintain morale, motivate people, control costs, communicate, and resolve problems. Supervision is provided by personal contact, meetings, and reports.

Every firm wants to continually motivate employees so as to harness their energy on behalf of the retailer and achieve its goals. **Job motivation** is the drive within people to attain work-related goals. It may be positive or negative. These questions can be used to help predict employee behavior, based on their motivation:

- Do you like the work you do? Does it give you a sense of accomplishment?
- Are you proud to say you work with us?
- Does the work expected from you influence your overall job attitude? How?
- Do physical working conditions influence your overall job attitude? How?
- Does the way you are treated by your boss affect your job attitude?
- Do you understand the firm's strategy?
- Do you see a connection between your work and the firm's strategic goals?[23]

Employee motivation should be approached from two perspectives: What job-related factors cause employees to be satisfied or dissatisfied with their positions? What supervision style is best for both the retailer and its employees? See Figure 11-12.

Each employee looks at job satisfaction in terms of minimum expectations ("dissatisfiers") and desired goals ("satisfiers"). A motivated employee requires fulfillment of both factors.

CAREERS IN RETAILING

Buyer Training

Retail buying is often viewed as an exciting job, especially when the goods bought for resale correspond to an employee's area of interest. For example, many fashion-oriented students are attracted to an apparel buying position and avid computer users may seek buying positions in electronics. Buyer training generally focuses on technical aspects of buying (such as how to evaluate the quality of hand-made carpets for a carpet buyer), negotiating skills (setting discounts, markdowns, and credit terms), and understanding open-to-buy calculations (that reconcile inventory and demand). Some retailers have formal training programs, others offer on-the-job training where junior buyers receive additional responsibilities over time.

What do you think are the attributes of a good retail buying program?

■

Minimum expectations relate mostly to the job environment, including a safe workplace; equitable treatment for those with the same jobs; some flexibility in company policies (such as not docking pay if a person is 10 minutes late); an even-tempered boss; some freedom in attire; a fair compensation package; basic fringe benefits (such as vacation time and medical coverage); clear communications; and job security. These elements can generally influence motivation in only one way—negatively. If minimum expectations are not met, an employee will be unhappy. If these expectations are met, they are taken for granted and do little to motivate the person to go "above and beyond."

Desired goals relate more to the job than to the work environment. They are based on whether an employee likes the job, is recognized for good performance, feels a sense of achievement, is empowered to make decisions, is trusted, has a defined career path, receives extra compensation when performance is exceptional, and is given the chance to learn and grow. These elements can have a huge impact on job satisfaction and motivate a person to go "above and beyond." Nonetheless, if minimum expectations are not met, an employee might still be dissatisfied enough to leave, even if the job is quite rewarding.

There are three basic styles of supervising retail employees:

▶ Management assumes that employees must be closely supervised and controlled and that only economic inducements really motivate. Management further believes that the average worker

FIGURE 11-12

Demotivated Employees Result in Lower Productivity

Today, many older adults work in retailing— to supplement their retirement benefits, to be active, and/or to be in a social setting. It is important that these workers be treated with respect and not be placed into menial, boring jobs that do not make use of their skill set. If they are unhappy, it may rub off on customers.

Source: Lisa F. Young/ Shutterstock. Reprinted by permission.

lacks ambition, dislikes responsibility, and prefers to be led. This is the traditional view of motivation and has been applied to lower-level retail positions.

▷ Management assumes employees can be self-managers and assigned authority, motivation is social and psychological, and supervision can be decentralized and participatory. Management also thinks that motivation, the capacity for assuming responsibility, and a readiness to achieve company goals exist in people. The critical supervisory task is to create an environment so people achieve their goals by attaining company objectives. This is a more modern view and applies to all levels of personnel.

▷ Management applies a self-management approach and also advocates more employee involvement in defining jobs and sharing overall decision making. There is mutual loyalty between the firm and its workers, and both parties enthusiastically cooperate for the long-term benefit of each. This is also a modern view and applies to all levels of personnel.

It is imperative to motivate employees in a manner that yields job satisfaction, low turnover, low absenteeism, and high productivity. Research in organizational behavior on employee motivation suggests that trade-offs among command, autonomy, respect for employees' need for self-determination and economic incentives can improve employee intrinsic motivation and performance. Some suggestions include: (1) Empower employees to solve problems. (2) Ask employees for their input. (3) Regularly communicate with employees about how they are doing. (4) Delegate tasks. (5) Encourage new ideas from employees. (6) Let employees learn from their mistakes without being unduly harsh. (7) Show employees what is needed for promotions. (8) Provide public recognition of good performance. (9) Seek employee input on company goals and how to achieve them.[24]

Chapter Summary

1. *To study the procedures involved in setting up a retail organization.* A retail organization structures and assigns tasks, policies, resources, authority, responsibilities, and rewards to satisfy the needs of its target market, employees, and management. There are five steps in setting up an organization: outlining specific tasks to be performed in a distribution channel, dividing tasks, grouping tasks into jobs, classifying jobs, and integrating positions with an organization chart.

   Specific tasks include buying, shipping, receiving and checking, pricing, and marking merchandise; inventory control; display preparation; facilities maintenance; research; customer contact and follow-up; and a lot more. These tasks may be divided among retailers, manufacturers, wholesalers, specialists, and customers.

   Tasks are next grouped into jobs, such as sales personnel, cashiers, inventory personnel, display personnel, customer service personnel, and management. Then jobs are arranged by functional, product, geographic, or combination classification. An organization chart displays the hierarchy of authority and the relationship among jobs, and it helps coordinates personnel.

2. *To examine the various organizational arrangements utilized in retailing.* Retail organization structures differ by institution. Small independents use simple formats with little specialization. Many department stores use a version of the Mazur plan and place functions into

store management, communications, merchandising, and financial accounting. The equal store format is used by numerous chain stores. Diversified firms have very complex organizations.

3. *To consider the special human resource environment of retailing.* Retailers are unique due to the large number of inexperienced workers, long hours, employee visibility, a diverse work force, many part-time workers, and variations in customer demand. There is a broad range of career opportunities available to women and minorities, although improvement is still needed.

4. *To describe the principles and practices involved with the human resource management process in retailing.* This process comprises several interrelated activities: recruitment, selection, training, compensation, and supervision. In applying the process, diversity, labor laws, and employee privacy should be kept in mind.

   Recruitment generates job applicants. Sources include educational institutions, channel members, competitors, ads, employment agencies, unsolicited applicants, employees, and Web sites (including social media).

   Personnel selection requires thorough job analysis, creating job descriptions, using application blanks, interviews, testing (optional), reference checking, and physical exams. After personnel are selected, they go through pre-training and job training. Good training identifies needs, uses proper methods, and assesses results. Training is usually vital for continuing, as well as new, personnel.

Employees are compensated by direct monetary payments and/or indirect payments. The direct compensation plans are straight salary, straight commission, and salary plus commission and/or bonus. Indirect payments involve such items as paid vacations, health benefits, and retirement plans.

Proper supervision is needed to sustain superior employee performance. A main task is employee motivation. The causes of job satisfaction/dissatisfaction and the supervisory style must be reviewed.

Key Terms

retail organization (p. 293)
hierarchy of authority (p. 297)
organization chart (p. 297)
Mazur plan (p. 298)
equal store organization (p. 300)
diversified retailer (p. 300)
human resource management (p. 301)

human resource management
      process (p. 305)
recruitment (p. 306)
job analysis (p. 306)
traditional job description (p. 307)
goal-oriented job description (p. 307)
application blank (p. 308)

weighted application blank (p. 308)
pre-training (p. 309)
onboarding (p. 309)
training programs (p. 309)
compensation (p. 310)
supervision (p. 311)
job motivation (p. 311)

Questions for Discussion

1. Cite at least five objectives a large fitness center chain should establish when setting up its organization structure.
2. Why are employee needs important in developing a retail organization?
3. Are the steps involved in setting up a retail organization the same for small and large retailers? Explain your answer.
4. Describe the greatest similarities and differences in the organization structures of small independents, chain retailers, and diversified retailers.
5. How can retailers attract and retain more women and minority workers?
6. How would small and large retailers act differently for each of the following?
   a. Diversity
   b. Recruitment
   c. Selection
   d. Training
   e. Compensation
   f. Supervision
7. Why are the job description and the application blank so important in employee selection?
8. What is the purpose of the document derived from the process of job analysis?
9. In a retail environment, how would you distinguish between pre-training and on-boarding? Why are they both necessary?
10. Distinguish between straight salary and straight commission, identifying the pros and cons of each form of compensation.
11. How would you describe the minimum expectations of an employee that are fundamental to their job satisfaction? Explain your answers.
12. If you were a retail store manager, what steps might you take to empower your workers?

Web-Based Exercise

Visit the career-based Web site that Debenhams has dedicated to graduate and non-graduate careers (http://debenhams-careers.com/). The department store chain has been operating for 200 years. What do you think of this site as a mechanism for attracting new graduates and non-graduates to the company?

12 Operations Management: Financial Dimensions

Retailers are always on the lookout for ways to improve their financial performance by more efficiently handling their operations. The intense competitive retail landscape, increasing consumer expectations for higher levels of service, and lower prices make financial budgeting for retail operations a critical function in squeezing out costs and improving productivity.

Two approaches to developing budgets are incremental and zero-based. With *incremental budgeting*, a retailer uses prior budgets as a base line and adjusts prior budget numbers to reflect inflation, competition, and other factors. In *zero-based budgeting*, every expense item needs to be justified. For example, a store renovation budgeted number would get high scrutiny on the basis of a number of questions. Financial managers would question the materials used, the need to close the store for renovations, whether carpeting can remain for another year, and so on.

Advocates for zero-based budgeting argue that it has several major advantages over incremental budgeting. A fundamental premise of incremental budgeting is that the initial

Chapter Objectives

1. To define operations management

2. To discuss profit planning

3. To describe asset management, including the strategic profit model, other key business ratios, and financial trends in retailing

4. To look at retail budgeting

5. To examine resource allocation

Source: suravid/Shutterstock. Reprinted by permission.

budget was prudent. This may not be the case, however. Zero-based budgeting elicits a cost containment, cost-conscious philosophy. A zero-based budget may arrive at new and innovative solutions as opposed to a "doing it the old way" mentality. Zero-based budgeting is an effective way of getting different functional areas (operations, buying, and finance) to work together and to better understand a business from a cross-functional perspective. Nonetheless, because of its ease of usage and lesser time commitment, many retailers continue to engage in incremental budgeting.

Overview

After devising an organization structure and a human resource plan, a retailer concentrates on **operations management**—the efficient and effective implementation of the policies and tasks necessary to satisfy the firm's customers, employees, and management (and stockholders, if a public company). This has a major impact on sales and profits. High inventory levels, long hours, expensive fixtures, extensive customer services, and widespread advertising may lead to higher revenues. But at what cost? If a store pays night-shift workers a 25 percent premium, is opening 24 hours a day worthwhile (i.e., do higher sales justify the costs and add to overall profit)?

This chapter covers the financial aspects of operations management, with emphasis on profit planning, asset management, budgeting, and resource allocation. The operational dimensions of operations management are explored in detail in Chapter 13. A number of posts about financial operations may be found at our blog (www.bermanevansretail.com).

PROFIT PLANNING

Learn more about the profit-and-loss statement (www.handsonbanking.org/biz/?p=212).

A **profit-and-loss (income) statement** is a summary of a retailer's revenues and expenses over a given period of time, usually a month, quarter, or year. It lets the firm review overall and specific revenues and costs for similar periods (such as January 1, 2016, to December 31, 2016, versus January 1, 2015, to December 31, 2015) and analyze profits. With frequent statements, a firm can monitor progress on goals, update performance estimates, and revise strategies and tactics.

In comparing profit-and-loss performance over time, it is crucial that the same time periods be used (such as the third quarter of 2016 compared with the third quarter of 2015) due to seasonality. Some fiscal years may have an unequal number of weeks (53 weeks one year versus 51 weeks another). Retailers that open new stores or expand existing stores between accounting periods should also take into account the larger facilities. Yearly results should reflect total revenue growth and the rise in same-store sales.

A profit-and-loss statement consists of several major components:

- ▶ **Net sales** The revenues received by a retailer during a given period after deducting customer returns, markdowns, and employee discounts.
- ▶ **Cost of goods sold** The amount a retailer pays to acquire the merchandise sold during a given time period. It is based on purchase prices and freight charges, less all discounts (such as quantity, cash, and promotion).
- ▶ **Gross profit (margin)** The difference between net sales and the cost of goods sold. It consists of operating expenses plus net profit.
- ▶ **Operating expenses** The cost of running a retail business.
- ▶ **Taxes** The portion of revenues turned over to the federal, state, and/or local government.
- ▶ **Net profit after taxes** The profit earned after all costs and taxes have been deducted.

Table 12-1 shows the most recent annual profit-and-loss statement for Donna's Gift Shop, an independent retailer. The firm uses a fiscal year (September 1 to August 31) rather than a calendar year in preparing its accounting reports. These observations can be drawn from the table:

- ▶ Annual net sales were $330,000—after deducting returns, markdowns on the items sold, and employee discounts from total sales.
- ▶ The cost of goods sold was $180,000, computed by taking the total purchases for merchandise sold, adding freight, and subtracting quantity, cash, and promotion discounts.

TABLE 12-1 Donna's Gift Shop, Fiscal 2016 Profit-and-Loss Statement

Net sales	$330,000
Cost of goods sold	$180,000
Gross profit	$150,000
Operating expenses	
Salaries	$ 75,000
Advertising	4,950
Supplies	1,650
Shipping	1,500
Insurance	4,500
Maintenance	5,100
Other	2,550
Total	$ 95,250
Other costs	$ 20,000
Total costs	$115,250
Net profit before taxes	$ 34,750
Taxes	$ 15,500
Net profit after taxes	$ 19,250

- Gross profit was $150,000, calculated by subtracting the cost of goods sold from net sales. This went for operating and other expenses, taxes, and profit.
- Operating expenses totaled $95,250, including salaries, advertising, supplies, shipping, insurance, maintenance, and other expenses.
- Unassigned costs were $20,000.
- Net profit before taxes was $34,750, computed by deducting total costs from gross profit. The tax bill was $15,500, leaving a net profit after taxes of $19,250.

Overall, fiscal 2016 was pretty good for Donna; her personal salary was $43,000 and the store's after-tax profit was $19,250. A further analysis of Donna's Gift Shop's profit-and-loss statement appears in the budgeting section of this chapter.

ASSET MANAGEMENT

Look at the Accounting Coach's balance sheet discussion (www.accountingcoach.com/balance-sheet/explanation).

Each retailer has assets to manage and liabilities to control. This section covers the balance sheet, the strategic profit model, and other ratios. A **balance sheet** itemizes a retailer's assets, liabilities, and net worth at a specific time—based on the principle that Assets = Liabilities + Net worth. Table 12-2 has a balance sheet for Donna's Gift Shop.

Assets are any items a retailer owns with a monetary value. Current assets are cash on hand (or in the bank) and items readily converted to cash, such as inventory on hand and accounts receivable (amounts owed to the firm). Fixed assets are property, buildings (a store, warehouse, etc.), fixtures, and equipment such as cash registers and trucks; these are used for a long period. The major fixed asset for many retailers is real-estate. Unlike current assets, which are recorded at cost, fixed assets are recorded at cost less accumulated depreciation. Thus, records may not reflect the true value of these assets. Many retailing analysts use the term **hidden assets** to describe depreciated assets, such as buildings and warehouses, that are noted on a retail balance sheet at low values relative to their actual worth.

Liabilities are financial obligations a retailer incurs in operating a business. Current liabilities are payroll expenses payable, taxes payable, accounts payable (amounts owed to suppliers), and short-term loans; these must be paid in the coming year. Fixed liabilities comprise mortgages and long-term loans; these are generally repaid over several years.

A retailer's **net worth** is computed as assets minus liabilities. It is also called owner's equity and represents the value of a business after deducting all financial obligations.

TABLE 12-2 A Retail Balance Sheet for Donna's Gift Shop (as of August 31, 2016)

Assets		Liabilities	
Current		Current	
Cash on hand	$ 19,950	Payroll expenses payable	$ 6,000
Inventory	36,150	Taxes payable	13,500
Accounts receivable	1,650	Accounts payable	32,100
Total	$ 57,750	Short-term loan	1,050
		Total	$ 52,650
Fixed (present value)			
Property	$187,500	Fixed	
Building	63,000	Mortgage	$ 97,500
Store fixtures	14,550	Long-term loan	6,750
Equipment	2,550	Total	$104,250
Total	$267,600	Total liabilities	$156,900
Total assets	$325,350		
		Net worth	$168,450
		Liabilities + net worth net worth	$325,350

In operations management, the retailer's goal is to use its assets in the manner providing the best results possible. There are three basic ways to measure those results: net profit margin, asset turnover, and financial leverage. Each component is discussed next.

Net profit margin is a performance measure based on a retailer's net profit and net sales:

$$\text{Net profit margin} = \frac{\text{Net profit alter taxes}}{\text{Net sales}}$$

At Donna's Gift Shop, fiscal year 2016 net profit margin was 5.83 percent—a very good percentage for a gift shop. To enhance its net profit margin, a retailer must either raise gross profit as a percentage of sales or reduce expenses as a percentage of sales.[1] It could lift gross profit by purchasing opportunistically, selling exclusive products, avoiding price competition through excellent service, and adding items with higher margins. It could reduce operating costs by stressing self-service, lowering labor costs, refinancing the mortgage, cutting energy costs, and so on. The firm must be careful not to lessen customer service to the extent that sales and profit would decline.

Asset turnover is a performance measure based on a retailer's net sales and total assets:

$$\text{Asset turnover} = \frac{\text{Net sales}}{\text{Total assets}}$$

Donna's Gift Shop had a very low asset turnover, 1.0143—meaning it averaged $1.01 in sales per dollar of total assets. To improve the asset turnover ratio, a firm must generate increased sales from the same level of assets or keep the same sales with fewer assets. A firm might increase sales by having longer hours, accepting online orders, training employees to sell additional products, or stocking better-known brands. None of these tactics requires expanding the asset base. Or a firm might maintain its sales on a lower asset base by moving to a smaller store, simplifying fixtures (or having suppliers install fixtures), keeping a lower inventory, and negotiating for the property owner to pay part of the costs of a renovation.

By looking at the relationship between net profit margin and asset turnover, **return on assets (ROA)** can be computed:

$$\text{Return on assets} = \text{Net profit margin} \times \text{Asset turnover}$$

$$= \frac{\text{Net profit after taxes}}{\text{Net sales}} \times \frac{\text{Net sales}}{\text{Total assets}}$$

$$= \frac{\text{Net profit after taxes}}{\text{Total assets}}$$

Ikea's Global Results

After 2 years of slow growth, Ikea sales rose 11.2 percent in its 2015 fiscal year. Sales grew fastest in China and Russia, with sales growth in Germany at a record level. Same-store U.S. sales growth was 4.5 percent. Of the 13 stores it opened in 2015, only one was in the United States. The remaining 12 were in China, Germany, France, South Korea, the Netherlands, Norway, Australia, and Poland. Despite being the world's largest furniture chain, Ikea's market is far from being saturated. With stores in 28 countries, Ikea still has no presence in many markets. Although online sales exceeded $1 billion Euros in 2015, Ikea currently offers online shopping in only 13 of its 28 country locations.

Discuss how Ikea should assess opportunities for new stores on a global basis.

Source: Based on material in the *Ikea Yearly Summary Fiscal Year 2015*, www.Ikea.com/us/en.

Donna's Gift Shop had an ROA of 5.9 percent (0.0583 × 1.0143 = 0.059). This return is below average for gift stores; the good net profit margin does not adequately offset low asset turnover.

Financial leverage is a performance measure based on the relationship between a retailer's total assets and net worth:

$$\text{Financial leverage} = \frac{\text{Total assets}}{\text{Net worth}}$$

Donna's Gift Shop's financial leverage ratio was 1.9314. Assets were just under twice the net worth, and total liabilities and net worth were almost equal. This ratio was slightly lower than the average for gift stores (a conservative group). The store is in no danger.

A retailer with a high financial leverage ratio has substantial debt. A ratio of 1 means it has no debt—assets equal net worth. If the ratio is too high, there may be an excessive focus on cost-cutting and short-run sales so as to make interest payments, net profit margins may suffer, and a firm may be forced into bankruptcy if debts cannot be paid. When financial leverage is low, a retailer may be overly conservative—limiting its ability to renovate and expand existing stores and to enter new markets. Leverage is too low if the owner's equity is relatively high; equity could be partly replaced by increasing short- and long-term loans and/or accounts payable. Some equity funds could be taken out of a business by the owner (stockholders, if a public firm).

The Strategic Profit Model

The relationship among net profit margin, asset turnover, and financial leverage is expressed by the **strategic profit model**, which reflects a performance measure known as **return on net worth (RONW)**. See Figure 12-1. The strategic profit model can be used to plan and/or control assets. Thus, a retailer could learn the major cause of its poor return on net worth is weak asset turnover or financial leverage that is too low. A firm can raise its return on net worth by lifting the net profit margin, asset turnover, or financial leverage. Because these measures are multiplied to determine return on net worth, doubling *any* of them would double the return on net worth.

This is how the strategic profit model can be applied to Donna's Gift Shop.

$$
\begin{aligned}
\text{Return on net worth} &= \frac{\text{Net profit after taxes}}{\text{Net sales}} \times \frac{\text{Net sales}}{\text{Total assets}} \times \frac{\text{Total assets}}{\text{Net worth}} \\
&= \frac{\$19,250}{\$330,000} \times \frac{\$330,000}{\$325,350} \times \frac{\$325,350}{\$168,450} \\
&= 0.0583 \times 1.0143 \times 1.9314 \\
&= 0.1142 = 11.4\%
\end{aligned}
$$

FIGURE 12-1
The Strategic Profit Model

TABLE 12-3 Application of Strategic Profit Model to Selected Retailers (2015 Data)

Retailer	Net Profit Margin	×	Asset Turnover	×	Financial Leverage	=	Return on Net Worth
Apparel Retailers							
TJX	7.61%		2.61		2.61		51.94%
Gap, Inc.	7.67%		2.14		2.58		42.31%
Consumer Electronics Retailers							
Best Buy	3.09%		2.64		3.05		24.92%
Drugstore Retailers							
Walgreens Boots	4.14%		1.50		2.23		13.87%
CVS Health	3.42%		1.64		2.52		14.08%
Food Retailers							
Publix	6.07%		1.98		1.32		15.80%
Safeway	0.03%		2.72		2.45		2.08%
General Merchandise Retailers							
Walmart	3.55%		2.37		2.37		19.90%
Target	−2.25%		1.75		2.96		−11.69%
Sears Holdings	−5.80%		2.36		−13.98		−191.53%
Costco	2.05%		3.47		3.15		22.39%
Macy's, Inc.	5.43%		1.31		3.99		28.36%
J. C. Penney	−6.29%		1.18		5.44		−40.28%
Home Improvement Retailers							
Home Depot	7.63%		2.08		4.29		68.06%
Lowe's	4.80%		1.77		3.19		27.07%
Office Supplies Retailers							
Staples	0.60%		2.18		1.94		2.53%
Office Depot	−2.02%		2.35		4.22		−21.71%

Note: There are small rounding errors.

Source: Computed by the authors based on data in company annual reports.

Overall, Donna's return on net worth was above average for gift stores.

Table 12-3 applies the strategic profit model to various retailers. It is best to compare firms within given retail categories. For example, net profit margins of general merchandise retailers have historically been higher than those of food retailers. Because financial performance differs each year, caution is advised in studying these data. Furthermore, the individual components of the strategic profit model must be analyzed, not just the return on net worth. For example,

Visit this site (www .inventorycurve.com/ Strategic_Profit_Model .html) to learn more about the strategic profit model.

▸ TJX had the highest return on net worth among all 17 retailers shown in Table 12-3. Its net profit margin was slightly lower than Gap, Inc., but its asset turnover was quite strong. TJX was also slightly more financially leveraged than Gap, Inc.

▸ Sears Holdings (including Sears and Kmart) had a very weak return on net worth. Its financial leverage and profit margin were especially weak.

▸ Staples outperformed Office Depot. It had a stronger profit margin and was not as leveraged.

Other Key Business Ratios

Additional ratios can also measure retailer success or failure in reaching performance goals. Here are several key business ratios—besides those covered in the preceding discussion:

▸ *Quick ratio:* Cash plus accounts receivable divided by total current liabilities, those due within one year. A ratio above 1-to-1 means the firm is liquid and can cover short-term debt.

The Census Bureau, online, provides more than a decade of gross profit (gross margin) percentage data by line of business (http://www2.census.gov/ retail/releases/current/arts/ gmper.xls).

► *Current ratio:* Total current assets (cash, accounts receivable, inventories, and marketable securities) divided by total current liabilities. A ratio of 2-to-1 or more is good.

► *Collection period:* Acounts receivable divided by net sales and then multiplied by 365. If most sales are on credit, a collection period one-third or more over normal terms (such as 40.0 for a store with 30-day credit terms) means slow-turning receivables.

► *Accounts payable to net sales:* Accounts payable divided by annual net sales. This compares how a retailer pays suppliers relative to volume transacted. A figure above the industry average indicates that a firm relies on suppliers to finance operations.

► *Overall gross profit:* Net sales minus the cost of goods sold and then divided by net sales. This companywide average includes markdowns, discounts, and shortages.[2]

For any retailer, large or small, the goal is to do as well as possible on these key business ratios. Areas of weakness must be identified and corrected for the firm to enhance its long-term results—and to avoid negative financial results. Table 12-4 describes ways to improve perfor mance for each of the preceding ratios, as well as asset turnover and return on net worth.

Financial Trends in Retailing

Several trends relating to asset management merit discussion: the state of the economy; funding sources (including initial public offerings); mergers, consolidations, and spin-offs; bankruptcies and liquidations; and questionable accounting and financial reporting practices.

Entrepreneur's "Finance" section (www.entrepreneur .com/topic/finance) has a lot of valuable advice for small businesses.

Many retailers are affected by the strength or weakness of the *economy*. During a strong economy, high consumer demand may mask retailer weaknesses. But when the economy is weak, sales stagnate, cash flow problems may occur, heavy markdowns may be needed (which cut profit margins), consumers are more reluctant to buy big-ticket items, and public firms may see their stock prices adversely affected.

The housing recession in 2008 and the shallow economic recovery that followed saw deep discounting by retailers to lure customers to stores and malls in order to increase revenues, which hurt profitability. It also conditioned shoppers to expect discounts every time they purchased or they would not shop at all. Many people have remained frugal despite the recovery and continue

TABLE 12-4 Selected Ways for a Retailer to Improve Its Key Business Ratios

Ratios	Causes of Poor Performance	Suggestions to Improve Performance
Quick ratio	Too low a quick ratio indicates too much current liabilities relative to cash and accounts receivable.	Reduce current liabilities by outsourcing delivery and installation, leasing equipment (instead of purchasing), and turning over inventory more quickly.
Current ratio	Too low a current ratio indicates too much current liabilities relative to cash, accounts receivable, inventories, and marketable securities	Reduce current liabilities. Consider outsourcing delivery and installation, as well as leasing equipment (instead of purchasing).
Collection period	Too long a collection period indicates too many slow-paying accounts.	Increase payment requirements for store-credit accounts and encourage marginal shoppers to use debit cards, layaway programs, and bank cards.
Accounts payable to net sales	Too high an accounts-payable-to-net-sales ratio indicates that a firm heavily relies on suppliers to finance inventories.	Increase inventory turnover of key items by reducing slow-turnover items, paying accounts payable on time, and purchasing more goods on consignment.
Overall gross profit margin	Too low an overall gross profit margin indicates a combination of low net sales and a high cost of goods sold.	Increase profit margins through better negotiation with vendors to reduce the cost of goods sold, lessen the use of discounting, avoid "meeting the price" of competition tactics, and better focus on merchandise with higher profit margins (such as private-label items).
Asset turnover	Too low an asset turnover indicates insufficient sales per dollar of assets.	Improve asset turnover by extending store hours, using central warehousing, outsourcing delivery and other services, and leasing instead of purchasing.
Return on net worth	Too low a return on net worth indicates insufficient profit as a percent of net worth.	Increase gross profit (through better negotiation and by selling a mix of more profitable goods) and lower operating expenses (by eliminating costly services that are not valued by consumers).

to trade down to lower-priced retailers, online retailing, and off-price and discount stores.[3] The disruptive effect of online retailing has further eroded retailer profitability. To stay competitive, many retailers are making investments in upgraded supply chains, digital marketing, information technology (both in-store and systemwide), and logistics to implement omnichannel strategies.[4] Margins remain under pressure from discounting, free shipping, price matching, greater expenses for ads, the high level of online returns, and expanded store hours.

Three sources of *funding* are important to retailers. First, because interest rates have remained low, many firms have sought to refinance their mortgages and leases—which can dramatically decrease their monthly payments. Even though funding has sometimes been tight, due to the tougher restrictions imposed by the financial markets, retailers retained some leverage. The weak economy led to many retail store vacancies and the rental marketplace has still not fully bounced back. Further, prior to the recession, retail developers overbuilt, which created even more vacancies. Although commercial property prices have been steadily increasing since 2008, they have now started to plateau despite tight supply.[5]

Second, shopping center developers often use a retail real-estate investment trust (REIT) to fund construction. With this strategy, investors buy shares in a REIT as they would a stock. Until the 2008 recession, investors favored REITs because property had historically been a good investment. Then, during the worst of the economic decline, many REITs struggled and their value fell. Nonetheless, the long-term forecast for REITs is good. Most REITS own strip malls and suburban shopping centers that fare better during recessions than tied to apartments or office space, and they typically have higher returns when domestic consumer spending rise. The limited supply of shopping center space in choice areas, the ability to raise rents, and the safe and relatively high yields of 2 to 4 percent that a typical REIT investor gets make them a desired investment vehicle.[6]

Third, a funding source that has gained retailing acceptance over the past 30 years is the initial public offering (IPO), whereby a privately-owned firm raises money by becoming public and selling stock. An IPO is typically used to fund expansion. What do investors look for in an IPO? Retailers with sustained high growth rates or profitability or preferably both, with unique goods or services, in markets with high barriers to entry are more likely to succeed. Retailers preparing to go public need to weigh the risks of public scrutiny of strategies, actions, and security regulations versus the rewards of such a move. In considering an IPO, retailers need to look beyond the current business landscape and evaluate the long-term profitability of being publicly traded. Despite a lackluster IPO market in 2015, retail IPOs performed better than the market average with such firms as Duluth Holdings, Etsy, Ollie's Bargain Outlet Holdings, Shopify, and Xcel going public.[7]

Mergers and consolidations represent a way for retailers to add to their asset base without building new facilities or waiting for new business units to turn a profit. They also present a way for weak retailers to receive financial transfusions. For example, in the last several years, Dick's Sporting Goods acquired Gaylan's, TD Bank acquired Commerce Bancorp, Dollar Tree acquired Family Dollar, and Foot Locker acquired Foot Action. These deals were driven by the relative weakness of the acquired firms. Typically, mergers and consolidations lead to some stores being shut, particularly those with trading-area overlap, and cutbacks among management personnel.

The leveraged buyout (LBO) is a type of acquisition in which a retail ownership change is mostly financed by loans from banks, investors, and others. The LBO phenomenon has had a big effect on retail budgeting and cash flow. At times, because debts incurred with LBOs can be high, some well-known retailers have had to focus more on paying interest on their debts than on investing in their businesses, run sales to generate enough cash to cover operating costs and buy new goods, and sell store units to pay off debt. Two major retailers involved with LBOs were weakened: Toys "R" Us and Barneys New York.

Retailers sometimes consolidate their businesses to streamline operations and improve profits. Winn-Dixie, Eddie Bauer, Kmart, Macy's, Pier 1, Michaels, Sears, and many others have shut underperforming stores. Other times, retailers use *spin-offs* to generate more money or to sell a division that no longer meets expectations. Many retailers (Macy's, Life Time Fitness, etc.) and restaurant chains (Darden, Bob Evans, etc.) spin off their real-estate to REITs or external investors and then lease them back.[8] Retailers may spin off a division for strategic reasons. For example, eBay spun off PayPal, its online payments division, because technology advances, growth opportunities, and challenges for the two business had diverged. As two standalone firms, each is now able to compete more effectively in its respective market.[9] Unlike a retail-estate spin-off, a business unit spin-off or split does not generate additional funds.[10] Hot Topic, a popular national retailer that sells music and pop culture-inspired clothes and accessories for young women spun off Torrid, which sells plus-size goth, rave, and punk clothing.[11] Supervalu, the grocery retailer is spinning off its discount retail chain Save-A-Lot.[12]

When they want to continue in business, weak retailers file Chapter 11. If they want to liquidate, they file Chapter 7 (www.uscourts .gov/services-forms/ bankruptcy).

To safeguard against mounting debts, as well as to continue in business, faltering retailers may seek *bankruptcy* protection under Chapter 11 of the Federal Bankruptcy Code (which was toughened in 2005). In November 2006, when the economy was quite strong, only 3.8 percent of the large retailers tracked by a turnaround consulting firm were facing a high possibility of bankruptcy or financial distress. By November 2008, the figure had risen to 25.8 percent.[13] Today, the figure is much lower (closer to pre-recession percentages), but rising in the retail sector.[14]

With bankruptcy protection, retailers can renegotiate bills, get out of leases, and work with creditors to plan for the future. Declaring bankruptcy has major ramifications: disruptions in supply (cash payment for stock purchased 20 days prior to bankruptcy); loss of key executives and demoralization of those who stay; short time frame to reorganize or sell stores; emergency liquidation of stock in stores that are trimmed; and the legal and financial advisory fees of bankruptcy protection. Chapter 11 bankruptcy fends off creditors and lets firms pay off debt and survive what may be a temporary upheaval. More than half of large store-based retailers who filed for bankruptcy since 2006 have been *liquidated*.[15] See Figure 12-2.

Since 2008, several large retailers have declared bankruptcy, with some ultimately going out of business. These include American Apparel (2015), Circuit City (2008), Linens 'n Things (2008), A&P (2015), Radio Shack (2015), Blockbuster (2010), Borders (2011), Sbarro (2011 and 2014), Friedman's (2008), Brookstone (2014), and Quiksilver (2015).[16]

American Apparel entered into a bankruptcy in which its secured lenders would receive shares in the reformed company in exchange for the bonds they held. Extra financing was also obtained from participating bondholders to enable American Apparel to keep its manufacturing operations functioning and its 130 U.S. stores open. The reorganization would wipe out the holdings of existing American Apparel stockholders.

Some retailers that focus on teenage consumers have recently struggled. In 2014, for example, Wet Seal, Bed Shops, Delia's, and Body Central declared bankruptcy. Many teenagers have switched to shopping with H&M, Zara, and other "fast-fashion" retailers that can quickly stock fast-selling fashion items from Asian suppliers.[17]

When a retailer goes out of business, it is painful for all parties: the owner/stockholders, employees, creditors, landlords (who then have vacant store sites), and customers. See Figure 12-3.

As with other sectors of business, over the last few years, some retailers have been heavily criticized for *questionable accounting and financial practices*. Sometimes, the practices have been illegal. For example, Sterling—which owns the Kay, Zales, Jared, and Signet jewelry chains—has been under scrutiny because it receives more revenue for sales made with extended-credit servicing plans provided by its own in-house facility. This may overstate revenues and profits and misleads investors.[18]

FIGURE 12-2

Bankruptcy and Contracts

One of the major reasons that a retailer declares bankruptcy is to be able to legally break existing contracts and then to negotiate new, more favorable contact terms with its creditors.

Source: Oleg Golovnev/ Shutterstock. Reprinted by permission.

FIGURE 12-3

Going Out of Business

Often, when retailers go out of business, it is because they are "missing the mark." They are not properly executing their strategies, they lose some key suppliers, their cash flow is poor, and they cannot attract enough loyal customers.

Source: iQoncept/Shutterstock. Reprinted by permission.

To avoid questionable or illegal practices, many larger retailers have enacted formal policies. At Home Depot, for example, there is a detailed "Code of Ethics for Senior Financial Officers," as shown here. The code applies to Home Depot's chief executive, chief financial officer, and other high-ranking personnel. Each of these executives must adhere to such practices as the following:

▸ Act in all financial and accounting matters in a way that shows honesty, integrity, and fairness.
▸ Do not let personal interests override company interests; and avoid conflicts of interest.
▸ Report data that have been recorded inaccurately.
▸ Be sure that all activities are lawful, accurate, complete, and not intended to mislead.
▸ Be proactive in promoting ethical behavior.
▸ Responsibly use company resources.[19]

BUDGETING

Why should a small business know about budgeting? Inc. shows you (http://www.inc.com/budgeting).

Budgeting outlines a retailer's planned expenditures for a given time based on expected performance. Costs are linked to satisfying target market, employee, and management goals. What should labor costs be to attain a certain level of customer service? What compensation will motivate salespeople? What operating expenses will reach intended revenue and profit goals?

There are several benefits from a retailer's meticulously preparing a budget:

▸ Expenditures are clearly related to expected performance, and costs can be adjusted as goals are revised. This enhances productivity.
▸ Resources are allocated to the right departments, product categories, and so on.
▸ Spending for various departments, product categories, and so on is coordinated.
▸ Because planning is structured and integrated, the goal of efficiency is prominent.

  CAREERS IN RETAILING | Retail Financial Analyst

Retail financial analysts are responsible for tasks relating to profit planning, asset management, and retail budgeting. These professionals typically have a degree in accounting, finance, or retail management. In addition to knowing both accounting and finance, retail financial analysts must be entrepreneurial, comfortable working with spreadsheets, and able to understand the operation of a retail business. These are a few long-term questions retail financial analysts must consider on a daily basis and in terms of long-range planning: What costs are associated with closing a store? How can asset turnover be improved? Will increased sales of private-label goods increase net profit?

What criteria would you use to answer these questions?

▷ Cost standards are set, such as advertising equals 5 percent of sales.
▷ A firm prepares for the future rather than reacts to it.
▷ Expenditures are monitored during a budget cycle. If a firm allots $50,000 to buy new merchandise, and it has spent $33,000 halfway through a cycle, it has $17,000 remaining.
▷ A firm can analyze planned budgets versus actual budgets.
▷ Costs and performance can be compared with industry averages.

A retailer should be aware of the effort involved in the budgeting process, recognize that forecasts may not be fully accurate (due to unexpected demand, competitors' tactics, and so on), and modify plans as needed. The process should not be too conservative (or inflexible) or simply add a percentage to each expense category to arrive at the next budget, such as increasing spending by 3 percent across the board based on anticipated sales growth of 3 percent. The budgeting process is shown in Figure 12-4 and described next.

Preliminary Budgeting Decisions

There are six preliminary decisions. First, budgeting authority is specified. In top-down budgeting, senior executives make centralized financial decisions and communicate them down the line to succeeding levels of managers. In bottom-up budgeting, lower-level executives develop departmental budget requests; these requests are assembled and a company budget is designed. Bottom-up budgeting includes varied perspectives, holds managers more accountable, and enhances employee morale. Many firms combine aspects of the two approaches.

Second, the time frame is defined. Most firms have budgets with yearly, quarterly, and monthly components. Annual spending is planned, and costs and performance are regularly reviewed. This responds to seasonal or other fluctuations. Sometimes, the time frame is longer than a year; other times it's shorter than a month. When a firm opens new stores over a 5-year period, it sets construction costs for the entire period. When a supermarket orders perishables, it has weekly budgets for each item.

Third, budgeting frequency is determined. Many firms review budgets on an ongoing basis, but most plan them yearly. In some firms, several months may be set aside each year for the budgeting process; this lets all participants have time to gather data and facilitates taking the budgets through several drafts.

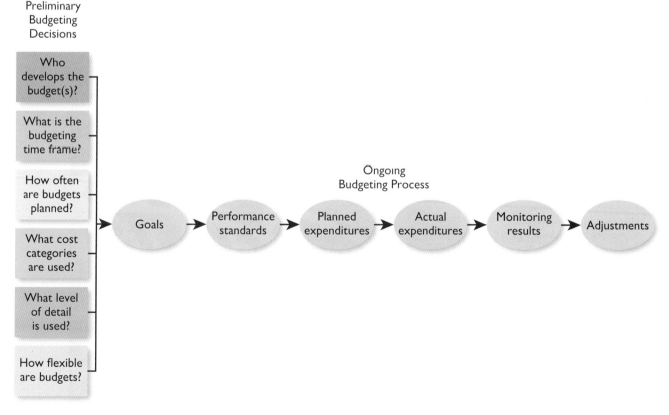

FIGURE 12-4
The Retail Budgeting Process

Fourth, cost categories are established:

▶ *Capital expenditures* are long-term investments in land, buildings, fixtures, and equipment. *Operating expenditures* are the short-term expenses of running a business.

▶ *Fixed costs*, such as store security, remain constant for the budget period regardless of the retailer's performance. *Variable costs*, such as sales commissions, are based on performance. If performance is good, these expenses often rise. Figure 12-5 shows that the clock is always ticking with regard to the timing of costs.

▶ *Direct costs* are incurred by specific departments, product categories, and so on, such as the earnings of department-based salespeople. *Indirect costs*, such as centralized cashiers, are shared by multiple departments, product categories, and so on.

▶ *Natural account expenses* are reported by the names of the costs, such as salaries, and not assigned by purpose. *Functional account expenses* are classified on the basis of the purpose or activity for which expenditures are made, such as cashier salaries.

Fifth, the level of detail is set. Should spending be assigned by department (produce), product category (fresh fruit), product subcategory (apples), and/or product item (McIntosh apples)? With a very detailed budget, every expense subcategory must be adequately covered.

Sixth, budget flexibility is prescribed. A budget should be strict enough to guide planned spending and link costs to goals. Yet, a budget that is too inflexible may not let a retailer adapt to changing market conditions, capitalize on new opportunities, or modify a poor strategy (if further spending is needed to improve matters). Budget flexibility is often expressed in quantitative terms, such as allowing a buyer to increase a quarterly budget by a certain maximum percentage if demand is higher than anticipated.

Ongoing Budgeting Process

After making preliminary budgeting decisions, the retailer engages in the ongoing budgeting process shown in Figure 12-4:

▶ Goals are set based on customer, employee, and management needs.

▶ Performance standards are specified, including customer-service levels, the compensation needed to motivate employees, and the sales and profits needed to satisfy management. Typically, the budget is related to a sales forecast, which projects revenues for the next period. Forecasts are usually broken down by department or product category.

▶ Expenditures are planned in terms of performance goals. In **zero-based budgeting**, a firm starts each new budget from scratch and outlines the expenditures needed to reach that period's goals.

FIGURE 12-5

Cash Flow and the Ticking Clock

One of the challenges that retailers must face is to best synchronize revenues and costs. The clock is always ticking with regard to retail buying, inventory on hand, personnel, and other costs relative to when revenues are received.

Source: iQoncept/Shutterstock. Reprinted by permission.

ETHICS IN RETAILING

Restrictive Loan Covenants

As a condition for obtaining a loan and maintain a line of credit, banks and other lenders commonly require specific covenants to a loan agreement. These may require the borrower to pay expenses promptly, submit financial statements, and maintain specific key ratios (such as current and quick rations, debt to net worth, and return on equity). Retailers not in compliance with these requirements can have their loan called in full by the bank or lender, face an increase in interest rates, or pay a penalty. Some retailers not complying with key ratio requirements have resorted to certain unethical practices. These include not marking down unsaleable inventories, disregarding bad debts, underestimating tax liabilities, charging expenses to future time periods, and deferring necessary building maintenance. In other instances, these retailers may choose to borrow additional funds without notifying the initial lender.

Discuss the ethics of these actions to avoid compliance issues.

All costs are justified each time a budget is done. With **incremental budgeting**, a firm uses current and past budgets as guides and adds to or subtracts from them to arrive at the coming period's spending. Most firms use incremental budgeting; it is easier, less time-consuming, and not as risky.

▷ Actual expenditures are made. The retailer pays rent and employee salaries, buys merchandise, places ads, and so on.

▷ Results are monitored: (1) Actual expenditures are compared with planned spending for each expense category, and reasons for any deviations are reviewed. (2) The firm learns if performance standards have been met and tries to explain deviations.

▷ The budget is adjusted. Revisions are major or minor, depending on how closely a firm has come to reaching its goals. The funds allotted to some expense categories may be reduced, while greater funds may be provided to other categories.

Table 12-5 compares budgeted and actual revenues, expenses, and profits for Donna's Gift Shop during fiscal 2016. The actual data come from Table 12-1. The variance figures compare

TABLE 12-5 Donna's Gift Shop, Fiscal 2016 Budgeted versus Actual Profit-and-Loss Statement (in dollars and percent)

	Budgeted		Actual		Variance[a]	
	Dollars	Percent	Dollars	Percent	Dollars	Percent
Net sales	$300,000	100.00	$330,000	100.00	+$30,000	—
Cost of goods sold	$165,000	55.00	$180,000	54.55	−$15,000	+0.45
Gross profit	$135,000	45.00	$150,000	45.45	+$15,000	+0.45
Operating expenses:						
Salaries	$ 75,000	25.00	$ 75,000	22.73	—	+2.27
Advertising	5,250	1.75	4,950	1.50	+$ 300	+0.25
Supplies	1,800	0.60	1,650	0.50	+$ 150	+0.10
Shipping	1,350	0.45	1,500	0.45	−$ 150	—
Insurance	4,500	1.50	4,500	1.36	—	+0.14
Maintenance	5,100	1.70	5,100	1.55	—	+0.15
Other	3,000	1.00	2,550	0.77	+$ 450	+0.23
Total	$ 96,000	32.00	$ 95,250	28.86	+$ 750	+3.14
Other costs	$ 18,000	6.00	$ 20,000	6.06	−$ 2,000	−0.06
Total costs	$114,000	38.00	$115,250	34.92	−$ 1,250	+3.08
Net profit before taxes	$ 21,000	7.00	$ 34,750	10.53	+$13,750	+3.53
Taxes	$ 9,000	3.00	$ 15,500	4.70	−$ 6,500	−1.70
Net profit after taxes	$ 12,000	4.00	$ 19,250	5.83	+$ 7,250	+1.83

There are small rounding errors.

[a] Variance in dollars is a positive number if actual sales or profits are higher than expected or actual expenses are lower than expected; variance is a negative number if actual sales or profits are lower than expected or actual expenses are higher than expected. Variance in percent depends upon the deviation of the actual percent of each budgeted item from the budgeted percent of each item.

TABLE 12-6 The Effects of Cash Flow

A.

A retailer has rather consistent sales throughout the year. Therefore, the cash flow in any given month is positive. This means no short-term loans are needed, and the owner can withdraw funds from the firm if she so desires:

Linda's Luncheonette, Cash Flow for January

Cash inflow:		
Net sales		$26,000
Cash outflow:		
Cost of goods sold	$9,500	
Operating expenses	8,000	
Other costs	2,500	
Total		$20,000
Positive cash flow		$6,000

B.

A retailer has highly seasonal sales that peak in December. Yet, to have a good assortment of merchandise on hand during December, it must order merchandise in September and October and pay for it in November. As a result, it has a negative cash flow in November that must be financed by a short-term loan. All debts are paid off in January, after the peak selling season is completed:

Dave's Party Favors, Cash Flow for November

Cash inflow:		
Net sales		$19,000
Cash outflow:		
Cost of goods sold	$22,500	
Operating expenses	3,000	
Other costs	2,100	
Total		$27,600
Net cash flow		−$8,600
Short-term loan (to be paid off in January)		$8,600

expected and actual results for each profit-and-loss item. Variances are positive if performance is better than expected and negative if it is worse.

As Table 12-5 indicates, in *dollar terms*, net profit after taxes was $7,250 higher than budgeted. Sales were $30,000 higher than expected; thus, the cost of goods sold was $15,000 higher. Actual operating expenses were $750 lower than expected, while other costs were $2,000 higher. Table 12-5 also shows results in *percentage terms*. This lets a firm evaluate budgeted versus actual performance on a percent-of-sales basis. In Donna's case, actual net profit after taxes was 5.83 percent of sales—better than planned. The higher net profit was mostly due to the actual operating costs percentage being lower than planned.

Learn more about cash flow here (www.entrepreneur .com/topic/cash-flow-management).

A firm must closely monitor **cash flow**, which relates the amount and timing of revenues received to the amount and timing of expenditures for a specific time. In cash flow management, the usual goal is to make sure revenues are received before expenditures are paid.[20] Otherwise, short-term loans may be needed or profits may be tied up in inventory and other expenses. For seasonal retailers, this may be unavoidable. Underestimating costs and overestimating revenues, both of which affect cash flow, are leading causes of new business failures. Table 12-6 has cash flow examples.

RESOURCE ALLOCATION

In allotting financial resources, the magnitude of various costs as well as productivity should be examined. Each has significance for asset management and budgeting.

To easily study the financial performance of publicly owned retailers, go to AnnualReports.com (www .annualreports.com), enter a company name, and download its annual report.

The Magnitude of Various Costs

As noted before, spending can be divided into two categories. **Capital expenditures** are long-term investments in fixed assets. **Operating expenditures** are short-term selling and administrative costs in running a business. It is vital to have a sense of the magnitude of various capital and operating costs.

These are a rough average of capital expenditures (for the basic building shell; heating, ventilation, and air conditioning; interior lighting; flooring; display fixtures; ceilings; interior and exterior signage; and roofing) for erecting the following single freestanding store for these retailers: big-box stores (including department stores), $5.65 million; supermarkets, $5.0 million; home centers, $2.7 million; and convenience stores—$685,000. Thus, a typical home center chain must be prepared to invest $2.7 million to build each new store (which averages more than 44,000 square feet industrywide), *not* including land and merchandise costs; the total could be higher if a bigger store is built.[21]

Remodeling can also be expensive. It is prompted by competitive pressures, mergers and acquisitions, consumer trends, the requirement of complying with the Americans with Disabilities Act, environmental concerns, and other factors.

To reduce their investments, some retailers insist that real-estate developers help pay for building, renovating, and fixture costs. These tenant demands reflect some areas' oversaturation, the amount of retail space available due to the liquidation of some retailers and mergers, and the interest of developers in gaining tenants that generate consumer traffic (such as category killers).

Operating expenses, usually expressed as a percentage of sales, range from 20 percent or so in supermarkets to more than 40 percent in some specialty stores. To succeed, these costs must be in line with competitors' costs. Costco has an edge over many rivals due to lower SGA (selling, general, and administrative costs as a percentage of sales): Costco, 10 percent; Walmart, 20 percent; Target, 20 percent; Kohl's, 23 percent; Dillard's, 25 percent; and Macy's, Inc., 30 percent.[22]

Resource allocation must also take into account **opportunity costs**—possible benefits a retailer forgoes if it invests in one opportunity rather than another. If a chain renovates 15 existing stores at a total cost of $3.5 million, it cannot open a new outlet requiring a $3.5 million investment. Financial resources are finite; consequently, firms often face either/or decisions.

Productivity

Look at the various ways in which retailers can assess their financial performance (www.bizfilings.com/ toolkit/sbg/finance/your-financial-position.aspx).

Due to erratic sales revenues, mixed economic growth, high labor costs, intense competition, and other factors, many retailers place great priority on their **productivity**, the efficiency with which a retail strategy is carried out. Productivity can be described in terms of costs as a percentage of sales, the time it takes a cashier to complete a transaction, profit margins, sales per square foot, inventory turnover, and so forth. The key question is: How can sales and profit goals be reached while keeping control over costs?

Because different retail strategy mixes have distinct resource needs as to store location, fixtures, personnel, and other elements, productivity must be based on norms for each type of strategy

---

 TECHNOLOGY IN RETAILING

Technology in Retailing: The Impact of Self-Scanning on Impulse Sales

According to some retail experts, front-end products that are sold near checkout registers account for 1 percent of supermarket sales but 4 percent of the store's gross profits. Retailers have embraced self-scanning due to labor-cost savings and the appeal to some customers; but the increased use of self-scanning has taken a toll on impulse sales. Customers at a self-scanning register have neither the time nor interest in impulse goods (such as magazines, beverages, candy, batteries, etc.). In addition, usually there are few impulse goods positioned near self-scanners. Supermarkets and drugstores need to carefully analyze the trade-off of

lower impulse sales and profits in self-scanning equipment with the reduction in labor costs. They also need to consider offering targeted coupons to self-scanning customers to increase future impulse purchases.

What are your conclusions about the self-scanning trade-offs? Why?

Source: Based on material in John Karolefski, "The Down Side of Supermarket Self-Checkout," February 9, 2015, www.progressivegrocer.com.

mix (such as department stores versus full-line discount stores). Sales growth should also be measured on the basis of comparable seasons, using the same stores. Otherwise, the data will be affected by seasonality and/or the increased square footage of stores.

There are two ways to enhance productivity: (1) A firm can improve employee performance, sales per foot of space, and other factors by upgrading training programs, increasing advertising, and so forth. (2) It can reduce costs by automating, having suppliers do certain tasks, and so forth. A retailer could use a small core of full-time workers during nonpeak times, supplemented with part-timers in peak periods.

Productivity must not be measured from a cost-cutting perspective alone. This may undermine customer loyalty. One of the more complex dilemmas omnichannel retailers face is how to handle online purchases returned to the store. To control the higher costs associated with processing online purchases in stores, some retailers have decided not to allow online purchases to be returned at their stores. This policy has upset a lot of customers and resulted in most of these firms changing their policies.

Here are two examples of strategies that diverse retailers have used to raise productivity:

> Many firms are using computer software to improve their allocation of shelf space to be more productive per square foot. The Winn-Dixie and ShopKo supermarket chains are among those that utilize SAS Retail Space Management software.

> Department store retailer Macy's, which also owns Bloomingdale's and BlueMercury, is relying on cost efficiencies and a flatter, more agile organizational structure to pursue growth and regain market share in its core omnichannel businesses. Measures include reducing the store portfolio and reinvesting resources online and with stores having the highest sales potential. Savings in labor costs will come through a 2 percent reduction in store personnel, back-office staff, and voluntary separation options for senior executives. Consolidating Macy's Inc. credit and consumer service facilities and reducing budgets for meetings and travel will further reduce costs.[23]

Tuesday Morning uses E-mail (www .tuesdaymorning.com/ email) to offer bargains to consumers and to reduce its costs by minimizing the need for printed circulars and newspaper ads.

It is vital that retailers, in their quest to become more productive, not alienate their customers and diminish the shopping experience. Increasing sales productivity by reducing costs is common, but the true challenge in a retailer's performance is to build productivity profitably.

Chapter Summary

1. *To define operations management.* Operations management involves efficiently and effectively implementing the tasks and policies to satisfy the retailer's customers, employees, and management. This chapter covered the financial aspects of operations management. Operational dimensions are studied in Chapter 13.

2. *To discuss profit planning.* The profit-and-loss (income) statement summarizes a retailer's revenues and expenses over a specific time, typically on a monthly, quarterly, and/or yearly basis. It consists of these major components: net sales, cost of goods sold, gross profit (margin), operating expenses, and net profit after taxes.

3. *To describe asset management, including the strategic profit model, other key business ratios, and financial trends in retailing.* Each retailer has assets and liabilities to manage. A balance sheet shows assets, liabilities, and net worth at a given time. Assets are items with a monetary value owned by a retailer; some appreciate and may have a hidden value. Liabilities are financial obligations.

The retailer's net worth, also called owner's equity, is computed as assets minus liabilities.

Asset management may be measured by reviewing the net profit margin, asset turnover, and financial leverage. Net profit margin equals net profit divided by net sales. Asset turnover equals net sales divided by total assets. By multiplying the net profit margin by asset turnover, a retailer can find its return on assets—which is based on net sales, net profit, and total assets. Financial leverage equals total assets divided by net worth. The strategic profit model incorporates asset turnover, profit margin, and financial leverage to yield the return on net worth. It allows a retailer to better plan and control its asset management. Other key ratios for retailers are the quick ratio, current ratio, collection period, accounts payable to net sales, and overall gross profit (in percent).

Important financial trends involve the state of the economy; funding sources; mergers, consolidations, and spin-offs; bankruptcies and liquidations; and questionable accounting and financial reporting practices.

4. *To look at retail budgeting.* Budgeting outlines a retailer's planned expenditures for a given time based on expected performance; costs are linked to goals. Six preliminary decisions are (a) Responsibility is defined by top-down and/or bottom-up methods. (b) The time frame is specified. (c) Budgeting frequency is set. (d) Cost categories are established. (e) The level of detail is ascertained. (f) Budgeting flexibility is determined.

The ongoing budgeting process then proceeds: goals, performance standards, planned spending, actual expenditures, monitoring results, and adjustments. With zero-based budgeting, each budget starts from scratch; with incremental budgeting, current and past budgets are guides. The budgeted versus actual profit-and-loss statement and the percentage profit-and-loss statement are vital tools. In all budgeting decisions, cash flow, which relates the amount and timing of revenues received with the amount and timing of expenditures, must be considered.

5. *To examine resource allocation.* Both the magnitude of costs and productivity need to be examined. Costs can be divided into capital and operating categories; both must be regularly reviewed. Opportunity costs mean forgoing possible benefits if a retailer invests in one opportunity rather than another. Productivity is the efficiency with which a retail strategy is carried out; the goal is to maximize sales and profits while keeping costs in check.

Key Terms

operations management (p. 316)
profit-and-loss (income) statement (p. 316)
net sales (p. 316)
cost of goods sold (p. 316)
gross profit (margin) (p. 316)
operating expenses (p. 316)
taxes (p. 316)
net profit after taxes (p. 316)
balance sheet (p. 317)

assets (p. 317)
hidden assets (p. 317)
liabilities (p. 317)
net worth (p. 317)
net profit margin (p. 318)
asset turnover (p. 318)
return on assets (ROA) (p. 318)
financial leverage (p. 319)
strategic profit model (p. 319)

return on net worth (RONW) (p. 319)
budgeting (p. 324)
zero-based budgeting (p. 326)
incremental budgeting (p. 327)
cash flow (p. 328)
capital expenditures (p. 329)
operating expenditures (p. 329)
opportunity costs (p. 329)
productivity (p. 329)

Questions for Discussion

1. What are net sales and costs of goods sold? What can be obtained by taking one figure from the other?
2. A retailer wants to use a series of performance ratios to assess financial wealth.
   a. What is the quick ratio?
   b. What is the current ratio?
   c. What is the collection period?
3. How can a retail store improve its overall gross profit margin?
4. Retailers can have a range of assets. Identify the main categories with examples.
5. What kind of financial pressures can an LBO cause?
6. A chain of stores selling smartphones and desktop computers has noted that the divergence in technology has had a major impact on the customer base and sales. They need to reorganize. What would you suggest to them?

7. What is zero-based budgeting? Why do most retailers utilize incremental budgeting, despite its limitations?
8. What is the value of a percentage profit-and-loss statement? The disadvantage?
9. How could a seasonal retailer improve its cash flow during periods when it must buy goods for future selling periods?
10. Distinguish between capital spending and operating costs. Why is this distinction important to retailers?
11. What factors should retailers consider when assessing opportunity costs?
12. How can these retailers improve their productivity?
    a. Fitness center
    b. Online bookstore
    c. Discount apparel store

Web-Based Exercise

Visit the Web site of QuickBooks (http://quickbooks.intuit .com/tutorials) to view many online tutorials. What are the benefits of a product such as this for a small retailer?

13 Operations Management: Operational Dimensions

Chapter Objectives

1. To describe the important role of operations management as a source of competitive advantage in the rapidly evolving omnichannel retail industry

2. To examine several specific aspects of operating a retail business: operations blueprint; store format, size, and space allocation; personnel utilization; store maintenance, energy management, and renovations; inventory management; store security; insurance; credit management; computerization; outsourcing; and crisis management

Digital technologies such as the Web, mobile devices, and social media influence virtually every aspect of retailing. Digital interactions accounted for 36 cents of every U.S dollar of approximately $22.5 trillion global retail sales in 2015.[1] Today, 12 percent of all digital retail buying now occurs through mobile devices. Most important are the rapid growth in technology-mediated retailing; the disruptive and irreversible pace of technological change; the strength of online-only retailers in some product categories; and the increasing expectations of the always-on omnichannel customer to pay, buy, and return anything, anywhere, at any time, using any device. These factors introduce additional opportunities and risks for retail managers and significant implications for retail store operations, which is the focus of this chapter.

How would you feel about paying with your face? Using a new system called MasterCard Identity Check, the credit-card provider will be able to use face recognition and fingerprint scans to better secure online shopping. Known as "selfie pay," this system uses an image of a shopper's face or fingerprint (instead of a password) to help fend off fraudsters. Users of selfie pay must take an initial photo that is converted into a string of 0s and 1s. Those opting to pay by "selfie" will have to blink to prove that an old photo is not being used to bypass the system. Advocates for selfie pay believe that although it's possible to change a compromised password, it is much harder—if not practically impossible—for most people to change their face or fingerprints.[2]

Source: Nomad_Soul/ Shutterstock. Reprinted by permission.

Overview

Operations management is the efficient and effective implementation of the policies and tasks that satisfy a retailer's customers, employees, and management (and stockholders, if it is publicly owned). Chapter 12 examined the financial dimensions of operations management; this chapter covers the operational aspects. This chapter covers the operational aspects of operations management.

For firms to succeed in the long term, operational areas need to be managed well. A decision to change a store format or to introduce new antitheft equipment must be carefully reviewed because these acts greatly affect performance. In running their businesses, retail executives must make a wide range of operational decisions, such as these:

For a good operations overview, go to this Web site (www.thebalance .com/retail-store-operations-4073841).

- What operating guidelines are used?
- What is the optimal format and size of a store? What is the relationship among shelf space, shelf location, and sales for each item in the store? How does the company's online store affect store size, assortment, and return policies?
- How can personnel best be matched to customer traffic flows? How do retailers optimize staff size to maximize productivity? What policies should retailers adopt to leverage or counter in-store showrooming? What impact do self-service and mobile payment have on revenues?
- What effect does the use of various building materials have on store maintenance? How can energy costs be better controlled? How often should facilities be renovated?
- How can inventory best be managed? How do online, order online and pick up in store, and mobile sales and returns impact inventory decisions? What is the optimal balance between satisfying customer needs and having too much selection?
- How can the personal safety of shoppers and employees be ensured?
- What levels of insurance (fire, flood, life insurance on key personnel, business interruption) are required?
- How can credit transactions be managed most effectively? How do mobile payment technologies affect purchase behavior?
- How can computer systems improve operating efficiency? How can retailers leverage mobile technology to enhance consumer experiences and purchase conversions in-store?
- Should any aspects of operations be outsourced (within the U.S. and/or abroad)?
- What crisis management plans should there be in an omnichannel, socially connected world?

OPERATING A RETAIL BUSINESS

We now look at the operations blueprint: store format, size, and space allocation; personnel utilization; store maintenance, energy management, and renovations; inventory management; store security; insurance; credit management; computerization; outsourcing; and crisis management.

Operations Blueprint

An **operations blueprint** systematically lists all operating functions to be performed, their characteristics, and their timing. When developing a blueprint, the retailer specifies, in detail, every operating function from the store's opening to closing—and those responsible for them.[3] For example, who opens the store? When? What are the steps (turning off the alarm, turning on power, setting up the computer, etc.)? The performance of these tasks must not be left to chance.

To encourage more compatibility among different retail hardware and software systems, the National Retail Federation has established its ARTS program (www.nrf-arts .org).

A large or diversified retailer may use multiple blueprints and have separate blueprints for such areas as store maintenance, inventory management, credit management, and store displays. When a retailer modifies its store format or operating procedures (such as relying more on self-service), it must also adjust the operations blueprint(s).

Figure 13-1 has an operations blueprint for a quick-oil-change firm. It identifies employee and customer tasks (in order) and expected performance times for each activity. Advantages of this blueprint—and others—are that it standardizes activities (in a location and between locations), isolates points at which operations may be weak or prone to fail (Do employees actually check transmission, brake, and power-steering fluids in one minute?), outlines a plan that can be evaluated for completeness (Should customers be offered different grades of oil?), shows personnel needs (Should one person change oil and another wash the windshield?), and helps identify

**Expected Average
Time per Activity**

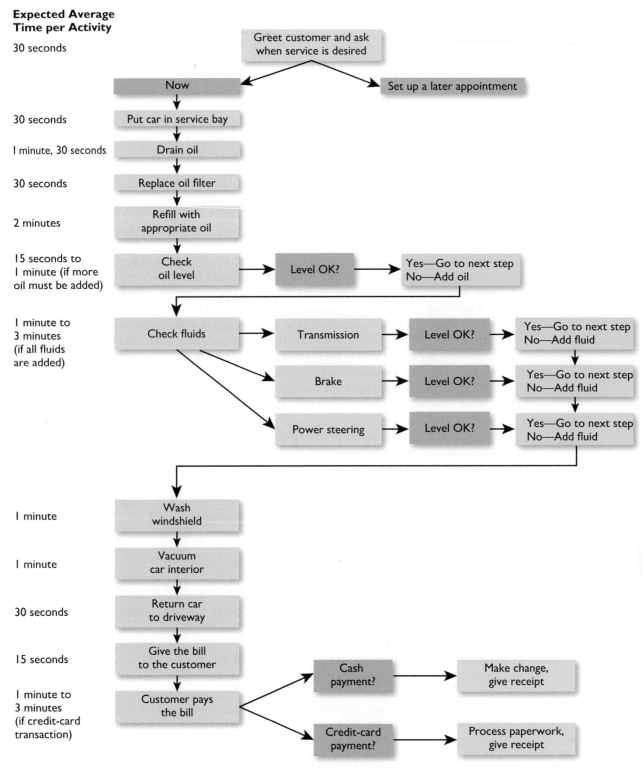

30 seconds — Greet customer and ask when service is desired

Now / Set up a later appointment

30 seconds — Put car in service bay

1 minute, 30 seconds — Drain oil

30 seconds — Replace oil filter

2 minutes — Refill with appropriate oil

15 seconds to 1 minute (if more oil must be added) — Check oil level → Level OK? → Yes—Go to next step / No—Add oil

1 minute to 3 minutes (if all fluids are added) — Check fluids → Transmission → Level OK? → Yes—Go to next step / No—Add fluid ; Brake → Level OK? → Yes—Go to next step / No—Add fluid ; Power steering → Level OK? → Yes—Go to next step / No—Add fluid

1 minute — Wash windshield

1 minute — Vacuum car interior

30 seconds — Return car to driveway

15 seconds — Give the bill to the customer

1 minute to 3 minutes (if credit-card transaction) — Customer pays the bill → Cash payment? → Make change, give receipt ; Credit-card payment? → Process paperwork, give receipt

Total expected time = 10 minutes to 14 minutes, 45 seconds

FIGURE 13-1

A Operations Blueprint for a Quick-Oil-Change Firm's Employees

productivity improvements (Should the customer or an employee drive a car into and out of the service bay?).

Store Format, Size, and Space Allocation

Store format decisions include site planning (such as a planned shopping center rather than an unplanned business district), construction choices (such as prefabricated materials), store size, store design, and store layouts. Some leading retailers use differentiated formats to align assortments to specific consumers and segments, to optimize space profitability, and to create a better customer destination. Multiformat apparel and accessories retailer Inditex has Massimo Dutti stores (personalized service for affluent men and women); Bershka (targeting a younger market with a store resembling a social meeting place); and its core brand Zara (targeting the mid-market, age group 20 to 35 with "cheap and chic" offerings). Some firms, including Target and Walmart (such as Walmart to Go) are using smaller format stores with lower operating costs (for rent, inventory, and lighting) and better access to locations in urban areas —in addition to their larger facilities.

The Benchmark Group (www.teamofchoice.com) has collaborated with a number of retailers to develop their stores.

A key store format decision for chain retailers is whether to use **prototype stores**, whereby multiple outlets conform to relatively uniform construction, layout, and operations standards. They make centralized management control easier, reduce construction costs, standardize operations, facilitate the interchange of employees among outlets, allow bulk purchases of fixtures and other materials, and convey a consistent chain image. Yet, a strict reliance on prototypes may lead to inflexibility, failure to adapt to or capitalize on local customer needs, and too little creativity. McDonald's, Pep Boys, Starbucks, and most supermarket chains have prototype stores.

Together with prototype stores, some chains use **rationalized retailing** programs to combine a high degree of centralized management control with strict operating procedures for every phase of business at all of their outlets. Rigid control and standardization make this technique easy to enact and manage, and a firm can add a significant number of stores in a short time. See Figure 13-2. Dunkin' Donuts, Old Navy, Toys "R" Us, and many major supermarket chains use rationalized retailing. They operate many stores that are similar in size, layout, and merchandising. Rationalized retailing also enables consumers to locate merchandise and to feel comfortable when visiting a new store.

FIGURE 13-2

Retailers Need to FORCE Their Efforts

In their short- and long-run operations, retailers continuously need to FORCE their efforts to be as efficient as possible.

Source: marekuliasz/ Shutterstock. Reprinted by permission.

Many retailers use one or both of two contrasting store-size approaches to be distinctive and to deal with high rents in some metropolitan markets. Home Depot, Barnes & Noble, Staples, Best Buy, and Dick's Sporting Goods have category-killer stores with huge assortments that try to dominate smaller stores. Food-based warehouse stores and large discount-oriented stores often situate in secondary sites, where rents are low and confidence is high that they can draw customers. Cub Foods (a warehouse chain) and Walmart engage in this approach. At the same time, some retailers believe large stores are not efficient in serving saturated (or small) markets; they have been opening smaller stores or downsizing existing ones because of high rents.

Getting the right store and shelf-space management strategy is key to driving traffic, retail sales revenues, and profitability. Retailers have to understand consumer needs, preferences, and purchase behavior across online and offline channels to better "curate" assortments and to optimize their space and assortments. They can use facilities productively by identifying the right amount of space, the right number of brands, and the placement of each product category to most profitably meet retailer and customer needs. Sometimes, retailers drop merchandise lines because they occupy too much space relative to sales, margins, and/or turnover. Today, many department stores focus more on apparel and cosmetics and less on electronics, appliances, and home furnishings (such as carpeting and window treatments).

The growth in cross-channel shopping allows retailers to leverage their Web sites as an "endless aisle" opportunity to extend their offerings without expanding physical space while lowering operating costs. This can support sales of long-tail SKUs (odd sizes, last season's colors, and so on) at full price, without sacrificing shelf space in stores. To ensure cross-channel coordination, Gap has been testing an "order-in-store" option in several locations, where store customers can place online orders from within the shops with free shipping—if the customer picks up from the store at a later date. This presents opportunities for additional purchases and cross-selling. At Bonobos stores, a men's clothing retailer, customers can purchase items, but they do not leave with merchandise in-hand; rather, it is shipped to them days later.

With a **top-down space management approach**, a retailer starts with its total available store space (by outlet and the overall firm, if a chain), divides space into categories, and then works on product layouts. In contrast, a **bottom-up space management approach** begins planning at the individual product level and then proceeds to category, total store, and overall company levels.

Measures by some retailers to improve store space productivity include vertical displays, which occupy less room and hang on walls and/or from ceilings. Formerly free space may have small point-of-sale displays and vending machines; sometimes, product displays are in front of stores. Open doorways, mirrored walls, and vaulted ceilings give small stores a larger appearance. Up to 75 percent or more of total space may be used for selling; the rest is for storage, rest rooms, and so on. Scrambled merchandising (with high-profit, high-turnover items) occupies more space in stores and at Web sites than before. By having longer hours, retailers can also use space better.

  RETAILING AROUND THE WORLD

Countries' Payment-Related Issues

In Canada and the United States, Visa, MasterCard, and American Express account for about 93 percent of all online payments. But in Mexico, these three credit-card companies account for only 44 percent of online payments; cash-based methods account for 24 percent; and bank transfers account for 22 percent. In addition, many Mexican credit cards are not enabled for cross-border purchases. As a consequence, retailers need to use a local bank if they do not have a payments processor with the necessary connections. In Germany, credit cards account for a relatively small market share: Visa, MasterCard, and American Express represent just one-quarter of online purchases; 35 percent come from a Europe-wide direct-debit system. Other popular methods include local payment companies Sofort and Giropay (16 percent combined) and U.S.-based PayPal (10 percent). Open invoices account for another 15 percent of payments.

What are the effects of these data on an online retailer seeking to expand in Mexico and Germany?

Source: Based on material in. "Clearing the Path to Purchase," *STORES Magazine,* August 2015. Reprinted by permission.

Personnel Utilization

According to the U.S. Bureau of Labor Statistics, millions of people work in retailing as salespersons, clerks, customer service representatives, cashiers, and other positions. From an operations perspective, efficiently utilizing retail personnel is vital:

1. Labor costs are high—the largest category of controllable, nonmerchandise costs for most retailers, with wages and benefits accounting for up to one-half of operating costs. Forthcoming state and city legislation to raise minimum wages will further lift labor costs.
2. High employee turnover means increased recruitment, training, and management costs.
3. Poor-performing personnel may have poor sales skills, mistreat shoppers, mis-ring transactions, and make other errors.
4. Productivity gains in technology have exceeded those in labor; yet some retailers are still labor intensive.
5. Labor scheduling is often subject to unanticipated demand. Retailers know they must increase staff in peak periods and reduce it in slow ones, but they may still be over- or understaffed if weather changes, competitors run specials, or suppliers increase promotions.
6. There is less flexibility for firms with unionized employees. Working conditions, compensation, tasks, overtime pay, performance measures, termination procedures, seniority rights, and promotion criteria are generally specified in union contracts.

Because online and mobile shopping account for a larger portion of sales revenues, the role of in-store sales personnel has evolved in response to shoppers' in-store expectations. Retailers are increasingly equipping in-store personnel with tablets and smartphones, as well as giving them access to customer accounts so they can update data on preferences and anticipated future purchases to enhance cross-selling efforts. Instead of resisting showrooming in their stores, some sales staff help customers find products, check product reviews, and compare prices using the retailers' mobile apps; order stockouts or irregular-sized products via the retailers' internal Web sites; and process payment using mobile POS on their tablets. All of this is may be done instead of shoppers lining up at the cashier. Increasingly, customer service personnel are expected to engage with, respond to, and solve customer concerns expressed on blogs, social media, and customer review Web sites.

Tactics to maximize personnel productivity include the following:

▸ *Hiring process.* By very carefully screening potential employees before they are offered jobs, turnover is reduced and better performance secured.

▸ *Workload forecasts.* For each time period, the number and type of employees are predetermined. A drugstore may have one pharmacist, one cashier, and one stockperson from 2:00 P.M. to 5:00 P.M. on weekdays and add a pharmacist and a cashier from 5:00 P.M. to 7:30 P.M. (to accommodate those shopping after work). In workload forecasts, costs must be balanced against the possibilities of lost sales if customer waiting time is excessive. The key is to be both efficient (cost-oriented) and effective (service-oriented). Many retailers use software in employee scheduling. Firms such as Invision (www.invisionwfm.com) have devised software to aid retailers in workload forecasting.

▸ *Job standardization and cross-training.* Through **job standardization**, the tasks of personnel with similar positions in different departments, such as cashiers in clothing and candy departments, are rather uniform. With **cross-training**, personnel learn tasks associated with more than one job, such as cashier, stockperson, and gift wrapper. A firm increases personnel flexibility, reduces employee boredom and the number of employees needed at any time by job standardization and cross-training. If one department is slow, a cashier could be assigned to a busy one; and a salesperson could process transactions, set up displays, and handle complaints. As consumers increasingly turn to mobile devices, in-store employees need to be trained to use mobile technology to enhance consumer experiences and improve purchase conversion and basket size.

▸ *Good communications.* Employees work best when they are clear about their responsibilities and well informed about policies and current company news. See Figure 13-3.

▸ *Employee performance standards.* Each worker is given clear goals and is accountable for them. Cashiers are judged on transaction speed and mis-rings, buyers on department revenues and markdowns, and senior executives on the firm's reaching sales and profit targets. Personnel are more productive when working toward specific goals.

Kronos' Workforce Scheduler (www.kronos.com/scheduling-software/scheduling.aspx) allows retailers to better manage employee scheduling.

FIGURE 13-3

Communicating Productively with Employees

From both cost and time perspectives, videoconferencing is quite an effective way to communicate. An executive at an offsite location can communicate interactively with retail personnel at a store or headquarters' location—at a convenient time and without travel. This approach is more personal than E-mail or other written formats.

Source: Andrey_Popov/ Shutterstock. Reprinted by permission.

> *Compensation.* Financial remuneration, promotions, and recognition that reward good performance will help motivate employees. A salesperson is motivated to "cross-sell" goods (ties and shirts with the purchase of a suit) if there is a bonus for related-item selling. Retailers using commission-based or two-tier compensation policies (low base pay plus commission on sales) may need to update their compensation policies to credit employees who persuade in-store shoppers to purchase from the retailer's Web site as more consumers engage in cross-channel shopping and in-store showrooming. For example, salespeople at Home Depot stores have an incentive to help customers learn how to use the Home Depot mobile app—a mobile-enabled sale anywhere within the ZIP code of their Home Depot store is credited to that store.

> *Self-service.* Self-service reduces personnel costs; however, there is less opportunity for cross-selling (whereby customers are encouraged to buy complementary goods they may not have been thinking about) and some shoppers may feel service is inadequate. Self-service requires investments in better displays, popular brands, ample assortments, and products with clear labels describing their specifications and features.

> *Length of employment.* Generally, full-time workers who have been with a firm for an extended time are more productive than those who are part-time or who have worked there for a short time. They are often more knowledgeable, are more anxious to see the firm succeed, need less supervision, are popular with customers, can be promoted, and adapt to the work environment. The superior productivity of these workers normally far outweighs their higher compensation.

Store Maintenance, Energy Management, and Renovations

Store maintenance encompasses all activities in managing physical facilities, including *exterior* (parking lot, points of entry and exit, outside signs and display windows, and common areas

  Security Personnel

Although inventory shrinkage is a major expense for all retailers, high-risk firms such as jewelry and luxury watch stores are particularly vulnerable. Large retail chains, especially department stores, typically have a high-level executive in charge of store security. An ongoing responsibility of the head of security is to conduct an annual security audit. This comprises evaluating security-based hardware such as alarm systems, the use of deadbolt locking mechanisms, closed-circuit camera coverage, and window gates; electronic article surveillance device usage on select items (such as small goods); store signage indicating that the store is under 24-hour video surveillance, that no cash is left in the store at closing, and that the retailer will undertake legal action to prosecute all offenders; security guard training, adequacy, and placement; and salesperson training on observing and reporting suspicious persons, and properly responding to a robbery.

How would the job description differ for a head of security of a store versus an online retailer?

FIGURE 13-4

A Checklist of Selected Store Maintenance Decisions

✓ What responsibility should the retailer have for maintaining outside facilities? For instance, does a lease agreement make the retailer or the property owner accountable for snow removal in the parking lot?

✓ Should store maintenance activities be done by the retailer's personnel or by outside specialists? Will that decision differ by type of facility (e.g., air-conditioning versus flooring) and by type of service (e.g., maintenance versus repairs)?

✓ What repairs should be classified as emergencies? How promptly should nonemergency repairs be made?

✓ What should be the required frequency of store maintenance for each type of facility (e.g., daily vacuuming of floors versus weekly washing of exterior windows)? How often should special maintenance activities be done (e.g., restriping spaces in a parking lot)?

✓ How should store maintenance vary by season and by time of day (e.g., when a store is open versus when it is closed)?

✓ How long should existing facilities be utilized before acquiring new ones? What schedule should be followed?

✓ What performance standards should be set for each element of store maintenance? Do these standards adequately balance costs against a desired level of maintenance?

adjacent to a store [e.g., sidewalks] and *interior* (windows, walls, flooring, climate control and energy use, lighting, displays and signs, fixtures, and ceilings). See Figure 13-4.

The quality of store maintenance affects consumer perceptions, the life span of facilities, and operating costs. Consumers do not like poorly maintained stores. This means promptly replacing burned-out lamps and periodically repainting room surfaces. Thorough, ongoing maintenance may extend current facilities for a longer period before having to invest in new ones. At home centers, the heating, ventilation, and air-conditioning equipment last an average of 15 years; display fixtures an average of 12 years; and interior signs an average of 7 years. Maintenance is costly.[4] In a typical year, a home center spends $15,000 on floor maintenance alone.

Retail companies spend almost $20 billion on energy every year; however, they have the potential to save $3 billion of that amount through effective energy management programs. A typical 50,000 square foot retail building in the United States spends around $90,000 each year on energy. On average, a store uses 14.3 kilowatt hours of electricity per year, resulting in a cost of $1.47 per square foot. Cutting energy costs by just 10 percent can result in a 1.2 to 1.6 percent increase in profit margins. The same reduction in an average supermarket would result in a 16 percent increase in net profit margins. The U.S. Environmental Protection Agency estimates that $1 in energy savings is equivalent to increasing sales by $59.[5]

Due to rising costs over the last 45-plus years, energy management is a major factor in retail operations. For firms with special needs, such as food stores, it is especially critical. To manage their energy resources more effectively, many retailers use a combination of short-term managerial practices and strategic, long-term decisions.

Shorter-term managerial actions include:

▸ *Turning things off.* Every kilowatt saved immediately increases profitability.
▸ *Using temperature control devices.* Adjust the interior temperature during nonselling hours.
▸ *Indoor lighting upgrades.* Replace fluorescent lights with LEDs or CFLs (which use only 20 to 25 percent of the energy of older fluorescents).
▸ *Parking lots.* Use lower wattage lighting in parking lots—but security may be an issue.
▸ *Changing HVAC filters regularly.* Old filters overwork equipment and use more energy.
▸ *Using sensor lighting.* Only utilize lighting when someone is in the room.
▸ *Using reflective paint on roof.* This keeps a building cool.
▸ *Cleaning and maintaining refrigerators.* This helps machinery operate more efficiently.

Strategic longer-term decisions include:

▸ *Structurally changing buildings.* This involves such as actions as energy-efficient windows and using glass instead of walls for natural light (which will also reduce cooling costs).

Visit this Web site (www .bltllc.com/products) to learn more about commercial flooring.

▶ *Air conditioning/heating.* Replace old systems with new energy-efficient units. Install special air-conditioning systems that control humidity levels in specific store areas, such as freezer locations. to minimize moisture condensation.

▶ *Installing computerized systems to monitor and coordinate temperature and lighting levels.* Some chains' systems even allow designated personnel to adjust the temperature, lighting, heat, and air conditioning in multiple stores from one office.

▶ *Insulating.* Through better insulation in constructing and renovating stores, heat and cool air are more efficiently controlled.

▶ *Demand-controlled ventilating.* Such a system senses carbon dioxide levels, detects how many people are in the store, and saves energy by adjusting ventilation accordingly.

▶ *Adding a building management system (BMS).* This system automatically controls and monitors building service performance and makes changes accordingly.

▶ *Energy auditing.* This entails partnering with an energy expert to assess current usage and implement a plan for savings.

▶ *Installing solar panels.* This involves an alternative form of energy.

▶ *Purchasing Energy Star–approved appliances.* These include energy-efficient refrigerators, air conditioning, vending machines, hot food cabinets, and so on.

This example shows how seriously some retailers take energy management: Lighting is a crucial, if seldom noticed, element in the selling atmosphere for LVMH (the parent company of Louis Vuitton, Fendi, Christian Dior, Donna Karan, Marc Jacobs, Bulgari, Sephora, and many others), which occupies nearly 11 million square feet of retail space. Seventy percent of its energy usage goes into stores, not factories or shipping. Optimal, directional lighting has a powerful visual impact that spotlights the aesthetics of luxury products. LVMH's lighting needs are so complex that the firm researched the best options for hue and those least likely to damage wines, and then signed agreements with 20 LED lighting suppliers. After measuring the energy used by escalators, air conditioning, lighting, and other uses, LVMH realized that computer and digital display screens were devouring almost as much as what the company was saving with the utilization of LED lightbulbs.[6]

Besides everyday maintenance and energy management, retailers need decision rules for renovations: How often are renovations necessary? What areas require renovations more frequently than others? How extensive will renovations be at any one time? Will the retailer be open for business as usual during renovations? How much money must be set aside in anticipation of future renovations? Will renovations result in higher revenues, lower operating costs, or both?

Inventory Management

Retailers use inventory management to maintain proper merchandise assortment while ensuring that operations are efficient and effective. See Figure 13-5. Channel boundaries are blurring for shoppers; they are demanding cross-channel service options such as ordering online with in-store pick-up, personalization of products, endless assortments and inventory, and no-cost returns across all channels. Most online-only retailers have optimized the location and number of distribution centers to be able to offer free 3-day delivery; however, many national retailers can leverage their network of stores to offer same-day pick-up if they modernize their inventory and

TECHNOLOGY IN RETAILING   Energy Management

Superior energy management can have a big impact on the bottom line. For example, if a store has a 5 percent profit margin, a 15 percent reduction in energy costs could increase its profit margin to 5.5 to 6 percent. However, retailers face difficult issues in attempting to reduce energy costs. Unlike offices and warehouses, stores can be open for over 90 hours per week, food retailers require refrigeration and freezer units, and some customers are intolerant of a store's reducing air-conditioner thermostats

below 72 degrees. One way to reduce energy usage on a long-term basis is to build new stores certified by LEED (Leadership in Energy & Environmental Design). As compared with traditional construction, a LEED-certified building can result in energy and water bill savings by as much as 40 percent.

Why do you think that many retailers do not insist on LEED construction?

FIGURE 13-5

Inventory Management and Retailing

For many retailers, the way they handle inventory management can mean the difference between success and failure. Inventory management decisions can be complex, based on the product assortment, speed of inventory turnover, order time, and more.

Source: Dusit/Shutterstock. Reprinted by permission.

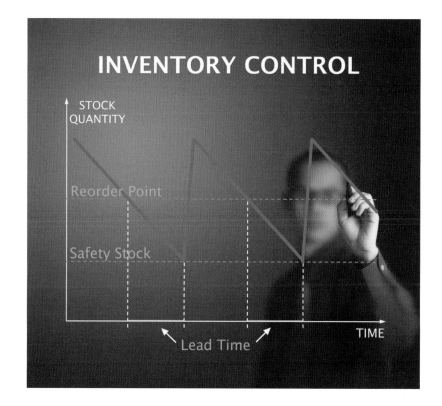

logistics for cross-channel visibility and transfers to prevent stockouts. The item is then likely to be closer to the customer so shipping from stores can be more cost-effective than single-item, direct-to-customer orders from distribution centers accustomed to larger orders bound for stores. Although the role of inventory management in merchandising is covered in Chapter 15, these are some operational issues to consider:

- How can the handling of merchandise from different suppliers be coordinated? In what situations is cross-docking suitable?
- Should drop shipping be employed (wherein manufacturers or wholesalers ship goods directly to consumers based on orders taken at a retail store or Web site)?
- How much inventory should be on the sales floor versus in a warehouse or storeroom?
- How often should inventory be moved from nonselling to selling areas of a store?
- What inventory functions can be done during nonstore hours?
- What are the trade-offs between faster supplier delivery and higher shipping costs?
- What supplier support is expected in storing merchandise or setting up displays?
- What level of in-store merchandise breakage is acceptable?
- Which items require customer delivery? When? By whom?

Store Security

Store security relates to two basic issues: personal security and merchandise security. Personal security is examined in this chapter. Merchandise security is covered in Chapter 15. Many shoppers and employees feel less safe at retail shopping locations than before. That is why companies such as ADT offer security support to retailers, including smaller ones (www.adt.com/business).

These are among the practices that retailers are utilizing to address this issue:

- Uniformed security guards provide a visible presence to reassure customers and employees, and they are a warning to potential thieves and muggers. Some shopping areas have horse-mounted guards or guards who patrol on motorized Segway Personal Transporters. As one security expert noted, "Standard practice is for guards to walk the floor to provide a visual reminder that they are there, and report unusual behavior to superiors or to police."[7]
- Undercover personnel are used to complement uniformed guards.

▸ Brighter lighting is used in parking lots, which are also patrolled more frequently by guards. These guards more often work in teams.

▸ TV cameras and other devices scan areas frequented by shoppers and employees.[8] See Figure 13-6. 7-Eleven stores have an in-store cable TVs and alarm monitoring systems, complete with audio.

▸ Some shopping areas have curfews for teenagers. This is a controversial tactic.

▸ Access to store backroom facilities (such as storage rooms) is tightened.

▸ Bank deposits are made more frequently—often by armed security guards.

Insurance

Among the types of insurance that retailers buy are workers' compensation; product liability; fire, accident, property (covering buildings, fixtures. and inventory); liability due to accidents on the premises; business interruption insurance (to cover lost earnings due to fire, floods, etc.); and crime (due to employees stealing cash and goods [inventory shrinkage]). Many firms also offer health insurance to full-time employees, but contributions to premiums differ across retailers. The Affordable Care Act requires employers with 50 or more employees to offer or assist in purchases of health insurance for those working more than 30 hours per week. Some firms still provide insurance coverage to eligible part-time employees, but others—such as Walmart and Target—have discontinued some coverage.

Insurance decisions can have a big impact on a retailer: (1) In recent years, premiums have risen dramatically. (2) Several insurers have reduced the scope of their coverage; they now require higher deductibles or do not provide coverage on all aspects of operations (such as the professional liability of pharmacists). (3) There are fewer insurers servicing retailers today than a decade ago; this limits the choice of carrier. (4) Insurance against environmental risks (such as leaking oil tanks) are more important due to government rules.

To protect themselves financially, retailers have often enacted costly programs aimed at lessening their vulnerability to employee and customer insurance claims from unsafe conditions, as well as to hold down premiums. These programs include no-slip carpeting, flooring, and rubber entrance mats; more frequent inspection of and mopping wet floors; doing more elevator and escalator checks; having regular fire drills; building more fire-resistant facilities; setting up separate storage areas for dangerous items; discussing safety in employee training; and keeping records showing proper maintenance activity.

FIGURE 13-6

Retail Security Means Vigilance

More retailers use video security cameras than ever before—partly because of declining equipment costs and partly due to the confidence that visible security measures have on customer perceptions of safety.

Source: Mats/Shutterstock. Reprinted by permission.

Credit Management

Operational decisions must be made in the area of credit management—for example:

▶ What form of payment is acceptable? A retailer may accept cash only, cash and personal checks, cash and credit card(s), cash and debit cards, mobile pay, or all of these.

▶ Who administers the credit plan? The firm can have its own credit system and/or accept major credit cards (such as Visa, MasterCard, American Express, and Discover). It may also work with PayPal, Apple Pay, and Google Checkout for store and online payments. One major innovation in credit management is the availability of free mobile payment apps and portable readers such as Square that plug into an iPod, iTouch, iPhone, or iPad that sales staff or consumers can use to reduce checkout lines at the cashier terminals.[9] Another possibility is Touch ID that uses fingerprints in instead of credit cards on selected iPhones and iPads.

▶ What are customer eligibility requirements for a check or credit purchase? With a check purchase, a photo ID might be sufficient. To open a new credit account, a customer must meet age, employment, income, and other conditions; an existing customer would be evaluated in terms of the outstanding balance and credit limit. Credit reports can be obtained from such firms as Transunion, Equifax, and Experian. These firms consolidate a consumer's credit risk using a FICO score.

▶ What credit terms will be used? A retailer with its own plan must determine when interest charges begin to accrue, the rate of interest, and minimum monthly payments.

▶ How are late payments or nonpayments to be handled? Some retailers with their own credit plans rely on outside collection agencies to follow up on past-due accounts.

The retailer must weigh the ability of credit to increase revenues against the costs of processing payments—screening, transaction, and collection costs, as well as bad debts. If a retailer completes credit functions itself, it incurs these costs; if outside parties (such as Visa) are used, the retailer covers the costs by its fees to the credit organization.

In the United States, there are 185 million credit-card holders. Total retail use of credit and debit cards exceeds $2 trillion. According to U.S. data from CardWeb.com, the average person has three bank-issued cards, four retail credit cards, and one debit card. Based on a survey by the American Bankers Association and Dove Consulting, payments by credit or debit card now account for 53 percent of purchases, versus 43 percent in 1999.

Credit-card fees paid by retailers typically range from 1.5 percent to 5.0 percent of sales for Visa, MasterCard, Discover, and American Express, depending on volume and card provider.[10] There may also be transaction and monthly fees. With retailers' own credit operations, they incur all the processing costs; but they also get to collect the interest on unpaid balances. Walmart and Sears seek to lower transaction fees by promoting consumer use of debit cards, which are less costly for retailers. Debit-card transactions now account for 29 percent of retail card activity versus 17 percent in 1999 according to the Nilson Report.[11]

Merchants need to monitor consumer preference for various payment methods—cash, debit, credit, check, mobile, and so forth—across generation and income levels. A Federal Reserve study from the Diary of Consumer Payment Choice found that the largest share of consumer transaction activity is payment by cash (40 percent), debit-card transactions (29 percent), and credit-card transactions at 17 percent.[12] Paper checks have become an antiquated form of payment. Younger consumers and seniors prefer cash or debit cards.

As just noted, many retailers—of all types—now place great emphasis on a **debit-card system**, whereby the purchase price is immediately deducted from a consumer's bank account and entered into a retailer's account by a computer terminal. The retailer's risk of nonpayment is eliminated, and costs are reduced with debit rather than credit transactions. The pre-paid gift card, a form of debit card, is also popular. For traditional credit cards, monthly billing is employed; with debit cards, monetary account transfers are made at the time of purchase. There is some resistance to debit transactions by those who like the delayed-payment benefit of conventional credit cards.

As the payment landscape evolves, new operational issues must be addressed:

▶ Retailers have more payment options. Online retailers offer many payment choices.[13] At store-based retailers, training cashiers is more complex due to all the payment formats, such as cash, third-party and retailer credit and debit cards, personal checks, gift cards, and more. Mobile payment systems introduce more complexity into the process.

Visa presents a lot of advice (https://usa.visa.com/support/merchant/library.html) for retailers through its online library.

The *Nilson Report* presents information on retail payment methods. At its site (www.nilsonreport.com), you can access highlights.

Click here (http://ww.deluxe.com/about-deluxe/company) to learn about one of the premier payment systems support companies for retailers.

> Visa and MasterCard have settled a lawsuit requiring retailers to accept both credit and debit cards, and charging higher interchange fees from retailers for debit cards.

> Nonstore retailers have less legal protection against credit-card fraud than store retailers that secure written authorization. By law, U.S. store retailers were required to update their POS terminals to accept chip-based credit and debit cards by October 1, 2015, or risk assuming liability for counterfeit cards and lost-and-stolen point-of-sale data.[14]

> Credit-card transactions on the Web must instantly take into account different sales tax rates and currencies (for global sales).

Technology and Computerization

CUSTOMER-FACING TECHNOLOGIES   Large and small retailers can use a **computerized checkout** to efficiently process transactions and monitor inventory. These UPC-based scanning systems and computerized registers instantly record and display sales, provide detailed receipts, and retain inventory data. They lower costs by shortening transaction time, employee training, misrings, and the need for item pricing. Retailers also have better inventory control, reduced spoilage, and improved ordering. They get item-by-item data, which aid in determining store layout and merchandise plans, shelf space, and inventory replenishment.

Recent technological developments include wireless scanners that let workers scan heavy items without lifting them, radio frequency identification tags (RFID) that emit a radio frequency code when placed near a receiver (which is faster than UPC codes and better for harsh climates), speech recognition (that can tally an order on the basis of a clerk's verbal command), and portable card readers. See Figure 13-7.

Retailers face two potential problems with computerized checkouts. First, UPC-based systems do not reach peak efficiency unless all suppliers attach UPC labels to merchandise; otherwise, retailers incur labeling costs. Second, because UPC symbols are unreadable by humans, some states have laws that require price labeling on individual items. This lessens the labor savings of posting only shelf prices.

Many retailers have upgraded to an **electronic point-of-sale system**, which performs all the tasks of a computerized checkout and verifies check and charge transactions, provides instantaneous sales reports, monitors and changes prices, sends intra- and inter-store messages, evaluates personnel and profitability, and stores data. A point-of-sale system is often used along with a retail information system. Point-of-sale terminals can stand alone or be integrated with an in-store or a headquarters computer. As noted in Chapter 2, another scanning option with retailer interest is **self-scanning**, whereby the consumer himself or herself scans items being purchased at a checkout counter, uses a portable retailer-provided barcode scanner (e.g., for gift registry), or uses the retailer's mobile app

Retail scanning equipment comes in a wide variety of models and price ranges (www.barcodediscount.com).

FIGURE 13-7

An Innovative Use of Checkout Technology

Portable credit- and debit-card readers make it easy for shoppers to checkout.

Source: Neil Speers/ Shutterstock.com. Reprinted by permission.

on a smartphone, and then pays by credit or debit card, and bags items. A potential problem with self-scanning involves the possibility for consumer theft by their leaving more expensive items in the shopping cart and scanning lower-priced items, or scanning items with the barcode covered by one's hand. Store personnel need to be alert to these and other consumer actions.[15]

Retailers are increasingly using telecommunications to aid operations via low-cost, secure, in-store transmissions. Retailers use beacon-based technology and applications to push targeted geo-tagged and time-sensitive notifications and promotions to mobile phones of customers in malls to encourage store visits and purchases. Many stores offer free Wi-Fi so customers may scan a barcode for checkout or to check inventory at a nearby location or retailer Web site when the item they are looking for is not in stock. Target's Cartwheel app allows customers to locate and page the nearest sales associate for help.

CAM Commerce Solutions (www.camcommerce.com) offers very inexpensive operations software to small retailers in the hope that as these retailers grow, they will upgrade to advanced software.

SUPPLY CHAIN MANAGEMENT TECHNOLOGIES   Depending on a retailer's market size and geography, omnichannel fulfillment can a daunting operation, particularly when customers (not the retailer) decide where and how they would like to receive their purchases among the options offered by the retailer. See Figure 13-8. Sometimes, a linear, pallet-based supply chain (customarily used for large orders bound for stores) can no longer be restricted to a distribution center. Sales associates and store cashiers need authority to send single-line, multiple-category, direct-to-consumer orders from demand-driven supply chains that provide store-shelf collaboration with store backrooms, distribution centers, and a supplier network. When using Amazon's DRS technology, customers can click Dash tags to order from various manufacturers and specialty retail partners with a simple button.[16]

Leading store-centric omnichannel retailers such as Lowes recognize the importance of demand-driven supply chains that increase product availability and inventory turnover while reducing cash-to-cash cycle times and costs to serve.[17] The focus is on meeting individual consumer demand across channels and on collaborating with suppliers to meet that demand cost effectively.

Cloud (or SaaS) inventory control and order-tracking services that enhance visibility in supply chains are making real-time product fulfillment possible for small and mid-sized retailers. For example, ADC's InterScale Scales Manager is a fully integrated software application that manages produce and fresh foods in supermarkets and convenience stores. The application identifies the true cost of goods sold and provides hourly forecasts and production plans in real time, thus reducing waste. It can accurately forecast demand for bakery and deli items, hot foods, seafood, produce, dairy, meat, frozen food, floral items, and more.[18]

FIGURE 13-8

How Computerization Improves Productivity

By having as much of their data computerized as possible, retailers can dramatically improve their productivity. They can automate personnel staffing, monitor inventory turnover in real time, and more.

Source: Glovatskiy/ Shutterstock. Reprinted by permission.

Corporate Responsibility at Target

Target has a well-conceived corporate responsibility program encompassing multiple activities. Since 1946, Target has donated 5 percent of its profits to charities; this amounts to over $4 million *weekly*. Annually Target publishes a Corporate Social Responsibility Report that describes its goals and its accomplishments relative to each goal. Among its recent goals were to increase organic food offerings, use more sustainable packaging on its private-label packages, increase Energy Star certifications in buildings, reduce waste via recycling, lessen greenhouse gas emissions, and improve transportation efficiencies (both inbound and outbound).

Why do you think other large retailers are not as socially conscious? What do you recommend for them?

Source: Based on material in Target Corporation, "Corporate Social Responsibility Report," https:corporate.target.com (August 21, 2016).

Polycom (www.polycom .com/solutions/solutions-by-industry/retail.html) has a variety of wireless communications products.

Retailers such as Home Depot, Walmart, and J. C. Penney use videoconferencing. This lets them link store employees with central headquarters, as well as interact with vendors. Videoconferencing can be done via satellite technology and by computer (with special hardware and software). Audio/video communications can be used to train workers, spread news, stimulate worker morale, and so on. Polycom, with its SpectraLink product line, is one of the firms marketing lightweight phones so workers can talk to each other anywhere in a store. Polycom clients have included Barnes & Noble, Giant Food, Ikea, Kmart, Neiman Marcus, Rite Aid, and Toys "R" Us.

Outsourcing

More retailers have turned to outsourcing for some of the operating tasks they previously performed themselves. With **outsourcing**, a retailer pays an outside party to undertake one or more of its operating functions. The goals are to reduce the costs and employee time devoted to particular tasks. For example, Limited Brands uses outside firms to oversee its energy use and facilities maintenance. Crate & Barrel outsources the management of its E-mail programs. Apple Stores, Payless Shoes, and Sports Chalet outsource their information technology services. Kmart uses logistics firms to consolidate small shipments and to process returned merchandise; it also outsources electronic data interchange tasks. Home Depot outsources most trucking operations. Retailers also outsource Web design, product delivery, processing of foreign currency transactions, and completion of tariff paperwork to specialized service providers.

Flagship Merchant Services (www.flagshipprocessing .com) handles credit operations for a number of retailers.

Outsourcing delivers operational competences and the ability to quickly respond to customer needs. To combat low margins and commoditization, high-performance retailers leverage outsourcing to increase operational effectiveness and lower costs. Outsourcing can range from IT infrastructure to business process applications. Many firms see outsourcing as a phased process, beginning with infrastructure and ending with business processes managed by a third party. The outsourcer can bring industrywide experience, along with specialist knowledge. Economies of scale drive down unit costs, as do shared resources. Unpredictable capital costs are replaced with variable operational costs.[19]

Crisis Management

Despite the best intentions, retailers may sometimes be faced with crisis situations that need to be managed as smoothly as feasible. Consumer responses to crises depend on the "locus of control"—whether they perceive the causes to be within or outside of the retailer's control.

Examples of crises brought on by factors *outside* a retailer's control include a storm that knocks out store power, unexpectedly high or low consumer demand for a good or service, a burglary, a sudden illness of the owner or a key employee, a sudden increase in a supplier's prices, or a natural disaster such as a flood or an earthquake. These can be addressed by good marketing communications. However, crises perceived to be *within* a retailer's control—such as an in-store fire or broken water pipe (poor maintenance), access to a store being partially blocked due to picketing by striking workers (poor employee relations), a car accident in the retailer's parking lot, or an in-store data breach compromising customer credit data—can lead to legal and financial penalties, undermine consumer trust, and damage a retailer's image.

Although many crises can be anticipated, and some adverse effects may occur regardless of retailer efforts, these principles are important:

1. There should be contingency plans for as many different types of crisis situations as possible. That is why retailers buy insurance, install backup generators, and prepare management succession plans. A firm can have a checklist to follow if there is an incident such as a store fire or a parking-lot accident.
2. A clear chain of command for decision making and external communications must be established and updated.
3. Essential information should be communicated to all affected parties, such as the fire or police department, employees, customers, and the media, as soon as a crisis occurs.
4. Cooperation—not conflict—among the involved parties is essential.
5. Responses should be as swift as feasible; indecisiveness may worsen the situation.
6. The firm needs to assess the need for appropriate insurance.

Crisis management is a key task for both small and large retailers. Hence, a thorough contingency plan for responding to a multitude of potential events can mitigate the reputational and financial risks of a crisis.[20]

Visit our blog site (www.bermanevansretail.com) for posts on crisis management.

Chapter Summary

1. *To describe the important role of operations management as a source of competitive advantage in the rapidly evolving omnichannel retail industry.* Operations management efficiently and effectively seeks to enact the policies needed to satisfy customers, employees, and management. In contrast to Chapter 12, which dealt with financial aspects, Chapter 13 covered operational facets.

2. *To examine several specific aspects of operating a retail business.* An operations blueprint systematically lists all operating functions, their characteristics, and their timing, as well as the responsibility for performing the functions.

Store format and size considerations include use of prototype stores and store dimensions. Firms often use prototype stores in conjunction with rationalized retailing. Some retailers emphasize category-killer stores; others open smaller stores. In space allocation, retailers deploy a top-down or a bottom-up approach. They want to optimize the productivity of store space.

Personnel utilization activities that improve productivity range from better screening applicants to workload forecasts to job standardization and cross-training. Job standardization routinizes the tasks of people with similar positions in different departments. In cross-training, people learn tasks associated with more than one job. A firm can advance its personnel flexibility and minimize the total number of workers needed at any given time by these techniques.

Store maintenance includes all activities in managing physical facilities. It influences people's perceptions of the retailer, the life span of facilities, and operating costs. Managerial actions and strategic planning are needed to control energy resources. Besides daily facilities

management, retailers need decision rules about frequency and manner of store renovations.

Good inventory management requires that retailers acquire and maintain the proper merchandise while ensuring efficient and effective operations. This encompasses everything from coordinating different supplier shipments to planning customer deliveries (if needed).

Store security measures protect both personal and merchandise safety. Retailers need to budget adequate resources for workers' compensation, product liability, fire, accident, property, officers' liability, and employee health insurance.

Most U.S. adults use credit cards. Check and credit payments generally mean larger transactions than cash payments. One-third of retail transactions are in cash, one-sixth by check, and one-half by credit or debit card. Retailers pay various fees to be able to offer noncash payment options to customers, and there is a wide range of payment systems available for retailers.

A growing number of retailers have computerized elements of operations. Computerized checkouts and electronic point-of-sale systems are quite useful. Self-scanning is gaining in popularity. Videoconferencing and mobile and wireless in-store telephone communications play a critical role in enhancing shopping experience.

With outsourcing, retailers pay another party to handle one or more operating functions. The goals are to reduce costs and better utilize employees' time.

Crisis management must handle unexpected situations as smoothly as possible. There should be contingency plans, information should be communicated to those affected, all parties should cooperate, responses should be swift, and the chain of command for decisions should be clear.

Key Terms

operations blueprint (p. 333)
prototype stores (p. 335)
rationalized retailing (p. 335)
top-down space management
    approach (p. 336)
bottom-up space management
    approach (p. 336)

job standardization (p. 337)
cross-training (p. 337)
store maintenance (p. 338)
debit-card system (p. 343)
computerized checkout (p. 344)

electronic point-of-sale system
    (p. 344)
self-scanning (p. 344)
outsourcing (p. 346)

Questions for Discussion

1. Present a brief operations blueprint for your college bookstore.
2. What are the pros and cons of prototype stores? For which kind of firms is this type of store *most* desirable?
3. What challenges do omnichannel retailers face in in job standardization and cross-training for their employees?
4. Comment on this statement: "The quality of store maintenance efforts affects consumer perceptions of the retailer, the life span of facilities, and operating expenses."
5. Talk to two local retailers and ask them what they have done to maximize their energy efficiency. Present your findings.
6. You own a sports goods store and offer personalization services. You are planning a complete renovation of the accessories department. What operations decisions must you make?
7. What steps can a retailer take to minimize their insurance costs in relation to safety issues?

8. Explain the steps that a retailer might take in offering a customer a credit account.
9. What are the key benefits to a retailer of installing modern electronic point-of-sale systems and linking them up to stock control, management, and re-ordering?
10. Explain how adopting an omnichannel system complicates the supply chain management of a retailer.
11. What does an outsourcer bring to the retailer in terms of advantages?
12. Outline the contingency plan a retailer could have in the event of each of these occurrences:
    a. A shopper accidentally setting off the burglar alarm.
    b. A flood in the store caused by a ruptured water pipe.
    c. A firm's Web site inadvertently making personal customer information available to a mailing list company.
    d. The bankruptcy of a key supplier.

Web-Based Exercise

Global Omnichannnel (http://globalomnichannel.com/) is one of a growing number of service providers supporting the global retail industry. They have expertise in helping retailers deliver customer service across the broadest range of channels. They create technologies for the retailer to offer a consistently high level of customer service, whether the customer is at the point of sales, online, or using mobile apps. Their systems help retailers to control their supply chains so they can ensure that all customers are handled in the right way.

Examine their solutions and customer base, and apply them to a local chain in your country.

PART 5 | Short Cases

Case 1: Assistant Store Manager *

Recently, a national discount apparel store chain posted a job listing for Assistant Store Manager. The applicant chosen would work in Oregon. Here is the position description placed at the National Retail Federation Job Board.

The Assistant Store Manager (ASM) is responsible for the management and supervision of all assigned departments and all nonexempt employees [non-managerial] in the store. The ASM will assist in managing and controlling store operations to ensure that all company standards and expectations are consistently met. The ASM will also supervise areas assigned by the Store Manager and follow the firm's philosophy and policies in regard to customers, store associates, and merchandising. The ASM is responsible for learning all phases of store operations. In the absence of the Store Manager, the Assistant Manager is responsible for the entire store operation and will execute the business plan and the associated programs that will deliver the desired sales and profit results, while maintaining good quality customer service.

These are the essential functions for the ASM: Execute customer service programs and merchandise presentation programs through store associates' training and program supervision. Supervise and coach retail associates in providing efficient and friendly service at the registers, the customer service desk, fitting rooms, the sales floor, and so on. Monitor the maintenance of customer service, sizing, and markdowns to reach corporate goals. Oversee merchandise processing, in-store marketing, and store appearance. Urgently approach processing merchandise to the selling floor within the company time frame. Ensure that merchandise is presented and organized utilizing the company's clear merchandising philosophy and guidelines. Ensure that markdowns are processed according to policy on an accurate and timely basis. Maintain a high standard of housekeeping with the help of contracted maintenance personnel and store associates. Manage store recovery to ensure a clean, neat, easy to shop environment.

In addition, the ASM will: Monitor inventory shortage programs in the store and ensure compliance with company policies. Understand company and store inventory results and goals. Assist in leading the annual inventory process, including preparation and execution of inventory guidelines. Assist with training store associates on loss prevention awareness and store shortage goals. Monitor the out-of-stock policy to ensure proper administration. Assist in analyzing monthly store reports to evaluate controllable expenses and overall store performance. Communicate any variances to company standards to the Store Manager. Ensure proper scheduling of employees to meet business objectives. Ensure that all associates understand and can execute emergency operating procedures. Accept special assignments as directed by management.

Finally, the ASM will: Assist in recruiting, hiring, training, and developing nonexempt store associates. Ensure compliance with personnel policies. Assist with employee relations issues by communicating any incidents to the Store Manager or District Managers. Maintain adherence to safety policies and ensure the safety of store associates and customers. Assist in facilitating monthly safety meetings. Ensure compliance with all government regulations. Assist in the management and continuous monitoring of actual spending to be within budget. Control payroll hours to plan and well as adjust to current business trends.

The ASM must meet several physical requirements, as well: Be able to stand for prolonged periods (up to 8 hours daily). Be able to raise or lower objects weighing up to 25 pounds, from one level to another (including upward). Be able to regularly bend, stoop, or crouch (varying per daily business need).

Questions

1. What are the pros and cons of delineating such a long list of specific activities for an ASM to perform?
2. Why is ASM a good starting point for a retail career?
3. What criteria would you use to determine how well an ASM is doing in his or her job?
4. What do you recommend that the retail employer should do to keep an ASM motivated?

Case 2: Manager, Training and Development *

Recently, a major global retail chain posted a job listing for the position of Manager of Training and Development. The applicant chosen would work in New Jersey. Following is the position description placed at the National Retail Federation Job Board.

The Manager of Training and Development (MTD) is responsible for designing, implementing, and sustaining best-in-class, innovative training and leadership programs that support and develop the company's talent within the Distribution Centers and within the Field/Store Leadership environment. The organizational development and learning team is high energy, creative, dynamic, and collaborative; it oversees talent development across the three business units of our company: retail, distribution, and global. The team is charged with providing training to develop and support high-performing, highly engaged diverse teams. The MTD reports to the Executive Director, Organizational Development and Learning.

Key responsibilities include: Lead, manage, create, and execute training that meets the strategic needs of the business within the field leadership environment. Oversee the design, development, and delivery of training programs, including new-hire training, leadership training, customer service, management skills, and operational training. Ensure high-quality training curriculum and instruction. Consult with line-of-business leaders to identify performance needs for talent enhancement in relation to attainment of business goals. Evaluate effectiveness

---

* Based on material in National Retail Federation, "Job Board," http://jobs.nrf.com (July 17, 2016). Reprinted by permission.

* Based on material in National Retail Federation, "Job Board," http://jobs.nrf.com (July 17, 2016). Reprinted by permission.

of learning and development programs, and providing direction. Assess, select, and manage vendor relationships. Translate identified needs into training design and development of solutions to address performance gaps. Collaborate with colleagues and subject-matter experts to share best practices involving various learning programs, skills, and technologies. Select proper instructional approaches and delivery platforms, and tailor the learning modalities to maximize learning opportunities.

In addition, the MTD would: Facilitate group interactions such as meetings, seminars, workshops, and team meetings, and lead classroom and distance-learning sessions. Use technology to deliver and track training solutions. Produce metrics and evaluations for the global resource center in terms of learning and development. Consistently seek out cutting-edge training methodologies and best practices to implement.

The successful MTD will have: A bachelor's degree. A graduate/advanced degree preferred. At least 7 years of work experience with solid career progression, including at least 3 years in learning program management, business, adult education, and/or consulting. Significant experience in developing, managing, delivering, and improving high-quality learning programs, including curriculum and materials design and program assessment tool. Effective problem-solving skills, an understanding of group and corporate dynamics, integrity, and the ability to employ sound judgment in complex situations. Excellent interpersonal and public communication and facilitation skills. Ability to work effectively with diverse clients at all levels in a large, complex, nonhierarchical firm, as well as ability to work with senior leaders in a corporate environment. Ability to influence leadership and work in a fast-pace environment. Demonstrate verbal and written communication skills and conflict resolution skills. Adaptability to changing priorities. Willingness to embrace creativity and new ideas. Strong project management experience with superb follow-up skills. Ability to design technology-based learning, self-study, virtual classrooms, and portal design. Reputation for commitment to building a high-performance culture.

Physical job requirements include: Most time spent sitting comfortably, with a frequent opportunity to move about. Occasionally requires walking for extended periods in the store and distribution center environment. Light lifting requirements. Requires overnight travel up to 20 percent of time.

Questions

1. Based on the information this case, what kind of career path would you expect an MTD to have? Why?
2. Using Figure 11-4 as an example, present a similarly formatted job description for an MTD.
3. How could an MTD improve a retailer's financial operations?
4. What are the greatest challenges facing an MTD?

Case 3: Senior Manager of Digital Operations *

Recently, a cosmetics firm posted a job listing for the position of Senior Manager of Digital Operations. This firm sells online, operates its own boutiques, and distributes via other retailers.

The applicant chosen would work in San Francisco. Here is the job description placed at the National Retail Federation Job Board. Reporting to the Vice-President of Digital Strategy, the Senior Manager of Digital Operations (SMDO) acts as an operational manager on the firm's Global Digital team, overseeing the team budget and spending, vendor selection, and contracts and renewals.

These are the SMDO's main duties and responsibilities: Stay in close partnership with other company executives. Develop and present an annual budget. Understand changes in the digital landscape that drive new investments, and provide analysis. Actively seek and identify ways to spend the team's money more wisely. Manage the digital budget on a monthly basis. Oversee the monthly digital P&L and report monthly on variances. Partner with project managers to approve any cost overruns and track underspends, revising and reallocating between expenses as needed to achieve overall goals. Develop charge-back guidance for geographic markets annually. Work with finance to ensure market charge-backs are processed in a timely and accurate manner. Create visibility on overall digital and project budgets for executives on the digital team.

He or she will also be involved with these activities: Assess new digital ideas, vendors, and potential solutions. Proactively identify areas where new solutions can support business objectives. Research and propose areas for operational savings based on knowledge of the digital landscape. Develop vendor scorecards and implement a process for improving the business performance of operational vendors, by leading vendor reviews with appropriate project managers. Provide proactive coaching and feedback on vendor performance, in order to drive quality and value from our business partners.

Last, the SMDO will do these tasks: Act as business owner for all team contracts, partnering with legal and purchasing departments. Work with project managers and purchasing to devise project request for proposals (RFPs), ensuring business and project needs are met. Identify optimal vendors for each job, given budget constraints and priorities. Work with project managers and purchasing to define vendor selection criteria for each major project. Partner with discipline leads to accurately reflect project scope and protect the business. Work with legal, bringing digital-specific savvy. Initiate timely renewal quotes and negotiations (in partnership with purchasing for larger contracts). Support other departments that sign digital-oriented contracts with advice about vendors and business terms based on experience. Document critical operational processes and practices across the digital team, including E-commerce, Web operations, customer service, etc. Substantiate business continuity procedures, manage vendor lists and communications, streamline emergency protocols, and participate in planning on behalf of the team to reduce business risk.

Job requirements include: Experience in operations management at a digital or high-tech company—or experience managing budgets and working in a project management role. 3+ years of experience managing a digital, tech, or agency budget and P&L. 3+ years of experience as a key reviewer/negotiator on statements of work and change orders. High level of familiarity with digital master agreements. Understanding and experience with these types of digital projects: photography/video production, Web or application development,

* Based on material in National Retail Federation, "Job Board," http://jobs.nrf.com (July 17, 2016). Reprinted by permission.

E-commerce systems, or software licensing. Strong spreadsheet skills and excellent communication skills. Proactive, detail oriented, with drive for fiscal responsibility and operational discipline. Bachelor's degree or equivalent experience preferred. Successfully pass an E-Verify check.

Questions

1. Based on the information this case, what kind of career path would you expect an SMDO to have? Why?
2. How could an SMDO have an impact on a retailer's cash flow?
3. How could an SMDO have an impact on a chain retailer's energy management systems?
4. How could an SMDO have an impact on a retailer's management of its own credit card?

Case 4: Retail Shrinkage: A Significant Problem *

A total of 100 retailers participated in the National Retail Federation's 2015 "National Retail Security Survey," representing more than 20 retail market categories. The largest sample (24 percent) came from retailers seeing $1 billion to $2.49 billion in sales.

"For some time we've been looking to compare where the shrinkage is coming from, and for the most part the highest amount has been internal theft," Richard Hollinger (the study's co-author) says. "For the first time, we're actually seeing shoplifting exceed the internal numbers." The efforts to combat shrinkage are substantial. Retailers use loss prevention systems "almost universally," but loss prevention budgets represented less than 1 percent of overall sales. Specialty apparel retailers spent an average of 0.63 percent of sales on loss prevention measures; grocery stores used 0.36 percent.

Almost all respondents are pursuing efforts to cut down on high-risk employees. Some 89 percent said they're conducting criminal conviction checks, 86 percent conduct multiple interviews, and 73 percent verify employment history. Men's and women's specialty apparel stores and supermarkets are pre-employment screening leaders, with 92 percent checking criminal convictions and 83 percent verifying past employment. Grocery stores and supermarkets reported 100 percent criminal background checks, with 83 percent test for drugs.

Training plays an important role, as do hotlines and incentives. Of those surveyed, 95 percent have an anonymous hotline and 88 percent use awareness posters; more than one-half offer a variety of training programs and notification systems. The leading program continues to be videos (72 percent), but

more than 55 percent use Internet-based systems and 54 percent offer "honesty incentives." Employee incentives offer great value to loss-prevention strategies, but retailers still must prove theft.

All respondents use burglar alarms and 93 percent use digital video recorders; 66 percent use live hidden closed-circuit television. More than 69 percent use point-of-sale data mining to help losses at the till. In-store deterrence—plain-clothes detectives (41 percent), receipt checkers (38 percent), and signage (36 percent)—are also gaining traction. One-third of department stores use acousto-magnetic electronic security tags, but *all* men's and women's specialty apparel stores and sporting goods retailers use them.

Hollinger believes the best programs are a combination of human resources and technology. "We've been seeing this for years: Hire the best people, train them as well as you can by making them aware of the impact of shrinkage, control your merchandise to make sure you know where it is and where it's going, and develop a range of technologies to apprehend those who are stealing from you," he says.

In human resources, loss-prevention staff can make a budget work and are leaders in diversity. One in four loss-prevention managers are women, slightly higher than the national trend that sees 22 percent of senior leadership roles filled by women. Almost 10 percent of loss-prevention managers are Hispanic.

The war against *Organized Retail Crime (ORC)* transcends the retail industry and is a national issue. Major cities from Minnesota to Utah are forming their own retail crime alliances. "The way we should be tackling crime as a whole is by making sure we come at it from an organized crime perspective," St. Paul Police Sergeant Charlie Anderson said after formation of the Twin Cities Organized Retail Crime Association.

Even with growth in regional and federal assistance, retailers have a responsibility to protect their merchandise and catch those who steal. What will loss prevention look like in 2020? "A major thing that we're going to see is a continuing emphasis on technology," Hollinger says. "There's a continued emphasis on trying to find better technologies to monitor and catch shoplifters and employed thieves."

Questions

1. What is the proper mix of humans and technology in preventing shrinkage losses?
2. How would a small retailer's theft avoidance strategy differ from that of a large strategy? Why?
3. Develop an operations blueprint (see Figure 13-1 for an example) to reduce retail theft.
4. What else could a retailer do to reduce shopper and employee theft? Explain your answer.

---

* Based on material in Fred Minnick, "Small and Significant," *STORES Magazine* (August 2015), pp. 66, 68. Reprinted by permission. Copyright 2016. STORES Magazine.

PART 5 Comprehensive Case

Predicting Retail Trends *

Introduction

Some predictions are a slam dunk. Retail will continue to be driven by technology. Science fiction is coming to life in the form of robotics and virtual reality. And the Internet will soon be embedded everywhere. Another truism: Change is exponential in retail. Accepting that is the easy part.

Trying to predict what's next in an industry that moves faster and faster—toppling norms and reimagining processes—is the hard part. In this case are several predictions for 2016. Let's see which ones turned out to be correct.

Predictions of 2016 Retailing Trends

In looking ahead to 2016, experts were asked to predict whether 2016 would be a "sweet" year for retailers. Would a handful of winning ideas drive industry objectives for 2016? Or was the idea of trying to predict what was just ahead for the industry our version of December insanity?

Economists seemed to agree that indicators pointed to a fairly solid 2016. Confidence data were encouraging, unemployment continued to dip, and there didn't appear to be any significant recession risks on the horizon. Presidential elections affect consumer sentiment, but historically they tend to have little impact on spending, which boded well for retailers.

Still, uncertainties remained. Goldman Sachs' sobering assessment of what was in store for 2016 boiled down to the phrase "flat is the new up." The investment bank forecast 2 to 4 percent growth and described economic recovery as "running in place."

With a nod to the NCAA basketball tournament's "Sweet 16," we came up with 16 predictions for the retail industry in 2016. No doubt some would deliver 'nothing but net'; others may have spun around the rim before dropping in, and a few may have turned out to be air balls. Still, there's something to be said for making it to the final 16.

Planning for this feature began in mid-July 2015. Every conference session, exhibit hall meeting, and phone briefing became fodder for determining what may have been on the horizon. A big "thank you" goes to all who shared their insight, took the time to teach us about new technology, or set aside a few minutes to share their retail vision. We simply couldn't have done it without you.

Convenience, Expedience the Fast Track to Shoppers' Hearts

With consumers able to summon a car ride with a few taps on a smartphone, the expectation that everything should be simple and frictionless is growing. Companies that save shoppers time, simplify routine tasks, and remove friction are capitalizing: Think Uber, Apple Pay, Instacart, and Amazon Prime.

Although some debate the popularity of subscription services, they continue to pop up—promising to simplify everything from the delivery of dinner to razors.

Same-day delivery was expected to move closer to critical mass in 2016 as more companies emerged to serve an increasing number of markets. For omnichannel retailers such as Macy's, same-day delivery was considered an important part of the value proposition.

Drones and 3D printing are topics du jour in retail circles, but were expected to continue to garner more talk than traction in 2016. Neither should be overlooked for the simple reason that both play to the desire for speed and convenience—two things that many consumers consider essential.

Personalization Is Mission-Critical

We live in the Age of the Consumer. Retailers need to explore every opportunity to raise the level and quality of contextual, personalized experiences. Investments in customer analytics are imperative, as is an understanding of where to apply personalization to deliver the biggest bang for the buck.

Shoppers expect tailored offerings, including their savings, merchandise, and service transactions. And personalization needs to be a consistent omnichannel effort. If retailers can't identify a shopper across various points of interaction, they're on thin ice.

Meanwhile, look for new "disruptors" to play the personalization card with aplomb. Stitch Fix is a prime example: By blending art, science, and a human touch, the personal stylist company projected $200 million in revenue for 2016.

A Digital Core Is Essential

Today's consumers are firmly in control; they choose how they will interact with the various retailers. And although we'd like to believe that shoppers can be forgiving, they're not. Responding to these instant gratification customers requires a digital pulse to sense and respond to their changing needs, and a digital pulse requires a digital core.

A digital core gives companies real-time visibility into all mission-critical business practices and processes around customers, suppliers, work force, big data, and the Internet of Things (IoT). It allows retail businesses to react in an agile and hyperaware fashion and enables them to predict, simulate, plan, and even anticipate future outcomes.

Experts report that only 37 percent of retailers currently have a strategy to create a 360-degree customer view. By 2020 (if not sooner), all retail store sales will be influenced by digital data. Retailers need a digital core to understand all the data that move in and out of the company.

Music versus Noise

Big data represent a $33 billion industry; and this is growing rapidly. Nine out of 10 retailers believe that big data are essential to their business operations. Still, it's how companies distill

* Based on material in Susan Reda, "Our Picks to Click," *STORES Magazine*, December 2015, pp. 22–24. Copyright 2016. STORES Magazine.

the data into meaningful insights that defines the value of the outcomes.

As the physical and virtual retail worlds more fully mesh, the challenge for retail companies will be to derive meaning from the intersection of multiple sources of data: stores, E-commerce, mobile, social, in-store sensors, and/or wearables. Connecting these data to deliver better customer service, improve the in-store experience, or design a more-engaging mobile app has become just basic table stakes.

Retailers that are truly obsessed with their customers, and their behavior and characteristics, will more aggressively invest in analytics efforts (and software), recognizing that both revenue growth and enhanced customer experiences depend on such actions.

Voice Technology to Be Worth Talking About

Have you spoken to Siri lately? How about Alexa, Google Now, or Cortana? Voice recognition software is dramatically changing shopper behavior; and this will be even more true in the future. If you're not listening, you risk being left out of the conversation.

Although solid data calculating the benefits of voice-activated search remain elusive by virtue of the so-far small sample size, the fact is that most consumers speak faster than they type. As advanced voice technology becomes more accepted by consumers, retailers will need to embrace its greater popularity as a search and information tool. Voice-recognition applications are simpler and require less effort for the shopper—a winning formula for those consumers who have shown time and again that they're willing to adopt technologies that help them sift through information or aid in a purchasing decision.

Generation Z to Disrupt Retail

While everyone was paying attention to Millennials, Generation Z has been honing their shopping chops. Fitch recently reported that by the year 2020 the people born in the late 1990s will be the largest group of shoppers worldwide, accounting for 40 percent of the United States, Europe, and Brazil, Russia, India, China (known as the BRIC countries) consumer base.

This group will disrupt retailers with a new set of attitudes, motivations, and behaviors. The Generation Z group is the most culturally diverse cohort, considered to be more self-reliant, solution-oriented, and ambitious than Millennials. It's also made up of impatient shoppers quick to dismiss companies that can't immediately and easily cater to their whims.

Which retailers have the upper hand with Gen Z? None of them do at the moment. It's all about who best meets their needs and who delivers something that is perceived to be unique—and how quickly the consumers can have what they want.

The Pursuit of "Frictionless" Payments

Consumers typically want payment processes to be simple, but delivering a seamless experience from aspiration to purchase requires heavy lifting by the supply chain (including retailers). Payment option iterations from Apple, Samsung, and Android have begun gaining traction, although usage has not been growing at anticipated rates. The key arbiter of what could be: 60 percent of consumers pay with smartphones because of loyalty benefits (e.g., nearly 15 percent of Starbucks customers pay with their phones).

Although not every payment innovation was expected to catch on, 2016 would find those consumers and retailers willing to wade through a sea of change. Biometrics such as fingerprint systems, facial recognition, and iris scanning are being introduced. Technology consulting firm Frost & Sullivan forecast that nearly half a billion people will be using smartphones equipped with biometric technology by 2017. MasterCard announced a program in October 2015 that would enable companies to add credit-card credentials to personal devices such as key fobs and smart rings.

Don't discount the possibilities of RFID (Radio Frequency Identification). The reality of paying by walking under an RFID-enabled archway is closer than ever. And resist the temptation to dismiss Bitcoin and other cryptocurrencies: They continue to drive home the message that the next generation thinks rather differently about money.

Say "Hi" to "Buy" Buttons on Social Sites

Social networks have moved way beyond their origins. Facebook, Pinterest, and others have all introduced Buy Buttons, but that's just the tip of the iceberg. Expect fringe platforms such as Snapchat, Instagram, and Medium—maybe even Periscope—to be nipping at their heels. [*Authors' note:* In mid-2016, Twitter decided to pull the plug on its Buy Button efforts. This was less than a year after Twitter had announced its program with great fanfare.]

Having Buy Buttons on some of the fastest-growing social networks means shoppers who are interested in Buy Buttons will no longer have to ask where to buy. And when retailers take away the friction of shopping, customers click to buy.

Even if you're not ready to leap into social shopping, don't overlook the power of these networks for marketing; Instagram's advertising revenue from direct viewer shopping was expected to exceed $1 billion in 2016.

Partnerships Will Thrive

Gone are the days when retailers kept all their cards close to their vest. Partnerships are now the new secret weapon for those committed to delivering on the promise of today's on-demand economy.

Walgreens, Target, Walmart, Costco, and 7-Eleven have been working with such delivery startups as Instacart, Doordash, and Postmates. Deliv, which billed itself as the bridge to the last-mile gap between retailers and their customers, secured a retailer roster that already includes Macy's, Neiman Marcus, and Williams-Sonoma.

On the other hand, some experts looked for retailer/designer collaborations to cool in year 2016 as more shoppers grew tired of this once-loved differentiation strategy, and more weary of the prevailing inventory management issues. In 2015, there was H&M with Balmain, Kohl's with Thakoon, and Target introducing Adam Lippes. All are top designers best known by just the 1 percent of shoppers who can actually afford their collections, not the masses who crave a designer label their friends will covet.

Year of the Mobile-Equipped Associate

Providing better customer service and generating more interaction with their shoppers can lead to greater retail sales. No longer an industry talking point, the concept of arming front-line associates with mobile technology has reached a critical mass.

Tech-empowered associates often have considerable insight into the available inventory across all stores and distribution centers; this can save a customer sale in just seconds. With their devices in hand, associates have the potential to better understand customer preferences based on actual past purchases or wish lists.

With great power comes great responsibility: Thus, retailers must better train their associates to be able to use and understand the technology tools, and realize that different people shop differently. Not every customer is tech savvy; many visit stores for the experience.

IoT Coming on PDQ

The Internet of Things (IoT) became "a thing" in 2014 and it's going to be much bigger as time goes on. The McKinsey Global Institute recently forecast that IoT could have a total economic impact of $11 trillion annually by 2025—less than a decade from now!

Even though much of the talk today is about the use of IoT in home appliances and smartphones, the technology really sets the stage for major big-data developments—specifically in the form of the improved levels of supply chain efficiency and inventory management. With IoT, products can communicate how they are actually being used, providing considerable insight into customer behavior and preferences.

Although this game-changing technology offers both potential cost savings and productivity enhancements, hurdles remain. Standards are imperative; the industry must work with technology vendors to provide connected, interoperable components and systems. Another significant obstacle involves security and privacy concerns—protecting both company and customer data.

Seeking the Mobile Toothbrush

Forrester Research reported that mobile technology would influence about $1 trillion in U.S. spending in the year 2016 as mobile search, shopping, and social interaction becomes the centerpiece of customers' "always-on" way of life. Meanwhile, eMarketer reported that 25 percent of all U.S. E-commerce sales would take place via mobile devices by the end of 2016.

According to Forrester, 4.8 billion people globally would be using smartphones by the end of 2016. The biggest challenge with this occurrence for retailers will be finding a way to effectively carve out a bit of real estate on those devices. Experts see mobile optimization eventually rivaling the importance of desktop optimization.

In 2016, "deep links" to apps were projected to become much more prevalent. Still, the success of mobile apps comes down to their ease of use and the speed of purchase. If an app is to have real value, it will need to pass the "toothbrush test": It has to prompt the consumer to use it every day.

That Shrinking Feeling

Macy's planned to shut as many as 40 of its stores in early 2016, after closing several dozen over the last few years. [*Authors' note:* In mid-2016, Macy's announced plans to close an additional 100 stores.] Forty stores were on the chopping block at

J. C. Penney, and Target was going to close 13 units at the end of January 2016. Along with these planned store closings, the industry will endure shrinking store counts as the office supply segment consolidates and Walgreens Boots Alliance swallows Rite Aid.

Experts point out that a leaner organization can often grow more profitably. Macy's Backstage locations have begun to debut, Walmart's Neighborhood Markets seem like compact supercenters, and Target is expanding its small-format stores, rebranding CityTarget and TargetExpress stores as Target. Kohl's plans to open between 5 and 10 smaller stores, as well.

One-size rarely fits all in apparel retailing. More retailers are realizing the same can be said of their real-estate strategy.

Soon We'll Have AI Make the Predictions

Retailers envision using the software algorithms that define artificial intelligence (AI)—including pattern recognition, deep-learning neural networks, and computer vision—to help generate the major decisions that help shape consumers' user experience. It can be used for product recommendations, dynamic pricing, and promotions, and it gets smarter over time, learning from the data.

While AI will become more rooted in the retail industry, virtual reality (VR) is also knocking on the door. The goal is to use VR to create more immersive, contextual experiences, customized to highlight every brand's assets and strengthen their customer relationships.

Regardless, it's time to test and explore. Even though the over-40 set may look askance at virtual reality, younger shoppers who have been immersed in videogaming since they were knee-high will be more inclined to embrace this new shopping experience, being dubbed *V-commerce*.

New Cybersecurity Threats Looming

The cat-and-mouse game between retailers and cybercriminals shows no signs of abating. Hackers will continue to find new ways to attack retailers' networks, and retailers will continue to do everything in their power to thwart these attempts.

Europay MasterCard and Visa chip-based credit cards will provide an additional line of defense against counterfeit card fraud, but expect a chorus of voices (including the NRF's) to continue to argue that not requiring a PIN to complete a transaction makes this a half-step forward at best.

Meanwhile, retailer and consumer concerns are shifting to other potentially unprotected opportunities for hackers. Merchant data warehouses, unencrypted data transmissions, and card-not-present transactions will be under greater scrutiny.

As the Internet of Things becomes more established, innovators need to keep an eye on protecting the growing number of smart devices. Wider adoption translates into stronger interest on the part of criminals looking to steal personal data captured by these devices.

The Rise of the Data Scientist

Success in 2016 was expected to boil down to smarter, more data-driven decision making. Intuition-based decisions will always play a role in retail, but true insight comes from combining different data sets—points of sale, weather reports, web traffic, competitors' pricing data, and even sensors.

Every merchant and marketer needs to be in sync with the ever-connected customer, and they're challenged to go above and beyond brand promises. That requires a continued emphasis on breaking down organizational silos and connecting data across and within the retail organization. Consider that the entire Uber experience is predicated on data science and algorithms—a high bar, indeed.

It's been said that understanding data science helps merchants speak a language that contributes to the bottom line from day 1. Although it's a huge opportunity, a considerable conundrum remains: There is a dearth of data scientists today and those retailers looking to tap into this expertise are finding that moving from aspiration to action is a longer process than anticipated.

Questions

1. What are the three most important trends cited in this case? Explain your answer.
2. To date, what are the three most accurate predictions cited in the case? Explain your answer.
3. To date, what are the three least accurate predictions cited in the case? Explain your answer.
4. How can retail employees be motivated in today's fast-changing marketplace?
5. Present a job description for one new retail job that will be created as a result of the trends cited in this case.
6. How will the trends cited in this case enable retailers to do a better job in profit planning?
7. On the basis of the trends discussed in this case, should retailers do more or less outsourcing of employee tasks? Why?

Part 6

Merchandise Management and Pricing

In Part Six, we present the merchandise management and pricing aspects of the retail strategy mix. Merchandise management consists of the buying, handling, and financial aspects of merchandising. Pricing decisions deal with the financial aspects of merchandise management and affect their interaction with other retailing elements.

Chapter 14 covers the development of merchandise plans. We begin by discussing the concept of a merchandising philosophy. We then look at buying organizations and their processes, as well as the major considerations in formulating merchandise plans. The chapter concludes by describing category management and merchandising software.

Chapter 15 focuses on implementing merchandise plans. We study each stage in the buying and handling process: gathering information, selecting and interacting with merchandise sources, evaluation, negotiation, concluding purchases, receiving and stocking merchandise, reordering, and re-evaluation. We also examine logistics and inventory management, as well as their effects on merchandising.

Chapter 16 concentrates on financial merchandise management. We introduce the cost and retail methods of accounting. The merchandise forecasting and budgeting process is also presented, as well as the unit control systems. The chapter concludes with the integration of dollar and unit financial inventory controls.

Chapter 17 deals with pricing. We review the outside factors affecting price decisions: consumers, government, suppliers, and competitors. A framework for developing a price strategy is then presented, including objectives, broad policy, basic strategy, implementation, and adjustments.

14 Developing Merchandise Plans

The basis of Chapter 14 is that merchandising plans and decisions must reflect target market desires, the retailer's intended marketplace positioning, and more. Utilized actively as a merchandising tool, the Internet can help retailers be better merchandisers and reach out in a dynamic way to their customers.

Amazon's Dash button is a device resembling a thumb drive that facilitates reordering frequently purchased consumables such as detergents and toilet paper. Consumers can put this wireless device near a washing machine or kitchen cabinet. Reordering is as simple as pressing a Dash button.

There are a number of positive elements of this strategy for consumers, Amazon, and manufacturers. Consumers can easily reorder goods and avoid carrying them from a local store. Since Dash is available only to Amazon Prime members, it serves as an incentive for

Source: Professional photography/Shutterstock. Reprinted by permission.

consumers to sign on to Prime. Companies pay Amazon $15 for each button deployed, as well as a 15 percent commission (above Amazon's traditional markup). Manufacturers of consumer goods generate additional sales due to the ease of shopping and the convenience of delivery. Despite its advantages, however, one study found that many consumers who purchase a Dash button use it just once every two months.[1]

Overview

Retail Detail Merchandising (www.rdmerchandising.com) is a third-party vendor of several merchandising services.

Retailers must have the proper product assortments and sell them in a manner consistent with their overall strategy. **Merchandising** consists of the activities involved in acquiring particular goods and/or services and making them available at the places, times, and prices and in the quantity that enable a retailer to reach its goals. Merchandising decisions can dramatically affect performance. Consider these observations—from two different perspectives:

> The biggest competitive advantages of an independent retailer is its ability to focus on and adapt to consumer needs—thus, offering superior expertise and a high level of customer service. In contrast, the big-box retailer is better at cutting costs and thereby offering lower prices (sometimes, extremely low prices) for shoppers. By virtue of their size, independent retailers can be nimble enough and have better insights to offer high-quality, specialty products that attract target customers who value quality, service, and a relaxed, friendly experience rather than just low prices. This can insulate a small retailer from price competition and lead to higher initial markups—which can make up for low volumes.[2]

> Department stores have typically appealed to consumers with broad product assortments based on demographics in their trading areas and relied on apparel as the traffic generator for their stores. Today, however, department stores are facing significant challenges due to declines in spending on apparel as a proportion of discretionary spending and consumers migrating to E-commerce and off-price retailers. Department store chains are retooling by enhancing their E-commerce offerings, introducing their own off-price brands and smaller store formats, and repositioning the store as a destination with experiential services—using social media and viral marketing tools to build a more loyal customer base. Specialty stores and smaller independent stores, such as Hot Topic and Torrid, that attract alternative shoppers are growing and increasingly becoming attractive to mall owners as tenants to replace traditional mall anchor tenants.[3]

In this chapter, the planning aspects of merchandising are discussed. The implementation aspects of merchandising are examined in Chapter 15. The financial aspects of merchandising are described in Chapter 16. And retail pricing is covered in Chapter 17. Visit our blog site (www.bermanevansretail.com) for a broad selection of posts related to merchandising strategies and tactics.

MERCHANDISING PHILOSOPHY

At Cost Plus World Market, you never know what you'll find (www.worldmarket.com).

A **merchandising philosophy** sets the guiding principles for all the merchandise decisions that a retailer makes. This encompasses every product decision, from what product lines to carry, to the shelf space allotted, to different products, to inventory turnover, to pricing. A retail merchandising philosophy can be product-based (using SKU proliferation data to find the most profitable products) and/or consumer-focused (tailoring assortments and merchandising plans to cater to the most profitable customers). *Product-focused merchandising* involves analyzing SKU-level sales performance and profitability metrics to find and invest in the most profitable products based on store size, volume, and sell-through for each category. *Consumer-focused merchandising* involves creating product assortments based on customer insights, their preferences, and their path to purchase based on an analysis of loyalty data, social network signals, shopping patterns, and other potential "big data" sources.

Astute retailers use customer segmentation data to identify the segments that are more profitable and have a higher lifetime value than others, and to invest in product assortments that reflect target market desires, the retailer's institutional type, marketplace positioning, the defined value chain, supplier capabilities, costs, competitors, product trends, and other factors. A merchandise plan must specify desired objectives in terms of revenue, gross profit, and inventory turnover in percentages and dollars by product groups.[4] See Figure 14-1.

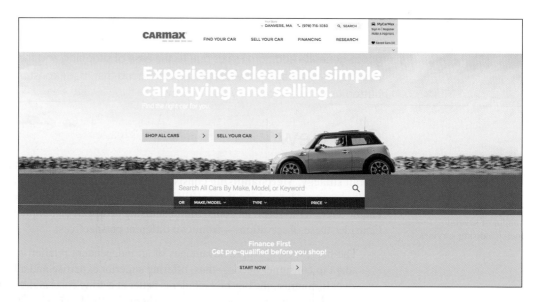

Costco, the membership club giant, flourishes with its individualistic merchandising philosophy, whereby it offers members very low prices on a limited selection, but broad assortment, of national and private brands. Costco's approach yields high sales revenue through quick inventory turnover. Furthermore, volume purchasing and efficient distribution through depots or warehouses (which reduces the handling of merchandise in no-frills, self-service warehouse facilities) stimulate profitable operations at significantly lower gross margins than most other traditional wholesalers, mass merchandisers, supermarkets, and supercenters. Costco carries an average of approximately 3,700 active stock-keeping units (SKUs) per warehouse, significantly less than other retailers. It limits specific items in each product line to fast-selling models, sizes, and colors and sells many consumable products in case, carton, and multiple-pack quantities only.[5]

In forming a merchandising philosophy, the scope of responsibility for merchandise personnel must be stated. Are these personnel involved with the full array of *merchandising functions*, both buying and selling goods and services (including selection, pricing, display, and customer transactions)? Or do they focus on the *buying function*, with others responsible for displays, personal selling, and so on? Many firms consider merchandising as the foundation for their success, and buyers (or merchandise managers) engage in both buying and selling tasks. Other retailers consider buyers to be skilled specialists who should not be active in the selling function, which is done by other skilled specialists. Store managers at full-line discount stores often have great influence on product displays but have little impact on whether to stock or promote particular brands.

With a merchandising-oriented philosophy, the buyer's expertise is used in selling, and his or her responsibility and authority are clear. The buyer ensures that items are properly displayed and that costs are reduced (fewer specialists). He or she is close to consumers due to selling involvement. When buying and selling are separate, specialized skills are applied to each task, the morale of store personnel goes up as they get more authority, selling is not viewed as a secondary task, salesperson–customer interaction is better, and buying and selling personnel are distinctly supervised. Each firm must see which format is best for it.

To capitalize on opportunities, more retailers now use micromerchandising and cross-merchandising. With **micromerchandising**, a retailer adjusts shelf-space allocations to respond to customer and other differences among local markets. Dominick's supermarkets assign shelf space to children's and adult's cereals to reflect demand patterns at different stores. Walmart allots space to product lines at various stores to reflect differences in demographics, weather, and shopping. Micromerchandising is easier today due to the data generated. Tilly's, a California-based specialty retailer of West Coast–inspired lifestyle apparel and accessories, enhances its micromerchandising strategy by leveraging customer data from stores, Web site browsing, and transactions, mobile apps, catalogs, and third-party data. This enables the retailer to monitor, identify, and address customer trends. Individual store profiles for every store in the portfolio are compiled to highlight the differences in brand performance, gender, and customer interests. By selecting

TECHNOLOGY IN RETAILING

Store Planning Software

ConceptDraw (www.conceptdraw.com), Symphony Gold (www .eyc.com), and SmartDraw (www.smartdraw.com) are examples of store planning software. Used by store designers, architects, and interior designers, the applications enable these design professionals to preview and assess alternate store layouts and designs in terms of optimal space utilization, visual impact, and cost considerations. The applications can also be applied to shelf display planograms. ConceptDraw includes templates for specific retailers. Its café and restaurant templates contain close to 300 objects (such as corner benches, square four-seat tables, a hostess podium, and even a salad bar) as well as templates for the kitchen area (such as food coolers and ranges with grills). Designers can easily rearrange the elements in these templates, as well as substitute different objects.

Discuss specific criteria to assess different store planning software packages.

relevant third-party and proprietary brands, styles, colors, sizes, and price points based on profiles, and then shipping products to its stores multiple times per week, Tilly's is able to dynamically adapt its merchandise allocation strategies to capitalize on individual store differences.[6]

In **cross-merchandising**, a retailer carries complementary goods and services to encourage shoppers to buy more. That is why apparel stores stock accessories and auto dealers offer extended warranties. Cross-merchandising, like scrambled merchandising, can be ineffective if taken too far. Yet, it has tremendous potential. Consider this from the perspective of pharmacies, which use cross-merchandising to increase revenues by making it easy for consumers to buy complementary items during the cold and flu season. Placing items such as cough drops, tissues, and medications close together in an aisle not only helps consumers easily find these items if they come in for one of them but it also generates in-store (impulse) purchases. Similarly, customers coming to a liquor store to buy spirits are more apt to also buy crackers, cheese, and/or glassware if placed together.[7] Cross-merchandising leverages customer preferences for one-stop shopping and the tendency to make impulse purchases—and increases the retailer's overall revenues. The impact of seasonality and competition on revenues is reduced.

BUYING ORGANIZATION FORMATS AND PROCESSES

A merchandising plan cannot be properly devised unless the buying organization and its processes are well defined: Who is responsible for decisions? What are their tasks? Do they have sufficient authority? How does merchandising fit with overall operations? Figure 14-2 highlights the range of organizational attributes from which to choose.

Level of Formality

With a *formal buying organization*, merchandising (buying) is a distinct retail task and requires the setup of a separate department. The functions involved in acquiring merchandise and making it available for sale are under the control of this department. A formal organization is most often used by larger firms and involves distinct personnel. In an *informal buying organization*, merchandising (buying) is not a distinct task. The same personnel handle both merchandising (buying) and other retail tasks; responsibility and authority are not always clear-cut. Informal organizations generally occur in smaller retailers.

Advantages of a formal organization are clarity of responsibilities and use of full-time, specialized merchandisers. The disadvantage is the cost of a separate department. Advantages of an informal format are low costs and flexibility. Disadvantages are less-defined responsibilities and less emphasis on merchandise planning. Both structures exist in great numbers. It is not critical for a firm to use a formal department, but it is crucial that it recognizes the role of merchandising (buying) and ensures that responsibility, activities, and operational relationships are defined and enacted.

Degree of Centralization

Chain retailers must choose whether to have a centralized buying organization or a decentralized one. In a *centralized buying organization*, all purchase decisions emanate from one office. A chain may have eight stores, with merchandise decisions made at the headquarters store. In a

FIGURE 14-2

The Attributes and Functions of Buying Organizations

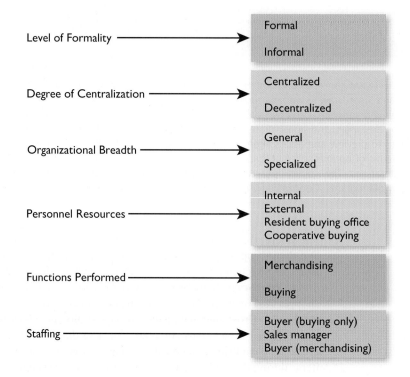

decentralized buying organization, purchase decisions are made locally or regionally. A 40-store chain may let each outlet select its own merchandise or divide branches into geographic territories (such as four branches per region) with regional decisions made by the headquarters store in each territory.

Advantages of centralized buying are the integration of effort, strict controls, consistent image, proximity to top management, staff support, and volume discounts. Possible disadvantages are the inflexibility, time delays, poor morale at local stores, and excessive uniformity. Decentralized buying has these advantages: adaptability to local conditions, quick order processing, and improved morale because of branch autonomy. Potential disadvantages are disjointed planning, an inconsistent image, limited controls, little staff support, and a loss of volume discounts.

Many chains combine the formats by deploying a centralized buying organization while also giving store managers some input. Inditex, the Madrid-based global parent company of retail chains such as Zara, Pull & Bear, Massimo Dutti, Bershka, Stradivarius, Oysho, Zara Home, and Uterqüe, has more than 7,000 stores in 88 countries and online stores in 29 countries. It uses centralized design, buying, and logistics centers for each concept while maintaining flexibility in adapting production to local market demand and customer preferences through 11 clusters that control the supply chain throughout the various stages of design, manufacture, and retailing.[8]

See what Zara's merchandisers think is "hot" (www.zara.com).

Organizational Breadth

In a general buying organization, one or several people buy all the merchandise for the firm. The owner of a small hardware store, however, will likely buy the merchandise for his or her store. With a specialized organization, each buyer is responsible for a product category. For example, a department store usually has separate buyers for girls', juniors', and women's clothes.

A general approach is better if a retailer is small or there are few products involved. A specialized approach is better if a retailer is large or carries many products. By specializing, there is greater expertise and responsibility is well defined; however, costs are higher and extra personnel are required.

Personnel Resources

A retailer can choose an inside or outside buying organization. An *inside buying organization* is staffed by a retailer's personnel, and merchandise decisions are made by permanent employees. See Figure 14-3. With an *outside buying organization*, a firm or personnel external to the retailer

FIGURE 14-3

Performing Merchandising Functions

Because merchandising encompasses such diverse functions, many retailers have multiple employees who participate in these functions—such as the young woman shown here. She is responsible for making sure that items are displayed properly and for monitoring inventory levels for each style and size in her department.

Source: michaeljung/ Shutterstock. Reprinted by permission.

are hired, usually on a fee basis. Most retailers use either an inside or an outside organization; some employ a combination.

An inside buying organization is most often used by large retailers and very small retailers. Large retailers do this to have greater control over merchandising decisions and to be more distinctive. They have the financial clout to employ their own specialists. At very small retailers, the owner or manager does all merchandising functions to save money and keep close to the market.

Ross Stores (www.rossstores.com), the off-price apparel chain that operates Ross Stores (1,210 stores in 33 states) and dd's Discounts (152 stores in 15 states), is an example of a retailer with an inside buying organization. The majority of merchandise in these stores are acquired through opportunistic purchases created by manufacturer overruns and canceled orders during season ("closeouts") and at the end of a season ("packaways"). Ross operates buying offices in two strategic locations, New York City and Los Angeles, the largest U.S. apparel markets. Its buyers are in the market daily, sourcing opportunities, negotiating purchases with vendors and manufacturers, and strengthening vendor relationships —a critical ingredient in the success of its off-price buying strategies. Ross has separate buying organizations for Ross Stores and dd's Discounts that employ 700 merchants, merchandise managers, buyers, and assistant buyers across both organizations, with an average of about 8 years of experience at other department stores or off-price retailers.[9]

Ross Stores has merchandising career opportunities (https://corp .rossstores.com/careers).

An outside organization is most frequently used by small or medium-sized retailers or those far from supply sources. It is more efficient for these retailers to hire outside buyers than to use company personnel. An outside organization has purchase volume clout in dealing with suppliers, usually services noncompeting retailers, offers research, and may sponsor private brands. Outside buying organizations may be paid by retailers that subscribe to their services or by vendors that give commissions. An individual retailer may set up its own internal organization if it feels its outside group is dealing with direct competitors or the firm finds it can buy items more efficiently on its own.

Learn more about the services provided by Doneger Group (www .doneger.com).

The Doneger Group (www.doneger.com), founded in 1946, is one of the leading outside buying firms, with hundreds of retailer clients. Through its Price Point Buying (PPB) division, Donegar identifies opportunistic buys and facilitates business relationships between its retail clients and vendors in the competitive, fast-changing, value-driven retail industry. It is the industry's leading source of global trend intelligence, creative design services, focused and seasonal merchandising direction, expert analysis of the retail business, trend forecasting, and comprehensive market information.[10]

A **resident buying office**, which can be an inside or outside organization, is used when a retailer wants to keep in close touch with key market trends and cannot do so through only the headquarters buying staff. Such offices are situated in vital merchandise centers and provide data and contacts. Worldwide, several specialized firms operate resident buying offices. For instance, the VIB Group, based in Milan, Italy, has a major resident buying office for international retailers. The VIB Fashion Consulting Buying office acts as a local representative of international clients providing a broad range of services, including market analysis, product portfolio reviews, assisting client company buying staff in making the right decisions in tune with local market preferences and intricacies, and developing relationships with vendors. VIB also acts in fulfilling supply requirements of clients in terms of price and contract negotiations, export documentation, compliance with import countries' legislation, and buying merchandise on their behalf.[11] Besides the large players, there are many smaller outside resident buying offices that assist retailers.

Today, independent retailers and small chains are involved with cooperative buying to a greater degree than before to compete with large chains. In **cooperative buying**, a group of retailers gets together to make quantity purchases from suppliers and obtain volume discounts. It is most popular among consumer electronics, food, hardware, and drugstore retailers. One such entity is BrandSource, which represents 4,500 member stores that together account for $14 billion in annual purchases.[12] In addition to major appliances, BrandSource-affiliated retailers sell consumer electronics, bedding, home furnishings, and floor coverings. The cooperative also plans and implements promotional programs, as well as wholesale and retail financing, for its members.

The Federation of Pharmacy Networks (www .fpn.org) provides many services for its members.

As another cooperative buying illustration, the Federation of Pharmacy Networks (FPN) comprises 22 member-buying groups across the United States. It represents more than 15,000 independent drugstore owners. Other consumer electronics buying groups (in the field of electronics) include Mega Group USA, Nationwide Marketing Group, and NATM Buying Corporation.

Functions Performed

At this juncture, the responsibilities and functions of merchandise and in-store personnel are assigned. With a "merchandising" view, merchandise personnel oversee all buying and selling functions, including assortments, advertising, pricing, point-of-sale displays, employee utilization, and personal selling approaches. With a "buying" view, merchandise personnel oversee the buying of products, advertising, and pricing, whereas in-store personnel oversee assortments, displays, employee utilization, and sales presentations. The functions undertaken must reflect the retailer's level of formality, the degree of centralization, and personnel resources.

Staffing

The last organizational decision involves staffing. What positions must be filled and with what qualifications? Firms with a merchandising viewpoint are most concerned with hiring good buyers. Firms with a buying perspective are concerned about hiring sales managers, as well. Many large firms hire college graduates, train them, and promote them to buyers and sales managers.

A **buyer** is responsible for selecting the merchandise to be carried by a retailer and setting a strategy to market that merchandise. He or she devises and controls sales and profit projections for a product category (generally for all stores in a chain); plans proper merchandise assortments, styling, sizes, and quantities; negotiates with and evaluates vendors; and often oversees in-store displays. He or she must be attuned to the marketplace and travel to the marketplace when needed, be able to bargain with suppliers, and be capable of preparing detailed plans. A **sales manager** typically supervises the on-floor selling and operational activities for a specific retail department. He or she must be a good organizer, administrator, and motivator. A *merchandising buyer* must possess attributes of each. Most retailers believe the critical qualification for good merchandisers is an ability to relate to customers and methodically anticipate future needs. In addition, to some extent, buyers are involved with many of the remaining tasks described in this and the next chapter.

Macy's, Inc. (www .macyscollege.com) has exciting career paths in both merchandising and operations.

Macy's, Inc., which operates the Macy's and Bloomingdale's department store chains, has career tracks that recognize the value of both merchandising and in-store personnel. Figure 14-4 shows two distinct career tracks.

DEVISING MERCHANDISE PLANS

Ikea (www.ikea.com) scours the globe for interesting new items that will be popular in its stores.

There are several factors to consider in devising merchandise plans, as discussed next. See Figure 14-5.

Forecasts

Forecasts are projections of expected retail sales for given periods. They are the foundation of merchandise plans and include overall company projections, product category projections, item-by-item projections, and store-by-store projections (if a chain). Consider L.L. Bean, a privately

FIGURE 14-4

Store Management versus Omni/ Digital Career Tracks at Macy's, Inc.: Selected Positions

Source: Figure fully developed by the authors based on information at "Careers After College," www.macyscollege.com/ Careers (August 30, 2016).

Store Management Track

Store Manager
Manages all aspects of operating a profitable store. Sets the tone and leads in driving sales, customer service, merchandise assortment and displays, expense control, employee development, and sales support.

Assistant Store Manager
Directs merchandise flow, store maintenance, expense management, shortage prevention, and sales support activities for a sales volume. Acts as Store Manager in his or her absence.

Sales Manager
Supervises the store activities in a specific product category. Includes merchandise displays, employee development, customer service, operations, and inventory control.

Store Management Executive Development
Eight-week program that provides an understanding of retail management, company philosophies for building partnerships and teams, leading and developing people, and driving customer service and sales.

Omni Buying/Digital Merchandising Track

Merchandise Manager
Responsible for planning, developing, and executing the assortment strategy across a larger product category while also managing a team of Buyers.

Buyer/Digital Merchant
Responsible for sales and profits for an entire category of business; involved with strategy formulation and execution. Leads and develops a team of Assistant and Associate Buyers.

Assistant/Associate Buyer
Assistant Buyer learns how to run a business and gets actual experience. Associate Buyer oversees sales and profits for an assigned product, and has responsibility to manage and train Assistant Buyers.

Merchant Executive Development
Provides overview of Macy's business model, and also covers technical and business skills required for merchant roles within and online businesses. Can become an Omni Buyer or a Digital Merchant*

* An Omni Buyer works across all purchasing channels, including Macy's stores and the macys.com Web site. A Digital Merchant focuses on the online assortment and merchandising to maximize online sales. These two buyers work together.

held apparel and outdoor retailer located in Freeport, Maine. L.L. Bean's reputation for outstanding customer service and speed of delivery for more than 140,000 products in various sizes, colors, and textures—some unchanged since 1928, others redesigned each year—is an important goal but a formidable task to achieve. Every year, L.L. Bean faces the strategic challenge of inventory and demand forecasting to invest in the right products for the coming year for its multiple channels

FIGURE 14-5

Considerations in Devising Merchandise Plans

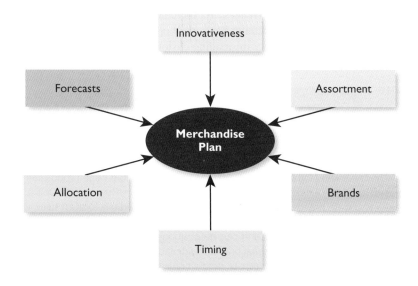

worldwide. These include catalogs (50 different versions in every U.S. state and in 170 countries); retail stores (28 stores and 10 outlets in the United States, 23 stores and outlets in Japan); Web sites (in 200 countries); Outdoor Adventures Programs (more than 150,000 U.S. customers); and corporate sales. L.L. Bean uses JDA Software's supply and demand optimization solutions, JDA Demand, to get a read on market trends and develop scalable, integrated multiyear plans for product design, assortment planning, logistics, and enterprise planning.[13]

In this section, forecasting is examined from a general planning perspective. In Chapter 16, the financial dimensions of forecasting are reviewed. When preparing forecasts, it is essential to distinguish among different types of merchandise. **Staple merchandise** consists of the regular products carried by a retailer. For a supermarket, staples include milk, bread, canned soup, and facial tissues. For a department store, staples include everyday watches, jeans, glassware, and housewares. Because these items have relatively stable sales (sometimes seasonal) and their nature may not change much over time, a retailer can clearly outline the quantities for these items. A **basic stock list** specifies the inventory level, color, brand, style category, size, package, and so on for every staple item carried by the retailer.

Assortment merchandise consists of apparel, furniture, autos, and other products for which the retailer must carry a variety of products in order to give customers a proper selection. These goods are harder to forecast than staples due to demand variations, style changes, and the number of sizes and colors carried. Decisions are two-pronged: (1) Product lines, styles, designs, and colors are projected. (2) A **model stock plan** is used to project specific items, such as the number of green, red, and blue pullover sweaters of a certain design by size. With a model stock plan, many items are ordered for popular sizes and colors, and small amounts of less popular sizes and colors fill out the assortment.

Fashion merchandise consists of products that may have cyclical sales due to changing tastes and lifestyles. For these items, forecasting can be hard because styles may change from year to year. "Hot" colors often change back and forth. **Seasonal merchandise** consists of products that sell well over nonconsecutive time periods. Items such as ski equipment and air-conditioner servicing have excellent sales during one season per year. Because the strongest sales of seasonal items usually occur at the same time each year, forecasting is straightforward.

With **fad merchandise**, high sales are generated for a short time. Often, toys and games are fads, such as *Star Wars* toys that flew off store shelves each time a related movie was released. It is hard to forecast whether such products will reach specific sales targets and how long they will be popular. Sometimes, fads turn into extended fads—and sales continue for a long period at a fraction of earlier sales. Trivial Pursuit board games are in the extended fad category.

In forecasting for best-sellers, many retailers use a **never-out list** to determine the amount of merchandise to purchase for resale. The goal is to purchase enough of these products so they are always in stock. Products are added to and deleted from the list as their popularity changes. Before a new James Patterson novel is released, stores order large quantities to be sure they meet anticipated demand. After it disappears from best-seller lists, smaller quantities are kept. It is a good strategy to use a combination of a basic stock list, a model stock plan, and a never-out list. These lists may overlap.

Innovativeness

The innovativeness of a merchandise plan depends on a number of factors. See Table 14-1. An innovative retailer has a great opportunity—distinctiveness (by being first to market) and a great risk (possibly misreading customers and being stuck with large inventories). By assessing each

  CAREERS IN RETAILING   Buying for a Retailer's Private-Label Program

Some retailers such as Gap, Limited, and Trader Joe's almost exclusively sell private brands. Others such as Costco, Sears, Amazon, Target, and Macy's use a mixed-brand strategy that features both national and private brands. In many respects, a buyer of private-brand goods has a more complex job than a national-brand buyer. For example, a private brand can be positioned below, at, or above the quality of a national brand. Private-label suppliers can be easily switched based on costs, product quality,

and delivery speed. Also, private-brand buyers must determine the value proposition behind the brand. Is it a better value due to lower cost? Or is it unique? Private-label buyers need to accurately forecast sales. Unlike national brands, private-brand orders cannot be canceled. There are also no markdown allowances associated with private brands.

As a private-label buyer of men's dress slacks for a membership club, develop your value proposition relative to national brands.

■

TABLE 14-1 Factors to Bear in Mind When Planning Merchandise Innovativeness

Factor	Relevance for Planning
Target market(s)	Evaluate whether the target market is conservative or innovative.
Goods/services growth potential	Consider each new offering on the basis of rapidity of initial sales, maximum sales potential per time period, and length of sales life.
Fashion trends	Understand vertical and horizontal fashion trends, if appropriate.
Retailer image	Carry goods/services that reinforce the firm's image. The level of innovativeness should be consistent with this image.
Competition	Lead or follow competition in the selection of new goods/services.
Customer segments	Segment customers by dividing merchandise into established-product displays and new-product displays.
Responsiveness to consumers	Carry new offerings when requested by the target market.
Amount of investment	Consider all the possible investments for each new good/service: product costs, new fixtures, and additional personnel (or further training for existing personnel).
Profitability	Assess each new offering for potential profits.
Risk	Be aware of the possible tarnishing of the retailer's image, investment costs, and opportunity costs.
Constrained decision making	Restrict franchisees and chain branches from buying certain items.
Declining goods/services	Delete older goods/services if sales and/or profits are too low.

factor in Table 14-1 and preparing a detailed plan for merchandising new goods and services, a firm can better capitalize on opportunities and reduce risks. As shown in Figure 14-6, some apparel retailers take innovativeness quite seriously—so do firms such as Brookstone and 7-Eleven:

Check out Brookstone's (www.brookstone.com) unique product offerings.

▶ Brookstone offers an eclectic mix of unique, functional, and distinctive consumer products—ranging from massage chairs to travel electronics to blood pressure monitors—through catalogs, Web sites, E-mail marketing, and its 200 retail stores in shopping malls, lifestyle centers, and airports. Brookstone provides a fun, interactive shopping experience and an opportunity to discover new and ingenious items where customers are encouraged to try products out for hands-on shopping.

▶ The convenience store format is quite innovative, as shown by 7-Eleven, which began as Southland Ice Company in 1927, selling milk, eggs, and bread. Today, 7-Eleven introduces new goods and services virtually every week based on the preferences of guests at each locale. Stores vary in size from 2,400 to 3,000 square feet and offer a selection of about 2,500 different goods and services, including food service offerings such as prepared-fresh-daily sandwiches; coffee and its popular Big Gulp fountain soft drink; a wide assortment of fruit,

FIGURE 14-6

Innovation in Retailing

In this apparel store, a unique in-store layout and unusual clothing displays highlight the innovativeness of merchandise to shoppers.

Source: Pavel L Photo and Video/Shutterstock. Reprinted by permission.

salads, and baked goods; wine; and automated money orders, automatic teller machines, phone cards and, where available, lottery tickets, 24 hours a day, 7 days a week at 7,800 U.S. stores.[14]

Retailers should assess the growth potential for each new good or service they carry: How fast will a new item generate significant sales? What are the most sales (dollars and units) to be reached in a season or year? Over what period will an item continue selling? One tool to assess potential is the **product life cycle**, which shows the expected behavior of a good or service over its life. The basic cycle comprises introduction, growth, maturity, and decline stages—shown in Figure 14-7 and described next.

During the *introduction* stage, a retailer should anticipate a limited target market. The good or service will probably be supplied in one basic version. The manufacturer (supplier) may limit distribution to "finer" stores. Yet, new convenience items such as food and housewares products are normally mass distributed. Items initially distributed selectively tend to have high prices. Mass-distributed products tend to involve low prices to foster faster consumer acceptance. Early promotion must be explanatory, geared to informing shoppers. At this stage, there are few possible suppliers.

As innovators buy a new product and recommend it to friends, sales increase rapidly and the *growth* stage begins. The target market includes middle-income consumers who are more innovative than average. The assortment expands, as do the retailers carrying a product. Price discounting is not widely used, but competitors offer a range of prices and customer service. Promotion is more persuasive and aimed at acquainting shoppers with availability and services. There are more suppliers.

In the *maturity* stage, sales reach their maximum, the largest part of the target market is attracted, and shoppers select from broad product offerings. All types of retailers (discount to upscale) carry a good or service in some form. Prestige retailers stress brand names and customer service, while others use active price competition. Price is more often cited in ads. Competition is intense.

Decline is brought on by a shrinking market (due to product obsolescence, newer substitutes, and boredom) and lower profit margins. The target market may be the lowest-income consumers and laggards. Some retailers cut back on the assortment; others drop the good or service. For retailers still carrying the items, promotion is reduced and geared to price. There are fewer suppliers.

Many retailers pay a lot of attention to new-product additions but not enough to decide whether to drop existing items. Yet, because of limited resources and shelf space, some items have to be dropped when others are added. Instead of intuitively pruning products, a retailer should use structured guidelines:

▷ Select items for possible elimination on the basis of declining sales, prices, and profits, as well as the appearance of substitutes.
▷ Gather and analyze detailed financial and other data about these items.

FIGURE 14-7
The Traditional Product Life Cycle

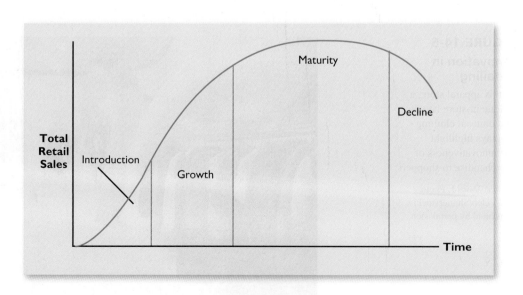

> Consider nondeletion strategies such as cutting costs, revising promotion efforts, adjusting prices, and cooperating with other retailers.
> After making a deletion decision, do not overlook timing, parts and servicing, inventory, and holdover demand.

Sometimes, a seemingly obsolete good or service can be revived. An innovative retailer recognizes the potential in this area and merchandises accordingly. Direct marketers heavily promote "greatest hits" recordings featuring individual music artists and compilations of multiple artists.

Apparel retailers must be familiar with fashion trends. A *vertical trend* occurs when a fashion is first introduced to and accepted by upscale consumers and then undergoes changes in its basic form before it is sold to the general public. This type of fashion goes through three stages: (1) distinctive—original designs, designer stores, custom-made, worn by upscale shoppers; (2) emulation—modification of original designs, finer stores, alterations, worn by middle class; and (3) economic emulation—simple copies, discount stores, mass-produced, mass-marketed.

With a *horizontal trend*, a new fashion is marketed to a broad spectrum of people at its introduction while retaining its basic form. In any social class, there are innovative customers who are opinion leaders. New fashions must be accepted by them, who then convince other members of the same social class (who are more conservative) to buy the items. Fashion is sold across the class and not from one class to another. Figure 14-8 has a checklist for predicting fashion adoption.

Assortment

An **assortment** is the selection of merchandise a retailer carries. It includes both the breadth of product categories and the variety within each category.

A firm first chooses merchandise quality. Should it carry top-line, expensive items and sell to upper-income customers? Or should it carry middle-of-the-line, moderately priced items and cater to middle-income customers? Or should it carry lesser-quality, inexpensive items and attract lower-income customers? Or should it try to draw more than one segment by offering a variety, such as middle- and top-line items? The firm must also decide whether to carry promotional products (low-priced closeout items or special buys used to generate store traffic). Several factors must be reviewed in choosing merchandise quality. See Table 14-2.

Dollar Tree is the largest single-price-point ($1.00) retailer in North America. Its overall visual merchandising strategy encourages a "treasure hunt" orientation to shopping with a selection of high-value, low-cost merchandise in attractively designed stores that are conveniently located. Dollar Tree provides a balanced selection of everyday consumables such as candy and food, health and beauty care; basic consumables such as paper products and household chemicals; variety merchandise such as toys, stationery, gifts, party goods, greeting cards, an soft goods; seasonal (Valentine's Day, Easter, Halloween, and Christmas merchandise); and closeout and promotional merchandise

FIGURE 14-8

A Selected Checklist for Predicting Fashion Adoption

✓ Does the fashion satisfy a consumer need?

✓ Is the fashion compatible with emerging consumer lifestyles?

✓ Is the fashion oriented toward the mass market or a market segment?

✓ Is the fashion radically new?

✓ Are the reputations of the designer(s) and the retailers carrying the fashion good?

✓ Are several designers marketing some version of the fashion?

✓ Is the price range for the fashion appropriate for the target market?

✓ Will appropriate advertising be used?

✓ Will the fashion change over time?

✓ Will consumers view the fashion as a long-term trend?

TABLE 14-2 Factors to Take into Account When Planning Merchandise Quality

Factor	Relevance for Planning
Target market(s)	Match merchandise quality to the wishes of the desired target market(s).
Competition	Sell similar quality (follow the competition) or different quality (to appeal to a different target market).
Retailer's image	Relate merchandise quality directly to the perception that customers have of a retailer.
Store location	Consider the impact of location on the retailer's image and the number of competitors, which, in turn, relate to quality.
Stock turnover	Be aware that high quality and high prices usually yield a lower turnover than low quality and low prices.
Profitability	Recognize that high-quality goods generally bring greater profit per unit than lesser quality goods; turnover may cause total profits to be greater for the latter.
Manufacturer versus private brands	Understand that, for many consumers, manufacturer brands connote higher quality than private brands.
Customer services offered	Know that high-quality goods require personal selling, alterations, delivery, and so on. Lesser-quality merchandise may not.
Personnel	Employ skilled, knowledgeable personnel for high-quality merchandise. Self-service may be used with lesser-quality merchandise.
Perceived goods/ services benefits	Analyze consumers. Lesser-quality goods attract customers who desire functional product benefits. High-quality goods attract customers who desire extended product benefits (e.g., status, services).
Constrained decision making	Face reality. a. Franchisees or chain store managers often have limited or no control over product decisions. b. Independent retailers that buy from a few large wholesalers are limited to the range of quality offered by those wholesalers.

Look at Dollar Tree's (www.dollartree.com) targeted merchandising approach. Click on "About Us" at the bottom of the screen.

all for $1 each! Consumables and variety goods each account for 45 percent of merchandise. Consumables encourage frequent store return visits and increase traffic and sales.[15]

After deciding on product quality, a retailer determines its width and depth of assortment. **Width of assortment** refers to the number of distinct goods/services categories (product lines) a retailer carries. **Depth of assortment** refers to the variety in any one goods/services category (product line) a retailer carries. As noted in Chapter 5, an assortment can range from wide and deep (department store) to narrow and shallow (box store). Figure 14-9 shows advantages and disadvantages for each basic strategy.

Assortment strategies vary widely. Web retailer Discount Art (www.discountart.com) says it is geared to "the artist who demands good-quality art materials, but also appreciates good prices." But even small retailers with a narrow product assortment, like the one in Figure 14-10, need a good selection to draw shoppers. KFC's thousands of worldwide outlets emphasize chicken and related products. They do not sell hamburgers, pizza, or many other popular fast-food items. Macy's department stores feature thousands of general merchandise items, and Amazon.com is an online department store with millions of items for sale. This is the dilemma that retailers may face in determining how big an assortment to carry. Creating the right merchandise assortment that is frequently refreshed, accurately tailored to local market and E-commerce customer preferences, and seasonal market demand is essential to maximizing ROI and growing top-line sales.[16]

Retailers should take several factors into account in planning their assortment: If variety is increased, will overall sales go up? Will overall profits? How much space is required for each product category? How much space is available? Carrying 10 varieties of cat food will not necessarily yield greater sales or profits than stocking 4 varieties. The retailer must look at the investment costs that occur with a large variety. Because selling space is limited, it should be allocated to those goods and services generating the most customer traffic and sales. The inventory turnover rate should also be studied.

Advantages	Disadvantages
Wide and Deep (many goods/service categories and a large assortment in each category)	
Broad market	High inventory investment
Full selection of items	General image
High level of customer traffic	Many items with low turnover
Customer loyalty	Some obsolete merchandise
One-stop shopping	
No disappointed customers	
Wide and Shallow (many goods/service categories and a limited assortment in each category)	
Broad market	Low variety within product lines
High level of customer traffic	Some disappointed customers
Emphasis on convenience customers	Weak image
Less costly than wide and deep	Many items with low turnover
One-stop shopping	Reduced customer loyalty
Narrow and Deep (few goods/service categories and a large assortment in each category)	
Specialist image	Too much emphasis on one category
Good customer choice in category(ies)	No one-stop shopping
Specialized personnel	More susceptible to trends/cycles
Customer loyalty	Greater effort needed to enlarge the size of the trading area
No disappointed customers	Little (no) scrambled merchandising
Less costly than wide and deep	
Narrow and Shallow (few goods/service categories and a limited assortment in each category)	
Aimed at convenience customers	Little width and depth
Least costly	No one-stop shopping
High turnover of items	Some disappointed customers
	Weak image
	Limited customer loyalty
	Small trading area
	Little (no) scrambled merchandising

FIGURE 14-9
Retail Assortment Strategies

A distinction should be made among scrambled merchandising, complementary goods and services, and substitute goods and services. With *scrambled merchandising*, a retailer adds unrelated items to generate more revenues and lift profit margins (such as a florist carrying umbrellas). Handling *complementary goods and services* lets the retailer sell both basic items and related offerings (such as stereos and CDs) via cross-merchandising. Although scrambled merchandising and cross-merchandising both increase overall sales, carrying too many *substitute goods and services* (such as competing brands of toothpaste) may shift sales from one brand to another and have little impact on overall retail sales.

These factors are also key as a retailer considers a wider, deeper assortment: (1) Risks, merchandise investments, damages, and obsolescence may rise dramatically. (2) Personnel may be spread too thinly over dissimilar products. (3) Both the positive and negative ramifications of scrambled merchandising may occur. (4) Inventory control may be difficult; overall turnover probably will slow down.

FIGURE 14-10

Product Assortment: A Key to Sales, Regardless of the Retailer

Specialty retailers, such as the chocolate store featured here, need to have a strong product assortment to attract shoppers and increase impulse purchases.

Source: Olga Popova/ Shutterstock. Reprinted by permission.

A retailer may not have a choice about stocking a full assortment within a product line if a powerful supplier insists that the retailer carry its entire line or it will not sell at all to that retailer. But large retailers—and smaller ones belonging to cooperative buying groups—are now standing up to suppliers, and many retailers stock their own brands next to those of the manufacturer.

Brands

As part of its assortment planning, a retailer chooses the proper mix of manufacturer, private, and generic brands—a challenge made more complex with the proliferation of brands. **Manufacturer (national) brands** are produced and controlled by manufacturers. They are usually well known, are supported by manufacturer ads, are somewhat pre-sold to consumers, require limited retailer investment in marketing, and often represent maximum quality to consumers.

Manufacturer brands dominate sales in many categories. Popular manufacturer brands include Apple, Coke, Gillette, Levi's, Microsoft, Nike, Revlon, and Samsung. The retailers likely to rely most heavily on manufacturer brands are small firms, Web firms, discounters, and others that want the credibility associated with well-known brands or that have low-price strategies (so consumers can compare the prices of different retailers on name-brand items). Although they face extensive competition from private brands, manufacturer brands remain the dominant type of brand, accounting for more than 80 percent of all retail sales worldwide.[17] See Figure 14-11.

The best-selling U.S. appliance brand (www .kenmore.com) is not GE or Whirlpool.

Private (dealer or store) brands contain names designated by wholesalers or retailers. They are more profitable to retailers, are better controlled by retailers, are not sold by competing retailers, are less expensive for consumers, and lead to customer loyalty to retailers. With most private brands, retailers must line up suppliers, arrange for distribution and warehousing, sponsor ads, create displays, and absorb losses from unsold items. This is why retailer interest in private brands is growing:

▶ In *dollar sales*, private brands account for about 17 percent of U.S. retail revenues; they account for 20 percent of *unit sales for consumer packaged goods*.[18] In Europe, the dollar sales figure for private brands at grocery stores ranges from 17 percent of retail store revenues in Italy to 53 percent in Switzerland.[19]

▶ Private brands are often priced 20 to 30 percent below manufacturer brands. This benefits consumers and retailers (whose costs are lower and whose revenues are shared by fewer

FIGURE 14-11

Auto Dealers and Manufacturer Brands

When shopping for an automobile, consumers place great importance on the brand(s) carried by a dealer. Most people are extremely brand-conscious about what automobile they ultimately buy. Pictured here are Fiat 500 models available at a Fiat dealer. Only people considering a Fiat would visit this dealer.

Source: 123rf.com. Reprinted by permission.

parties). In general, gross profits are higher for private brands than manufacturer brands, despite their lower prices.

➤ At Gap, Old Navy, Limited, Uniqlo, McDonald's, Aldi, Trader Joe's, and many other retailers, private brands represent most or all of company revenues.

➤ At virtually all large retailers, both private brands and manufacturer brands are strong. Amazon.com has plans to sell private-label nuts, teas, spices, coffees, baby foods, and vitamins along with millions of manufacturer-branded items. It plans to use such brand names as Happy Belly, Wickedly Prime, Presto!, and Mama Bear for its private-label products and to restrict purchases to its Amazon Prime customers who pay $99 per year for the service.[20] Take our private brand challenge in Table 14-3.

In the past, private brands were only discount versions of mid-tier products. Today, shoppers around the world are more conscious of value and increasingly read ingredient labels on products to impute quality. Recognizing that price is not the single differentiator for all shoppers, retailers have invested in developing a wider variety of competitive private-brand offerings. Multitiered private label brands target shoppers at the premium, standard, and value price points. In some categories, differentiated features of the higher-priced premium private label products make them the most expensive and innovative product.[21]

For example, a *premium private brand* offered by Harris Teeter (the supermarket chain) is H.T. Traders, which is exclusive to the chain. Harris Teeter applies global food and flavor trends to its premium private-label products such as olive oil and aromatic gourmet coffee to convey superior quality and to cater to consumers who seek quality, novelty, and adventure in their everyday grocery food purchases.[22]

RETAILING AROUND THE WORLD

Young Chinese Favor Global Brands

By sheer numbers, China's Gen-Y (born in the 1980s to mid-1990s) and Gen-Z (born in the mid-1990s to 2000s) are equal to the whole population of the United States. No doubt, then, that they represent a massive market not only in China itself but for global retailers and brands too. In the past, Chinese consumers would have favored domestic brands; perhaps they could only access these particular ones at the time, and for the most part, global brands would have been too expensive as

alternatives. The Gen-Y and Gen-Z groups grew up in a prosperous China. This is a new China that had—to some extent—opened its doors and was truly international and connected. Gen-Yers favor Apple, Alipay, Taobao, Adidas, and Zara. The slightly younger Gen-Zers want Nike, Adidas, UNIQLO, Converse, Zara, and Xiaomi.

Suggest why the new generations of Chinese consumers seem to favor global brands over domestic ones.

◼

TABLE 14-3 The Berman/Evans/Chatterjee Private Brand Test

Do you think you know a lot about private brands? Then take our test. Match the retailers and the brand names. The answers are at the bottom of the table. No peeking.

Please note: Retailers may have more than one brand on the list.

Retailer	Brand
1. Amazon	a. Alfani men's apparel
2. Best Buy	b. America's Choice jellies
3. Costco	c. Croft & Barrow swim apparel
4. Kmart	d. Greenway organics
5. Macy's	e. Insignia electronics
6. J.C. Penney	f. Jaclyn Smith female clothing
7. Kohl's	g. Kenmore appliances
8. Sears	h. Kindle tablet
9. Target	i. Kirkland Signature coffee
10. Walmart	j. Mossimo women's apparel
	k. Ol' Roy dog food
	l. Roadhandler tires
	m. Tools of the Trade kitchen implements
	n. Worthington apparel

Answers: 1—h, e; 2—e; 3—i; 4—f; 5—a, m; 6—n; 7—c; 8—g, l; 9—j; 10—k

Care must be taken in deciding how much to emphasize private brands. As previously noted, many consumers are loyal to manufacturer brands and would shop elsewhere if those brands are not stocked or their variety is pruned. See Figure 14-12.

Generic brands feature products' generic names as brands (such as canned peas); they are a form of private, no-frills goods stocked by some retailers. These items usually get secondary shelf locations, have little or no promotion support, may be of less quality, are stocked in limited assortments, and have plain packages. Retailers control generics and price them well below other brands. In supermarkets, generics account for under 1 percent of sales. For prescription drugs, where the quality of manufacturer brands and generics is similar, generics provide 60 percent of sales.

FIGURE 14-12

Private Branding Challenges

Although private brands may offer many benefits—such as exclusivity, customer loyalty, retailer control of store positioning and pricing, and so on—it can be challenging to develop and oversee these brands. The retailer needs to persuade consumers that these sometimes unknown brands are trustworthy, of good quality, and a proper value for the price.

Source: Chatchawan/Shutterstock. Reprinted by permission.

The competition between manufacturers and retailers for shelf space and profits has led to a **battle of the brands**, whereby manufacturer, private, and generic brands fight each other for more space and control. Nowhere is this battle clearer than for mature product categories such as paper products at large grocery stores or office products retail chains.[23]

Timing

For new products, the retailer must decide when they are first purchased, displayed, and sold. For established products, the firm must plan the merchandise flow during the year. The retailer should take into account its forecasts and other factors: peak seasons, order and delivery time, routine versus special orders, stock turnover, discounts, and the efficiency of inventory procedures.

Some goods (e.g., winter coats) and services (snow plowing) have peak seasons. These items require large inventories in peak times and less stock during off seasons. Because some people like to shop during off seasons, the retailer should not eliminate the items.

With regard to order and delivery time, how long does it take the retailer to process an order request? After the order is sent to the supplier, how long does it take to receive merchandise? By adding these two periods together, the retailer can get a good idea of the lead time to restock shelves. If it takes a retailer 7 days to process an order and the supplier another 14 days to deliver goods, the retailer should begin a new order at least 21 days before the old inventory runs out.

Routine orders involve restocking staples and other regularly sold items. Deliveries are received weekly, monthly, and so on. Planning and problems are minimized. Special orders involve merchandise not sold regularly, such as custom furniture. They need more planning and cooperation between retailer and supplier. Specific delivery dates are usually arranged.

Stock turnover (how quickly merchandise sells) greatly influences how often items must be ordered. Convenience items such as milk and bread (which are also highly perishable) have a high turnover rate and are restocked quite often. Shopping items such as refrigerators and televisions have a lower turnover rate and are restocked less often.

In deciding when and how often to buy merchandise, the availability of quantity discounts should be considered. Large purchases may result in lower per-unit costs. Efficient inventory procedures, such as electronic data interchange and quick response planning procedures, also decrease costs and order times while raising merchandise productivity.

Allocation

The last part of merchandise planning is the allocation of products. A single-unit retailer chooses how much merchandise to place on the sales floor, how much to place in a stockroom, and whether to use a warehouse. A chain also apportions products among stores. Allocation is covered further in Chapter 15.

Some retailers rely on warehouses as distribution centers. Products are shipped from suppliers to these warehouses, and then they are assigned and shipped to individual stores. Other retailers, including many supermarket chains, do not rely as much on warehouses. They have at least some goods shipped directly from suppliers to individual stores.

It is vital for chains, whether engaged in centralized or decentralized merchandising, to have a clear store-by-store allocation plan. Even if merchandise lines are standardized across the chain, store-by-store assortments must reflect the variations in the size and diversity of the customer base, in store size and location, in the climate, and in other factors.

ETHICS IN RETAILING   What's a Fair Return Policy?

Retailers with liberal return policies may be setting themselves up for fraud. Return fraud by consumers can take various forms: used merchandise represented as new; merchandise intended to be returned at the time of purchase (a costly camera for use on a vacation); merchandise bought on sale but returned at full price; merchandise bought at other stores; stolen merchandise; and more. Fraudulent returns may occur more frequently at holiday periods when retailers are overwhelmed with requests. In response, some retailers have restocking fees (unless a good is defective), monitor customer return frequency to stop frequent offenders, and insist on sales receipts or other proof of purchase.

How would you deter fraud at a fine jewelry store, which suspects that a high proportion of heavy customers return goods directly after use on a special occasion?

CATEGORY MANAGEMENT

As noted in Chapter 2, **category management** is a merchandising technique that some firms—including supermarkets, drugstores, hardware stores, and general merchandise retailers—use to improve productivity. It is a way to manage a retail business that focuses on the performance of product category results rather than individual brands. It arranges product groupings into strategic business units to better meet consumer needs and to achieve sales and profit goals. Retail managers make merchandising decisions that maximize the total return on the assets assigned to them.

Retailers implement category management by recognizing the interrelatedness of products in a category; they then focus on improving the performance of whole product categories rather than the performance of individual brands. Some examples might be cheese, clothes, detergent, skin care, small animal foods, and athletic wear. Under category management, traditional brand-(vendor-) oriented buyers are replaced with category managers who are responsible for integrating procurement, pricing, and merchandising of all brands in a category. These category managers jointly develop and implement category-based plans with manufacturers to enhance the outcomes for both parties, which is conducive to more collaborative relationships and information sharing. Sometimes, the category management leader might be a representative of the dominant supplier in the category—for example, cheese (Kraft Food Group); clothes detergent (P&G); skin care (L'Oréal); and so on. Suppliers are expected to propose actions (such as new products or promotions) and be rated on their ability to increase total category sales (not just their own brands) and shopper satisfaction.[24]

According to the A.C. Nielsen research firm, good category management involves these steps:

1. Define the category based on the needs of the target market.
2. Assign a role to the category based on several questions: How important is the category to the consumer? How important is the category to the retailer? How important is the category to the retailer's competitors? What is the category's outlook in the marketplace?
3. Assess the category to find opportunities for improvement.
4. Set performance targets and measure progress with a category scorecard.
5. Create a marketing strategy that draws the overarching picture of how to achieve the category role and scorecard targets.
6. Choose tactics for category assortment, pricing, promotion, merchandising, and supply chain strategies.
7. Roll out the plan.
8. Review performance regularly and adjust as needed.[25]

A fundamental premise is that a retailer must empower specific personnel to be responsible for the financial performance of each product category. As with micromerchandising, category management means adapting merchandise for each store or region to best satisfy customers. In deciding on the space per product category, there are several crucial measures of performance. Comparisons can be made by studying company data from period to period and by looking at categorical statistics in trade publications:

- ▸ *Sales per linear foot of shelf space:* Annual sales divided by the total linear footage devoted to the product category.
- ▸ *Gross profit per linear foot of shelf space:* Annual gross profit divided by the total linear footage devoted to the product category.
- ▸ *Return on inventory investment:* Annual gross profit divided by average inventory at cost.
- ▸ *Inventory turnover:* The number of times during a given period, usually one year, that the average inventory on hand is sold.
- ▸ *Days' supply:* The number of days of supply of an item on the shelf.
- ▸ *Direct product profitability (DPP):* An item's gross profit less its direct retailing costs (warehouse and store support, occupancy, inventory, and direct labor, but not general overhead).

Some collaborative aspects of category management are working well, whereas other aspects are not—due to the differing roles of manufacturers and retailers in the channel of distribution:[26]

What Manufacturers Think about Retailers

SUCCESSFUL APPLICATIONS OF CATEGORY MANAGEMENT

▷ Retailers act as equal partners.
▷ Retailers get input from manufacturers so they put the best possible plan together.
▷ Retailers are open minded and willing to change.
▷ Retailers that give manufacturers proper lead time—and timely goals and suggestions— receive the highest-quality work.

UNSUCCESSFUL APPLICATIONS OF CATEGORY MANAGEMENT

▷ Different goals among the retailers' senior managers, category managers, and operations managers impede the process.
▷ Retailers have a "template fixation." Yet, a template alone cannot explain why shoppers choose a given product or category.
▷ Retailers expect manufacturers to do more than their share or to pay more than their share for gathering and analyzing data.

What Retailers Think about Manufacturers

SUCCESSFUL APPLICATIONS OF CATEGORY MANAGEMENT

▷ Manufacturers gather data on consumer purchases and make recommendations to retailers.
▷ Manufacturers with clearly defined and supported plans are viewed favorably.
▷ Manufacturers help the retailers understand how to get more out of shopper traffic and build shopper loyalty, incremental volume, and return on merchandising assets.

UNSUCCESSFUL APPLICATIONS OF CATEGORY MANAGEMENT

▷ Manufacturers make recommendations that consistently favor their brands.
▷ Manufacturers just drop a completed template off with their retailers.
▷ Manufacturers do not maintain confidentiality for shared data or recommendations.

Figure 14-13 indicates how a retailer could use category management to better merchandise manufacturer and private brands in a category. The vertical axis relates to direct product

FIGURE 14-13
Applying Category Management

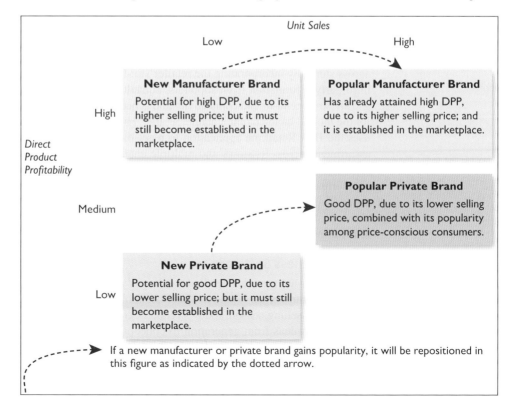

profitability. The horizontal axis classifies brands in terms of unit sales (an indicator of inventory turnover). A new manufacturer brand in a category has the potential for high DPP but is not yet selling well, whereas a popular manufacturer brand in a category has both high DPP and high unit sales. The goal is to move the new manufacturer brand into the upper-right quadrant. A new private brand has the potential for good DPP if it can emulate a popular private brand in the category. The goal is to improve DPP based on sales by moving to the right-center quadrant. If both new brands succeed, while the existing ones stay popular, then sales and profits for the whole category will rise.

MERCHANDISING SOFTWARE

One of the most significant advances in merchandise planning is the widespread availability of computer software that gives retailers an excellent support mechanism to systematically prepare forecasts, try various assortment scenarios, coordinate data for category management, and so forth. In an era when many retailers carry thousands of items, merchandising software is a part of every-day business life. See Figure 14-14.

Some merchandising software is provided by suppliers and trade associations at no charge—as part of the value delivery chain and relationship retailing. Other software is sold by marketing firms, often for $1,500 or less (although some software sells for $25,000 or more). Let's discuss the far-reaching nature of merchandising software.

General Merchandise Planning Software

Some retailers prefer functionally driven software; others use integrated software packages. The Container Store, the national storage and organization specialty retail pioneer, is an example of the latter. It utilizes MicroStrategy (www.microstrategy.com), a mobile-enabled platform that empowers store employees with real-time business intelligence from inventory systems. The data help analyze various store operations, sales performance, customer insights, and customer loyalty through easily configured mobile dashboards—without the need for information technology support. This enables Container Store leadership to access information throughout the firm's entire network of stores and its supplier interface through a MicroStrategy dashboard named "The Score" (using the game analogy). Store personnel thus gain insights into trends and data that can be used to monitor, maximize, and benchmark performance against store and company goals.[27]

Forecasting Software

Many retailers use big data (culled from customer insights, loyalty card information, and interaction across multiple channels) and advanced analytical systems to make merchandise forecasts. JDA Software (www.jda.com) is one of the firms that offers a wide range of products. Its Retail. me solution is designed to help retailers forecast, plan, and develop highly localized assortments across stores by incorporating the retailer's in-house customer and supply chain data along with third-party information from suppliers, consultants, and the industry. Retail.me is cloud-hosted and allows for end-to-end connectivity and synchronization with multiple organizational processes for the mobile-enabled omnichannel retailer. Hibbett Sports, a chain with more than 1,000 stores, uses the JDA Retail.me application to meet the challenge of planning and managing localized assortments across its stores and multiple channels, including mobile apps, to deliver its target ROI.[28]

Firms such as SAS (www.sas.com) offer sophisticated software for retail forecasting purposes. This software can be used to analyze and forecast events that occur over time. Retailers are able to discern trends that were not previously noticeable, and they can anticipate ups and downs to better plan future activities.[29]

Innovativeness Software

Today's software provides detailed data rapidly, thereby allowing retailers to monitor and more quickly react to trends. Processes that once took months are now done in weeks or days. Instead of missing a selling season, today's retailers are prepared for the latest craze by crowdsourcing new product ideas from generation to concept testing. With crowdsourcing, retailers can raise funds online from small investors who do not receive any ownership.

As part of Macy's (www.macys.com) retail innovation strategy to provide a frictionless omni-shopping experience for Macys.com and Bloomingdales.com customers, Macy's Idea Labs is a

FIGURE 14-14

The Many Uses of Computer Software

With the substantial advances in merchandising software, retailers can do such tasks as examine merchandise selections from different suppliers online, reduce inventory shortages, integrate merchandising plans, coordinate information across the company and stores, draw/sketch new product ideas for suppliers, review results in real time, and more.

Source: Shutterstock. Reprinted by permission.

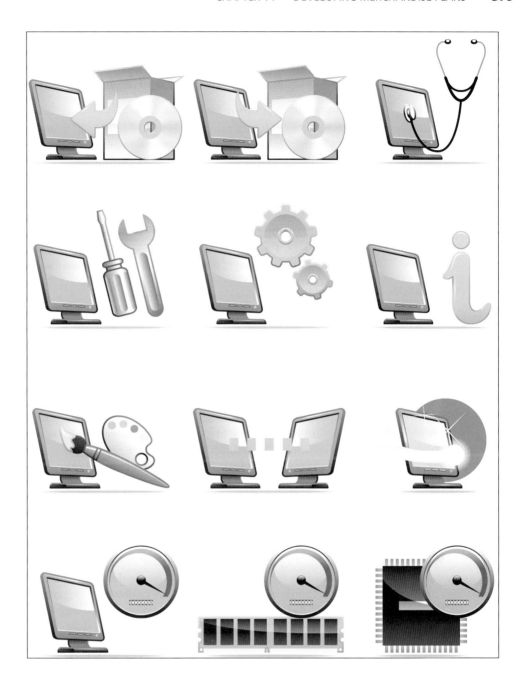

central online hub for idea generation, discussion, analysis, and experimentation. It is supported by the SpigitEngage platform, a social collaboration product from Spigit (www.spigit.com), which encourages Employees and external stakeholders across multiple functional areas and locations are encouraged to embrace disruption, crowdsource innovation funding, and execute technology excellence in acquiring and retaining Macy's customers.[30]

Assortment and Allocation Software

A number of retailers employ merchandising software to better plan assortments. Leading footwear and accessories retailer DSW has to ensure that its merchandise assortment keeps pace with fashion and style trends. Among its goals are that it has the right sizes in appropriate quantities (or packs) delivered at the right time during the fashion cycle to each of its more than 375 stores, E-commerce warehouse, and 345 leased departments in U.S. retailers under the Affiliated Business Group banner.

Learn more about SAS retail software (www.sas .com/industry/retail).

SAS Merchandise Intelligence Solutions software (which includes SAS Size Profiling and Pack Optimization) helps DSW managers determine location-specific size and pack optimization for each shoe style and for unit replenishment orders in a way that results in fewer markdowns while also reducing stockouts. This is particularly effective with seasonal items such as sandals that have a shorter shelf life than dress shoes. Store managers have greater confidence in ordering few quantities of hot seasonal styles while achieving good sales performance and avoiding end-of-season liquidation. Vendors wary of markdowns and the effect this has on their brand equity are cooperative because they are alerted well in advance to the need for different pack sizes.[31]

Category Management Software

Harbor Wholesale supports its convenience stores, grocery stores, restaurants, and drugstores with a category management team (www.harborwholesale.com/solutions/category-experts).

A wide range of software programs is available to help manufacturers and retailers deal with category management's complexities. A few retailers have even developed their own software. Programs typically base space allocation on sales, inventory turnover, and profits at individual stores. Because data are specific to each store, space allocations reflect actual sales. Here are some examples of category management software:

- SAP for Retail (http://go.sap.com/solution/industry/retail.html) from SAP
- Symphony GOLD (www.eyc.com/gold) from Symphony EYC
- Shelf Logic Enterprise (www.shelflogic.com/enterprise-edition.html) and Shelf Logic Master (www.shelflogic.com/master-edition.html); the Enterprise version is $4,995 and the Master version is $995.
- JDA Space Planning (www.jda.com/solutions).

Chapter Summary

1. *To demonstrate the importance of a sound merchandising philosophy.* Developing and implementing a merchandise plan is a key element in a successful retail strategy. Merchandising consists of the activities involved in a retailer's buying goods and services and making them available for sale. A merchandising philosophy sets the guiding principles for all merchandise decisions and must reflect the desires of the target market, the retailer's institutional type, its positioning, its defined value chain, supplier capabilities, costs, competitors, product trends, and other factors.

2. *To study various buying organization formats and the processes they use.* The buying organization and its processes must be defined in terms of its formality, degree of centralization, organizational breadth, personnel resources, functions performed, and staffing.

    With a formal buying organization, merchandising is a distinct task in a separate department. In an informal buying organization, the same personnel handle both merchandising and other retail tasks. Multiunit retailers must choose whether to have a centralized or a decentralized buying organization. In a centralized organization, all purchases emanate from one office. In a decentralized organization, decisions are made locally or regionally. For a general organization, one person or a few people buy all merchandise. For a specialized organization, each buyer is responsible for a product category.

    An inside buying organization is staffed by a retailer's personnel and decisions are made by its permanent employees. An outside buying organization involves a company or personnel external to the retailer. Most retailers use either an inside or an outside buying organization; some employ a combination. A resident buying office, which can be an inside or outside organization, is used when a retailer wants to keep in close touch with

key markets and cannot do so through the headquarters buying staff. Independents and small chains often use cooperative buying to compete with large chains.

If a retailer has a "merchandising" view, merchandise personnel oversee all buying and selling functions. If it has a "buying" view, merchandise personnel oversee buying, advertising, and pricing, while store personnel oversee assortments, displays, personnel deployment, and sales presentations.

A buyer is responsible for selecting merchandise and setting a strategy to market that merchandise. He or she devises and controls sales and profit projections for a product category; plans assortments, styling, sizes, and quantities; negotiates with and evaluates vendors; and oversees store displays. A sales manager supervises the on-floor selling and operational activities for a specific retail department. He or she must be a good organizer, administrator, and motivator.

3. *To outline the considerations in devising merchandise plans: forecasts, innovativeness, assortment, brands, timing, and allocation.* Forecasts are projections of expected retail sales; they form the foundation of merchandise plans. Staple merchandise consists of the regular products a retailer carries. A basic stock list specifies the inventory level, color, brand, and so on for every staple item carried. Assortment merchandise consists of products for which there must be a variety so customers have a proper selection. A model stock plan projects levels of specific assortment merchandise. Fashion merchandise has cyclical sales due to changing tastes and lifestyles. Seasonal merchandise sells well over nonconsecutive periods. With fad merchandise, sales are high for a short time. When forecasting for best-sellers, many retailers use a never-out list.

A retailer's innovativeness is related to the target market(s), product growth potential, fashion trends, the retailer's image, competition, customer segments, responsiveness to consumers, investment costs, profitability, risk, constrained decision making, and declining goods and services. Three issues are of particular interest: How fast will a new good or service generate sales? What are the most sales to be achieved in a season or a year? Over what period will a good or service continue to sell? A useful tool is the product life cycle.

An *assortment* is the merchandise selection carried. The retailer first chooses the quality of merchandise. The assortment is then determined. *Width of assortment* refers to the number of distinct product categories carried. *Depth of assortment* refers to the variety in any category. As part of assortment planning, a retailer chooses its mix of brands. Manufacturer brands are produced and controlled by manufacturers. Private brands contain names designated by wholesalers or retailers. Generic brands feature generic names as brands and are a form of private brand. Competition between manufacturers and retailers is called *the battle of the brands*.

For new goods and services, it must be decided when they are first to be displayed and sold. For established goods and services, the firm must plan the merchandise flow during the year. In deciding when and how often to buy merchandise, quantity discounts should be considered. A single-unit retailer chooses how much merchandise to allocate to the sales floor and how much to the stockroom, and whether to use a warehouse. A chain also allocates items among stores.

4. *To discuss category management and merchandising software.* Category management is a technique for managing a retail business that focuses on product category results rather than the performance of individual brands. It arranges product groups into strategic business units to better address consumer needs and meet financial goals. Category management helps retail personnel make the merchandising decisions that maximize the total return on the assets. There is now plentiful PC- and Web-based merchandising software available for retailers, in just about every aspect of merchandise planning.

Key Terms

merchandising (p. 359)
merchandising philosophy (p. 359)
micromerchandising (p. 360)
cross-merchandising (p. 361)
resident buying office (p. 363)
cooperative buying (p. 364)
buyer (p. 364)
sales manager (p. 364)
forecasts (p. 364)

staple merchandise (p. 366)
basic stock list (p. 366)
assortment merchandise (p. 366)
model stock plan (p. 366)
fashion merchandise (p. 366)
seasonal merchandise (p. 366)
fad merchandise (p. 366)
never-out list (p. 366)
product life cycle (p. 368)

assortment (p. 369)
width of assortment (p. 370)
depth of assortment (p. 370)
manufacturer (national) brands (p. 372)
private (dealer or store) brands (p. 372)
generic brands (p. 374)
battle of the brands (p. 375)
category management (p. 376)

Questions for Discussion

1. Outline the key aspects of consumer-focused merchandising as far as it impacts on the retailer.
2. Explain how a retailer can make use of customer segmentation data.
3. Is cross-merchandising a good approach? Why or why not?
4. A chain of food stores across a country has decentralized buying. Is this a good idea?
5. Global retailer Marks and Spencer runs a 12-to-18-month graduate merchandising program. Research it and suggest what the course content should be.
6. Suggest what would be included in the staple, basic, and assortment lists for a busy city-center coffee shop.
7. Under what circumstances could a retailer carry a wide range of merchandise quality without hurting its image? When should the quality of merchandise carried be quite narrow?
8. How could a major appliance repair service apply the product life-cycle concept?
9. What are the trade-offs in a retailer's deciding how much to emphasize private brands rather than manufacturer brands?
10. Present a checklist of five factors for a chain retailer to review in determining how to allocate merchandise among its stores.
11. What is the basic premise of category management? Why do you think that supermarkets have been at the forefront of the movement to use category management?
12. What do you think are the risks of placing too much reliance on merchandising software? Do the risks outweigh the benefits? Explain your answer.

Web-Based Exercise

Visit this section of the TXT Retail Web site (http://txtretail.txtgroup.com/solutions/assortment-planning-buying/). Review the merchandise planning information described there. How would you recommend that a retailer use this information?

15 Implementing Merchandise Plans

Chapter Objectives

1. To describe the steps in the implementation of merchandise plans: gathering information, selecting and interacting with merchandise sources, evaluation, negotiation, concluding purchases, receiving and stocking merchandise, reordering, and re-evaluation

2. To examine the prominent roles of logistics and inventory management in the implementation of merchandise plans

When enacting merchandise plans, many retail managers have a mantra: "Organize, Optimize, Synchronize." American Eagle Outfitters' (AEO) new distribution center in Hazelton, Pennsylvania, was specifically designed to handle both E-commerce and store fulfillment with maximum efficiency. Before the facility was constructed, the company maintained two separate distribution centers, neither of which was optimized for the company's growing E-commerce sales. One facility in Kansas provided direct-to-consumer order fulfillment and in-store replenishment (handling all women's AEO and Aerie-branded products); the other, near Pittsburgh, exclusively served bricks-and-mortar locations (handling all men's products and footwear and accessories for both genders).

The logistics capabilities of direct-to-consumer order fulfillment and in-store replenishment differ greatly as a result of the order size. "Most distribution centers cannot economically ship small orders to final consumers. We needed a facility that could serve both and do it more efficiently," says Christine Miller, AEO director of operations. "We also needed redundant capabilities for the direct [to store] business."[1]

Source: Bilan 3D/Shutterstock. Reprinted by permission.

Overview

Enter the 7-Eleven Web site (http://corp.7-eleven .com) and click on "News Room" to find out what this creative retailer is doing.

This chapter builds on Chapter 14 and covers the implementation of merchandise plans, including logistics and inventory management. Sometimes, it is simple to enact merchandise plans. Other times, it requires a lot of hard work. A big challenge that retailers face is reaching the proper balance between out-of-stock (OOS) and too much stock.

Out-of-stocks cost U.S. retailers more than $634 billion in lost retail sales. Overstocks account for $472 billion in lost revenues due to markdowns on excess inventory, which hurts margins. Increasing online sales, online returns, and order-online/pickup-in-store sales further complicate inventory management for omnichannel retailers. A lack of supplier collaboration in terms of their flexibility in pack sizes can further constrain retailers. Retailers can leverage customer data and advanced supply-chain solutions to develop accurate forecasts, which should also consider the impact of external factors such as weather, seasonality, and supplier constraints.[7]

IMPLEMENTING MERCHANDISE PLANS

The implementation of merchandise plans comprises the eight sequential steps shown in Figure 15-1 and discussed next.

Gathering Information

After overall merchandising plans are set, more information about target market needs and prospective suppliers is required before buying or rebuying merchandise. In gathering data *about the marketplace*, a retailer has several possible sources. The most valuable is the consumer. By regularly researching target-market demographics, lifestyles, product preferences, and potential shopping plans, a retailer can learn about consumer demand directly. Loyalty programs and social-media comments are especially useful in tracking consumer purchases and interests.

Other information sources can be used when direct consumer data are insufficient. Suppliers (manufacturers and wholesalers) usually do their own sales forecasts and marketing research (such as test marketing). They also know how much outside promotional support a retailer will get. In closing a deal with the retailer, a supplier may present charts and graphs, showing forecasts and promotional support. Yet, the retailer should remember that it is the party with direct access to the target market and its needs.

Retail sales and display personnel interact with consumers and can pass their observations along to management. A **want book (want slip)** system is a formal way to record consumer requests for unstocked or out-of-stock merchandise. It is very helpful to a retailer's buyers. Aside from customers, salespeople may provide the most useful information for merchandising decisions.

See how mySimon (www .mysimon.com) can help retailers track competitors.

Competitors represent another information source. A risk-averse retailer may not stock an item until competitors do and may employ comparison shoppers to study the offerings and prices of competitors. The most sophisticated comparison shopping involves the use of Web-based

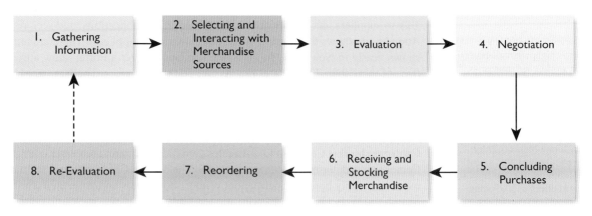

FIGURE 15-1
The Process for Implementing Merchandise Plans

FIGURE 15-2

A Competition Shopping Report

COMPETITION SHOPPING REPORT

Store # _____   Date _____

Dept. # _____   Qualified Competition Shopped:

1. _____
2. _____

Our Style No.	Mfr. Model or Style	Description	Our Price	1st Compet. Price	2nd Compet. Price	Store's Recom. Price	Buyer's Recom. Price

Item Seen at Our Competitor's Store Which We Should Carry:					
Manufacturer	Mfr. Model or Style	Description	Reg. or List Price	Sale Price	Buyer's Comments

Signature of Shopper   _Store Manager_

shopping bots (Web robots) such as mySimon.com, whereby competitors' offerings and prices are tracked electronically. Rakuten.com, for one, constantly checks its prices to make sure that it is not undersold. In addition, trade publications report on trends in each aspect of retailing and provide another way of gathering data from competitors. Figure 15-2 is an example of a competition shopping report.

In addition, government sources indicate unemployment, inflation, and product safety data; independent news sources conduct their own consumer polls and do investigative reporting; and commercial data can be purchased.

To learn about the attributes of *specific suppliers* and their merchandise, retailers can do the following:

▶ Talk to suppliers, get specification sheets, read trade publications, and seek references.

Learn why High Point (www.highpointmarket.org) is a world-class trade show.

▶ Attend trade shows that feature numerous exhibitors (suppliers). There are hundreds of trade shows yearly in New York. In Paris, the semiannual Prêt à Porter show attracts representatives of more than 700 apparel brands and 50,000 attendees. The National Hardware Show in Las Vegas has 2,800 exhibitors and 30,000 attendees each year. The High Point Furniture Market in North Carolina has semiannual shows that attract more than 2,000 manufacturers and 75,000 attendees—from all 50 states and 110 countries.

California Market Center (www.californiamarketcenter.com) offers a lot of online information for retailers.

▶ Visit year-round merchandise marts such as AmericasMart Atlanta (www.americasmart.com); California Market Center in Los Angeles (www.californiamarketcenter.com); Dallas Market Center (www.dallasmarketcenter.com); and The Mart in Chicago (http://themart.com). These marts have daily hours for permanent vendor showrooms and large areas for trade shows.

▶ Search the Web. One newer application is GoExhibit (www.goexhibit.com). A trade show coordinator can use this Web-based application to create a 3D virtual reality environment of a trade show on a Web site. Like a physical trade show, the coordinator can add and design booths, modify the exhibit hall layout, and manage exhibit hall features. In addition, the coordinator can view and analyze trade-show chatter among attendees, as well as traffic counts and flow at exhibits—which are difficult to do at a traditional trade show. Attendees can access product information visit booths and chat with exhibitors and other attendees. Other technology allows exhibitors to stream on-demand webinars 24/7 anywhere in the world.[3]

Whatever information acquired, a retailer should feel comfortable that it is sufficient for good decision making. For routine decisions (staple products), limited information may be adequate. On the other hand, new fashions' sales fluctuate widely and require extensive data for forecasts.

Selecting and Interacting with Merchandise Sources

The next step is to select merchandise sources and to interact with them. Three major options exist:

▶ *Company-owned:* A large retailer owns a manufacturing and/or wholesaling facility. A company-owned supplier handles all or part of the merchandise the retailer requests.

▶ *Outside, regularly used supplier:* This supplier is not owned by the retailer but used regularly. A retailer knows the quality of merchandise and the reliability of the supplier from its experience.

▶ *Outside, new supplier:* This supplier is not owned by the retailer, nor has the retailer bought from it before. The retailer may be unfamiliar with merchandise quality and supplier reliability.

A retailer can rely on one kind of supplier or use a combination (the biggest retailers often use all three formats). The types of outside suppliers (regularly used and new) are described in Figure 15-3. In choosing vendors, the criteria listed in the Figure 15-4 checklist should be considered.

Big Lots places emphasis on supplier relations (www .biglots.com/corporate/ vendors).

Big Lots, which buys merchandise to stock its national chain of closeout stores, can attest to the complicated process of choosing suppliers. An important competitive advantage of its business model is to opportunistically purchase quality brand-name merchandise directly from manufacturers, vendors, and, in some cases, bankruptcies, liquidations, and insurance claims at substantially lower prices than those paid by traditional retailers. It buys significant quantities of a vendor's closeout merchandise in specific product categories and controls distribution in accordance with vendor instructions. In addition, purchases are supplemented with direct import and domestically sourced merchandise in some departments. The firm purchases 24 percent of merchandise directly from overseas vendors, including 20 percent from vendors in China.[4]

Retailers and suppliers often interact well together, as highlighted in Figure 15-5. Other times, there are conflicts. As noted earlier, relationship building can be invaluable. Yet, there remain sore points between retailers and suppliers. On the one hand, many retailers have beefed up their use of private brands because they are upset when suppliers such as Gucci open their own stores in the same shopping centers. Most Gucci sales now come from company-owned and franchised shops. On the other hand, many suppliers are distressed by what they believe is retailers' excessive use of **chargebacks**, whereby retailers, at their sole discretion, make deductions in their bills for infractions ranging from late shipments to damaged and expired goods. Some suppliers have even taken their retailers to court over the practice. Attain Consulting Group divides chargebacks into three categories:[5]

▶ *Intentional deductions* are offered by manufacturers to retailers with the goal of increasing the revenue of the manufacturers. Examples are discounts, rebates, advertising, and markdown allowances that provide retailers with an extra incentive to promote products.

▶ *Unauthorized deductions* are not foreseen by manufacturers. Examples are retailer chargebacks for alleged merchandise shortages, customer returns to the retailer, and allegations of price discrepancies from what the retailer agreed to pay. Some retailers are aggressive in applying unauthorized deductions.

▶ *Preventable deductions* can be avoided by manufacturers through better performance. These deductions are due to suppliers not fully complying with retailers' rules as to order fulfillment, shipper routing, container labeling, shipment documentation, or E-commerce practices. For example, a retailer might require that shipments be labeled with a specific barcode or that every item be folded and marked with the suggested retail price.

Selecting merchandise sources must be viewed as a two-way street. Given the growth of E-commerce, many manufacturers sell products online directly to customers. Most manufacturers

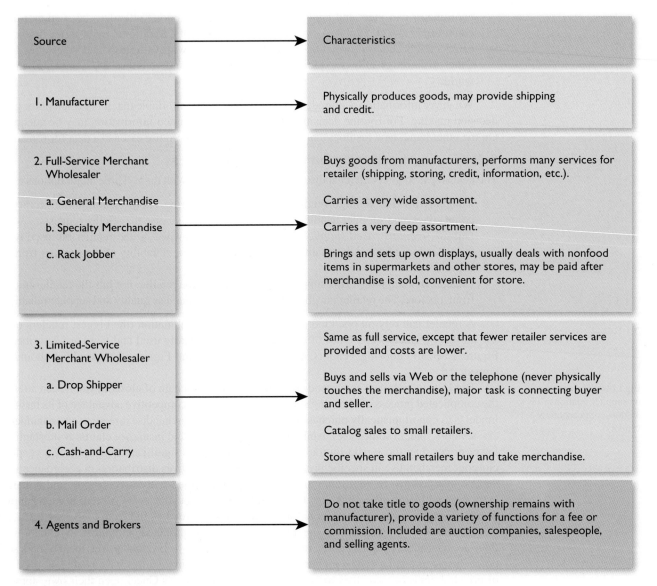

FIGURE 15-3
Outside Sources of Supply

take into account their retailers' or resellers' commercial interests and keep prices on their direct E-commerce sites high enough so retailers can still be competitive. Some manufacturers do not, however; prices on those manufacturer Web sites may be equal to or lower than retailers' wholesale prices. The retailer has to pay for logistics, warehousing, rent, and employee salaries and may not be able to be competitive.[6] Many retailers are able to counter the entry of manufacturer flagship stores by offering enhanced services and product add-ons.

Evaluating Merchandise

Whatever source is chosen, there must be a procedure to evaluate the merchandise under consideration. Three procedures are possible: inspection, sampling, and description. The technique depends on the item's cost, its attributes, and purchase regularity.

Inspection occurs when every single unit is examined before purchase and after delivery. Jewelry and art are examples of expensive, rather unique purchases for which the retailer carefully inspects all items.

Sampling is used with regular purchases of large quantities of breakable, perishable, or expensive items. Because inspection is inefficient, items are sampled for quality and condition. A retailer ready to buy several hundred light fixtures, bunches of bananas, or inexpensive watches does not inspect each item. A number of units are sampled, and the entire selection is bought if the sample

FIGURE 15-4

A Checklist of Points to Review in Choosing Vendors

✓ Reliability—Will a supplier consistently fulfill all written promises?

✓ Price–quality—Who provides the best merchandise at the lowest price?

✓ Order-processing time—How fast will deliveries be made?

✓ Exclusive rights—Will a supplier give exclusive selling rights or customize products?

✓ Functions provided—Will a supplier undertake shipping, storing, and other functions, if needed?

✓ Information—Will a supplier pass along important data?

✓ Ethics—Will a supplier fulfill all verbal promises and not engage in unfair business or labor practices?

✓ Guarantee—Does a supplier stand behind its offerings?

✓ Credit—Can credit purchases be made from a supplier? On what terms?

✓ Long-term relationships—Will a supplier be available over an extended period?

✓ Reorders—Can a supplier promptly fill reorders?

✓ Markup—Will markup (price margins) be adequate?

✓ Innovativeness—Is a supplier's line innovative or conservative?

✓ Local advertising—Does a supplier advertise in local media?

✓ Investment—How large are total investment costs with a supplier?

✓ Risk—How much risk is involved in dealing with a supplier?

is okay. An unsatisfactory sample might cause a whole shipment to be rejected (or a discount negotiated). Sampling may also occur upon receipt of merchandise.

Description buying is used with standardized, nonbreakable, and nonperishable merchandise. Items are not inspected or sampled; they are ordered in quantity based on a verbal, written, or pictorial description. A stationery store can order paper clips, pads, and printer paper from a catalog or Web site. After it receives an order, only a count of those items is conducted.

Negotiating the Purchase

Next, a retailer negotiates purchase terms. A new or special order usually leads to a negotiated contract, and a retailer and a supplier carefully discuss all aspects of the purchase. A regular order or reorder often involves a uniform contract, because terms are standard or have already been set and the order is handled routinely.

FIGURE 15-5

Every Link Must Be Strong in Supplier-Retailer Relationships

So long as every member of a retail distribution channel is on the same page, they will interact well and cooperate to reach the same goal—to satisfy the customer. If one party disappoints, the retailer and the customer will not be satisfied.

Source: cosma/Shutterstock. Reprinted by permission.

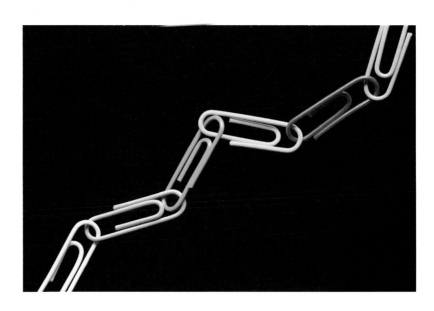

Off-price retailers and other deep discounters may require negotiated contracts for most purchases. These firms employ **opportunistic buying**, by which especially low prices are negotiated for merchandise whose sales have not lived up to expectations, end-of-season goods, items consumers have returned to the manufacturer or another retailer, and closeouts. TJX is different from typical retailers that place merchandise orders well in advance of the selling season. Its buying organization has more than 1,000 associates in 15 buying offices in 11 countries and executes an opportunistic buying strategy depending on market conditions. This allows TJX to have better insights into fashion and market trends, as well as pricing—and it provides more flexibility to expand or contract product categories since TJX buys closer to the time merchandise is sold, thus reducing the need for markdowns. It acquires merchandise on an ongoing basis from many sources so as to offer a desirable and rapidly changing mix of branded designer and other quality merchandise for less than the regular prices for comparable merchandise at department and specialty stores.[7]

Several purchase terms must be specified, whether a negotiated or a uniform contract is involved. These include the delivery date, quantity purchased, price and payment arrangements, discounts, form of delivery, and point of transfer of title, as well as special clauses.

Delivery dates and quantity purchased must be clear. A retailer should be able to cancel an order if either provision is not fulfilled. The purchase price, payment arrangements, and permissible discounts must also be addressed. What is the retailer's cost per item (including handling)? What forms of payment are permitted (cash and credit)? What discounts are given? Retailers' purchase prices are often discounted for early payments ("2/10/net 30" means there is a 2 percent discount if the full bill is paid in 10 days; the full bill is due in 30 days); support activities (setting up displays); and quantity purchases. Stipulations are needed for the form of delivery (truck, rail, and so on) and the party responsible for shipping fees (FOB factory—free on board—means a supplier places merchandise with the shipper, but the retailer pays the freight). Last, the point of transfer of title—when ownership changes from supplier to buyer—must be stated in a contract.

To learn more about the slotting allowance controversy, visit this Web site (www.customdirect .com/slotting-fees-expensive-battle-shelf-space).

Special clauses may be inserted by either party. Sometimes, they are beneficial to both parties (such as an agreement about the advertising support each party provides). Other times, clauses are inserted by the more powerful party. A major disagreement between vendors and large retailers is the latter's increasing use of **slotting allowances**—payments that retailers require of vendors for providing shelf space, which varies based on number of product facings, prominence on a shelf or location within the store. Slotting fees were investigated by the Senate and Federal Trade Commission (FTC) in the 1990s, since they reduce product variety for customers and is anti-competitive, a disadvantage for new or small manufacturers. The proprietary nature of negotiations on slotting allowances and the ensuing vertical contracts made it difficult for the FTC to ban slotting allowances because of lack of empirical evidence.[8]

Unlike many other retailers, industry leader Walmart does not charge any slotting allowances and often gets new products first from suppliers as a result of this policy.

Concluding Purchases

Many medium-sized and large retailers use computers to complete and process orders (based on electronic data interchange [EDI] and quick response [QR] inventory planning), and each purchase is fed into a computer data bank. Smaller retailers often write up and process orders manually, and purchase amounts are added to their inventory in the same way. Yet, with the advances in computerized ordering software, even small retailers may have the capability of placing orders electronically—especially if they buy from large wholesalers that use EDI and QR systems.

There is EDI/QR software (http://edi.gxs.com) to fit almost any budget.

Multiunit retailers must determine whether the final purchase decision is made by central or regional management or by local managers. Advantages and disadvantages accrue to each approach.

Several alternatives are possible regarding the transfer of title between parties. The retailer's responsibilities and rights differ in each of these situations:

▷ The retailer takes title immediately on purchase.
▷ The retailer assumes ownership after items are loaded onto the mode of transportation.
▷ The retailer takes title when a shipment is received.
▷ The retailer does not take title until the end of a billing cycle, when the supplier is paid.
▷ The retailer accepts merchandise on consignment and does not own the items. The supplier is paid after merchandise is sold.

CAREERS IN RETAILING

Opportunistic Buying by Discounters

Buyers for membership (warehouse) clubs and off-price chains such as Burlington Coat Factory (now known simply as Burlington) and Marshall's often engage in opportunistic buying. Buyers for specialty stores and department stores—who buy much of their merchandise from traditional sources—purchase merchandise 8 to 10 weeks ahead of the selling season, purchase a full range of sizes and colors, and are strictly governed by open-to-buy restrictions. In contrast, opportunistic buyers purchase goods from a variety of nonrecurring sources, often acquire end-of-season merchandise, may purchase odd lots (broken sizes), and are less constrained by budgets developed at the beginning of a year. Opportunistic buying results in retail prices so low that many shoppers can't resist, even though an item was not on their shopping list.

Evaluate the pros and cons of an opportunistic buyer's purchasing end-of-season merchandise versus broken lots (unequal size distributions) for men's clothing.

■

A consignment or memorandum deal may be possible if a vendor is in a weak position and wants to persuade retailers to carry its items. In a **consignment purchase**, a retailer has no risk because title is not taken; the supplier owns the goods until sold. An electronic version (scan-based trading) is being tried at some supermarkets. It saves time and money for all parties due to paperless steps in a purchase. In a **memorandum purchase**, risk is still low, but a retailer takes title on delivery and is responsible for damages. In both cases, retailers do not pay for items until they are sold, and they can return them.

Receiving and Stocking Merchandise

The retailer is now set to receive and handle items. This involves receiving and storing, checking and paying invoices, price and inventory marking, setting up displays, figuring on-floor assortments, completing transactions, arranging delivery or pickup, processing returns and damaged goods, monitoring pilferage, and controlling merchandise. See Figure 15-6. Good distribution management is key.

Items may be shipped from suppliers to warehouses (for storage and disbursement) or directly to retailers' store(s). The Walgreens drugstore chain has fully automated warehouses that stock thousands of products and speed their delivery to stores. Amazon.com uses U.S. and international fulfillment centers and warehouses that it operates itself, as well as fulfillment centers that are operated under co-sourcing arrangements.

One important emerging technology that may greatly advance the merchandise tracking and handling process for retailers involves an **RFID (radio frequency identification)** system—a method of storing and remotely retrieving data using devices called RFID tags or transponders. In an RFID system, information is sent via RFID tags by a reader that uses radio waves. In a *passive system*, which is the most often utilized, an RFID reader provides the power for the tag to

FIGURE 15-6

Receiving and Verifying Inventory

Every time merchandise orders are received by the retailer, they must be verified in terms of the quantity, assortment, and condition of the goods.

Source: Marcin Balcerzak/Shutterstock. Reprinted by permission.

communicate with the reader. In an *active system*, a battery in the RFID tag boosts the effective geographic range of the tag and supports other features not available with passive tags, such as sensing temperature changes in the environment. Data from RFID tags go through communication interfaces to host computers in a manner similar to that involving barcode labels—with data sent to computer systems to interpret, store, and act upon.

In comparison to a barcode, an RFID system has greater range and speed. An RFID tag can be read from many feet between the tag and a scanner. In addition, unlike a barcode, the RFID tag does not have to be passed along the line of sight of the scanner. There are two types of RFID tags: passive and active. *Passive tags* have unpowered chips that are programmed with data. These tags must be near a hand-held or fixed-position reader to be read. With passive RFID tags, the tags and reader can be purchased from different manufacturers. *Active tags* are internally powered, and can be read from a range of several hundred feet and located in a single central location. These tags and machinery are proprietary and must be purchased from the same manufacturer.

One study found that 78 percent of retailers received at least some RFID tagged merchandise (mostly apparel and footwear). On average, 40 percent of items made by apparel and general merchandise manufacturers have RFID tags.[9] Suppliers are responsible for most of the work and costs. The costs for an RFID system include computer equipment, network configuration, backup systems, software, cabling, and installation. Fortunately, the price of RFID tags has dropped to 10 cents for a basic passive RFID tag and $15 to $20 for an active RFID tag.[10]

Macy's is aware that, even though the accuracy of inventory data is 95 percent or better at the warehouse level, it's very different at the store level. Because of such factors as pilferage and errors associated with the checkout procedure (a cashier can scan the same shirt three times, when a customer purchases three different colors), inventory accuracy at the store level can be 60 to 70 percent during the holiday season. Macy's began using RFID technology in 2011, initially to maintain inventory information on a group of products (denim, men's basics, and women's intimate apparel) that accounted for 30 percent of sales. Due to the RFID success with these goods, Macy's now uses RFID tags to allow fulfillment of omnichannel orders where only one unit is shown to be available in-store. Prior to RFID adoption, inventory counts—especially when only one unit was listed as being in inventory—were not reliable.[11]

At present, RFID use is still somewhat limited. It is too early to predict how widespread RFID use will be or how long it will take to be accepted by most retailers and their suppliers. Suppliers are responsible for most of the work and costs. The current costs for an RFID system range from under $100,000 to $300,000 for a small or medium-sized supplier to several million dollars for a large supplier. Both retailers (such as Macy's, Lululemon, and Athletica) and suppliers (such as Levi Strauss and Co.) benefit from using RFID systems.

Item-level RFID tagging at the source improves inventory accuracy by up to 80 percent, stock visibility and availability, and loss prevention, and allows identification of an item throughout an entire supply chain of an omnichannel retailer. RFID tags in apparel retailing can typically cut out-of-stocks by up to 50 percent, saving 80 percent of the time needed for inventory management. Item-level RFID tagging by suppliers at source also reduces chargebacks, efficiently audits every item in cartons without opening them, and reduces inventory audit and packing times.[12]

As orders are received, they must be checked for completeness and product condition. Invoices must be reviewed for accuracy and payments made as specified. This step cannot be taken for granted.

Seagull Scientific (www.seagullscientific.com) markets popular labeling software.

At this point, prices and inventory information are marked on merchandise. Supermarkets estimate that price marking on individual items costs them an amount equal to their annual profits. Marking can be done in various ways. Small firms may hand-post prices and manually keep inventory records. Some retailers use their own computer-generated price tags and rely on pre-printed UPC data on packages to keep records. Others buy tags, with computer- and human-readable price and inventory data, from outside suppliers. Still others expect vendors to provide source tagging. An inventory system works best when there are more data on labels or tags. With portable devices, UPC-based labels can be printed and connected to store computers.

Store displays and on-floor quantities and assortments depend on the retailer and products involved. Supermarkets have bin-and-rack displays and place most inventory on the sales floor. Traditional department stores have all kinds of interior displays and place a lot of inventory off the sales floor. See Figure 15-7. Displays and on-floor merchandising are discussed in Chapter 18.

FIGURE 15-7

On-Floor Assortments and Men's Shirts

On-floor inventory planning is complicated for items such as men's shirts—due to the choices that must be offered and the various sizes that must be readily available.

Source: Rob Bouwman/ Shutterstock. Reprinted by permission

Merchandise handling is not complete until the customer buys and receives it from a retailer. This means order taking, credit or cash transactions, packaging, and delivery or pickup. Automation has improved retailer performance in each of these areas.

A procedure for processing returns and damaged goods is needed. A retailer must determine the party responsible for customer returns (supplier or retailer) and situations in which damaged goods would be accepted for refund or exchange (such as the length of time a warranty is honored).

As discussed later in the chapter, more retailers are taking aggressive actions to monitor and reduce inventory losses. This is a major problem due to the high costs of merchandise theft.

Merchandise control involves assessing sales, profits, turnover, inventory shortages, seasonality, and costs for each product category and item carried. Control is usually achieved by preparing computerized inventory data and doing physical inventories. A physical inventory must be adjusted to reflect damaged goods, pilferage, customer returns, and other factors. See Figure 15-8. A discussion of this topic appears in Chapter 16.

Merchandise receiving and handling is discussed further later in this chapter.

Reordering Merchandise

Four factors are critical in reordering merchandise that the retailer purchases more than once: order and delivery time, inventory turnover, financial outlays, and inventory versus ordering costs.

How long does it take for a retailer to process an order and a supplier to fulfill and deliver it? It is possible for delivery time to be so lengthy that a retailer must reorder while having a full inventory. On the other hand, overnight delivery may be available for some items.

How long does it take for a retailer to sell out inventory? A fast-selling product gives a retailer two choices: (1) order a surplus of items and spread out reorder periods or (2) keep a low inventory and order frequently. A slow-selling item may let a retailer reduce its initial inventory and spread out reorders.

What are the financial outlays under various purchase options? A large order, with a quantity discount, may require a big cash outlay. A small order, although more expensive per item, results in lower total costs at any one time because less inventory is held.

There are trade-offs between inventory holding and ordering costs. A large inventory fosters customer satisfaction, volume discounts, low per-item shipping costs, and easier handling. It also means high investments; greater obsolescence and damages; and storage, insurance, and

FIGURE 15-8

Automated Inventory Management

Through an automated inventory management system, retailers can efficiently and continuously track inventory in any store or warehouse. This system would be complemented by a semiannual or annual physical inventory.

Source: NAN728/ Shutterstock. Reprinted by permission.

opportunity costs. Placing many orders and keeping a small inventory mean a low investment, low opportunity costs, low storage costs, and little obsolescence. Yet, there may be disappointed customers if items are out of stock, higher unit costs, adverse effects from order delays, a need for partial shipments, service charges, and complex handling. Retailers try to hold enough stock to satisfy customers yet not having a high surplus. Quick response inventory planning lowers inventory and ordering costs via close retailer–supplier relationships.

Re-evaluating on a Regular Basis

A merchandising plan should be re-evaluated regularly, with management reviewing the buying organization and that organization assessing the implementation. The overall procedure, as well as the handling of individual goods and services, should be monitored. Conclusions during this stage become part of the information-gathering stage for future efforts.

LOGISTICS

Logistics is the total process of planning, implementing, and coordinating the physical movement of merchandise from manufacturer (wholesaler) to retailer to customer in the most timely, effective, and cost-efficient manner possible. Logistics regards order processing and fulfillment, transportation, warehousing, customer service, and inventory management as interdependent functions in the value delivery chain. If a logistics system works well, firms reduce stockouts, hold down inventories, and improve customer service—all at the same time. See Figure 15-9.

Logistics can also be quite challenging. Consider the case of Supervalu, the largest public grocery wholesaler in the U. S. as well as a retailer that owns the Cub Foods, Farm Fresh, Save-A-Lot, Fresh Market, and other chains. Supervalu is the primary grocery supplier to more than 2,000 single-store and independent grocers and the military. Its network of 18 distribution centers and more than 11 million square feet of facilities is part of a multitiered logistics system that provides order accuracy and strong service while meeting tight delivery schedules. The distribution centers offer support for grocery products across a range of categories, including meat, deli, bakery, grocery, frozen foods, and dairy, as well as home-and-beauty-care items, general merchandise, and pharmacy items. Customer service professionals work around the clock to support distribution customers. The center in Denver handles more than 100,000 customer contacts monthly.[13]

In this section, we discuss these logistics concepts: performance goals, the supply chain, order processing and fulfillment, transportation and warehousing, and customer transactions and customer service. Inventory management is covered in the final section of this chapter.

CHAPTER 15 • IMPLEMENTING MERCHANDISE PLANS   **393**

FIGURE 15-9

The Multifaceted Nature of Logistics

Logistics has a lot of pieces that must be coordinated and timed right to be effective.

Source: Login/Shutterstock. Reprinted by permission.

Performance Goals

Bon-Ton (http://logistics .bonton.com) is serious about maximizing logistics performance.

Among retailers' major logistics goals are to:

▸ Match the costs incurred to specific logistics activities, thereby fulfilling all activities as economically as possible, given the firms' other performance objectives.
▸ Place and receive orders as easily, accurately, and satisfactorily as possible.
▸ Minimize the time between ordering and receiving merchandise.
▸ Coordinate shipments from various suppliers.
▸ Have enough merchandise on hand to satisfy customer demand, without having so much inventory that heavy markdowns will be necessary.

  ETHICS IN RETAILING   Upcycling—a Form of Green Marketing

In recycling (also known as "downcycling"), a product is broken down and then reconstituted as another product. This process requires the expenditure of energy. "Upcycling" transforms an otherwise disposable good into something of higher quality. Looptworks (www.looptworks.com) is an example of a firm engaged in upcycling. It makes fashion accessories, gear, and apparel from textile waste fabrics that would otherwise be burned or placed in garbage dumps. Looptworks partners with major brands and corporations by providing ecologically based solutions to handle those firms' excess capacity. Among the items made from "pre-consumer excess" materials is its MotoTri-Fold wallet that is upcycled from materials that were used in motorcycle jackets.

Why haven't more firms engaged in upcycling?

▶ Place merchandise on the sales floor efficiently.
▶ Process customer orders efficiently and in a manner satisfactory to customers.
▶ Work collaboratively and communicate regularly with other supply chain members.
▶ Handle returns effectively and minimize damaged products.
▶ Monitor logistics performance.
▶ Have backup plans in case of breakdowns in the system.

Innovel Solutions, formerly called Sears Logistics Services (SLS), is the sole point of contact for virtually all logistical activity at Sears and Kmart. It transports apparel and other products from manufacturers' facilities to store shelves and manages other transportation and warehousing services. The nationwide home-delivery business for appliances, electronics, furniture, and home improvement goods from 106 delivery hubs in the Sears network is a profit center for the retailer. Its 1,100-truck delivery service provides the same service for some rivals, such as Costco.[14]

Supply Chain Management

The **supply chain** is the logistics aspect of a value delivery chain. It comprises all the parties that participate in the retail logistics process: manufacturers, wholesalers, third-party specialists (shippers, order-fulfillment houses, and so forth), and the retailer. For posts related to supply chain management, visit our blog site (www.bermanevansretail.com).

The CPFR Committee (www.vics.org/committees/cpfr) is actively working to expand the use of integrated supply chain planning.

Many retailers and suppliers are seeking closer logistical relationships. One technique for larger retailers is **collaborative planning, forecasting, and replenishment (CPFR)**—a holistic approach to supply-chain management among a network of trading partners. According to the Voluntary Interindustry Commerce Standards Association, hundreds of leading manufacturers, service providers, and retailers (including Best Buy, Kohl's, Macy's, J. C. Penney, QVC, Staples, Target, Walgreens, and Walmart) have participated in CPFR programs.

Yet, retailers implementing CPFR must take into account the challenges associated with total implementation costs and determine whether they are at a competitive disadvantage. Aligning business goals and making internal changes can be challenging. Collaborative relationships mean that practices benefiting one party must be discontinued or modified if they are not rewarding to a partner. Examples include "channel stuffing" or "trade loading," wherein a retailer is persuaded to periodically absorb larger-than-needed replenishment orders to help a supplier. Trust is a major hurdle in implementing CPFR, as many retailers and suppliers may be unwilling to share information that reduces their ability to negotiate.[15]

Omnichannel retailers often rely on third-party logistics (3PL), sometimes called outsourcing. Third-party logistics companies work closely with retail businesses of all sizes to provide such supply chain processes as warehouse management, transportation of goods, reporting and forecasting, and managing return logistics without long-term or inflexible capital costs, leases, or staffing. For example, many retailers (including online firms) with cyclical or uneven sales, rapid sales growth, or a weak logistics infrastructure rely on UPS Supply Chain Solutions, a division of United Parcel Service, as their logistics specialist. This allows the retailers to focus on their retail strategy, stay competitive, and be able to maintain profit margins. Logistics specialists can optimize distribution and transportation networks, and streamline global supply chains.[16]

Target's Partners Online program (www.partnersonline.com) is a proactive relationship retailing activity.

The Web is a growing force in supplier–retailer communications. A number of manufacturers and retailers have set up dedicated sites exclusively to interact with their channel partners. For confidential data exchanges, passwords, and secure encryption technology are utilized. Target Corporation has a very advanced Web site called Partners Online, which took several years to develop and test. At the Web site, vendors can access sales data and inventory reports, accounts payable figures, invoices, and report cards on their performance. There are also manuals and newsletters.

Order Processing and Fulfillment

To optimize order processing and fulfillment, many firms now engage in **quick response (QR) inventory planning**, by which a retailer reduces the amount of inventory it holds by ordering more frequently and in lower quantity. A QR system requires a retailer to have good relationships with suppliers, coordinate shipments, monitor inventory levels closely to avoid stockouts, and regularly communicate with suppliers by electronic data interchange (via the Web or direct PC connections) and other means.

For the retailer, a QR system reduces inventory costs, minimizes the space required for storage, and lets the firm better match orders with market conditions—by replenishing stock more quickly. For the manufacturer, a QR system can also improve inventory turnover and better match supply and demand by giving the vendor the data to track actual sales. These data were less available in the past. In addition, an effective quick response system makes it more unlikely that a retailer would switch suppliers. The most active users of QR are department stores, full-line discount stores, apparel stores, home centers, supermarkets, and drugstores. Among the firms using QR are Dillard's, Giant Food, Home Depot, Limited Brands, Macy's, J. C. Penney, Sears, Target Corporation, and Walmart.

A QR system works best in conjunction with floor-ready merchandise, lower minimum order sizes, properly formatted store fixtures, and electronic data interchange (EDI). **Floor-ready merchandise** refers to items received at the store that are pre-tagged, with a UPC ticket marked with necessary information specified by the retailer such as style, size, type, color, and price (retailer price or suggested retail price or both) and placed on hangers so the items can be put directly on display without any preparation by retail workers. For example, Nordstrom requires that all merchandise displayed on hangers on the selling floor be shipped on floor-ready hangers, packed to prevent wrinkling. Nordstrom's requirements for floor-ready merchandise differ for its full-line stores versus Nordstrom Rack stores. Suppliers must also be able to receive or transmit an EDI purchase order. Nordstrom charges an expense offset fee for merchandise not in compliance, so merchandise can be moved to the selling floor quickly with minimal handling.[17]

Quick response also means suppliers need to rethink the minimum order sizes they will accept. Although a minimum order size of 12 for a given size or color was once required by sheet and towel makers, minimum order size is now as low as 2 units. Also, minimum orders for men's shirts have been reduced from six to as few as two units. The lower order sizes have led some retailers to refixture in-store departments. Previously, fixtures were often set up on the basis of a retailer's stocking full inventories. Today, the retailer must make a visual impact with smaller inventories.

Electronic data interchange (described in Chapter 8), allows retailers to do QR inventory planning efficiently—via a paperless, computer-to-computer relationship between retailers and vendors. Research suggests that retail prices could be reduced by an average of 10 percent with the industrywide usage of QR and EDI. Lean supply chain management uses Web-based tools to implement collaborative, real-time synchronization of product transfers; exchange vital marketplace information; utilize logistics delivery capabilities for faster responses to consumer demand; and increase profitability for supply chain partners. Rigorously identifying and eliminating waste (all non-necessary activities that do not add value) to continuously improve processes is a vital function in lean supply-chain management. Major retailers such as Costco and Walmart—as well as their suppliers—use lean supply-chain management to drive down costs and pass savings to customers.[18]

ECR Europe (www.gs1 .ch/en/prozesse/studies/ ecr-europe) has taken a lead role in trying to popularize this business tool.

Many firms in the food sector of retailing are using **efficient consumer response (ECR)** planning, which permits supermarkets to incorporate aspects of quick response inventory planning, electronic data interchange, and logistics planning. Efficient customer response focuses on developing a responsive, consumer-driven system in which manufacturers, brokers, and distributors work together to maximize consumer value and minimize supply chain costs by better transferring data, automating administration processes, and unifying replenishment cycles. Although ECR has enabled supermarkets to cut tens of billions of dollars in distribution costs, applying it has not been easy. Many supermarkets are unwilling to trade their ability to negotiate short-term purchase terms with vendors in return for routine order fulfillment without special deals.[19]

Retailers are also addressing two other aspects of order processing and fulfillment. (1) With *advanced ship notices*, retailers that utilize QR and EDI receive an alert when bills of lading are sent electronically as soon as a shipment leaves the vendor. This gives the retailers more time to efficiently receive and allocate merchandise. (2) Because more retailers are buying from multiple suppliers, from multilocation sources, and from overseas, they must better coordinate order placement and fulfillment. Home Depot, among others, has added an import logistics group to coordinate overseas forecasting, ordering, sourcing, and logistics; and Supervalu is addressing the complexity of buying products from so many different countries around the globe.

Transportation and Warehousing

Several transportation decisions are necessary:

- ► How often will merchandise be shipped to the retailer?
- ► How will small order quantities be handled?
- ► What shipper will be used (the manufacturer, the retailer, or a third-party specialist)?
- ► What transportation form will be used? Are multiple forms required (such as manufacturer trucks to retailer warehouses and retailer trucks to individual stores)? See Figure 15-10.
- ► What are the special considerations for perishables and expensive merchandise?
- ► How often will special shipping arrangements be necessary (such as rush orders)?
- ► How are shipping terms negotiated with suppliers?
- ► What delivery options will be available for the retailer's customers? This is a critical decision for nonstore retailers, especially those selling through the Web.

Transportation effectiveness is influenced by the caliber of the logistics infrastructure (including access to refrigerated trucks, airports, waterway docking, and superhighways), traffic congestion, parking, and other factors. Retailers operating outside the United States must come to grips with the logistical problems in many foreign countries, where the transportation network and the existence of modern technology may be severely lacking.

Some retailers focus on warehouses as central or regional distribution centers. Products are sent from suppliers to these warehouses, and then allotted and shipped to individual stores. Claire's Stores has its central buying and store operations offices, as well as its North American distribution center, in Hoffman Estates, Illinois. The distribution facility has over 370,000 square feet of space. Toys "R" Us has separate regional distribution centers for the U.S. stores and its international stores. Most centers are owned; some are leased.

HighJump (www.highjump .com) offers integrated DSD software. Click on "Solutions."

Other retailers, including many supermarket chains, do not rely as much on central or regional warehouses. Instead, they have at least some goods shipped right from suppliers to individual stores through **direct store delivery (DSD)**. This approach works best with retailers that also utilize electronic data interchange. It is a way to move high turnover, high bulk, perishable products from the manufacturer directly to the store. The items most apt to involve DSD (such as beverages, bread, and snack foods) typically have shelf lives of 60 days or less, whereas warehoused items have an average shelf life of one year or more. More than one-quarter of the typical supermarket's sales are from items with DSD. Manufacturers or suppliers assume costs and responsibility for demand-driven delivery, inventory management, and merchandising; DSD trucks are "mobile warehouses" that reduce retailers' operating costs.[20]

The advantages of central warehousing are the efficiency in transportation and storage, mechanized processing of goods, improved security, efficient merchandise marking, ease of returns,

FIGURE 15-10

Shipping Possibilities

A lot of merchandise is transported by at least two types of transportation—such as train and truck or air and truck. These shipments must be delivered as scheduled for the retail supply chain to operate well. With the growth of foreign suppliers, this is tougher to accomplish.

Source: Digital Genetics/ Shutterstock. Reprinted by permission.

TECHNOLOGY IN RETAILING   Taking Steps to Fight Shrinkage

Retailers have been fighting against inventory shrinkage for decades. But when the "National Retail Security Survey" was published every year, they'd see only marginal improvements. Not recently, however: The retail industry has seen good improvements, although retailers still report tens of billions of dollars in losses. "It's a pretty remarkably low number, which is good news for the retailers," says Richard Hollinger, an author of the study and professor of sociology, criminology, and law at the University of Florida. "Not all retailers report their shrinkage, so it's not a complete examination of every retailer, but in general it's a good trend."

How would you encourage employees to help reduce retail inventory shrinkage even further?

Source: Based on material in Fred Minnick, "Small and Significant," *STORES Magazine,* August 2015. Reprinted by permission. Copyright 2016. STORES Magazine.

and coordinated merchandise flow. Key disadvantages are the excessive centralized control, extra handling of perishables, high costs for small retailers, and potential ordering delays. Centralized warehousing may also reduce the capability of QR systems by adding another step.

Direct store delivery offers retailers the opportunity to grow, increase stock turnover, improve cash flow, and drive higher volumes and margins. Suppliers provide value-added services in the form of in-store forecasting, shelf-sensing, demand-driven replenishment, trade promotions, and co-op funds. A direct-to-store model can help mitigate risks for high-value goods such as jewelry that are challenged with security issues and product theft. However, DSD delivery trucks cannot be used for products that require pallet display execution or for delivery to small-format convenience stores. Tight control of delivery times and customer service to ensure there are no stock-outs require a lot of scheduling precision, which means that all DSD channel members must have real-time access to all relevant interactions, information, and applications— from product availability, to scheduling, to sales data, to demand-generating activities. Determining the optimal routes for deliveries to multiple retail outlets can be complicated. There are many variables to consider, such as traffic patterns, speed limits, distance, and time calculations.[21]

Customer Transactions and Customer Service

Retailers must plan for outbound logistics (as well as inbound logistics): completing transactions by turning over merchandise to customers. This can be as simple as having a shopper take an item from a display area to the checkout counter or driving his or her car to a loading area. It can also be as complex as concluding a Web transaction that entails shipments from multiple vendors to the customer. A shopper's purchase of a computer, a tablet, and a refrigerator from Rakuten.com may result in three separate shipments. That is why UPS, Federal Express, and others are doing more home deliveries of packages. They can readily handle the diversity of shipping requests that retailers often cannot.

Even basic deliveries can have a breakdown. Think of the local pharmacy whose high school delivery person fails to come to work one day—or the pizzeria that gets no customer orders between 2:00 P.M. and 5:00 P.M. and 25 delivery orders between 5:00 P.M. and 7:00 P.M.

There are considerable differences between store-based and nonstore retailers. Most retail stores know that the customer wants to take the purchase or pick it up when it is ready (such as a new car). All direct marketers, including Web retailers, are responsible for ensuring that products are delivered to the shopper's door or another convenient nearby location.

Customer service expectations are affected by logistical effectiveness. That is why Amazon .com emphasizes excellent logistics and fulfills orders at different levels of service to its direct customers (Prime versus regular) to meet its goal of delighting every customer. In the United States, its Fulfillment by Amazon service provides storage, packing, and shipping for independent merchants selling products on Amazon's Web site. In 2015, Amazon opened up four university brick-and-mortar bookstores and started operating 43 urban U.S. distribution facilities (Prime Now hubs and Fresh Delivery stations) to enable click-to-door delivery in 60 minutes or less. International fulfillment is outsourced or cosourced through delivery networks of third-party logistics firms and digital delivery. Amazon even owns French package delivery service Colis Prive to serve European customers. Its proposed Global Supply Chain initiative will set up a global delivery network controlling the flow of goods from factories in China and India to customer doorsteps in the United States and Europe.[22]

INVENTORY MANAGEMENT

As part of its logistics efforts, a retailer utilizes **inventory management** to acquire and maintain a proper merchandise assortment while ordering, shipping, handling, storing, displaying, and selling costs are kept in check. First, a retailer places an order based on a sales forecast or actual customer behavior. Both the number of items and their variety are requested when ordering. Order size and frequency depend on quantity discounts and inventory costs. Second, a supplier fills the order and sends the merchandise to a warehouse or directly to the store(s). Third, the retailer receives the products, makes items available for sale (by removing them from packing, marking prices, and placing them on the sales floor), and completes customer transactions. Some transactions are not concluded until the items are delivered to the customer. The cycle starts anew as a retailer places another order. Let's look at these aspects of inventory management: retailer tasks, inventory levels, merchandise security, reverse logistics, and inventory analysis.

Retailer Tasks

Due to the comprehensive nature of inventory management, and to be more cost-effective, some retailers now expect suppliers to perform more tasks or ship *floor-ready* merchandise, or they outsource at least part of their inventory management activities rather than accept warehouse-ready merchandise as in the 1990s. Today, and in the future, more manufacturers will shift to *consumer-ready* manufacturing where the links between producer and consumer will be more direct.[23] Here are some examples:

> ▶ Walmart and other retailers count on key suppliers to participate in their inventory management programs. Industrywide, this practice is known as **vendor-managed inventory (VMI)**. Procter & Gamble even has its own employees stationed at Walmart headquarters to manage the inventory replenishment of that manufacturer's products.[24]

> ▶ Target Corporation is at the forefront of another trend—store-based retailers doing their own customer order fulfillment for their online, especially mobile, businesses (as those businesses grow) or partnering with on-demand logistics companies such as Instacart to provide a menu of flexible services to customers. Services include regular online delivery, online with 1- to 2-hour delivery, ship from store, curbside pickup, and Target subscriptions for repeat purchasers. Target's Cartwheel and Curbside mobile apps account for 40 percent of digital orders and go beyond providing promotional discounts to serving in-store customer assistants, creating a personalized in-store experience, or offering an ordering portal that provides drive-thru service.[25]

The National Association for Retailing Merchandising Services offers a national online "JobBank" (www.narms.com/jobbank.html) by category and job location.

> ▶ According to the National Association for Retail Merchandising Services (www.narms.com), well over $3 billion annually in retail merchandising services—ranging from reordering to display design—are provided by specialized firms. An example is New Concepts in Marketing, which has provided ordering and inventory control, promotional selling, display placement, and other services for such clients as Babies "R" Us, Kmart, Publix, and Sam's Clubs.

One contentious inventory management activity involves who is responsible for tagging: the manufacturer or the retailer? In *source tagging*, antitheft tags are put on items when they are made, rather than at the store. Although both sides agree on the benefits of this, in terms of reduced costs and floor-readiness of merchandise, there are disagreements about who should pay for the tags.

Inventory Levels

Having the proper inventory on hand is a difficult balancing act:

1. The retailer wants to be appealing and never lose a sale by being out of stock. Yet, it does not want to be "stuck" with excess merchandise that must be marked down drastically.
2. The situation is more complicated for retailers that carry fad merchandise, handle new items for which there is no track record, and operate in new business formats where demand estimates are often inaccurate. Thus, inventory levels must be planned in relation to the products involved: staples, assortment merchandise, fashion merchandise, fads, and best-sellers.
3. Customer demand is *never* completely predictable—even for staple items. Weather, special sales, and other factors can have an impact on even the most stable items.
4. Shelf space allocations should be linked to current revenues, which means that allocations must be regularly reviewed and adjusted.

One of the advantages of QR and EDI is that retailers hold "leaner" inventories because they receive new merchandise more often. Yet, when merchandise is especially popular or the supply chain breaks down, stockouts may still occur. A Food Marketing Institute study found that even supermarkets, which carry more staples than most other retailers, lose 3 percent of sales due to out-of-stock goods.

Inventory level planning is discussed further in the next chapter.

Merchandise Security

Each year, tens of billions of dollars in U.S. retail sales—are lost due to **inventory shrinkage** caused by employee theft, customer shoplifting, vendor fraud, organized crime, and administrative errors. According to the National Retail Security Survey 2015, shoplifting accounts for 38 percent of overall shrinkage, employee theft 34.5 percent, administrative and paperwork errors 16.5 percent, vendor fraud or error 6.8 percent, and unknown loss 4.2 percent.[26]

The overall shrinkage for the United States is about 1.4 percent of sales. This means a small store with $500,000 in annual sales might lose up to $7,000 or more due to shrinkage, and a large store with $20 million in sales might lose up to $280,000 or more due to shrinkage. Thus, some form of merchandise security is needed by all retailers. Theft prevention devices include smart tagging (which uses radio frequency identification to track stolen goods), exit sensors (that make loud sounds when a thief exits the store), and source tagging (tags sewn into garments).

To reduce merchandise theft, there are three key points to consider: (1) Loss-prevention measures should be incorporated as stores are designed and built. The placement of entrances, dressing rooms, and delivery areas is critical. (2) A combination of security measures should be enacted, such as employee background checks, in-store guards, electronic security equipment, and merchandise tags. (3) Retailers must communicate the importance of loss prevention to employees, customers, and vendors—and the actions they are prepared to take to reduce losses (such as firing workers and prosecuting shoplifters).

The following activities are reducing losses from merchandise theft:

Sensormatic (www .sensormatic.com) is a leader in electronic security.

▷ Product tags, guards, video cameras, point-of-sale computers, employee surveillance, and burglar alarms are being used by more firms. Storefront protection is also popular. See the left side of Figure 15-11.

▷ Many general merchandise retailers and some supermarkets use **electronic article surveillance**—whereby special tags are attached to products so that the tags can be sensed by electronic security devices at store exits. If the tags are not removed by store personnel or desensitized by scanning equipment, an alarm goes off. Retailers also have access to nonelectronic tags. These are snugly attached to products and must be removed by special detachers; otherwise products are unusable. Dye tags permanently stain products, if not removed properly. See the right side of Figure 15-11.

▷ A number of retailers do detailed background checks for each prospective new employee. Some use loss-prevention software that detects suspicious employee behavior.

▷ Various retailers have employee training programs and offer incentives for reducing merchandise losses. Others use written policies on ethical behavior that are signed by all personnel, including senior management. Target has enrolled managers at problem stores in a Stock

RETAILING AROUND THE WORLD

Processing Foreign Credit Cards

A major problem for Web-based merchants with foreign sales is the need to process purchases made by foreign shoppers. A number of firms specialize in redeeming sales paid for in multiple foreign currencies. Authorize.Net (www.authorize.net) is the largest online payment gateway. In addition to online transactions, Authorize.Net is able to accept foreign credit cards and E-checks used in a retail store. It also offers fraud detection, is synchronized with QuickBooks, and handles automated recurring billing for subscription-based customers. Authorize.Net charges a transaction fee of 2.9 percent plus $.30. There is also a nominal one-time set up fee of $49 and a monthly gateway fee of $25.

Assess the value of Authorize.net to a small retailer seeking additional international sales.

FIGURE 15-11

Store and Merchandise Security

Above left: Retailers are concerned about store security during the hours when they are closed. Above right: They also want to make sure that individual items of merchandise are protected from theft.

Sources: (A) Alis Leonte/Shutterstock. Reprinted by permission. (B) Alexander Mazurkevich/Shutterstock. Reprinted by permission.

Shortage Institute. Neiman Marcus has shown workers a film with interviews of convicted shoplifters in prison to highlight the problem's seriousness.

▶ More retailers are apt to fire employees and prosecute shoplifters involved with theft. Courts are imposing stiffer penalties; in some areas, store detectives are empowered by police to make arrests. In more than 40 states, there are civil restitution laws; shoplifters must pay for stolen goods or face arrests and criminal trials. In most states, fines are higher if goods are not returned or are damaged. Shoplifters must also contribute to court costs.

▶ Some mystery shoppers are hired to watch for shoplifting, not just to research behavior.

Figure 15-12 presents a list of tactics retailers can use to combat employee and shopper theft, by far the leading causes of losses.

When devising a merchandise security plan, a retailer must assess the plan's impact on its image, employee morale, shopper comfort, and vendor relations. By setting strict rules for fitting rooms (by limiting the number of garments) or placing chains on very expensive coats, a retailer may cause some shoppers to avoid this merchandise—or visit another store.

Reverse Logistics

The term **reverse logistics** encompasses all merchandise flows from the customer and/or the retailer back through the supply channel. It typically involves items returned because of a shopper's second thoughts (also called *shopper's remorse*), damaged or defective products, or retailer overstocking. In the United States, customer returns alone are estimated by the National Retail Federation at about 8 percent of total retail merchandise sales, with $16 billion of returns being fraudulent. Sometimes, retailers may use closeout firms that buy back unpopular merchandise (at a fraction of the original cost) that suppliers will not take back; these firms then resell the goods at a deep discount. To avoid channel conflicts, conditions for reverse logistics should be specified in advance. U.S. firms spend more than $50 billion per year for handling, transportation, and processing costs associated with returns.[27]

These are among the decisions that must be made for reverse logistics:

The Reverse Logistics Association (www .reverselogisticstrends.com) presents a lot of helpful information on this topic at its Web site.

▶ Under what conditions (the permissible time, the condition of the product, etc.) are customer returns accepted by the retailer and by the manufacturer?

▶ What is the customer refund policy? Is there a fee for returning an opened package?

A. Employee Theft
- Use honesty tests as employee screening devices.
- Lock up trash to prevent merchandise from being thrown out and then retrieved.
- Verify through cameras and undercover personnel whether all sales are rung up.
- Centrally control all exterior doors to monitor opening and closing.
- Divide responsibilities—have one employee record sales and another make deposits.
- Give rewards for spotting thefts.
- Have training programs.
- Vigorously investigate all known losses and fire offenders immediately.

B. Shopper Theft While Store Is Open
- Use uniformed guards.
- Set up cameras and mirrors to increase visibility—especially in low-traffic areas.
- Use electronic article surveillance for high-value and theft-prone goods.
- Develop comprehensive employee training programs.
- Offer employee bonuses based on an overall reduction in shortages.
- Inspect all packages brought into store.
- Use self-locking showcases for high-value items such as jewelry.
- Attach expensive clothing together.
- Alternate the direction of hangers on clothing near doors.
- Limit the number of entrances and exits to the store, and the dollar value and quantity of merchandise displayed near exits.
- Prosecute all individuals charged with theft.

C. Employee/Shopper Theft While Store Is Closed
- Conduct a thorough building check at night to make sure no one is left in store.
- Lock all exits, even fire exits.
- Utilize ultrasonic/infrared detectors, burglar alarm traps, or guards with dogs.
- Place valuables in a safe.
- Install shatterproof glass and/or iron gates on windows and doors to prevent break-ins.
- Make sure exterior lighting is adequate.
- Periodically test burglar alarms.

FIGURE 15-12

Ways Retailers Can Deter Employee and Shopper Theft

▹ What party is responsible for shipping a returned product to the manufacturer?
▹ What customer documentation is needed to prove the date of purchase and the price paid?
▹ How are customer repairs handled (an immediate exchange, a third-party repair, or a refurbished product sent by the manufacturer)?
▹ To what extent are employees empowered to process customer returns?

Inventory Analysis

Inventory status and performance must be analyzed regularly to gauge the success of inventory management. Recent advances in computer software have made such analysis much more accurate and timely. According to surveys of retailers, these are the elements of inventory performance that are deemed most important: gross margin dollars, inventory turnover, gross profit percentage, gross margin return on inventory, the weeks of supply available, and the average in-stock position.

Inventory analysis is discussed further in the next chapter.

Chapter Summary

1. *To describe the steps in the implementation of merchandise plans.*

    (a) Information is gathered about target market needs and prospective suppliers. Data about shopper needs can come from customers, suppliers, personnel, competitors, and others. A want book (want slip) is helpful. To acquire information about suppliers, the retailer can talk to prospects, attend trade shows, visit merchandise marts, and search the Web.

    (b) The retailer chooses firm-owned; outside, regularly used; and/or outside, new supply sources. Relationships may become strained with suppliers because their goals differ from those of retailers.

    (c) The merchandise under consideration is evaluated by inspection, sampling, and/or description. The method depends on the product and situation.

    (d) Purchase terms may be negotiated (as with opportunistic buying) or uniform contracts may be used. Terms must be clear, including delivery date, quantity bought, price and payment arrangements, discounts, form of delivery, and point of transfer. There may be special provisions.

    (e) The purchase is concluded automatically or manually. Sometimes, management approval is needed. The transfer of title may take place as soon as the order is shipped or not until after merchandise is sold by the retailer.

    (f) Handling involves receiving and storing, price and inventory marking, displays, floor stocking, customer transactions, delivery or pickup, returns and damaged goods, monitoring pilferage, and control. Radio frequency identification is an emerging technology.

    (g) Reorder procedures depend on order and delivery time, inventory turnover, financial outlays, and inventory versus ordering costs.

    (h) Both the overall merchandising procedure and specific goods and services must be reviewed.

2. *To examine the prominent roles of logistics and inventory management in the implementation of merchandise plans.* Logistics includes planning, implementing, and coordinating the movement of merchandise from supplier to retailer to customer. Logistics goals are to relate costs to activities, accurately place and receive orders, minimize ordering/receiving time, coordinate shipments, have proper merchandise levels, place merchandise on the sales floor, process customer orders, work well in the supply chain, handle returns effectively and minimize damaged goods, monitor performance, and have backup plans.

    A supply chain covers all parties in the logistics process. Collaborative planning, forecasting, and replenishment uses a holistic approach. Third-party logistics is more popular than before. Many manufacturers and retailers have Web sites to interact with channel partners.

    Some retailers engage in quick-response inventory planning. Floor-ready merchandise is received at the store ready to be displayed. Electronic data interchange lets retailers use QR planning through computerized supply chain relationships. Numerous supermarkets use efficient consumer response. Several transportation decisions are needed, as are warehousing choices. Certain retailers have goods shipped by direct store delivery. Retailers must also plan outbound logistics, which involves completing transactions by turning over merchandise to the customer.

    As part of logistics, a retailer uses inventory management. Due to its complexity, and to reduce costs, retailers may expect suppliers to perform more tasks or they may outsource some inventory activities. Vendor-managed inventory is growing in popularity.

    Having a proper inventory is a balancing act: A retailer does not want to lose sales from being out of stock nor does it want to be stuck with excess goods. Yearly, tens of billions of dollars in U.S. retail sales are lost due to employee theft, customer shoplifting, vendor fraud, and errors. Many retailers use electronic article surveillance, with tags attached to products.

    Reverse logistics involves all merchandise flows from the customer and/or the retailer back through a supply channel. It includes returns due to damages, defects, or poor retail sales.

    Inventory performance must be analyzed regularly.

Key Terms

want book (want slip) (p. 383)
chargebacks, (p. 385)
opportunistic buying (p. 388)
slotting allowances (p. 388)
consignment purchase (p. 389)
memorandum purchase (p. 389)
RFID (radio frequency identification) (p. 389)
logistics (p. 392)

supply chain (p. 394)
collaborative planning, forecasting, and replenishment (CPFR) (p. 394)
quick response (QR) inventory planning (p. 394)
floor-ready merchandise (p. 395)
efficient consumer response (ECR) (p. 395)

direct store delivery (DSD) (p. 396)
inventory management (p. 398)
vendor-managed inventory (VMI) (p. 398)
inventory shrinkage (p. 399)
electronic article surveillance (p. 399)
reverse logistics (p. 400)

Questions for Discussion

1. What information should a department store gather before adding a new jewelry brand to its product mix?
2. As a new retailer, how would you research the attributes of a specific supplier?
3. To keep up with current trends and demands, a supermarket has to mix its merchandising sources. Suggest five product lines from each of the following categories.
   a. Company-owned.
   b. Outside, regularly used.
   c. Outside, new.
4. Why is inspection and sampling necessary for some categories of products being supplied to a retailer?
5. What type of retailer would tend to take advantage of an opportunistic buying situation?
6. A fast-food retailer rarely holds much stock, as their product lines and ingredients sell out fast. What are their options?

7. Distinguish between *logistics* and *inventory management*. Give an example of each.
8. What are the benefits of quick-response inventory planning? What do you think are the risks?
9. Why are some retailers convinced that distribution centers must be used as the shipping points for merchandise from manufacturers while other retailers favor direct store delivery?
10. How could a neighborhood pizzeria be prepared for the variations in customer demand for home delivery during the day?
11. What is vendor-managed inventory? How do both manufacturers and retailers benefit from it?
12. Present a seven-item checklist for a retailer to use with its reverse logistics.

Web-Based Exercise

Visit the "Business" section of the Hermes Web site (https://www.myhermes.co.uk/). Describe the services offered that are appropriate for retailers. Where does Hermes operate, and where is its central headquarters?

16 Financial Merchandise Management

Chapter Objectives

1. To describe the major aspects of financial merchandise planning and management

2. To explain the cost and retail methods of accounting

3. To study the merchandise forecasting and budgeting process

4. To examine alternative methods of inventory unit control

5. To integrate dollar and unit merchandising control concepts

Unanticipated markdowns and reductions from planned selling prices can have a devastating effect on profits. Alternatives to markdowns, such as holding goods until the end of a selling season in the hope of selling them at full price, can result in a lack of fresh merchandise, and a need for higher markdowns to sell goods late in the season. Here are some strategies to minimize markdowns:

▶ Carefully monitor sales throughout the selling season to determine slow-selling goods. Consider the maxim, "Early markdowns are the cheapest."

▶ Employ drop shipping, by sending orders directly to customers from suppliers. This enables a retailer to increase sales with no inventory or warehousing expenses of its own.

▶ Favor suppliers with quick delivery capability. Domestic suppliers may have an edge over imported goods on this criterion.

▶ Negotiate markdown allowances with major suppliers.

▶ Monitor sales across channels and locations. Cross-channel redistribution can avoid markdowns.

▶ Respond quickly to unexpected sales declines, such as a warm season for coats.

▶ Remember that price matching programs count as markdowns.

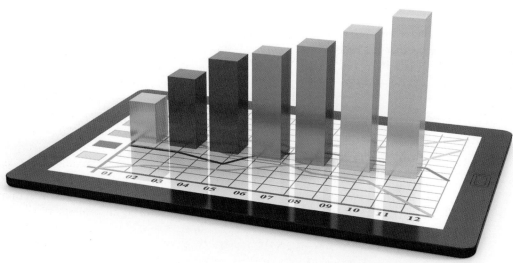

Source: pedrosek/Shutterstock. Reprinted by permission.

Overview

Sage (www.sage.com/us/erp/sage-300) is one of many firms that offer integrated accounting software that is widely used by retailers.

Through **financial merchandise management**, a retailer specifies which products (goods and services) are purchased, when products are purchased, and how many products are purchased. **Dollar control** involves planning and monitoring a retailer's financial investment in merchandise over a stated period. **Unit control** relates to the quantities of merchandise a retailer handles during a stated period. Dollar investment is determined before assortment decisions are made.

Well-structured financial merchandise plans offer these benefits:

- The value and amount of inventory in each department and/or store unit during a given period are delineated. Stock is balanced, and fewer markdowns may be necessary.
- The amount of merchandise (in terms of investment) a buyer can purchase during a given period is stipulated. This gives a buyer direction.
- The inventory investment in relation to planned and actual revenues is studied. This improves the return on investment.
- The retailer's space requirements are partly determined by estimating beginning-of-month and end-of-month inventory levels.
- A buyer's performance is rated. Various measures may be used to set standards.
- Stock shortages are determined, and bookkeeping errors and pilferage are uncovered.
- Slow-moving items are classified—leading to increased sales efforts or markdowns.
- A proper balance between inventory and out-of-stock conditions is maintained.

Inventory management at multiproduct, multibrand, and multichannel retailers is extremely complicated. However, poor inventory control leads to wasted working capital for unsold goods on store shelves or warehouses. Selecting the right inventory management software is very important, keeping in mind the industry type, company size, and preference for software type: on-premise system, software-as-a-service (SaaS) system, and/or a cloud-hosted system.[1]

This chapter divides financial merchandise management into four areas: methods of accounting, merchandise forecasting and budgeting, unit control systems, and financial inventory control. The hypothetical Handy Hardware Store illustrates the concepts.

INVENTORY VALUATION: THE COST AND RETAIL METHODS OF ACCOUNTING

This site (www.clearlyinventory.com/inventory-basics) has a guide on inventory management.

Retail inventory accounting systems can be complex because they entail a great deal of data (due to the number of items sold). A typical retailer's dollar control system must provide such data as the sales and purchases made by that firm during a budget period, the value of beginning and ending inventory, markups and markdowns, and merchandise shortages.

Table 16-1 shows a profit-and-loss statement for Handy Hardware Store for January 1, 2016, through June 30, 2016. The sales amount is total receipts over this time. Beginning inventory was computed by counting merchandise in stock on January 1, 2016—recorded at cost. Purchases (at cost) and transportation charges (costs incurred in shipping items from suppliers to the retailer) were derived by adding invoice slips for all merchandise bought by Handy in the period.

Together, beginning inventory, purchases, and transportation charges equal the cost of **merchandise available for sale**. The **cost of goods sold** equals the cost of merchandise available for sale minus the cost value of ending inventory. Sales less cost of goods sold yields **gross profit**, and **net profit** is gross profit minus retail operating expenses. Because Handy does a physical inventory twice yearly, ending inventory was figured by counting the items in stock on June 30, 2016—recorded at cost (Handy codes each item).

Retailers have data needs that are different from those of manufacturers. Assortments are larger. Costs cannot be printed on cartons unless coded (due to customer inspection). Stock shortages are higher. Sales are more frequent. Retailers require monthly, not quarterly, profit data.

Two inventory accounting systems are available: (1) The cost accounting system values merchandise at cost plus inbound transportation charges. (2) The retail accounting system values merchandise at current retail prices. Let's study both methods in terms of the frequency with which data are obtained, the difficulties of a physical inventory and record keeping, the ease of settling insurance claims (if there is inventory damage), the extent to which shortages can be computed, and system complexities.

TABLE 16-1 Handy Hardware Store Profit-and-Loss Statement, January 1, 2016–June 30, 2016

Sales		$417,460
Less cost of goods sold:		
Beginning inventory (at cost)	$44,620	
Purchases (at cost)	289,400	
Transportation charges	2,600	
Merchandise available for sale	$336,620	
Ending inventory (at cost)	90,500	
Cost of goods sold		246,120
Gross profit		$171,340
Less operating expenses:		
Salaries	$70,000	
Advertising	25,000	
Rental	16,000	
Other	26,000	
Total operating expenses		137,000
Net profit before taxes		$34,340

At our blog site (www.bermanevansretail.com), there are posts related to retail accounting and inventory valuation.

The Cost Method

With the **cost method of accounting**, the cost to the retailer of each item is recorded on an accounting sheet and/or is coded on a price tag or merchandise container. As a physical inventory is done, item costs must be learned, the quantity of every item in stock counted, and total inventory value at cost calculated. One way to code merchandise cost is to use a 10-letter equivalency system, such as M = 0, N = 1, O = 2, P = 3, Q = 4, R = 5, S = 6, T = 7, U = 8, and V = 9. An item coded with STOP has a cost value of $67.23. This technique is useful as an accounting tool and for retailers that allow price bargaining by customers (profit per item is easy to compute).

A retailer can use the cost method as it does physical or book inventories. A physical inventory means an actual merchandise count; a book inventory relies on record keeping.

A PHYSICAL INVENTORY SYSTEM USING THE COST METHOD In a **physical inventory system**, ending inventory—recorded at cost—is measured by counting the merchandise in stock at the close of a selling period. Gross profit is not computed until ending inventory is valued. A retailer using the cost method along with a physical inventory system derives gross profit only as often as it performs a full merchandise count. Because most firms do so just once or twice yearly, a

CAREERS IN RETAILING

Retailing Accounting Careers

Although small retailers generally hire accountants or accounting firms to prepare financial statements, larger retailers have staff accountants and even dedicated accounting departments. There are several advantages to an accountant's working full-time with a major retailer as opposed to working for a CPA firm. There is some seasonality with accounting work at a retailer (associated with preparing quarterly and annual reports), but it is nothing like a traditional CPA firm with a tax-preparation practice. Many retail accountants begin their careers with CPA firms and decide to switch to retailing-based positions. And even though a large

retailer's controller may have earned a CPA, this may not be a requirement for lower-level positions. Accountants working for retailers may need to rethink some of their methods. Unlike manufacturers that value inventories at cost, most retailers value inventories at retail value. As a staff accountant for a retailer, much attention has to be given to calculating deductions from retail value—such as markdowns, stock shortages, and employee discounts.

Discuss the advantages of a retailer-based career for a CPA working at an accounting firm.

physical inventory system alone imposes limits on planning. In addition, a firm might be unable to compute inventory shortages (due to pilferage and unrecorded breakage) because ending inventory value is set by adding the costs of all items in stock. It does not compute what the ending inventory *should be*.

A BOOK INVENTORY SYSTEM USING THE COST METHOD   A **book (perpetual) inventory system** avoids the problem of infrequent financial analysis by keeping a running total of the value of all inventory on hand at cost at a given time. End-of-month inventory values can be computed without a physical inventory, and frequent financial statements can be prepared. In addition, a book inventory lets a retailer uncover stock shortages by comparing projected inventory values with actual inventory values through a physical inventory.[2]

A book inventory is kept by regularly recording purchases and adding them to existing inventory value; sales are subtracted to arrive at the new current inventory value (all at cost). Table 16-2 shows Handy Hardware's book inventory system for July 1, 2016, through December 31, 2016; the beginning inventory in Table 16-2 is the ending inventory from Table 16-1. Table 16-2 assumes that merchandise costs are rather constant and monthly sales at cost are easy to compute. Yet, suppose merchandise costs rise. How would inventory value then be computed?

FIFO and LIFO are two ways to value inventory. The **FIFO (first-in-first-out) method** logically assumes old merchandise is sold first, while newer items remain in inventory. The **LIFO (last-in-first-out) method** assumes new merchandise is sold first, while older stock remains in inventory. FIFO matches inventory value with the current cost structure—the goods in inventory are the ones bought most recently, whereas LIFO matches current sales with the current cost structure—the goods sold first are the ones bought most recently. When inventory values rise, LIFO offers retailers a tax advantage because lower profits are shown.

In Figure 16-1, the FIFO and LIFO methods are illustrated for Handy Hardware's snow blowers for 2016; the store carries only one model of snow blower. Handy knows that it sold 220 snow blowers in 2016 at an average price of $320. It began 2016 with an inventory of 30 snow blowers, purchased for $150 each. During January 2016, it bought 100 snow blowers at $175 each; from October to December 2016, Handy bought another 150 snow blowers for $225 apiece. Because Handy sold 220 snow blowers in 2016, as of the close of business on December 31, it had 60 units remaining.

With the FIFO method, Handy assumes its beginning inventory and initial purchases were sold first. The 60 snow blowers remaining in inventory would have a cost value of $225 each, a total cost of goods sold of $42,250, and a gross profit of $28,150. With the LIFO method, Handy assumes the most recently purchased items were sold first and the remaining inventory would consist of beginning goods and early purchases. Of the snow blowers remaining in inventory, 30 would have a cost value of $150 each and 30 a cost value of $175 apiece, resulting in a total cost of goods sold of $46,000 and a gross profit of $24,400. The FIFO method presents a more accurate picture of the cost of goods sold and the true cost value of ending inventory. The LIFO method indicates a lower profit, leading to the payment of lower taxes but an understated ending inventory value at cost.

There is a large assortment of software (www.capterra.com/inventory-control-software) that facilitates inventory calculations.

At its Web site, Accounting Tools provides good background information on LIFO (http://www.accountingtools.com/lifo-method).

TABLE 16-2 Handy Hardware Store Perpetual Inventory System, July 1, 2016–December 31, 2016*

Date	Beginning-of-Month Inventory (at Cost)	+	Net Monthly Purchases (at Cost)	−	Monthly Sales (at Cost)	=	End-of-Month Inventory (at Cost)
7/1/16	$90,500		$ 40,000		$ 62,400		$ 68,100
8/1/16	68,100		28,000		38,400		57,700
9/1/16	57,700		27,600		28,800		56,500
10/1/16	56,500		44,000		28,800		71,700
11/1/16	71,700		50,400		40,800		81,300
12/1/16	81,300		15,900		61,200		36,000
		Total	$205,900		$260,400		(as of 12/31/16)

* Transportation charges are not included in computing inventory value in this table.

FIGURE 16-1

Applying FIFO and LIFO Inventory Methods to Handy Hardware, January 1, 2016–December 31, 2016

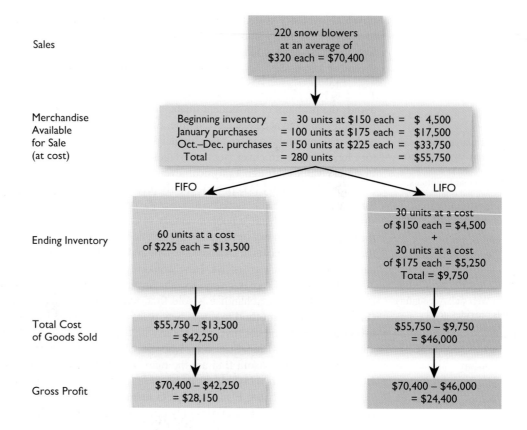

The retail method of inventory, which combines FIFO and LIFO concepts, is explained shortly.

DISADVANTAGES OF COST-BASED INVENTORY SYSTEMS   Cost-based physical and book systems have significant disadvantages. First, both require that a cost be assigned to each item in stock (and to each item sold). When merchandise costs change, cost-based valuation systems work best for firms with low inventory turnover, limited assortments, and high average prices—such as car dealers.

Second, neither cost-based method adjusts inventory values to reflect style changes, end-of-season markdowns, or sudden surges of demand (which may raise prices). Thus, ending inventory value based on merchandise cost may not reflect its actual worth. This discrepancy could be troublesome if inventory value is used in filing insurance claims for losses.

Despite these factors, retailers that make the products they sell—such as bakeries, restaurants, and furniture showrooms—often keep records on a cost basis. A department store with these operations can use the cost method for them and the retail method for other areas.

The Retail Method

With the **retail method of accounting**, closing inventory value is determined by calculating the average relationship between the cost and retail values of merchandise available for sale during a period. Although the retail method overcomes the disadvantages of the cost method, it requires detailed records and is more complex because ending inventory is first valued in retail dollars and then converted to compute gross margin (gross profit).

The three basic steps to determine ending inventory value by the retail method are:

1. Calculating the cost complement
2. Calculating deductions from retail value
3. Converting retail inventory value to cost

CALCULATING THE COST COMPLEMENT   The value of beginning inventory, net purchases, additional markups, and transportation charges are all included in the retail method. Beginning inventory and net purchase amounts (purchases less returns) are recorded at both cost and retail

TABLE 16-3 Handy Hardware Store, Calculating Merchandise Available for Sale at Cost and at Retail, July 1, 2016–December 31, 2016

	At Cost	At Retail
Beginning inventory	$ 90,500	$139,200
Net purchases	205,900	340,526
Additional markups	—	16,400
Transportation charges	3,492	—
Total merchandise available for sale	$299,892	$496,126

levels. Additional markups represent the extra revenues received when a retailer increases selling prices, due to inflation or unexpectedly high demand. Transportation charges are the retailer's costs for shipping the goods it buys from suppliers to the retailer. Table 16-3 shows the total merchandise available for sale at cost and at retail for Handy Hardware from July 1, 2016, through December 31, 2016, using the costs in Table 16-2.

By using Table 16-3 data, the average relationship of cost to retail value for all merchandise available for sale by Handy Hardware—the **cost complement**—can be computed:

$$\text{Cost complement} = \frac{\text{Total cost valuation}}{\text{Total retail valuation}}$$

$$= \frac{\$299,892}{\$496,126} = 0.6045$$

Because the cost complement is 0.6045 (60.45 percent), on average, 60.45 cents of every retail sales dollar went to cover Handy Hardware's merchandise cost.

CALCULATING DEDUCTIONS FROM RETAIL VALUE   The ending retail value of inventory must reflect all deductions from the total merchandise available for sale at retail. Besides sales, deductions include markdowns (for special sales and end-of-season goods), employee discounts, and stock shortages (due to pilferage and unrecorded breakage). Although sales, markdowns, and employee discounts can be recorded throughout an accounting period, a physical inventory is needed to learn about stock shortages.

From Table 16-3, it is known that Handy Hardware had a retail value of merchandise available for sale of $496,126 for the period from July 1, 2016, through December 31, 2016. As shown in Table 16-4, this was reduced by sales of $422,540 and recorded markdowns and employee discounts of $14,034. The ending book value of inventory at retail as of December 31, 2016, was $59,552.

To compute stock shortages, the retail book value of ending inventory is compared with the actual physical ending inventory at retail. If book inventory exceeds physical inventory, a shortage exists. Table 16-5 shows the results of Handy's physical inventory. Shortages were $3,082 (at retail), and book value was adjusted accordingly. Although Handy knows the shortages were

TABLE 16-4 Handy Hardware Store, Computing Ending Retail Book Value, as of December 31, 2016

Merchandise available for sale (at retail)		$496,126
Less deductions:		
Sales	$422,540	
Markdowns	11,634	
Employee discounts	2,400	
Total deductions		436,574
Ending retail book value of inventory		$ 59,552

TABLE 16-5 Handy Hardware Store, Computing Stock Shortages and Adjusting Retail Book Value, as of December 31, 2016

Ending retail book value of inventory	$59,552
Physical inventory (at retail)	56,470
Stock shortages (at retail)	3,082
Adjusted ending retail book value of inventory	$56,470

from pilferage, bookkeeping errors, and overshipments not billed to customers, it cannot learn the proportion of shortages from each factor.

Occasionally, a physical inventory may reveal a stock overage—an excess of physical inventory value over book value. This may be due to errors in a physical inventory or in keeping a book inventory. If overages occur, ending retail book value is adjusted upward. Inasmuch as a retailer has to conduct a physical inventory to compute shortages (overages), and a physical inventory is usually taken only once or twice a year, shortages (overages) are often estimated for monthly merchandise budgets.

CONVERTING RETAIL INVENTORY VALUE TO COST The retailer must next convert the adjusted ending retail book value of inventory to cost so as to compute dollar gross profit (gross margin). The ending inventory at cost equals the adjusted ending retail book value multiplied by the cost complement. For Handy Hardware, this was:

$$\text{Ending inventory (at cost)} = \text{Adjusted ending retail book value} \times \text{Cost complement}$$

$$= \$56,470 \times 0.6045 = \$34,136$$

This computation does not yield the exact inventory cost. It shows the average relationship between cost and the retail selling price for all merchandise available for sale.

The adjusted ending inventory at cost can be used to find gross profit. As Table 16-6 shows, Handy's 6-month cost of goods sold was $265,756, resulting in gross profit of $156,784. By deducting operating expenses of $139,000, Handy learns that the net profit before taxes for this period was $17,784.

TABLE 16-6 Handy Hardware Store Profit-and-Loss Statement, July 1, 2016–December 31, 2016

Sales		$422,540
Less cost of goods sold:		
Total merchandise available for sale (at cost)	$299,892	
Adjusted ending inventory (at cost)[a]	34,136	
Cost of goods sold		265,756
Gross profit		$156,784
Less operating expenses:		
Salaries	$ 70,000	
Advertising	25,000	
Rental	16,000	
Other	28,000	
Total operating expenses		139,000
Net profit before taxes		$ 17,784

[a] Adjusted ending inventory
(at cost) = Adjusted retail book value × Cost complement = $56,470 × 0.6045 = $34,136

Go here (http://goo
.gl/09QMOi) to download
a good discussion on "How
to Get to the Numbers That
Matter in Retail."

ADVANTAGES OF THE RETAIL METHOD Compared with other techniques, there are several advantages to the retail method of accounting:

▶ Valuation errors are reduced when conducting a physical inventory because merchandise value is recorded at retail and costs do not have to be decoded.

▶ Because the process is simpler, a physical inventory can be completed more often. This lets a firm be more aware of slow-moving items and stock shortages.

▶ The physical inventory method at cost requires a physical inventory to prepare a profit-and-loss statement. The retail method lets a firm set up a profit-and-loss statement based on book inventory. The retailer can then estimate the stock shortages between physical inventories and study departmental profit trends.

▶ A complete record of ending book values helps determine insurance coverage and settle insurance claims. The retail book method gives an estimate of inventory value throughout the year. Because physical inventories are usually taken when merchandise levels are low, the book value at retail lets retailers plan insurance coverage for peak periods and shows the values of goods on hand. The retail method is accepted in insurance claims.

LIMITATIONS OF THE RETAIL METHOD The greatest weakness is the bookkeeping burden of recording data. Ending book inventory figures can be correctly computed only if the following are accurately noted: the value of beginning inventory (at cost and at retail), purchases (at cost and at retail), shipping charges, markups and markdowns, employee discounts, transfers from other departments or stores, returns, and sales. Although personnel are freed from taking many physical inventories, ending book value at retail may be inaccurate unless all required data are precisely recorded. With computerization, this potential problem is lessened.

Another limitation is that the cost complement is an average based on the total cost of merchandise available for sale and total retail value. The ending cost value only approximates the true inventory value. This may cause misinformation if fast-selling items have different markups from slow-selling items or if there are wide variations among the markups of different goods.

Familiarity with the retail and cost methods of inventory is essential for understanding the financial merchandise management material described in the balance of this chapter.

MERCHANDISE FORECASTING AND BUDGETING: DOLLAR CONTROL

As we noted earlier, dollar control entails planning and monitoring a firm's inventory investment over time. Figure 16-2 shows the six-step dollar control process for merchandise forecasting and budgeting. This process should be followed sequentially since a change in one stage affects all the stages after it. If a sales forecast is too low, a firm may run out of items because it does not plan to have enough merchandise during a selling season and planned purchases will also be too low.

Designating Control Units

Merchandise forecasting and budgeting requires the selection of **control units**, the merchandise categories for which data are gathered. Such classifications must be narrow enough to isolate opportunities and problems with specific merchandise lines. A retailer wishing to control goods within departments must record data on dollar allotments separately for each category.

Knowing that total markdowns in a department are 20 percent above last year's level is less valuable than knowing the specific merchandise lines in which large markdowns are being taken. A retailer can broaden its control system by combining categories that comprise a department. However, a broad category cannot be broken down into components.

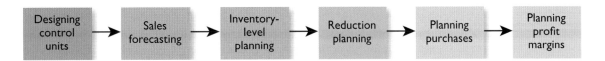

FIGURE 16-2

The Merchandise Forecasting and Budgeting Process: Dollar Control

Markdown Allowances

Retailers with strong buying power often negotiate markdown allowances from vendors. These allowances reimburse retailers for markdowns incurred due to goods sold at less than full retail suggested price. Types of markdowns include short-term allowances to compensate for lost profits during a special sale period; allowances for price reductions from full list price for end-of-season merchandise; allowances for price reductions due to product defects; and allowances for the short life expectancy of perishable goods. Critics of markdown allowances feel that large chains may be able to negotiate better deals than smaller independent retailers. This raises antitrust issues. Others say these allowances may be nothing more than an additional discount. And since these allowances may not be properly recorded in a retailer's financial statements, they may overstate profits.

Discuss the advantages and disadvantages associated with the use of markdown allowances from a vendor's perspective.

It is helpful to use control units consistent with company and trade association data. Internal comparisons are meaningful only if categories are stable. Classifications that shift over time do not permit comparisons. External comparisons are not meaningful if control units are dissimilar for a retailer and its trade associations. Control units may be based on departments, classifications in departments, price-line classifications, and standard merchandise classifications. A discussion of each follows.

The broadest practical classification for financial records is the department, which lets a retailer assess each general merchandise grouping or buyer. Even small Handy Hardware needs departmental data (tools and equipment, supplies, housewares, and so on) for buying, inventory control, and markdown decisions. For more financial data, **classification merchandising** can be used, with each department subdivided into further categories for related types of merchandise. In planning its tools and equipment department, Handy Hardware can keep financial records on both overall departmental performance and the results of such categories as lawn mowers/snow blowers, power tools, hand tools, and ladders.

A special form of classification merchandising uses *price line classifications*—sales, inventories, and purchases are analyzed by price category. This helps if distinct models of a product are sold at different prices to dissimilar target markets (such as Handy's having $50 power tools for do-it-yourselfers and $135 models for contractors). Retailers with deep assortments most often use price line control.

To best contrast its data with industry averages, a firm's merchandise categories should conform to those cited in trade publications. The National Retail Federation devised a *standard merchandise classification* with common reporting categories for a range of retailers and products. Specific classifications are also popular for some retailers. *Progressive Grocer* regularly publishes data based on standard classifications for supermarkets.

Once appropriate dollar control units are set, all transactions—including sales, purchases, transfers, markdowns, and employee discounts—must be recorded under the proper classification number. Thus, if house paint is Department 25 and brushes are 25-1, all transactions must carry these designations.

Sales Forecasting

A retailer estimates its expected future revenues for a given period by *sales forecasting*. Forecasts may be companywide, departmental, and for individual merchandise classifications. Perhaps the most important step in financial merchandise planning is accurate sales forecasting, because an incorrect projection of sales throws off the entire process. That is why many retailers use state-of-the-art forecasting software. Unified Grocers has dramatically improved its inventory productivity by using such software from SAS.[3]

SAS software is widely used in retailing (www.sas.com/en_us/industry/retail.html).

Larger retailers often forecast total and department sales by techniques such as trend analysis, time-series analysis, and multiple regression analysis. A discussion of these techniques is beyond the scope of this book. Small retailers rely more on "guesstimates," projections based on experience. Even for larger firms, sales forecasting for merchandise classifications within departments (or price lines) relies on more qualitative methods. One way to forecast sales for narrow categories is first to project sales on a company basis and then by department, and finally to break down figures judgmentally into merchandise classifications.

External factors, internal company factors, and seasonal trends must be anticipated and taken into account. Among the external factors that can affect projected sales are consumer trends, competitors' actions, the state of the economy, the weather, and new supplier offerings. For example, Planalytics offers a patented methodology to analyze and forecast the relationship among consumer demand, store traffic, and the weather.[4] Internal company factors that can affect future sales include additions and deletions of merchandise lines, revised promotion and credit policies, changes in hours, new outlets, and store remodeling. With many retailers, seasonality must be considered in setting monthly or quarterly sales forecasts. Handy's yearly snow blower sales should not be estimated from December sales alone.

A sales forecast can be developed by examining past trends and projecting future growth (based on external and internal factors). Table 16-7 shows a sales forecast for Handy Hardware. It is an estimate, subject to revisions. Various factors may be hard to incorporate when devising a forecast, such as merchandise shortages, consumer reactions to new products, the rate of inflation, and new government legislation. That is why a financial merchandise plan needs some flexibility.

After a yearly forecast is derived, it should be broken into quarters or months. In retailing, monthly forecasts are typical. Jewelry stores know December accounts for nearly one-quarter of annual sales, whereas drugstores know December sales are slightly better than average. Stationery stores and card stores realize that Christmas and other holiday cards generate more than 30 percent of seasonal greeting card sales, and Valentine's Day cards are second with about 15 percent.[5]

To acquire more specific estimates, a retailer could use a **monthly sales index** that divides each month's actual sales by average monthly sales and multiplies the results by 100. Table 16-8 shows Handy Hardware's 2016 actual monthly sales and monthly sales indexes. The store is seasonal, with peaks in late spring and early summer (for lawn mowers, garden supplies, and so on), as well as December (for lighting fixtures, snow blowers, and gifts). Average monthly 2016 sales were $70,000 ($840,000/12). Thus, the monthly sales index for January is 67[($46,800/$70,000) × 100]; other monthly indexes are computed similarly. Each monthly index shows the percentage deviation of that month's sales from the average month. A May index of 160 means May sales are 60 percent higher than average. An October index of 67 means sales in October are 33 percent below average.

After monthly sales indexes are determined, a retailer can forecast monthly sales, based on the yearly sales forecast. Table 16-9 shows how Handy's 2017 monthly sales can be forecast if average monthly sales are expected to be $73,423.

Inventory-Level Planning

Supply Chain Guru software (www.llamasoft.com/solutions/inventory-optimization) enhances inventory planning.

At this point, a retailer plans its inventory. The level must be sufficient to meet sales expectations, allowing a margin for error. Techniques to plan inventory levels are the basic stock, percentage variation, weeks' supply, and stock-to-sales methods.

With the **basic stock method**, a retailer carries more items than it expects to sell over a specified period. There is a cushion if sales are more than expected, shipments are delayed, or

TABLE 16-7 Handy Hardware Store: A Simple Sales Forecast Using Product Control Units

Product Control Units	Actual Sales 2016	Projected Growth/ Decline (%)	Sales Forecast 2017
Lawn mowers/snow blowers	$200,000	+10.0	$220,000
Paint and supplies	128,000	+3.0	131,840
Hardware supplies	108,000	+8.0	116,640
Plumbing supplies	88,000	−4.0	84,480
Power tools	88,000	+6.0	93,280
Garden supplies/chemicals	68,000	+4.0	70,720
Housewares	48,000	−6.0	45,120
Electrical supplies	40,000	+4.0	41,600
Ladders	36,000	+6.0	38,160
Hand tools	36,000	+9.0	39,240
Total year	$840,000	+4.9*	$881,080

* There is a small rounding error.

TABLE 16-8 Handy Hardware Store, 2016 Sales by Month

Month	Monthly Actual Sales	Sales Index[a]
January	$46,800	67
February	40,864	58
March	48,000	69
April	65,600	94
May	112,196	160
June	103,800	148
July	104,560	149
August	62,800	90
September	46,904	67
October	46,800	67
November	66,884	96
December	94,792	135
Total yearly sales	$840,000	
Average monthly sales	$70,000	
Average monthly index		100

[a] Monthly sales index = (Monthly sales/Average monthly sales) × 100

customers want to select from a variety of items. It is best when inventory turnover is low or sales are erratic over the year. Beginning-of-month planned inventory equals planned sales plus a basic stock amount:

$$\text{Basic stock (at retail)} = \text{Average monthly stock at retail} - \text{Average monthly sales}$$

$$\begin{array}{l}\text{Beginning-of-month} \\ \text{planned inventory level} = \text{Planned monthly sales} + \text{Basic stock} \\ \text{(at retail)}\end{array}$$

TABLE 16-9 Handy Hardware Store, 2017 Sales Forecast by Month

Month	Actual Sales 2016	Monthly Sales Index	Monthly Sales Forecast for 2017[*]
January	$46,800	67	$73,423 × 0.67 = $ 49,193
February	40,864	58	73,423 × 0.58 = 42,585
March	48,000	69	73,423 × 0.69 = 50,662
April	65,600	94	73,423 × 0.94 = 69,018
May	112,196	160	73,423 × 1.60 = 117,477
June	103,800	148	73,423 × 1.48 = 108,666
July	104,560	149	73,423 × 1.49 = 109,400
August	62,800	90	73,423 × 0.90 = 66,081
September	46,904	67	73,423 × 0.67 = 49,193
October	46,800	67	73,423 × 0.67 = 49,193
November	66,884	96	73,423 × 0.96 = 70,486
December	94,792	135	73,423 × 1.35 = 99,121
Total sales	$840,000		Total sales forecast $881,080[†]
Average monthly sales	$70,000		Average monthly forecast $73,423

[*] Monthly sales forecast = Average monthly forecast × (Monthly index/100). In this equation, the monthly index is computed as a fraction of 1.00 rather than 100.
[†] There is a small rounding error.

If Handy Hardware, with an average monthly 2017 forecast of $73,423, wants extra stock equal to 10 percent of its monthly forecast and expects January 2017 sales to be $49,193:

$$\text{Basic stock (at retail)} = (\$73,423 \times 1.10) - \$73,423 = \$7,342$$

Beginning-of-January
planned inventory level $= \$49,193 + \$7,342 = \$56,535$
(at retail)

In the **percentage variation method**, beginning-of-month planned inventory during any month differs from planned average monthly stock by only one-half of that month's variation from estimated average monthly sales. This method is recommended if stock turnover is more than six times a year or relatively stable, since it results in planned inventories closer to the monthly average than other techniques:

Beginning-of-month   Planned average monthly stock at retail
planned inventory level $= \times 1/2$ [1 $+$ (Estimated monthly sales/
(at retail)   Estimated average monthly sales)]

If Handy Hardware plans average monthly stock of $80,765 and November 2017 sales are expected to be 4 percent less than average monthly sales of $73,423, the store's planned inventory level at the beginning of November 2017 would be:

Beginning-of-November
planned inventory level $= \$80,765 \times 1/2$ [1 $+$ ($\$70,487/\$73,423$)] $= \$79,150$
(at retail)

Handy Hardware should not use this method due to its variable sales. If it did, Handy would plan a beginning-of-December 2017 inventory of $94,899, less than expected sales ($99,121).

The **weeks' supply method** forecasts average sales weekly, so beginning inventory equals several weeks' expected sales. It assumes inventory is in proportion to sales. Too much merchandise may be stocked in peak periods and too little during slow periods:

Beginning-of-Month   Average estimated   Number of weeks
planned inventory level $= \dfrac{\text{Average estimated}}{\text{weekly sales}} \times \dfrac{\text{Number of weeks}}{\text{to be stocked}}$
(at retail)

If Handy Hardware forecasts average weekly sales of $10,956.92 from January 1, 2017, through March 31, 2017, and it wants to stock 13 weeks of merchandise (based on expected turnover), beginning inventory would be $142,440:

Beginning-of-January
planned inventory level $= \$10,956.92 \times 13 = \$142,440$
(at retail)

TECHNOLOGY IN RETAILING   ## Point-of-Sale (POS) Systems

A major development with point-of-sale (POS) systems is their evolution from being used as cash registers to being interconnected with other software systems and portable data storage devices. Many retailers use POS systems to manage inventory within a single channel or across multiple channels. In addition, some POS systems capture relevant data for employee management (based on customer activity by time of day and day of week) and secure customer data used in market research. TouchBistro (www.touchbistro.com) has features needed by specific types of retailers, such as food establishments. TouchBistro lets the wait staff E-mail the chef with an order via an iPad, denotes shared meals, applies discounts, and enables credit-card processing on an iPad. The Shopkeep POS system (www.shopkeep.com) accepts all types of payments (including Apple Pay), automatically tracks inventory, keeps a record of the hours worked by each employee, and identifies top-performing employees. This information can be tracked on all devices at all times.

Discuss a restaurant's unique POS system requirements.

With the **stock-to-sales method**, a retailer wants to maintain a specified ratio of goods on hand to sales. A ratio of 1.3 means that if Handy Hardware plans sales of $69,018 in April 2017, it should have $89,723 worth of merchandise (at retail) available during the month. Like the weeks' supply method, this approach tends to adjust inventory more drastically than changes in sales require.

Yearly stock-to-sales ratios by retail type are provided by sources such as *Industry Norms & Key Business Ratios* (New York: Dun & Bradstreet) and *Annual Statement Studies* (Philadelphia: RMA). These sources will allow a retailer to compare its ratios with those of other firms.

Reduction Planning

Besides forecasting sales, a firm should estimate its expected **retail reductions**, which represent the difference between beginning inventory plus purchases during the period and sales plus ending inventory. Planned reductions incorporate anticipated markdowns (discounts to stimulate sales), employee and other discounts (price cuts to employees, senior citizens, and others), and stock shortages (pilferage, breakage, and bookkeeping errors):

$$\text{Planned reductions} = \begin{aligned}&\text{(Beginning inventory} + \text{Planned purchases)}\\ &- \text{(Planned sales} + \text{Ending inventory)}\end{aligned}$$

Reduction planning revolves around two key factors: estimating expected total reductions by budget period and assigning estimates monthly. The following should be considered in planning reductions: past experience, markdown data for similar retailers, changes in company policies, merchandise carryover from one budget period to another, price trends, and stock-shortage trends.

Past experience is a good starting point. The data can then be compared with the performance of similar firms—by reviewing data on markdowns, discounts, and stock shortages in trade publications. A retailer with higher markdowns than those of its competitors could investigate and correct the situation by adjusting its buying practices and price levels or improve the training of sales personnel.

A retailer must consider its own procedures in reviewing reductions. Policy changes often affect the quantity and timing of markdowns. If a firm expands its assortment of seasonal and fashion merchandise, this would probably lead to a rise in markdowns.

Merchandise carryover, price trends, and stock-shortage trends also affect planning. If such items as gloves and antifreeze are stocked in off seasons, markdowns are often not used to clear out inventory. Yet, the carryover of fad items merely postpones reductions. Price trends of product categories have a strong impact on reductions. Many full computer systems now sell for less than $1,000, down considerably from prior years. This means higher-priced computers must be marked down. Recent stock shortage trends (comparing prior book and physical inventory values) can be used to project future reductions due to employee, customer, and vendor theft; breakage; and bookkeeping mistakes. If a firm has stock shortages of less than 2 percent of annual sales, it is usually deemed to be doing well. Figure 16-3 shows a checklist to reduce shortages from clerical and handling errors. Suggestions for reducing shortages from theft were covered in Chapter 15.

After determining total reductions, they must be planned by month because reductions as a percentage of sales are not the same during each month. Stock shortages may be much higher during busy periods, when stores are more crowded and transactions happen more quickly.

Planning Purchases

The formula for calculating planned purchases for a period is:

$$\begin{aligned}\text{Planned purchases} \\ \text{(at retail)}\end{aligned} = \begin{aligned}&\text{Planned sales for the month} + \text{Planned reductions for the month}\\ &+ \text{Planned end-of-month stock} - \text{Beginning-of-month stock}\end{aligned}$$

If Handy Hardware projects June 2017 sales to be $108,666 and total planned reductions to be 5 percent of sales, plans end-of-month inventory at retail to be $72,000, and has a beginning-of-month inventory at retail of $80,000, planned purchases for June are:

$$\begin{aligned}\text{Planned purchases}\\ \text{(at retail)}\end{aligned} = \$108,666 + \$5,433 + \$72,000 - \$80,000 = \$106,099$$

FIGURE 16-3

A Checklist to Reduce Inventory Shortages Due to Clerical and Handling Errors

Answer yes or no to each of the following questions. A no means corrective action must be taken.

Buying

1. Is the exact quantity of merchandise purchased always specified in the contract?
2. Are special purchase terms clearly noted?
3. Are returns to the vendor recorded properly?

Marking

4. Are retail prices clearly and correctly marked on merchandise?
5. Are markdowns and additional markups recorded by item number and quantity?
6. Does a cashier check with a manager if a price is not marked on an item?
7. Are old price tags removed when an item's price changes?

Handling

8. After receipt, are purchase quantities checked against the order?
9. Is merchandise handled in a systematic manner?
10. Are items sold in bulk (such as produce, sugar, candy) measured accurately?
11. Are damaged, soiled, returned, or other special goods handled separately?

Selling

12. Do sales personnel know correct prices or have easy access to them?
13. Are mis-rings by cashiers made on a very small percentage of sales?
14. Are special terms noted on sales receipts (such as employee discounts)?
15. Are sales receipts numbered and later checked for missing invoices?

Inventory Planning

16. Is a physical inventory conducted at least annually and is a book inventory kept throughout the year?
17. Are the differences between physical inventory and book inventory always explained?

Accounting

18. Are permanent records on all transactions kept and monitored for accuracy?
19. Are both retail and cost data maintained?
20. Are inventory shortages compared with industry averages?

Because Handy Hardware expects 2017 merchandise costs to be about 60 percent of retail selling price, its plan is to purchase $63,659 of goods at cost in June 2017:

$$\begin{array}{c}\text{Planned purchases} \\ \text{(at cost)}\end{array} = \begin{array}{l}\text{Planned purchases at retail} \\ \times \text{ Merchandise costs as a percentage of selling price}\end{array}$$

$$= \$106{,}99 \times 0.60 = \$63{,}659$$

Open-to-buy is the difference between planned purchases and the purchase commitments already made by a buyer for a given period, often a month. It represents the amount the buyer has left to spend for that month and is reduced each time a purchase is made. At the beginning of a month, a firm's planned purchases and open-to-buy are equal if no purchase commitments have been made before that month starts. Open-to-buy is recorded at cost.

MY OTB Software (http://myotbplan.com) is easy-to-use, reasonably priced software.

At Handy Hardware, the buyer has made purchase commitments for June 2017 in the amount of $55,000 at retail. Accordingly, Handy's open-to-buy at retail for June is $51,099:

$$\begin{array}{c}\text{Open-to-buy} \\ \text{(at retail)}\end{array} = \begin{array}{l}\text{Planned purchases for the month} \\ - \text{ Purchase commitments for that month}\end{array}$$

$$= \$106{,}099 - \$55{,}000 = \$51{,}099$$

To calculate the June 2017 open-to-buy at cost, $51,099 is multiplied by Handy Hardware's merchandise costs as a percentage of selling price:

$$\frac{\text{Open-to-buy}}{\text{(at cost)}} = \frac{\text{Open-to-buy at retail}}{\times \text{ Merchandise costs as a percentage of selling price}}$$

$$= \$51,099 \times 0.60 = \$30,659$$

The open-to-buy concept has two major strengths: (1) It maintains a specified relationship between inventory and planned sales, which avoids overbuying and underbuying and (2) it lets a firm adjust purchases to reflect changes in sales, markdowns, and so on. If Handy revises its June 2017 sales forecast to $120,000 (from $108,666), it automatically increases planned purchases and open-to-buy by $11,334 at retail and $6,800 at cost.

It is advisable for a retailer to keep at least a small open-to-buy figure for as long as possible—to take advantage of special deals, purchase new models when introduced, and fill in items that sell out. An open-to-buy limit sometimes must be exceeded due to underestimated demand (low sales forecasts). A retailer should not be so rigid that merchandising personnel are unable to have the discretion (employee empowerment) to purchase below-average-priced items when the open-to-buy is not really open.

Planning Profit Margins

In preparing a profitable merchandise budget, a retailer must consider planned net sales, retail operating expenses, profit, and retail reductions in pricing merchandise:

$$\frac{\text{Required initial}}{\text{markup percentage}} = \frac{\text{Planned retail expenses} + \text{Planned profit} + \text{Planned reductions}}{\text{Planned net sales} + \text{Planned reductions}}$$

The required markup is a firmwide average. Individual items may be priced according to demand and other factors, as long as the average is met. The concept of initial markup is introduced here for continuity in the description of merchandise budgeting. A fuller discussion on markup can be found in Chapter 17.

Handy has an overall 2017 sales forecast of $881,080 and expects annual expenses to be $290,000. Reductions are projected at $44,000. The total net dollar profit margin goal is $60,000 (6.8 percent of sales). Its required initial markup is 42.6 percent:

$$\frac{\text{Required initial}}{\text{markup percentage}} = \frac{\$290,000 + \$60,000 + \$44,000}{\$881,080 + \$44,000} = 42.6\%$$

$$\frac{\text{Required initial markup percentage (all factors expressed as a percentage of net sales)}}{} = \frac{32.9\% + 6.8\% + 5.0\%}{100.0\% + 5.0\%} = 42.6\%$$

UNIT CONTROL SYSTEMS

Smart Sheet (www.smartsheet.com/free-excel-inventory-templates) offers unit control capabilities in its free spreadsheet-based software.

Unit control systems deal with quantities of merchandise in units rather than in dollars. Information typically reveals:

▸ Items selling well and those selling poorly
▸ Opportunities and problems in terms of price, color, style, size, and so on
▸ The quantity of goods on hand (if book inventory is used); minimizes overstocking and understocking
▸ An indication of inventory age, highlighting candidates for markdowns or promotions
▸ The optimal time to reorder merchandise
▸ Experiences with alternative sources (vendors) when problems arise
▸ The level of inventory and sales for each item in every store branch (This improves the transfer of goods between branches and alerts salespeople as to which branches have desired products. Also, less stock can be held in individual stores, reducing costs.)

Physical Inventory Systems

A *physical inventory unit control system* is similar to a physical inventory dollar control system. However, the latter is concerned with the financial value of inventory, whereas a unit control system looks at the number of units by item classification. With unit control, inventory levels are monitored either by visual inspection or actual count. See Figure 16-4.

In a visual inspection system, merchandise is placed on pegboard (or similar) displays, with each item numbered on the back or on a stock card. Minimum inventory quantities are noted, and sales personnel reorder when inventory reaches the minimum level. This is accurate only if items are placed in numerical order on displays (and sold accordingly). The system is used in the house-wares and hardware displays of various discount and hardware stores. Although easy to maintain and inexpensive, it does not provide data on the rate of sales of individual items. And minimum stock quantities may be arbitrarily defined and not drawn from in-depth analysis.

The other physical inventory system, actual counting, means regularly compiling the number of units on hand. This approach records—in units—inventory on hand, purchases, sales volume, and shortages for specified periods. A stock-counting system requires more clerical work but lets a firm obtain sales data for given periods and stock-to-sales relationships as of the time of each count. A physical system is not as sophisticated as a book system. It is more useful with low-value items having predictable sales. Handy Hardware could use the system for its insulation tape:

	Number of Rolls of Tape for the Period 12/1/16–12/31/16
Beginning inventory, December 1, 2016	100
Total purchases for period	70
Total units available for sale	170
Closing inventory, December 31, 2016	60
Sales and shortages for period	110

Perpetual Inventory Systems

A *perpetual inventory unit control system* keeps a running total of the number of units handled by a retailer through record keeping entries that adjust for sales, returns, transfers to other departments or stores, receipt of shipments, and other transactions. All additions to and subtractions from beginning inventory are recorded. Such a system can be applied manually, use merchandise tags processed by computers, or rely on point-of-sale devices such as optical scanners.

FIGURE 16-4

The Time-Consuming Nature of Physical Inventory Systems

Conducting a physical inventory can be extremely time consuming. Think about how much effort an apparel and accessories retailer with a large merchandise mix, such as the one depicted here, would have to exert.

Source: kedrov/Shutterstock. Reprinted by permission.

Point-of-sale systems—which are widely used today, even by many small retailers—feed data from merchandise tags or product labels directly to in-store computers for immediate data processing. Computer-based systems are quicker, more accurate, and of higher quality than manual ones. A manual system requires employees to gather data by examining sales checks, merchandise receipts, transfer requests, and other documents. Data are then coded and tabulated. A merchandise tagging system relies on pre-printed tags with data by department, classification, vendor, style, date of receipt, color, and/or material. When an item is sold, a copy of the tag is removed and sent to a tabulating facility for computer analysis. Since pre-printed tags are processed in batches, they can be used by smaller retailers that subscribe to service bureaus and by branches of chains (with data processed at a central location).

Want to look up a UPC code? Go here (www.upcdatabase.com/itemform.asp).

Current POS systems are easy to network; they have battery backup capabilities and run with standard PCs and software. Many of these systems use optical scanners to transfer data from products to computers by wands or other devices that pass over sensitized strips on the items. Figure 16-5 shows how barcoding works. As noted earlier, the UPC is the dominant format for coding data onto merchandise. This is how to interpret a barcode:

1. The *numbering system* contains two (or possibly three) digits to identify the nation (or region) that assigns the manufacturer codes in that geographic area. In the typical UPC code, the initial number digit is 0—which is not shown on a label.
2. The *manufacturer code* is a series of distinctive numbers assigned to specific manufacturers by the coding authority of the nation or region. All of a given company's products get the same manufacturer code—which is usually five numbers.
3. The *product code* is determined by each manufacturer—which can assign any five-digit product codes that it wants to designate different products by that company.
4. The *check digit* is an additional number that helps verify that a specific barcode is scanned accurately. It is based on the other digits of a barcode.[6]

Many retailers combine perpetual and physical systems, whereby items accounting for a high proportion of sales are controlled by a perpetual system and other items are controlled by a physical inventory system. Attention is properly placed on the retailer's most important products.

Unit Control Systems in Practice

Conducting a physical inventory is extremely time consuming and labor-intensive. It is also crucial: *Having too much stock, or too little, is costly.* The consulting firm, First Insight, has found that each year U.S. retailers lose about $280 billion due to holding excessive inventory.[7] And the costs of not having sufficient inventory on hand are estimated to be more than $50 billion annually.

Retailers need to determine the "real" cost of excess, unsold inventory—which means considering not just the invoice and freight costs but also the cost of capital (the funds invested in unsold inventory), inventory-carrying costs (insurance and the cost of occupied space in warehouses or selling areas), handling costs, theft rates, product obsolescence if items are not sold quickly, and the opportunity cost of lost sales. Together, these inventory-related costs can mount up and

FIGURE 16-5

How Does a UPC-Based Scanner System Work?

As described by eHow (www.ehow.com), a store scanner reads, decodes, and charges customers in seconds. The scanner has a laser beam light that converts the UPC's binary code into its proper price. The UPC code is identified from a retailer's database.

Source: florin oprea/Shutterstock. Reprinted by permission.

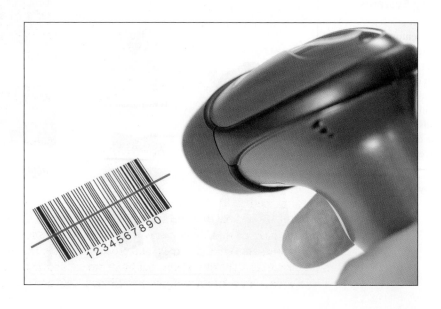

Gray Market Sourcing

Unlike counterfeit products, gray market goods are authentic and sourced through nontraditional channels that are not authorized by manufacturers. In gray marketing, retailers analyze price differences for goods sold worldwide, and buy the goods where the price differential between normal wholesale price levels and foreign market prices is big enough to compensate them for shipping, inventory holding costs, and product servicing expenses

(most manufacturers will not provide warranty-related repairs on gray market products). Gray market goods also do not qualify for cooperative advertising allowances, rebates, or coupon offers. Aside from watches, there is a large gray market presence in cosmetics, college textbooks, perfumes, and camera equipment.

As a retailer of fine watches selling from $2,000 to $20,000, explain the financial implications of reselling gray market products.

have a big impact on profits. Having too much inventory can be as big a problem (or worse) than running out of merchandise, due to both the costs and the markdowns that might be necessary to move inventory. In some product categories, the marked-down inventory can cannibalize sales of full-price products.[8] When all additional costs are taken into account, the total cost can be 25 to 30 percent more than the unit-cost value of the excess inventory.[9]

FINANCIAL INVENTORY CONTROL: INTEGRATING DOLLAR AND UNIT CONCEPTS

Until now, we have discussed dollar and unit control separately. In practice, they are linked. A decision on how many units to buy is affected by dollar investments, inventory turnover, quantity discounts, warehousing and insurance costs, and so on. Three aspects of financial inventory control are covered next: stock turnover and gross margin return on investment, when to reorder, and how much to reorder.

Oracle (www.oracle.com/ industries/retail/index .html) markets sophisticated inventory analysis software.

Stock Turnover and Gross Margin Return on Investment

Stock turnover represents the number of times during a specific period, usually 1 year, that the average inventory on hand is sold. It can be measured by store, product line, department, and vendor. With high turnover, inventory investments are productive on a per-dollar basis; items are fresh; there are fewer losses due to changes in styles; and interest, insurance, breakage, and warehousing costs are reduced. A retailer can raise stock turnover by reducing its assortment, eliminating or having little inventory for slow-selling items, buying in a timely way, applying quick response (QR) inventory planning, and using reliable suppliers.

Stock turnover can be computed in units or dollars (at retail or cost). The choice of a formula depends on the retailer's accounting system:

$$\text{Annual rate of stock turnover (in units)} = \frac{\text{Number of units sold during year}}{\text{Average inventory on hand (in units)}}$$

$$\text{Annual rate of stock turnover (in retail dollars)} = \frac{\text{Net yearly sales}}{\text{Average inventory on hand (at retail)}}$$

$$\text{Annual rate of stock turnover (at cost)} = \frac{\text{Cost of goods sold during the year}}{\text{Average inventory on hand (at cost)}}$$

In computing turnover, average inventory for the entire period needs to be reflected. Turnover rates are invalid if the true average is not used, as occurs if a firm mistakenly views the inventory level of a peak or slow month as average. Table 16-10 shows turnover rates for various retailers. Gas stations, convenience stores, and grocers have the highest rates. They rely on sales volume for their success. Jewelry stores, hardware stores, and some clothing stores have very low rates. They require larger profit margins on each item sold and maintain a sizable assortment.

TABLE 16-10 Annual Median Stock Turnover Rates for Selected Types of Retailers, 2016

Type of Retailer	Annual Median Stock Turnover Rate (Times)
Car dealers (new)	5.1
Convenience stores	29.1
Department stores	4.3
Family clothing stores	2.6
Florists	9.5
Furniture stores	3.5
Gasoline stations with convenience stores	51.6
Gift, novelty and souvenir stores	3.7
Hardware stores	2.7
Home centers	5.5
Household appliance stores	4.7
Jewelry stores	1.3
Lumber and other materials dealers	6.7
Men's clothing stores	2.8
Online retailers	5.4
Pharmacy and drug stores	13.7
Supermarkets and grocery stores	15.0
Women's apparel stores	3.4

Source: Extracted and compiled by the authors. Copyright 2016, The Risk Management Association (www.rmahq.org). All rights reserved. Used by permission.

Despite the advantages of high turnover, buying items in small amounts may also result in the loss of quantity discounts and in higher transportation charges. Because high turnover might be due to a limited assortment, some sales may be lost, and profits may be lower if prices are reduced to move inventory quickly. The return on investment depends on both turnover and profit per unit.

Learn more about GMROI (www.jewelerprofit.com/ GMROI_Worksheet.html).

Gross margin return on investment (GMROI) shows the relationship between the gross margin in dollars (total dollar operating profits) and the average inventory investment (at cost) by combining profitability and sales-to-stock measures:

$$\text{GMROI} = \frac{\text{Gross margin in dollars}}{\text{Net sales}} \times \frac{\text{Net sales}}{\text{Average inventory at Cost}}$$

$$= \frac{\text{Gross margin in dollars}}{\text{Average inventory at cost}}$$

The gross margin in dollars equals net sales minus the cost of goods sold. The gross margin percentage is derived by dividing dollar gross margin by net sales. A sales-to-stock ratio is derived by dividing net sales by average inventory at cost. That ratio may be converted to stock turnover by multiplying it by $[(100 - \text{Gross margin percentage})/100]$.

Gross margin return on investment is a useful concept for several reasons:

▷ It shows how diverse retailers can prosper. A supermarket may have a gross margin of 20 percent and a sales-to-stock ratio of 15—a GMROI of 300 percent. A women's clothing store may have a gross margin of 50 percent and a sales-to-stock ratio of 6—a GMROI of 300 percent. Both firms have the same GMROI due to the trade-off between item profitability and turnover.

▷ It is a good indicator of a manager's performance because it focuses on factors controlled by that person. Interdepartmental comparisons can also be made.

▷ It is simple to plan and understand, and data collection is easy.

▷ It can be determined if GMROI performance is consistent with other company goals.

The gross margin percentage and the sales-to-stock ratio must be studied individually. If only overall GMROI is reviewed, performance may be assessed improperly.

When to Reorder

One way to control inventory investment is to systematically set stock levels at which new orders must be placed. Such a stock level is called a **reorder point**, and it is based on three factors.

1. **Order lead time** is the period from the date an order is placed by a retailer to the date merchandise is ready for sale (received, price-marked, and put on the selling floor).
2. **Usage rate** refers to average sales per day, in units, of merchandise.
3. **Safety stock** is the extra inventory that protects against out-of-stock conditions due to unexpected demand and delays in delivery. It depends on the firm's policy toward running out of items.

The formula for a retailer that does not plan to carry safety stock is shown here. It believes customer demand is stable and that its orders are promptly filled by suppliers:

$$\text{Reorder point} = \text{Usage rate} \times \text{Lead time}$$

If Handy Hardware sells 10 paintbrushes a day and needs 8 days to order, receive, and display them, it has a reorder point of 80 brushes. It would reorder brushes when the inventory on hand reaches 80. By the time brushes from that order are placed on shelves (8 days later), stock on hand will be zero, and the new stock will replenish the inventory.

This strategy is proper when Handy has a steady customer demand of 10 paintbrushes daily and it takes exactly 8 days to complete all stages in the ordering process. This does not normally occur. If customers buy 15 brushes per day in a month, Handy would run out of stock in 5-1/3 days and be without brushes for 2-2/3 days. If an order takes 10 days to process, Handy would have no brushes for 2 days, despite correctly estimating demand. Figure 16-6 shows how stockouts may occur.

For a retailer interested in keeping a safety stock, the reorder formula becomes:

$$\text{Reorder point} = (\text{Usage rate} \times \text{Lead time}) + \text{Safety stock}$$

Suppose Handy Hardware decides on safety stock of 30 percent for paintbrushes; its reorder point is $(10 \times 8) + (0.30 \times 80) = 80 + 24 = 104$. Handy still expects to sell an average of

FIGURE 16-6

How Stockouts May Occur

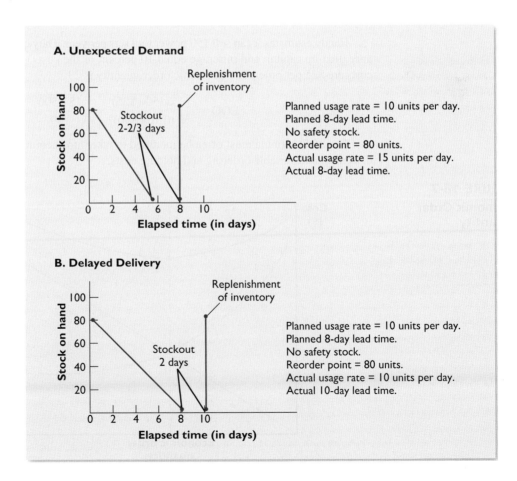

10 brushes per day and receive orders in an average of 8 days. The safety stock of 24 extra brushes is kept on hand to protect against unexpected demand or a late shipment.

By combining a perpetual inventory system and reorder point calculations, ordering can be computerized and an **automatic reordering system** can be mechanically activated when stock-on-hand reaches the reorder point. However, intervention by a buyer or manager must be possible, especially if monthly sales fluctuate greatly.

How Much to Reorder

A firm placing large orders generally reduces ordering costs but increases inventory-holding costs. A firm placing small orders often minimizes inventory-holding costs while ordering costs may rise (unless EDI and a QR inventory system are used).

Economic order quantity (EOQ) is the quantity per order (in units) that minimizes the total costs of processing orders and holding inventory. Order-processing costs include computer time, order forms, labor, and handling new goods. Holding costs include warehousing, inventory investment, insurance, taxes, depreciation, deterioration, and pilferage. Economic order quantity calculations can be done by large and small firms.

As Figure 16-7 shows, order-processing costs drop as order quantity (in units) goes up because fewer orders are needed for the same annual quantity. Inventory-holding costs rise as the order quantity goes up because more units must be held in inventory and they are kept for longer periods. The two costs are summed into a total cost curve. Mathematically, the economic order quantity is:

$$EOQ = \sqrt{\frac{2DS}{IC}}$$

where

EOQ = quantity per order (in units)

D = annual demand (in units)

S = costs to place an order (in dollars)

I = percentage of annual carrying cost to unit cost

C = unit cost of an item (in dollars)

Handy estimates it can sell 150 power tool sets per year. They cost $90 each. Breakage, insurance, tied-up capital, and pilferage equal 10 percent of the costs of the sets (or $9 each). Order costs are $25 per order. The economic order quantity is 29:

$$EOQ = \sqrt{\frac{2(150)(\$25)}{(0.10)(\$90)}} = \sqrt{\frac{\$7,500}{\$9}} = 29$$

The EOQ formula must often be modified to take into account changes in demand, quantity discounts, and variable ordering and holding costs.

FIGURE 16-7

Economic Order Quantity

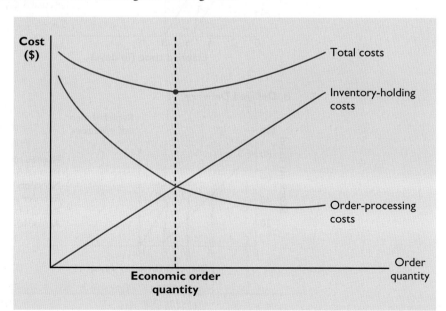

Chapter Summary

1. *To describe the major aspects of financial merchandise planning and management.* The purpose of financial merchandise management is to stipulate which products are bought by the retailer, when, and in what quantity. Dollar control monitors inventory investment, whereas unit control relates to the amount of merchandise handled. Financial merchandise management encompasses accounting methods, merchandise forecasts and budgets, unit control, and integrated dollar and unit controls.

2. *To explain the cost and retail methods of accounting.* The two accounting techniques for retailers are the cost and retail methods of inventory valuation. Physical and book (perpetual) procedures are possible with each. Physical inventory valuation requires counting merchandise at prescribed times. Book inventory valuation relies on accurate bookkeeping and a smooth data flow.

   The cost method obligates a retailer to have careful records or to code costs on packages. This must be done to find the exact value of ending inventory at cost. Many firms use LIFO accounting to project that value, which lets them reduce taxes by having a low ending inventory value. In the retail method, closing inventory value is tied to the average relationship between the cost and retail value of merchandise. That more accurately reflects market conditions but can be complex.

3. *To study the merchandise forecasting and budgeting process.* This is a form of dollar control with six stages: designating control units, sales forecasting, inventory-level planning, reduction planning, planning purchases, and planning profit margins. Adjustments require all later stages to be modified.

   Control units—merchandise categories for which data are gathered—must be narrow to isolate problems and opportunities with specific product lines. Sales forecasting may be the key stage in the merchandising and budgeting process. Through inventory-level planning, a firm sets merchandise quantities for specified periods through the basic stock, percentage variation, weeks' supply, and/or stock-to-sales methods. Reduction planning estimates expected markdowns, discounts, and stock shortages. Planned purchases are linked to planned sales, reductions, and ending and beginning inventory. Profit margins depend on planned net sales, operating expenses, profit, and reductions.

4. *To examine alternative methods of inventory unit control.* A unit control system involves physical units of merchandise. It monitors best-sellers and poor-sellers, the quantity of goods on hand, inventory age, reorder time, and so on. A physical inventory unit control system may use visual inspection or stock counting. A perpetual inventory unit control system keeps a running total of the units handled through record keeping entries that adjust for sales, returns, transfers, and so on. A perpetual system can be applied manually, by merchandise tags processed by computers, or by point-of-sale devices. Virtually all larger retailers conduct regular complete physical inventories; two-thirds use a perpetual inventory system.

5. *To integrate dollar and unit merchandising control concepts.* Three aspects of financial inventory management integrate dollar and unit control concepts: stock turnover and gross margin return on investment, when to reorder, and how much to reorder. Stock turnover is the number of times during a period that average inventory on hand is sold. Gross margin return on investment shows the relationship between gross margin in dollars (total dollar operating profits) and average inventory investment (at cost). A reorder point calculation—when to reorder—includes the retailer's usage rate, order lead time, and safety stock. The economic order quantity—how much to reorder—shows how big an order to place, based on both ordering and inventory costs.

Key Terms

financial merchandise management (p. 405)
dollar control (p. 405)
unit control (p. 405)
merchandise available for sale (p. 405)
cost of goods sold (p. 405)
gross profit (p. 405)
net profit (p. 405)
cost method of accounting (p. 406)
physical inventory system (p. 406)
book (perpetual) inventory system (p. 407)

FIFO (first-in-first-out) method (p. 407)
LIFO (last-in-first-out) method (p. 407)
retail method of accounting (p. 408)
cost complement (p. 409)
control units (p. 411)
classification merchandising (p. 412)
monthly sales index (p. 413)
basic stock method (p. 413)
percentage variation method (p. 415)
weeks' supply method (p. 415)
stock-to-sales method (p. 416)

retail reductions (p. 416)
open-to-buy (p. 417)
stock turnover (p. 421)
gross margin return on investment (GMROI) (p. 422)
reorder point (p. 423)
order lead time (p. 423)
usage rate (p. 423)
safety stock (p. 423)
automatic reordering system (p. 424)
economic order quantity (EOQ) (p. 424)

Questions for Discussion

1. What are the two key disadvantages for a retailer opting to use a manual physical inventory system? Explain your answer.
2. Cost-based physical and book systems have significant disadvantages. What are these disadvantages, and what steps might a retailer take to overcome them? Which types of retailer are more likely to use them?
3. Compared with other techniques, there are several advantages to the retail method of accounting. What are they?
4. Why might a store selling power tools decide to use a special form of classification merchandising with price line classifications?
5. How might an ice cream parlor use monthly sales index figures to predict demand for their products?
6. How do you calculate the stock-to-sales ratio, and what does it mean?
7. Present two situations in which it would be advisable for a retailer to take a markdown instead of carry over merchandise from one budget period to another.
8. A retailer has yearly sales of $900,000. Inventory on January 1 is $360,000 (at cost). During the year, $660,000 of merchandise (at cost) is purchased. The ending inventory is $325,000 (at cost). Operating costs are $90,000. Calculate the cost of goods sold and net profit, and set up a profit-and-loss statement. There are no retail reductions in this problem.
9. A retailer has beginning monthly inventory valued at $100,000 at retail and $61,000 at cost. Net purchases for the month are $190,000 at retail and $115,000 at cost. Transportation charges are $10,500. Sales are $225,000. Markdowns and discounts equal $30,000. A physical inventory at the end of the month shows merchandise valued at $15,000 (retail) on hand. Compute the following:
   a. Total merchandise available for sale—at cost and at retail
   b. Cost complement
   c. Ending retail book value of inventory
   d. Stock shortages
   e. Adjusted ending retail book value
   f. Gross profit
10. The sales of a specialty store are listed. Calculate the monthly sales indexes. What do they mean?

January	$300,000	July	270,000
February	315,000	August	330,000
March	315,000	September	360,000
April	360,000	October	300,000
May	360,000	November	390,000
June	330,000	December	510,000

11. If the planned average monthly stock for the discount store in Question 10 is $420,000 (at retail), how much inventory should be planned for August if the retailer uses the percentage variation method? Comment on this retailer's choice of the percentage variation method.
12. The store in Questions 10 and 11 knows its cost complement for all merchandise purchased last year was 0.61; it projects this to remain constant. It expects to begin and end December with inventory valued at $140,000 at retail and estimates December reductions to be $18,000. The firm already has purchase commitments for December worth $50,000 (at retail). What is the open-to-buy at cost for December?

Web-Based Exercise

Visit the benchmarking section of the Retail Owners Institute Web site (http://retailowner.com/Benchmarks). Describe how a department store executive could use the information found at the site in its financial merchandise management efforts. Describe how a gift store could use the information found at the site.

17 Pricing in Retailing

Retail price setting can take one of several approaches. Some retailers offer deep discounts and no-frills shopping (think Costco), others offer everyday low pricing (think Walmart), others offer mid-level prices and promote special sales (think Macy's), and still others set prices that are rarely discounted (think Apple stores). A new entrant to the retail pricing mix is the "real-time deal," whereby online firms—usually driven by social media—offer deals for consumers willing to make a purchase during a defined, short time period.

The balance of power in terms of pricing information has shifted from the retailer to the consumer due to the Web. A consumer can use such sites as True Car (www.truecar.com) for new car pricing, Travelocity (www.travelocity.com) for airline and hotel pricing, Trivago (www.trivago.com) for hotel pricing, and mySimon.com (www.mysimon.com) for pricing data on a wide range of goods. Thus, consumers can enter a store knowing the range of prices offered by local retailers and Web-based firms. If they forget to come prepared with these data, they can usually use a retailer's Wi-Fi to easily obtain pricing information on their smartphones.

These retailing tactics need to be considered as a response to consumers' requests for matching lower prices: Make it easier for salespeople to verify lower price offers. Obtain special model numbers that are unique to a given store. Stress private-label products. Sell brands that are not typically discounted. Charge additional fees for services that may not offered by discounters such as delivery and installation.

Chapter Objectives

1. To describe the role of pricing in a retail strategy and to show that pricing decisions must be made in an integrated and adaptive manner

2. To examine the impact of consumers; government; manufacturers, wholesalers, and other suppliers; and current and potential competitors on pricing decisions

3. To present a framework for developing a retail price strategy: objectives, broad policy, basic strategy, implementation, and adjustments

Source: convisum/123RF.
Reprinted by permission.

Learn about the complexities of setting prices (www.ehow.com/how_4473994_set-retail-prices.html).

Overview

Goods and services must be priced in a way that achieves profitability for the retailer and satisfies customers. A pricing strategy must be consistent with the retailer's overall image (positioning), sales, profit, and return on investment goals.

There are three basic pricing options for a retailer:

1. A *discount orientation* uses low prices as the major competitive advantage. A low-price image, fewer shopping frills, and low per-unit profit margins mean a target market of price-oriented customers, low operating costs, and high inventory turnover. Off-price retailers and full-line discount stores are in this category.
2. With an *at-the-market orientation*, the retailer has average prices. It offers solid service and a nice atmosphere to middle-class shoppers. Margins are moderate to good, and average- to above-average quality products are stocked. This firm may find it hard to expand its price range, and it may be squeezed by retailers positioned as discounters or prestige stores. Traditional department stores and many drugstores are in this category.
3. Through an *upscale orientation*, a prestigious image is the retailer's major competitive advantage. A smaller target market, higher expenses, and lower turnover mean customer loyalty, distinctive services and products, and high per-unit profit margins. Upscale department stores and specialty stores are in this category.

Nordstrom is one of the world's largest online shoe retailers (http://shop.nordstrom.com/c/shoes), with its usual upscale prices and service.

A key to successful retailing is offering a good *value* in the consumer's mind—for the price orientation chosen. Every customer, whether buying an inexpensive $4 ream of paper or a $40 ream of embossed, personalized stationery, wants to feel his or her purchase represents a good value. The consumer is not necessarily looking only for the best price. He or she is often interested in the best value—which may be reflected in a superior shopping experience. See Figures 17-1 and 17-2.

Consider the universal appeal and consistency of H&M's strategy. This retailer offers customers affordable, sustainable, fashionable, and trendy apparel at more than 3,900 stores in 60 cities around the world. To fulfill customer needs, H&M follows a two-tier pricing strategy that includes offering everyday-low-price products and higher-priced collections in partnership with top designers such as Karl Lagerfeld and Balmain. H&M maintains low prices by offering basic customer service with minimal store staff.[1]

Another factor shaping today's pricing environment for retailers of all types is the ease by which a shopper can compare prices on the Web. When the only way a consumer could do price comparisons was by visiting individual stores, the process was time consuming, which limited many people's willingness to shop around. Now, with a few clicks of a computer mouse, a shopper can quickly gain online price information from several retailers in just minutes—without leaving home. Web sites such as PriceGrabber.com, NexTag, Shopping.com, and mySimon.com make

FIGURE 17-1

Good Prices AND Customer Service

Many shoppers are not only interested in good prices but also in customer service, especially for big-ticket items such as cars. The shopping experience is tied to the concept of "value."

Source: goodluz/123RF.com. Reprinted by permission.

FIGURE 17-2

Feeling Ripped Off

Consumers do not like feeling overcharged, whether it's for a gallon of gas or a new house or a lawn care service. They want to believe that they are treated fairly and not being gouged.

Source: Heather A. Craig/ Shutterstock. Reprinted by permission.

comparison shopping very simple. Price-comparison mobile apps such as RedLaser, ShopSavvy, BuyVia, and Purchx save shoppers money and they predict prices, the likelihood of price cuts, and the timing of product releases. Most apps need consumers to snap a photo of a barcode or type a SKU to perform a price-comparison search across retailer stores and Web sites.[2]

The interaction of price with other retailing mix elements can be illustrated by BE's Toy City, a hypothetical discounter. It has a broad strategy consisting of:

▷ A target market of price-conscious families that shop for inexpensive toys ($9 to $12)
▷ A limited range of quality (mostly end-of-season closeouts and manufacturer overruns)
▷ Self-service in an outlet mall location
▷ A good assortment supported by quantity purchases at deep discounts from suppliers
▷ An image of efficiency and variety

In this chapter, we divide retail pricing into two major sections: the external factors affecting a price strategy and the steps in a price strategy. At our blog site (www.bermanevansretail.com), there are posts with information on setting a price strategy.

EXTERNAL FACTORS AFFECTING A RETAIL PRICE STRATEGY

Several factors have an impact on a retail pricing strategy, as shown in Figure 17-3. Sometimes, the factors have a minor effect. In other cases, they severely restrict a firm's pricing options.

The Consumer and Retail Pricing[3]

Retailers should understand the **price elasticity of demand**—the sensitivity of customers to price changes in terms of the quantities they will buy—because there is often a relationship between price and consumer purchases and perceptions. If small percentage changes in price lead to substantial percentage changes in the number of units bought, demand is *price elastic*. This occurs when the urgency to purchase is low or there are acceptable substitutes. If large percentage

FIGURE 17-3

Factors Affecting a Retail Price Strategy

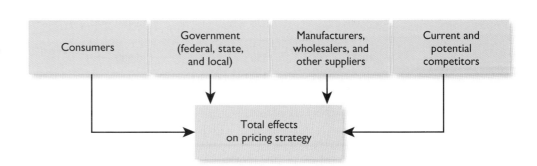

changes in price lead to small percentage changes in the number of units bought, demand is *price inelastic*. Then purchase urgency is high or there are no acceptable substitutes (as takes place with brand or retailer loyalty). *Unitary elasticity* occurs when percentage changes in price are directly offset by percentage changes in quantity.

Price elasticity is computed by dividing the percentage change in the quantity demanded by the percentage change in the price charged. Because purchases generally decline as prices go up, elasticity tends to be a negative number:

One look at Godiva's Web site (www.godiva.com) and you'll know why demand for its products is inelastic.

$$\text{Elasticity} = \frac{\dfrac{\text{Quantity 1} - \text{Quantity 2}}{\text{Quantity 1} + \text{Quantity 2}}}{\dfrac{\text{Price 1} - \text{Price 2}}{\text{Price 1} + \text{Price 2}}}$$

Table 17-1 shows price elasticity for a 1,000-seat movie theater (with elasticities converted to positive numbers) that offers second-run films. Quantity demanded (tickets sold) declines at each price from $6.00 to $10.00. Demand is inelastic from $6.00 to $7.00 and $7.00 to $8.00; ticket receipts rise since the percentage price change exceeds the percentage change in tickets sold. At $8.00 to $9.00, demand is unitary; ticket receipts are constant since the percentage change in tickets sold exactly offsets the percentage price change. Demand is elastic from $9.00 to $10.00; ticket receipts fall since the percentage change in tickets sold is more than the percentage change in price.

For our movie theater example, total ticket receipts are highest at $8.00 or at $9.00. But what about total revenues? If patrons spend an average of $4.00 each at the concession stand, the best price is $6.00 (total overall revenues of $10,000). This theater is most interested in total revenues because its operating costs are the same whether there are 1,000 or 550 patrons. But typically, retailers should evaluate the costs, as well as the revenues, from serving additional customers.

In retailing, computing price elasticity is difficult. First, as with the movie theater, demand for individual events or items may be hard to predict. One week, the theater may attract 1,000 patrons to a movie, and the next week it may attract 400 patrons to a different movie. Second, many retailers carry thousands of items and cannot possibly compute elasticities for every one. As a result, they usually rely on average markup pricing, competition, tradition, and industrywide data to indicate price elasticity.

Dell (http://www.dell.com/en-us) appeals to multiple consumer segments—from novice to advanced computer user, with prices set accordingly.

Price sensitivity varies by market segment, based on shopping orientation. After identifying potential segments, retailers determine which of them form their target market:

▶ *Economic consumers:* They perceive competing retailers as similar and shop around for the lowest possible prices. This segment has grown dramatically in recent years.

TABLE 17-1 A Movie Theater's Elasticity of Demand

Price	Tickets Sold (Saturday Night)	Total Ticket Receipts	Elasticity of Demand[a]
$6.00	1,000	$6,000	
			E = 0.68
7.00	900	6,300	
			E = 0.79
8.00	810	6,480	
			E = 1.00
9.00	720	6,480	
			E = 2.54
10.00	550	5,500	

$$\text{Computation example (\$6.00 to \$7.00 price range)} = \frac{\dfrac{1{,}000 - 900}{1{,}000 + 900}}{\dfrac{\$6.00 - \$7.00}{\$6.00 + \$7.00}} = 0.68$$

[a] Expressed as a positive number.

Game Stores, Africa's Largest Discounter

The first outlet of Game Stores (www.game.co.za) opened in South Africa during 1970 and offered a wide variety of national brands, from electronics to foods (nonperishables and dry groceries), at discount prices. In 1998, the 28-store chain was acquired by Massmart (www.massmart.co.za), a wholesale-and-retail conglomerate. In 2011, Walmart purchased a 51 percent stake in Massmart. Especially attractive to Walmart was the high growth in sub-Saharan African retail markets. By 2016, Game Stores operated 135 stores in South Africa and other major African markets—including Botswana, Ghana, Kenya, Mozambique, Namibia, Nigeria, Uganda, and Zambia.

Although Game Stores has been known for its aggressive pricing, it has received significant competition in groceries from South Africa's Shoprite and Pick 'n Pay. These competitors have prevented Game Stores from selling food items in shopping malls where they have stores. Lease clauses give these competitors the exclusive right to sell food in these malls.

Do a Google search and determine the potential of Africa for Game Stores.

Sources: Authors' research and material in Andile Ntingi, "Analyst Warns of Walmart Pull Out in Massmart," *Forbes,* May 4, 2016.

▷ *Status-oriented consumers:* They perceive competing retailers as quite different. They are more interested in upscale retailers with prestige brands and strong customer service than in price.

▷ *Assortment-oriented consumers:* They seek retailers with a strong selection in the product categories being considered. They want fair prices.

▷ *Personalizing consumers:* They shop where they are known and feel a bond with employees and the firm itself. These shoppers will pay slightly above-average prices.

▷ *Convenience-oriented consumers:* They shop because they must, want nearby stores with long hours, and may use TV shopping or the Web. These people will pay more for convenience.

The Government and Retail Pricing

Three levels of government may affect domestic retail pricing decisions: federal, state, and local. When laws are federal, they apply to interstate commerce. A retailer operating only within the boundaries of one state may not be restricted by some federal legislation. Major government rules relate to horizontal price fixing, vertical price fixing, price discrimination, minimum price levels, unit pricing, item price removal, and price advertising. For retailers operating outside their home countries, a fourth level of government comes into play: international jurisdictions.

HORIZONTAL PRICE FIXING   An agreement among manufacturers, among wholesalers, or among retailers to set prices is known as **horizontal price fixing**. Such agreements are illegal under the Sherman Antitrust Act and the Federal Trade Commission Act, regardless of how "reasonable" prices may be. It is also illegal for retailers to get together regarding the use of coupons, rebates, or other price-oriented tactics.

Although few large-scale legal actions have been taken in recent years, the penalties for horizontal price fixing can be severe. A recent horizontal price-fixing case involved Apple and five book publishing companies and alleged that together the companies conspired to raise the price of E-books to consumers. The judge ruled that the price-fixing conspiracy was a *per se* violation of Section 1 of the Sherman Act. The publishers promptly settled the case but Apple decided to appeal the decision to the Supreme Court. In March 2016, the Supreme Court held that it would not consider Apple's appeal. The $450 million case action settlement against Apple is in effect.[4]

VERTICAL PRICE FIXING   When manufacturers or wholesalers seek to control the retail prices of their goods and services, **vertical price fixing** occurs. Until 2007, retailers in the United States could not be forced to adhere to *minimum retail prices* set by manufacturers and wholesalers. Federal laws banning this practice were intended to encourage price competition among retailers and lower prices for consumers. However, as a result of a 2007 Supreme Court ruling, the situation changed significantly. The Supreme Court decision stated that minimum resale price restrictions should be judged on a case-by-case basis. Among the factors to be considered are the effect on competition, consumer benefits, and other issues.

Minimum resale price agreements are most likely to be found to be anticompetitive if these agreements facilitate price fixing at one level of the channel such as at the retailer level. Proof of a retail-level agreement often includes evidence that two or more retailers have communicated among themselves, and then asked a common supplier to set minimum resale prices or to punish competing retailers that cut prices. In addition, minimum resale price maintenance is not permitted when a dominant retailer uses it to hurt competitors.

Today, even though manufacturers and wholesalers may be able to enforce minimum prices at the retail level if they choose, most suppliers opt not to do so since they do not want to eliminate business with discounters such as Walmart, Target, and Costco.

Manufacturers and wholesalers can also legally control retail prices by one of these methods: (1) They can screen retailers. (2) They can set realistic list prices. (3) They can pre-print prices on products (which retailers do not have to use). (4) They can set regular prices that are accepted by consumers (such as 75 cents for a newspaper). (5) They can use consignment selling, whereby the supplier owns items until they are sold and assumes costs normally associated with the retailer. (6) They can own retail facilities. (7) They can refuse to sell to retailers that advertise discount prices in violation of written policies. (8) A supplier has a right to announce a policy for dealer pricing and can refuse to sell to those that do not comply. (9) It cannot use coercion to prohibit a retailer from advertising low prices.

PRICE DISCRIMINATION   The **Robinson-Patman Act** bars manufacturers and wholesalers from discriminating in price or purchase terms (such as advertising allowances) in selling to individual retailers if these retailers are purchasing products of "like quality" and the effect of such discrimination is to injure competition. The intent of this act is to stop large retailers from using their power to gain discounts not justified by the cost savings achieved by suppliers due to big orders. There are exceptions that allow justifiable price discrimination when:

► Products are physically different.
► The retailers paying different prices are not competitors.
► Competition is not injured.
► Price differences are due to differences in supplier costs.
► Market conditions change—costs rise or fall or competing suppliers shift their prices.

Discounts are not illegal, so long as suppliers follow the preceding rules, make discounts available to competing retailers on an equitable basis, and offer discounts sufficiently graduated so small retailers can also qualify. Discounts for cumulative purchases (total yearly orders) and for multistore purchases by chains may be hard to justify.

Although the Robinson-Patman Act restricts sellers more than buyers, retailers are covered under Section 2(F): "It shall be unlawful for any person engaged in commerce, in the course of such commerce, knowingly to induce or receive a discrimination in price which is prohibited in this section." Thus, a retail buyer must try to get the lowest prices charged to any competitor, yet not bargain so hard that discounts cannot be justified by acceptable exceptions. The act applies to purchases but not to services or leases.[5]

MINIMUM-PRICE LAWS   Nearly one-half of the states have **minimum-price laws** that prevent retailers from selling certain items for less than their cost plus a fixed percentage to cover overhead. Besides general laws, some state rules set minimum prices for specific products. For instance, in New Jersey and Connecticut, the retail price of liquor cannot be less than the wholesale cost (including taxes and delivery charges).

Minimum-price laws protect small retailers from **predatory pricing**, in which large retailers seek to reduce competition by selling goods and services at very low prices, thus causing small retailers to go out of business. In one case, three Arkansas pharmacies filed a suit claiming Walmart had sold selected items below cost in order to reduce competition. Walmart agreed it had priced some items below cost to meet or beat rivals' prices but not to harm competitors. The Arkansas Supreme Court ruled Walmart did not use predatory pricing since the three pharmacies were still profitable.

With **loss leaders**, retailers price selected items below cost to lure more customer traffic to their stores. Supermarkets and other retailers advertise loss leaders to induce customers to visit a store or Web site. When the customers are at the store, they will also buy additional items that have higher margins, thus increasing overall sales and profits. The loss leader products may result in no profit being made but will be made up through the sale of other goods/services that may or may not be related to the product. Implementing the loss leader strategy can be risky. Price-sensitive customers may not make additional purchases, hence some loss leaders may be conditional bargains requiring customers to meet a minimum purchase limit. Pervasive use of loss leaders by retailers can lead to downward pressure on prices, so using it to penetrate the market needs to be carefully considered.[6]

UNIT PRICING   In some states, the proliferation of package sizes has led to **unit-pricing** laws, whereby some retailers must express both the total price of an item and its price per unit of measure. Food stores are most affected by unit-price rules because grocery items are more regulated than nongrocery items.[7] There are exemptions for firms with low sales. The aim of unit pricing is to enable consumers to compare prices of products available in many sizes. Thus, a 5-ounce can of tuna fish priced at $1.35 would also have a shelf label showing this as 27 cents per ounce. And a person learns that a 20-ounce bottle of soda selling for $1.00 (5 cents per ounce) costs more than a 67.6-ounce (2-liter) bottle for $1.49 (2.2 cents per ounce).

Retailer costs include computing per-unit prices, printing product and shelf labels, and keeping computer records. These costs are influenced by the way prices are attached to goods (by the supplier or the retailer), the number of items subject to unit pricing, the frequency of price changes, sales volume, and the number of stores in a chain.

Unit pricing can be a good strategy for retailers to follow, even when not required. At many supermarkets, the unit-pricing system more than pays for itself because of decreased price-marking errors, better inventory control, and improved space management.

ITEM PRICE REMOVAL   The boom in computerized checkout systems has led many firms, especially supermarkets, to push for **item price removal**—whereby prices are marked only on shelves or signs and not on individual items. Instead of the costly price marking of individual items, retailers want to rely on scanning equipment that reads pre-marked product codes and enters price data at the checkout counter. Their efforts have been successful; in 2011, Michigan removed its law—leaving Massachusetts as the only place in the United States with a statewide ban on some forms of item price removal. Shelf pricing is now more widely accepted.

Why have retailers opposed item pricing laws? They insist that electronic or manual shelf labeling and checkout scanners make prices on individual items redundant. Instead of serving customers, salesperson hours are wasted ticketing items with a sticker gun and increased employee expenses. Consumerists support them because price tags help customers shop and help them verify the prices they are charged at checkout. They also help cashiers reduce checkout errors.[8]

PRICE ADVERTISING   The Federal Trade Commission (FTC) has guidelines pertaining to advertising price reductions, advertising prices in relation to competitors' prices, and bait-and-switch advertising.

A retailer cannot claim or imply that a price has been reduced from some former level (a suggested list price) unless the former price was one that the retailer had actually offered for a good or service on a regular basis during a reasonably substantial, recent period of time.

When a retailer says its prices are lower than its competitors' prices, it must make certain that its comparisons pertain to firms selling large quantities in the same trading area. A somewhat controversial, but legal, practice is price matching. For the most part, a retailer makes three assumptions when it "guarantees to match the lowest price" of any competing retailer: (1) This guarantee gives shoppers the impression that a firm always offers low prices or else it would not make such a commitment. (2) Most shoppers will not return to a store after a purchase even if they see a lower price advertised elsewhere. (3) The guarantee may exclude most deep discounters and online firms by stating that they are not really competitors.

Bait-and-switch advertising is an illegal practice in which a retailer lures a customer by advertising goods and services at exceptionally low prices. When the customer contacts the retailer (by entering a store, calling a toll-free number, or going to a Web site), he or she is told the good/service of interest is out of stock or of inferior quality. A salesperson (or Web script) tries to convince the person to buy a more costly substitute. The retailer does not intend to sell the advertised item. In deciding if a promotion uses bait-and-switch advertising, the FTC considers how many transactions are made at the advertised price, whether sales commissions are excluded on sale items, and total sales relative to advertising costs.

Manufacturers, Wholesalers, and Other Suppliers—and Retail Pricing

There may be conflicts between manufacturers (and other suppliers) and retailers in setting final prices; each would like some control. Manufacturers usually want a certain image and to enable all retailers, even inefficient ones, to earn profits. Most retailers want to set prices based on their image, goals, and so forth. A supplier can best control prices through exclusive distribution, not selling to price-cutting retailers, or being its own retailer. A retailer can best gain control by being a vital customer, threatening to stop carrying items, stocking private brands, or selling gray-market goods (defined soon).

Trust and Fairness in Revenue Management

Revenue management systems seek to maximize a retailer's profits by constantly changing the mix of prices. An airline might have multiple prices for adjacent seats on the same plane based on when the seats were purchased. A restaurant might offer selective discounts on its Web site at times when its reservation schedule indicates a low table utilization rate. In contrast, there may be no discount seats—on the plane or at the restaurant—if a major convention is in town. The popularity of the Web has increased the opportunities for revenue management strategies by efficiently enabling a retailer to monitor low and high sales periods, and to adjust prices accordingly. A retailer's revenue management policies might undermine a consumer's trust, based on the retailer's desire to maximize profits and to use customer satisfaction concepts that stress the lifetime revenue per loyal customer. Trust can also be undermined by two customers paying disparate prices for a comparable item.

How would you satisfy bother retailers and consumers in using revenue management tactics?

Many manufacturers set prices to retailers by estimating final retail prices and then subtracting required retailer and wholesaler profit margins. In men's apparel, the common retail markup is 50 percent of the final price. Thus, a man's shirt retailing at $50 can be sold to a retailer for no more than $25. If a wholesaler is involved, the manufacturer's wholesale price must be far less than $25.

Retailers sometimes carry manufacturers' brands and place high prices on them so rival brands (such as private labels) can be sold more easily. This is called "selling against the brand" and is disliked by manufacturers because sales of their brands are apt to decline. Some retailers also sell **gray-market goods**, brand-name products bought in foreign markets or goods transshipped from other retailers. Manufacturers dislike gray-market goods because they are often sold at low prices by unauthorized dealers. They may sue gray-market goods resellers on the basis of copyright and trademark infringement.

When suppliers are unknown or products are new, retailers may seek price guarantees. For example, to get its radios stocked, a new supplier might have to guarantee the $30 suggested retail price. If the retailers cannot sell the radios for $30, the manufacturer pays a refund. Should the retailers have to sell the radios at $25, the manufacturer gives back $5. Another guarantee is one in which a supplier tells the retailer that no competitor can buy an item for a lower price. If anyone does, the retailer gets a rebate. The relative power of the retailer and its suppliers determines whether such guarantees are provided.

A retailer also has other suppliers: employees, fixtures manufacturers, landlords, and outside parties (such as ad agencies). Each has an effect on price because of its costs to the retailer.

Competition and Retail Pricing

See how Auto-by-Tel (www.autobytel.com) and CarsDirect.com (www.carsdirect.com) approach the selling of cars.

Market pricing occurs when shoppers have a large choice of retailers. In this instance, retailers often price similarly to each other and have less control over price because consumers can easily shop around. Supermarkets, fast-food restaurants, and gas stations may use market pricing due to their competitive industries. Demand for specific retailers may be weak enough so that some customers would switch to a competitor if prices are raised much.

With *administered pricing*, firms seek to attract consumers on the basis of distinctive retailing mixes. This occurs when people consider image, assortment, service, and so forth to be important and they are willing to pay above-average prices to unique retailers. Upscale department stores, fashion apparel stores, and expensive restaurants are among those with unique offerings and solid control over their prices.

Most price-oriented strategies can be quickly imitated. Thus, the reaction of competitors is predictable if the leading firm is successful. This means a price strategy should be viewed from both short-run and long-run perspectives. If competition becomes too intense, a price war may erupt—whereby various firms continually lower prices below regular amounts and sometimes below their cost to lure consumers from competitors. Price wars are sometimes difficult to end and can lead to low profits, losses, or even bankruptcy for some competitors. This is especially so for Web retailers.

DEVELOPING A RETAIL PRICE STRATEGY

As Figure 17-4 shows, a retail price strategy has five steps: objectives, policy, strategy, implementation, and adjustments. Pricing policies must be integrated with the total retail mix, which occurs in the second step. The process can be complex due to the often erratic nature of demand, the number of items carried, and the impact of the external factors already noted.

Retail Objectives and Pricing

A retailer's pricing strategy has to reflect its overall goals and be related to sales and profits. There must also be specific pricing goals to avoid such potential problems as confusing people by having too many prices, spending too much time bargaining with customers, offering frequent discounts to stimulate customer traffic, having low profit margins, and placing too much focus on price.

OVERALL OBJECTIVES AND PRICING   Sales goals may be stated in terms of revenues and/or units. An aggressive strategy, known as **market penetration pricing**, is used when a retailer seeks large revenues by setting low prices and selling many units. Profit per unit is low, but total profit is high if sales projections are met. This approach is proper if customers are price sensitive, low prices discourage actual and potential competition, and retail costs do not rise much with volume.

With a **market skimming pricing** strategy, a firm sets premium prices and attracts customers less concerned with price than service, assortment, and prestige. It usually does not maximize sales but achieves high profit per unit. It is proper if the targeted segment is price insensitive, if new competitors are unlikely to enter the market, and if added sales will greatly increase retail costs. See Figure 17-5.

Return on investment and early recovery of cash are other possible profit-based goals for retailers using a market skimming strategy. *Return on investment* is sought if a retailer wants profit to be a certain percentage of its investment, such as 20 percent of inventory investment. *Early recovery of cash* is used by retailers that may be short on funds, wish to expand, or be uncertain about the future.

BE's Toy City, the discounter we introduced earlier in this chapter, may be used to illustrate how a retailer sets sales, profit, and return-on-investment goals. The firm sells inexpensive toys and overruns to avoid competing with mainstream toy stores, has one price for all toys (to be set within the $9 to $12 range), minimizes operating costs, encourages self-service, and carries a good selection. Table 17-2 has data on BE's Toy City pertaining to demand, costs, profit, and return-on-inventory investment at prices from $9 to $12. The firm must select the best price within that range. Table 17-3 shows how the figures in Table 17-2 were derived. Several conclusions can be drawn from Table 17-2:

- ▶ A sales revenue goal would lead to a price of $10. Total sales are highest ($1,040,000).
- ▶ A dollar profit goal would lead to a price of $11. Total profit is highest ($132,000).
- ▶ A return-on-inventory investment goal would lead to a price of $10. Return on inventory investment is 127 percent.
- ▶ Although the most items can be sold at $9, that price would lead to the least profit ($55,600).
- ▶ A price of $12 would yield the highest profit per unit ($1.92) and as a percentage of sales, but total dollar profit is not maximized at this price.
- ▶ The highest inventory turnover (9.5 times at $9.00) would not lead to the highest total profits.

Margin note (left column):

Revionics software (www.revionics.com/ pricing-software.html) can assist retailers in price optimization.

SecondSpin.com (www .secondspin.com) sells used CDs and DVDs at a discount. Tiffany (www .tiffany.com) has great jewelry—although it can be a little pricey.

FIGURE 17-4

A Framework for Developing a Retail Price Strategy

FIGURE 17-5

Organic Food and a Market-Skimming Approach

Because consumers who buy organic food believe that it is healthier for you and more natural than traditional food, they are willing to pay extra for the organic food—sometimes, significantly extra!

Source: CoolR/Shutterstock. Reprinted by permission.

As a result, BE's Toy City decides on a price of $11 because it would earn the highest dollar profits, while generating good profit per unit and good profit as a percentage of sales.

SPECIFIC PRICING OBJECTIVES Figure 17-6 lists specific pricing goals other than sales and profits. Each retailer must determine its relative importance for its situation—and plan accordingly. Some goals may be incompatible, such as "to not encourage shoppers to be overly price-conscious" and a "we-will-not-be-undersold" philosophy.

Broad Price Policy

Kalibrate (www.kalibrate.com) offers a lot of software solutions that enable gas stations and convenience stores to better integrate their price strategies.

Through a broad price policy, a retailer generates an integrated price plan with short- and long-run perspectives (balancing immediate and future goals) and a consistent image (vital for chains and franchises). The retailer interrelates price policy with the target market, the retail image, and the other elements of the retail mix. These are some price policies from which a firm could choose:

▶ No competitors will have lower prices, no competitors will have higher prices (for prestige purposes), or prices will be consistent with competitors' prices.

TABLE 17-2 BE's Toy City: Demand, Costs, Profit, and Return on Inventory Investment[a]

Selling Price ($)	Demand (units)	Total Sales Revenue ($)	Average Cost of Goods ($)	Total Cost of Goods ($)	Total Operating Costs ($)	Total Costs ($)	Average Total Costs ($)	Total Profit ($)
9.00	114,000	1,026,000	7.60	866,400	104,000	970,400	8.51	55,600
10.00	104,000	1,040,000	7.85	816,400	94,000	910,400	8.75	129,600
11.00	80,000	880,000	8.25	660,000	88,000	748,000	9.35	132,000
12.00	60,000	720,000	8.75	525,000	80,000	605,000	10.08	115,000

Selling Price ($)	Profit/ Unit ($)	Markup at Retail (%)	Profit/ Sales (%)	Average Inventory on Hand (units)	Inventory Turnover (units)	Average Inventory Investment at Cost ($)	Inventory Turnover ($)	Return-on-Inventory Investment (%)
9.00	0.49	16	5.4	12,000	9.5	91,200	9.5	61
10.00	1.25	22	12.5	13,000	8.0	102,050	8.0	127
11.00	1.65	25	15.0	14,000	5.7	115,500	5.7	114
12.00	1.92	27	16.0	16,000	3.8	140,000	3.8	82

Note: The average cost of goods reflects quantity discounts. Total operating costs include all retail operating expenses.
[a] Numbers have been rounded.

TABLE 17-3 Derivation of BE's Toy City Data

Column in Table 17-2	Source of Information or Method of Computation
Selling price	Trade data, comparison shopping, experience
Demand (in units) at each price	Consumer surveys, trade data, experience
Total sales revenue	Selling price × Quantity demanded
Average cost of goods	Supplier contacts, quantity discount structure, estimates of order sizes
Total cost of goods	Average cost of goods × Quantity demanded
Total operating costs	Experience, trade data, estimation of individual retail expenses
Total costs	Total cost of goods + Total operating costs
Average total costs	Total costs/Quantity demanded
Total profit	Total sales revenue − Total costs
Profit per unit	Total profit/Quantity demanded
Markup (at retail)	(Selling price − Average cost of goods)/Selling price
Profit as a percentage of sales	Total profit/Total sales revenue
Average inventory on hand	Trade data, inventory turnover data (in units), experience
Inventory turnover (in units)	Quantity demanded/Average inventory on hand (in units)
Average inventory investment (at cost)	Average cost of goods × Average inventory on hand (in units)
Inventory turnover (in $)	Total cost of goods/Average inventory investment (at cost)
Return-on-inventory investment	Total profit/Average inventory investment (at cost)

▸ All items will be priced independently, depending on the demand for each, or the prices for all items will be interrelated to maintain an image and ensure proper markups.
▸ Price leadership will be exerted, competitors will be price leaders and set prices first, or prices will be set independently of competitors.
▸ Prices will be constant over a year or season, or prices will change if costs change.

FIGURE 17-6

Specific Pricing Objectives from Which Retailers May Choose

✓ To maintain a proper image
✓ To encourage shoppers not to be overly price-conscious
✓ To be perceived as fair by all parties (including suppliers, employees, and customers)
✓ To be consistent in setting prices
✓ To increase customer traffic during slow periods
✓ To clear out seasonal merchandise
✓ To match competitors' prices without starting a price war
✓ To promote a "we-will-not-be-undersold" philosophy
✓ To be regarded as the price leader in the market area by consumers
✓ To provide ample customer service
✓ To minimize the chance of government actions relating to price advertising and antitrust matters
✓ To discourage potential competitors from entering the marketplace
✓ To create and maintain customer interest
✓ To encourage repeat business

Price Strategy

See how retailers can improve pricing decisions (http://fso.cpasitesolutions .com/Premium/BS/fg/ fg-Pricing.html).

In **demand-oriented pricing**, a retailer sets prices based on consumer desires. It determines the range of prices acceptable to the target market. The top of this range is the demand ceiling—the most that people will pay for a good or service. With **cost-oriented pricing**, a retailer sets a price floor, the minimum price acceptable to the firm so it can reach a specified profit goal. A retailer usually computes merchandise and operating costs and adds a profit margin to these figures. For **competition-oriented pricing**, a retailer sets its prices in accordance with those of its competitors. The price levels of key competitors are studied and applied.

As a rule, retailers should combine these approaches in enacting a price strategy. The approaches should not be viewed as operating independently.

DEMAND-ORIENTED PRICING   Retailers use demand-oriented pricing to estimate the quantities that customers would buy at various prices. This approach studies customer interests and the psychological implications of pricing. Two aspects of psychological pricing are the price–quality association and prestige pricing.

According to the **price–quality association** concept, many consumers believe high prices connote high quality and low prices connote low quality. This association is especially important if competing firms or products are hard to judge on bases other than price, consumers have little experience or confidence in judging quality (as with a new retailer), shoppers perceive large differences in quality among retailers or products, and brand names are insignificant in product choice. Although various studies have documented a price–quality relationship, research also indicates that if other quality cues—such as retailer atmospherics, customer service, and popular brands—are involved, these cues may be more important than price in a person's judgment of overall retailer or product quality.

Prestige pricing—which assumes that consumers will not buy goods and services at prices deemed too low—is based on the price–quality association. Its premise is that consumers may feel too low a price means poor quality and status. Some people look for prestige pricing when selecting retailers and do not patronize those with prices viewed as too low. Saks Fifth Avenue and Neiman Marcus do not generally carry low-end items because their customers may believe such items are inferior. Prestige pricing does not apply to all shoppers. Some people may be economizers and always shop for bargains; and neither the price–quality association nor prestige pricing may be applicable for them.

COST-ORIENTED PRICING   One form of cost-oriented pricing, markup pricing, is the most widely used pricing technique. In **markup pricing**, a retailer sets prices by adding per-unit merchandise costs, retail operating expenses, and desired profit. The difference between merchandise costs and selling price is the **markup**. If a retailer buys a desk for $200 and sells it for $300, the extra $100 covers operating costs and profit. The markup is 33-1/3 percent at retail or 50 percent at cost. The markup level depends on a product's traditional markup, the supplier's suggested list price, inventory turnover, competition, rent and other overhead costs, the extent to which the product must be serviced, and the selling effort.

Markups can be computed on the basis of retail selling price or cost but are usually calculated using the retail price. Why? (1) Retail expenses, markdowns, and profit are always stated as a percentage of sales. Thus, markups as a percentage of sales are more meaningful. (2) Manufacturers quote selling prices and discounts to retailers as percentage reductions from retail list prices. (3) Retail price data are more readily available than cost data. (4) Profitability seems smaller if expressed on the basis of price. This can be useful in communicating with the government, employees, and consumers.

This is how a **markup percentage** is calculated. The difference is in the denominator:

$$\frac{\text{Markup percentage}}{\text{(at retail)}} = \frac{\text{Retail selling price } - \text{ Merchandise cost}}{\text{Retail selling price}}$$

$$\frac{\text{Markup percentage}}{\text{(at cost)}} = \frac{\text{Retail selling price } - \text{ Merchandise cost}}{\text{Merchandise cost}}$$

Table 17-4 shows several markup percentages at retail and at cost. As markups go up, the disparity between the percentages grows. Suppose a retailer buys a watch for $20 and considers

TABLE 17-4 Markup Equivalents

Percentage at Retail	Percentage at Cost
10.0	11.1
20.0	25.0
30.0	42.9
40.0	66.7
50.0	100.0
60.0	150.0
70.0	233.3
80.0	400.0
90.0	900.0

whether to sell it for $25, $40, or $100. The $25 price yields a markup of 20 percent at retail and 25 percent at cost, the $40 price a markup of 50 percent at retail and 100 percent at cost, and the $100 price a markup of 80 percent at retail and 400 percent at cost.

The following three examples indicate the usefulness of the markup concept in planning:

1. A discount clothing store can buy a shipment of men's long-sleeve shirts at $12 each and wants a 30 percent markup at retail.[9] What retail price should the store charge to achieve this markup?

$$\text{Markup percentage (at retail)} = \frac{\text{Retail selling price} - \text{Merchandise cost}}{\text{Retail selling price}}$$

$$0.30 = \frac{\text{Retail selling price} - \$12.00}{\text{Retail selling price}}$$

$$\text{Retail selling price} = \$17.14$$

2. A stationery store desires a minimum 40 percent markup at retail.[10] If standard envelopes retail at $7.99 per box, what is the maximum price the store should pay for each box?

$$\text{Markup percentage (at retail)} = \frac{\text{Retail selling price} - \text{Merchandise cost}}{\text{Retail selling price}}$$

$$0.40 = \frac{\$7.99 - \text{Merchandise cost}}{\$7.99}$$

$$\text{Merchandise cost} = \$4.794$$

3. A sporting goods store has been offered a closeout purchase for bicycles. The cost of each bike is $105, and it should retail for $160. What markup percentage at retail would the store obtain?

$$\text{Markup percentage (at retail)} = \frac{\text{Retail selling price} - \text{Merchandise cost}}{\text{Retail selling price}}$$

$$= \frac{\$160.00 - \$105.00}{\$160.00} = 34.4$$

A retailer's markup percentage may also be determined by examining planned retail operating expenses, profit, and net sales. Suppose a florist estimates yearly operating expenses to be $55,000. The desired profit is $50,000 per year, including the owner's salary. Net sales are forecast to be $250,000. The planned markup percentage would be:

$$\text{Markup percentage (at retail)} = \frac{\text{Planned retail operating expenses} + \text{Planned profit}}{\text{Planned net sales}}$$

$$= \frac{\$55,000 + \$50,000}{\$250,000} = 42$$

If potted plants cost the florist $8.00 each, the retailer's selling price would be:

$$\text{Retail selling price} = \frac{\text{Merchandise cost}}{1 - \text{Markup}}$$

$$= \frac{\$8.00}{1 - 0.42} = \$13.79$$

The florist must sell about 18,129 plants (assuming this is the only item it carries) at $13.79 apiece to achieve sales and profit goals. To reach these goals, all plants must be sold at the $13.79 price.

Because it is rare to sell all items in stock at their original prices, initial markup, maintained markup, and gross margin should each be computed. **Initial markup** is based on the original retail value assigned to merchandise less the costs of the merchandise. **Maintained markup** is based on the actual prices received for merchandise sold during a time period less merchandise cost. Maintained markups relate to actual prices received, so they can be hard to predict. The difference between initial and maintained markups is that the latter reflect adjustments for markdowns, added markups, shortages, and discounts.

The initial markup percentage depends on planned retail operating expenses, profit, reductions, and net sales:

$$\begin{array}{l}\text{Initial markup} \\ \text{percentage} \\ \text{(at retail)}\end{array} = \frac{\begin{array}{c}\text{Planned retail operating expenses} + \text{Planned profit} \\ + \text{ Planned retail reductions}\end{array}}{\text{Planned net sales} + \text{Planned retail reductions}}$$

If planned retail reductions are 0, the initial markup percentage equals planned retail operating expenses plus profit, both divided by planned net sales. To resume the florist example, suppose the firm projects that retail reductions will be 20 percent of estimated sales, or $50,000. To reach its goals, the initial markup and the original selling price would be:

$$\begin{array}{l}\text{Initial markup} \\ \text{percentage} \\ \text{(at retail)}\end{array} = \frac{\$55,000 + \$50,000 + \$50,000}{\$250,000 + \$50,000} = 51.7$$

$$\text{Retail selling price} = \frac{\text{Merchandise cost}}{1 - \text{Markup}} = \frac{\$8.00}{1 - 0.517} = \$16.56$$

The original retail value of 18,129 plants is about $300,000. Retail reductions of $50,000 lead to net sales of $250,000. Thus, the retailer must begin by selling plants at $16.56 apiece if it wants an average selling price of $13.79 and a maintained markup of 42 percent.

The maintained markup percentage is:

$$\begin{array}{l}\text{Maintained markup} \\ \text{percentage} \\ \text{(at retail)}\end{array} = \frac{\text{Actual retail operation expenses} + \text{Actual profit}}{\text{Actual net sales}}$$

or

$$\begin{array}{l}\text{Maintained markup} \\ \text{percentage} \\ \text{(at retail)}\end{array} = \frac{\text{Average selling price} - \text{Merchandise cost}}{\text{Average selling price}}$$

Gross margin is the difference between net sales and the total cost of goods sold (which adjusts for cash discounts and additional expenses):

$$\text{Gross margin (in \$)} = \text{Net sales} - \text{Total cost of goods}$$

The florist's gross margin (the dollar equivalent of maintained markup) is roughly $105,000.

TECHNOLOGY IN RETAILING | Oracle Markdown Software

Markdown planning is complicated. A markdown made too early in a selling season results in less time to sell an item at full price, resulting in low profit margins. On the other hand, delaying markdowns until late in an item's selling season can require large markdowns, and also results in stale, slow-selling goods. Oracle's retail markdown optimization software was designed to take much of the guesswork out of markdown planning. This software recommends candidates for markdowns and specifies recommended price reductions based on the inventory risk at the end of a selling season. Recommendations are based on an item's product's life cycle, seasonality, price elasticity, and in-season performance—using advanced predictive and simulation techniques. According to Oracle, this software is capable of increasing a retailer's gross margin, overall sales, and inventory turnover.

Comment on the choice of an early versus a late markdown policy.

Sources: Authors' research and material in "Oracle Retail Markdown Optimization," January 1, 2015, www.slideshare.net/OLBEConsulting/oracle-retail-markdown-optimization

Although a retailer must set a companywide markup goal, markups for categories of merchandise or individual products may differ—sometimes dramatically. At many full-line discount stores, maintained markup as a percentage of sales ranges from under 20 percent for consumer electronics to as much as 30 to 40 percent or more for jewelry and watches.

With a **variable markup policy**, a retailer purposely adjusts markups by merchandise category.

▶ A variable markup policy recognizes that costs of different goods/services categories may fluctuate widely. Some items require alterations or installation. Even within a product line, expensive items may require greater end-of-year markdowns than inexpensive ones. The high-priced line needs a larger initial markup.

▶ A variable markup policy allows for differences in product investments. For major appliances, where the retailer orders regularly from a wholesaler, lower markups are needed than with fine jewelry, where the retailer must have a complete stock of unique merchandise.

▶ A variable markup policy accounts for differences in sales efforts and merchandising skills. For example, a feature-laden food processor may require a substantial effort, whereas a standard toaster involves much less effort.

▶ A variable markup policy may help a retailer to generate more customer traffic by advertising certain products at deep discounts. This entails leader pricing (discussed later in the chapter).

One way to plan variable markups is **direct product profitability (DPP)**, a technique that enables a retailer to find the profitability of each category of merchandise by computing adjusted per-unit gross margin and assigning direct product costs for such expense categories as warehousing, transportation, handling, and selling. The proper markup for each category or item is then set. Direct product profitability is used by some supermarkets, discounters, and other retailers. However, it is complex to assign costs.

Figure 17-7 illustrates DPP for two items with a selling price of $20. The retailer pays $12 for Item A; per-unit gross margin is $8. Since the retailer gets a $1 per unit allowance to set up a special display, the adjusted gross margin is $9. Total direct retail costs are estimated at $5. Direct product profit is $4 (20 percent of sales). The retailer pays $10 for Item B; per-unit gross margin is $10. There are no special discounts or allowances. Because Item B needs more selling effort, total direct retail costs are $6. The direct profit is $4 (20 percent of sales). To attain the same direct profit per unit, Item A needs a 40 percent markup (per-unit gross margin/selling price), and Item B needs 50 percent.

Cost-oriented (markup) pricing is popular among retailers. It is simple, because a retailer can apply a standard markup for a product category more easily than it can estimate demand at various prices. The firm can also adjust prices according to demand or segment its customers. Markup pricing has a sense of equity given that the retailer earns a fair profit. When retailers have similar markups, price competition is reduced. Markup pricing is efficient if it takes into account competition, seasonal factors, and the intricacies in selling some products.

COMPETITION-ORIENTED PRICING A retailer can use competitors' prices as a guide. That firm might not alter prices in reaction to changes in demand or costs unless competitors alter theirs. Similarly, it might change prices when competitors do, even if demand or costs remain the same.

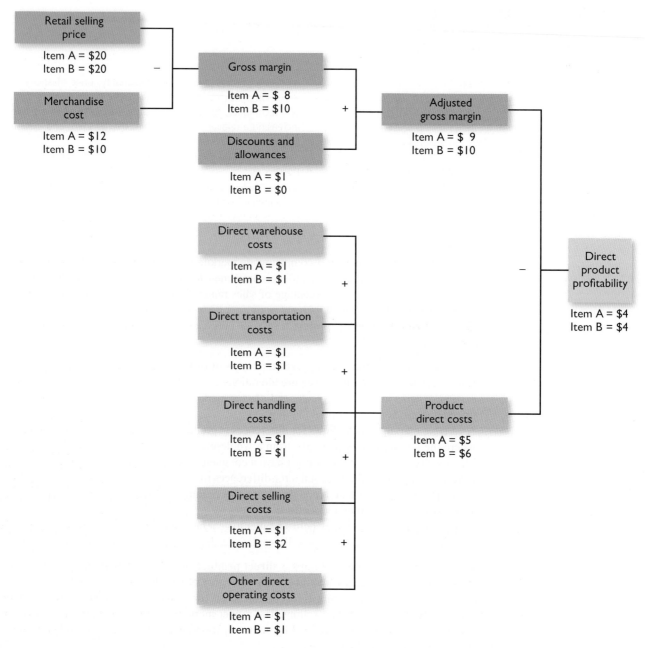

FIGURE 17-7

How to Determine Direct Product Profitability

As shown in Table 17-5, a competition-oriented retailer can price below, at, or above the market. A firm with a strong location, superior service, good assortments, a favorable image, and exclusive brands can set prices above competitors. However, above-market pricing is not suitable for a retailer that has an inconvenient location, relies on self-service, is not innovative, and offers no real product distinctiveness.

Competition-oriented pricing does not require calculations of demand curves or price elasticity. The average market price is assumed to be fair for both the consumer and the retailer. Pricing at the market level does not disrupt competition and therefore does not usually lead to retaliation.

INTEGRATION OF APPROACHES TO PRICE STRATEGY To properly integrate the three approaches—demand-oriented pricing, cost-oriented pricing, and competition-oriented pricing—questions such as these should be addressed:

▶ If prices are reduced, will revenues increase greatly? (Demand orientation)

TABLE 17-5 Competition-Oriented Pricing Alternatives

Retail Mix Variable	Alternative Price Strategies		
	Pricing Below the Market	Pricing at the Market	Pricing Above the Market
Location	Poor, inconvenient site; low rent	Close to competitors, no location advantage	Few strong competitors, convenient to consumers
Customer service	Self-service, little salesperson support, limited displays	Moderate assistance by sales personnel	High levels of personal selling, delivery, etc.
Product assortment	More emphasis on best-sellers	Medium or large assortment	Small or large assortment
Atmosphere	Inexpensive fixtures, racks for merchandise	Moderate atmosphere	Attractive and pleasant decor
Innovativeness in assortment	Follower, conservative	Concentration on best-sellers	Quite innovative
Special services	Not available	Not available or extra fee	Included in price
Product lines carried	Some name brands, private labels, closeouts	Selection of name brands, private labels	Exclusive name brands and private labels

    ▸ Should different prices be charged for a product based on negotiations with customers, seasonality, and so on? (Demand orientation)
    ▸ Will a given price level allow a traditional markup to be attained? (Cost orientation)
    ▸ What price level is needed for an item with special buying, selling, or delivery costs? (Cost orientation)
    ▸ What price levels are competitors setting? (Competitive orientation)
    ▸ Can above-market prices be set due to a superior image? (Competitive orientation)

NEW USES FOR CREDIT AND DEBIT CARDS According to a leading research and consulting firm, the sales of pre-paid credit and debit cards grew from $12 billion in 2007 to more than $235 billion in 2015 and accounted for 4 percent of all payment card purchases with retailers.[11] This high growth rate can be explained by two developments: the increase in the gift card market and the greater number of consumers who do not have traditional bank accounts.

Firms such as Home Depot (www.homedepot.com), Gap (www.gap.com), and Nike (www.nike.com) offer closed-loop (firm-specific) gift cards. Visa (www.visa.com), MasterCard (www.mastercard.com), Discover (www.discovercard.com), and American Express (www.americanexpress.com) offer open-loop gift cards that can be redeemed by any merchant.

The growth in pre-paid cards and gift cards has encouraged convenience stores to enter the banking business. Stripes (www.stripesstores.com), which operates about 700 convenience stores—primarily in New Mexico, Oklahoma, and Texas—offers a pre-paid credit card in conjunction with nFinanSe (www.nfinanse.com), a financial services company. For a $2.95 monthly fee, Stripes customers can participate in the firm's credit-card programs. This fee entitles users to an unlimited number of purchase transactions, no-cost direct deposit of payroll checks, and 24/7 customer support. The card is particularly attractive to Stripes because it operates in markets where a high percentage of consumers do not have traditional bank accounts. Stripes is now a subsidiary of Energy Transfer Partners, the parent company of Sunoco.[12]

Implementation of Price Strategy

Implementing a price strategy involves a variety of separate but interrelated specific decisions, in addition to those broad concepts already discussed. A checklist of selected decisions is shown in Figure 17-8. In this section, the specifics of a pricing strategy are detailed.

Bi-Lo (www.bi-lo.com), the Southeast supermarket chain, offers both everyday low prices and regular promotions.

CUSTOMARY AND VARIABLE PRICING With **customary pricing**, a retailer sets prices for goods and services and seeks to maintain them for an extended period. Examples of items with customary prices are newspapers, candy, arcade games, vending machine items, and foods on restaurant menus. In each case, the retailer wants to establish set prices and have consumers take them for granted.

A version of customary pricing is **everyday low pricing (EDLP)**, in which a retailer strives to sell its goods and services at consistently low prices throughout the selling season. Low prices

FIGURE 17-8

A Checklist of Selected Specific Pricing Decisions

✓ How important is price stability? How long should prices be maintained?

✓ Is everyday low pricing desirable?

✓ Should prices change if costs and/or customer demand vary?

✓ Should the same prices be charged to all customers buying under the same conditions?

✓ Should customer bargaining be permitted?

✓ Should odd pricing be used?

✓ Should leader pricing be utilized to draw customer traffic? If yes, should leader prices be above, at, or below costs?

✓ Should consumers be offered discounts for purchasing in quantity?

✓ Should price lining be used to provide a price range and price points within that range?

✓ Should pricing practices vary by department or product line?

are set initially, and there are few or no advertised specials, except on discontinued items or end-of-season closeouts. The retailer reduces its advertising and product re-pricing costs, and this approach increases the credibility of its prices in the consumer's mind. On the other hand, with EDLP, suppliers may eliminate special trade allowances designed to encourage retailers to offer price promotions during the year. Walmart, McDonald's, and Ikea are among the retailers successfully using everyday low pricing. See Figure 17-9.

In many instances, a retailer cannot or should not use customary pricing. A firm *cannot* hold constant prices if costs are rising. A firm *should not* keep prices constant if customer demand varies. Under **variable pricing**, a retailer alters its prices to coincide with fluctuations in costs or consumer demand. Variable pricing may offer excitement due to special sales opportunities for customers.

Cost fluctuations can be seasonal or trend-related. Supermarket and florist prices vary over the year due to the seasonal nature of many food and floral products. When seasonal items are scarce, the cost to the retailer goes up. If costs continually rise (as with luxury cars) or fall (as with computers), the retailer must change prices permanently (unlike temporary seasonal changes).

Demand fluctuations can be place- or time-based. Place-based fluctuations exist for retailers selling seat locations (such as concert halls) or room locations (such as hotels). Different prices can

FIGURE 17-9

Everyday Low Pricing

Everyday low pricing is an appealing approach for consumers who want to be assured that the retailer continuously places its focus on low prices. Besides the retailers noted in the text, Costco, Target, T. J. Maxx, and Amazon .com utilize everyday low pricing as a competitive advantage.

Source: Infomages/ Shutterstock. Reprinted by permission.

be charged for different locales, such as tickets close to the stage commanding higher prices. Time-based fluctuations occur if consumer demand differs by hour, day, or season. Demand for a movie theater is greater on Saturday than on Wednesday. Prices should be lower in periods of less demand.

Yield management pricing is a computerized, demand-based, variable pricing technique whereby a retailer (typically a service firm) determines the combination of prices that yield the greatest total revenues for a given period. It is widely used by airlines and hotels. A key airline decision is how many first-class, full-coach, and discount tickets to sell on each flight. With this approach, an airline has fewer discount tickets in peak periods than in off-peak times. The airline has two goals: fill as many seats as possible on every flight and sell as many full-fare tickets as it can. (An airline doesn't want to sell a seat for $199 if someone will pay $599!) Yield management pricing may be too complex for small firms and requires software

It is possible to combine customary and variable pricing. A movie theater can charge $5 each Wednesday night and $9 every Saturday. A bookstore can lower prices by 20 percent for best sellers that have been on shelves for three months.

ONE-PRICE POLICY AND FLEXIBLE PRICING   Under a **one-price policy**, a retailer charges the same price to all customers buying an item under similar conditions. This policy may be used together with customary pricing or variable pricing. With variable pricing, all customers interested in a particular section of concert seats would pay the same price. This approach is easy to manage, does not require skilled salespeople, makes shopping quicker, permits self-service, puts consumers under less pressure, and is tied to price goals. One-price policies are the rule for most U.S. retailers, and bargaining is often not permitted.

Flexible pricing lets consumers bargain over prices; those who are good at it obtain lower prices. Jewelry stores, car dealers, and others use flexible pricing. They post "list prices" but shoppers who are able to haggle can purchase at lower prices. Shoppers need prior knowledge to bargain well. Flexible pricing encourages consumers to spend more time, gives an impression the firm is discount-oriented, and generates high margins from shoppers who do not like haggling. It requires high initial prices and good salespeople.[13]

A special form of flexible pricing is **contingency pricing**, whereby a service retailer does not get paid until after the service is performed and payment is contingent on the service being satisfactory. In some cases, such as real-estate, consumers like contingency payments so they know the service is done properly. This represents some risk to the retailer because a lot of time and effort may be incurred without payment. A real-estate broker may show a house 25 times, not sell it, and, therefore, not be paid.

ODD PRICING   In **odd pricing**, retail prices are set at levels below even dollar values, such as $0.49, $4.98, and $199. The assumption is that people feel these prices represent discounts or that the amounts are beneath consumer price ceilings. Odd pricing is a form of psychological pricing.[14] Realtors hope consumers with a price ceiling of less than $350,000 are attracted to houses selling for $349,500. See Figure 17-10.

Odd prices that are 1 cent or 2 cents below the next highest even price ($0.29, $0.99, $2.98) are common up to $10.00. Beyond that point and up to $50.00, 5-cent reductions from the highest even price ($19.95, $49.95) are more usual. For more expensive items, prices are in dollars ($399, $4,995).

Looking to bargain? Go to eBay (http://pages.ebay.com/live-auctions/about.html) or uBid (www.ubid.com).

CAREERS IN RETAILING   Carol Meyrowitz of TJX

TJX (www.tjx.com) is the largest off-price retailer specializing in apparel and home fashions Carol Meyrowitz, now the executive chair of the firm, was the chief executive of TJX from January 2007 until January 2016. She was a member of the firm's board of directors for a decade. Meyrowitz's career includes holding senior management positions with former divisions of TJX, consulting work for a private-equity firm, and serving as an executive vice president of TJX. Her experience encompasses a broad understanding of distribution, real-estate, finance, and international operations. In 2015, her total compensation was $18 million, of which $1.575 million was base salary and $10 million for stock options. TJX's companywide strategy is to price its fashionable, brand-name merchandise at 20 to 60 percent less than at department and specialty stores.

Sources: Authors' research and 2016 material from TJX.com, *Fortune*, *Forbes*, and Bloomberg.com.

FIGURE 17-10

Odd Pricing: A Popular Retail Tactic Worldwide

Around the globe, regardless of the currency, odd pricing is a popular retailing tactic. (Top) In U.S. dollars; (Bottom Left) in European euros; (Bottom Right) in Japanese yen.

Sources: little Whale/ Shutterstock; aleksandr hunta/Shutterstock; and Claudio Divizia/Shutterstock. Reprinted by permission.

LEADER PRICING   In **leader pricing**, a retailer advertises and sells selected items in its goods/ services assortment at less than the usual profit margins. The goal is to increase customer traffic for the retailer so that it can sell regularly priced goods and services in addition to the specially priced items. This is different from bait-and-switch, in which sale items are not sold.

Leader pricing typically involves frequently purchased, nationally branded, high-turnover goods and services because it is easy for customers to detect low prices. Supermarkets, home centers, discount stores, drugstores, and fast-food restaurants are just some of the retailers that utilize leader pricing to draw shoppers. There are two kinds of leader pricing: loss leaders and sales at lower than regular prices (but higher than cost). Loss leaders are regulated in some states under minimum-price laws.

MULTIPLE-UNIT PRICING   With **multiple-unit pricing**, a retailer offers discounts to customers who buy in quantity or who buy a product bundle. By pricing items at two for $0.75, a retailer attempts to sell more products than at $0.39 each. There are three reasons to use multiple-unit pricing: (1) A firm could seek to have shoppers increase their total purchases of an item. (If people buy multiple units to stockpile them, instead of consuming more, the firm's overall sales do not increase.) (2) This approach can help sell slow-moving and end-of-season merchandise. (3) Price bundling may increase sales of related items.

In **bundled pricing**, a retailer combines several items in one basic price. A digital camera bundle could include a camera, batteries, a telephoto lens, a case, and a tripod for $259. This approach increases overall sales and offers people a discount over unbundled prices. However, it is unresponsive to the needs of customers who vary in their needs and preferences. Many retailers offer hybrid bundles that combine complementary products(s) and service(s) for a single price; home improvement stores may charge a single price for floor tiles, installation, and disposal of previous flooring materials. As an alternative, many retailers use **unbundled pricing**—they charge separate prices for each product or service sold. A TV rental firm could charge separately for TV set rental, home delivery, and a monthly service contract. This closely links prices with costs and gives people more choice. Unbundled pricing may be harder to manage and may lead to people buying fewer related items.[15]

With its many hotel brands (http://www.marriott .com/marriott-brands.mi), Marriott International really knows how to use price lining.

PRICE LINING Rather than stock merchandise at all different price levels, retailers often employ **price lining** and sell merchandise at a limited range of price points, with each point representing a distinct level of quality. Retailers first determine their price floors and ceilings in each product category. They then set a limited number of price points within the range. Department stores generally carry good, better, and best versions of merchandise consistent with their overall price policy—and set individual prices accordingly. See Figure 17-11.

Price lining benefits both consumers and retailers. If the price range for a box of handkerchiefs is $6 to $25 and the price points are $6, $15, and $25, consumers know that distinct product qualities exist. However, should a retailer have prices of $6, $7, $8, $9, $10, $11, $12, $13, $14, $15, $16, $17, $18, $19, $20, $21, $22, $23, $24, and $25, the consumer may be confused about product differences. For retailers, price lining aids merchandise planning. Retail buyers can seek suppliers carrying products at appropriate prices and better negotiate with suppliers. They can automatically disregard products not fitting within price lines and thereby reduce inventory investment. Also, stock turnover goes up when the number of models carried is limited.

Difficulties do exist in price lining: (1) Depending on the price points selected, price lining may leave excessive gaps. A parent shopping for a graduation gift might find a $30 briefcase to be too cheap and a $200 one to be too expensive. (2) Inflation can make it tough to keep price points and price ranges. (3) Markdowns may disrupt the balance in a price line, unless all items in a line are reduced proportionally. (4) Price lines must be coordinated for complementary product categories, such as blazers, skirts, and shoes.

Price Adjustments

Retailers needs to be focused in making price adjustments (www .bizmove.com/general/ m6h4.htm).

Price adjustments enable retailers to use price as an adaptive mechanism. Markdowns and additional markups may be needed due to competition, seasonality, demand patterns, merchandise costs, and pilferage. Figure 17-12 shows a price change authorization form.

A **markdown** from an item's original price is used to meet the lower price of another retailer, adapt to inventory overstocking, clear out shopworn merchandise, reduce assortments of odds and ends, and increase customer traffic. An **additional markup** increases an item's original price because demand is unexpectedly high or costs are rising. In today's competitive marketplace, markdowns are applied much more frequently than additional markups.

A third price adjustment, the *employee discount*, is noted here because it may affect the computation of markdowns and additional markups. Although an employee discount is not an adaptive mechanism, it influences morale. Some firms give employee discounts on all items and also let workers buy sale items before they are made available to the general public.

COMPUTING MARKDOWNS AND ADDITIONAL MARKUPS Markdowns and additional markups can be expressed in dollars or percentages.

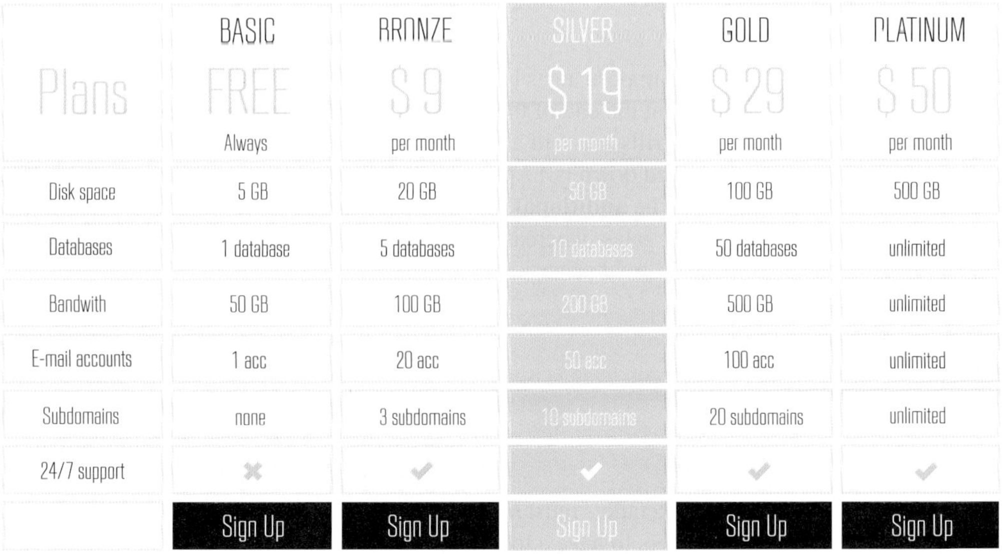

FIGURE 17-11
Price Lining

The Web developer highlighted here offers five different monthly plans depending on customer needs. These inexpensive plans range from basic (free) to platinum ($50 per month). These prices are best suited for individuals or small businesses wanting a Web presence.

Source: Antun Hirsman/ Shutterstock. Reprinted by permission.

Plans	BASIC FREE Always	BRONZE $9 per month	SILVER $19 per month	GOLD $29 per month	PLATINUM $50 per month
Disk space	5 GB	20 GB	50 GB	100 GB	500 GB
Databases	1 database	5 databases	10 databases	50 databases	unlimited
Bandwith	50 GB	100 GB	200 GB	500 GB	unlimited
E-mail accounts	1 acc	20 acc	50 acc	100 acc	unlimited
Subdomains	none	3 subdomains	10 subdomains	20 subdomains	unlimited
24/7 support	✗	✓	✓	✓	✓
	Sign Up	Sign Up	Sign Up	Sign Up	Sign Up

FIGURE 17-12
A Price Change Authorization Form

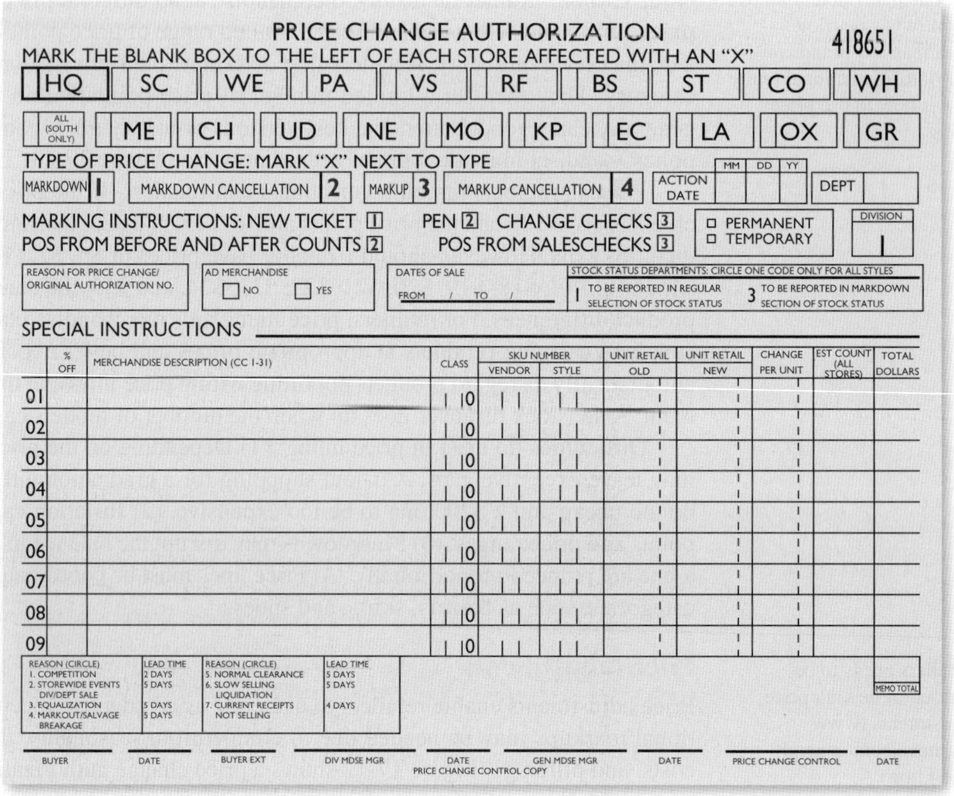
PRICE CHANGE AUTHORIZATION 418651
MARK THE BLANK BOX TO THE LEFT OF EACH STORE AFFECTED WITH AN "X"
HQ SC WE PA VS RF BS ST CO WH
ALL (SOUTH ONLY) ME CH UD NE MO KP EC LA OX GR
TYPE OF PRICE CHANGE: MARK "X" NEXT TO TYPE
MARKDOWN 1 MARKDOWN CANCELLATION 2 MARKUP 3 MARKUP CANCELLATION 4 ACTION DATE MM DD YY DEPT
MARKING INSTRUCTIONS: NEW TICKET 1 PEN 2 CHANGE CHECKS 3 □ PERMANENT □ TEMPORARY DIVISION 1
POS FROM BEFORE AND AFTER COUNTS 2 POS FROM SALESCHECKS 3
REASON FOR PRICE CHANGE/ ORIGINAL AUTHORIZATION NO. | AD MERCHANDISE □ NO □ YES | DATES OF SALE FROM / TO / | STOCK STATUS DEPARTMENTS: CIRCLE ONE CODE ONLY FOR ALL STYLES 1 TO BE REPORTED IN REGULAR SELECTION OF STOCK STATUS 3 TO BE REPORTED IN MARKDOWN SECTION OF STOCK STATUS
SPECIAL INSTRUCTIONS

	% OFF	MERCHANDISE DESCRIPTION (CC 1-31)	CLASS	SKU NUMBER VENDOR	SKU NUMBER STYLE	UNIT RETAIL OLD	UNIT RETAIL NEW	CHANGE PER UNIT	EST COUNT (ALL STORES)	TOTAL DOLLARS
01			10							
02			10							
03			10							
04			10							
05			10							
06			10							
07			10							
08			10							
09			10							

REASON (CIRCLE)	LEAD TIME	REASON (CIRCLE)	LEAD TIME
1. COMPETITION	2 DAYS	5. NORMAL CLEARANCE	5 DAYS
2. STOREWIDE EVENTS DIV/DEPT SALE	5 DAYS	6. SLOW SELLING LIQUIDATION	5 DAYS
3. EQUALIZATION	5 DAYS	7. CURRENT RECEIPTS NOT SELLING	4 DAYS
4. MARKOUT/SALVAGE BREAKAGE	5 DAYS		

MEMO TOTAL
BUYER DATE BUYER EXT DIV MDSE MGR DATE GEN MDSE MGR DATE PRICE CHANGE CONTROL DATE
PRICE CHANGE CONTROL COPY

The **markdown percentage** is the total dollar markdown as a percentage of net sales (in dollars). Although it is simple to compute, this formula does not enable a retailer to learn the percentage of items that are marked down relative to those sold at the original price:

$$\text{Markdown percentage} = \frac{\text{Total dollar markdown}}{\text{Net sales (in \$)}}$$

A complementary measure is the **off-retail markdown percentage**, which looks at the markdown for each item or category of items as a percentage of original retail price. The markdown percentage for every item can be computed, as well as the percentage of items marked down:

$$\text{Off-retail markdown percentage} = \frac{\text{Original price} - \text{New price}}{\text{Original price}}$$

Suppose a gas barbecue grill sells for \$400 at the beginning of the summer and is reduced to \$280 at the end of the summer. The off-retail markdown is 30 percent [(\$400 − \$280)/\$400]. If 100 grills are sold at the original price and 20 are sold at the sale price, the percentage of items marked down is 17 percent, and the total dollar markdown is \$2,400.

The **additional markup percentage** looks at total dollar additional markups as a percentage of net sales, whereas the **addition to retail percentage** measures a price rise as a percentage of the original price:

$$\text{Additional markup percentage} = \frac{\text{Total dollar additional markups}}{\text{Net sales (in \$)}}$$

$$\text{Additional to retail precentage} = \frac{\text{New price} - \text{Original price}}{\text{Original price}}$$

Retailers must realize that many more customers would have to buy at reduced prices for those retailers to have a total gross profit equal to that at higher prices. A retailer's judgment regarding price adjustments is affected by operating costs at various sales volumes and customer price elasticities. The true impact of a markdown or an additional markup can be learned from this formula:

$$\begin{matrix} \text{Unit sales required to} \\ \text{earn the same total} \\ \text{gross profit with a} \\ \text{price adjustment} \end{matrix} = \frac{\text{Original markup (\%)}}{\begin{matrix}\text{Original markup (\%)}\\ +/- \text{ Price change (\%)}\end{matrix}} \times \begin{matrix}\text{Expected unit}\\\text{sales at}\\\text{original price}\end{matrix}$$

Suppose a Brother printer with a cost of $50 has an original retail price of $100 (a markup of 50 percent). A retailer expects to sell 500 units over the next year, generating a total gross profit of $25,000 ($50 × 500). How many units does the retailer have to sell if it reduces the price to $85 or raises it to $110—and still earn a $25,000 gross profit? Here are the answers:

$$\frac{\text{Unit sales required}}{\text{(at \$85)}} = \frac{50\%}{50\% - 15\%} \times 500 = 1.43 \times 500 = 714$$

$$\frac{\text{Unit sales required}}{\text{(at \$110)}} = \frac{50\%}{50\% + 10\%} \times 500 = 0.83 \times 500 = 417$$

MARKDOWN CONTROL   Through markdown control, a retailer evaluates the number of markdowns, the proportion of sales involving markdowns, and the causes. The control must be such that buying plans can be altered in later periods to reflect markdowns. A good way to evaluate the cause of markdowns is to have retail buyers record the reasons for each markdown and then examine them periodically. Possible buyer notations are "end of season," "to match the price of a competitor," and "obsolete style."

Through markdown control, a retailer can monitor policies, such as the way items are displayed. Careful planning may also enable a retailer to avoid some markdowns by running more ads, training workers better, shipping goods more efficiently among branch units, and returning items to vendors.

The need for markdown control should not be interpreted as meaning that all markdowns can or should be minimized or eliminated. In fact, too low a markdown percentage may indicate that a retailer's buyers have not assumed enough risk in purchasing goods.

TIMING MARKDOWNS   There are different perspectives among retailers about the best markdown timing sequence, but much can be said about the benefits of an *early markdown policy*: It requires lower markdowns to sell products than markdowns late in the season. Merchandise is offered at reduced prices while demand is still fairly active. Early markdowns free selling space for new merchandise. The retailer's cash flow position can be improved. The main advantage of a *late markdown policy* is that a retailer gives itself every opportunity to sell merchandise at original prices. Yet, the advantages associated with an early markdown policy cannot be achieved under a late markdown policy.

Retailers can also use a *staggered markdown policy* and discount prices throughout a selling period. One pre-planned staggered markdown policy is an *automatic markdown plan*, in which the amount and timing of markdowns are controlled by the length of time merchandise remains in stock.

A *storewide clearance*, done once or twice a year, is another way to time markdowns. It often takes place after peak selling periods such as Christmas and Mother's Day. The goal is to clear out merchandise before taking a physical inventory and beginning the next season. The advantages of a storewide clearance are that a longer period is provided for selling items at original prices and that frequent markdowns can destroy a consumer's confidence in regular prices: "Why buy now, when it will be on sale next week?" Clearance sales limit bargain hunting to once or twice a year.

In the past, many retailers would introduce merchandise at high prices and then mark down many items by as much as 60 percent to increase store traffic and improve inventory turnover. This caused customers to wait for price reductions and treat initial prices skeptically. Today, more retailers start out with lower prices and try to run fewer sales and apply fewer markdowns than before. Nonetheless, a big problem facing some retailers is that they have gotten consumers too used to buying when items are discounted.

One interesting example of markdown management support is Markdown Manager software that eBay offers as a service for its sellers (http://pages.ebay.com/help/sell/items_on_sale.html).

Chapter Summary

1. *To describe the role of pricing in a retail strategy and to show that pricing decisions must be made in an integrated and adaptive manner.* Pricing is crucial to a retailer because of its interrelationship with overall objectives and the other components of the retail strategy. A price plan must be integrated and responsive—and provide a good value to customers.

2. *To examine the impact of consumers; government; manufacturers, wholesalers, and other suppliers; and current and potential competitors on pricing decisions.* Before designing a price plan, a retailer must study the factors affecting its decisions. Sometimes, the factors have a minor effect on pricing discretion; other times, they severely limit pricing options.

    Retailers should be familiar with the price elasticity of demand and the different market segments that are possible. Government restrictions deal with price fixing, price discrimination, minimum prices, unit pricing, item price removal, and price advertising. There may be conflicts about which party controls retail prices; and manufacturers, wholesalers, and other suppliers may be asked to provide price guarantees (if they are in a weak position). The competitive environment may foster market pricing, lead to price wars, or allow administered pricing.

3. *To present a framework for developing a retail price strategy: objectives, broad policy, basic strategy,* *implementation, and adjustments.* This framework consists of five stages: objectives, broad price policy, price strategy, implementation of price strategy, and price adjustments.

    Retail pricing goals can be chosen from among sales, dollar profits, return on investment, and early recovery of cash. Next, a broad policy outlines a coordinated series of actions, consistent with the retailer's image and oriented to the short and long run.

    A good price strategy incorporates demand, cost, and competitive concepts. Each of these orientations must be understood separately and jointly. Psychological pricing; markup pricing; alternative ways of computing markups; gross margin; direct product profitability; and pricing below, at, or above the market are among the key aspects of strategy planning.

    When enacting a price strategy, specific tools can be used to supplement the broad base of the strategy. Retailers should know when to use customary and variable pricing, one-price policies and flexible pricing, odd pricing, leader pricing, multiple-unit pricing, and price lining.

    Price adjustments may be required to adapt to internal and external conditions. Adjustments include markdowns, additional markups, and employee discounts. It is important that adjustments are controlled by a budget, causes of markdowns are noted, future company buying reflects prior performance, adjustments are properly timed, and excessive discounting is avoided.

Key Terms

price elasticity of demand (p. 429)
horizontal price fixing (p. 431)
vertical price fixing (p. 431)
Robinson-Patman Act (p. 432)
minimum-price laws (p. 432)
predatory pricing (p. 432)
loss leaders (p. 432)
unit pricing (p. 433)
item price removal (p. 433)
bait-and-switch advertising (p. 433)
gray-market goods (p. 434)
market penetration pricing (p. 435)
market skimming pricing (p. 435)
demand-oriented pricing (p. 438)
cost-oriented pricing (p. 438)
competition-oriented pricing (p. 438)

price–quality association (p. 438)
prestige pricing (p. 438)
markup pricing (p. 438)
markup (p. 438)
markup percentage (p. 438)
initial markup (p. 440)
maintained markup (p. 440)
gross margin (p. 440)
variable markup policy (p. 441)
direct product profitability (DPP) (p. 441)
customary pricing (p. 443)
everyday low pricing (EDLP) (p. 443)
variable pricing (p. 444)
yield management pricing (p. 445)
one-price policy (p. 445)

flexible pricing (p. 445)
contingency pricing (p. 445)
odd pricing (p. 445)
leader pricing (p. 446)
multiple-unit pricing (p. 446)
bundled pricing (p. 446)
unbundled pricing (p. 446)
price lining (p. 447)
markdown (p. 447)
additional markup (p. 447)
markdown percentage (p. 448)
off-retail markdown percentage (p. 448)
additional markup percentage (p. 448)
addition to retail percentage (p. 448)

Questions for Discussion

1. Why is it important for retailers to understand the concept of price elasticity even if they are unable to compute it?
2. Comment on each of the following from the perspective of a large retailer as well as from the perspective of a smaller, single-outlet retailer.
   a. discount orientation
   b. at-the-market orientation
   c. upscale orientation
3. Which target markets of consumers are more likely to be price sensitive?
4. Distinguish between market skimming and market penetration, and provide examples of each.
5. A beauty supply retailer wants to receive a 35 percent markup (at retail) for all merchandise. If a magnifying mirror retails for $11, what is the maximum cost that the retailer would be willing to pay for a magnifying mirror?
6. A sandwich-and-snack store had a revenue of $66,798 in a week, of which 60 percent was profit. In that week, the retailer sold 9,822 individual items. What is the profit per unit?
7. A gift store charges $25.00 for a ceramic figurine; its cost is $14.00. What is the markup percentage (at cost and at retail)?

8. A firm has planned operating expenses of $200,000, a profit goal of $130,000, and planned reductions of $35,000, and it expects sales of $700,000. Compute the initial markup percentage.
9. At the end of the year, the retailer in Question 8 determines that actual operating expenses are $160,000, actual profit is $120,000, and actual sales are $650,000. What is the maintained markup percentage? Explain the difference in your answers to Questions 8 and 9.
10. What are the pros and cons of everyday low pricing to a retailer? To a manufacturer?
11. Under what circumstances do you think unbundled pricing is a good idea? A poor idea? Why?
12. A retailer buys items for $65. At an original retail price of $89, it expects to sell 1,000 units.
   a. If the price is marked down to $79, how many units must the retailer sell to earn the same total gross profit it would attain with an $89 price?
   a. If the price is marked up to $99, how many units must the retailer sell to earn the same total gross profit it would attain with an $89 price?

Web-Based Exercise

Before China's economic slowdown, some of the upmarket brands were reporting that up to 35 percent of their global sales came from China. Look up the article titled "Luxury Brands Must Redefine the Way They Do Business" at *The Guardian*'s Web site. What steps are the global retailers taking, and are they doing it right?

PART 6 Short Cases

Case 1: Buyer of Sports Equipment*

Recently, a sporting-goods retail chain posted a job listing for the position of Buyer of Sports Equipment. The applicant chosen would work in Pittsburgh. Following is the position description placed at the National Retail Federation Job Board.

Pittsburgh has transformed itself into one of the best "made over towns," evolving from steel to science, and was recently declared the "#1 Most Livable City" for the second time in the last three years! With a national average of 40 percent lower cost of living, Pittsburgh is also sixth in the United States for job growth. There are about 3,200 high-tech companies; and 36 colleges and universities surround the area. With its low crime rate, arts and leisure, and sports teams, Pittsburgh appeals to audiences of all ages.

This full-line sporting-goods retailer offers a broad assortment of branded sporting-goods equipment, apparel, and footwear in a specialty store environment. The firm also has a golf specialty retailer, E-commerce Web sites, and catalog operations. At this company, the buyer owns a product category; this includes creating assortments, developing strategies and ads, and maintaining an omnichannel experience within all channels of the firm's businesses for its customers. The person maximizes vendor relationships.

These are the major job duties and responsibilities: Achieve sales, profit, and inventory turnover plans by creating, driving, and ensuring the execution of merchandising strategies. Build a visual merchandising strategy and E-commerce experience that will support the sales, margin, and turnover objectives. Devise, market, and review consumer trends. Assortment creation includes selecting and buying merchandise by type, and creating and managing merchandise assortments by category, with existing and new brands that align with quality, source, timing, delivery, mix, and promotions. Management of assortments includes the continual evaluation of pricing, demand, forecasting, and product flow. Analyze economic, financial, market, competitive/noncompetitive, and industry data to assess current business strategies or identify future business opportunities. Assume the customer's perspective and ensure merchandising strategies will meet customer needs (current and future). Ensure execution of regional marketing and pricing strategies to showcase the current assortment to drive customer traffic and increase sales. Leverage relationships with vendors and the product development team to deliver exclusive products to all channels of the business.

Also included in the manager's duties will be: Work closely with product team members to ensure feedback, performance management, and career development conversations. Interview candidates and make hiring decisions. Build and manage relationships with vendors and cross-functional teams. Leverage vendor relationships to gain knowledge and data as pertains to the product category. Utilize established relationships in product selection and pricing negotiations. Shop at the firm's national and global store branches, as well as other comparative retail stores, to identify new trends and opportunities, evaluate the merchandise mix, evaluate competition, and translate findings into executable product plans.

These are the minimum job requirements: Education—Bachelor's degree in marketing, merchandising, or other business-related field. Experience—Seven to 10 years, with a background in a leadership/management role. Knowledge, Skills, and Abilities—Excellent written and verbal communication skills; customer-service oriented; strong interpersonal and client consultation skills; self-motivated and results oriented; strong presentation skills; supervisory and leadership capabilities; problem solving and troubleshooting capabilities and execution skills; project management knowledge; ability to drive projects and manage project teams, and to work well in a team environment; in-depth analytical skills, strong detail orientation, and superior organizational abilities; process and procedure oriented; and willingness to travel.

Questions

1. Present a merchandising philosophy for this sporting-goods retailer.
2. Why do you think this retailer would prefer an inside buying organization, rather than an outside one?
3. If this buyer position is responsible for tennis equipment, what decisions would he or she have to make?
4. As described in the case, would a buyer of sporting goods for this retailer be a category manager?

Case 2: Adapting to the Internet of Things (IoT)*

In an era where *customization* and *personalization* are the operative words in retailing, the challenge to build closer connections with shoppers has never been greater. Ubiquitous Internet connectivity is driving radical transformation of a retail world whose epicenter of consumer intelligence, long entrenched in the front end and back office, has given rise to a new ecosystem of data derived from interconnected devices, many of which enable consumers to shop for just about anything without ever entering a store.

Not only is it now possible for people to shop for groceries without leaving their kitchens; but their refrigerators have the ability to make up the shopping lists. "We live in a hyperconnected world, where every device, from the phone to the fridge, is becoming connected to the Internet," says Betty DeVita, of MasterCard Labs, a partner with Samsung in developing its Family Hub refrigerator. This "smart fridge" is equipped with the Groceries by MasterCard app, which "shows a major enhancement to the Smart Home environment by bringing consumers a simple and convenient way to shop for groceries directly from their kitchen."

The Family Hub may be a game-changer for traditional grocery retailers, such as Wakefern Foods, which has been at the forefront with its popular online delivery and click-and-collect

*Based on material in National Retail Federation, "Job Board," August 29, 2016, http://jobs.nrf.com. Reprinted by permission.

*Based on material in Jim Dudlicek and Meg Major, "Fridge's Dare," *Progressive Grocer,* February 2016, pp. 24–33. Reprinted by permission.

services. The supermarket cooperative—whose members operate 250 ShopRite supermarkets in New Jersey, New York, Pennsylvania, Connecticut, Delaware, and Maryland—has teamed up with MasterCard to integrate its online grocery shopping service, ShopRite from Home, with Groceries by MasterCard, which is preloaded in new Samsung Family Hub refrigerators and allows consumers to order directly from the fridge using a built-in screen.

ShopRite customers can use the appliance's integrated tablet to order groceries from their own kitchens by scheduling in-store pickups or at-home delivery with a few taps on the Family Hub refrigerator. Using the Groceries app's secure, easy-to-navigate interface, customers also have the ability to add products to a ShopRite shopping basket and pay online. Items are added to a cart and paid for in a simple, single checkout experience that accepts any U.S.-issued credit and debit cards. Orders are delivered directly by the merchants and aren't dependent on a third-party or concierge service, making shopping more efficient.

DeVita notes that features such as cameras within the fridge and a companion mobile app will allow consumers to view contents and shop on the go using the device most convenient to them, with the highest level of security. "Multiple members of the family can add to the shopping list and build a single cart over the week. Final approval and submission of the cart is secured through a four-digit PIN to allow more control and avoid ordering duplicate items. Virtual-aisle shopping technology allows consumers to search for their favorite brands across multiple grocers. Since the app directly connects grocers, consumers are able to access deals and coupons, and there is no markup on delivery charges."

The family cart is intelligent and learns from shopping habits, and MasterCard is continuing to work with partners to create simple and convenient experiences. "Consumers appreciate the convenience, and merchants value having another way to engage with customers and build their brands," DeVita observes.

Groceries by MasterCard was developed in a partnership between MasterCard Labs and Samsung. At the 2016 refrigerator launch, consumers were able to shop and select their needed items and favorite brands from leading online grocer and key integration partner FreshDirect, as well as from ShopRite. Groceries by MasterCard is creating a new channel of consumer engagement for fellow online launch partners FreshDirect and MyWebGrocer, whose respective executives are equally pumped about the prospects for seamless consumer convenience.

Questions

1. As a retail buyer, what criteria would you use in deciding whether your chain should carry the new Samsung Family Hub refrigerator?
2. What kind of support would you require from Samsung with regard to training you (as the buyer) and the on-floor sales personnel?
3. Discuss the logistics of the new refrigerator from the perspective of the retailer.
4. What retail price would you set for the new refrigerator? How would you come up with this price?

Case 3: High Marks by Suppliers and Wholesalers for Convenience Stores*

On a broad scale, 2015 was an interesting year for the United States and, with the presidential election, 2016 promised to be every bit as exciting. The same can be said about the convenience store industry. Based on the results of an outlook survey conducted in early November 2015 by the National Association for Business Economics, the average forecast for growth in 2016 was 2.6 percent, down slightly from 2.7 percent in its previous survey conducted in September 2015.

The panel of 49 business economists expected the jobs market to continue strengthening in 2016, with unemployment dropping to 4.7 percent by the end of 2016, down from 5 percent in December 2015. The experts lowered their earlier forecasts on a variety of measures of economic health, including housing starts and industrial production. Looking further down the road, two-thirds of the business economists surveyed expect potential economic growth of between 2 percent and 2.5 percent over the next 5 years.

When it comes to convenience and fuel retailing, at least one side of the equation entered 2016 with an upbeat attitude. As part of the Industry Forecast Study, *Convenience Store News* conducted its first Supplier Forecast Study to complement the Retailer Forecast Study. The majority of convenience-store suppliers and wholesalers that participated had a favorable outlook when it came to the 2016 economic picture.

Notably, 41.7 percent had a "very positive" view of the overall conditions of the U.S. economy, 28.6 percent had a "positive" view, and 10.4 percent had a "slightly positive" view. On the other hand, at the beginning of that year, only a combined 12.8 percent viewed the U.S. economy of 2016 negatively.

When asked about their particular product categories, the supply side of convenience retailing did hedge bets a little. Although overwhelmingly positive, those indicating they were very positive about their particular product category dipped to 35.5 percent, followed by 28.7 percent who were positive and 16.4 percent who were slightly positive. No respondents from either the supplier or wholesaler communities said they were very negative on their product category, and only 6.5 percent said they were slightly negative.

Stacking up the convenience channel against the other retail channels they serve, c-store suppliers and wholesalers gave convenience high marks for performance. A whopping 86.7 percent of respondents placed convenience in the positive column when asked to rate conditions in the retail channels where they work. This rating placed convenience squarely in front of all competing channels, with drugstores coming in second at a 65.4-percent positive rating. See Table 1.

The Supplier Forecast Study also asked participants to weigh in on what the key factors for retailers' success in 2016 would be. New product development, an uptick in consumer spending, and growth in store count were the top factors cited. The study also asked c-store suppliers and wholesalers to list their top concerns for 2016. Although some mentioned fad brands and private-label brands, the issues weighing most

*Material based on "A Full Stock of Optimism," *Convenience Store News,* January 2016, pp. 48–50. Reprinted by permission. Convenience Store News © 2016 (www.csnews.com)

TABLE 1 Suppliers' Rating of Retail Channels

Rate conditions in each of the following retail channels your company works with:

	Positive	Neutral	Negative
Convenience	86.7%	13.3%	0.0%
Drug	65.4%	23.1%	11.5%
Mass merchandise	57.1%	32.1%	10.8%
Grocery	50.0%	30.8%	19.2%

Source: "Convenience Store News Supplier Forecast Study", 2016. Reprinted by permission. Convenience Store News © 2016 (www.csnews.com)

widely on their minds were government regulation, political events, consumer confidence, gas prices, and rising costs. Here were their top reasons for optimism: innovation and new products, new or remodeled store locations, a strong business pipeline, growth across small-format channels, and category upticks.

Questions

1. What are your overall conclusions about the information presented in this case?
2. Do the data highlighted in the case affect both suppliers and retailers? Explain your answer.
3. Comment on the results shown in Table 1.
4. What criteria should suppliers use in rating the retailers with which they do business? Why?

Case 4: Data-Driven Pricing*

Retailers are under pressure to improve profitability and gain a greater percentage of spending, so it's not surprising that more firms realize the value of price optimization to increase same-store sales and improve their competitive position. But how can retailers best optimize pricing? Experts advise them to move away from a "gut-feel" approach to a data-driven pricing strategy. That should lead to the right offer, at the right location, at the right price, with the right range of products to gain a greater share of shoppers' wallets.

Karen Dutch of Revionics (a provider of price optimization solutions), comments, "Pricing needs to be strategically driven and technology-enabled. Demand-based optimization provides a granular view of shopper and competitor behavior, blended with business and financial strategy and rules, enabling retailers to surgically execute competitive positions while maximizing profit opportunities."

One retailer that has validated its approach to price optimization is Roundy's Supermarkets, the $4 billion operator of 150 stores in Wisconsin and Illinois under four banners: Mariano's, Metro Market, Copps, and Pick 'n Save. "We're looking to increase sales and margins, while improving price perception," states Laura Roehl, vice-president of pricing. "Those goals can be at odds with each other, particularly in

the short term. This is where we saw the need for a data-driven tool. We also wanted to improve price integrity and consistency."

Roehl cites five lessons from Roundy's price optimization work with Revionics, which enabled its stores "to thrive in hypercompetitive markets":

▸ For a smooth transition, pre-work and setup are crucial prior to implementation.
▸ A review suggests details using knowledge (promotional plans, etc.) to complement pricing strategy.
▸ Fine-tune the tool after initial installation for better results.
▸ Document and measure results for management review.
▸ Price optimization provides visibility to elasticity in a way that was previously unavailable.

"Roundy's effectively uses the solution with a customer-focused approach," notes consultant Mark Kelso, of Price Revolution, who spoke with Roehl at FMI Connect. "Their process has resulted not only in improvements in unit movement, sales, and gross margin, but has also reduced the amount of time spent on developing price recommendations."

SAS lists several other retailers that have benefited from deploying a price optimization strategy:

▸ A midsize North American grocer integrates regular price and promotional price activity, letting the firm take into account promotional activity across a timeline to achieve overall pricing goals.
▸ A European grocer uses price optimization as part of its category review process. It was able to identify a combination of price increases and price decreases to meet category financial objectives.
▸ A North American regional grocer used localized segmentation and promotion optimization to develop new circulars customized to neighborhood markets, leading to an increased revenue of 3 to 5 percent.

Howard Langer, of Dunnhumby, advocates customer-centric pricing because consumers respond to prices differently. Thus, he notes that retailers need to understand which customers buy which products, and then set pricing strategies from there. "Instead, most retailers evaluate what competitors are doing with pricing and product costs. This compare-and-contrast strategy will no longer work, as it no longer resonates with the consumer—who expect personalized experiences. Until

---

*Based on material in John Karolefski , "Deploying a Data-Driven Pricing Strategy," *Progressive Grocer 2016 Category Management Handbook,* September 2015, pp. 156–160. Reprinted by permission.

grocery retailers customize pricing based on their customers' behavior and shopping habits, they'll continue to fail to meet the consumers' needs."

According to NCR's Todd Michaud, the biggest mistake a retailer can make is adopting price management and optimization systems without a price strategy known, understood, and thought through before, during, and after implementation. He says pricing systems are typically underused by firms, with most using only a fraction of available technology, due to a "lack of comprehensive pricing strategies." This can include competitive and loyalty-pricing strategies, private label positioning, cannibalization policies, zone nuances, ending-numbers price thresholds for changes, and category-specific strategies.

Questions

1. What retailer activities are involved with a price optimization strategy?
2. Why don't more retailers use price optimization strategies?
3. How does price optimization relate to the concept of category management?
4. How could a small retailer engage in a price optimization strategy?

PART 6 Comprehensive Case

Knocking Off the Knockoffs?*

Introduction

As E-commerce numbers grow, counterfeiters are heading online. Producers of knockoff merchandise are busy all year long, but the holiday season of 2015 may have set records for the sheer volume of bogus goods that entered the marketplace, with E-commerce earning the dubious distinction of leading the way.

"The growth of counterfeit merchandise available can be directly attributed to the growth of online sales," says Andrew Brodsky, commercial director of NetNames, a firm specializing in online brand protection and anticounterfeiting services.

"It's harder for the counterfeiters to get their products into the supply chain headed for bricks-and-mortar stores, but the Internet makes it possible for counterfeiters to flourish, as they're hiding behind the anonymity of a Web site or online marketplace."

"Sophisticated" Web Sites

As retailers ramped up for the holiday selling season, so did the counterfeiters targeting shoppers who were searching for tremendous deals, suggests Charlie Abrahams, senior vice-president at MarkMonitor, another firm engaged in enterprise brand protection.

"I think [consumers] are more on the lookout for bargains and there is no question that searching for 'cheap brand X' or 'sale brand X' plays right into the counterfeiters' hands, who regularly purchase domain names and paid search ads with that sort of nomenclature," Abrahams says. "Talking to the luxury brands in particular, they are unlikely to take properties such as 'cheap brand *x*.'"

MarkMonitor, in conjunction with research firm Opinium, produces an annual survey of consumer online shopping habits. Its most recent survey found that nearly one-quarter (24 percent) of consumers have bought a product online that turned out to be fake.

According to the *2015 MarkMonitor Online Barometer: Global Consumer Shopping Habits Survey,* "Younger consumers are more likely to have bought counterfeit goods or said they

would be willing to do so in the future." Therefore, the "prevalence of buying counterfeit items online looks set to increase for the foreseeable future due to those younger consumers." Nearly 40 percent of the survey respondents aged 18 to 34 had previously purchased counterfeit items and 42 percent said that they would purchase counterfeit items again.

The survey further found that as consumers' online shopping increases during the holiday season—stepping up by about 15 percent, on average—counterfeiters display "a high level of sophistication in developing Web sites," so "it can be very difficult to recognize a genuine site over one selling a counterfeit one." The result is that in the E-commerce channel, "which has again broken records" for holiday season selling, "we would expect the level of counterfeit sales online to have matched that," Abrahams says. Between Black Friday and Christmas Eve, 2015, retail sales (excluding automobiles and gasoline) rose 7.9 percent, while E-commerce sales increased 20 percent compared to the prior year, according to MasterCard Advisors' research data.

In addition to the various types of luxury-branded apparel and accessories—typically among the most counterfeited goods that are sold in the Web and through the mobile marketplace—NetNames found that IO Hawk hoverboards and Stars Wars merchandise, including an app-enabled BB-8 and the Jedi Master Lightsaber, were among the most popular fakes during the 2015 holiday season. This was discouraging to retailers selling authentic merchandise. See Table 1.

"Our general rule of thumb is that the most popular items are the ones that are the most likely to be counterfeited," says Brodsky. "Some [genuine] products are faked enough to even have YouTube videos about them explaining how to tell if [the consumers] have gotten a fake or the real thing."

The situation can sometimes be dire for sellers of authentic merchandise. For example, when NetNames looked into the hoverboards, says Brodsky, "we found that less than one percent of all of the online marketplace listings which made reference to the 10 Hawk hoverboard brand name actually represented genuine products."

"A Growth Industry"

There is no end to what can be counterfeited, says Marcella Ballard, a former prosecutor and intellectual property partner at the

*Based on Material in David P. Schulz, "Following The Sales," STORES Magazine, February 2016, pp. 53–56. Reprinted by permission. Copyright 2016. STORES Magazine.

TABLE 1 Searches for Various IO Hawk-Related Product Types on Select Major Marketplace Sites (Official IO Hawk listed at $1,799.99 on the IO Hawk Web site)

Site	Search Term	Product	Category	Approx. # of Listings	Price Range
DHgate.com	(B2B)	IO Hawk	All	1,251	$162–$1,620
Alibaba.com	(B2B)	IO Hawk	All	11,524	$ 50–$ 350
eBay.com	(B2C)	IO Hawk	All	124	$285–$1,159
eBay.co.uk	(B2C)	IO Hawk	All	275	$130–$ 801
eBay.fr	(B2C)	IO Hawk	All	62	$271–$ 761
eBay.de	(B2C)	IO Hawk	All	13	$411–$1,411
Taobao.com	(B2C)	IO Hawk	All	7	$ 8–$ 127

Source: STORES research, conducted December 2015. Reprinted by permission. Copyright 2016. STORES Magazine.

Venable law firm in New York. "Mouthwash, batteries, clothing, pharmaceuticals, brake pads," she says, "every consumer product imaginable is a target of counterfeiters."

To illustrate her point, she refers to a case involving a cigarette-paper manufacturer that makes its products in one facility in France and involves a number of unusual materials, including flax fiber and natural gum arabic. Last summer, her firm successfully executed seizure orders on both the retailers and wholesalers found to be selling counterfeit Zig-Zag paper products.

Aside from such incidents, Ballard agrees with Brodsky and Abrahams that E- and M-commerce [mobile] is where the counterfeiters' attention is really focused today. "It's a growth industry," she says. "Chinese counterfeiters have huge global auction sites such as Alibaba where they can get their products to consumers." According to Brodsky, "An astounding amount of counterfeit and gray-market goods comes from China, which is responsible for approximately 70 percent of worldwide seizures of these goods, with little evidence that this tidal wave is being stemmed." He says that counterfeit goods are likely to be available on E-commerce marketplaces, "either independent sites specifically set up to market fakes or on platforms such as Taobao or AliExpress."

China manufactures goods in so much volume "that it is not surprising that a lot of counterfeit merchandise originates there," Abraham says. "When it is sold via Web sites or online marketplaces, it will generally be shipped direct to the consumer in individual packages, which is what makes it so hard for governments to track and intercept. "The trend toward online shopping and direct shipping has severely impacted traditional anticounterfeiting physical enforcement programs, which have relied on intercepting large shipments of fake merchandise at points of entry into a country," he comments.

The Notorious Markets List

One anticounterfeiting program is the Notorious Markets List (www.stopfakes.gov/article?id=Notorious-Market-Lists), which contains the names of businesses where the U.S. government has determined that much counterfeit merchandise selling and copyright infringement occurs. Alibaba Group (which is the operator of a number of global Web sites including Aliexpress.com, Taobao.com, and Tmall.com, which are among China's largest E-commerce sites) narrowly escaped being relisted on the Notorious Markets List released in December 2015 by the Office of the U.S. Trade Representative (USTR).

The U.S. government sent a strong warning to Alibaba; what it said was, clean up your sites, show us the results, and

do it soon," Juanita Duggan, president and chief executive of the American Apparel and Footwear Association, said when the 2016 list was released. "The USTR told Alibaba to make serious reforms and get rid of the rampant counterfeit problem on its sites; and the American Apparel & Footwear Association (AAFA) agrees." The USTR criticized Alibaba's enforcement system, saying it is "too slow, difficult to use, and lacks transparency." The AAFA advocated Alibaba's inclusion on the Notorious Markets list, noting that its apparel and shoe manufacturing members "face enormous difficulty working with Taobao in solving the problem of counterfeits," said Duggan. "Meanwhile, illegal merchandise continues to proliferate."

Taobao was removed from the Notorious Markets list in December 2012, with the USTR saying then that Taobao "worked with rights holders to significantly decrease the list of infringing products for sale at its Web site, and committed to continue to streamline its complaint procedures to further reduce listings of counterfeit products." Alibaba spent a reported $460,000 on lobbying to have Taobao removed from list.

In response to the most recent criticism from the USTR, Alibaba hired a former U.S. Justice Department prosecutor and experienced anticounterfeiting executive who had previously worked with Pfizer and Apple on fake and pirated goods. At the time of Matthew Bassiur's hiring, the Alibaba executive chairman and co-founder Jack Ma said in a statement, "We will continue to be relentless in our long-term commitment to protect both consumers and intellectual property rights owners." Although Alibaba Group is based in China, it is publicly traded with shares listed on the New York Stock Exchange.

Alibaba's anticounterfeiting efforts notwithstanding, in early 2016, a court in Beijing allowed Louis Vuitton to proceed with a lawsuit against three individuals alleged to have offered counterfeit merchandise for sale on Taobao. That the ruling was in China may herald a new era in prosecuting counterfeiting cases.

The U.S. Government's STOPfakes.gov Program**

According to the U.S. government's STOPfakes Web site (www.stopfakes.gov), "STOPfakes.gov was launched to serve as a one-stop shop for U.S. government tools and resources on intellectual property rights (IPR). The federal agencies behind STOPfakes.gov have developed a number of resources to

---

**The material in this section is from the Stopfakes.gov Web site operated by several U.S. government agencies. It is NOT from *STORES* magazine.

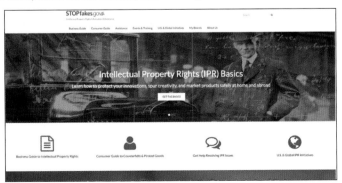

FIGURE 1

Intellectual property theft has an adverse impact on the innovation and commercialization of new products, and on overall economic success. Law-abiding retailers and other supply chain members are especially at a distinct disadvantage from fakes and counterfeit merchandise from unscrupulous foreign retailers and suppliers.

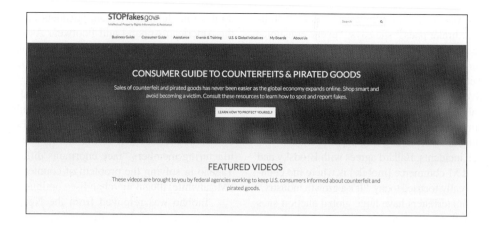

FIGURE 2

In the consumer guide section of the STOPfakes.gov Web site, there are ten tips for consumers to protect themselves from counterfeiting and piracy. Go to this site (http://goo.gl/NdHdPq), abbreviated for ease of use, to see all of the tips.

educate and assist businesses, particularly small and medium-sized enterprises (SMEs), as well as consumers, government officials, and the general public."

As shown in Figures 1 and 2, resources are available in five main categories:

► *Business Guide to IPR:* STOPfakes is dedicated to helping companies protect their innovations and safely market products at home and overseas. Here are guidance and resources to help understand how to register your firm and protect it from counterfeiting and piracy.

► *Consumer Guide to Counterfeits & Pirated Goods:* Sales of counterfeit and pirated goods have never been easier as the global economy expands online. Shop smarter and do not become a victim. Consult the resources to learn how to spot and report fakes.

► *Assistance: Need Help with an IPR Issue?:* Several U.S. agencies are charged with protecting intellectual property rights. Here are key Web sites, phone numbers, and E-mail addresses of offices ready to help answer questions.

► *Events and Training:* Online events and training are noted here that cover a range of topics, from commercializing innovations to strategies for protecting intellectual property rights when exporting to foreign markets.

► *U.S. & Global IPR Initiatives:--* The U.S. and partner governments, private-sector groups, and international organizations have developed tools and resources to help businesses protect intellectual property globally.

Questions

1. Present a five-item ethics code that a retailer could impose on its suppliers with regard to fake and counterfeit merchandise.
2. As the buyer for a retail chain, what would you do if you found out that one of your long-time suppliers had been passing on counterfeit goods as authentic? Why?
3. Visit the www.stopfakes.gov Web site and click on the business guide tab. Comment on what you learn from this guide.
4. Visit the www.stopfakes.gov Web site and click on the consumer guide tab. Comment on what you learn from this guide.
5. Would you match the online price of a competitor that offered a deep discount on products you were carrying if you were not sure that the competitor's products were authentic? Explain your answer.
6. As discussed in Chapter 17, what are gray-market goods? How do they differ from counterfeit merchandise?
7. Do you think that it is okay for a retailer to purchase and resell gray market goods? Explain your answer.

Part 7

Communicating with the Customer

Source: nasirkhan/Shutterstock. Reprinted by permission.

In Part Seven, the elements involved in how a retailer communicates with its customers are discussed. First, we look at the role of a retail image and how it is developed and sustained. Various aspects of a promotional strategy are then detailed.

Chapter 18 discusses the importance of communications for a retailer. We review the significance of image in the communications effort and the components of a retailer's image. The creation of an image depends heavily on a retailer's atmosphere—which is comprised of all its physical characteristics, such as the store exterior, the general interior, layouts, and displays. This applies to both store and nonstore retailers. Ways of encouraging customers to spend more time shopping and the value of community relations are also described.

Chapter 19 focuses on the promotional strategy, specifically how a retailer can inform, persuade, and remind the target market about its strategic mix. In the first part of the chapter, we deal with the four basic types of retail promotion: advertising, public relations, personal selling, and sales promotion. The second part describes the steps in a promotional strategy: objectives, budget, mix of forms, implementation of mix, and review and revision of the plan.

18 Establishing and Maintaining a Retail Image

Chapter Objectives

1. To show the importance of communicating with customers and to examine the concept of retail image

2. To describe how a retail store image is related to the atmosphere it creates via its exterior, general interior, layout, and displays, and to look at the special case of nonstore atmospherics

3. To discuss ways of encouraging customers to spend more time shopping

4. To consider the impact of community relations on a retailer's image

A retailer must have a strong communications strategy to properly position itself in customers' minds—and to nurture their shopping behavior. As soon as customers are attracted, the retailer must strive to create a proper shopping mood for them.

Customer expectations keep rising, especially when it comes to in-store shopping. A comfortable retail shopping environment that more than satisfied customers several years ago is now expected. Today's on-demand shoppers want to create their own unique shopping experiences, according to a *Stores'* story on TimeTrade's "Annual State of Retail Survey," which gathered responses from 5,000 consumers and 100 senior retail executives.

That study suggests that there's a lot of room for improving the in-store customer experience. Only 27 percent of consumers feel big-name retailers try to provide VIP-like service; when shopping in-store, consumers most highly value "prompt service" (54 percent), "personalized experience" (30 percent), and "smart recommendations" (30 percent). Lack of prompt assistance drives the majority of consumers (85 percent) to leave a dressing room—and the store—and abandon their intended purchases. And 59 percent of respondents would like store associates to know the items in their online shopping carts, yet only 24 percent of retailers have that ability.[1]

Source: Oleksiy Mark/Scanrail1/ Shutterstock. Reprinted by permission.

Overview

A retailer needs a superior communications strategy to properly position itself in customers' minds, as well as to nurture their shopping behavior. When customers have been attracted, the retailer must strive to create an engaging shopping experience for them. Various physical and symbolic cues can be used to do this. See Figure 18-1. It is imperative to maximize the total retail experience for shoppers.

There are many trade associations in the retail image arena. Visit a few online (http://vmsd.com/associations).

For example, researchers have found that shoppers' experiences at online retailer Web sites drive their expectations of the shopping experience in stores. It is important for retailers to maintain "digital parity" in stores by ensuring that the stores are well stocked; providing location-enabled, easy-to-use, in-store technology to locate and learn about products; and helping customers to seamlessly view in-store and online inventory to meet their shopping goals. Retailers need to leverage the tangible strengths of physical stores to create interactive and inspired social experiences through theatrical product displays, as well as professional assistance by knowledgeable and friendly store associates to maximize the total retail experience for shoppers.[2]

This chapter describes how to establish and maintain an image. Retail atmosphere, storefronts, store layouts, and displays are examined. We also explore the challenge of how to encourage people to spend more time shopping and the role of community relations. Chapter 19 focuses on the common promotional tools available to retailers: advertising, public relations, personal selling, and sales promotion.

Although our discussion looks more at store retailers, the basic principles apply to nonstore retailers as well. For a mail-order firm, the catalog cover is its storefront, and the interior layouts and displays are the pages devoted to product categories and the individual items within them. For a Web retailer, the home page is its storefront, and interior layouts and displays are represented by links within the site.

THE SIGNIFICANCE OF RETAIL IMAGE

Design: Retail (www.designretailonline.com) deals with retail image topics from a store design perspective.

Image refers to how a retailer is perceived by customers and others, and *positioning* refers to how a firm devises its strategy so as to project an image relative to its retail category and its competitors—and to elicit a positive consumer response. To succeed, a retailer must communicate a distinctive, clear, and consistent image. Once its image is established in consumers' minds, a retailer is placed in a niche relative to competitors. For global retailers, it can be challenging to convey a consistent image worldwide, given the different backgrounds of consumers.

Today's extensive use of social media by all parties—including customers, the general public, the media, suppliers, brands, and retailers themselves—must be thoroughly understood by retailers and proper strategies proactively enacted. No firm, of any size or type, is immune from the impact of social media content—pro and con—on its image. **Social media** encompass online

FIGURE 18-1

Positioning and Retail Image

Through its colorful displays and quality serapes, this Mexican retailer positions itself as an inviting and warm place for shoppers to visit and browse. The look is quite eye-catching.

Source: holbox/Shutterstock. Reprinted by permission.

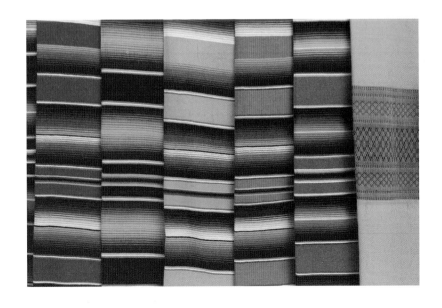

technology tools that allow vast numbers of people to easily communicate with one another via the Web and mobile devices. With social media, messages, audio, video, photos, podcasts, and other multimedia communications are possible. Social media are discussed further in Chapter 19.

Components of a Retail Image

Many factors contribute to a retailer's image; it is the totality of them that forms an overall image. See Figure 18-2. We studied these factors in earlier chapters: target market, retail positioning, customer service, store location, merchandise attributes, and pricing. Our focus in this chapter and Chapter 19 is attributes of physical facilities, shopping experiences, community service, advertising, public relations, personal selling, and sales promotion.

TECHNOLOGY IN RETAILING	3D Afoot

It's pretty clear that three-dimensional (3D) printing has reached an inflection point and is poised to revolutionize many businesses, one of which is the shoe business. Adidas recently unveiled a 3D-printed prototype shoe with a sole composed of latticed layers. This 3D shoe can accurately replicate the individual shapes of wearers' feet. It takes into account specific pressure points and requirements to create more supportive running shoes. Although still in the prototype stage, Adidas hopes foot-scanning technology will allow consumers to buy running shoes that are highly customized and produced in-store. Think about that—retailers will be able to customize an item and manufacture it in the store, on the spot. When talk turns to reinvention of the store, this technology needs to be on the short list.

List three other goods that apply use in-store manufacturing of customized goods using 3D scanning and printing technology.

Sources: Based on material in Susan Reda, "3D Afoot," *STORES Magazine*, March 2016, https://nrf.com/news/stores-trends-march-2016. Reprinted by permission. Copyright 2016. STORES Magazine.

The Dynamics of Creating and Maintaining a Retail Image

Creating and maintaining a retail image is a complex, multistep, ongoing process. It encompasses far more than store "atmosphere," which is discussed shortly. Furthermore, with so many people having little time for shopping and others having less interest in it, more retailers understand that they may have to *entertain* shoppers to draw their business. Here are three examples.

FIGURE 18-2

The Elements of a Retail Image

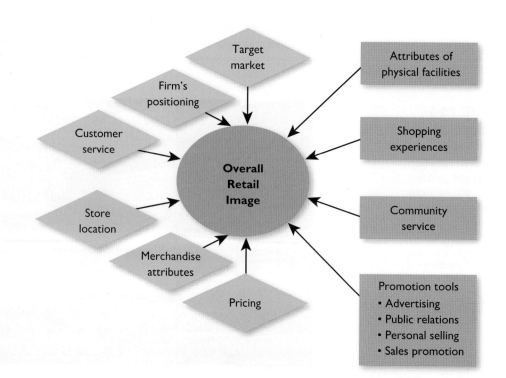

As Bass Pro Shops' image has evolved, so has its Web site (www.basspro.com).

Consider the 145,000-square-foot Bass Pro Shops Outdoor World store in Altoona, Iowa, that includes entertainment features such as archery ranges, miniature shooting ranges, aquariums, and a 3,500-square-foot area with themed artifacts, antiques, pictures, and memorabilia of hunting, fishing, camping, and outdoor recreation. It also has a 15,000-square-foot bowling area—"Uncle Buck's Fishbowl and Grill"—with 12 10-pin lanes and underwater scenery of sharks, stingrays, and sea turtles that glow in the dark when guests bowl "under the ocean." A separate upscale "Black Widow Billiards Parlor" features a fireplace with a screen displaying a black widow spider spinning its web. All Pro Bass shops strive to be destination stores with a museum, art gallery, antique store, aquarium, education center, and conservation and entertainment center. The stores engage local communities and customers with taxidermy and wildlife tours, community and Boys Scout events, and seminars and workshops on safely experiencing outdoor adventures.[3]

Jungle Jim's International Market, with stores in Ohio (Fairfield and Cincinnati), has grown from a simple roadside stand to two stores, with more than 200,000-square-feet for each store. These stores are food amusement parks and tourist destinations, with over 150,000 different items from over 75 countries around the globe; each store employs an average of 350 employees. Jungle Jim's has one of the largest wine collections in the United States, live seafood tanks, an in-store cooking school, a monorail in its huge parking lot, a gated wildlife preserve with fiberglass animals, and a 1,000-person Oscar Event Center. Scattered around the stores are telephone poles disguised as giraffes that enable customers to speak to a customer service agent. Approximately 80,000 shoppers, known as "Foodies," visit the stores each week to interact with the animatronic robots that dispense or move products or sing and tell stories about the food in their sections.[4]

Nordstrom's new stores have open floor plans with no segregation between departments, designers, or price points, allowing customers to browse seamlessly from one merchandise category to another. These stores are wired for a full digital experience. In-store customers will be able to use a smartphone app to send apparel to a fitting room without having to search through racks. Nordstrom is testing smart fitting-room mirrors with a virtual dressing feature—the mirrors show shoppers how they would look in the clothes without physically wearing them. The mirrors can recommend accessories, such as a scarf to match a dress. The fitting rooms provide videos and side-by-side comparisons of the apparel a shopper tries on. Similar to online retailers, the mirrors can collect data on shopper preferences and how they make decisions if customers opt-in to the feature.[5]

Retailers can be classified as occupying the following retail image positions based on their leadership on six dimensions (price, location, store interior, product quality, selection, and service): [6]

- ▸ *Price leaders:* These retailers focus on low prices and are more apt to offer self-service and a functional store environment. At these retailers, in-store shopping does not go much beyond what consumers can experience online. Examples are Walmart and CVS.
- ▸ *Location leaders:* These retailers are situated at convenient locations; they make their merchandise and services available where customers need them most. Often, they do not offer liberal return policies or present innovative products or displays but that does not concern their customer base. Examples are Dollar General and a local grocery store.
- ▸ *Atmospherics leaders:* These retailers offer an outstanding in-store experience. The firms typically do not carry a wide range of product lines, and prices are higher, commensurate with their image. Examples are Tiffany and Abercrombie & Fitch.
- ▸ *Product quality leaders:* These retailers offer unique, high-quality merchandise and attractive, appealing displays. Examples are Whole Foods and Hallmark/Gold Crown.
- ▸ *Selection leaders:* These retailers offer good value on the wide range of items they sell and are an interesting place to shop. However, they are typically not as exciting as *atmosphere leaders*. They add new items on a regular basis and encourage shoppers to spend more time. They do a good job in coordinating in-store and online shopping experiences. Examples are Kohl's and Bed Bath & Beyond.
- ▸ *Service leaders:* These retailers are conveniently located and offer shoppers good customer service. The sales staff has some product expertise, and information is easy to acquire. This type of retailer does not have a very exciting in-store environment. It is a good place to buy items that are planned in advance. Examples are AutoZone and Lowe's.

Figure 18-3 shows the image presented by a membership (warehouse) store. Retailers in this category are price leaders.

FIGURE 18-3

A Warehouse Store Image

Not only do warehouse stores intentionally present an austere look (so that customers believe these stores do everything possible to cut costs), many also offer a deep assortment in the product lines that they carry to encourage people to be in the stores longer.

Source: Pressmaster/ Shutterstock. Reprinted by permission.

A key goal for chain retailers, franchisors, and global retailers is to maintain a consistent image among all branches and with the Web site. Yet, despite the best planning, a number of factors may vary widely among branch stores and affect the image. They include management and employee performance, consumer profiles, competitors, convenient locations, parking, safety, the ease of finding merchandise, language and cultural diversity among customers in different countries, and the qualities of the surrounding area. Sometimes, retailers with good images receive negative publicity. This must be countered in order for them to maintain their desired standing with the public.

ATMOSPHERE

VMSD design galleries (http://vmsd.com/projects) provides many examples of excellence in retail atmospherics.

A retailer's image depends heavily on its "atmosphere," the psychological feeling a customer gets when visiting that retailer. It is the personality of a store, catalog, vending machine, or Web site. "Retail image" is a much broader and all-encompassing term relative to the communication tools a retailer uses to position itself. For a store-based retailer, **atmosphere (atmospherics)** refers to the store's physical characteristics that project an image and draw customers. For a nonstore-based firm, *atmosphere* refers to the physical characteristics of catalogs, vending machines, Web sites, and so forth. A retailer's sights, sounds, smells, and other physical attributes all contribute to customer perceptions.

A retailer's atmosphere often influences people's shopping enjoyment, as well as their time spent browsing, willingness to converse with personnel, tendency to spend more than originally planned, and likelihood of future patronage. Many people even form impressions of a retailer before entering its facilities (due to the store location, storefront, easy accessibility, and other factors) or just after entering (due to displays, width of aisles, indoor temperature, and other things). They often judge the firm prior to examining merchandise and prices.

When a retailer takes a proactive, integrated atmospherics approach to create a certain "look"—properly displayed products, stimulating shopping behavior, and enhanced physical environment—it engages in **visual merchandising**. This includes such factors as the in-store layout, the type of fixtures, store display windows, and aisle width—as well as how merchandise is visually organized, the types of lighting, in-store signage, the choice of background music, the paint on walls and graphics, the type of flooring, and the use of videos on in-store screens—that encourage the target customer to shop longer. The goal of visual merchandising is to increase the sales per square foot.[7] The best retailers recognize that they should periodically refresh their visual merchandising. See Figure 18-4.

Check out the use of augmented reality (www .marxentlabs.com/ar-video-examples/retail/) in planning atmospherics.

Visit our blog site (www.bermanevansretail) for visual merchandising posts.

A Store-Based Retailing Perspective

Store atmosphere (atmospherics) can be divided into these key elements: exterior, general interior, store layout, and displays. Figure 18-5 contains a detailed breakdown of them.

FIGURE 18-4

Visual Merchandising and Shopping Centers

Not only is visual merchandising important to the individual retailer but it is also important in the shopping centers in which retailers are located. Appealing atmospherics add to the shopping experience. Shown here is a musical fountain in a Hong Kong shopping center.

Source: Cheuk-king Lo/ Pearson Education Ltd. Reprinted by permission.

EXTERIOR A store's exterior has a powerful impact on its image and should be planned accordingly.

A **storefront** is the total physical exterior of the store itself. It includes the marquee, entrances, windows, lighting, and construction materials. With its storefront, a retailer can present a conservative, trendy, upscale, discount, or other image. Consumers who pass through an unfamiliar business district or shopping center often judge a store by its exterior. Besides the storefront itself, atmosphere can be enhanced by trees, fountains, and benches in front of the store. These intensify consumer feelings about shopping and about the store by establishing a relaxed environment. There are various alternatives in planning a basic storefront. Here are a few of them:

 ▸ *Modular structure:* A one-piece rectangle or square that may attach several stores.
 ▸ *Prefabricated (prefab) structure:* A frame built in a factory and assembled at the site.
 ▸ *Prototype store:* Used by franchisors and chains to foster a consistent atmosphere.
 ▸ *Recessed storefront:* Lures people by being recessed from the level of other stores. Customers must walk in a number of feet to examine the storefront.
 ▸ *Unique building design:* A round or pyramid-shaped structure, for example.

A **marquee** is a sign that displays the store's name. It can be painted or a neon light, printed or script, and set alone or mixed with a slogan (trademark) and other information. The marquee should attract attention, as El Corte Ingles' distinctive logo on the front of each of its department stores does. See Figure 18-6. Image is influenced because a marquee can be gaudy and flashy or subdued and subtle. The world's best known marquee is McDonald's golden arches.

FIGURE 18-5

The Elements of Atmosphere

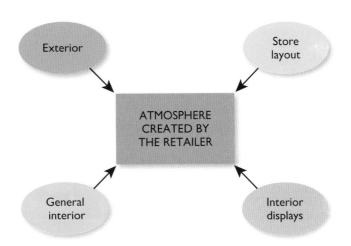

FIGURE 18-6

Using a Storefront and Marquee to Generate a Powerful Retail Image

El Corte Ingles (www .elcorteingles.eu) has a large department store in Barcelona, Spain. Its name is clearly shown near the top of the distinctive store façade, which also benefits from its size and the corner influence of this location.

Source: Jules Selmes/Pearson Education Ltd. Reprinted by permission.

Store entrances require three major decisions. First, the number of entrances is determined. Many small stores have only one entrance. Department stores may have four to eight or more entrances. A store hoping to draw both vehicular and pedestrian traffic may need at least two entrances (one for pedestrians, another near the parking lot). Because front and back entrances serve different purposes, they should be designed separately. A factor that may limit the number of entrances is potential pilferage.

Second, the type of entrance(s) is chosen. The doorway can be revolving; electric, self-opening; regular, push-pull; or climate-controlled. The latter is an open entrance with a curtain of warm or cold air, set at the same temperature as inside the store. Entrance flooring can be cement, tile, or carpeting. Lighting can be traditional or fluorescent, white or colors, and/or flashing or constant. At the bakery depicted in Figure 18-7, the exterior entrance and displays are inviting and designed to reinforce its image for freshness.

Third, walkways are considered. A wide, lavish walkway creates a different atmosphere and mood than does a narrow one. Large window displays may be attractive, but customers would not be pleased if there is insufficient space for a comfortable entry into the store.

Display windows have two main purposes: (1) to identify the store and its offerings and (2) to induce people to enter. By showing a representative merchandise offering, a store can create an overall mood. By showing fashion or seasonal goods, it can show it is contemporary. By showing sale items, a store can lure price-conscious consumers. By showing eye-catching displays that

FIGURE 18-7

An Enticing Entranceway

A pâtisserie is a type of French or Belgian bakery that specializes in pastries and sweets. To draw in customers, this pâtisserie in Châlons en Champagne, France, places beautiful fresh, pink flowers near the entranceway.

Source: Handan Erek/Pearson Education Ltd. Reprinted by permission.

CAREERS IN RETAILING

Joseph Bona's Design Career Path

Joseph Bona recently co-founded MoseleyBona Retail (www .moseleybonaretail.com), a firm "Integrating the Business of Retail with the Art of Design" for the food, beverage, and convenience store sectors of retailing. Previously, Bona was a founding partner of retail design firm GroupRed, which was merged with CBX in 2006. From 2007 to 2015, Bona was president of the retail division of CBX (www.cbx.com), a firm specializing in store design. As head of this division, he was responsible for leading a team of designer professionals who worked with many different retail formats—from convenience stores to apparel and lifestyle-based retailers. At CBX, Bona's mission was to communicate a retailer's image from the store's exterior. Bona's educational background includes an architecture degree from Fullerton College

and advanced classwork at the National Academy of Design. At graduation, he became a retail planner and project manager at Hickory Farms (www.hickoryfarms.com), a specialty food retailer of fruits, nuts, cheeses, and sausages. He later worked for CDI Group (www.cdigroupinc.com), a design consulting and project management company, for more than 20 years.

What characteristics should someone possess to become a good retail designer?

Sources: MoseleyBona Retail, "Joe Bona," www.moseleybonaretail .com/5-east-end (Accessed September 20, 2016); and "Joseph Bona," www.linkedin.com/in/joseph-bona-02890014 (Accessed September 20, 2016).

have little to do with its merchandise offering, a store can attract pedestrians' attention. By showing public service messages (such as a sign for the Special Olympics), the store can indicate its community involvement.

A lot of planning is needed to develop good display windows, which leads many retailers to hire outside specialists. Decisions include the number, size, shape, color, and themes of display windows—and the frequency of changes per year. Retailers in shopping malls may not use display windows for the side of the building facing the parking lot; there are solid building exteriors. These retailers believe that vehicular patrons are not lured by expensive outside windows; they invest in displays for storefronts inside the malls.

Exterior building height can be disguised or nondisguised. With disguised building height, part of a store or shopping center is beneath ground level. Such a building is not as intimidating to people who dislike a large structure. With nondisguised building height, the entire store or center can be seen by pedestrians. An intimate image cannot be fostered with a block-long building, nor can a department store image be linked to a small site.

Few firms succeed with poor visibility. This means storefronts or marquees must be clearly visible to pedestrian and/or vehicular traffic. A store located behind a bus stop has poor visibility for vehicular traffic and pedestrians across the street. Many retailers near highways use billboards to attract attention from those drivers who go by quickly.

In every case, the goal is to have the store or center appear unique and catch the shopper's eye. A distinctive storefront, an elaborate marquee, recessed open-air entrances, decorative windows, and unusual building height and size are one set of features that could attract consumers by their uniqueness. Nonetheless, uniqueness may not be without its shortcomings. An example is the multilevel "shopping-center-in-the-round." Because this center (which often occupies a square city block) is round, parking on each floor level makes the walking distances very short. Yet, a rectangular center may have greater floor space on a lot of the same size, on-floor parking may reduce shopping on other floors, added entrances increase chances for pilferage, many people dislike circular driving, and architectural costs are higher.

As a retailer plans its exterior, the nearby stores and the surrounding area should be studied. Nearby stores present image cues due to their price range, level of service, and so on. The surrounding area reflects the demographics and lifestyles of those who live nearby. An overall area image rubs off on individual retailers because people tend to have a general perception of a shopping center or a business district. An unfavorable atmosphere would exist if vandalism and crime are high, people living near the store are not in the target market, and the area is rundown.

Parking facilities can add to or detract from store atmosphere. Plentiful, free, nearby parking creates a more positive image than scarce, costly, distant parking. Some potential shoppers may never enter a store if they must hunt for available parking. Other customers may rush in and out of a store to finish shopping before parking meters expire. A related potential problem is that of congestion. Atmospherics are diminished if the parking lot, sidewalks, and/or entrances are jammed. Consumers who feel crushed in the crowd spend less time shopping and are in poorer moods than those who feel comfortable.

GENERAL INTERIOR   When customers are in a store, various elements affect their perceptions. Retailers must plan accordingly:

► At Anthropologie, owned by parent company Urban Outfitters, every location has its own visual display team to select and place each element on site to create an unique atmosphere reflecting the "cool home" their customers want. Antique furniture and fixtures, carefully sourced from around the world, enhance the sense of stability and entrenchment that customers seek to replicate in their own homes, thus driving purchases in-store and online.[8]

► Apple has been redesigning some stores to feel more like a town square, replete with trees and a courtyard, a fountain, free Wi-Fi, and seating outside the store for up to 200 people that will always be open and will host acoustic concerts. These stores will be a destination where Millennials want to meet and not just a place to shop. To reflect openness and make customers invited, aisles are wider and feature a single Apple product or a facet of the Apple lifestyle. There is an open space for classes and presentations, an arboretum, and leather benches where customers sit while customer service agents ("geniuses") repair their products.[9]

► Abercrombie & Fitch wants its branded multisensory in-store experience to attract its choosy teen customer base and get them to linger longer and buy more products. The retailer uses research that shows that people's sense of smell triggers emotional responses by introducing its own line of men's fragrance "Fierce," which is sprayed in stores to exude a "cool, good-looking" image that appeals to both male and female teenagers. This is to encourage purchases based on how they feel about the products rather than price. Loud club music is used, based on research that shows teenagers can withstand loud club music longer while older customers avoid it—further accentuating a youthful image. Rapid tempo in club music has also been shown to lead to sensory overload, thus weakening self-control and increasing impulsive purchases.[10]

The general interior elements of store atmosphere were cited in Figure 18-5. They are described next.

Popular flooring types used by retailers include carpet, various types of tile, and wood. Atmosphere, ease of maintenance, and initial cost are important considerations.[11] A plush, thick carpet creates one kind of atmosphere and a concrete floor another. A recent development in retail flooring is new printing techniques that allow images (such as company logos) to be transferred onto ceramic tile. This enables retailers to have the same design on porcelain tile and less-costly vinyl tile. Another development is the use of faux wood floors that resemble wood but have higher durability.

Bright, vibrant colors contribute to a different atmosphere than light pastels or plain white walls. Lighting can be direct or indirect, white or colors, constant or flashing. See Figure 18-8.

Maxey Hayse Design Studios (www.maxeyhayse .com/design_portfolio.html) has designed interiors for a variety of retailers. Several are profiled here.

FIGURE 18-8

The Impact of Lighting and Flooring

At this fashion- forward apparel store, the distinctive lighting and tile flooring both contribute to the upscale store ambience — as do the fixtures and displays.

Source: fiphoto/Shutterstock. Reprinted by permission.

A teen-oriented apparel boutique might use bright colors and vibrant, flashing lights to foster one atmosphere, and a maternity dress shop could use pastel colors and indirect lighting to form a different atmosphere. Sometimes, when colors are changed, customers may be initially uncomfortable until they get used to the new scheme.

Scents and sounds influence the customer's mood. A restaurant can use aromas to increase people's appetites. A cosmetics store can use perfume scents to attract shoppers. A pet store can let animals' natural scents and sounds woo customers. A beauty salon can play soft music or rock, depending on its customers. Slow-tempo music in supermarkets encourages people to move more slowly.

Store fixtures can be planned on the basis of both their utility and aesthetics. Pipes, plumbing, beams, doors, storage rooms, and display racks and tables should be considered part of interior decorating. An upscale store usually dresses up its fixtures and disguises them. A discount store might leave fixtures exposed because this portrays the desired image.

Wall textures enhance or diminish atmospherics. Prestigious stores often use raised wallpaper. Department stores are more apt to use flat wallpaper, while discount stores may have barren walls. Chic stores might have chandeliers, whereas discounters will likely have fluorescent lighting.

The customer's mood is affected by the store's temperature and how it is achieved. Insufficient heat in winter and no air conditioning in summer can shorten a shopping trip. And image is influenced by the use of central air conditioning, unit air conditioning, fans, or open windows.

Wide, uncrowded aisles create a better atmosphere than narrow, crowded ones. People shop longer and spend more if they are not pushed while walking or looking at merchandise. Although in-store kiosks have proven very popular, they sometimes cause overcrowding in tight retail spaces or create customer lines if there are not enough kiosks to handle the number of shoppers.

Dressing facilities can be elaborate, plain, or nonexistent. An upscale store has carpeted, private dressing rooms. An average-quality store has linoleum-floored, semiprivate rooms. A discount store has small stalls or no facilities. For some apparel shoppers, dressing facilities are a factor in store selection.

Multilevel stores must have vertical transportation: elevator, escalator, and/or stairs. Larger stores may have a combination of all three. Traditionally, finer stores relied on operator-run elevators and discount stores on stairs. Today, escalators are quite popular. They provide shoppers with a quiet ride and a panoramic view of the store. Finer stores decorate their escalators with fountains, shrubs, and trees. Stairs remain important for some discount and smaller stores.

Light fixtures, wood or metal beams, doors, rest rooms, dressing rooms, and vertical transportation can cause **dead areas** for the retailer. These are awkward spaces where normal displays cannot be set up. Sometimes, it is not possible for such areas to be deployed profitably or attractively. However, retailers have learned to use dead areas better. Mirrors are attached to exit doors. Vending machines are located near restrooms. Ads appear in dressing rooms. One creative use of a dead area involves the escalator. It lets shoppers view each floor, and sales of impulse items go up when placed at the escalator entrance or exit. Many firms plan escalators so customers must get off at each floor and pass by appealing displays to get to the next level.

Polite, well-groomed, knowledgeable personnel generate a positive atmosphere. Ill-mannered, poorly groomed, uninformed personnel engender a negative one. A store using self-service minimizes its personnel and creates a discount, impersonal image. A store cannot develop an upscale image if it is set up for self-service. Some malls and retailers use robots with facial recognition technology matched with social media feeds to greet shoppers by name as they walk by.[12]

The merchandise a retailer sells influences its image. Top-line items yield one kind of image, and lower-quality items yield another. The mood of the customer is affected accordingly.

Price levels foster a perception of retail image in consumers' minds, and the way prices are displayed is a vital part of atmosphere. Upscale stores have few or no price displays, rely on discrete price tags, and place cash registers in inconspicuous areas behind posts or in employee rooms. Discounters accentuate price displays, show prices in large print, and locate cash registers centrally, with signs pointing to them.

A store with state-of-the-art technology impresses people with its operations efficiency and speed. One with slower, older technology may have impatient shoppers. A store with a modern building (new storefront and marquee) and new fixtures (lights, floors, and walls) fosters a more favorable atmosphere than one with older facilities. Remodeling can enhance store appearance, update facilities, and reallocate space. It often results in strong sales and profit increases after completion.

Hyatt Hotels Promotes Global Social Responsibility

Hyatt Hotels Corporation (www.hyatt.com) has established a global sustainability and community service operation called Hyatt Thrive (www.thrive.hyatt.com/en/thrive.html). This program uses a common platform to promote local efforts among Hyatt's employees, investors, business partners, and guests. Hyatt Thrive is tied to colleague satisfaction, diversity and inclusion, respecting human rights, investing in communities, responding to disasters, and environmental sustainability. To underscore its worldwide commitment to these goals, Hyatt publishes separate reports on

its goals and levels of achievement in the Americas, Europe and Africa, Asia Pacific, and Southwest Asia and the Middle East. Since 2006, Hyatt has reduced energy consumption by 10 percent in the Americas, by 20 percent in Asia Pacific, and by 14 percent in Europe, Africa, and the Middle East. By 2020, it wants to reduce energy consumption by 25 percent.[14]

Explain why many other hotel chains have not adopted similar practices, including transparency in their reaching goals.

Last, but certainly not least, there must be a plan for keeping the store clean. No matter how impressive the exterior and interior, an unkempt store will be perceived poorly. Customers associate clean stores with overall store quality and, in the case of stores selling or serving food, the ability to sell food safely. Unclean and messy facilities can give customers a reason not to buy.[13]

STORE LAYOUT The specifics of store layout are now *sequentially* planned and enacted.

ALLOCATION OF FLOOR SPACE Each store has a total amount of floor space to allot to selling, merchandise, personnel, and customers. Without this allocation, the retailer would have no idea of the space available for displays, signs, rest rooms, and so on:

- *Selling space* is used for displays of merchandise, interactions between salespeople and customers, demonstrations, and so on. Self-service retailers apportion most space to selling.
- *Merchandise space* is used to stock nondisplayed items. At a traditional shoe store, this area takes up a large percentage of total space.
- *Personnel space* is set aside for employees to change clothes and to take lunch and coffee breaks, and for rest rooms. Because retail space is valuable, personnel space is strictly controlled. Yet, a retailer should consider the effect on employee morale.
- *Customer space* contributes to the shopping mood. It can include a lounge, benches and/or chairs, dressing rooms, rest rooms, a restaurant, a nursery, parking, and wide aisles. Discounters are more apt to skimp on these areas.

More firms now use planograms to assign space. A **planogram** is a visual (graphical) representation of the space for selling, merchandise, personnel, and customers—as well as for product categories. It also lays out the retailer's in-store placement. A planogram may be hand-drawn or computer-generated.

Visit Shelf Logic (www.shelflogic.com/planogram-case-studies.html) for examples of planograms to learn more about this tool.

CLASSIFICATION OF STORE OFFERINGS A store's offerings are next classified into product groupings. Many retailers use a combination of groupings and plan store layouts accordingly. Special provisions are needed to minimize shoplifting and pilferage. This means placing vulnerable products away from corners and doors. Four types of groupings (and combinations of them) are most common:

- **Functional product groupings** display merchandise by common end use. A men's clothing store might group shirts, ties, cuff links, and tie pins; shoes, shoe trees, and shoe polish; T-shirts, undershorts, and socks; suits; and sports jackets and slacks.
- **Purchase motivation product groupings** appeal to the consumer's urge to buy products and the amount of time he or she is willing to spend on shopping. A committed customer with time to shop will visit a store's upper floors; a disinterested person with less time will look at displays on the first floor. Look at the first level of a department store. It includes impulse products and other rather quick purchases. The third floor has items encouraging and requiring more thoughtful shopping.
- **Market segment product groupings** place together various items that appeal to a given target market. A women's apparel store divides products into juniors', misses', and ladies'

apparel. A music store separates CDs into rock, jazz, classical, R&B, country, and other sections. An art gallery places paintings into different price groups.

▶ **Storability product groupings** may be used for products needing special handling. A supermarket has freezer, refrigerator, and room-temperature sections. A florist keeps some flowers refrigerated and others at room temperature as do a bakery and a fruit store.

DETERMINATION OF A TRAFFIC-FLOW PATTERN   The traffic-flow pattern of the store is then set. A **straight (gridiron) traffic flow** places displays and aisles in a rectangular or gridiron pattern, as shown in Figure 18-9. A **curving (free-flowing) traffic flow** places displays and aisles in a free-flowing pattern, as shown in Figure 18-10.

A straight traffic pattern is often used by food retailers, discount stores, drugstores, hardware stores, and stationery stores. It has several advantages:

▶ An efficient atmosphere is created.
▶ More floor space is devoted to product displays.
▶ People can shop quickly.
▶ Inventory control and security are simplified.
▶ Self-service is easy, thereby reducing labor costs.

The disadvantages are the impersonal atmosphere, more limited browsing by customers, and rushed shopping behavior.

A curving traffic pattern is used by department stores, apparel stores, and other shopping-oriented stores. This approach has several benefits:

▶ A friendly atmosphere is presented.
▶ Shoppers do not feel rushed and will browse around.
▶ People are encouraged to walk through the store in any direction or pattern.
▶ Impulse or unplanned purchases are enhanced.

FIGURE 18-9

How a Supermarket Uses a Straight (Gridiron) Traffic Pattern

Supermarkets are known for their use of a straight (gridiron) traffic pattern. This pattern efficiently directs shoppers throughout the store and makes shopping quicker. As indicated in the top photo, the rectangular aisles are easy to follow. The layout of shelf displays, shown in the bottom photo, also facilitates the traffic flow.

Source: (Top) Monkey Business Images/ Shutterstock. Reprinted by permission. (Bottom) gurza/123rf.com. Reprinted by permission.

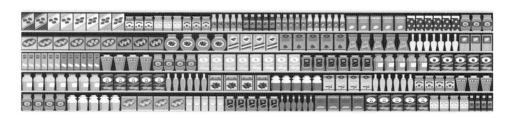

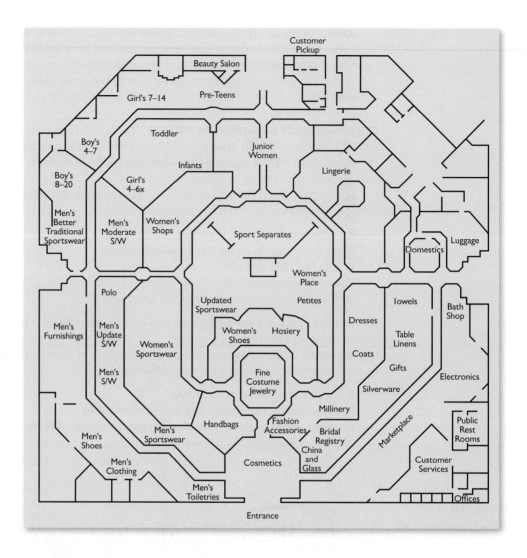

The disadvantages are the possible customer confusion, wasted floor space, difficulties in inventory control, higher labor intensity, and potential loitering. Also, the displays often cost more.

DETERMINATION OF SPACE NEEDS The space for each product category is calculated, with both selling and nonselling space considered. There are two different approaches: the model stock method and the space–productivity ratio.

The **model stock approach** determines the floor space necessary to carry and display a proper merchandise assortment. Apparel stores and shoe stores are among those using this method. The **sales–productivity ratio** assigns floor space on the basis of sales or profit per foot. Highly profitable product categories get large chunks of space; marginally profitable categories get less. Food stores and bookstores are among those that use this technique.

MAPPING OUT IN-STORE LOCATIONS At this juncture, department locations are mapped out. For multilevel stores, that means assigning departments to floors and laying out individual floors. What products should be on each floor? What should be the layout of each floor? A single-level store addresses only the second question. These are some questions to consider:

- ▶ What items should be placed on the first floor, on the second floor, and so on?
- ▶ How should groupings be placed relative to doors, vertical transportation, and so on?
- ▶ Where should impulse products and convenience products be situated?
- ▶ How should associated product categories be aligned?
- ▶ Where should seasonal and off-season products be placed?
- ▶ Where should space-consuming categories such as furniture be located?
- ▶ How close should product displays and stored inventory be to each other?

▶ What shopping patterns do consumers follow once they enter the store?

▶ How can the overall appearance of store crowding be averted?

ARRANGEMENT OF INDIVIDUAL PRODUCTS   The last step in store layout planning is arranging individual products. The most profitable items and brands could be placed in the best locations, and products could be arranged by package size, price, color, brand, level of personal service required, and/or customer interest. End-aisle display positions, eye-level positions, and checkout counter positions are the most likely to increase sales for individual items. Continuity of locations is also important; shifts in store layout may decrease sales by confusing shoppers. The least desirable display position is often knee or ankle level, because consumers do not like to bend down.

Although large retailers may sometimes use video-tracking equipment to study shoppers' in-store traffic patterns, that is not feasible for small retailers. Retail store staff can visually track shoppers' behavior in the store. Point-of-sale systems give merchants the ability to track customer purchase patterns and allow them to experiment with alternative merchandise placements and displays.[15]

Retailer goals often differ from those of manufacturers. The latter want to maximize their brands' sales and push for eye-level, full-shelf, end-aisle locations, but retailers seek to maximize total store sales and profit, regardless of brand. Self-service retailers have special considerations. Besides using a gridiron layout to minimize shopper confusion, they must clearly mark aisles, displays, and merchandise.

Consider some of the tactics that supermarkets have employed:

▶ The area just past the entrance at most supermarkets is a relaxed zone with coffee shops, flowers, and bakeries with eye-catching displays and inviting scents to lift customer mood.

▶ The bullseye or "thigh to eye" zone is typically occupied by profitable products and brands, with specialty brands on the top and store brands at the bottom.

▶ "Cereal theory" means placing boxes on lower shelves, which are at eye level for children.

▶ Most stores have an "aisle of value" so customers walking past the "superspecials" make additional purchases.

▶ Store brands do better when located to the left of manufacturer brands since consumers read left to right.

▶ Dairy, fruits, and vegetables are located at the store perimeter, so customers walking through the store are exposed to nonessential items and put items in their carts.

▶ Virtually all stores place smaller impulse-type items near cash registers so customers waiting to pay are enticed to purchase candy, soft drinks in refrigerated cases, and magazines.[16]

INTERIOR (POINT-OF-PURCHASE) DISPLAYS   After the store layout is fully detailed, a retailer devises its interior displays. Each **point-of-purchase (POP) display** provides shoppers with information, adds to store atmosphere, and serves a substantial promotional role. Advantages of using retail displays include:

Cahill specializes in creative retail displays (www.cahilldisplay.com).

▶ *Displays are persuasive.* When located near checkout counters, displays can induce unplanned or impulse purchases after the customer has finished grocery shopping but before the customer has paid for purchases. There is no need for a salesperson or sales pressure.

▶ *Displays create the proper placement for new products or promotions.* Almost 30,000 new SKUs are launched just in supermarkets every year. Manufacturers use displays and in-store media to get retailers to display new products prominently to draw attention and educate consumers about product availability and attributes. Displays can help customers visualize how product benefits can improve their experience and increase of the product being purchased. Some new products don't have to compete for shelf space and can stand out from competitors.[17]

▶ *Displays offer flexibility in messaging and placement.* Displays can convey the same overall strategic message in multiple languages to varying audiences and can be placed in different parts of the store throughout the life cycle of the product. Newer plastic, semitransparent, interactive displays allow customers to see and feel the difference in product attributes.[18]

▶ *Displays enhance the overall shopping experience.* Displays can help shape a retail store's image, re-direct store traffic, and bolster merchandising plans.[19]

At this site (http://
buyersguide
.designretailonline.com),
retailers can choose
from many display firms
in a variety of product
categories.

Several types of displays are described here. Most retailers use a combination of them.

An **assortment display** exhibits a wide range of merchandise. With an *open assortment*, the customer is encouraged to feel, look at, and/or try on products. Greeting cards, books, magazines, and apparel are the kinds of products for which retailers use open assortments. In addition, food stores have expanded their open displays for fruit, vegetables, and candy; some department stores have open displays for cosmetics and perfume. With a *closed assortment*, the customer is encouraged to look at merchandise but not touch it or try it on. Computer software, CDs, and DVDs are pre-packaged items that cannot be opened before buying. Jewelry is usually kept in closed glass cases that employees must unlock.

A **theme-setting display** depicts a product offering in a thematic manner and sets a specific mood. Retailers often vary their displays to reflect seasons or special events; some even have employees dress for the occasion. All or part of a store may be adapted to a theme, such as Presidents' Day, Valentine's Day, or another concept. Each special theme seeks to attract attention and make shopping more fun.

With an **ensemble display**, a complete product bundle (ensemble) is presented—rather than showing merchandise in separate categories (such as a shoe department, sock department, pants department, shirt department, and sports jacket department). Thus, a mannequin may be dressed in a matching combination of shoes, socks, pants, shirt, and sports jacket, and these items would be available in one department or adjacent departments. Customers like the ease of a purchase and envisioning an entire product bundle.

A **rack display** has a primarily functional use: to neatly hang or present products. It is often used by apparel retailers, housewares retailers, and others. This display must be carefully maintained because it may lead to product clutter and shoppers returning items to the wrong place. Current technology enables retailers to use sliding, disconnecting, contracting/expanding, lightweight, attractive rack displays. A **case display** exhibits heavier, bulkier items than racks hold. Books, DVD sets, pre-packaged goods, and sweaters typically appear in case displays.

A **cut case** is an inexpensive display that leaves merchandise in the original carton. Supermarkets and discount stores frequently use cut cases, which do not create a warm atmosphere. A **dump bin**—also lacking any comforting atmosphere—is a case that holds piles of sale clothing, marked-down books, or other products. Dump bins have open assortments of roughly handled items. Both cut cases and dump bins reduce display costs and project a low-price image.

Posters, signs, and cards can dress up all types of displays, including cut cases and dump bins. They provide information about product locations and stimulate customers to shop. A mobile (a hanging display with parts that move in response to air currents) serves the same purpose—but stands out more. Electronic displays are also widely used today. They can be interactive, tailored to individual stores, provide product demonstrations, answer customer questions, and incorporate the latest in multimedia capabilities. These displays are much easier to reprogram than traditional displays are to remodel.

A Nonstore-Based Retailing Perspective

Try out these demo E-stores
(http://demo.themegrill
.com/estore/demos) to
experience many of the
components of online
retailing.

Many atmospherics principles apply to both store and nonstore retailers. However, there are also some distinctions. Let's look at the storefront, general interior, store layout, displays, and checkout counter from the vantage point of one type of direct marketer, the Web retailer.

STOREFRONT   The storefront for a Web retailer is the home page. Thus, it is important that the home page has certain appealing characteristics (see Figure 18-11):

▶ Prominently shows the company name and indicates the positioning of the firm
▶ Be inviting (a "virtual storefront" must encourage customers to enter)
▶ Makes it easy to go into the store
▶ Shows the product lines carried
▶ Uses graphics as display windows and icons as access points
▶ Have a distinctive look and feel
▶ Includes the retailer's E-mail address, mailing address, and phone number
▶ Indicates that the retailer is involved with social media
▶ Be listed at various search engines

FIGURE 18-11

The Importance of Web Site Design

This photo shows a highly stylized view of an online shopping experience. The customer is enticed by the colorful online assortment of products and the ease of shopping for current and novel merchandise.

Source: Shutterstock. Reprinted by permission.

GENERAL INTERIOR As with store retailers, a Web retailer's general interior sets a shopping mood. Colors run the gamut from plain white backgrounds to stylish black backgrounds. Some firms use audio to generate shopper interest. "Fixtures" relate to how simple or elaborate the Web site looks. "Width of aisles" means how cluttered the site appears and the size of the text and images. The general interior also involves these elements:

- Instructions about how to use the site
- Information about the company
- Product icons
- News items
- The shopping cart (how orders are placed)
- A product search engine
- Locations of physical stores (for multichannel and omnichannel retailers)
- A shopper login for firms that use loyalty programs and track their customers

STORE LAYOUT A Web retailer's store layout has two components: the layout of each individual Web page and the links to move from page to page. Web retailers spend a lot of time planning the traffic flow for their stores. Online consumers want to shop efficiently, and they get impatient if the "store" is not laid out properly.

Some online firms use a gridiron approach, whereas others have more free-flowing Web pages and links. Web retailers often have a directory on the home page indicating product categories. Shoppers click on an icon to enter the area of the site housing the category (department) of interest. Many retailers encourage customers to shop for any product from any section of the Web site by having an interactive search engine, whereby a person types in the product name or category and is automatically sent to the relevant Web page. As with physical stores, online retailers allocate more display space to popular products and brands—and give them a better position. On pages that require scrolling down, best-sellers usually appear at the top and slower-sellers at the bottom.

DISPLAYS Web retailers can display full product assortments or let shoppers choose from tailored assortments. This decision affects the open or cluttered appearance of a site, the level of choice, and possible shopper confusion. Online firms often use special themes, such as Valentine's Day. It is easy for them to show ensembles—and for shoppers to interactively mix and match to create their own ensembles. Through graphics and photos, a site can give the appearance of cut cases and dump bins for items on sale.

CHECKOUT COUNTER   The checkout process at a Web site can be complex: (1) Online shoppers worry more about the security and privacy of purchase transactions than those buying in a store. (2) Online shoppers often work harder to complete transactions. They must carefully enter the model number and quantity, as well as their shipping address, E-mail address, shipping preference, and credit card number. They may also be asked for their phone number, job title, and so on, because some retailers want to build their data bases. (3) Online shoppers may feel surprised by shipping and handling fees, if these fees are not revealed until they go to checkout.

To simplify matters, Amazon.com has a patented checkout process—a major competitive advantage. Amazon.com's "1-Click" program lets shoppers securely store their shipping address, preferred shipping method, and credit card information. Each purchase requires just one click to set up an order form.

SPECIAL CONSIDERATIONS   Let's examine two other issues: how to set up a proper Web site and the advantages and disadvantages of Web atmospherics versus those of traditional stores.

New online retailers often have little experience with Web design or the fundamentals of store design and layout. These firms typically hire specialists to design their sites. When business grows, they may take Web design in-house. These are a few of the many firms that design online stores for small retailers: Easy Store Creator (www.easystorecreator.com); Volusion (www.volusion.com/ecommerce-web-design); Webfodder (www.webfodder.com); and Wix (www.wix.com/ecommerce/website). Wix design and hosting costs for an E-commerce store (www.wix.com/upgrade/website) are as low as $17 monthly (if one year is paid in advance).

Compared with physical stores, online stores have several advantages. A Web site:

- Has a huge amount of space (memory) to present product assortments, displays, and information
- Can be tailored to the individual customer
- Can be modified daily (or even hourly) to reflect changes in demand, new offerings from suppliers, and competitors' actions
- Can promote cross-merchandising and impulse purchases with little shopper effort
- Enables a shopper to enter and exit an online store in a matter of minutes
- Is a good gateway to company-run social media sites

Online stores also have potential disadvantages. A Web site:

- Can be confusing. How many clicks must a shopper make from the time he or she enters a site until a purchase is made?
- Cannot display the three-dimensional aspects of products as well as physical stores.
- Requires constant updating to reflect stockouts, new merchandise, and price changes.
- Is more likely to be exited without a purchase. It is easy to visit another Web site.
- Can be slow for shoppers with poor Internet connections. In this case, the situation worsens as more graphics and video clips are added. [*Note:* With the widespread use of broadband connections, this is not much of an issue today.]

ENCOURAGING CUSTOMERS TO SPEND MORE TIME SHOPPING

Paco Underhill, a pioneer in retail anthropology, advises retailers to encourage consumers to spend more time at the store because shopping time (excluding the time spent waiting in a line) is directly related to total spending. This insight has been supported by a variety of studies with online and store-based retailers that have tried to slow the shopping trip through experiential events and shopping environments.[20] Our blog site (www.bermanevansretail.com) has posts on this topic.

Among the tactics to persuade people to spend more time shopping are experiential merchandising, solutions selling, an enhanced shopping experience, retailer co-branding, and wish-list programs.

The aim of **experiential merchandising** is to convert shopping from a passive activity into a more interactive one, by better engaging customers. See Figure 18-12. For example, customers

Learn how Amazon.com enables shoppers to use "1-Click Settings" for easy ordering (https://techboomers.com/t/amazon-one-click-ordering).

Underhill's Envirosell company (www.envirosell.com) is a leader in shopping behavior research.

FIGURE 18-12

Making the Shopping Experience More Entertaining and Interactive

One way that retailers can greatly enhance the shopping experience—and get customers to spend a lot more time in the store—is to have events such as the fashion show highlighted here.

Source: 123rf.com. Reprinted by permission.

at the stores of British-based fashion retailer TopShop can enjoy the London Fashion show using Occulus Rift headsets and then buy from the TopShop Collection.[21]

Origins, owned by Estee Lauder, has been remodeling its stores to encourage customers to sample new products, take selfies, and linger in comfortable chairs. Williams-Sonoma hosts cooking classes, and A. C. Moore offers weekly craft classes for customers. A local beauty store could have a makeup artist come in to show customers how to apply cosmetics and new products. Free food samples (Trader Joe's), live music (Urban Outfitters Inc.), and product demos (Lush) can entice customers and keep them in the spending mood. Some stores spray aromas in various parts of their stores.[22]

Solutions selling takes a customer-centered approach and presents "solutions" rather than "products." It goes a step beyond cross-merchandising. At holiday times, some retailers group gift items by price ("under $25, under $50, under $100, $100 and above") rather than by product category. This provides a solution for the shopper who has a budget to spend but a fuzzy idea of what to buy. Many supermarkets sell fully prepared, complete meals that just have to be heated and served. This solves the problem of "What's for dinner?" without requiring the consumer to shop for meal components.

An *enhanced shopping experience* means the retailer does everything possible to minimize annoyances and to make the shopping trip pleasant. Given all the retail choices facing consumers, retailers must do all they can so that shoppers do not have unpleasant experiences. Customers at some Nestle Nespresso boutiques can experience a redesigned, enhanced, personal one-on-one coffee shopping experience with open spaces and Nespresso Coffee Specialists who share their expertise, providing tastings, and personally advising customers. These specialists use mobile technology to recommend and prepare beverages based on each customer's prior purchase history, the occasion, and their mood to help them explore and expand their coffee experience. Each of these boutiques also uses RFID technology so customers can conveniently purchase *Nespresso* coffee sleeves without any staff interaction and offers pick-up desks for online and mobile orders.[23]

Retailers can also provide an enhanced shopping experience by setting up wider aisles so people do not feel cramped, adding benches and chairs so those accompanying the main shopper can relax, using kiosks to stimulate impulse purchases and answer questions, having activities for children (such as Ikea's playroom), and opening more checkout counters. What decades-old shopping accessory is turning out to be one of the greatest enhancements of all? It is the humble shopping cart, as highlighted in Figure 18-13.

Scanner-enhanced shopping carts provide shrinkage-free mobile self-checkout for retailers and convenience to customers. A customer can scan each product using the retailer's app on her or his mobile phone before placing it in the online cart. The scanner on the shopping cart finds the price associated with the item name and displays the item name and price, and links the cart to the customer's loyalty/mobile app account. This information is sent via Bluetooth, and the cart

See how retailers can create an enhanced shopping experience (http://merchandiseconcepts .com/anne-obarskis-blog-insights).

FIGURE 18-13

The Shopping Cart's Role in an Enriched Shopping Experience

Consider shopping in a large supermarket (or home center or discount store) and NOT finding a shopping cart to assist with the in-store experience. Many people would spend less time in the store and buy fewer items.

Source: Lisa S./Shutterstock. Reprinted by permission.

and mobile app automatically sync all scanned items. If the customer removes an item, the cart will remove the item from the scanned items list and deduct the price from the total price. The app on a phone is also be updated accordingly. Pressure sensors at the bottom of the cart prevent customers from placing items into the cart without first scanning them; a buzzer will keep beeping to remind shoppers to scan the items.[24]

More firms participate in *co-branding*, whereby two or more well-known retailers situate under the same roof (or at one Web site) to share costs, stimulate consumers to visit more often, and attract people shopping together who have different preferences. Here are several examples: Subway in Walmart stores, Starbucks in Barnes & Noble stores, joint Dunkin' Donuts and Baskin-Robbins outlets, and numerous small retailers that sell their merchandise through Amazon.com. Multiple branded-food retailers that share the same space attract customers who enjoy the ability to order food from different menus at one location instead of selecting a stand-alone chain. Coffee shops and restaurants in department stores can enhance the overall shopping experience, increase the in-store time of shoppers who take a break from their shopping without leaving the store, and enhance the potential for unplanned purchases and more sales per square foot.[25]

Another tactic being implemented by a growing number of retailers is the *wish-list program*. It is a technique that expands on the long-standing concept of a wedding registry, and it can be used with virtually any products or life events. Wish lists are being used to great effect by Web retailers (and multichannel/omnichannel retailers) to enable customers to prepare shopping lists for gift items they'd like to receive from a particular store or shopping center. Amazon.com customers use its wish list as a memory aid. Some customers use wish lists to store possible alternatives so they can easily evaluate and winnow them before making their selection. Others use it as

ETHICS IN RETAILING | Product Reviews on the Web |

Consumers seeking to purchase a good or service often seek product reviews from such apps as TripAdvisor (www.tripadvisor .com); Yelp (www.yelp.com); Open Table (www.opentable.com); and Zagat (www.zagat.com). In addition, many consumers search product reviews from such firms as Amazon (www.amazon.com) and Home Depot (www.homedepot.com), as well as specialty retailer sites such as Whole Latte Love (www.wholelattelove.com). Despite their popularity, there are some ethical issues associated with these product reviews. Although some sites verify that a person actually purchased the reviewed item, others do not. This

enables a competitor to place an unjustified negative review about another retailer or product. Many product reviews are based on few observer comments. Reviewers are typically not self-ranked by such criteria as light versus heavy shoppers or novice versus expert. There is typically no oversight in reviewing service recovery strategies made by a manufacturer or retailer in response to negative reviews. Readers cannot determine whether the negative reviewer was contacted or a replacement product issued.

Develop a policy for placing consumers' product reviews on an electronics chain's Web site.

a "save for later" list for a future shopping session. Yet others create wish lists explicitly to send to friends and family by E-mail or to post a link on Facebook or Twitter to give them gift ideas. Amazon disaggregates wish-list data to develop personalized recommendations for future wish lists and also analyzes aggregate data to apply in predictive analysis for its merchandising decisions.[26]

COMMUNITY RELATIONS

The way retailers interact with the communities around them can have a significant impact on both their image and performance. Their stature can be enhanced by engaging in such community-oriented actions as these:

- ▸ Making sure that stores are barrier-free for disabled shoppers and strictly enforcing handicapped parking rules
- ▸ Showing a concern for the environment by recycling trash and cleaning streets
- ▸ Supporting charities and noting that support at the company Web site
- ▸ Participating in antidrug programs
- ▸ Employing area residents
- ▸ Running special sales for senior citizens and other groups
- ▸ Sponsoring Little League and other youth activities
- ▸ Cooperating with neighborhood planning groups
- ▸ Donating money and/or equipment to schools.
- ▸ Carefully checking IDs for purchases with age minimums

Each year, 7-Eleven makes substantial charitable contributions of cash and goods to support programs addressing issues such as literacy, reading, crime, and multicultural understanding. It also donates hundreds of thousands of pounds of food to local food banks throughout the United States. Walmart, Kmart, and Big Lots are among the numerous retailers participating in some type of antidrug program. Barnes & Noble, Target, and others participate in national literacy programs. Giant Food is just one of the supermarket chains that give money or equipment to schools in their neighborhoods.

As with any aspect of retail strategy planning, community relations efforts can be undertaken by retailers of any size and format. Many retailers use cause-related marketing to differentiate themselves and their products and build customer loyalty in highly competitive markets. Retailers may choose a complementary nonprofit partner or charitable cause that their customers are likely to support, such as supermarkets with food banks and pet stores with no-kill animal shelters. Sometimes, the charitable organizations give retailers access to their members and the retailers donate a percentage of sales or profits to the charities.

Some cause-related marketing efforts by retailers may be met with skepticism by their customers. Research shows that utilitarian appeals made individually (such as a cashier asking a shopper to donate money to a charity during the checkout process) are met with more skepticism than more collective appeals (such as using the store's pubic announcement system to ask shoppers to buy tickets for a walkathon or golf outing).[27] Massachusetts-based Jordan's Furniture has partnered with a nonprofit organization to host an annual Adoption Option picnic event at its stores; families can meet children in state foster care and learn more about adopting them. The firm also sponsors clothing drives and furniture collection events throughout the year for other nonprofits.[28]

Chapter Summary

1. *To show the importance of communicating with customers and to examine the concept of retail image.* Customer communications are crucial for a store or nonstore retailer to position itself in customers' minds. Various physical and symbolic cues can be used.

Presenting the proper image—the way a firm is perceived by its customers and others—is an essential aspect of the retail strategy mix. And the growing impact of social media on a retailer's image must be appreciated. The components of a firm's image are its target market characteristics, retail positioning and reputation, store location, merchandise assortment, price levels, physical facilities, shopping experiences, community service, advertising, public relations, personal selling, and sales promotion. A retail image requires a multistep, ongoing approach. For chains, there must be a consistent image among branches.

2. *To describe how a retail store image is related to the atmosphere it creates via its exterior, general interior, layout, and displays, and to look at the special case of nonstore atmospherics.* For a store retailer, atmosphere (atmospherics) is based on the physical attributes of the store utilized to develop an image; it is composed of the exterior, general interior, store layout, and displays. For a nonstore firm, physical attributes of such factors as catalogs, vending machines, and Web sites affect image.

The store exterior is comprised of the storefront, marquee, entrances, display windows, building height and size, visibility, uniqueness, surrounding stores and area, parking, and congestion. It sets a mood before a prospective customer even enters a store.

The general interior of a store encompasses its flooring, colors, lighting, scents and sounds, fixtures, wall textures, temperature, width of aisles, dressing facilities, vertical transportation, dead areas, personnel, self-service, merchandise, price displays, cash register placement, technology/modernization, and cleanliness. An upscale retailer's interior is far different from a discounter's interior—reflecting the image desired and the costs of doing business.

In laying out a store interior, six steps are necessary: (a) Floor space is allocated among selling, merchandise, personnel, and customers based on a firm's overall strategy. More firms now use planograms. (b) Product groupings are set, based on function, purchase motivation, market segment, and/or storability. (c) Traffic flows are planned, using a straight or curving pattern. (d) Space per product category is computed by a model stock approach or sales–productivity ratio. (e) Departments are located. (f) Individual products are arranged within departments.

Interior (point-of-purchase) displays provide information for consumers, add to the atmosphere, and have a promotional role. Interior display possibilities include assortment displays, theme displays, ensemble displays, rack and case displays, cut case and dump bin displays, posters, mobiles, and electronic displays.

For Web retailers, many principles of atmospherics are similar to those for store retailers. There are also key differences. The home page is the storefront. The general interior consists of site instructions, company information, product icons, the shopping cart, the product search engine, and other factors. The store layout includes individual Web pages, as well as the links that connect them. Displays can feature full or more selective assortments. Sales are lost if the checkout counter does not function well. There are specialists that help in Web site design. Compared with traditional stores, Web stores have various pros and cons.

3. *To discuss ways of encouraging customers to spend more time shopping.* To persuade consumers to devote more time with the retailer, these tactics are often employed: experiential merchandising, solutions selling, enhancing the shopping experience, retailer co-branding, and wish-list programs.

4. *To consider the impact of community relations on a retailer's image.* Consumers react favorably to retailers involved in such activities as establishing stores that are barrier-free for persons with disabilities, supporting charities, and running special sales for senior citizens.

Key Terms

social media (p. 461)
atmosphere (atmospherics) (p. 464)
visual merchandising (p. 464)
storefront (p. 465)
marquee (p. 465)
dead areas (p. 469)
planogram (p. 470)
functional product groupings (p. 470)
purchase motivation product
    groupings (p. 470)

market segment product groupings
    (p. 470)
storability product groupings (p. 471)
straight (gridiron) traffic flow (p. 471)
curving (free-flowing) traffic flow
    (p. 471)
model stock approach (p. 472)
sales–productivity ratio (p. 472)
point-of-purchase (POP) display
    (p. 473)

assortment display (p. 474)
theme-setting display (p. 474)
ensemble display (p. 474)
rack display (p. 474)
case display (p. 474)
cut case (p. 474)
dump bin (p. 474)
experiential merchandising
    (p. 476)
solutions selling (p. 477)

Questions for Discussion

1. Why is it sometimes difficult for a retailer to convey its image to consumers? Give an example of a restaurant with a fuzzy image.
2. How could a store selling new computers project a value-based retail image? How could a store selling used computers project such an image?

3. Define the concept of *atmosphere.* How does this differ from that of *visual merchandising?*
4. Which aspects of a store's exterior are controllable by a retailer? Which are uncontrollable?
5. What is meant by *selling, merchandise, personnel,* and *customer space?*

6. Present a planogram for a nearby bank.
7. How would a retailer develop a market-segment product grouping for their products and services?
8. Which stores should not use a straight traffic flow layout? Explain your answer.
9. Some online retailers are streamlining their checkouts. Why is this the case? What concerns do customers have about online checkouts?
10. What is the purpose of experiential merchandising, and where would you see it?
11. Suggest some methods that a department store could employ to enhance the shopping experience of their customers. Why would these methods be suitable?
12. Present a community relations program for a pharmacy chain.

Web-Based Exercise

Visit the Web site of Lush Cosmetics (https://uk.lush.com/). How would you rate the atmospherics and ambience of this site? What do you like most and least about the site? Explain your answers.

19 Promotional Strategy

Chapter Objectives

1. To explore the scope of retail promotion

2. To study the elements of retail promotion: advertising, public relations, personal selling, and sales promotion

3. To discuss the strategic aspects of retail promotion: objectives, budgeting, the mix of forms, implementing the mix, and reviewing and revising the plan

For retailers, the main elements of their promotion strategy are advertising, public relations, personal selling, and sales promotion—topics we cover in this chapter.

Chris Tuff, executive vice-president and director of business development and partnerships at 22squared (www.22squared.com), says that marketers looking for the next hot platform should consider experimenting with the Imgur, Kik, YikYak, and Venmo social media apps. Tuff believes that a campaign created on one of these hot apps can provide a first-mover publicity boost.

Imgur (http:imgur.com) lets users upload any kind of media files and share them seamlessly with sites such as Reddit (https://www.reddit.com). This app also hosts content. Kik (www.kik .com), a messaging app, sends texts and content such as videos to friends and groups. YikYak (www.yikyak.com) is an anonymous posting board, popular on college campuses, and Venmo (http://venmo.com) is a personal finance app that lets users send money instantly over the Internet.

About 40 percent of U.S. teens use Kik, and millions of consumers use Imgur. YikYak users can be found at over 2,000 U.S. college campuses. Venmo is especially popular to make and share payments (such as splitting a taxi fare).[1]

Source: Stuart Miles/
Shutterstock. Reprinted
by permission.

Overview

Sephora, the European and U.S. beauty chain, has a well-integrated promotion plan—from its colorful Web site (www.sephora.com) to its stores.

Retail promotion includes any communication by a retailer that informs, persuades, and/or reminds the target market about any aspect of that firm. In the first part of this chapter, the elements of retail promotion are detailed. The second part centers on strategic aspects of promotion.

Consider the importance of promotion strategy to the brand equity of the second largest pizza company in the world—Domino's Pizza. Its approach to retail promotions is largely influenced by its retail positioning strategy and the competitive marketplace. Domino's reinforces its brand in the consumer's mind with extensive advertising at various media channels and strengthens it by marketing affiliations with well-known brands such as Coca-Cola. Its U.S. franchise- and company-owned stores invest about $300 million annually in national, cooperative, and local advertising. Domino's domestic stores are required to contribute 6 percent of their annual retail sales to fund national marketing and advertising campaigns. These funds are used for media buys, market research, field communications, public relations, commercial production, talent payments, and other activities to promote the brand. In addition to the national and market-level advertising contributions, domestic stores spend additional funds on local store marketing activities.[2]

ELEMENTS OF THE RETAIL PROMOTIONAL MIX

Advertising, public relations, personal selling, and sales promotion are the elements of promotion. In this section, we discuss each in terms of goals, advantages and disadvantages, and basic forms. A good plan integrates these elements—based on the overall strategy. For example, a movie theater concentrates on ads and sales promotion (food displays), whereas an upscale specialty store stresses personal selling. See Figure 19-1.

This site (www.managementhelp.org/marketing/advertising) provides an overview on promotion planning. Click on a topic.

Retailers devote significant sums to promotion. A typical department store, for instance, spends up to 4 to 5 percent of sales on ads and 8 to 10 percent on personal selling and support services. And most department store chains also invest heavily in sales promotions and use public relations to generate favorable publicity and reply to media information requests. We have several posts related to the retail promotion mix at our blog (www.bermanevansretail.com).

Advertising

Advertising is paid, nonpersonal communication transmitted through out-of-store mass media by an identified sponsor. Four aspects of this definition merit clarification:

1. *Paid form:* This distinguishes advertising from publicity (an element of public relations), for which no payment is made by the retailer for the time or space used to convey a message.
2. *Nonpersonal presentation:* A standard message is delivered to the entire audience, and it cannot be adapted to individual customers (except with the Web).
3. *Out-of-store mass media:* These include newspapers, radio, TV, the Web, and other mass channels, rather than personal contacts. In-store communications (such as displays) are considered sales promotion.
4. *Identified sponsor:* The sponsor's name is clearly divulged, unlike publicity. See Figure 19-2.

Amazon has the highest annual dollar advertising expenditures among U.S. retailers—nearly $4 billion. However, this represents just 3.5 percent of U.S. sales. Amazon relies on targeted online advertising, television advertising, public relations, its Associates program (where participants get commissions when their customer referrals result in product sales), cooperative advertising with vendors, and price promotions such as percentage discounts off current purchases and inducement offers for discounts on future purchases subject to a minimum current purchase.[3] Table 19-1 shows advertising ratios for several retailing categories.

DIFFERENCES BETWEEN RETAILER AND MANUFACTURER ADVERTISING STRATEGIES   Retailers—other than national chains and online firms—usually have more geographically concentrated target markets than do manufacturers. This means they can adapt better to local needs, habits, and preferences. However, those retailers cannot utilize national media as readily as manufacturers. Only the largest retail chains and franchises can advertise on national TV programs. An exception is direct marketing (including the Web) because trading areas for even small firms can then be geographically dispersed.

Retail ads stress immediacy. Individual items are placed for sale and advertised over short time periods. Manufacturers are more often concerned with developing favorable attitudes.

FIGURE 19-1

The Retail Promotion Mix in Action

As this montage shows, the retail promotion mix is wide reaching and includes customer relations (A), advertising (B), personal selling (C), sales promotion (D), and more.

Sources: (A) Steve Mann/Shutterstock.com. Reprinted by permission. (B) iQoncept/Shutterstock.com. Reprinted by permission. (C) Corepics VOF/Shutterstock. Reprinted by permission. (D) iQoncept/Shutterstock.com. Reprinted by permission.

Many retailers stress prices in ads, whereas manufacturers usually emphasize key product attributes. In addition, retailers often display several different products in one ad, whereas manufacturers are likely to minimize the number of products mentioned in a single ad.

FIGURE 19-2

Advertising and Marc Jacobs

Marc Jacobs, the U.S.-based retailer that also operates in China, France, Italy, Japan, and Great Britain, uses all kinds of advertising media to get out its messages—including a billboard ad on the side of a Hong Kong bus

Source: Coleman Yuen/Pearson Education Ltd. Reprinted by permission.

TABLE 19-1 Selected U.S. Advertising-to-Sales Ratios by Type of Retailer

Type of Retailer	Advertising Dollars as Percentage of Sales Dollars[a]	Advertising Dollars as Percentage of Margin[b]
Amusement parks	6.2	13.0
Apparel and accessories stores	3.5	9.3
Auto and home supply stores	1.2	2.5
Department stores	4.2	12.7
Drug and proprietary stores	0.4	2.0
Eating places	2.5	9.5
Family clothing stores	2.1	5.8
Food stores	2.3	6.6
Grocery stores	0.8	3.0
Hobby, toy, and game shops	3.3	8.6
Hotels and motels	1.4	5.2
Jewelry stores	5.5	11.5
Lumber and other building materials—retail	1.4	4.0
Miscellaneous furniture and fixtures	0.5	1.0
Radio, TV, and consumer electronics stores	1.8	7.8
Real-estate agents and managers	4.7	14.1
Shoe stores	2.3	6.4
Variety stores	0.9	3.3
Video rental	9.4	11.1

[a] Advertising dollars as percentage of sales = Advertising expenditures/(Net company sales).
[b] Advertising dollars as percentage of margin = Advertising expenditures/(Net company sales – Cost of goods sold).

Source: Based on material in Schonfeld & Associates, "2015 Advertising-to-Sales Ratios and Budgets." Reprinted by permission.

Media rates tend to be lower for retailers. Because of this, and the desire of many manufacturers and wholesalers for wide distribution, the costs of retail advertising are sometimes shared by manufacturers or wholesalers and their retailers. Two or more retailers may also share costs. Both of these approaches entail **cooperative advertising**.

Find out how to devise good ads (www.inc.com/advertising).

OBJECTIVES   A retailer would select one or more of these goals and base advertising efforts on it (them):

- To grow short-term sales
- To increase customer traffic
- To develop and/or reinforce a retail image
- To inform customers about goods and services and/or company attributes
- To ease the job for sales personnel
- To stimulate demand for private brands

ADVANTAGES AND DISADVANTAGES   The major advantages of advertising are:

- A large audience is attracted. For print media, circulation is supplemented by the passing of a copy from one reader to another.
- The costs per viewer, reader, or listener are low.
- A number of alternative media are available (including social media), so a retailer can match a medium to the target market.
- The retailer has control over message content, graphics, timing, and size (or length), so a standardized message in a chosen format can be delivered to the entire audience.
- In print media, a message can be studied and restudied by the target market.
- Editorial content (a TV show, a news story, etc.) often surrounds an ad. This may increase its credibility or the probability it will be read.

Omnichannel Promotions Manager

Multichannel promotion managers are often responsible for promotional planning and implementation in only one channel: either in-store or Web based. In contrast, the omnichannel promotion manager is involved with both channels. A major responsibility of the omnichannel manager is to ensure that shoppers receive a seamless experience throughout their purchase journey. This is accomplished through common logos, the same prices, and a single customer database that shows the customer's purchase history in both stores as well as on the Web. Omnichannel promotion managers need to better integrate promotion activity across channels by using Web ads clearly listing inventory availability, aisle location, and store hours at a local retail store. They may also strive to get heavy online customers to shop at a local store via mobile couponing; give store personnel sales commissions on orders placed by them at an in-store kiosk; and offer a common customer loyalty program that acknowledges all customer purchases regardless of channel.

Describe the pros and cons of using separate promotion managers for in-store versus online.

► Self-service or reduced-service operations are possible because a customer becomes aware of a retailer and its offerings before shopping.

The major disadvantages of advertising are:

► Standardized messages lack flexibility (except for the Web and its interactive nature). They do not focus on the needs of individual customers.
► Some media require large investments. This may reduce the access of small firms.
► Media may reach large geographic areas, and for retailers, this may be wasteful. A small supermarket chain might find that only 30 percent of an audience resides in its trading area.
► Some media require a long lead time for placing ads. This reduces the ability to advertise fad items or to react to some current events themes.
► Some media have a high throwaway rate. Circulars may be discarded without being read.
► A 30-second TV commercial or small newspaper ad does not have many details.

The preceding are broad generalities. The pros and cons of specific media are covered next.

MEDIA Retailers can choose from the media highlighted in Table 19-2 and described here.

Papers (dailies, weeklies, and shoppers) represent the preferred medium for many retailers, having the advantages of proper market coverage, short lead time, reasonable costs, flexibility, longevity, graphics, and editorial association (ads near columns or articles). Disadvantages include the possible waste (circulation to a wider area than necessary), the competition among retailers, the black-and-white format, and the appeal to fewer senses than TV. To maintain a dominant position, many papers have revamped their graphics, and some run color ads. Free-distribution shopper papers ("penny savers"), with little news content and delivery to all households in a geographic area, are popular today.

TV ads, which have grown in importance due to the rise of national and regional retailers, are far behind papers in retail promotion expenditures and have a lot of competition from digital (Web) advertising. Among the advantages are the dramatic effects of messages, large market coverage, creativity, and program affiliation (for sponsors). Disadvantages include high minimum costs, audience waste, a need for brevity and repetition, and limited availability of popular times for nonsponsors. Because cable TV is more focused than conventional stations, it appeals to local retailers.

From an advertising perspective, online retailers use Web ads to stimulate awareness and E-commerce. For store retailers, the Web provides information to customers about locations, describes products carried, lets people order catalogs, and so forth. Retailers have two opportunities to reach customers: advertising on search engines and other firms' Web sites; and communicating with customers at their own sites. Web-based advertising has been growing at a fast pace—and will continue to do so for the foreseeable future. See Figure 19-3.

In a White Pages phone directory (in print or online), retailers get free alphabetical listings along with all other phone subscribers, commercial and noncommercial. The major advantage of the White over the Yellow Pages (in print or online) is that those who know a firm's name are

TABLE 19-2 Advertising Media Comparison Chart

Medium	Market Coverage	Particular Suitability
TV	Definable market area surrounding the station	Retailers of goods and services with wide appeal
Daily papers	Single community or entire metro area; local editions may be available	All larger retailers
Weekly papers	Usually single community; may be a metro area	Retailers with a strictly local market
Shopper papers	Most households in one community; chain shoppers can cover a metro area	Neighborhood retailers and service businesses
Web	Broad, even global	All types of goods and service-oriented retailers
Phone directories	Geographic area or occupational field served by a directory	All types of goods and service-oriented retailers
Direct mail	Controlled by the retailer	New and expanding firms, those using coupons or special offers, mail order
Radio	Definable market area surrounding the station	Retailers focusing on identifiable segments
Transit	Urban or metro community served by transit system	Retailers near transit routes, especially those appealing to commuters
Outdoor	Entire metro area or single neighborhood	Amusement and tourist-oriented retailers, well-known firms
Local magazines	Entire metro area or region, zoned editions sometimes available	Restaurants, entertainment-oriented firms, specialty shops, mail-order firms
Flyers/circulars	Single neighborhood	Restaurants, dry cleaners, service stations, and other neighborhood firms
Social Media	Broad, even global	All types of goods and service-oriented retailers
Mobile in-app advertising	Local and geo-targeted areas	All types of goods and service-oriented retailers

The online Yellow Pages (www.yellowpages.com) remains a key medium for small retailers.

not exposed to competitors. The major disadvantage, in contrast with the Yellow Pages, is the alphabetical rather than type-of-business listing. A person unfamiliar with repair services will usually look in the Yellow Pages under "Repair." In the Yellow Pages, firms pay for listings (and display ads, if desired) in their category. Most retailers advertise in the Yellow Pages. The advantages include widespread usage by people ready to shop, and the long life (one year or more) of the Yellow Pages. The disadvantages are that retailer awareness may not be gained and there is a lengthy lead time for new ads. *Note:* There has been a dramatic shift to online directories and away from printed ones.

With direct mail, retailers send catalogs or ads to customers by the mail (including E-mail) or private delivery firms. Advantages are a targeted audience, tailored format, controlled costs, quick feedback, and tie-ins (including ads with bills). Among the disadvantages are the high throwaway rate ("junk mail"), poor image to some people, low response rate, and outdated mailing lists (addressees may have moved).

Radio is still used by a variety of retailers. Advantages are the relatively low costs, its value as a medium for car drivers and passengers, its ability to use segmentation, its rather short lead time, and its wide reach. Disadvantages include no visual impact, the need for repetition, the need for brevity, and waste. The use of radio by retailers has increased in recent years.

Transit advertising is used in areas with mass transit systems. Ads are displayed on buses and in trains and taxis. Advantages are the captive audience, mass market, high level of repetitiveness, and geographically defined market. Disadvantages are the ad clutter, distracted audience, lack of availability in small areas, restricted travel paths, and graffiti. Many retailers also advertise on their delivery vehicles.

At the Outdoor Advertising Association Web site (www.oaaa.org), type in "Retail."

Outdoor (billboard) advertising is sometimes used by retailers. Posters and signs may be displayed in public places, on buildings, and alongside highways. Advantages are the large size

FIGURE 19-3

Using the Internet to Draw New Customers

Retailers such as real-estate brokers, hotel chains, repair services, restaurants, and others find Web advertising to be a very good way to attract new customers.

Source: iQoncept/Shutterstock.com. Reprinted by permission

Take a look at the site of the Outdoor Advertising Association Web site (www.oaaa.org).

of the ads, the frequency of exposure, the relatively low costs, and the assistance in directing new customers. Disadvantages include the clutter of ads, a distracted audience, the limited information, and some legislation banning outdoor ads.

Magazine usage (in print and online) is valuable for three reasons: the number of larger retail chains, the creation of regional and local editions, and the use by nonstore and omnichannel retailers. Advantages are tailoring to specific markets, creative options, editorial associations, message longevity, and color. Disadvantages include long lead time, less sense of consumer urgency, waste, and declining readership.

Single-page (flyers) or multiple-page (circulars) ads are distributed in parking lots or to consumer homes. Advantages include the targeted audience, low costs, flexibility, and speed. Among the disadvantages are the level of throwaways, the poor image to some, and clutter. Flyers are good for smaller firms; circulars are best used by larger ones.

Social media have become the digital hub for many retailers' Web sites. Furthermore, social media such as Facebook may provide the sole digital presence for many small retailers that do not have a Web site. Advantages include developing interactive relationships with customers; creating excitement and suggestion selling through sharing of images (Instagram, Pinterest), videos (YouTube), and information and promotions (Facebook, Twitter); and providing customer service (Yelp), identifying new customers based on their social media profiles (Facebook and Linkedin). Disadvantages include the intense competition for customer "likes," the possibility of negative comments, and the lack of methods to measure the impact on sales.

Mobile apps are now being developed by retailers or third-party retail intermediaries (such as OpenTable), and then downloaded by customers from iPhones, Android phones, and Windows phones. Advantages include the ability to drive traffic to stores; to provide personalized, geo-targeted information and time-sensitive promotions (SMS text, Snapchat); to enhance in-store experiences (Home Depot, Nordstrom); to provide out-of-store product interaction opportunities; and to complete ordering, payments, and purchases through a smartphone without the need for retail salesperson interaction. Disadvantages include technological limitations and privacy implications.

Many smartphone-only innovations such as MikMak, the first mobile shopping video network app, are redefining impulse buying. MikMak creates 30-second videos ("minimercials") for its retail clients. The videos combine humor and music, and enable one-touch ordering and payment from the app and shipping from the sellers.[4] Retailers are experimenting with E-commerce chatbots integrated into social media messenger apps such as WhatsApp, Facebook Messenger, Slack, and WeChat (China). Chatbots simulate human conversation to help customers search products, to suggest alternatives, and to offer in-app ordering and payment help to complete purchases.[5]

TYPES   Advertisements can be classified by content and payment method. See Figure 19-4. *Pioneer ads* have awareness as a goal and offer information (usually on new firms, products, or locations). *Competitive ads* have persuasion as a goal. *Reminder ads* are geared to loyal customers and stress attributes that have made retailers successful. *Institutional ads* seek to keep retailer names before the public without emphasizing the sale of goods or services. Public service messages are institutional.

Channel Fusion (http:// channel-fusion.com .dnnmax.com) is a leader in cooperative promotions.

Retailers may pay their own way or seek cooperative ventures in placing ads. Firms paying their own way have total control and incur all costs. With cooperative ventures, two or more parties share costs and decision making.[6] Billions of dollars are spent yearly on U.S. cooperative ads, most in vertical agreements.

In a **vertical cooperative advertising agreement**, a manufacturer and a retailer or a wholesaler and a retailer share an ad. Responsibilities are specified contractually, and retailers are typically not reimbursed until after the ads run. Vertical cooperative ads are subject to the Robinson-Patman Act; similar arrangements must be offered to all retailers on a proportional basis. Advantages to a retailer are reduced ad costs, assistance in preparing ads, greater market coverage, and less planning time. Disadvantages to a retailer include less control, flexibility, and distinctiveness. Some retailers are concerned about the eligibility requirements to participate and the emphasis on the supplier's name in ads. In response, manufacturers and other suppliers are now more flexible and understanding.

Carol Wright (www .carolwright.com) is a leader in horizontal cooperative promotions.

With a **horizontal cooperative advertising agreement**, two or more retailers share an ad. A horizontal agreement is most often used by small noncompeting retailers (such as independent hardware stores), retailers in a shopping center, and franchisees of a firm. Advantages and disadvantages are similar to those in a vertical agreement. Two further benefits are the bargaining power of retailers in dealing with the media and the synergies when multiple retailers work together.

When planning a cooperative strategy, these questions should be considered:

▸ What ads qualify, in terms of merchandise and special requirements?
▸ What percentage of advertising is paid by each party?
▸ When can ads be run? In what media?

FIGURE 19-4
Types of Advertising

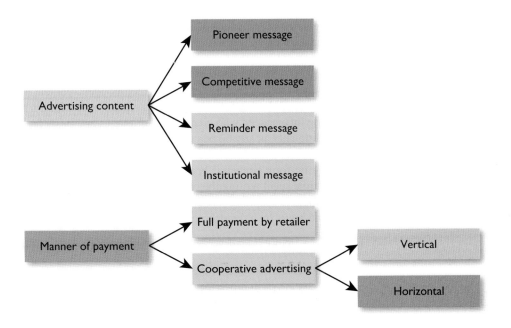

> ► Are there special provisions regarding message content?
> ► What documentation is required for reimbursement?
> ► How does each party benefit?
> ► Do cooperative ads obscure the image of individual retailers?

Public Relations

At Wendy's (www.wendys
.com/en-us/about-wendys),
public relations means
community relations. Click
on "Responsibility."

Public relations entails any communication that fosters a favorable image for the retailer among its publics (consumers, investors, government, channel members, employees, and the general public). It may be nonpersonal or personal, paid or nonpaid, and sponsor controlled or not controlled. **Publicity** is any nonpersonal form of public relations whereby messages are transmitted through mass media, the time or space provided by the media is not paid for, and there is no identified commercial sponsor.

The basic distinction between advertising and publicity is that publicity is nonpaid. Thus, it is not as readily controllable. A story on a store opening may not appear, appear after the fact, or not appear in the form desired. Yet, to shoppers, publicity is often more credible and valuable. Advertising and publicity (public relations) should complement one another. Therefore, on some occasions, it may be a good idea to try to gain positive publicity before placing ads.

Public relations can benefit both large and small retailers. Although the former often spend a lot of money to publicize events such as the Macy's Thanksgiving Day Parade, small firms can creatively generate attention on a limited budget. They can feature book signings by authors, sponsor school sports teams, donate goods and services to charities, and so forth.

Social media now have a huge impact on a retailer's public relations efforts and on the publicity it receives. Consider the influence of highly interactive blogging sites (some operated by retailers themselves), which now number as many as 300 million worldwide and rapidly spread information. Bloggers as influencers may represent real customers who reach a targeted audience and whose storytelling and opinions are trusted by their followers. They may generate active engagement, influence purchase decisions, and help drive return on investment in a way that complements other marketing activities of the retailer. The business of blogging has become more formalized and is sometimes referred to as "influencer marketing." Blogger behavior is changing in response to the increased accountability of retailers and the availability of improved metrics, as evidenced by findings from recent blogger surveys: [7]

> ► Blogging was often just a hobby; today, it is sometimes a career option, with successful bloggers earning a good income. More bloggers post during normal business hours than at other times or days. Although small (16 percent), some bloggers write more posts for clients than for themselves. More than half of bloggers post content on behalf of clients. Bloggers can be classified as hobbyists, professional bloggers, company bloggers who blog on behalf of firms for whom they work, and entrepreneurs who blog on behalf of their own firms.
> ► Several blogger influence measurement services such as Alexa.com, Blogmetrics (www.blogmetrics.org), and others document that competition among bloggers is fierce. A small percentage of viewed posts has an inordinate effect on the overall traffic and followers for top-ranked bloggers.
> ► Most active bloggers post at least weekly, and some write for more than one blog. Collaborating, contributing, and responding to other bloggers' content is mutually beneficial–by sharing content and sharing followers. For example, Pottery Barn's holiday catalog is sent to several strong influencers, who create a set of images and posts for different channels.
> ► Traditionally, nearly 60 percent of blog posts have been between 500 and 1,000 words. However, longer posts (more than 1,000 words) are often more effective in generating conversions; and long-form content is becoming more popular.
> ► The time spent writing the typical blog post is more than 2.5 hours per post, with 16 percent of bloggers spending more than 4 hours per post and 6 percent of bloggers spending more than 6 hours on a typical blog post.

OBJECTIVES Public relations seeks to accomplish one or more of these goals:

> ► To increase awareness of the retailer and its strategy mix
> ► To maintain or improve the company image
> ► To show the retailer as a contributor to the community's quality of life

   ▷ To demonstrate innovativeness
   ▷ To resent a favorable message in a highly believable manner
   ▷ To minimize total promotion costs

ADVANTAGES AND DISADVANTAGES   The major advantages of public relations are:

   ▷ An image can be presented or enhanced.
   ▷ A more credible source presents the message (such as a good restaurant review).
   ▷ There are no costs for message time or space.
   ▷ A mass audience is addressed.
   ▷ Carryover effects are possible (if a retailer is perceived as community-oriented, its value positioning is more apt to be perceived favorably).
   ▷ People pay more attention to independent (third-party) sources than to clearly identified ads.

The major disadvantages of public relations are:

   ▷ Some retailers do not believe in spending any funds on image-related communication.
   ▷ There is little retailer control over a publicity message and its timing, placement, and coverage by a given medium (particularly with social media).
   ▷ It may be more suitable for short-run, rather than long-run, planning.
   ▷ Although there are no media costs for publicity, there are costs for a public relations staff, planning activities, and the activities themselves (such as store openings).
   ▷ The Web can quickly turn a negative local story into a worldwide media blitz.

TYPES   Public relations can be planned or unexpected and image enhancing or image detracting. With planned public relations, a retailer outlines its activities in advance, strives to have media report on them, and anticipates certain coverage. Community services, such as donations and special sales; parades on holidays (such as the Macy's Thanksgiving Day Parade); the introduction of "hot" new goods and services; and a new store opening are activities a retailer hopes will gain media coverage. The release of quarterly sales figures and publication of the annual report are events a retailer knows will be covered.

When unexpected publicity occurs, media report on a company without giving it advance notice. TV, newspaper, magazine, Web, and other reporters may anonymously visit retail stores and Web sites or call customer service representatives to rate their performance and quality. A fire, an employee strike, or other newsworthy event may be mentioned in a story. Investigative reports on company practices—such as using suppliers with under-age workers—may appear.

There is positive publicity when media reports are complimentary, with regard to the excellence of a retailer's practices, its community efforts, and so on. However, the media may also provide negative publicity. A story could describe a store opening in less than glowing terms, rap a firm's environmental record, or otherwise be critical. That is why public relations must be viewed as a component of the promotion mix, not as the whole mix.

Personal Selling

The communication tips at this Web site (www.inc.com/guides/sales/23032.html) are quite helpful.

Personal selling involves oral communication with one or more prospective customers for the purpose of making a sale. Retail salespeople include anyone who interacts face-to-face (or via the phone) with the shopper in a way that encourages that shopper to make a purchase. The level of personal selling used by a retailer depends on the image it wants to convey, the products sold, the amount of self-service, and the interest in long-term customer relationships—as well as customer expectations. Retail salespeople may work in a store, visit consumer homes or places of work; engage in telemarketing; or engage in real-time online chat.

Customer-service–oriented retailers believe in training superior sales associates. Why? First, higher levels of selling are needed to reinforce the retailer's image as customer-centric. Unlike self-service discounters, full-service retailers want their sales staff to frequently interact with and advise customers. Second, many retailers want to stimulate cross-selling, whereby associates recommend related items to customers. Third, sales associates may be able to "save the sale" by suggesting that customers who return merchandise try different colors, styles, or quality. And last, salespeople can help foster customer loyalty. Figure 19-5 highlights sales associate tips.

FIGURE 19-5

Tips for Retail Sales Personnel

✓ Have the right state of mind and exhibit extreme politeness.
✓ Be knowledgeable about product features, alternative suggestions, prices, company policies, and so on.
✓ Understand your ability to utilize employee empowerment—and be helpful whenever you can.
✓ Always greet the customer and make him or her feel comfortable in communicating with you.
✓ Ask the customer what he or she is looking to purchase and LISTEN to the answer.
✓ Tailor your sales approach to the individual customer and his or her needs.
✓ When appropriate, try to cross-sell related items.
✓ Do not be "pushy."
✓ Be honest and ethical in all customer interactions.
✓ Never argue with the customer or lose your temper.
✓ If you interact with more than one customer at a time, make sure all customers see that you are fair with your attention to each one.
✓ Wrap merchandise carefully.
✓ Maintain the appearance of the department; clean up when necessary.
✓ Be pleasant when customers return products and make the experience as "hassle-free" as possible.

OBJECTIVES The goals of personal selling are:

▸ To persuade customers to buy (since they often enter a store after seeing an ad)
▸ To stimulate sales of impulse items or products related to customers' basic purchases
▸ To complete customer transactions
▸ To feed information back to company decision makers
▸ To provide proper levels of customer service
▸ To improve and maintain customer satisfaction
▸ To create awareness of items also marketed through the Web, mail, and telemarketing

ADVANTAGES AND DISADVANTAGES The advantages of selling relate to its personal nature:

▸ A salesperson can adapt a message to the needs of the individual customer.
▸ A salesperson can be flexible in offering ways to address customer needs.
▸ The time commitment of the customer is higher than with advertising.
▸ There is less audience waste than with advertising; most people who walk into a store are potential customers.
▸ Customers respond more often to personal selling than to ads.
▸ Immediate feedback is provided.

The major disadvantages of personal selling are that:

▸ Only a limited number of customers can be handled at a given time.
▸ The costs of interacting with each customer can be high.
▸ Customers are not initially lured into a store or onto a Web site through personal selling.
▸ Self-service may be discouraged.
▸ Some customers may view salespeople as unhelpful and as too aggressive.

TYPES Most sales positions involve either order taking or order getting. An **order-taking salesperson** performs routine clerical and sales functions—setting up displays, stocking shelves, answering simple questions, and ringing up sales. This type of selling is most likely in stores that are strong in self-service but also have some personnel on the floor. An **order-getting salesperson** is actively involved with informing and persuading customers and in closing sales. This is a true "sales" employee. Order getters usually sell higher-priced or complex items, such as real-estate, autos, and consumer electronics. They are more skilled and better paid than order takers. See Figure 19-6.

A manufacturer may sometimes help fund personal selling by providing **PMs (promotional or push monies)** for retail salespeople selling its brand. This is in addition to regular salesperson compensation. Many retailers dislike this practice because their salespeople may be less

FIGURE 19-6

Personal Selling: Catering to the Customer

Even in a mostly self-service store, an appropriate level of personal selling and good customer service are essential—especially in a small store.

Source: Tyler Olson/ Shutterstock. Reprinted by permission.

responsive to actual customer desires (if customers desire brands that do not yield PMs for the salespeople).

FUNCTIONS   Store sales personnel may be responsible for all or many of the tasks shown in Figure 19-7 and described next. Nonstore sales personnel may also have to generate customer leads (by knocking on doors in residential areas or calling people who are listed in a local phone directory).

On entering a store or a department in it (or being contacted at home), a salesperson greets the customer. Typical in-store greetings are: "Hello, may I help you?" "Hi, is there anything in particular you are looking for?" With any greeting, the salesperson seeks to put the customer at ease and build rapport.

The salesperson next finds out what the person wants: Is the person just looking, or is there a specific good or service in mind? For what purpose is the item to be used? Is there a price range in mind? What other information can the shopper provide to help the salesperson?

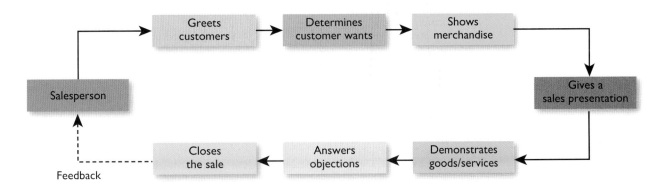

FIGURE 19-7

Typical Personal Selling Functions

At this point, the salesperson may show merchandise. He or she selects the product most apt to satisfy the customer. The salesperson may try to trade up (discuss a more expensive version) or offer a substitute (if the retailer does not carry or is out of the requested item).

The salesperson now makes a sales presentation to motivate the customer to purchase. The **canned sales presentation** is a memorized, repetitive speech given to all customers interested in a particular item. It works best if shoppers require little assistance and sales force turnover is high. The **need-satisfaction approach** is based on the principle that each customer has different wants; thus, a sales presentation should be geared to the demands of the individual customer. It is being used more in retailing.

A demonstration can show the utility of an item and allow customer participation. Demonstrations are often used with sound systems, autos, health clubs, and watches.

A customer may have questions, and the salesperson must address them. After all questions are answered, the salesperson tries to close the sale and get the shopper to buy. Typical closing lines are: "Will you take it with you or have it delivered?" "Cash or charge?" "Would you like this gift wrapped?"

For personal selling to work well, salespeople must be enthusiastic, knowledgeable, interested in customers, and good communicators. Figure 19-8 cites several ways that retail sales can be lost through poor personal selling and how to avoid these problems.[8]

Sales Promotion

Sales promotion encompasses the paid communication activities other than advertising, public relations, and personal selling that stimulate consumer purchases and dealer effectiveness. The purpose of a promotional campaign is to build sales in the short term—or sometimes as a long-term strategy of constant promotional pushes to reach sales goals. It includes displays, contests, sweepstakes, coupons, frequent shopper programs, prizes, samples, demonstrations, referral gifts, and other limited-time selling efforts outside of the ordinary promotion routine.

The main priority of a sales promotional strategy should be to maximize profit by selling as many units as possible at full price within the "prime season," and then to sell the remaining units at lower price. A retail promotion calendar is often based on sales history and a projection of the assortment plan for the current period. Then, the retailer plans to use various promotional tools to drive greater revenues by creating excitement, urgency, or price satisfaction at various times during the selling period. At the start of a season, full-margin sales can be driven by "prime" promotions—displays, upsells, and campaigns designed to promote and sell the intrinsic value and unique selling attributes of merchandise. As the season progresses, actual performance is tracked, with both better and worse results than planned taken into account. More promotions may then be used—such as loss leaders, markdowns, and deals (buy pants to get a polo T-shirt free) to stimulate sales while holding margins.[9]

The SmartSource portfolio owned by News America Marketing provides retailers and brand managers with the ability to reach their consumers through home-delivered, in-store, sampling,

The Sales Promotions Web site (http://salespromotions.org) is a leading source of information about sales promotion.

FIGURE 19-8

Selected Reasons Retail Sales Are Lost—and How to Avoid Them

X *Poor qualification of the customer.* ✓ Obtain information from the customer so the sales presentation is properly tailored.

X *Salespersons not demonstrating the good or service.* ✓ Show the good or service in use so that benefits are visualized.

X *Failure to put feeling into the presentation.* ✓ Encourage salespeople to be sincere and consumer-oriented.

X *Poor knowledge.* ✓ Train salespeople to know the major advantages and disadvantages of the goods and services, as well as those of competitors, and be able to answer questions.

X *Arguing with a customer.* ✓ Avoid arguments in handling customer objections, even if the customer is wrong.

X *No suggestion selling.* ✓ Attempt to sell related items (such as service contracts, product supplies, and installation).

X *Giving up too early.* ✓ Try again if an attempt to close a sale is unsuccessful.

X *Inflexibility.* ✓ Be creative in offering alternative solutions to a customer's needs.

X *Poor follow-up.* ✓ Be sure that orders are correctly written, that deliveries arrive on time, and that customers are satisfied.

as well as via digital and mobile media. In-store media placed in more than 61,000 food, drug, mass, and office supply stores, reach up to 75 million households monthly. SmartSource provides information, coupons, recipes, rebates, and sweepstakes forms in the store. It also supplies samples that generate trial use for nonbrand or noncategory customers, or that influence "switchers" to buy the advertised brand over others of which they are aware., or that remind loyal users to buy the product. Mobile solutions include the SmartSource Direct2Card that is integrated into a retailer mobile app so consumers can download offers to their loyalty cards and then present the cards at checkout to have the savings automatically applied.[10]

OBJECTIVES   Sales promotion goals are:

- ▶ To increase short-term sales volume
- ▶ To maintain customer loyalty
- ▶ To emphasize novelty
- ▶ To complement other promotion tools

ADVANTAGES AND DISADVANTAGES   The major advantages of sales promotion are that:

- ▶ It often has eye-catching appeal.
- ▶ Themes and tools can be distinctive.
- ▶ The consumer may receive something of value, such as coupons or free merchandise.
- ▶ It helps draw customer traffic and maintain loyalty to the retailer.
- ▶ Impulse purchases are increased.
- ▶ Customers can have fun, particularly with promotion tools such as contests and demonstrations.

The major disadvantages of sales promotion are that:

- ▶ It may be hard to terminate certain promotions without adverse customer reactions.
- ▶ The retailer's image may be hurt if trite promotions are used.
- ▶ Frivolous selling points may be stressed rather than the retailer's product assortment, prices, customer services, and other factors.
- ▶ Many sales promotions have only short-term effects.
- ▶ It should be used mostly as a supplement to other promotional forms.

Visit the site of Shop!, the leading point-of-purchase trade association (www .shopassociation.org).

TYPES   Figure 19-9 describes the major types of sales promotions. Each is explained here. Point-of-purchase promotion consists of in-store displays designed to lift sales. Displays may remind customers, stimulate impulse behavior, facilitate self-service, and reduce retailer costs if manufacturers provide the displays. See Figure 19-10. These data show the extent of displays:

- ▶ We estimate that U.S. manufacturers and retailers together annually spend more than $20 billion on in-store displays, with retailers using about two-thirds of all displays provided by manufacturers.
- ▶ Virtually all retailers have some type of point-of-purchase display.
- ▶ Restaurants, apparel stores, music/video stores, toy stores, and sporting goods stores are among the retail categories with above-average use of in-store displays.

ETHICS IN RETAILING   Using Promotional Goods

Some retailers purchase goods especially for promotions during key periods such as pre-Christmas sales, Black Friday, and Cyber Monday. Many shoppers defer purchasing items at other times, preferring to buy during these special sales—anticipating that retailers will offer especially attractive prices at these times. Some retailers feature promotional goods that are especially produced for these times. For example, although a promotional good could be produced by a well-respected television manufacturer, it may

have a lower resolution monitor and less powerful speakers. There are advantages to selling promotional goods for retailers. The goods enable retailers to achieve high levels of store traffic, to generate high inventory turnover on these goods, and to maintain traditional profit margins. These goods also provide retailers with an opportunity to trade up consumers to more costly items.

Discuss the pros and cons of promotional goods from a *consumer* perspective.

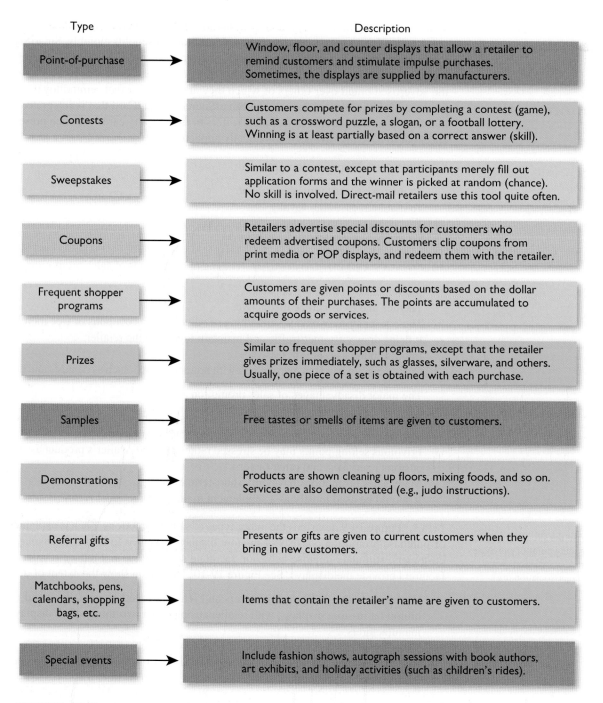

Type	Description
Point-of-purchase	Window, floor, and counter displays that allow a retailer to remind customers and stimulate impulse purchases. Sometimes, the displays are supplied by manufacturers.
Contests	Customers compete for prizes by completing a contest (game), such as a crossword puzzle, a slogan, or a football lottery. Winning is at least partially based on a correct answer (skill).
Sweepstakes	Similar to a contest, except that participants merely fill out application forms and the winner is picked at random (chance). No skill is involved. Direct-mail retailers use this tool quite often.
Coupons	Retailers advertise special discounts for customers who redeem advertised coupons. Customers clip coupons from print media or POP displays, and redeem them with the retailer.
Frequent shopper programs	Customers are given points or discounts based on the dollar amounts of their purchases. The points are accumulated to acquire goods or services.
Prizes	Similar to frequent shopper programs, except that the retailer gives prizes immediately, such as glasses, silverware, and others. Usually, one piece of a set is obtained with each purchase.
Samples	Free tastes or smells of items are given to customers.
Demonstrations	Products are shown cleaning up floors, mixing foods, and so on. Services are also demonstrated (e.g., judo instructions).
Referral gifts	Presents or gifts are given to current customers when they bring in new customers.
Matchbooks, pens, calendars, shopping bags, etc.	Items that contain the retailer's name are given to customers.
Special events	Include fashion shows, autograph sessions with book authors, art exhibits, and holiday activities (such as children's rides).

FIGURE 19-9

Types of Sales Promotion

- Retailers spend one-sixth of their sales promotion budgets on displays.
- Display ads appear on shopping carts in most U.S. supermarkets. And thousands of supermarkets have electronic signs above their aisles promoting well-known brands.

Contests and sweepstakes are similar; they seek to attract customers who participate in events with large prizes. A contest requires a customer to show some skill. A sweepstakes only requires participation, with the winner chosen at random. Disadvantages of contests and sweepstakes are their costs, customer reliance on these tools for continued patronage, the customer effort, and entries by nonshoppers. Together, we project that U.S. manufacturers and retailers spend $2 billion yearly on contests and sweepstakes.

FIGURE 19-10

Best Sales Promotion Theme?

For value-conscious customers, it's hard to top this in-store promotion—unless the retailer loses money.

Source: Lena Pan/ Shutterstock. Reprinted by permission.

Each year, hundreds of billions of dollars in coupons—discounts from regular selling prices—are distributed in the United States, with grocery products accounting for two-thirds of them. Consumers redeem $4 billion in coupons annually; retailers receive several hundred million dollars for processing coupon redemptions. Coupons are offered through freestanding inserts in Sunday papers and placements in daily papers, direct mail, Web sites, smart phones, regular magazines, and Sunday newspaper magazines. They are also put in or on packages and dispensed from store machines.[11]

Coupons have four key advantages: (1) In many cases, manufacturers pay to advertise and redeem them. (2) According to surveys, about 85 percent of consumers redeem coupons at least once during the year. (3) They contribute to the consumer's perception that a retailer offers good value. (4) Effectiveness can be measured by counting redeemed coupons. Disadvantages include the possible negative effect on the retailer's image, consumers shopping only if coupons are available, the low redemption rates, coupon clutter, retailer and consumer fraud, and handling costs. Due to the large number of coupons distributed, less than 3 percent of them are redeemed by consumers.

Frequent shopper programs foster customer relationships by awarding discounts or prizes for continued patronage. In most programs, customers accumulate points (or the equivalent) that are redeemed for cash, discounts, or prizes. Programs following these principles are most apt to succeed in the following ways:

1. Customer data are regularly collected. This enables the retailer to personalize rewards based on customer preferences and past purchases. When there are many "lapsed customers" in the database, it may be a good tactic to offer an instant reward to encourage these former shoppers to return. According to one survey, discounts on merchandise are the most important motivator.[12]

2. A loyalty program's format, rewards, and manner of communications have to be crafted to be relevant to the specific customer group. Loyalty programs offered through mobile apps can be personalized based on the individual shopper's purchase history and browsing behavior.

3. A membership card in a shopper's wallet can be a constant reminder of the benefits of the loyalty program of a given retailer.

4. A good loyalty program builds excitement by letting customers know exactly what rewards they can expect, how to earn them, and how they are progressing to a reward goal.

5. For a loyalty program to reach a high level of customer participation, rewards should be readily obtainable and incremental to transform more customers from low value to high value.

6. When intangible and exclusive services and experiences are provided at higher levels of rewards, customers will brag about reaching special membership status. This will propel even more repeat business and may politely nudge those who are in a lower reward category.

7. A loyalty program can be used as part of regular digital communications with customers. Retailers can send follow-up messages after each purchase and communicate frequently to introduce new perks and special offers.[13]

All sorts of retailers participate in online loyalty programs; e-Rewards is a good example (www.e-rewards.com).

The advantages of frequent shopper programs for retailers are the loyalty (customers amass points only by shopping at a specific firm or firms), the increased shopping, and the competitive edge for a retailer similar to others. However, some consumers feel these programs are not really free and would rather shop at lower-priced stores without loyalty programs. These shoppers believe it will take too long to gather enough points to earn meaningful gifts, and retail profit margins may be smaller if firms with these programs try to price competitively with those without the programs.

Prizes are similar to frequent shopper programs, but they are given with each purchase. They are most effective when sets of glasses, silverware, dishes, place mats, and so on are distributed one at a time to shoppers. These encourage loyalty. Problems are the cost of prizes, the difficulty of termination, and the possible impact on image.

Free samples (food tastings) and demonstrations (cooking lessons) can complement personal selling. We estimate that more than $2.5 billion is spent annually on sampling and demonstrations by U.S. stores—mostly at supermarkets, membership clubs, specialty stores, and department stores. They are effective because customers become involved and impulse purchases increase. Loitering and costs may be problems.

Referral gifts may encourage existing customers to bring in new ones. Direct marketers, such as book and music clubs, often use this tool. It is a technique that has no important shortcomings and recognizes the value of friends in influencing purchases.

Matchbooks, pens, calendars, and shopping bags may be given to customers. They differ from prizes because they promote retailers' names. These items should be used as supplements. The advantage is longevity. There is no real disadvantage.

Retailers may use special events to generate consumer enthusiasm. Events can range from store grand openings to fashion shows. When new McDonald's stores open, there are typically giveaways and children's activities, and there is a guest appearance by Ronald McDonald (a human in a costume). Generally, in choosing a special event, the potential increase in consumer awareness and store traffic needs to be weighed against that event's costs. See Figure 19-11.

FIGURE 19-11

Driving Business through Special Events

Many types of retailers run Halloween-themed special events every year. Painted pumpkins are colorful and eye-catching—and can drive higher store traffic. Often the pumpkins themselves can even be sold.

Source: Jules Selmes/Pearson Education Ltd. Reprinted by permission.

PLANNING A RETAIL PROMOTIONAL STRATEGY

A systematic approach to promotional planning is shown in Figure 19-12 and explained next. Our blog site (www.bermanevansretail) has posts related to promotional strategy, including word of mouth.

Determining Promotional Objectives

A retailer's broad promotional goals are typically drawn from this list. In developing a promotional strategy, the firm must determine which of these are most important:

- ▸ Increase sales.
- ▸ Stimulate impulse and reminder buying.
- ▸ Raise customer traffic.
- ▸ Get leads for sales personnel.
- ▸ Present and reinforce the retailer image.
- ▸ Inform customers about goods and services.
- ▸ Popularize new stores and Web sites.
- ▸ Capitalize on manufacturer support.

FIGURE 19-12

Planning a Retail Promotional Strategy

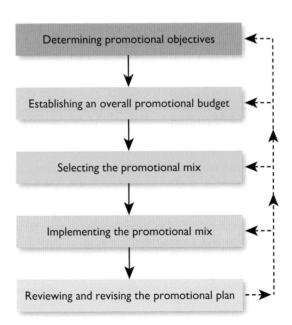

> Enhance customer relations.
> Maintain customer loyalty.
> Have consumers pass along positive information to friends and others.

It is vital to state goals as precisely as possible to give direction to the choice of promotional types, media, and messages. Increasing sales is not a specific goal. However, increasing sales by 10 percent is directional, quantitative, and measurable. With that goal, a firm would be able to prepare a thorough promotional plan and evaluate its success.

Perhaps the most vital long-term promotion goal for any retailer is to gain positive **word of mouth (WOM)**, which occurs when one consumer talks to others—in person, on the phone, by E-mail, through social media, or in some other format. If a satisfied customer refers friends to a retailer, this can build into a chain of customers. No retailer can succeed if it receives extensive negative WOM (such as "The hotel advertised that everything was included in the price. Yet it cost me another $50 to play golf"). Negative WOM will cause a firm to lose substantial business.

Both goods- and services-oriented retailers must have positive word of mouth to attract new customers and retain existing customers. It has even greater importance given the widespread use of social media, where a single negative post or tweet can undo years of careful brand building.[14] For example, many Netflix lapsed members who rejoin the service hear or read word-of-mouth messages by existing members. If Netflix does not satisfy existing members, it may not be able to attract new members, and the ability to maintain and grow the business will be adversely affected.[15]

See what activities facilitate good word of mouth (http://wommapedia.org).

Establishing an Overall Promotional Budget

There are five main procedures for setting the size of a retail promotional budget. Retailers should weigh the strengths and weaknesses of each technique in relation to their own requirements and constraints. To assist firms in their efforts, there is now computer software available.

With the **all-you-can-afford method**, a retailer first allots funds for each element of the retail strategy mix except promotion. The remaining funds go to promotion. This is the weakest technique. Its shortcomings are that little emphasis is placed on promotion as a strategic variable; expenditures are not linked to goals; and if little or no funds are left over, the promotion budget is too small or nonexistent. The method is used predominantly by small, conservative retailers.

The **incremental method** relies on prior promotion budgets to allocate funds. A percentage is either added to or subtracted from one year's budget to determine the budget for next year. If this year's promotion budget is $100,000, next year's would be calculated by adjusting that amount. A 10 percent rise means that next year's budget would be $110,000. This technique is useful for a small retailer. It provides a reference point. The budget is adjusted based on the firm's feelings about past successes and future trends. It is easy to apply. Yet, the budget is rarely tied to specific goals; rather, "gut feelings" are generally used.

With the **competitive parity method**, a retailer's promotion budget is raised or lowered based on competitors' actions. If the leading competitor raises its budget, other retailers in the area may follow. This method, often employed by both small and large firms, uses a comparison

RETAILING AROUND THE WORLD

Burberry's Chinese Promotional Strategy

Thirty-eight percent of Burberry's sales are to Chinese customers as compared to 30 percent for its major competitors. As a result, winning over Chinese customers is a key part of Burberry's (www.burberry.com) promotional strategy. To build market share at a time when the Chinese economy is slowing down, Burberry has equipped its stores in China with touchscreens and iPads. They display special collections, fashion shows, and Burberry-produced special events. Burberry also uses WeChat (www.wechat.com), a popular Chinese social media site, as an online source of information on its luxury goods, such as material on its classic collections and new styles, as well as a link to Burberry's Web site. In a recent campaign, WeChat users were eligible to win Burberry New Year's envelopes that were only available for in-store pickup.

Discuss how Burberry can adapt these promotional strategies worldwide.

Sources: Corinne Grether and Janice Kew, "Burberry, Richemont Say Mainland China Luxury Sales Rebound," January 14, 2016, www.bloomberg.com; and Yuyu Chen, "How Burberry, Coach and Chanel Win Over WeChat," June 1, 2016, http://digiday.com

point and is market-oriented and conservative. It also is imitative, takes for granted that tough-to-get competitive data are available, and assumes competitors are similar (as to years in business, size, customers, location, merchandise, prices, etc.). That last point is critical because competitors often need very different promotional budgets.

In the **percentage-of-sales method**, a retailer ties its promotion budget to revenue. A promotion-to-sales ratio is developed. Then, during succeeding years, this ratio remains constant. A firm could set promotion costs at 10 percent of sales. If this year's sales are $600,000, there is a $60,000 promotion budget. If next year's sales are estimated at $720,000, a $72,000 budget is planned. This process uses sales as a base, is adaptable, and correlates promotion and sales. Nonetheless, there is no relation to goals (for an established firm, sales growth may not require increased promotion); promotion is not used to lead sales; and promotion drops during poor periods, when increases might be helpful. This technique provides excess financing in times of high sales and too few funds in periods of low sales.

Under the **objective-and-task method**, a retailer clearly defines its promotion goals and prepares a budget to satisfy them. A goal might be to have 70 percent of the people in its trading area know a retailer's name by the end of a one-month promotion campaign, up from 50 percent. To do so, it would determine the tasks and costs required to achieve that goal:

Objective	Task	Cost
1. Gain awareness of working women.	Use eight 1/4-page ads in four successive Sunday editions of two area papers.	$20,000
2. Gain awareness of motorists.	Use twenty 30-second radio ads during prime time on local radio stations.	$12,000
3. Gain awareness of pedestrians.	Give away 5,000 shopping bags.	$15,000
	Total budget	$47,000

The objective-and-task method is the best budgeting technique. Goals are clear, spending relates to goal-oriented tasks, and performance can be assessed. However, it can be time consuming and complex to set goals and specific tasks, especially for small retailers.

Selecting the Promotional Mix

After a budget is set, the promotional mix is determined: the retailer's combination of advertising, public relations, personal selling, and sales promotion. A firm with a limited budget may rely on store displays, Web site traffic, flyers, targeted direct mail, and publicity to generate customer traffic. One with a large budget may rely more on newspaper and TV ads. Retailers often use an assortment of forms to reinforce each other. A melding of media ads and point-of-purchse displays may be more effective than either form alone. See Figure 19-13.

The promotional mix is affected by the type of retailer involved. In supermarkets, sampling, frequent shopper promotions, theme sales, and bonus coupons are among the techniques used most. At upscale stores, there is more attention to personal selling and less to advertising and sales promotion as compared with discounters. Table 19-3 shows a number of small-retailer promotional mixes.

In reacting to a retailer's communication efforts, consumers often go through a sequence of steps known as the, **hierarchy of effects**, which takes them from awareness, to knowledge, to liking, to preference, to conviction, to purchase. Different promotional mixes are needed in each step. Ads and public relations are best to develop awareness; personal selling and sales promotion are best in changing attitudes and stimulating desires. This is especially true for expensive, complex goods and services. See Figure 19-14.

Implementing the Promotional Mix

The implementation of a promotional mix involves choosing which specific media to use (such as Newspaper A and Newspaper B), timing, message content, the makeup of the sales force, specific sales promotion tools, and the responsibility for coordination.[16]

MEDIA DECISIONS The choice of specific media is based on their overall costs, efficiency (the cost to reach the target market), lead time, and editorial content. The retailer's promotion budget

Freestanding inserts offer retailers many possibilities. Visit Valassis and see some examples (www.valassis.com/print-advertising/newspaper-ads#flyers).

Is 3D shopping on the Web ahead of its time or on target (www.ardzan.com)?

FIGURE 19-13

An Integrated Promotional Approach

In today's vast multimedia communication environment, two things are quite clear for retailers. First, the message, look, image, and other communication factors must be consistent and integrated across all the media platforms that a given retailer chooses. There cannot be a disconnect; otherwise, shoppers will become confused. Second, the effects of different media need to be carefully monitored. In particular, a retailer cannot ignore social media; it needs to embrace them and regularly post there.

Source: Rawpixel/Shutterstock. Reprinted by permission.

TABLE 19-3 The Promotional Mixes of Selected Small Retailers

Type of Retailer	Favorite Media	Personal Selling Emphasis	Special Considerations	Promotional Opportunities
Apparel store	Weekly papers; direct mail; radio; Web; exterior signs	High	Cooperative ads available from manufacturers	Fashion shows for community groups and charities; social media
Auto supply store	Local papers; Yellow Pages; POP displays; Web; exterior signs	Moderate	Cooperative ads available from manufacturers	Direct mail
Bookstore	Local papers; Yellow Pages; radio; Web; exterior signs	Moderate	Cooperative ads available from publishers	Author-signing events; retailer blog
Coin-operated laundry	Yellow Pages; flyers in area; local direct mail; exterior signs	None	None	Coupons in newspaper ads
Gift store	Weekly papers; Yellow Pages; direct mail; Web; exterior signs	Moderate	None	Special events; Web ads
Hair grooming/ beauty salon	Yellow Pages; mentions in feature articles; exterior signs	Moderate	Word-of-mouth communication key	Participation in fashion shows; free beauty clinics
Health food store	Local papers; shoppers; POP displays; Web; exterior signs	Moderate	None	Display windows
Restaurant	Newspapers; radio; Web; Yellow Pages; entertainment guides; exterior signs	Moderate	Word-of-mouth communication key	Write-ups in critics' columns; special events

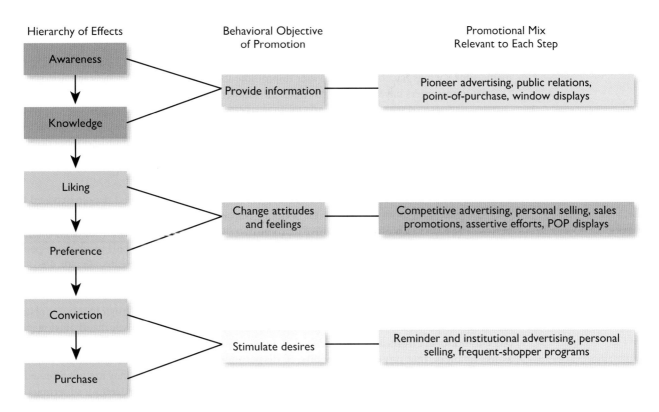

FIGURE 19-14

Promotion and the Hierarchy of Effects

is important since heavy use of one expensive medium may preclude a balanced promotional mix, and a firm may not be able to repeat a message in a costly medium.

A medium's efficiency relates to the cost of reaching a given number of target customers. Media rates are often expressed in terms of cost per 1,000 readers, watchers, or listeners:

$$\text{Cost per thousand} = \frac{\text{Cost per message} \times 1{,}000}{\text{Circulation}}$$

A newspaper with a circulation of 400,000 and a one-page advertising rate of $10,000 has a per-page cost per thousand of $25.

In this computation, total circulation is used to measure efficiency. Yet, because a retailer usually appeals to a limited target market, only the relevant portion of circulation should be considered. If 70 percent of readers are target customers for a particular firm (and the other 30 percent live outside the trading area), the real cost per thousand is:

$$\text{Cost per thousand (target marked)} = \frac{\text{Cost per page} \times 1{,}000}{\text{Circulation} \times \dfrac{\text{Target market}}{\text{Circulation}}}$$

$$= \frac{\$10{,}000 \times 1{,}000}{400{,}000 \times 0.70} = \$35.71$$

Different media require different lead times. A newspaper ad can be placed shortly before publication and an online ad can sometimes go "live" almost immediately, whereas a print magazine ad sometimes must be placed months in advance. In addition, the retailer must decide what kind of editorial content it wants near ads (such as a sports story or a personal-care column).

Media decisions are not simple. Despite spending billions of dollars on TV and radio commercials, banner ads at search engines, and other media, many Web retailers have found the most valuable medium for them is E-mail. It is fast, inexpensive, and targeted. Consider the following example.

To generate greater *awareness* of Web retailers, costly advertising may be necessary in today's competitive and cluttered landscape. Netflix has a broad mix of marketing and public relations programs, including digital and television advertising, affiliates and device partners, and social media sites such as Facebook and Twitter to promote its service to potential new members.[17]

After customers have visited a Web site, the retailer can use explicit opt-in marketing to help sustain relationships with the customer. *Opt-in marketing* involves the customer giving permission for the retailer to send marketing materials, which leads to higher receptivity to marketing messages. Astute marketers collect preference information, so that content and promotional offers in an E-mail newsletter are relevant to the customer. This leads to an ongoing, evolving relationship between the retailer and the customer.[18]

TIMING OF THE PROMOTIONAL MIX   **Reach** refers to the number of distinct people exposed to a retailer's promotion efforts in a specific period. **Frequency** is the average number of times each person reached is exposed to a retailer's promotion efforts in a specific period. A retailer can advertise extensively or intensively. *Extensive media coverage* often means ads reach many people but with relatively low frequency. *Intensive media coverage* generally means ads are placed in selected media and repeated frequently. Repetition is important, particularly for a retailer seeking to develop an image or sell new goods or services.

Decisions are needed about how to address peak selling seasons and whether to mass or distribute efforts. In peak seasons, all elements of the promotional mix are usually utilized; in slow periods, promotional efforts are often reduced. A **massed promotion effort** is used by retailers, such as toy retailers, that promote seasonally. A **distributed promotion effort** is used by retailers, such as fast-food restaurants, that promote throughout the year. Although they are not affected by seasonality in the same way as other retailers, massed advertising is practiced by supermarkets; many use Wednesday or Thursday for weekly newspaper ads. This takes advantage of the fact that a high proportion of consumers make their major shopping trip on Friday, Saturday, or Sunday.

Sales force size can vary by time (morning versus evening), day (weekdays versus weekends), and month (December versus January). Sales promotions also vary in their timing. Store openings and holidays are especially good times for sales promotions (and public relations).

CONTENT OF MESSAGES   Whether written or spoken, personally or impersonally delivered, message content is important. Advertising themes, wording, headlines, use of color, size, layout, and placement must be selected. Publicity releases must be written. In personal selling, the greeting, sales presentation, demonstration, and closing need to be applied. With sales promotion, the firm's message must be composed and placed on the promotional device.

The CarMax (www .carmax.com) message— "Experience clear and simple car buying and selling"—is easy to understand. Scroll down to see "Why buy or sell with us."

To a large extent, the characteristics of the promotional form influence the message. A shopping bag often contains no more than a retailer's name, and a billboard (seen at 55 miles per hour) is good for visual effect but can hold only limited information. Yet, a salesperson may be able to hold a customer's attention for a while. A number of shopping centers use a glossy magazine—in print and online—to communicate a community-oriented image, introduce new stores to consumers, and promote the goods and services carried at stores in the center. Cluttered ads displaying many products suggest a discounter's orientation, whereas fine pencil drawings and selective product displays suggest a specialty store focus.

TECHNOLOGY IN RETAILING | Smartphone Couponing

There are many advantages to the use of mobile coupons as compared to the traditional paper format. Mobile coupons do not have to be cut, organized, and searched for while in a store. They can be redeemed by displaying the coupons on a customer's smartphone. Retailers can use mobile couponing in conjunction with geo-fencing applications, whereby the retailers can offer select coupon offers to customers within a given distance of a store. The redemption rate for mobile coupons can be as much as 10 percent or more. Effective mobile coupons should be capable of being redeemed without printing. They also should be based on a customer's purchase history. A retailer can offer special coupons to lapsed customers, brand-loyal customers, or customers with special purchase histories (such as those that favor organics, prepared foods, local produce).

Distinguish between retailer and consumer goods manufacturer-based mobile coupons.

Some retailers use comparative advertising to contrast their offerings with those of their competitors. These ads help position a retailer relative to competitors, increase awareness of the firm, maximize the efficiency of a limited budget, and offer credibility. Yet, they provide visibility for competitors, may confuse people, and may lead to legal action. Fast-food and off-price retailers are among those using comparative ads.

MAKEUP OF SALES FORCE   Qualifications of sales personnel must be detailed, and these personnel must be recruited, selected, trained, compensated, supervised, and monitored. Personnel should also be classified as order takers or order getters and assigned to the appropriate departments.

SALES PROMOTION TOOLS   Specific sales promotion tools must be chosen from among those that were cited in Figure 19-9. The combination of tools depends on short-term goals and the other aspects of the promotion mix. If possible, cooperative ventures should be sought. Tools inconsistent with the firm's image should never be used; and retailers should recognize the types of promotions that customers really want.

RESPONSIBILITY FOR COORDINATION   Regardless of the retailer's size or format, someone must be responsible for the promotion function. Larger retailers often assign this job to a vice-president who oversees display personnel, works with the firm's ad agency, supervises the firm's advertising department (if there is one), and supplies branch outlets with POP materials. In a large retail store, personal selling is usually under the jurisdiction of the store manager. For a promotional strategy to succeed, its components have to be coordinated with other retail mix elements. Sales personnel must be informed of special sales and know product attributes; featured items must be received, marked, and displayed; and accounting entries must be made. Often, a shopping center or a shopping district runs theme promotions, such as "Back to School." In those instances, someone must coordinate the activities of all participating retailers.

Reviewing and Revising the Promotional Plan

An analysis of the success of a promotional plan depends on its objectives. Revisions should be made if pre-set goals are not achieved. Here are some ways to test the effectiveness of a promotional effort:

Examples of Retail Promotion Goals	Approaches for Evaluating Promotion Effectiveness
Inform current customers about new credit plans; acquaint potential customers with new offerings.	Study company and product awareness before and after promotion; evaluate size of audience.
Develop and reinforce a particular image; maintain customer loyalty.	Study image through surveys before and after public relations and other promotion efforts.
Increase customer traffic; get leads for salespeople; increase revenues above last year's; reduce customer returns from prior years.	Evaluate sales performance and the number of inquiries; study customer intentions to buy before and after promotion; study customer trading areas and average purchases; review coupon redemption.

Although it may at times be tough to assess promotion efforts (e.g., increased revenues might be due to several factors, not just promotion), it is crucial for retailers to systematically study and adapt their promotional mixes. Walmart provides suppliers with store-by-store data and sets up-front goals for cooperative promotion programs. Actual sales are then compared against the goals. Lowe's, the home center chain, applies computerized testing to review thousands of different ideas affecting the design of circulars and media mix options. In a suburb of Minneapolis, Supervalu runs a "lab store," a model store not open to the public where the company can test how new products look on its shelves and experiment with seasonal displays. Retailers such as Kohl's are testing the effectiveness of newspaper circulars versus digital flyers on in-store sales and profitability.[19]

Smart Brief (www .smartbrief.com/industry/ marketing-advertising/ digital) presents insights on the current status of online advertising.

Chapter Summary

1. *To explore the scope of retail promotion.* Retail promotion is any communication by a retailer that informs, persuades, and/or reminds the target market about any aspect of the retailer through ads, public relations, personal selling, and sales promotion.

2. *To study the elements of retail promotion: advertising, public relations, personal selling, and sales promotion.* Advertising involves paid, nonpersonal communication. It has a large audience, low costs per person, many alternative media, and other factors. It also involves message inflexibility, high absolute costs, and a wasted portion of the audience. Key advertising media are papers, TV, the Web, phone directories, direct mail, radio, transit, outdoor, magazines, and flyers/circulars. Especially useful are cooperative ads, in which a retailer shares costs and messages with manufacturers, wholesalers, or other retailers.

   Public relations includes all communications fostering a favorable image. It may be nonpersonal or personal, paid or nonpaid, and sponsor controlled or not controlled. Publicity is the nonpersonal, nonpaid form of public relations. Public relations creates awareness, enhances the image, involves credible sources, and has no message costs. It also has little control over messages, is short term, and can entail nonmedia costs. Publicity can be expected or unexpected and positive or negative.

   Personal selling uses oral communication with one or more potential customers and is critical for persuasion and in closing sales. It is adaptable, flexible, and provides immediate feedback. The audience is small, per-customer costs are high, and shoppers are not lured into the store. Order-taking and/or order-getting salespeople can be employed. Functions include greeting the customer, determining wants, showing merchandise, making a sales presentation, demonstrating products, answering objections, and closing the sale.

   Sales promotion comprises paid communication activities other than advertising, public relations, and personal selling. It may be eye-catching, unique, and valuable to the customer. It also may be hard to end, negatively affect image, and rely on frivolous points. Tools include point-of-purchase displays, contests and sweepstakes, coupons, frequent shopper programs, prizes, samples, demonstrations, referral gifts, matchbooks, pens, calendars, shopping bags, and special events.

3. *To discuss the strategic aspects of retail promotion: objectives, budgeting, the mix of forms, implementing the mix, and reviewing and revising the plan.* There are five steps in a promotion strategy: (a) Goals are stated in specific measurable terms. Positive word of mouth is an important long-term goal. (b) An overall promotion budget is set on the basis of one of these methods: all you can afford, incremental, competitive parity, percentage of sales, and objective and task. (c) The promotional mix is outlined, based on the budget, the type of retailing, the coverage of the media, and the hierarchy of effects. (d) The promotional mix is enacted. Included are decisions involving specific media, promotional timing, message content, sales force composition, sales promotion tools, and the responsibility for coordination. (e) The retailer systematically reviews and adjusts the promotional plan, consistent with pre-set goals.

Key Terms

retail promotion (p. 483)
advertising (p. 483)
cooperative advertising (p. 485)
vertical cooperative advertising
    agreement (p. 489)
horizontal cooperative advertising
    agreement (p. 489)
public relations (p. 490)
publicity (p. 490)
personal selling (p. 491)

order-taking salesperson (p. 492)
order-getting salesperson (p. 492)
PMs (promotional or push monies)
    (p. 492)
canned sales presentation (p. 494)
need-satisfaction approach (p. 494)
sales promotion (p. 494)
word of mouth (WOM) (p. 500)
all-you-can-afford method
    (p. 500)

incremental method (p. 500)
competitive parity method (p. 500)
percentage-of-sales method (p. 501)
objective-and-task method (p. 501)
hierarchy of effects (p. 501)
reach (p. 504)
frequency (p. 504)
massed promotion effort (p. 504)
distributed promotion effort
    (p. 504)

Questions for Discussion

1. What are the four different elements of advertising? Are all of them appropriate to an average retailer in most markets?
2. Retailers may have a wide variety of different advertising objectives. Suggest four options.
3. What are the major advantages of public relations? Why is it used?
4. How do you distinguish between an order taker and an order getter?
5. Suggest the four main objectives that a retailer might choose when launching a sales promotion.
6. How might a point-of-purchase promotion significantly contribute to retail sales?
7. What are the pros and cons of coupons?
8. Develop sales promotions for each of the following:
    a. A nearby strip shopping center
    b. A new restaurant
    c. An upscale discount online furniture retailer
9. Which method of promotional budgeting should a small retailer use? A large retailer? Why?
10. Explain the hierarchy of effects from a retail perspective. Apply your answer to a consumer electronics store that is just opening.
11. Develop a checklist for a chain of large sporting goods stores to coordinate its promotional plan.
12. For each of these promotional goals, explain how to evaluate promotional effectiveness:
    a. To increase impulse purchases of candy
    b. To project a reliable image
    c. To increase customer loyalty rates

Web-Based Exercise

Visit this Web site (www.entrepreneur.com/article/241607). What could a small store-based retailer learn by visiting this site?

PART 7 Short Cases

Case 1: Keep It Simple*

"In this omnichannel shopping era, it is more important than ever to deliver a simplified shopping experience. Retail brands that can deliver the most streamlined experience will drive the highest levels of long-term customer loyalty."

That was the message in branding firm Siegel and Gale's sixth annual Global Brand Simplicity Index, based on responses from 12,000+ adults across eight countries. The survey asked consumers to rank leading retail brands based on how simple they are, why disrupters are gaining ground, and the benefits of simplifying customer experiences. "Brands delivering value through streamlined customer experiences are learning that simplicity pays off," says Brian Rafferty, global director of insights at Siegel and Gale.

This could be a turning point for companies that have historically struggled with how to connect with the omnichannel shopper. By definition, the omnichannel retailing model enables shoppers to seamlessly hop across a brand's physical and digital touchpoints and procure merchandise just as easily. It has also conditioned shoppers to expect to shop across a "brand," rather than individual "channels." Retailers must adopt and integrate multiple customer touchpoints—whether via Web-based kiosks, smartphones, tablets, or mobile apps—to ensure real-time engagement with customers during their path to purchase.

Merchants must ensure that ordered merchandise can be shipped to shoppers' homes or their desired store for pickup. This calls for new fulfillment options designed to make it simple to receive orders. "The pace of technology is changing in terms of customer expectations, but retailers must keep up and seamlessly coordinate channels and operations," Rafferty says. "Retailers need to personalize shopping experiences, and give shoppers exactly what they want, when they want it. This experience needs to be invisible to the customer. They are not interested in processes—they just want a top-notch experience."

Only a handful of retailers are making strides in customers' eyes— especially in the United States. Grocery chain Publix is one of them: Jumping 20 spots in one year and landing third on the U.S. simplicity list, Publix touts an "easily navigated layout and pays close attention to the customer experience," the study reported.

Publix aside, unconventional sources are outpacing customary ones in this area. Shoppers ranked Google as the top U.S. retailer choice due to its providing instant information when making purchase decisions. Netflix was second, and Amazon.com and Zappos.com were fourth and sixth, based on free shipping.

For firms on the fence about the power of the simplified, informational shopping experience, consider this: 63 percent of people are willing to pay more for simpler experiences, and 69 percent are more apt to recommend a brand because it provides simpler experiences and communications, according to the report.

Already inundated with information from conventional sources such as point-of-sale stations, the omnichannel business model is producing unprecedented levels of unstructured data from Web sites, social media, and electronic customer touchpoints, including kiosks and mobile devices. That "big data" contain intricate nuggets like customer preferences and merchandise consumption patterns.

There is no better place for retail brands to find customer-specific information than in their own loyalty program databases. Understanding what Dunkin' Donuts shoppers want makes it easier for the marketing team to "focus on fewer bigger things," John Costello, CMO of Dunkin' Brands, says. "We get people to focus on the three to five things in their area that make a difference," he said. "Find out what makes a difference, and eliminate the little things that create clutter." Keeping a keen eye on these ever-changing factors has helped Dunkin' Donuts claim the seventh spot in the U.S. Simplicity Index.

Questions

1. From a retailer perspective, how would you exhibit "simplicity" in an omnichannel world?
2. From a consumer perspective, what does "simplicity" mean to you? Is it important? Explain your answer.
3. Should every kind of retailer—small, large; discount, upscale; and so on—strive to be "simplistic"? Why or why not?
4. Based on this case, what lessons would you recommend for your college bookstore?

Case 2: More than Price*

A study released in 2016 by Deloitte, the Food Marketing Institute, and the Grocery Manufacturers Association shows that more than half of Americans surveyed weigh "evolving drivers" in their purchasing decisions—health and wellness, safety, social impact experience, and transparency—in addition to the traditional drivers of taste, price, and convenience.

"Price is always going to be important; so is quality. But what we're seeing here is a shift from value to values," says Tom Compernolle, principal in the retail practice at Deloitte Consulting. "Some chains have hired registered dietitians to provide food and nutrition information. Others have showed innovation in their organic private-label programs. Even dollar stores and other small-store formats use signage to drive home environmental and health and wellness messaging."

Jack Ringquist, global leader of consumer products at Deloitte, says today's supermarket shoppers behave differently than even 3 years ago—and their preferences are becoming more fragmented than the food industry may have anticipated. "At one time health and wellness might have been considered outlying values," he says, but "that's no longer true. Technology has made information so pervasive that shoppers are making more informed choices about the foods they eat."

Viewpoints differ when the conversation turns to Millennials, and the changes this cohort are likely to spur in the channel. Still, whether folks argue that they'll abandon traditional supermarkets or drag them kicking and screaming into the next

* Based on material in Deena M. Amato-Mccoy, "Keep It Simple," *STORES Magazine,* March 2016, pp. 54–58. Reprinted by permission. Copyright 2016. STORES Magazine.

* Based on material in Susan Reda, "Supermarket Showdown," *STORES Magazine,* April 2016, p. 26. Reprinted by permission. Copyright 2016. STORES Magazine.

decade, there remain a few truisms. Millennials do not have a reputation for loading up their pantry; they're more inclined to think about what they're going to eat when they get hungry. The idea of three traditional meals a day doesn't mesh with their lifestyle; sometimes a protein bar is just right for breakfast, and on other days it's perfect for dinner.

"Millennials don't bring a lot of preconceived notions about foods and meals to the table," says Phil Lempert, food industry analyst. "They like the idea of buying meats at a butcher shop. They are passionate about food but short on time, so home delivery and meal kits suit them fine. They're changing the dynamics of food retailing because they're not encumbered by all the reasons why they can't" do things differently.

"The reinvention happening in this space is being driven by the consumer[s]. They've pushed the traditional supermarket operators to ask themselves, 'How can I be iconic and different?'" says Farla Efros, president of HRC Advisory, Hilco's global retail advisory practice. "Consumers are … time-starved, they like online ordering, they prefer to pick [food] up at the store on the way home from wherever. It's up to the traditional supermarkets to figure out how to make that happen."

Prosper Insight and Analytics' consumer research consistently shows that customers choose to shop at certain supermarkets based on a handful of qualities: In order of importance, they are price, location, selection, quality, and fresh produce. Price is cited by 73 percent of shoppers, location by 70 percent. "Keep in mind that while new concepts and formats are springing up, nearly 20 percent of shoppers make Walmart their top choice for groceries—and price is the main driver," says Phil Rist, principal and executive vice-president of strategy at Prosper. "At other stores, loyalty cards, fuel/gas rewards, and coupons could be significant drivers. The takeaway is really the need for marketers to understand what's important to their customers—and what's not—and to use that to carve their niche."

Because price is important to many shoppers, value supermarkets such as Aldi can expect growth rates 55 percent higher than for premium chains and 228 percent higher than mainstream supermarkets.

Questions

1. How would you promote a proactive health-and-wellness theme as a drugstore chain?
2. What does "transparency" mean with regard to the information provided by retailers? What grade would you give to the retailers you patronize? Why?
3. How would you advertise differently to Millennials than to Baby Boomers?
4. Describe the role of in-store displays in terms of the material presented in this case.

Case 3: Enhancing the In-Store Experience through Facial Recognition Software*

The best way to understand what eyeQ is trying to do is to compare it to a conventional digital display. Unless it's a specialized store, that display can't show shoppers a significant portion of

a store's assortment, so it might instead show a variety: lots of fast fades and dissolves, and maybe some panning video of the aisles or the escalators. The idea is to keep it moving, so if a shopper stands there long enough he or she will see something of interest

The digital sign in eyeQ's system is connected to a camera, a lot of proprietary facial recognition software, and—via IBM's cloud service—Watson. When a shopper stops to look at an eyeQ digital sign, the sign looks back at him or her. Then, based on facial features and appearance, eyeQ tailors its content to the viewer's age and gender. Men between the ages of 35 and 45 might see suits, top-end cameras, or fly fishing rods; women between the ages of 18 and 30 might see jewelry or clothes.

"When somebody approaches the screen," says Doug Bain, the chief revenue officer of eyeQ Insights, "the screen is already aware of the baseline information—the age and gender of the person—and is ready to make product recommendations." There's more, though: If the shopper gives the system his or her Twitter user name, Watson can capture the most recent 200 tweets, run them through its natural language processing capabilities, and slot him or her into one of a selection of basic personality types. Not only can the system change the products being recommended but it can also change the whole experience—background colors, video, music, whatever it's got.

The most recent version of eyeQ's system can even register emotion. "It's categorizing the person's expression as happy, sad, angry, surprised—and to what degree," says Bain. "Is the expression changing dramatically when he or she gets to a certain point in the video, or a certain page, or when he or she touches the screen? It's another data point to determine the effectiveness of the content."

As it develops, eyeQ has been working closely with retail marketing agency TPN. Manolo Almagro, TPN's senior managing director for digital and retail technologies, notes that the system, even without a consumer opting in or providing her or his own information, can identify a repeat visitor by the unique media access control address her or his mobile device sends out to find available Wi-Fi. "We don't know the individual's name," he says, "but we know it's the same 40-year-old woman who was in on Tuesday."

Almagro adds that further development of the technology requires some care. "I know you're interested in a certain type of product, I know your age and gender, and I know your personality type. This is a level of depth we've never had before, and we have to ask ourselves, 'How much personalization is too much?' I want to give enough to make the experience more convenient for you, but not so much that it becomes creepy. That's a kind of fine line we have to walk."

At the moment, one retailer has a prototype in place, and several consumer package goods companies are experimenting with prototypes in the retail space. Shortly, eyeQ expects to have a prototype implementation robust enough to start to generate some real feedback. Bain says early signs are encouraging. "We have data that demonstrate that increased engagement with the system does indeed mean increased sales."

---

* Based on material in Peter Johnston, "Eye Know You!" *STORES Magazine,* December 2015, pp. 58–60. Reprinted by permission. Copyright 2016. STORES Magazine.

Questions

1. As an apparel retailer, would you be excited by utilizing eyeQ displays to tailor products to specific customers?
2. As a one-way system—no questions are asked of shoppers—how accurate do you think eyeQ would be in identifying customer characteristics and their desires?
3. What promotion mix would you use to let shoppers know about eyeQ? Explain your answer.
4. Comment on the privacy issues involved with eyeQ.

Case 4: Revitalizing Customer Loyalty*

There are many ways to maintain customer loyalty, but experts say consistent and clear pricing may be the most important. Moreover, getting the price right across all products all the time is a key ingredient in strengthening shopper loyalty. The trick is to do so profitably. "Today's retailers have a unique opportunity to leverage price management and optimization tools to make the most profitable decisions," explains Cindy Kim, vice-president of global marketing for Revionics, a Texas-based provider of price optimization solutions. "But the advantage is being able to tap into the vast amounts of market, competitive, and customer data to effectively manage and execute those pricing decisions without killing their margins."

According to Kim, intelligent data can provide a lot of value in terms of the types of assortments by stores, demand, sensitivity to price, and shopper purchasing behavior and preferences, as well as understanding how competitors are pricing, which can affect the shopper at the product level.

Jim Sills, president and CEO of software and services provider Clear Demand, agrees, adding that customer loyalty is driven by price and experience. "It's a service equation that has to be informed by using pricing intelligence, which ensures an interconnected and consistent shopping experience. You must have rational line structures automated with a rules engine, which ensures products are priced rationally—that is, not in a way that forces shoppers to trade down because the gap between brands is too large. If loyalty really matters to a retailer, consistent, rational pricing strategies must be maintained."

Also necessary is a better understanding of shopper behavior than that of the competition, asserts Guru Hariharan, CEO of Boomerang Commerce, which advises retailers on how to make smart pricing decisions to boost profits. What's more, retailers need recommendations based on knowing where to hold prices, even when a rival drops its prices. "It's vital—the balance of knowing what price differential your customer will allow before making a decision that takes them elsewhere. If a competitor changes prices at lunchtime, you know the recommendation and act on it—not just for individual products, but across interrelated products."

Todd Michaud, vice-president of NCR global enterprise, merchandising, and supply chain solutions, focuses on the link between pricing and the ability of retailers to give customers personalized offers based on shopping history and preferences, which he believes is key to effective loyalty programs. He says firms must understand, interpret, and act on shopping data to offer the right price or promotion to drive behavior.

Michaud adds that price management systems also must integrate into loyalty systems to consume special pricing and offers, managing the related complexities, to ensure proper price execution. Increasingly important in an omnichannel world is "that a customer's purchase history considers purchases across all channels, not just online or in store," he states.

Experts point to shoppers' desire for value as another link between pricing and customer loyalty. This is important regardless of the price sensitivity of various customer segments. "All customers are cognizant of value," explains Alan Lipson, global retail marketing manager at SAS, a provider of business analytics software and services. "Pricing plays a role in communicating a firm's value proposition. It is vital to understand which products need to be priced appropriately to communicate their value to customer segments. Customers will not be loyal to a firm that does not provide value, however value is defined."

Mark Kelso, president of consultancy Price Revolution, says, "Price management is the glue that merges each component of the retail mix—product assortment, promotion, and the merchandising message—into one cohesive offering, improving the overall value as perceived by the retailer's customers."

Questions

1. For a deep discounter, should price be the only element of the retailer's strategy that is promoted? Explain your answer.
2. In advertising prices, does Walmart have to enact the same prices for items sold in all of its stores throughout the United States and on online? Why or why not?
3. As a consultant to Macy's department stores, how much emphasis would you recommend that the retailer place on the sales staff versus offering low prices? Why?
4. What sales promotions would be appropriate for the Walgreens drugstore chain? Which would be inappropriate? Why?

---

* Based on material in John Karolefski, "The Price of Customer Loyalty," *Progressive Grocer*, February 2016, pp. 114–116. Reprinted by permission.

Comprehensive Case

Inside the Mind of Shake Shack's Founder*

Introduction

Danny Meyer is an extremely creative and proactive business thinker and entrepreneur. He has demonstrated this throughout his career—especially with the introduction and expansion of the growing Shake Shack chain. Shake Shack serves a menu of premium burgers, hot dogs, crinkle-cut fries, shakes, frozen custard, beer, and wine. With its fresh and simple, high-quality food, Shake Shack is a fun and lively gathering place with widespread appeal.

Meyer's Basic Philosophy

"People want the highest quality food, but they don't want the fancy experience anymore," said Danny Meyer, the chief executive officer (CEO) of Union Square Hospitality Group and the founder of Shake Shack. According to Meyer, some diners are saying, "We like our food better when it's at a hole in the wall."

Union Square Hospitality Group's restaurant portfolio runs the gamut from such tony New York City eateries as the Gramercy Tavern and The Modern at the Museum of Modern Art (MoMA), to the classy-casual barbecue joint Blue Smoke, to the fast-growing Shake Shack, which started as a hot dog stand in New York City's Madison Square Park and had grown to more than 90 locations worldwide by mid-2016. According to Shake Shack's Web site (www.shakeshack.com), at that time, it had outlets in 15 states and the District of Columbia, as well as in four foreign countries and the Middle East.

Danny Meyer was a special guest at the 2016 Convenience Store News Foodservice Summit, held March 15–16, 2016, in partnership with Tyson Convenience, where he participated in an interactive roundtable discussion with about a dozen other leading foodservice executives.

The trailblazing restaurateur noted that in his many travels around the world, the best croissant he's ever tasted was at a gas station in Uruguay. "People like to be surprised by high/low experiences like that. It's a wonderful trend for you all," he said, gesturing to the convenience foodservice retail executives and chefs gathered around the table.

Meyer, whose restaurants and chefs have earned an unprecedented 25 James Beard Awards, had breakfast with the convenience store (c-store) retailers after they spent the previous day visiting unique food concepts throughout the Big Apple on CSNews' Taste of Manhattan Tour, which included a stop at Meyer's Shake Shack outlet, his uber-successful hamburger chain. "We started Shake Shack as a hot dog cart in Madison Square Park in 2000," Meyer recounted, relating how the creation of the fast-casual chain was "a great experiment in combining capitalism with philanthropy."

Meyer, then spearheading the rehabilitation of Madison Square Park, which had fallen into great disrepair, was asked to supervise the operation of a hot dog cart inside an art exhibit that was part of the park's renewal effort. Already operating several upscale restaurants near the park and elsewhere in New York City, Meyer decided to use the hot dog stand to examine "the meaning of hospitality and what that means outside of a fancy restaurant."

Selling Chicago-style hot dogs (hot dogs topped with yellow mustard, chopped onions, pickle relish, a dill pickle spear, tomato slices, pickled peppers, and celery salt.), the single food stand became extremely successful, drawing lines that numbered more than 100 people at a time. Four years later, the city asked Meyer to operate a permanent 20-foot by 20-foot kiosk in Madison Square Park. Interestingly, that original Shake Shack kiosk focused on milkshakes, not on the hamburgers. "I had no idea it would become so famous for its burgers," said Meyer. "Every year, we had to renovate the kitchens to increase space for burgers." In addition to burgers, the restaurant's menu included its eponymous milkshakes and French fries, and even a 'Shroom Burger. Since the beginning, Meyer has wanted "everything at Shake Shack to be 'craveable'."

He eventually donated the original building, which cost $1 million to build, to the park and continues to operate the Shake Shack unit as a tenant. The Madison Square Park location's sales continue to grow today. During the summertime, the line typically reaches to outside the park and the wait time for service can be an hour or more. A Web cam on the Shack's homepage shows the length of the current line in real time for that location.

Unlike more aggressive entrepreneurs, Danny Meyer waited 5 years before opening a second Shake Shack, this time on Manhattan's Upper West Side. "Shake Shack is the first time we did anything for the second time," commented Meyer, whose other restaurants are mainly single-unit locations.

Although he eventually expanded Shake Shack to additional locations in New York, as well as in Connecticut, Washington, D.C., Florida, Georgia, Illinois, Maryland, Massachusetts, New Jersey, Nevada, Pennsylvania, and Texas, Meyer felt that it was important to make every location unique. "We're proud to be a chain, but who wrote the rule that every link in the chain has to be the same?" he asked.

Twenty percent of the menu at every Shake Shack unit is localized; and none of the units look the same, he noted, pointing to the seats at the New Haven, Connecticut, Shake Shack that look like the seats at the city's historic Yale Bowl football stadium. Each Shake Shack unit also carries a wide selection of craft beers local to that particular area.

At the 2016 CSNews Foodservice Summit, Meyer had just returned from the grand opening of the first California Shake Shack in West Hollywood in Los Angeles. With international partners, Shake Shack also operates in such locales as Tokyo, London, Istanbul, Moscow, Beirut, Dubai, Abu Dhabi, Doha, Kuwait City, Riyadh, and Jeddah.

Chick'n Shack Hatched

As Shake Shack has expanded, so too has its menu, leading to the recent introduction of the restaurant's first chicken sandwich, the Chick'n Shack—a skinless, marinated chicken breast that arrives vacuum-packed to the store and is then freshly battered and fried, and served with bib lettuce, pickles, and a buttermilk herb mayo.

---

* Based on information in Don Longo, "Inside the Mind of Food Visionary Danny Meyer," *Convenience Store News,* May 2016, pp. 24–32. Reprinted by permission. Convenience Store News (c) 2016 (www.csnews.com).

The Chick'n Shack has been an immediate hit. "In Los Angeles, we had our busiest opening day in our history," said Meyer, "and the chicken sandwich sold at 80 percent of the beef burger."

At the Foodservice Summit, Meyer asked the c-store retailers to share what they saw and experienced during the Taste of Manhattan tour. He agreed with them that the eateries on the tour illustrated many of the key trends in the foodservice sector, such as the popularity of local, fresh ingredients; the importance of being authentic; and the opportunity to "make food be theater." Several of the retailer attendees told Meyer they were impressed with the upbeat spirit shown by the young people working at many of the restaurants featured on the tour.

"Even though we call it 'work,' hospitality is a team sport," remarked Meyer, whose first business book, *Setting the Table* (Harper Collins, 2006), was a *New York Times* bestseller. It examines the power of warm and sincere hospitality in restaurants, business, and life. "If you think about what sports has in common with hospitality, you notice that ballplayers don't say they're going to work today. They say they're going to play to win. That's all part of our approach to servant leadership. It's the belief that the power flows from the bottom up, not the top down," he said.

"Lately, we've been challenging our teams to think about what it would be like if we had no prices for the food on the menu and the guest gets a check for how much they enjoyed the entire experience," Meyer continued. "That's not to diminish the importance of food innovation, but if we take food out of the equation, how did we make the guest feel?"

Hospitality Included

Meyer made headlines in 2015 with the institution of a "no-tipping" policy at his restaurant The Modern at New York's MoMA; and he planned to expand the policy to all his eateries by the end of 2016. A number of observations and personal experiences over the past 20 years led Meyer to launch the paradigm-changing policy on November 15, 2015.

[*Authors' note:* In the following paragraphs, Meyer's no tipping plan is discussed in detail to highlight the many issues involved. However, after just a short time, in 2016, Meyer backed off the no-tipping policy due to customer and employee dissatisfaction. It turned out that many customers wanted to provide tips to ensure the best possible dining service; and the waitstaff wanted to earn the tips for giving customers their outstanding service.]

"I travel around the world to learn about food, and the U.S. culture of tipping is unusual," Meyer relayed to the group. "There's no tipping in Asia, and much less in Europe. Tipping came about in the U.S. because we wanted to be more like Europe—150 years ago, when really rich people tipped the help. It was a power thing."

A couple of years ago, the adjusted minimum wage for tipped employees in New York City became $7.50 per hour. The National Restaurant Association intends to make sure no legislation changes that. Meyer, by the way, paid his waitstaff $9 per hour at that time, $1.50 above the city minimum. [*Authors' note:* Today, there are ongoing legislative battles throughout the country about what the minimum wage hourly rate should be in the future.]

"It's troubled me for the past 20 years. And now, the last 2 years, we are in the midst of the greatest labor crisis in New York City history," he said. "The disparity between the wages of tipped employees and non-tipped employees is huge. The average tip in New York City is about 21 percent, which is great for tipped employees, but we can't find enough skilled cooks to staff our kitchens."

Meyer reached his own personal tipping point, so to speak, when he found out that he had more Culinary Institute of America–trained chefs working for him as servers than working in his kitchens because they couldn't make enough money as cooks. "Because of that, and the fact that I never liked the master/servant relationship that tipping implies, I decided that someone has to take a stand and do something about it," he said.

So, Meyer enacted the following steps at The Modern, and shortly thereafter at Maialino, a Roman trattoria at the Meyer-owned Gramercy Park Hotel:

➤ He gave all cooks a $2-per-hour raise and built a career ladder for them.

➤ Menu prices were adjusted upward by about 20 percent and the policy was branded as "Hospitality Included." Guest receipts no longer had a tipping line.

➤ He announced the restaurant would share 13.5 percent of its top-line revenues with all employees—tipped and non-tipped workers.

➤ He unfurled the most comprehensive communications program in company history, getting input and feedback from all employees, holding town hall meetings, and conducting one-on-ones with affected employees. He shared with the employees what they would have made under the old tipping system and what they were making under the new no-tipping policy.

The bottom line: Cooks were happier with the wage increase and tipped employees were "kept whole," according to Meyer. Guests pay about the same. [*Authors' note:* Again, many customers and tipped employees were not at all happy with the new plan.]

After Meyer introduced "Hospitality Included" at The Modern, at least eight other top chefs and restaurants in New York City have followed suit with similar no-tipping policies. [*Authors' note:* The number of restaurants switching to a no-tipping policy has been quite small.] Nonetheless, one expert who has been a no-tipping critic, points out some downsides in Figure 1.

World-Class Service

Even before the no-tipping experiment, Union Square Hospitality Group was renowned for its world-class customer service. The c-store retailers who participated in the 2016 roundtable were interested in learning how Meyer's restaurants are able to achieve such a superior level of service from the employees, and, perhaps more importantly, how practical is it to think convenience stores could achieve a superior level of customer service with many of its employees making minimum wage or just slightly higher?

In response, Meyer shared his hiring philosophy, which is to hire people based on their emotional skills, or by having what he calls a high "hospitality quotient." "We don't view high labor costs as something happening to us," he said. "It's

FIGURE 1

Tipping Point—and Counterpoint

Source: Reprinted by permission. Convenience Store News (c) 2016 (www.csnews.com)

> ✓ One restaurant critic who originally supported a "service included" policy is now having second thoughts. The *New York Post's* Steve Cuozzo, a food writer who has long called for the end of tipping, acknowledges that it's far too early to judge results, but he has some concerns.
> ✓ "Owners say customers will pay the same amount as before because slightly higher prices to reimburse staff will work out to the same amount as tips," Cuozzo wrote recently. "But not so fast. Diners will surely pay more because tax will now be based on the higher amount."
> ✓ Cuozzo also points out potential legal issues related to transparency for those restaurants who pledge to share revenues with employees, in lieu of tips.
> ✓ And he even sees problems for restaurant owners whose lease arrangements require them to pay rent based on an agreed-upon percentage of revenue over a certain point.
> ✓ "None of this means we should give up on getting rid of tipping," concluded Cuozzo. "It's a rotten practice of which Americans are irrationally fond. But every restaurant should take a long, hard look before they dive into a pool that might not have a bottom."

something we are choosing to do. We feel that it actually drives higher sales volume." Managers at Meyer's restaurants are trained to look for six "emotional skills" when interviewing potential new hires. These skills (see Figure 2), with Meyer's commentary, are:

▶ Kindness & Optimism: "Skeptics don't tend to thrive in the hospitality business."

▶ Curiosity: "Every day is an opportunity to learn something new."

▶ Work Ethic: "I can't teach you to care about doing things right."

▶ Empathy: "What kind of wake do you leave in your path as you go through life?"

▶ Self-Awareness: "Do you know your own personal weather report?"

▶ Integrity: "The judgement to do the right thing even if it's not in your self-interest."

In addition, Meyer offered some final words of wisdom and encouragement to the foodservice executives. "The smartphone has given people so many choices today. With just the touch of their phone, they can communicate, get car service, get directions, and order food," he said. "About the only thing it doesn't do is cook food for you or fill your tank with gas."

The restaurateur acknowledged what he calls "captive dining" is a thing of the past. "There are a huge number of places to eat. … Today, if I'm eating excellent food in every other channel of my life, why wouldn't I want that quality at every place I eat?" He recalled one of his first experiences with restaurant-quality food at a convenience store. "I was traveling to Penn State University and had read that Sheetz actually cared about the food experience. It didn't disappoint. Clearly, Sheetz didn't view food as a captive audience experience."

To the group of c-store retailers, Meyer said, "I've probably done business with most of your companies before just traveling around the country, and I really admire what you are doing and how your industry is changing, and all of our industries are changing. There's more and more interest in food and how you make your place so much more than what it once was. I think it is a fascinating thing to grapple with." Based on what he's seen of convenience stores' improved foodservice around the country, he concluded, "You guys are on the right track with foodservice, and people are not going to go back to accepting lower-quality food at a gas station."

Who Is Danny Meyer?

Danny Meyer is CEO of New York-based Union Square Hospitality Group, which includes Union Square Café, Gramercy Tavern, Blue Smoke, Jazz Standard, Shake Shack, The Modern,

FIGURE 2

The Hospitality Quotient

Source: Reprinted by permission. Convenience Store News (c) 2016 (www.csnews.com)

When interviewing potential new hires, managers at all of Danny Meyer's restaurants are trained to look for six "emotional skills." These skills, according to Meyer, add up to what he calls having a high "hospitality quotient." The six skills are:

Kindness & Optimism   Empathy
Curiosity   Self-Awareness
Work Ethic   Integrity

Maialino, Untitled, North End Grill, Marta, Union Square Events, and Hospitality Quotient, a learning and consulting business.

Meyer was born and raised in St. Louis, worked for his father as a tour guide in Rome during college, and then returned to Rome to study international politics. After graduating from Trinity College in Hartford, Connecticut, in 1980 with a degree in political science, he worked in Chicago for John Anderson's 1980 independent presidential campaign. He later gained his first restaurant experience in 1984 as an assistant manager at an Italian seafood restaurant in New York City, before returning to Europe to study cooking in both Italy and France. He opened his first restaurant, Union Square Café, in 1985 at age 27.

An active national leader in the fight against hunger, Meyer has long served on the boards of Share Our Strength and City Harvest. He is equally active in civic affairs, serving on the boards of NYC & Co., Union Square Partnership, and the Madison Square Park Conservancy.

Questions

1. Based on the information presented in this case, how would you describe Shake Shack's retail image?

2. How would you describe the store atmosphere that Shake Shack seeks to maintain?

3. The Grammercy Tavern is more upscale than Shake Shack. Explain how you would expect its retail strategy to differ.

4. From a retail positioning point of view, what are the pros and cons of this statement: "Twenty percent of the menu at every Shake Shack unit is localized; and none of the units look the same."

5. As a restaurant patron, what would you think of a strategy that permits no tipping of the waitstaff? As a member of the waitstaff, what would you think?

6. Develop a five-point promotion mix plan for Shake Shack. Which factors would you include? Exclude? Why?

7. Visit the Shake Shack Web site (www.shakeshack.com). Where should this site fit in the chain's overall promotion mix? What functions does it perform?

Part 8

Putting It All Together

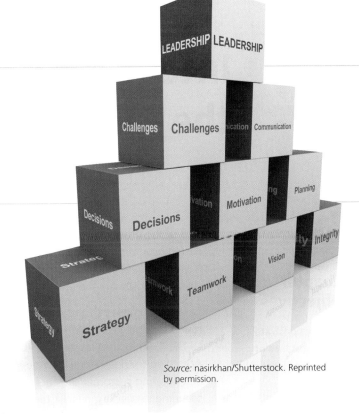

In Part Eight, we "put it all together."

Chapter 20 connects the elements of a retail strategy that have been described throughout this book. We examine planning and opportunity analysis, productivity, performance measures, and scenario analysis. The value of data comparisons (benchmarking and gap analysis) is highlighted. Strategic control via the retail audit is covered.

20 Integrating and Controlling the Retail Strategy

Chapter Objectives

1. To demonstrate the importance of integrating a retail strategy

2. To examine four key factors in the development and enactment of an integrated retail strategy: planning procedures and opportunity analysis, defining productivity, performance measures, and scenario analysis

3. To show how industry and company data can be used in strategy planning and analysis (benchmarking and gap analysis)

4. To show the value of a retail audit

One of the greatest challenges that retailers face with social media relates to negative customer postings. Such postings can rapidly spread, whether true or not, and they can have an impact on a retailer's image and performance. So, both the ramifications of negative customer posts and the proper strategy to handle them must be understood.

Research compiled by the American Customer Satisfaction Index (www.theacsi.org) (ACSI), found that the year 2015 was characterized by lower customer satisfaction across the board. Of the 43 industries tracked by ACSI, 5 improved, 30 declined, and 8 were unchanged. According to Claes Fornell, founder of ACSI, "There are exceptions, but the overall trend of deteriorating customer satisfaction encompasses nearly every industry and is holding consumer spending in check, forcing retailers into steeper or more extended discounts."

Source: iQoncept/Shutterstock. Reprinted by permission.

Three of the five industries that improved were Web-based. Social media and online travel services also saw improvement in user satisfaction last year. The online travel service industry was up 1.3 percent to 78, led by a gain for the combination of smaller travel Web sites, which includes the online presence of hotels and airlines. Big gainers in the retail space included Amazon, Chick-fil-A, and Nordstrom: All scored 86 on ACSI's 100-point scale.[1]

Overview

This site (www.bizmove .com/marketing/m2c. htm) raises a lot of good questions for retailers to think about in integrating their strategies.

This chapter focuses on integrating and controlling a retail strategy. We tie together the material detailed previously, show why retailers need coordinated strategies, and describe how to assess performance.

By integrating and regularly monitoring their strategies, firms of any size or format can take a proper view of the retailing concept and create a superior total retail experience. Consider how Dick's Sporting Goods uses a three-pronged retail strategy to stay competitive against the pure online players such as Amazon.com and nimble and niche "athleisure" retailers such as Lululemon and Athleta, while its competitors Sports Authority and Sports Chalet have failed.

At Dick's, increased exclusive private-label offerings sold under established brands such as Umbro and Maxfli increase store traffic and allow more pricing flexibility. Partnering with athletic apparel brands to offer store-within-a-store shops such as Nike Field House and Under Armour All-American stores increases store traffic, while reducing operating costs since interior design and fixtures are provided by the brands. Opening smaller, less-capital-intensive specialty stores such as Field and Stream (focused on hunting and fishing gear) and Chelsea Collective (targeting the female customer) that offer unique, tailored, brand experiences helps attract the fast-growing and less price-sensitive customer segments.[2]

As today's retailers look to the future, they must deal with new strategic choices due to the globalization of world markets, economic uncertainty, evolving consumer lifestyles, competition among formats, and rapid technology changes such as the advances in mobile and social media. See Figure 20-1.

FIGURE 20-1

The Need to Evolve

To succeed in the long run, retail formats and individual retailers need to evolve. The retail life cycle is not static; new retail concepts regularly enter the marketplace as other retail concepts mature or fade away. Being open-minded, proactive, and flexible are essential for retailers to survive and thrive.

Source: iQoncept/ Shutterstock. Reprinted by permission.

Retailers would also be wise to study the strategies of successful firms such as Dick's Sporting Goods and those facing significant challenges. Consider Sports Authority, once the largest U.S. sporting goods chain. Its failure to rightsize itself and to formulate a more focused strategy to respond to the competitive threats of E-commerce and omnichannel rivals led to its demise in 2016. Sports Authority grew in size and scale through mergers, each with distinct cultures, images and positioning, and overlapping markets, which resulted in inefficiencies, lower profits, and lower sales. Sports Authority's strategy to counter the disruptive threat of Amazon was simply to match prices offered by online retailers, and reduce investments to modernize its store experience and merchandise or to enhance in-store sales support. Instead, it incentivized store shoppers to order merchandise online at considerable discounts and with free shipping. Although sporting goods shoppers came to stores armed with the latest information for the specific products and services best suited to their needs and purchase occasions, Sports Authority used mass marketing, which meant simplified assumptions regarding its merchandising assortment, product availability, and pricing to deal with the true desires of its customers. This muddled strategy met neither the needs of sporting enthusiasts—because the merchandise assortment and in-store experience were not specialized enough—nor was Sports Authority a destination store for occasional shoppers who found it cheaper and more convenient to shop online or at rivals such as Dick's, Modell's, and athleisure retailers.[3]

INTEGRATING THE RETAIL STRATEGY

A major goal of *Retail Management* has been to describe the relationships among the elements of a retail strategy and show the need to act in an integrated way. Figure 20-2 highlights the integrated strategy of TJX, the off-price apparel retailer. TJX has been cited as a "high performance retailer"—and it outperforms most retailers. From fiscal 2011 through fiscal 2016, TJX's sales rose every year. And, despite price pressures from the weak economy, its gross margins and profits remained strong.[4] At our blog site (www.bermanevansretail.com), there are posts on integrated retail strategies.

Four fundamental factors especially need to be taken into account in devising and enacting an integrated retail strategy: planning procedures and opportunity analysis, properly defining productivity, performance measures, and scenario analysis. These factors are discussed next.

Planning Procedures and Opportunity Analysis

Planning procedures are enhanced by undertaking three coordinated activities. The process is then more systematic and reflects input from multiple parties:

1. Senior executives outline the firm's overall direction and goals. This provides written guidelines for middle- and lower-level managers, who get input from various internal and external sources. These managers are encouraged to generate ideas at an early stage.
2. Top-down plans and bottom-up or horizontal plans are combined.
3. Specific plans are enacted, including checkpoints and dates.

Opportunities need to be studied with regard to their impact on overall strategy and not in an isolated manner. See Figure 20-3. The growth strategy of retailers expanding globally has often been via brick-and-mortar stores. With many global retail markets maturing and significant technological disruptions impacting domestic and international markets, retailers need to consider whether they prioritize digital or brick-and-mortar expansion or use an omnichannel bricks-and-clicks approach. Retailers can be successful with any or all of these approaches, but the strategy development process must include understanding the digital potential and brick-and-mortar potential of each market, and how it is evolving over time. Retailers must analyze and understand their company business models, capabilities, priorities, and preferences before finalizing channel strategy decisions.[5]

A useful retailer tool for evaluating opportunities is the **sales opportunity grid**, which rates the promise of new and established goods, services, procedures, and/or store outlets across a variety of criteria. Opportunities can be rated in terms of the integrated strategies the firms would follow if those options are pursued. Computer software makes it easy to use such a grid.

Table 20-1 shows a sales opportunity grid for a supermarket deciding which of two salad dressings to stock. Brand A is established; Brand B is new. Due to newness, the store believes Brand B sales would initially be lower, but first-year sales would be similar. The brands would be priced the same and occupy identical space. Brand B requires higher display costs but offers

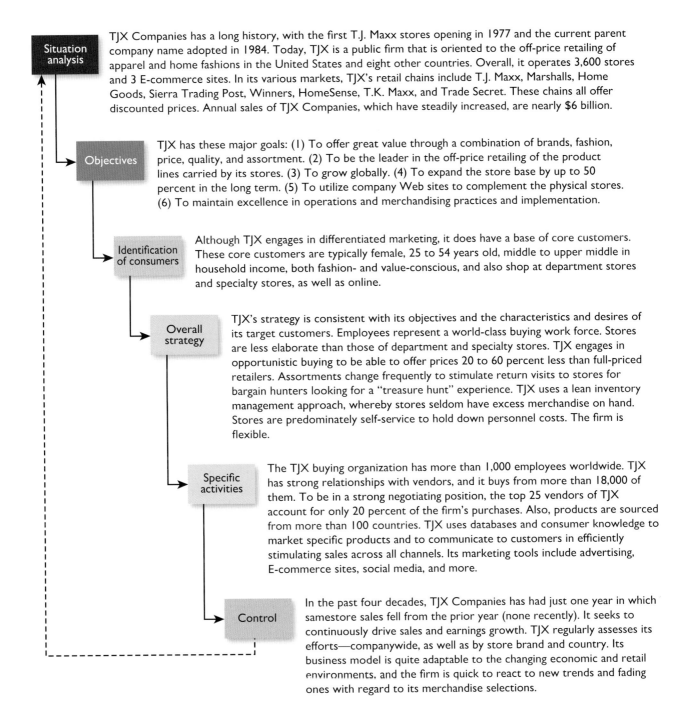

Situation analysis

TJX Companies has a long history, with the first T.J. Maxx stores opening in 1977 and the current parent company name adopted in 1984. Today, TJX is a public firm that is oriented to the off-price retailing of apparel and home fashions in the United States and eight other countries. Overall, it operates 3,600 stores and 3 E-commerce sites. In its various markets, TJX's retail chains include T.J. Maxx, Marshalls, Home Goods, Sierra Trading Post, Winners, HomeSense, T.K. Maxx, and Trade Secret. These chains all offer discounted prices. Annual sales of TJX Companies, which have steadily increased, are nearly $6 billion.

Objectives

TJX has these major goals: (1) To offer great value through a combination of brands, fashion, price, quality, and assortment. (2) To be the leader in the off-price retailing of the product lines carried by its stores. (3) To grow globally. (4) To expand the store base by up to 50 percent in the long term. (5) To utilize company Web sites to complement the physical stores. (6) To maintain excellence in operations and merchandising practices and implementation.

Identification of consumers

Although TJX engages in differentiated marketing, it does have a base of core customers. These core customers are typically female, 25 to 54 years old, middle to upper middle in household income, both fashion- and value-conscious, and also shop at department stores and specialty stores, as well as online.

Overall strategy

TJX's strategy is consistent with its objectives and the characteristics and desires of its target customers. Employees represent a world-class buying work force. Stores are less elaborate than those of department and specialty stores. TJX engages in opportunistic buying to be able to offer prices 20 to 60 percent less than full-priced retailers. Assortments change frequently to stimulate return visits to stores for bargain hunters looking for a "treasure hunt" experience. TJX uses a lean inventory management approach, whereby stores seldom have excess merchandise on hand. Stores are predominately self-service to hold down personnel costs. The firm is flexible.

Specific activities

The TJX buying organization has more than 1,000 employees worldwide. TJX has strong relationships with vendors, and it buys from more than 18,000 of them. To be in a strong negotiating position, the top 25 vendors of TJX account for only 20 percent of the firm's purchases. Also, products are sourced from more than 100 countries. TJX uses databases and consumer knowledge to market specific products and to communicate to customers in efficiently stimulating sales across all channels. Its marketing tools include advertising, E-commerce sites, social media, and more.

Control

In the past four decades, TJX Companies has had just one year in which samestore sales fell from the prior year (none recently). It seeks to continuously drive sales and earnings growth. TJX regularly assesses its efforts—companywide, as well as by store brand and country. Its business model is quite adaptable to the changing economic and retail environments, and the firm is quick to react to new trends and fading ones with regard to its merchandise selections.

FIGURE 20-2

The Integrated Strategy of TJX

Sources: Figure fully developed by the authors based on data from various TJX Company Inc. materials, including "Background Information 2016," "Our Company," "Growing a Global, Off-Price Value Company," "How We Do It," *TJX Companies, Form 10Q July 30, 2016*; TJX Companies Inc. 2015 *Annual Report*; and the firm's Web site, www.tjx.com/index.html (September 17, 2016).

Klipfolio (www.klipfolio .com/resources/ kpi-examples/retail) shows how to improve a retailer's productivity.

a larger markup. Brand B would have a greater gross profit and net profit by the end of the first year. Based on the overall grid, Brand B is selected. Yet, if the store is more concerned about a quick profit, Brand A might be chosen.

Defining Productivity in a Manner Consistent with the Strategy

As we noted in Chapters 12 and 13, productivity refers to the efficiency with which a retail strategy is carried out; it is in any retailer's interest to reach sales and profit goals while keeping control over costs. On the one hand, a retailer looks to avoid unnecessary costs. It does not want eight

FIGURE 20-3

Opportunity Analysis with the Small Business Administration

Go to www.sba.gov/starting-business/how-start-business and learn more about the opportunities and challenges in starting and running a business.

Source: U.S. Small Business Administration.

salespeople working at one time if four can satisfactorily handle all customers. And it does not want to pay high rent for a site in a regional shopping center if customers would willingly travel a few miles farther to a less costly site. On the other hand, a firm is not looking to lose customers because there are insufficient sales personnel to handle the rush of shoppers during peak hours. It also does not want a low rent site if this means a significant drop in customer traffic. See Figure 20-4.

Potential trade-offs often mean neither the least expensive strategy nor the most expensive one is the most productive strategy; the former approach might not adequately service customers and the latter might be wasteful. An upscale retailer could not succeed with self-service, and it would be unnecessary for a discounter to have a large sales staff. The most productive approach applies a specific integrated retail strategy (such as a full-service jewelry store) as efficiently as possible.

Food Lion (part of the Brussels-based Ahold Delhaize Group) is a leading U.S. retailer—with nearly 1,100 supermarkets in 10 Southeast and Mid-Atlantic states. It carries 28,000 nationally

    **CAREERS IN RETAILING**   Retail Audit Personnel

Many retailers pay a lot of attention to developing strategies, but strategy implementation is equally important. Retail auditing measures the extent to which plans are implemented. This process can be conducted by either an in-house staff or outsourced to firms such as Field Agent (www.fieldagent.net) or Customer Impact (www.customerimpactinfo.com). In-house auditing is commonly used by large chains and franchises. Some retailers may prefer to outsource this activity to ensure an impartial, objective, and thorough audit. Common topics that are audited include inventory availability (particularly out-of-stock situations), compliance with planograms, pricing accuracy, proper use of displays, cashier-related waiting times,

and staff satisfaction. These areas are often assessed by observation. Other reviews, such as customer feedback and staff reviews, are based on interviews and surveys. These can be disguised (mystery shoppers assessing a salesperson's performance) or nondisguised (customer satisfaction surveys). Auditing needs to adapt to the type of retailer. A restaurant audit would critically evaluate the kitchen area to ensure compliance with health codes. In contrast, the audit of an appliance retailer would need to evaluate a salesperson's knowledge of the features of different model dishwashers.

Develop a job description for a retail auditor for a major retail coffee chain.

■

TABLE 20-1 Supermarket's Sales Opportunity Grid for Two Brands of Salad Dressing

Criteria	Brand A (established)	Brand B (new)
Retail price	$2.58/8-ounce bottle	$2.58/8-ounce bottle
Floor space needed	8 square feet	8 square feet
Display costs	$10.00/month	$20.00/month for 6 months
		$10.00/month thereafter
Operating costs	$0.12/unit	$0.12/unit
Markup	19%	22%
Sales estimate		
During first month		
Units	250	50
Dollars	$645	$129
During first six months		
Units	1,400	500
Dollars	$3,612	$1,290
During first year		
Units	2,500	2,750
Dollars	$6,450	$7,095
Gross profit estimate		
During first month	$123	$28
During first six months	$686	$284
During first year	$1,226	$1,561
Net profit estimate		
During first month	$83	$2
During first six months	$458	$104
During first year	$806	$1,051

Example 1:
Gross profit estimate = Sales estimate − [(1.00 − Markup percentage) × (Sales estimate)]
Brand A gross profit estimate during first six months = $3,612 − [(1.00 − 0.19) × ($3,612)] = $686

Example 2:
Net profit estimate = Gross profit estimate − (Display costs + Operating costs)
Brand A net profit estimate during first six months = $686 − ($60 + $168) = $458

and regionally advertised brand name products, as well as high-quality private-label products—as key element of its well-integrated strategy. Its supermarkets are directly owned or affiliates in a wide variety of store formats—supermarkets, online food delivery, and online order pick-up points. Food Lion stores recently underwent extensive remodeling, rebranding ("Easy, Fresh, and Affordable"), and a new three-tier pricing scheme that includes weekly "hot sale" items available to holders of its MVP loyalty card, "WOW" prices on key best-sellers, and "low prices" on essential items throughout the store.[6]

Ahold Delhaize Group's U.S. chains include Giant Carlisle, Giant Landover, Hannaford, Martin's, and Stop & Shop (New England and New York)—each with a distinct go-to-market strategy. Systemwide, the company has responded to a fast-changing retail environment shaped by customer trends, increased penetration of online and mobile usage in-store, higher acceptance of E-commerce (through ownership of the leading online grocer Peapod), and the fresh and organic food concept brand bfresh.[7]

Performance Measures

By outlining relevant **performance measures**—the criteria used to assess effectiveness—and setting standards (goals) for each of them, a retailer can better develop and integrate its strategy. Among the measures frequently used by retailers are total sales, average sales per store, sales by goods/service category, sales per square foot, gross margins, gross margin return on investment, operating income, inventory turnover, markdown percentages, employee turnover, financial ratios, and profitability.

FIGURE 20-4

The Delicate Balance with Activities Intended to Improve Productivity

Cut costs too much and shoppers will surely notice and not be happy with fewer salespeople, longer checkout lines, less clean restrooms, and so forth. Cut costs too little and the retailer may have to raise prices or suffer low profits.

Source: Lisa S./Shutterstock. Reprinted by permission.

A retailer can gain insights on benchmarking from this site (www .rbabenchmarking.com).

Learn about best practices in retailing (www.crmsearch.com/ retailbestpractices.php).

To properly gauge a strategy's effectiveness, a firm should use **benchmarking**, whereby the retailer sets standards and measures its performance based on the achievements of its sector of retailing, specific competitors, high-performance firms, and/or the prior actions of the firm itself. It is necessary to look at internal as well as external standards. The goal of benchmarking is to use peer operating results to generate ideas for improving processes, approaches, considering technologies to reduce costs, strengthen customer satisfaction and loyalty and increase profits.[8]

A good free source is the "Monthly & Annual Retail Trade" section of the U.S. Census Bureau's Web site (www.census.gov/retail). It shows about 25 years of data involving a monthly comparison of sales, purchases, gross margins, inventories, and inventory-to-sales ratios by retail category. In addition to monthly and annual store data, quarterly E-commerce data are reported.

Retailers of varying sizes—and in different goods or service lines—can also obtain comparative data from such sources as the Small Business Administration, the Internal Revenue Service, *Progressive Grocer, Stores, Chain Store Age, Retailing Today*, BizMiner, Dun & Bradstreet, the National Retail Federation, Risk Management Association, and annual reports. Those retailers can then compare their performance with others.

Table 20-2 contains revenue, expense, and income benchmarking data for small retailers in 14 different business categories. The cost of goods sold as a percentage of revenues is highest for

TABLE 20-2 Benchmarking through Annual Operating Statements of Typical Sole Proprietors, 2013 (Expressed in Terms of Total Revenues = 100%)

Type of Retailer	Total Revenues	Gross Profit	Cost of Goods Sold	Total Operating Expenses	Net Profit
Apparel and accessories stores	100.0	48.0	52.0	32.9	15.1
Building materials stores	100.0	37.9	62.1	24.9	13.0
Electronics and appliance stores	100.0	33.4	66.6	23.4	10.0
Food and beverage stores	100.0	29.0	71.0	22.8	6.2
Furniture and home furnishings stores	100.0	43.7	56.3	31.2	12.5
Gas stations	100.0	13.8	86.2	11.3	2.5
General merchandise stores	100.0	32.7	67.3	20.7	12.0
Health and personal care stores	100.0	41.7	58.3	27.0	14.7
Miscellaneous stores	100.0	52.4	47.6	31.6	20.8
Nonstore retailers	100.0	53.0	47.0	29.7	23.3
Sporting goods, hobby, book, and music stores	100.0	37.6	62.4	25.5	12.1

Source: Computed by the authors from U.S. Internal Revenue Service data, www.bizstats.com

gas stations and food and beverage stores, gross profit is greatest for nonstore retailers, operating expenses are the most for apparel and accessories stores, and net income is highest for nonstore retailers.

A popular, independent, ongoing benchmarking survey is the American Customer Satisfaction Index (ACSI; www.theacsi.org), briefly discussed earlier in the chapter. It addresses two questions: (1) Are customer satisfaction and evaluations of quality improving or declining in the United States? (2) Are they improving or declining for particular sectors of industry and for specific companies? The index is based on a scale of 0 to 100. A national sample of more than 70,000 people takes part in phone interviews, with 250 interviews of current customers for each firm studied. In 2015, these were the satisfaction scores for some leading retailers: Amazon.com, 83; Nordstrom, 82; Costco and Priceline, 81; Applebee's, 79; Bed Bath & Beyond, 75; Home Depot, 73; McDonald's, 69; and Abercrombies & Fitch, 65.[9]

There is now great interest in benchmarking service retailers. One well known measurement tool is SERVQUAL, which lets service retailers assess their quality by asking customers to react to a series of statements in five areas of performance:[10]

► *Reliability*. Provide services as promised. Dependably handle service problems. Perform services right the first time and when promised. Maintain error-free records.
► *Responsiveness*. Keep customers informed about when services will be done. Give prompt service. Be willing to help customers. Be ready to act on customer requests.
► *Assurance*. Employees must instill customer confidence and make customers feel safe in transactions. Employees must always be courteous and have the knowledge to answer questions.
► *Empathy*. Give customers individual attention in a caring way. Have the customer's best interest at heart. Employees should understand customer needs. Provide convenient business hours.
► *Tangibles*. Use modern equipment. Provide visually appealing facilities and materials associated with the service. Employees must have a neat, professional appearance.

In reviewing the performance of others, firms should look at the *best practices* in retailing—whether involving companies in their own business sector or other sectors. For example, the Tompkins Supply Chain Consortium (www.supplychainconsortium.com) includes a number of retailers. By joining the consortium, member companies get information to help them address issues such as:

► How their *economic impact* compares to that of their competitors and the needed areas of improvement
► How the competitiveness of their *cost structures* compare to that of their peers and if they are focusing on the right initiatives to optimize results
► How their *operations* compare to their peers' operations in terms of efficiency, and what processes (including outsourcing) and technologies are used by leading high-performance companies
► How their peers measure *supply-chain performance* and how these peers are overcoming obstacles and challenges in the supply chain
► How *performance metrics* compare to those of their peers and how well they are meeting their objectives
► How their *organization structures* compare to those of their peers.[11]

For those retailers expanding internationally, A. T. Kearney (www.atkearney.com), the consulting firm, has devised a **Global Retail Development Index (GRDI)**. It measures the retail prospects in emerging countries with regard to four factors: market attractiveness, country risk, market saturation, and time pressure. According to the 2015 GRDI, China, Uruguay, Chile, Qatar, Mongolia, and Georgia were rated highest. These factors are equally weighted in computing a global retail development index score:[12]

► *Market attractiveness:* Based on retail sales per capita, population size, the level of urbanization, and the ease of doing business
► *Country risk:* Based on political risk, economic performance, debt indicators, and credit ratings, as well as the business costs of crime, violence, and corruption

Why Do Poor Ethics Occur?

Retailers can indirectly encourage salespeople to make questionable ethical decisions. Let's look at some tactics that may encourage unethical behavior. Many retail salespeople are paid on a sales commission; this motivates them to recommend more costly products than a customer needs. Car dealers often compensate salespeople based on gross profit, rather than sales volume; this inspires salespeople to take advantage of a customer's poor bargaining skills, immediate need for a new car, and/or lack of knowledge of a car's trade-in value. Sometimes, high sales commissions are given for paid services such as extended warranties for appliances and electronics. Retailers may knowingly have salespeople sell low-priced brands with poor quality reputations. Salespeople may be told to "do whatever it takes" to achieve a sale—even make promises they cannot fulfill.

Discuss how a retailer can avoid these and other unethical selling practices.

▶ *Market saturation:* Based on the share of retail sales made through a modern distribution format, and the number of international retailers and their market share

▶ *Time pressure:* Based on how rapidly sales through modern retail formats have grown, which is an indicator of the time until the market is saturated

What makes a good retail Web site? Companies can close the gap by looking at these excellent sites (www.awwwards.com/20-of-the-very-best-e-commerce-websites.html).

A retailer can also benchmark its own internal performance, conduct gap analysis, and plan for the future. Through **gap analysis**, a company compares its actual performance against its potential performance and then determines the areas in which it must improve. As Figure 20-5 indicates, gap analysis has four main steps.

Let us apply gap analysis to a hypothetical company, ABC Stores. Table 20-3 indicates its financial results for fiscal years that ended in December 31, 2013, through December 31, 2016. The data in the table may be used to benchmark ABC Stores in terms of its own performance. Between 2013 and 2016, ABC Stores saw sales growth rise, fall, and then rise again. The gross margin as a percent of sales remained strong, while operating expenses as a percent of sales declined, but saw an increase in 2016. Profitability declined initially and then rose. The current ratio declined. Inventory turnover fluctuated, but return on invested capital steadily improved. Sales per square foot steadily despite the volatility in its average sale per transaction; and comparable store stores grew consistently. Overall, ABC Stores' 2013–2016 performance was positive. This signals that the ABC Stores Company was successful in addressing gaps in its performance in the near term, and is regaining momentum.

To ensure gaps are minimized in relationship retailing, firms should do these tasks:

1. *Customer insight:* Analyze consumer data, such as sales, cost, and profits by segment.

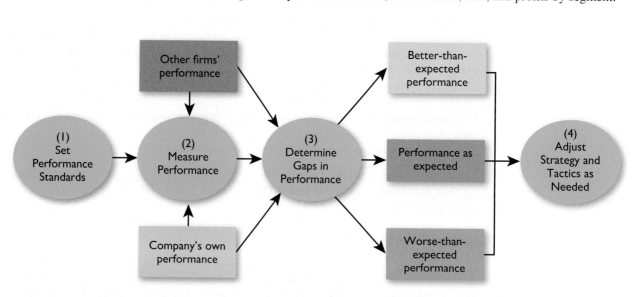

FIGURE 20-5 Utilizing Gap Analysis

TABLE 20-3 ABC STORES: Internal Benchmarking and Gap Analysis

	2016	2015	2014	2013
Statement of Earnings Data				
Net sales (in $000)	$58,219	$52,590	$53,821	$ 50,750
Gross margin (% of sales)	27.5	27.1	28.2	28.0
Total operating expenses (% of sales)	21.6	20.9	23.5	24.0
Net earnings (% of sales)	5.8	4.2	4.7	5.0
Balance Sheet Data and Financial Ratios				
Current ratio (times)	1.42	1.39	1.47	1.50
Inventory turnover (times)	5.2	4.9	5.1	4.8
Return on invested capital (%)	25.3	24.0	21.6	18.1
Customer and Store Data				
Average sale per transaction	$159.55	$145.56	$178.12	$ 157.92
Comparable-store sales change over prior year (%)	+5.9	+5.1	+6.2	+4.9
Sales per square foot	$ 389	$ 365	$ 367	$ 323

2. *Customer profiling:* Collect and merge transaction and lifestyle data to better understand individual shoppers. Identify noncustomers who fit the profile of the firm's best segment.
3. *Customer life-cycle model:* Analyze shopper behavior at various life stages, and review demographics by segment.
4. *Extended business model:* Based on steps (3) and (4), determine which customers to center on, how best to interact with them, and the best way to build and sustain relationships.
5. *Relationship planning:* Engage in all points of contact (in person, pickup, delivery, kiosk, phone, fax, computer, mobile, tablet) to interact with customers.
6. *Implementation:* Integrate all aspects of the retail strategy.[13]

At our blog (www.bermanevansretail.com), we have posts related to benchmarking and gap analysis.

Scenario Analysis

Visit this site (www.toolshero.com/strategy/scenario-planning) for an in-depth look at scenario planning.

In **scenario analysis**, a retailer projects the future by studying factors that affect long-run performance and then forms contingency ("what if") plans based on alternate scenarios (such as low, moderate, and high levels of competition). Given the rapid pace of change in the industry, this is an important tool for retailers and one that is used extensively to make projections for the future. Retail managers face the challenge of accomplishing their short-term goals while still anticipating disruptions that could alter established processes in the future.[14] The significant number of recent store closings and bankruptcies are an indication of dramatic shifts in consumer buying habits and preferences, slow growth in consumer spending despite low unemployment rate, fierce price competition, and the pervasive impact of social, mobile, and Internet of Things technology in retail processes that benefit nimble, online firms at the expense of traditional retailers.[15]

Some traditional retailers are downsizing and restructuring to better integrate their supply chain so as to provide consistent omnichannel shopping experiences, quality customer service both in-store and online, and faster production of merchandise in response to customer trends. Lord & Taylor is partnering with quick-time supplier Xcel, which owns proprietary brands and labels and provides nimble sourcing to cut delivery time from 9 months to 6 weeks. J. C. Penney will place fewer initial orders of its private-label brands with suppliers in Bangladesh at the start of the season, use consumer data early in the selling season to identify winners, and place additional orders for winners only with Central American suppliers who can deliver in 6 weeks. This approach can help retailers sell more goods at full price similar to fast-fashion retailers such as Zara.[16]

RETAILING AROUND THE WORLD

Best Buy's Failure In China

Best Buy entered the Chinese market in 2006 after buying a majority interest in Jiangsu Five Star Appliance, a local retailer. In 2011, it closed its 184 Chinese stores, and in 2014, Best Buy sold its Chinese operations to a real-estate company. According to one analysis, a key reason for Best Buy's failure was its store rental and channel strategy. Unlike in the United States and elsewhere, Chinese retailers more closely resemble real-estate firms that rent space to manufacturers. Manufacturers selling goods in China more closely resemble retailers in that they manage inventories, supervise and motivate salespeople, and pay for rent-related expenses. Also, unlike in the United States, an appliance maker selling in China would place all of its products (such as dishwashers, air conditioners, and microwaves) in the same retail space. Best Buy's strategy of operating its own stores as in other parts of the world was unfamiliar to Chinese consumers, created supply chain conflicts, and resulted in higher prices to a cost-conscious market.

Explain how Best Buy could have avoided these issues.

Sources: Authors' analysis; and Rakesh Sharma, "Why Best Buy Failed in China," *Investopedia*, July 23, 2015, www.investopedia.com

---

In planning for its future, Kohl's (www.kohls.com) has a clear strategic plan. Here are selected elements of that plan:

▶ *Organizational mission and positioning.* Kohl's is positioned as a family-focused, value-oriented department store chain with an E-commerce Web site (www.Kohls.com). It offers moderately priced apparel, footwear, and accessories for women, men, and children, as well as beauty aids and home goods. Stores have a consistent product assortment with some regional differences. It features private and exclusive brands ("Only at Kohl's"), and national brands.

▶ *Goals.* Kohl's believes several goals are necessary for long-term success. Its strategic framework, referred to as "the Greatness Agenda," has five initiatives: "amazing product, incredible savings, easy experience, personalized connections, and winning teams." These initiatives are expected to increase store and online customer traffic.

▶ *Basic strategy.* Kohl's has clean, bright stores that offer an easy and desirable shopping experience. New mobile and tablet platforms offer an improved in-store digital experience. In 2015, Kohl's launched "buy online, pick-up in store" (BOPUS) in all stores, thus offering convenience and driving incremental sales.

▶ *Merchandising.* About one-half of Kohl's annual sales are from private and exclusive brands; the other one-half is from national brands. In the early 2000s, 75 percent of Kohl's sales were from national brands, which have higher selling prices, but lower gross margins, than private and exclusive brands. Its private brands (Croft & Barrow, Sonoma Goods for Life, and others) are well-established and represent the best value in stores. Despite having lower selling prices, private brands generally have higher gross margins. The exclusive brands are developed and marketed through license agreements with recognized brands such as Food Network, Simply Vera by Vera Wang, and others. Their prices are lower than national brands but higher than private-label brands, and gross margins are higher than national brands but lower than private brands.

▶ *Marketing.* Kohl's has a unique "nine-box merchandising grid" ("lifestyle matrix") to focus its offerings and promotion strategy in a way that relates to both consumer lifestyles and price points.[17]

Posts related to scenario analysis and future planning may be found on our blog (www.bermanevansretail.com).

Predicting the future is not simple (www.futurist.com/blog).

CONTROL: USING THE RETAIL AUDIT

After a retail strategy is devised and enacted, it must be continuously assessed and necessary adjustments made. A vital evaluation tool is the **retail audit**, which systematically examines and evaluates a firm's total retailing effort or a specific aspect of it. The purpose of an audit is to study what a retailer is presently doing, appraise performance, and make recommendations for the future. An audit investigates a retailer's objectives, strategy, implementation, and organization. Goals are reviewed and evaluated for their clarity, consistency, and appropriateness. The strategy and the methods for deriving it are analyzed. Also, the application of the strategy and how it is received by customers are reviewed. The organizational structure is analyzed with regard to lines of command and other factors.

Good auditing includes these elements: (1) Audits are conducted regularly. (2) In-depth analysis is involved. (3) Data are amassed and analyzed systematically. (4) An open-minded, unbiased perspective is maintained. (5) There is a willingness to uncover weaknesses to be corrected, as well as strengths to be exploited. (6) After an audit is completed, decision makers are responsive to the recommendations made in the audit report.

Undertaking an Audit

There are six steps in retail auditing. See Figure 20-6 for an overview of the retail auditing process, which is described next: (1) Determine who does an audit. (2) Decide when and how often an audit is done. (3) Establish the areas to be audited. (4) Develop audit form(s). (5) Conduct the audit. (6) Report to management.

DETERMINING WHO DOES THE AUDIT   One or a combination of three parties can be involved: a company audit specialist, a company department manager, and/or an outside auditor.

FIGURE 20-6
The Retail Audit Process

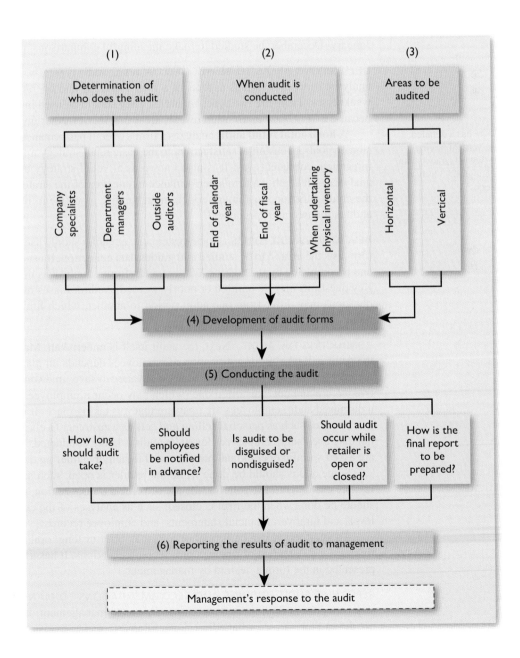

A *company audit specialist* is an internal employee whose prime responsibility is the retail audit. The advantages of this person include the auditing expertise, thoroughness, level of knowledge about the firm, and ongoing nature (no time lags). Disadvantages include the costs (especially for retailers that do not need full-time auditors) and the auditor's limited independence.

A *company department manager* is an internal employee whose prime job is operations management; that manager may also be asked to participate in the retail audit. The advantages are that there are no added personnel expenses and that the manager is knowledgeable about the firm and its operations. Disadvantages include the manager's time away from the primary job, the potential lack of objectivity, time pressure, and the complexity of companywide audits.

An *outside auditor* is not a retail employee but a paid consultant. Advantages are the auditor's experience, objectivity, and thoroughness. Disadvantages are the high costs per day or hour (for some retailers, it may be cheaper to hire per-diem consultants than full-time auditors; the opposite is true for larger firms), the time lag while a consultant gains familiarity with the firm, the failure of some firms to use outside specialists continuously, and some employees' reluctance to cooperate.

DETERMINING WHEN AND HOW OFTEN THE AUDIT IS CONDUCTED Logical times for auditing are the end of the calendar year, the end of the retailer's annual reporting year (fiscal year), or when a complete physical inventory is conducted. Each of these is appropriate for evaluating a retailer's operations during the previous period. An audit must be done at least annually, although some retailers desire more frequent analysis. It is important that the same period(s), such as January–December, be studied to make meaningful comparisons, projections, and adjustments.

DETERMINING AREAS TO BE AUDITED A retail audit typically includes more than financial analysis; it reviews various aspects of a firm's strategy and operations to identify strengths and weaknesses. There are two types of audits. They should be used in conjunction with one another because a *horizontal audit* often reveals areas that merit further investigation by a *vertical audit*.

This site has a detailed online vertical pricing audit (www.bizmove.com/marketing/m2y3.htm) for retailers.

A **horizontal retail audit** analyzes a firm's overall performance, from the organizational mission, to goals, to customer satisfaction, to the basic retail strategy mix and its implementation in an integrated, consistent way. It is also known as a "retail strategy audit." A **vertical retail audit** analyzes—in depth—a firm's performance in one area of the strategy mix or operations, such as the credit function, customer service, merchandise assortment, or interior displays. A vertical audit is focused and specialized.

DEVELOPING AUDIT FORMS To be systematic, a retailer should use detailed audit forms. An audit form lists the area(s) to be studied and guides data collection. It usually resembles a questionnaire and is completed by the auditor. Without audit forms, analysis is more haphazard and subjective. Key questions may be omitted or poorly worded. Auditor biases may appear. Most significantly, questions may differ from one audit period to another, which limits comparisons. Examples of retail audit forms are presented shortly.

CONDUCTING THE AUDIT Next, the audit itself is undertaken. Management specifies how long the audit will take. Prior notification of employees depends on management's perception of two factors: the need to compile some data in advance to save time versus the desire to get an objective picture and not a distorted one (which may occur if employees have too much notice). With a disguised audit, employees are unaware that it is taking place. It is useful if the auditor investigates an area such as personal selling and acts as a customer to elicit employee responses. With a nondisguised audit, employees know an audit is being conducted. This is desirable if employees are asked specific operational questions and to help in gathering data.

Some audits should be done while the retailer is open, such as assessing parking adequacy, in-store customer traffic patterns, the use of vertical transportation, and customer relations. Others should be done when the firm is closed, such as analyses of the condition of fixtures, inventory levels and turnover, financial statements, and employee records.

An audit report can be formal or informal, brief or long, oral or written, and a statement of findings or a statement of findings plus recommendations. It has a better chance of acceptance if presented in the format desired by management.

REPORTING AUDIT FINDINGS AND RECOMMENDATIONS TO MANAGEMENT The last auditing step is to present findings and recommendations to management. It is the role of management—not the auditor—to see what adjustments (if any) to make. Decision makers must read the report thoroughly, consider each point, and enact the needed strategic changes. They should treat each audit seriously and react accordingly. No matter how well an audit is done, it is not a worthwhile activity if management fails to enact recommendations.

Responding to an Audit

TJX (www.tjx.com/ about) is very open about its performance. Click "Our Businesses" and see how much information is available about the firm's plans and results.

After management studies audit findings, appropriate actions are taken. Areas of strength are continued and areas of weakness are revised. The actions must be consistent with the retail strategy and noted in the firm's retail information system (for further reference).

Retailers with multiple Web sites and/or a large number of brands or stores are dependent on many interconnected processes to ensure optimal customer experience and successful performance. The best way of acting upon the results of retail audits is to tailor actions to local market conditions and demographics, incorporate variations in product assortment as necessary, engage in retail consolidation if appropriate, better handle a new or mature distributor and wholesaler network, and tweak go-to-market approaches if appropriate.[18]

Possible Difficulties in Conducting a Retail Audit

AuditNet (www.auditnet .org/audit-library) has a number of good resources on auditing.

Several obstacles may occur in doing a retail audit. A retailer should be aware of them:

- An audit may be costly.
- It may be quite time consuming.
- Performance measures may be inaccurate.
- Employees may feel threatened and not cooperate as much as desired.
- Incorrect data may be collected.
- Management may not be responsive to the findings.

At present, many retailers—particularly small ones—still do not understand or perform systematic retail audits. But this must change if they are to assess themselves properly and plan correctly for the future.

Illustrations of Retail Audit Forms

Here, we present a management audit form and a retailing effectiveness checklist to show how small and large retailers can inexpensively, yet efficiently, conduct retail audits. An internal or external auditor (or department manager) could periodically complete one of these forms and then discuss the findings with management. The examples noted are both horizontal audits. A vertical audit would involve an in-depth analysis of any one area in the forms.

A MANAGEMENT AUDIT FORM FOR SMALL RETAILERS   Under the auspices of the U.S. Small Business Administration, a *Marketing Checklist for Small Retailers* was devised. Although written for small firms, it is a comprehensive horizontal audit applicable to all retailers. Figure 20-7 shows selected questions from this audit form. "Yes" is the desired answer to each question. For questions answered negatively, the firm must learn the causes and adjust its strategy.

 TECHNOLOGY IN RETAILING   Retail Planning Using Excel

One of the most useful parts of Microsoft's Office suite is EXCEL spreadsheet software. Retail personnel can use EXCEL as a planning tool. By entering different assumptions for inventory levels, inventory turnover, prices and gross margins, and more, retailers can compute return on sales, return on assets, and retail on equity. In addition, by using "if, then" or "what, if" assumptions, retail managers can estimate the impact of planned markdowns on inventory turnover and inventory holding costs. EXCEL is also a helpful tool in demand forecasting, assortment planning, and monitoring and updating a retailer's open-to-buy position. These activities can be done on a buyer, department, merchandise classification, store, and overall chain level. Because EXCEL calculations are often computed on a buyer level, it promotes bottom-up planning. A major advantage of bottom-up planning is the use of a buyer's specialized knowledge. Bottom-up planning also elevates buyer morale.

What are the potential difficulties associated with using EXCEL as a planning tool?

Planning
1.   Have you thought about the long-term direction of your business?   _____
2.   Have you developed a realistic set of plans for the year's operations?   _____
3.   Do your plans provide methods to deal with competition?   _____
4.   Is there a system for auditing your objectives?   _____

Customer Analysis (Who are your target customers and what are they seeking from you?)
1.   Have you profiled your customers by age, income, education, occupation, etc.?   _____
2.   Are you aware of the reasons why customers shop with you?   _____
3.   Do you ask your customers for suggestions on ways to improve your operation?   _____
4.   Do you know what goods and services your customers most prefer?   _____

Organization and Human Resources
1.   Are job descriptions and authority for responsibilities clearly stated?   _____
2.   Have you an effective system for communication with employees?   _____
3.   Do you have a formal program for motivating employees?   _____
4.   Have you taken steps to minimize shoplifting and internal theft?   _____

Operations and Special Services
1.   Do you monitor every facet of your operations in terms of specific goals?   _____
2.   Do you provide time-saving services for greater customer convenience?   _____
3.   Do you have a policy for handling merchandise returned by customers?   _____
4.   Do you get feedback through customer surveys?   _____

Financial Analysis and Control
1.   Do your financial records give you the information to make sound decisions?   _____
2.   Can sales be broken down by department?   _____
3.   Do you understand the pros and cons of the retail method of accounting?   _____
4.   Have you taken steps to minimize shoplifting and internal theft?   _____

Buying
1.   Do you have a merchandise budget (planned purchases) for each season that is broken
     down by department and merchandise classification?   _____
2.   Does it take into consideration planned sales, planned gross margin, planned inventory
     turnover, and planned markdowns?   _____
3.   Do you plan exclusive or private brand programs?   _____
4.   Do you take advantage of cash discounts and allowances offered by your vendor/supplier?   _____

Pricing
1.   Have you determined whether to price below, at, or above the market?   _____
2.   Do you set specific markups for each product category?   _____
3.   Do you know which products are slow-movers and which are fast?   _____
4.   Have you developed a markdown policy?   _____

Atmospherics
1.   Are the unique appeals of your business reflected in your image?   _____
2.   Have you figured out the best locations for displays?   _____
3.   Do you know which items are bought on "impulse"?   _____
4.   Do you use signs to aid your customers in shopping?   _____

Promotion
1.   Are you familiar with the strengths and weaknesses of various promotional methods?   _____
2.   Do you participate in cooperative advertising?   _____
3.   Do you ask customers to refer your business to friends and relatives?   _____
4.   Do you make use of community projects or publicity?   _____

FIGURE 20-7

A Management Audit Form for Small Retailers—Selected Questions

These questions cover areas that are the basis for retailing. You can use this form to evaluate your current status and, perhaps, to rethink certain decisions. Answer YES or NO to each question.

Source: Adapted by the authors from Michael W. Little, *Marketing Checklist for Small Retailers* (Washington, DC: U.S. Small Business Administration, Management Aids Number 4.012).

A RETAILING EFFECTIVENESS CHECKLIST Figure 20-8 has another type of audit form to assess performance and prepare for the future: a retailing effectiveness checklist. It can be used by small and large firms alike. The checklist is more strategic than the *Management Audit for Small Retailers*—which is more tactical. Unlike the yes–no answers in Figure 20-7, the checklist lets a retailer rate its performance from 1 to 5 in each area; this provides more in-depth information. However, a total score should not be computed (unless items are weighted), because all items are not equally important. A simple summation would not be a meaningful score.

✓ A long-term organizational mission is clearly articulated. _____
✓ The current status of the firm is taken into consideration when setting future plans. _____
✓ Sustainable competitive advantages are actively pursued. _____
✓ Company weaknesses have been identified and minimized. _____
✓ The management style is compatible with the firm's way of doing business. _____
✓ There is a logical short-run and long-run approach to the firm's chosen line of business. _____
✓ There are specific, realistic, and measurable short- and long-term goals. _____
✓ These goals guide strategy development and resource allocation. _____
✓ The characteristics and needs of the target market are known. _____
✓ The strategy is tailored to the chosen target market. _____
✓ Customers are extremely loyal. _____
✓ There are systematic plans prepared for each element of the strategy mix. _____
✓ All important uncontrollable factors are monitored. _____
✓ The overall strategy is integrated. _____
✓ Short-, moderate-, and long-term plans are compatible. _____
✓ The firm knows how each merchandise line, for-sale service, and business format stands in
   the marketplace. _____
✓ Tactics are carried out in a manner consistent with the strategic plan. _____
✓ The strategic plan and its elements are adequately communicated. _____
✓ Unbiased feedback is regularly sought for each aspect of the strategic plan. _____
✓ Information about new opportunities and threats is sought out. _____
✓ After enacting a strategic plan, company strengths and weaknesses, as well as successes and
   failures, are studied on an ongoing basis. _____
✓ Results are studied in a manner that reduces the firm's chances of overreacting to a situation. _____
✓ Strategic modifications are made when needed and before crises occur. _____
✓ The firm avoids strategy flip-flops (that confuse customers, employees, suppliers, and others). _____
✓ The company has a well-executed Web site or plans to have one shortly. _____

FIGURE 20-8

A Retailing Effectiveness Checklist

Rate your company's effectiveness in each of these areas on a scale of 1 to 5, with 1 being strongly agree (excellent effort) and 5 being strongly disagree (poor effort). An answer of 3 or higher signifies that improvements are necessary.

Chapter Summary

1. *To demonstrate the importance of integrating a retail strategy.* This chapter shows why retailers need to plan and apply coordinated strategies, and it describes how to assess success or failure. The stages of a retail strategy must be viewed as an ongoing, integrated system of interrelated steps.

2. *To examine four key factors in the development and enactment of an integrated retail strategy: planning procedures and opportunity analysis, defining productivity,* *performance measures, and scenario analysis.* Planning procedures can be optimized by adhering to a series of specified actions, from situation analysis to control. Opportunities must be studied in terms of their impact on overall strategy. A sales opportunity grid is good for comparing various strategic options.

   To maximize productivity, retailers need to define exactly what productivity represents to them when they enact their strategies. Although firms should be efficient, this does not necessarily mean having the lowest possible operating costs (which may lead to customer dissatisfaction) but rather keying spending to the performance standards required by a retailer's chosen niche (such as upscale versus discount).

By applying the right performance measures and setting standards for them, a retailer can better integrate its strategy. Measures include total sales, average sales per store, sales by goods/services category, sales per square foot, gross margins, gross margin return on investment, operating income, inventory turnover, markdown percentages, employee turnover, financial ratios, and profitability. A. T. Kearney's Global Retail Development Index is good for reviewing the retailing prospects in developing countries.

With scenario analysis, a retailer projects the future by examining the major factors that will have an impact on its long-term performance. Contingency plans are then keyed to alternative scenarios. This is not easy.

3. *To show how industry and company data can be used in strategy planning and analysis (benchmarking and gap analysis).* With benchmarking, a retailer sets its own standards and measures performance based on the achievements of its sector of retailing, specific competitors, the best companies, and/or its own prior actions. Through gap analysis, a retailer can compare its actual performance against its potential performance and see the areas in which it must improve.

4. *To show the value of a retail audit.* A retail strategy must be regularly monitored, evaluated, and fine-tuned or revised. The retail audit is one way to do this. It is a systematic, thorough, and unbiased review and appraisal.

The audit process has six sequential steps: (1) determining who does the audit, (2) deciding when and how often it is conducted, (3) setting the areas to be audited, (4) preparing forms, (5) conducting the audit, and (6) reporting results and recommendations to management. After the right executives read the audit report, necessary revisions in strategy should be made.

In a horizontal audit, a retailer's overall strategy and performance are assessed. In a vertical audit, one element of a strategy is reviewed in detail. Among the potential difficulties of auditing are the costs, the time commitment, the inaccuracy of performance standards, the poor cooperation from some employees, the collection of incorrect data, and unresponsive management. Some firms do not conduct audits; thus, they may find it difficult to evaluate their positions and plan for the future.

Two audit forms are presented in the chapter: a management audit for retailers and a retailing effectiveness checklist.

Key Terms

sales opportunity grid (p. 518)
performance measures (p. 521)
benchmarking (p. 522)
Global Retail Development Index (GRDI) (p. 523)

gap analysis (p. 524)
scenario analysis (p. 525)
retail audit (p. 526)

horizontal retail audit (p. 528)
vertical retail audit (p. 528)

Questions for Discussion

1. Today's retailers look to the future, as they must deal with new strategic choices. What are the key areas they need to address, and why?
2. Develop a solution for a physical store to expand its digital offering in order to take advantage of new trends in customer research and purchase.
3. Some retailers use benchmarking through tools such as SERVQUAL. What are the five areas of performance measurement?
4. What are the most commonly used performance measurements used by retailers to assess effectiveness? List five of them.
5. Assess a country and region of your choice using the global retail development index.
6. How are the terms *gap analysis* and *scenario analysis* interrelated?

7. Distinguish between horizontal and vertical retail audits. Develop a vertical audit form for an auto repair retailer.
8. What are the attributes of good retail auditing?
9. Distinguish among these auditors. Under what circumstances would each be preferred?
   a. Outside auditor
   b. Company audit specialist
   c. Company department manager
10. Under what circumstances should a disguised audit be used?
11. How should management respond to the findings of an audit? What can happen if the findings are ignored?
12. Why do many retailers not conduct any form of retail audit? Are these reasons valid? Explain your answer.

Web-Based Exercise

Visit the Web site of the Singapore Management University, home of the Customer Satisfaction Index of Singapore (http://ises.smu.edu.sg/). Click on "Downloads of Past CSIG Results" and find the results that pertain to retail. What do you conclude from reviewing these scores? Comment on both the most recent results and how these results have changed.

PART 8 Short Cases

Case 1: Envision the Future: Part 1*

Note: Following are findings from a study encompassing an industrywide retailer survey and interviews by Meridian-NorthStar Partners and *Progressive Grocer*; a similar supplier survey and interviews; a Web-based survey of 1,000 shoppers across age groups by Carbonview Research, a division of Stagnito Business Information + Edgell Communications; a review of industry learning; and incorporation of "real-world" in-market experience.

Changes—including new shopper purchase/delivery options, information sources, preferences for Millennials and others, and blurring of channels, including retail/"e-tail"—are redefining "requirements for success," as noted by 91 percent of retailers and 95 percent of suppliers in an industrywide study.

Market changes are creating entirely new challenges and an unprecedented demand for new thinking and solutions. "Brick-and-mortar retailers need to come up with a better proposition to lure shoppers into their stores," Chicago-based business consultancy Alix Partners told the *New York Times*. "'Stack it high and let it fly' doesn't work anymore. They have to figure out how to make shopping fun again."

The first challenge is *Differentiation and Relevance*. Expanding shopper options—for meal solutions, health and beauty, pet, and other categories—are a source of competition, especially with Millennials. Up to one-third of all shoppers and almost half of Millennials, shop in specialty stores, and online creates further challenges. These options are changing requirements for success. "We traditionally look at market basket and traffic," said one retailer responding to our survey, "But our more fundamental need is differentiation and relevance in a world with more shopping options."

A second challenge is *Physical/Virtual Balance*. Will the store be seen by shoppers, and Millennials in particular, as relevant 5 years from now? The answer is yes, but with a caveat: The store must elevate its game. First, the good news: Shoppers, and Millennials specifically, feel online shopping will grow over the next 5 years, but the physical store will continue to play a big role for shopping and pickup. "Shoppers want both options—physical and virtual—and the ability to move between them," another retailer responded.

Now, the caveat: A physical store must link to virtual shopping options, but not diminish focus on the first challenge—differentiation, relevance, and ability of the store to attract and excite people. As one retailer put it, "Focus on the store in an omnichannel environment is critical to our long-term survival." A food supplier said, "We are projecting huge online growth, but even by 2020, this will only be 3 percent of our sales."

Category management has played a key role for decades and will continue to do so, but today there is also need for an approach above this: to address the higher-level needs of shoppers and total-store needs of retailers. Shoppers' needs aren't confined by traditional category boundaries. For retailers, a gap exists between solutions developed across 150-plus categories and their need to prioritize and integrate these into a unified whole to excite and engage shoppers, and differentiate overall operations.

Suppliers and retailers both recognize there are limitations to category management for future shopper and store management needs. "Category management is important, but it's the price of entry, and by definition is more limited in scope and the kind of solutions it can provide," a retailer responded. "You can't win with this." This higher-level shopper/store approach impacts the type and depth of insights that are developed, as well as the application of these insights.

While virtually all suppliers today have shopper insights, retailers express the need for broader business insights that are developed to more fully address both shopper and store needs. In addition to deeper and more developed insights, there's a need for applications that identify "white space" beyond category definitions, in terms of shopper need states and also retail execution.

Questions

1. What do you think about the methodology used to gather the data for this case? Explain your answer.
2. "The first challenge is Differentiation and Relevance." Why is this true for retailers of all types and sizes? Why will this be even more difficult in the future?
3. "A second challenge is Physical/Virtual Balance." Why is this true for retailers of all types and sizes? Why will this be even more difficult in the future?
4. What are the pros and cons of optimistic planning about the growth of online revenues?

Case 2: Envision the Future: Part 2*

Note: Following are findings from a study encompassing an industrywide retailer survey and interviews by Meridian-NorthStar Partners and *Progressive Grocer*; a similar supplier survey and interviews; a Web-based survey of 1,000 shoppers across age groups by Carbonview Research, a division of Stagnito Business Information + Edgell Communications; a review of industry learning; and incorporation of "real-world" in-market experience.

Winning in today's environment demands more, given the blurring of channels, both physical and virtual; the need to focus on not just consumer needs but also shopper needs; the retailers' needs to address these in a compelling way; and a shift in the industry's perceived "moment of truth," from when a shopper is in front of a shelf with products to a much earlier point when the shopper considers which channel/retailer to shop.

The 2Es are critical today as differentiators—to excite and engage shoppers, and address the retailer need for a differentiated image and relevance. Excitement: When shoppers walk by a section of the store, does it create a "wow"? An emotional

*Based on material in "Envision the Future," *Progressive Grocer,* March 2016, pp. 38–41. Reprinted by permission.

*Based on material in "Envision the Future," *Progressive Grocer,* March 2016, pp. 38–41. Reprinted by permission.

connection? Does it make them need to enter and check it out? Does it provide a compelling alternative to specialty outlets? Engagement: The tactic of promotion focuses on communication to the shopper, but engagement focuses on dialog originating from the shopper. To compete with restaurant takeout, for example, where shoppers often use a mobile device to call ahead, is the same option available for your prepared food section? With other sections of the store, is there opportunity for dialog before, in, and after the store?

Only 50 percent of shoppers indicated that they're "fully or pretty loyal" to their primary grocery store; only 51 percent said that they have "high or somewhat high enjoyment" in the shopping experience; 41 percent said that it's "not organized to the way I shop"; and 30 percent said, "I don't think they focus on shopper needs when organizing products." The 2Es have the potential to change the game. The "treasure hunt" of club stores and the "fun/excitement" in many specialty stores, noted in various studies, provide a helpful reference point. In our study, more than three-quarters of shoppers indicated that they'd be likely to shift "back" to their regular store if it offered a more engaging shopping experience.

In a very different business environment, it's also instructive to revisit industry "truths" in two areas. The first is perceptions of the perimeter and the center store. The perimeter has unique elements, but also several others that can be broadly applied, such as category integration, visual appeal, information/news, "stations," and more.

The second is perception of a "common look" across the store. "Common look can be more weakness than strength," another retailer asserted. "Why should the pet aisle look the same as household cleaning or snacks or HBC? These sections need to connect with shoppers, not just provide products. A pet is a family member. Beverages provide purity, variety, enjoyment. OTC meets treatment and preventive needs." Creating a more exciting, engaging retail experience must take a broader approach than trying to solve center store problems with center store tactics, or maintaining a common look across the store.

Look at a top-five grocery retailer to illustrate certain opportunities, but observations and implications also apply to other channels. The store has a typical perimeter, and the center store has 24 aisles. There's a numbered sign at the end of each aisle that lists seven to eight product types found in that aisle, or almost 200 categories. Signs are the same shape and color, and aisles generally use the same "fixturing" and other elements. Certain product types (e.g., beverages) occupy three entire aisles, but aren't next to one another. Other product types (e.g., HBC, pet, general merchandise) are typically their own aisles. End-aisle displays are used, often for items that typically don't align with the product types stocked in the aisles adjacent to them.

Questions

1. Explain why the 2Es are so important for forward-looking retail planning.
2. What's the last retailer—physical store or online store—that excited you? Describe what excited you. Did this encourage you to buy more or pay a quick return visit? Why or why not?
3. As a shopper, do you want the retailer to engage with you? Based on your answer, what should the retailer do to cultivate your continuing business?
4. What are the pros and cons of a supermarket radically redesigning its store interior and layout?

PART 8 Comprehensive Case

Achieving Excellence in Retailing*

Introduction

The 2016 A. T. Kearney Achieving Excellence in Retail Operations (AERO) study uncovers both the good and the bad in this new era of store operations. The good: a clear and consistent trend of "smarter" retail. Survey responses from executives at more than 100 global retailers reveal that companies are aligning store operations strategies and metrics to the new omnichannel environment and are investing heavily in providing support. Pilots and trials are evolving more rapidly and more fulfillment options are quickly becoming available across all retail sectors.

The bad: AERO points to the many challenges retailers face in effectively adopting these smarter strategies and metrics. Although technology is the number-one retail investment today, there's limited visibility on the return on investment. Amid the noise of technology investment and omnichannel integration, store associates are often overlooked as crucial conduits for improved store performance. And importantly, the study points to a misalignment between consumer expectations and retailer offerings, with retailers investing in services that customers may not want, need, or expect, particularly in terms of fulfillment, in-store technology, and social engagement. In seeking to be all things to all people, are retailers driving unnecessary cost and complexity in their operations?

The 2016 AERO study probes these key trends in retail today, offers insightful case studies, and shares our thoughts on potential solutions By understanding the new rules of the game, improved retail operations can be a path to success in this new retail era.

A Smarter Way to Manage Retail Operations

Omnichannel has ushered in the next wave of growth in retail. But defining what it exactly is depends on who you're talking to. Is it uniform messaging across channels? Seamless fulfillment across channels? Consistent pricing across channels? All of the above? Regardless of how it is defined, any retailer will tell you that its impact on retail operations has been incredible.

The AERO findings point to major changes already in place in stores to support omnichannel. Eighty-six percent of retailers have aligned store strategies and metrics to support an omnichannel environment. Store associates are being trained on cross-platform engagement, incentivized to sell through E-commerce channels, and rewarded for in-store fulfillment.

Training on consumer engagement, education, and sales is evolving as retail leaders rethink their stores' role into showrooms, mini-distribution centers, education centers, and the like. Gone are the days when a store's success was based solely on the revenue generated within the four walls, with store profit and incentive structures refined to include its surrounding

E-commerce business. This has also fundamentally changed how store associates need to think about their customers.

Retailers are also getting smarter about when, where, and how they test their new concepts in stores. In our 2013 survey, we found that 19 percent of retailers had an active pilot program; today, the number is above 30 percent. This year's survey finds some retailers are well down the path to a store operations toolset to be successful.

JOHN LEWIS CASE STUDY John Lewis, a 150-year-old U.K. department store, found a smarter way to manage technology and ultimately provide a differentiated service offering to consumers. The success started with several pilot programs. It used online technologies to pilot an "omnichannel store" that offered the full assortment of John Lewis products in a smaller format. Its app gave consumers access to 250,000 products, product reviews, price matches, wish lists, and videos. In-store iPads and computers gave consumers access to thousands of products not currently in the store, along with fulfillment options to a home or a store. And a click-and-collect program allowed customers to buy a range of products from John Lewis and other subsidiary brands, from clothing to homewares, online and then collect in one trip.

John Lewis' offering has proved successful. Today, one-third of sales are from online purchases, worth roughly $1.5 billion, with growth in that channel of 25 percent. Its click-and-collect orders have reached 6 million per year, a 17-fold increase from 350,000 in 2008, its first year.

Aligning Consumer Expectations and Retailer Offerings

Despite the wave of exciting activity to support omnichannel, many bets that retailers are placing in store operations aren't necessarily bringing desired results. Our study points to misalignment between retail offerings and consumer expectations. As retailers take leaps forward toward "omnichannel nirvana," consumers are only demanding small steps.

While we expect expectations to shift as more options become available and known, the findings point to the need for simply getting this basic capability right; more than a third of respondents say their company falls short.

For example, we've also seen the race to near immediate shipping times—from next-day to same-day to one-hour shipping. Despite this focus, more than three-quarters of consumers surveyed say they merely expect two days or more for shipping. Consumers say they are more interested in retailers fulfilling their promises—getting products when they were told they would—rather than on getting the product immediately. See Figure 1.

These issues have dramatic implications on retail operations—the need for new capabilities, skill sets, and tools, and for workflow and incentives to meet omnichannel expectations. The missed opportunity is when a retailer's offering and the investments needed to produce it are far separated from customer expectations. What consumers value should underpin omnichannel investments in store operations—and not merely a retailer's "omnichannel vision." This will help avoid unnecessary cost and complexity, and ultimately reduce consumer confusion.

---

*Based on material in Joel Alden, Dean Hillier, Pierre-Alexandre Koch, Adam Pressman, Ryan Fisher, and John Rabenhorst, "2016 Achieving Excellence in Retail Operations (AERO®) Study— Retail Operations: People Are Still the Best Investment," A. T. Kearney, 2016, pp. 1–8. Reprinted by permission.

FIGURE 1

As the Race to Faster Shipping Times Heats Up, Most Customers Are Happy with Two-Day Shipping

Source: A. T. Kearney, 2016. Reprinted by permission.

In general, what do you believe to be an acceptable E-commerce order shipping time for a non-urgent purchase?

% of respondents

100%

13%	Same day
12%	1 day
19%	2 days
24%	3 days
9%	4 days
16%	5 days
7%	More than 5 days

When you make an E-commerce purchase, which is more important to you regarding delivery?

% of respondents

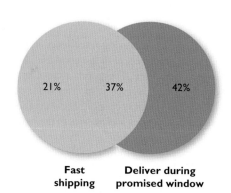

21% 37% 42%

Fast shipping   **Deliver during promised window**

Technology: Hopes and Frustrations

This year's study finds once again that retailers are investing heavily in technology, yet are still struggling with figuring out its value. Technology is the number-one area of investment according to respondents in our 2016 study, with nearly every respondent saying they will invest in it. Yet nearly 60 percent surveyed say their company struggles with executing and measuring its return on investment. These results are slightly better than the findings in 2013, yet still quite low. See Figure 2.

So what's going on here? Why are retailers continuing year after year to toss money at technology in an effort to chase after the next big thing in retail, yet coming up short?

We believe the answer lies with the focus of these investments. Ninety percent or so of retail sales still happen within the four walls of a physical store. Yet almost none of the investments we see today are about helping store associates do their jobs better. Instead, most focus on consumer-facing technology, even though 80 percent of consumers say they experience poor service when directly interacting with in-store technology. Just because there is a poor service experience today doesn't mean to stop trying. Focusing investments on tools and information that enable the employee to better engage with customers and meet true customer needs will remain valuable. There is an opportunity to close the information gap regarding in-store customer interactions (such as preferences based on in-store activities), but that will require a greater sense of trust and willingness to share information than we have today.

The retailers that are investing in technology are successfully using it to help store associates. It helps ease the burden of execution also, as associates are incentivized to learn, adopt, and implement new technology solutions to boost productivity, sales, and potentially their own commissions.

Social Currency

Another focus area in the age of omnichannel is social media, and the value retailers can generate from getting it right. The 2016 survey, however, reveals a gulf between what the consumers actually expect and what retailers are offering on social media. More than 60 percent of retailers say they still focus on mining social media to generate value. Two-thirds of consumers, on the other hand, say they are not engaging with retailers on social media at all; for those that do, the primary reason is to get a coupon or a discount. See Figure 3.

Is this another case of misalignment between the retailer's offering and consumer expectations? Consider that more than 85 percent of consumers say that social-media interactions do not lead to store visits; and when asked to rank a number of touch points with retailers, consumers ranked social media the least valuable out of 13 listed. Store location, product selection, and store cleanliness topped the list.

This does not mean that retailers should stop investing so much time and effort in social media. Rather, they must refocus on doing it right. Retailers that have pulled ahead of the pack when it comes to social media engagement and the value they're generating from it are interacting with customers online and creating a sense of community.

WARBY PARKER CASE STUDY   Warby Parker's eyeglass customers are more highly engaged on social media than those of typical retailers. Its strong social mission makes it popular with the younger population. The company also maintains a consistent, recognizable look across eyewear, Web site content, and store experience.

It succeeds in its social mission by regularly promoting unique and exclusive events that are apt to be shared on social media. It encourages interfacing with social media over the "try-on" period. Its #warbyhometryon hashtag gives the company an "expert" opinion of what its customers think of their eyewear.

Store Associates: The Unsung Heroes of Retail

So much focus today is on the consumer of the future, on new and exciting technologies, and on social media engagement, but the AERO findings show that the real heroes of store operations

FIGURE 2
Retailers Are Making Technology Investments across Nearly Every Major Area of Store Operations

Source: A. T. Kearney, 2016. Reprinted by permission.

Please indicate your current investment outlook with regard to the following technology over the next two years:

% of respondents

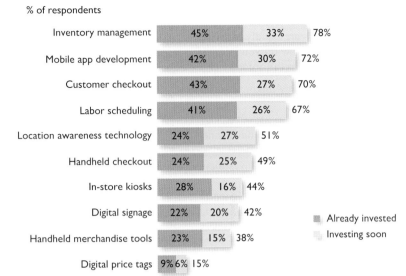

	Already invested	Investing soon	Total
Inventory management	45%	33%	78%
Mobile app development	42%	30%	72%
Customer checkout	43%	27%	70%
Labor scheduling	41%	26%	67%
Location awareness technology	24%	27%	51%
Handheld checkout	24%	25%	49%
In-store kiosks	28%	16%	44%
Digital signage	22%	20%	42%
Handheld merchandise tools	23%	15%	38%
Digital price tags	9%	6%	15%

are in-store associates, and they are often being overlooked. Customers say that experience and service have the greatest impact on productivity. Yet we consistently find that store associates get little investment focus.

Nearly one-half of retailer respondents said employee training programs could be "significantly improved." More than 70 percent of retailers expect spans of control to widen in the immediate future. And nearly all express concern regarding their workforce's ability to adapt to a new omnichannel

environment. In our opinion, it's not that retailers have had store associates with poor skill sets, but rather that they have not had the right focus on what it takes to properly support in-store staff.

Store associates are the most important assets retailers have; they are central to the future of any store. Investments should focus on the core fundamentals of what it takes to support store associates: training, incentives, career progression, and corporate support to meet expectations. Interestingly, about three-quarters of retailers plan to invest in more training and

FIGURE 3
For Customers, Social Media Do Not Drive Store Visits, But Is Instead Used for Discounts

Source: A. T. Kearney, 2016. Reprinted by permission.

% of consumers highly satisfied

Store location	49%
Product selection	43%
Store cleanliness	41%
Register wait times	39%
Staff knowledge	38%
Store layout	36%
Inventory depth	33%
Loyalty program	32%
Social media	13%

% of consumers who say digital media leads to store visits

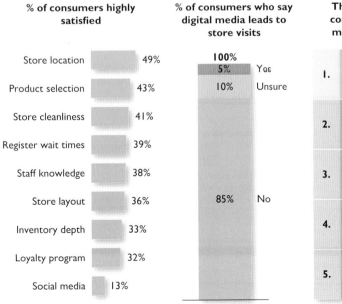

- 100%
- 5% Yes
- 10% Unsure
- 85% No

The top five reasons consumers use social media with retailers

1. To get a discount
2. To support a retailer I like
3. To receive regular updates
4. To research products
5. To participate in contests

labor; but right now, the workforce needs more support to do its most critical task: deliver superior customer service.

Driving to "Smarter" Retail

With the omnichannel age here, retailers are rapidly evolving store operations capabilities to support. How do you know if your retail organization is ready to realize its full value?

▶ Do you have a defined business strategy linking metrics across channels and store formats?

▶ Do you use learning stores and pilots for trying out change programs to understand the impact of your omnichannel investments?

▶ How well are you measuring the return on investment (ROI) for your retail technology expenditures?

▶ Are your online order delivery service levels aligned to effectively deliver to your customer when promised?

▶ How can you drive more value for you and your customers from social media?

▶ How are you investing in your in-store associates to set them up for success?

The truth is, many retailers are starting to answer these questions affirmatively. New strategies are seeking to meet consumer expectations, new metrics are more properly measuring and incentivizing store staff, and focused and more frequent store pilots are getting answers faster.

However, in their chase for "omnichannel nirvana," retailers need to get better at the basics of omnichanne—a dedicated focus on what the customer wants and needs; support to ensure that investments improve store performance; clear reviews about returns on investment; and an understanding of how in-store associates can be supported. Retail remains a people business. Getting that part right remains a critical ingredient for success.

Research Methodology

ABOUT THE STUDY A. T. Kearney's Achieving Excellence in Retail Operations (AERO) study provides insights into how

retailers globally can improve their operations. This year's study captured more than 100 responses from senior retail executives in the Americas, Europe, and Asia Pacific, offering a view of emerging global best practices in store operations. It covers multiple sectors, including apparel, health and personal care, mass-market and hypermarket, electronics, food and grocery, and cash and carry.

Besides the retailer perspective, this year's study also brings in the consumer view. We surveyed nearly 800 North American consumers across demographic backgrounds, and their responses provide a clear view of the consumer's opinion of store operations. In the study, we compare and contrast retailer perspectives with those of consumers, identifying what is truly important to today's retail environment.

The study is based on A. T. Kearney's Store Operations Framework; see Figure 4. This framework, which was also used to pioneer the 2010 study, evaluates operations across setting strategic direction, delivering core value, optimizing expenses, and driving lasting change.

Questions

1. What overall conclusions do you draw from this case? Explain your answer.

2. What is the biggest "disconnect" between retailers and their customers today? How could this be fixed?

3. What could other retailers learn from John Lewis and Warby Parker?

4. Describe the findings shown in Figure 1. Are you surprised by the results? What are the implications of these findings for retailers?

5. Describe the findings shown in Figure 2. Are retailers doing well in their technology investments? Explain your answer.

6. Describe the findings shown in Figure 3. Are you surprised by the results? Why or why not? What are the implications of these findings for retailers?

7. Comment on the methodology used for the AERO study. Discuss how you would improve it.

FIGURE 4
A. T. Kearney's Store Operations Framework Forms the Basis for the AERO Study

Source: A. T. Kearney, 2016. Reprinted by permission.

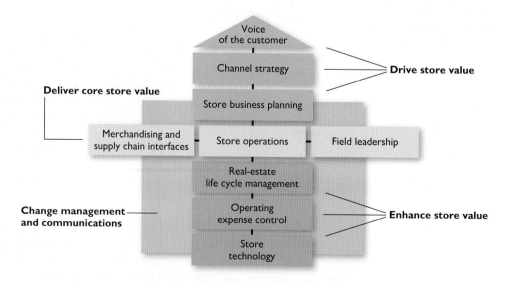

Appendix   Careers in Retailing

Overview

A person looking for a career in retailing has two broad possibilities: owning a business or working for a retailer. One alternative does not preclude the other. Many people open their own retail businesses after getting experience as employees. A person can also choose franchising, which has elements of both entrepreneurship and managerial assistance (as discussed in Chapter 4).

Regardless of the specific retail career path chosen, recent college graduates often gain personnel and profit-and-loss responsibilities faster in retailing than in any other major sector of business. After an initial training program, an entry-level manager supervises personnel, works on in-store displays, interacts with customers, and reviews sales and other data on a regular basis. An assistant buyer helps in planning merchandise assortments, interacting with suppliers, and outlining the promotion effort. Our blog (www.bermanevansretail.com) has loads of career-related materials: We

- Have a table describing dozens of positions in retailing.
- Present career paths for several leading retailers across a variety of formats.
- Offer advice on résumé writing (with a sample résumé), interviewing, and internships.
- Highlight retailing-related information from the *Occupational Outlook Handbook*.
- Present links to a number of popular career sites.

THE BRIGHT FUTURE OF A CAREER IN RETAILING

The U.S. Bureau of Labor Statistics predicts that employment in retailing will grow by about 7 percent between 2014 and 2024.[1] In addition to new positions being available, there will be opportunities to advance in a retail career via designated career paths. For example, many employees who started as a retail salesperson have progressed to department level sales managers.

According to the Bureau of Labor Statistics, the largest retail employers are general merchandise stores (including warehouse clubs, supercenters, dollar stores, and variety stores), and food and beverage stores. The next largest employers include motor vehicle and parts dealers, and clothing and clothing accessory stores.

The National Retail Federation offers a lot of valuable advice and resources at its "Retail Careers Center" Web site (www.nrf.com/career-center).

OWNING A BUSINESS

Owning a retail business is popular, and many opportunities exist. Most retail outlets are sole proprietorships; and many of today's giants began as independents, including Walmart, Home Depot, J.C. Penney, McDonald's, Sears, Cheesecake Factory, and Mrs. Fields.

Too often, people overlook the possibility of owning a retail business. Initial investments can be quite modest (several thousand dollars). Direct marketing (both mail order and online retailing), direct selling, and service retailing often require relatively low initial investments—as do various franchises. Financing may also be available from banks, suppliers, store-fixture firms. and equipment companies. Furthermore, owning a business gives the operator opportunity to be flexible in choosing among retail formats, to serve unique niches, to be independent of stockholders and other publics. In many cases, there are few or no licensing standards.

OPPORTUNITIES AS A RETAIL EMPLOYEE

As we've noted before, in the United States, tens of millions of people are employed by traditional retailers, as well as others who are employed by firms such as banks, insurance companies, and airlines. More people work in retailing than in any other industry.

Career opportunities are plentiful because of the number of new retail businesses that open and the labor intensity of retailing. Thousands of new outlets open each year in the United States, and certain segments of retailing are growing at particularly rapid rates. Many large retailers also plan to open many new stores in foreign markets. The increased employment from new store openings and the sales growth of retail formats (such as supercenters) also mean there are significant opportunities for personal advancement for talented retail personnel. Every time a chain opens a new outlet, there is a need for a store manager and other management-level people.

Selected retailing positions, career paths, and compensation ranges are described next.

Types of Positions in Retailing

Employment is not confined to buying and merchandising. Retail career opportunities also encompass advertising, public relations, credit analysis, marketing research, warehouse management, information technology, human resource management, accounting, and real-estate. Look at our Web site for a list and description of a wide range of retailing positions. Some highly specialized jobs may be available only in large retail firms.

The type of position a person seeks should be matched with the type of retailer likely to have such a position. Chain stores and franchises typically have real-estate divisions. Department stores and chain stores usually have large human resource departments. Mail-order firms often have advertising production departments. Franchises and fast-growing retailers commonly have large real-estate departments. And online firms have Web site design, Web analytics, and large order fulfillment departments. If one is interested in travel, a buying position or a job with a retailer having geographically dispersed operations should be sought.

Career Paths and Compensation in Retailing

For college graduates, executive training programs at larger retailers offer good learning experiences and advancement potential. These firms often offer careers in both merchandising and nonmerchandising areas.

Here is how a new college graduate could progress in a career path at a typical department store or specialty store chain: He or she usually begins with a training program (lasting from three months to a year or more) on how to run a merchandise department. That program often involves on-the-job and classroom experiences. On-the-job training includes working with records, reordering stock, planning displays, and supervising salespeople. Classroom activities include learning how to evaluate vendors, analyze computer reports, forecast fashion trends, and administer store policy.

After initial training, the person becomes an entry-level operations manager (often called a sales manager, assistant department manager, or department manager—depending on the firm) or an assistant buyer. An entry-level manager or assistant buyer works under the direction of a seasoned department (group) manager or buyer and analyzes sales, assists in purchasing goods, handles reorders, and helps with displays. The new manager supervises personnel and learns store operations; the assistant buyer is more involved in purchases than operations. Depending on the retailer, either person may follow the same type of career path, or the entry-level operations manager may progress up the store management ladder and the assistant buyer up the buying ladder.

During this time, responsibilities and duties depend on the department (group) manager's or buyer's willingness to delegate and teach. When a manager or buyer has authority to make decisions, the entry-level manager or assistant buyer will usually have more responsibility. If a firm has centralized management, a manager (buyer) is more limited in his or her responsibilities, as is the entry-level manager or assistant buyer. Further, an assistant buyer will gain more experience if he or she is in a firm near a wholesale market center and can make trips to the market to buy merchandise.

The next step in a department store or specialty store chain's career path is promotion to department (group) manager or buyer. This position is entrepreneurial—running a business. The manager or buyer selects merchandise, develops a promotional campaign, decides which items to reorder, and oversees personnel and record keeping. For some retailers, *manager* and *buyer* are synonymous. For others, the distinction is as just explained for entry-level positions. Generally, a person is considered for promotion to manager or buyer after two years.

Large department store and specialty store chains have additional levels of personnel to plan, supervise, and assess merchandise departments. On the store management side, there can be group

TABLE 1 10 Retail Positions with Unique Responsibilities

▶ *Stacey Cavin, Local Forager, Whole Foods Market* – Cavin is charged with seeking out local products for the stores she supports in suburban Los Angeles. Her expertise includes guiding local suppliers through Whole Foods' stringent quality standards application and approval process.

▶ *Sarah Hutnick, Spirit Director, Drybar* – Through selective recruitment and manager training, Hutnick's goal is for every guest to be given the most amazing, over-the-top customer service. She also supports customers' causes and seeks ways for Drybar to give back to local neighborhoods.

▶ *Frank Youngman, BrainCoach, Marbles: The Brain Store* – A BrainCoach takes the reins, maximizing sales and sparking customer engagement utilizing Marbles' customer interaction cycle. BrainCoaches are trained on matters of the brain and make personal recommendations with these benefits in mind.

▶ *Michael Phillips Moskowitz, Global Chief Curator, eBay Inc.* – Moskowitz says he's working to develop a catalytic, original, approachable, and living editorial voice for eBay. "They wanted a curatorial approach: How can we paint vivid, vibrant portraits, or mosaics — mosaics of merchandise that tell a story or convey a sense of soul?"

▶ *Seth Goldman, President and TeaEO, Honest Tea* – Goldman oversees the nation's top-selling organic bottled tea. Under his leadership, Honest Tea has expanded distribution to more than 100,000 outlets. He also develops partnerships with organic and Fair Trade Certified suppliers.

▶ *Hillary Jacobson, Manager of Joy Fulfillment, PIRCH* – It's Jacobson's job to deliver on the promises made to customers of the home goods retailer and to seamlessly facilitate the moments imagined in its showrooms — from product procurement to logistical fulfillment to joy achievement.

▶ *Stephen Hultquist, Chief Evangelist, RedSeal* – Hultquist communicates RedSeal's value and benefits to customers and partners through training and other education and by speaking, writing, and working with the press and analysts.

▶ *Tawni Cranz, Chief Talent Officer, Netflix* – Cranz leads a team that maintains the firm's unique corporate culture, hires new talent, and keeps the organization lean and flexible despite enormous growth.

▶ *David Pomije, Chief Fun Officer, Halo* – The head of the videogame company summarizes his mission on LinkedIn thusly: "Taking journeys that begin at the intersection of the impossible, wind through the improbable, endorsed by the few, but in the end loved by humanity."

▶ *Chade-Meng Tan, Jolly Good Fellow, Google* – Tan is a Google pioneer, an award-winning engineer, a *New York Times* best-selling author, a thought leader, and a philanthropist. He endeavors to enlighten minds, open hearts, and create world peace.

Source: Based on material in *STORES magazine*. Susan Reda, "Chief Concerns," *STORES Magazine* (June 2015). Reprinted by permission. Copyright 2016. STORES Magazine.

managers, store managers, branch vice-presidents, and others. On the buying side, there can be divisional managers, merchandising vice-presidents, and others.

At many firms, advancement is indicated by specific career paths. This lets employees monitor their performance, know the next career step, and progress in a clear manner. Selected retail career paths are shown in the careers section of our Web site.

As an illustration of the diversity in retail career paths, Table 1 lists 10 retail positions with unique responsibilities. Table 2 lists compensation ranges for personnel in various retailing positions.

TABLE 2 Typical Compensation Ranges for Personnel in Selected Retailing Positions

Position	Compensation Range
Operations	
Customer service representative	$ 25,000–$ 50,000+
Department manager—soft-line retailer	$ 30,000–$ 35,000+
Store management trainee	$ 30,000–$ 35,000+
Department manager—department store	$ 30,000–$ 35,000+
Department manager—mass merchandiser	$ 30,000–$ 35,000+
Department manager—hard-line retailer	$ 30,000–$ 35,000+
Warehouse director	$ 30,000–$ 90,000+

Continued

TABLE 2 Typical Compensation Ranges for Personnel in Selected Retailing Positions (continued)

Position	Compensation Range
Store manager—specialty store, home center, drugstore	$ 32,000–$ 70,000+
Store manager—soft-line retailer	$ 35,000–$ 100,000+
Customer service supervisor	$ 40,000–$ 60,000+
Security director	$ 42,000–$ 70,000+
Store manager—department store	$ 45,000–$ 85,000+
Human resource manager	$ 50,000–$ 80,000+
Operations director	$ 60,000–$ 100,000+
Supply chain manager	$ 65,000–$ 100,000+
Merchandising	
Assistant buyer	$ 25,000–$ 40,000+
Buyer—specialty store, home center, drugstore, department store	$ 35,000–$ 80,000+
Buyer—discount store	$ 35,000–$ 85,000+
Buyer—national chain	$ 45,000–$ 85,000+
Divisional merchandise manager	$ 60,000–$ 100,000+
General merchandise manager—drugstore, home center	$ 65,000–$ 100,000+
General merchandise manager—specialty store, department store	$ 70,000–$ 125,000+
General merchandise manager—discount store, national chain	$ 70,000–$ 125,000+
Senior merchandising executive	$ 80,000–$ 250,000+
Marketing Research and Information Technology	
Market research junior analyst	$ 30,000–$ 35,000+
Market research analyst	$ 30,000–$ 45,000+
Market research senior analyst	$ 40,000–$ 55,000+
Web site developer	$ 45,000–$ 75,000+
Market research assistant director	$ 45,000–$ 65,000+
Market research director	$ 55,000–$ 75,000+
Database administrator	$ 60,000–$ 100,000+
Top Management	
Senior human resources executive	$ 60,000–$ 140,000+
Senior advertising executive	$ 65,000–$ 110,000+
Senior real-estate executive	$ 65,000–$ 120,000+
Senior financial executive	$ 85,000–$ 200,000+
President	$250,000–$ 3,000,000+
Chairman of the board	$350,000–$10,000,000+
Other	
Public relations specialist	$ 35,000–$ 85,000+
Retail sales analyst	$ 38,000–$ 90,000+
Supply chain specialist	$ 40,000–$ 60,000+

Source: Estimated by the authors from various sources.

GETTING YOUR FIRST POSITION AS A RETAIL PROFESSIONAL

The key steps in getting your first professional position in retailing are the search for opportunities, interview preparation, and the evaluation of options. You must devote sufficient time to these steps so your job hunt progresses as well as possible.

Searching for Career Opportunities in Retailing

Various sources should be consulted. These include your school placement office, company directories and Web sites (such as www.linkedin.com), ads in your local newspapers, Web networking and job sites, and networking (with professors, friends, neighbors, and family members). Here are some hints to consider:

▶ *Incorporate internships into your college experience.* This lets you try out different types of positions, different types of retailers, different goods/service categories, and different size firms. Internship sponsors also can directly see your job-related skills and motivation.

▶ *Do not "place all your eggs in one basket."* Do not rely too much on friends and relatives. They may be able to get you an interview but not a guaranteed job offer.

▶ *Be serious and systematic in your career search.* Plan in advance and do not wait until the recruiting season starts at your school to generate a list of retail employers.

▶ *Use directories with lists of retailers and current job openings.* Online listings include Career-Builder.com Retail Jobs (http://careerbuilder.com/jobs-retail) AllRetailJobs.com (www.allretailjobs.com), Work in Retail.com (www.workinretail.com), and I Hire Retail (www.ihireretail.com). Also visit our blog (www.bermanevansretail.com).

▶ *Rely on the "law of large numbers."* In sending out résumés, you may have to contact at least 10 to 20 retailers to get just two to four interviews.

▶ *Make sure your résumé and cover letter highlight your best qualities.* These may include school honors, officer status in an organization, work experience, computer skills, and the proportion of college tuition you paid. Also aim your résumé and cover letter to each specific potential employer. Our Web site shows a sample résumé for an entry-level position in retailing.

▶ *Show your résumé to at least one professor, your college's placement office manager, or other advisor.* Be receptive to their constructive comments. Remember, their goal is to help you get the best possible first job.

▶ *Be professional at social media sites.* Companies may look you up at Facebook, LinkedIn, and other social media sites. Be careful what you have posted—including the pictures you display.

Preparing for the Interview

The initial and subsequent interviews for a position, which may last for 20 to 30 minutes or longer, play a large part in determining if you get a job offer. Thus, you should prepare for all interviews:

▶ *Adequately research each firm.* Be aware of its goods/service category, current size, overall retail strategy, competitive developments, and so on.

▶ *Anticipate questions and plan general responses.* "Tell me about yourself." "Why are you interested in a retailing career?" "Why do you want a job with us?" "What are your major strengths?" "Your major weaknesses?" "What do you want to be doing five years from now?" "What would your prior boss say about you?" In preparation, role-play your answers to these questions with someone.

▶ *Treat every interview as if it is the most important one.* Otherwise, you may not be properly prepared if the position turns out to be more desirable than you originally thought. And remember that you represent both your college and yourself at all interviews.

▶ *Be prepared to raise your own questions when asked to do so in the interview.* They should relate to career paths, training, and opportunities for advancement.

▶ *Dress appropriately and be well groomed.*

▶ *Verify the date and place of the interview.* Be prompt.

▶ *Have a pen and pad (or PDA/smartphone) to record information after an interview is over.*

▶ *Write a note to the interviewer within a week to thank him or her for spending time with you and to express a continuing interest in the company.*

Evaluating Retail Career Opportunities

Job seekers often place too much emphasis on initial salary or the firm's image in assessing career opportunities. Many other factors should be considered, as well:

▶ What activities do you like?

▶ Would you regard the position as fulfilling?

- ▶ What are your personal strengths and weaknesses?
- ▶ What are your current and long-term goals?
- ▶ Do you want to work for an independent, a chain, or a franchise operation?
- ▶ Does the opportunity offer an acceptable and clear career path?
- ▶ Does the opportunity include a formal training program?
- ▶ Will the opportunity enable you to be rewarded for good performance?
- ▶ Will you have to relocate?
- ▶ Will each promotion in the company result in greater authority and responsibility?
- ▶ Is the compensation level fair relative to other offers?
- ▶ Can a dedicated and hard-working employee move up the career path much faster than an average one?
- ▶ If owning a retail firm is a long-term goal, which opportunity is the best preparation?

UPWARD MOBILITY IN YOUR CAREER: THE CHIEFS OF RETAILING[2]

While it's become more common to hear about new "chief" roles, determining the specifics of what each is responsible for can be tricky. When an employer, a headhunter, or a colleague learns someone is a CFO – chief financial officer – a reasonably clear picture of that person's role emerges. If the title is chief experience officer, however, the definition is far less clear.

Susan Hart, co-leader of Spencer Stuart's global executive search and leadership consulting practice, admits that finding the right candidate for these jobs often requires a deep dive into the employers' exact qualifications, but it's not all that different from other jobs the company is asked to fill. "Every company is somewhat unique, so it's up to us to probe how they operate, how they expect this candidate to interface with others in the company, what's the structure of the job," she says. "We start with a diagnostic, then work to zero in on the right person."

She says chief digital officers are currently in high demand, and it is a position that could be a breeding ground for future retail CEOs. "The 21st-century retail CEO needs to be fluent in all things digital, E-commerce, and marketing," she says. "They need to know how to use data to gain customer insight. Oftentimes, much of that is what the chief digital officer is working on today."

Maryam Morse, national retail practice leader for Hay Group, believes some retailers are working through hiccups as they carve out a course for the newly named chiefs to follow. "Firms are making the leap by designating a chief digital officer, but most say they're paving the path as they go." In the past, retail "celebrated and rewarded individual accountability. Now, leaders are asked to think differently (to apply companywide thinking to every task) to keep the customer at the center."

That was exactly the case for Kathy Doyle Thomas of Half Price Books. Thomas logged several years as vice-president of marketing and development before being named chief strategy officer. "Decisions to elevate someone to 'chief' are grounded in the importance of a certain business objective — whether that be digital or innovation or whatever," she says. "There are a lot of VPs in retail, and as that organizational structure progressed the need to designate a chief became more apparent."

Thomas views "chief" titles as indicative of executives who are being called upon for more big-picture thinking. "As chief strategy officer, I'm charged with exploring any new opportunities for the company—ranging from new revenue-generating opportunities to exploring outside partnerships," she says. "I'm being asked to come up with new ideas that will increase sales rather than focusing my attention on the nuts and bolts of one portion of the company."

Will those functions and responsibilities be understood and valued outside Half Price Books, were she to move on? "That's hard to say," Thomas admits. "I would imagine the responsibilities of the chief strategy officer would be different from one company to the next. Still, in this role, my job is to encourage and to help make things happen, but I don't necessarily get credit for that. For example, I can push for certain divisions to carry different merchandise, but if and when they do, that's something a buyer would be rewarded for. So much of this comes down to recognizing how different retail is now from what it looked like even just a few years ago."

Many experts feel the inclination to name more retail chiefs is a positive trend, but they're guarded about the staying power of the titles. "I see these chief titles as catalytic roles at a point in time," Eamonn Kelly, a director with Deloitte Consulting, says. "They're trying to make a connection between advances in digital and customer and technology. If a firm gets that right and embraces customer-centric thinking—that's a success, and these roles wouldn't be needed five years later. What really matters is the ability to combine a deep understanding of the customer with an understanding of how digital technology will drive new sources of customer value. Then everyone wins—the customer, the retailer and the industry."

Glossary

Additional Markup Increase in a retail price above the original markup when demand is unexpectedly high or costs are rising.

Additional Markup Percentage Looks at total dollar additional markups as a percentage of net sales:

$$\text{Additional markup percentage} = \frac{\text{Total dollar additional markups}}{\text{Net sales (in \$)}}$$

Addition to Retail Percentage Measures a price rise as a percentage of the original price:

$$\text{Addition to retail percentage} = \frac{\text{New price} - \text{Original price}}{\text{Original price}}$$

Advertising Paid, nonpersonal communication transmitted through out-of-store mass media by an identified sponsor.

Affinity Exists when the stores at a given location complement, blend, and cooperate with one another, and each benefits from the others' presence.

All-You-Can-Afford Method Promotional budgeting procedure in which a retailer first allots funds for each element of the strategy mix except promotion. The funds that are left go to the promotional budget.

Americans with Disabilities Act (ADA) Mandates that persons with disabilities be given appropriate access to retailing facilities.

Analog Model Computerized site selection tool in which potential sales for a new store are estimated based on sales of similar stores in existing areas, competition at a prospective location, the new store's expected market share at that location, and the size and density of a location's primary trading area.

Application Blank Usually the first tool used to screen applicants. It provides data on education, experience, health, reasons for leaving prior jobs, outside activities, hobbies, and references.

Assets Any items a retailer owns with a monetary value.

Asset Turnover Performance measure based on a retailer's net sales and total assets. It is equal to net sales divided by total assets.

Assortment Selection of merchandise carried by a retailer. It includes both the breadth of product categories and the variety within each category.

Assortment Display An open or closed display in which a retailer exhibits a wide range of merchandise.

Assortment Merchandise Apparel, furniture, autos, and other products for which the retailer must carry a variety of products in order to give customers a proper selection.

Atmosphere (Atmospherics) Reflection of a store's physical characteristics that are used to develop an image and draw customers. The concept is also applicable to non-store retailers.

Attitudes (Opinions) Positive, neutral, or negative feelings a person has about different topics.

Augmented Customer Service Encompasses the actions that enhance the shopping experience and give retailers a competitive advantage.

Automatic Reordering System Computerized approach that combines a perpetual inventory and reorder point calculations.

Bait-and-Switch Advertising Illegal practice in which a retailer lures a customer by advertising goods and services at exceptionally low prices and then tries to convince the person to buy a better, more expensive substitute that is available. The retailer has no intention of selling the advertised item.

Balanced Tenancy Occurs when stores in a planned shopping center complement each other as to the quality and variety of their product offerings.

Balance Sheet Itemizes a retailer's assets, liabilities, and net worth at a specific time—based on the principle that assets equal liabilities plus net worth.

Basic Stock List Specifies the inventory level, color, brand, style category, size, package, and so on for every staple item carried by a retailer.

Basic Stock Method Inventory level planning tool wherein a retailer carries more items than it expects to sell over a specified period:

$$\text{Basic stock} = \begin{array}{l}\text{Average monthly stock at retail} \\ -\text{Average monthly sales}\end{array}$$

Battle of the Brands The competition between manufacturers and retailers for shelf space and profits, whereby manufacturer, private, and generic brands fight each other for more space and control.

Benchmarking Occurs when the retailer sets its own standards and measures performance based on the achievements in its sector, specific competitors, high-performance firms, and/or its own prior actions.

Bifurcated Retailing Denotes the decline of middle-of-the-market retailing due to the popularity of both mass merchandising and niche retailing.

Book Inventory System (Perpetual Inventory System) Keeps a running total of the value of all inventory at cost as of a given time. This is done by recording purchases and adding them to existing inventory value; sales are subtracted to arrive at the new current inventory value (all at cost). It is also known as a perpetual inventory system.

Bottom-Up Space Management Approach Exists when planning starts at the individual product level and then proceeds to the category, total store, and overall company levels.

Box (Limited-Line) Store Food-based discounter that focuses on a small selection of items, moderate hours of operation (compared with supermarkets), few services, and limited manufacturer brands.

Budgeting Outlines a retailer's planned expenditures for a given time based on expected performance.

Bundled Pricing Involves a retailer combining several elements in one basic price.

Business Format Franchising Arrangement in which the franchisee receives assistance in site location, quality control, accounting, startup practices, management training, and responding to problems—besides the right to sell goods and services.

Buyer Person responsible for selecting the merchandise to be carried by a retailer and setting a strategy to market that merchandise.

Canned Sales Presentation Memorized, repetitive speech given to all customers interested in a particular item.

Capital Expenditures Retail expenditures that are long-term investments in fixed assets.

Case Display Interior display that exhibits heavier, bulkier items than racks hold.

Cash Flow Relates the amount and timing of revenues received to the amount and timing of expenditures made during a specific time.

Category Killer (Power Retailer) Very large specialty store featuring an enormous selection in its product category and relatively low prices. It draws consumers from wide geographic areas.

Category Management Merchandising technique that improves productivity. It focuses on product category results rather than the performance of individual brands or models.

Census of Population Supplies a wide range of demographic data for all U.S. cities and surrounding vicinities. These data are organized on a geographic basis.

Central Business District (CBD) Hub of retailing in a city. It is synonymous with "downtown." The CBD has the greatest density of office buildings and stores.

Chain Retailer that operates multiple outlets (store units) under common ownership. It usually engages in some level of centralized (or coordinated) purchasing and decision making.

Channel Control Occurs when one member of a distribution channel can dominate the decisions made in that channel by the power it possesses.

Channel of Distribution All of the businesses and people involved in the physical movement and transfer of ownership of goods and services from producer to consumer.

Chargebacks Practice of retailers, at their discretion, making deductions in the manufacturers' bills for infractions ranging from late shipments to damaged and expired merchandise.

Class Consciousness Extent to which a person desires and pursues social status.

Classification Merchandising Allows firms to obtain more financial data by subdividing each specified department into further categories for related types of merchandise.

Cognitive Dissonance Doubt that occurs after a purchase is made, which can be alleviated by customer after-care, money-back guarantees, and realistic sales presentations and advertising campaigns.

Collaborative Planning, Forecasting, and Replenishment (CPFR) Emerging technique for larger firms whereby there is a holistic approach to supply chain management among a network of trading partners.

Combination Store Unites supermarket and general merchandise sales in one facility, with general merchandise typically accounting for 25 to 40 percent of total sales.

Community Shopping Center Moderate-sized, planned shopping facility with a branch department store and/or a category killer store, in addition to several smaller stores. About 20,000 to 100,000 people, who live or work within 10 to 20 minutes of the center, are served by this location.

Compensation Includes direct monetary payments to employees (such as salaries, commissions, and bonuses) and indirect payments (such as paid vacations, health and life insurance benefits, and retirement plans).

Competition-Oriented Pricing Approach in which a firm sets prices in accordance with competitors'.

Competitive Advantages Distinct competencies of a retailer relative to competitors.

Competitive Parity Method Promotional budgeting procedure by which a retailer's budget is raised or lowered based on competitors' actions.

Computerized Checkout Used by large and small retailers to efficiently process transactions and monitor inventory. Cashiers ring up sales or pass items by scanners. Computerized registers instantly record and display sales, customers get detailed receipts, and inventory data are stored in a memory bank.

Concentrated Marketing Selling goods and services to one specific group.

Consignment Purchase Items not paid for by a retailer until they are sold. The retailer can return unsold merchandise. Title is not taken by the retailer; the supplier owns the goods until sold.

Constrained Decision Making Limits franchisee involvement in the strategic planning process.

Consumer Behavior The process by which people determine whether, what, when, where, how, from whom, and how often to purchase goods and services.

Consumer Cooperative Retail firm owned by its customer members. A group of consumers invests in the company, elects officers, manages operations, and shares the profits or savings that accrue.

Consumer Decision Process Stages a consumer goes through in buying a good or service: stimulus, problem awareness, information search, evaluation of alternatives, purchase, and post-purchase behavior. Demographics and lifestyle factors affect this decision process.

Consumerism Involves the activities of government, business, and other organizations that protect people from practices infringing on their rights as consumers.

Consumer Loyalty (Frequent Shopper) Programs Reward a retailer's best customers, those with whom it wants long-lasting relationships.

Contingency Pricing Arrangement by which a service retailer does not get paid until after the service is satisfactorily performed. This is a special form of flexible pricing.

Control Phase in the evaluation of a firm's strategy and tactics in which a semiannual or annual review of the retailer takes place.

Controllable Variables Aspects of business that the retailer can directly affect (such as hours of operation and sales personnel).

Control Units Merchandise categories for which data are gathered.

Convenience Store Well-located food-oriented retailer that is open long hours and carries a moderate number of items. It is small, with average to above-average prices and average atmosphere and services.

Conventional Supermarket Departmentalized food store with a wide range of food and related products; sales of general merchandise are rather limited.

Cooperative Advertising Occurs when manufacturers or wholesalers and their retailers, or two or more retailers, share the costs of retail advertising.

Cooperative Buying Procedure used when a group of retailers make quantity purchases from suppliers.

Core Customers Consumers with whom retailers seek to nurture long relationships. They should be singled out in a firm's database.

Corporation Retail firm that is formally incorporated under state law. It is a legal entity apart from individual officers (or stockholders).

Cost Complement Average relationship of cost to retail value for all merchandise available for sale during a given time period.

Cost Method of Accounting Requires the retailer's cost of each item to be recorded on an accounting sheet and/or coded on a price tag or merchandise container. When a physical inventory is done, item costs must be learned, the quantity of every item in stock counted, and total inventory value at cost calculated.

Cost of Goods Sold Amount a retailer has paid to acquire the merchandise sold during a given time period. It equals the cost of merchandise available for sale minus the cost value of ending inventory.

Cost-Oriented Pricing Approach in which a retailer sets a price floor, the minimum price acceptable to the firm so it can reach a specified profit goal. A retailer usually computes merchandise and retail operating costs and adds a profit margin to these figures.

Cross-Merchandising Exists when a retailer carries complementary goods and services so that shoppers are encouraged to buy more.

Cross-Shopping Occurs when consumers shop for a product category through more than one retail format during the year or visit multiple retailers on one shopping trip.

Cross-Training Enables personnel to learn tasks associated with more than one job.

Culture Distinctive heritage shared by a group of people. It passes on beliefs, norms, and customs.

Curving (Free-Flowing) Traffic Flow Presents displays and aisles in a free-flowing pattern.

Customary Pricing Used when a retailer sets prices for goods and services and seeks to maintain them for an extended period.

Customer Loyalty Exists when a person regularly patronizes a particular retailer (store or nonstore) that he or she knows, likes, and trusts.

Customer Satisfaction Occurs when the value and customer service provided through a retailing experience meet or exceed consumer expectations.

Customer Service Identifiable, but sometimes intangible, activities undertaken by a retailer in conjunction with the basic goods and services it sells.

Cut Case Inexpensive display in which merchandise is left in the original carton.

Database Management Procedure a retailer uses to gather, integrate, apply, and store information related to specific subject areas. It is a key element in a retail information system.

Database Retailing Way to collect, store, and use relevant information on customers.

Data Mining Involves the in-depth analysis of information so as to gain specific insights about customers, product categories, vendors, and so forth.

Data Warehousing Advance in database management whereby copies of all the databases in a company are maintained in one location and accessible to employees at any locale.

Dead Areas Awkward spaces where normal displays cannot be set up.

Debit Card System Computerized process whereby the purchase price of a good or service is immediately deducted from a consumer's bank account and entered into a retailer's account.

Demand-Oriented Pricing Approach by which a retailer sets prices based on consumer desires. It determines the range of prices acceptable to the target market.

Demographics Objective, quantifiable, easily identifiable, and measurable population data.

Department Store Large store with an extensive assortment (width and depth) of goods and services that has separate departments for purposes of buying, promotion, customer service, and control.

Depth of Assortment The variety in any one goods/service category (product line) with which a retailer is involved.

Destination Retailer Firm that consumers view as distinctive enough to become loyal to it. Consumers go out of their way to shop there.

Destination Store Retail outlet with a trading area much larger than that of a competitor with a less unique appeal. It offers a better merchandise assortment in its product category(ies), promotes more extensively, and/or creates a stronger image.

Differentiated Marketing Aims at two or more distinct consumer groups, with different retailing approaches for each group.

Direct Marketing Form of retailing in which a customer is first exposed to a good or service through a nonpersonal medium and then orders by mail, phone, or fax—and increasingly by computer, phone, or tablet.

Direct Product Profitability (DPP) Method for planning variable markups whereby a retailer finds the profitability of each category or unit of merchandise by computing adjusted per-unit gross margin and assigning direct product costs for such expenses as warehousing, transportation, handling, and selling.

Direct Selling Includes both personal contact with consumers in their homes (and other nonstore locations such as offices) and phone solicitations initiated by a retailer.

Direct Store Delivery (DSD) Exists when retailers have at least some goods shipped directly from suppliers to individual stores. It works best with retailers that also utilize EDI.

Discretionary Income Money left after paying taxes and buying necessities.

Distributed Promotion Effort Used by retailers that promote throughout the year.

Diversification Way in which retailers become active in business outside their normal operations—and add stores in different goods/service categories.

Diversified Retailer Multiline firm with central ownership. It is also known as a retail conglomerate.

Dollar Control Planning and monitoring the financial merchandise investment over a stated period.

Downsizing Unprofitable stores closed or divisions sold off by retailers unhappy with performance.

Dual Marketing Involves firms engaged in more than one type of distribution arrangement. This enables those firms to appeal to different consumers, increase sales, share some costs, and maintain a good degree of strategic control.

Dump Bin Case display that houses piles of sale clothing, marked-down books, or other products.

Ease of Entry Occurs due to low capital requirements and no, or relatively simple, licensing provisions.

Economic Base Area's industrial and commercial structure—the companies and industries that residents depend on to earn a living.

Economic Order Quantity (EOQ) Quantity per order (in units) that minimizes the total costs of processing orders and holding inventory:

$$EOQ = \sqrt{\frac{2DS}{IC}}$$

Efficient Consumer Response (ECR) Form of order processing and fulfillment by which supermarkets are incorporating aspects of quick response inventory planning, electronic data interchange, and logistics planning.

Electronic Article Surveillance Involves special tags that are attached to products so that the tags can be sensed by electronic security devices at store exits.

Electronic Banking Includes both automatic teller machines (ATMs) and the instant processing of retail purchases.

Electronic Data Interchange (EDI) Lets retailers and suppliers regularly exchange information through their computers with regard to inventory levels, delivery times, unit sales, and so on, of particular items.

Electronic Point-of-Sale System Performs all the tasks of a computerized checkout and also verifies check and charge transactions, provides instantaneous sales reports, monitors and changes prices, sends intra- and inter-store messages, evaluates personnel and profitability, and stores data.

Employee Empowerment Way of improving customer service in which workers have discretion to do what they feel is needed—within reason to satisfy the customer, even if this means bending some rules.

Ensemble Display Interior display whereby a complete product bundle (ensemble) is presented rather than showing merchandise in separate categories.

Equal Store Organization Centralizes the buying function. Branch stores become sales units with equal operational status.

Ethics Involves activities that are trustworthy, fair, honest, and respectful for each retailer constituency.

Evaluation of Alternatives Stage in the decision process where a consumer selects one good or service to buy from a list of alternatives.

Everyday Low Pricing (EDLP) Version of customary pricing whereby a retailer strives to sell its goods and services at consistently low prices throughout the selling season.

Exclusive Distribution Takes place when suppliers enter agreements with one or a few retailers to designate the latter as the only firms in specified geographic areas to carry certain brands or product lines.

Expected Customer Service Level of service that customers want to receive from any retailer, such as basic employee courtesy.

Experiential Merchandising Tactic whose intent is to convert shopping from a passive activity into a more interactive one, by better engaging the customer.

Experiment Type of research in which one or more elements of a retail strategy mix are manipulated under controlled conditions.

Extended Decision Making Occurs when a consumer makes full use of the decision process, usually for expensive, complex items with which the person has had little or no experience.

External Secondary Data Available from sources outside a firm.

Factory Outlet Manufacturer-owned store selling its closeouts, discontinued merchandise, irregulars, canceled orders, and, sometimes, in-season, first-quality merchandise.

Fad Merchandise Items that generate a high level of sales for a short time.

Family Life Cycle How a traditional family moves from bachelorhood to children to solitary retirement.

Fashion Merchandise Products that may have cyclical sales due to changing tastes and lifestyles.

Feedback Signals or cues as to the success or failure of part of a retail strategy.

FIFO (First In, First Out) Method Logically assumes old merchandise is sold first, while newer items remain in inventory. It matches inventory value with the current cost structure.

Financial Leverage Performance measure based on the relationship between a retailer's total assets and net worth. It is equal to total assets divided by net worth.

Financial Merchandise Management Occurs when a retailer specifies exactly which products (goods and services) are purchased, when products are purchased, and how many products are purchased.

Flea Market Location where many vendors offer a range of products at discount prices in plain surroundings. Many flea markets are located in nontraditional sites not normally associated with retailing.

Flexible Pricing Strategy that lets consumers bargain over selling prices; those consumers who are good at bargaining obtain lower prices than those who are not.

Floor-Ready Merchandise Items that are received at the store in condition to be put directly on display without any preparation by retail workers.

Food-Based Superstore Retailer that is larger and more diversified than a conventional supermarket but usually smaller and less diversified than a combination store. It caters to consumers' complete grocery needs and offers them the ability to buy fill-in general merchandise.

Forecasts Projections of expected retail sales for given time periods.

Franchising Contractual arrangement between a franchisor (a manufacturer, a wholesaler, or a service sponsor) and a retail franchisee, which allows the franchisee to conduct a given form of business under an established name and according to a given pattern of business.

Frequency Average number of times each person who is reached by a message is exposed to a retailer's promotion efforts in a specific period.

Fringe Trading Area Includes customers not found in primary and secondary trading areas. These are the most widely dispersed customers.

Full-Line Discount Store Type of department store with a broad, low-priced product assortment; all of the range of products expected at department stores; centralized checkout service; self-service; private-brand nondurables and well-known manufacturer-brand durables; less fashion-sensitive merchandise; relatively inexpensive building, equipment, and fixtures; and less emphasis on credit.

Functional Product Groupings Categorize and display a store's merchandise by common end use.

Gap Analysis Enables a company to compare its actual performance against its potential performance and then determine the areas in which it must improve.

Generic Brands No-frills goods stocked by some retailers. These items usually receive secondary shelf locations, have little or no promotion support, are sometimes of less quality than other brands, are stocked in limited assortments, and have plain packages. They are a form of private brand.

Geographic Information System (GIS) Combines digitized mapping with key locational data to graphically depict such trading-area characteristics as the demographic attributes of the population; data on customer purchases; and listings of current, proposed, and competitor locations.

Global Retail Development Index (GRDI) Measures the retail prospects in emerging countries with regard to four factors: market attractiveness, country risk, market saturation, and time pressure.

Goal-Oriented Job Description Enumerates a position's basic functions, the relationship of each job to overall goals, the interdependence of positions, and information flows.

Goods Retailing Focuses on the sale of tangible (physical) products.

Goods/Service Category Retail firm's line of business.

Graduated Lease Calls for precise rent increases over a stated period of time.

Gravity Model Computerized site selection tool based on the premise that people are drawn to stores that are closer and more attractive than competitors'.

Gray-Market Goods Brand-name products bought in foreign markets or goods transshipped from other retailers. They are often sold at low prices by unauthorized dealers.

Gross Margin Difference between net sales and the total cost of goods sold. It is also called *gross profit*.

Gross Margin Return on Investment (GMROI) Shows the relationship between total dollar operating profits and the average inventory investment (at cost) by combining profitability and sales-to-stock measures:

$$GMROI = \frac{\text{Gross margin in dollars}}{\text{Net sales}}$$
$$\times \frac{\text{Net sales}}{\text{Average inventory at cost}}$$
$$= \frac{\text{Gross margin in dollars}}{\text{Average inventory at cost}}$$

Gross Profit Difference between net sales and the total cost of goods sold. It is also known as *gross margin*.

Hidden Assets Depreciated assets, such as store buildings and warehouses, that are reflected on a retailer's balance sheet at low values relative to their actual worth.

Hierarchy of Authority Outlines the job interactions within a company by describing the reporting relationships among employees. Coordination and control are provided.

Hierarchy of Effects Sequence of steps a consumer goes through in reacting to retail communications, which leads him or her from awareness to knowledge to liking to preference to conviction to purchase.

Horizontal Cooperative Advertising Agreement Enables two or more retailers (most often small, situated together, or franchisees of the same company) to share an ad.

Horizontal Price Fixing Agreement among manufacturers, among wholesalers, or among retailers to set certain prices. This is illegal, regardless of how "reasonable" prices may be.

Horizontal Retail Audit Analyzes a retail firm's overall performance, from mission to goals to customer satisfaction to basic retail strategy mix and its implementation in an integrated, consistent way.

Household Life Cycle Incorporates the life stages of both family and nonfamily households.

Huff's Law of Shopper Attraction Delineates trading areas on the basis of the product assortment carried at various shopping locations, travel times from the shopper's home to alternative locations, and the sensitivity of the kind of shopping to travel time.

Human Resource Management Recruiting, selecting, training, compensating, and supervising personnel in a manner consistent with the retailer's organization structure and strategy mix.

Human Resource Management Process Consists of these interrelated activities: recruitment, selection, training, compensation, and supervision. The goals are to obtain, develop, and retain employees.

Hypermarket Combination store pioneered in Europe that blends an economy supermarket with a discount department store. It is even larger than a supercenter.

Image Represents how a given retailer is perceived by consumers and others.

Impulse Purchases Occur when consumers buy products and/or brands they had not planned to before entering a store, reading a catalog, seeing a TV shopping show, turning to the Web, and so forth.

Incremental Budgeting Process whereby a firm uses current and past budgets as guides and adds to or subtracts from them to arrive at the coming period's expenditures.

Incremental Method Promotional budgeting procedure by which a percentage is either added to or subtracted from one year's budget to determine the next year's.

Independent Retailer that owns one retail unit.

Infomercial Program-length TV commercial (most often, 30 minutes in length) for a specific good or service that airs on cable television or on broadcast television, often at a fringe time. It is particularly worthwhile for products that benefit from visual demonstrations.

Information Search Consists of two parts: determining alternatives to solve the problem at hand (and where they can be bought) and learning the characteristics of alternatives. It may be internal or external.

Initial Markup (at Retail) Based on the original retail value assigned to merchandise less the merchandise costs, expressed as a percentage of the original retail price:

$$\text{Initial markup percentage (at retail)} =$$

$$\frac{\text{Planned retail operating expenses} + \text{Planned profit} + \text{Planned retail reductions}}{\text{Planned net sales} + \text{Planned retail reductions}}$$

Intensive Distribution Takes place when suppliers sell through as many retailers as possible. This often maximizes suppliers' sales and lets retailers offer many brands and product versions.

Internal Secondary Data Available within a company, sometimes from the data bank of a retail information system.

Internet Global electronic superhighway of computer networks that use a common protocol and that are linked by telecommunications lines and satellite.

Inventory Management Process whereby a firm seeks to acquire and maintain a proper merchandise assortment while ordering, shipping, handling, storing, displaying, and selling costs are kept in check.

Inventory Shrinkage Encompasses employee theft, customer shoplifting, vendor fraud, and administrative errors.

Isolated Store Freestanding retail outlet located on either a highway or a street. There are no adjacent retailers with which this type of store shares traffic.

Issue (Problem) Definition Step in the marketing research process that involves a clear statement of the topic to be studied.

Item Price Removal Practice whereby prices are marked only on shelves or signs and not on individual items. It is banned in several states and local communities.

Job Analysis Consists of gathering information about each job's functions and requirements: duties, responsibilities, aptitude, interest, education, experience, and physical tasks.

Job Motivation Drive within people to attain work-related goals.

Job Standardization Keeps tasks of employees with similar positions in different departments rather uniform.

Leader Pricing Occurs when a retailer advertises and sells selected items in its goods/service assortment at less than the usual profit margins. The goal is to increase customer traffic so as to sell regularly priced goods and services in addition to the specially priced items.

Leased Department Site in a retail store—usually a department, discount, or specialty store—that is rented to an outside party.

Liabilities Financial obligations a retailer incurs in operating a business.

Lifestyle Center An open-air shopping site that typically includes 150,000 to 500,000 square feet of space dedicated to upscale, well-known specialty stores.

Lifestyles Ways that individual consumers and families (households) live and spend time and money.

LIFO (Last In, First Out) Method Assumes new merchandise is sold first, while older stock remains in inventory. It matches current sales with the current cost structure.

Limited Decision Making Occurs when a consumer uses every step in the purchase process but does not spend a great deal of time on each of them.

Logistics Total process of planning, enacting, and coordinating the physical movement of merchandise from supplier to retailer to customer in the most timely, effective, and cost-efficient manner possible.

Loss Leaders Items priced below cost to lure more customer traffic. Loss leaders are restricted by some state minimum-price laws.

Maintained Markup (at Retail) Based on the actual prices received for merchandise sold during a time period less merchandise cost, expressed as a percentage:

$$\text{Maintained markup percentage (at retail)} = \frac{\text{Actual retail operating expenses} + \text{Actual profit}}{\text{Actual net sales}}$$

or

$$\frac{\text{Average selling price} - \text{Merchandise cost}}{\text{Average selling price}}$$

Maintenance-Increase-Recoupment Lease Has a provision allowing rent to increase if a property owner's taxes, heating bills, insurance, or other expenses rise beyond a certain point.

Manufacturer (National) Brands Produced and controlled by manufacturers. They are usually well known, supported by manufacturer ads, somewhat pre-sold to consumers, require limited retailer investment in marketing, and often represent maximum product quality to consumers.

Markdown Reduction from the original retail price of an item to meet the lower price of another retailer, adapt to inventory overstocking, clear out shopworn merchandise, reduce assortments of odds and ends, and increase customer traffic.

Markdown Percentage Total dollar markdown as a percentage of net sales (in dollars):

$$\text{Markdown percentage} = \frac{\text{Total dollar markdown}}{\text{Net sales (in \$)}}$$

Marketing Research in Retailing Collection and analysis of information relating to specific issues or problems facing a retailer.

Marketing Research Process Embodies a series of activities: defining the issue or problem, examining secondary data, generating primary data (if needed), analyzing data, making recommendations, and implementing findings.

Market Penetration Pricing Strategy in which a retailer seeks to achieve large revenues by setting low prices and selling a high unit volume.

Market Segment Product Groupings Place together various items that appeal to a given target market.

Market Skimming Pricing Strategy wherein a firm charges premium prices and attracts customers less concerned with price than service, assortment, and status.

Markup Difference between merchandise costs and retail selling price.

Markup Percentage (at Cost) Difference between retail price and merchandise cost expressed as a percentage of merchandise cost:

$$\text{Markup Percentage (at cost)} = \frac{\text{Retail selling price} - \text{Merchandise cost}}{\text{Merchandise cost}}$$

Markup Percentage (at Retail) Difference between retail price and merchandise cost expressed as a percentage of retail price:

$$\text{Markup Percentage (at retail)} = \frac{\text{Retail selling price} - \text{Merchandise cost}}{\text{Retail selling price}}$$

Markup Pricing Form of cost-oriented pricing in which a retailer sets prices by adding per-unit merchandise costs, retail operating expenses, and desired profit.

Marquee Sign used to display a store's name and/or logo.

Massed Promotion Effort Used by retailers that promote mostly in one or two seasons.

Mass Marketing Selling goods and services to a broad spectrum of consumers.

Mass Merchandising Positioning approach whereby retailers offer a discount or value-oriented image, a wide and/or deep merchandise selection, and large store facilities.

Mazur Plan Divides all retail activities into four functional areas: merchandising, communications, store management, and financial accounting. [modern view]

Megamall Enormous planned shopping center with at least 1 million square feet of retail space, multiple anchor stores, up to several hundred specialty stores, food courts, and entertainment facilities.

Membership (Warehouse) Club Appeals to price-conscious consumers, who must be members to shop.

Memorandum Purchase Occurs when items are not paid for by the retailer until they are sold. The retailer can return unsold merchandise. However, it takes title on delivery and is responsible for damages.

Merchandise Available for Sale Equals beginning inventory, purchases, and transportation charges.

Merchandising Activities involved in acquiring particular goods and/or services and making them available at the places, times, and prices and in the quantity to enable a retailer to reach its goals.

Merchandising Philosophy Sets the guiding principles for all the merchandise decisions a retailer makes.

Mergers The combinations of separately owned retail firms.

Micromarketing Application of data mining whereby the retailer uses differentiated marketing and focused strategy mixes for specific segments, sometimes fine-tuned for the individual shopper.

Micromerchandising Strategy whereby a retailer adjusts its shelf-space allocations to respond to customer and other differences among local markets.

Minimum-Price Laws State regulations preventing retailers from selling certain items for less than their cost plus a fixed percentage to cover overhead. These laws restrict loss leaders and predatory pricing.

Model Stock Approach Method of determining the amount of floor space necessary to carry and display a proper merchandise assortment.

Model Stock Plan Planned composition of fashion goods, which reflects the mix of merchandise available based on expected sales. It indicates product lines, colors, and size distributions.

Monthly Sales Index Measure of sales seasonality that is calculated by dividing each month's actual sales by average monthly sales and then multiplying the results by 100.

Motives Reasons for consumer behavior.

Multichannel Retailing A distribution approach whereby a retailer sells to consumers through multiple retail formats (points of contact). Multichannel retailing is characterized by having few linkages among the channel alternatives.

Multiple-Unit Pricing Discounts offered to customers who buy in quantity or who buy a product bundle.

Mystery Shoppers People hired by retailers to pose as customers and observe their operations, from sales presentations to how well displays are maintained to service calls.

Need-Satisfaction Approach Sales technique based on the principle that each customer has a different set of wants; thus, a sales presentation should be geared to the demands of the individual customer.

Neighborhood Business District (NBD) Unplanned shopping area that appeals to the convenience shopping and service needs of a single residential area. The leading retailer is typically a supermarket or a large drugstore, and it is situated on the major street(s) of its residential area.

Neighborhood Shopping Center Planned shopping facility with the largest store being a supermarket or a drugstore. It serves 3,000 to 50,000 people within a 15-minute drive (usually less than 10 minutes).

Net Lease Calls for all maintenance costs, such as heating, electricity, insurance, and interior repair, to be paid by the retailer.

Net Profit Equals gross profit minus retail operating expenses.

Net Profit after Taxes The profit earned after all costs and taxes have been deducted.

Net Profit Margin Performance measure based on a retailer's net profit and net sales. It is equal to net profit divided by net sales.

Net Sales Revenues received by a retailer during a given time period after deducting customer returns, markdowns, and employee discounts.

Net Worth Retailer's assets minus its liabilities.

Never-Out List Used when a retailer plans stock levels for best-sellers. The goal is to purchase enough of these products so they are always in stock.

Niche Retailing Enables retailers to identify customer segments and deploy unique strategies to address the desires of those segments.

Nongoods Services Area of service retailing in which intangible personal services are offered to consumers—who experience the services rather than possess them.

Nonprobability Sample Approach in which stores, products, or customers are chosen by the researcher—based on judgment or convenience.

Nonstore Retailing Utilizes strategy mixes that are not store-based to reach consumers and complete transactions. It occurs via direct marketing, direct selling, and vending machines.

Objective-and-Task Method Promotional budgeting procedure by which a retailer clearly defines its promotional goals and prepares a budget to satisfy them.

Objectives Long-term and short-term performance targets that a retailer hopes to attain. Goals can involve sales, profit, satisfaction of publics, and image.

Observation Form of research in which present behavior or the results of past behavior are observed and recorded. It can be human or mechanical.

Odd Pricing Retail prices set at levels below even dollar values, such as $0.49, $4.98, and $199.

Off-Price Chain Features brand-name apparel and accessories, footwear, linens, fabrics, cosmetics, and/or housewares and sells them at everyday low prices in an efficient, limited-service environment.

Off-Retail Markdown Percentage Markdown for each item or category of items computed as a percentage of original retail price:

$$\frac{\text{Off-retail markdown}}{\text{percentage}} = \frac{\text{Original price} - \text{New price}}{\text{Original price}}$$

Omnichannel Retailing Delivers a consistent, uninterrupted, and seamless brand experience regardless of channel or device (store, laptop computer, iPad, smartphone, etc.)

Onboarding The process of integrating new employees into an organization and its culture and having them better understand the expectations of their new jobs.

One-Hundred Percent Location Optimum site for a particular store. A location labeled as 100 percent for one firm may be less than optimal for another.

One-Price Policy Strategy wherein a retailer charges the same price to all customers buying an item under similar conditions.

Open Credit Account Requires a consumer to pay his or her bill in full when it is due.

Open-to-Buy Difference between planned purchases and the purchase commitments already made by a buyer for a given time period, often a month. It represents the amount the buyer has left to spend for that month and is reduced each time a purchase is made.

Operating Expenditures (Expenses) Short-term selling and administrative costs of running a business.

Operations Blueprint Systematically lists all the operating functions to be performed, their characteristics, and their timing.

Operations Management Process used to efficiently and effectively enact the policies and tasks to satisfy a firm's customers, employees, and management (and stockholders, if a publicly owned company).

Opportunistic Buying Negotiates low prices for merchandise whose sales have not met expectations, end-of-season goods, items returned to the manufacturer or another retailer, and closeouts.

Opportunities Marketplace openings that exist because other retailers have not yet capitalized on them.

Opportunity Costs Possible benefits a retailer forgoes if it invests in one opportunity rather than another.

Option Credit Account Form of revolving account that allows partial payments. No interest is assessed if a person pays a bill in full when it is due.

Order-Getting Salesperson Actively involved with informing and persuading customers, and in closing sales. This is a true "sales" employee.

Order Lead Time Period from when an order is placed by a retailer to the date merchandise is ready for sale (received, price marked, and put on the selling floor).

Order-Taking Salesperson Engages in routine clerical and sales functions, such as setting up displays, placing inventory on shelves, answering simple questions, filling orders, and ringing up sales.

Organizational Mission Retailer's commitment to a type of business and a distinctive marketplace role. It is reflected in the attitude to consumers, employees, suppliers, competitors, government, and others.

Organization Chart Graphically displays the hierarchical relationships within a firm.

Outshopping When a person goes out of his or her hometown to shop.

Outsourcing Situation whereby a retailer pays an outside party to undertake one or more operating tasks.

Overstored Trading Area Geographic area with so many stores selling a specific good or service that some retailers will be unable to earn an adequate profit.

Owned-Goods Services Area of service retailing in which goods owned by consumers are repaired, improved, or maintained.

Parasite Store Outlet that does not create its own traffic and has no real trading area of its own.

Partnership Unincorporated retail firm owned by two or more persons, each with a financial interest.

Perceived Risk Level of risk a consumer believes exists regarding the purchase of a specific good or service from a given retailer, whether or not the belief is actually correct.

Percentage Lease Stipulates that rent is related to a retailer's sales or profits.

Percentage-of-Sales Method Promotional budgeting method in which a retailer ties its budget to revenue.

Percentage Variation Method Inventory level planning method where beginning-of-month planned inventory during any month differs from planned average monthly stock by only one-half of that month's variation from estimated average monthly sales. Under this method:

$$\begin{array}{l}\text{Beginning-of-month} \\ \text{planned inventory} \\ \text{level (at retail)}\end{array} = \begin{array}{c}\text{Planned average monthly} \\ \text{stock at retail} \times 1/2 \\ [1 + (\text{Estimated monthly sales/} \\ \text{Estimated average monthly sales})]\end{array}$$

Performance Measures Criteria used to assess effectiveness, including total sales, sales per store, sales by product category, sales per square foot, gross margins, gross margin return on investment, operating income, inventory turnover, markdown percentages, employee turnover, financial ratios, and profitability.

Personality Sum total of an individual's traits, which make that individual unique.

Personal Selling Oral communication with one or more prospective customers to make sales.

Physical Inventory System Actual counting of merchandise. A firm using the cost method of inventory valuation and relying on a physical inventory can derive gross profit only when it does a full inventory.

Planned Shopping Center Group of architecturally unified commercial facilities on a site that is centrally owned or managed, designed and operated as a unit, based on balanced tenancy, and accompanied by parking.

Planogram Visual (graphical) representation of the space for selling, merchandise, personnel, and customers—as well as for product categories.

PMs Promotional money, push money, or prize money that a manufacturer provides for retail salespeople selling that manufacturer's brand.

Point of Indifference Geographic breaking point between two cities (communities), so that the trading area of each can be determined. At this point, consumers would be indifferent to shopping at either area.

Point-of-Purchase (POP) Display Interior display that provides shoppers with information, adds to store atmosphere, and serves a substantial promotional role.

Positioning Enables a retailer to devise its strategy in a way that projects an image relative to its retail category and its competitors, and elicits consumer responses to that image.

Post-Purchase Behavior Further purchases or re-evaluation based on a purchase.

Power Center Shopping site with (1) up to a half dozen or so category killer stores and a mix of smaller stores or (2) several complementary stores specializing in one product category.

Predatory Pricing Involves large retailers that seek to reduce competition by selling goods and services at very low prices, thus causing small retailers to go out of business.

Prestige Pricing Assumes consumers will not buy goods and services at prices deemed too low. It is based on the price-quality association.

Pre-Training Indoctrination on the history and policies of the retailer and a job orientation on hours, compensation, the chain of command, and job duties.

Price Elasticity of Demand Sensitivity of customers to price changes in terms of the quantities bought:

$$\text{Elasticity} = \frac{\dfrac{\text{Quantity 1} - \text{Quantity 2}}{\text{Quantity 1} + \text{Quantity 2}}}{\dfrac{\text{Price 1} - \text{Price 2}}{\text{Price 1} + \text{Price 2}}}$$

Price Lining Practice whereby retailers sell merchandise at a limited range of price points, with each point representing a distinct level of quality.

Price–Quality Association Concept stating that many consumers feel high prices connote high quality and low prices connote low quality.

Primary Data Those collected to address the specific issue or problem under study. This type of data may be gathered via surveys, observations, experiments, and simulation.

Primary Trading Area Encompasses 50 to 80 percent of a store's customers. It is the area closest to the store and possesses the highest density of customers to population and the highest per capita sales.

Private (Dealer, Store) Brands Contain names designated by wholesalers or retailers, are more profitable to retailers, are better controlled by retailers, are not sold by competing retailers, are less expensive for consumers, and lead to customer loyalty to retailers (rather than to manufacturers).

Probability (Random) Sample Approach whereby every store, product, or customer has an equal or known chance of being chosen for study.

Problem Awareness Stage in the decision process at which the consumer not only has been aroused by social, commercial, and/or physical stimuli, but also recognizes that the good or service under consideration may solve a problem of shortage or unfulfilled desire.

Productivity Efficiency with which a retail strategy is carried out.

Product Life Cycle Shows the expected behavior of a good or service over its life. The traditional cycle has four stages: introduction, growth, maturity, and decline.

Product/Trademark Franchising Arrangement in which the franchisee acquires the identity of the franchisor by agreeing to sell the latter's products and/or operate under the latter's name.

Profit-and-Loss (Income) Statement Summary of a retailer's revenues and expenses over a particular period of time, usually a month, quarter, or year.

Prototype Stores Used with an operations strategy that requires multiple outlets in a chain to conform to relatively uniform construction, layout, and operations standards.

Publicity Any nonpersonal form of public relations whereby messages are transmitted by mass media, the time or space provided by the media is not paid for, and there is no identified commercial sponsor.

Public Relations Any communication that fosters a favorable image for the retailer among its publics (consumers, investors, government, channel members, employees, and the general public).

Purchase Act Exchange of money or a promise to pay for the ownership or use of a good or service. Purchase variables include the place of purchase, terms, and availability of merchandise.

Purchase Motivation Product Groupings Appeal to the consumer's urge to buy products and the amount of time he or she is willing to spend in shopping.

Quick Response (QR) Inventory Planning Enables a retailer to reduce the amount of inventory it keeps on hand by ordering more frequently and in lower quantity.

Rack Display Interior display that neatly hangs or presents products.

Rationalized Retailing Combines a high degree of centralized management control with strict operating procedures for every phase of business.

Reach Number of distinct people exposed to a retailer's promotional efforts during a specified period.

Recruitment Activity whereby a retailer generates a list of job applicants.

Reference Groups Influence people's thoughts and behavior. They may be classified as aspirational, membership, and dissociative.

Regional Shopping Center Large, planned shopping facility appealing to a geographically dispersed market. It has at least one or two full-sized department stores and 50 to 150 or more smaller retailers. The market for this center is 100,000+ people who live or work up to a 30-minute drive time from the center.

Regression Model Computerized site selection tool that uses equations showing the association between potential store sales and several independent variables at each location under consideration.

Reilly's Law of Retail Gravitation Traditional means of trading-area delineation that establishes a point of indifference between two cities or communities, so the trading area of each can be determined.

Relationship Retailing Exists when retailers seek to establish and maintain long-term bonds with customers, rather than act as if each sales transaction is a completely new encounter with them.

Rented-Goods Services Area of service retailing in which consumers lease and use goods for specified periods of time.

Reorder Point Stock level at which new orders must be placed:

$$\text{Reorder point} = (\text{Usage rate} \times \text{Lead time}) + \text{Safety stock}$$

Resident Buying Office Inside or outside buying organization used when a retailer wants to keep in close touch with market trends and cannot do so with just its headquarters buying staff. Such offices are usually situated in important merchandise centers (sources of supply) and provide valuable data and contacts.

Retail Audit Systematically examines the total retailing effort or a specific aspect of it to study what a retailer is presently doing, appraise how well it is performing, and make recommendations.

Retail Balance The mix of stores within a district or shopping center.

Retail Information System (RIS) Anticipates the information needs of managers; collects, organizes, and stores relevant data on a continuous basis; and directs the flow of information to proper decision makers.

Retailing Business activities involved in selling goods and services to consumers for their personal, family, or household use.

Retailing Concept An approach to business that is customer-oriented, coordinated, value-driven, and goal-oriented.

Retail Institution Basic format or structure of a business. Institutions can be classified by ownership, store-based retail strategy mix, and nonstore-based, electronic, and nontraditional retailing.

Retail Life Cycle Theory asserting that institutions—like the goods and services they sell—pass through identifiable life stages: introduction (early growth), growth (accelerated development), maturity, and decline.

Retail Method of Accounting Determines closing inventory value by calculating the average relationship between the cost and retail values of merchandise available for sale during a period.

Retail Organization How a firm structures and assigns tasks, policies, resources, authority, responsibilities, and rewards so as to efficiently and effectively satisfy the needs of its target market, employees, and management.

Retail Promotion Any communication by a retailer that informs, persuades, and/or reminds the target market about any aspect of that firm.

Retail Reductions Difference between beginning inventory plus purchases during the period and sales plus ending inventory. They encompass anticipated markdowns, employee and other discounts, and stock shortages.

Retail Strategy Overall plan guiding a retail firm. It influences the firm's business activities and its response to market forces, such as competition and the economy.

Return on Assets (ROA) Performance ratio based on net sales, net profit, and total assets:

$$\frac{\text{Return on}}{\text{assets}} = \frac{\text{Net profit}}{\text{Net sales}} \times \frac{\text{Net sales}}{\text{Total assets}} = \frac{\text{Net profit}}{\text{Total assets}}$$

Return on Net Worth (RONW) Performance measure based on net profit, net sales, total assets, and net worth:

$$\frac{\text{Return on}}{\text{net worth}} = \frac{\text{Net profit}}{\text{Net sales}} \times \frac{\text{Net sales}}{\text{Total assets}} \times \frac{\text{Total assets}}{\text{Net worth}}$$

Reverse Logistics Encompasses all merchandise flows from the customer and/or the retailer back through the supply channel.

Revolving Credit Account Allows a customer to charge items and be billed monthly on the basis of the outstanding cumulative balance.

RFID (Radio Frequency Identification) A method of storing and remotely retrieving data using devices called RFID tags or transponders.

Robinson-Patman Act Bars manufacturers and wholesalers from discriminating in price or purchase terms in selling to individual retailers if these retailers are purchasing products of "like quality" and the effect of such discrimination is to injure competition.

Routine Decision Making Takes place when a consumer buys out of habit and skips steps in the purchase process.

Safety Stock Extra inventory to protect against out-of-stock conditions due to unexpected demand and delays in delivery.

Sales Manager Person who typically supervises the on-floor selling and operational activities for a specific retail department.

Sales Opportunity Grid Rates the promise of new and established goods, services, procedures, and/or store outlets across a variety of criteria.

Sales–Productivity Ratio Method for assigning floor space on the basis of sales or profit per foot.

Sales Promotion Encompasses the paid communication activities other than advertising, public relations, and personal selling that stimulate consumer purchases and dealer effectiveness.

Saturated Trading Area Geographic area with the proper amount of retail facilities to satisfy the needs of its population for a specific good or service, as well as to enable retailers to prosper.

Scenario Analysis Lets a retailer project the future by studying factors that affect long-term performance and then forming contingency plans based on alternate scenarios.

Scrambled Merchandising Occurs when a retailer adds goods and services that may be unrelated to each other and to the firm's original business.

Seasonal Merchandise Products that sell well over nonconsecutive time periods.

Secondary Business District (SBD) Unplanned shopping area in a city or town that is usually bounded by the intersection of two major streets. It has at least a junior department store and/or some larger specialty stores—in addition to many smaller stores.

Secondary Data Those gathered for purposes other than addressing the issue or problem currently under study.

Secondary Trading Area Geographic area that contains an additional 15 to 25 percent of a store's customers. It is located outside the primary area, and customers are more widely dispersed.

Selective Distribution Takes place when suppliers sell through a moderate number of retailers. This lets suppliers have higher sales than in exclusive distribution and lets retailers carry some competing brands.

Self-Scanning Enables the consumer himself or herself to scan the items being purchased at a checkout counter, pay electronically by credit or debit card, and bag the items.

Semantic Differential Disguised or nondisguised survey technique, whereby a respondent is asked to rate one or more retailers on several criteria; each criterion is evaluated along a bipolar adjective scale.

Service Retailing Involves transactions in which consumers do not purchase or acquire ownership of tangible products. It encompasses rented goods, owned goods, and nongoods.

Simulation Type of experiment whereby a computer program is used to manipulate the elements of a retail strategy mix rather than test them in a real setting.

Single-Channel Retailing A distribution approach whereby a retailer sells to consumers through one retail format.

Situation Analysis Candid evaluation of the opportunities and threats facing a prospective or existing retailer.

Slotting Allowances Payments that retailers require of vendors for providing shelf space in stores.

Social Class Informal ranking of people based on income, occupation, education, and other factors.

Social Media Encompass online technology tools that allow vast numbers of people to easily communicate with one another via the Internet and mobile devices. With social media, messages, audio, video, photos, podcasts, and other multimedia communications are possible.

Social Responsibility Occurs when a retailer acts in society's best interests—as well as its own. The challenge is to balance corporate citizenship with fair profits.

Sole Proprietorship Unincorporated retail firm owned by one person.

Solutions Selling Takes a customer-centered approach and presents "solutions" rather than "products." It goes a step beyond cross-merchandising.

Sorting Process Involves the retailer's collecting an assortment of goods and services from various sources, buying them in large quantity, and offering to sell them in small quantities to consumers.

Specialog Enables a retailer to cater to the specific needs of customer segments, emphasize a limited number of items, and reduce catalog production and postage costs.

Specialty Store Retailer that concentrates on selling one goods or service line.

Staple Merchandise Consists of the regular products carried by a retailer.

Stimulus Cue (social or commercial) or a drive (physical) meant to motivate or arouse a person to act.

Stock-to-Sales Method Inventory level planning technique wherein a retailer wants to maintain a specified ratio of goods on hand to sales.

Stock Turnover Number of times during a specific period, usually one year, that the average inventory on hand is sold. It can be computed in units or dollars (at retail or cost):

$$\text{Annual rate of stock turnover (in units)} = \frac{\text{Number of units sold during year}}{\text{Average inventory on hand (in units)}}$$

$$\text{Annual rate of stock turnover (in retail dollars)} = \frac{\text{Net yearly sales}}{\text{Average inventory on hand (at retail)}}$$

$$\text{Annual rate of stock turnover (at cost)} = \frac{\text{Cost of goods sold during year}}{\text{Average inventory on hand (at cost)}}$$

Storability Product Groupings Used for products that need special handling.

Storefront Total physical exterior of a store, including the marquee, entrances, windows, lighting, and construction materials.

Store Maintenance Encompasses all the activities in managing a retailer's physical facilities.

Straight (Gridiron) Traffic Flow Presents displays and aisles in a rectangular or gridiron pattern.

Straight Lease Requires the retailer to pay a fixed dollar amount per month over the life of a lease. It is the simplest, most direct leasing arrangement.

Strategic Profit Model Expresses the numerical relationship among net profit margin, asset turnover, and financial leverage. It can be used in planning or controlling a retailer's assets.

Strategy Mix Firm's particular combination of store location, operating procedures, goods/services offered, pricing tactics, store atmosphere and customer services, and promotional methods.

String Unplanned shopping area comprising a group of retail stores, often with similar or compatible product lines, located along a street or highway.

Supercenter Combination store blending an economy supermarket with a discount department store.

Supermarket Self-service food store with grocery, meat, and produce departments and minimum annual sales of $2 million. The category includes conventional supermarkets, food-based superstores, combination stores, box (limited-line) stores, and warehouse stores.

Supervision Manner of providing a job environment that encourages employee accomplishment.

Supply Chain Logistics aspect of a value delivery chain. It comprises all of the parties that participate in the retail logistics process: manufacturers, wholesalers, third-party specialists, and the retailer.

Survey Research technique that systematically gathers information from respondents by communicating with them.

Tactics Actions that encompass a retailer's daily and short-term operations.

Target Market Customer group that a retailer seeks to attract and satisfy.

Taxes The portion of revenues turned over to the federal, state, and/or local government.

Terms of Occupancy Consist of ownership versus leasing, the type of lease, operations and maintenance costs, taxes, zoning restrictions, and voluntary regulations.

Theme-Setting Display Interior display that depicts a product offering in a thematic manner and portrays a specific atmosphere or mood.

Threats Environmental and marketplace factors that can adversely affect retailers if they do not react to them (and sometimes, even if they do).

Top-Down Space Management Approach Exists when a retailer starts with its total available store space, divides the space into categories, and then works on in-store product layouts.

Total Retail Experience All the elements in a retail offering that encourage or inhibit consumers during their contact with a retailer.

Trading Area Geographical area containing the customers and potential customers of a particular retailer or group of retailers for specific goods or services.

Trading-Area Overlap Occurs when the trading areas of stores in different locations encroach on one another. In the overlap area, the same customers are served by both stores.

Traditional Department Store Type of department store in which merchandise quality ranges from average to quite good, pricing is moderate to above average, and customer service ranges from medium levels of sales help, credit, delivery, and so forth to high levels of each.

Traditional Job Description Contains each position's title, supervisory relationships (superior and subordinate), committee assignments, and the specific ongoing roles and tasks.

Training Programs Used to teach new (and existing) personnel how best to perform their jobs or how to improve themselves.

Unbundled Pricing Involves a retailer's charging separate prices for each item sold.

Uncontrollable Variables Aspects of business to which the retailer must adapt (such as competition, the economy, and laws).

Understored Trading Area Geographic area that has too few stores selling a specific good or service to satisfy the needs of its population.

Unit Control Looks at the quantities of merchandise a retailer handles during a stated period.

Unit Pricing Practice required by many states, whereby retailers (mostly food stores) must express both the total price of an item and its price per unit of measure.

Universal Product Code (UPC) Classification for coding data onto products via a series of thick and thin vertical lines. It lets retailers record information instantaneously on a product's model number, size, color, and other factors when it is sold, as well as send the information to a computer that monitors unit sales, inventory levels, and other factors. The UPC is not readable by humans.

Unplanned Business District Type of retail location where two or more stores situate together (or nearby) in such a way that the total arrangement or mix of stores is not due to prior long-range planning.

Usage Rate Average sales per day, in units, of merchandise.

Value Embodied by the activities and processes (a value chain) that provide a given level of value for the consumer—from manufacturer, wholesaler, and retailer perspectives. From the customer's perspective, it is the perception the shopper has of a value chain.

Value Chain Total bundle of benefits offered to consumers through a channel of distribution.

Value Delivery System All the parties that develop, produce, deliver, and sell and service particular goods and services.

Variable Markup Policy Strategy whereby a firm purposely adjusts markups by merchandise category.

Variable Pricing Strategy wherein a retailer alters prices to coincide with fluctuations in costs or consumer demand.

Variety Store Outlet that handles a wide assortment of inexpensive and popularly priced goods and services, such as apparel and accessories, costume jewelry, notions and small wares, candy, toys, and other items in the price range.

Vending Machine Format involving the cash- or card-operated dispensing of goods and services. It eliminates the use of sales personnel and allows around-the-clock sales.

Vendor-Managed Inventory (VMI) Practice of retailers counting on key suppliers to actively participate in their inventory management programs. Suppliers have their own employees stationed at retailers' headquarters to manage the inventory replenishment of the suppliers' products.

Vertical Cooperative Advertising Agreement Enables a manufacturer and a retailer or a wholesaler and a retailer to share an ad.

Vertical Marketing System All the levels of independently owned businesses along a channel of distribution. Goods and services are normally distributed through one of three types of systems: independent, partially integrated, and fully integrated.

Vertical Price Fixing Occurs when manufacturers or wholesalers seek to control the retail prices of their goods and services.

Vertical Retail Audit Analyzes—in depth—performance in one area of the strategy mix or operations.

Video Kiosk Freestanding, interactive, electronic computer terminal that displays products and related information on a video screen; it often uses a touch screen for consumers to make selections.

Visual Merchandising Proactive, integrated approach to atmospherics taken by a retailer to create a certain "look," properly display products, stimulate shopping, and enhance the physical environment.

Want Book Notebook in which retail store employees record requests for unstocked or out-of-stock merchandise.

Want Slip Slip on which retail store employees enter requests for unstocked or out-of-stock merchandise.

Warehouse Store Food-based discounter offering a moderate number of food items in a no-frills setting.

Weeks' Supply Method An inventory level planning method wherein beginning inventory equals several weeks' expected sales. It assumes inventory is in direct proportion to sales. Under this method:

$$\begin{array}{c}\text{Beginning-of-month}\\\text{planned inventory}\\\text{level (at retail)}\end{array} = \begin{array}{c}\text{Average estimated weekly sales}\\\times \text{ Number of weeks}\\\text{to be stocked}\end{array}$$

Weighted Application Blank Form whereby criteria best correlating with job success get more weight than others. A minimum total score becomes a cutoff point for hiring.

Wheel of Retailing Theory stating that retail innovators often first appear as low-price operators with low costs and low profit margins. Over time, they upgrade the products carried and improve facilities and customer services. They then become vulnerable to new discounters with lower cost structures.

Width of Assortment Number of distinct goods/service categories (product lines) a retailer carries.

Word of Mouth (WOM) Occurs when one consumer talks to others—in person, on the phone, by E-mail, through social media, or in some other format.

World Wide Web (Web) Way of accessing the Internet, whereby people work with easy-to-use Web addresses and pages. Users see words, colorful charts, pictures, and video and hear audio.

Yield Management Pricing Computerized, demand-based, variable pricing technique whereby a retailer (typically a service firm) determines the combination of prices that yield the greatest total revenues for a given period.

Zero-Based Budgeting Practice followed when a firm starts each new budget from scratch and outlines the expenditures needed to reach that period's goals. All costs are justified each time a budget is done.

Endnotes

Chapter 1

1. Shelly Banjo, "Today Looks Good for Walmart, Tomorrow Not So Much," *Bloomberg Gadfly*, May 19, 2016, http://www.bloomberg.com/gadfly/articles/2016-05-19/walmart-earnings-online-sales-growth-slowing.
2. "U.S. Retail Sales to Near $5 Trillion in 2016," *eMarketer*, December 21, 2015, http://www.emarketer.com/Article/US-Retail-Sales-Near-5-Trillion-2016/1013368.
3. Estimated by the authors from data in "U.S. Census Bureau News: Quarterly Retail E-commerce Sales, 1st Quarter 2016," https://www.census.gov/retail/mrts/www/data/pdf/ec_current.pdf (May 26, 2016).
4. Estimated by the authors from data in Deloitte, "Global Powers of Retailing 2016," https://www2.deloitte.com/content/dam/Deloitte/global/Documents/Consumer-Business/gx-cb-global-powers-of-retailing-2016.pdf.
5. PricewaterhouseCoopers LLP, "The Economic Impact of the U.S. Retail Industry," October 2014, Reported in "Retail Means Jobs," *The National Retail Federation*, https://nrf.com/who-we-are/retail-means-jobs.
6. The Retail Owners Institute, http://retailowner.com.
7. Estimated by authors from "Walmart 10K for the Fiscal Year Ended January 31, 2016."
8. "Supermarket Facts," *Food Marketing Institute*, http://www.fmi.org/research-resources/supermarket-facts.
9. The Home Depot 10-K for the Fiscal Year Ended January 31, 2016.
10. The material in this section is drawn from various Home Depot sources, including http://corporate.homedepot.com, http://investors.homedepot.com; http://pressroom.homedepot.com; www.homedepot.com; *Home Depot Corporation 2015 Annual Report;* 2015 Home Depot Investor and Analyst Conference Transcripts, "Home Depot Corporation," www.hoovers.com (June 25, 2015); *Home Depot, Inc. MarketLine Company Profile,* January 8, 2015; *Trefis Analysis for Home Depot Corporation* (Boston: Insight Guru Inc., May 25, 2016); Kevin Hofmann, senior vice president and president of the online business of The Home Depot (HD) update to analysts on June 18, 2015, at the Goldman Sachs dotCommerce Day 2015; and May Hongmei Gao, "Culture Determines Business Models: Analyzing Home Depot's Failure in China from a Communication Perspective," *Thunderbird International Business Review,* 55(2), March/April 2013, pp. 173–191.
11. "Best Retail Brands 2015," www.interbrand.eu/en/BestRetailBrands/2011.aspx.
12. C. L. Esmark, S. M. Noble, J. E. Bell, and D. A. Griffith, "The effects of behavioral, cognitive, and decisional control in co-production service experiences," *Marketing Letters*, 2015, pp. 1–14.
13. Adapted from Kristin Copeland, "Build-A-Bear Workshop Unveils New Store Design at Flagship Mall of America® Store in Next Phase of Brand Refresh," *BusinessWire,* September 1, 2015, http://www.businesswire.com/news/home/20150901006548/en/Build-A-Bear-Workshop-Unveils-Store-Design-Flagship-Mall and "Build-A-Bear Workshop, Inc.," March 2, 2012, www.buildabear.com/html/en_US/aboutus/ourcompany/factSheet.pdf.

Chapter 1 Appendix

1. Doug Short, "Real Median Household Income Growth Stalls in April," *Advisor Perspectives* (May 26, 2014), http://www.advisorperspectives.com/dshort/updates/Median-Household-Income-Update.
2. Susan Milligan, "Census Bureau: U.S. Poverty, Incomes Stay Stagnant," *U.S. News.com,* September 16, 2015, http://www.usnews.com/news/articles/2015/09/16/poverty-income-stay-stagnant-census-bureau-says.
3. Michael Hiltzik, "America's Explosion of Income Inequality, in One Amazing Animated Chart," *Los Angeles Times,* March 20, 2016, http://www.latimes.com/business/hiltzik/la-fi-hiltzik-ft-graphic-20160320-snap-htmlstory.html.
4. "Distribution of Family Index," *The CIA World Factbook,* 2016, https://www.cia.gov/library/publications/the-world-factbook/rankorder/2172rank.html.
5. Christopher Ingraham, "If You Thought Income Inequality Was Bad, Get a Load of Wealth Inequality," *The Washington Post*, May 21, 2015, https://www.washingtonpost.com/news/wonk/wp/2015/05/21/the-top-10-of-americans-own-76-of-the-stuff-and-its-dragging-our-economy-down/.
6. Heather Long, "Why Doesn't 4.9 Percent Unemployment Feel Great?" *Money,* February 6, 2016. http://money.cnn.com/2016/02/06/news/economy/obama-us-jobs/.
7. Efraim Levy, "Industry Surveys: Multiline Retail," *S&P Capital IQ,* March 2016.
8. "U.S. Personal Savings Rate, 5.4 Percent for April 2016," https://ycharts.com/indicators/personal_saving_rate.
9. Richard Curtin, "Final Results for May 2016," *Surveys of Consumers*, University of Michigan, http://www.sca.isr.umich.edu/.
10. Michael Gerrity, "1.1 Million U.S. Foreclosure Filings in 2015, Down 3 Percent From 2014," *World Property*

Journal, January 14, 2016, http://www.worldproperty journal.com/author/michael-gerrity/.

11. "Subdued Demand, Diminished Prospects," *World Economic Outlook, International Monetary Fund,* January 2016, http://www.imf.org/external/pubs/ft/ weo/2016/update/01/.

12. Ibid.

13. James Hogarth and Holly Felder Etlin, "Results of Retail Bankruptcy Study: Plan or Perish," *AIRA Journal* 29(4), 2015, pp. 5–7.

14. Tom Hals, Supriya Kurane, and Yashaswini Swamynathan, "A&P: Bankruptcy Again," *Reuters,* July 10, 2015, http://www.reuters.com/article/ greatatlantic-bankruptcy-idUSL3N1003U52015072.

15. "Navigating Store Choice Among Small-Box Retail Formats," *Nielsen,* January 27, 2016, http://www .nielsen.com/us/en/insights/news/2016/navigating-store-choice-among-small-box-retail-formats.html.

16. Efraim Levy, "Industry Surveys: Multiline Retail," *S&P Capital IQ,* March 2016.

17. 2K16 Valassis Coupon Intelligence Report, "Savvy Shoppers Provide Reality Check," https://www2 .nchmarketing.com/ResourceCenter/assets/0/22/28/82/ 367/0f7d539900a74b80af71bf6eb60df6b1.pdf.

18. 2016 NCH Marketing Services, Inc., Full-Year 2015.

19. "Industry Coupon Facts and Trends. 2014" *Coupon Trends Highlights,* http://couponpros.org/resources/ industry-coupon-facts-and-trends/ (Accessed June 19, 2016).

20. Andrea Woroch, "Mobile Coupon Trends for 2016, Plus Ways to Make Savings Easier," *LTP,* March 29, 2016, https://letstalkpayments.com/mobile-coupon-trends-for-2016-plus-ways-to-make-saving-easier/.

Chapter 2

1. Huanzhang Wang, Kyung Hoon Kim, Eunju Ko, and Honglei Liu, "Relationship between Service Quality and Customer Equity in Traditional Markets," *Journal of Business Research*, 69(9), September 2016, pp. 3827–3834.

2. Susan Reda, "STORES Trends: MARCH 2016," *STORES Magazine,* March 2016, https://nrf.com/ news/stores-trends-march-2016 (Based on material from STORES magazine. Reprinted by permission.)

3. Ibid. (Based on material from STORES magazine. Reprinted by permission.)

4. Peter Johnston, "Eye Know You!" *STORES Magazine,* December 2015, https://nrf.com/news/eye-know-you (Based on material from STORES magazine. Reprinted by permission.)

5. Susan Reda, "STORES Trends: MARCH 2016," *STORES Magazine,* March 2016, https://nrf.com/ news/stores-trends-march-2016 (Based on material from STORES magazine. Reprinted by permission.)

6. *GameStop Corp. 10Q for Quarter Ended April 30, 2016.* (Based on information collected by the authors at www.gamestop.com).

7. Susan Reda, "STORES Trends: MARCH 2016," *STORES Magazine,* March 2016, https://nrf.com/ news/stores-trends-march-2016 (Based on material from STORES magazine. Reprinted by permission.)

8. J. Zhang and J. M. M. Bloemer, "The Impact of Value Congruence on Consumer-Service Brand Relationships," *Journal of Service Research,* 11(2), (2008),pp. 161–178.

9. R. Sethuraman and K. Gielens, "Determinants of Store Brand Share," *Journal of Retailing*, 90(2), pp. 141–153.

10. Hansen Lieu, "Customer Satisfaction and Customer Loyalty: It's Like 'Like vs. Love,'" October 20, 2011, www.business2community.com/loyalty-marketing.

11. Craig Guillot, "Millennial Moment," STORES Magazine, January 2016, https://nrf.com/news/ millennial-moment (Based on material from STORES magazine. Reprinted by permission.)

12. Sunil Gupta and Donald R. Lehman, *Managing Customers as Investments: The Strategic Value of Customers in the Long Run* (Upper Saddle River, NJ: Pearson, 2005).

13. Adapted by the authors from http://corporate. homedepot.com/about and ACSI: Retail Customer Satisfaction Drops Despite Improvement for Online Shopping, February 18, 2015, https://www.theacsi .org/news-and-resources/press-releases/press-2015/ press-release-retail-2014.

14. Edwin J. Nijssen, Jeroen J. L. Schepers, and Daniel Belanche, "Why Did They Do It? How Customers' Self-Service Technology Introduction Attributions Affect the Customer-Provider Relationship," *Journal of Service Management*, 27(3), 2015, pp. 276–298, http://www.emeraldinsight.com/doi/abs/10.1108/ JOSM-08-2015-0233.

15. Rose Otieno, Chris Harrow, and Gaynor Lea-Greenwood, "The Unhappy Shopper, A Retail Experience: Exploring Fashion, Fit, and Affordability," *International Journal of Retail & Distribution Management*, 33(4), 2005, pp. 298–309.

16. "Customer Satisfaction Survey," June 17, 2016, http://www.statpac.com/online-surveys/customer_ satisfaction_survey.htm.

17. V. Melnyk and T. Bijmolt, "The Effects of Introducing and Terminating Loyalty Programs," *European Journal of Marketing*, 49(3-4), 2015, pp. 398–419.

18. C. Lembregts and M. Pandelaere, "Are All Units Created Equal? The Effect of Default Units on Product Evaluations," *Journal of Consumer Research*, 39(6), 2013, pp. 1275–1289.

19. C. Ashley, E. A. Gillespie, and S. M. Noble, "The Effect of Loyalty Program Fees on Program Perceptions and Engagement," *Journal of Business Research*, 69(2), 2015, pp. 964–973.

20. Lars Meyer Waarden and Christophe Benavent, "Rewards That Reward," September 18, 2008, http://online.wsj.com/article/SB122160028857244783.html.

21. DD Perks Rewards Program, https://www.dunkindonuts.com/dunkindonuts/en/responsive/ddperks/splashpage.html.

22. "Customer Service," https://customerservice.starbucks.com/app/answers/detail/a_id/3949/kw/gold%20status%20benefits.

23. "Becoming a Wal-Mart or Sam's Club Supplier," June 17, 2016, http://corporate.walmart.com/suppliers.

24. "Ace Hardware Stores," June 17, 2016, http://www.acehardware-vendors.com/locations/ace_vendor_manuals/ace_warehouse_supplier/index.asp.

25. Leonard L. Berry, "Relationship Marketing of Services—Growing Interest, Emerging Prospects," *Journal of the Academy of Marketing Science*, 23, 1995, pp. 237–238. See also Charlene Pleger Bebko, "Service Intangibility and Its Impact on Consumer Expectations of Service Quality," *Journal of Services Marketing*, 14(1), 2000, pp. 9–26.

26. "Statistic Brain," May 2, 2016, www.statisticbrain.com/atm-machine-statistics/.

27. "Smart Card FAQ," http://www.smartcardalliance.org/smart-cards-faq/ (Accessed June 24, 2016).

28. "Contactless Payments Resources," http://www.smartcardalliance.org/activities-councils-contactless-payments-resources/ (Accessed June 24, 2016).

29. "Definition of Self-Checkout," February 3, 2012, www.pcmag.com/encyclopedia_term/0,2542,t=self-scanning+checkout&i=51072,00.asp.

30. "Mobile Self-Checkout Solutions for Retail—Scandit" http://www.scandit.com/products/mobile-app-suite-retail/self-checkout/ (Accessed June 24, 2016).

31. Gift Card Statistics, http://www.giftcards.com/gift-card-statistics (Accessed June 24, 2016).

32. "How to Exchange Gift Cards and Get the Most Cash," *Consumer Reports*, December 26, 2016, http://www.consumerreports.org/holiday-shopping/how-to-exchange-gift-cards/ http://www.thergca.org/us-shoppers-love-gift-cards-which-translates-to-more-revenue-for-retailers.

33. "Global Interactive Kiosks Market 2015 is Poised to Reach $2.88 Billion by 2022," http://netdugout.com/2015/10/global-interactive-kiosks-market-2015-is-poised-to-reach-2-88-billion-by-2022/ (Accessed June 24, 2016).

34. Amazon Locker and International Pickup Points. http://www.amazon.com/gp/help/customer/display.html?nodeId=200689010 (Accessed June 22, 2016).

35. ChainDrugStore.net. https://hub.pharmacyfocus.com/ (Accessed June 21, 2016).

36. Direct Marketing Association's Guidelines for Ethical Business Practices, http://thedma.org/wp-content/uploads/DMA_Guidelines_January_2014.pdf (revised January 2014).

37. Ronald McDonald House Charities, http://rmhcny.org (Accessed September 8, 2016).

38. "Walmart Highlights Progress in 2015 Global Responsibility Report," http://corporate.walmart.com/_news_/news-archive/2015/04/22/walmart-highlights-progress-in-2015-global-responsibility-report.

39. Plangger, Kirk, and Richard T. Watson. "Balancing Customer Privacy, Secrets, and Surveillance: Insights and Management." *Business Horizons,* 58/6 (November-December 2015),: 625-633.

40. Giant Food, public relations.

41. Wireless Customer Bill of Rights. https://newsroom.t-mobile.com/news-and-blogs/bill-of-rights.htm (March 28, 2016).

Chapter 2 Appendix

1. Estimated by the authors based on data from The SBDC National Clearinghouse, http://www.sbdcnet.org/small-business-research-reports.

2. Micah Solomon, "Four Steps From Customer Anger to Customer Loyalty: The Expert Service Recovery Method," *Forbes,* July 16, 2014, http://www.forbes.com/sites/micahsolomon/2014/07/16/customer-service-recovery/#a7d06eb12c4c.

3. Barry Berman and Anil Mathur, "Planning and Implementing Effective Service Guarantee Programs," *Business Horizons,* 57(1), January 2014, pp. 107–116.

4. Greg Petro, "Dynamic Pricing: Which Customers Are Worth the Most: Amazon, Delta Airlines and Staples Weigh In," *Forbes,* April 17, 2015, http://www.forbes.com/sites/gregpetro/2015/04/17/dynamic-pricing-which-customers-are-worth-the-most-amazon-delta-airlines-and-staples-weigh-in/#3bef5587b516

5. The material in this section is drawn from Bill Taylor, "How One Fast-Food Chain Keeps Its Turnover Rates Absurdly Low," *Harvard Business Review,* January 26, 2016, https://hbr.org/2016/01/how-one-fast-food-chain-keeps-its-turnover-rates-absurdly-low; and Leigh Buchanan, "Training the Best Damn Fry Cooks (and Future Leaders) in the U.S., *Inc.,* April 23, 2014, http://www.inc.com/audacious-companies/leigh-buchanan/pals-sudden-service.html.

Chapter 3

1. Based on material in Susan Reda, "Store Trends," *STORES Magazine,* April 2016. Reprinted by permission.

2. "Create Your Business Plan," https://www.sba.gov/starting-business/write-your-business-plan/how-make-your-business-plan-stand-out.

3. "About Amazon.com.," http://www.amazon.com/exec/obidos/subst/misc/company-info.html Cached version: http://web.archive.org/web/20000229045453/http://www.amazon.com/exec/obidos/subst/misc/company-info.html.

4. Amazon.com 2015 Annual Report, April 6, 2016, file:///C:/Users/chatterjeep/Downloads/2015%20 Annual%20Report%20(1).pdf.

5. Amazon Company Facts, http://phx.corporate-ir.net/ phoenix.zhtml?c=176060&p=irol-factSheet (Accessed June 25, 2016).

6. For additional information about business ownership formats, go to SBA*Inc.*'s "Know Your Options: Choosing a Corporate Form" site (https://www.sba .gov/starting-business/choose-your-business-structure) (Accessed on June 26, 2016).

7. Ameen Khwaja, "Choose Your Business Structure," *Entrepreneur,* January 6, 2016, www.entrepreneur.com/ article/38822.

8. Estimated by the authors from data in *2012 Statistical Abstract of the United States*, www.census.gov/ compendia/statab.

9. Kroger Form 10-K, January 30, 2016.

10. "Bebe's Spring 2016 Collection," February 1, 2016, http://investorrelations.bebe.com/press-release/other/ bebes-spring-2016-collection and "Rock the Vote Announces Partnership with Bebe to Engage Young Women in the 2016 Election," November 8, 2015, http://investorrelations.bebe.com.

11. "Our Story," http://www.traderjoes.com/our-story (Accessed June 28, 2016).

Chapter 3 Appendix

1. "The 2015 Global Retail Development Index: Global Retail Expansion; An Unstoppable Force," https:// www.atkearney.com/consumer-products-retail/ global-retail-development-index/2015.

2. Ibid.

3. Toys "R" Us, 10K for the Fiscal Year Ending January 30, 2016.

4. McDonald's Corporation, 10K for the Fiscal year Ending December 31, 2015; and Pamela Engel, "I Went to McDonald's in France and Discovered How the U.S. is Doing It All Wrong," *Business Insider,* April 13, 2015, http://www.businessinsider.com/ mcdonalds-in-france-is-better-than-in-america-2015-4.

5. "Luxottica Group on Forbes Lists," http://www.forbes .com/companies/luxottica-group/.

6. Clint Engel, "IKEA Says U.S. Sales Hit $5 Billion in Fiscal Year," *Furniture Today,* December 14, 2015, http://www.furnituretoday.com/article/526626-ikea- says-us-sales-hit-5-billion-fiscal-year.

Chapter 4

1. Elon Musk, "Tesla Approach to Distributing and Servicing Cars," *Tesla Blog,* October 22, 2012, https:// www.teslamotors.com/de_AT/blog/tesla-approach- distributing-and-servicing-cars and Trefis Team, "Is the Direct Sales Model Critical for Tesla Motors?" *Forbes,* March 3, 2016, http://www.forbes.com/sites/ greatspeculations/2016/03/03/is-the-direct-sales- model-critical-for-tesla-motors/#5c17b70f685f.

2. *2012 Statistical Abstract of the United States*, www .census.gov/compendia/statab.

3. For example, see Tajeddini, Kayhan, Ulf Elg, and Myfanwy Trueman. "Efficiency and Effectiveness of Small Retailers: The Role of Customer and Entrepreneurial Orientation," *Journal of Retailing and Consumer Services* 20.5 (2013): 453–462.

4. Lynn Voss, "Ten Truths That All Small Business Owners Should Know," *Business Sense*, Georgia SBDC Network. Brent Underwood, "The 8 Unexpected Rules of Business That No One Teaches but Everyone Should Know," *Observer Business and Tech,* January 11, 2016, http:// observer.com/2016/01/the-8-unexpected-rules-of- business-that-no-one-teaches-but-everyone-should-know/.

5. For a good overview of franchising and franchising opportunities, see *Entrepreneur's* "Annual Franchise 500" issue (www.entrepreneur.com/franchise500), which appears each January.

6. The material in this section is estimated by the authors based on data in "Franchise Business Economic Outlook: 2016," http://www.franchise. org/research. For more information on trends about strategy, see Alexander Rosado Serrano, "Store in Store Franchising Strategy: The Trend in Franchising Negotiation," *Neumann Business Review*, 2(1), 2016, pp. 20–37.

7. For more information on leased departments, see Kinshuk Jerath and Z. John Zhang, "Store Within a Store," *Journal of Marketing Research*, 47, August 2010, pp. 748–763.

8. Ashlee Kieler, "CVS Unveils First Store-Within-Store Pharmacies at Target," *Consumerist,* February 3, 2016, https://consumerist.com/2016/02/03/cvs-unveils-first- store-within-store-pharmacies-at-target/ and Katie Sershon, "What's the Real Estate Diagnosis for the CVS and Target Deal?" *JLL Real Views,* June 18, 2015, http://www.jllrealviews.com/industries/whats- the-diagnosis-for-the-cvs-and-target-pharmacy-deal/.

9. Sanjana Saluja, "Stores-within-Stores Enhance the Shopping Experience," *JLL Views,* August 4, 2015, http://www.jllrealviews.com/industries/ stores-within-stores-enhance-the-shopping-experience.

10. Post Wire Report, "Sears Pockets $114M in Stores Deal," *New York Post*, April 13, 2015, http://nypost .com/2015/04/13/sears-pockets-114m-in-stores-deal/.

11. Andy Brownfield, "Macy's Partners with Major Eyewear Retailer for Store-within-Store," *Cicinatti Business Courier,* November 12, 2015, http://www .bizjournals.com/cincinnati/news/2015/11/11/macys- partners-with-major-eyewear-retailer-for.html.

12. *Sherwin-Williams 2015 Annual Report*, http://investors .sherwin-williams.com/pdf/annual-reports/2015_ annual_report.pdf.

13. For more information on cooperatives, visit these Web sites: National Cooperative Business Association

(www.ncba.coop); National Cooperative Grocers Association (http://ncga.coop); and Go.coop (www .go.coop).

Chapter 4 Appendix

1. "Tariq Farid's Bio," http://www.ediblearrangements. com/About/tariq-farid-ceo-edible-arrangements.
2. Adam Jones, "Dunkin' Donuts' Unit Growth Is More Aggressive in U.S. Market, Market Realist, April 3, 2015, http://marketrealist.com/2015/04/ dunkin-donuts-unit-growth-aggressive-us-market/.
3. "National Franchise Mediation Program," maret .franchise/org/NationalFranchiseMediation.pdf.

Chapter 5

1. The pioneering works on the wheel of retailing are Malcolm P. McNair, "Significant Trends and Developments in the Postwar Period," in A. B. Smith (Ed.), *Competitive Distribution in a Free High Level Economy and Its Implications for the University* (Pittsburgh: University of Pittsburgh Press, 1958), pp. 17–18; and Stanley Hollander, "The Wheel of Retailing," *Journal of Marketing*, 25, July 1960, pp. 37–42. For further analysis of the concept, see Stephen Brown, "The Wheel of Retailing: Past and Future," *Journal of Retailing*, 66, Summer 1990, pp. 143–149; Stephen Brown, "Postmodernism, the Wheel of Retailing, and Will to Power," *International Review of Retail, Distribution, and Consumer Research*, 5, July 1995, pp. 387–414; Don E. Schultz, "Another Turn of the Wheel," *Marketing Management,* March– April 2002, pp. 8–9; Susan D. Sampson, "Category Killers and Big-Box Retailing: Their Historical Impact on Retailing in the USA," *International Journal of Retail & Distribution Management*, 36(1), 2008, pp. 17–31; Victor J. Massad, Mary Beth Nein, and Joanne M. Tucker, "The Wheel of Retailing Revisited: Toward a 'Wheel of E-Tailing,'" *Journal of Management and Marketing Research*, 8, September 2011, www.aabri.com/manuscripts/11838.pdf; and Mert Tokman, R. Glenn Richey, and George D. Deitz. "A Strategic Choice Theory Taxonomy of Retailers' Strategic Orientations." *Journal of Marketing Theory and Practice*, 24(2), 2016, pp. 186–208.
2. John Kotter, Clayton Christensen, Renee A. Mauborgne, and W. Chan Kim, "Introduction," *Leading Change—Harvard Business Review Leadership and Strategy Boxed Set*, May 17, 2016; and Amy Merrick, "Where the Middle Class Shops," *New Yorker,* February 6, 2014, www.newyorker.com/ business/currency/where-the-middle-class-shops.
3. See Jonathan Reynolds, Elizabeth Howard, Christine Cuthbertson, and Latchezar Hristov, "Perspectives on Retail Format Innovation: Relating Theory and Practice," *International Journal of Retail & Distribution*

Management, 35(8), 2007, pp. 647–660; Lai Ngun Sun, Robert Kay, and Matthew Chew, "Development of a Retail Life Cycle: The Case of Hong Kong's Department Store Industry," *Asia Pacific Business Review*, 15, January 2009, pp. 107–121; and Gérard Cliquet and Pierre-Alain Guillo, "Retail Network Spatial Expansion: An Application of the Percolation Theory to Hard Discounters." *Journal of Retailing and Consumer Services,* 20(2), 2013, 173–181.
4. "15 Best Flash Sale Sites You Don't Know But Should," Retail-Me-Not, www.retailmenot.com/blog/ flash-sale-sites.html.
5. Leena Rao, "Why Flash Sales Are in Trouble," *Fortune,* December 16, 2015, http://fortune. com/2015/12/16/flash-sales-trouble/.
6. Kari Hamanaka, "Gilt Testing Personal Closet Service," *Women's Wear Daily*, April 28, 2015, http://wwd.com/fashion-news/fashion-scoops/ gilt-testing-personal-closet-service-10116908/.
7. See www.kioskmarketplace.com for an overview of kiosks; and "IHL Survey: Sales Via Self-Service Kiosk Expected to Grow to $1 Trillion in 2015," www.retailtouchpoints.com.
8. "Last Catalog Showroom Retailer Now in Liquidation," *Knight Ridder/Tribune Business News,* February 3, 2002; and Home Retail Group, *Annual Report and Financial Statements 2016—Argos Key Facts*, p. 13.
9. "Retailing: General," *Standard & Poor's Industry Surveys,* November 24, 2011, pp. 11–12.
10. "Fact Sheets," NACS, December 31, 2015, http:// www.nacsonline.com/Research/FactSheets/Pages/ default.aspx.
11. *Marathon Petroleum Corporation 2015 Annual Report,* p. 15.
12. "C-Store Sales Surge in 2016," Convenience Store Decisions, July 7, 2016, http://www.cstoredecisions.com.
13. "83rd Annual Report of the Grocery Industry," *Progressive Grocer,* April 2016, p. 34. Reprinted by permission; "Facts & Figures," www.fmi.org/facts_figs; and author's estimates.
14. Ibid.
15. Ibid.
16. Ibid.
17. Ibid.
18. "Sephora," May 2016, www.sephora.com/about-us.
19. "Multiline Retail," *Standard & Poor's Industry Surveys,* March 2016, p. 33.
20. Estimated by the authors from Walmart and Target company Web sites (Accessed July 29, 2016).
21. Estimated by the authors from Dollar General, Dollar Tree, and Big Lots company Web sites (Accessed July 29, 2016).
22. Linda Humphers, "2015 State of the Outlet Industry," *Value Retail News*, August 2015, pp. 10–12.
23. Estimated by the authors from Costco and Sam's Club company Web sites (Accessed July 29, 2016).

Chapter 6

1. Based on material from David P. Schulz "Top 100 Retailers 2015," *STORES Magazine,* July 2015. Reprinted by permission.
2. "Most Small Businesses Are Discovered Online First," *eMarketer*, www.emarketer.com (Accessed June 1, 2016).
3. Oliver Emrich and Peter C. Verhoef, "The Impact of a Homogenous Versus a Prototypical Web Design on Online Retail Patronage for Multichannel Providers," *International Journal of Research in Marketing*, 32(4), May 26, 2015.
4. Authors' estimates, based on information from "Web-Influenced Retail Sales in the United States from 2012–2017, By Segment," www.statista.com/statistics/368309/us-webinfluenced-retail-sales/.
5. John Deighton and Peter A. Johnson, "The Value of Data 2015: Consequences for Insight, Innovation and Efficiency in the U.S. Economy," http://thedma.org/wp-content/uploads/Value-of-Data-Summary.pdf.
6. Ibid.
7. Ibid.
8. Based on material in David P. Schulz, "Top 100 Retailers 2015," *STORES Magazine,* July 2015. Reprinted by permission.
9. "QVC Fact Sheet," February 24, 2016. http://corporate.qvc.com.
10. Federation of European Direct and Interactive Marketing, www.fedma.org and Indian Direct Marketing Association, www.idsa.co.in/ (Accessed June 23, 2016).
11. "Where to Complain and Get Help," *Consumers—A Helpful Guide*, www.dmaconsumers.org/wheretocomplainandgethelp.html (Accessed July 26, 2016).
12. "2015 Growth and Outlook Report: Direct Selling in 2015," www.dsa.org; and WFDSA Annual Report 2016, June 22, 2016.
13. Authors' estimates based on *Vending Times 2014: Census of the Industry*, www.vendingtimes.com; and "Annual Report: Vending Operators Punch Through Last Year's Revenue," *Automatic Merchandiser*, June 2015, pp. 24–31.
14. "Internet World Stats: Usage and Population Statistics," www.internetworldstats.com/stats.htm (Accessed August 3, 2016).
15. Matt Linder, "U.S. Online Sales Will Surpass $530 Billion by 2020," *Internet Retailer,* May 2, 2016.
16. "Retail E-Commerce Sales Worldwide from 2014 to 2019," *Statista*, www.statista.com (Accessed July 24, 2016).
17. "Retail E-Commerce Sales in the United States from 2013 to 2019," *Statista*, www.statista.com (accessed July 24, 2016).
18. "Mobile Retail E-Commerce Sales in the United States from 2013 to 2020," *Statista*, www.statista.com (accessed July 24, 2016).
19. Quarterly Retail E-Commerce Sales—1st Quarter 2016," *U.S. Census Bureau News,* May 17, 2016, www.census.gov/retail/mrts/www/data/pdf/ec_current.pdf.
20. Paul Demery, "Mobile Shopping Accounts for a Larger Share of Online Sales," June 8, 2015, *InternetRetailer.com*, www.internetretailer.com.
21. Based on material in Sandy Smith," The Future in Now," *Stores Magazine*, April 2016. Reprinted by permission.
22. Weiling Zhuang and Barry J. Babin, "The Influence of E-Service-Quality on Customer Value Perception and Satisfaction: The Case of Third-Party Web Sites." *Marketing Dynamism & Sustainability: Things Change, Things Stay the Same* (City: Springer, 2015), pp. 114–117.
23. Andreas Liedtke, Mirko Warschun, Sophie Glusac, and Felix Krusenbaum, "10 Steps to Reach Online Sales Excellence," A. T. Kearney, 2015, https://goo.gl/r5RkOq.
24. David Swift, "Studies on Cart Abandonment and Email Retargeting," February 25, 2016, www.swifterm.com.
25. Ginny Marvin, "Mobile Is Converting: Accounts for More Than 30 Percent of US Ecommerce Transactions In Q2," *Marketing Land*, June 25, 2015, http://marketingland.com.
26. Based on multiple sources, including "Mobile Retail App and Sites: Designing a Better Experience for Shoppers," http://snip.ly (Accessed April 2, 2016); and "How and When You're Losing Your App Users," *Localytics*, December 12, 2014, http://info.localytics.com/blog.
27. Estimated by the authors from data in first name Deloitte, "Global Powers of Retailing 2016," http://www2.deloitte.com/global/en.html (Accessed June 26, 2016).
28. *Amazon.com 2015 Annual Report.*
29. "SeamlessWeb," www.seamless.com (Accessed July 25, 2016).
30. CarMax Web site, https://www.carmax.com (Accessed August 2, 2016).
31. Authors' estimates, based on information from www.kioskmarketplace.com and others sources (July 23, 2016); and Lee Holman and Greg Buzek, *Market Study: North American Self-Service Kiosks* (Franklin, TN: IHL Group, March 1, 2016).
32. "Interactive Kiosks," July 23, 2016, www.wirespring.com/Solutions/interactive_kiosks.html.
33. "2015 Kiosks in Retail 101," *Kioskmarketplace.com,* www.kioskmarketplace.com (Accessed July 23, 2016).
34. Authors' estimates, based on a variety of sources, including "Know Your Total Cost of Ownership," June 1, 2015, *KioskMarketplace.com*, www.kioskmarketplace.com; and BCC Research, "Global Self-Service Tech Markets on the Rise; Galloping CAGR in Kiosk Market," June 21, 2016, www.bccresearch.com.
35. Authors' estimates, based on 2015 ACI Annual World Airport Traffic Report, www.aci.aero; and *Airport*

Revenue News 2015 Fact Book, www.airportrevenue news.com.

36. "Duty Free Retailing Market Worth $73.6 Billion by 2019," *RnR Market Research, April 22, 2015,* http:// prnewswire.com.

37. "The ARK Readies for fall Opening," *Airport Revenue News,* July 2016, www.airportrevenuenews.com.

38. "Regional Airports Look to Shopping Malls for Inspiration," June 29, 2016, http://milanamos.com/ airports-shopping-malls/; and "Airport Shopping— The Sixth Continent," *Economist*, May 10, 2014, www.economist.com.

Chapter 6 Appendix

1. "Which Omnichannel Retailing Services Need Improvement?" *eMarketer,* April 28, 2016, www .emarketer.com.

2. Based on material in David P. Schulz, "Top 100 Retailers 2015," *STORES Magazine* (July 2015). Reprinted with permission.

3. Barry Berman, "Planning and Implementing Effective Mobile Marketing Programs," *Business Horizons,* 59(4), September/October 2016.

4. Lisa Gevelber, "Winning Omnichannel Shoppers in Their Micro-Moments," *Thinkwithgoogle.com,* October, 2015, www.thinkwithgoogle.com.

5. Jonathan Sockell, "Retail Omnichannel: Tying the Knot with Your Most Valuable Customers," August 18, 2014, http://blog.medallia.com/.

6. "Luxury Retailers Go Omnichannel," *Livingmalls .com,* January 27, 2015, http://thrivingmalls.com.

7. Lisa Gevelber, "Winning Omnichannel Shoppers in Their Micro-Moments," *Thinkwithgoogle.com,* October 2015, www.thinkwithgoogle.com.

8. Wayne Usie, "Removing Omnichannel Silos Creates Competitive Advantage," *Supply Chain Nation,* February 23, 2016, http://blog.jda.com/.

Chapter 7

1. Based on material in Susan Reda, "Supermarket Showdown," *STORES Magazine,* April 2016. Reprinted by permission.

2. Federal Reserve Bank of St. Louis, "Real Median Household Income in the United States," October 21, 2015, https://research.stlouisfed.org.

3. United States Department of Labor, "Women in the Labor Force—Data & Statistics," 2016, www.dol.gov/ wb/stats/stats_data.htm.

4. "Educational Attainment in the United States: 2015," *US Census Bureau,* 2016, www.census.gov.

5. Authors' estimates based on data from the U.S. Census Bureau (www.census.gov); and "ACS Demographic and Housing Estimates," http:// factfinder.census.govduct (Accessed April 23, 2016).

6. "Millennial Dads Take on Household Grocery Shopping," *Convenience Store News*, June 22, 2016, www.csnews.com.

7. Ashley Lutz, "This Clothing Company Whose CEO Is Richer than Warren Buffett Is Blowing the Competition Out of the Water, *Business Insider,*June 13, 2015, www.businessinsider.com.

8. Hanna Ehrnrooth Christian Gronroos, "The Hybrid Consumer: Exploring Hybrid Consumption Behaviour," *Management Decision*, 51(9), 2013, pp. 1793–1820; and Mercedes Martos-Partal, Oscar González-Benito, and Mariana Fustinoni-Venturini, "Motivational Profiling of Store Brand Shoppers: Differences across Quality Tiers," *Marketing Letters*, 26(2), 2015, pp. 187–200.

9. Laura Layden, "Boston Proper Returns Catalog, Online Sales for Women's Apparel," *Naples Daily News,* January 21, 2016.

10. Alexander Campbell Howe, "How Latinas Are Influencing the Retail Industry," *NBC News,* July 1, 2015, www.nbc.com.

11. Nielsen My Best Segments, https:// segmentationsolutions.nielsen.com/mybestsegments/.

12. *Toys "R" Us 10K for Fiscal Year Ended January 30, 2016.*

13. Kim K. P. Johnson et al., "Keeping Customers Shopping in Stores: Interrelationships among Store Attributes, Shopping Enjoyment, and Place Attachment," *International Review of Retail, Distribution and Consumer Research*, 25(1), 2015, pp. 20–34; Cathy Hart, Andrew M. Farrell, Grazyna Stachow, Gary Reed, and John W. Cadogan, "Enjoyment of the Shopping Experience: Impact on Customers' Repatronage Intentions and Gender Influence," *Service Industries Journal*, 27, July 2007, p. 599.

14. Jun Yao and Harmen Oppewal, "Unit Pricing Matters More When Consumers are under Time Pressure," *European Journal of Marketing*, 50(5-6), 2016, pp. 1094–1114.

15. Kim, Kyoungmi, Arthur W. Allaway, and Alexander E. Ellinger. "Retail Assortment Size and Customer Choice Overload: The Influence of Shopping Enjoyment and Time Pressure," *Marketing Dynamism & Sustainability: Things Change, Things Stay the Same* (New York: Springer International Publishing, 2015), p. 139; and Hye-Young Kim and Youn-Kyung Kim, "Shopping Enjoyment and Store Shopping: The Moderating Influence of Chronic Time Pressure Modes," *Journal of Retailing and Consumer Services*, 15, September 2008, p. 417.

16. Efraim Levy, "Retailing: Multiline," *Standard & Poor's Industry Surveys,* March 24, 2016, p. 18; and "Retailing: Specialty," *Standard & Poor's Industry Surveys,* April 2016, p. 39.

17. Amy Ding, Shibo Li, and Patrali Chatterjee, "Learning User Real-Time Intent for Optimal Dynamic Webpage

Transformation," *Information Systems Research*, 26(2), 2015, pp. 339–359.

18. Spangenberg, E. R., A.E. Crowley, and P.W. Henderson, "Improving the Store Environment; Do Olfactory Cues Affect Evaluations and Behavior?" *Journal of Marketing* Vol. 60, No. 2 (1996), pp. 67-80.

19. Lelly Green Atkins, Archana Kumar, and Youn-Kyung Kim, "Smart Grocery Shopper Segments," Journal of International Consumer Marketing, 28, January 2016, pp. 42–53; Arne De Keyser, Jeroen Schepers, and Umut Konuş, "Multichannel Customer Segmentation: Does the After-Sales Channel Matter? A Replication and Extension," *International Journal of Research in Marketing,* 32(4), 2015, pp. 453–456; Marta Frasquet, Alejandro Mollá, and Eugenia Ruiz, "Identifying Patterns in Channel Usage Across the Search, Purchase and Post-Sales Stages of Shopping," *Electronic Commerce Research and Applications*, 14(6), 2015, pp. 654–665; and Mike Reid, "Give Me the Money . . . Or Maybe the Deal: Does Sales Promotion Proneness Influence Consumers' Willingness to Switch from Price to Non-Price Promotions?" *Marketing in Transition: Scarcity, Globalism, & Sustainability* (New York: Springer International Publishing, 2015), pp. 24–28.

20. Mercedes Martos-Partal, Oscar González-Benito, and Mariana Fustinoni-Venturini, "Motivational Profiling of Store Brand Shoppers: Differences across Quality Tiers." *Marketing Letters*, 26(2), 2015, pp. 187–200; and "A. C. Nielsen Private-Label Powerhouses: Europe and North America," December 8, 2014, www.nielsen.com.

21. "Smartphones Are (Still) for Shopping, Not Buying," *eMarketer,* October 27, 2015, www.emarketer.com.

22. Jessica Wohl, "Brands Acting on Impulse to Fill the In-Store Checkouts Void," *Advertising Age*, November 9, 2015, http://adage.com.

23. Kate Kaylor, "The 'Impulse Buy' Is Dying—Here's How Companies are Trying to Revive It," *Business Insider*, November 23, 2015, www.businessinsider.com.

24. Adapted by the authors from Joanna Lord, "Five Types of Loyalty and What Marketers Need to Know," *Big Door Blog*, April 24, 2014, http://bigdoor.com.

25. Rakhi Thakur, "Understanding Customer Engagement and Loyalty: A Case of Mobile Devices for Shopping," *Journal of Retailing and Consumer Services*, 32, September 2016, pp. 151–163.

26. *Walgreens Boots Alliance 10-K for the Year Ended August 31, 2015.*

27. *Kohl's 10-K for the Year Ended January 30, 2016.*

28. *Dollar Tree Stores Inc., 10K for Fiscal Year Ended January 30, 2016.*

29. "Company Overview of Claire's Stores Inc.," August 4, 2016, www.bloomberg.com.

30. *Foot Locker 10K for the Fiscal Year Ending January 30, 2016.*

31. *Gap Inc., 10 K for the Fiscal Year Ended January 30, 2016.*

Chapter 8

1. Based on material in Susan Reda, "STORES Trends," *STORES Magazine,* February 2016. Reprinted by permission.

2. eMarketer, "Retailers Eye Value in Beacon Data," August 11, 2015, www.emarketer.com.

3. Dale Allardyce, "Top 4 Supply Chain Challenges Facing Today's Multichannel Retailers," *News from Allen Austin*, March 30, 2016, www.allenaustin.com.

4. "Making Sense of Retail Link Data,"2016, www .walmartvendor.com.

5. Authors' estimates based on "IT Spending & Staffing Benchmarks, 2016/2017," *Consumer Economics*, 2016).

6. "Retail Pro International Increases Worldwide Reach by 15% in 4 Months," Press Release, May 18, 2016, www.retailpro.com.

7. "MicroStrategy Enterprise Analytics Platform," August 1, 2016, https://www.microstrategy.com.

8. "Single Customer View," *Pitney Bowes Annual Report 2015*, www.pitneybowes.com; and "Customer and Marketing Analytics," August 4, 2016, www.pitney bowes.com.

9. Checklist developed by the authors, with some items drawn from "Data Management Checklist: The Long Version," , May 2, 2012, http://dataservices.gmu.edu.

10. For example, this material is drawn from "Data Warehousing," www.osc.nc.gov. See also Margaret Rouse, "Definition Data Warehouse," August 4, 2016, http://searchsqlserver.techtarget.com.

11. Margaret Rouse, "Data Warehouse as a Service (DWaaS)," http://searchdatamanagement.techtarget. com (Accessed August 2, 2016).

12. Teradata: Retail, www.teradata.com (Accessed August 5, 2016).

13. "Family Dollar Program: Collaboration through Data Analytics," *RSi Retail Solutions*, April 30, 2016, www .retailsolutions.com.

14. John Karolefski, "Not Ready for Prime Time," *Progressive Grocer*, April 2016, pp. 134, 136.

15. "Universal Product Code," 2016, www.gs1us.org.

16. "Frequently Asked Questions," *GS1 US Mobile Scan*, August 5, 2016, https://sites.gs1us.org/mobilescan/faqs.

17. "How EDI Streamlines Processes in the Retail Industry," February 15, 2016, http://boldvan.com/blog).

18. Joe Nguyen, "Connect to Large Retailers with Commerce EDI," March 1, 2016, www.shipwire.com.

19. Based on material in CSN Staff, "Bring Your 'A' Game," *Convenience Store News*, February 2016, pp. 24–28. Reprinted with permission.

20. "Mystery Shopping?" July 19, 2016, www.gfk.com; "Becoming a Video Mystery Shopper," *Insight*, May 3, 2016, www.insightmarketresearch.co.uk; and Rachel Chen and Clayton W. Barrows, "Developing a Mystery Shopping Measure to Operate a Sustainable Restaurant Business: The Power of Integrating

with Corporate Executive Members' Feedback." *Sustainability*, 9, 2015, pp. 12279–12294.

21. "Case Study HMD Eye Tracking: Virtual Shopper Journey," www.smivision.com (Accessed August 5, 2016).

Chapter 9

1. Marianne Wilson, "Aldi Steps Out—Into the Mall,"August–September, www.chainstoreage.com; Heather Cherone, "Aldi, Ross to Anchor Huge Center Set to Replace Empty Bank at Six Corners," February 18, 2016, https://www.dnainfo.com; and "Aldi Strengthens Senior Management Team As Fast-Paced Us Expansion Continues," March 8, 2016, https://corporate.aldi.us.

2. American Marketing Association, "Dictionary," May 30, 2016, www.ama.org.

3. "What Is Geographic Information Systems (GIS)?" July 27, 2016, http://gisgeography.com; also see "Web-based GIS," January 3, 2016, http://gislounge.com for more information about the technical aspects of geographic information systems and "Commercial GIS Software: List of Commercial Mapping Software," August 10, 2016, http://gisgeography.com.

4. TIGERweb Overview, August 15, 2016, https://tigerweb.geo.census.gov.

5. TIGER Products, August 15, 2016, https://www.census.gov/geo/maps-data/data/tiger.html.

6. "Starbucks: Brewing Up a Data Storm!" November 21, 2015, https://digit.hbs.org.

7. Heather Clancy, "Why Walgreens Uses Interactive Maps Plus Analytics to Evaluate Store Locations," October 22, 2015, www.fortune.com.

8. "GFK GeoMarketing," August 9, 2016, http://www.gfk.com/solutions/geomarketing.

9. For a good overview of trading-area analysis, see Jean-Paul Rodrigue, "Market Areas Analysis," https://people.hofstra.edu/geotrans/eng/methods/ch7m2en.html (July 6, 2016). Click on the images on the right side of this Web site.

10. William J. Reilly, *Method for the Study of Retail Relationships*, Research Monograph No. 4 (Austin: University of Texas Press, 1929), University of Texas Bulletin No. 2944. See also MacKenzie S. Bottum, "Reilly's Law," *Appraisal Journal*, 57, April 1989, pp. 166–172; Michael D. D'Amico, Jon M. Hawes, and Dale M. Lewison, "Determining a Hospital's Trading Area: An Application of Reilly's Law," *Journal of Hospital Marketing*, 8(2), 1994, pp. 121–129; att T. Rosenberg, "Gravity Models," April 25, 2016, http://geography.about.com; and Thomas Wuerzer and Susan G. Mason, "Retail Gravitation and Economic Impact: A Market-Driven Analytical Framework for Bike-Share Station Location Analysis in the United States." *International Journal of Sustainable Transportation*, 10(3), 2016, pp. 247–259.

11. Debayan Nandi, "Is Reilly's Law of Retail Gravitation Pertinent in Sub-Urban Areas of West Bengal?—A Study," *International Educational Scientific Research Journal*, 2(5), 2016.

12. David L. Huff, "Defining and Estimating a Trading Area," *Journal of Marketing*, 28, July 1964, pp. 34–38; and David L. Huff and Larry Blue, *A Programmed Solution for Estimating Retail Sales Potential* (Lawrence: University of Kansas, 1966). See also David Huff and Bradley M. McCallum, "Calibrating the Huff Model Using ArcGIS Business Analyst," September 25, 2008, www.esri.com/library; Pan-Jin Kim1, Wanki Kim, Won-Ki Chung, and Myoung-Kil Youn, "Using New Huff Model for Predicting Potential Retail Market in South Korea," March 4, 2011, www.academicjournals.org/AJBM; Les Dolega, Michalis Pavlis, and Alex Singleton, "Estimating Attractiveness, Hierarchy and Catchment Area Extents for a National Set of Retail Centre Agglomerations," *Journal of Retailing and Consumer Services*, 28, 2016, pp. 78–90.

13. David A. Gautschi, "Specification of Patronage Models for Retail Center Choice," *Journal of Marketing Research*, 18, May 1981, pp. 162–174; Glen E. Weisbrod, Robert J. Parcells, and Clifford Kern, "A Disaggregate Model for Predicting Shopping Area Market Attraction," *Journal of Retailing*, 60, Spring 1984, pp. 65–83; David R. Bell, Teck-Hua Ho, and Christopher S. Tang, "Determining Where to Shop: Fixed and Variable Costs of Shopping," *Journal of Marketing Research*, 35, August 1998, pp. 352–369; David S. Rogers, "Developing a Location Research Methodology," *Journal of Targeting, Measurement & Analysis for Marketing*, 13, March 2005, pp. 201–208; Rajagopal, "Determinants of Shopping Behavior of Urban Consumers," *Journal of International Consumer Marketing*, 23(2), 2011, pp. 83–104; and Les Dolega, Michalis Pavlis, and Alex Singleton, "Estimating Attractiveness, Hierarchy and Catchment Area Extents for a National Set of Retail Centre Agglomerations," *Journal of Retailing and Consumer Services* 28, 2016, pp. 78–90.

14. Mark Belko, "Duluth Trading Sets Sights on Pittsburgh," *Pittsburgh Post-Gazette*, January 20, 2016, www.post-gazette.com; and Judy Newman, "Profits Grow for Duluth Trading Co.," *Wisconsin State Journal*, April 11, 2016, www.duluthnewstribune.com.

15. Jeff Bounds, "Modern Magic: How Data Is Changing Site Selection," July 27, 2016, http://www.dallasinnovates.com.

16. Gail MarksJarvis, "Furniture Retailers on a Chicago-area Expansion Kick," February 4, 2016, www.chicagotribune.com.

17. Bob Pisani, "Macy's Finally Starts Addressing the Overstored Retail Landscape," August 11, 2016, www.cnbc.com.

18. Michael Johnsen, "Rite Aid Targeting Net New Store Growth for the Future," *Drug Store News*, May 28, 2015, www.drugstorenews.com; *Rite Aid 10Q Quarterly Report*, July 5, 2016, www.riteaid.com and "Rite Aid Pharmacy Acquisitions," August 10, 2016, www.riteaid.com.

Chapter 10

1. Jeff Hainer, "The Renaissance of the American Shopping Mall," *Colliers International Knowledge Leader*, August 27, 2015, http://knowledge-leader.colliers.com.
2. "Five Tips for Retail Sites Selection," May 15, 2011, www.progressivegrocer.com. See also Michael Coretz, "21 Questions to Your New Tucson Commercial Real Estate Lease," July 5, 2016, http://commercial-real-estate-tucson.com.
3. *Compare Retail Portfolios*, August 12, 2016, https://theretailplanet.com/AnalyticsCompareRetail Portfolios.aspx.
4. Al Berry and Gary Faitler, "The 10 Common Mistakes in Retail Site Selection," Pitney Bowes Software, August 15, 2016, www.pb.com.
5. "Miami Retail: Reinventing Itself," December 2015, www.cushmanwakefield.com.
6. "Surging Demand for Urban Retail," September 9, 2015, http://www.cbre.us; Ryan Briggs, "Revitalizing Philadelphia's Market Street," February 12, 2016, http://urbanland.uli.org; and Suzette Pamley, "Thanks to Philly Millennials, Center City Undergoing a Radical Change," August 1, 2016, http://articles.philly.com.
7. Nick DeLuca, "Should Faneuil Hall Marketplace Become a Draw for Locals?" July 8, 2015, http://bostinno.streetwise.co (July 8, 2015); "Neighborhood Guide: Faneuil Marketplace," May 28, 2016, http://faneuilhallmarketplace.com; and "Faneuil Hall Marketplace," August 11, 2016, www.faneuilhall marketplace.com.
8. Author projections, based on International Council of Shopping Centers' data in "2013 Economic Impact of Shopping Centers," www.icsc.org.
9. "The Mall at Partridge Creek," June 16, 2016, www.shoppartridgecreek.com/about_us.
10. *Simon 2015 Annual Report*, January 29, 2016, http://nasdaqomx.mobular.net.
11. "North Jersey Malls Try New Programs in Search for Loyalty," April 24, 2016, www.northjersey.com.
12. Suzanne Kapner, "Macy's Reignites Retail Worries," May 2, 2016, *Wall Street Journal*, p.A2.
13. *International Council of Shopping Centers, "2013 Economic Impact of Shopping Centers," June 2016*, www.icsc.org; and *International Council of Shopping Centers, "U.S. Shopping-Center Classification and Definitions," June 2016*, www.icsc.org.
14. *International Council of Shopping Centers, "2013 Economic Impact of Shopping Centers," June 2016*, www.icsc.org.

15. *Ibid.*, and *International Council of Shopping Centers,* "U.S. Shopping-Center Classification and Definitions," June 2016, www.icsc.org.
16. Guitar Center, Inc. Corporate Relations, March 26, 2016, www.guitarcenter.com/pages/company-information; and Corporate Capital Trust, *2015 Annual Report*, www.corporatecapitaltrust.com.
17. *Apple Inc. 2015 Annual Report.*
18. *Home Depot 2015 Annual Report.*
19. See "3 Different Types of Commercial Real Estate Leases," July 27, 2016, https://42floors.com/edu/basics/types-of-commercial-real-estate-leases.
20. "New York's Upper Fifth Avenue World's Most Expensive Retail Street," November 18, 2015, www.cushmanwakefield.ca.
21. "Keeping Commercial Space Affordable for Local Businesses," May 20, 2016, https://ilsr.org; and "Store Size Caps," March 15, 2012, https://ilsr.org (March 15, 2012).

Chapter 11

1. Bon Phibbs, " Reasons Why Your Retail Turnover Is So High," February 14, 2014, www.retaildoc.com/blog.
2. Greatly adapted and updated by the authors to reflect 21st-century practices from Paul M. Mazur, *Principles of Organization Applied to Modern Retailing* (New York: Harper & Brothers, 1927). See also Shirley M. Stretch and Shelley S. Harp, "Retail Internships: An Experiential Learning Challenge," *Marketing Education Review*, 1(2), 1991, pp. 66–75; Steve Wood, "Organisational Rigidities and Marketing Theory: Examining the U.S. Department Store 1910–1965," *Service Industries Journal*, 31(5), 2011, pp. 747–770; and John Donnellan, *Merchandise Buying and Management*, 4th ed. (London: Bloomsbury Academic, 2013).
3. Rachel Feintzeig, "Full-Time Hires Buck the Trend at Fast-Food, Retail Chains," April 26, 2016, www.wsj.com.
4. "Target Careers: Culture," https://corporate.target.com/careers/culture (Accessed August 14, 2016); and *Target Inc. 2015 Annual Report.*
5. "Why Us," http://jobs.jobvite.com/zappos/p/why (Accessed August 14, 2016).
6. "100 Best Companies to Work For 2016," *Fortune*, March 3, 2016, http://fortune.com/best-companies/wegmans-food-markets-4/.
7. "What Makes Working Here Different," http://www.wegmans.com (Accessed August 14, 2016).
8. "Welcome," https://careers.homedepot.com/ and "Military Commitment," https://careers.homedepot.com (Accessed August 15, 2016).
9. Tracy Benson, "Motivating Millenials Takes More than Flexible Work Policies," February 11, 2016, *Harvard Business Review*, https://hbr.org/2016/02/

motivating-millennials-takes-more-than-flexible-work-policies.

10. Adapted from Tracy Benson, "Motivating Millennials Takes More than Flexible Work Policies," February 11, 2016, https://hbr.org and Ariana Ayu, "The Quick Guide to Motivating Millennials," February 19, 2015, www.inc.com.

11. "Steady Gains Made by Women on Fortune 1000 Company Boards," *2020 Women on Boards,* November 19, 2015, www.2020wob.com.

12. Lauaren Indivik, "Meet the Female CEOs Running Fashion's Biggest Brands," January 14, 2016, http://fashionista.com and Valentina Zarya, "The Percentage of Female CEOs in the Fortune 500 Drops to 4%," June 6, 2016, http://fortune.com.

13. "The World's 100 Most Powerful Women," www.forbes.com/power-women (Accessed June 6, 2016).

14. "Most Powerful Women in Business 2015," *Fortune,* www.fortune.com (Accessed August 15, 2016); "Global Leadership," www.enterpriseholdings.com (Accessed August 15, 2016); and "Pamela M. Nicholson," January 2016, www.enterpriseholdings.com.

15. "100 Best Companies to Work For," 2016, www.fortune.com/best-companies.

16. "Carmax: Our Core Values," www.carmax.com/about-carmax/culture-diversity (Accessed August 18, 2016).

17. "Supplier Diversity," http://corporate.walmart.com/suppliers/supplier-diversity (Accessed August 8, 2016).

18. "Walgreens Supplier Diversity: Clear Policy, Firm Commitment" www.walgreens.com/topic/sr/sr_supplier_diversity_home.jsp (Accessed August 10, 2016).

19. For a good illustration of the testing resources available for retailers, visit the Web site of Employee Selection & Development Inc. (www.employeeselect.com/selectTests.htm).

20. "Getting On Board: A Model for Integrating and Engaging New Employees," May 2008, www.boozallen.com and Retail Employee Onboarding Checklist, www.process.st (Accessed August 4, 2016).

21. "Our Employee First Culture," October 30, 2015, http://standfor.containerstore.com and "Careers with Heart: New Store Training," http://standfor.containerstore.com (Accessed June 7, 2016).

22. Adam Silverman, "Endless Aisle Capabilities Drive Incremental Demand for Retailers," April 7, 2015, http://blogs.forrester.com/category/clienteling.

23. Adapted by the authors from Anthony J. Rucci, Steven P. Kirn, and Richard T. Quinn, "The Employee-Customer-Profit Chain at Sears," *Harvard Business Review*, 76, January–February 1998, pp. 82–97; and Lars Grønholdt and Anne Martensen, "The Service-Profit Chain," *15th International Marketing Trends Conference*, 2016.

24. Adapted by the authors from from Ed Sykes, "Jump Start Your Employee Motivation," October 9, 2011, www.thesykesgrp.com. See also Maria Falk Mikkelsen, Christian Bøtcher Jacobsen, and Lotte Bøgh Andersen, "Managing Employee Motivation: Exploring the Connections between Managers' Enforcement Actions, Employee Perceptions, and Employee Intrinsic Motivation," *International Public Management Journal,* 2015, pp. 1–23 and Julia Weiherl and Doris Masal, "Transformational Leadership and Followers' Commitment to Mission Changes," *International Journal of Public Administration,* 2016, pp. 1–11.

Chapter 12

1. See "Profit Margin," www.shopify.ca/encyclopedia/profit-margin (Accessed August 16, 2016); and "Technology Retail Industry Profitability Ratios," http://csimarket.com (Accessed August 9, 2016).

2. *Industry Norms & Key Business Ratios* (New York: Dun & Bradstreet, 2013–14); and "Retail Sector Profitability Ratios," http://csimarket.com (Accessed August 9, 2016).

3. *Retail Monitor*, March 2016, http://goo.gl/VUESB1.

4. Tom Ryan, "Study: E-Commerce Is Eroding Retail Profitability," May 10, 2016, http://www.retailwire.com.

5. Peter Grant, "Turning Point? U.S. Commercial-Property Sales Plunge in February," March 22, 2016.

6. Liam Peven, "Shopping-Center REITs are on Many Investors' Lists," March 8, 2016, www.wsj.com.

7. "How to Cash in on IPOs," January 2010, www.kiplinger.com; "IPO Central," April 29, 2012, www.hoovers.com; and Debra Worchardt, "Retail-Related IPOs Perform Relatively Well in 2015," December 24, 2015, http://campfire-capital.com.

8. Gregory Andre, "Stores for Sale! Retailers and Restaurant's Spin Off Real-Estate," September 9, 2015, www.klgates.com.

9. "eBay & PayPal to Become Independent Companies in 2015," September 30, 2014, www.ebayinc.com; Tandherese Poletti, "eBay Investors Lose Patience as PayPal Spin-off Takes a Bite Out of Earnings," January 28, 2016, www.marketwatch.com.

10. Lauren Silva Laughlin, "eBay-PayPal Spin-off: Why Shareholders Are Loving It," September 30, 2014, http://fortune.com.

11. Alicia Stice, "Plus-Size Hot Topic Spinoff Torrid Signs Columbia Mall Lease," www.columbiatribune.com (February 27, 2016).

12. Jon Springer, "Sav-A-Lot files for Potential Spin-off," January 7, 2016, http://supermarketnews.com.

13. Rachel Dodes, Ann Zimmerman, and Jeffrey McCracken, "Retailers Brace for Major Change—Chain Stores See a Future with Fewer Outlets, Brands—and Thinner Profits," December 27, 2008, www.wsj.com.

14. "First Quarter Bankruptcy Filings Down 5 Percent from 2015, Commercial Filings Increase 24 Percent," April 5, 2016, www.abi.org.

15. "Alix Partners Bankruptcy Study," October 26, 2015, www.alixpartners.com; and Steven Church, "U.S. Stores Face Win-Or-Die Sprint When They File for Bankruptcy," November 2, 2015, www.bloomberg.com.

16. Barbara Farfan, "All Bankrupt Retailing Companies: 2015 Chapter 11 and Chapter 7 Filings," www.thebalance.com (July 11, 2016).

17. Hiroko Tabuchi, "American Apparel Files for Bankruptcy," October 5, 2015, www.nytimes.com.

18. Linette Lopez, "The Company That Sells Wedding Rings to Much of America Is in Big Trouble," www.businessinsider.com (June 13, 2016).

19. Based on material from "Business Code of Conduct and Ethics," http://ir.homedepot.com (Accessed August 25, 2016).

20. See Jared Hecht, "The 5 Worst Cash-Flow Mistakes Small-Business Owners Make," September 25, 2015, www.entrepreneur.com; and "Five Cash Flow Problems Faced by Offline Retailers and How to Manage Them," www.storediscoveryoptimisation.com (June 8, 2016).

21. Computed by the authors based on data in "2013 Store Construction & Outfitting Survey," 2013, www.chainstoreage.com.

22. Company annual reports.

23. "Macy's, Inc. Outlines Cost Efficiency Initiatives and Lists Store Locations to Be Closed," www.businesswire.com (July 6, 2016).

Chapter 13

1. "Navigating the New Digital Divide—Capitalizing on Digital Influence in Retail," December 2015, http://www2.deloitte.com; and "US Retail Sales to Near $5 Trillion in 2016," December 21, 2015, www.emarketer.com.

2. Based on material in Susan Reda, "STORES Trends," *STORES Magazine,* April 2016. Reprinted by permission.

3. See Mary Jo Bitner, Amy L. Ostrom, and Felicia N. Morgan, "Service Blueprinting: A Practical Technique for Service Innovation," *California Management Review*, 50, Spring 2008, pp. 66–94; and *Izac Ross, Lauren Chapman Ruiz, and Shahrzad Samadzadeh,* "Service Blueprints: Laying the Foundation," August 20, 2014, www.cooper.com/journal.

4. Marian Wilson, "Annual Store Construction and Outfitting Survey," 2011, www.chainstoreage.com; and Marian Wilson, "Costs Going Up: Annual Study Tracks Costs of Building and Outfitting Stores," 2013, www.chainstoreage.com.

5. "2015 Retail Sustainability Management Report," 2015, http://www.rila.org; and "Retail Store Fact Sheet: Energy Management for Your Business," July 21, 2016, www.pge.com.

6. Christine Binkley, "Stores That Sell Luxury Get Stingy About Energy Costs," April 15, 2015, www.wsj.com.

7. David Bodamer, "Talking Points," *Retail Traffic,* January 2008, p. 23.

8. "Hidden Cameras and Retail Loss Prevention," September 3, 2014, www.brickhousesecurity.com.

9. Square Magstripe Reader. "Small Credit Card Reader, Big Possibilities," https://squareup.com (Accessed August 22, 2016).

10. "Average Debit Card Interchange Fee by Payment Card Network," www.federalreserve.gov (Accessed August 22, 2016).

11. Ari Weinberg, "Credit Versus Cash," March 17, 2016, http://abcnews.go.com.

12. Melissa Johnson, "The True Cost of Debit Card Transactions," March 9, 2015, www.merchantmaverick.com; and Jim Marous, "Cash Beats Debit, Credit, Checks, and Mobile as Payment Choice," May 6, 2014, http://thefinancialbrand.com.

13. Sofia, "What Do More Payment Options Mean and Why Online Retailers Need to Have Them," November 17, 2015, https://letstalkpayments.com.

14. John Stewart, "While EMV and Mobile Captivate the Industry, Big Retailers Express Frustrations," *Digital Transactions: Trends in the Digital Exchange of Value,* April 1, 2015, http://digitaltransactions.net.

15. Malay Kundu, "How to Stop Those Self-Checkout Thieves," August 12, 2014, www.retailtouchpoints.com.

16. Mark Wilson, "Inside-Amazons-Quest-to-Brand-Your-Home," April 2, 2015, www.fastcodesign.com.

17. Dan Berthiaume, "Supply and Demand—Lowe's, Home Hardware Align Supply Chain with Consumer Demand," March 6, 2015, www.chainstoreage.com.

18. "IDC—InterScales Scale Manager," April, 2015, www.applieddatacorp.com.

19. Evan Puzey, Kewill, "Outsourcing and the Need for Increased Supply Chain Visibility," January 8, 2015, www.chainstoreage.com.

20. Bill Turner, "From Alarm Monitoring to Crisis Management," *LP Magazine*, May 16, 2015, http://lpportal.com; and Miglė Šontaitė-Petkevičienė, "Crisis Management to Avoid Damage for Corporate Reputation: The Case of Retail Chain Crisis in the Baltic Countries," *Procedia—Social and Behavioral Sciences*, 156, November 26, 2014, pp. 452–457.

Chapter 14

1. Sharon Terlep and Greg Bensinger, "Amazon to Expand Buttons for Ordering," June 27, 2016, *Wall Street Journal*, pp. B1–B2.

2. Pam Danzinger, "Small Is the Next Big Story in Retail," October 9, 2015, http://blog.marketresearch.com.

3. Suzette Parmley, "Department Store Anchors at Malls Face a New Demographic of Shoppers," www.twincities.com (Accessed January 26, 2016); and Anne D'innocenzio, "Department Stores Hope to Recapture Appeal, Be Destinations," http://bigstory.ap.org (Accessed August 11, 2016).

4. Scott Welty, "Retail 20/20: A Vision for the Digital Age, Part II," September 5, 2015, http://blog.jda.com.

5. *Costco 2015 Annual Report,* http://phx.corporate-ir.net.

6. *Tilly's, Inc. 2015 Annual Report (10-K).* http://phx.corporate-ir.net.

7. "Four Merchandising Opportunities You're Missing Out On," December 3, 2015, www.breakthrubev.com.

8. *Inditex Annual Report 2015,* www.inditex.com.

9. *Ross Stores 2015 Annual Report,* http://investors.ross stores.com.

10. "Our Services," www.doneger.com/services.html (Accessed August 26, 2016).

11. "Fashion Consulting Buying Office," www.vibitalia.com (Accessed August 20, 2016).

12. "About BrandSource," www.joinbrandsource.com (26, 2016).

13. "L.L. Bean: Partnering to Improve Forecast Accuracy," https://jda.com (Accessed February 2016); and "Company Information," www.llbean.com (Accessed August 28, 2016).

14. "About Brookstone," www.brookstone.com (Accessed August 27, 2016); and "7-Eleven Profile," http://corp.7-eleven.com (Accessed August 27, 2016).

15. *Dollar Tree, Inc. Form 10-K,* http://files.shareholder.com.

16. Oracle, "Retail Assortment Planning," www.oracle.com (December 8, 2015).

17. Carolyn Heneghan, "Retailers Overhaul Private Label Brands, Challenging Manufacturers' Dominance," www.fooddive.com (February 24, 2016).

18. Elaine Watson, "CPG Industry Sales Trends Are 'Stagnant,' with Dollar Sales Growth Being Largely Driven by Price Increases, Says IRI," www.food navigator-usa.com (January 22, 2015).

19. "Private Label Today: Popularity Keeps Growing," www.plmainternational.com (July 2016).

20. Elizabeth Weise, and Eli Blumenthal, "Amazon Hoping Private Labels Hit Millennials' Sweet Spot," May 17, 2016, *USA Today,* p. 2B.

21. "Private Label's Market Share Climbs in 13 of 20 Countries across Europe," www.plmainternational.com (Accessed June 13, 2016); and Lynn Dornblaser, "Top Trends in Global Private Brands Innovation," http://fmi16.mapyourshow.com (Accessed June 22, 2016).

22. "H. T. Traders: Our Stores," www.harristeeter.com (Accessed August 26, 2016).

23. *Jabel Parayil,* "U.S: Battle for Value and Volume Growth Heats Up in Mature Market," www.tissue worldmagazine.com (Accessed May 16, 2016).

24. Gordon Wade, "Category Management Mastery: The Key to Growth!" http://catman.global (Accessed June 2016).

25. Al Heller, "Consumer-Centric Category Management a Fresh Spin on Maximizing Performance," Fourth Quarter 2015, www.acnielsen.com.

26. Information Resources, Inc., "Manufacturer and Retailer Report Cards," *NeoBrief.* Issue 1, 1999, pp. 3–6.

27. "The Container Store Equips Store Teams to Make Better Decisions," www.microstrategy.com (Accessed August 26, 2016).

28. "Hibbett Sport- JDA Real Results," https://jda.com (Accessed August 20, 2016).

29. "SAS Demand Forecasting for Retail,"www.sas.com (Accessed August 20, 2016).

30. Arwen Heredia, "Innovation Pipelines Are Built on Logic, Not Luck," March 17, 2015, http://blog.mindjet.com.

31. "DSW Supplies a Shoe That Fits- DSW Integrates Merchandise Planning with Other Systems for the Perfect Fit," www.sas.com/en_us/customers/dsw-customization.html (Accessed August 30, 2016).

Chapter 15

1. Based on material in Craig Guillot, "Organize, Optimize, Synchronize," *STORES Magazine,* February 2016. Reprinted by permission.

2. Kristina Gustafson, "Retailers Are Losing $1.75 Trillion Over This," CNBC, November 30, 2015, www.cnbc.com.

3. "Real 3-D Virtual Trade Shows," August 31, 2016, www.goexhibit.com; and "Total Retail—Virtual Conference and Expo," August 31, 2016, http://virtualshow.mytotalretail.com/.

4. *Big Lots 2015 Annual Report.*

5. "2016 State of Retailer-Vendor Supply Chain Relationships," November 20, 2015, www.compliance networks.com.

6. "Tech Retailers Insist They're Smiling at UAE Apple Store Opening," November 2, 2015, http://7days.ae; and Kris Hiiemaa, "Retailers: How to Beat Manufacturers and Online?" March 11, 2016, https://erply.com.

7. *TJX Companies 2015 Annual Report.*

8. "Sherwin-Williams/Valspar: FTC Likely to Closely Scrutinize Wholesale Level Competition; Potential Post-Merger Wholesale Price, Slotting Fee, Contract Incentive Effects," May 9, 2016, https://thecapitolforum.com; and "3 Factors to Consider Before Selling to Big-Box Retailers," June 28, 2016, www.cit.com.

9. Claire Swedberg, "GS1 U.S. Survey Finds Strong RDID Adoption," *RFID Journal,* www.rfidjournal.com (Accessed June 30, 2016).

10. Thomas Watson, "Simple Cost Analysis for RFID Options—Choice Must Fit the Organization's Needs and Budget," *Information Technology Asset Knowledge,* April 28, 2015, www.itak.iaitam.org.

11. Claire Swedberg, "Macy's Launches Pick to the Last Unit Program for Omnichannel Sales," *RFID Journal,* January 16, 2016, www.rfidjournal.com; and Bob Trebilcock, "RFID: The Macy's Way," *Modern Materials Handling,* June 1, 2013, www.mmh.com.

12. "Not Just for Retailers: Four Ways RFID Can Benefit Retail Brands," February 17, 2016, http://cybra.com;

"Leaders Representing Retail and Apparel Industries to Discuss RFID's Benefits at RFID Journal Live!2016," March 31, 2016, www.rfidjournal.com; and Michelle Russell, "UK Apparel Market Realising Real Benefits of RFID," April 26, 2016, www.just-style.com.

13. *2016 Super Valu Annual Report.*

14. *2015 Annual Report Sears Holding Corporation*; and Lisa Fickenscher, "Sears Finds a New Way to Rake in Cash," July 14, 2015, http://nypost.com.

15. Jerry Andrews, "CPFR: Considering the Options, Advantages, and Pitfalls," April–May, 2008, www.sdcexec.com; and "CPFR Guidelines and Resources," September 2, 2016, www.gs1us.org.

16. "United Problem Solvers," September 2, 2016, https://solvers.ups.com.

17. "Voluntary Guidelines for Hanger Specifications for Floor-Ready Merchandise," May 19, 2016, www.gs1us.org; and "Nordstrom Full Line and Rack—Nordstrom Supplier Compliance Manual," July 29, 2016, http://nordstromsupplier.com.

18. Kim Souza, "The Supply Side: Walmart Tells Suppliers to Expect 'Healthy Tensions' in 2016," February 25, 2016, http://talkbusiness.net; and "Why You Need Lean Supply Chain Management," September 2, 2016, www.usanfranonline.com.

19. Martin Hingley, Adam Lindgreen, and David B. Grant, "Intermediaries in Power-Laden Retail Supply Chains: An Opportunity to Improve Buyer–Supplier Relationships and Collaboration," *Industrial Marketing Management*, 50, 2015, pp. 78–84.

20. Bill O'Boyle, "Direct Store Delivery (DSD) Powers Growth: Visibility Powers DSD," June 8, 2016, www.dmwandh.com.

21. Ibid; and Josh Sosland and Joanie Spencer, "Hostess 2.0," February 12, 2016, www.foodbusinessnews.net.

22. Dan Gilmore, "Amazon—The Most Audacious Logistics Plan in History?" February 18, 2016, www.scdigest.com; and *Amazon.com 2015 Annual Report.*

23. Davide Sher, "Ultimaker Listens to Its Consumers with Upgraded 3D Printers at CES," January 5, 2016, https://3dprintingindustry.com.

24. See Stan Aronow, Mike Burkett, Jim Romano, and Kimberly Nilles, "The Art and Science of Supply Chain Leadership," September 21, 2015, www.supplychain247.com.

25. Tim O'Reilly, "How On Demand Logistics Could Save Brick and Mortar Retail," September 17, 2015, https://medium.com; and John Waldron, "Target's Omnichannel Two-App Tactic," May 10, 2016, http://etaileast.wbresearch.com.

26. "National Retail Security Survey 2015," June 30, 2016, https://nrf.com.

27. "2015 Customer Returns in the Retail Industry," December 17, 2015, https://nrf.com; and Kyle Hagerty, "Reverse Logistics: The Hidden Cost of E-Commerce," July 27, 2016, www.bisnow.com.

Chapter 16

1. "Inventory Management System," July 19, 2016, https://sales-software.financesonline.com/c/inventory-management-software.

2. For more information on inventory valuat ion, visit the Investopedia.com Web site, http://www.investopedia.com/articles/02/060502.asp.

3. John Karolefski, "The Future of Demand Forecasting," November 15, 2015, www.progressivegrocer.com.

4. "Weather-Driven Demand Planning," November 15, 2015, www.planalytics.com.

5. "Greeting Card Publishers—Industry Facts and Trends—Hoovers," March 9, 2016, www.hoovers.com/industry-facts.greeting-card-publishers.1464.html.

6. Adapted by the authors from "EAN-13 Background Information," April 18, 2012, www.barcodeisland.com; and "Express Guide to Retail Barcodes," October 8, 2016, www.gs1ie.org.

7. First Insight, "Weeding Out the Weak: Real-Time Insight from Customers Who Know," Fall 2011, www.firstinsight.com.

8. "First Insight, "Improved David's Bridal Forecast Accuracy by More than 20%," http://info.firstinsight.com (Accessed September 5, 2016).

9. Eric Jensen, "What Is the Real Cost of Dead Inventory?" June 6, 2016, www.inddist.com/article/2016/06/what-real-cost-dead-inventory.

Chapter 17

1. Boby Kurlani, "H&M plans to Enter India's E-tail Sector," *Times of India*, September 11, 2015, http://timesofindia.indiatimes.com.

2. Chandra Steele, "The 11 Best Shopping Apps to Compare Prices," November 23, 2015, www.pcmag.com/slideshow/story/290959.

3. See, for example, Kyle B. Murray, *The American Retail Value Proposition: Crafting Unique Experiences at Compelling Prices* (Toronto: University of Toronto Press, 2016).

4. Jeff John Roberts, "Supreme Court Won't Hear Apple's Appeal in E-Books Price Fixing Case," *Fortune*, March 7, 2016, www.fortune.com.

5. "Price Discrimination: Robinson-Patman Violations," www.ftc.gov/tips-advice/competition-guidance/guide-antitrust-laws/price-discrimination-robinson-patman (Accessed September 10, 2016).

6. Matsushima, Noriaki, and Akira Miyaoka, "The Effects of Resale-Below-Cost Laws in the Presence of a Strategic Manufacturer," *Quantitative Marketing and Economics,* Vol. 13, No.1 (2015), pp. 59-91.

7. See "New Best Practices Guide Shows Unit Pricing Is a Great Deal," www.nist.gov/news-events/news/2015/02/new-best-practices-guide-shows-unit-pricing-great-deal, (February 3, 2015); and "A Guide to Retail Pricing Laws and Regulations," www.nist.gov/pml/wmd/metric/pricing-laws.cfm (Accessed December 15, 2011).

8. Ken Clark, "Sticker Shock," *Chain Store Age* (September 2000), p. 88. See also David C. Wyld, "Back to the Future? Why 'Old School' Item Pricing Laws May Hold Back the Use of RFID in Retail Settings," www.coastal.edu (Spring 2008).

9. Selling price may also be computed by transposing the markup formula into.

$$\text{Retail selling price} = \frac{\text{Merchandise cost}}{1 - \text{Markup}} = \$17.14$$

10. Merchandise cost may also be computed by transposing the markup formula into.

$$\text{Merchandise cost} = (\text{Retail selling price})(1 - \text{Markup}) = \$4.794$$

11. "Prepaid Card Buying Guide," www.consumerreports .org (March 2016).

12. *Source:* "About Stripes Convenience Stores," www .stripesstores.com/about-us/news.cms/2016 (accessed September 12, 2016).

13. See "How to Negotiate a New Car Price Effectively Do Your Homework Before You Go to the Dealership," *Consumer Reports,* www.consumerreports.org (March 2016).

14. See James Wilkie, Kenneth Manning, David Sprott, and Galen Bodenhausen ,"The 'Even-Odd Effect' in Consumers' Reactions to Prices." *Advances in Consumer Research*, Vol.43 (2015), pp. 738–739.

15. See Jeffrey Meyer and Venkatesh Shankar, "Pricing Strategies for Hybrid Bundles: Analytical Model and Insights," *Journal of Retailing*, Vol. 92, No. 2 (2016), pp. 133–146 and Ruiliang Yan and Subir Bandyopadhyay, "The Profit Benefits of Bundle Pricing of Complementary Products," *Journal of Retailing and Consumer Services*, Vol. 18 (2011), pp. 355–361.

Chapter 18

1. Based on material in Susan Reda, "STORES Trends: March 2016," *STORES Magazine*, March 2016, https://nrf.com/news/stores-trends-march-2016. (Reprinted by permission).

2. Micah Solomon, "The Future of the Retail Customer Experience: Experts Discuss Trends and Engagement," February 12, 2016, www.forbes.com.

3. "Bass Pro Shops, Altoona, IA," www.basspro.com (Accessed September 18, 2016).

4. Matt Siegel, "Jungle Jim's and the Art of the Tourist-Attraction Grocery Store," May 23, 2016, www.epicurious .com/expert-advice/jungle-jims-grocery-store-ohio-article; and "Jungle Jim's International Market," www.junglejims. com (Accessed September 20, 2016).

5. Mary Beth Quick, "Neiman Marcus, Nordstrom & Other Retailers Trying Out Smart Fitting Room Mirrors," May 11, 2015, https://consumerist.com; and Christina Binkley, "Store Wars," August 8, 2016, www.wsj.com.

6. Harmen Oppewal and Harry Timmermans, "Retailer Self-Perceived Store Image and Competitive Position," *International Review of Retail, Distribution and Consumer Research*, 7(1), 1997; and Dan Berthiaume, "Autozone Revs Up Network," January 25, 2016, www.chainstoreage.com.

7. Humayun Khan, "Visual Merchandising 101: How to Create Store Designs with High-Converting Displays" May 2, 2016, www.shopify.ca.

8. David Talton, "Top 5: Retail Store Interiors," January 7, 2016, http://culturescenemag.com.

9. "Apple's New In-Store Innovation? Trees," May 20, 2016, www.pymnts.com.

10. Humayun Khan, "How Retailers Manipulate Sight, Smell, and Sound to Trigger Purchase Behavior in Customers," April 25, 2016, www.shopify.com.

11. C. C. Sullivan and Barbara Horwitz-Bennett, "Emerging Trends in Commercial Flooring," *Building Design + Construction*, July 2, 2014, www .bdcnetwork.com.

12. Melanie, "Using Retail Technology to Create a Personalized In-Store Experience," May 25, 2016, http://awgadvertising.com.

13. Traci Dawn Carneal, "Why Restrooms Matter," February 12, 2016, www.cstoredecisions.com.

14. "Hyatt 2015/2016 Corporate Responsibility Scorecard," http://thrive.hyatt.com.

15. Brian Sutter, "Keeping Up with the Competitors: With Small Business It's Personal," May 2, 2016, www .waspbarcode.com.

16. "Supermarket Savvy: Layout, Placement and Price," March 3, 2016, www.fitnessbox.co.nz; and Tiffany Craig, "Grocery Store Secrets: Dissecting the Supermarket Layout," May 20, 2016, www.khou.com.

17. "Key Trends in Plastic, Semi-Transparent Merchandising Displays," July 7, 2014, www.kdmpop.com.

18. *Ibid.*

19. "Trends in Retail Displays," July 21, 2016, www. retailcustomerexperience.com.

20. For example, see Paco Underhill, *Why We Buy: Updated and Revised* (New York: Simon & Schuster, 2009); Ellen Byron, "The Slower You Shop, the More You Spend," October 20, 2015, www.wsj.com; and "Why We Buy," March 18, 2016, http://news.fitnyc.edu.

21. TopShop Creates VR Catwalk at Flagship London Store," http://oculusrift-blog.com/topshop-creates-virtual-catwalk-flagship-london-store/2705 (Accessed September 16, 2016).

22. Byron, "The Slower You Shop, the More You Spend"; and "Craftsy Classes," www.acmoore.com/classes/ (Accessed September 17, 2016).

23. "*Nespresso* Announces New Boutiques with Re-Designed Shopping Experience," November 2015, www.nestle-nespresso.com.

24. "New York Company Debuts Pure Mobile-Only Grocery Checkout," January 18, 2016, www.mobile paymentstoday.com; "Shoprite Mobile Scan,"

www.shoprite.com/mobilescan/ (Accessed September 18, 2016); and "Expresscart," January 2016, http://devpost.com/software/expresscart.

25. Annelise Kleinbaum, "Restaurants in Retail Stores Lure Hungry Shoppers," May 27, 2014, https://www.specialtyfood.com.

26. Marianne Wilson, "Amazon Expands Deal with Twitter to Include 'Wish List'," September 24, 2014, www.chainstoreage.com; and Ellis Welner, "An Important Notice from Amazon," March 21, 2015, www.newyorker.com.

27. Chun-Tuan Chang and Zhao-Hong Cheng, "Tugging on Heartstrings: Shopping Orientation, Mindset, and Consumer Responses to Cause-Related Marketing," *Journal of Business Ethics*, 127(2), 2015, pp. 337–350.

28. Bob Negen, "Retail with a Cause," November 30, 2015, http://retailernowmag.com.

Chapter 19

1. Based on material in Susan Reda, "STORES Trends," *STORES Magazine,* February 2016. Reprinted by permission.

2. *Domino's Pizza 2016 Annual Report.*

3. Computed by the authors from data in "Leading National Advertisers Index," June 26, 2016, http://adage.com; and *2015 Amazon Annual Report.*

4. MikMak, www.mikmak.tv (Accessed September 26, 2016); and Jordan Crook, "MikMak Is the Smartphone-Based Reinvention of the Infomercial," May 12, 2015, https://techcrunch.com.

5. Sarah Halzak, "The Chatbots Are Coming—And They Want to Help You Buy Stuff," April 13, 2016, www.washingtonpost.com.

6. Guiomar Martín-Herrán and Simon P. Sigué, "An Integrative Framework of Cooperative Advertising: Should Manufacturers Continuously Support Retailer Advertising?" *Journal of Business Research,* July 31, 2016.

7. "State of the Blogosphere 2011," November 4, 2011, http://technorati.com; Andy Crestodina, "Research Reveals Success Tactics of Top Bloggers: 11 Trends," Sepember 2015, www.orbitmedia.com/blog; and Jessica Hibbard, "Customers Are the New Celebrities," January 17, 2016, https://nrf.com.

8. See also Mark Smock, "Don't Make These Top 10 Selling Mistakes!" May 3, 2012, www.woopidoo.com/articles/smock/selling-mistakes.htm.

9. "Retail Calendar and Sales Promotions," October 27, 2015, www.vm-unleashed.com; "How Discount Culture Is Shaping the Sales Promotion Industry," January 7, 2016, www.promorati.com/blog/how-discount-culture-is-shaping-the-sales-promotion-industry/; and Humayun Khan, "3 Time-Tested Retail Sales Promotions That Drive Foot Traffic and Build Loyalty," May 3, 2016, www.shopify.com.

10. "In-Store," www.newsamerica.com/products-services/instore (Accessed September 26, 2016).

11. For much more information, see Brandon Carter, "Coupon Statistics, The Ultimate Collection," September 2, 2016, http://blog.accessdevelopment.com/ultimate-collection-coupon-statistics.

12. "Getting to the Core," *Convenience Store News*, January 2016, p. 106.

13. "Loyalty Marketing: Creating Stickiness in a Distracted World," August 2016, www.emarketer.com.

14. Thorsten Hennig-Thurau, Caroline Wiertz, and Fabian Feldhaus, "Does Twitter Matter? The Impact of Microblogging Word of Mouth on Consumers' Adoption of New Movies," *Journal of the Academy of Marketing Science,* 43(3), 2015, pp. 375–394.

15. *Netflix 2015 Annual Report*, p. 8.

16. George G. Panigyrakis and Cleopatra A. Veloutsou, "Brand Manager's Planning Role for Fast Moving Consumer Good Products," *Global Perspectives in Marketing for the 21st Century* (Switzerland: Springer International Publishing, 2015), pp. 182–185.

17. *Netflix 2015 Annual Report*, p. 26.

18. Eliza Fisher, "E-Mail Marketing Best Practices: Are You In or Out?" October 21, 2015, www.socialannex.com/blog.

19. "The Circular Revolution," October 2015, https://cloud.oracle.com; and "Supervalu," http://hga.com/work/supervalu (Accessed September 25, 2016).

Chapter 20

1. Based on material from Susan Reda, "STORES Trends," February 2016. (Reprinted by permission).

2. Denise Lee Yohn, "What Sports Authority and Dick's Sporting Goods Indicate about the State of the Retail Industry," March 30, 2016, www.forbes.com.

3. Phil Rosenthal, "Sports Authority in Classic Retail Struggle with Size, Strategy, Debt," March 2, 2016, www.chicagotribune.com; Grace L. Williams, "Sports Authority's Pain, Whose Gain?" March 2, 2016, www.forbes.com; and Robert Cross, "Lessons from Sports Authority's Demise," March 24, 2016, http://revenueanalytics.com.

4. *The TJX Companies Inc. 2016 Annual Report/10 K.*

5. "Designing a Global Channel Strategy to Accelerate Growth; All Channels Are Not Created Equally," March 16, 2016, http://www2.deloitte.com.

6. Marianne Wilson, "Food Lion Continues Remodeling Push," March 9, 2016, www.chainstoreage.com; and Food Lion, www.aholddelhaize.com (Accessed September 28, 2016).

7. Ibid.

8. Thomas O'Connor, "How to Implement Effective Benchmarking in Your Retail Supply Chain," May 19, 2016, www.gartner.com.

9. "Benchmarks by Industry," www.theacsi.org/customer-satisfaction-benchmarks/benchmarks-by-industry (Accessed September 30, 2016).

10. Parasuraman, Valarie A. Zeithaml, and Leonard L. Berry, "Alternative Scales for Measuring Service Quality: A Comparative Assessment Based on Psychometric and Diagnostic Criteria," *Journal of Retailing*, 70, Fall 1994, pp. 201–230. See also François A. Carrillat, Fernando Jaramillo, and Jay P. Mulki, "The Validity of the SERVQUAL and SERVPERF Scales," *International Journal of Service Industry Management*, 18, December 2007, pp. 472–490; Riadh Ladhari, "Developing E-Service Quality Scales: A Literature Review," *Journal of Retailing and Consumer Services*, 10, 2010, pp. 464–477; Hokey Min and Hyesung Min, "Benchmarking the Service Quality of Fast-Food Restaurant Franchises in the USA: A Longitudinal Study," *Benchmarking: An International Journal*, 18, April 2011, pp. 282–300; Nor Atiqah Aima Roslan, Norasmiha Mohd Nor, and Eta Wahab, "Service Quality: A Case Study Using SERVQUAL Model," *Advanced Science Letters*, 21(6), 2015, pp. 2159–2162; and Seema Sharma, "Using SERVQUAL to Assess the Customer Satisfaction Level: A Study of an Urban Cooperative Bank," *Journal of Economics and Public Finance*, 2(1), 2016, pp. 57–85.

11. "How Supply Chain Excellence Creates Economic Value," October 19, 2015, www.supplychainconsortium.com.

12. "The 2015 A. T. Kearney Global Retail Development Index," www.atkearney.com (Accessed September 27, 2016).

13. Extracted from material in Austen Mulinder, "Hear Today . . . Or Gone Tomorrow? Winners Listen to Customers," September 1999, *Retailing Issues Letter*, p. 5.

14. Walter Loeb, "Why Retailers Must Restructure In 2016," January 4, 2016, www.forbes.com.

15. Efraim Levy, "Industry Surveys: Multiline Retail," March 2016, *Standard & Poor's Industry Surveys*, p. 35.

16. Suzanne Kapner, "Fast-Fashion Tricks Are on Display at Department-Store Chains," September 29, 2016, www.wsj.com.

17. Information based on authors' review of many sources, including *Kohl's 2016 Annual Report*.

18. Liz Sandwith, "Is the Retail Sector Unclear about the Role of Internal Audit?" August 5, 2016, www.iia.org.uk.

Appendix

1 U.S. Bureau of Labor Statistics, "Employment by Major Industry Sector," www.bls.gov/news.release/ecopro.t02.htm, December 8, 2015.

2 Based on material in Susan Reda, "Chief Concerns," *STORES Magazine*, June 2015, pp. 22-25. (Reprinted by permission).

Name Index

Subject Index

technology and, 62, 145
typical services, 53
Customer space, 470
Cut cases, 474

D

Database management
  data mining and micromarketing,
    219–220
  data warehousing, 218–219
  explanation of, 217–218
  UPC and EDI data, 220–221
Database retailing, 156
Dead area, 469
Debit-card system, 343
Decentralized buying organization, 362
Delivery
  as customer service, 53
  in direct marketing, 161
Demand fluctuations, 444–445
Demand-oriented pricing,
    438, 442, 443
Demographics, 190–192, 194–196
Department stores, traditional
  merchandising in, 359
  organizational structure of, 298–300
  retail strategy mix, 138, 143–144
Depth of assortment, 370
Description buying, 387
Destination retailers, 131, 248
Differentiated marketing
  explanation of, 84, 206
  strategy examples, 208
Direct costs, 326
Direct mail advertising, 487
Direct marketing
  advantages/disadvantages of, 155
  customer database for, 156
  domain of, 156
  explanation of, 154
  key issues in, 161
  measuring results of, 160–161
  strategy for, 159–161
  trends in, 156–158
Direct product profitability (DPP), 441
Direct selling, 161–163
Direct store delivery (DSD),
    396–397
Discount orientation, 428
Discretionary income, 190
Disguised surveys, 227
Displays
  in E-retailing, 475–476
  in traditional stores, 473–474
Display windows, 466–467
Dissociative group, 192
Distributed promotion effort, 504

Distribution channel. *See* Channel of
    distribution
Diversified retailers
  explanation of, 136
  organizational structure of, 300–301,
    302
Diversity
  in consumers, 189
  in employment, 305
Dollar control, 405, 411, 419
Dollar discount stores, 146
Domestic vs. global sourcing, 373
Downsizing, 137
Downtown revitalization, 267–268
DPP (direct product profitability), 441
DSD (direct store delivery), 396–397
Dual marketing, 122
Dump bins, 474
DWcodes, 220

E

Early markdown policy, 449
Early recovery of cash, 435
Ease of entry, 112
Easy Analytic Software, 258
Economic base, 253, 258–259
Economic consumers, 430
Economic order quantity (EOQ), 424
Economy
  current U.S. climate, 40–42
  global, 98
  impact on retailing, 41, 321
  recession (2008), 321–322
  retailing impact on, 25–26
  retailing strategies and, 42–43
  as uncontrollable variable, 88
ECR (efficient consumer response), 395
EDI. *See* Electronic data interchange
Editor & Publisher Market Guide,
    258–259, 260
EDLP (everyday low pricing), 443–444
Efficient consumer response (ECR), 395
Electronic article surveillance, 399
Electronic banking, 60
Electronic data interchange (EDI),
    220–221, 388, 395, 399
Electronic point-of-sale systems, 344
Electronic retailing. *See* E-retailing
Employee benefits, 296, 311, 342
Employee discounts, 447
Employee Polygraph Protection Act, 308
Employees
  communicating with, 337, 338
  compensation of, 310–311, 338
  diversity in, 305
  efficient use of, 337–338
  empowerment of, 51

merchandising functions of, 360, 364
motivation of, 311–313
needs of, 293
performance standards for, 337
productivity of, 337–338
recruitment of, 306
selection process for, 306–309
store atmosphere and, 469
supervision of, 311–313
women, 304–305
Employee scheduling, 337
Employee space, 470
Employee theft, 399, 401
Employee training, 309–310, 337
Employee turnover, 292–293,
    301–303, 337
Empowerment, of employees, 51
Energy management, 339–340
Enhanced shopping experience, 477
Ensemble displays, 474
Environmental factors, 208
EOQ (economic order quantity), 424
Equal store organization, 300, 301
E-retailing
  advantages/disadvantages of,
    167–168, 476
  examples of, 170–171
  factors to consider, 167–170
  global index of, 165, 166
  mobile apps for, 170
  online grocery business, 188–189
  role of Web in, 164
  sales tax and, 158
  scope of, 165–166
  "store" atmosphere, 474–476
  Web user characteristics, 167
Ethics. *See also* Consumerism;
    Social responsibility
  ADA requirements and, 64
  in bargaining power, 147
  codes of, 63
  in customer returns, 375
  employment benefits and, 296
  in franchising, 121
  gentrification and, 254
  in loan covenants, 327
  markdown allowances and, 412
  online customer reviews and, 478
  in pricing, 89, 434
  promotional goods and, 495
  in relationship retailing, 62–63
  in sales personnel, 524
  security breaches and, 215
  in selling add-ons, 195
  shopping center leases and, 268
  social responsibility and, 346
  in upcycling, 393